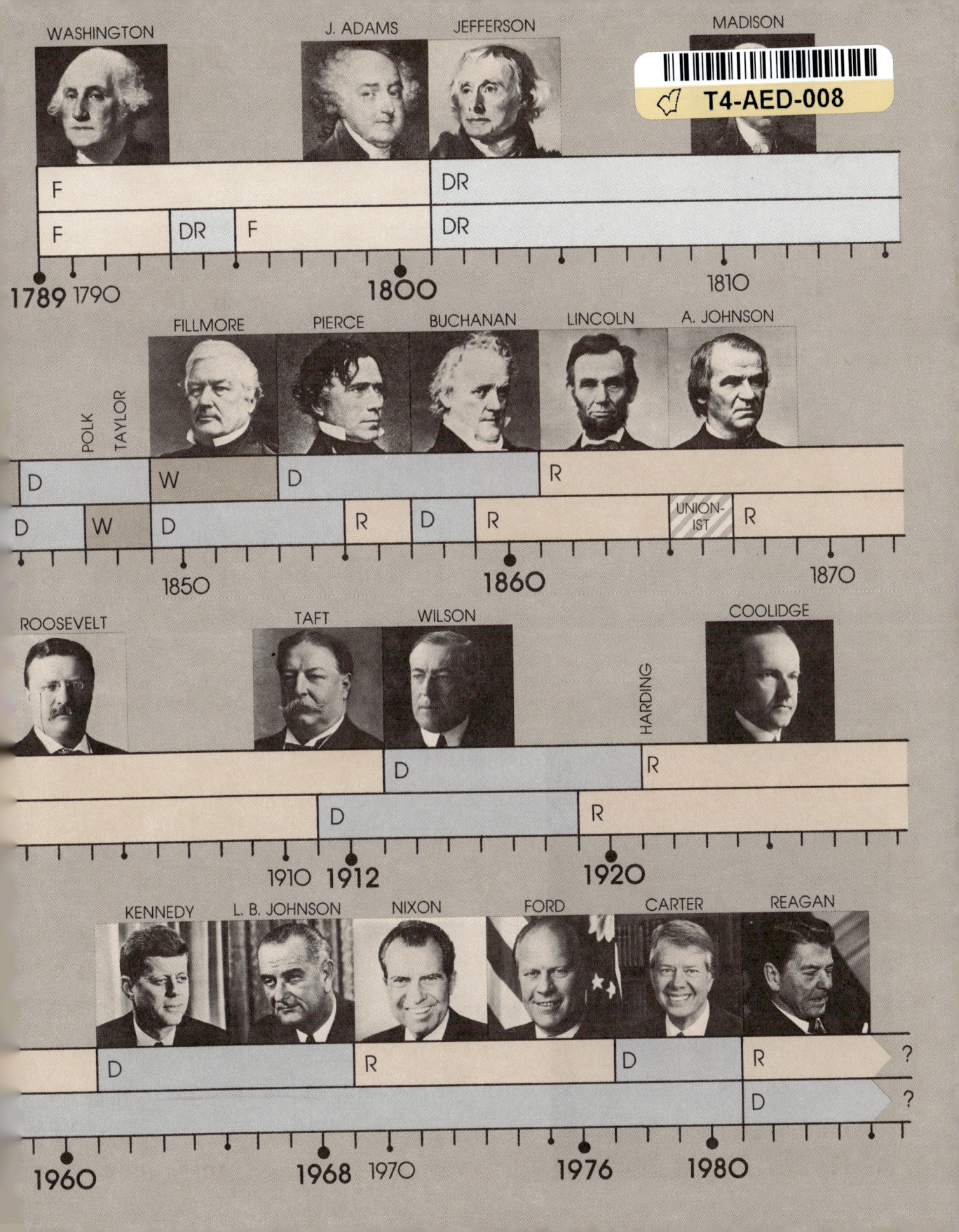

UNDERSTANDING AMERICAN POLITICS

THE DORSEY SERIES IN POLITICAL SCIENCE
Consulting Editor SAMUEL C. PATTERSON The University of Iowa

Understanding American Politics

GROVER STARLING
University of Houston
at Clear Lake City

1982

THE DORSEY PRESS
Homewood, Illinois 60430

Cover photos: Mary Jo Flagg Boyd *(color inset);*
Maje Waldo/Stock, Boston, Inc. *(background)*

Endpaper photos: Jack Kightlinger/The White House *(President Reagan);*
Library of Congress *(others)*

© THE DORSEY PRESS, 1982

All rights reserved. No part of this publication may be reproduced, stored in a retrieval system, or transmitted, in any form or by any means, electronic, mechanical, photocopying, recording, or otherwise, without the prior written permission of the publisher.

ISBN 0-256-02453-7
Library of Congress Catalog Card No. 81–70952
Printed in the United States of America

1 2 3 4 5 6 7 8 9 0 H 9 8 7 6 5 4 3 2

To Terry and Gregory

Preface

If I told you the aim of this book is to provide a comprehensive yet concise introduction to American politics, I would not be the first to make that claim. While I do not know what other writers might mean by the expression "comprehensive yet concise," I know what I mean. My explanation boils down to this: What can be omitted and what cannot?

Faced with the menacing mountain of facts, figures, and theories about American politics that the experts have produced, students might wonder how they can ever appropriate more than a smattering of that knowledge. Yet students in every field of study have faced similar situations. In each case, the same thing happened. Much of what was thought indisputable knowledge was, in a matter of decades, proven false.

But there are even better grounds for not trying to become an expert in order to understand a subject. An intimate knowledge of details can distract us from the essential issues at hand. For this reason, an architect need not know all about the tensile strength of steel to design a building; nor does a movie critic need to know all about camera angle to analyze a film; nor does a president need to know every detail of a law to be an effective, even a great, president. In each instance too much knowledge can cloud understanding. More simply put, one cannot see the forest for the trees.

In writing an introduction to American politics, the danger is that this line of reasoning will result in a kind of digest or outline. Authors take out everything that anybody might find offensive, erroneous, or difficult. Eventually, they arrive at the bare bones, the bottom line—the basics. This goes too far. To properly understand a subject, one still must know the accepted truths, the disputed problems, and the favored methods.

What else should not be omitted from an introduction to American politics? One major function of an introductory treatment should be to organize what we know. It should order our thinking and reduce the chaos of events in the news. It should map out how all these events are related. Another function is to sharpen critical faculties. Though it cannot teach us the truth, still it can teach us the direction in which truth lies. It can teach us what is probable and what is less so, what is needed for proof of a point, what is lacking in a theory, and what is likely to follow from a particular action.

Language plays a decisive role in this critical function. The language of politics abounds with words and phrases contrary to fact. Yet they are clung to because they sound familiar and look plausible. When we hear them, we have the warm sense of recognition. Words that might serve as examples include *obscene, fascism, racism,* and *crisis.* Phrases include, "the truth probably lies somewhere in the middle," "the reason America has failed to create a good and just society is the ability of a small segment of the population to dominate power," and "government needs to get at the root cause of this problem."

Now, such words and phrases, in certain instances, are correct. But they are often used indiscriminantly. When we have been initiated into a set of attitudes rather than trained to think, this invariably happens.

To summarize, the aim of this book is to provide a comprehensive yet concise introduction to American politics. In pursuing it, I have made several important assumptions. To properly understand a subject, one must know the accepted truths (even though these may one day pass), the disputed problems (even though this may complicate the picture), and the favored methods. But an introduction to American politics should do more than provide a body of common knowledge. It should also provide the channels through which the right part of it can be brought to bear on the issue at hand. This requires that the knowledge be organized or mapped and that the critical function be enhanced.

How, specifically, is this book going to do all this? Consider, for example, the following eight features: In Chapter 1, the relation between politics and other major fields of study (including not only history and economics but biology and systems analysis) is clearly and fully laid out. The student gets the full import of Aristotle's observation that politics is the master science.

Chapter 2 evaluates the role of ideas in shaping the political history and political future of American and world politics. In a free society full of rights, how can we accept the notion that ideas do not matter? Though fights and scandals enliven the television news, I have tried to make ideas enliven at least some of this text.

Chapter 4 considers the acquisition, exercise, and maintenance of power.

On the assumption that not many students will ever have a case argued before the Supreme Court, Chapter 9 focuses on much more than the policymaking role of the Supreme Court. For this reason, it is entitled "A Citizen's Guide to the Judiciary."

At the end of Chapter 10 appears a short discussion of how to cope with bureaucracy. Its purpose is blatantly practical.

The output of the federal government is approximately 400 separate programs. Even if one could discuss all these—clearly impossible in anything less than an encyclopedia—it would not be enough. New programs are constantly being added; old ones are being phased out. The only solution is to teach a general method for analyzing any public policy. This is the aim of Chapter 12.

It would be hard to find an observer of the American political scene who would deny the profound interrelationship of politics and economics. Rather than skim over economics, I have tried to treat its most relevant parts in Chapter 13.

While this book gives as much attention to foreign and defense policy as other texts, Chapter 14 contains several interesting features. Among these are the historical background of American foreign policy; a region-by-region survey of the globe, highlighting potential hot spots; a classification of approaches to foreign policy; how a nuclear war can start and how it can be prevented; and how military strength is measured.

Most who read this book will spend over a third of their lives in the 21st century. While we cannot *know* the future, we can spot trends and speculate. Each activity is, I think, worthwhile. To give the reader more of a sense of the future, I have integrated into the text 10

Future Files. These deal with the following subjects:

- Creeping Capitalism?
- American Political Culture in Transition
- Is the Party Over?
- Was the 1980 Election a "Critical Election"?
- Congress 2001
- Delegalizing America
- Reagan and the Supreme Court
- Urban Catastrophe or Urban Renaissance?
- Persistence of Poverty in Less Developed Countries
- Where Is American Technology Headed?

As previously noted, the study of politics must include critical analysis as well as information acquisition. It must be an active as well as a passive endeavor. For that reason, I have also integrated a number of quizzes into the text to encourage the reader to think. For example, at the end of Chapter 12, the reader is asked to apply the methods of policy analysis to a proposal to legalize marijuana in order to see what the consequences of such action might be.

To enhance the scholarly and pedagogical value of this book, several other features have been added:

- Each chapter begins with a picture that serves to crystallize in the reader's mind the central theme of that chapter.
- Each chapter builds around five to seven focus questions. Each of these questions is briefly addressed in the Chapter Keys at the end of each chapter.
- The critical terms to be introduced in a chapter appear at the front of the chapter. These are defined in a glossary at the end of the book.
- To help the reader see how all the topics work together, a chart showing the organizational framework of the book is introduced in Chapter 1 and repeated at the start of each of the book's four parts.
- Appendixes containing the Constitution, *Federalist Papers* Nos. 10 and 51, and a list of useful addresses are provided.

In an undertaking such as this, one perhaps should combine the good points of divergent schemes, or better yet, the contributions of several authors. Such an approach may provide a hedge against failure and better surface finish. But what is given up is unity of conception. I hope that the reader deems the trade-off I have made justified.

Eric Partridge, the late lexicographer, liked to say, "He who never makes mistakes makes nothing." Though many people have taken the trouble to read either parts or all of the manuscript and offer perceptive criticism and advice, I am not sure they were always able to save me from my errors and outright follies. Regrettably, it is quite impossible for me to thank individually all those who have been helpful. But I do owe a special thanks to my friend and colleague Albert C. Hyde of the University of Houston at Clear Lake City, to Michael Binford of Georgia State University, and to Richard Hardy of the University of Missouri at Columbia.

Grover Starling

Contents

1. **What Is Politics? 2**

    Preliminary Definitions, 4
    Why Study Politics? 16
    How This Book Is Organized, 24

PART 1
Foundations

2. **Architecture of a Republic: The Constitution, 32**

    The American Revolution, 35
    The Critical Period and Its Aftermath, 41
    Basic Design Features of the Constitution, 48

3. **The Force of Ideas, 66**

    The Role of Ideas in Politics, 68
    Shaping the Declaration of Independence and the Constitution, 70
    Shaping Contemporary American Politics, 78
    Shaping Global Politics, 92

4. **The Craft of Politics, 104**

    The Role of Power in American Politics, 106
    Who Are the Powerful? 109
    Sources of Power, 115
    Political Strategy and Tactics, 119
    Resolving Conflict through Negotiations, 130
    Political Language and Symbols, 134
    Concluding Observations: The Necessity of Power, 140

PART 2
Inputs for the Political System

5. **Public Opinion and Political Action in an Electronic Age, 146**

    Taking the Pulse of the People, 148
    A Simple Model for Analysis of Individual Political Behavior, 152
    Political Socialization, 153
    Political Culture, 157
    Mass Media, 166
    Voting, 171
    Other Forms of Political Action, 177

6. **Interest Groups and Political Parties, 182**

    Interest Groups, 184
    Political Parties, 199
    Electing a President, 205

PART 3
Government Institutions

7. **The Executive Branch: Presidential Leadership and Bureaucratic Management, 224**

    The Existential Presidency, 227
    The Structure of the Presidency, 244
    Presidential Policymaking, 255

xii CONTENTS

8. The Congressional Balance, 262

Congress and the President, 264
What Congress Is, 265
Congress in Action, 271
Power within Congress, 283

9. The Judiciary: A Citizen's Guide, 298

What the Law Is, 301
The Structure and Operations of the Judiciary, 305
The Adversary Process, 318
The Judiciary and Paradoxes of Political Power, 331

10. Government at the Grass Roots, 338

Federalism: Pro and Con, 342
What States Do, 344
The Concept of Intergovernmental Relations, 346
Institutional Modernization, 352

CODA: Coping with Government, 367

PART 4
Outputs of the Political System

11. Civil Liberties and Civil Rights, 378

Civil Liberties: The Quest for Freedom, 381
Civil Rights: The Quest for Equality, 394
Equality in Freedom: An Assessment of America in the 1980s, 406

12. How to Analyze Public Policy, 414

1. What Is the Problem? 418
2. What Should the Goals Be? 424
3. What Are the Alternative Strategies that Will Help Attain These Goals? 426
4. What Are the Total Costs and Benefits of Each Alternative? 429
5. Who Pays? Who Benefits? 432
6. What Are the Risks? 434
7. Select an Alternative or Set of Alternatives, 436
8. Is the Policy Politically Feasible? 439
9. What Are the Possible Implementation Problems? 441
10. How Will Results Be Evaluated? 443

13. The Government and the Economy, 454

Rediscovering the Links between Politics and Economics, 457
Measuring America's Wealth, 458
How the American Economic Engine Works—and Fails to Work, 467
How Government Manages the Economy, 471
The American Economy in the 1980s: Issues and Ideas, 477
The Global Connection, 486

14. America in an Interdependent World, 498

The Political Connection, 502
Making Sense of American Reaction to World Events, 510
Regional Survey, 513
The Strategic Connection, 519

EPILOGUE, 536

APPENDIX A: The Constitution of the United States, A-1

The Bill of Rights, A-7
Pre-Civil War Amendments, A-8
Civil War Amendments, A-8
Twentieth-Century Amendments, A-9

APPENDIX B: Two Selections from *The Federalist*, B-1

No. 10, B-1
No. 51, B-6

APPENDIX C: Acquiring Information More Efficiently, C-1

APPENDIX D: A Brief Guide to Federal Statutory Forms and Judicial Reports, D

Glossary, G

Notes, N

To Explore Further, T-1

Index, i

1 | What Is Politics?

After studying this chapter you should be able to answer these questions:

1. What are the identifying characteristics of politics?
2. What are the major forms of government?
3. What are the major types of economies?
4. How are politics and economics related?
5. How does the study of politics draw on other academic disciplines?
6. Why study politics?

Terms you should know:*

authority
authoritarian
behavioral science
capitalism
command economies
conflict
consensus
correlation
democratic
economic system
institutions
government
market economies
mean

median
mixed economy
political science
political system
power
programs
public policy
socialism
sociobiology
statistics
systems analysis
survey research
totalitarian
welfare state

---

* All terms are defined in the text and in the glossary at the end of the book.

Because I want to begin in the simplest possible terms, I do so with the ancient parable of the cave. In this cave, men are chained with their faces to the wall and their backs to a fire. They have been there all their lives. They cannot turn around. Behind them, their captors pace back and forth, holding up various objects so that the shadows of these objects fall on the wall. All that the men in chains can see, of course, are the shadows of these objects. But the men in chains think the shadows are the real things.

Now assume that one man throws off the chains and turns around. There, for the first time, he sees the full-blooded objects of the real world. What would happen if he tried to tell the other prisoners about his discovery? Very likely, he would seem to his fellow creatures even crazier than before.[1]

This parable was told by Plato, one of the philosophers of ancient Greece who laid the foundations of Western philosophy. I have used it to try to suggest that our picture of American politics is all too often a dim reflection of reality, a world of mere shadows.

Is it possible that this inability to understand the political world we inhabit can be overcome? Can a single volume on American politics accomplish that?

Perhaps, if we expand the meaning of the expression "the study of politics" to encompass clear and logical thought as well as information acquisition, some of the mystery of politics that now confronts us would be resolved. Perhaps, if we clear our minds of clichés, we can get rid of half-baked notions and unsupportable opinions. Finally, perhaps, if we view politics from a variety of perspectives and steadfastedly refuse to become the captives of any one academic tradition, we can arrive at a deeper, richer, less one-dimensional understanding of our subject. The only thing for us to do is try. Then we shall see.

PRELIMINARY DEFINITIONS

In America, the word *politics* has fallen on bad times. In public esteem, those who practice politics for a living—the politicians—are probably half a percentage point ahead of Howard Cosell and used car dealers, but a long way behind joggers, chiropractors, magicians, and florists. Public opinion polls make dreary reading for politicians.

Yet politics cannot be ignored. In the first place, it is the master science from which all other fields of study take their cue; so Plato's pupil Aristotle said over two thousand years ago. This means that the ends of politics are the ultimate ends of every art and science. The politics of a society—more than anything else—determines how the knowledge from the other arts and sciences will be used, if at all. Politics even determines which sciences are to be studied in school, and by whom and to what extent.

A second reason politics cannot be ignored is that it is a universal activity. Any set of people—families, clubs, corporations, universities, hospitals, even circuses—that chance or choice has brought together have their politics. Though many would sharply disagree, one leader of the women's movement, Kate Millett, has argued that relations between men and women are basically political, since all societies at present are patriarchies (that is, headed by males). Meanwhile, in the office and factory, workers are increasingly demanding some freedom to perform their jobs outside the traditional top-down lines of control imposed by managers.

Third, politics cannot be ignored because those political institutions we call states profoundly shape everyone's future. The rates of inflation and unemployment, the quality of health care and transportation, war and peace are all the direct result of political decisions.

Finally, politics helps explain who in a society gets what, when, and how. I would only add to this marvelously concise definition the words "and who pays the bill."

The Identifying Characteristics of Politics

Politics is concerned with human relationships involving conflict, consensus (or agreement), and power. If we examine each of these special properties, we can study American politics with a better understanding of the fundamental questions it seeks to answer.

Conflict. Perhaps the most conspicuous attribute of politics is that it involves **conflict** over values. In other words, unless different individuals, groups, or countries are pursuing their basic interest, a situation is not political. What might these basic interests be? Harold D. Lasswell of Yale University suggests eight values over which people will have conflicts: power, enlightenment, wealth, health, skill, affection, justice, and respect. Thus, in a fundamental sense, American politics is an arena in which people struggle for the allocation of these values.

Stanley J. Forman/*Boston Herald American*

Politics involves, among other things, conflict—that is, struggle over values. Outraged by court-ordered busing in 1976, rioting Boston students attack a black lawyer with Old Glory. Stanley Forman's photo won the 1977 Pulitzer Prize.

Conflict is not new in American politics. Thomas Paine accused George Washington of betraying his cause when he became head of the new federal government. Paine addressed Washington as follows in an open letter:

> As to you, sir, treacherous in private friendship . . . and a hypocrite in public life, the world will be puzzled to decide whether you are an apostate or an imposter; whether you have abandoned good principles or whether you ever had any.[2]

Other opponents abused Washington by calling him "crocodile," "hyena," "traitor."

Conflicts also occur when individuals interpret and seek justice in different ways. When he had become assistant secretary of the navy under President McKinley, Theodore Roosevelt called the president a "white-livered cur" for thinking twice before attacking the Spaniards in Cuba. And political campaigns are nowadays almost pure conflict. Among the more recent and vivid was President Carter's assertion that, if Senator Edward Kennedy chose to run against him, "I'll whip his ass."[3] (Kennedy later joked, "I always knew the White House would stand behind me, but I didn't realize how close they would be.")

In the last example, the struggle over values is not hard to see. But this is not the usual case. Consider the recent conflicts between environmentalists and industrialists. What exactly are the values sought by environmentalists? At first blush, one might be inclined to answer, clean air, clean water, better land use management, solid waste disposal, and so forth. Unfortunately, these values conflict with other values, such as jobs. Stricter environmental laws can lead to a leveling off of the economy and loss of manufacturing jobs. To a great extent, environmentalists are professionals who are relatively independent of industry; thus they are less concerned about losing these jobs than those in the lower echelons of society are. Some environmentalists may actually prefer less economic growth; it means fewer people climbing the economic ladder and interfering with their lifestyles—trying to move into the suburbs, crowding the beaches, buying ski cabins, etc. By blocking development and working against broadening material consumption, some environmentalists may have begun reviving the old conflict between the haves and have-nots. This line of analysis may or may not be correct. But it should at least help to remind us that the true values at stake in a political conflict are not necessarily the professed ones.

It would be wrong to conclude that the foregoing conflicts—Paine versus Washington, Roosevelt versus McKinley, Carter versus Kennedy, environmentalists versus industrialists (and factory workers)—are undesirable in a democracy. Conflict gives a society a safety valve through which grievances can be aired. As Senator Daniel P. Moynihan correctly noted, the quick and easy way to see how much democracy a country has is to look at its newspapers. If they are full of praise for the government, you are not likely in a real democracy. But if the papers are ripe with criticism, you have probably landed in one. Moreover, a society without conflict is a petrified society; conflict is the chief generator of progress of any kind. Martin Luther King, Jr., described this essential function well: "Nonviolent direct action seeks to create such a crisis and foster such a tension that a community which has constantly refused to negotiate is forced to confront the issue. It seeks so to dramatize the issue that it can no longer be ignored."[4]

Consensus. Conflict, however, can only fulfill this important function in a democracy if there is a preexisting **consensus** that sets the bounds for the conflict: No one ever described better the dire conditions that result when conflict goes unrestricted and uncontrolled than 17th-century English philosopher Thomas Hobbes:

> There is no place for industry, because the fruit thereof is uncertain: and consequently no culture of the earth; no navigation, nor use of the commodities that may be imported by sea; no commodious building; no instruments of moving and removing such things as require much force; no knowledge of the face of the earth; no account of time; no arts; no letters; no society; and which is worst of all, continual fear, and danger of violent death; and the life of man, solitary, poor, nasty, brutish, and short.[5]

Consensus means that, despite differences over specific values, people will hold similar views on how collective decisions will be made. For example, a legislature is the scene of multiple conflicts. But all of its members pretty much agree on the basics of how any law should be passed. Consensus, though, really means more than adherence to a formal set of rules. It also means following unwritten "rules of the games." For example, keep your word, practice self-restraint and courtesy during debates, and do not be a publicity hound.

Similarly, members of society as a whole must share basic beliefs. What might these be? Of particular importance is the notion that the government is legitimate. Legitimacy means that government deserves our support and obedience because of custom or tradition and because of law or fear of punishment. Equally important is a belief in the "rules of the democratic game." Such rules include majority rule, equality, rule of law, sanctity of human life, competitive political parties, unrestricted discussion of issues, and peaceful displacement of officials defeated in elections.

Power. In politics, a relationship in which one or more persons can alter the behavior of others involves **power** (from the Latin root meaning "to be able to"). But why should B go along with the wishes of A? Why should B do something that he or she would not otherwise have done simply because of A?

In the study of politics, these questions are not trivial. The obvious answer is force. In other words, because A makes certain threats ("Do this or else . . .") or promises ("If you do this, then I'll do this for you."), B conforms to the wishes of A. But some commands gain obedience without the implied use of naked force. Such commands rely on a special kind of power or right, called **authority**; it is granted to A because of his or her rank or office. For example, the centurion in St. Matthew's Gospel both possessed authority and served under it: "I am a man under authority, having soldiers under me: and I say to this man go, and he goes; and to another come and he comes; and to my servant do this, and he does it."

Finally, a few theorists would point to manipulation as yet another basis for power. By giving, withholding, or distorting information, A can exercise power over B.

Whatever the source of power—force, authority, or manipulation—one thing is clear: B takes some action because of A's power. Politics is an activity designed to bring about some result. (It may be a change in air quality standards, the replacement of a mayor, or the ending of a war.) Therefore it *requires* knowledge of how to produce or cause certain actions in others. Once this fact is grasped, it is not hard to see why power (which we defined as the ability to alter the actions of others) is a basic characteristic of politics.

Indeed, some political scientists have gone so far as to suggest that the concept of power is as important to them as the concept of money is to economists. Money is the generalized medium of economic exchange between buyer and seller; power is the generalized medium of exchange between citizen and government.

Government and Its Forms

Government and political system defined. Politics, to repeat, is concerned with human relationships involving conflict, consensus, and power. When such relationships exist over time, the individuals who are involved begin to take on roles. In other words, they share roughly similar expectations about how to behave in particular situations. Whenever a country is complex and stable, political roles develop. Persons who create, interpret, and enforce rules that are binding on other citizens—that is to say, legislators, judges, and bureaucrats—are perhaps in the most obvious political roles. These roles are offices. The collection of offices in a country is what constitutes the **government** of that country.

From this definition, it should be clear why government is not the same as politics. Though individuals or groups may be deeply involved in politics, they may not be part of government. An individual may serve as a fund raiser for a U.S. senator, or a labor union leader may have considerable political influence, but neither can create, interpret, and enforce rules that are binding on the rest of us.

Fortunately, we have a term that covers political actors such as fund raisers, labor leaders, and government officials but excludes human relationships that are political but unrelated to government. That term is **political system.** Broadly defined, it includes the government plus all components in a society that have frequent interaction with that government. The relationship among politics, political system, and government is shown schematically in the accompanying figure.

Forms of government. The most common and convenient way to classify governments is according to the structure and placement of power. Using this classification, we can pinpoint all nations somewhere along a line or continuum. At one end are **democratic** governments, where ultimate political power is vested in the people. (The word *democracy* derives from the Greek word *demos*, the people, and *kratos*, authority.)

Democracy may be direct, as practiced in

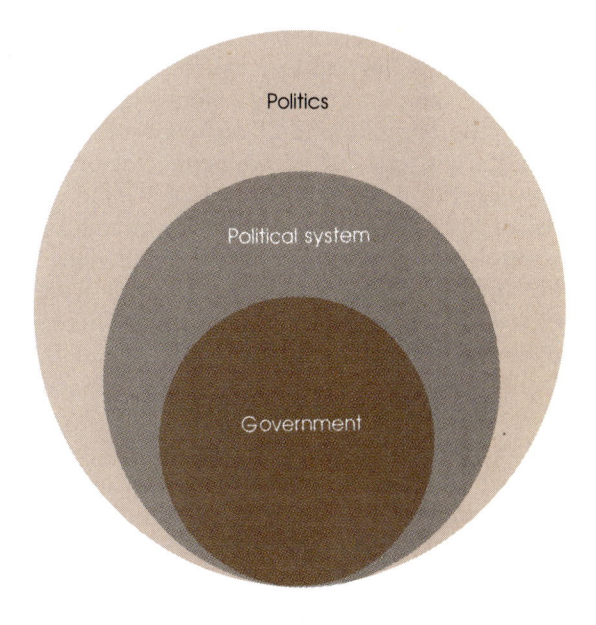

Alexander Calder, *Streetcar.* Collection of The Art Institute of Chicago

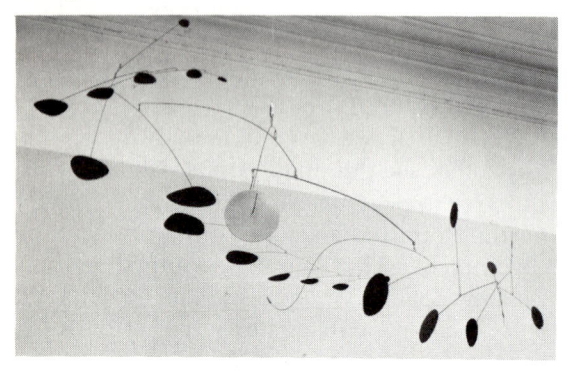

A *system* may be defined as a collection of recognizable units that hang together like a Calder mobile. If you disturb one unit, you affect the others. Political systems, though, consist of political units rather than sheet aluminum and are connected by political processes, not steel wire.

ancient Greece or in New England town meetings; or it may be representative, as practiced in most Western industrialized countries. Although decision making tends to follow the principle of majority rule, minority rights are protected. In order to make the political right of voting meaningful, civil liberties are considered indispensable. (Civil liberties include guarantees of freedom of speech, press, religion, and assembly, the right to complain to government officials, and equality before the law.)

At the opposite end of our continuum are **totalitarian** forms of government. Not only is power concentrated in the hands of one individual or a small group but the government also controls nearly every aspect of the individual's life. Such governments do not tolerate activities of individuals or groups unless clearly directed towards the government goals. In place of the freedom and openness associated with democracies, the totalitarian government offers secret police, propaganda, and repression. Trials of "public enemies" and fears of foreign military threats also help maintain national unity.

The concept of totalitarian government presupposes total control over the flow of information in a society and completely centralized political power. Because of this, totalitarianism is seldom achieved in practice. Therefore, it is useful to introduce a third type of government to place somewhere between democracy and totalitarianism.

This third type of government is called **authoritarian.*** Here the voice of the people is muted, to be sure. But authoritarian governments generally do not try to intrude into every facet of life (e.g., religion). They do not erase the distinction between areas of private judgment and public control. Another characteristic is more than one center of power in government. (For example, there may be industrial managers, rivals in the party, and generals.)

The words totalitarian and authoritarian are seldom used with clinical precision in the game of international politics. "Totalitarian" is to the free-world vocabulary what "imperialist" is to communist terminology.

Dictators friendly to the free world are "paternalistic"; totalitarian governments necessary to the defense of the free world are "authoritarian." Such distinctions help explain why Iran under Shah Mohammed Riza Palevi, who had taken only limited steps towards greater freedom and political liberalization, was not considered—at least officially considered—authoritarian.

Despite this imprecision, the distinction between totalitarian and authoritarian governments is useful. Figure 1–1 attempts to array all nations of the world on a democratic–authoritarian–totalitarian scale.

---

* The term *totalitarianism* was adopted in the 1930s by defenders of constitutional democracy to convey the common traits of evil they percieved in the political systems of fascism, nazism, and communism. In her *Origins of Totalitarianism* (New York: Harcourt, Brace & World, new edition, 1966), Hannah Arendt made the term academically respectable. Jerry F. Hough's update of Merle Fainsod's *How the Soviet Union Is Governed* (Cambridge, Mass.: Harvard University Press, 1979) takes the position that, because there are several sources of power in the USSR, the totalitarian model is too simplistic. Hough has little to say, however, about the role of the police and concentration camps in Soviet life. For further discussion of how these words are used in everyday politics, see William Safire's *Political Dictionary* (New York: Random House, 1978).

FIGURE 1-1
Approximate Distribution of Selected Nations Along a Continuum of Democracy and Totalitarianism

Democracy ←─────────────────────────── *(Authoritarian)* ──→ *Totalitarianism*

Australia				Indonesia	China
Austria				Kenya	Cuba
Canada	Greece	Brazil		South Korea	Jordan
Costa Rica	India	El Salvador		Nicaragua	Saudi Arabia
Ireland	Israel	Mexico		Panama	Haiti
Sweden	Italy	Nigeria		Poland	Iran
Great Britain		Columbia		Chile	USSR
United States		Jamaica		Hungary	Albania
	France	Spain		South Africa	Bulgaria
	Germany	Peru		Syria	Ethiopia
	Japan	Ecuador	Honduras	Yugoslavia	Kampuchea
	Venezuela				North Korea
					Vietnam
					Afghanistan

Source: Based on the annual report *Comparative Survey of Freedom*, January–February 1981, by Freedom House, a New York-based, nonpartisan human rights organization.

The survey uses about two dozen criteria to determine whether a country allows its citizens to exercise civil rights. The major criteria include political rights such as forming or belonging to "alternative political parties" and "the fairness of the process of naming choices or voting in elections and the yielding of power to those elected." It also takes into account the impartiality of the judiciary, freedoms of press, assembly, and religion, and freedom from harsh and unusual punishments and torture.

Economic Systems

Economics and political systems. Societies, like biological organisms, must fulfill certain basic functions in order to survive. For example, both need some mechanism for attaining goals. The mechanism that steers a society towards its collective goals is, of course, government. To speak of "steering a society towards its collective goals" is just a complicated way of saying that governments make public policy.

But what is a **public policy?** It is a list of goals in some order of priority. For instance, the National Environmental Act of 1969 certainly qualifies as a policy. It was an authoritative statement of America's general goals in regard to the problem of pollution. **Plans** and **programs** are more specific means for achieving the goals of a policy.

Can you now think of any functions other than attaining goals that are essential to a society's survival? Consider this: Every society requires *(a)* some mechanism of producing goods and services for its people and *(b)* some mechanism to distribute those goods and services among them. It is not hard to figure out what component in society carries out that twofold task—the economy.

Different countries have developed different types of economies, just as they have developed types of governments. Knowledge of **economic systems** in other parts of the world can help us understand the American economic system better. Such knowledge may also help us avoid confusing economic systems with political systems. However, the two systems in a given country are related in important ways. But more about these relationships in a minute.

For now let us again think of a line upon which we can pinpoint any country's economic system. At one end we can put **market economies.** In such systems the primary means of production are privately owned; goods and services are distributed through a market in which producers agrees to sell to buyers at a mutually agreed-upon price. Another word for this economic system is, of course, **capitalism.**

Looking now at the other end of our continuum, we see **command economies.** In such economic systems, the primary means of production are publicly owned; goods and services are distributed through some centralized mechanism. (More than likely that mechanism is a government agency). Another word for this economic system is **socialism.**

In today's world, most Western industrial nations (including Japan) are capitalist; socialism is common among the developing nations of Asia and Africa and the Communist bloc nations. One hundred years ago, the American government exercised little control over the economy. Individuals made almost all economic decisions in the market. Today, things have become much more complicated; but Americans still exercise much economic choice.

As Figure 1–2 indicates, ownership in basic American industries remains largely in private hands. The figure, it should be emphasized, shows only 11 basic industries. It might appear that a country like Sweden has little private ownership and should be considered socialist. Such is not the case. In that country, 90 percent of *total* industry is privately owned. Moreover, cooperative enterprises (that is, business-government partnerships) account for about half of the rest; only the remaining 5 percent is entirely in public hands.

No country today meets exactly the criteria of capitalism. Therefore many Western economists call the American economy a **mixed economy.**

Finally, it is important that we distinguish socialism from **welfare state.** The latter is an essentially capitalistic country in which government has assumed responsibility for protecting and promoting the social security and welfare of its citizens. It does so through various programs of medical care, unemployment insurance, old-age pensions, family allowances, public housing, and the like. In a welfare state, a large percentage of the total value of goods and services produced by a nation's economy in a year can go into the government's treasury to pay for the kinds of programs listed above. But the government interference in the economy comes chiefly *after* the goods and services have been produced, not before, as in a socialistic nation.

How economics and politics are related. Now we come to the really interesting question: What is the relationship, if any, between market and command economies on the one hand and democratic and authoritarian political systems on the other? Market economies can be democratic, as in the United States, or somewhat more authoritarian, as in Spain. The converse, however, is less true; socialist economies can be authoritarian but seldom appear alongside a democractic political system. Suppose we rather strictly define democracy as any system that appears on the left side of the scale used in Figure 1–1. Then we find that no democratic countries have socialist economic systems. Table 1–1 attempts to classify all nations with respect to the form of government and economy they have.

Another interesting question is, How do political decisions influence the American economy? To answer that question will require an entire chapter (see Chapter 13). For now, let

FIGURE 1–2

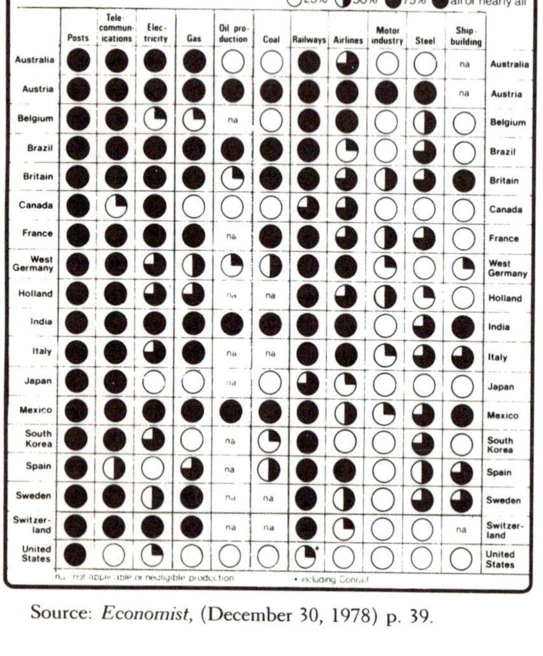

Source: *Economist*, (December 30, 1978) p. 39.

TABLE 1-1
The Relationship Between Political and Economic Systems

	Political System	
Economic system	*Democratic*	*Authoritarian*
Market-oriented systems	All countries appearing on left side of Figure 1-1.	Most of the world's systems, including most of Latin America, new African nations, the Middle East except Israel, and all of noncommunist Asia except Japan
Centralized authority	*	Communist systems; also Nazi-Germany

* The temporary arrangements for wartime economic mobilization made by the United Kingdom, the United States, and other Western democracies in World War II might be placed in the otherwise empty box.

Source: Adapted from Charles E. Lindblom, *Politics and Markets* (New York: Basic Books, 1977), p. 161.

us simply say that, since World War II, American government has assumed a greater and greater responsibility for managing the economy. And because politicians run the government, purely political consideration can sometimes push economic theory aside.

Political Science

The study of politics has a long tradition that runs at least as far back as Plato's *Republic*, from which the parable of the cave was taken. Today the systematic study of politics, applying scientific methods of analysis, is widely referred to as **political science**. In the 13 chapters that follow you will learn quite a bit about political science as well as American politics. Fortunately, not everything you learn will be entirely new. If you have done previous work in economics, history, philosophy, statistics, behavioral science, systems analysis, or biology, you are already on the road to understanding American politics.

This book is probably more eclectic than most treatments of American politics. Therefore, I feel obliged to sketch briefly how each of the seven disciplines just mentioned can be brought to bear on politics (Figure 1-3).

Economics: The dismal science. Given the many ailments plaguing the American economy today, economics has never seemed more of a "dismal science." That title was conferred upon economics in the 19th century by T. R. Malthus. He began putting forward his theory that population would grow to the limit of resources and would be checked only by misery, war, or starvation.

Today's dismal theories have to do with inflation, unemployment, and sluggish growth. In Chapter 8, we shall see how the management of the economy has been one of the touchstones of presidential leadership. In Chapter 12, we shall even see how economic tools can help us get a surer grasp of how social programs work. In Chapter 13 we shall explore in some depth how certain economic theories have surged into political debate almost overnight.

History: An indispensible part of political education. The contribution of history to the study of politics cannot be overemphasized. Yet, in our time, it seems particularly underemphasized. Not long ago, David Broder of the *Washington Post*, an outstanding political reporter, spent several months at the Institute of Politics at Harvard. When he returned to the real world of politics, he was asked about his views on the students. Broder's comment was remarkable: "They don't care about anything that happened more than five years ago."[6] What a Harvard student happens to think may not be a great national concern. But what political leaders and their advisers think certainly is.

Incidents such as the following are indeed cause for concern:

> When Russian troops entered Afghanistan in 1980, President Carter called the action the greatest threat to peace since World

**FIGURE 1-3
Politics as the Master Science**

(Pie chart showing Politics at center, surrounded by: Biology, Economics, History, Philosophy, Statistics, Behavioral science, Systems analysis)

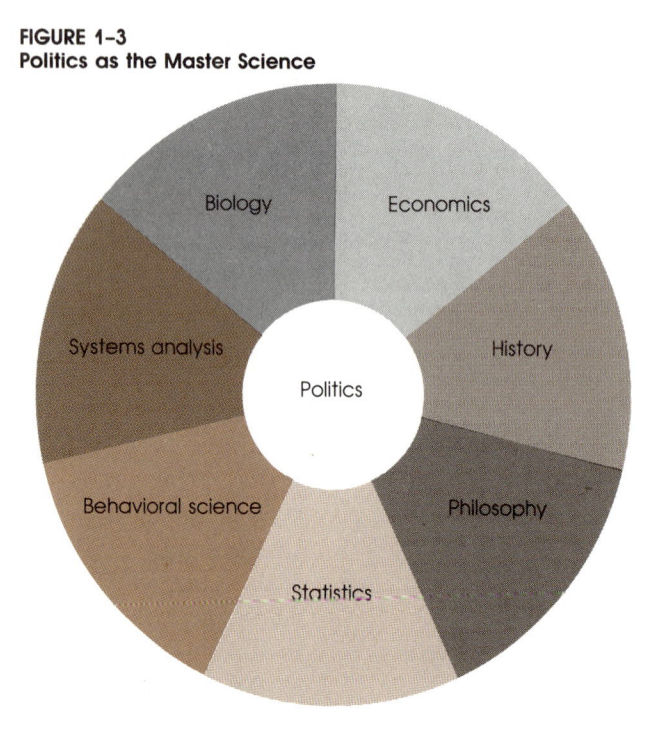

War II. But what of the Berlin blockade in 1948 and the Cuban missile crisis in 1962? (Events discussed in Chapter 14.)

When the Shah of Iran was brought down by the religious establishment rather than progressive army officers, American experts were surprised. But historians were not. They saw a direct line of descent from successful political opposition mounted by the 19th-century religious establishment to the recent struggle of Khomeini against the Shah's regime.

During the 1980 campaign, Ronald Reagan liked to recall those days when American pioneers conquered the continent, "settling the prairies and crossing the mountains without help of the federal government." "They did it themselves," he said. "They didn't need an urban renewal program or community development block grant." While this may be a great applause line, historians know better. The U.S. government, through its armed forces, Indian agents, explorers, surveyors, road builders, physicians, and mail carriers, was essential to the winning of the West. Since Reagan once played General George Armstrong Custer in a movie, he should have known. One wonders: Who did Reagan think paid Custer? General Electric?

In short, history gives us a basis for making predictions about contemporary events. It enhances our awareness of the complex way events unfold. It forces us to acknowledge more fully the consequences, often unanticipated, that flow from major public decisions. It puts us on guard for politicians who seek to interpret history for partisan purposes. And finally, history helps us to distinguish between important and inconsequential, lasting and fleeting political experiences.

Michael Oakeshott, a British professor of politics with a keen appreciation of the contribution history can make to his field, put it well: "Nothing appears on the present surface of a tradition of political activity which has not its roots deep in the past, and that not to observe it coming into being is often to be denied the clue to its significance; and for this reason genuine historical study is an indispensable part of a political education."[7]

Philosophy: A return to the heart of things. Why does generation after generation leave college with so little understanding of the issues that shape their lives? One major reason is that textbooks, especially in the social sciences, *fail to address the ideas behind the events.* The purpose of philosophy in the study of politics is to clarify the issues involved in the problems that confront government. This does not mean that it tells us what decision to make. Rather, it means that philosophy can help us make decisions with a fuller, clearer understanding of what is at stake. For these reasons, one entire chapter of this book has been devoted to political philosophy (Chapter 3).

Statistics: A kind of lie or a prerequisite for citizenship? Benjamin Disraeli, the great 19th-century British statesman, once remarked, "There are three kinds of lies: lies, damned lies, and statistics." But a few years later, his countryman H.G. Wells was to observe, "Statistical thinking will one day be as necessary for efficient citizenship as the ability to read and write."

These statements are complementary, not contradictory. The numbers thrown around in discussions of public policy can be very misleading, it is hard for a citizen to hold an informed position without some knowledge of statistical inference.

Essentially, **statistics** is the collection, organization, and interpretation of numerical data. Much of statistics involves analyzing the traits of a large population by inference from a small "sample." To understand politics, we must understand that our experience is quite limited.

Here statistics plays an important role. It gets us thinking not in terms of subjective, isolated cases ("I once knew a Republican, and he wasn't very nice."), but in terms of objective, aggregate data ("A survey of 1,200 Democrats reveals that 48 percent believe that . . ."). The method that political scientists use to learn things about large populations is called **survey research.** It involves asking questions and collecting data about a small group (a sample) that has been chosen to be representative of the larger group.

We must also guard against the *post hoc ergo propter hoc* fallacy. In other words, just because one event comes after another does not necessarily mean the former caused the latter.

The point cannot be overemphasized. We like sequences of cause and effect. The news media, in particular, like to connect unrelated phenomena by conditional verbs and label it "one possible explanation." They sometimes also eliminate the conditional tense and replace "one possible" with "the." We, as knowledge consumers, must be alert to this tendency. The statistical measure of the strength of a relationship between two factors (e.g., level of education and tendency to vote) is called **correlation.**

For obvious reasons, data on the progress of minority groups, such as blacks, attract considerable attention. To properly interpret these data, one must respect the principles of statistical inference (see box).

Behavioral science: Political science's first cousin. The intellectual roots of political science, psychology, and sociology cross at many points. Therefore, it has not been hard for contemporary political scientists to develop working relationships with behavioral scientists. This alliance has allowed political scientists to use the scientific method to postulate hypotheses about individual and group political action, then verify them by observation and experimentation.

One of the earliest and most influential attempts to apply psychoanalytical theory by an

The Numbers Game

Imagine a small community of nine families. Seven have an annual income of $25,000 each, but two have an income of $1 million. Add up all these incomes and divide by the nine families. We find that the average or **mean** income is $241,667.

Now imagine yourself going to almost anyone in the community and stating that the average income is $241,667. You will have a 78 percent chance of being laughed at or run out of town—or worse. This is because $241,667 is almost 10 times as much as seven out of the nine families make.

A much better measure here would be the **median**. To calculate this measure, simply list the incomes from lowest to highest and pick the middle one:

$ 25,000
25,000
25,000
25,000
(25,000)
25,000
25,000
1,000,000
1,000,000

Now when you go downtown and announce that you have calculated their average salary to $25,000, 78 percent of the citizens will nod in agreement.

American political scientist was by Harold Lasswell. Power seekers, he argued, pursue power as a means of compensating for psychological deprivations suffered during childhood. (For example, Churchill was virtually ignored as a child by his always on-the-go parents.) Like adult sexuality, political inclinations seem to have a developmental history.

One recent example of the application of psychology to politics is David Barber's theory that a president, like all of us, draws on his past to shape his future.[8] The degree and quality of a president's emotional involvement in an issue are powerful influences in many ways. How does he define the issue itself? How much attention does he pay to it? Which facts and people does he see as relevant to its resolution? And finally, what principles and purposes does he associate with the issue?*

---

* Although it is a fairly common practice—and was before Barber wrote his book—to report on a candidate's background, family, and associates, many people have reservations about pushing this into the realm of character analysis. Alexander George of Stanford University contends that Barber's methods are too poorly worked out to predict anything meaningful. He says that Barber's Nixon could "conceivably" become another Harry Truman.

Barber places presidents into four categories:

Active-positives are active ("want to change the world") and enjoy their job. When faced with opposition, they go around it or wait until it subsides. (Examples: Jefferson, Franklin Roosevelt, Truman, and, to a lesser extent, Kennedy.)

Active-negatives are also active but in a compulsive way ("trying to make up for something or to escape from anxiety into hard work"). Tending to persevere rigidly in a disastrous policy, they often end their careers in tragedy—as did Wilson, Lyndon Johnson, and Nixon.

Passive-positives respond to rather than shape events. They are open, compliant personalities. As President Taft's father said of him, it was good he was not a girl or he would have always been pregnant. Other presidents are unable to resist the pressures of friendship. Harding once confided to Kansas editor William Allen White, "My God, this is a hell of a job! I can take care of my enemies. But my damn friends, my goddamn friends,

White. They're the ones that keep me walking the floor at night!"

Passive-negatives pose the danger of drift, letting opportunities go by (e.g., Coolidge). Under certain circumstances, however, they can provide a welcome breathing spell (e.g., Eisenhower).

Having accurately assessed Nixon well before Watergate, one cannot help but ask, How does Barber assess Reagan? Given Reagan's 9-to-5 approach to the governorship of California, Barber sees him as passive. Given his infectious optimism—an obvious contrast to Nixon—Barber sees Reagan as positive. Barber does not see Reagan as too rigid (as some of Reagan's critics fear). Quite the contrary, the danger is that he might give in too readily to his advisers. Consequently, the effectiveness of the Reagan administration might turn on the quality of his advisers.

Systems analysis: The youngest contribution. The systems approach, or **systems analysis**, really began during World War II. The basic idea is to look at a complex problem as a system (a term we encountered earlier) or a model (i.e., a highly simplified version of the real thing). Systems analysis can help policymakers better understand the nature of a public policy by seeing how all the components interact. It can also help us, as students of American politics, to grasp in broad outline how the entire American political system operates. (At this point, you may want to turn ahead to Figure 1–5.)

We shall make frequent use of the systems approach in the book. Therefore a few more features of systems ought to be noted. For convenience we can lump these into structural and functional aspects. The former concerns the organization in space of the components of the system; the latter, concerns the dependence on time (e.g., exchange, flow, and growth).

The principal structural traits of every system are:[9]

1. The boundaries of the system (e.g., the borders of a country).
2. The components (e.g., institutions, people, and money).
3. A communication network that permits the exchange of energy and information among the components of the system.

The principal functional traits of every system are:

1. Flows of information, or elements that circulate through the system. Flows of elements are represented symbolically by heavy black arrows; flows of information are indicated by dotted-line arrows.
2. Valves that control the volume of various flows. Each valve is a center of decision that receives information and transforms it into action. Their symbolic representation is that of a valve:

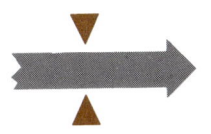

3. Feedback loops that play a decisive part in the behavior of a system. There are two kinds: positive (do more of what you are doing) and negative (do less).

Biology: Pretender to the throne? There are three reasons the influence of biology seems to have been felt in political science more than in other social sciences. First, a knowledge of biology is essential to government in order to deal effectively with such major problems as population, resources, health, and the environment. Second, recent advances in biology are already presenting society with hard ethical choices that can only be resolved in the political arena. Among these hard choices are what limits, if any, to put on creating new life forms through genetic engineering and what international restrictions to accept on "sea farming" projects. Harold Lasswell coined the term *somatarchy* to describe a state in which drugs might be used to control behavior of the people to assure stability.

Few political scientists would object to the first two reasons. The third reason for the influence of biology on politics, however, is more controversial. Some scholars, among them three Nobel Prize winners in biology, have suggested that studies of animal behavior (or ethology or **sociobiology**) can help explain political behavior.

Assume that from some distant galaxy the Chlorophyll People, Pod People, or whatever come to visit earth. From their perspective, human art, history, and politics would likely be viewed as specialized branches of biology. In other words, at some level of analysis, all animal behavior has certain things in common and these are biologically based. Advocates of this position would have biology replace politics as the master science.

But one need not go that far to concede that through the study of animal behavior we can gain insight into one's own political behavior. In recent years, writers have used such ethological concepts as territoriality, male bonding, personal space, dominance, aggression, and communalism to analyze human political behavior. Robin Fox, an anthropologist at Rutgers, offers this explanation of why human beings are not as free as they think they are:

> If a group of children were plunked on a remote island and left there, they would develop kinship patterns, an incest taboo, male initiation rites, totemism, ritual, exogamy, intergenerational male conflict, and an attempt by some males to dominate the mating system. The pattern can take a lot of stretching, but ultimately it must hold. Because it not only constrains us, it is us.[10]

This view is not without its critics.* It builds on the theory of evolution of species by means of natural selection. This theory accounts in general terms for an enormous range of natural phenomena—including the history, structure, and behavior of every species that has existed on earth, from lowly bacteria to humans. Figure 1–4 expresses this unity of life far better than words.

WHY STUDY POLITICS?

Let us face facts. Unlike selling real estate or raising earthworms, the scholarly investigation of politics is not a guaranteed money-making enterprise. But surely there are other grounds for undertaking such a study. In this section, I want to suggest four.

1. The study of politics develops critical thinking.
2. It reveals how power is acquired and exercised.
3. It helps us contend with a complex, ever-changing government.
4. It prepares us to make more effective decisions.

The Study of Politics Develops Critical Thinking

Most introductions to an academic discipline aim to give the student some factual knowledge and a modest ability to theorize. This book is

---

* Objections to sociobiology are threefold. First, with the exception of some very simple reflexes, there is scant evidence for a genetic basis for human behavior. Second, because it could be used to forgive ourselves for and even to justify violence and greed, sociobiology is politically dangerous. And third, to say that human beings are no more than very clever animals is to deny the spiritual dimension of human life. How, in other words, can a biologist ever explain Bach's *St. Matthew Passion?*

Still, recent anthropological thinking (as typified in Donald Johanson and Maitland Edey's *Lucy*) does suggest the social nature of human evolutionary history. Data from animal experiments indicate that animals are biologically predisposed to learn some responses much more quickly than others. The logic of evolution suggests that the same should hold for human beings. Furthermore, behavior-genetic studies have demonstrated genetic influences on such socially relevant characteristics as extraversion, activity level, and impulsivity.

FIGURE 1-4
Comparison of the Embryos of Vertebrate Species at Three Stages of Development

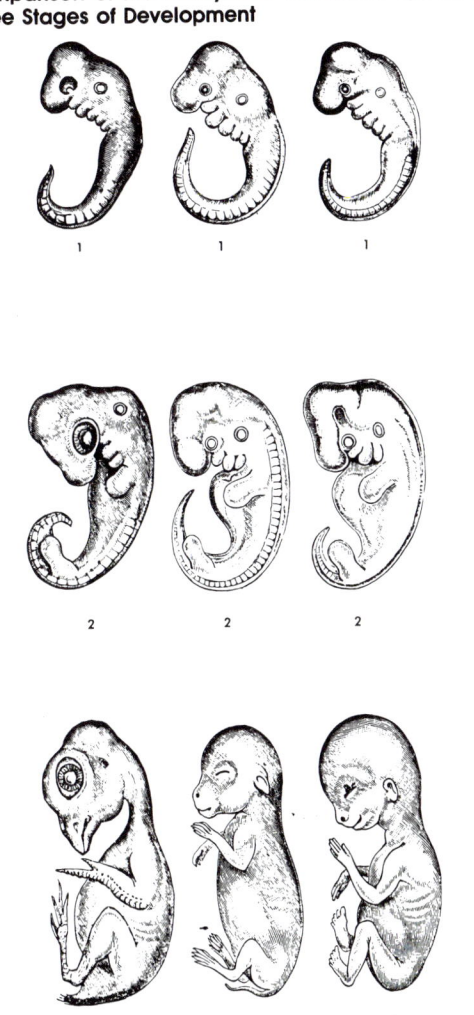

chick   rabbit   man

Sociobiology is far less anthropocentric than the other social sciences, which place humankind in a special place in a catalog of the social species on earth. Sociobiologists view each living form as an evolutionary experiment. They attempt to compare these species and construct general principles of social behavior.

Source: William T. Keeton, *Biological Science*, 2d ed. (New York: W. W. Norton, 1972).

no exception. Both goals are necessary and proper.

Unfortunately, these two goals do not always serve the best interest of the student who does not plan to go on to major in political science.

What such students need most is an introductory course aimed at developing a capacity for critical thought with respect to reports about political events in their everyday lives. That, after all, was the point of the parable of the cave with which we opened this chapter.

Outside of school we are exposed to more kinds of information, more masses of data, more multimedia stimuli than any previous generation. Take a moment to look at the Quiz. What is going on here? This information pours in electronically—unorganized and, worst of all, unevaluated.

Who among us is brilliant enough to specialize in all the fields of study suggested in this Niagara of political information? The possibility passed long ago. We can acquire certain skills that are applicable across a wide range of subjects. One such skill that the comprehensively educated man or woman will certainly need is critical analysis. Politics can serve as a sound introduction to that skill. The study of politics (to borrow what one of its great teachers said in a different context) "demands from us the boldness implied in the resolve to regard the average opinions as the extreme opinion which are at least as likely to be wrong as the most strange or the least popular opinions."[11]

The Study of Politics Reveals How Power Is Acquired and Exercised

Theodore Roosevelt was born of a prosperous New York family. After graduation from Harvard in 1880, he studied law for two years, then dropped it to enter the New York state legislature. For a well-to-do youth like Roosevelt, this was at the time considered a bizarre act. As his friends pointed out, his associates would be horse trainers, liquor dealers, and low politicians. His answer was characteristically direct: "In that case, they belong to the governing class, and you do not. I mean, if I can, to be one of the governing class."[12]

Several generations later, another young, well-to-do Harvard graduate faced the same

Why Is Mickey Mouse Cute?

As Mickey Mouse became increasingly well behaved over the years, his appearance became more youthful. As can be seen from the drawings below, his development revealed a larger relative head size and large eyes. These are all traits of juvenility.

Why did Disney make these changes? Biologists have spent a great deal of time trying to learn what features appeal to people and animals. According to one of the world's leading animal behaviorists, Konrad Lorenz, features of juvenility trigger "innate releasing mechanisms" for affection and nurturance in adult humans. The usefulness of this response can scarcely be questioned; we have nurtured babies to preserve the human species. Many animals happen to possess some features also shared by human babies but not by human adults. Lorenz thinks that, because of this similarity, we cultivate them as pets and admire them in the wild. Thus, most of us are attracted to the animals in the left column of the illustration below.

SOURCE: Stephen Jay Gould, "Mickey Mouse Meets Konrad Lorenz," *Natural History* (May 1979).

---

problem. After winning his first hard political election, John F. Kennedy became impatient with his Ivy League friends and professors, who regarded his pursuit of political power as distasteful. Why get out of bed in darkness on a freezing morning to shake hands at a factory gate or deal with unsavory district leaders in a smoke-filled room? This is the way he answered them.

> In America, politicians are looked down upon because of their free and easy compromises. However, I do think it is well for us to understand that politicians are dealing with human beings, with all their varied ambitions, desires, and backgrounds, and many of these compromises are unavoidable. We must recognize that if we do not take an interest in our political life we can easily lose at home what so many young men have so bloodily won abroad.[13]

Few today are so frank about their quest for power as Roosevelt or Kennedy. A need for achievement or higher income is acceptable. But we distrust people who openly seek power. Yet power, which we defined as the ability to influence the behavior of others, provides the basis for the attainment of the most noble and worth social goals. Its absence is invariably marked by immobility. When reformers fragment power by parceling it out to independent city boards and commissions, not enough power

1 / WHAT IS POLITICS?   19

United Press International Photo

United Press International Photo

World Wide Photos

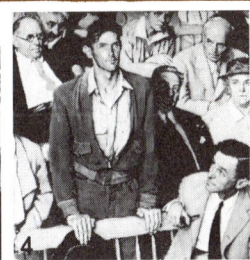

The Metropolitan Museum of Art, George A. Hearn Fund, 1952

The Blame!

What is going on here?

Reprinted by permission of the Chicago Tribune-New York News Syndicate, Inc.

J. Ross Baughman/Visions

United Nations/Y. Nagata

Quiz

Who said it and why?

8. "Syrian peace-keeping troops pounded right-wing Christian militias in and around Beirut yesterday in the worst explosion of fighting since the Lebanese civil war that supposedly ended almost two years ago."

Allen Green

9. "My goal is a budget deficit less than half what it was when I was running for office."

10. "Northeast Ohio Regional Sewer District."

11. "The fact that no member of the general public has been injured by nuclear power in over 25 years of nuclear plant operation made the utility industry too sanguine about potential risks."

Et cetera

12. Who is this man (left) and what is he doing?

13. How do you get a passport for traveling?

14. What can you do if you think you have been turned down for a job because of race or sex?

15. Can a state bar anyone from voting because of age? Can you lose your right to vote if you refuse to pay taxes?

16. If the government wants to build a highway through your bedroom, will you have to find another place to sleep?

17. Your neighbor's dog barks, keeping you awake. You have spoken to the neighbor but the dog continues to bark. What do you do now?

18. If you want an aerial photograph of your hometown (like the one of San Francisco that appears at the beginning of Chapter 11), to whom do you write?

19. How could you get a $5,000 loan for your record store at less than half the interest rate your bank charges? Could you get a similar amount to put on a stage play?

20. This summer you plan to visit a nearby national forest. You want to know when the camping season is, whether reservations are required, how much it will cost to stay, and a lot more. What do you do?

21. For the first time in your life, you find yourself unemployed. What do you do?

22. You have a term paper to do on solar energy. Library holdings are meager. How do you go about getting government information on this subject cheap?

23. And, while you are getting the solar information, you decide to also get government information on yourself. How would you find out what the government has found out about you?

* Answers on p. 27.

Courtesy of Harvard University Archives

The 26th president of the United States as an undergraduate, age 21. Not ambivalent about the pursuit of power, Theodore Roosevelt used it to win the Nobel Peace Prize in 1906.

remains for the city to deliver needed services. Despite awesome formal powers, the president can be as much a victim of bureaucratic inertia as anyone. "I sit here all day," President Truman once said, "trying to persuade people to do the things they ought to have sense enough to do without my persuading them. . . . That's all the power of the president amounts to."[14]

And what holds true for presidents, mayors, and community organizations also holds true for business managers. Research clearly shows that one distinguishing feature of managerial work compared with other professions (such as medicine and computer science) is its dependence on the activities of other people—superiors, subordinates, colleagues, suppliers, customers, competitors, union officials, government bureaucrats, etc. Few realize how this requires skill in acquiring and exercising power and how many management failures are the result of deficiencies in this skill.

I do not want to be misunderstood. Power, as used here, does not involve dominance and submission; it does not mean the bending of one human being's will at the expense of another's self-esteem. Rather, the exercise of power entails such things as taking the time to develop friendly relationships with key people outside your own organization, whose support you will need to do your job; it entails recognizing the importance of timing, accurate information, and perceptions in the successful completion of a job; and it entails much more.

If one accepts the idea that power is a social necessity, the problem then becomes how to learn about its exercise. One answer is to learn on the job through trial and error. Obviously, this has disadvantages. Why not learn from the past actions of those who have made their marks in politics? Isn't the modern science of management only a continuation of the old art of government? When we study management theory side by side with political theory, and management case histories side by side with political history, we very quickly see that we are only studying two very similar branches of the same subject. Each illuminates the other. But we have much more political history to draw upon. Therefore management situations are illuminated more often.

The Study of Politics Helps Us Contend with a Complex, Ever-Changing Government

Like it or not, few of us can avoid dealing with federal, state, and local governments. And none can avoid the effects of what these governments do. The last 10 questions in the Quiz make that clear enough.

Still, the study of politics is not going to give you specific answers to all such questions. Political science is not concerned with zip codes. But one thing it is concerned with is the struts and cables of that contraption called government. To the extent you learn that, you become a little more savvy about where to go for answers.

Unfortunately, the machinery is always being changed; government programs and organization are constantly being phased in and out. The full implication of the preceding statement should be layed on the table, preferably under Klieg lights.

Government has such a large, pervasive influence on society and, at the same time, is constantly changing. Therefore the study of politics becomes, in a profound sense, the study of the future—your future. Let me illustrate with a few examples:

The quality of air going into your lungs as you read this book is largely determined by government policy. Thanks to the passage by Congress of a series of tough clean air laws through the 1970s, the overall trend in most urban areas in the United States was towards continued improvement. Such improvements translate into reduced health risks. (According to some research, as much as 90 percent of all cancer is environmentally related.)

The nature of information going into your brain is partially determined by government policy. In the view of communications experts, the Communications Act of 1934 was fashioned when the telegraph was the industry backbone and telephone and radio were still in infancy. The dizzying array of innovations fostered by the marriage of computers and telecommunications and the explosion in home entertainment systems has left the act hopelessly out of date. Now Congress and the Federal Communications Commission are redesigning the old law to promote greater diversity and competition. The following are among the planned proposals: Remove restrictions from the cable television industry; limit total commercial time; and increase the number of TV and radio stations. These changes, in turn, could foster even more profound changes. Fifty video channels could be available to the average household; long-distance calls could cost less; and more home work centers could be linked by telecommunications with a central office.

Politics affects home life in controversial ways. Does home childbirth, which is a growing trend, constitute "child abuse"? In 1978, three couples in three separate states, who had opted to have their children born in their homes rather than in a hospital, were accused of child abuse. In one case, the police, acting on an obstetrician's complaint, forcibly took the woman from her home while she was in labor and transported her to a hospital. In another case, a woman wanted natural childbirth and refused an injection to hasten her labor; the hospital tried to get a court order forcing her to accept the drug.

The government can determine whether it is legal to kill a fetus. It can decide whether a 12-year-old child who wants to live in the United States can be ordered to return to the Soviet Union with his parents. And it can decide whether the words "Thou shalt not kill" may be posted in Kentucky schoolrooms. (Answers: yes, yes, no.)

The government determines how much money you have. The obvious way is through taxes. According to the Tax Foundation, Inc., a research group based in Washington, D.C., the average American working an eight-hour day spends two hours and 52 minutes to earn enough to pay his or her taxes. But government also determines how much money you have in slightly less direct ways—namely, through inflation. In Chapter 13, we shall see the decisive effect government actions can have on the level of inflation in society.

Some people who think they are winners in the inflation game might be surprised. Look at this example:

	1974	1979
Gross income	$20,000	$29,280
Federal taxes	3,282	5,434
Aftertax income	16,718	23,946
Aftertax income in 1974 dollars	16,716	16,301

In other words, if you made $20,000 in 1974 and almost $30,000 in 1979, you might have reason to feel good. But as the figures above show, you are actually worse off in 1979. Your added dollars are worth 30 percent less, and you are in a higher tax bracket. Result: Your purchasing power declines by $415. Your $10,000 raise is an illusion, like shadows on the wall of the cave. Imagine where you would be if you had not gotten that large raise. As you can see in Table 1–2, in 1979, only four groups out of 46 were winners in the government-run inflation game.

Government is the most expensive purchase you will probably ever make in your lifetime. Today government takes twice as much of the average American's income as mortgage payments do. But unlike house payments, which end in 30 or so years, payments to the government never stop. As *New York Times* columnist Russell Baker has recently pointed out, even after you die you are expected to continue those payments—via the inheritance tax.

Finally, what will happen if the Equal Rights Amendment eventually does pass? Almost certainly, women could be drafted and assigned to combat. Men would still have to pay alimony and child support to women who need it; but women in some cases would have to pay their ex-husbands. Single-sex schools would probably no longer receive public funds. Contrary to what ERA's extreme opponents claim, it would not legalize prostitution, require coed restrooms, or destroy the family. Its ratification would represent more a social evolution than social revolution.

The Study of Politics Prepares Us to Make More Effective Decisions

For most Americans, democracy amounts to voting every four years for one of two presidential candidates who sound very much the same.

TABLE 1-2
Gainers and Losers in Real Pay in 1979

	Change in Real Weekly Pay After Allowing for Higher Prices, Taxes*		Change in Real Weekly Pay After Allowing for Higher Prices, Taxes*
Those Keeping Up:			
Farm operators	+$17.13	Lumber workers	−8.17
Meatpackers	+6.86	Furniture workers	−8.22
Metal miners	+4.23	Chemical workers	−8.33
Aluminum workers	+3.22	Shoe-factory workers	−8.33
Those Falling Back:		Oil-refinery workers	−8.56
Social security recipients	−0.59	Printing-and-publishing workers	−9.19
Steelworkers	−1.50	Sporting-goods workers	−9.42
Aircraft workers	−2.89	Electrical-equipment workers	−9.73
Toy-factory workers	−2.89	Local bus drivers	−10.19
Retired Federal workers	−3.20	Federal workers	−10.39
Oil and gas-production workers	−3.70	Schoolteacher	−11.78
Coal miners	−4.74	Construction workers	−12.09
Bank employees	−4.87	Telephone workers	−13.71
Textile workers	−5.05	Brewery workers	−13.71
Retail clerks	−5.92	Electric and gas-utility workers	−13.99
Fully disabled veterans	−6.87	Tire-factory workers	−18.56
Medical-supplies workers	−8.09	Auto workers	−23.58

Note: Latest available weekly pay usually June 1979. Farm operators often include family members instead of individual workers.

* Figures on change in real pay are changes after federal income and social security taxes and adjustment for the rise in consumer prices. Assumes a family of four for tax purposes, except for retired federal workers, who are assumed to be married couples. Social security recipients and fully disabled veterans pay no taxes.

Sources: *U.S. News & World Report* table—basic data: U.S. Departments of Labor, Agriculture, and Health, Education, and Welfare; Veterans' Administration; Office of Personnel Management; National Education Association.

If the Equal Rights Amendment to the Constitution is ever adopted it would be another example of how government affects our lives. Already, 16 states have passed their own equal rights amendments, and the U.S. Air Force has awarded wings to women pilots. Second Lieutenant Marilyn Koon, one of the first, is shown here walking away from her T-38 after a training flight.

Between elections, as the major issues are actually resolved, democracy is reduced to crude speculations of opinion polling (see Chapter 5).

What, then, is the alternative? Should all the people be absorbed all the time by public affairs? Charles Peters, editor of the *Washington Monthly*, thinks not. To Peters, true democracy in contemporary America means

> enlisting the judgment, understanding, and common sense of the public on the issues that affect the nation rather than leaving those decisions to vaguely accountable legislators, and the technicians they employ.
>
> As a first step toward this kind of democracy, the schools must do a better job of preparing for us for the choices we have to make. . . . Students needn't be told what kind of health care system is best—but they should understand the full consequences of our present approach, and of the five or six possible alternatives. They should be helped to see how costs add up in our various programs of income support. And they should be prepared to deal with problems we haven't even heard of yet.[15]

That may sound like an awfully tall order. But it is not quite as tall as it seems. The kind of democracy for which Peters calls really amounts to no more than remembering a few principles about government policies. The most important principles, in a simplified form, might be briefly noted.

The first principle is that *the biggest costs of a policy are often the indirect ones*. Consider the proposal to bring back the draft. Military conscription is actually a form of taxation. Conscription simply imposes the costs of national defense on youth rather than the general public. If you have to pay very high wages to attract volunteers, then you know that defense is very costly. Conscription does not avoid those costs; it simply shifts the burden. Or take President Carter's 1979 plan to spend $88 billion to develop synthetic fuels, such as oil from coal, shale, tar sands, and biomass. The $88 billion could easily double if one considered the horrendous cost escalation on most plants of this kind and the environmental costs. Getting a half million barrels a day from shale would involve disposing of 250,000 tons of waste a year. The shale contains cancer-causing pollutants, and extracting its oil would require 5 percent of Colorado's river water.

The quest for a cleaner, safe automobile has hidden costs—as well as obvious benefits. A 1978 Chevrolet that listed for $9,674 would have cost less than $5,000 five years earlier. According to the Bureau of Labor Statistics, inflation accounts for only $1,500 of the $4,600 increase. Regulatory costs—safety rules, management costs, pollution controls, new plant facilities, safety regulations, and noise abatement—account for the $3,100 discrepancy. Moreover, fuel economy standards coming into effect in the early 1980s could add another $800 to the average retail price of cars.*

I want to stress that the foregoing analysis does not tell us that the draft, the synthetic fuels plan, or automobile regulation are wrong. The purpose of the examples is to suggest that, when making decisions about public policy, all costs need to be recognized.

The second principle is to *avoid isolating and particularizing public policy decisions.* We want the best equipment money can buy in *our* hospital. We want the best services and professional care available for *our* family and friends who are disabled. Without repudiating such sentiments, the second principle challenges us also to look as these problems in the aggregate and in comparison with other worthy programs. Suppose the federal government should, as a matter of public policy, provide your uncle with a kidney dialysis machine. This might cost taxpayers in the aggregate at least a billion dollars a year (others have uncles, too). That means the government has a billion dollars *less* to spend on something else—say, a cancer detection program or new judgeships (to reduce delays in bringing people to trial).

The third principle is that *most government programs are shaped like a brontosaurus.* At the start, they resemble the tip of the tail. But in the end they take on the girth of the brontosaurus torso. The Pentagon has shamelessly exploited both congressional and public ignorance of this principle with their foot-in-the-door financing proposals. "Well, just give us a meager $10 million to discuss the feasibility of a $2 billion submersible aircraft carrier."

The fourth principle is that *not all relationships between spending and services are linear.* In other words, doubling the funding of a program does not necessarily mean that services delivered will also double. And let me add a corollary: Government does not do everything equally well. It collects taxes, explores the moon, and promotes equal opportunity better than it stops crime, creates jobs, and (lately) educates children.

Principles like these will not tell you clearly and directly which policy is the correct one. What is correct and incorrect policy will depend—perhaps more than anything else—on our values. The paramount virtue of the principles is this: They help us avoid separating means and ends and thus supporting policies we are not prepared to pay for. In a democracy, wishful thinking abounds. The cardinal vice is that we demand many things for which we are not willing to pay the bill. We are much too disposed, political commentator Walter Lippmann once wrote, "to grandiose policies based on bluffing, to words that are not really meant, to clever tactics and ingenious stratagems."[16]

HOW THIS BOOK IS ORGANIZED

The remainder of this book consists of 13 chapters grouped into four separate but closely related parts (Figure 1–5).

Part 1: Fundamentals

Chapter 2 introduces you to the document that embodies the ideas upon which American politics is conducted—the Constitution. It is a remarkably brief, general statement by the founding fathers of how to solve one great political question: What form of government will best

---

* The figures on the extra cost of a Chevrolet appeared in *Time,* June 5, 1978. Trying to measure the total costs to business and consumers of government regulation has itself become a minor industry. The U.S. Congress Joint Economic Committee's *Special Study on Economic Change* provides a relatively objective survey of the state of the art. Murray L. Weidenbaum's *Business, Government and the Public* (Englewood Cliffs, N.J.: Prentice-Hall, 1981) provides a thorough view of the effect of government and public interest groups on the operations of business firms.

**FIGURE 1-5
The Key to This Book**

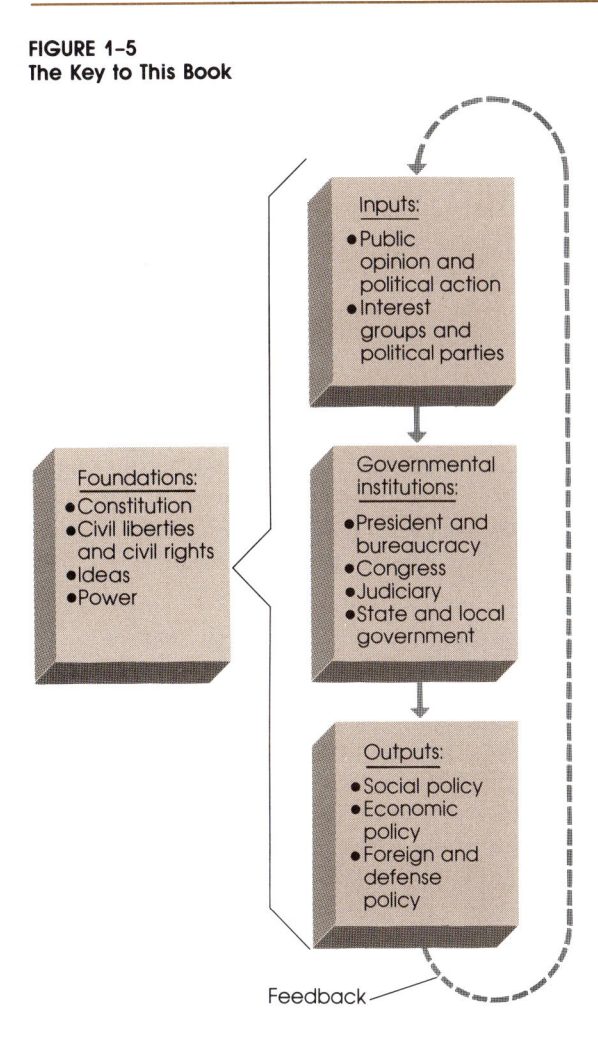

Foundations:
- Constitution
- Civil liberties and civil rights
- Ideas
- Power

Inputs:
- Public opinion and political action
- Interest groups and political parties

Governmental institutions:
- President and bureaucracy
- Congress
- Judiciary
- State and local government

Outputs:
- Social policy
- Economic policy
- Foreign and defense policy

Feedback

protect individual rights and long-term national interest against the temporary passions of a majority of the people yet preserve the spirit and form of popular government? The answer was to balance power carefully between the states and federal government and then among the three branches of the federal government (namely, the president, Congress, and the Supreme Court). The whole system is devised to see to it that, in fundamental matters affecting the liberties and property of individuals and the rights of local communities, the will of the people shall be thoroughly known before great changes are finally adopted.

Chapter 3 takes us even deeper into the realm of ideas. Here we consider one of the cornerstones of American politics—the ideal of equality in freedom. It is most forcefully expressed in the Declaration of Independence and the Bill of Rights (the first 10 amendments to the Constitution).

One does not consider such weighty matters as "equality in freedom" for very long without encountering some of the perennial questions of political theory. For example: What is human nature? What is the relationship between liberty and equality? Why obey government? Who should rule? Chapter 3, therefore, traces how some of the most powerful minds from Plato and Aristotle to a small but provocative group of modern thinkers have attempted to resolve such questions. (For a bird's-eye view of the family tree of political theory, look inside the back cover.) Chapter 4 should provide more than just a deeper understanding of the ideas of Chapter 2 and 3. It should also help you think through with greater clarity many of today's political controversies.

Chapter 4 deals with another fundamental concept that should advance our understanding of American politics—power. That chapter begins by considering why power has been relatively neglected in the literature of political science. Next, it addresses the issue of how to define and assess the distribution of political power in the United States. Then it considers the conditions under which power is likely to be employed by political leaders. The chapter will also explore the subject of how power is used and maintained. The chapter concludes by discussing the implications of a power perspective for understanding how governments work and fail to work.

Part 2: Inputs for the Political System

The term *inputs* refers to all those individual and group activities that affect the decision makers in government and, ultimately, public policy.

An important assumption of this book is that a relationship exists between the political ideas explored in Chapter 3 and political action. But, if ideas shape political behavior, the reverse is also true: Events in the political arena spark thought.

Chapter 5 examines how individuals form their political opinions. The chapter places particular emphasis on the role of television and other mass media in this process of opinion formulation. But there are other influences—family, schools, culture, etc. We shall explore these as well. The conclusion of the chapter focuses on how opinion manifests itself in political action. This action can take many forms: voting (the most common), donating money, writing letters, helping a political party, protesting, etc.

Chapter 6 considers the two major institutions through which citizens can collectively influence government—political parties and interest groups. (For a bird's-eye view of the history of American political parties, see the diagram inside the front cover.) The conclusion of the chapter focuses on the machinery by which the political community selects individuals for key leadership roles in the government. That machinery is complicated and antiquated. Yet somehow it continues to work like some enormous grandfather clock. Political scientists call this wheezy contraption the electoral system.

Part 3: Government Institutions

An **institution** is a well-established and structured pattern of relationships that exists over time. In Part 3 of this book, we shall focus on several fundamental institutions of the American political system.

The president and the bureaucracy that he tries to manage are the subjects of Chapter 7; Congress, Chapter 8; the courts, Chapter 9; and state and local governments, Chapter 10. Unlike most introductory treatments of these institutions, this book aims to emphasize how the citizen can cope with them. Rather than provide encyclopedia knowledge of how they operate, the book will zero in on the essential features. (For a bird's-eye view of the major institutions of American national government, look inside the back cover, right-hand page.)

Chapters 7 through 10 will also give some thought to how each of these institutions might be transformed in the next two decades. The vehicle for this effort is a series of "Future Files" that appears throughout Part 3.

Part 4: Outputs of the Political System

If the output of a widget factory is widgets, what can we say the output of this trillion-dollar outfit called government is? The answer, in short, is public policy.

One can classify public policies in a variety of ways. Perhaps the simplest—if not the most elegant or thorough—is to say that most public policy affects one of four things: individual rights, social problems (unemployment, welfare, crime, health care, education, housing, transportation, telecommunications, energy, and ecology), the economy (which includes the business community), and global relations. Chapter 11 looks at individual rights; Chapter 12 will focus on social policy; Chapter 13, economic management; and Chapter 14, foreign relations and national defense.

Admittedly, these four categories are broad. But they are at least concrete and readily identifiable. (For an indication of how spending in these areas has shifted in the last several years, see the inside of the back cover.)

Chapter Key

Broadly defined, politics is concerned with human relationships involving conflict, consensus (or agreement), and power. This book focuses, however, only on those relationships that are associated with the running of American government.

Any government can be placed somewhere along a continuum that runs from democracy through increasingly authoritarian states to totalitarianism. Although there are many ways to classify governments—monarchies (rule by one), aristocracies (rule by the entitled few), plutocracies (rule by the rich), direct democracy, representative democracy, etc.—the use of this continuum is probably the most basic.

Economic systems also can be placed on a continuum. At each end is an "ideal type"—that is, a form that exists only as a model and is never perfectly achieved in the real world. At one end is a market-based system (capitalism); at the other is a command system (socialism). Most systems in the world today are mixed; that is, they combine features of both.

A democratic nation can have any type of economy, as can an authoritarian nation. However, a survey of the world's nearly 170 nations reveals that democracy, wherever found, appears to ride on the back of capitalism. If Poland had continued its drift towards democracy without altering its economic institutions, it could have proven the exception.

The title of this book signals its aim—to advance your understanding of politics as practiced in the United States. In the pursuit of this objective, I shall draw heavily upon the literature of political science. The systematic study of politics is one of the oldest of human endeavors. For that reason perhaps it draws quite a lot on other disciplines—in particular, economics, history, philosophy, statistics, behavioral science, systems analysis, and biology.

This introductory chapter tried to peak your interest in politics and show how your income and well-being plainly depend more and more on political choices. But it never presented a more forceful argument for studying politics than the one Aristotle mounted a long, long time ago. What makes politics important is that it produces the conditions necessary for a really civilized life. Man, Aristotle wrote, is distinctively a political animal, the only being that subjects himself to law. To live beyond politics, a being must be either a beast or a god.

Answers to Quiz

What is going on here?
1. To protest certain "anti-Indian" legislation introduced in Congress, many American Indians in 1978 participated in a 3,000-mile march to the nation's capital. This "spiritual journey" illustrates the ability of the

news media to shape the presentation of issues and the perception of those issues by the public. The real purpose of the journey was to promote the cause of *one* element of the Indian people—those opposed to established tribal governments—against another element—those elected to represent Indian people through such governments. As Wilcomb E. Washburn, director of the Office of American Studies at the Smithsonian Institution, points out: "To provide a focus so rich with visual symbolism unwittingly honors not the Indian leaders elected by the tribes but those who have sought unsuccessfully to depose them."

2. Major candidates for president ardently woo rock stars, movie stars, Nashville pickers, and popular singers. The reason is that, while individual campaign contributions are limited to $1,000, there is no limit on the amount that can be raised at a benefit appearance. In 1980, Jimmy Carter pursued country-western singer Willie Nelson; Ronald Reagan enlisted the support of Frank Sinatra. Governor Edmund G. Brown, Jr. (shown on left in picture) had a little help from his friend singer Linda Ronstadt (shown with him); his strong stand against nuclear power brought him additional support from Jane Fonda.

3. Understanding politics means realizing that presidents, especially in hard times, always appeal to certain symbols. In the picture, President Harry S Truman is decorating General Douglas MacArthur during a meeting on Wake Island. The ostensible purpose of the meeting was to settle U.S. policy toward the Korean War, which had just began. Some suggest that the trip, intended to insure that MacArthur clearly understood Truman's decision, was at least influenced by less lofty aims. With congressional elections at hand, Truman reasoned that he could capture valuable press attention by a dramatic meeting with MacArthur. At the time the general had become, in effect, a popular symbol. In short, the meeting may have been only "presidential theater."

4. Democracy in action? The reality of town meetings is not quite what this idealized picture by Norman Rockwell would lead you to believe. To the extent that such meetings are dominated by special interests—e.g., land developers—they are something less than representative of the entire community.

5. When faced with an apparently intractable crisis, politicians tend to follow an old maxim: Elevate the crisis to the level of "war." This maxim has been scrupulously adhered to in the face of a continuing U.S. energy crisis. It is not clear precisely who or what the enemy is in the war the public is requested to support. In 1979, President Carter's aides wanted him to name OPEC the villain. Rather than make an enemy of someone who can give you more trouble than you can handle, the president decided to identify Congress and the oil companies. They were pushovers. Public trust in Congress was less than in the president, and nobody loves rich oil executives. Not surprisingly, both were quick to point the finger of suspicion back to the president.

6. Politics is values in conflict. The picture shows a group of feminists on a tour of Times Square pornographic attractions—prostitutes, bookstores, topless bars, and X-rated movies. They argue that the portrayal of sexual violence tends to encourage the use of aggression among people exposed to it; at a minimum, pornography exploits women. Some legal scholars object on the grounds that obscenity and pornography are rights protected by the First Amendment (discussed in Chapter 12). Women who would have the government ban sexist material are, they charge, censors. In any event, understanding politics requires a sensitivity to legitimate differences in values across social groups.

7. Behind the sober conversations and elegant dinners at the delegates lounge at the U.N. building in New York City is a world where the business of intelligence gathering is an assumed way of life. Spying, in fact, is so pervasive that some diplomats call the United Nations "the stock exchange of global intelligence operations."

Who said it?

8. From the beginning of a report in the *Washington Post* on the battle in Lebanon. The terms have little relation to reality. How can an invasion of one country by another be a "civil war"? How can invasion forces be "peacekeeping troops"? Why are people defending Lebanon's constitutional arrangements called "right-wing Christians"? The quote is a clear-cut example of what Fred C. Iklé of the RAND Corporation terms "semantic infiltration." Simply put, it means we come to adopt the language of our adversaries in describing political reality. Thus Afghans fighting against the Soviet invasion are "rebels"; communist-led rebel movements are "national liberation fronts"; Soviet hard-liners are "conservatives."

9. From a 1978 white paper on the federal budget. It is a good example of what William Safire calls "weasel words"—that is, ambiguous speech, deliberately fuzzy phraseology. Why didn't Carter say, "When I became president"? Simple. "When I was running for office" pushes the comparison back eight months, to a time when economic policy required a high deficit to bring down unemployment.

10. In 1979 the Cleveland Regional Sewer District asked the court permission to change its name. But the district was not bothered by the word "sewer" (which some euphemistically call "wastewater" treatment). The word *sewer* was all right; the word that had to go was *Cleveland*. Why? The sewer district periodically sells bonds to the investing public. Some investors were leery of putting their money into anything with the "Cleveland" label.

11. The Kemeny Commission's report on the Three Mile Island nuclear accident was a sober, careful, and objective assessment of nuclear dangers. The report is a good example of how, in politics, different points of view are sometimes neither right nor wrong; they are partially correct and useful within limits. The principal effect of the accident on humans, according to the commission, was "mental stress," partly caused by misinformation put out by government officials.

Et cetera

12. A dynamic young congressman striding purposefully to his office? Not quite. It is Bernard Shapiro, chief of staff of the Joint Committee on Taxation. A tax proposal is seldom considered until he passes on it—a claim very few members of Congress could make. Though congressional staffs are little known outside Washington, their power is considerable. So, to understand American politics, remember the iceberg theorem: Seven eighths of everything can't be seen.

For answers to questions 13 through 23, refer to Appendix C.

Must not a critic of society understand something? Is every ignorant carper to be dignified into social critic? Significant criticism is a form of appreciation; appreciation requires understanding.

But the critical art may require more, even, than perceptiveness and understanding. Just as there is something strange about an art critic who does not love art, so there is something strange—and even fraudulent—about the critic of society, of politics, of government, who does not love the object of his critical attention. Burke says somewhere that one must approach the flaws in his society as one would approach the wounds of a parent. It may be difficult, these days, to know how to do either, but what is required are understanding and love.

Joseph Tussman (1977)

PART 1 Foundations

THE KEY TO THIS BOOK

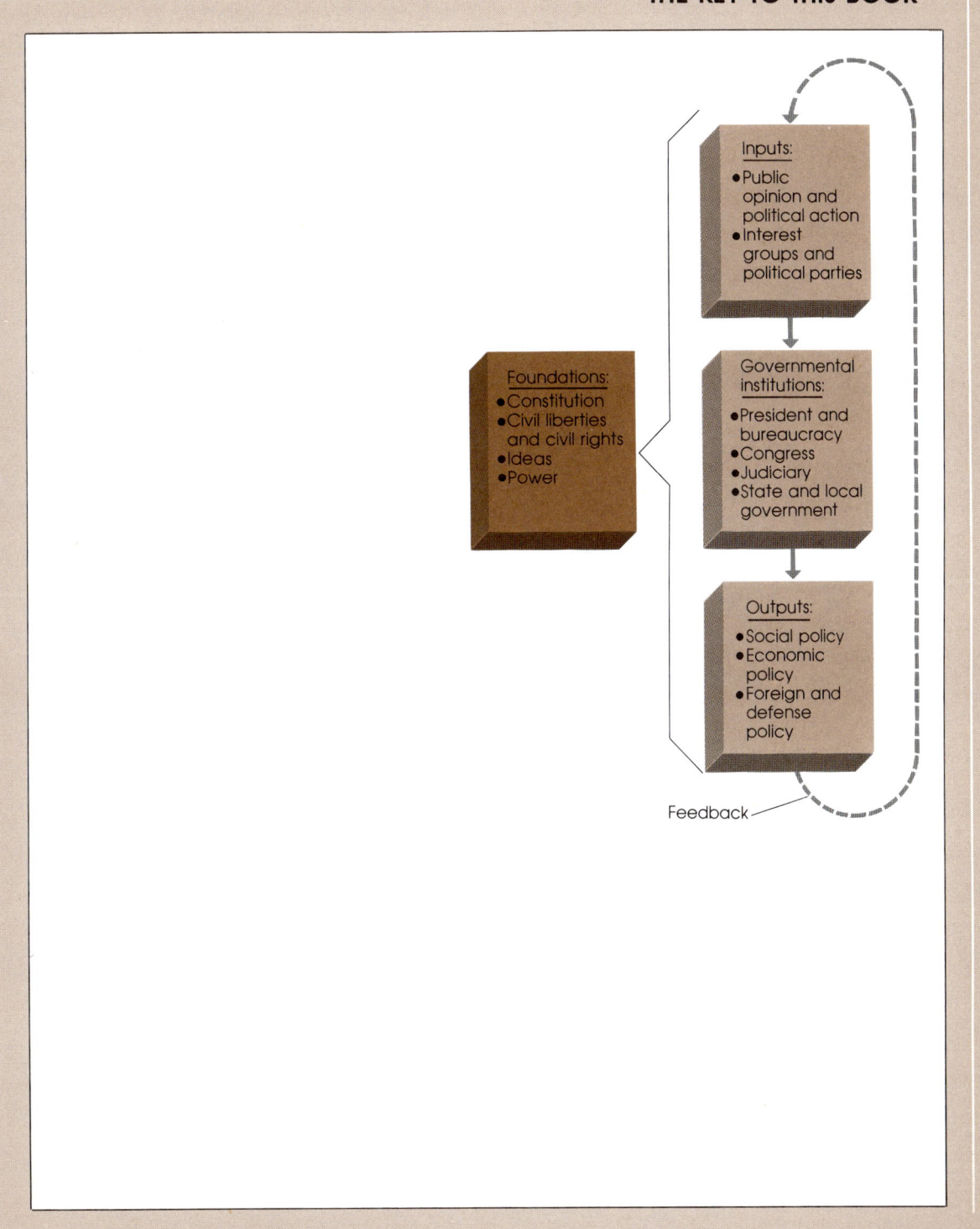

Inputs:
- Public opinion and political action
- Interest groups and political parties

Foundations:
- Constitution
- Civil liberties and civil rights
- Ideas
- Power

Governmental institutions:
- President and bureaucracy
- Congress
- Judiciary
- State and local government

Outputs:
- Social policy
- Economic policy
- Foreign and defense policy

Feedback

United Press International Photo

2 | Architecture of a Republic: The Constitution

After studying this chapter, you should be able to answer these questions:

1. What were the major events leading to the colonies' break with Great Britain? Do they form a pattern?
2. Was the American Revolution a true revolution?
3. What are the strengths and weaknesses of the Articles of Confederation?
4. What were the major compromises at the Constitutional Convention of 1787?
5. What are the main features of the U.S. Constitution?
6. How does the Constitution separate and balance power?
7. How can the Constitution be changed?

Terms you should know:

Antifederalists
Articles of Confederation
Bill of Rights
commerce clause
concurrent powers
Connecticut Compromise
delegated or expressed power
"doctrine of nullification"
elastic clause
enumerated powers
executive interpretation
executive privilege
expressed powers
federalism
Federalists
"full faith and credit"
impeachment
implied powers

inherent powers
judicial review
Marbury v. *Madison* (1803)
McCulloch v. *Maryland* (1910)
"necessary and proper clause"
New Jersey Plan
ratification
republican government
representative government
reserved powers
separation of power
Shay's Rebellion
sovereignty
supremacy clause
10th Amendment
unitary system
Virginia Plan
Youngstown Sheet and Tube Co. v. *Sawyer* (1952)

Samuel Eliot Morison, historian and seaman, died a month before America celebrated its bicentennial with an armada of "tall ships." Sometime earlier Morison made this observation about American clipper ships:

> Their architects, like poets who transmute nature's message into song, obeyed what wind and wave had taught them, to create the noblest of all sailing vessels, and the most beautiful creations of man in America. With no extraneous ornament except a figurehead, a bit of carving and a few lines of gold leaf, their one purpose of speed over the great ocean routes was achieved by perfect balance of spars and sails to the curving lines of the smooth black hull; and this harmony of mass, form and color was practiced to the music of dancing waves and of brave winds whistling in the rigging. These were our Gothic cathedrals, our Parthenon. . . .[1]

I quote this brief passage because the metaphor of state as ship is so apt. And well it should be. The word *government* itself comes from an ancient Greek word meaning "to direct a ship" (see box). In this chapter, we shall see how a relatively small group of extraordinary men became architects for a new nation. The beauty of their creation had much in common with the beauty Morison saw in the clipper ship.

The plans for the new nation are contained in a document now on display in the National Archives Building in Washington, D.C. (Russians embalm dead leaders, like Lenin, and put them on display. Americans encase old documents and put them on display.) It is the U.S. Constitution. It has no extraneous ornaments and can be read and comprehended by any bright high school student in a single sitting. Designed for speed over great routes, it has sailed through two centuries and into a third.

This feat was accomplished by carefully balancing all the parts in a *republican* or representative form of government. The Constitution is a kind of framework that assigns power and duties to various institutions and holds those who govern accountable to the governed.

The U.S. Constitution is not a work of art. The artist, animated by fancy and guided by taste, attempts to duplicate the characters and passions of the human spirit. The authors of the Constitution, guided by an abiding faith in reason, sought to check human passions, to protect freedom from the "thirst of power, from rapacious and ambitious passions." Nor is the Constitution a work of engineering. The engineer, directed by a few general and even mechanical rules, attempts merely to construct a useful, functional edifice. The authors of the Constitution aimed higher. They sought—as does the architect—to relate human requirement and available resources to furnish a practical and aesthetic balance.

This chapter is in three sections. The first

Etymology and Political Science

Political scientists can—though few do—make language itself a major focus of investigation. They can inquire into what is meant by what is said and how syntax either generates or constrains political thought. By going to roots of human language, they can condense today's words into primal nodes of truth.

Take the Greek word *kybernates*, which means the steersman or helmsman of a ship. The Greek word for govern was *kybernan*. In Latin, this became *gubernare* (to steer, to govern). And eventually it appeared in old French as *governer*. Not only do the words *governor* and *government* derive from this term, but so does the word for the modern science of communication and control, *cybernetics*. I cannot imagine a more compact explanation of government than "steersman."

briefly retells the story of how it came to pass that 13 loosely related colonies, with a population of about 3 million free people, could break their ties with a powerful mother country (Great Britain) and create a new nation. The aim here must be more than to tell a good story, however. In particular, I want to show how political events that often seem to unfold so gradually, so inexorably, are actually kicked along by the skill (or incompetence) of key participants.

The second section reviews the efforts of the colonies, once freed from Great Britain, to design a government structure that would provide protection from external threats and tranquility at home. We shall see how they eventually settled on the Constitution through trial and effort.

The last section takes a close look at the principal features of that document.

THE AMERICAN REVOLUTION

Differences with Great Britain Mount

The government of the early American colonies was in the hands of the British king and his advisers. For over 100 years, the colonists found this arrangement satisfactory. To be sure, the king sent his governors to the colonies, but the British did not interfere much with personal freedom. They allowed colonists, through elected representatives, to decide about taxes, public improvements, and other important matters.

Between 1754 and 1765, with British imperial power in North America at its height, some changes began to occur. The British became engaged in a war with France, which spilled over into North America. The French, with their Indian allies, fought against the British, with their colonial allies. By 1763 the French were beaten.

The British government had spent large sums of money in fighting a war on two sides of the Atlantic. Now it tried to collect (for services rendered) part of the cost of the war from the colonists. Therefore, it proceeded in 1765 to put a heavy stamp tax on all kinds of business in the colonies. Part of the revenue would go for internal improvements; the rest would go to the mother country. Even today we accept stamps on bottles of liquor and decks of cards. But the colonists were displeased. The real issue was not the money but the principle; they were being *taxed without representation*. So what was wrong with that? Simply, it ran counter to a rather old English right of voting for or against the plan of taxation. The colonists had no representatives sitting in the British Parliament; and their own elected assemblies had never been consulted.

Over the next 10 years, grumbles turn into resistance. But the government of King George III always managed to find new ways of interfering. Why had the king not managed the conflict better? Some recent medical investigation suggests that George III was the victim of the hereditary disease prophyria, which produced great pain, paralysis, overactivity, and delirium. Whatever the problem, his own minister considered him quite mad.

In the colonies, each of his new initiatives was countered. We need not recount every thrust and counterthrust here. (Some of the more important ones appear in Figure 2–1.) The important point is that, between 1763 and July 4, 1776, the tempo of the match between the mother country and her colonies increased. Why was this so? The deficiencies of the British government in conflict management are only half of the story. The other half is the amazing ability of the colonial leaders to use each provocative British action to help convince the people that their rights to self-government were being lost. The "Boston Massacre" is an excellent example of how the technique worked (see boxed material).

By the summer of 1774, the situation had deteriorated to the point where delegates from the colonies were meeting as a **Continental**

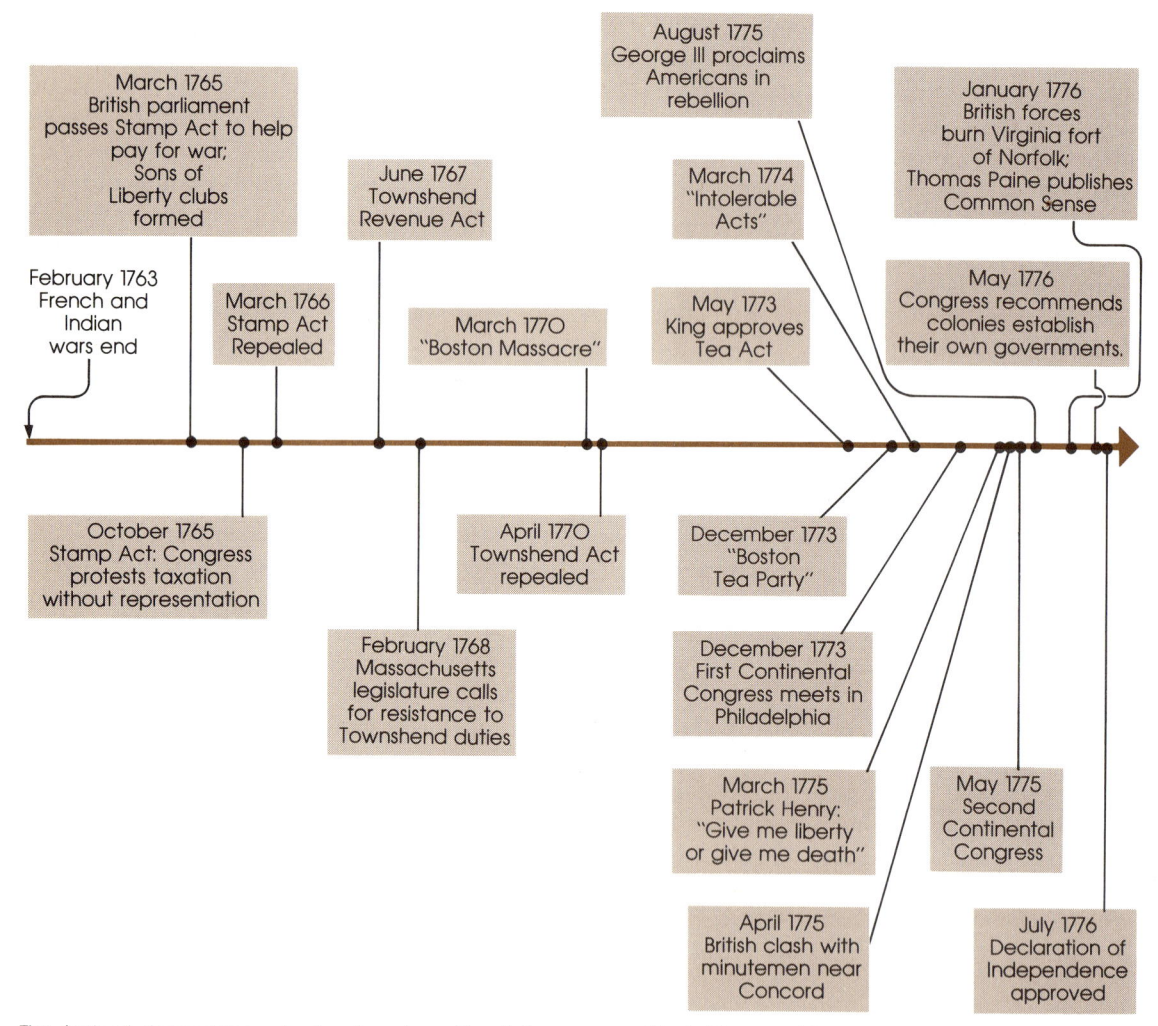

FIGURE 2-1
Events Leading to Independence: Thrust and Counterthrust

March 1765 British parliament passes Stamp Act to help pay for war; Sons of Liberty clubs formed

June 1767 Townshend Revenue Act

August 1775 George III proclaims Americans in rebellion

March 1774 "Intolerable Acts"

January 1776 British forces burn Virginia fort of Norfolk; Thomas Paine publishes Common Sense

February 1763 French and Indian wars end

March 1766 Stamp Act Repealed

March 1770 "Boston Massacre"

May 1773 King approves Tea Act

May 1776 Congress recommends colonies establish their own governments.

October 1765 Stamp Act; Congress protests taxation without representation

April 1770 Townshend Act repealed

December 1773 "Boston Tea Party"

February 1768 Massachusetts legislature calls for resistance to Townshend duties

December 1773 First Continental Congress meets in Philadelphia

March 1775 Patrick Henry: "Give me liberty or give me death"

May 1775 Second Continental Congress

April 1775 British clash with minutemen near Concord

July 1776 Declaration of Independence approved

The task of determining why the American Revolution occurred is fruitless and impossible. But we do know how and when loyalty to England began to decline in the colonies. We also know who the main participants were and what they did.

The year 1763 marked the beginning of a 13-year period in which the seeds of independence began to germinate. Grievances about taxes turned to grumbles about lack of political representation. Throughout the period, London set the pace. But colonial leaders used provocative British actions to radicalize American politics. One of the earliest such actions was the Stamp Act of 1765. Soon the grumbles turned to resistance. By 1770 the issue of taxation had been replaced by a more fundamental one: Could the English Parliament make laws enforceable in the colonies? In the end, resistance and isolated riots had turned into open rebellion.

Events and colonial leaders had conspired to destroy what had been a workable arrangement between England and the colonies. This was hardly what the leaders of the mother country had intended.

Congress in Philadelphia. They had hoped to get fairer treatment by sending a petition to the king. The session's most important act was to proclaim the severing of commercial relations with Great Britain. Though most people still considered themselves English, some were willing to fight to get away from Great Britain. The king was not amused.

What could he do? Though radical colonists revealed a sense of independence already felt by many Americans, an 18th-century imperial mind could not grasp its significance any more than it could understand the photoelectric effect. The word *revolution*—at least in the sense that it would come to be known shortly—did not even exist. Still, the king and his advisers did know matters were not going quite right. If, on the one hand, they resorted to overt force, they could antagonize the more moderate colonists. On the other hand, they could not back down on the issue of **sovereignty**—that is, who had supreme power over the body politic. The 18th-century imperial mind did not work that way either.

As already noted, the war that ended in 1763 left Great Britain the most powerful nation in the world. In contemplating a war against this great power, the colonists had to remember that they were divided into 13 separate groups, confined to a narrow north-south strip between the Allegheny Mountains and the Atlantic, and loosely joined by a new Congress of delegates having no real authority (to raise money, for example). The colonies had no well-trained soldiers and no real armies. They had been successfully fighting against the Indians for over a hundred years. Now these farmers, trappers, and traders would be fighting on regular battlefields against well-drilled soldiers who had learned their trade on the most famous battlefields of Europe.

That, at any rate, was the strategic situation in April 1775, when a detachment of British soldiers marched up to Lexington, Massachusetts, where the colonists had begun to gather arms and fired what every American schoolchild knows was "the shot heard around the world." The colonists were now more or less in a war. Their leaders slowly became convinced that only complete independence from Great Britain would rally an effective resistance. The result was the Declaration of Independence,

What Is Going on Here?

(a) Wholesale slaughter of innocent civilians by redcoated stormtroopers
(b) A terrible breakdown in communications
(c) Skillful use of political propaganda

Library of Congress

Answer

On March 5, 1770, British troops stationed in Boston fired into a crowd and killed five men—three died on the spot, two died later of wounds. Paul Revere and Samuel Adams attacked the incident as wanton British brutality. Revere's interpretation of the incident he calls a "bloody massacre, perpetrated by the king" was one of the most widely circulated pieces of propaganda before the Revolution. The funeral of the victims was the occasion for a great patriot demonstration.

This interpretation, along with Revere's engraving, has lasted marvelously well over the last two centuries. Today both are pretty much standard fare in American history texts. Revere's engraving is especially evocative. But, as we saw in the opening chapter of this book, in the arena of politics things are not always quite what they seem on the surface.

What had actually happened was this. Behind the scenes, Samuel Adams had been using his able pen in colonial newspapers and pamphlets to stir up sentiment against the British. By March 1770 conditions in Boston were ripe for an incident that could be another weapon for maximum publicity. After several days of individual confrontations, on the cold night of March 5, three separate crowds converged on King Street. Led by clever radical organizers, armed with cudgels, and spoiling for trouble, the mob began to taunt, snowball, and threaten some British troops.

One isolated young sentry was surrounded near the Customs House by a group of rowdies. The sentry had to be rescued. Eight nervous British soldiers, defying the mob, tried to reach him. General Thomas Gage, commander in chief of the British army in America gives this account of what happened next:

> This party as well as the sentinel was immediately attacked, some throwing bricks, stones, pieces of ice and snowballs at them, whilst others advanced up to their bayonets, and endeavored to close with them, to use their bludgeons and clubs; calling out to them to fire if they dared, and provoking them to it by the most opprobrious language.
>
> Captain Preston stood between the soldiers and the mob, parleying with the latter, and using every conciliating method to persuade them to retire peaceably. Some amongst them asked him if he intended to order the men to fire, he replied by no means, and observed he stood between the troops and them. All he could say had no effect, and one of the soldiers, receiving a violent blow, instantly fired. Captain Preston turned round to see who fired, and received a blow upon his arm, which was aimed at his head; and the mob, at first seeing no execution done, and imagining the soldiers had only fired powder to frighten, grew more bold and attacked with greater violence, continually striking at the soldiers and pelting them, and calling out to them to fire. The soldiers at length perceiving their lives in danger, and hearing the word fire all round them, three or four of them fired one after another, and again three more in the same hurry and confusion. [The Annals of America, vol. 2. (Chicago: Encyclopedia Britannica, 1968), p. 205.]

In addition to this account, we also have the deathbed confession of Patrick Carr that the townspeople had been the aggressors and the soldiers had fired in self-defense. This recantation by one of the martyrs who Samuel Adams had already sanctified could have proved fatal to the patriots' cause. Adams began, therefore, to blast Carr's testimony. John C. Miller writes, "After Sam Adams had finished with Patrick Carr, even the (pro-British) Tories did not dare quote him to prove Bostonians were responsible for the Massacre."

One footnote to this tragic moment of the pre-Revolutionary period: Out of this incident came one of the finest moments in the annals of the American judicial system. John Adams, later to be president, and Josiah Quincy successfully defended the soldiers against the outcries of an enraged citizenry bent on retribution.

which appeared a year and a month after the shots at Lexington.

The Declaration of Independence

The colonists' original idea was to persuade the British to respect their rights and treat them better by showing a willingness to fight if necessary. In short, they were bluffing. But as the war wore on, this idea transformed itself into something quite different. They began to favor complete separation.

To that end, the Continental Congress on June 11, 1775 appointed a committee of five to draw up a **Declaration of Independence.** Like any good committee, the actual job of writing was delegated to the youngest member—Thomas Jefferson. The document would serve to explain and, they hoped, convince the rest of the world that separation was necessary and right.

The first draft after revision by the rest of the committee, which included Ben Franklin and John Adams, was sent to the Congress, where it was again changed. On July 4, 1776, Congress adopted the final document. Almost a month passed, however, before the Declaration was signed by the 56 delegates. The British government viewed these signers and their families as traitors. As Benjamin Franklin said, as the document was being signed, "We must indeed all hang together, or most assuredly we shall hang separately."

The Declaration of Independence proclaimed that the colonies were from that day forward independent states. They were no longer under any allegiance or obligation to the British king. The argument for separation rested on two premises:

> All human beings have rights that cannot be taken away.

THE AUTHOR OF THE DECLARATION OF INDEPENDENCE: A BRIEF PROFILE: What was young Jefferson trying to accomplish in this document? Professor Carl L. Becker resolves the question concisely as follows:

Library of Congress

> The primary purpose . . . was to convince a candid world that the colonies had a moral and legal right to separate from Great Britain. . . . Accordingly, the idea around which Jefferson built the Declaration was that the colonies were not rebels against established political authority, but a free people maintaining long-established and imprescriptible rights against a usurping king. . . . The king is represented as exclusively aggressive, the colonists are represented as essentially submissive. In this drama the king alone acts—he conspires, incites, plunders; the colonists have the passive part, never lifting a hand to burn stamps or destroy tea; they suffer while evils are sufferable. It is a high literary merit of the Declaration that by subtle contrasts Jefferson contrives to conjure up for us the virtuous and long-suffering colonists standing like martyrs to receive on their defenseless heads the ceaseless blows of the tyrant's hand. [*The Declaration of Independence* (New York: Harcourt, Brace, 1922), p. 203.]

One of the minor, unresolvable matters in the story of the American Revolution is why Congress let a young man of 33 compose the draft of the Declaration instead of wise old men like Adams and Franklin. According to Adams, the explanation was that Jefferson was a felicitous writer whom nobody as yet disliked.

By any measure, he was a remarkable man: statesman, philosopher, inventor, scientist, architect, educator. At a White House dinner honoring American Nobel Prize winners, President Kennedy announced: "This is the most extraordinary collection of talent . . . that has ever gathered together at the White House—with the possible exception of when Thomas Jefferson dined alone."

The British Empire is a voluntary federation of independent states.

Jefferson did not dream up these premises in a moment of divine inspiration or cosmic consciousness. Both ideas were commonplace at the time. Indeed, one of the great strengths of the Declaration was that it said what most colonists were already thinking. And no one understood this better than Thomas Jefferson himself. As he patiently explained a number of years later, his task in writing the Declaration had not been to find out new principles or new arguments never before thought of, not merely to say things that had never been said before, but to place before mankind the common sense of the subject in terms so plain and firm as to command their assent.

Debate by Battle

The Second Continental Congress, which met the month following the gunfire at Lexington, did perhaps the best thing it could have done. It chose by unanimous vote George Washington of Virginia to be the commander of the colonial army.

Why had Congress chosen Washington? A number of delegates differed on his appointment, and Washington himself was touting a General Andrew Lewis for the post. The best answer is that New England had cut a deal with Virginia. If you will support the New England army in this conflict, then we will offer you the chief command.

It was Washington's fame and this strange new idea of a colony fighting for freedom that began to attract help from Europe. From France came the Marquis de Lafayette, who persuaded the government of Louis XVI to send a 6,000-man expeditionary army to aid the colonists. Lafayette was given command of an army in Virginia and was hailed as "the hero of two worlds." From Poland came Thaddeus Kosciusko, who took part in fortifying West Point, conducted a lengthy blockade of Charleston, and, at the end of the war, took U.S. citizenship. From Germany came Baron von Steuben, whose professional experience in military training, organization, and administration proved invaluable in the war.

During the five-year-long war, the American cause was repeatedly near complete disaster. But Washington's strength of character, ability to instill confidence, energy in organizing raw volunteers, and sound judgment (rather than any Napoleonic battlefield brilliance) helped to keep the dubious enterprise afloat. Historians debate how much difference a single individual

National Park Service, U.S. Department of the Interior

On the morning of July 2, 1776 nearly 50 men sat at the ground-floor meeting room of the State House (Independence Hall) on Walnut Street in Philadelphia. Since it was raining outside, the windows were kept closed. The room steamed—but at least the horseflies from a nearby stable were excluded.

Later that day, with the city awash, they would vote to sever the 169-year-old political ties of the American colonies with England. Two days later, on July 4, the Congress would endorse an extraordinary document, a Declaration that stated the colonies' reasons for taking such action. While the week's events seemed startling in their sudden finality, we know from Figure 2-1 that they had been months, even years, in coming.

can make in shaping the course of events. But it is not difficult to imagine some other general, placed in this crucial position, failing. To keep such an ill-fed, ill-clothed, and ill-equipped army from breaking up and going home required more than the usual qualities of generalship.

The British conduct of the war was not up to their usual standards—fortunately for the Americans. Above all, the complete lack of good military and political leadership prevented Great Britain from delivering a quick, crushing blow to what at first was only a thinly supported revolt. The observations of one of England's most illustrious modern commanders, General Bernard Montgomery, might be of some interest here.

> It is a nice point which were the worse equipped and the worse led: the American troops or the British. However, George Washington matured as a leader although he was never more than a mediocre soldier, and the Americans adapted themselves better to fighting in the type of country involved. Whereas the British troops fought in red coats and drill formations, the Americans camouflaged themselves in green and fought largely as irregulars.[2]

In addition to generalship problems, the intervention of France, followed by Spain and the Dutch United Provinces, meant that Britain was fighting a world war. In 1781, after finding his sea communication cut and Washington's large army behind him, General Charles Cornwallis was compelled to surrender at Yorktown. His troops, the main British force in America, marched in good order to surrender, and the band played "The World Turned Upside Down."

In accordance with the terms of the wartime alliance with France, Congress had instructed the peace commissioners not to negotiate with the British without French cooperation. But, as the commission soon learned, France sought terms that would keep America dependent on France. In order to end the war and drive a wedge between France and America, Great Britain shrewdly offered the Americans very generous peace terms. The commissioners, not being ones to pass up a good deal, ignored French objections and congressional instruction. On September 3, 1783 they signed a separate treaty with Great Britain; Congress quickly approved it.

Now an independent nation, the 13 colonies had the problem of designing a government agreeable to all. They were free but in an unfriendly world and without a real central government. They were free, but in debt (thanks to the war) and without money. The period from 1783 to 1789 is accurately named "The Critical Period."

THE CRITICAL PERIOD AND ITS AFTERMATH

Articles of Confederation: An Underrated Innovation in Political Architecture

The period from the Declaration of Independence to the final implementation of the federal government under the Constitution includes several events less familiar in history but significant to American politics. In 1781 came two events—the final ratification of the **Articles of Confederation** in March and the final victory of the Revolution at Yorktown in October.

Of these two, the Yorktown event is the more widely recognized. But as a milestone in the experiment in government that became the United States of America, the quiet event at Philadelphia in March 1781 may be more significant in constitutional history. With that event—the final adoption by the 13 states of the Articles of Confederation—the American people moved toward identity as a nation. This was the vital transitional step from the ad hoc Continental Congress to "the United States in Congress assembled" to the ultimate drafting of the Constitution and "the more perfect union" of a federal form of government.

The Articles were the first constitution to create a system of **federalism** in the United States. And federalism—that careful allocation of power between individual states and a central national government—is the glue that holds the American system together. The Articles also set out many proposed powers of government that were to be repeated in the later Constitution.* The Articles also made it possible for Congress to score three notable achievements. The first was the final peace with Great Britain of 1783. This peace was made by Congress's negotiators and ratified by Congress—not by the states, since Congress had exclusive authority in foreign affairs. It was the greatest treaty that Americans ever ratified. Second, the Articles made possible the establishment of a public-land policy for newly acquired territory after the states turned over their western land claims to Congress. These were to prove to be the guidelines for a great many years. Third, and most important, under the Articles' authority, in 1787 the Northwest Ordinance was enacted. This was a perpetual compact that set up regulations for the government of territories and provided for their ultimate admission as states *on equal footing* with the original 13 states.[3]

As innovative as the Articles were in many respects, they contained several fatal flaws. The biggest crack in the foundation was a provision in Article VIII. It provided that all expenses of government were to be paid from a "common treasury, which shall be supplied by the several states." The legislature of each state would presumably levy special taxes to meet its proportionate share of the costs. If this were not enough to impede the national government, the sixth clause of Article IX took away most of what appeared to be granted by the first five clauses. That clause stated that, in conducting or financing national defense, Congress was not to act without the consent of at least 9 of the 13 states.

Slowly matters got worse as the states began

---

* For example, full faith and credit, jurisdiction over interstate commerce, power of coinage, operation of a postal service, authority to set standards of weights, and measures, even training and disciplining of military forces (saving various state prerogatives).

Courtesy of The Henry Francis du Pont Winterthur Museum

By the Treaty of Paris (1783), Great Britain formally acknowledged the independence of the United States. The treaty required months of tortuous negotiations in which the American representatives acquitted themselves so well that their achievement has been labeled "the greatest triumph in the history of American diplomacy." This painting, showing the American representatives Jay, Adams, Ben Franklin, Laurens, and William Franklin, was never finished (some speculate, because the British representatives refused to sit for the artist).

to drift apart and distrust one another. Recognizing what was happening and the danger it entailed, some of the leaders of the states began to argue for a stronger central government with enough authority to force states to obey its laws.

But words alone cannot always lead to action. As we shall see time and time again in our study of politics, a crucial event is sometimes required to galvanize people into action. For those calling for stronger central government, **Daniel Shays' Rebellion** of 1786 was just such an event. The rebellion involved farmers in western Massachusetts seeking relief from debts and possible foreclosures of mortgages. Armed bands, led by Shays, forced the closing of several courts to prevent debt processes and foreclosures. Open warfare between the rebels and state troops lasted about six weeks.

Some leaders urged Washington to use his influence to quiet the troubles. But Washington snapped back: "Influence is no Government. . . . If they have *real* grievances, redress them. . . . If they have not, employ the force of government against them at once." While Washington was outraged by the very idea of a rebellion against the new American republic, he was also outraged by the fact that the rebels had their voting rights taken away. This seemed to him as much an abuse of power as the failure to use power effectively against them in the first place.

Shays' Rebellion was a timely event coming against a background of piracy, Indian uprisings, lack of good roads, and a postwar economic depression (linked to currency problems stemming from the independence of the individual states). It helped drive home the point that the advocates of a stronger central government had been making: The Articles of Confederation left Americans too weak to deal with major problems.

The Constitutional Convention of 1787: Back to the Drawing Board

Congress was still the only central group for the representatives of the 13 states. Now it was in a position to suggest a convention to change and strengthen the Articles of Confederation. The states could, if they wished move toward "a more perfect union."

The individual state governments named more than 70 delegates to attend the Convention; only 55 came. Rhode Island sent no one. Few of the radical leaders of the Revolution were present. Jefferson was in Paris as American minister. Patrick Henry refused to attend, believing the Convention a potential threat to state sovereignty (which indeed it was!). Samuel Adams, who had drafted a protest against the Stamp Act and helped bring about the Boston Massacre with his anti-British writings, was not chosen. Who then attended?

Well, the founding fathers were probably the most civilized revolutionaries the world has ever seen. Twenty-nine were college graduates. Their average age was 42, just a little beyond the average life span of the time.

Conflict, consensus, compromise. Although most of the men who attended the Convention were friends of property and business, they still came from different groups. Each was loyal to his own state. Their opinions on how large and small states should be represented in the new government were not unconnected to the state from which they came. There were also sharp difference between representatives of the merchants and cities. Each delegate also had to consider the ways of living, customs of government, and many smaller group interests in his state. And finally, not all delegates were rich.

Given such fundamental differences, agreement could only be reached if there was some underlying consensus and a willingness to compromise. Fortunately, both were present when the delegates met at Philadelphia on May 5, 1787.

One of the major sticking points was the worry of the smaller states that disproportionate power would go to the larger states. For example, the **Virginia Plan,** submitted by Edmund Randolph of Virginia, had called for a two-house legislature, based on state population or wealth, and a national executive and judiciary. The legislature, invested with broad power over matters of national concern, would have power to reject state legislation. The smaller states and the states' rights advocates, therefore, backed a counterproposal by William Paterson of New Jersey. Under the **New Jersey Plan,** Congress would be a single house in which each state, no matter how large or small, had an equal vote.

As a battle line began to appear, with supporters of the New Jersey Plan on one side and supporters of the Virginia Plan on the other, a compromise was put forward. Why not let each state be represented in the House of Representatives according to population and in the Senate represented equally? The **Connecticut Compromise,** also called the **Great Compromise,** made it possible for the smaller states to agree to the establishment of a strong central government as called for in the Virginia Plan. Accepting this bit of the New Jersey Plan (equal representation in one house) was the "price of union." The smaller states were also able to limit the power of the central government to acting directly on individuals—rather than through the states (as the Virginia Plan had called for).

There were also several other compromises by which different groups of states were given certain special rights in exchange for giving up other rights. But in the end, they all agreed to a plan for a central government that would be strong enough to make them act together and form a single nation.

Ratification. After a long summer of work, the Convention asked Gouverneur Morris to write the final draft of the Constitution. It was ready to signing on September 17, 1787. Only 39 of the 55 members signed. Some were absent, but others refused to sign. Now one hurdle remained: to send copies of the Constitution to each of the 13 states for ratification. Each state ratifying convention subjected it to mi-

---

The Question of Black Americans

The Great Compromise was closely tied to a number of other compromises. The southern states wanted to count slaves for representation in Congress; northern states did not want to count them at all. It was even suggested that, since the South thought of blacks as property, the North should be able to count horses and cattle. After bitter debate, another compromise was reached. Slaves would count for representation but not as whole persons. The Constitutional Convention chose to count a slave as three fifths of a person.

In the summer of 1974, Barbara Jordan, a black Congresswoman from Houston, gripped the attention of the American public watching on television the House Judiciary Committee's debate on the impeachment of President Richard M. Nixon. In a clear, concise, and implacable voice she said:

> We the people—it is a very eloquent beginning. But when the Constitution of the United States was completed on the 17th of September in 1787, I was not included in that "We the people." I felt for many years that somehow George Washington and Alexander Hamilton just left me out by mistake. But through the process of amendment, interpretation, and court decision, I have finally been included in "We the people."
>
> Today, I am an inquisitor. I believe hyperbole would not be fictional and would not overstate the solemnness that I feel right now. My faith in the Constitution is whole. It is complete. It is total. I am not going to sit here and be an idle spectator to the diminution, the subversion, the destruction of the Constitution. [Barbara Jordan, *A Self-Portrait* (New York: Doubleday, 1979).]

United Press International Photo

nute examination. During this period, Hamilton, Madison, and Jay wrote a penetrating series of articles to win over the people of New York. These articles, *The Federalist Papers,* are perhaps the only literature from the United States that can stand with any of the world's classics of political theory. (Two selections from this work appear in Appendix B.)

The struggle was sometimes bitter. The supporters of the new government artfully called themselves **Federalists** to emphasize their fundamental commitment to a government in which the states still shared in power. The Federalists, again artfully, tagged the opposition to the new government **Antifederalists.** They thereby highlighted the negative character of those who opposed ratification.

By June 1788, nine states had ratified. This was the number necessary to place the Constitution into operation. Elections were held, and New York became the temporary capital of the nation. George Washington was sworn in as president on April 30, 1789. A new government was lauched. She would show, again and again, by the beauty of her motion, in the roughest of seas, the skill of her builders.

Influences. In framing this new government, the founding fathers, as these men came to be known, borrowed ideas from a variety of sources. Perhaps most significant of all was their experience with British government. This simple fact is too often forgotten.

Those who had called for revolution 12 years earlier had no passion for national unity. They never argued that America had institutions, ideas, or culture superior to that of the British. Historian Daniel Boorstin's view is that the major issue of the American Revolution was, in fact, the true constitution of the British Empire.[4] The revolutionaries' position was that the British by their treatment of the American colonies were being untrue to the ancient spirit of their own institutions. The slogan "Taxation without representation is tyranny" was clearly founded on a British assumption. The colonists were fighting not so much to establish new rights as to preserve old ones: "for the preservation of our liberties . . . in defence of the freedom that is our birthright, and which we ever enjoyed till the late violation of it" (Declaration of Causes of Taking Up Arms, July 6, 1775). From the colonists' point of view, until 1776 it was Parliament that had been revolutionary, by exercising a power for which there was no warrant in English constitutional precedent (see box).

Now, reluctantly, they had to reexamine the experience of the British government, reclaiming what was deemed useful, sloughing off what was not. The British had a constitution (albeit unwritten) that provided a great deal more personal liberty than in most European countries, and the people had the right to elect certain members to Parliament (the British legislative body). British law courts gave fairer trials than in any other country. These ideas served as standards that guided the founding fathers.

The Declaration of Independence also guided them. That document had declared that government must get its power from the people. It had protested against specific wrongs committed by the British government. (In fact, over half the document is devoted to that purpose.) It had declared that all men are created equal and have the right to live, be free, and work for happiness. It proclaimed the duty of the government to preserve these rights of the people.

There were 13 state constitutions in 1789. When the colonies renounced their allegiance to Great Britain, they also declared themselves to be independent states. Each of the colonial groups then wrote its own state constitution. In doing so, it borrowed ideas from the older colonial charters. In Philadelphia, the founders studied the plans of government that had been set up by these state constitutions and found some of them very helpful in guiding their work.

One of the great secrets of American history, which most high school textbooks are not about to give away, is that the founders were intellectuals. The Constitutional Convention was more

The Meanings of Revolution

The word *revolution* implies two elements. First is the change by movement; the second is a motion that returns to its starting point. The first usage, which originated with the French Revolution, is today closer to what we mean when we speak of revolution. The second usage, which appeared with Copernicus' theory of the movement of the stars, might more accurately apply to the American Revolution. In astronomy, revolution indicates the orbital movement of the planets.

Application of the term *revolution* to the overthrow of the British rule by the American colonies seems, in this second sense, justified. The change that took place was a revolution because it represented a return to the true old constitution of England and as such closed a cycle. In contrast, the French Revolution was fought over not a few legal points but "liberty, equality, fraternity." It promised not merely freedom but a new society. Change was so sweeping that even the calendar was altered.

Yet it would be wrong to think that the American revolution showed no signs of forward movement. Afterward, England could no longer dictate the terms of trade with the colonies. The implications of this change were to echo through the next two centuries, as countries of Asia, Africa, and Latin America successfully struggled against foreign domination. Furthermore, the colonies were to go on to design a feasible system of government that, while resting on many principles of English law, contained several quite innovative features.

Historical Pictures Service, Inc., Chicago

SOURCE: Based on Felix Gilbert, "Revolution," in *Dictionary of History of Ideas*, vol. 4 (New York: Scribner's Sons, 1973), pp. 152–67.

than a product of compromises and political tinkering. The founders knew of and were influenced by the great political thinkers of the western world. For example, it was a French writer, Baron de Montesquieu, whose writings suggested to Gouverneur Morris and others the idea of dividing the power among three branches—legislative, executive, and judicial. (In the British system then, as today, these powers tend to be less clearly divided.) Chapter 3 will provide a closer look at how such ideas influenced the founding fathers. It will show the degree to which the document is grounded in the political philosophy of the period. To neglect this intellectual history is to miss the spirit of the Constitution and to run the risk of making the document appear no more than a jerry-built collection of rules and regulations.

Assessment. Modern scholars largely agree that the debates and the Constitution were carried on at an intellectual level that is rare in politics. Scholars also agree that the Constitution itself is one of the world's masterpieces of practical politics. The British philosopher and mathematician Alfred North Whitehead stated the view well:

> I know of only two occasions in history when the people in power did what needed to be done about as well as you can imagine its being possible. One was the framing of your American Constitution. They were able statesmen; they had access to a body of good ideas; they incorporated these general principles into the instrument without trying to particularize too explicitly how they should be put into effect; and they were men of immense practical experience themselves.[5]

But on other aspects of the Convention, scholars disagree. Charles A. Beard's *An Economic Interpretation of the Constitution of the United States*, which appeared in 1913, concluded that the founding fathers' support for or opposition to the Constitution could best be explained in terms of their pocketbooks. Beard did not say that the document was written exclusively for their personal benefit. But he did maintain that their political behavior reflected their financial interests. For Beard, the Constitution was "essentially an economic document" written by a small and active group of men "who were with a few exceptions, immediately, directly, and personally interested in, and derived economic advantages from, the establishment of the new system."

Farrect McDonald, in his *E Pluribus Unum: The Formation of the American Republic*, which appeared in 1965, out-Beards Beard. According to McDonald, the critical compromise that made the Constitution possible was a secret deal between Connecticut land speculators and South Carolina planters.

The preponderance of historical research goes against this interpretation. Scholars have pointed out that in 1787 (as probably today) *everyone* was interested in protecting property—not just the wealthy. Furthermore, differences over the merits of the Constitution were associated more with an individual's political views than with his economic status. For much the same reason, contemporary political figures like Senator Edward M. Kennedy do not vote their pocketbooks.

The case of Alexander Hamilton is also illustrative. Few founding fathers are more closely associated with property and business interests than he. Yet in his strivings as the first secretary of the Treasury, Hamilton clashed repeatedly with entrenched commercial interests. Among them were the speculators who trafficked in the wildly fluctuating bonds issued to finance the Revolutionary War. Even more formidable than the speculators were the handful of landed, intermarried families that monopolized power in America then. In particular, he singled out the Virginians (namely Madison, Monroe, and Jefferson) as opponents of all change and champions of an agrarian life whose economy was based on slavery and inherited wealth. Hamilton worked to devise an economic program that would destroy that system of privilege, replacing it with one based on individual merit and competition. Not surprisingly, Jefferson came to regard Hamilton as his enemy.

Perhaps Beard and, to a greater extent, McDonald have committed what one historian terms the "furtive fallacy." This is the erroneous idea

> that facts of special significance are dark and dirty things and that history itself is a story of causes mostly insidious and results most invidious. It begins with the premise that reality is a sordid, secret thing; and that history happens on the back stairs a little after midnight.... The furtive fallacy ... combines a naive ... assumption that things are never what they seem to be, with a firm attachment to the doctrine of original sin. There is a little furtive fallacy in us all—enough to sustain the common truth ... that facts, like sinners, gain something from an unsavory reputation.[6]

Probably closer to the mark was the founding fathers' image of themselves as moderate republicans standing between political extremes. They were impelled by class motives more than pietistic writers like to admit. But they were also controlled, as Professor Beard himself was later to emphasize, by a statesmanlike sense of moderation and a scrupulously republican philosophy.

Ultimately, we must judge the Constitution like any creative work—in terms of itself and not the artists' motives. The fact that a poet was sexually repressed or a painter was a religious fanatic should not diminish our appreciation of their work. When the British stateman William Gladstone paid tribute to the Constitution in 1878, he was speaking as an art critic not as an amateur psychologist: "I have always regarded that Constitution as the most remarkable work known to me in modern times to have been produced by the human intellect at a single stroke (so to speak), in its application to political affairs."[7]

BASIC DESIGN FEATURES OF THE CONSTITUTION

Thus far we have spoken only in general terms about the substance of the Constitution. The box gives you an idea of how it is organized. (Appendix A gives the entire document.) Many of the chapters ahead are devoted to explaining the meaning of the seven articles and 26 amendments highlighted in the box. Therefore, let us limit ourselves here to grasping only the basic features, not paragraphs, clauses, and commas.

Federalism

Why federalism? One of the great architectural feats of the 1787 Convention was the fragmentation of political power between two layers of government—national and state. With one master stroke, the Articles of Confederation were replaced with a tighter, stronger, more effective central government, yet the independence of the states was preserved. This system of government, in which **sovereignty** or supreme political authority is divided between central and regional governments, is called **federalism**.

Federalism is a compromise between a confederation and a **unitary system** in which the central government is supreme and allocates power, as necessary, to regional governments. French government today is a prime example of a unitary system. All officials except mayors and municipal councils are appointed and controlled by Paris. Nations claiming a federal system govern more than half the world's land area. Besides the United States, the following nations might be cited: Switzerland (one of the oldest), Germany, Australia, Brazil, India, and Nigeria.

There were good reasons for rejecting the unitary system and preserving some state power.

National Park Service, U.S. Department of the Interior

The assembly room of the State House (Independence Hall) is the most historic political meeting place in the United States. Here the Declaration of Independence was debated and adopted in 1776, the Articles of Confederation were ratified in 1781, and the federal Constitution was framed in 1787. The room has been restored to its appearance in that period. A delegate described it at the time as "neat but not elegant," true to the Quaker spirit of the host city.

The Constitution in Brief

Preamble
Explains the purposes of the people in adopting the Constitution:

> We the People of the United States, in Order to form a more perfect Union, establish Justice, insure domestic Tranquility, provide for the common defence, promote the general Welfare, and secure the Blessings of Liberty to ourselves and our Posterity, do ordain and establish this Constitution for the United States of America.

Article I
All power to make laws lies in a Congress composed of two houses, the Senate and the House of Representatives. Their authority and limitations are set forth. Today the Senate consists of 100 members (two from each state) and the House of 435 members (with the number from each state determined by population).

Article II
Provides for the election of a president and vice-president with defined powers and for the appointment of other officials. Today an enormous establishment surrounds the president. Directly serving the president is the Executive Office, which includes the White House Office, the Office of Management and Budget, and the National Security Council. The executive branch also includes the 13 executive departments that together make up the cabinet. As with the Executive Office, the Constitution makes no provision for a cabinet. All of the executive departments have been created by acts of Congress, the most recent additions being the Department of Energy (1977) and the Department of Education (1979).

Article III
Sets up a Supreme Court, authorizes the Congress to set up other courts, and defines their power. Over the years, Congress has created a structure of lower federal courts made up of the U.S. circuit courts of appeals and the U.S. district courts.

Article IV
Defines relationships between the federal government and the states and between the states themselves. Section I requires states to honor the civil rulings of other states: "Full **faith and credit** shall be given in each state to the public acts, records, and judicial proceedings of every other state."

Article V
Tells how the Constitution can be changed.

Article VI
Declares that the Constitution, constitutional laws, and treaties are the supreme law of the land; provides that all public officers must take an oath to support the Constitution.

Article VII
Declares that ratification by nine states will put the Constitution into effect.

Amendments 1–10: Bill of Rights
Lists human rights (not stated elsewhere in the document) that cannot be infringed upon by the government. Provides for protection of freedom of expression, the rights of property, and rights of accused. The 10th Amendment embodies the principle of federalism, which reserves for the states the residue of powers not granted to the federal government or withheld from the states.

Amendments 11–26
Modifies or clarifies the Constitution in a variety of ways: restriction of judicial power (11th) election of president and senators, vice-president (12th and 17th), abolition of slavery (13th), protection of citizenship rights from abridgement by states (14th), suffrage (15th, 19th, and 23d), authorization of income taxes (16th), presidential terms of office and succession (20th, 22d, and 25th), elimination of poll tax (24th), and voting age (26th).

First, partially independent states would help to check the power of national government. Significantly, one of the primary objectives of the Constitution of the German Federal Republic, which was drafted in 1948, was to resist any drive toward militarism or dictatorship by making it federal. Accordingly, the German states (Lands) control the police, administer much national legislation, and have charge of education and schools.

Second, whatever else the founders might have been, they were practical. They knew the struggle to get the new Constitution ratified would be fierce; to propose a unitary system to the 13 states would be hopeless.

Third, federalism made geographic sense. In other words, to allow some degree of decentralization seemed a reasonable way to administer such a large heterogenous area with so many local interests. For the same reason, Nigeria—an incredibly diverse African nation with 300 tribes and a Moslem North and Christian South—now has a federal system that operates more or less as America's founding fathers had envisioned for the United States.

Federalism has been compared to a heavy mortgage. Meeting the payments may be agonizing, but the house would not be possible without it. One major cost of federalism is found in the chaotic arrangement of thousands of governments—one national government, 50 state governments, then scores of cities, counties, and special-purpose districts.

Distributing the power. In Chapter 12, we shall review in detail federalism as practiced in the United States today. But here it is appropriate that we note how the pattern of American federalism is established by the Constitution.

Because it makes federalism work, the best place to begin is with the **supremacy clause.** One of the major problems under the Articles of Confederation had been the inability of the national government to get states to accept its legislation. Article VI, the supremacy clause, makes it clear. Within its field of powers, the national government is supreme. State courts are bound to uphold its supremacy. Any provision of a state constitution or any state law is null and void if it conflicts with the federal Constitution ("the highest law").

The Constitution gives two basic types of power to the national government: **delegated** (also called **expressed**) **powers** and **implied powers.** Delegated powers are named in the Constitution; implied powers are derived from the **necessary and proper** (also called **elastic**) **clause** of Article I, Section 8. For example, the Constitution gives Congress the expressed power to raise an army and navy; but it says nothing about the draft. That power is justified by the "necessary and proper" clause.

In the field of foreign affairs, powers exercised by the national government that are neither expressed nor implied in the Constitution are called **inherent powers.** They are derived from the concept that, since the United States exists in a world of many nations, it must have powers to act to protect the security and well-being of the American people. For example, just like other nations in the international family, the United States may acquire territory by occupation even though the Constitution is silent on such acquisitions.

Next, **concurrent powers,** such as to tax and spend, are granted to both the national government and the states. All remaining powers are **reserved** to the states. Figure 2–2 gives examples of three kinds of powers—implied, concurrent, and reserved—as well as certain limitations placed on government. (In Chapter 11, we shall return to examine these limitations in detail.)

By way of conclusion, it might be noted that federalism today poses little serious restraint on the powers of the national government. But these limitations, these provisions designed to protect the liberties of the people, do. Those provisions designed to preserve the powers of the individual state governments, which once came together to form the union, have been largely anesthetized.

FIGURE 2-2
The Federal System: Where the Power Lies

A. Powers of the Federal Government
(those delegated to it)

To control relations with foreign nations
To punish crimes against the United States
To establish post offices
To coin money and regulate its value
To keep up an army, a navy, and an air corps
To declare war and make peace
To set standards for weights and measures
To regulate commerce among the states and with foreign countries
To make uniform laws about naturalization and bankruptcy
To protect authors and inventors by giving copyrights and patents
To admit new states and to control the territory of the United States
To make all laws necessary and proper for carrying into effect the expressly stated powers and all other powers granted by the United States Constitution.

B. Concurrent Powers

To borrow money
To collect taxes
To build public works
To charter banks
To establish courts
To help agriculture and industry
To protect the public health

C. Prohibited Powers

To deny civil rights (such as freedom of speech, press, religion, and assembly)
To pass laws that make illegal something that has already been done legally and honestly
To pass a law that finds any person guilty without trial

D. Powers of the States ("reserved powers")

To authorize the establishment of local governments
To establish and keep up schools
To regulate city government groups
To provide for a state militia
To regulate commerce within the borders of the state
To regulate labor, industry, and business within the state
To provide care for orphans and paupers, and for blind, crippled, insane, and other helpless persons
To make laws on all other subjects not prohibited to the states by the federal or state constitutions, and not delegated to the federal government

E. Implied Powers

"To make all Laws which shall be necessary and proper for carrying into Execution the foregoing Powers, and all other Powers vested by this Constitution in the Government of the United States, or in any Department or Officer thereof."
(Article 1, Section 8, 18.)

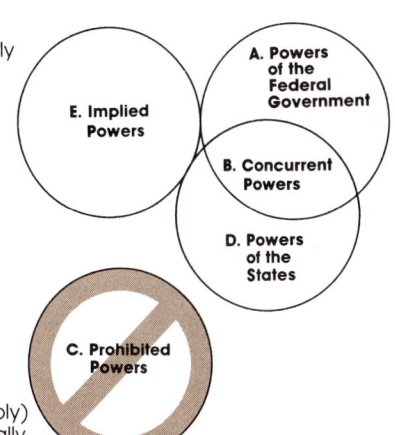

Separation of Powers

The founders essentially viewed politics not as some cooperative enterprise but as an enduring conflict of opposed interests. With a sailor's sure sense of equilibrium and instinct for balanced tension in the rigging, John Adams regarded the chief architectural problem of Constitution making as the establishment of "a multitude of curious and ingenious inventions to balance in their turn all those powers (legislative, executive, and judicial), to check the passions peculiar to them, and to control them from rushing into the exorbitances to which they are most addicted." Like a ship, government had to make prudent accommodations to turbulent forces she could not defy and had to obey.

In devising a solution, as Herbert J. Storing of the University of Chicago points out, the founders faced two difficulties. First, to merely divide government powers was unlikely to be a very effective restraint if each of the separate parts were similar in outlook and interests. For example, how could they give that part of a government that was basically popular (i.e., elected by the people) an attitude, a spirit that was something more than that of an adding machine? The second difficulty was how to prevent a government of checks and balances from reaching such a perfect equilibrium that it could not act at all. Columbia, the Gem of the Ocean, must be made for movement.

The solution to both difficulties was the presidency. Professor Storing thinks that this institution—far more than federalism—represents the founders' real achievement and their challenge:

> The president was to be part of the system of checks and balances and the chief counterweight to the legislative branch. But he was also to be the primary source of energy and direction for the government as a whole.... The system was designed to leave the president free from a dependence on any other branch of the government; for this was to be no subservient administrator, no timeserver, no mere doer of the will of Congress or the people. On the wisdom and courage of the president, on his capacity to guide the people when they were confused, encourage them when they were right, and stand against them—at least to demand that they think again—when they were wrong, would depend the excellence of the American government, the effectiveness of its protection of liberty, and the greatness to which it might aspire. The presidency was the crucial feature of the Constitution, and in spite of many changes it remains so, because the duty of the holder of this office is the most difficult in any popular government: to reconcile the wants of the people and the needs of the Republic.[8]

While this reconciliation of wants and needs was to be primarily the job of the president, other institutions were established for the same purpose. Special care was taken to keep these institutions politically independent of one another and to insulate them as much as possible from the momentary passions of the voters. Elected officials were given terms of different lengths. House members serve two-year terms; senators serve six-year terms; presidents and vice presidents serve four-year terms. This greatly minimizes the possibility of a takeover of all other centers of power in a single election year by a wave of popular feeling that may reflect the wants of the people but not the needs of the republic.

What if it happened anyway? The founding fathers provided for that contingency by establishing a Supreme Court, with its judges appointed for life. (As former Chief Justice Earl Warren told his friends, he would prefer to sit in the center of the Supreme Court than in the White House. Why? "There have been 34 presidents, but only 13 chief justices.") In such a situation, it could provide a stabilizing influence.

Each institution serves as a check on the accumulation of excessive power by any other part. For example:

Congress makes the nations laws, but these can be vetoed (rejected) by the president or voided as unconstitutional by the Supreme Court.

The president and his officers administer the laws, but they can be called to account by the Court and are closely watched over by congressional committees and staffs. The ultimate check on the president is held by Congress: removal from office through **impeachment.**

The Court, the supreme interpreter of the Constitution, must rely on both the president and Congress to appoint and confirm its members and to provide funds for its operations.

The bureaucracy looks to the president for leadership but must turn to the Congress for the authority to start new programs and the money to run them.

Figure 2–3 shows how these and other *checks and balances* keep the American system in balance. As should be apparent from the figures, power in the system is not really separated as much as shared by separate institutions. Each

FIGURE 2-3
American National Government Keeping All the Parts in Balance

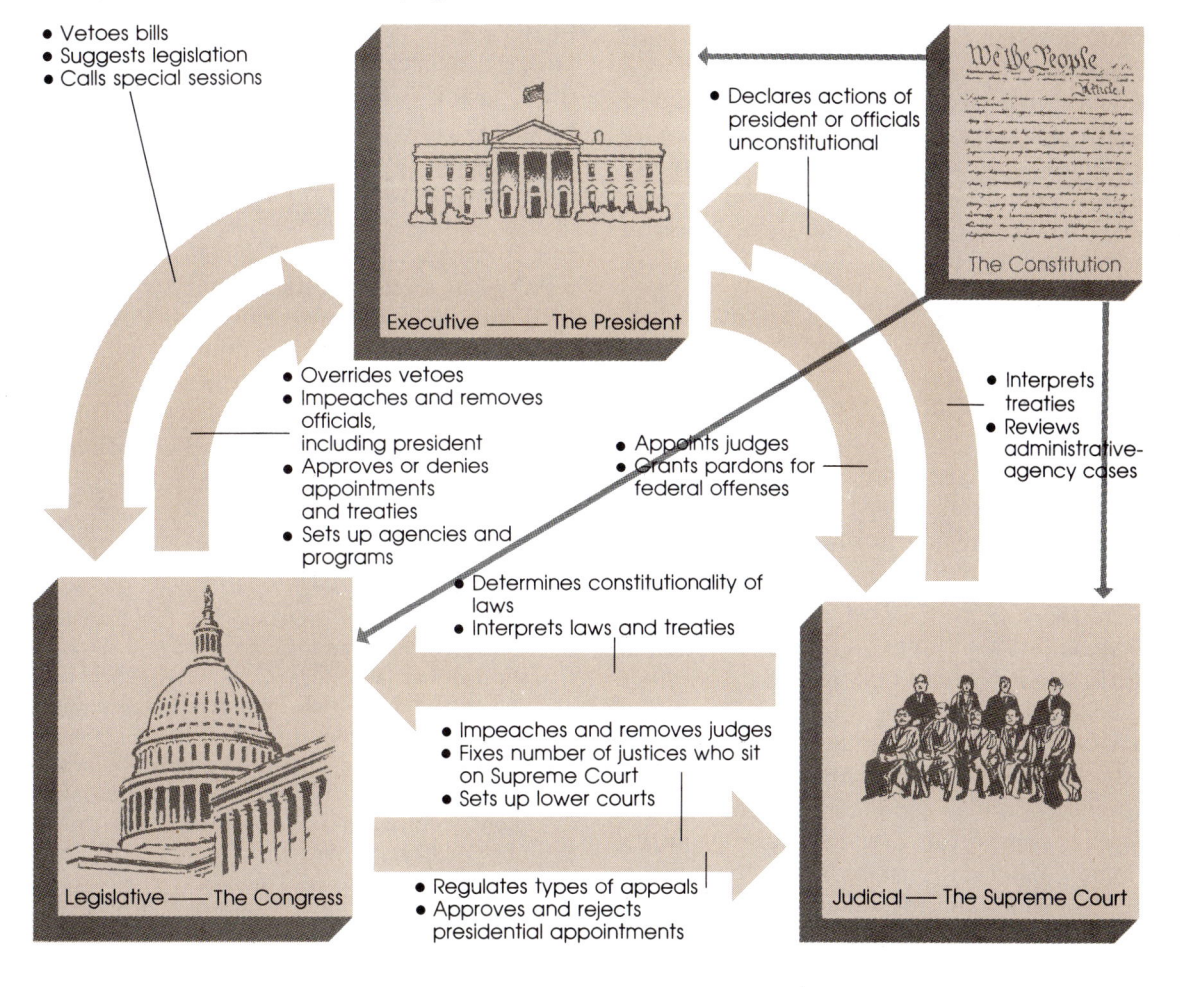

Executive — The President
- Vetoes bills
- Suggests legislation
- Calls special sessions

The Constitution
- Declares actions of president or officials unconstitutional
- Interprets treaties
- Reviews administrative-agency cases

Legislative — The Congress
- Overrides vetoes
- Impeaches and removes officials, including president
- Approves or denies appointments and treaties
- Sets up agencies and programs

- Appoints judges
- Grants pardons for federal offenses

- Determines constitutionality of laws
- Interprets laws and treaties

- Impeaches and removes judges
- Fixes number of justices who sit on Supreme Court
- Sets up lower courts

- Regulates types of appeals
- Approves and rejects presidential appointments

Judicial — The Supreme Court

institution has a voice in the business of others.

The federal judiciary plays a particularly important role in this system of checks and balances. Certainly, the design of the Constitution gives judges more power, more independence than can be found in the British system. This independence has been reinforced by the power of **judicial review,** the third basic feature of the Constitution.

Judicial Review

Judicial review is the power of judges to interpret the Constitution and to refuse to enforce those measures they consider in conflict with the Constitution. All courts, both state and national, may exercise this authority; the final decision, however, is held by the Supreme Court.

Actually, the Constitution never mentioned explicitly judicial review; the Supreme Court itself asserted the power in 1803 in *Marbury v. Madison,* a remarkable case we shall consider more closely in Chapter 4. In doing so, the Court based its power on the three powerful assumptions:

First, the Constitution is the supreme law (as indicated in Figure 2–3).

Second, legislation or presidential actions contrary to it are void (without legal force).

And third, the judiciary has the duty to serve as the bulwark against such legislative and executive encroachments.

A good illustration of the lasting influence of *Marbury* is the case of the *United States v. Nixon* (1974). This case grew out of a refusal by President Nixon to release tape recordings and documents involving conversations relating to Watergate. The Court held that the president's claim of **executive privilege** (that is, the principle by which the president can withhold sensitive papers from Congress) cannot justify withholding of information bearing on a pending criminal trial. In making its ruling, the Court went back to the language of the groundbreaking 1803 case:

> It is, emphatically, the province and duty of the judicial department, to say what the law is. Those who apply the rule to particular cases must of necessity expound and interpret that rule. . . . If a law be in opposition to the constitution; if both the law and the constitution apply to a particular case, so that the court must either decide that case, conformably to the law, disregarding the constitution, or conformably to the constitution, disregarding the law; the court must determine which of these conflicting rules governs the case; this is of the very essence of judicial duty.

Wisely, the Supreme Court has used this power sparingly since 1803. Only a little over one hundred federal laws and several hundred state laws have been declared unconstitutional. I say "wisely" because too frequent use of this power can backfire, generating disrespect for the Court. It is just not very smart in a democracy to roll out too often the doctrine that five out of nine unelected individuals can thwart the collective will of 535 elected representatives of the people—no matter how philosophically sound it happens to be. Of course, declaring a single law unconstitutional can effectively deter a long line of similar legislation. Again the sailing metaphor leaps to mind. The words Woodrow Wilson used to express his idea of prudent statecraft may be used with equal effect to express the idea of prudent adjudication.

> We say of a boat skimming the water with light foot, "How free she runs," when we mean, how perfectly she is adjusted to the force of the wind, how perfectly she obeys the great breath out of the heavens that fills her sails.
>
> Throw her head into the wind and see how she will halt and stagger, how every sheet will shiver and her whole frame be shaken, how instantly she is "in irons," in the expressive phrase of the sea. She is free only when you let her fall off again and have recovered once more her nice adjustment to the forces she must obey and cannot defy.[9]

Most judges accept the notion that they do not have a roving commission to interpret the Constitution whenever or however they wish.

Rather, they operate subject to certain limitations. For example, courts must wait for someone to bring the case before them. And not every social problem translates into a case. There must be an actual conflict with two parties having adverse interests. Hence the courts cannot give opinions on the constitutionality of *proposed* laws or executive actions.

In addition to requiring conflict, a case or controversy must *not* involve political questions. When does a case or controversy involve a political question? The short answer is, when the Court says it does. The better answer, however, is, when Congress or the president has made a decision involving global relations or when satisfactory illegal criteria for a judicial determination is not readily apparent. A recent example was the ruling of a federal appeals court that the president had the right to check visas of Iranian students and deport those who are in the United States illegally. In overturning a lower court ruling, the three-judge circuit court declared, "Certainly, in a case such as the one presented here, it is not the business of courts to pass judgment on the decision of the president in the field of foreign policy."

This does not mean, however, that there are no constitutional limits to what the president can do to safeguard the security of the nation. During the Korean War, President Harry S Truman, acting under his inherent power as chief executive and commander in chief, had authorized seizure of the steel mills and their operation by the government during a strike. In *Youngstown Sheet and Tube Co.* v. *Sawyer* (1952), the Court held that the president has no authority under the Constitution to seize private property unless authorized by Congress. The Constitution, in short, does not allow the president to legislate; Truman was, in effect, legislating.

Representative Government

The fourth feature is perhaps the most obvious: The Constitution was *republican*. Article IV, Section 4 of the Constitution provides that the national government "shall guarantee to every state in this union a republican form of government." That is, the government will operate through elected representatives of the people. To that stripped-down definition, the founding fathers added two further requirements:

> The term of office should be for a limited time and only during good behavior.
>
> Trust should be placed not in a few but a number of office holders.

Neither the Declaration of Independence nor the Constitution mentions "democracy," and examples of pure or direct democracy in today's political system are limited. Perhaps the classic example is the *town meeting*. This is an annual event throughout New England and many midwestern townships. In them small-town residents gather to vote on budgets, make rules, and decide the conduct of their daily lives. Several state constitutions provide for initiative, referendum, and recall action by the people. These are essentially electoral devices that allow interested citizens to propose legislation or constitutional amendments directly, to veto a bill passed by their legislature, or to remove an elected official from office before his or her term expires.

The founders had two objections to a direct democracy. First a democracy where people meet and exercise the government in person would have to be confined to a small spot; a republic could be extended over a large region. Second, they viewed pure democracies as turbulent and contentious, incompatible with personal security or the rights of property, and "as short in their lives as they have been violent in their deaths."[10]

The founding fathers deliberately denied that the opinion of any temporary majority is to be regarded as the will of the people. The ultimate authority is of course the people. But that will is not to be confused with the opinions of 50 percent of the voters at any particular moment. Therefore, they devised a system that required the will of the people be thoroughly known before any fundamental decisions could be made. But the founding fathers did not make that system so cumbersome that the Constitution could not develop and thereby continue to serve changing needs.

Adaptability

Amendment process. Article V of the Constitution provides two different ways changes can be *proposed* to the states and two different ways the states can then *approve* such changes. Thus, there are four routes to a formal change in the Constitution. In Figure 2–4, these appear as A to B, A to D, C to B, and C to D. Making these changes is the amendment process.

Of the 26 amendments, all except one was first proposed by Congress and then adopted by state legislatures (the A to B route). In the case of the 21st Amendment, the single exception, Congress directed each state to call together its own convention to vote its decision (the A to D route).

As you know from the box outlining the parts of the Constitution the first 10 amendments make up what is usually called the **Bill of Rights.** These amendments stated a long list of rights that the people already had and that the federal government was forbidden to take away. A large portion of Chapter 11 is devoted to an examination of these.

The states ratified the Bill of Rights in 1791. Over the next 189 years, only 16 more amendments have been added. Or, more accurately, only 14 have been added, since the 18th and

FIGURE 2–4
Four Routes to a New Amendment to the Constitution

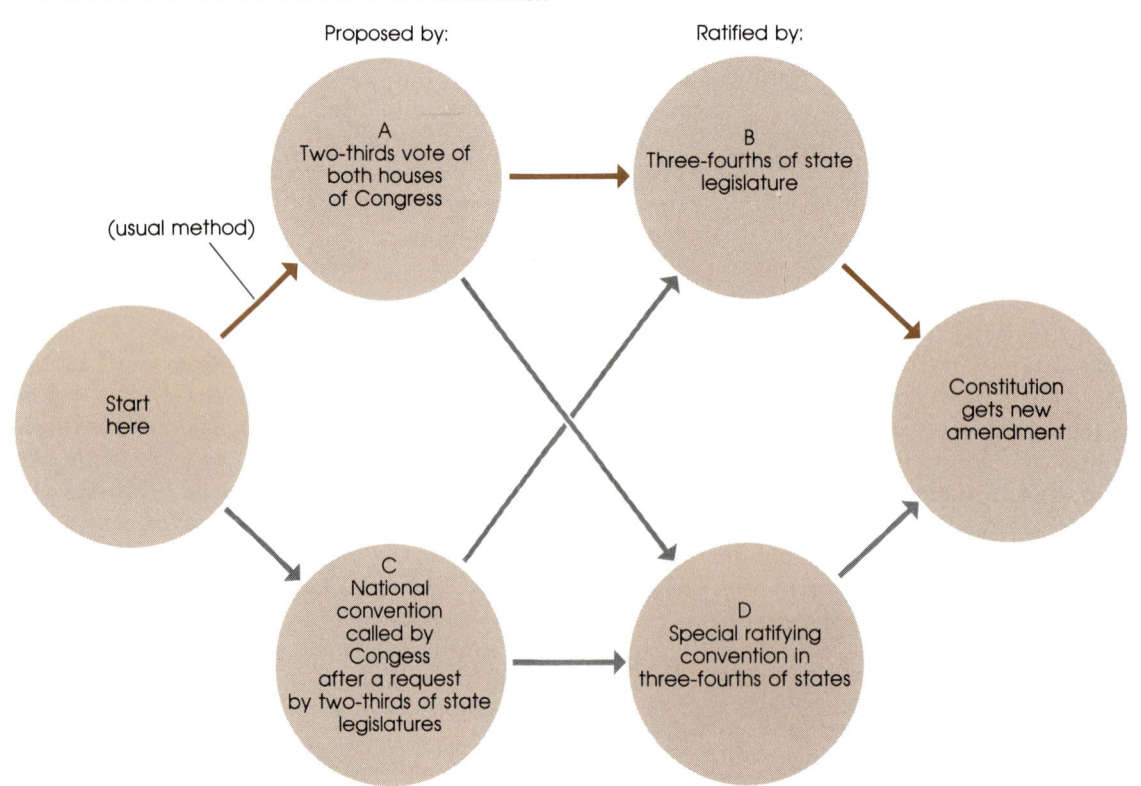

Wide World Photos

In addition to the scores of suggested amendments still in Congress, two have already been proposed to the states. The rally above was held in Chicago, Ill., in 1980 to gather support for one of these, the Equal Rights Amendment (ERA). The other amendment proposed that the District of Columbia be treated as a state for purposes of congressional representation and presidential elections.

21st cancel one another out. The former prohibited the sale of intoxicating liquors; the latter repealed that prohibition 16 years later. Only 14 amendments in 189 years would seem to indicate that amending the Constitution is hardly a favorite American pastime.

Or is it? Scores of suggested amendments are every year on the calendars of the House and Senate Judiciary Committees. At first blush, one gets the impression that almost every self-respecting member of Congress has some plan to improve the Constitution. But on closer investigation, one learns that the subjects dealt with really come down to a dozen or so: abortion, capital punishment, school prayer, school busing, and a single six-year term for the president and vice president. But heading the list are various proposals to balance the federal budget. Some of these do no more than say that the government should not spend more than it takes in. Others set various ceilings on the percentage of the gross national product (ranging from 15 percent to $33\frac{1}{3}$ percent) that government can spend.

What makes the call for the balanced budget amendment interesting and even frightening to some students of constitutional development is the manner in which it is being proposed. Under Article V of the Constitution, "Congress . . . shall call a convention for proposing amendments" if it is demanded by two thirds (or 34) of the state legislatures. With 26 states already aboard, only eight more are needed.

Almost nothing is known with any certainty about the procedures that would govern such a constitutional convention. Remember, there has been no convention since the founding meeting of 1787 in Philadelphia—although the threat of one often has been used to stir Congress to act. It was a call for such a convention that prompted Congress to propose the prohibition amendment.

The real concern of some is what the scope of such a convention would be once assembled. With all kinds of half-baked proposals waiting in the wings, the result could be a constitutional free-for-all. If it came to that, who would play the roles of Madison, Hamilton, Franklin, Wilson, and Washington? The candidates seem to be few. As Richard Rovere, a long-time observer of American politics, wrote:

> There is a case against a budget-balancing amendment that has nothing to do with the economic wisdom of any specific proposal or with the hidden dangers of a convention. It is simply that the amendment process should be used as sparingly as a surgeon's knife, and only as a legislative tool of last resort.[11]

Fortunately, there are at least three alternatives to the radical surgery suggested by the amendment process: judicial interpretation, **executive interpretation,** and custom and practices of political parties. In the paragraphs that follow, we shall consider these three alternatives. To conclude this chapter, we shall explore the more general issue of whether the Constitution should be interpreted strictly or loosely.

Judicial interpretation. One reason we have federal courts is to explain or interpret the Constitution. As we shall see in the next chapter, the constitutional language on which Supreme Court justices have based many of their important decisions affecting personal autonomy and lifestyles is rarely self-revealing. And, as we have already seen, it can be silent on important matters, such as **judicial review.** Then, too, the words used in the Constitution change with time. Not even Franklin could have imagined the need for laws to regulate telegraph, telephone, radio, computerization of records, cable television, electronic spying equipment, and communications satellites. Yet the Supreme Court has decided that such laws—when they are drawn up in agreement with the basic principles given in the Constitution—are constitutional. Such decisions, and the laws they approve, apply the principles of the Constitution to new realities.

Two parts of the Constitution have been the chief technical instruments for the Court in this context: the **commerce clause** (Article I, Section 8) and the equal protection clause (Section 1 of the 14th Amendment). Chapter 11 deals with the equal protection clause; here we shall only consider the commerce clause to see how courts adapt the Constitution over time.

The commerce clause granted Congress the power to "regulate commerce among the several states." The obvious purpose was to promote trade between the states. With only these terse words, the Court has nullified (i.e., deprived of legal force) state tax laws and regulations that hamper interstate commerce.

Building on this groundwork layed by the Marshall Court early in the 19th century, Congress gradually took over regulation of parts of the economy that states had formerly policed. Two milestones of this period were the Interstate Commerce Act of 1887 and the Sherman Anti-Trust Act of 1890. Both will be discussed in later chapters.

Around 1910, state governments began to impose restrictions on the employment of children. Since states that had such laws were at a competitive disadvantage, pressure increased for national legislation. Eventually, legislation banning products produced using child labor from interstate commerce passed; the Supreme Court, though, struck it down in 1918 (*Hammer* v. *Dagenhart*). Over the next several years, efforts at getting a constitutional amendment adopted proved unsuccessful. In 1938, Congress passed the Fair Labor Standards Act. This act, among other things, prohibited child labor. But this time, the Supreme Court decided to interpret the commerce clause differently; in *U.S.* v. *Darby* (1941) it upheld the power of Congress to regulate child labor.

Since then, the Court has supported even more far-reaching applications of the commerce clause by Congress. *Wickard* v. *Filburn* (1942) is perhaps the most striking example. In that case the Court decided the commerce clause gave the federal government authority to say to an Ohio farmer, "You cannot grow wheat on your own farm to feed your own chickens and cows and to make flour with which to make biscuits for you and your family to eat in your own home. If you do, the Secretary of Agriculture can make you pay a penalty." What has that got to do with interstate commerce? Well, the Court said, "If we assume [Mr. Filburn's wheat] is never marketed, it supplies a need of a man who grew it which would otherwise be reflected by purchases in the open market." That is, if Mr. Filburn is not allowed to raise any wheat, he will have to buy his chicken feed at the store. The store will buy it from a feed mill, which, in turn, will perhaps buy its grain in Chicago.

Executive interpretation. Relations with other nations are under the joint control of the president and the Senate. The Constitution provides that the president "shall have power, by and with the advice and consent of the Senate, to make treaties, provided two thirds of the senators present concur." When the president and Senate together agree with a foreign nation upon a treaty, this often helps to clarify and expand the meaning of the Constitution.

Many examples could be given to show how treaties help to develop the meaning of the Constitution. The Constitution does not say whether aliens living in this country can own land, so you might think the states would decide this matter. But the president and the Senate have made treaties with foreign governments in which the right to own land in the United States was granted to the citizens of the foreign countries. The Constitution gives Congress the power to "provide and maintain" a navy. The Congress has usually decided how large the navy should be by controlling the amount of money spent for it. But the United States has made treaties with foreign nations in which it agreed to limit the size of its navy.

Furthermore, rules made by government agencies help to clarify and expand the plan of government outlined in the Constitution. Many of the acts passed by the Congress are rather general; they do not take care of all the details necessary to put the laws into effect. This responsibility is delegated to some government department, bureau, or commission. Often the agencies that put the laws into effect have to make rules to fill in the details. These rules have the same general effect as acts of the Congress if they interpret the law and do not go beyond it. In this way, the rules made by government agencies help to develop the plan of government outlined in the Constitution.

Custom and practices of political parties. Even though the way of choosing officers to whom the people may delegate authority is part of the plan of government built on the foundation of the Constitution, American political parties are nowhere mentioned in the Constitution. Yet they nominate candidates for national offices, and neither the Constitution nor the federal laws give any standards to regulate such nominations.

Sometimes custom is stronger than written law. It is a custom that the president shall in most cases appoint members of his own political party to head the executive departments of the federal government. This has proved to be a good way to reach the objective of Article II of the Constitution—the setting up of an effective executive branch to put the laws into effect.

Constitutional change in perspective. In sum, the Constitution has grown through both regular amendments and informal methods. As one of the great chief justices of the Supreme Court, John Marshall, said when the Constitution was still in adolescence: "We must never forget that it is a Constitution . . . intended to *endure* for ages to come, and, consequently, to be *adapted* to the various *crises* of human affairs."

Here we come to one of the really fundamental questions of American politics. In adapting the Constitution to changing circumstances, how far should presidents, Congress, and the judiciary go? Some favor a loose or liberal construction of constitutional phrases; others favor a strict interpretation. The difference in these two positions on constitutional construction hinges largely on how one feels about broad grants of power to national government (loose construction) as opposed to the retention of as much power as possible in the states (strict construction). The issue first arose in the case of *McCulloch* v. *Maryland* (1819). Did the national government have *implied* powers in addition to those expressly delegated to it? Chief Justice Marshall answered yes. Thus the principle of and necessity for a loose construction was established (see box).

That "necessity" is perhaps best seen in the

McCulloch v. Maryland

In 1819 the Supreme Court, under Chief Justice John Marshall, announced an opinion that has had as much influence on American politics as any deed by president or Congress. The opinion concerned the Second Bank of the U.S., which had been approved by Congress in 1816 and allowed to establish branches in large towns.

During the depression of 1818–19 feelings ran high against the Second Bank. Several state legislatures decided to tax the bank's branches with the hope of destroying its business. When the Baltimore branch decided to ignore the law, the state of Maryland brought suit against the cashier, James McCulloch. It won in a state court. McCulloch appealed.

The lawyer for the state of Maryland argued that the U.S. Constitution came not from the people but from "sovereign and independent states." Any power that the national government exercised had been delegated to it by the states, who alone possessed supreme power. This was also the view of Thomas Jefferson and, several decades later, the Southern Confederacy. But it was not the view of Marshall.

It would be difficult, he wrote, to support this proposition. Although the Constitutional Convention of 1787 was elected by state legislatures, the document that they produced was a mere proposal. True, these people had assembled in their several states. But where else should they have assembled? The measures they adopted do not cease to be the measures of the people themselves just because they happened to decide inside

Participants in *McCulloch* v. *Maryland (1819):* (left) John Marshall, Chief Justice of the Supreme Court; (right) Daniel Webster, attorney for the United States government.

these states. The Constitution derives its whole authority from these groupings of *people*, not from the states. "The government of the Union, then . . . is emphatically and truly a government of the people." If the people and not separate states are sovereign (i.e., have supreme power), then it follows that the states do not have the right to nullify (i.e., to deprive of legal force) an act of Congress.

Having demolished the doctrine of "states rights," Marshall next attacked the doctrine of "strict construction."

The argument against the bank had been simple: The power to charter it was not expressly granted by the Constitution and cannot be inferred from Article I, Section 8. A national bank, Jefferson had said, is clearly not necessary, even if some people may consider it useful. In meeting this argument, Marshall made two statements that profoundly shaped America's constitutional growth.

The first statement concerned the implied powers of Congress. "Let the end be legitimate, let it be within the scope of the Constitution, and all means which are plainly adapted to that end, which are not prohibited, but consist with the letter and spirit of the Constitution, are constitutional. In other words, even if the word "bank" did not appear in the Constitution, the power to manage money is. Congress is to lay and collect taxes, issue a currency, and borrow funds. To carry out these **enumerated powers**, Congress may reasonably decide that chartering a bank is "necessary and proper."

But who is to decide whether the end is "within the scope of the Constitution" and whether the means "are plainly adapted to that end"? Marshall's answer is clear and logical:

> Should Congress, in the execution of its powers, adopt measures which are prohibited by the Constitution; or should Congress, under the pretext of executing its powers, pass laws for the accomplishment of objects not entrusted to the government, it would become the painful duty of this tribunal, should a case requiring such a decision come before it, to say that such an act was not the law of the land. But where the law is not prohibited, and is really calculated to effect any of the objects entrusted to the government, to undertake here to inquire into the degree of its necessity would be to pass the line which circumscribes the Judicial Department, and to tread on legislative ground. This court disclaims all pretensions to such a power.

Unfortunately, the decision did not quite settle the issue of states' rights versus national supremacy once and for all. Only a few years later John C. Calhoun of South Carolina would be expounding the **doctrine of nullification.** Calhoun's view was that, since the Constitution was a compact among states, each state was free to nullify any federal law that state considered unauthorized. How would it do that? By simply refusing to enforce the law within its boundaries. It took the Civil War to destroy this doctrine.

---

case of Jefferson, who had preached long and hard the gospel of strict construction—that is, until he was confronted with the opportunity to purchase the entire Louisiana Territory at a wholesale price. Finding nothing in the Constitution specifically allowing such a transaction, he swallowed hard and bought. Still, not all presidents, courts, or Congresses have agreed with Jefferson that "as new discoveries are made, new truths disclosed, and manners and opinions changed . . . institutions must advance also, and keep pace with the times."

What then is the other side of the argument? Strict constructionists are found quoting Washington's Farewell Address:

> If in the opinion of the people the distribution or modification of the constitutional powers be in any particular wrong, let it be corrected by an amendment in the way by which the Constitution designates. But let there be no change by usurpation; for though this in one instance may be the instrument of good, it is the customary weapon by which free governments are destroyed.

Similarly, Justice Hugo Black, in his dissent in *Harper* v. *Virginia Board of Elections* (1966), puts the case for strict construction this way:

> When a political theory embodied in our Constitution becomes outdated, a majority of the nine members of this Court are not only without constitutional power, but are far less qualified to choose a new constitutional political theory than the people of this country proceeding in the manner provided by Article V.

Like so many controversies, the best course of action probably lies somewhere between two extremes. In a modern world, strict construction would result in a Constitution barnacled with hundreds of amendments. Some states have followed this line in changing their own constitutions. The results have not been altogether good. For example, the Texas Constitution has over 200 amendments streaming along after it like the tail of a comet.

For the loose constructionist, the goal line was probably marked off by Charles Evan Hughes in a speech made long before he became chief justice: "The Constitution is what the judges say it is."*

To shed light on the drawbacks in this position, it is useful to return to the metaphor of architecture. Some experts (Vincent Scully of Yale, for example) have speculated that the mobile home is the germ of tomorrow's architecture. Not only shall we have prefabricated, fully equipped houses in the factory. We also shall have a more mobile lifestyle. "The automobile, although more a vehicle than a home, displays what will be the new architecture's basic characteristics." Rudolf Arnheim contrasts this brave new architecture to what has gone before.

> The traditional house, rooted in the ground, has always served the productive role of counterpoint to human mobility. In opposing the one-sidedness of a nomadic lifestyle, the stable home establishes a richer pattern of being and dwelling pitted against moving, acting, and changing. When everything changes constantly, change loses much of its creative power. Architecture, therefore, has always acted as a tangible symbol of what is given, what can be relied upon, but also what must be reckoned with as a constant condition.[12]

Paraphrase is not hard here. In a whirl of technological change and social upheaval, the hallmarks of the last half of the 20th century, a stable Constitution serves an important role. It provides the modicum of underlying stability that is the prerequisite for creativity and sanity. The ship of state the founding fathers designed in 1787 was not, as one early critic charged, "all sails." They had given the American republic an anchor, too.

---

* While this statement is used with great delight by the loose constructionist for discounting the significance of the Constitution, it is taken out of context. The point Hughes was trying to make was that, the Constitution, like all other laws, is not self-enforcing; therefore, we should select judges who respect it and who will give it correct interpretation.

Chapter Key

The peaceful, mutually beneficial relationship between Britain and the American colonies began to come apart after the French and Indian Wars. During the 1760s, King George and his prime minister forced laws through Parliament designed to raise British revenues from the colonies and to restrict severely the colonists' rights as English citizens. The colonists reacted to each action more sharply than the British government had expected. More British repressions led to the gathering of the First Continental Congress in September 1774 and, ultimately, to open hostility.

The Second Continental Congress on July 2, 1776, appointed a committee to write a Declaration of Independence, expressing the colonists' rights as human beings and defending actions already taken. Thomas Jefferson, drawing on the "sentiments of the day," wrote the first draft of the Declaration. He concentrated on three principles: human rights, political participation, and limited government.

From 1781 until 1787, the colonies were loosely united under the Articles of Confederation. The Articles created a government dominated by the individual states rather than a central national government. The national legislature had few powers, and there was no national executive. The economic instability of this period was the principal factor prompting delegates from the states to call for a convention.

The Constitutional Convention was attended by 55 men of democratic and republican convictions. They met in Philadelphia in May 1787 to draft a constitution to present to the states for ratification. The Continental Congress had wished to limit the convention to a revision of the Articles. But devoted nationalists such as James Madison and Alexander Hamilton turned their ideas into actions. The delegates went well beyond revision of the Articles. They established a national government, republican in form and employing the concept of federalism. Among the plans introduced at the convention were the Virginia Plan (which offered a sovereign national government able to deal directly both with the people and with states) and the New Jersey Plan (which offered a system in which the states were sovereign). The delegates eventually adopted the Connecticut Compromise (also known as the Great Compromise). This agreement set up a federation—a mixture of state and national sovereignty.

The Federalists supported ratification of the Constitution. James Madison, Alexander Hamilton, and John Jay wrote *The Federalist Papers* explaining the Constitution and supporting ratification. Influential men such as George Mason, Richard Henry Lee, Patrick Henry, and Samuel Adams opposed ratification for various reasons. Many criticized the lack of a Bill of Rights. Within 11 months after being submitted to the states, the Constitution had been ratified by the necessary nine states.

The U.S. Constitution, the first written constitution in the world, embodies these major principles of government:

Federalism—sharing of political power between the national and state governments, though federal law is supreme in areas where the federal government has power.

Separation of powers—division of power into executive, legislative, and judicial branches, with checks and balances and sharing among the branches.

Judicial review—the authority of the Supreme Court to review laws and declare them to be invalid if they are in conflict with the Constitution.

Representative government—the people rule through the representatives they choose in free elections.

The Constitution is not static; it is flexible. It has changed over time. In many places, its language is deliberately vague. This allows differing interpretations by public officials, especially the Supreme Court. The Constitution can also be amended by one of several methods. The basic requirement is that three fourths of the states concur with the change. Since 1788, 26 amendments have been added to the Constitution. The first 10, the Bill of Rights, were adopted by the first Congress.

The Tate Gallery, London

3 | The Force of Ideas

After studying this chapter you should be able to answer the following questions:

1. What role did ideas play in shaping the thinking of the founding fathers?
2. Why is democracy hard to achieve in practice?
3. How are the ideas of equality and liberty related?
4. What is a conservative?
5. What did Marx believe?
6. Discuss the problems of contemporary communism?

Terms you should know:

alienation
aristocracy
bourgeois
civil disobedience
citizenship
conservatism
constitutionalism
democracy
empirical
Enlightenment
equality
fascism
justice
tyranny
government of laws
Gulag
historical materialism

ideology
imperialism
labor theory of values
liberalism
liberty
Maoism
monarchy
natural laws
oligarchy
participatory democracy
property
proletariat
radicalism
social contract
state of nature
utilitarianism
utopian

We can never know exactly when Thomas Jefferson became a champion of freedom. But it is safe to assume that by the time he entered politics, he had become deeply committed to the idea that human reason and freedom were essential to the good life. Jefferson did not hold this idea alone; it was a part of the intellectual climate in which he dwelled. That climate is commonly described as the **Enlightenment**.

If we must find a starting point for the Enlightenment, we can say it was ushered in by Sir Isaac Newton (1642–1727). In 1793, William Blake, the English poet and engraver, portrayed Newton in a large graphic as a kind of great architect, measuring the boundaries of the heavens with his compass. What a look of concentration! Here is one of the most intelligent men who ever lived. Newton's work in science began quickly to have an impact in other fields. His law of gravity in particular came to be regarded as the ultimate example of exploratory science. Phenomena of any kind, it was believed, could and should be explained in terms of certain fundamental or **natural laws**. The scientific method and careful observation of Newton could and should be extended to all fields of human endeavors.

Jefferson did not introduce the Enlightenment into the colonies. But he, along with Ben Franklin, became its chief apostles on their side of the Atlantic. They always clung to its major tenets. What were these tenets? In addition to those already mentioned—natural laws, careful observation, the scientific method—there were these: the ultimate importance of the individual, opposition to superstition and absolute dogma, a faith in progress, a hostility to arbitrary power of any sort, a belief in toleration, and a reliance on the general improvement of the human condition through reason. (Blake put it this way: "Peace and plenty and domestic happiness is the source of sublime act. . . . Enjoyment and not abstinence is the food of intellect.")

The political credo of the founding fathers is encapsulated in the Declaration of Independence and the Constitution. It was based on the intellectual optimism of the Enlightenment. The respect for the individual and toleration of differences, which constituted liberty as they understood it, was seen as a primary political good. If one only knew enough science, any intelligent person could see this goodness.

In the ninth *Federalist Paper*, Hamilton spoke of a new "science of politics." Although previous republics had sometimes failed, progress in political science could overcome this tendency. He wrote: "The science of politics . . . like most other sciences, has received great improvement. The efficacy of various principles is now well understood, which were either not known at all or imperfectly known to the ancients." Hamilton went on to cite as examples of "new discoveries" the various constitutional institutions with which we dealt in the last chapter: separation of powers, the system of checks and balances (how mechanistic, how Newtonian a concept), representation of the people in the legislature, the independent judiciary, and so on.

THE ROLE OF IDEAS IN POLITICS

The point of the preceding discussion of Newton, the Enlightenment, and the founding fathers is that *ideas do matter*. To paraphrase a well-known quote by British economist John Maynard Keynes, the ideas of political philosophers and economists are more powerful than is commonly understood. Indeed, little else rules the world. Practical men and women who consider themselves quite immune to intellectual influences are usually the slaves of some deceased political philosopher. Political leaders who think they act on instinct in truth are drawing their thoughts from some intellectual scribbler of a few years back. Even the power of special interest groups, which has been such a great and long-standing concern to observers of American politics, is exaggerated compared with the gradual force of ideas.

The thesis of this chapter is that ideas do matter. To put it negatively: If we ignore the role of ideas in politics, then our view of past political events is obscured and our understanding of current (and future) issues shallow.

Without some grasp of how political theory evolved, it would be impossible to make sense of many terms and phrases that dominate the oratory, pamphleteering, and key documents of the revolutionary period. What is meant by "natural law" and "natural rights"? What is the justification for the rule of law? What is the "state of nature"? The contract theory of government? What did the founders mean by the "pursuit of happiness"? By the expression "all men are created equal"? Similarly, when Martin Luther King, Jr., urged the tactic of passive resistance—blacks, he said, should meet "physical force with an even stronger force, namely, soul force"—what did he mean? To deny the influence of previous ideas on the founders and on King is to drain much of the meaning out of the American Revolution and the nonviolent protest movement. The Constitution becomes no more than the product of various compromises and artful political tinkering. King's letter from the Birmingham jail, written from his cell on April 16, 1963, and containing his answer to charges by a group of Birmingham clergymen that he was in their city as an "outside agitator," becomes only an incident in a morality play. The letter, as we shall see later in the chapter, is actually a minor classic of political philosophy.

Political theory also helps us clarify the perennial issues of politics. Leaders today may be less philosophical than those in the past and citizens may be less well schooled in the inner principles of their institutions. But political ideas still abound in America today. Countless academics, artists, and media stars regularly peddle ideas to the public. But there is no Consumer Protection Agency for ideas. Purveyors of intellectual untruth, therefore, enjoy virtual immunity. To select from this harvest must always be hazardous. What can and should be

University of Virginia Information Services

Wide World Photos

John Ruskin, the 19th-century English art critic, said: "Great nations write their autobiographies in three manuscripts, the book of their deeds, the book of their words and the book of their art. Not one of these books can be understood unless we read the others, but of the three the only trustworthy one is the last." Ruskin might be right. If one wants to know whether Thomas Jefferson's preference for clarity, elegance, symmetry, and repose was true, one need only look at the Rotunda of the University of Virginia (above). There is no better record of the elusive spirit of the American Revolution than the colonnades and high porticos of Jefferson's Rotunda. It is the spirit of the Roman republic, of individual freedom against monarchical control. Even in the harsh glare of today, it attests to the founding fathers' profound feeling that Roman architecture (below) and their own bold adventure were related.

done about this seems fairly clear. The greater our familiarity with political philosophy, the less we shall be at the mercy of plausible but mistaken analogy; the less we shall be tempted by a false or irrelevant model; and the less likely we shall be to embrace the illusions that wait for the ignorant and unwary.

One of Bill Brock's favorite dictums while he was chairman of the Republican party was that politics is a "battle of ideas." I would not argue that the 1980 presidential election can be understood purely as a battle of ideas. But I would submit that the perspective of ideas is useful. Behind all the reporting on Ronald Reagan's style, personality, ability to communicate, and stand on the issues (e.g., government regulation, foreign policy, spending, and unemployment) were the ideas he was affirming. If one wants to understand how Reagan perceives, feels, and deals with public policy issues, one must get to the level of ideas.

President Reagan says he is a conservative. But what does this mean? In this chapter, we shall explore the roots of this concept. We shall try to sort out different versions of it and compare and contrast it with liberalism.

Turning to Reagan's opponent in the 1980 contest, Jimmy Carter, what role did ideas play in his defeat? It could be argued that, behind all the reporting on Carter's style and personality, behind all the accomplishments and failures of his four years in office, were the ideas he was affirming. In the waning days of his reelection campaign, he reiterated day after day the old, once-successful ideas that the Democrats had used to conquer the Depression and create the good life for the average American.

One interpretation of the election, then, is this: Middle-class audiences found the ideas Carter was expounding less relevant than in past elections. Today many leading Democrats believe their party has been coasting on old ideas. Some of them think the party needs to develop and publicize what had been lacking in the 1980 election—new ideas about governing and pursuing the traditional Democratic goals of social and economic justice.

Ideas probably play an even more vital role in world politics. One quick example. The Soviet Union's problem in Eastern Europe has been the failure of ideas. In 1944 and 1945, the Soviet leaders might reasonably have thought that their ideas and institutions would prevail. This was not merely because they had soldiers and secret agents in the East European countries to impose what they wanted. It was because Russia's Marxism-Leninism seemed a new and vital system. Leninist Russia won the war, had vanquished Nazism, and dominated Central Europe. Moreover, the societies it now occupied seemed to belong to a discredited past. But this proved untrue. The Eastern European nations reestablished ideas from their pasts and stubbornly resisted the Soviet idea. Thirty-five years later, the Soviet Union has made few converts. Ideas can only be defeated by antithetical ideas; this is the gist of what is happening in Eastern Europe today. The Soviet Union remains in Eastern Europe only by force of arms—not by force of ideas.

We can wrap up the preceding discussion by simply saying that ideas help us to understand past and present American and world politics. If true, this makes ideas very important in understanding politics. To see just how true, we need to take a closer look at how ideas have shaped each kind of politics—American and world, past and present.

SHAPING THE DECLARATION OF INDEPENDENCE AND THE CONSTITUTION

From Legal Quibbles to Natural Rights

Obviously, the colonists did not think of themselves as crass opportunists, striking at Britain once the French and Indian threat was removed. They were unwilling to accept the ancient notion that might makes right. They would act in the name of justice, nothing less.

But to hold this view, the colonists had to find something other than taxation without representation as the basis for revolt. Few men are willing to die for disputes in public finance. Who is going to storm a fort full of redcoats because the British Parliament set customs duties too high?

By the time Thomas Jefferson wrote the Declaration of Independence, the Revolutionary leaders had hit upon the right moral basis. They would present their case to King George and, more important, to the world in terms of the loftiest of ideas: natural or universal law, individual rights, and political equality. Eleven years later, when the founding fathers met in Philadelphia, they would face the difficult challenge of designing a government that would embody, that would institutionalize, these abstract ideas.

The founding fathers' job was made less difficult by their being comfortable with ideas. Questions about natural law, individual rights, and political equality could not be answered by lawyers and textbooks. But they could be handled by statesmen who deeply believed in them. The founding fathers, therefore, saw their job clearly: Create an independent nation based squarely on these ideas.

Whence Did These Ideas Arise?

One does not resolve the perennial issues of politics such as we discussed above by flipping through a world almanac or by spending an afternoon in the computer center. These issues do not raise questions of fact, such as, Are there alligators in North Dakota? Nor do they lend themselves to resolution by applying certain principles of mathematics or logic. These issues are philosophical; one just does not know where to look for their answers.

Well, not exactly. We can, as the founding fathers did, look to some of the thinkers who have already discussed them. They are worth our attention because they have managed to restate the questions in a way that makes certain answers seem at least plausible. These philosophers dig into the presuppositions of our thinking; they investigate and bring to light the buried assumptions hidden in the terms we use. And, because we use them, they get smuggled into our conclusions and therefore into our beliefs and actions.

A journey through 2,400 years of political theory may seem a frightening prospect. It really is not. One of the greatest philosophers of modern times, Bertrand Russell, once explained why the central visions of the great philosophers are essentially simple. What can make them seem so difficult is not their visions of politics nor their terms of explanation. It is their elaborate efforts to defend these conceptions from the objections of other philosophers. Fortunately, in the remainder of this chapter, we need not concern ourselves with this elaborate armament designed to fend off every possible adversary. We cannot fit their philosophies on a bumper sticker, but we can present their central vision with clarity and simplicity.

Aristotle (384–322 B.C.). Although Aristotle studied under Plato, he had a more practical bent. Though he journeyed through all of Plato's ideas, Aristotle departs far less from common experience than his master. Where Plato is inspired, Aristotle is sober. Where Plato aims for utopia, Aristotle settles for a constitution. Our study of Aristotle can be advantageously divided into three topics: (1) **citizenship,** (2) the **rule of law,** and (3) **constitutionalism.**

Citizenship. To Aristotle, the good human being and the good citizen are one and the same in the ideal state. It follows that the end of the state should be to produce the highest moral type. Unless a citizen actually shares in the power of the political community, however, this is not possible.

A dividend of this wider political participation is increased self-sufficiency of the community. But the main payoff for Aristotle is the expectation that participation allows citizens to

In the center of Raphael's *School of Athens*, Plato and Aristotle are found. Plato points heavenward, signifying his belief that political authority should be placed in the hands of a philosopher-king, who would know the ideal way to run a government.

Aristotle rejected the notion that one could determine this otherworldly ideal. Thus, he extends his arm in an earthly gesture signifying his more mundane approach. He focused his political philosophy on insuring that certain democratic procedures were followed in running the government.

The philosophers on the left, by Plato, are those representing the theoretical approach. Those on the right, by Aristotle, are the more practical, empirical thinkers.

develop their capacities to the fullest. Indeed, because individuals gain through participation, they have not only the right but also the obligation to take part in affairs of state. Man is, he wrote, "a political animal"; the solitary man is either a beast or a God.

The rule of law. Aristotle proclaimed that there were two sorts of laws—the particular and the universal. The former is the law defined and declared by each community for its members. The latter, however, is the law of nature or **natural law.** Like Plato, Aristotle believed that there existed a natural form of the just and unjust (that is, common to all human beings, no matter where they reside).

It is a natural law that Antigone of Sophocles' play has in mind when she insists that it is just to bury her brother in spite of the king's decree to the contrary. According to natural law and Antigone, some acts are *naturally* just: "Not of today or yesterday its force: It springs eternal: No man knows its birth."

It is natural law that Thomas Jefferson had in mind when he listed several "self-evident" truths in the second paragraph of the Declaration of Independence. It is a concept that underpins most of Abraham Lincoln's political thought.

> What constitutes the bulwark of our own liberty and independence? It is not frowning battlements, our bristling sea coasts, our army and our navy. These are not our reliance against tyranny . . . our reliance in the love of liberty which God has planted in us. Our defense is in the spirit which prized liberty as the heritage of all men, in all lands everywhere.[1]

After a long history, 17th- and 18th-century philosophers, such as Hobbes and Kant, began to criticize the notion of natural law. By the 19th century, it had begun to fade. Today, however, we are once again asking whether there are certain actions that, no matter what the particular laws or extenuating circumstances of the land, can be—must be—called unjust. An inventory of such actions might include genocide, torture, and terrorist tactics (e.g., the taking of innocent hostages).

Constitutionalism. To discover what political arrangement will best insure justice along with stability, Aristotle made an elaborate study of 158 constitutions and the causes for changes in constitutions. Because he grounded his generalizations in observation rather than abstract reasoning alone, we say his method was **empirical**. The results of his study appear, somewhat modified, in Figure 3–1.

According to Aristotle, the first governments were kingships. In time, many persons of equal merit arose. They began to desire a commonwealth with a constitution. But this ruling class, or **aristocracy**, soon begins to deteriorate and enrich itself out of the public treasury. As riches became the path to honor, oligarchies naturally grew up.

Because the love of gain in the ruling classes tended to diminish their number, the masses where strengthened. So, oligarchies eventually pass into democracies.

FIGURE 3–1
Aristotle's Political Life Cycle (modified)

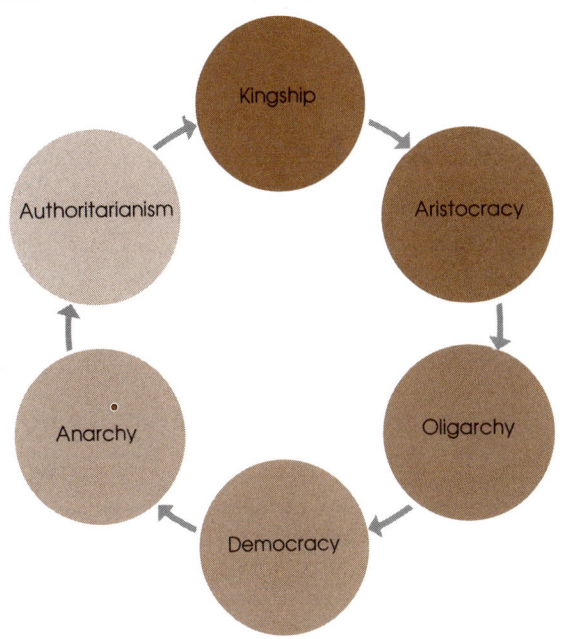

In democracies the passion for greater equality and less restraint leads to an extreme form of democracy, egalitarianism (absolute social and political equality) or anarchy (absence of all government control over individuals).

People cannot tolerate "life at random" for long. In time, the opportunity becomes ripe for the emergence of a "strong man on a white horse," a Napoleon, who will restore stability. But the temporary savior becomes a permanent one, and the tyranny becomes a kingship. How well do you think Aristotle's theory of political cycles applies to modern nation-states?

Some claim Aristotle to be the initiator of constitutionalism. He recognized that politics was a conflict-resolving activity and sought to distribute power among the upper, middle, and lower classes within a framework of laws. Plato had advocated placing all power in a specially trained philosopher-king. The good society to Aristotle was pluralistic and dynamic. He writes:

> There is a point at which a state may attain such a degree of unity as to be no longer a state, or at which without actually ceasing to exist, it will become an inferior state, like harmony passing into unison, or rhythm which has been reduced to a single note.

Aristotle looked upon freedom of speech as a means of attaining political truth. There are no all-knowing philosopher-kings here. "The ability to raise searching difficulties on both sides of a subject will make us detect more easily the truth and error about the several points that arise." Four centuries later, St. Paul, in his travels up and down the coast of Asia Minor, was mobbed, imprisoned, and beaten—everywhere but in Athens. There he was brought into a great assembly of the citizens, the Arcopagus, and asked, "May we know what this new teaching is?"

To conclude our discussion of Aristotle, let us return to the Declaration of Independence's reference to each person's right to pursue happiness. You may not be aware that the term *happiness* has acquired a meaning—under the influence of some 18th- and 19th-century philosophers we shall meet shortly—quite different from the original meaning. Today we tend to mean by "happiness" something like pleasure or satisfaction. This meaning was hardly what Jefferson and the signers had in mind.

Aristotle can help us understand this crucial term as it appears in one of America's two most important political documents. He was closer to the mark than the pop thinkers of the 1980s. Happiness to him was the good life; that is, "the exercise of vital powers along lines of excellence in a life affording scope." To Aristotle and his fellow Greeks, happiness was not the pursuit of some floating, thrill-seeking life. It was one carefully concerned with doing well at the task of living a *human* existence. I am afraid the mere passage of time does not always usher in improvements in human thought and life.

Judaic and Christian heritage. Judaic and Christian thought produced no systematic philosophical discussion of political principles on the order of Aristotle. This thought, however, cannot be ignored. It provided symbols and psychological assumptions that deeply influenced subsequent political thinking.

Take the Judaic sense of the "chosen people," the people led by God through the wilderness because they had an enduring purpose. This model undoubtedly influenced later political theorists when they argued that the people should have a voice in the appointment of a king or a regime or that the king had a duty to the people.

The words of the New Testament had a more direct influence. Jesus' submission to Roman authority ("Render unto Caesar the things that are Caesar's") undoubtedly made a doctrine of resistance hard to develop in the West. But the emphasis on heaven and soul fostered a sense of privacy and individualism. The emphasis on the brotherhood of man strengthened the idea of common human nature. As St. Paul wrote:

> There are varieties of gifts, but the same Spirit. There are varieties of service, but the same Lord. There are many forms of work, but all of them, in all men, all the work of the same God. In each of of us the Spirit is manifested in one particular way, for some useful purpose.[2]

Centuries later, Martin Luther King in his "Letter from Birmingham Jail" would appeal to theological sources—namely, St. Augustine, one of the Latin fathers in the early Christian Church—to justify civil disobedience. "The answer lies," he wrote, "in the fact that there are two types of laws: just and unjust. I would be the first to advocate obeying just laws. One has not only a legal but a moral responsibility to obey just laws. Conversely, one has a moral responsibility to disobey unjust laws. I would agree with St. Augustine that 'an unjust law is no law at all.'" To King, one could not be moral by obeying immoral laws. But the troublesome question is, How does one determine whether a law is just or unjust?

In the following passage, which represents his best reasoning on the subject, King appealed to the authority of Catholic, Protestant, and Jewish theologians to support his understanding of how one identifies unjust laws:

> A just law is a man-made code that squares with the moral law or the law of God. An unjust law is a code that is out of harmony with the moral law. To put it in the terms of St. Thomas Aquinas: An unjust law is a human law that is not rooted in eternal law and natural law. Any law that uplifts human personality is just. Any law that degrades human personality is unjust. All segregation statutes are unjust because segregation distorts the soul and damages the personality. It gives the segregator a false sense of superiority and the segregated a false sense of inferiority. Segregation, to use the terminology of the Jewish philosopher Martin Buber, substitutes an 'I-it' relationship for an 'I-thou' relationship and ends up relegating persons to the status of things. Hence segregation is not only politically, economically, and sociologically unsound, it is morally wrong and sinful. Paul Tillich has said that sin is separation. Is not

segregation an existential expression of man's tragic separation, his awful estrangement, his terrible sinfulness? Thus it is that I can urge men to obey the 1954 decision of the Supreme Court, for it is morally right; and I can urge them to disobey segregation ordinances, for they are morally wrong.

As Peter J. Paris, professor of ethics and society at Vanderbilt Divinity School, points out in his book *Black Leaders in Conflict* (Pilgrim Press, 1978), King occasionally called upon biblical examples to strengthen his justification of civil disobedience—for example, the refusal of Shadrach, Meshach, and Abednego to obey the laws of Nebuchadnezzar because of their loyalty to a higher moral law and the refusal of the early Christians to compromise their faith with the laws of the Roman Empire.

John Locke (1632–1704). A remarkably persistent belief in Western history was that kings were part of a divinely ordered chain of command. Break that chain and chaos would be king. You may shake your heads at this notion. But how would you refute it if you happened to live in a monarchy that believed it?

This is the solution that Locke chalked out in his *Two Treatises of Government* (1690). He began by looking backward to a peaceable state of nature. To Locke and many philosophers who followed him, the best way to understand political power is to consider the natural condition of men. So he tried to imagine a state of perfect freedom and equality, when they could do as they saw fit without asking anyone's permission.

These frontier conditions are hardly perfect. But they are better than life in an absolute monarchy. The **state of nature** is "full of fear and continual danger." (In the absence of a common judge, each individual holds a kind of authority over all those who may be violating the law of nature.) But it is far less harsh than the state of nature suggested by Thomas Hobbes (1588–1679). In the Hobbesean world, doors are battered down and the threat of violent death is just around the next corner. But in the Lockean world, men seem rational and sociable. They understand the law of nature, which is to say they know the difference between liberty and license.

Why then would anyone want to leave this Lockean world? His answer reveals the common sense that runs through so much of his political philosophy. While men do understand natural law, they are also egoistic and aggressive. For this reason, they form a contract to enter political society. No longer can each man be judge; the legislative function of society now has that responsibility. But this new collective political power is not absolute. If it were, who would ever want to leave the reasonable calm of the state of nature? Who would ever wish to be cast into a situation where **property,** which he or she has labored to produce, could be taken away without consent?

A limited political power, however, is another matter; that is exactly what Locke is offering. Such a political power would have the right to make laws with penalties, to regulate and preserve property, to employ force to execute the laws, and to defend the commonwealth from foreign invasion. In sum, the authority of government *derives* from the contract between the rulers and the people, and it binds both parties. Rulers exercise public power only in accordance with established laws; they do so only for "the peace, safety, and public good of the people."

Thus, Locke vindicates the responsibility of government to the governed, the rule of law, and the toleration of speculative opinion. His writings are a milestone on the road to liberal democracy and an unending source of discomfort to advocates of the totalitarian state.

The idea that people enter into **social contracts** and form governments to protect their property runs from Locke's writings to the Declaration of Independence and on through the Constitution and *The Federalists Papers* like a steel thread.

The reasoning is as follows: Each person is born into the state of nature in a condition

How Much Did Jefferson Rely on Locke?

In his widely acclaimed *Inventing America*, Garry Wills argues that the Declaration of Independence can be understood without reference to Locke. But a careful reading of his *Second Treatise* and *An Essay Concerning Human Understanding* makes it clear that Wills is wrong. In diction, terms ("consent," "usurpations," "dissolution," etc.), structure, and, of course, ideas, the resemblance is striking. Consider the following parallels with the first printed version of the Declaration of Independence. You be the judge. Exerpts from Locke's *Essay on Human Understanding* (1690) and *Second Treatise* (1681):

"As therefore the highest perfection of intellectual nature, his in a careful and constant pursuit of true and solid happiness. . . . The stronger ties we have to an unalterable *pursuit of happiness* in general. . . ." (Compare lines 11 and 12 below)

"For till the mischief be grown general, and all the ill-designs of the rulers become visible, or their attempts sensible to the greater part. The people who are more disposed to suffer than right themselves by resistance are not apt to stir." (Compare lines 19–22)

But if a long train of abuses, prevarications, and artifices, all tending the same way, make the design visible to the people . . . it is not to be wondered that they should then rouse themselves. . . ." (Compare lines 22–25)

The entire Declaration of Independence revolves around this Lockean emphasis on the "legislative power." Over half the document itself is devoted to listing the king's offenses against that power in the colonies. (Compare lines 32–99)

"Whensoever . . . the legislative shall transgress this fundamental rule of society, and either by ambition, fear, folly, or corruption, endeavour to grasp themselves, or put into the hands of any other, an absolute power over their lives, liberties, and estates of the people, by this breach of trust they forfeit the power the people had put into their hands . . . and it devolves upon the people, who have a right to resume their original liberty, and by the establishment of a new legislative . . . provide for their own safety and security." (Compare lines 104–14)

In CONGRESS, July 4, 1776.

A DECLARATION

By the REPRESENTATIVES of the

UNITED STATES OF AMERICA,

In GENERAL CONGRESS assembled.

WHEN in the Course of human Events, it becomes necessary for one People to dissolve the Political Bands which have connected them with another, and to assume among the Powers of the Earth, the separate and equal Station to which the Laws of Nature and of Nature's God entitle them, a decent Respect to the Opinions of Mankind requires that they should declare the causes which impel them to the Separation.

We hold these Truths to be self-evident, that all Men are created equal, that they are endowed by their Creator with certain unalienable
10 Rights, that among these are Life, Liberty, and the Pursuit of Happiness—That to secure these Rights, Governments are instituted among Men, deriving their just Powers from the Consent of the Governed, that whenever any Form of Government becomes destructive of these Ends, it is the Right of the People to alter or to abolish it, and to institute new Government, laying its Foundation on such Principles, and organizing its Powers in such Form, as to them shall seem most likely to effect their Safety and Happiness. Prudence, indeed, will dictate that Governments long established should not be changed for light and transient Causes; and accordingly all Experience hath shewn,
20 that Mankind are more disposed to suffer, while Evils are sufferable, than to right themselves by abolishing the Forms to which they are accustomed. But when a long Train of Abuses and Usurpations, pursuing invariably the same Object, evinces a Design to reduce them under absolute Despotism, it is their Right, it is their Duty, to throw off such Government, and to provide new Guards for their future Security. Such has been the patient Sufferance of these Colonies; and such is now the Necessity which constrains them to alter their former Systems of Government. The History of the present King of Great-Britain is a History of repeated Injuries and Usurpations, all having in direct Object
30 the Establishment of an absolute Tyranny over these States. To prove this, let Facts be submitted to a candid World.

He has refused his Assent to Laws, the most wholesome and necessary for the public Good.

He has forbidden his Governors to pass Laws of immediate and pressing Importance, unless suspended in their Operation till his Assent should be obtained; and when so suspended, he has utterly neglected to attend to them.

He has refused to pass other Laws for the Accommodation of large Districts of People, unless those People would relinquish the Right of
40 Representation in the Legislature, a Right inestimable to them, and formidable to Tyrants only.

He has called together Legislative Bodies at Places unusual, uncomfortable, and distant from the Depository of their public Records, for the sole Purpose of fatiguing them into Compliance with his Measures.

HE has dissolved Representative Houses repeatedly, for opposing with manly Firmness his Invasions on the Rights of the People.

HE has refused for a long Time, after such Dissolutions, to cause others to be elected; whereby the Legislative Powers, incapable of Annihilation, have returned to the People at large for their exercise; the State remain-
50 ing in the mean time exposed to all the Dangers of Invasion from without, and Convulsions within.

HE has endeavoured to prevent the Population of these States; for that Purpose obstructing the Laws for Naturalization of Foreigners; refusing to pass others to encourage their Migrations hither, and raising the Conditions of new Appropriations of Lands.

HE has obstructed the Administration of Justice, by refusing his Assent to Laws for establishing Judiciary Powers.

HE has made Judges dependent on his Will alone, for the Tenure of their Offices, and the Amount and Payment of their Salaries.

60 HE has erected a Multitude of new Offices, and sent hither Swarms of Officers to harrass our People, and eat out their Substance.

HE has kept among us, in Times of Peace, Standing Armies, without the consent of our Legislatures.

HE has affected to render the Military independent of and superior to the Civil Power.

HE has combined with others to subject us to a Jurisdiction foreign to our Constitution, and unacknowledged by our Laws; giving his Assent to their Acts of pretended Legislation:

FOR quartering large Bodies of Armed Troops among us:

70 FOR protecting them, by a mock Trial, from Punishment for any Murders which they should commit on the Inhabitants of these States:

FOR cutting off our Trade with all Parts of the World:

FOR imposing Taxes on us without our Consent:

FOR depriving us, in many Cases, of the Benefits of Trial by Jury:

FOR transporting us beyond Seas to be tried for pretended Offences:

FOR abolishing the free System of English Laws in a neighbouring Province, establishing therein an arbitrary Government, and enlarging its Boundaries, so as to render it at once an Example and fit Instrument for introducing the same absolute Rule into these Colonies:

80 FOR taking away our Charters, abolishing our most valuable Laws, and altering fundamentally the Forms of our Governments:

FOR suspending our own Legislatures, and declaring themselves invested with Power to legislate for us in all Cases whatsoever.

HE has abdicated Government here, by declaring us out of his Protection and waging War against us.

HE has plundered our Seas, ravaged our Coasts, burnt our Towns, and destroyed the Lives of our People.

HE is, at this Time, transporting large Armies of foreign Mercenaries to compleat the Works of Death, Desolation, and Tyranny, already
90 begun with circumstances of Cruelty and Perfidy, scarcely paralleled in the most barbarous Ages, and totally unworthy the Head of a civilized Nation.

HE has constrained our fellow Citizens taken Captive on the high Seas to bear Arms against their Country, to become the Executioners of their Friends and Brethren, or to fall themselves by their Hands.

HE has excited domestic Insurrections amongst us, and has endeavoured to bring on the Inhabitants of our Frontiers, the merciless Indian Savages, whose known Rule of Warfare, is an undistinguished Destruction, of all Ages, Sexes and Conditions.

100 IN every stage of these Oppressions we have Petitioned for Redress in the most humble Terms: Our repeated Petitions have been answered only by repeated Injury. A Prince, whose Character is thus marked by every act which may define a Tyrant, is unfit to be the Ruler of a free People.

NOR have we been wanting in Attentions to our British Brethren. We have warned them from Time to Time of Attempts by their Legislature to extend an unwarrantable Jurisdiction over us. We have reminded them of the Circumstances of our Emigration and Settlement here. We have appealed to their native Justice and Magnanimity, and we have conjured them by the Ties of our common Kindred to disavow
110 these Usurpations, which, would inevitably interrupt our Connections and Correspondence. They too have been deaf to the Voice of Justice

Library of Congress

John Locke

and of Consanguinity. We must, therefore, acquiesce in the Necessity, which denounces our Separation, and hold them, as we hold the rest of Mankind, Enemies in War, in Peace, Friends.

WE, therefore, the Representatives of the UNITED STATES OF AMERICA, in GENERAL CONGRESS, Assembled, appealing to the Supreme Judge of the World for the Rectitude of our Intentions, do, in the Name, and by Authority of the good People of these Colonies, solemnly Publish and Declare, That these United Colo-
120 nies are, and of Right ought to be, FREE AND INDEPENDENT STATES; that they are absolved from all Allegiance to the British Crown, and that all political Connection between them and the State of Great-Britain, is and ought to be totally dissolved; and that as FREE AND INDEPENDENT STATES, they have full Power to levy War, conclude Peace, contract Alliances, establish Commerce, and to do all other Acts and Things which INDEPENDENT STATES may of right do. And for the support of this Declaration, with a firm Reliance on the Protection of divine Providence, we mutually pledge to each other our Lives, our Fortunes, and our sacred Honor.

Signed by ORDER *and in* BEHALF *of the* CONGRESS,
JOHN HANCOCK, PRESIDENT.

ATTEST.
CHARLES THOMSON, SECRETARY.

PHILADELPHIA: PRINTED BY JOHN DUNLAP.

of absolute independence from every other person. This equal independence forms a "title to perfect freedom" for each person. It is this equal, perfect freedom which we leave behind when we enter the social contract that gives us our equal "unalienable rights" in the political community.

Even the ideas of a written constitution entered into voluntarily by sovereign states and the division of powers within a federal system can be traced to Locke's writings. While the idea of separation of powers and checks and balances can be traced to several sources (e.g., the 18th-century French philosopher Montesquieu), Locke was probably the most important source. Last but not least, the idea of representative government—as opposed to direct democracy—owed a debt to Locke.

SHAPING CONTEMPORARY AMERICAN POLITICS

In the preceding section, we saw that the intellectual roots of the Declaration of Independence and Constitution run deep. We did not explore every facet of the philosophical origins of these two fundamental documents. But we did note three: Aristotle, the Judaic and Christian heritage, and Locke.

What was true in 1776 and 1787 is equally true today. Ideas continue to influence the American political debate. The best way to see this is to consider six contemporary concepts: **democracy, equality, liberty, justice, liberalism,** and **conservativism.** These are terms that all of us use. But what do they mean? How have modern philosophers tried to clarify them?

Democracy. Who should rule? To say "the people" is a tidy but really quite insufficient answer. It tells us little about where exactly the supreme power resides. Take a relatively simple issue: building a highway through St. Louis. Who exactly should have the authority to accept or reject the project? Assuming one is of the democratic persuasion, we can safely eliminate any faceless board of experts (traffic engineers, city planners, civil engineers, etc.). The next question becomes whether to let elected representatives of the people or the people themselves decide (perhaps through a referendum). In either case, one then faces a geographic question. Will it be all the people in the communities surrounding St. Louis? They surely will be affected by the project and even expected to help pay for it. In deciding on this project, is it right to ignore the interests of the people of Missouri or those in Illinois who might be even more affected?

The subtleties do not end there. Where would an advocate of world government say the locus of decision on the St. Louis highway project resides? With a world minister of transportation? And even if one could come up with a way out of this geographic muddle, there is the demographic problem of how the interests of future generations, still too young to vote or yet unborn, should be factored into the decision. Is it "democratic" to exclude those who in the long run will be the chief users of the highway and, quite possibly, also the chief financiers?[3]

The authors of *The Federalist Papers* definitely show their preference for "popular government." However, as you know from Chapter 2, they usually refer to it as a "republic" rather than as a democracy.

In recent years, research into voting habits, public opinion, interest groups, and political parties has revealed voter apathy, uninformed citizens, and a disproportionate influence of small numbers on important issues. These findings have led to attempts by the late Joseph Schumpeter, Robert A. Dahl of Yale University, and others to rethink the concept of modern democracy.[4]

Schumpeter argued that the classical theory of democracy did not describe the political situation as we know it. Why pretend, as the 18th century did, that the democratic method realizes the common good by letting the people decide issues through their elected representatives. Schumpeter viewed the idea that representatives carry out the people's will as an elaborate fiction. He preferred a new defintion of the democratic method: "an institutional arrangement for arriving at political decisions in which individuals acquire the power to decide by means of a competitive struggle for the people's vote."[5] This, Schumpeter said, implied nothing less than that "democracy is the rule of the politicians."

In another critique of the classical theory of democracy, Dahl argued that one of the influences of the Constitution on American thought has been that it "hindered realistic and precise thinking about the requirements of democracy." For Dahl, the possibility of majority rule on any specific policy is negligible. The election itself is "the critical technique for insuring that government leaders will be relatively responsive to non-leaders." But elections are "quite ineffective as indicators of majority preference." Specific policies tended to be the products of "minorities rule."

Dahl saw majority rule, in the sense that the founding fathers had used the term, as largely a myth. In most societies, minorities frustrate and tyrannize majorities.

If the constitution is not a principal device for protecting one group in society against another, what was it useful for? Dahl thought it significant mostly for determining "what particular groups are to be given advantages or handicaps in the political struggle." In Dahl's view, the reason the American Constitution had survived was not that the founding fathers had constructed such a delicate mechanism for guaranteeing a political balance. It was that the Constitution was frequently altered to fit a changing social balance of power. It was the American love of bargaining that made the whole political process work.

In the early 1960s, the term **participatory democracy** gained wide acceptance and added a new dimension to American attitudes towards self-government. The essential and initial meaning was to give power directly to those people most affected by government policy. The first application was in the community action agencies of President Johnson's War on Poverty. Bureaucrats in the agencies took the "maximum feasible participation" specified in the act to mean that the beneficiaries of the program would have a say in the planning and operations of the program. The participatory idea continues to have a profound effect in contemporary American politics. Samuel Beer of Harvard University writes:

> In qualified form the formula requiring participation was incorporated in many Great Society programs and has become a normal ingredient of program structure. It would be difficult today to find a program involving regulation or delivery of services in such fields as health, education, welfare, and the environment that does not provide for "community input." In a more diffuse, but more important way, the participatory idea has affected attitudes toward the whole process of representative government. It was a powerful influence on the McGovern reforms of the methods of selecting delegates to the Democratic National Convention. It has legitimized and stimulated the increasingly populistic style of campaigns for public office. Recent reforms of Congress, which also serve to break down cohesion and hierarchy, are in harmony with this outlook. Indeed, the immense new structure of intergovernmental relations based on federal grants, which inserts state and local governments between the central government and the impact of programs, has been presented as forwarding the cause of participation. Many forces, ideal and material, have been reshaping American attitudes toward political action. But the idea of participatory democracy, drawing on old themes of political romanticism, has given a sharp new twist to the democratic values of the American political tradition and to any future public philosophy.[6]

Equality. What do we mean when we speak of equality? To the founders, Lincoln, Martin Luther King, Jr., and many Americans today, it means "equal opportunity." But, as we shall see in later chapters of this book, another notion about equality has been advanced—equality of results or outcome. It is referred to by a variety of names—positive rights, cultural equality, entitlements, equality of results. We shall simply refer to it as *social rights*.

According to Daniel Bell, a Harvard sociologist, it is the "central value problem" of America today.[7] More to the point, the idea is having increasing influence on government policymakers. There is good reason for singling out equality, for giving it special attention.

Like the realization of democracy, the realization of equality is a difficult—even frustrating—matter (See box, "Cutting a Cake

---

Cutting a Cake *Equally*

Our concern here is to sketch the main sorts of things that the innocent contention that government *should*, somehow, treat its subjects as equals may suggest, and to consider some of the ways these may contradict one another. To begin, let us take something much smaller and much less complex than the state. Consider the banal (and pejoratively "philosophical") problem of cutting a cake equally. We may plausibly begin, as does Isaiah Berlin, by supposing that there is a single egalitarian solution, that is, slicing the cake into as many identical pieces as there are guests. But as we shall see, there are alternative routes to equality, even for so simple an occasion as this notional tea party. By looking at these in a simple context, we can point out some main difficulties that most certainly will arise in the livelier and more intricate world of politics and the state. If these alternatives seem strained in relation to a philosopher's cake, please forgive that much and rejoice in their clarity: momentarily, politics will complicate them. Here are five types of complications to the cutting of a hypothetical cake.

1. The cake, cut in equal slices, is served at a party to which our host has invited ten persons—but *only* ten. What, we may wonder, do the equal slices for this inner circle mean to those left out altogether? Perhaps the most basic inequality has been inflicted *before* the cake is sliced or served.

2. Imagine that the guests belong to different castes or classes. Three of the ten are, perhaps, black, and our party occurs in Cape Town. Or, they are English dons, four of whom speak with "high" Oxford accents, the others, with accents different and "lower." It would be one thing to divide the cake (or, more interesting, conversational deference) equally among persons; it would be another to divide these equally among the blocs formed by race or class. It is one thing to ask: Did our host listen to Smith the same way he listened to Jones? It is another to ask: Did our host listen to blacks the same way he listened to whites? At our imaginary banquet, the difference between these questions is perhaps second-rate; in life itself, the difference is first-rate.

3. The cake in question turns out to be the last of seven courses. Two of our guests have distinguished themselves over the first six courses. Herr Grobrain has eaten nearly all of the shrimp, consumed the best pieces of the duck, and helped himself to the tip of each asparagus shoot as the dish was passed, leaving the stalks for others. He has more than held his own in every dish save the parsnips, which he modestly urged on the others. Frau Magrian, seated beside our gluttonous friend, has been governed by an over-polite denial of appetite. She is the sort of person who never quite manages her share of good things, and she finishes six courses with hunger gnawing at her stomach. It would be one thing for our host to cut the cake in equal slices for Grobrian and Magrian (forgetting, in effect, about the other courses). It would be another to cut the cake to bring about *overall* equal meals for these two diners. These two views lead to equalities that are very different from one another indeed.

4. Our guests are again alike in caste and class, and the cake is the only course to be served. But imagine a chocolate cake served in equal measure to a guest who loathes the taste of it;

> or an angelfood cake served to a woman who is violently allergic to eggwhite; or a boysenberry fudge cake palatable only to our host, served in equal and generous slices to all. Slices of equal size will accomplish equality in one sense: no guest who despises the cake will wish he had gotten somebody else's slice. But those who like the cake, or at least have no allergy to it, will be getting more value from their slices than the others; equal slices, unequal value. The difference between the underlying notions of equality here is important.
>
> 5. We have so far assumed a divisible, homogeneous cake, implying that equality (at least of a literal sort) is possible. But suppose, like Solomon's baby, the cake became worthless when cut into pieces. Or suppose the cake to be so small as to contain fewer than ten worthwhile bites. Under these circumstances, and many such others, the host might issue equal forks, not equal slices of the actual cake, and let his guests fight it out with these equal implements. Or, quite differently, he might draw names from a hat so that each guest has the same chance of winning a slice. The forks correspond to one view of "equal opportunity," and the names in a hat correspond to a radically different conception. Which, if either, corresponds to the form of equality best pursued by the state when actual equality is impossible or undesirable?
>
> It is clear that these alternatives would be quite silly if we really meant to think about private entertaining. Yet, in the case that acutally concerns us—the egalitarian state—every one of the objections made to each alternative is important and has important consequences for practice.
>
> SOURCE: Douglas Rae, "The Egalitarian State." Reprinted by permission of *DAEDALUS, Journal of the American Academy of Arts and Sciences* 108, no. 4 (Fall 1979), Cambridge, Mass., pp. 39–40.

Equally"). For example, proponents of equality of opportunity tend to disagree with earmarking access to jobs and public funds for the disadvantaged or members of minority groups. But let us assume that they have been won over by the proponents of equality of outcome. The crux of the problem now becomes one of setting priorities.

White women are likely to be in direct competition with black men. The latter are likely to contend that the former are far more privileged—better home environment, more education, more contacts in the business world, etc.—and do not require the same sort of help that they do. As Robert Lewis, vice president of the National Association of Black Manufacturers, argues: "This society treats its mothers, sisters, and wives far better than its ex-slaves. Racism is a greater evil than sexism."[8] Nancy S. Barrett, an economist at the Urban Institute, disagrees: "The labor market still functions as a man's world where women are expected to take a secondary role. No one says that a black man does not need a job because he has a working spouse, or that he'll work for lower pay, and no one asks a black man about his baby sitting problem."[9]

Liberty. The issue of liberty is much more complicated than it at first seems. The Bill of Rights restricts the power of the majority to limit the freedom of expression and assembly. But is it the justification for those who wish to "do their own thing" whenever and wherever they please? Does freedom means absence of restraint?

Or is it true that every law restrains *some* liberty for *some*, but in so doing, may establish some liberty for some others—or indeed for all? Does liberty then become a kind of linear programming problem in which a society seeks to maximize liberty subject to certain essential constraints? Or, are certain freedoms never to be constrained? If you burn *Mein Kampf* and *The Communist Manifesto* today, what might you burn tomorrow?

Tale of the Slave

As a libertarian, Robert Nozick is concerned about the vast panoply of powers that the modern *democratic* state has over its citizens. To better understand the essential nature of such a state and its relationships with its citizens, Nozick asks us to consider the following sequences of cases and imagine it is about us.

1. There is a slave completely at the mercy of his brutal master's whims. He often is cruelly beaten, called out in the middle of the night, and so on.

2. The master is kindlier and beats the slave only for stated infractions of his rules (not fulfilling the work quota, and so on). He gives the slave some free time.

3. The master has a group of slaves, and he decides how things are to be allocated among them on nice grounds, taking into account their needs, merit, and so on.

4. The master allows his slaves four days on their own and requires them to work only three days a week on his land. The rest of the time is their own.

5. The master allows his slaves to go off and work in the city (or anywhere they wish) for wages. He requires only that they send back to him three sevenths of their wages. He also retains the power to recall them to the plantation if some emergency threatens his land; and to raise or lower the three-sevenths amount required to be turned over to him. He further retains the right to restrict the slaves from participating in certain dangerous activities that threaten his financial return, for example, mountain climbing, cigarette smoking.

6. The master allows all of his 10,000 slaves, except you, to vote, and the joint decision is made by all of them. There is open discussion, and so forth, among them, and they have the power to determine to what uses to put whatever percentage of your (and their) earnings they decide to take; what activities legitimately may be forbidden to you, and so on.

Let us pause in this sequence of cases to take stock. If the master contracts this transfer of power so that he cannot withdraw it, you have a change of master. You now have 10,000 masters instead of just one; rather you have one 10,000-headed master. Perhaps the 10,000 even will be kindlier than the benevolent master in case 2. Still, they are your master. However, still more can be done. A kindly single master (as in case 2) might allow his slave(s) to speak up and try to persuade him to make a certain decision. The 10,000-headed master can do this also.

7. Though still not having the vote, you are at liberty (and are given the right) to enter into the discussions of the 10,000, to try to persuade them to adopt various policies and to treat you and themselves in a certain way. They then go off to vote to decide upon policies covering the *vast* range of their powers.

8. In appreciation of your useful contributions to discussion, the 10,000 allow you to vote if they are deadlocked; they commit themselves to this procedure. After the discussion you mark your vote on a slip of paper, and they go off and vote. In the eventuality that they divide evenly on some issue, 5,000 for and 5,000 against, they look at your ballot and count it in. This has never yet happened; they have never yet had occasion to open your ballot. (A single master also might commit himself to letting his slave decide any issue concerning him about which he, the master, was absolutely indifferent.)

9. They throw your vote in with theirs. If they are exactly tied your vote carries the issue. Otherwise it makes no difference to the electoral outcome.

The question is: Which transaction from case 1 to case 9 made it no longer the tale of a slave?

SOURCE: Robert Nozick, *Anarchy, State, and Utopia.* Copyright © 1974 by Basic Books, Inc. By permission of Basic Books, Inc., publishers, New York.

What does a society do when legitimate rights conflict? Consider these cases:

- How can society balance the right of an adopted child to know his biological parents with the right of the natural parents not to have reopened past events that led to putting a child up for adoption?
- How does society balance the fundamental right of patients to choose, obtain, and use desired health-care drugs with the government's compelling interest in preserving the structure of the federal laws and preventing self-destructive behavior or conduct seriously affecting the health and safety of its citizens? More specifically, should the Federal Drug Administration deter some cancer patients from relying upon laetrile and encourage them to seek treatment within the confines of the medical establishment?
- How can society weigh your "right" to read this book in quiet with the "right" of your neighbors to play their stereo or of demonstrators outside your window to express their convictions about baby seals, Soviet aggression, punk rock, or nuclear power?
- Should the state regulate the contents of books, magazines, and movies when many feminists regard the content as "genocidal propaganda" and a new form of "terrorism" and say it must be banned? Should the state ban the use of the name "Sambo's" by a restaurant chain, when a coalition of black and civil rights activists claim that the word "Sambo's" is offensive to blacks? Should the state remove the book *Little Black Sambo* from school libraries?
- Do American Nazis have the right to march through a largely Jewish suburb—where thousands of residents are survivors of Nazi death camps—to celebrate der Fuhrer's birthday?
- Should news organizations disclose the fact that a public official is having an extramarital affair? Or that the official is an alcoholic? Should they publish the names of rape victims? Of young people under 16 who have committed crimes?
- Has the federal government become too open for its (and our) good? No other democracy has ventured so far in assuring access to the billions of secret documents that form one of the bulwarks of bureaucratic power. Looking for something to do on a dull weekend? For $4.50 you can order from the Nuclear Regulatory Commission a booklet entitled *Barrier Penetration Database*. It tells how you and a few adventurous friends could break into a top-secret plutonium plant. Under the Freedom of Information Act, adopted in 1967 and substantially toughened by Congress in 1974, even a foreigner can petition for files sequestered in the Pentagon, State Department, and CIA. But probably the most serious charge against the Freedom of Information Act is that it impairs the work of law enforcement agencies. Undercover contacts are said to be reluctant to confide anything that might turn up in a document accessible to the wrong eyes. Lincoln gave a superb formulation of the dilemma this issue presents for American politics: "Must a government, of necessity, be too strong for the liberties of its own people, or too weak to maintain its existence?"

Thus far, we have been talking about political liberties. Now we need to consider the idea of economic liberty.

Some modern supporters of the democratic idea forget that not only democracy and liberty assisted the beginning of industrialization; commerce and a free market have also tended to play an important part in maintaining democracy. One cannot really understand American politics without grasping the many ways free markets and political democracies nourish,

THE QUINTESSENTIAL LIBERAL: John Stuart Mill (1806–1873) was a lifelong advocate of political and social reforms, such as the emancipation of women. When his wife Harriet Taylor died, he dedicated to her his famous classic statement of freedom in society, *On Liberty,* on which they had worked together. Some key passages are found below:

Library of Congress

The sole end for which mankind are warranted, individually or collectively, in interfering with the liberty of action of any of their number, is self-protection. . . . The only purpose for which power can be rightfully exercised over any member of a civilised community, against his will, is to prevent harm to others.

Chap. 1

The . . . most cogent reason for restricting the interference of government is the great evil of adding unnecessarily to its power. Every function superadded to those already exercised by the government causes its influence over hopes and fears to be more widely diffused, and converts, more and more, the active and ambitious part of the public into hangers-on of the government, or of some party which aims at becoming the government.

Chap. 5

If all mankind minus one, were of one opinion, and only one person were of the contrary opinion, mankind would be no more justified in silencing that one person, than he, if he had the power, would be justified in silencing mankind.

Chap. 2

We can never be sure that the opinion we are endeavoring to stifle is a false opinion; and if we were sure, stifling it would be an evil still.

Chap. 2

guide, and restrain one another. When all industry, all newspapers, and all universities are branches of government, the preservation of democracy becomes an uphill struggle.

If everyone worked for the state, where could people whom some senator indiscriminately accused of being communists have found work? If the government had owned the *Washington Post,* how could the Watergate scandal have been uncovered? Private enterprise, along with unions, churches, and other organizations, help to provide a balance to government power.

For government to replace capitalism with socialism would invariably require coersion and hence a diminution of liberty. For socialism to work, capitalists acts between consenting adults would have to be outlawed. In practice, real political freedom is more difficult when human beings are not free to make their own economic choices about their labor, earnings, investments, and purchases.

The classic case for the market is Adam Smith's *Wealth of Nations,* which appeared in 1776. Smith's crucial insight was that, in a free market, an exchange between two parties will not occur unless both parties believe they will benefit from it. The motive is not myopic selfishness but rational self-interest. Critics see these market transactions as impersonal, alienating, purely monetary acts. But the impersonality of the market makes it an equalizer and teacher of tolerance. Wherever the market goes, customs and prejudices must yield to new forms of openness, mobility, and tolerance. I have never met a man or woman from a third world country (members of the educated elite excluded) who did not want to work for a multinational corporation.

It can be argued, however, that great concentrations of wealth and property in the hands of relatively few people is not conducive to a democratic system. Great disparities breed re-sentiment and eventually instability. For that reason, most modern democracies do not allow capitalism to operate without restrictions. Wealth has been redistributed and businesses regulated (see Chapters 12 and 13).

Marxists like to argue that markets, especially labor markets, are only "formally" free. In reality, they say, workers remain "wage slaves" and are treated like "commodities."

But workers have proven to be far from inert masses. They migrate, organize, take jobs and quit them, seize opportunites to improve their condition, upgrade their skills, treat the economy as a ladder, and (in good proportion) educate their children to surpass their own attainments.

Justice

Preliminaries. Although I wish to look at justice as a contemporary issue, it is useful to use Aristotle for a basis of discussion. Aristotle regarded justice as embracing many, if not all, the other virtues. To him it was the supreme political idea. As love binds members of a family together, justice binds the citizens of a state together.

Justice reconciles liberty and equality. Aristotle thought we should have as much liberty as possible. The state and other citizens should do nothing to impede or obstruct our pursuit of happiness—nothing that might interfere with or prevent our pursuit of a good life. But we should have only as much freedom or liberty as justice allows. Anything more would be harmful to others. Similarly, Aristotle said we should have as much equality as justice requires. The welfare of the community affects the pursuit of happiness by its members. A good society, a society in which the common good of the people is served and advanced, contributes to the good life of its individuals.

Justice, then, is the proper balance between liberty and equality. For reasons that will be clear in a moment, it is helpful to think of this reconciliation of liberty and equality graphically. A society that had an excess of liberty (point A) or equality (point B) would not be just, according to Aristotle. The just society would find the proper balance between these two extremes (point C). As we shall see below, not all contemporary political philosophers would reconcile liberty and equality in quite the same way as Aristotle.

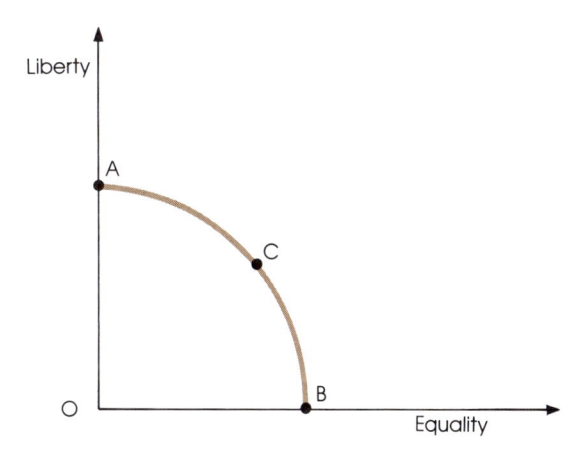

Rawls: "A Theory of Justice" (1972).[10] Imagine you are one of a group of men and women who do not belong to any particular society yet. It is a situation not unlike Locke's state of nature. You have gathered together in a kind of constitutional convention, as did the founders in 1787, to decide upon the fundamental rules for a government.

To make matters interesting, try to imagine that you and the others do not know who you are. That is, you do not know if you are male or female, young or old, black or white, intelligent or stupid, healthy or sickly, affluent or poor. Nor do you even know what values—security, wealth, liberty, truth, opportunity, respect, love, etc.—are important to you. Everyone then has acute amnesia.

This bizarre situation was devised by John Rawls to help discover the rules of a just society. According to Rawls, if everyone under such circumstances acted in his or her own self-interest, the resulting constitution would be just.

What might it look like? First, Rawls tells

us everyone would have basic liberties in the greatest amount *consistent with everyone having the basic liberties equally.* (These basic liberties are, more or less, those found in the U.S. Constitution.) Second, unless differences in wealth benefit the worst-off group in society, they will not be permitted. Every change in society must therefore benefit the worst-off group. Third, the first principle has priority over the second.

You may disagree with these rules. But would you if you were actually in the original position described before? Rawls seems to suggest that you would probably want to play it safe and support the second principle, which puts a floor beneath the worst you can be. The core idea of Rawls' idea of justice is fairness. He argues that this second principle has for us a deep, intrinsic appeal.

Ronald Dworkin: "Taking Rights Seriously" (1977). Dworkin sees a shortcoming in the Rawls theory.[11] Is it really true, he asks, that once the minimum economic conditions of life are met, everyone would choose liberty over any further improvement in material wealth? Would you give up your right to a free press for a beach house in the Bahamas and a private plane to get there on cold winter weekends? It is not too hard to imagine that thousands (millions?) of Americans might make this exchange eagerly.

According to Dworkin, we do not need to make any trade-off between liberty and economic equality. The two are connected; they are mutually supportive: "Equality is the motor of liberalism, and every defense of liberalism is also a defense of equality." What connects liberty and equality is the more fundamental concept that for liberty to be meaningful the individual must enjoy a certain amount of economic independence. Dworkin does not want freedom at the cost of all other values. Would a state be "free" if it gave orphans, the blind, widows, and the sick the liberty to sleep under bridges?

Dworkin offers an updated version of the natural rights theory that guided the founding fathers. He argues that an individual has a natural right "to be treated as an equal," or to be accorded respect, dignity, and equal consideration by society. He insists that the parties in a court case are often entitled to more consideration than is explicitly written down as "the law." He feels that judges should be encouraged to range widely. They should ask fundamental questions and apply ethical principles as well as written legal rules to the case.

For example, a qualified white has no inherent right to be admitted to medical school ahead of a less qualified minority member. Nobody has a basic right to a medical education. But the university does have a right to determine its own admissions policy based on many factors, including intelligence, reduction of racial tension, and redress of historical inequities. Whites and blacks are owed equal respect and consideration. But "the right to be treated as an equal" does not always mean "the right to equal treatment." It does always mean, however, that competing interests will be considered in the decision-making process. In short, according to Dworkin, judges should act imaginatively when they feel that a minority is threatened with moral and social prejudice.

Dworkin's philosophy is also an attack on the 18th- and 19th-century theory that laws should provide for the "greatest happiness of the greatest number." Dworkin faults this theory, **utilitarianism,** because it can be used by a democracy to justify disregarding minority rights; minorities, by definition, are not "the greatest number." The issue of obscenity provides an example of how Dworkin's theory would work in practice. Laws to ban pornography, though voted for by a majority of the citizens, are wrong.

Laws should not be founded on personal moral judgments. Pornographers, Dworkin argues, carry issues of principle, though they may lack principles themselves. Etiquette is a more ac-

Law vs. Justice

By the time he was 25, Harry Fred Palmer III had been a Vietnam infantryman, a drunk and a busy house burglar. He was serving 10 years in an Indiana prison when the Superior Court judge in his case, a cowboy-booted maverick named William Bontrager, released Palmer after only a year on the condition that he repay his victims. Palmer did just as he was told and then settled down to a clean life in Elkhart. That was three years ago. Today Palmer is back in prison, the judge has been fined for contempt of court, and some people in Indiana wonder whether justice has been sacrificed to the fine print of the law.

Palmer's unusual case began as a string of garden-variety housebreakings in 1976. After the Elkhart police caught him, Palmer confessed to a dozen crimes, a record that then carried a mandatory jail term of 10 to 20 years. But Bontrager decided to bend the rules a bit. First he treated Palmer like a felon and gave him the full sentence. Then he suspended all but the first year and started a reclamation project. "My object was to give him a solid dose of maximum security and then bring him back while there still was time to work with him," said Bontrager. Even before Palmer got out of jail, he appeared to have changed. "I picked up the Bible," he explains. "It was the only thing I had."

Labor. Palmer returned to Elkhart as the first adult participant in a restitution program run by a local group called PACT (Prisoner and Community Together). The PACT program required Palmer to meet with his victims and work out a repayment plan. Some homeowners were reluctant at first; one who had had all his wedding presents stolen wanted to bring a shotgun to the session. But ultimately Palmer met with four of his victims, paid back $650, and completed considerable manual labor. He also made some converts for PACT: Randy Yohn, a police officer whose house Palmer burgled, was so impressed that he has become the group's board chairman.

Elkhart deputy prosecutor Max K. Walker, Jr. wasn't impressed. He asked the Indiana Supreme Court to reverse Bontrager's sentence, arguing that the judge violated the law in suspending a mandatory jail term. "It wasn't like Palmer was a boy scout," said Walker. "He committed a dozen serious crimes." Bontrager, arguing that he could not in good conscience return the rehabilitated father of two to prison, eventually withdrew from the case. Another judge, Richard Sproull, took over. After listening to five witnesses describe the new Palmer, Sproull reluctantly resentenced him, but left him free on an appeal bond. Finally in January the state Supreme Court ordered Palmer back to prison. In February the Court also found Bontrager in contempt and fined him $500.

Palmer's only hope for an early release now is a Federal court reversal or a clemency writ from Indiana Governor Robert D. Orr. "I did what the judge gave me and I thought that was the end of it," said Palmer. "I don't see why I'm being punished again." The people at PACT see Palmer's case as an example of legality pitted against justice, particularly because the Indiana law has been changed so that all burglars are not automatically sentenced to prison. (The new statute is not retroactive to the time when Palmer was breaking and entering.) Furthermore, PACT's restitution program is well accepted in Elkhart. "Judge Bontrager offered a sense of justice which was not consistent with the letter of the law," says PACT's executive director, Mark Umbreit. "Instead of a pound of flesh, the state got an ounce. Justice was served but the law was violated. What message do we take from that?" To Palmer, the message is clear. "I don't think there is justice at all in this system," he says.

SOURCE: *Newsweek* (May 25, 1981).

ceptable basis for legislation than morality. In other words, "It's the wrong time and place" is acceptable; "There's no place" is not.

Dworkin further asserts that individuals must be allowed to decide for themselves which valid laws they will obey and which they will disobey. The decision, though, should be based on sincere convictions, not greedy impulses. But what if this right of **civil disobedience** harms the general welfare—that is, causes many people to suffer? To Dworkin, it makes no difference. Such rights are necessary to protect equality.

Robert Nozick: "Anarchy, State and Utopia" (1974). Nozick, like Dworkin, believes individuals have absolute rights.[12] Dworkin's emphasis seems largely on the right to break the law (that is, civil disobedience). Nozick is interested in property rights as well as civil liberties. The state may not do anything except act as a kind of night watchman. Today this view is commonly referred to as "libertarian."

But suppose a government wants to do more than support police and similar services? Suppose it wants to tax everyone, then redistribute that wealth in a more "just" pattern? As soon as the state's back is turned, millions of people start giving away part of their "just" earnings to see Reggie Jackson hit home runs, hear the Rolling Stones play, or obtain a widget warmer made in some entrepreneur's garage. In time, the original just pattern of distribution has been distroyed. Jackson, the Stones, and our widget king are all far richer than they deserve to be. Therefore, Nozick writes, "the socialist society would have to forbid capitalist acts between consenting adults."

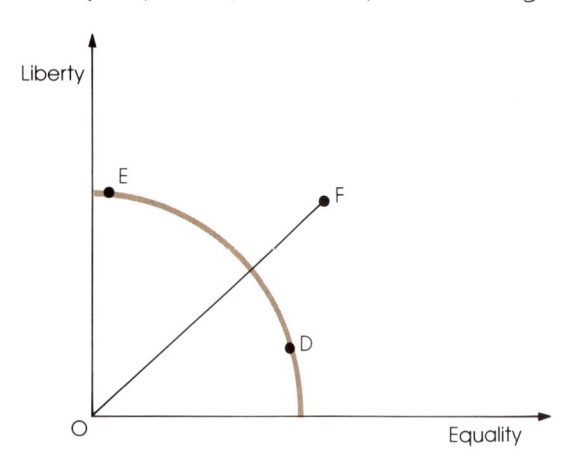

In place of government prohibition, Nozick proposes an entitlement theory of justice that depends on a process, not an end result. Everyone is entitled to everything he or she has gained by a legitimate process. As far as Nozick is concerned, government—*democratic* government—is already powerful enough. It has no business hindering "capitalist acts."

Now let us compare and contrast our discussion of Rawls, Dworkin, and Nozick. Rawls seeks a compromise between two competing liberal values: liberty and equality. When they conflict, his preference is for the latter. (He would prefer point D over point E.) Dworkin denies that liberty and equality are competing values. Individual rights are necessary to equality, and vice versa. The real question for the liberal, in Dworkin's view, is not, How much liberty must we give up for equality? It is rather, Is this liberty necessary to protect equality? (He believes that trade-offs are not always necessary, that a point F actually exists.) Nozick's position is the most clear-cut. Liberty is everything. He opposes the use of state power to take care of the needy; they should be cared for by purely voluntary means. He also opposes drug laws, seat-belt laws, and restrictions on imports, and taxing the rich only a dime per year. (Therefore he would accept point E over point D.)

Is there any common theme running through these three theories of liberalism? Fortunately, there is. They all reject the idea that the state has any moral or spiritual function. Herein lies the difference between modern liberals and conservatives.

Conservatism

One facet of American liberalism is convervatism. That statement may seem strange, since we are so used to speaking of conservatives versus liberals. But useful distinctions in the world of practical politics are not necesarily accurate distinctions in the world of political philosophy. Let us first see how conservatism is like liberalism. Then we will see how it is different.

The first similarity is a basic acceptance of a market-based economy. To a 19th-century liberal, restrictions on trade were almost as bad as restrictions of civil liberties. By the middle of the 20th century, this view was considerably modified. All sorts of regulations of commerce and controls over the national economy were in place. To the modern liberal, these regulations and economic controls represent not a rejection of the market system but a means of *saving* that system.

Since World War II, conservatives have come to accept—though with greater reluctance than liberals—the welfare state. Liberals and conservatives differ as to its size, scope, and effectiveness. But they both recognize the desirability of a government that attempts to meet various human needs over and above the physical safety of its citizens (e.g., health, housing, food, social security, and unemployment benefits). There are solid reasons for this support, though not all American conservatives are able to see them. Conservatism is about the conservation of certain values and institutions. But the existence of a permanent underclass, brutalized by its environment, makes the survival of institutions like the family and values like gentleness and lawfulness difficult.

A third similarity between conservatives and liberals is a respect for the individual as opposed to the state. Both desire to permit the free development and blossoming of the individual. Politics of differing interests—or conciliation—is the means by which democratic government is made possible. All builders of utopias—from Plato to Marx—and all worshipers of the community or the state—such as Rousseau—are directed in the final analysis against the individual. In their dreams, utopians and statists want to destroy the personality. Pursuing perfection, they reject politics as "untruth." Liberal societies, in contrast, accept politics and thus imperfection; to do otherwise is to destroy the individual.

There are a few issues partially shared by conservatives and liberals, though more closely associated with the former. Among such issues, full-scale military preparedness and less government regulation are worth noting.

Both liberals and conservatives more or less accept the market system, the welfare state, and democratic politics. Both admire Aristotle and respect Locke. Because of these facts, they can be taken together and contrasted with the radical position. But what are the differences between conservatives and liberals? I see two fundamental differences. The first deals with the rate of change in a society. The second deals with the degree to which the government should be concerned with the values of its citizens.

Neither liberal nor conservative opposes change. But conservatives want to go much slower than liberals. The only question is, Why?

With extravagant language and lamentable vagueness, Edmund Burke still gave the best answer. He thought the governments were trustees for previous generations and for posterity. Therefore, the freedom of each generation to act is limited by the expectations of the past and the interests of the future. Burke had championed the Americans against the arbitrary powers of the British crown while a member of the British Parliament. But he was horrified by the actions of the French revolutionaries. In 1796, he condmened as immoral such radical, fundamental change.

> Society is indeed a contract. Subordinate contracts for objects of mere occasional interest may be dissolved at pleasure—but the state ought not to be considered as nothing better than a partnership agreement in a trade of pepper and coffee, calico or tobacco, or some other such low concern, to be taken up for a little temporary interest, and to be dissolved by the fancy of the parties. It is to be looked upon with other reverence; because it is not a partnership in things subservient only to the gross ani-

mal existence of a temporary and perishable nature. It is a partnership in all science, a partnership in all art; a partnership in every virtue, and in all perfection. As the ends of such a partnership cannot be obtained in many generations, it becomes a partnership not only between those who are living, but between those who are to be born.[13]

Now I must remind you that Burke is speaking as a philosophical conservative. Americans who oppose change merely because the status quo has been good to them and they do not want the boat rocked often call themselves conservative. But in the deeper philosophical sense of the word, the title is not warranted. Who would not prefer being called conservative to being called greedy or fearful?

True conservatism has been more concerned with preserving ethical and religious values than with conserving the wealth of the affluent. Indeed, the second way to distinguish the conservative position from the liberal involves this concern with the values of the citizens. Conservatives claim that every open society must have a public philosophy that proclaims its commitment to fundamental moral and political concepts as well as rejects the legitimacy of some beliefs. (For example, intolerance of political organizations preaching racism and fascism demonstrates a society's commitments to equality and democracy.)

Again, we turn to Burke for a justification of this position. "Society," he wrote, "cannot exist, unless a controlling power upon will and appetite be placed somewhere; and less of it there is within, the more there must be without." Politics, writes George Will, one of America's leading conservative columnists, "should be about the cultivation and conservation of character."[14] Without principles, nations, like individuals, are guided by impulse and appetite.

Conservatives believe that civilization is under attack in an America where the sole remaining growth industry in the country's largest city is pornography, where the music praises the advantages of the YMCA for picking up young boys, where television and cinema extol gratuitous violence, where decades of striving after more and more material goods has imprinted many faces with worry and even depression, and where leaders of business and politics practice the old army axiom "Anything is OK as long as you don't get caught." Conservatives ask, Is this liberation?

But liberals believe that how the individual lives is something for him or her to decide. They recall how the Athenians, in their Golden Age, condemned Socrates to death for his views and how the Roman emperor Marcus Aurelius, perhaps the most cultivated man of his age, persecuted Christians. If citizens and leaders so great can be so wrong, how can *we* know we are right in proscribing certain values and practices today? Therefore, liberals want no political theory that holds out a particular life for the individual, however noble.

THE GODFATHER OF CONSERVATISM: Edmund Burke was the original exponent of long-lived constitutional conventions and the idea of the political party. More generally, he remains the most persuasive spokesperson for conservative principles such as the limited role of government in the life of society. That the problems of society are difficult has been known for a long time. Burke gave this cautionary advice to those prepared to redesign society:

Library of Congress

An ignorant man, who is not fool enough to meddle with his clock, is, however, sufficiently confident to think he can safely take to pieces and put together, at his pleasure, a moral machine of another guise, importance and complexity, composed of far other wheels and springs and balances and counteracting and cooperating powers. Men little think how immorally they act in rashly meddling with what they do not understand. [From W. J. Bate, ed., *Selected Writing of Edmund Burke* (New York: Modern Library, 1960).]

The Trial of Socrates

In the *Apology*, Plato gives an account of the last days of the life of his teacher, Socrates. A lifetime of questioning and his outspoken criticism of the Athenian democracy (with its presumption that any man can fill any office) had brought Socrates to a death sentence imposed by his fellow Athenians.

At this trial, Socrates gives free rein to his irony. He asks the judges to bear with his unlegal way of talking. He explains why he spent his time debunking pretence to wisdom. He tells the court that his duty is to fulfill the gods' order to search into himself and other men, even at the risk of displeasing the state. He was the original gadfly. Throughout the trial he concentrated on convincing the judges and steadfastedly refused to plead for mercy by bringing his weeping children there.

In prison, he rejected efforts by his friends to save his life by escaping. A voice, he said, kept murmuring in his ears, warning him that in escaping he would betray the laws under which he had always lived. At the end, he calmed his weeping friends and drank the poisonous hemlock brought by the executioner. His sense of duty and obligation to the very city-state that had sentenced him to death kept him from escaping. He was the personification of what Pericles applauded as the capacity for *both* questioning and acting.

What is your opinion of Socrates' refusal to escape his death by explaining to his friends that, while he believed the law that condemned him unjust, he had lived his whole life under the protection of the laws of Athens and would not then defy its laws?

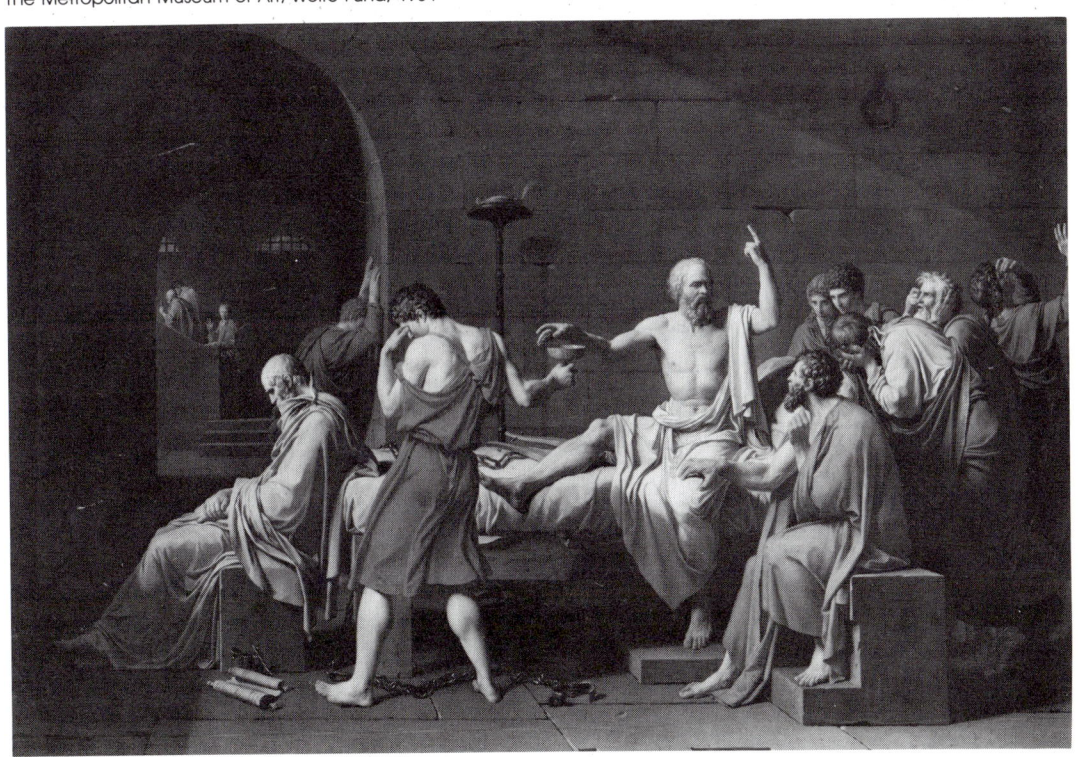

The Metropolitan Museum of Art, Wolfe Fund, 1931

Why not? Because the liberal believes the answer to the question of how human beings should live must be given by each person for himself or herself; it is an insult for society to attempt to decide that question for individuals. Therefore, a liberal such as Dworkin views a recent Supreme Court decision allowing the cutoff of public funding for abortion as wrong. The state has no business enforcing a moral judgment on a minority.

Conservatives would argue that that line of argument does not square well with reality; government is already concerned with the mind of its citizens. Consider, they say, the vast public school system, the Federal Communications Commission (which regulates what we see and hear), public universities, research grants, even the regulation of free speech. (As Burke remarked: "We govern speech in order that we may govern ourselves by speech.")

This chapter is built on the assumption that ideas *do* matter. The study of politics creates, or at least gives shape to, general ideas. The problems with which politicians must struggle and the laws they pass are formed from those general ideas. Political theories form a sort of intellectual atmosphere breathed by both governors and governed in society. Unwittingly, all derive from it the principles of their action.* From this explanation, very practical conclusions follow. If one wants to gain some sense of future political action—for example, what laws will be passed in the next few years—then it is towards the arena of ideas that he or she needs to look.

SHAPING GLOBAL POLITICS

Enemies of the Open Society

Classifying political philosophies is frankly impossible. Few great political thinkers can be pigeonholed. Yet, if one wanted to trace the evolution of political theory from ancient Greece and Rome to the present, a road map would help. Accepting the fact that classification is worth the risks, I can think of no surer guide than Sir Karl Popper. Many consider him to be the greatest philosopher of science ever.[15]

Popper regards living as above all else a process of problem solving. Therefore he prefers forms of society that permit the free assertion of different alternatives, followed by criticism, and, if warranted, the genuine possibility of change. Democracies are particularly well-organized for problem solving. These kinds of societies he calls *open societies*.

But, from the time of Plato onward, there have been gifted individuals opposed to a society's becoming more "open." They have wanted to go back to a tribal society or forward to a utopia—in either case, to the womblike security of a society that was more "closed." To put it crudely, they fear the messiness and disorder of the open society.

Among these enemies of the open society, Popper would include Plato, Hobbes, Rousseau, and Marx. Among the philosophers of the open society, he would include many we have already considered, including Locke and Mill. Both streams of political philosophy have manifested themselves in the 20th century. Schematically, and greatly simplified, the pattern might look something like this:

Plato	(4th century B.C.)	Aristotle
↓		↓
	(1st century B.C.)	Cicero
		↓
Hobbes	(17th century)	Locke
↓		↓
Rousseau	(18th century)	Montesquieu
↓		↓
Marx	(19th century)	Mill
↓		↓
radicalism	(20th century)	liberalism

Speaking very loosely, we can note two major **ideologies,** or belief systems, that have domi-

---

* It is uncertain how many, if any, American political leaders and judges read the philosophers mentioned in this chapter. More likely, their ideas come to them via cultural osmosis, from publicists and journalists.

nated the 20th century: radicalism and liberalism. The focus of this concluding section will be on the former.

Radicalism embraces a broad spectrum of political tendencies. Despite the variety, one common theme appears in them all. This is a deep dissatisfaction with a society that has not lived up to its ideals and dreams of perfection; it is also a willingness to take action—whatever action—necessary to change this state of affairs. Those espousing radicalism want a quick escape from the present. It could be to the glorious past (Plato) or to the **utopian** future (Marx).

Fascism is a political ideology and mass movement that acquired considerable power in Europe between World Wars I and II. Because of its emphasis on order and extensive government planning we can consider it one of the political tendencies included under the heading of radicalism. Because fascism also emphasizes nationalism (i.e., devotion to interests of one's own nation), probably the only nations meeting this definition today are some of the newer African nations. But it is unlikely the leaders of these nations would accept that label.

Movements, parties, and governments that follow the view of **liberalism** tend to tolerate imperfections (diversity, conflict, unpredictable and uncontrollable change, insecurity, etc.); these are thought of as the inevitable price of an open society. In the past, the principle justification for such tolerance—which includes minority rights, civil liberties, open elections—was natural law. Since the Enlightenment, another justification for such toleration has grown increasingly important. It is the belief that only through the free and open criticism of ideas and public policies can knowledge and society advance. To shut off dissent in the name of some higher good would, in the liberal's view, freeze a society. This brings us back to Popper.

A great deal of international politics can be explained in terms of the clash between these two great systems of ideas or ideologies. Advocates of each ideology try to sell, defend, or impose its way of economic, political, and social life to others. In Chapter 14 we shall examine the history and intensity of this struggle. In this chapter our aims are to understand what the struggle is fundamentally about.

Because earlier parts of this chapter have considered liberalism, what follows focuses chiefly on radicalism. And there is simply no way to approach that topic except through writings of the most influential philosopher of the last century—Karl Marx.

Marx: The Core Ideas

The extraordinary personal achievement of Karl Marx (1818–1883) has few parallels in history. He was hardly known in his lifetime to even educated people. Yet within just 70 years of his death, a third of the entire human race had adopted forms of society that called themselves by his name. An understanding of today's world is simply not possible without some knowledge of his political and social thought.

Marx had three core ideas. While no idea was particularly original, his synthesis was masterful.

Historical materialism. Let us begin with **historical materialism**. This theory of history attempts to explain why feudalism gave way to capitalism and why capitalism must eventually give way to socialism. According to Marx, people in every society have a certain set of productive forces: skills, technology, and natural resources. Those productive forces, which Marx called the "economic structure of society," determine *everything* else in society—religion, politics, law, philosophy, and class structure. As people develop new ways of extracting a living from their environment, these new forces come into conflict with the existing class structure.

More specifically, the old ruling class, which is based on older production forces, comes into conflict with the rising class, which is based on the newer means of production. Results? Class struggle, revolution, and victory for the new class. According to this theory of history, a new rising class (the workers or **proletariat**) would inevitably replace the older middle class.

Labor theory of value. The second core idea was his **labor theory of value.** Marx maintained that the true value of a commodity is determined by the amount of labor required to make it. To explain capitalism's exploitation of workers, Marx said the capitalist pays the workers just enough for their survival. The value of the commodities the workers produce, however, is greater than this amount. The difference is profit or, in Marxian terms, surplus value.

Before talking about the third core idea, let us pause to consider the first two. As a forecaster, few philosophers have fared as badly as Marx. The most advanced capitalist countries were, according to his theory, the most likely to go communist; the less developed countries, the least. What happened was, of course, the exact opposite. Beginning with Russia in 1917—the most agricultural and least capitalist of all European countries—all countries that have gone communist (except for Czechoslovakia) have been preindustrial. One wonders with the French political analyst Raymond Aron why "the Western obsession with Marxism" persists when history has failed to vindicate any of Marx's major predictions.*

Marx's labor theory of value is riddled with problems, as many contemporary Marxists admit. The theory ignores entrepreneurship and risk taking. If these did not exist, labor unions would rush to buy out companies, take over the management function, and pass on the surplus value to the workers. Nor does Marx satisfactorily explain why the amount of labor alone determines value. Can making a giant knot, which might take weeks to do, really be more valuable than making a dress, which might take only a half day.

---

* Kenneth Minogue agrees with Aron. According to Minogue, the Polish worker strikes of the early 1980s may be taken as "a finally decisive piece of evidence that nobody who has to live Marxism actually believes the stuff anymore. It survives only as a hobby among some intellectuals who inhabit the protected academic reservations of Europe and America." (*Policy Review*, Winter 1981.)

Alienation. Marx's third basic idea was that, under capitalism, workers experience **alienation** because they have lost control over the processes of work and over the product of their labor. Workers become things. In his later, more mature works, Marx focuses not on the individual worker but on social organization and class relations. The term *alienation* no longer appears; it has been replaced by *exploitation*. Nonetheless, in an effort to present a more hu-

Drawing by David Levine. Reprinted with permission from *The New York Review of Books*. Copyright © 1972 NYREV, Inc.

By the late 1960s, the picture of Marx as the morose, forboding philosopher muttering imponderables like historical materialism and labor theory of value was not playing well in the West. Moreover, historical materialism had been used to justify the Bolshevik use of terror. Thus, neo-Marxists had good reason to go back to Marx's early writings on alienation to find a warmer, trendier image.

manist version of Marx's thought, neo-Marxists in the 1950s and 1960s resurrected the term *alienation*.

Some indication of alienation in American society is evident in the responses obtained in 1978 to six statements designed to elicit feelings of alienation (Figure 3–2). These responses cannot be regarded as a precise measure of alienation. But they at least suggest the prevalence of substantial feelings of mistrust and hostility; over half of the respondents expressed agreement with five of the six items presented. Over three fourths of the respondents agreed that "The rich get richer and poor get poorer"; at the other end of the scale, only 29 percent agreed that "You're left out of things going on around you."

Contemporary difficulty with Marx's theory of alienation grows out of doubts about whether it is the nature of the work (dull, repetitive, etc.) or the ownership of the business that causes alienation. Does a Russian putting headlights on tractors all day in a Kiev factory feel less alienated than a Californian coating silicon chips in a Palo Alto electronics plant? The Russian may "know" that he "owns the means of production," but does that cheer him up? With the possible exception of Yugoslavia, most of the advances in worker participation have occurred in nonsocialistic countries.

Marx, Newton, and the founding fathers. As a "scientific philosopher," Marx had a weaker grasp of the nature of science than many philosophers. He believed that he had discovered scientific laws that govern the development of human society. He thought that Newton had discovered natural laws that govern the motions of matter in space and that he (Marx) had made parallel discoveries about the movements of societies.

Yet there is a crucial difference between the kind of theory building Marx engaged in and that carried out by Newton and the founding fathers. The concepts of representative government and separation of powers are much closer to Newton's theory of gravity than Marx's dialetical materialism. Marx throught science meant absolute certainty. It does not.

Newton and the founding fathers developed concepts to hold together a body of experience, the one physical and the other political. Each set of concepts gives order and meaning to the whole body of conduct, physical or political. Representative government and separation of

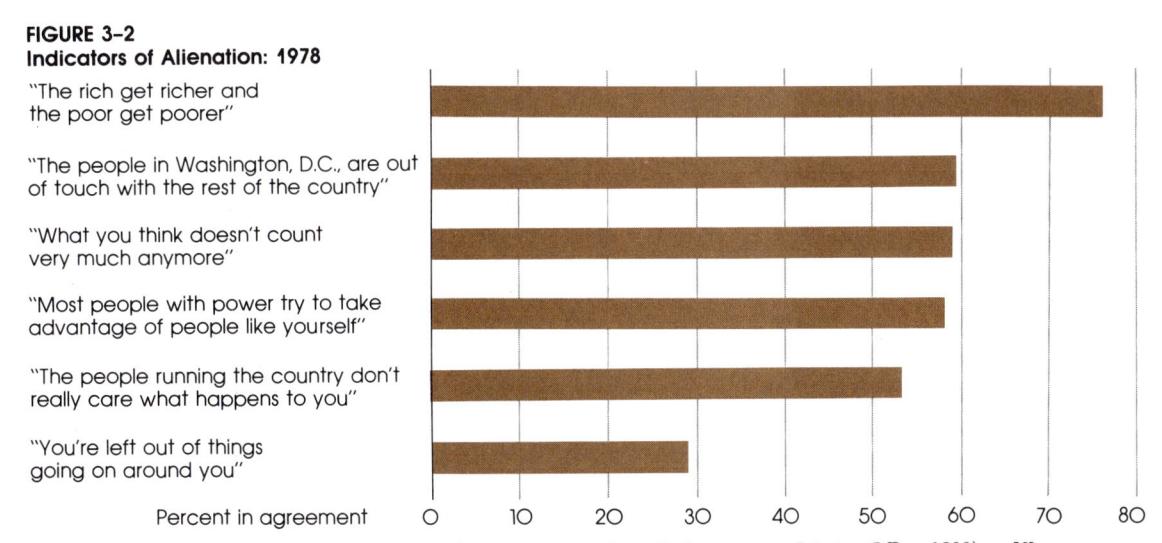

FIGURE 3–2
Indicators of Alienation: 1978

Statement	Percent in agreement
"The rich get richer and the poor get poorer"	~77
"The people in Washington, D.C., are out of touch with the rest of the country"	~60
"What you think doesn't count very much anymore"	~60
"Most people with power try to take advantage of people like yourself"	~58
"The people running the country don't really care what happens to you"	~53
"You're left out of things going on around you"	~29

Source: Bureau of Census, *Social Indicators III.* (Washington, D.C.: U.S. Government Printing Office, 1980), p. XL.

powers are concepts that the founding fathers derived from their own experience and reading of history; the theory of gravity was derived from the gyrations of the moon and earth. Neither requires a higher sanction; *neither calls for an absolute end to further inquiry.*

Science is the activity of making concepts—that is, general pictures of relationships. The concept of gravity says only that the world can be both stable and capable of change. But no concept is final. Concepts are made and remade in the natural sciences as they are in the social sciences. Einstein refined and widened Newton's theory of gravity; modern political theorists (such as Dahl and Schumpeter) are refining and widening some of the founding fathers' political concepts.

Marx, in effect, says, "I can solve all your problems (exploitation, injustice, alienation, and so forth). But I'm afraid you'll have to put yourself completely in my power. Nothing else will do." This intellectual arrogance is light years from Newton, who late in his life said to a nephew:

> I do not know what I may appear to the world; but to myself I seem to have been only like a boy, playing on the sea shore, and diverting myself, now and then finding a smoother pebble or a prettier shell than ordinary, whilst the great ocean of truth lay all undiscovered before me.

Science or not, Marxism remains an effective device for seizing political power. It provides an intellectual justification for dismissing all rival groups as delusions. It replaces **government of laws** by government by men. Kenneth Minogue sums up its approach in one sentence: "Either you agree with what I am telling you, or you must admit yourself to be nothing else but a victim of **bourgeois** [liberal] ideology."

To summarize, science is a guide to action. The truth at which it arrives is neither absolute nor perfect. Rather, it is something that we can act upon with reasonable certainty. To dictate by the authority of science, as Marx did, is fundamentally a refusal to understand the glorious adventure of science.

Fragmentation of Marxism

The ideas associated with Karl Marx have been widely adopted in countries where communists have come to power (see box). But what impact has Marx had in the noncommunist West?

Not all parties and movements in the West that advocate radical social change are Marxist. But their intellectual debt to Marx is not small. This debt is perhaps most clearly revealed in their critique of the capitalist system. Much of their terminology—**imperialism,** superstructure, class conflict, exploitation, alienation, etc.—has roots in Marx's writings.

Still, distinctions can and ought to be drawn. Neo-Marxists are more likely than, say, Soviet Marxists and Maoists to think that social institutions can develop in a peaceful, orderly way and to subscribe to democratic processes. They are more likely to emphasize the earlier works of Marx. They find these writings more relevant and acceptable to the problems of advanced technological societies. They are also more likely to emphasize participatory control of economic institutions, more decentralized decision making in the political arena, government control of major industries, and a far-reaching redistribution of wealth.

We can see these tendencies by considering the emergence of the New Left in the United States. This movement began in the early 1960s with the civil rights movement. But it became increasingly militant with the escalation of the Vietnam War in the late 1960s. The radical Students for a Democratic Society (SDS), the predominantly black Student Non-Violent Coordinating Committee, and the Weathermen, all called vaguely for an overthrow of the "system." Despite later efforts to expand its political basis to including working-class elements, the New Left remained essentially an idealistic, upper-middle class student movement.

By the mid-1970s, the New Left had for

Marxism After Marx

Leninism is based on the beliefs of Vladimir Ilich Ulyanov, known as Lenin (1870–1924), who provided the first divergence from "orthodox Marxism." Lenin knew that Russian workers could not develop by themselves and bring about an overthrow of government. They needed an organization tightly controlled by professional revolutionaries. In October 1917, Lenin and his party, the Bolsheviks, overthrew not the czar (who had already been disposed of) but a democratic republic and founded a dictatorship of the proletariat. Another important idea in Leninism was the theory of **imperialism** as the last stage of a decaying capitalism. This formed the philosophical basis for the communists' seizing power in underdeveloped countries and for the communist perception of the world as a struggle between imperialism and socialism.

Wide World Photos

Stalin

great emphasis on action—e.g., enforced collectivization of agriculture and industrialization in the Soviet Union. To ensure these goals, Stalin expanded police controls and forced labor camps. At the same time, he presented a picture of himself as a kindly ruler protecting his people from hostile "capitalist encirclement." Some communists in the West view Stalin's tactics as an aberration from true communism. But Lenin had paved the way for Stalinism by forbidding all political opposition in 1921. Furthermore, efforts made by Khrushchev in the late 1950s to repudiate the "errors of Stalin" have since been minimized in the USSR.

Library of Congress

Lenin

Stalinism is based on the beliefs of Joseph Stalin (1879–1953), who gradually took over power in the Soviet Union after Lenin's death in 1924. Under the name of Marxism-Leninism, it provides the doctrinal basis of European communist parties. Marx expected final victory to come primarily from the intellectual development of the working class; Stalin believed that what counted were the immediate results. Therefore, he placed

Library of Congress

Trotsky

Trotskyism is based on the view expressed by Stalin's opponent, Leon Trotsky (1879–1940). Trotsky held that revolutions cannot be carried out in isolation. Therefore, the communists' struggle must be worldwide and permanent. Stalin believed that communism could be built in one country.

Maoism is based on the thought of Mao Zedong (1893–1976), who took over power in China in 1949. Mao was fascinated by contradictions. First is the contradiction between the people and their enemies (the imperialists). This is resolved by revolutionary action in the form of guerrilla warfare in the countryside. Second are the contradictions between the socialist government and the people. These are resolved by vigorous fraternal criticism and self-criticism. Another essential element in Maoism is the notion of permanent revolution. For Mao, the people must be mobilized into a permanent movement in order to carry forward the revolution and to prevent the ruling group from turning into complacent, middle-class bureaucrats. In short, it was important to keep things stirred up. In 1979, the Chinese Communist party began to criticize this policy (called the Cultural Revolution) harshly and admitted that mistakes were made during Mao's 27-year rule.

Titoism was developed after the Yugoslav communists, led by Josip Broz Tito (1891–1979), broke with the Soviet Union in 1948. This event was significant because it showed that the communist world was not a monolith. It emphasized the struggle against bureaucracy—even the withering away of the state—and the need for workers' control of the factories. It rejects the national chauvinism (Soviet-style) and refuses allegiance to any power bloc in foreign affairs. The Communist party in Yugoslavia does not operate in every sphere of social and economic life; it does not, however, permit any political opposition.

Wide World Photos

Tito

United Press International Photo

Mao

Castroism is a mixture of Marxism and Latin American revolutionary tradition created by Fidel Castro (1927–). Unlike Titoism, it is highly nationalistic and closely aligned with the Soviet Union. Unlike Leninism and Stalinism, it opposes dogmatism and bureaucracy. Castroism is based more on the personal charisma of Castro than on the impersonal mystique of the party. Instead of waiting for Marxist conditions for revolution to ripen, it proposes creating them by starting guerrilla movements.

all intents and purposes ceased to exist. Its leaders drifted into established political organizations, law, and government; some even went to work for corporations. Others such as Tom Hayden tried to build more broadly based coalitions around the issue of nuclear energy.*

Enter Solzhenitsyn

Undoubtedly, one of the severest blows to the Left in both the United States and Western Europe was the writing of Alexander Solzhenitsyn, especially his *Gulag Archipelago*. The word **GULAG** is an acronym for the department of the Soviet Security Police responsible for administering the forced labor system. These huge camps are scattered islands of Gulag territory and exist throughout the Soviet Union. Solzhenitsyn therefore chose the metaphorical title *Gulag Archipelago*.

Solzhenitsyn was hardly the first to say "Yes, there are concentration camps in the Soviet Union." But no one said it with such literary power. Moreover, he was no mere reporter of events. He had a message and it cut deeply into the radical ideology: Oppression is *inherent* in Marxist theory. Radicals in general and Marxists in particular seek an entirely new world, one that is truly beautiful and humane; therefore, virtually any short-term sacrifice seems just. Sentiments about responsibilities to individual human beings cannot be allowed to bridle efforts to free the world once and for all from ugliness and injustice. While constitutional democracy has difficulty imposing common social purposes, a government with utopian aims has to become authoritarian. The reason is that it views people who oppose its policies not as individuals who happen to disagree but as "enemies of the people."

Fundamentally, Solzhenitsyn is saying that there is nothing special about the Soviet system. It is merely the inevitable outcome of a radical political theory put into practice. It is not even

United Press International Photo

Alexander Solzhenitsyn, a Nobel Prize winner in literature, was exiled from the Soviet Union in 1974 for publication of his *Gulag Archipelago* abroad.

Mike Peters in *Dayton Daily News*

---

* To historians of the New Left this is ironic, since the movement in its early days was pro-nuclear. Hayden's "Port Huron Statement," for example, declared: "With nuclear energy whole cities can easily be powered . . ." and "Atomic power plants must spring up to make electrical energy available." Political analysts would probably explain this reversal on nuclear energy in terms of the Left's need to maintain its cohesion and effectiveness in the post-Vietnam era.

the most brutal regime. (Cambodia would probably win that dubious title.) Nor is it the least. (Yugoslavia has a good claim to that one.) It is just another example of what Solzhenitsyn views as an inevitable pattern.

To be sure, radical thinkers in the West object to this line of analysis. "Marxist theory," they say, "is being perverted." To Solzhenitsyn—and I suppose, anyone at all familiar with the scientific method—this is a fallacy. If a theory fails to work in practice time and time again, something is wrong with the theory.

FUTURE FILE

Creeping Capitalism?

Despite Marxist theory, a growing number of communist and communist-leaning countries have embraced the market system or profit motive. In each case, the governments involved were grasping for ways to fight inflation and unemployment while maintaining economic growth.

In Cuba, Fidel Castro's regime is encouraging state-run enterprises to turn a profit and offering workers incentive pay for superior performance. Cuban wholesalers have been allowed, for the first time since the island nation went communist, to select consumer goods they want to order from producers. This is a marked relaxation of the tight grip the government has kept on the economy. The country has not adopted a completely open-market economy. But the profit test is being used to evaluate management performance and possibly even to determine whether some state-run enterprises would survive.

Yugoslavia has removed price controls from a broad range of products as part of a package of economic reforms that include tax cuts and increased welfare benefits. But lifting controls, thus allowing market forces to set prices, is seen as a further departure from the centrally planned economies of Yugoslavia's Soviet-dominated neighbors in Eastern Europe.

Several years of struggle took place within the Communist party to determine what sort of China its revolution should create. That struggle apparently ended in 1976 with the death of Mao and the accession to power of Chairman Hua and his followers. That group would turn China outward, not inward, in order to make it a modern industrialized economic power. The Hua group, of course, is thoroughly communistic in its ideas on political organization. It believes in tight control of the country by the party and tight control of the party by the Politburo leadership. The Hua group also proclaims itself Marxist in its economic thinking. That is, it professes the doctrine that the whole economy of a huge nation not only should be but can be controlled by a central planning apparatus. But China seems to be Marxist with a difference. Its communist leaders talk much of studying Marx's, Lenin's and Mao Zedong's thoughts, but they do not let that thought blindly dictate their actions.

In a word, the Chinese are pragmatic. Thus their policy is this. If modernizing China means opening up to the West, open up. If it means joint ventures with Western business, make them. If it means a little "creeping capitalism" in rewarding peasants for more farm production, let it creep. If it means applying capitalistic ideas about costs, profits, or capital investment, let them be applied. If it means letting their scientists, technicians, and intellectuals have freer access to Western ideas, let them have it.

Pragmatism is also characteristic of Robert Mugabe, once a Marxist "terrorist," now the prime minister of Zimbabwe. For all but a tiny handful or intellectuals in Mugabe's government, "Marxism" is only a code word for general egalitarian goals for social change and a casting off of oppression. It is not a systematic ideology. In trying to change the capitalist system of what was once Rhodesia, Mugabe has exercised caution and patience. The result is probably less radical than he would have wished.

Mugabe's behavior is not difficult to understand. He also had the negative example of neighboring guerrilla movements, especially that of Mozambique. That nation is still paying the economic price for its overnight nationalizations and its disregard for the virtues of small-scale private enterprise.

Why are communist nations flirting with an economic theory that is the antithesis of communism? First, they are eager to trade with the more prosperous and technologically advanced West. Second, they cannot help but be concerned lest their economic failings lead to social unrest. That apprehension must have been sharpened by events in Poland. If the seeds of capitalism are allowed to take root in communist lands, they might in the long term prove beneficial to East-West relations. But of equal potential significance could be their liberizing influence on the authoritarian systems that are selectively substituting some of Adam Smith's teachings for those of Karl Marx.

Robert L. Heilbroner has written recently,

As an imaginable institutional arrangement, socialism has become a word almost without content. If it means the nationalization of industry or private-public planning, it can be seen—at least, so I suggest—as the extension of capitalism. As a deindustrialization of society it holds forth the specter of a catastrophic decline in living standards. As a vast extension of worker participation, it suffers from a complete lack of any economic and political institutions—or conception of such institutions—within which workers' autonomy could be expressed. In the underdeveloped world it is all too likely that socialist revolutions will usher in narrow, inefficient, and xenophobic regimes.

Hence there is little enthusiasm for socialism today, always excepting the burning desire of oppressed peoples or abused workers to throw off cruel or simply sclerotic regimes. After that, the realities of the industrial process, the impatient expectations of the masses, the contagion of Western ideas and goods must somehow be accommodated. ["The Demand for the Supply Side," *The New York Review of Books* (June 11, 1981), p. 41.]

It should be noted that Heilbroner is no greater admirer of capitalism. He is a sharp critic of moral emptiness and environmental pollution. Moreover, looking at current economic policy in the United States, he concludes that the next stage of economic history will not be a pleasant one (see Chapter 13).

So we arrive at the end of survey of political ideas. But we are not through with ideas. For example, in Chapter 5 we shall see how ideas influence political behavior. In Chapters 6 and 8 we shall find the two major American political parties asking themselves what, if anything, they believe in. How well each answers that question will largely determine how much power the American electorate will trust it with in the decades ahead.

In Chapters 12 and 13 we shall see the importance of ideas in shaping social and economic policy. In Chapter 14 we shall examine the global war of ideas and try to determine what message the United States offers the rest of the world. In Asia and Africa, in the Middle East and Latin America, who is reading Aristotle, Locke, and Jefferson? But who is *not* reading Marx, Lenin, Mao, Ho Chi Minh, and Che Guevara? If a nation wins the whole world and loses the battle of the mind, it has won nothing.

In other chapters—but especially Chapters 4 and 7—we learn what happens when public officials come into office without some undergirding political philosophy. They are unable to give clarity, consistency, and coherence to their politics. They have no "vision." Without vision, they become the crudest sorts of pragmatists, striving to be whatever the polls say they should be. As Norman Mailer, an uninhibited and irreverent observer of American politics, puts it:

> Leaders today are much less philosophically oriented than they used to be. They lack the sense that there is a world beneath the world of appearances.
>
> To be philosophical, you need to have some sense of responsibility to matters other than the immediate social problems before you. You need to see what you do in perspective against a historical framework or social setting rather than just act as a technician who is tightening nuts and changing gaskets.[16]

Today, there is much talk—and much of it is true—about how people are increasingly alienated from their political institutions. For institutions to continue to stand, they must be built upon the foundations of political philosophy. Unfortunately, the public who are using these institutions today are not being taught, and no longer adhere to, the inner principles of these institutions. Overcoming this alienation will require repairing this rupture between the public and the philosophical underpinnings of its institutions. I close this chapter with a beautiful line that appears in the Constitution of North Carolina: "The frequent recurrence to fundamental principles is absolutely necessary to preserve the blessings of liberty."

Chapter Key

Jefferson declared that basic human rights entitled all men to be treated equally under the law. He was drawing chiefly on ideas expressed by Aristotle and John Locke. But these ideas had become a part of American common sense. Jefferson maintained that the colonists possessed the "inalienable" rights that had developed over the centuries in English common law. He argued that the colonists had obtained them from their "creator"—not as gifts from the English government. Jefferson changed Locke's "life, liberty, and property" to "life, liberty, and the pursuit of happiness"; however, the delegates to the Congress probably equated the pursuit of happiness with the right to possess property.

Jefferson stated the ideals of political participation in a republican form of government. For this he used Locke's social contract as well as the colonial experience of representative government and the independent, representative traditions built among colonial preachers. Jefferson also turned to Locke and colonial religious traditions when he wrote that government should be limited to expressing the will of the people. If government becomes arbitrary or violates existing law regarding the rights of its citizens, the people have the right and the duty "to alter or abolish it."

In practice, the idea of democracy is not easily achieved. The founding fathers knew it was not feasible for a large geographic area. Therefore they designed a republican or representative system. But even in local politics pure democracy is problematic. Not all citizens are willing to devote equal amounts of time to the process of continuous, collective decision making. Moreover, who exactly are the "people"? That is, should the people most affected by a public decision have more of a say than those only slightly affected?

Aristotle used justice to reconcile liberty and equality. He thought citizens should have as much liberty, or freedom, *as justice allows*. This means that, in their pursuit of the good life, citizens should not do anything harmful to one another. Similarly, Aristotle maintained that citizens should have as much equality *as justice requires*. Contemporary philosophers, such as Rawls, Dworkin, and Nozick, have also tried to show how equality and liberty are reconciled in the just state.

In a philosophical sense, conservativism is very close to liberalism. In everyday American politics, however, it is useful to distinguish the two. Both liberals and conservatives would emphasize liberty (as did John Stuart Mill in the 19th century). But conservatives are more apt than liberals are to extend its application to personal property and limit its application to free speech. A true conservative also believes (as did Edmund Buke at the end of the 18th century) that tradition carries a certain wisdom. Therefore, the burden of proof should always be on those who advocate change.

Marx believed that under capitalism the labor of workers is expropriated by owners. Furthermore, because the workers do not own the means of production, they are alienated. Marx believed that he had discovered the laws of historical change. Eventually, the capitalist system would collapse; socialism and, later, communism would inevitably emerge.

This prediction proved quite wrong. Capitalism proved amazingly adaptable. Meanwhile, where communism did emerge, that emergence was more the product of the Soviet army than any "laws of history." Due to the writings of Solzhenitsyn and increasing economic difficulties, Marxism lacks much of the appeal it had 10 or 20 years ago.

Culver Pictures

4 The Craft of Politics

After studying this chapter you should be able to answer the following questions:

1. What is power?
2. What are the leading theories of how to measure power in society?
3. What are the major sources of power?
4. What are the strategies used in the exercise of political power?
5. When power fails, how can conflict be resolved?
6. What is the role of language and symbols in the maintenance of power?
7. Why is power necessary?

Terms you should know:

access points
backlash
bargaining chip
blue ribbon panel
charisma
coalition building
compromise
cooling-off period
co-optation
elite theory
finesse
hatchetman
honeymoon period
image
incrementalism
Iron Law of Oligarchy
leadership
leak

leverage
Lion and the Fox
logrolling
machine
military-industrial complex
nonviolence
ploy
pluralism
policy agenda
power base
referent power
targeting
The New Class
step-by-step negotiating
strategy
writ of mandamus
zero-sum game

The thought of the Italian political philosopher Niccolo Machiavelli (1469–1527) has always outraged many of his readers. What makes his vision of politics so disturbing is his notion of politics-as-perpetual-conflict. A prince, Machiavelli wrote, must imitate both the **lion and the fox**. The lion is not clever and prudent enough to recognize traps; the fox is not strong and valiant enough to frighten the wolves. It is not coincidental that, when the first political biography of Franklin Roosevelt appeared, it was subtitled "The Lion and the Fox."

It is true that Americans are wary of strong-willed presidents. But it is also true that they do not want ineffective ones either. I cannot say for sure why Franklin Roosevelt is considered a better president than Jimmy Carter. The margin of difference surely does not lie in intelligence or in loftiness of purpose. Is it possible that the difference might be that Roosevelt was not reluctant to acquire, maintain, and exercise power? As Machiavelli wrote, "Where the willingness is great, the difficulties cannot be great."

Nor can I say why George Washington still seems to stand out even among that illustrious group of early American leaders. He had none of the legal acumen of James Madison, economic genius of Alexander Hamilton, intellectual curiosity of Thomas Jefferson, intellectual passion of Thomas Paine, or creativity of Benjamin Franklin. The margin of difference was, I suspect, Washington's understanding of power. In this respect, he left them all behind— as he did the British generals who opposed him. Edmund S. Morgan, Sterling Professor of History at Yale University, gives this assessment:

> Washington's genius lay in his understanding of power, both military power and political power, an understanding unmatched by that of any of his contemporaries. At a time when the United States needed nothing quite so much as military power but had very little, this hitherto obscure Virginia planter knew how to make the best possible use of what there was.

Library of Congress

And after securing independence, when the United States was trying to establish itself in a war-torn world, he knew how to deal with foreign countries to the maximum advantage of his own. He was not a bookish man. He contributed nothing to the formal political thought of the American Revolution, nor did he produce any treatises on military strategy or tactics. But he did understand power in every form.[1]

THE ROLE OF POWER IN AMERICAN POLITICS

Power Defined

Let us agree from the start that the concept of power, at least in the social sciences, is not easily defined. Nevertheless, we need a working definition, and Robert A. Dahl provides one good enough for our purposes. According to Dahl, when A can get B to do something that B would probably not have otherwise done, then we can say that A has power over B.

If we put this definition of power alongside Harold Lasswell's definition of politics, it is easy to come to the conclusion that politics is power. Lasswell defined politics as "who gets what, when, how." "The study of politics," he wrote, "is the study of influence and the influential. The influential are those who get the most of what there is to get." He then goes on to define political science as "the shaping and sharing of power."

Perhaps this is going a little too far. A more moderate conclusion would be to say, as we did in Chapter 1, that politics involves the use of power to get something done. Power might be the oil in the machinery of government, but it is not the whole works.

One might object to Dahl's definition of power on the grounds that it puts undue emphasis on interpersonal relationships (A and B, for example). Don't institutions (e.g., the Federal Bureau of Investigation) and groups (e.g., the National Organization of Women) also have power? Only in a superficial sense can one speak of the power of an institution or group. To do so conceals the fact that that institution or group has conferred decision-making power upon certain individuals. The more effective the organization is, the more likely this is to be the case. Power is, in the final analysis, an attribute of individuals. To put this even more sharply, power cannot exist without a holder. Abstract concepts of power—disembodied from living men and women—cannot take us far.

Robert Michels, in his study entitled *Political Parties* (originally published in 1915), understood this. He suggested that all parties, no matter how democratic their principles, eventually turn into organizations run by an inner circle. Michels called this tendency the **Iron Law of Oligarchy**.

President John Kennedy understood this intuitively. Theodore White, in his *The Making of the President, 1960*, explains:

> Politics, in his [Kennedy's] conversation, were groups of men led by other men. To know who the leaders were and understand them was to know and understand how the group worked.
>
> . . . .
>
> The root question of American politics is always: Who's the Man to See? To understand American politics is, simply, to know people, to know the relative weight of names—who are heroes, who are straw men, who controls, who does not. But to operate in American politics one must go a step further—one must build a bridge to such names, establish a warmth, a personal connection.[2]

Nor was the point lost on Kennedy's vice president. When someone warned Lyndon Johnson in 1960 not to exchange the vast power of the majority leader of the Senate for the emptiness of the vice presidency, Johnson said: "Power is where power goes." One might say Johnson turned the principle into an art form.

First, there was what came to be known as "The Treatment." Rowland Evans and Robert Novak describe it thus:

> The Treatment could last 10 minutes or four hours. It came, enveloping its target, at the LBJ Ranch swimming pool, in one of LBJ's offices, in the Senate cloakroom, on the floor of the Senate itself—wherever Johnson might find a fellow Senator within his reach. Its tone could be supplication, accusation, cajolery, exuberance, scorn, tears, complaint, the hint of threat. It was all of these together. It ran the gamut of human emotions. Its velocity was breathtaking, and it was all in one direction. Interjections from the target were rare. Johnson anticipated them before they could be spoken. He moved in close, his face a scant millimeter from his target, his eyes widening and narrowing, his eyebrows rising and falling. From his pockets poured dippings, memos, statistics. Mimicry, humor, and the genius of analogy made The Treatment an almost hypnotic experience and rendered the target stunned and helpless.[3]

Then, there were the eyes. As President Johnson told his staff, "Watch their eyes, watch their hands." With the careful observation—if not sensitivity—of a Rembrandt, Johnson related how Bobby Kennedy's Adam's apple went up and down when he barred Kennedy from the vice presidential ticket in 1964. When a TV reporter offended Johnson, he told an aide, "He's a wall eye. My daddy said never trust a mule or a man who is wall-eyed." Absurd? Per-

Wide World Photos

Some theories of politics tend to obscure the fact that power ultimately is personal. Above President Johnson eyes Soviet Premier Alexsei N. Kosygin in 1967 at the Glassboro (New Jersey) summit meeting. Below, Secretary of State Haig sizes up Soviet Ambassador Dobrynin at a Washington banquet.

United Press International Photo

haps. But the most successful presidents have been those who tried to explore the minds and manners of men and women in power.

A Few Distinctions

The term *power* cannot be precisely defined. But it can and should be distinguished from a few other terms often used in political analysis.

To begin with, power or holding power is not synonymous with true **leadership.** Powerholders are primarily interested in fulfilling their own power objectives. That—and not their followers' needs and motivations—is the primary concern of a power wielder. True leaders, as FDR biographer James MacGregor Burns has pointed out,

> emerge from, and always return to, the wants and needs of their followers. They see their task as the recognition and mobilization of their followers' needs. . . . The effective leader mobilizes new, "higher" needs in his followers. The *truly* great or creative leader do something more—they induce new, more activist tendencies in their followers; they arouse hopes, and aspirations, and expectations.[4]

Leaders, then, must be concerned with power, and power is an element of leadership. But leadership is more than power. Leadership is power plus the transcendent task Burns so well describes.

Some scholars would define power as persuasion, authority, or something else. In every instance, they are not so much wrong as they are guilty of the fallacy of composition. That is to say, they have taken what might be true of a part and alleged, on that account alone, that it must be true for the whole. For example, a scholar will focus on selected presidents or selected incidents and quotes from one administration, then conclude they have found the "essence" of presidential power. But presidential power—indeed, all power—has a number of complex sources. Among these are the ability to persuade and the reliance on formal authority. But, as we shall see in this chapter, these are sources not the "essence."

Finally, we might ask, What is the difference between power and force? In the world of physics, these terms have precise meanings. If we simply say that force is the *intensity of power,* we can be fairly consistent with the way physicists understand the term. More important, we shall have managed to untangle power from yet another term and reduce conceptual fuzziness.

Importance of Power: Past, Present, Future

The concept of power, like ideas, is a major building block in our understanding of American politics.

It requires no mental gymnastics to interpret the U.S. Constitution almost entirely in terms of power. The word appears 16 times in the Constitution. In Chapter 2 we saw how the founding fathers delegated certain powers to the national government. For example, Article I, Section 8 of the Constitution provides a fairly lengthy list of specific powers that are expressly delegated to Congress. There are also a number of restrictions placed on the power of the national and state governments.

Today, the act of governance is to a large degree an exercise in interinstitutional management. That is to say, American government is neither a monolith nor a collection of self-contained parts. Interdependence is a political fact of life. What happens to one part of government affects what happens to other parts. The vast majority of government programs are joint activities tying many participants together. If there was not such interdependence, there would be far less need for political actors to have and use power.

It is unlikely that the need for power among political actors will lessen anytime soon. For one thing, scarce resources and slower economic growth increase the need for power. This is because such conditions increase the conflict among groups in society. Conversely, when resources are plentiful and the economic pie large, the potential for conflict is reduced.

Another factor that increases conflict is the increasing heterogeneity of American society. We shall take a closer look at this trend in later chapters. Suffice it for now to note the increased immigration from Mexico, Southeast Asia, Cuba, and other nations. At the same time, individuals are more resistant to displays of formal authority. Thus managers, both public and private, will need to become more flexible and skillful in their exercising of power.

Finally, as the locus of decision making drifts more and more from individuals, the family, and voluntary associations of various sorts towards government, as more and more vital decisions are made in Washington, more attention will be paid to the actions of government officials. This means that, if they are to be effective in their jobs, they must be particularly sensitive to the nuances of power.

If citizens want officials who can perform, then citizens must look at experience and skill from the perspective of power. The ability to gain, use, and keep power—along with honesty, intelligence, and noble goals—must be a criterion for the selection of American political leaders.

The remainder of this chapter is devoted to four aspects of power: its assessment, its sources, its strategy and tactics, and its institutionalization. We shall also consider the resolution of conflict through negotiations when the exercise of power fails to produce the desired ends.

WHO ARE THE POWERFUL?

It is easy to accept the notion that political power is unevenly distributed within organizations, communities, and nations. But it is difficult to decide just how. Over the years, two competing theories—I am inclined to say stereotypes—have emerged. They are **pluralism** and **elite theory**. In this section, we shall consider both. Particular attention will be given to elite theory.

The first theory of how power is distributed is called pluralism. Its advocates contend that power in the United States is divided up among many groups. (A few of these groups we shall look at in Chapter 6.) Each group has sufficient power to protect its vital interests, but none has sufficient power to dominate the others.

The second theory is quite different. Instead

of large numbers of plural interests, all in a kind of magnificent balance, power resides in the hands of a ruling elite. Advocates of elite theory contend that a relatively small interlocking group shapes public policy. The idea is not new (see our discussion of Marx in Chapter 3). The chief popularizer of the modern version was American sociologist C. Wright Mills.

Mills and the Power Elite Hypothesis

C. Wright Mills was both a social researcher and social critic. His book *The Power Elite* (1956) offers a sociological view of the structure of political leadership in the United States along with a moral criticism of American society. Mills held that the U.S. elite is made up of a tightly knit ruling group. This group is self-centered and devoid of social responsibility. In Mills' view, this small group of business, political, and military leaders dominate and rule the United States. This elite has power over all the "important" decisions.

As might be expected, Mills' theory generated controversy when it appeared in the 1950s. Today it attracts less attention. One reason is that more careful research revealed that Mills had oversimplified the elite structure. Another reason for the decline in interest was the changing interests of activist intellectuals. Morris Janowitz of the University of Chicago explains:

> The rise of black power and women's liberation movements found this symbolism of limited pertinence; their leaders had different notions of the power elite. The spokesmen for these movements were more interested in enlarging the power elite than in analyzing its members moral behaviors.[5]

Moreover, an increasing body of evidence seems to indicate that, even if there was once a power elite, the trend for the last half century has been towards increasing differentiation (see box). That is, we don't find a cohesive structure; we have fragmented business elites, political elites, military elites, education elites, professional elites, media elites, and so forth. Unlike Mills' power elite, the individuals in these elites have varied social and educational background. This line of research seems to suggest that between the theories of a power elite and pluralism might be the reality of a "pluralistic elite."

It All Depends

Elite theory and pluralism provide one-dimensional, overstated explanations of American politics. Advocates of elite theory, for instance, are clearly on to something when they claim that elites hold power far out of proportion to their members. But making either their case or the pluralist case requires full fidelity to the nuances of power and full awareness of the varying motives of power-holders.

Theodore Lowi has suggested that different kinds of policy might be decided in different ways.[6] Some would be decided by the interaction envisioned by pluralists, others by elites. Here are three types of public policies and the political processes Lowi identifies with them.

First, distributive policies are government actions that provide tangible benefits to individuals, groups, or corporations. Included here are most contemporary public land and resource

> ### Thirty-eight Years of Studying American Political Elites
>
> *1937* In *Middletown in Transitions*, Robert and Helen Lynd pointed out the dispersion of power in a community during the 1930s as the influence of trade unionism, local voluntary associations, and local political managers grew.
>
> *1953* In *Community Power Structure*, Floyd Hunter showed how the rise to political power of the black community in Atlanta produced a separation between wealth and political power.
>
> *1961* In *Who Governs: Democracy and Power in the American City*, Robert A. Dahl observed the shift of political power from the men of wealth to politicians from lower-status and minority groups, then to the professional political leaders.
>
> *1975* In "Change and Continuity in the Recruitment of the U.S. House Leaders, 1789–1975," Garrison Nelson concluded that an increased "democratization" of social recruitment produced more minority-group members and women in House of Representatives.

policies; rivers and harbors ("pork barrel") programs; defense procurement and research and development; labor, business, and agricultural "clientele" services; and the traditional tariff. Distributive policies benefit individuals and single firms. Therefore most participants in this kind of policymaking are *small groups* acting independently and quietly in congressional committees (see Chapter 8).

It is significant that the modern president with the most distinguished military background, Eisenhower, himself warned of **a military-industrial complex,** that is, an alliance of generals, industrialists, and politicians whose interests are furthered by government defense spending. (And Ike knew that more defense spending did not always mean more national security.)

Second, regulatory policies are also specific and individual in their impact, though not quite to the extent that distributive policies are. The laws are stated in general terms ("Arrange the transportation system efficiently"; "Thou shalt not show favoritism in pricing"). However, the impact of regulatory decisions is clearly one of directly raising costs and/or reducing or expanding the alternatives of private individuals. It is only in this area, Lowi argues, that what the pluralist call "interest group activity" actually takes place. The struggle usually occurs on the House or Senate floor.

Third, redistributive policies involve a conscious attempt by the government to manipulate the allocation of wealth, property rights, or some other value among broad categories of private individuals in society. But the effects, Lowi stresses, are much broader than those involved in regulatory policies. These issues, which include such matters as the income tax and various welfare programs, tend to be defined along class lines—the haves versus the have-nots. Redistributive policies, Mills would argue, are made by the power elite. The pluralists would argue that such policies are decided by the interplay of powerful interest groups. But Lowi maintains that the decisions are made by broad ideological groupings. For example, he points to social classes and "peak associations" such as the AFL–CIO and the Chamber of Commerce.

Critique of pluralism and elite theory. As the preceding discussion indicates, advocates of pluralism are harder pressed to explain how some policies were decided than others. Monetary policy (i.e., how much money is in circulation and how high interest rates are) is the most clear-cut example. There is no question but that monetary policy is set by a small group. Similarly, the vast majority of foreign policy decisions (e.g., recognition of the People's Republic of China) and national defense (e.g., suspension or resumption of the neutron bomb project) tend not to be the result of the interaction of various groups. They are decisions made in high places by a handful of like-minded people.

Furthermore, elites are more evident in some jurisdictions than others. Dallas is a city that would delight C. Wright Mills. At least it would to the extent that it has, until recent years, fitted his theory about as well as any American city could. Probably more than any other major city, Dallas was run by business leaders. Its entrepreneurs, bankers, executives, and developers were cheerily confident that they knew what was best for the 850,000 people who live in Dallas.

The business leaders of Dallas left few matters of any importance to the whims of the voters. Decisions were more often announced than debated. Public projects rejected by taxpayers had a way of sneaking back on the ballot until they were passed. As late as 1979, the city government did not even bother to ask the taxpayers before starting to build them a $35 million arena to house professional basketball and hockey teams. Dallas's business leaders were so dominant that they were able to tell the elected county commission and the public-hospital board to stop their short-term borrowing. And it was a group of business leaders, not the elected school board, that drafted the city's school desegregation plan.

Elite theory is also deeply flawed. As a scientific theory, it cannot be disproved. Elite theory tells us that the visible leaders of a community are not the real ruling elite. Behind them is a set of covert leaders pulling the strings. (Why a president or mayor cannot simply say no to an elite is an interesting question that I shall let pass.) What if careful investigation reveals that this set of covert leaders did not in fact determine public policy? Then the theory tells us that there is yet another covert elite lurking behind the first. I do not know what to call this line of reasoning. But I am sure it is not social science.

A bright 10-year-old might enter a more direct objection. How can we say small elites rule in a country with open, periodic elections determined by simple majorities? An advocate of elite theory would probably reply patiently that the elite determine who the candidates will be. But this answer is not wholly satisfactory. In picking presidential candidates, the influence of party bosses is today slight. Moreover, there is a jumble of other candidates from which to choose.

Advocates of elite theory are also confronted with a long list of legislation designed to improve the living conditions of a great number of people. According to the theory, all these measures—social security, health care, affirmative action, pollution control, etc.—are only to help the elite maintain its dominance. But these arrangements represent, in effect, a new economic arrangement in which many groups have a powerful voice. Elite theory fails to make clear just how far would an elite have to go in making concessions before its dominance disappears. Furthermore, dismissing all this social legislation as only a clever ploy by power-holders to mollify the masses causes other problems. Elite theorists fail to explain the fanatic public opposition to it by business executives.

One further point about all this welfare legislation: It tends to blur all roles in America. Is a machinist who buys a two-story house with a federally insured loan a worker or a landlord? During the 1930s, economic issues deeply divided the country along lines of occupation (unskilled workers, skilled workers, managers, etc.) and income. Consistently, the richer you were the more likely you were to oppose liberal policies. By the late 1970s, this pattern had disappeared. Political opinions among higher- and lower-income groups were similar. For example, according to Roper Reports (1978), 34 percent of those making under $7,000 a year had an unfavorable opinion of big business; 32 percent of those making over $25,000 a year had an unfavorable opinion. Roper also found the same percentage (39 percent) among *both* groups in opposition to wage and price controls. But, as you can see in Figure 4–1, there are social and cultural divisions. They are rooted, not in income but education.

Finally, there is the problem that those who we are supposed to consider members of the elite do not agree with the normal elite position. Senator Edward M. Kennedy is a millionaire several times over but hardly the champion of the rich; quite the contrary. One study of DuPont by three political scientists in 1963 even found a number of sharp divisions over public policy decisions *within* that company. For this reason, one must exercise caution when examining a chart like Figure 4–2. It makes interesting and, in many respects, illuminating reading. But it implies that all corporate executives think alike, that there *is* a "pro-business" position.

It is not that simple. Within each industry there are tensions between rising segments (based on more advanced technologies) and declining segments, especially over the issue of government regulation.

What then does Figure 4–2 tell us? Merely this: One of the best and least obtrusive ways of exercising power is to control which issues surface in the first place. Or, to put it in the language of political science, they control which issues get on the **policy agenda.** Peter Bachrach and Morton S. Baratz recognized this application of powers when they wrote:

> Of course power is exercised when A participates in the making of decisions that affect B. But power is also exercised when A devotes his energies to creating or reinforcing social and political values and institutional practices that limit the scope of the political process to public consideration of only those issues which are comparatively innocuous to A . . . to the extent that a person or group—consciously or unconsciously—creates or reinforces barriers to the public airing of policy conflicts, that person or group has power.[7]

The Paradox of Elite Theory

Strangely enough, elite theory plays equally well with liberal and conservative audiences. At the same time, Mills (political left) was arguing that a power elite made up of business tycoons, politicians, and generals was shutting intellectuals and liberal politicos out of the policymaking process, William F. Buckley, Jr. (political right) was saying that an establishment of intellectuals and liberal politicos was shutting out conservatives.

Today, more than a few political scientists and sociologists continue to argue that somewhere in America sinister meetings are always under way. Because so little can actually be known about them, these meetings are especially menacing. Who are the powerful today, as seen by the political left? Chief executive officers of the giant grain and pharmaceutical companies, Catholic bishops and Jewish bond salesmen, television evangelists, David Rockefeller and Richard Milhous Nixon, and nuclear-minded generals. But the conservatives' elite theory has also been updated. They point to the emergence of a widespread **new class.** Who belongs to this new class? The university educated, employed mainly in swollen government agencies, the nonprofit sector, or the media. They have little use for business enterprise and seek a disproportionate influence over all Americans so as to achieve their ideals of a more just and equal social order.

FIGURE 4-1
The New Social and Cultural Divisions

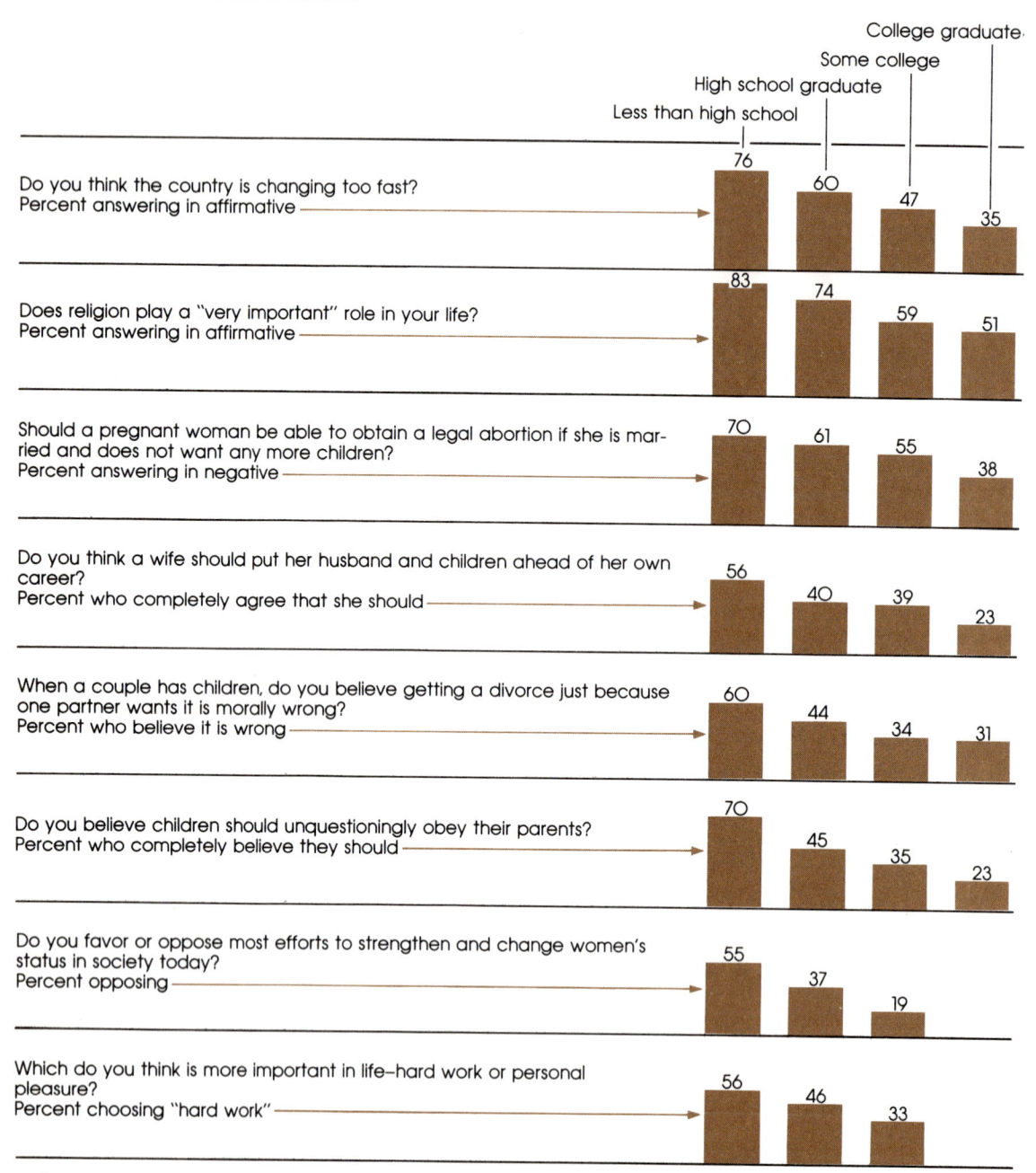

Question	Less than high school	High school graduate	Some college	College graduate
Do you think the country is changing too fast? Percent answering in affirmative	76	60	47	35
Does religion play a "very important" role in your life? Percent answering in affirmative	83	74	59	51
Should a pregnant woman be able to obtain a legal abortion if she is married and does not want any more children? Percent answering in negative	70	61	55	38
Do you think a wife should put her husband and children ahead of her own career? Percent who completely agree that she should	56	40	39	23
When a couple has children, do you believe getting a divorce just because one partner wants it is morally wrong? Percent who believe it is wrong	60	44	34	31
Do you believe children should unquestioningly obey their parents? Percent who completely believe they should	70	45	35	23
Do you favor or oppose most efforts to strengthen and change women's status in society today? Percent opposing	55	37	19	
Which do you think is more important in life—hard work or personal pleasure? Percent choosing "hard work"	56	46	33	

Sources: *Time*/Yankelovich, Skeliv, and White, 1977–78; General Social Survey, National Opinion Research Center, 1978; Roper Reports, 1978; and the Los Angeles *Times*, 1978.

FIGURE 4-2
A Theory of Interlocking Elites

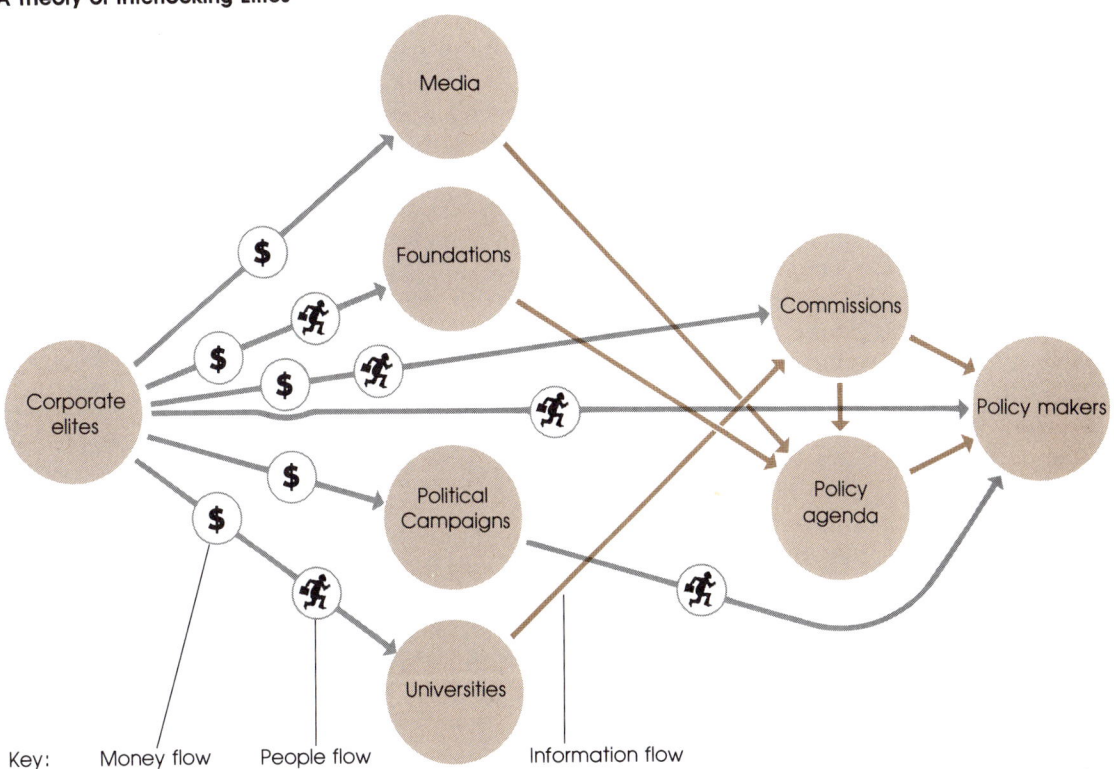

Key: Money flow   People flow   Information flow

Corporate executives can influence public policy either directly or indirectly. The direct route is when a president appoints an executive to a policymaking position in government. There are, however, several indirect routes. Corporate executives give advertising dollars to the media; funds and people (usually to sit on boards) to foundations (like the Ford and Rockefeller Foundations) and universities; and financial contributions to political campaigns. These four institutions in turn influence both commissions, which study and make recommendations about policy issues, and the policy agenda, which is the list of issues under active consideration by policymakers.

SOURCES OF POWER

To repeat our working definition, when A can get B to do what B would not otherwise have done, we say A has power over B. It is important to note that exactly how A goes about this can vary. This is because there are a variety of bases of individual power.

We shall begin with the most Machiavellian base, then gradually move towards the moral high ground. Nevertheless, it is crucial to recognize that effective political actors do not rely on any one base; they probably use them all at one time or another.

Coercive Powers

Coercive power derives from a leader's ability to threaten punishment and deliver penalties. Its strength depends on two factors. First is the magnitude of punishment, real or imagined, that the leader controls. Second is the other party's estimate of the probability that A will in fact mete punishment (e.g., undesirable work assignments, reprimands, and dismissal) if necessary.

For example, in 1981, the Reagan White House staff punished Charles Percy, chairman of the Senate Foreign Relations Committee.

Percy had opposed Ernest Lefever, who had been nominated by Reagan to be assistant secretary of state for human rights. Percy's punishment was to have his choice for U.S. attorney in Chicago held up indefinitely.

Connection Power

Connection power derives from a leader's personal ties with important people inside or outside an organization. A junior aide on the president's staff telephones a senior cabinet member and begins by saying "This is the White House calling. . . ." He is using connection powers. (Bad grammar, too, since buildings do not call anyone.)

Connection power also derives from one's knowledge of **access points.** These are the times and places in the policymaking process that are especially good for promoting one's point of view. (What do you consider the most important access points in Congress? See Chapter 8.)

Expert Power

Expert power derives from a leader's reputation for special knowledge, expertise, or skill in a given area. Lobbyists, who maintain their credibility with members of the legislature, find this kind of power far more effective than the preceding two. Thomas P. ("Tip") O'Neill, Jr., provides us with a good illustration of how David Stockman as director of the Office of Management of Budget (Chapter 7) used expert power. "Every time a cabinet secretary comes up here, he brings a battery of assistants and refers everything to them," O'Neill said. "This guy comes in all by himself and ticks them off boom, boom. I've never seen anybody who knows the operation like this kid—he's something else, believe me."[8] Using expert power, Stockman was able very early in the Reagan administration to almost totally eclipse the secretary of treasury. Later, revealing doubts about Reagan's economic policy, Stockman lost credibility with Congress, undermining that power.

Dependence Power

Dependence power derives from a people's perception that they are dependent on the leader either for help or protection. Leaders create dependence through finding and acquiring resources that others need to do their jobs. For instance, they gain: authority to make certain decisions; access to important people; and control of money, equipment, office space information, and subordinates.

Obligation Power

Obligation power derives from a leader's efforts to do favors for people he or she expects will feel an obligation to return those favors. Also, a leader develops true friendships with those on whom they depend.

Obligation power is used frequently in the legislative process and goes by the name of **logrolling.** Representatives trade votes in support of each other's bill. (For example, A votes for a dam in B's district, with the tacit understanding that B will vote for a new post office in A's.)

Legitimate Power

Legitimate power derives from the formal position held by the leader. In recent years, textbooks on the president have tended to emphasize a theory of presidential power based on persuasion. Richard M. Pious attacks this bit of wisdom. Ability to pursuade, he argues, affects power at the margins, but it does not determine its use or set its limits. The key to understanding presidential power, Pious says, "is to concentrate on the constitutional authority that the president asserts unilaterally through various rules of constitutional construction and interpretation in order to resolve crises or important issues facing the nation."[9]

Although persuasion is an important tool, it has limits. To make it work requires time and people who listen. But both conditions are sometimes absent, and there is little a political leader can do about it.

Referent Power

Referent power derives from the identification of others with the leader. This identification can be established if the leader is greatly like, admired, or respected. John P. Kotter of Harvard Business School writes:

> Managers develop power based on others' idealized views of them in a number of ways. They try to look and behave in ways that others respect. They go out of their way to be visible to their employees and to give speeches about their organizational goals, values, and ideals.[10]

When Martin Luther King, Jr., gave his famous "I Have a Dream" speech, he was fostering the listener's subconscious identification with his dream.

One could also get a good idea of what referred power is by watching certain classical conductors rehearse an orchestra for a week. Unlike Toscanini, Pierre Monteux never stamped his feet or made threats. Nonetheless through referent power, Richard Sennett reports, Monteux was able to impose as rigid a discipline as the fearsome Toscanini. Sennett writes:

> His baton movements were restricted within a box he imagined in front of him, a box about eighteen inches wide and a foot high. The audience saw little of the stickwork going on inside that box, but the orchestra was intensely aware of it. A movement of an inch upward was the sign of a crescendo; a movement of ten inches indicated a massive outpouring of sound. Most of the cueing (the indication of a player's entrance) was done with Monteux's eyes. The French horns, always a difficult group to cue, received signals from a raised eyebrow; for the strings, simply a glance from the conductor was enough.
>
> The key to his success was his self-assurance, which prompted others "to think it only natural to yield to him."[11]

Theodore Roosevelt probably relied on referent power as much as any president. For those who fell under his spell, he could raise great hopes and dreams. The Kansas editor William Allen White, who was to serve and love Roosevelt for many years, recalled his first meeting with Roosevelt:

> I met Roosevelt. I went hurrying home from our first casual meeting . . . to tell Sallie of the marvel. . . . I had never known such a man as he and never shall again. He overcame me. And in the hour or two we spent that day at lunch, and in a walk down F Street, he poured into my heart such visions, such ideals, such hopes, such a new attitude toward life and patriotism and the meaning of things, as I had never dreamed men had. . . . It was youth and the new order calling youth away from the old order.[12]

A few political leaders do appear to possess certain extraordinary qualities that followers think give them (the leaders) special authority. In the everyday language of politics—if not the more technical vocabulary of sociology—we say such leaders have **charisma.** It is certainly a source of power.

Reward Power

Reward power derives from the leader's ability to make followers believe that their compliance will lead to pay, promotion, recognition, or other rewards. When General George Patton asked his troops how they would answer when their grandchildren ask them what they did in the war, in a particularly sophisticated application of reward power, he suggested that they could either say they shoveled manure in the states or rode through Europe with Patton's Third Army.

Ronald Reagan may be genial in public, but he can play hardball in private. One liberal eastern Democratic congressman who opposed the president's programs in 1981 was turned down 22 times for White House tour passes for constituents. In fact, he never got a pass.

On Using the Sources of Power Successfully

According to John Kotter, managers who successfully exercise power tend to share a number of characteristics. They are sensitive to what others consider legitimate uses of power and the "obligation of power." Consequently, they know when, where, and with whom to use the various types of power. Nor do they rely on any one type of power.

They use all their resources to develop still more power. In effect, they "invest" in power. For example,

> By asking a person to do him two important favors, a manager might be able to finish his construction program one day ahead of schedule. That request may cost him most of the obligation-based power he has over that person, but in return he may significantly increase his perceived expertise as a manager of construction projects in the eyes of everyone in his organization.[13]

Finally, they recognize that use of power is not a **zero-sum game**. That is, when the leader has more power, the follower need not have less. Some research indicates that, in organizations where there is a greater amount of power at all levels, the organization is likely to be more effective and members more satisfied.

This chapter opened by noting that Machiavelli, the first philosopher to look at politics with cold realism, has become in modern times the philosopher many love to hate. The reason for the contemporary animus is nowhere more obvious than in one particular short passage in *The Prince*. In it he examines the question of whether it is better to be loved or feared. You can probably already guess his answer. Men love the rule of their own free will, but fear at the will of the prince. Thus it follows that "a wise prince must rely on what is in his power and not on what is in the power of others." In short, fear works better than warm feelings.

Machiavelli's theory may never really have been true; today it would surely not hold true. One of the best ways that successful political leaders can generate power in their relationships with others is to create a sense of obligation in them. Thus successful political leaders make an effort to do favors, large and small, for people who they expect will feel an obligation to reciprocate.

There is an important corollary to this rule: Be sure you are the sole dispenser of every favor possible. Thus, after the defeat of his newly formed Progressive party in the elections of 1912, Theodore Roosevelt dismissed the idea that a new major party had been founded. When someone spoke hopefully to Roosevelt, he was answered coldly:

> I thought you were a better politician. The fight is over. We are beaten. There is only one thing to do and that is to go back to the Republican party. *You can't hold a party like the Progressive party together. . . . There are no loaves and fishes.*[14]

As can be seen in the following example, Lyndon Johnson was very skilled at identifying opportunities for doing favors that cost them very little but that others appreciate very much. In 1956, Senate Majority Leader Johnson decided to bring Senator John F. Kennedy closer to his orbit of influence. At one point a single vacancy on the prestigious Foreign Relations Committee appeared. Johnson was determined that it would go to Kennedy over Johnson's old foe, Estes Kefauver of Tennessee. The rub was that Kefauver had seniority over Kennedy.

Johnson, therefore, telephoned Senator Clinton Anderson, for whom he had performed a considerable favor two years earlier. (He had made Anderson chairman of the Joint Atomic Energy Committee.) Johnson asked Anderson if he was still as interested in a seat on the Foreign Relations Committee as he had been several years ago. Anderson was puzzled; his campaign for such a seat had ended when he got his JAEC chairmanship. Before he could answer, Johnson rushed on: "You have seniority over Kennedy. But if you don't claim it, Kefauver will."

Anderson saw he and Kefauver both had equal seniority. If they both applied for the one seat, Johnson would have to throw up his hands in mock frustration. Then Johnson could declare a standoff—and give the seat to Kennedy. Anderson went along with this neat strategy; Kennedy got his seat; Johnson had Kennedy in his orbit of influence.[15]

To conclude, a second corollary is worth noting. It is so obvious I hesitate to enter it. Yet I must. Never, never treat supporters shabbily.

The morning after Richard Nixon's overwhelming reelection in 1972, the good feeling of the White House staff was shattered. At 11 A.M., Nixon strode into a staff meeting. Grim and remote, he thanked them in a perfunctory manner and then left, turning the meeting over to his assistant, Bob Haldeman. Haldeman ordered all members of the staff to submit their resignation immediately. Nixon would announce his personnel decisions for the new term within a month.

This was an appalling performance. It wounded and humiliated a hard-working group of supporters. Surely Nixon deprived himself of much sympathy and support when, not long after, the Watergate troubles began to descend upon him.

POLITICAL STRATEGY AND TACTICS

In discussing the sources of power in the preceding section, an assumption was made. Although power of a political actor is largely a function of his or her position within an organization, there are still strategies and tactics that could enhance the power of the political actor. This section describes some of the strategies and tactics that are employed in politics to acquire and exercise power.

The purpose of this section is not to show you how to acquire power. That ability depends on your motives and personality. This section aims to make you more aware of it. We can identify at least six rules for its use.

Keep Goals in Sight

Above all, the effective exercise of power requires the participants to keep their goals firmly and continuously in sight. All tactics should be tested against this simple question: If I take this action, will it further or hinder my ultimate goals. Many students of American politics and government are infatuated with sports images; therefore these goals are sometimes referred to as "game plans."

Regardless of the label, few politicians were more religious practitioners of this principle than Winston Churchill. A remark by Churchill to his private secretary just before Nazi Germany invaded the Soviet Union illustrates this laser-straight sense of purpose. How, the secretary asked, can you—the leading British anticommunist—reconcile yourself to being on the same side as the Soviets? Is it not embarrassing? Churchill's reply was clear and unequivocal. "Not at all. I have only one purpose, the destruction of Hitler, and my life is much simplified thereby. If Hitler would invade Hell, I would make at least a favorable reference to the Devil in the House of Commons."

Churchill could swallow his distaste for communism. Lincoln could swallow his distaste for that abominable institution, slavery. Like Churchill, Lincoln did not lose sight of his goals. In 1862, in his famous letter to the publisher Horace Greeley, Lincoln wrote:

> My paramount purpose is to save the Union, and is not either to save or destroy slavery. If I could save the Union without freeing any slave, I would do it; and if I could save it by freeing all slaves, I would do it; and if I could save it by freeing some and leaving others alone, I would do that.

In 1960, the first televised debates between presidential candidates occurred. Nixon debated Kennedy as if a board of judges were scoring points; he rebutted and refuted systematically the inconsistencies and errors of his opponent. But Kennedy had a different goal. He wanted to address himself to the audience. Here was Nixon, before the largest audience of Americans in history, trying to score debating points. At the same time, Kennedy, cool and undisturbed, was trying to offer his vision of the future to millions of voters.

In sum, keeping goals in sight—whether in economic, social, or foreign policy—breeds consistency, and consistency in decision making helps political leaders dominate policymaking. Idiosyncrasies in decision making indicate a loss of power.

Marshal Resources

In economics, when we speak of resources, we traditionally think of land, capital, technology, and workers. With minor modifications, the same holds true in politics.

First, there are *people*. They may be full-time staff or merely volunteers. Gerald M. Rafshoon, President Carter's media adviser, compiled a master list of prominent opinion leaders inside and outside the government. These people could be used to rebut editorial and public criticism of the president's policies on subjects from the strategic arms treaty to the 1980 budget. Similarly, the late Richard Daley, mayor of Chicago, was upset when the Johnson administration chose to reroute antipoverty funds to his city. The idea was that someone other than Daley would hand out the funds. For the same reason, one of Ed Koch's first acts after becoming mayor of New York City was to assume greater control over antipoverty funds.

Second, there is *money*. As we shall see in Chapter 6, money is perhaps the most vital ingredient in a political campaign.

Next, there is *knowledge*. Whether of a technical or political nature, knowledge is an important source of power. For example, in many American cities, the policies of institutions like the city water board, the public-service commission, or the planning and zoning commission, have routinely been accepted; it is assumed that occupants are the only people in town who know enough to make decisions. Citizens who go to the trouble of understanding, say, procedures of water-main extension or comparative utility rates are, merely by their knowledge, in a position to have some impact on public policy. Franklin Roosevelt's understanding of the public mood was based not on some sixth sense but it was, according to biographer, "in a solid, day-to-day accumulation of facts on what people were thinking. Roosevelt read half a dozen newspapers a day."[16]

Unlike his predecessors, Senate Majority Leader Johnson was constantly probing to discover what senators were really thinking. For that he used his "intelligence system," which was frighteningly efficient. One evening late in the 1950s, one Republican senator had dinner with a group of reporters. Thinking the meeting was off the record, he talked about division in his party. The reporters, who worked as a team, had a reputation for observing confidentiality. Yet, a few days later, one of the reporters called on Johnson in his office. Johnson chided the reporter for always writing about divisions in the Democratic party while ignoring those in the Republican party. To prove his point, Johnson pulled out a memorandum on the "confidential" dinner session.[17]

A final source of power is the *formal authority* vested in the office. Recently, political scientist Richard M. Pious has challenged the usual textbook picture of presidential power.

> The fundamental and irreducible core of presidential power rests not on influence, persuasion, public opinion, elections, or party, but rather on the successful assertion of constitutional authority to resolve crises and significant domestic issues.[18]

I think any political scientist would be hard-pressed to argue that great presidents have been timid about interpreting their powers as restricted to the specific ones listed in Article II of the Constitution. Theodore Roosevelt, for instance, led the United States into the responsibilities of a world power at the turn of the century. Bypassing the Senate, he sent the whole fleet into the Pacific, then around the world on a "practice cruise." Congress then either had to pay the bills or allow the ships to rot quietly in some foreign port.

In his witty book *Power,* Michael Korda argues that offices in the corner of an office are particularly desirable in terms of power. For one thing, they tend to be larger. The floor plan of the main floor of the west wing of the White House supports Korda's thesis (see Figure 4–3). He writes:

> The closer one is to the center, the less powerful one is, just as the offices in the middle of a row are less powerful than the ones at either end of it. Power therefore tends to communicate itself from corner to corner in an X-shaped pattern, leaving certain areas as dead-space in power terms, even though they may contain large and comfortable offices with outside windows.

In the floor plan in Figure 4–3, Korda's "power dead space" has been shaded. Certainly, few Washington observers would disagree that Baker and Meese are the two most powerful members of Reagan's White House staff. In the Carter White House, special security adviser Zbigniew Brzezinski had occupied Meese's office. As the Korda "theory" would predict, Brzezinski exercised much more influence than Reagan's first national security adviser, Richard Allen—who was located in the *basement* of the West Wing.

How resources are used is as important as their magnitude. Sometimes availability of resources determines strategy. As labor organizer Saul Alinsky has pointed out when, Lenin returned to Russia during World War I, he advocated a strategy of peace and reformation through the ballot. Similarly, Mahatma Gandhi advocated one of change through passive resistance. But, if either had possessed guns, Alinsky maintains, it would have been through the bullet. In any event, those naive about the use of power were surprised when another great Indian apostle of nonviolence and a protégé of Gandhi ordered the armed invasion of tiny Goa. In 1961, Jawaharlal Nehru had the bullets.[19]

How and when resources are concentrated is also important. Generals know that a little army can beat a bigger army provided the little army concentrates its full force at the right time and place. Evidence mounts that the U.S. attempt to rescue the American hostages in Teheran failed because planners violated this maxim. Consider the size of the assault force. Ninety men were assigned to overwhelm an enclosed compound defended by 150 well-armed and disciplined terrorists. At Entebbe in 1976, an Israeli unit of more than 100 select troops was employed against only seven Palestinian terrorists and a scattered number of predictably late-reacting and confused Ugandan soldiers. That was concentration of forces. The German recapture of a hijacked Lufthansa airliner in Mogadishu in 1977 involved a strike force of about 90 commandos against only four or five terrorists. That was concentration of forces. In terms of both men and machines, the U.S. attempt to free its hostages in Teheran appears to have been severely "underfunded." It allowed little margin for error or for the unexpected event (see box).

In a political campaign, to marshal resources is called **targeting**. Since it is impossible to reach every voter in every precinct, a campaign manager needs to target voter contact programs so that they *persuade* those who are undecided and *turn out* on election day those who favor his or her candidate.

In the marshalling of resources, a couple of ploys are worth noting. (A **ploy** is simply a maneuver to achieve an objective without revealing the ultimate goal or true intent. Because politics is rife with ploys, skillful politicians are generally skeptical people. See examples, p. 128.) One ploy is the **leak** or **trial balloon,** that is, the disclosure of information concerning

"There's No Such Thing as a Little Force"

On the night of April 24, 1980 an elite American commando team lifted off the deck of the carrier U.S.S. *Nimitz* in the Arabian Sea in an effort to rescue 52 American hostages held in Teheran. But three of their helicopters were crippled en route or in the desert staging area. President Carter then called off the mission. As the team prepared to evacuate, a helicopter collided with a transport plane, killing eight Americans. Ayotallah Khomeini threatened to kill the hostages if Carter tried another such "silly maneuver." U.S. Secretary of State Cyrus Vance resigned in protest against the raid.

In 1958, when President Eisenhower sent American troops to Lebanon, he sent an overwhelming 14,000. He explained: "When you appeal to force, there's just one thing you must never do—lose. . . . Remember this: there's no such thing as a little force. You have to use it overwhelmingly."

While one hesitates to lecture Eisenhower on the use of power, note that *certain circumstances* call not for the use of overwhelming force, but for **finesse**. This means that one uses just enough power to accomplish the goal. In general, finesse is called for when there is a risk of inducing a counterattack from one's opponents. For a classic example of finesse, see how Chief Justice John Marshall handled President Jefferson (pp. 124–25).

SOURCE: Eisenhower material from William Bragg Ewald, Jr., *Eisenhower the President* (Englewood Cliffs, N.J.: Prentice-Hall, 1981).

---

news-worthy government activity through unofficial channels. This allows government officials to test public reaction without committing themselves to a particular course of action.*

Another ploy is the use of a **hatchetman**. When a president fires a well-respected subordinate or attacks the opposition, he stands to lose some of his political capital. He might appear cruel or insensitive. Accordingly, presidents generally prefer to avoid such risky chores and delegate them to associates.

To conclude, I want to stress that the second rule, like the other six, applies to virtually any management situation. Resources can be used, or "invested," to develop still more power. Political scientist Edward Banfield reports that successful politicians take risks; they invest their power in decisions and actions in hopes of getting a high return.[20] Is this not true of successful managers as well? For example, to finish a project ahead of schedule, Manager A might ask manager B for a favor. The favor, of course, costs A some of his obligation-based power over B. But an early completion of the project might raise A's perceived expertise in the organization. (Remember: Power is not just what you have. It is also what others perceive you to have.)

Use Political Jujitsu

Jujitsu or judo literally means "the gentle art." It is based on the principle of defeating ones' opponents by yielding to them and using their own strength. According to a legend, it was discovered through watching the snow fall on the branches of trees. On the branches of rigid trees, the snow piles up until they crack beneath the weight. But on the branches of thin, springy trees, the branches do not break; they simply yield and throw the snow to the ground. So much for trees in the wintertime. Let us see how the principle applies in the sweaty arena of politics.

First, the opposition must be singled out

---

* Not all leaks are favorable to the government's cause. Sometimes insiders, dissatisfied with its policies, give sensitive, unflattering information to the press in order to discredit those policies.

FIGURE 4-3
The "Geography" of Power in the White House

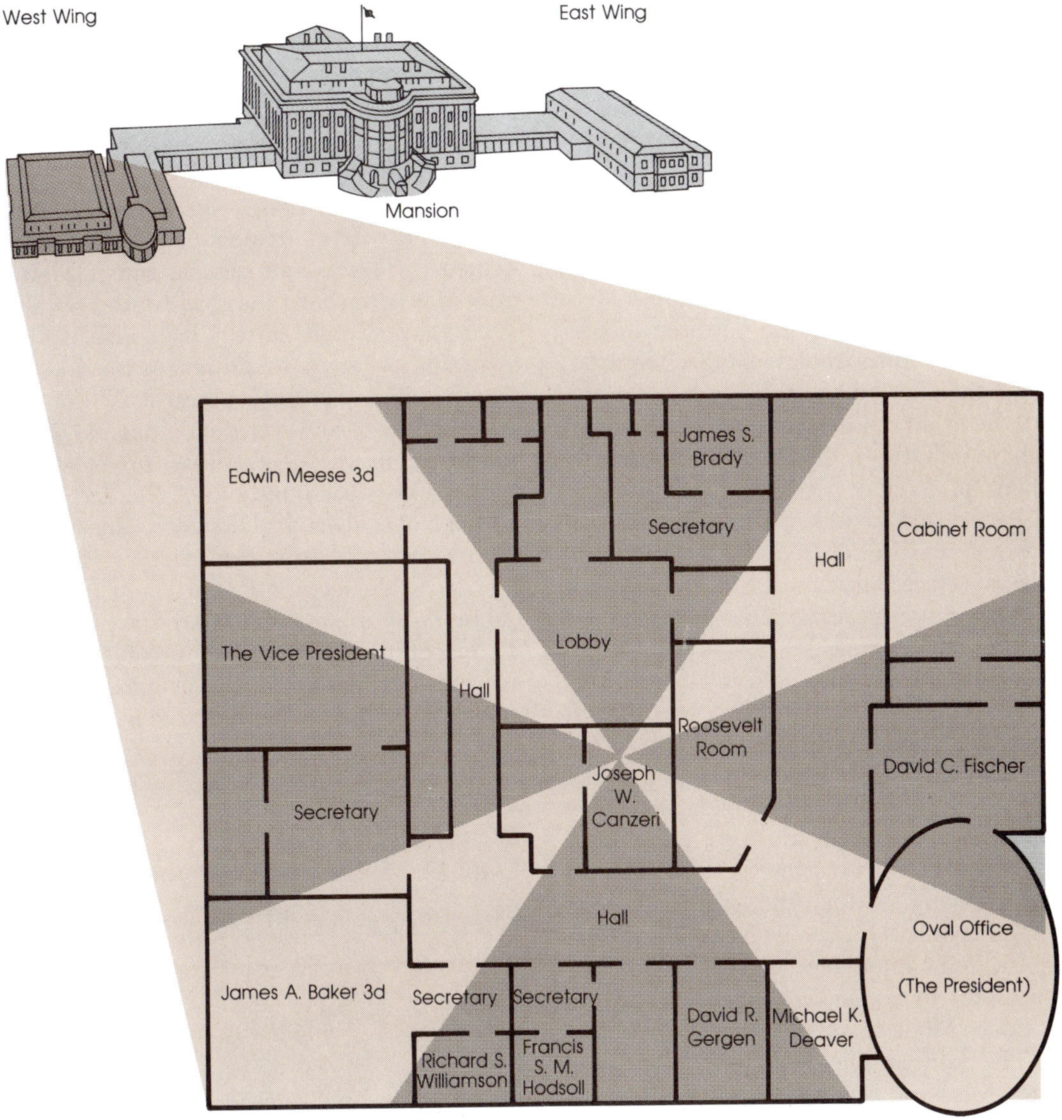

quite clearly. If it is a mayor, he or she should not be allowed to shift responsibility to a committee. If it is a giant corporation, it is hard to talk about corporate power in the abstract. Because Ralph Nader recognized this, he focused on what he believed to be the lethal design of the Corvair. If it is a political party, separate leaders from the rank and file. (The exception to the rule is when the leader is popular, as Eisenhower was.)

Sooner or later, the opposition attempts a ploy or verbal attack. At that moment, when things become fierce and stormy, the skillful politician calmly uses jujitsu. Some examples follow.

Marbury v. Madison. Now we come to one of the most important cases in American constitutional history. In deciding the case, Chief Justice John Marshall displayed more than just a keen mind. He showed a knack for suddenly turning a defense against the opposition into an attack on the opposition.

In 1800, Thomas Jefferson defeated incumbent President John Adams. Unlike Jefferson, Adams and his fellow Federalists generally supported the courts and favored judicial review (see Chapter 2). But in 1800 the issue of exactly who had this review power was still unclear.

To insure that at least part of the government would remain in Federalists' hands, Congress hastily created dozens of new judicial positions. Adams also gave the chief justiceship to Jefferson's deep enemy, John Marshall. Needless to say, Jefferson and his party were something less than delighted to find one branch of government securely in control of anti-Jefferson forces.

They were so annoyed, in fact, that they repealed the act creating the new judgeships. They also refused to deliver the commissions of four new judges, which the Adams administration had not had time to deliver. Not surprisingly, the four appointees applied to the Supreme Court to *compel* the new secretary of state, James Madison, to deliver their commissions. The name of one of the appointees was William Marbury; the case became known as *Marbury* v. *Madison*.

Marbury based his case on Section 13 of the Judiciary Act of 1789. This act authorized the Supreme Court "to issue writs of mandamus, in cases warranted by the principles and usages of law, to . . . persons holding office, under the authority of the United States." A **writ of mandamus** is a court order directing an official to perform a certain act. Marbury asked the Supreme Court to issue a writ of mandamus to force Madison to deliver the commission.

To John Marshall, the case turned on three essential questions. First, did Marbury have a right to the commission? The Court said yes. Second, did the laws provide a remedy for the violations of this right? The Court again said yes. (The writ of mandamus was the proper remedy.) Third—and here is where Marshall gave the Jeffersonians a good tumble—did the Court have the authority to issue such an order? This authority was found not in the Constitution but in an act of Congress passed in 1789. Marshall held, however, that Congress was not permitted by the Constitution to give the Supreme Court such authority. The act, at least in part, was invalid. Therefore, the Supreme Court could not issue the order.

Marshall's decision is worth replay, in slow motion. By saying that Marbury had a right to the commission, Marshall was able to admonish President Jefferson. By saying that the Supreme Court had no authority to issue an order,

Architect of the Capitol

At the age of 32, John Marshall, was a delegate to the Constitutional Convention and helped turn back the antifederalist challenge in the Virginia ratification convention. Later he served as chief justice of the Supreme Court for 34 years. His court handed down many landmark decisions that established the power of the judicial branch.

Marshall was able to combine a seeming passivity with a real assertion of power. He was affirming for the first time that the Supreme Court might declare an act of Congress to be unconstitutional. Marshall had laid the basis for the Supreme Court's power of judicial review of acts of Congress. Jefferson and his supporters, landing on their backs, were in no position to counter.

Fort Sumter. Before Lincoln took office, seven states of the deep South had seceded. The Union could now be preserved only through an aggressive war. But few in the North wanted such a war. An unprovoked attack upon the South would alienate too many people in the North and the world. Lincoln's achievement was to use a thrust by the South to move the North from the defensive to the offensive.

Fort Sumter was a fort belonging to the United States but located in the mouth of Charleston harbor. It was already running short of supplies and the South was demanding its evacuation. To reinforce it would subject Union ships to Confederate gunfire. To order an evacuation would be to acknowledge the legality of secession and boost southern morale. To try a military assault to bring relief to the fort would be dangerous. The only solution to the dilemma was to let the Confederates themselves bring matters to a head by attacking Fort Sumter.

Lincoln carefully began to make his moves. The navy was ordered to prepare a relief expedition. The governor of South Carolina was told an attempt would be made to supply the fort *with provisions only* but not with arms. He was also told that, as long as the relief attempt was not resisted, no secret attempt would be made at some future date to supply the fort with arms.

Few in the North could disagree with that. But the Confederates were put on the horns of a dilemma. If the relief attempt was resisted, the Union would use force. If it was not resisted, then the Confederates must accept indefinite occupation by Union forces. This would weaken their causes in the South and in Europe. Note well what Lincoln had done. He had taken the burden from his shoulders and put it on the southerners. No matter what the South decided to do, he would be master of the situation.

Before the navy's relief expedition arrived, the Confederates demanded from the fort's commander a prompt evacuation. The commander refused. At dawn on April 12, 1861, the Confederate shore batteries began to bombard Fort Sumter. These were the first shots of the Civil War.

It would be a gross misinterpretation of events to say that Lincoln had manoeuvered the Confederates into firing the first shots. His overriding concern was to preserve the Union, but not at any cost. Federal property could not be given up at the behest of Confederate authorities. As he had told the South in his first inaugural address: "The government will not assail you. You can have no conflict without being yourselves the aggressors. You have no oath registered in Heaven to destroy the government, while I shall have the most solemn one to preserve, protect and defend it . . ."

Lincoln knew that he must take a stand against the South somewhere. Fort Sumter was as good a place as any. With it he was able to keep his inaugural pledge and let the South—by its own choosing—play the aggressor. Now he was in a much stronger position to call upon the state governors for troops. As he informed Congress when it met on July 4: "Then and thereby the assailants of the Government began the conflict of arms."

Protest at Selma. The Reverend Martin Luther King Jr., and his colleagues applied political jujitsu during their 1965 direct action campaign in Selma, Alabama. The campaign resulted in the passage of the Federal Voting Rights Act. The technique was to provoke deliberately—but nonviolently—severe, even lethal, violence from white southern racists.[21] This, in turn, would attract the press and

Wide World Photos

During racial demonstrations in Birmingham, Alabama, in 1963 this photograph of a police dog attacking a black was taken and flashed around the world. It was frequently referred to in congressional debates on the Civil Rights Act of 1964. The effect and its lesson was not lost on Martin Luther King, Jr., two years later.

thereby influence public opinion to bring pressure on the government for passage of the Voting Rights Act. Dr. King explained the technique of **nonviolence** this way:

1. Nonviolent demonstrators go into the streets to exercise their constitutional rights.
2. Racists resist by unleashing violence against them.
3. Americans of conscience in the name of decency demand federal intervention and legislation.
4. The administration, under mass pressure, initiates measures of immediate intervention and remedial legislation.[22]

The essence of political jujitsu is to turn your opponent's strength into weakness and your weaknesses into strength. It is hard to survive in politics without this ability. When Benjamin Disraeli, the great 19th-century British statesman, saw he was about to be fiercely attacked by his opponents in Parliament, he just tipped his top hat over his eyes and pretended to slumber. Any attack, no matter how strong, will be blunted if it is addressed to a hat. Commentator Jeff Greenfield gave the following example of how California's Senator S.I. Hayakawa turns his weakness into strength:

> When S.I. Hayakawa told a questioner, "I don't give a goddamn about dog racing," that was political jujitsu in action. Instead of bluffing an answer about something he knew nothing about, Hayakawa took the aggressive question and attacked it as unworthy. The effect was very much like running full tilt toward a closed door in an attempt to knock it down, only to have it flung open at the point of impact. It is the lack of resistance that sends the attacker completely off balance.[23]

Finally, not to be overlooked as a gentle but effective counter to the opposition's thrusts is humor. Few American politicians could use this weapon any more devastatingly than John Kennedy. During the 1960 presidential campaign, each blow struck at him by Nixon seemed to offer him opportunity for a humorous parry. Theodore White gives this example:

> In the South, where Nixon had been preaching the doctrine that he, not Democrat Kennedy, was the true heir of Thomas Jefferson, Kennedy parried with a quotation from one of Jefferson's contemporaries on the great Virginian.
> "'He (said the contemporary of Jefferson) is a gentleman of 32 who can plot an eclipse, survey a field, plan an edifice, break a horse, play the violin, dance the minuet.' Now what," Kennedy would challenge the Southern audience, "has he got in common with Mr. Nixon?"—and the audience would roar back: "Nothing."[24]

Maintain Equanimity

Author Hermann Hesse, in *The Glass Bead Game*, wrote:

> A man can be a star of the first magnitude in gifts, willpower and endurance, but so well balanced that he turns with the system to which he belongs without any friction or waste of energy. Another may have the same great gifts, or even finer ones, but the axis does not pass precisely through the center and he squanders half his strength in eccentric movements which weaken him and disturb his surroundings.

What traits might characterize the type of individual Hesse so eloquently describes? I should like to suggests three: self-control (what Hemingway called "grace under pressure"), efficiency (accomplishes goals with minimum expenditure of resources), and a healthy skepticism (but not cynicism).

Again, we come back to George Washington. How he kept his troops in the field—so poorly fed, paid, and clothed—is one of the real puzzles of history. Part of the answer must be found in the supreme self-control that kept him on a steady course and made him someone others could rally around. As Machiavelli wrote, "Where the willingness is great, the difficulties cannot be great."

For Washington, this was as true in war as it was peace. As you may recall from Chapter 2, Washington presided over the Constitutional Convention for four months. During that time, he spoke only once (upon a quite minor point). Yet his weight of character and his steadiness probably did more than anything else to bring the convention to an agreement.

Lincoln too had remarkable self-control. Ten days before his inauguration he met with delegates from 21 states who had gathered in a hope of finding some way of avoiding war. One delegate heatedly told Lincoln, "It is for you, sir, to say whether the whole nation shall be plunged into bankruptcy, whether the grass shall grow in the streets of our commercial cities." A sad but stern expression swept over Lincoln's face. Then, without raising his voice and in carefully measured tones, he replied:

> I do not know that I understand your meaning, nor do I know what my acts or my opinions may be in the future, beyond this. If I shall ever come to the great office of President of the United States, I shall take an oath. I shall swear that I will . . . to the best of my ability, preserve, protect, and defend the Constitution of the United States. . . . It is not the Constitution as I would like to have it, but as it *is*, that is to be defended. The Constitution will not be preserved and defended unless it is enforced and obeyed in every part of every one of the United States. it must be so respected, obeyed, enforced, and defended, let the grass grow where it may.[25]

A. Philip Randolph, the first national labor leader among American blacks, forged the Pullman porters into a powerful union. He even managed to obtain concessions from Presidents Franklin Roosevelt and Harry Truman on crucial civil rights issues (banning discrimination in defense industries and armed forces). One of the keys to Randolph's power was his ability

United Press International Photo

A. Philip Randolph speaking before a House committee in 1969 at age 80.

to exert pressure without getting personally involved. As he used to say, "Don't get emotional."

The great leaders and the great executives in politics work *efficiently*. That is to say, they do not try to cook everyone's dinner and sew the buttons on everyone's shirt. They have an instinct for the jugular, striking only at the vital points of a problem. They let others take care of the details. Simplicity and concentration produce efficiency. That in turn produces power.

Yet some details *are* important. Especially important are those that involve the ambitions and hopes of the countless other people upon whom a political leader must rely for implementing his or her decisions. Most White House staffs are geared for this purpose. A memo to Franklin Roosevelt during one of his campaigns from one of his assistants read:

> 1. Dan Tobin needs a little pat on the back. What do you think of taking him along on the New England trip? . . .
> 2. Jim (Farley) suggests the possibility of taking John J. O'Connor up through New England since he's an old Massachusetts man—nose a bit out of joint, etc.
> 3. Jim thinks the Connecticut trip should include Meriden. It is Frank Maloney's home town. . . .[26]

Finally, the professionals are skeptical, Jimmy Carter went to court to overturn a suspected rigged election in Georgia when he made his first bid for election to the state senate in 1962. He had been beaten by voters who were dead, jailed, or never at the polls on election day. If Carter had accepted the first count in that Georgia election, he very likely would never have become president of the United States. His start in politics would have been blunted and discouraged.

That same year, President Kennedy asked Henry Kissinger to brief West German Chancellor Konrad Adenauer on the military policies of the new administration. Adenauer, crusty and professional, at one point interrupted Kissinger. He asked Kissinger how he *knew* what he was presenting was true. Kissinger replied that he had been briefed by a general. "Was he wearing a uniform?" Adenauer asked. Kissinger confessed he could not recall. The German chancellor suggested that Kissinger ask the general to repeat his briefing in civilian clothes and, if still impressed, let him know.[27]

Consider Timing

No one ever defined the importance of good timing to the political leader better than Shakespeare in *Julius Caesar*. I cannot resist quoting it here:

> There is a tide in the affairs of men,
> Which, taken at the flood, leads on to fortune.
> Omitted, all the voyage of their life
> Is bound in shallows and in miseries.[28]

No American political leader ever took this bit of advice to heart quite the way Franklin Roosevelt did. No president has ever taken better advantage of that period of high public expectation, popular support, and cordial congressional relations at the beginning of his first term. (This period is often called the **honeymoon period**—for obvious reasons.)

Roosevelt's timing also seemed intuitive. But it too was largely calculated. Essential in his timing was the care he took not to confront his political opposition when it was mobilizing and moving hard and fast. He believed, for example, that presidents could expect to lose some popular support during congressional sessions. Therefore the president should wait until Congress adjourns before seizing the offensive again. Sometimes he moved fast, before the opposition could mobilize. "I am like a cat," Roosevelt said once. "I make a quick stroke and then relax." More often, he waited for the crest of the opposition to subside, then he acted. In the 1936 campaign he was under intense pressure from his political advisers to attack Alf Landon when the Republican tide was running strong in early summer. He refused, telling Samuel L. Rosenman (a member of his staff) that tides turned quickly in politics. He recognized a shiftiness and moodiness in certain sectors of public opinion that have since been tested and proved in opinion and voting studies.[29]

In close elections, timing is critical in order that the candidate does not peak too early. Ideally, a candidate's popularity should build to a crescendo 48 hours before the election. For that reason, sophisticated candidates do not run a flat-out or scrambling campaign but a carefully paced one.

Some experts think that Nixon may have peaked too soon in 1960, giving the victory to Kennedy. In contrast, Hubert Humphrey probably did not peak soon enough in 1968. Had the election been held a few days later, he might have defeated Nixon. (When Nixon announced a year before the 1972 election that Henry Kissinger would visit China, one punster in his administration, worried about the reaction of U.S. conservatives, asked, "Peking too soon?")

In crisis situations, timing is particularly critical. But in exactly what way, the experts disagree. Disagreement turns on the question of how fast to apply pressure to an adversary. To escalate the pressures too rapidly could create a **backlash,** widening the scope of the conflict and causing additional parties to become involved. On the other hand, increasing pressure drop by drop, as was done in Vietnam under President Johnson and in Iran under President Carter, allows the adversary time to adjust to worsening conditions.

Build Institutions

Political leaders seek to multiply their power by building organizations, which are only collections of individuals. Except for Superman, Spiderman, the Hulk, and other superheroes who occupy my children's world, individuals must work through institutions if they want to be powerful. Skillful politicians, therefore, are able

Reprinted by permission *The Wall Street Journal*

"Ms. Ryan, send me in a scapegoat."

Leaders who treat supporters well take the blame when things go wrong. Such candor generates public sympathy and, more important, respect. Looking for scapegoats diminishes power because it undermines loyalty among supporters.

to **build coalitions** by combining two or more factions for the purpose of achieving some political goal.

Ralph Nader does not matter today because he wrote *Unsafe at Any Speed*. He matters because he built the organization shown in Figure 6–1. Although Mexican-Americans form a majority in San Antonio, they were relatively powerless for a long time at city hall. Then Ernesto Cortes, Jr., working with some young Roman Catholic priests, put together a federation of organizations to form Communities Organized for Public Service (COPS). Three years later, any list of the most powerful institutions in San Antonio would have to include, among the bankers and real estate developers, COPS.

Candidates win election not only on issues and personality but also through campaign organization. Virtually every major campaign needs a publicity director to handle the media, a campaign director to direct day-to-day operations, a treasurer to raise funds and file financial reports, and a field staff to contact voters directly. When a state or local party organization is centrally led and is able to consistently reward members with material benefits and get its candidates elected, it is called a **machine**. Whether candidates have machine backing or not, they should try to build a foundation of support. One of the most curious things about President Carter was his apparent lack of any hardcore support or **power base.**

RESOLVING CONFLICT THROUGH NEGOTIATIONS

Sometimes A cannot get B to do what A wants. Perhaps A lacks the necessary sources of power or applies the power ineptly. In any event, B does not budge. Assuming that the matter at hand is fairly important to A, what should be done now? The answer is that A needs to switch from trying to exercise power to negotiating the best deal possible with B.

In his 1960 inauguration speech, President Kennedy said: "Let us begin anew, remembering on both sides that civility is not a sign of weakness, that sincerity is always subject to proof. Let us never negotiate out of fear. But let us never fear to negotiate." These are fine, even stirring words. But I am afraid they are often forgotten in public affairs.

In 1979, a Chicago transit workers' strike stranded a million commuters and disrupted the city's economy. For the first time in the city's history, firefighters voted to strike. And the school system was on the verge of bankruptcy. "The city that works" had never been so close to breakdown.

In his 22 years as mayor, Richard J. Daley faced many strikes but never feared to negotiate. But the current mayor Jane Byrne was more combative. Rather than sitting down with unions and other groups to seek a compromise, Mayor Byrne's approach was to attack. She had threatened to bring in strikebreakers if the transit workers walked out. She called in the parties to the dispute and announced a settlement before it was actually made. In the sometimes obtuse language of social science, we would say Mayor Byrne was not very good at conflict resolution. Daley, though no social scientist, would have understood.

When the Constitutional Convention of 1787 was over, Alexander Hamilton said that no one's ideas were further from the plan than his. But, he added, it seemed preferable to anarchy. Hamilton was a proud and arrogant man. He had one great virtue, however—magnanimity. He could lose gracefully. He was also willing to believe that his opponents were as honorable as he and could even be right. Swallowing many strongly held beliefs, he wrote more than 40 brilliant essays in *The Federalist* in order to convince others to ratify the Constitution. He knew the meaning of compromise and, I suspect, conflict resolution.

Regardless of what you do—manage, sell, counsel, purchase, teach, work on a team, deal with government, etc.—you are involved in conflicts of one sort or another every day. Few if any of us can avoid for long disagreements, misunderstandings, stubbornness, gamesmanship, anger, intimidation, and resentment of one form or another. Handling these problems successfully requires skill in conflict resolution.

This penultimate section takes a look at how political leaders handle conflict. First, we shall see how they pinpoint the real causes of conflict. Then we shall examine what techniques they use to resolve it.

Pinpointing the Real Issues

To resolve the conflict, one must know what the other side's needs are. How does one do this? I can assure you that merely asking them will not do much good. In the heat of conflict, people are not as open as usual. Figure 4–4 suggests an answer. One tries to see the current strike, riot, or whatever as part of a *process*.[30] One must think in terms of when and how it started.

As Figure 4–4 shows, when we think of a current conflict we must look at actually far more than the obvious open conflict. We must

FIGURE 4-4
The Anatomy of Conflict

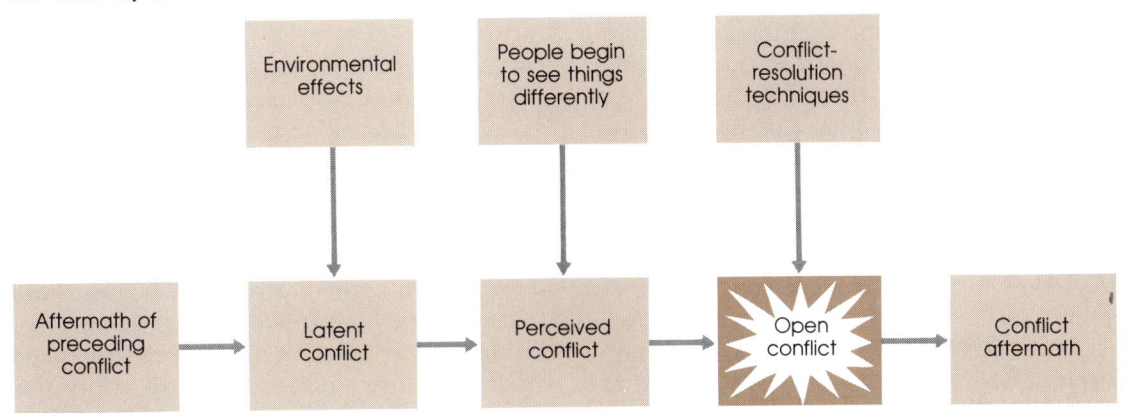

look to its origins, which probably can be traced back to perceived conflict, latent conflict, and, finally, the previous open conflict. Figure 4-4 also tells us that, for open conflict to occur, at least two things must take place. First, changes in the environment cause latent conflict. Second, changes in the way people view their situation cause the actual incident (open conflict).

Conflict in politics occurs for a variety of reasons: disagreement about the facts in a situation (often rooted in communication failure), about the appropriate means to be used, about the appropriate goals to be attained, and about the appropriate values to guide the enterprise (e.g., independence and personal autonomy). But probably the most important source of political conflict in the 1980s will be economic—that is, competition for limited resources.

In such cases, the essence of successful negotiation lies in pinpointing what the other side *really* wants, then showing it a way to get it while you get what you want. In other words, try to turn a zero-sum game into a "win/win game."* For example, a member of Congress might refuse to support transportation legislation unless it provides $20 million for his district. Sponsors of the legislation offer $13 million, $16 million, $19 million. The congressman refuses to budge. Only after several days—by asking questions and attentively listening—does it dawn on the sponsors that one of the congressman's political rivals, from the same state but a different district, would get $20 million for *her* district. Suddenly, the sponsors realize that the congressman had needs other than money. They work out terms that do not increase the total cost of the transportation measure but allow the congressman to feel he has done better than his political rival.

Techniques of Conflict Resolution

The basics. Pride and selfishness react upon one another in a vicious circle. Each one greatly enlarges the other's capacity to destroy negotiations. Pride causes one to view all issues in the negotiations from a limited, individual viewpoint. If one is the center of the universe, everything belongs to that person. A certain amount of humility, therefore, is absolutely necessary if one is to be an effective negotiator. In fact, to grow up means, to throw away the notion that the world exists to provide you with whatever you need.

---

* In the technical language of game theory, this is called a **variable-sum game**. It is the opposite of a zero-sum game, where one person's gain is another person's loss.

Mature adults know how to assert their opinions without devaluing others. They are not afraid to ask for help and say they do not understand. They know to confront the other side with reality, with the facts gently—not brusquely. When the other side begins to manipulate or intimidate them, they know how to be firm. In sum, they know how to get what they want without attacking others as human beings. They focus on the problem at hand; they don't focus on the character flaw of the opposition.

Good negotiators are persistent. As one expert observed, persistence is to power as carbon is to steel. Persistence, along perhaps with his ability to get personal commitments from Egypt's President Anwar Sadat, explains how President Carter was able to get Sadat and Israel's Menachem Begin to agree to a framework for a peace treaty in 1978. He kept them at the presidential retreat at Camp David five long days. This privacy was important because it kept each side from taking public stands that tend to make the other side feel boxed in. In the month that followed, representatives of Egypt and Israel met repeatedly to negotiate the treaty itself. When the negotiations began to break down, Carter again intervened by inviting himself to Egypt for further long, grueling talks. He had gone what his press secretary called "that final, extra mile." The final treaty was signed in Washington with a worldwide television audience of about 100 million watching. The issues separating the two countries had been as wide as the Red Sea; the history of conflict between them was centuries old. Carter's persistence had paid off.

Avoidance. This technique does not completely remove the basic conflict. The negotiator tries to emphasize the positive—that is, the issues upon which agreement is more likely. The thorniest issues are set aside for later. The negotiators proceed cautiously, **step-by-step.** They seek small agreements from each other rather than a sudden, comprehensive solution.

This is precisely what was done at Camp David with respect to the issue of what to do about the Palestinians living within Israeli jurisdiction. (When Israel was founded after World War II to provide a homeland for the Jews, Palestinians were displaced from theirs. Today millions of Palestinians live in camps within Israel's border. See Chapter 14.)

This step-by-step approach to diplomacy is criticized by those who call for a "comprehensive solution."

Strategic concessions. Politics has been called the "art of the possible." In other words, one can seldom attain the ideal but must cut a deal. This means horse trading and compromising. For example, presidential nominees often do not select their ideal choice for vice president. Rather they pick someone else in

Michael Evans/The White House

A skillful negotiator strives to foster a positive climate at the outset. In a relaxed Camp David atmosphere, marked by horseback rides and a barbecue, Ronald Reagan and Jose Lopez Portillo laid the basis for an unprecedented working relationship between the United States and Mexico. While policy disputes persisted after the two presidents' talked, Lopez Portillo reported that relations, "for the first time," no longer were tense. Reagan used Spanish—"*Mi casa es su casa;* my house is your house"—in a toast that caused Lopez Portillo to remark that he had never been so moved.

Jimmy Carter's persistence paid off at Camp David. Egypt's Sadat (right) and Israel's Begin (left) were able to reduce some historical tensions between their two countries.

return for the pledge of the active support from a certain sector of the party.

Few negotiations are without time limits. As one side's deadline approaches, it is increasingly inclined to make concessions. Henry Kissinger, who has had some experience at negotiating, warns:

> In managing the conclusion of any crisis, perhaps the most critical moment occurs when the opponent appears ready to settle; then it is the natural temptation to relax. This is almost always a mistake; the time for conciliation is after the crisis is surmounted and a settlement or modus vivendi has been reached. Otherwise moderation may abort the hopeful prospects by raising last-minute doubts as to whether the cost of settlement need be paid. Stopping offensive military actions in Korea in 1951 when cease-fire talks started almost surely prolonged the talks.[31]

Thus, skillful negotiators try to conceal their deadlines and try to learn the deadline of the other side. (One way to find out is to peek at their airline tickets.)

In arms control negotiations, some weapons systems such as the B-1 bomber and Trident submarine are called **bargaining chips.** The theory is that they can be traded for concessions that the other side might not otherwise make. In 1977, Carter was sharply criticized by the Republicans for canceling the neutron bomb on the grounds that it would have been a good bargaining chip. Unfortunately, the pursuit of too many chips can intensify the arms race and prove to be very expensive.

Skilled negotiators generally start low in terms of what they offer and high in terms of what they expect. This, they think, gives them more room to maneuver and lowers the other side's expectations. From that point forward, they try to avoid making too many concessions too quickly. Concession makes demands escalate. This does not mean one should make his or her moves in driblets and try to look tough. Going too slowly can be self-defeating. It encourages the other side to hold on to see what the next concession will be, even when one has reached his or her rock-bottom position.

Co-optation. There are a variety of ways for dealing with the other side. The most typical perhaps is **compromise,** in which each side gives a little. For example, a labor union lowers its initial wage demands while management raises its initial offer.

Dealing with the opposition by absorption has been called **co-optation.** In the United States, the two major political parties are often able to suffocate third parties by adopting their issues and reaching out to their membership. Similarly, bureaucracy enfolds protest groups by putting them on special "advisory panels."

Nonresolutions. Sometimes one may not want to negotiate. When financier J. Pierpont Morgan received word in 1902 that the government planned to prosecute his company for illegalities, he hurried to Washington. He said to Theodore Roosevelt, "If we have done anything wrong, send your man [meaning the attorney general] to my man [meaning one of his lawyers] and they can fix it up." To which Roosevelt answered: "We don't want to fix it up; we want to stop it."

At other times it may be a good idea to change the negotiators. (Personal chemistry is important.) Or perhaps breaking off temporarily will help. This is to get matters back into better focus and clear the air for further negotiations. Such postponements (especially of forceful action) during conflict resolution are sometimes called **cooling-off periods.**

Finally, one should beware of "winning" one set of negotiations and losing larger, longer-term interests. Pressing too hard and winning a quick victory can lead to the loss of allies and other costs. In 1791, George Washington was about to appoint Gouverneur Morris as minister to France. He warned Morris against seeking to obtain favorable treaties from countries in distress. Unless treaties are mutually beneficial to the parties, it is in vain to hope for a continuance of them beyond the moment when the one which conceives itself to be overreached is in a situation to break off the agreement. A treaty had to match the powers and interests of the parties making it. Otherwise, it would be just a scrap of paper. Today we would say Washington knew the value of a variable-sum game.

We began this discussion of conflict resolution with a quote by John Kennedy. We will close with a quote that he himself picked out for special praise from a book he once reviewed. The book was *Deterrent or Defense* by British military historian B.H. Liddell Hart. What Kennedy liked was a remarkably concise set of recommendations for negotiation in crisis.

> Keep strong if possible. In any case, keep cool. Have unlimited patience. Never corner an opponent, and always assist him to save his face. Put yourself in his shoes—so as to see things through his eyes. Avoid self-righteousness like the devil—nothing is so self-blinding.

POLITICAL LANGUAGE AND SYMBOLS

The Symbolic Use of Politics

Once a political actor has decided on a course of action, he or she must justify it. Here, as Murray Edelman points out, language plays an important role: "Political argument, when it is effective, calls the attention of a group with shared interests to those aspects of their situation which make an argued-for line of action consistent with the furthering of their interests."[32] In this way, political leaders build broad-based coalitions.

According to Edelman, language can substitute for the use of brute force. Clearly this was what Lincoln was trying to do in his first inaugural address (quoted earlier in this chapter). In his speech he called up the "mystic chords of memory, stretching from every . . . patriot grave to every living heart and hearthstone." It was a last-ditch effort to bring southern dissidents back to the Union before any shots were fired.

But political language serves other purposes than legitimizing certain courses of action or avoiding force of arms. Edelman argues, correctly I think, that political language can cloud our efforts to make a rational assessment of a situation. It can dull rather than sharpen our critical faculties. It can provide symbols rather than substance, shadows rather than reality.

Some of the most noble and worthy uses of English prose can be found in political speeches. But the fact remains that many speeches—and perhaps parts of every speech—are designed to be evocative and motivating. Citizens interested in a more clearheaded assessment of their self-interest and the national interest might want to familarize themselves with the mechanics of the political speech (see Table 4–1).

Earlier in the chapter, we saw that information is one of the major resources that political leaders can draw upon to build their power. It follows that controlling the production, processing, and flow of information is important. E.E. Schattschneider asserts that "the definition of the alternatives is the supreme instruments of power."

> The choice of conflicts explains some things about politics that have long puzzled scholars. Political conflict is not like an intercollegiate

debate in which the opponents agree in advance on a definition of the issues. As a matter of fact, *the definition of the alternatives is the supreme instrument of power;* the antagonists can rarely agree on what the issues are because power is involved in the definition. He who determines what politics is about runs the country, because the definition of the alternatives is the choice of conflicts, and the choice of conflicts allocates power.[33]

TABLE 4-1
Political Speech Writing from A to Z

Device	Definition	Examples
Alliteration	The use in a phrase or sentence of words beginning with or containing the same letter or sound. In ordinary expository writing, it serves little purposee and indeed may divert attention from the subject.	In 1952, the Republicans attacked the Democratic administration with the slogan "Korea, Communism, and Corruption." In 1961, John F. Kennedy wrote, "Words can do more than convey policy. They can also convey and create a mood, an attitude, an atmosphere—or an awakening." In 1963, President Johnson addressed a joint session of Congress five days after the Kennedy assassination with these effective words: "I profoundly hope that the tragedy and the torment of these terrible days will bind us together. . . ."
Catchword	A word that crystallizes an issue or sparks a response.	In 1941, Franklin Roosevelt used the phrase "days of infamy" to describe the Japanese attack on the Pearl Harbor naval base. In 1964, Lyndon Johnson's "Let us continue" built on Kennedy's "Let us begin." In 1980, Ronald Reagan ask voters "are you better off today than you were four years ago" (when Carter took office)
Cant	A parrotlike appeal to principles, moral or political, that the speaker is not really thinking about.	"Strenuous" as in "the strenuous life" (Theodore Roosevelt). "Vigor" pronounced with a Boston accent (John F. Kennedy). "Deeds" (Dwight Eisenhower). "Simplistic" (Jimmy Carter).
Code words	A phrase, innocuous in itself, intended to transmit a hidden message which may be quite biting.	In 1972, President Nixon spoke of "work ethic" when he wanted to talk about "those who get something for nothing." In the 1980 campaign for the Democratic presidential nomination, President Carter spoke of how he did not "panic in a crisis." Carter said this to remind voters about Senator Edward Kennedy's accident in which a young woman was killed.
Contrapuntal phrases	The use of repeated rhythm with an inversion of words for emphasis.	Abraham Lincoln: "The world will little note nor long remember what we say here: but it can never forget what they did here." Adlai Stevenson: "Shouting is not a substitute for thinking, and reason is not the subversion but the salvation of freedom." John F. Kennedy: "Let us never negotiate out of fear, but let us never fear to negotiate."

TABLE 4-1 *(continued)*

Device	Definition	Examples
"I See" constructions	A device to outline a vision of the future.	In 1940, Franklin Roosevelt used the "I see" construction as follows: I see an America where factory workers are not discarded after they reach their prime. . . . I see an America whose rivers and valleys and lakes . . . are protected as the rightful heritage of all the people. I see an America where small business really has a chance to flourish and grow. I see an America of great cultural and educational opportunity for all its people. In 1963, at the Lincoln Memorial during the march on Washington, the Reverend Martin Luther King, Jr., used one variation of this device: I have a dream that one day on the red hills of Georgia the sons of former slaves and the sons of former slaveowners will be able to sit down together at the table of brotherhood. . . . I have a dream that my four little children will one day live in a nation where they will not be judged by the color of their skin, but by the content of their character. . . .
Metaphor	A figure of speech in which a word or phrase implies a comparison or identity.	"Square deal" was the card game metaphor Theodore Roosevelt used as a campaign slogan (originally directed against the trusts). "Iron curtain" was the metaphor Winston Churchill used in 1946 to describe the barrier to communication between Eastern Europe and the West by the communists regimes to permit them to operate in isolation from Western criticism.
Oxymoron	The combining in one expression of two terms that are ordinarily contradictory, and whose exceptional coincidence is therefore arresting.	"Loyal opposition": The role of the political opposition in a republican form of government, implying the responsibility to oppose with patriotic motives. "Unthinkable thought": Proposals too mind-boggling to discuss, such as those concerning nuclear war. "Waging peace": Eisenhower's phrase to describe a foreign relations bared on ideological—not military—competition.
Pointer phrases	Verbal signals that underscore the essential point in a speech.	"Let me make one thing perfectly clear." (Nixon used this so much it became an object of ridicule.) "My point is this." "Let me be quite blunt." "It all comes down to this." "In plain words."

TABLE 4-1 (concluded)

Device	Definition	Examples
Rhetoric	As used today in politics, high-flying oratory, bombast, promises unlikely to be fulfilled.	"Law and order" "Peace at home and abroad" "The crisis of the cities" "The erosion of moral values" "The erosion of America's prestige abroad" "Rebuilding the urban and slum areas"
Sneer words	Adjectives used to malign high-sounding nouns.	"Self-appointed" "So-called" "Self-styled"
Zinger	A stirring conclusion to a speech; peroration.	In 1865, in his second inaugural address, Lincoln began his ending with these famous lines: With malice toward none; with charity for all; with firmness in the right, as God gives us to see the right, let us strive on to finish the work we are in; to bind up the nation's wounds; to care for him who shall have borne the battle, and for his widow, and his orphan—to do all which may achieve and cherish a just and lasting peace among ourselves, and with all nations.

Sources: John Bartlett, *Familiar Quotations* (Boston: Little, Brown, 1982); Theodore M. Bernstein, *The Careful Writer* (New York: Atheneum, 1967); H. W. Fowler, *Modern English Usage* (New York: Oxford, 1965); and William Safire, *Safire's Political Dictionary* (New York: Random House, 1978).

Nonverbal Communication

A mistake in trying to understand the exercise of power is to assume that all communication is verbal—that is, strings of words with periods after them. To be sure, in political campaigns the statement of issues is usually verbal. (For example, "To bring inflation under control, we need a balanced budget.") But, at the same time, messages are being sent in other ways. Some nonverbal communication can be very powerful indeed. No matter what Senator Kennedy said when congratulating President Carter on his renomination at the Democratic National Convention in 1980, the real message was Kennedy's raised fist in the air (see picture).

During a political speech, hand gestures are an important part of the verbal delivery. The beating of the hand indicates the important points being made. Posture indicates the mood of the speaker. For example, in negotiation, a most welcome gesture is when the hands are held out in the handshake position. This reflects the urge to stretch out and touch the listener. "The predominant mood," author Desmond Morris writes, "appears to be a strong desire to bridge the gap between speaker and listener—to 'reach' the other person's mind with the idea being expressed in words."

In contrast, the tight fist signals iron determination and strength of thought. This gesture is so well-known that it is the most likely one to be used as a deliberate, contrived act—especially by someone who is indecisive and confused. Much more aggressive is the fist in the air (as in the picture).

When the hand chops the air like an ax,

© John Chao/Woodfin Camp & Associates

The raised fist tells it all.

the speaker is also being aggressive but wants his or her ideas to cut through the confusion of the situation to an important solution. An entirely different mood is expressed when the hand is extended with the palm up. It is the imploring hand of the beggar. The speaker is begging the listener to agree. The palm down is the restraining hand of the cool-headed. It urges listeners to reduce their emotional intensity. When the palm is turned back towards the speaker, it reflects an attempt to embrace the idea under discussion or to pull the listener closer to the speaker.[34]

Image. Though you may deplore the fact, the truth is that candidates do not win exclusively on the basis of issues. **Image** counts, too.

During the presidential debates of 1976 and 1980, television audiences judged the candidates as much by the images they projected as by what they said. Assume that one of the candidates is the incumbent; just the sight of the challenger standing side by side with the president carries quite a visual punch. To many who watched the 1960 debate between Nixon and Kennedy, Nixon looked like the sharp Eastern railroad lawyer who tries to finagle dirt farmers out of their land; Kennedy looked like the handsome young sheriff.

Some analysts think the three debates held in 1976 gave Jimmy Carter his narrow margin of victory over President Ford. Carter did seem to smile too much when speaking about deadly serious issues. But Ford's statement that the Soviet Union did not dominate Eastern Europe hurt him badly in the second debate. Carter also benefited from his ability to convince voters, especially from the rural South, that he was "one of them." (One could argue that it was Thomas Dewey's almost total lack of this ability that caused his loss to Truman in 1948. Many voters saw Dewey not as "one of us" but as an outsider. When one pundit said he looked like "the little man on top of a wedding cake," his fate was sealed.)

Research seems to indicate that television debates do not convert large numbers of people. But debates can affect small groups of people who have not made of their minds. Though these groups are small, in a close election they can be important. In general, however, debates merely reinforce previously held beliefs.

The importance of both a good image and an attractive issue did not dawn with the age of television. Abraham Lincoln never hesitated to remind farmers of his own frontier origins. The image of "the rail splitter" while it had a factual basis, was artfully capitalized on. (But, of course, Lincoln also had the issues.)

Symbols. Symbols also help candidates and political leaders get their messages across. A senator from Ohio campaigns with a loaf of bread under his arm to dramatize what inflation is doing to food prices. A young woman runs for city council in Los Angeles by handing out small cakes of soap to dramatize the need to clean up city government. And a president gives a "fireside chat" on the energy problem wearing a sweater to dramatize the need to conserve. Even Franklin Roosevelt's cigarette holder, held at a jaunty upward angle with clenched teeth, was a symbol during the depths of the Great Depression that America would persevere. If you snicker at these examples, you are forgetting that *all* human communication is through symbols.

The real problem is whether the symbols

On Projecting the Gift of Command

The American republic does not confer royalty. But it does confer certain privileges. Because presidents must often lead by persuasion, these privileges are a resource for power.

For example, before taking office, Jimmy Carter had wanted to divest himself of the presidential retreat at Camp David. Two years later, this remote setting provided the ideal setting for the historic peace agreement between Egypt and Isreal.

While difficult to measure, it is possible that breaking precedent by walking from his inauguration and engaging in other "unpresidential" activities lowers a president's political capital. It is doubtful that the American people would today want a president as aloof as George Washington. But they probably expect a president to speak and act in a manner that at once communicates "his own common humanity and his uncommon mastery of turmoil and complication" (as Edmund S. Morgan put it).

United Press International Photo

Wide World Photos

---

used are correctly interpreted by both the sender and receiver. Take, for example, the picture of President Carter and his brother munching a sandwich at Billy's gas station. It might be interpreted quite differently in Paris, Bonn, and London than in the Piney Woods of Arkansas. The same is true for the picture of President Carter and his wife Rosalynn walking hand-in-hand from his 1976 inauguration. In trying to influence people's judgments, effective political leaders pay considerable attention to the "trappings" of power and to their own reputation and images. Without any trappings of power, a president can become just a good ole boy who happens to own a blue suit and a shoeshine.

Finally, symbolic language may serve to deflect opposition or generate support. Appointing a few minority-group members to highly visible positions in an administration can direct attention away from high levels of unemployment among minority youth. Creating regulatory agencies "to protect the public interest" and special commissions or **blue ribbon panels** (composed of well-known and respected individuals) to "study the problem" may convince some groups that progress is being made.

Perception. If others think you have it, you have it. Saul D. Alinsky, a community organizer who died in 1972, describes how to stage a "cinch fight" to build the confidence of one's followers in their leader and in themselves. In the late 1930s, one poor area of Chicago was plagued with a high rate of infant mortality. Alinsky knew medical service was available from the Infant Welfare Society for the asking, since the community itself had started the service about a decade earlier. Keeping this bit of information to himself, Alinsky called a meeting to plan strategy. They would march into the office of the Infant Welfare Society and demand medical service. Alinsky explains what happened a few days later:

> With this careful indoctrination we stormed into the Infant Welfare Society downtown, identified ourselves and began a tirade consisting of militant demands, refusing to permit them to say anything. All the time the poor woman was desperately trying to say, "Why of course you can have it. We'll start immediately." But she never had a chance to say anything and finally we ended up in a storm of "And we will not take 'No' for an answer!" At which point she said, "Well, I've been trying to tell you . . ." and I cut in demanding, "Is it yes or is it no?" She said, "Well, of course it's yes." I said, "That's all we wanted to know." And we stormed out of the place.[35]

CONCLUDING OBSERVATIONS: THE NECESSITY OF POWER

If one accepts the premise that occasional change in politics is good, that governments occasionally do need reform and innovation, then one must face the dilemma Machiavelli so elegantly stated in Book III of *The Prince*. The cards are all stacked against change. The intrinsic merit of a new idea will not alone overcome the resistance it is bound to face. Something else is required—power.

> It ought to be remembered that there is nothing more difficult to take in hand, more perilous to conduct, or more uncertain in its success, than to take the lead in the introduction of a new order of things. Because the innovator has for enemies all those who have done well under the old conditions, and lukewarm defenders in those who may do well under the new. This coolness arises partly from fear of opponents, who have the laws on their side, and partly from the incredulity of men, who do not readily believe in new things until they have had a long experience of them. Thus it happens that whenever those who are hostile have the opportunity to attack they do it like partisans, whilst the others defend lukewarmly, in such wise that the prince is endangered along with them.
>
> It is necessary, therefore, if we desire to discuss this matter thoroughly, to inquire whether these innovators can rely on themselves or have to depend on others: that is to say, whether, to consummate their enterprise, have they to use prayers or can they use force? In the first instance they always succeed badly, and never compass anything; but when they can rely on themselves and use force, then they are rarely endangered. Hence it is that all armed prophets have conquered, and the unarmed ones have been destroyed.

Power is nothing more than the ability of getting a job done; it is a *means* to an end. St. Igantius, the founder of the Jesuit order, recognized this when he wrote, "To do a thing well a man needs power and competence." When civil rights leader Jesse Jackson talks about young blacks lifting themselves up by their bootstraps, he is talking about power. When President Eisenhower, however, sent the 101st Airborne Division to Little Rock in 1957 in defense of the civil rights of schoolchildren, he was *using* power.

The importance of understanding how power is acquired, exercised, and maintained is probably best seen by focusing on one example, the women's movement. Because of culture and past discrimination, not as many women as men have backgrounds in the administration of power. Yet, if women are to continue to progress in the world of politics and business, particular attention will have to be paid to skills such as jockeying for position, exercising leadership, and developing personal relationships. In her recent book *In the Running: Women as*

Political Candidates, Ruth Mandel points out that one reason women feel they have to work harder than men is that they are excluded from "male networks." To combat this ostracism, women are weaving networks of their own. Their actions far better than my words say why power is necessary.

"Justice without power is impotent," French philosopher Blaise Pascal observed. But then he added something important: "Power without justice is tyranny." Pascal was saying that not all power is the same. Depending on why and how it is used, we can make distinctions. The place to begin is with the ambitions of the people exercising power.

The first kind of ambition we might note is that of people who are anxious to enlarge their own influence in the community so that they can get more of the economic pie and satisfy their swollen egos. This kind of power is, of course, vulgar and degenerate. The second kind of ambition is that of people who strive to enlarge the power of their community, district, state, country, or cause. While this kind is more dignified than the first; it is not less covetous. But, if one were to endeavor to renew and enlarge the power of mankind in general, this third set of ambition would be both more sound and noble. The ambition of all political leaders who have passed across the stage of American politics can be placed somewhere between the extremes of the first and third kind.

Allow me a second generalization, one I did not discover: When a political leader fails to "take charge," someone else will. *Natura abhorret a vacuum ("Nature abhors a vacuum").* When a president fails to exercise his power in making foreign policy, that power flows to Congress or the media. When a president fails to exercise his power in making economic policy, it flows to Congress or the Federal Reserve Board (see Chapter 13). When the president and Congress fail to use their power in making all citizens equal, it flows to Congress. When states fail to use their power to protect children in labor policy, it flows to Washington. In politics, the concept of power is unavoidable.

Good presidents are not squeamish about the exercise of power when they deem its exercise justified. Eisenhower sent the 101st Airborne Division to Little Rock in defense of the civil rights of black high school students.

Chapter Key

When A can get B to do what B would not otherwise have done, we say that A has power over B. The source of that power may be raw strength (coercive power); it may be who A knows (connection power) or what A knows (expert power); it may be what B owes A (obligation power); it may be the authority A has (legitimate power), the resources A might control (dependence power), or the character of A (referent power); or it may be what A can do for B (reward power).

The Constitution begins "We the people. Despite this, most of us realize that power in society is unevenly distributed.

One theory of how to measure how power is distributed in society is elitism. It says that the United States is governed not by the people or even majorities but by tiny elites. The elites are found not only in government. They are also in corporations and other large, powerful institutions. Proponents of elitist theory, such as C. Wright Mills, argue that relatively small groups of people control these large organizations and also control policymaking. In the 20th century, these theorists say that the power of elites has grown as the power of a few large institutions has increased. Since the 1880s, power in the United States has become concentrated; a few large institutions (public and private) have replaced many smaller ones and have come to dominate society. Elite power, say these theorists, is further increased by a system of interlocking elites and by consensus among elites on the most important issues.

Pluralist theory provides an alternative prospective. Its proponents contend that neither a popular majority nor an elite governs America. Instead, policy is determined as a result of competition among a large number of organized groups. Pluralist theory argues that the complexity of the U.S. political system promotes participation by many groups. Competing interests try to influence policy by contacts with the executive branch, the legislature, or the courts. Large institutions check and balance one another's influence. Unorganized groups need only get organized to make their voices heard.

Neither theory can fully explain all public policy decisions. In some cases, elites do seem to operate; in others, groups prevail. But in all cases it is important to recognize that *within* effective groups, however large and democratically structured, it is ultimately a small group of individuals who will wield power.

In exercising power, skilled politicians employ a variety of strategies. They keep their goals in sight while others become confused or distracted. They marshal or direct their resources at the crucial time and place. They turn attacks by their opponents back on the attackers (as did Chief Justice Marshall in *Marbury* v. *Madison* and Martin Luther King, Jr., in Selma, Alabama). And finally, they generally exhibit a high degree of self-control, accomplish goals with little wasted motion, and are not easily misled.

To resolve a conflict, one needs to know what the other sides really needs. This in turn requires looking at the conflict as part of a longer process, searching for the origins of the conflict. Ideal negotiators are mature and persistent. They try to emphasize the positive and set aside the thorniest issues for later. They know the value of compromise and co-optation.

Language and symbols are important tools in the play of political power. Correctly used, they can legitimize new course of action and motivate others to action.

This chapter has not been about "looking out for number one," "winning through intimidation," or "manipulating other people before they manipulate us." It has tried to show you how, in the world of politics, power is acquired, exercised, and maintained. When people are powerless, when they fail to recognize their options, it is bad for everyone in the political community. Why? Because the powerless do one of two things. They become hostile and try to tear down existing institutions; or they become apathetic and shun all participation in public affairs. Neither seems particularly desirable.

> Our ordinary citizens, though occupied with the pursuits of industry, are still fair judges of public matters; for, unlike any other nation, regarding him who takes no part in these duties not as unambitious but as useless, we Athenians are able to judge at all events if we cannot originate, and, instead of looking on discussion as a stumbling block in the way of action, we think it an indispensable preliminary to any wise action at all.
>
> Pericles (431 B.C.)

PART 2 | Inputs for the Political System

THE KEY TO THIS BOOK

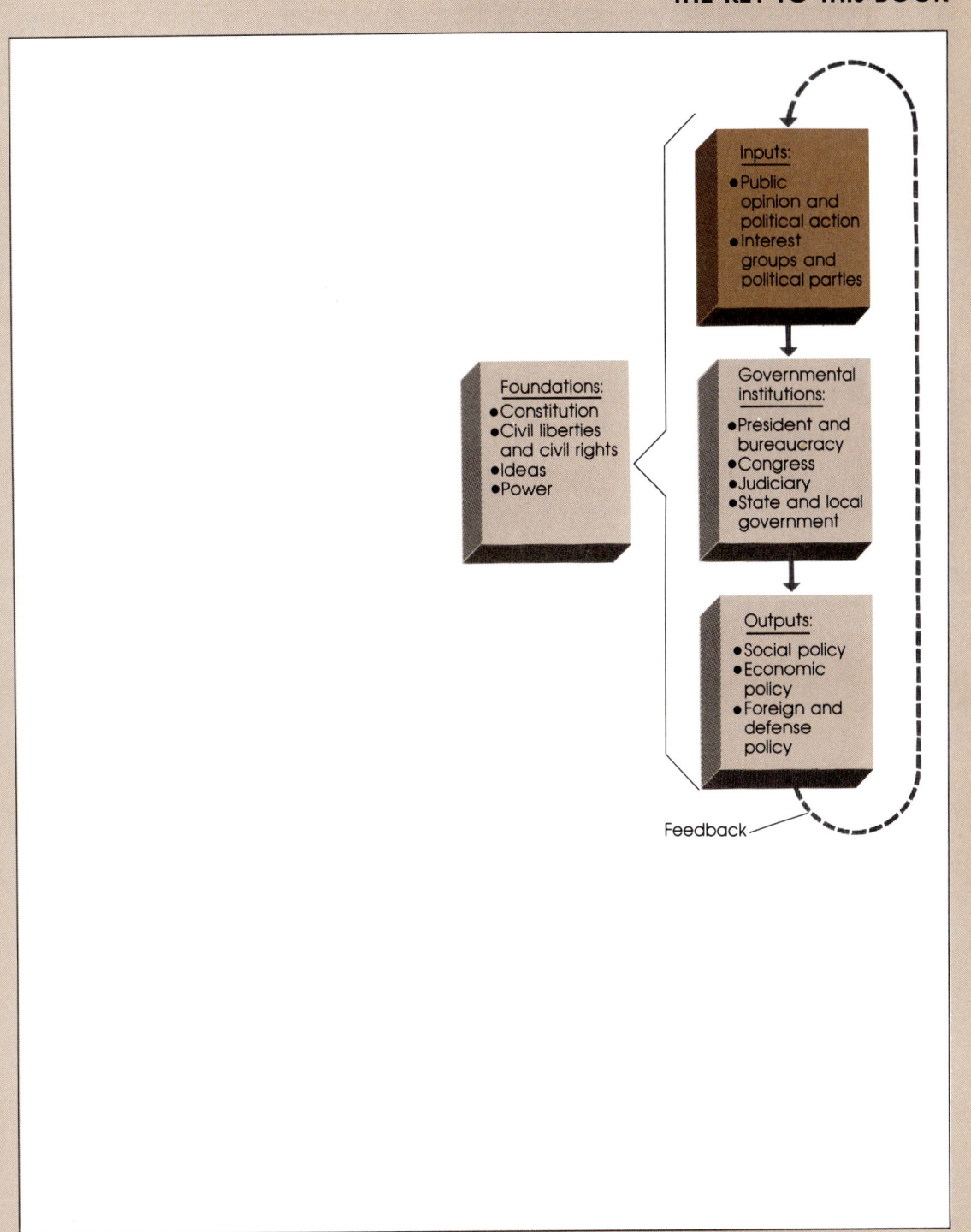

Inputs:
- Public opinion and political action
- Interest groups and political parties

Foundations:
- Constitution
- Civil liberties and civil rights
- Ideas
- Power

Governmental institutions:
- President and bureaucracy
- Congress
- Judiciary
- State and local government

Outputs:
- Social policy
- Economic policy
- Foreign and defense policy

Feedback

© 1981 Gerard Murrell, New York

5 Public Opinion and Political Action in an Electronic Age

After studying this chapter you should be able to answer the following questions:

1. How should we interpret public opinion polls?
2. How do we come to have our political attitudes?
3. What are the major features of American political culture? How might they change in your lifetime?
4. What are the limitations of the electronic media in reporting political events? What can you, as an individual, do about it?
5. What effect do the media have on politics?
6. Who votes and why?
7. What are the various types of political participation?

Terms you should know:

absentee requirements
activists
agenda
Baker v. *Carr*
constituency
gate keeper
initiative
lobbying
managed news
mass media
melting pot
model
opinion leader
partisanship
party identification

patronage
political culture
political socialization
pseudo-event
public opinion
public opinion poll
random sample
recall
referendum
registration
sampling error
volatility
voter turnout
Wesbury v. *Sanders*

Chapter 3, you will recall, was devoted to the intellectual context of American politics. There we surveyed the ideas that shaped the Constitution and that are shaping the political future. Powerful though such ideas are, they do not provide a very good guide to what the average American is thinking about politics. Perhaps a far better guide is the collective television interview, which has become an electronic version of an older social form—conversation. How then can we begin to make sense out of the complex, cacophonous, and contrary opinions held by the 160 million voting-age Americans as well as the more famous citizens who effectively exploit the medium nightly?

For starters, we shall have to shift our focus from relatively abstract concepts, such as checks and balances, federalism, liberty, equality, and power, to the nitty gritty of politics. What people think about politicis is about as fundamental as we can get. You may be aware by now that the American system of government is something less than a pure democracy. You should also be equally aware that no set of political leaders can govern for very long nor govern very effectively without a certain amount of support from the people.

What the people are thinking is a major concern of social scientists. We shall begin, therefore, by taking a look at how social scientists use survey research and public opinion polls to learn what people think and how they perceive the political world. Later we shall see how individual opinions are learned and shaped. In the later parts of this chapter and in the chapter that follows, we shall see how thoughts are transformed into political behavior that attempts to influence government.

TAKING THE PULSE OF THE PEOPLE

When chefs want to know if the chili contains enough green pepper, they do not eat the whole pot—they take a sip. Similarly, when a presidential candidate wants to know if America contains enough support to elect him or her, the candidate does not ask every one of the 160 million potential voters. Rather, candidates take a sample. They ask a small group of people whose views should be representative of those who are not polled.

Today political organizations and business pay firms like Gallup, Harris, Yankelovich, and Roper large fees to find out how people think on a topic. Fortunately, you and I do not have to pay these fees. Still, we need to know a few things about polling.

How Public Opinion Influences Political Leaders

When opinion polls were introduced into politics, Winston Churchill and Harry Truman dismissed them. The late Ernest Bevin, a prominent British Labor politician, spoke for many when he explained many years ago why he could not accept polls: "They take the poetry out of politics." Today, given the emphasis placed on polls by the news media, candidates and government officials find it prudent to watch them.

Research seems to indicate that public opinion *does* influence government's actions. The influence, though, varies with the topic and the time. For example, for 20 years, American opinion opposed the admission of the People's Republic of China into the United Nations, as did government policy. But public opinion has sharply disagreed with government policy regarding school prayer and busing. Opinion on other topics (e.g., capital punishment for murder) varies from year to year. In Vietnam, Lyndon Johnson tried to pay only the "minimum necessary price" of stopping a takeover of South Vietnam by Hanoi. As the price went up, he glumly kept paying it. Finally over 500,000 Americans were in Vietnam, and the American people decided that the minimum was getting too high. Johnson followed public opinion. As it shifted, he shifted.

A few other generalizations about the influence of polls might be made. The safest one is that public opinion does not influence the details of most public policies; it does, though, set limits within which policymakers must operate. That is to say, government officials will usually try to satisfy a widespread demand; they will at least take it into account when shaping their policies.

A second generalization is that polls are less useful as a way of dictating a politician's precise position than as a way of determining which positions—*already taken*—should be emphasized or deemphasized (soft-pedaled). For example, a candidate's pollster looks at the computer sheets and discovers that the candidate's supporters are uncomfortable with his strong military stands. So the pollster recommends airing a series of commercials emphasizing the candidate's role as a supporter of arms control. The pollster can also advise the candidate whether he or she needs to respond to attacks by opponents. Without polling, a lot of money can be wasted responding to charges that will not affect the electorate.

Our third generalization is perhaps the most intriguing: Polling is becoming a part of running the federal government. Experts in survey research, or pollsters, help politicians identify issues, goals, and principles in the polity. By studying polling results, pollsters believe they can tell what public views on what questions are likely to be important at a given time in the future (say, six to nine months ahead). In this way, they help politicians decide how to proceed.

Thus polling can do more than tell politicians who is ahead and who is slipping in a political campaign. It can actually help them govern more effectively by allowing them to see what issues are emerging. This way elected officials can stay on top of the issues and even help set the **agenda** for what will be discussed and how. President Reagan has a particularly sophisticated team of pollsters, along with media experts, to help him appeal directly to the people when Congress is reluctant to follow his pro-

grams or when the mass media reports unfavorably on these programs.* For much the same reason, many members of Congress conduct polls (unscientific, to be sure) by mailing questionnaires to their **constituents,** the voters in their state or district.

A final generalization is that, when leaders rely too much on polls, they cease to be leaders—at least in the full sense of the word. This is not to say political leaders ignore polls. Favorable public opinion is a source of power that effective leaders cultivate. But, and this is crucial, they cultivate popularity only to eventually spend it on some hard decision. John F. Kennedy brilliantly cultivated his popularity. But it seemed to become an end in itself. He seldom made an unpopular decision. Thus civil rights legislation, which would anger the South, was deferred.

Interpreting the Polls

Like any powerful tool, polling should be used carefully. Below we shall discuss five topics that professional politicians as well as ordinary citizens need to keep in mind when interpreting the findings of polling experts.

Sample size. How many people should the pollster ask? Well, the sample size depends on the precision desired. For many purposes, a sample of a few hundred is adequate—if it is chosen randomly. A **random sample** is one in which each person has an equal chance of being selected.

The classic example of what can go wrong when a sample is not random occurred in 1936.

---

* As Sidney Blumenthal has observed, these experts have new language as well as new methods. They speak about *open windows* ("the relative openness of public opinion to presidential initiatives"), *targets of opportunity* ("events or issues that can be quickly taken advantage of"), *sequencing* ("the timing and order of a series of actions"), *resistance ratios* ("the degree to which the public accepts Reagan and what he is doing"), and the need to be *proactive* rather than *reactive.* For more on how Reagan uses his team of pollsters and public-opinion survey analysts, see Blumenthal's "Marketing the President," *New York Times Magazine,* September 31, 1981, p. 42ff.

In that year, a magazine that for many years had accurately predicted the results of presidential elections claimed that Alf Landon would defeat President Franklin D. Roosevelt, a Democrat. Soon after Roosevelt's record-breaking majority, the *Literary Digest* was out of business. The magazine's fatal mistake was to think that the 2.4 million people it asked were representative of the whole electorate. Most of the names were drawn from the magazine's subscription list and from automobile registration records. Because this group was relatively prosperous, the poll exaggerated the Republican vote.

Many people express dismay that most national polls include the opinions of only about 1,500 people. Nevertheless, statisticians have determined that 95 percent of the time a random survey of 1,500 people will produce results that have a margin of error of plus or minus 3 percent. For example, a survey of 1,500 people showing that 49 percent favor a return to the draft means that the "real" support is almost certainly somewhere between 46 and 52 percent. Increasing the size of a sample will not reduce this sampling error of plus or minus 3 percent very much. Therefore, most national surveys use a sample of 1,500 to 2,700 people.

Types of questions. The way the questions are worded may cause great variation in the opinion expressed by the same population about the same issue. For example, whether American opinion supports the Strategic Arms Limitation Talks (SALT) can vary anywhere from 26 to 87 percent. It all depends on how the question is asked. For a high positive response, be general. Ask the public if they support an arms treaty between the United States and Russia. For a lower positive response, be more specific. Ask the public if they support the treaty called SALT. For an even higher positive response define the treaty as limiting *nuclear* weapons rather than *military* weapons. Similarly, suppose you wish to find a lot of people willing to make compromises on the First Amendment. Ask them if they favor *not allowing* speeches against democracy rather than *forbidding* such speeches. A recent *New York Times*/CBS News survey demonstrates the point. It found that only 29 percent of respondents said they favored a constitutional amendment "prohibiting abortion." But fully 50 percent said they favored an amendment "protecting the life of an unborn child"—which amounts to the same thing.

No matter how thoughtfully pollsters phrase a question, they still must face the problem that many words mean different things to different people. Labels like *liberal* and *conservative*, for example, are neither simple nor clearcut. To see a little better why this is so, consider one group of Americans, the leaders of the women's movement. Surveys find them quite "liberal" on most social issues. Yet when it comes to controlling pornography, prosecuting rapists, or respecting individual merit, they tend to be "conservative." (A 1976 *Washington Post* poll found that 64 percent of the leaders of the women's movement "strongly" disagreed with the statement that government should limit the amount of money a person is allowed to earn.)

Volatility. In November 1979, according to the polls, Jimmy Carter seemed to be the worst leader of a Western nation since Ethelred the Unready tried to rule England in the 10th century.* Two months later, according to the polls, Jimmy Carter was a very good president. How can someone's "approval" rating go from 2-to-1 negative to 2-to-1 positive in two months?

Volatility is characteristic of certain kinds of public opinions. Dramatic change often comes about as a result of events. When a foreign country is invaded by the Soviet Union, people rally around the president and his popularity rises sharply. Conversely, when the presi-

---

* I exaggerate, of course. But an earlier ABC News-Harris survey (in June 1979) did find that Americans rated Carter negatively on the overall job he was doing, 73 percent to 25 percent. This was the lowest score ever accorded any president—including Richard Nixon—in modern political history.

Copyright 1980 G. B. Trudeau. Reprinted with permission of Universal Press Syndicate. All rights reserved.

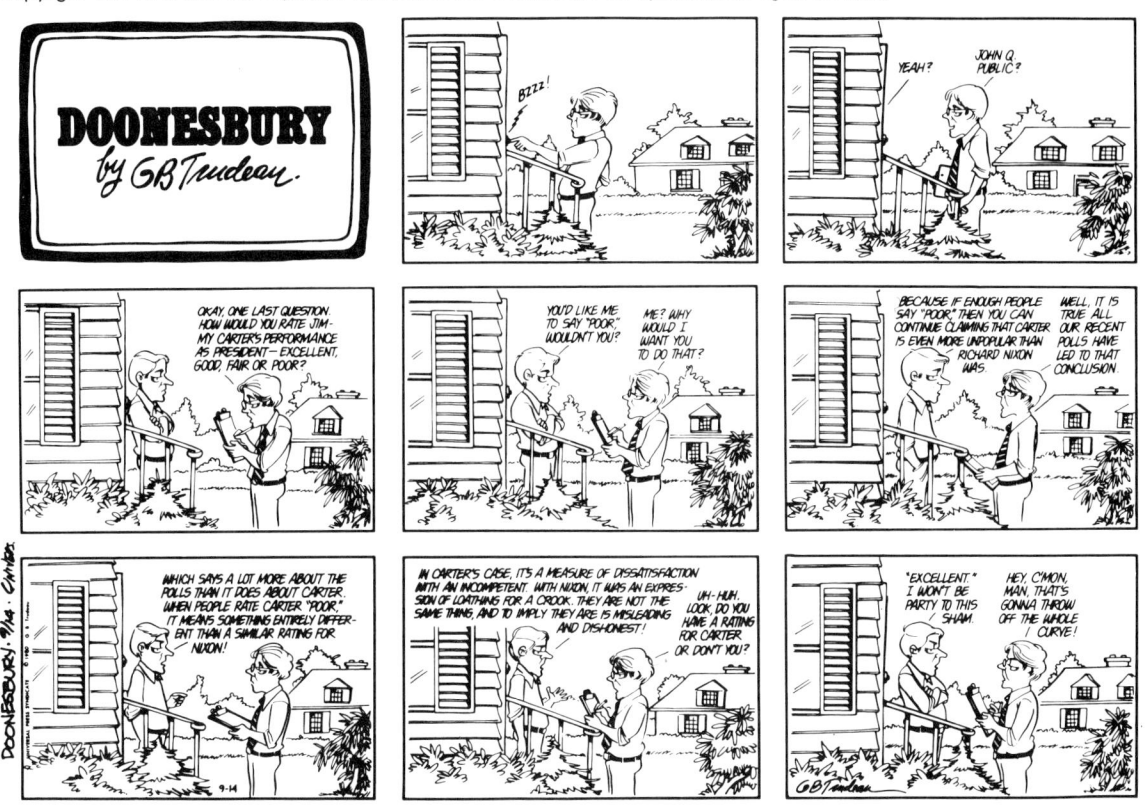

dent appears to be compromising the truth, it plummets (as it did for Nixon in 1974). When gas lines lengthen, the energy issue comes on like War Admiral in the stretch. When the inflation rate hits double digits, the economy surges back into the lead as the most important issue facing the country.

One might argue that the electronic media account for some of this volatility. What does one see on television? News tends to be biased towards the dramatic. An analysis of international trade problems is dull and static; footage of a demonstration is not. Progress in increasing the capability of the armed services is virtually invisible; the shooting of a president is not. Moreover, by its nature, television has no memory. It tends to present a new world every day. Last but not least, the electronic media benefits by rapidly changing polls, which themselves are news.

Not all attitudes are volatile. For instance, the set of opinions concerning the place and right of women in society has changed only slowly. Likewise, party affiliations change only slowly (see Figure 5–4 on page 174).

The closet vote. There is some evidence that a "closet" or hidden vote exists for certain candidates or issues. For example, 14 percent of the black vote actually went to Ronald Reagan; but only 7 percent of black voters leaving the polling booths admitted to having voted for him. Reagan often scored better in telephone polls than in polls taken face to face. Similarly, men tend more often to voice support for the Equal Rights Amendment when polled by women than by men.

Does the poll deal with personal experience? Polls that ask people about, say, economic aid to Katmandu (the capital of Nepal, in case you forgot), or how many intercontinental missiles the United States needs, should be given little credence. The reason is they do not deal with the *personal experience* of most of those being asked the question. Conversely, when questions in a poll focus on topics close to the lives of individuals, their expressed opinions tend to be well considered.

To see how this works, let us go back to the very start of the book. There I cited a poll showing a great drop in the confidence people had in politicians. I could have shown you other polls showing a similar drop in confidence regarding institutions generally—business, labor, government, and so forth. Reading these polls together, you would likely think that the United States is ripe for revolution.

But ask people about their personal lives—their job opportunities, their children, etc.—and they tend to be quite positive. Similarly, if you ask them about Congress in general, the response is negative. But if you ask them about their own congressional representative, you get overwhelmingly positive responses.

A SIMPLE MODEL FOR ANALYSIS OF INDIVIDUAL POLITICAL BEHAVIOR

So far, we have been discussing how social scientists classify and describe the diversity of individual opinions and how they try to make them comprehensible to political leaders. Now we need to think about the constituents of public opinion. More specifically, we want to understand why individual citizens hold the beliefs, attitudes, and perceptions they do. Such an understanding can be doubly beneficial. Not only will it give us a look at the roots of public opinion. It will also help us explain why people perform some political acts and not others.

Figure 5–1 shows a conceptual diagram that is useful for thinking about the causes of political behavior. Before going any further, however, it should be emphasized that the model shown in Figure 5–1 is not a scientific theory. Rather, it is merely a way of explaining how individual and group political activity influence the government institutions that produce public policy. The test is not whether the **model** can be verified in a laboratory. It is whether it can clarify in a commonsense way important political relationships.

Political behavior can take many forms, as we shall see later in the chapter. The most common is voting. But there are others: communicating with public officials, working with an interest group or political party, giving money to a candidate during a campaign, joining a protest or demonstration, and so on.

Political behavior, unlike sneezing, is a conscious, voluntary act. That means such behavior originates with the thoughts or opinions in our heads. A central concern of this chapter will be to discover how these are formed. Figure 5–1 suggests four factors.

First is the direct perception of events. We find that the price of peanut butter is higher than it was last week, and conclude that the cost of living is getting higher. We find that our house has been robbed, and conclude that the crime rate is up. In either case, the thoughts in our heads are rearranging themselves.

Of course a great deal of what we know about the world comes not through direct observation but through the **mass media**. This term refers to any means of communication that has a large audience, such as newspapers and television. The importance of the mass media cannot be overemphasized. In the past, it was commonplace for political scientists to view the American political community in terms of three basic elements: the politician; the voter; and, in between, a cluster of intermediate agencies. The function of these intermediate agencies—which include most significantly the party organization but also the trade association, the labor union, the farm organization, and the ethnic brotherhood—was to negotiate between the politician and the voter. These agencies inter-

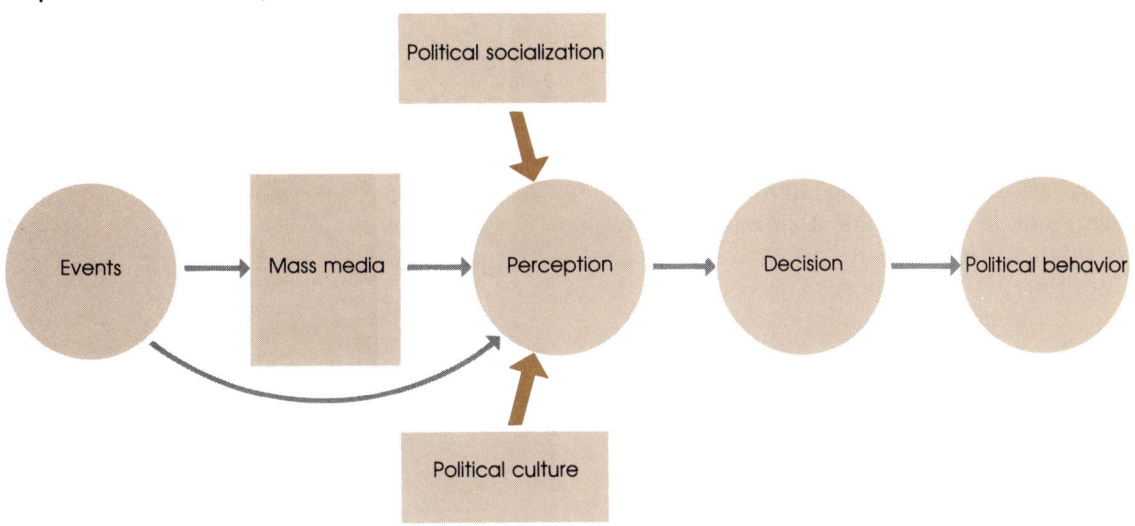

FIGURE 5-1
Simplified Model for Analysis of Factors Affecting Individual Political Behavior

Events → Mass media → Perception → Decision → Political behavior

Political socialization → Perception
Political culture → Perception
Events → Perception (curved arrow)

ceded for politician and voter. Thereby they provided the links that held the system together.

The electronic revolution has weakened this mediating function. Television presents the politician directly to the voters. The voters make their judgments more on what the screen shows and tells than on what the party leaders say. Some research says that television has become the main source not just of information but of reality for the voter.

The electronic revolution has, however, wrought more than John Chancellor and David Brinkley. It also makes possible computerized opinion polling that presents the voter directly to the politician. Today's politicians judge opinion more by what the polls show them than by what party leaders tell them. Similarly, computerized mailing provides a way of raising funds outside the party organization. Clearly, the electronic revolution has transformed American politics. The only questions are, How much? and How permanently?

But our minds are not blank slates upon which external events write themselves out. Rather, our past experiences and heredity (remember the sociobiologists in Chapter 1) influence how we interpret and arrange those events. Some events, in fact, we even ignore. The point, then, is this: We are each *predisposed* to select and structure environmental events in a certain way.

To understand this predisposition, we need to consider a couple of other closely related concepts: **political socialization** and **political culture.** The former refers to the process by which young people learn basic political beliefs in the family, school, church, and the like. Political culture refers to the basic values, attitudes, myths, and traditions of a nation and its government. They make up the political atmosphere breathed by all citizens and linger generation after generation.

The remainder of this chapter will elaborate on the model in Figure 5–1.

POLITICAL SOCIALIZATION

This section considers one of the four major influences found in Figure 5–1 that shape public opinion. Political socialization, as we defined earlier, is the process by which we learn basic political beliefs while growing up. This section will expand that definition considerably.

How the Family Socializes

How do we learn English? Not by learning the alphabet, studying grammar textbooks, or memorizing words lists. Learning our native language begins not in school but at home, when we are infants. The same is true of our political education. It begins as soon as we begin to observe and imitate the behavior of our parents. Long before children know the difference between Republicans and Democrats, they have an inclination to idealize important national figures and the country as a whole, its history and institutions. Without that home-grown knowledge, it would be hard to ever make sense of political parties or a book like the one you are now reading.

The greater part—and perhaps the most important part—of our political socialization we acquire at home. A few concrete examples may give you a better idea of how this haphazard, almost invisible process takes place. Look at the photograph that shows two Iranians using an American flag to haul a load of trash away from the occupied U.S. embassy compound in Teheran. If that photograph causes a reaction in you, it is not because of any book you have read. It results from countless incidents—now mostly forgotten but nonetheless significant—that you experienced as a child: flags out on July Fourth; pictures of your father in uniform during one or another war; climbs up the steps of a historic shrine; prayers for America heard in church; and perhaps most of all, comments by parents while watching television ("Thank God we're Americans," "It's lucky we live where we do," etc.).

If the photograph elicits no negative reaction in you, it should not be inferred that you have escaped political socialization. It has just taken other forms. According to Kenneth Keniston, the eminent MIT psychologist, many middle-class college students *like* to protest.[1] This type

Wide World Photos

United Press International Photo

comes from a family in which the dominant ethos is egalitarian, permissive, and "democratic"—a family in which the kids are encouraged to express themselves. They do a lot of talking back to their parents at the dinner table.

The experiences of poor, black children are likely to be different. Yet there are many unforgettable events in their lives that definitely help to shape their attitudes toward their nation and its political authority. Look now at the picture of Governor George Wallace blocking the doorway of the University of Alabama in opposition to federally supported integration of the school in 1963. How would a black child of 10, whose father is a tenant farmer in the Mississippi Delta, react to that? Here is an actual remark from just such a child: "I don't like the teachers; they say bad things to us. They're always calling us names; they make you feel no good. We saw the man on the television, the governor, and he wasn't good either."[2] As psychologist Robert Coles observes,

> When a child of 10 links the governor of his state with the schoolteachers who look down upon him in a rural, still all-black elementary school, he is making a significant judgment—one which ought to be explored if we are to understand how and when various political viewpoints begin to take shape.[3]

Although the influence is not as great as researchers once believed, the family influences political party identification. When asked, grade-school children refer to party affiliation as almost a family characteristic. As one 10-year-old girl remarked: "All I know is *we're not Republican*." One study found that over one half of fifth graders in the Chicago area claimed a party preference.

How the School Socializes

Schools further the process in a variety of ways: civics and history courses; the pledge of allegiance to the flag; elections for class offices;

Bradford Bachrach

Perhaps the most important political influence of parents on their children does not involve political beliefs or party identification but the basic personality. Here, in 1934, Joseph P. Kennedy, Sr., is shown with his sons (left to right) Edward, John, Joseph, Jr., and Robert. No doubt Joseph, Sr., created psychic conditions—a need to achieve and to serve—that influenced his sons' remarkable political careers. (Joseph, Jr., supposedly the most promising politician in the family, was killed in World War II.)

celebrating holidays such as Thanksgiving; pictures of Washington, Lincoln, King, and other national figures hanging in the classroom; and so forth. The role of the school in political socialization was particularly important when the United States was trying to assimilate millions of immigrants in the years 1880 through 1920.

Political socialization does not necessarily end when a young person leaves school and family. Some research seems to indicate that, in recent years, college has had a liberalizing influence. Polls shows that the percent of self-designated liberals in a freshman class (28 percent) is roughly the same as in the general population; but it becomes higher in later years—40 percent for seniors and 63 percent for graduated students.

There are two basic explanations of how colleges socialize. The first traces the students' liberalism to what they studied. Since professors tend to be considerably more liberal than the general population, their lectures and assigned readings reflect this bias. As one San Francisco lawyer put it, "It's the academic world's revenge for how it feels it has been treated by the business community. For the businessman who invests $20,000 a year in his child's education, what's his return? An architect who votes Democratic."[4]

The other explanation is that political opinion does not come from the effect of particular courses. It comes from the general, open atmosphere of college (more peers, free inquiry, few restriction, etc.).

The problem with both explanations is the same. How do you untangle the multitude of experiences associated with four years in college and say *this* is what is causing the leftward shift? Perhaps the safest conclusion is to say that college has a liberalizing influence. Period.

Political Socialization as Never-Ending Process

In the broadest sense, political socialization is a lifetime process. Perhaps some of us escape the indoctrinating influences of parents, teachers, and professors. But we never escape the potential effects of what I shall term "significant events." It is hard to conceive, for example, how a 35-year-old woman living in America in 1930 could not have had her political views reshaped, at least a little, by the Great Depression; or how a 19-year-old serving in the Marines in the late 1950s could have escaped socialization.

Think of the millions of Americans who became politically aware during the period from 1965 to 1975. Riots, a disastrous foreign war, and a presidential resignation were just some of the ingredients for a terrible recipe for citizenship. Like all political socialization, significant events leave their mark. Why was President Carter booed before the 1980 Democratic convention for just a passing reference to draft registration? Many of the delegates seated before him had become politically conscious when hating one's country was highly fashionable. (Compare that group to the 1935–45 group!)

If this line of analysis is correct, then the profile of the citizenry is like a rock formation with geological stratifications every three to five years. Table 5–1 might serve as a guide to political rock hounds.

Ideally, representative government requires two things of public opinion. First is the ability of the people to transcend their casual experi-

TABLE 5–1
Significant Events That Have Influenced National Thinking

Assuming that 10 is the age at which an event makes a lasting impression on a person's memory, then in 1980 . . .

96 percent of Americans do not remember the start of the federal income tax (1913).

94 percent have no recollection of World War I (1914–18).

92 percent are too young to remember when women couldn't vote.

86 percent cannot recall Charles Lindbergh's solo flight to Paris.

85 percent do not remember the stock-market crash.

74 percent are unable to remember the Great Depression.

68 percent cannot recollect World War II.

65 percent cannot remember life before the start of the TV era.

59 percent do not remember the Korean War.

53 percent are not old enough to remember Russia's launching of its first Sputnik.

44 percent do not remember the assassination of President Kennedy.

32 percent are too young to remember when man first landed on the moon.

Source: Based on *U.S. News & World Report*, January 14, 1980, pp. 56–57.

ence and prejudice. Second is the ability to hold a reliable picture of the world.

If a self-governing people lack the first, the trouble can be traced back to the failure of families, schools, and churches to develop in them the machinery to organize and creatively think about what they learn. If a self-governing people lack the second, the trouble can be traced to the mass media. As we shall see in a later section, the mass media at times show a preference for the curious and trivial against the dull but important.

Here we are touching the raw nerves of popular government. What, if anything, can be done about this defect? If one cares to make the effort, here is a prescription, simple and direct. *Go beyond the mass media and explore the publications opinion leaders read* (see box).

POLITICAL CULTURE

In addition to the socializing influences of family, school, college, and significant events, public opinion is also influenced by the political culture in which people grow up. Contrary to what you might think, you do not view the world just as it is but rather in terms defined largely by your culture. To recognize this is almost as difficult as it is for fish to recognize that their environment is water. But if a fish is tossed ashore it will get the idea very quickly. Similarly, if we visit another culture, we will come to understand that there are quite different ways of viewing reality. What seems natural and inevitable to a Arab may seem bizarre to an American—and vice versa.

As might be expected, foreigners have had an advantage in describing the American political culture. Alexis de Tocqueville, the early 19th-century French visitor cited in the previous chapter, was one of the earliest and most perceptive observers. In 1944, the Swedish economist Gunnar Myrdal continued the Tocqueville tradition by trying to describe "the American creed."

Earlier, the assertion was made that public opinion in America varies greatly, that it is complex, cacophonous, and often contradictory. Despite this, it does not follow that American citizens have no basic attitudes in common. There are a few general beliefs that most Americans share. We refer to this set of beliefs about the political system and the individual's role in it as the American political culture.

Political culture and public opinion are related. In particular, political culture helps the citizen determine what issues are important and what demands upon government are legitimate. In short, political culture determines the context of public opinion.

Since the beginning of public opinion polls, one of the most frequently heard questions has been whether Americans are basically liberal or conservative. If the question is posed in terms of how people perceive themselves, a majority would classify themselves as either middle-of-the-road or conservative (see Figure 5–2). But for most citizens the terms have no concrete meaning. A more useful approach is to pose the question as a series of issues to be answered. Such an approach will reveal just how inconsistent Americans are in their political thinking.

What beliefs do Americans share? Civil libertarians would no doubt like to be able to list the Bill of Rights, but alas, support for that particular set of values is soft. Witness a 1972 survey by CBS. It found that 5 of the 10 rights guaranteed by the Bill of Rights are not supported by a majority of Americans. (The five failing to generate a majority were peaceful assembly, free press, free speech; trial by jury; protection against unreasonable and unwarranted search and seizure; public trial; and confronting witnesses.)

Yet surveying the last two decades, civil libertarians can find plenty to cheer about. Public opinion polls have registered a steady increase in the number who believe that blacks should not be discriminated against, that women deserve equal educational and job opportunities outside the home, and that more liberal life-

How to Know *Almost* as Much as Opinion Leaders

Opinion leaders are individuals who are able to influence other individuals' attitudes or behavior in a desired way with relative frequency. Where do they get *their* opinions? Or, more accurately, where do they get the basic facts and ideas out of which they form their opinions?

Some of this input comes from the intellectual grapevine. That is, it comes through personal communication at conferences, cocktail parties, on panels and task forces, by telephone and mail, and on the job. Fortunately, a great deal of their input is more accessible. It consists solely of printed material available at most newstands or through subscription.

The following is a quick peek over the shoulders of individuals who must certainly be considered opinion leaders. You note no mention of the *New York Times* or *Time*. That is because we can assume that most of them read both. (Few, though, admit to the latter publication.)

Courtesy of The Leadership Network

Some publications were mentioned by several opinion leaders. But to keep the list short, I have eliminated these repeaters.

Theodore H. White, historian and journalist: *Washington Monthly* ("It's the only thing that reports on the doing of the bureaucracy"), *U.S. News & World Report* ("It's got more facts than any other magazine"), *Foreign Affairs*, *Public Interest* ("cutting edge of new ideas"), *National Review*, *Reader's Digest* ("You gotta know what the people of the country are thinking, too"), *Daedalus* ("because whatever *Daedalus* is saying now, the editors of the country will be saying three years from now"), *New Republic*, and *Village Voice*.

David Garth, political media consultant who headed John Anderson's 1980 run for the presidency: *Congressional Quarterly*, to keep up on legislation; the *Barron's* letter, for "political gossip on what's happening in different states around the country"; and *E.P.O.: The Magazine for Elected Public Officials*, for "information on the problems officeholders face staying or getting in office—which is very specific to our business."

John Kenneth Galbraith
THE NEW YORK REVIEW OF BOOKS

Theodore H. White
COLUMBIA JOURNALISM REVIEW

I.M. Pei
TECHNOLOGY REVIEWS

Anthony Lewis, political columnist for the *New York Times* and author of *Gideon's Trumpet:* the British publication *Economist* ("because it has very good coverage of obscure parts of the world and very up-to-date material") and *New Society* ("a sociological magazine with a lot of statistics and comments . . . on race relations, health care, etc.")

Stewart Brand, creator of the *Whole Earth Catalog: Science* (published weekly by the American Association for the Advancement of Science), the British magazine *New Scientist,* and *Science News.*

Charlotte Curtis, an editor for the *New York Times: Public Policy, The Nation, Texas Monthly,* and *The Wilson Quarterly.*

Ralph Nader, consumer activist: *Consumer Reports,* the *Bulletin of the Atomic Scientists,* and scores of government reports published by various agencies and congressional committees.

Warren Bennis, management expert and former president of the University of Cincinnati: *The Wall Street Journal, Newsweek, Business Week, Scientific American, Manas* ("an idiosyncratic charmer tending toward philosophy and history of ideas"), *Brain/Mind* ("a model of less-is-more with a neat four-page format containing almost as much information as one issue of *Psychology Today*"), a monthly report on U.S. economy officed by the Morgan Guaranty Trust Co. in New York, and a monthly *Statistical Bulletin* published by Metropolitan Life Insurance Company ("tracing important demographic trends and their consequences").

SOURCE: Lists based on interview by Sue Mittenthol, *Esquire* (June 5, 1979).

FIGURE 5-2
Where Americans Place Themselves Ideologically

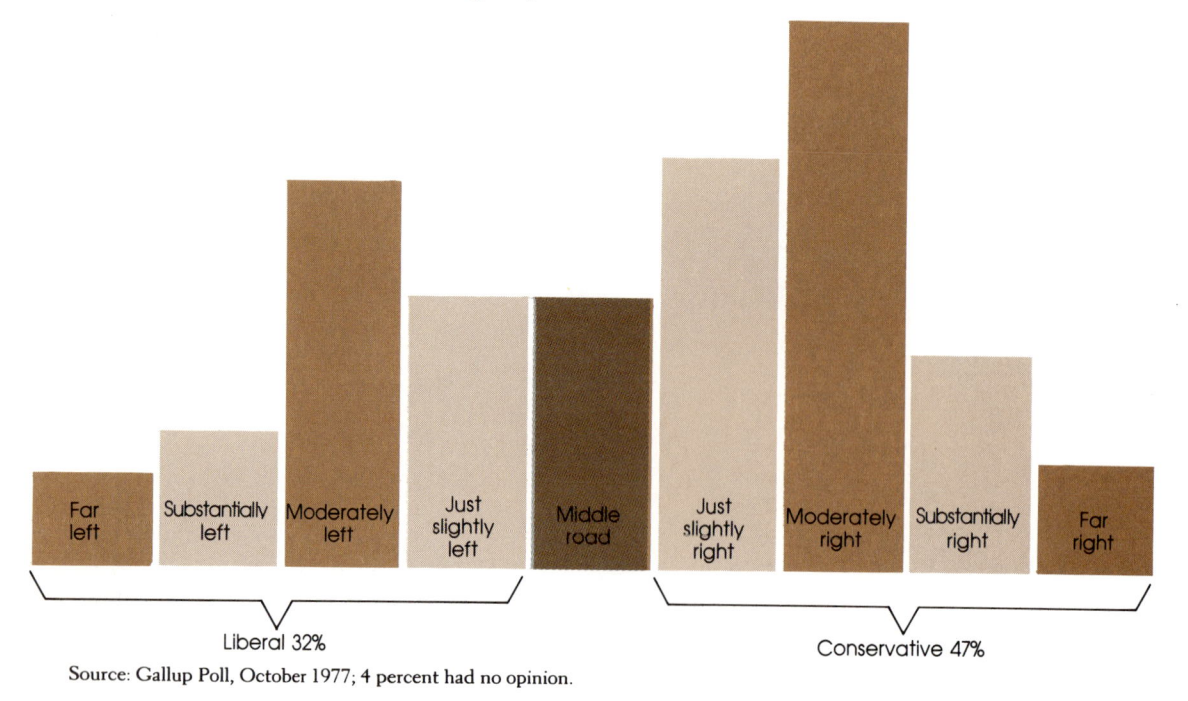

| Far left | Substantially left | Moderately left | Just slightly left | Middle road | Just slightly right | Moderately right | Substantially right | Far right |

Liberal 32% — Conservative 47%

Source: Gallup Poll, October 1977; 4 percent had no opinion.

styles are permissible—so long as they are not flaunted. In 1968, for example, 32 percent of whites in a national survey said that whites have a right to keep blacks from living in their neighborhoods. By 1978, support for the proposition had dwindled to 5 percent of the white population. Conversely, the number of whites saying that blacks have a right to live anywhere they can afford jumped from 63 to 93 percent. Between 1958 and 1978, Gallup found a similar rise from 42 percent to 81 percent in the number who say they would be willing to vote for a black as president.

Surveys about civil liberties have found liberalizing changes of much the same nature. In 1954, for example, only 28 percent said that an admitted communist should be allowed to speak in their communities; 38 percent would permit an antireligious speech. By 1977, tolerance of such oratory had grown to over half of those surveyed—57 percent in the case of the communist, 63 percent in the case of the atheist. Journalists Ben J. Wattenberg and David Gergen write:

> One can counter that changes in reality have not kept pace with these changes in attitude (the Klan is still with us, as are black slums and riots), but the significant point is that among the public at large, there is a much greater climate of acceptance and even an eagerness for social diversity than existed two decades ago.[5]

On the other hand, the public has been very firm over these same years in rejecting other social changes that directly challenge traditional American values. (Drugs, violence, obscenity, and promiscuity are examples of such changes.)

Public attitudes have also changed towards government and the economy. By the late 1970s, the public was telling the pollsters that they wanted to halt the growth of government: Stopping inflation was more important than starting a new spending program. Government had suddenly become the villain. Between 1959 and 1978 those who thought that "big government" was the prime cause of inflation leapt upwards from 14 to 51 percent. Between 1964 to 1976, those who said that the people running the government "don't seem to know what they are doing" rose from 28 to 53 percent. By 1978, 76 percent said that Washington had become too powerful; 84 percent said that it was spending too much.

Rather than try to summarize any further the characteristics of contemporary American political culture, I would like to consider how it might change in the decades ahead. For this excursion into the future, we shall be looking at another of the Future Files that appear throughout this book.

FUTURE FILE

American Political Culture in Transition

Commitments to Tradition and Values
Everett C. Ladd, Jr., of the University of Connecticut, has examined recent opinion poll data to see whether there is continuity in values held in common by most Americans. Ladd's four key values in American political culture are individualism, equality of opportunity, property rights, and progress ("Traditional Values Regnant," Public Opinion, March/April 1978).

Let us be clear about what these terms mean. According to Alexis de Tocqueville, the United States actually invented the concept of *individualism*. While other cultures had known such concepts at self-centeredness or selfishness, the United States was the first to assert that the task of society was to allow the individual a chance to pursue happiness or, more accurately, the good life. The thrust of the Constitution was more towards protecting individual wants than towards providing collective needs.

In Chapter 3, we saw how fundamental the commitment to *equality of opportunity* has been to American politics. The idea that people should be judged or rewarded on the basis of performance—not social class or ethnic background—is rooted, along with the individualism, in the political culture.

Ladd distinguished two more values there: *private property* and *progress*. In American political culture, the right to hold property and do with it as one wishes is seen as making individualism possible. The modern concept of progress, which began with the Enlightenment (Chapter 3), meant that more goods and services along with more opportunities for individuals were obtainable through the use of reason. Moreover, because they were desirable ends, progress was a value to be sought.

Drawing on survey research, Ladd argues that these four values, central to any description of contemporary American political culture, are still alive and well. For example, a great deal has been said in the last few years about how Americans have stressed self-fulfillment as more important than obligations to others (including their children and parents). Writer Tom Wolfe called the 1970s the "Me-decade." But Ladd maintains that this attitude is really just a newer version of individualism. In any event, it is the antithesis of collectivism.

Despite the intellectual ferment over equality of results (examined in Chapter 3), American political culture appears remarkably untouched by it. In the spring of 1977, Seymour Martin Lipset and Ladd presented this choice to the group one would expect to have changed the most—college professors: "Here are two ways to deal with inequality. Which do you prefer?"

> Equality of opportunity: giving each person an equal chance for a good education and to develop his or her ability.

> Equality of results: giving each person a relatively equal share of income and status regardless of education and ability.

Eighty-five percent of the professors opted for the "opportunity" standard; just 7 percent chose "results"; 8 percent were in the middle. Research among working-class Americans also reveals a tolerance of economic inequality, provided it is based on merit.

Nevertheless, the public does draw a distinction between "compensatory action" and "preferential treatment" (or equality of results). The former includes programs designed to compensate for past discrimination through special training programs. Because such programs are seen as being consistent with equality of opportunity, they are accepted. But preferential treatment is not. In fact, the entire spectrum of leadership groups in the United States rejects equality of results (Table 5–2).

Similarly, Ladd reports a solid commitment to the concept of private property—despite all the criticism of large corporations. About 95 percent of Americans maintain that "We must be ready to make sacrifices if necessary to preserve the free enterprise system" (Yankelovich, Skelly and White, survey in January 1976).

Ladd argues that Americans continue to value progress. To support this, he cites research

TABLE 5–2
Responses of Leaders to Questions of Equality

Here are two ways to deal with inequality; which do you prefer:

	Equality of Opportunity?	Equality of Results?
Businessman	85%	2%
Feminists	82	7
Students at prestige colleges	84	6
Blacks	81	7
Party leaders	90	4
Intellectuals	88	3
Media	94	1

Note: The data are from the Leadership Survey, a joint project of the *Washington Post* and the Harvard University Center for International Affairs, conducted in the spring of 1976. Percentages do not add up to 100 because some respondents chose an "in-between" position.

showing that Americans almost invariably see themselves moving upward in the future. Without disputing the data, I think it only fair to note that the idea of progress is today challenged as never before. Robert Nisbet recently (in *History of the Idea of Progress*) put forward this premise:

> Disbelief, doubt, disillusionment and despair have taken over—or so it would seem from our literature, art, philosophy, theology, even our scholarship and science. What is in all ways most devastating, however, is the . . . decline in America and Europe . . . of faith in the value and promise of Western civilization. What has succeeded faith is, on the vivid and continually enlarging record, guilt, alienation and indifference.

According to Nisbet, many factors have contributed to this decline in faith in progress. One is the waning respect for knowledge and the fast-spreading preoccupation with the bizarre, exotic, and occult. Another is "a disenchantment with or more ominously an outright hostility toward economic growth . . . rising fear that we and our planet are doomed unless we bring this growth to a halt." Many new projects are viewed as too big or too dangerous.

New Values and Attitudes

There is scattered evidence that, in the last couple of decades, new attitudes have emerged. Whether these attitudes are to be considered a part of the American political culture, I am not prepared to say. But the evidence is worth noting, beginning with the strongest.

The documentation for the rise in distrust of political and public administration institutions is thorough. But such popular attitudes are accompanied by a somewhat contradictory impulse—*a rise in the belief that government must be more active* rather than less in the solution of societal "problems." In 1974, a National Opinion Research Center Survey found that 85.9 percent of the population believed the "government in Washington ought to see to it that everybody who wants to work can find a job." Yet, in January 1977, 39 percent of the population labeled "big government" the *greatest* threat to the nation.

From approximately the middle of the 1930s, when data was first available, another important trend has been continued *decline in expressed prejudice against minority groups*. Even the outburst of racial violence between 1964 and 1969 did not interrupt this trend.

But these trend data describe only verbal attitudes expressed in a semipublic interview. Since respondents may have simply learned to conceal their prejudices, research that probes more deeply is still needed. Furthermore, this decline in intergroup prejudice has been accompanied by growth of distrust in government (cited in Chapter 1) and a weakening of the electoral process (cited in this chapter). Therefore, it cannot be viewed as effectively strengthening the values of mutual respect required for a democratic society. In other words, if indifference causes this decline in prejudice, one can hardly say that political process are strengthened.

A related long-term trend that cannot be ignored is *the role of women* in American society. In 1947, only one fifth of married women were in the labor force; by 1977, nearly half were. In 1950, less than 10 percent of the married women in the labor force were in professional or technical jobs; by 1977, over 17 percent were. In 1937, only 31 percent of Americans said they would vote for a woman for president; by 1967, the percentage had risen to 57; and by 1978, it had reached 76 percent.

Besides the decline in prejudice towards minorities and women, a second trend worth noting concerns changing symbols of success. Stanford Research Institute has identified past and emerging symbols of success. It has found them evolving from the group toward the individual, from abundance toward sufficiency, and from quantity toward quality. Past symbols included fame, five-figure salary, college degree, executive position, live-in servants, new car every year, and club membership. Future symbols include free time any time, recognition as a creative person, oneness of work and play, rewarded less by money than by honor and affection, philosophical independence, easy laughter, and unembarrassed tears.

Trends in Population and Social Structures

Exactly how values change or continue over time is a problem that has long puzzled sociologists. We can hardly solve that puzzle here. But it does seem fairly obvious that changes in the population (age, ethnic mix, region) and social structures (family and church) of a society can lead to changes in shared values.

Age structure. Richard Easterlin is a demographer at the University of Pennsylvania. His specialty is "cohort analysis"—that is, studying the number of people born (the cohort) in a given year. (Discussion based on Easterlin's presidential address before the Population Association of America, "What Will 1984 Be Like?" April 1978.) Particularly important is the ratio of elderly (over 65) to younger (18 to 64) people. As Figure 5-3 shows, the size of the elderly population in relation to the working age population has risen steadily over the decades and is projected to climb from 17 per hundred in 1970 to 31 per hundred by 2025.

What do those numbers mean? To Easterlin, they mean the greater the number of young people entering the work force, the less opportunity there will be for each of them to succeed. And when there is less opportunity, there will be greater malaise and alienation—measured by increased crime, suicide, and divorce rates, and reduced birth rates, voting participation, and college entrance examination scores. In other words, because of the baby boom of the late 1940s and early 1950s, a frustrated generation inevitably came of age in the late 60s and 70s. But precisely because of the frustration and pessimism of those cohorts, people born between, say, 1946 and 1956 are having very few children themselves.

But the cohorts about to come of age—the next generation of teenagers and young adults—are quite small in number. They will have many more work opportunities and be more optimistic. Thus the indicators of malaise will decrease. Easterlin thinks, therefore, times will simply be better.

Hispanics. Another demographic trend that could possibly affect the American political culture in the decades ahead is the tide of immigration (unequaled since the turn of the century) and high birth rate among residents

FIGURE 5-3
The Changing Age Structure in the United States

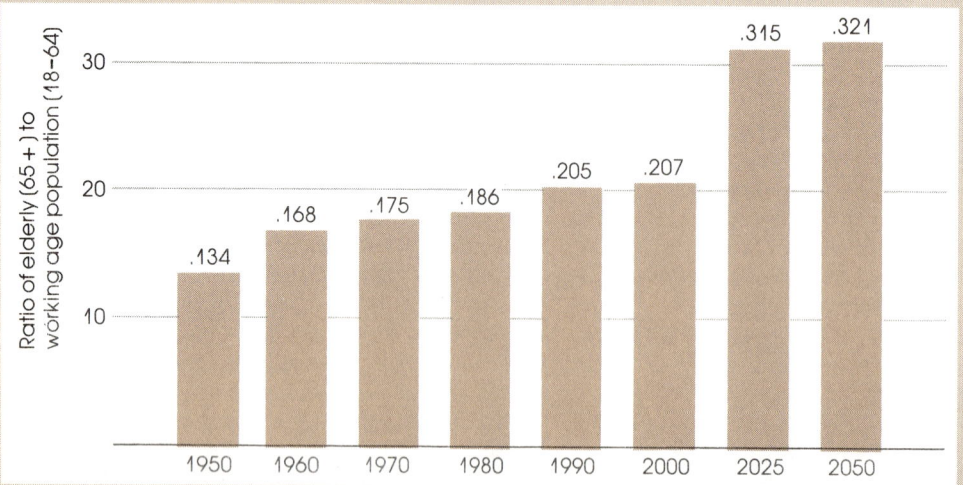

Year	Ratio of elderly (65+) to working age population (18-64)
1950	.134
1960	.168
1970	.175
1980	.186
1990	.205
2000	.207
2025	.315
2050	.321

Source: Calculated from U.S. Bureau of the Census, *Current Population Reports*, series P-25. Projected data assumes "replacement level" fertility (i.e., the level of fertility at which the population would exactly replace itself in the absence of net migration).

of Hispanic origin. During the 1970s, while the proportion of blacks in the U.S. population rose from 11.1 to 11.7 percent, Hispanic population jumped from 4.5 to 6.4 percent of the total. These trends are making Hispanic people the fastest-growing minority. Some demographers expect them to overtake blacks as the nation's predominant minority during the 1980s.

It is too early to appraise precisely the long-term implications of that rapid increase in Hispanic population. But their growing presence is already beginning to have a broad impact on the economic, social and cultural life of mainstream America. (According to a food industry study, Mexican restaurants have supplanted Chinese restaurants as America's second most popular ethnic restaurant—after Italian.) All this change has occurred despite a tendency to remain behind a formidable barrier to assimilation—the Spanish language. Indeed, a few analysts have suggested that the most devisive issue to face the American politics in the late 1980s will be the clash over bilingual rights.

Above all, political analysts will have to avoid thinking in terms of a "Hispanic bloc," for political attitudes vary. Fiercely anti-Castro Cubans in Miami gave Ronald Reagan more than 80 percent of their vote in 1980; staunchly Democratic Mexican-Americans in Texas gave Jimmy Carter 70 percent of theirs.

Sun Belt newcomers. What happens when a young man or woman moves from a state in the Northeast to one in the South or West? It is unclear with which party the migrants will affiliate. Since Democrats overwhelmingly outnumber Republicans nationally, it is reasonable to assume this is true of the migrants. But the GOP hold on Sun Belt voters has grown in recent years. No matter which party profits, the trend toward conservative views on such things as curbing big government and reducing spending is likely to accelerate.

A variety of polls indicate that these newcomers increase the political traditions of the nation's fastest-growing region.

What are those traditions? The label conservative is probably less accurate than traditionalism. In other words, the political culture of the Sun Belt is better described in terms of traditional values such as family and patriotism than that constellation of beliefs described in Chapter 3 as conservative.

Of course, in terms of practical politics the results are pretty much the same. That is to say, traditionalism has more in common with conservatism than liberalism. Therefore, the growth population in the Sun Belt helps conservative politicians more than liberal ones.

For the first time in American history, according to the Census Bureau, more than half of the nation's voters now live in the South and West. The 1980 presidential election was the first with both candidates from those regions.

NYT Pictures

Demographics are people. This young man is a living lesson in Sun Belt demographics. Despite the 10-gallon hat and python-skin boots, he is a native of Indiana who moved to Waco, Texas, in 1970. Adopting a new way of life, he abandoned his home state's devotion to Democratic politicians and decided to vote for Republican Reagan in 1980.

MASS MEDIA

One day at the White House, President Franklin Roosevelt noticed a radio reporter holding a microphone that bore unfamiliar initials. Roosevelt stopped and asked: "CBS? What's that?" Some 40 years later, President Richard Nixon believed that CBS and other news organizations were doing what no other single institution, group, or combination of institutions and groups had done before in American history: forcing out of office a president who had been elected by an overwhelming popular majority. Clearly, something had happened in between. What precisely that was forms the subject of this section.

Our discussion is to two parts. We begin by noting the three functions that the mass media serves in the American political systems. Then we shall evaluate how well the media performs those functions.

The Unwritten Electronic Amendment

The Constitution says nothing about radio, television, cinema, and the popular press. Yet the electronic age is reshaping American politics. Today, as never before, the instant dissemination of word or image to millions of people is possible. By 1976, a survey conducted by the Roper organization found television was by far the American public's main source of news. Sixty-four percent of those polled said they obtained most of their news from TV; in 1959, the figure was 51 percent.

During political campaigns, citizens are electronically bombarded by commercials. These come perilously close to sounding like soft drink jingles. In the comfort of their livingrooms, citizens watch the attempted assassinations of presidents on instant replay. They see police dogs attack civil rights demonstrators. They see urban rioters burn and loot American cities, a bloody war far away, and flickering images of mobs in Teheran mugging for camera crews.

Regulator of information flow about politics. The mass media is situated at a crucial position in the political life of America. Every day millions of facts, propaganda, rumor, suspicion, clues, hopes, and fears arrive at the offices of the mass media. These institutions have the power to determine each day what out of this incredible medley shall seem important and what shall be neglected. The "news" is literally what the media executives say is news. Because they determine what material will be included in print and in broadcast news, these executives have been called **gatekeepers**. They have the power to shape public opinion. They can determine reality. If certain words and events are not reported, they may as well have never occurred. When Walter Cronkite used to say, "And that's the way it is," we should have kept this in mind.

One quick example. In the spring of 1968 the communist side in Vietnam launched an offensive during Tet (the Vietnamese new year celebration). Militarily the offensive, whose aim was to provoke a "general uprising" in the cities, was a complete failure. Not only was their objective unattained; their forces were so badly mauled by American and South Vietnamese forces, they were unable to mount any attack for several months. Yet, according to Peter Braestrip's two-volume study, *The Big Story*, the American media virtually single-handedly turned the event into a defeat for the Americans and South Vietnamese. It was at this point that public support for the war began to slip rather rapidly.

Adversary. At its best, the media is a servant and guardian of political institutions. The adversary relationship between politicians and media must exist. The latter helps the former improve its own performance. At its worst, the media exploits events, avoids issues, and bends the truth. Free men and women cannot govern themselves with information obtained from 21 minutes of episodes, incidents, and eruptions driven across their attention span each day.

They need a human mind that explains what it means.

Has this adversarial relationship changed in recent years? Some political scientists think so. For example, Samuel P. Huntington of Harvard University sees this adversarial relationship between the media and the government as a new conflict comparable to the old cleavages between political parties, between state and local governments, and among the three branches of the federal government.[6]

Selector of political candidates. Another political scientist, James David Barber of Duke University, opens his most recent book on the presidency with this startling observation:

> A revolution in presidential politics is underway. No longer do the Democratic and Republican parties control the choice of standard bearers. In their place a new set of King makers has arisen: the journalists. For it is in the newspapers, the magazines and on television screens that the presidential candidacies are created and destroyed.[7]

To a degree this line of analysis would seem to apply to the 1980 presidential election. The hard look the media took at Senator Edward Kennedy certainly kept him from getting off to a fast start against President Carter. Conversely, the press gave John Anderson coverage far beyond what his final vote-getting ability would seem to justify.

As we shall see in the next chapter, television has given the ordinary citizen a new sense of importance in the political process. Presidential nominations are no longer settled by party leaders in smoke-filled rooms. They are settled by primaries and caucuses at the grassroots. Political conventions have become ceremonies of ratification.

Television stimulates political activism. Every candidate knows about "photo opportunities" and schemes to get himself or herself on camera. What Sam Lubell has called the "struggle for political visibility" is the means by which

United Press International Photo

At its best, the media is a servant and guardian of political institutions. In 1954, Sen. Joseph McCarthy (see Chapter 8) was at his height of political power, terrorizing the nation with wild charges that nearly every branch of government had been infiltrated by communists. While many feared to attack him lest they appear "soft on communism," Edward R. Murrow struck one of the first and most deadly blows when he spoke out on his famous television program, "See It Now." On a later broadcast, Murrow delivered his last word on the subject: "It is my devotion to the principles upon which this nation rests—justice, freedom and fairness—which sets me apart from Senator McCarthy. . . . When the record is finally written, as it will be one day, it will answer the question: Who has helped the communist cause and who has served his country better—Senator McCarthy or I? I would like to be remembered by the answer to that question." (Quote from Joseph Wershba, "Murrow v. McCarthy: See It Now," *New York Times Magazine,* March 4, 1979).

a new candidate presses his or her claims. All this has further weakened party identification and intensified the distrust of politicians and organizations.

In addition, the party organization is losing its control over campaigns. Television and polling have bred a new profession of electronic manipulators. Assembled in election management firms, the media specialists, working indifferently for one party or the other, reduce campaigns to displays more of technique than of issues. If the media does help in the selection of political candidates it is mainly by following certain institutional or economic imperatives—not by favoring a particular party or ideology.

Criticisms of the Mass Media

The powers that be?[8] Worth keeping in mind is the elementary fact that the mass media are businesses. Because they are, the mass media must, like any other business, continue to make profits to survive. According to Ben Bagdikian, average profits of the media industry are 76 percent higher than those of other American industries. There is nothing incompatible about profits and democracy. But one need not be a radical to suspect that the necessity of profits influences what the news will be. The editor of the *Washington Post* once gave a "respectable if rather dull story" the terse dismissal "its a room emptier." The need for profits also makes it difficult to expand television news coverage. (At CBS there was a standing insider's joke that if Moses came down from the mountain the evening news lead would be: "Moses today came down from the mountain with the Ten Commandments, the two most important of which are . . .") This influence of profit is a topic to which we shall return in a moment.

What has concerned a number of students of the mass media even more than profits is the trend toward concentration, especially among the newspapers, in this industry. At first blush, to speak of concentration in the mass media might seem strange. After all, there are 6,700 commercial radio stations, 700 commercial television stations, and about 1,750 daily newspapers. Why worry?

The answer is that the restraining influence of competition is disappearing, especially among the newspapers. Today, there are fewer than 45 cities with two or more competing daily newspapers; about 1,500 cities have a noncompetitive daily press. Each year, more and more noncompetitive dailies are being swallowed up by the large corporate chains.

Moreover, to a remarkable degree, two newspapers—the *New York Times* and the *Washington Post*—dominate the treatment of the news. They shape the agenda not only for the New York-based television networks (ABC, NBC, and CBS) and weekly newsmagazines (*Time* and *Newsweek*) but also for the hundreds of papers that subscribe to the *Times* or *Post* news services.

But there are potentially important countertrends, some fostered by the electronics revolution itself. Increased competition among the networks suggests that hour-long newscasts are not long off. Candidates in 1980 who tended to be fuzzy on the issues did considerably less well than such candidates did in 1976. Finally, there are signs that the *mass* media might be in the early stages of decline as a new information system is being born. The place of the great mass-circulation magazine is being taken by hundreds of smaller, more specialized magazines. Cheap copying machines make every individual a "publisher." Cable television and video cassettes increase the number of channels and of different messages. The news, instead of being mass machined at a few centers, then mass distributed to passive citizens, might take on a new richness and variety.

Accuracy. How unbiased a view of the world does the media present? Consider the cinema as a part of the mass media. An increasing number of Americans seem to have difficulty distinguishing fact from fiction. If one relied entirely on the motion pictures and television entertainment shows, they would certainly have a somewhat lopsided view of American life. Not all motion pictures express a left-of-center view. But many of the most successful ones do: *The Parallax View, The Candidate, Coming Home, The China Syndrome, Cuba, Three Days of the Condor, WUSA, The Electric Horseman,* and *Reds.*

The television image of business executives in such popular programs as *Baretta, Kojak, Hawaii Five-O,* and *Columbo* invariably connects them to the Mafia, murderers, drug pushers, etc. Even in TV comedies, business executives play highly unflattering roles. Ben Stein writes:

> Often they are con men. They promise the money-starved regular characters a way out of their poverty. Then, having bilked our lovable favorites, they disappear without a trace. Sometimes they simply appear as pompous fools, bullying and overbearing our regulars until a devastating joke blows them off the set.[9]

Stein provides numerous examples. Here are two:

> On *Good Times*, a banker approached J.J., the teenage son in the poverty-stricken black family, and asked him to paint a mural for a new bank branch. After J.J. had painted it, putting his heart, soul, and hopes into it, the banker refused to pay him.
>
> On *The Mary Tyler Moore Show*, in the valedictory episode, a hard-headed businessman was brought in to salvage the ratings of WJM, the fictional television station where the most appealing human beings on earth worked and played. He fired Mary and all her friends.[10]

Compounding the problem is the difficulty that some Americans have in distinguishing fact from fiction. Even college professors report of students citing film and television shows as "sources" of information.

Another source of inaccuracy has little to do with the personal opinion of reporters. The press tends not to write about places where it is not allowed to go. Consequently, despite a death toll of several million from shootings, starvation, and forced labor, the American press largely ignored the holocaust in Cambodia. At the same time, however, one alleged beating by Isreali police of an Arab can gain front-page coverage for several days.

In his book, *Terrorism*, Walter Lacqueur points out that the media act as a selective magnifying glass. They are enormously attracted to terrorism because of its mystery, quick action, tension, and drama. Thus, there is a symbiotic relationship between terrorism—indeed, all violent actions (e.g., kidnapping, and prison riots)—and the mass media.

This unrelenting search for drama also affects how political campaigns—especially for the presidency—are covered. As a rule, the media focuses little on a candidate's personal qualifications or stands on the issues (inflation, welfare, Russia and energy). What they do focus on are the "horse-race" aspect of the campaign. Is the candidate gaining or losing ground? Is X going to support Y? Rather than an urbane discussion of the issues, we have a horse race.

Finally, in recent years much attention has been focused on the liberties taken in the name of so-called New Journalism, which became popular in the mid-1960s (see box).

In 1981, the credibility of the *Washington Post*, one of the nation's most distinguished newspapers, received a severe blow, dealt by one of its own reporters. The case involved Janet Cooke, who had won a Pultizer Price for her report on an 8-year-old heroin addict. Unfortunately for the *Post*, the story was a fake. Ironically, it was the *Post* that had made many of the exposures in the Watergate affair (Chapter 7) and thus helped propel the media to an unusually high confidence level in the 1970s. That confidence—thanks to Janet Cooke, her editors, and others—has gradually eroded to the point where only 13 percent of the public have "very much" trust in their newspaper (Harris Survey, June 30, 1981) and 33 percent think that reporters "often make things up" (Gallup Organization, April 22–23, 1981). These figures are disturbing to the extent that believable news media is a crucial ingredient in a free society.

What Is the New Journalism?

One cannot examine the objectivity of the press without noting the rise of the "New Journalism." It is based on the theory that the responsibility of the press is to discover the truth not merely the facts. In some variations of this new type of journalism, reporters are encouraged to indicate and further their points of view in their news stories. Objectivity is ridiculed as being impossible to attain. Reporters even become participants in events. Perhaps no one has practiced this form of journalism with greater élan than Hunter A. Thompson of *Rolling Stone*.

Unfortunately, the doctoring of quotes and the invention of vivid detail ("said the secretary of state across the bowl of asparagus") is only a short hop from making it up. And this is exactly what *Washington Post* reporter Janet Cooke did in an article about an eight-year-old heroin addict. After she was awarded the Pulitzer Prize, the hoax was revealed.

Photograph © 1981 by Jill Krementz

News management. Where do journalists obtain their information about American politics? According to Herbert J. Gans, they get it from what they themselves read in the papers (mainly the *New York Times*), from what they learn from relations and friends, and most important, from public officials.[11] One survey cited by Gans shows that 78 percent of the stories in the *New York Times* and the *Washington Post* came from public officials.

Furthermore, presidents and their advisers can manipulate the kinds of information that will be made available to reporters and the forums in which that information is given to them. For example, trips are planned where reporters have only access to government officials and must therefore accept the official version of what is going on. White House officials are likely to evaluate reporters on how favorable their stories are. On a 1964 letter to his press secretary from Dan Rather requesting permission to film the White House staff at work, Lyndon Johnson noted in the margin, "This man and CBS are out to get us. . . . Tell him you have much more work than you can handle and these men are workers on routine, not actors."[12]

Finally, politicians can contrive news. That is to say, they can create or manufacture an event to generate publicity. It may be a headquarters opening, a "spontaneous" touch football game, or a press conference to announce that an important announcement is forthcoming. Daniel Boorstin, now librarian of Congress, provides a useful phrase to cover such happenings, the **pseudo-event**. As he puts it, a pseudo-event "is not a train wreck or an earthquake but an interview."[13]

Wide World Photos

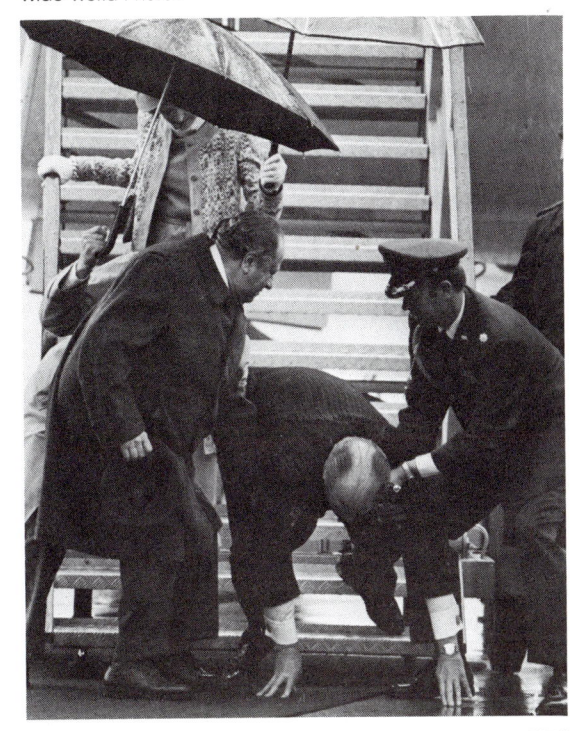

President Gerald Ford's media problems began in 1975 when he tumbled down the steps of Air Force One on arrival in Austria. The image was perpetuated by news reports, photographs, and film clips that magnified every Ford stumble. It is unlikely that this bumbling image caused his defeat to Jimmy Carter in 1976. There was, after all, the Nixon pardon and a rather conservative economic policy. Still, one wonders why this fall made big news.

Now you have some ideas of how citizens perceive the political world. We can turn to how these thoughts are mobilized and focused on government. There are several mechanisms to provide that linkage: elections, participation, interest groups, and political parties.

Before we plunge into the details surrounding these four mechanisms, it is vitally important to see them in broad perspective. In particular, what function do they play in the American political system? The answer is that they serve to simplify the complex, cacophonous, and contrary opinions suggested in the photograph that appears on the title page of this chapter. But simplify for whom? For all those individuals who run the government—presidents, governors, mayors, bureaucrats, legislators, council members, and even judges.

VOTING

Of all the forms of political action, voting is the most common. This section addresses the questions, Who votes and why? Who does not vote and why? and What are the implications of low voter turn out?

Since most of the discussion in this section will center on voting for candidates, we should perhaps note at the outset that sometimes citizens can achieve direct legislation through the voting process. For example, the **recall** permits voters to remove a public official from office. A rarely used but very effective devise, recall was wielded by voters in Madison, Wisconsin, in 1977 to remove from office a local judge who had made what many considered to be offensive remarks about women during a rape case.

Some states and localities provide for the **initiative.** When enough voters sign a petition requesting it, election officials must put a proposed law on the ballot for a vote by the general public. If it passes, it is law—regardless of what the legislature might want.

Closely related to the initiative is the **referendum.** In this case, the legislature itself decides (sometimes with prompting by a citizen petition) to put action it has taken to a popular vote for ratification (approval).

In the 1980 election, besides voting for the president and state and local officials, many Americans faced tough decisions on a wide array of issues. Except for gambling, most proposals were defeated. Among them: measures to extend civil rights, limit rents, reduce litter, and ban smoking in many public places. Some concerns were more specialized. Miami area residents, in an apparent backlash against the flood of Cuban refugees, voted to stop providing

Anchorperson: Second Generation

In 1981, when Walter Cronkite retired from CBS News he marked the end of a line of radio-TV newsmen that stretched back to Edward R. Murrow. What made this generation of newsmen different than the second generation was this: They had a background in print journalism. They were reporters who covered a story, wrote it, and analyzed its meaning. They were doing this before they became personalities in the electronic media.

The second generation is different. TV news stars are hired because they are attractive or because they give the program the right "mix." Generally, at least on the local level, they do not write their own copy; they just read it. They do not write books or even articles.

But the second generation is well rewarded. CBS offered Dan Rather $8 million over five years. This is a contract more comparable to TV entertainers like Johnny Carson ($3 million a year) than to Edward R. Murrow.

Wide World Photos

Spanish translations of public documents. Voters in Nye County, Nevada, voted to preserve the status quo by endorsing a proposition to continue legalized prostitution.

Who Votes and Why

Institutional setting. In Chapter 11, we shall trace the gradual expansion of the right to vote in the United States, but the high points may be summarized here. The 15th Amendment (1870) forbade the states to deny or limit the franchise because of "race, color, or previous condition of servitude." This amendment was reenforced by the Voting Rights Act of 1965. The 19th Amendment (1920) extended the vote to women; the 26th Amendment (1971) gave the vote to 18-year-olds. The Supreme Court's *Baker* v. *Carr* decision (1962) required that the boundaries of state legislative districts be drawn so that they are nearly equal in population. In *Wesberry* v. *Sanders* (1964) the Court ruled that Georgia must redraw the borders of congressional districts so they would be nearly equal in population. These two Supreme Court decisions helped to advance the concept of one person, one vote implicit in Article I of the Constitution. Finally, the 24th Amendment (1964) forbade the states from requiring voters to pay a special tax, or poll tax, to vote.

Despite these steps, election turnout remains surprisingly low. In the past half century, the proportion of voting-age population who actually voted for the president has never been higher than 65 percent. In the off-year congressional elections, which come two years after each presidential election, the average is under 42 percent casting a ballot.

Even more amazing, note in Table 5–3 percentage of voting-age population that actually pick a president.[14] Never in the history of the

TABLE 5-3
Picking Presidents: The Tradition of Low Turnouts

Year	Winner	Winner's Percent of Total Vote	Winner's Percent of Voting-Age Population	Percent of Voting-Age Population Casting Vote for any Candidate
1960	John Kennedy	49.7%	31.2%	62.8%
1964	Lyndon Johnson	61.1	37.8	61.9
1968	Richard Nixon	43.4	26.4	60.9
1972	Richard Nixon	60.7	33.7	55.5
1976	Jimmy Carter	50.1	27.2	54.3
1980	Ronald Reagan	51.0	26.7	51.8

Source: *Statistical Abstract of the United States, 1980*, p. 498.

United States has a majority of all adults elected a president. Instead, the votes of as few as 11.4 percent of voting-age Americans have placed men in the White House. In 1912, for example, a mere 11.7 percent elected Woodrow Wilson. (Remember, women did not gain universal suffrage until 1920.)

How does this turnout compare with other democracies. It is lower than most, which range from 95 percent of the population in Australia to 73 percent in Great Britain and Japan. The U.S. turnout is, however, about the same as that of what some call the world's oldest democracy—Switzerland. That country had a 52 percent turnout in its most recent national election.

One of the main reasons for these differences is institutional—specifically, **registration** and **absentee ballot** requirements. When cutoff dates are set well in advance of the election, people may forget to register in time. Moreover, registration and obtaining an absentee ballot can be bothersome and time-consuming. In Minnesota, any eligible voter can register at the polling place on election day; turnout was 61.5 percent in the 1980 election. South Carolina has a deadline a month before the election, and voter interest is low; the turnout in that election was 39.8 percent.

Characteristics of voters. What kinds of people are best represented in the turnout figures cited above? The two most important factors are education and age. Table 5-4 examines these and other characteristics.

When the founding fathers considered the idea of ordinary citizen participation in government, they assumed that those less well off would use the electoral process to secure gains from the rich. As Table 5-4 suggests, that never happened. In fact, it is the groups with the most social and economic advantages that have been most inclined to vote.

TABLE 5-4
Who the Voters Are

More Likely to Vote	Percent	Less Likely to Vote	Percent
Middle-aged people (45-65 years old)	58.5%	Young (18-24 years old)	20.1%
College educated	57.3	Grade-school educated	34.6
Whites	47.3	Blacks	37.2
Northerners or Westerners	48.9	Southerners	39.6
Men	46.6	Women	45.3
Jews		Catholics	
White-collar workers		Blue-collar workers	
Republicans		Democrats	

Source: *Statistical Abstract of the United States, 1980*, p. 520. Percentages are for national election in 1978.

How voters make up their minds. For over a generation American political scientists have been diligently trying to discover why people vote the way they do. A broad conclusion to this research is that how a person votes is largely a function of three factions: party affiliation, candidate appeal, and the issues. The relative importance of each factor will vary depending on the individual and the election.

As you will hear in the next chapter, there is much talk about the decline in political parties. Much of it is exaggerated. As Figure 5-4 shows, **party identification,** or **partisanship,** among the electorate has remained remarkably consistent since 1952. But what about the bulge in independents that can be seen in recent years? Is this not a sign of party loyalists converting to independents? The best explanation is that the rise in independents is the result of a higher percentage of young people in the voting population than existed in 1952. Traditionally, young people have been less likely than other groups to exhibit party loyalty.

The extent to which people who identify with a party vote with that party can be seen by examining the vote in presidential and House elections. Party-line votes (i.e., votes by party identifiers for the candidate of their party) have remained between 82 and 69 percent from 1956 to 1978. The rate of defection in the 1976 presidential election was no higher than in 1952: 15 percent. In the 1980 election, however, defection were higher. Twenty-five percent of Democrats voted Republican; 6 percent of Republicans voted Democrat. (If independent candidate John Anderson is considered,

FIGURE 5-4
Continuity in Party Identification in the United States, 1952-1978

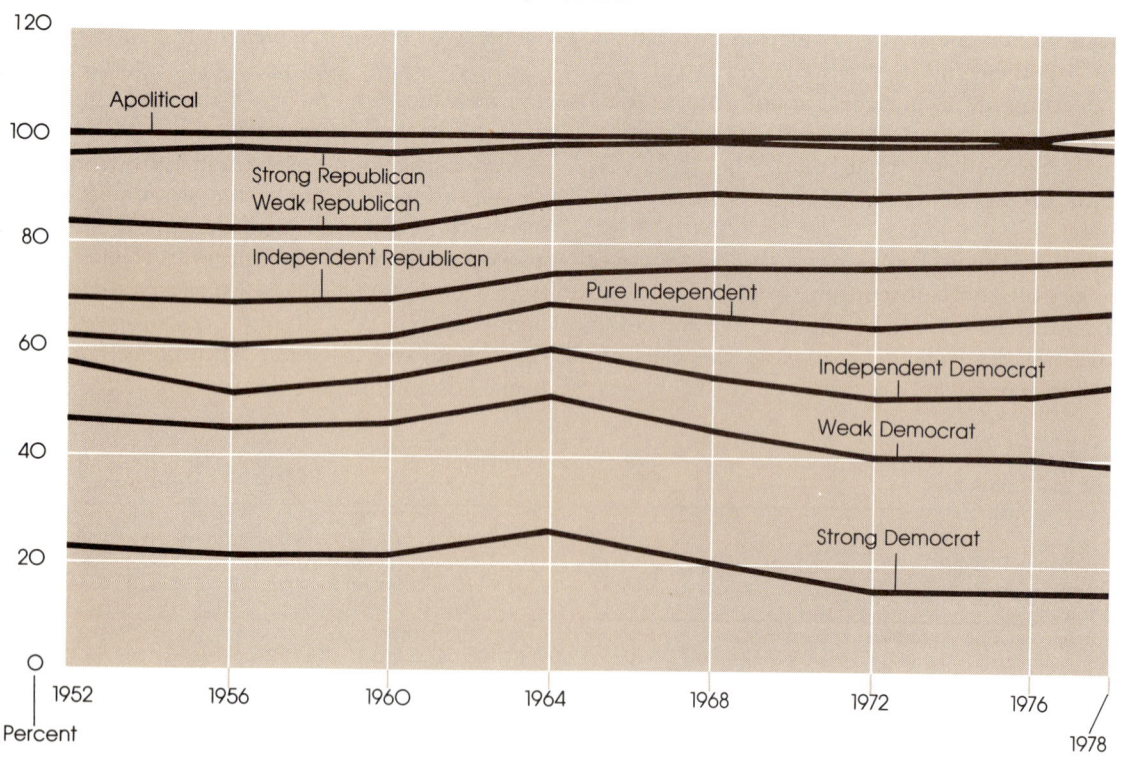

Data source: 1952 through 1978 SRC/CPS Election Studies; graph by author.

the rate is even higher: 7 percent of Democrats and 5 percent of Republicans voted for Anderson.) The conclusion is that, while there has been some decline in straight party voting, party affiliation remains a strong indicator of how a person will vote.

The positive or negative appeal of a candidate is one cause for party defection. The personal appeal of Dwight D. Eisenhower enabled him to get the vote of most of the independents and a significant fraction of Democrats. He was the only president since World War II to serve two full terms. In the 1960 election, John F. Kennedy's wit and vigorous style undoubtedly helped him edge out Richard M. Nixon who could provoke hostility without even trying. In 1980, Jimmy Carter hoped to get the voters to view Ronald Reagan as they had Barry Goldwater. Lyndon Johnson had beaten Goldwater badly in 1964 by branding him an extremist and a warmonger. Though Reagan and Goldwater were both conservatives, the ploy never worked because of Reagan's genial style. Goldwater's somewhat quick, tight, bitter style, however, seemed to many voters consistent with the Johnson charge.

V. O. Key's *The Responsible Electorate*, published posthumously in 1966, was a reaction to the initial readings of the public opinion polls that had started to study the minds of the voters. The picture of the democratic process that had emerged from these studies was not a pretty one. Most voters mindlessly pulled the level of party loyalty; elections were often decided by the whims of the least motivated and least informed voters. Key rereading the same polls to focus on why voters changed from one party to other. In so doing, he was able to draw a picture of "an electorate moved by concern about central and relevant questions of public policy, of governmental performance, and of executive personality." His theme was that "voters are not fools."

More recent research tends to rate the influence of issues somewhat lower than Key did. Many voters do not have sharply defined opinions on issues. They don't care how much unemployment is tolerable in order to get the inflation rate down or whether the United States needs a B-1 bomber. They don't think about who should run job training programs or whether abortions are the taking of life. They don't consider how to stop drug pushers or what additional measures need to be taken to insure equal opportunity for all. Even if one does have a well thought-out position on each issue (which requires an investment of time few voters are willing or able to make), candidates can blur the issues, as Carter did in the 1976 campaign. Or candidates can take essentially identical positions, as Reagan and George Bush did during the race for the Republican presidential nomination in the spring of 1980. And finally, what does the voter do if the voter agrees with candidate A on four issues and candidate B on six issues? Since all issues are not of equal importance, choosing between A and B is hardly a matter of simple addition.

Nonvoting: A Sign of Decay or Health?[15]

Every election year civic groups and the media launch a vigorous campaign to get out the vote. The premise of those pushing people to vote is that a large **voter turnout** indicates a strong, healthy democracy. That is undoubtedly true.

And an opposite proposition is also true. A large voter turnout can indicate strong totalitarianism. Albania (a country you might recall from Figure 1–1) reported that only one registered voter failed to show up for its November 1978 general elections. North Korea counts on a full 100 percent voter turnout. Romania and East Germany hover somewhere over 99 percent. Sierra Leone set a new world record in June 1977 when 2,215,586 votes were cast by an electorate of 2,152,454 for a stunning 103 percent turnout.

But there is another, seldom considered premise. High voter turnout denotes high voter discontent and a sign of stress—not health—in the body politic. During tranquil times people turn to commerce, recreation, the arts, or whatever. They usually do not turn to politics. As Walter Lippmann once wrote, "Politics and government are secondary and subsidiary, not goods and ends in themselves." Most free people concentrate on primary "goods and ends." They become politically engaged only as these are threatened. Hence high voter turnout may be taken as a distress signal.

Data bear out theory here. During this century's presidential elections, the highest proportion (above 61 percent) of those eligible voted in the following cases: on the eve of America's involvement in ongoing world wars (1916 and 1940); amidst the Great Depression (1936); during the Korean war (1952); and at the time of recession and scares over Cuba and China (1960). The lowest voter turnout (under 55 percent of those eligible) is consistently recorded for times of relative peace and prosperity (1920 and 1924, 1948, 1976). People do seem to vote their resentments and fears. When there is a relative dearth of each, people simply vote less.

Does this lesser voting hurt the country? In a general, gut-feeling sense, yes. Good citizenship demands that each adult at least vote, and everyone favors good citizenship. (Remember the arrows in Figure 5–1 are two-directional.) In a more particular, empirical sense, perhaps not. Low turnout may not deprive the country of much collective wisdom.

Marginal voters—those going to the polls more out of guilt and pressure than will and patriotism—are those marginally interested in and marginally informed about politics. This common sense hypothesis is backed by data in the American Enterprise Institute book *The Myth of the Independent Voter*. During the past five presidential elections, individuals who say they voted less frequently (63 percent of the time versus 87 percent for others) were less frequently very interested in the ongoing election (28 percent versus 57 percent). They were less knowledgeable on even such an elementary matter as which party had the most seats in Congress (54 percent versus 74 percent). Arguably, a higher proportion of voters may not serve the collective good if this necessitates, as it does, a much higher proportion of uninformed voters.

The same principle does not hold true, however, for private interests. We shall look at those in the next chapter. The leaders of farmers, fundamentalists, businessmen, and blacks have good cause to get out the vote among their members. High turnout yields greater political power and furthers their group interests. But these are special interests. They are to be equated with the public-interest motivation to "get out the vote" that civic groups and the media dwell upon.

Moreover, studies of the last few elections have shown that, as Edward Costikyan sums up the evidence, "There is no wide gulf between voters and non-voters. There are no deep-seated ideological schisms."[16] In the case of the 1980 election, a *New York Times*/CBS post-election poll estimated that a 100 percent voter turnout would have resulted in a still decisive 5 percent win for Reagan (45 percent to 40 percent for Carter).[17]

The question raised earlier in this section still lingers: Why the low voter turnout in the United States? Besides the argument of political theorists that people simply care more about other things, there is the one of political economists: Casting an informed vote is usually irrational for anyone to do. Anthony Downs has analyzed individual voting in terms of whether marginal benefits outweigh marginal costs. Examined in this way, "We reach the startling conclusion that it is irrational for most citizens to acquire political information for purposes of voting [however much each citizen] might benefit substantially if the whole electorate were well informed." For an individual, the bother of finding out who the candidates are, what they are saying on the issues, and whether they are right entails costs that are not worth the benefits, to the person or the society, of one additional informed vote. "Hence ignorance of politics is not a result of unpatriotic apathy;

rather it is a highly rational response to the facts of life in a large democracy," Downs concludes.

OTHER FORMS OF POLITICAL ACTION

For millions of Americans, voting is not enough. Therefore, they take part in a variety of other political activities (Table 5-5). Their reasons are varied: to increase their influence over policy; to increase their chances of receiving **patronage** (i.e., a government job, franchise, contract, or favor awarded on a partisan basis); or to enjoy the friendship and prestige.

Many of the activities indicated in Table 5-5 are discussed elsewhere in the book. This concluding section will highlight only one of the items on the list—contacting a state or national official. A reporter once asked President Harry Truman, "Would you be against lobbyists who are working for your program?" Truman replied, "We would call them citizens appearing in the public interest."[18] The reply reflects how uncomfortable most Americans are with the word **lobbying**.

Steve Groer/*Rocky Mountain News*

Political participation takes a variety of forms, as Table 5-5 makes clear. Among these is protest, which itself comes in many guises. Here poet Allen Ginsberg (third from left) and friends go "Ommm" to protest nuclear weapons. While the author does not recommend the Ginsberg method, political protest can be an important and effective method of participation for certain groups.

TABLE 5-5
How Americans Participate in Politics

	Mode of Participation	Percentage	Where Discussed in This Book
1.	Active in at least one organization involved in community problems	32	Chapter 7 and 11
2.	Have worked with others trying to solve some community problems	30	Chapter 7
3.	Have attempted to persuade others how to vote	28	Chapter 4
4.	Have ever actively worked for a party or candidate during an election	26	Chapter 7
5.	Have ever contacted a local government official about some issue or problem	20	Chapter 11
6.	Have attended at least one political meeting or rally in last three years	19	Chapter 7
7.	Have ever contacted a state or national government official about some issue or problem	18	Chapter 6, 9, and 11
8.	Have ever formed a group or organization to attempt to solve some local community problem	14	Chapter 4
9.	Have ever given money to a party or candidate during an election campaign	13	Chapter 6
10.	Presently a member of a political club or organization	8	Chapter 7

Sources: Sidney Verba and Norman H. Nie, *Participation in America* (New York: Harper & Row, 1972), p. 31; Lester W. Milbrath and M. L. Goel, *Political Participation*, 2d ed. (Chicago: Rand McNally, 1977), p. 22.

Yet attempts by private citizens and groups to influence government decisions—particularly the content of pending legislation and the outcome of legislative voters—by directly speaking with government officials are as old as the practice of legislating itself. (The word came into use in the mid-17th century when the large anteroom near where the English Parliament met became known as the lobby.) Not only is the practice old; it is guaranteed: "Congress shall make no law . . . abridging . . . the right of the people peaceably . . . to petition the government" (First Amendment). We shall have more to say about lobbying as a method of political communication in the next chapter.

Lobbying is not the only way citizens can communicate with public officials. They can write letters. What can be said about writing a letter? Every literate person can write a letter, presumably. True enough. But there are letters and there are effective letters. Congressman Morris K. Udall of Arizona has provided some valuable suggestions on how to make sure what we write falls into the latter category (see the box entitled "How to Write a Member of Congress").

How to Write a Member of Congress

Surprisingly few people ever write their Congressman. Perhaps 90 percent of our citizens live and die without ever taking pen in hand and expressing a single opinion to the man or woman who represents them in Congress—a person whose vote may decide what price they will pay for the acts of Government, either in dollars or in human lives.

This reluctance to communicate results from the typical and understandable feelings that Congressmen have no time or inclination to read their mail, that a letter probably will not be answered or answered satisfactorily, that one letter will not make any difference anyway. Based on my own 16 years' experience, and speaking for myself, I can state flatly that most of these notions are wrong. On several occasions a single, thoughtful, factually persuasive letter did change my mind or cause me to initiate a review of a previous judgment.

Some Fundamentals

Here are some suggestions that apply to all congressional mail:

Address it properly: "Hon. _____, House Office Building, Washington, D.C. 20515." Or "Senator _____, Senate Office Building, Washington, D.C. 20510." This may seem fundamental, but I once received a letter addressed like this: "Mr. Morris K. Udall, U.S. Senator, Capitol Building Phoenix, Arizona. Dear Congressman Rhodes. . . ."

Identify the bill or issue: About 20,000 bills are introduced in each Congress; it's important to be specific. If you write about a bill, try to give the bill number or describe it by popular title ("clean air," "minimum wage," etc.). The letter should be timely: Sometimes a bill is out of committee, or has passed the House, before a helpful letter arrives. Inform your Congressman while there is still time to take effective action.

Concentrate on your own delegation: The representative of your district and the senators of your State cast your votes in Congress and want to know your views.

Be reasonably brief: Your opinions and arguments stand a better chance of being read if they are stated as concisely as the subject matter will permit.

Do's

Write your own views—not someone else's: A personal letter is far better than a form letter or signature on a petition.

Give your reasons for taking a stand: Statements like "Vote against H.R. 100; I'm bitterly opposed" don't help me much. But a letter which says "I'm a small hardware dealer, and H.R. 100 will put me out of business for the following reasons . . ." tells me a lot more.

Be constructive: If a bill deals with a problem you admit exists, but you believe the bill is the wrong approach, tell what the right approach is. If you have expert knowledge, share it with your Congressman: Of all the letters pouring into a Congressman's office every morning, perhaps one in a hundred comes from a constituent who is a real expert in that subject. The opinions expressed in the others are important, and will be heeded, but this one is a real gold mine for the conscientious member.

Say "well done" when it's deserved: Congressmen are human, too, and they appreciate an occasional "well done" from people who believe they have done the right thing.

Don'ts

Don't make threats or promises: Congressmen usually want to do the popular thing, but this is not their only motivation; nearly all the Members I know want, most of all, to do what is best for the country. Occasionally a letter will conclude by saying, "If you vote for this monstrous bill, I'll do everything in my power to defeat you in the next election." A writer has the privilege of making such assertions, of course, but they rarely intimidate a conscientious Member, and they may generate an adverse reaction. He would rather know why you felt so strongly. The reasons may change his mind; the threat probably won't.

Don't berate your Congressman: You can't hope to persuade him of your position by calling him names. If you disagree with him, give reasons for your disagreement. Try to keep the dialogue open.

Don't pretend to wield vast political influence: Write your Congressman as an individual—not as a self-appointed spokesman for your neighborhood, community, or industry. Unsupported claims to political influence will only cast doubt upon the views you express.

Do not demand a commitment before the facts are in. If you have written a personal letter and stated your reasons for a particular stand, you have a right to know my present thinking on the question. But writers who "demand to know how you will vote on H.R. 100" should bear certain legislative realities in mind: (1) On major bills there usually are two sides to be considered, and you may have heard only one; (2) The bill may be 100 pages long with 20 provisions in addition to the one you wrote about, and I may be forced to vote on the bill as a whole, weighing the good with the bad; (3) It makes little sense to adopt a firm and unyielding position before a single witness has been heard or study made of the bill in question; and (4) A bill rarely becomes law in the same form as introduced. It is possible that the bill you write me about you would oppose when it reached the floor.

SOURCE: Excerpted from, "The Right to Write," address by the Honorable Morris K. Udall of Arizona in the House of Representatives, Wednesday, November 2, 1977. *Congressional Record*, November 3, 1977. p. E6822.

The piece by Udall is doubly valuable. Not only does it tell how to write an effective letter. It also dispels the notion that letters do not matter, that they are never read. To drive home the point I shall cite probably the most famous letter from a private citizen to a public official in recent American history. In 1939, Danish atomic physicist Niels Bohr brought news to Einstein that a German refugee physicist had split the uranium atom. Though these experiments were performed in Copenhagen, they were inspired by experiments already done by scientists in Germany. Both saw these events as evidence that an atomic bomb might be feasible. With war in Europe imminent, fears that the Nazi scientists might build such a weapon first were natural. Einstein, therefore, wrote a letter which was delivered to President Franklin

Roosevelt by Alexander Sachs, an intimate of the president. At the meeting with Roosevelt, Sach read aloud his covering letter. It emphasized the same ideas as the Einstein communication but stressed the need for funds. As the interview drew to a close, Roosevelt remarked, "Alex, what you are after is to see that the Nazis don't blow us up." Then he called in an aide and announced: "This requires action."[19]

Chapter Key

Essentially, the purpose of political action is to influence government and thereby affect public policy. The root of this action, however, is public opinion.

As the photograph from the "Dick Cavett Show" found at the beginning of the chapter suggests, expressing opinions is a popular American pastime. Moreover, those opinions tend to be complex and varied. Surveys purporting to measure "approval" or "disapproval" of an issue or of an individual are, accordingly, blunt instruments. The cautious reader of polls will, therefore, want to know, Was the sample size random and sufficiently large? Were the questions objective and related to the personal experience of the respondent? The poll reader will also recognize that even the best polls are not predictions but snapshots in time. In a word, some polls can be quite volatile.

Individuals are not assigned opinions like social security numbers or X and Y chromosomes. Opinions are formed through a combination of four major influences: socialization, political culture, mass media, and personal experience. Socialization goes on in the family, the school, the church. It also occurs among peers and continues throughout life. Early experiences, though, are probably most lasting.

Political culture determines the context of public opinion. To varying degrees, Americans believe in civil liberties and civil rights. But at a more fundamental level, they believe in individualism, equality of opportunity, private property, and progress.

Three basic demographic trends that might shape the future evolution of the American political culture are fewer young people, more Hispanics, and the southern and western migration.

Like socialization and political culture, the mass media help shape public opinion. In fact, the modern media not only regulate the flow of information in the polity, they also serve as a check on political institutions and play a role in the selection of political candidates. Individuals who rely primarily on the mass media for news should keep in mind that these organizations are money-making enterprises with varying degrees of fidelity to accuracy. Moreover, their chief source of news is what public officials tell them.

What troubles a number of media watchers is the extent to which political reporting focuses on personalities and political maneuvering as opposed to public policy issues. Instead of fully explaining issues, the media cover fragments of them as they pop to the surface on a given day. This makes understanding complex national issues difficult for many people.

The most fundamental and popular way citizens participate in politics is by voting. For those citizens who think voting is not enough, a variety of other forms of participation are available: community action, campaign work, lobbying, writing letters, giving money, membership in political organization, and protesting. Generally, voters and the politically active tend to be older, college educated, white, from the North or West, and white-collar.

Collection of the Boatmen's National Bank of St. Louis

6 | Interest Groups and Political Parties

After studying this chapter you should be able to answer the following questions:

1. What are the major trade and professional associations, labor, business, and public interest groups? What are their special interests?
2. What are the major minority groups in America? What issues do they raise?
3. What are the various tactics used by these groups in their relations with Congress, the public, the bureaucracy, and the courts?
4. What functions do American political parties perform? Which do you consider the most important?
5. What is the organizational makeup and the principal activities of the national party organizations?
6. What are the major phases of a presidential campaign?
7. What trends are shaping the party system?

Terms you should know:

caucus
class action
closed primary v. open primary
cross-cutting cleavages
electoral college
enfranchisement
Federal Election Campaign Act
delegates
general election
GOP
interest groups
lame duck
litigation
melting pot
multiparty system
national chairman
national convention

platforms
plurality vote
political action committees
political parties
populism
precincts
primary
progressivism
proportional representation
"public interest" group
runoff primary
single-issue politics
statutes of limitations
suffrage
third parties
trade association

More than any other artists in the 19th century, George Caleb Bingham captured the vitality and diversity of the democratic process in America. In *The County Election*, he gives us a glimpse of politics in the raw. Bingham, a politician as well as artist, had no legal fine points to make, no social issues to illuminate. All he wanted to show was the range of the American electorate—rowdy boatmen, tophatted drunkards, and a few hecklers.

The founders believed that the Constitution could somehow balance this volatile mixture of humanity and produce a workable, self-governing whole. But it quickly became apparent that the institutions they had established for this purpose would not carry the load alone. Congress, the presidency, the Supreme Court, the electoral college, and federalism would be yoked to a pair of institutions never mentioned in the Constitution—interest groups and political parties. Along with voting, these two institutions serve as major vehicles by which citizens can influence public policy. This chapter, by focusing on them, will round out our discussion of Figure 5–1.

Interest groups, or pressure groups as they are sometimes called, try to influence public policy in ways favorable to their membership. They do this by persuading government decision makers, by supporting or opposing political candidates, by fighting in court (litigation), and by shaping public opinion. **Political parties,** by contrast, are chiefly interested in influencing public policy by getting their members elected or appointed to government offices.

As you know from the last chapter, there are millions of citizens expressing political demands. Obviously, there is no effective way each of these demands can be communicated directly to government officials. Rather, they must be aggregated and filtered through groups, political parties, and the mass media. Basically the process looks like the diagram below.[1]

Because of these overlapping functions, the strength of political parties is related to the strength of interest groups. One of the principal objectives of this chapter will be to examine the proposition that the growth in power of interest groups has led to a decline in the power of political parties. We shall also want to ask what the larger implications of this proposition might be for the democratic process.

We shall begin by looking at the types of interest groups Americans have organized. Next we shall consider the tactics they use when trying to influence public policy. Particular emphasis will be placed on those groups that represent minority interests.

This review of interest groups in American politics is followed by a similar review of political parties. That phase of our inquiry opens with an analysis of the two-party system; the focus will be on Democrats and Republicans. However, the place of third parties in American political history will not be ignored. Then we shall look at the organizational structure and operations of each major party. The chapter closes with a quick glance at how the electoral system operates.

INTEREST GROUPS

Criticisms and Contributions

James Madison and the other founding fathers were well aware of the pernicious effects that interest groups (or "factions") could have on liberty and equality if left unchecked. So they took precautions. Specifically, they designed a government with central power divided not only among states but also among three branches of the federal government. If an interest group was bent on seizing all the levers of government—well, it had a lot of grabbing to do. Chances of success for such a group did not seem bright.

Why all this fear of interest groups? First, they tend to attract the better educated and wealthy. Therefore interest groups do not represent all the people in the American political community. Second, interest groups tend to be organized along bureaucratic lines. Someone has to be at the top running things. This means interest groups are run by small groups of men and women who take positions sometimes inconsistent with the views of rank-and-file members.* Finally, because they are engaged in constant competition and compromise, interest groups can hamstring government policy. For example, a president, his advisers, and a congressional majority may have a fairly clear idea about what they want to do regarding air pollution. If affected industries want to raise the standards, they can employ a variety of tactics to block the proposed policy. If environmental groups want to lower standards, they can use similar tactics to block any loosening of standards.

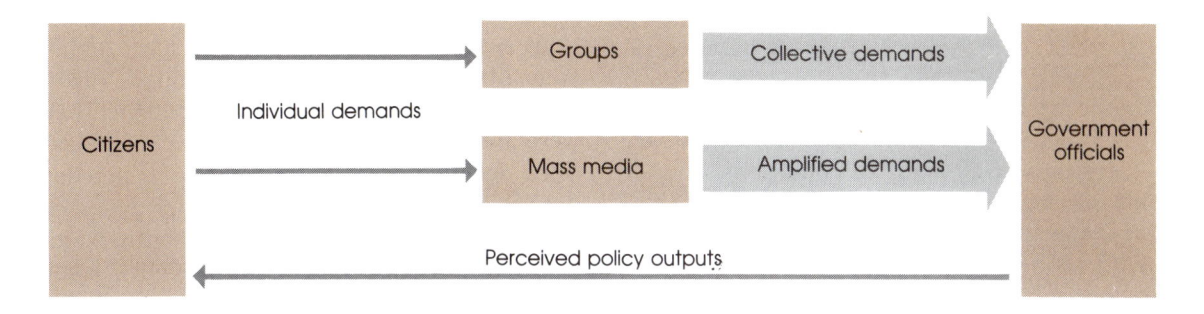

How can relatively small groups thwart overwhelming majorities. One answer is purely economic. Assume that a group of 5,000 citizens benefits from a $100 million government program. The benefit to this group is about $20,000 per citizen; the average *cost* of the program, though, is less than 50 cents per person in the United States. Obviously, the added cost to the individual taxpayer is so low that he or she has little incentive to let out a cry of protest. Who is going to camp out in front of the White House for a measly 50 cents? But if one stands to lose $20,000, one can become very, very vociferous.

These criticisms must be weighed, however, against several important contributions. Most important, interest groups are one of the major links between citizens and their government. Indeed, they actually *encourage* political participation. For candidates, they raise money and help get out the vote. For government officials, they provide valuable information about existing and future public policies. And, despite my disparaging remarks a moment ago about incessant competition and conflict, they help resolve social conflicts in a civilized, albeit sometimes messy, manner.

These criticisms also must be weighed against the phenomenon of cross-cutting pressures almost every American citizen faces. For example, a citizen may be a Catholic, a black, a woman, a physician, and an ex-army officer. On any given issue, it is not easy to predict which group affiliation, if any, will determine her position. Political scientists have a term for the variety of factors that can affect the voting of such individuals in conflicting ways. The term is **cross-cutting cleavages.**

---

* A striking example was the $85,000 grant given by the World Council of Churches in 1978 to the Patriotic Front guerrillas in Zimbabwe, who by terrorism were seeking to overthrow the interim regime there. Though the money was ostensibly for "humanitarian" assistance, no effort was made to monitor its use; council leaders admitted that it was intended as a "political statement." As if to underscore its political intent, the council then gave $125,000 to the SWAPO guerrillas in South West Africa (Namibia). By terror tactics SWAPO is seeking to prevent a transition to majority rule. The WCC grants precipitated a lively debate in religious circles and raised two basic questions: For whom do the council's leaders speak? Do the rank and file really want to side with radical forces in the Third World? The same question might be asked of groups such as the Moral Majority (to be discussed later in this chapter). According to Gallup polls, evangelical Christians are as politically divided as most Americans. It would appear that the leaders of such groups are as far to the *right* of their members as the leaders of the World Council of Churches are to the left of theirs.

Types

Americans are joiners. This was true in the 1830s, when Alexis de Tocqueville wrote, "Americans of all ages, all conditions, and all dispositions, constantly form associations."[2] Today 74 percent of all American adults belong to at least one organization. Fifty-seven percent are active in at least one organization.

People under all governments form interest groups. But Americans seem to have a special affinity for interest groups. Over 14,600 nonprofit national organizations were enumerated as of 1979. That was 16 percent above the count recorded in 1973 and 42 percent more than 1968. Trade, business, and commercial associations have constituted the largest single type of organization. Their proportion of the total, though, dropped from 27 percent to 20 percent between 1968 and 1979. During this 11-year period, the most significant increases in numbers of national organizations have occurred in public affairs, health, social welfare, educational, cultural, and scientific, engineering, and technical fields of endeavor (see Figure 6–1).

Membership in various groups and organizations between 1974 and 1978 was most highly concentrated in church-affiliated groups. Nevertheless, the share of respondents indicating they were members of religious-oriented organizations declined from 42 percent to 36 percent during this short time span. Other types of groups in which participation was fairly widespread were sports groups (20 percent), labor unions (15 percent), and school service groups (14 percent).

Given the social diversity of the country, so apparent in Bingham's painting, it is hardly surprising that one can probably find more interest groups in the United States than anywhere else. The constitutional arrangement also encourages the proliferation of interest groups. For example, some interest groups have sprung up around state or regional concerns; other interest groups concentrate their efforts on the courts.

Business. One does not have to think very hard to discover why business groups tend to be powerful. Consider, for example, the big oil companies. They have tremendous economic resources, sophisticated public relations people, geographic dispersion (which means more members of Congress representing them),

FIGURE 6–1
Selected National Organizations, by Type: 1968, 1973, and 1979

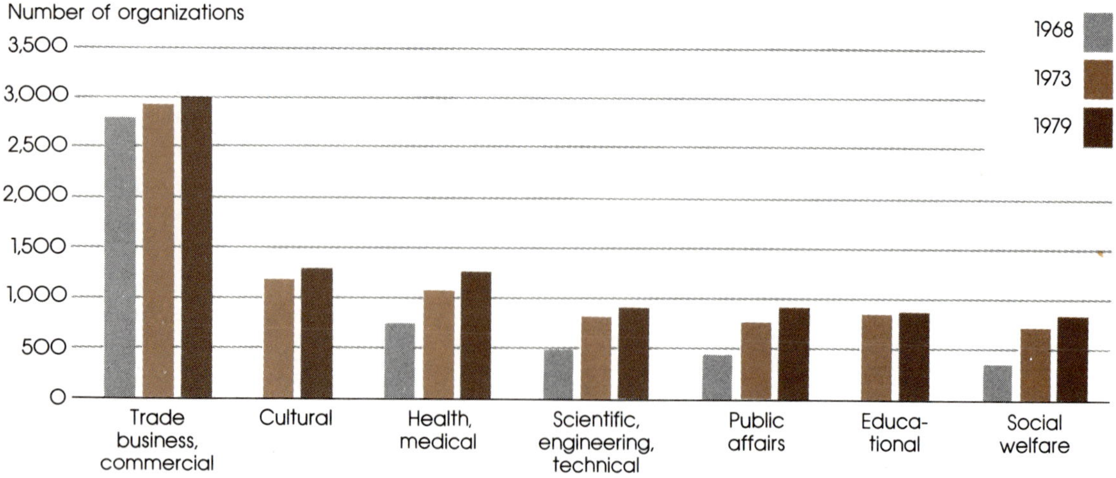

Source: Bureau of the Census, *Social Indicators III* (Washington, D.C.: U.S. Government Printing Office, 1980), p. 511.

Drawing by Whitney Darrow, Jr.; © 1968 The New Yorker Magazine, Inc.

"Well, if you feel so left out, why don't you join one of those Citizens Concerned About Something groups?"

and access to information critical to policymaking.

Nor does one have to walk very far down K Street to learn how well business is represented in the nation's capital. Indeed, if one wants to get the flavor of today's statecraft, such a walk would be almost as valuable as reading the Constitution. While not every company has its own Washington lobbyist, virtually every company, both large and small, is represented through one or more **trade associations.** Some have obscure-sounding names, such as the Porcelain Enamel Institute; others are more earthy, like the Envelope Manufacturers Association. The Washington, D.C., yellow pages contain thousands of such listings for those who prefer not to take the K Street walk.

As the examples in the illustration indicate, business groups cover a wide range of interests. Many interests, however, lead to conflict: small business versus big business; advocates of free trade versus advocates of high restrictions on imports; regulated companies wanting to preserve the status quo versus aggressive, new companies that want to compete. But there are certain issues that virtually all business share—e.g., lowering the minimum wage. Thus there are umbrella-type organizations, such as the Chamber of Commerce and the National Association of Manufacturers. They have large memberships, which include many interest groups and trade associations. Smaller, less well known, but still influential are the Conference Board, a kind of economic think tank, and the Business Roundtable, an association of the heads of major corporations. The former conducts research on public policy issues; the latter seeks to ensure that the views of big business are heard in Washington.

Labor. Labor unions have come a long way in the American polity since John Mitchell and his United Mine Workers organized the anthracite miners in Pennsylvania between 1897 and 1900. At that time, it managed to win a modest wage increase. But the union was still outlawed. So, in 1902, the miners struck again for better wages and union recognition. At the time, the average wage was a little more than $500 a year; the accident rate was terrifying; and worker's compensation was unheard of. As one owner explained: "Mining was a business . . . not a religious, sentimental, or academic proposition." The interests of the miners would be safe in the hands of "the Christian men to whom God in his infinite wisdom has given the control of the property interests of this country." The mine workers' case was so bad that leaders in other industries sided with President Theodore Roosevelt when he finally intervened.

Today organized labor is highly influential on a variety of economic and civil rights issues. On these, the labor leaders take a liberal position. But on foreign policy they are generally conservative. The largest group is the American Federation of Labor–Congress of Industrial Organizations (AFL–CIO). It represents about 14 of the 25 million workers in the labor movement and is headed by Lane Kirkland. Neither the United Mine Workers nor the United Auto Workers is affiliated with the AFL–CIO.

In recent years, as the role of heavy industry

George Tames/NYT Pictures

1604 K Street N.W.
National Small Business Association

1608 K Street
American Legion

1612 K Street
American Association of Port Authorities
American Electronics Association
American Industrial Health Council
American Maritime Association
City of San Jose
Control Data Corporation
International Trade and Investment
Korean Institute for Democracy and Unification
National Association of State Alcohol and Drug Abuse Directors
National Engineering Service
Rafshoon Communications
Rocky Mountain Energy and Trade Group

1625 K Street
American Institute of Merchant Shipping
American Recreation Coalition
Council of American Flag Ship Operators
Kerr McGee Corporation
National Association for Milk Marketing Reform
National Petroleum Council

1627 K Street
Armour & Company
Coca-Cola Company
Greyhound Corporation
Richard Helms
Institute of Scrap Iron and Steel
Wilbur D. Mills
National Newspaper Association
Northern Illinois Gas Company

1629 K Street
American Society of Home Inspectors
Americans for Energy Independence
Applied Conservation
National Federation of the Blind
U.S. Hide, Skin and Leather Association
Carnation Company
E.I. du Pont de Nemours & Company
Friends of China
General Mills
Hershey Foods Corporation
International Chemical Company
Minority Resources
Montana Power Company
Nabisco
National Association of Black Broadcast Owners
National Association of Insured Persons
National Association of School Psychologists
National Independent Retail Jewelers
National Institute of Graduate Studies
National Investor Relations Institute
National Law and Order Committee
National Organization of State Conservative Parties
National Space Club
Pflow Industries
South Dakota Industrial Development and Expansion Agency
Spra Kleen Company
Tiara Oil Company

1666 K Street
Bell Aerospace Company
Bell Helicopter Company Textron
Wilmer, Cutler & Pickering
National Police Conference

(steel, autos, coal, railroads, etc.) has shrunk in the U.S. economy, so too has labor's role. As late as 1970, about a third of the work force in the private sector was unionized. Now it is just over a quarter.

For awhile, the rapid growth of unions in the public sector slowed that shrinkage. Indeed, the fastest growing big union in the AFL–CIO is the Federation of State, County and Municipal Workers. But lately, the turn of public opinion against government as a whole has hurt public service unions. Mayors across the country (from Edward Koch in New York City to Tom Bradley in Los Angeles) reinforced their popularity by taking tough lines with municipal unions, as did President Reagan when he literally destroyed the Professional Air Traffic Controllers Organization.

Ironically, rank-and-file union members helped elect many conservative Republicans in 1980, including Ronald Reagan. A *New York Times*/CBS survey of voters leaving the polls found that Reagan got an unusually high 44 percent of the union vote. This statistic was interpreted by labor's critics as evidence of an ideological gap between members and union leaders (who supported Carter).

The year 1980 may have been a discouraging year for unions. Their membership as a percentage of total work force declined through the 1970s. They lacked, for the first time in 50 years, an inner pipeline to the national leadership. But only a poor student of history would say the American labor's future is dim. In the early years of the Depression, membership had slipped badly and the outlook seemed bad. Yet, within a year, the unions were surging ahead on the crest of Franklin Roosevelt's legislative program. By 1938, the membership had doubled.

Professional associations. Today some professional groups are experiencing the same explosive growth that the unions did in the 1930s. This is not surprising. The U.S. work force is becoming more white-collar and less blue-collar. (This trend has not escaped notice of labor unions who will be scrambling throughout the 1980s to organize white-collar workers.)

An outstanding example of the rise of professional organizations is the National Education Association (NEA). It has 1.8 million members, an annual budget of nearly $50 million, and a staff in Washington alone of over 500 people. It must be considered one of the heavyweights on the lobbyists' row. Its most decisive victory was probably getting President Carter to push for and obtain a new Department of Education in 1979.

Organizations such as the American Medical Association and the American Bar Association, meanwhile, continue to look after the economic well-being of physicians and lawyers.

"Public interest" groups. The distinguishing characteristic of these groups is that they supposedly seek goals that do not directly benefit their membership. Certainly members of the American League to Abolish Capital Punishment (ALACP) are not trying to escape the hangman's noose.

But for other groups purporting to speak in the public interest, the definition fits less neatly. The Sierra Club might advocate policies that promote clean air. Certain business groups might advocate policies that promote jobs expansion. Which good—clean air or jobs—is in the public interest, or is it really in the eye of the beholder?

One of the largest and best known public interest groups is Common Cause. In the 1970s, John W. Gardner founded this group to fix the leaking pipes of American government. Like many Americans, Gardner was disturbed by the disproportionate influence special interst groups have in the political system. (Remember the earlier illustration of how the average citizen has little incentive to fight back.)

As any amateur plumber knows, tapping and tinkering with the pipes can spring new leaks. Consider these reforms by Common Cause and their unintended consequences:[3]

Reform 1—Limit the amount an individual can contribute to a political candidate to $1,000. *Results*—The American Civil Liberties Union, one of the country's oldest public interest groups, charged that this reform is a blatant attack on the right of free speech. Candidates trying to unseat a member of Congress charged that putting a limit on how much they can spend favors the incumbent, since incumbents are generally better known than challengers. The Supreme Court ruled that independent *groups* cannot be prevented from spending money on a campaign so long as there is no collaboration between the private organization and the candidate; thus, political action committees (PACs) have grown rapidly. (PACs will be discussed in greater depth later.)

Reform 2—Change the seniority system in Congress; committee chairs will no longer be automatically appointed on the basis of seniority. *Results*—Today the chair no longer goes automatically to those who have been in office longest. But the authority in Congress is much more fragmented, and many members admit that it functions more poorly than it did before the reforms.

Reform 3—Open to the public the markup or bill-writing sessions. *Result*—Today a majority of the committees are now open to the public. But most of the people who attend are not public-spirited citizens; they are representatives of the special interest groups. Legislators find it harder to vote their consciences when lobbyists from their home states are only a few feet away.

We can also include among the public interest groups all those organizations that attempt to protect the consumer. Ralph Nader appeared on the national scene in 1965 with his book *Unsafe at Any Speed* (which focused on the Corvair, a General Motors Chevrolet model). Until then, the idea of linking consumer advocacy with political activity of average citizens was virtually unknown. From safety in automobiles, Nader moved on to a variety of other concerns. Today he himself presides over the GM of citizen action organizations (see Figure 6–2).

Public interest groups have had difficulties in organizing and maintaining dues-paying membership. They also pay relatively low salaries to their staff (which creates a high turnover). Despite this, public interest groups had considerable success in the 1970s. Some high points:

- In 1970, the Environmental Protection Agency was established to coordinate and manage federal pollution-control programs. The Occupational Safety and Health Act set federal air pollution and safety standards for the workplace.
- The federal Water Pollution Control Act of 1972 and the Safe Drinking Water Act of 1974 set standards for cleaning up the nation's water resources. As a result, the Potomac River is safe for swimming again. Lake Erie is coming back to life. And even Ohio's Cuyahoga River, which once caught fire when petroleum wastes in it ignited, shows signs of improvement.
- The Endangered Species Act of 1973 now protects American plant and animal species threatened with extinction.

Other groups. Other important interest groups can only be mentioned in passing. Groups organized to promote farm interests began to appear after the Civil War. Their most powerful voice in this century has been the American Farm Bureau Federation. Former members of the armed forces and their families are represented by the American Legion and Veterans of Foreign Wars. The Association of Community Organizations for Reform Now (A-CORN) is a community-based political action group that is active in 14 states and claims 23,000 members.

FIGURE 6–2
The Nader Network

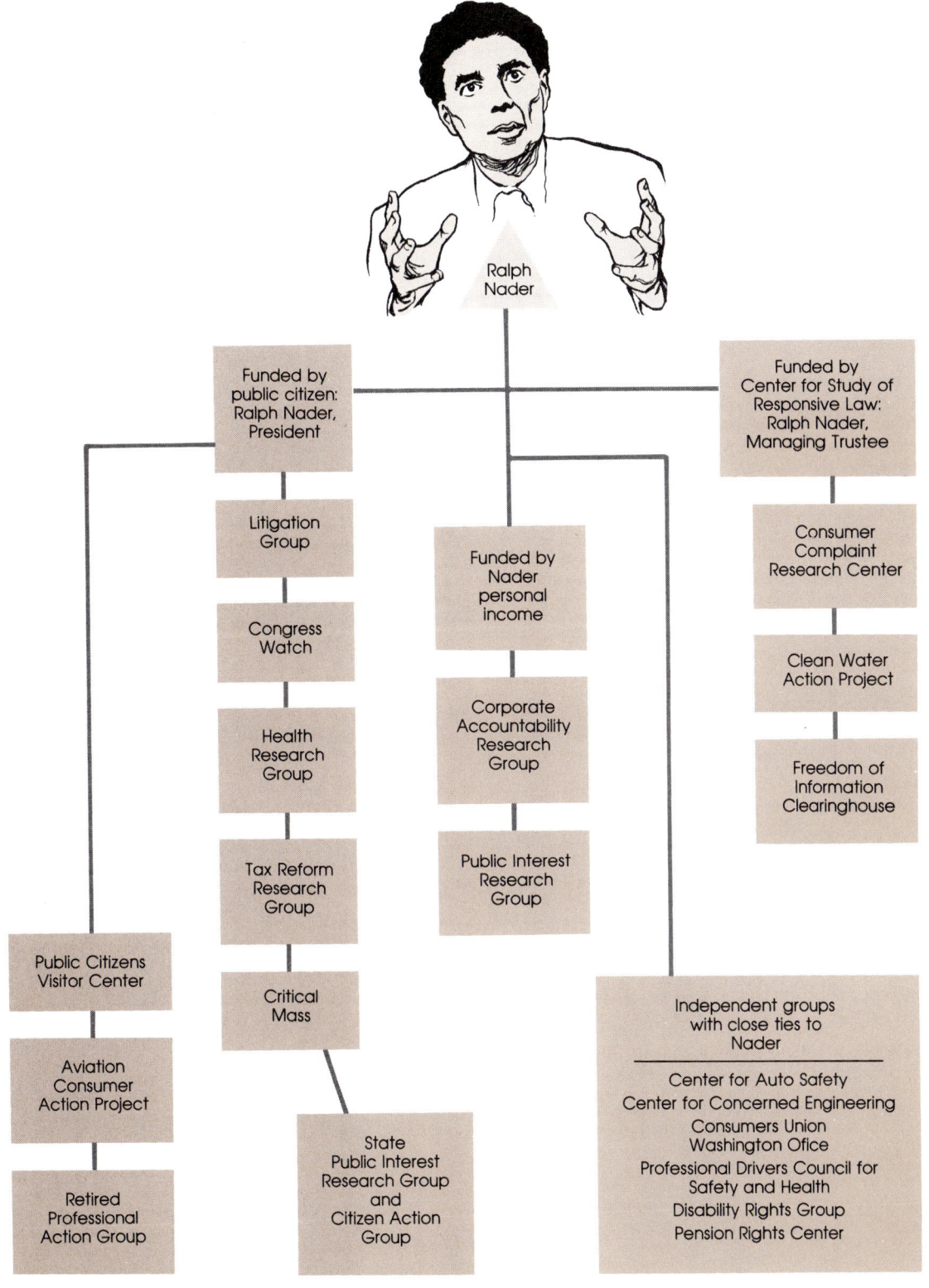

Ralph Nader

Funded by public citizen: Ralph Nader, President
- Litigation Group
- Congress Watch
- Health Research Group
- Tax Reform Research Group
- Critical Mass

- Public Citizens Visitor Center
- Aviation Consumer Action Project
- Retired Professional Action Group

Funded by Nader personal income
- Corporate Accountability Research Group
- Public Interest Research Group

- State Public Interest Research Group and Citizen Action Group

Funded by Center for Study of Responsive Law: Ralph Nader, Managing Trustee
- Consumer Complaint Research Center
- Clean Water Action Project
- Freedom of Information Clearinghouse

Independent groups with close ties to Nader
- Center for Auto Safety
- Center for Concerned Engineering
- Consumers Union Washington Office
- Professional Drivers Council for Safety and Health
- Disability Rights Group
- Pension Rights Center

Source: Randy Jones, © 1978, *New York Times*.

United Press International Photo

One of the oldest special interest groups are the farmers. In 1979, the American Agricultural Movement converged on Washington to ask for financial aid. Demonstrating with tractors, many of which were new and quite expensive, failed to arouse the compassion of the public. As pointed out in Chapter 1, there is a basic consensus in the U.S. that issues can and ought to be resolved by coalition building and compromise, not by confrontation. The consensus says that you do not ride expensive tractors down Constitution Avenue to win specific farm prices.

Representing elected governments and officials below the national level are groups that either seek assistance from the federal government on some issues or advocate that they be left free of federal interference on certain issues. Five independent organizations form the backbone of this lobby: the National Governors' Conference, the National Conference of State Legislatures, the National League of Cities, the U.S. Conference of Mayors, and the National Association of Counties.

Recently, evangelicals, or fundamentalist Christians, have abandoned their historical tendency to shy away from involvement in politics. They established a political action group known as the Moral Majority. In 1980, it registered over 2 million to vote in the fall election and its leader clearly favored Ronald Reagan, who had taken positions favored by most of their members. Finally, we must consider the special interest groups sponsored by ethnic organizations. Their influence and unique role merits a close look.

Groups Representing Minorities

Bingham's *County Election* exhibits all the social diversity of the American Political community of the early 19th century. But to the modern eye it is a remarkably incomplete picture. It contains neither women nor blacks. As this section tries to make clear, things have changed considerably.

The subject of how a political community allows for representation of its minorities and disadvantaged is particularly important. If progress is to be made in the realization of such ideals as equality and liberty (see Chapter 3), then the acid test will not be how big business and big labor are treated but rather how minorities are treated. An assessment of how well the American Republic has performed in that respect must wait until later (see Chapters 11 and 12). Below, our aim is only to describe some of the organizations that represent minorities in the political system.

Strictly speaking, any segment of the population that is not a majority (i.e., over 50 percent) is a minority. In this sense, even white Anglo-Saxon Protestants are a minority; they are only 14 percent of the population. (This is not much larger than the German-Americans' 13 percent and the blacks' 11 percent.) But because of intermixture over generations, such ethnic distinctions are probably sharper in rhetoric than in reality. For example, about 40 percent of Japanese-American men marry women who are not Japanese-American. And according to one leading social historian, tens of millions of white Americans have at least one black ancestor.[4]

Therefore, we shall use the word *minority* not in a sociological sense but rather a *political* one. Setting the numbers aside, the term *minorities* refers to blacks, Hispanics, Native Americans, and even women—who are 51 percent of the U.S. population and outnumber men by over 5 million. That might seem like a long list. But a case could be made for extending it even further to include children, old people, the handicapped, and homosexuals. For the sake of length only, we shall not.

Blacks. The statistics tell quite well the effect of the Voting Rights Act of 1965. In 1964 only 41 percent of adult blacks in the South reported ever having voted; in 1972 black registration in the South was 64 percent. Blacks, who now vote nationwide at about 90 percent of the rate of whites, are a decisive force in all presidential elections. (At comparable levels of income and education as whites, they participate *more* than their white counterparts.)

Moreover, black representation, both in elective office and top levels of government administration, has increased dramatically since 1964. There were virtually no elected black officials in 1965. Blacks now elect about 4,000 annually; there are 16 in Congress. But representation still remains proportionately small.

The long struggle for civil rights produced organizations as well as laws such as the Voting Rights Act of 1965. The first major black organization established in this century was the National Association for the Advancement of Colored People (NAACP) in 1909. Two years later the Urban League was established. In 1942, the Congress of Racial Equality was formed to concentrate on nonviolent direct action. In 1955, a black woman named Rosa Parks took a seat in the "whites only" front section of a public bus in Montgomery, Alabama. When she was arrested, Martin Luther King, Jr., and a coalition of church groups called the Southern Christian Leadership Conference (SCLC) organized a yearlong bus boycott.

The civil rights struggle also produced more radical protest groups, such as the Student Nonviolent Coordinating Committee, which was organized in 1960, and the black power movement of the 1960s. The latter included the black nationalism of the late Malcolm X and the armed militancy of the Black Panthers. More recent developments include black self-help movements, such as those under the Reverend Jesse Jackson, once a lieutenant of Dr. King. To Jackson, educational achievement is indispensable to the black struggle for equality. When campaigning among poor blacks his message is: "We have to pull ourselves up by our brains." For example, his program called PUSH for Excellence attempts to bring parents into the educational process in inner city schools.

By the early 1980s, it appeared that a new matrix of black leadership was developing. The traditional civil rights leaders and legislators continue to apply political pressure. But also, management-oriented blacks tend the social and economic needs of the community. And innovators like Jackson advise blacks to prepare for developing opportunities.

Hispanics: The weak giant. The term *Hispanic* is a label of convenience that includes Mexican-Americans (60 percent of the total), Puerto Ricans, Cubans, and Latin Americans. Some, like Cubans and Latin Americans, came to the United States as political exiles and refugees. Others, like Mexican-Americans, can claim ancestors who were in what is the United States before the colonists.

Some of these subgroups that go under the Hispanic label are themselves made up of differing factions. Mexican-Americans divide into those of Spanish, those of Indian, and those of long-established Mexican-American descent. This group also divides along the lines of those who call themselves *Chicano* and those who will not.* Puerto Ricans range in color from

---

* The major complaint against *Chicano*, a title that had its heyday in the "brown power" movement of the 1960s, is that it is offensive and derogatory—a term used only by lower-class Mexican-Americans. Some resent being lumped into a class of people that includes uneducated farm workers and street people. The origins of the term are not clear. But one theory suggests that it evolved out of the Spaniards' efforts to degrade the natives by referring to them as *chicos* (meaning small boys).

Whatever the origin, I know of no simpler term to refer to a person who is a native of the United States but whose ancestry can be traced to Mexico. Moreover, the contemporary Mexican term used derogatorily to describe Mexicans who are Americanized is not *Chicano* but *rocho*.

Wide World Photos

The focus of groups in the black struggle for equality has become more diverse in recent years. Black-owned banks provide mortgage loans to blacks; older organizations, such as the NAACP, continue to press political demands; and social innovators like Jesse Jackson (second from right, demonstrating in front of the White House) provide moral leadership, help prepare poor blacks for new opportunities, and demand more jobs from government. Demonstrations by interest groups are almost a daily occurrence in Washington, D.C.

blond to black—and discriminate among themselves accordingly.

Whatever the difficulty in finding a single voice, the fact is that Hispanics are the nation's youngest and fastest-growing minority. They will soon outnumber blacks. Today, one in five Texans is of Mexican origin; in some counties, their proportion is as high as 98 percent. The second largest "Mexican" city after Mexico City itself is not Monterrey or Guadalajara; it is Los Angeles, with 1.5 million Mexican-Americans. According to some projections, Mexican-Americans should constitute a majority of California's population by the end of the 1980s. The growth in Hispanics is not, however, a phenomenon of the Southwest. More Hispanics live in New Jersey than Arizona; and there are more Spanish-speaking people in Massachussetts than there are blacks. Despite these impressive figures, representation in both national and state government remains weak.

Several organizations represent Hispanics. The League of United Latin American Citizens (LULAC), founded in 1929, seeks assimilation into the mainstream of American life. The 3,000-member Mexican-American Political Association (MAPA) was founded in the 1960s. The La Raza Unida Party, founded in 1969, stresses chicanoismo rather than assimilation. No Hispanic Martin Luther King has yet appeared. But probably their best-known leader is Ceasar Chavez, who organized the United Farm Workers in California.

Because of the high birth and immigration rates, Hispanic political power is almost certain to increase. Already Hispanics swing many important elections. Some argue that, to the extent they delivered Texas to Carter in 1976, they made his presidential victory possible. Still, their voting runs about half the rate of *anglos*.

Hispanics take the blacks' progress in political and economic life as a model. But because Hispanics were never enslaved and oppressed like the blacks, the nation as a whole cannot as easily be made to feel responsible. For the second minority in line, help from government and sympathy from fellow citizens is less forthcoming. The hardship of the migrant farmworker or dishwasher simply does not fix the national attention like the distant echo of a whip on a man's back and the disease, famine, and extermination of Indians.

Native Americans. When the Pilgrims arrived at Plymouth Rock in 1620, millions of Indians were in the United States; by 1900, only 245,000 remained. What had happened during those 280 years is not an uplifting story.

Today the birthrate is back up, and there are probably about one million Indians in the United States. About half of these live around the 267 reservations that occupy 2 percent of the United States land.

On June 30, 1980, the Supreme Court of the United States awarded $122.5 million to the Sioux people because in 1877 Congress had taken 7 million acres in the Black Hills region of South Dakota from the Sioux without fair compensation.* The event was not unusual for Indians have become legal activists.

The event was interesting from a legal standpoint. When the average American buys a house, he or she must have a title search. This means that a lawyer looks back through the records of the last few decades, but certainly not to 1877. Why not? The answer is found in the **statutes of limitations.** Several decades is considered sufficient lapse of time to invalidate any claims automatically. But tribal Indian claims are exempt from the statutes of limitations. Their claims are based on the historical fact that Indians exercised independent sovereignty before the United States took control of their territory.

It is useful to think of the relationship between the federal government and Indians as evolving through several phases.[5] The first phase was one of *autonomy;* that is, tribes were allowed to exist as small self-governing nations. Since Indians did present a serious military threat at the time, this policy made some sense. But that threat ended ignominiously in the fall of 1890 near the reservation town of Pine Ridge, South Dakota. There, the Seventh Cavalry—the same regiment that was destroyed 14 years earlier under the command of General George Armstrong Custer at Little Bighorn—annihilated a band of 200 Sioux, including women and children.

In the second phase, *assimilation,* the federal government began to view the tribal Indians as primitive, childlike wards. Indian reservations were chopped up for sale to whites. Indian children were enrolled in schools designed to turn them from their ancestral ways.

The third phase, begun in the Eisenhower years (1953–61), was one of *termination.* Special programs and benefits by the Bureau of Indian Affairs (BIA) and privileges stemming from tribal status were cut back. Native Americans, so the reasoning ran, had learned to live in white society.

The fourth phase is *activism.* Tribes have begun to seek aggressively long-lost rights and legal distinctions. At the same time, they have reemphasized their ancestry. The long-range result of this latest phase could be the emergence of geographically separate enclaves, sometimes operating contrary to national goals. For example, in 1977 some tribes, settling on reservations rich in national resources (e.g., timber, oil, coal, uranium, and water), began direct discussion with OPEC nations. The white man had pushed the Indian onto this land, where few white men could possibly survive. But the Indian had fooled him. He survived and, in the last few years, began to prosper.

How far can Indians go in exploiting these assets? Will the federal government allow for enclaves of quasi-international communities to exist at a time of increasing scarcity? Who should be responsible for the cost of righting ancient wrongs? Should thousands of non-Indians have to face the possibility of losing their homes or business as federal courts decide the merits of complicated Indian land claims? Clearly, some balance must be found between these claims. In addition, the federal government must develop policies to accommodate the differing aspirations of Indians. Not all find the idea of going back to the reservation very attractive.

Women. The women's movement for equality did not begin with quite the explosive force of a cannon. But it can be said to have begun in 1776. Abigail Adams, married to a man who played a leading part in the American Revolution and who became the second president of the United States, exemplified what it meant to be a woman, an American, and a revolutionary. As her thousands of letters show, she was an independent married woman. She reflected constantly and carefully on her life and the life of her country. Her conclusion: Women in republican America had an impor-

---

* Some time earlier the Sioux had taken that land from the Cheyenne, presumably without compensation.

tant and special role, different from the European notion of womanhood.

Abigail Adams urged her husband John in writing a new code of laws to "remember the ladies and be more generous and favorable to them than your ancestors."[6] She urged the founding fathers to promote education and equality for women. **Enfranchisement,** though—i.e., acquisition of the rights of citizenship (especially voting rights)—seemed to her beyond reasonable hope. And then she gave a warning: "If particular care and attention is not paid to the ladies, we are determined to foment a rebellion, and will not hold ourselves bound by any laws in which we have no voice, or representation."[7]

In the early history of the republic, the main thrust of the women's movement was towards the abolition of slavery, then towards **suffrage**—i.e., the right to vote. The first breakthrough came shortly after the Civil War, when Wyoming granted suffrage to women. Unfortunately for the suffragettes, as they were called, few states followed suit. Agitation intensified in the early part of the 20th century, culminating in the 19th Amendment in 1920.

Today, voting turnout among women is about equal to that of white men, except in the South. Nationwide, however, women hold only 5 percent of all elective offices; in the federal government they hold only 2.3 percent of high-level jobs.

The woman's movement now consists of a variety of organizations. The National Congress of Neighborhood Women is made up of poorer women, predominantly from cities. In contrast, the National Organization of Women (NOW) was established in 1966 and consists mostly of white middle-class women. NOW is particularly concerned with the adoption of the Equal Rights Amendment (ERA) and elimination of job and pay discrimination.

In the early 1980s, the women's movement began to shift its forces quietly from these traditional concerns to the effects of the nation's economic problems—inflation, unemployment, and recession (see Chapter 13)—on women. The adoption of the ERA does remain a central theme for women's groups. But its leaders think economic strains affect women more adversely than men. Consequently, they require greater attention. Some groups—such as the National Women's Political Caucus and the Women's Legal Defense Fund—see federally financed abortions as an economic issue.

Not all women's groups are of like mind on these issues. A number of women, especially those active in politics, would like to see the abortion issue muted. Phyllis Schlafly is national chairman of Stop ERA, the major opposition to the Equal Rights Amendment.

Tactics

From the preceding discussion, you probably already have some notion of how interest groups try to influence public policy. The paragraphs below will highlight these tactics and possibly introduce you to some nuances you were not aware of.

Litigation. Despite periodic fuel shortages along the East Coast, the last major refinery built there was in 1957. Oil companies have tried and failed more than 30 times. The reason is that interest groups have become skilled at using **litigation** in the forms of court action against the companies.

The Environmental Defense Fund works to prevent cancer by identifying carcinogens and eliminating the public's exposure to them. EDP has sued the Environmental Protection Agency to compel its implementation of the Safe Drinking Water Act and to control discharge of 65 toxic chemicals into U.S. waterways. It has obtained a court order requiring the EPA to meet a deadline in setting standards for the disposal of highly toxic chemical wastes.

Such groups often file *amicus curiae* (friend of the court) briefs to assist the court in arriving at a decision. The **class action** lawsuit makes it possible for a citizen to bring a case into court on behalf of *all* persons who would directly benefit from the court decision. Many interest groups have been quick to take advantage of this tactic. Suppose, for example, you think your utility company is overcharging you. Not many lawyers would take your case; there is no money in it. But if you bring a class action suit against the utility on behalf of 5,000 citizens who have been overcharged, lawyers might see matters differently. (One of the most famous class action cases was the 1954 *Brown* school desegregation decision of the Supreme Court, discussed in Chapter 11.)

Public relations campaign. The better-financed interest groups, and here we must certainly include those representing various business interests, can conduct campaigns to influence public opinion in directions favorable to their cause. After using names that obscure the sponsors, they advertise and provide speakers and films. For example, critics of the oil industry called several years ago for the big companies to be split up; the American Petroleum Institute provided counterarguments based on economic analysis.

Grass-roots pressure. A number of interest groups encourage their members to exert pressure on government policymakers by mail, telegraph, telephone, and visits. The right combination of these approaches will presumably convince the political representatives that the groups cause has broad appeal.

Major U.S. corporations are becoming increasingly active politically as they seek to influence federal decisions bearing on their business interests. There are many examples. A $1.6 billion manufacturing company sends mailings to its thousands of shareholders asking them to write their congressmen on specific political issues. A tire and rubber company tells its managers that so-called grassroots political activity has become part of their job, to be included in future appraisals of their performance.

Lobbying. Most interest groups have full-time employees who concentrate on trying to speak directly and convincingly to government policymakers at both state and federal levels in both executive and legislative branches. Once they gain access, what do they say? They try to get people sympathetic to their cause appointed to administrative positions. And they provide arguments for legislation they favor and against legislation they oppose. Success in these endeavors is a function of the size of the group, the narrowness of focus, the geographic distribution of its members (the wider, the better), and the quality of information it provides.

The term *lobbying* has a slightly evil connotation. But lobbyists do interject information and new ideas into the policymaking process. Therefore, they are probably essential to the proper working of government. For that reason, we shall take a closer look at the subject of lobbying in Chapter 8.

Political campaign activity. Along with lobbying, the other principal tactic of interest groups is to help the "right" people get elected.

In 1974, Common Cause and other reform-minded groups got Congress to pass legislation to regulate campaign financing. The result was the **Federal Election Campaign Act,** also known as the Campaign Reform Act. Two years later, the Supreme Court declared a few of the act's provisions unconstitutional. (For instance, limits were set on the amount an individual could contribute to his or her own campaign.)

Here is what the act, with subsequent amendments, does. First, it sets up a federal election commission to enforce the law. Second, the act limits the contributions of individual citizens to $1,000 in each federal election or primary and to no more than $25,000 altogether. Groups can contribute up to $5,000 to a candidate in any election. Third, it provides public financing for presidential elections and general elections; and if a candidate accepts this aid, the act limits their campaign expenditure. Finally, the act requires periodic reports to the federal election commission, listing who contributed how much.

Although the act reduced the amount wealthy individuals could contribute, it in effect encouraged the explosive growth of **political**

action committees (PACs). Technically, a PAC is the political arm of an interest group. It is legally entitled to raise funds, on a voluntary basis, from members, stockholders, or employees. These funds are then given to candidates or political parties. The general idea is to help elect candidates who view favorably the groups' goals. But this is not always the case. Often the idea is simply to keep the lines of communications open, to insure access. Thus business groups will contribute to certain influential members of Congress whose record is anything but pro-business.

In the 1980 election, business interests dominated campaign contributions to both Democratic and Republican congressional leaders. They far surpass the donations of the once-dominant labor interests. According to the federal election commission, business interests in 1980 gave close to $30 million to all congressional candidates. That was double what labor gave. Only four years earlier, labor political action committees outspent business interests, $8.2 million to $7.1 million. This proliferation of business-related PACs is evident in Figure 6–3.

FIGURE 6–3
Political Action Committee Growth

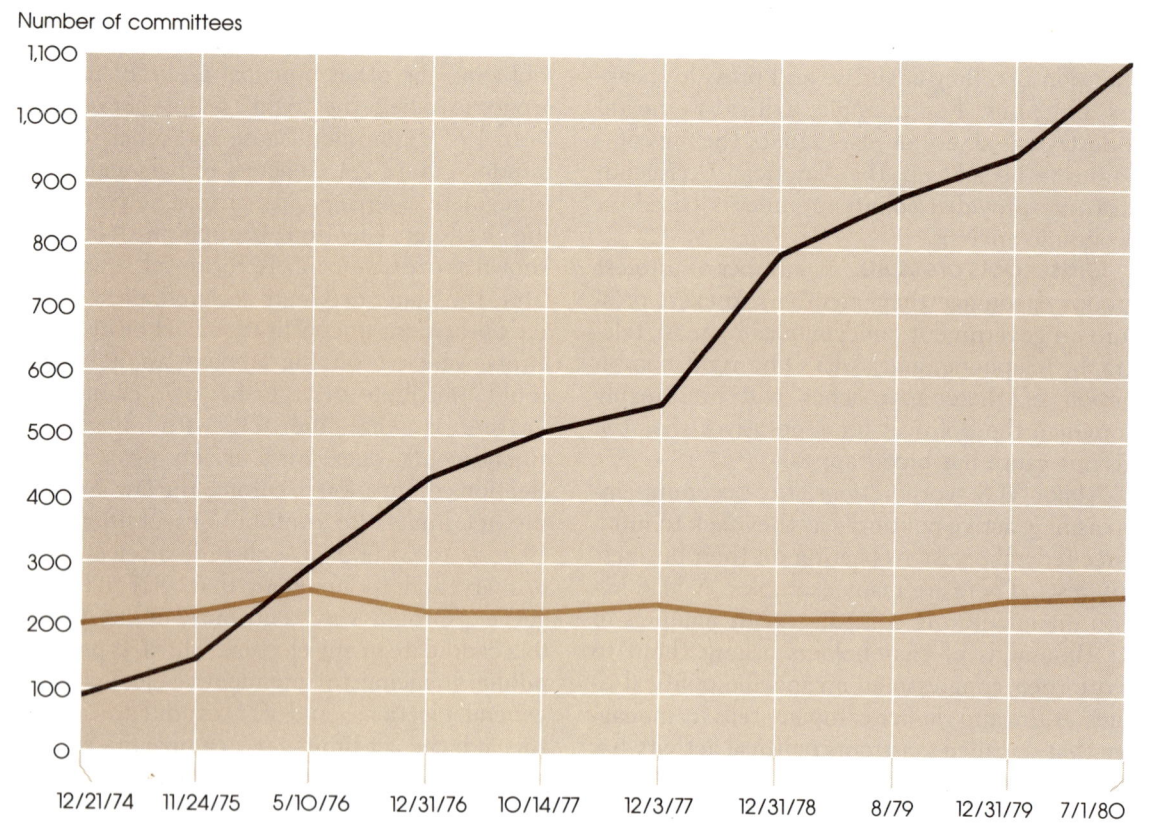

Key: Black line = business; color line = labor.
* Date of Federal Election Commission ruling allowing use of corporate funds to set up and operate political action committees.
Source: Federal Election Commission data.

This section described the various types of interest groups. We also examined the tactics these groups employ and the power they wield. A major criticism of these groups, noted at the start, is that they tend to fragment government along narrow, specialized issues. In such a system, unorganized segments of the population lack fair representation.

There is more than a shred of truth in this criticism. But a couple of points should be kept in mind. First, American politics has been shaken by special interests at a number of points throughout its history—by abolitionist, suffragettes, prohibitionists, and others. Special interest politics is really nothing new. Second, those people who are unrepresented by interest groups still can look to other, less fragmented institutions in the American political system.

Three of these—the president, the bureaucracy, and the courts—will be the subject of later chapters. But one of them is the subject of the next section—the political party.

POLITICAL PARTIES

Functions

One could argue that parties are inseparable from free government to the extent they help organize public opinion. Without parties, citizens would face a long, confusing list of candidates at election time. Parties provide labels for candidates and define the policies those candidates stand for; they make it easier to choose (see box).

Republicans and Democrats—Is There Any Difference?

The labels *Democrat* or *Republican* are sometimes poor guides to the opinion of candidates who wear them. The failure of voters to perceive any sharp differences between the two has probably contributed to the weakening of both parties.

Since Franklin Roosevelt was elected in 1932, the Democratic party generally has been thought to stand for an active government role in managing the economy and providing welfare. The Republican party, or Grand Old Party (G.O.P.), has generally been thought to stand for a limited government role in managing the economy and providing social services. To let the parties speak for themselves, one need only turn to the **platforms**. These are statements of principles (or "planks") trumpeted by a party that are used during a campaign to win votes. The Democratic party, according to its 1956 platform, "is marked by a strong belief in the power of collective action to promote social justice, equality, humanitarianism, and economic planning." The Republican party "is distinguished by faith in the wisdom of the natural competitive process and in the supreme virtue of individuals, 'character,' self-reliance, frugality, and independence from government." The platforms 24 years later had become even more sharply divergent. Summaries of the major planks appear below.

If asked, "What is the major fault of your party?" how might a candid Republican or Democrat respond? The former might admit that the Republican party has failed to establish a rapport with enough other groups in society. The percentage of blacks professing to be Republican should be cause for a close self-examination. If the G.O.P. is not the party of the privileged, many certainly perceive it to be.

The problems of the Democratic party are of a different sort. After nearly a half century as the governing party, it seems at the moment lost, without a purpose or philosophy. The problem is not unrecognized—which is good. Indeed, the guests you see with Dick Cavett (beginning of Chapter 5) are all Democrats discussing whether the party still has a philosophy.

		Democratic Platform	*Republican Platform*
1.	The economy	"The need to guarantee a job for every American who is able to work . . . is our highest domestic priority."	"Unless taxes are reduced and federal spending is restrained, our nation's economy faces continued inflation, recession and economic stagnation."
2.	Energy	"Conservation is the cheapest form of energy production."	Emphasizes energy production over conservation.
3.	Welfare	Propose that the federal government assume the state and local burden of welfare costs, reject reductions in programs for the needy.	"The Democratic Congress has produced a jumble of degrading, dehumanizing, wasteful, overlapping, and inefficient programs that invite waste and fraud but inadequately assist the needy poor."
4.	Defense	Pledges a 3 percent increase in defense spending.	They commit themselves to achieving "military and technological superiority over the Soviet Union" and will "accept no arms control agreement . . . which locks the U.S. into a position of military inferiority."
5.	Women's rights	The party vows to ensure passage of the Equal Rights Amendment and opposes efforts to rescind earlier ratification.	Ratification is now in the hands of state legislatures, which have a "constitutional right to accept or reject [it] without federal interference or pressure."
6.	abortion	Rejects any constitutional amendment banning abortion and opposes restrictions that deny poor women government funding for abortions.	Calls for a constitutional amendment to protect "the right to life for unborn children" and supports curbs on public funding for abortion.

Later in the chapter we shall be looking at how political parties select presidential candidates through the nomination process. In the two chapters that follow, we shall see how parties provide a mechanism for coordinating both within and between the executive and legislative branches.

Accepting the premise that parties are particularly effective—if not the only effective—way of organizing public opinion, the question becomes why two rather than, say, six parties. The answer is that, when a nation always has one major party in power and another one out, the chances for turnover in government tend to increase; an inherent cleaning process is set in motion. Moreover, the party out of power can be expected to be always watching—that is, keeping honest and responsive—the party in power. The "outs" will also be advancing new programs and ideas in the hopes of regaining office.

The question of why two rather than five or six parties can also be answered in a negative way. Two-party systems increase the chances that the party in power will have sufficient popular support to rule. When the citizens' support is spread too thinly, the party in power finds its ability to advance bold solutions to big new problems severely restricted.

Why the Two-Party System?

Origins. The founding fathers viewed parties with suspicion. The Constitution is silent about them. To James Monroe, the fifth president, parties were "the curse of the country."

Nevertheless, Americans formed political alliances with the founding of the republic. Today's Democratic party can trace its roots to Jefferson's Democratic-Republicans, who opposed Hamilton's Federalists (see Figure 6–4). At Jefferson Day dinners, however, modern Democrats do not quote Jefferson's definitive statement on parties: "If I could not go to

FIGURE 6-4
The Evolution of American Parties—"Building Coalitions in the Sand"

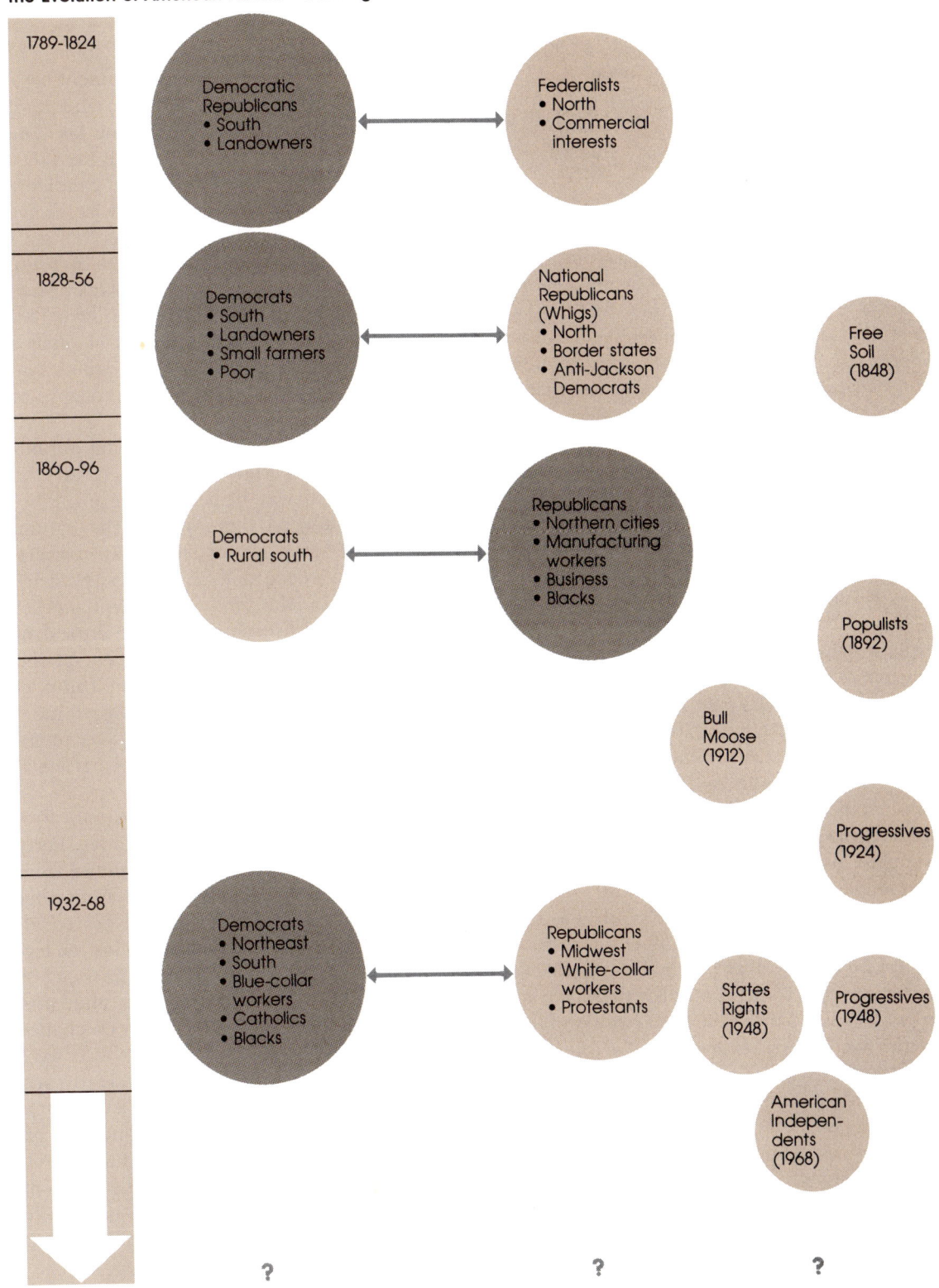

1789-1824

Democratic Republicans
- South
- Landowners

↔

Federalists
- North
- Commercial interests

1828-56

Democrats
- South
- Landowners
- Small farmers
- Poor

↔

National Republicans (Whigs)
- North
- Border states
- Anti-Jackson Democrats

Free Soil (1848)

1860-96

Democrats
- Rural south

↔

Republicans
- Northern cities
- Manufacturing workers
- Business
- Blacks

Populists (1892)

Bull Moose (1912)

Progressives (1924)

1932-68

Democrats
- Northeast
- South
- Blue-collar workers
- Catholics
- Blacks

↔

Republicans
- Midwest
- White-collar workers
- Protestants

States Rights (1948)

Progressives (1948)

American Independents (1968)

? ? ?

Note: Darker circle indicates the dominant party.

Heaven but with a party, I would not go there at all." The Republican party, meanwhile, can trace its roots back to 1854 and the turmoil over slavery. Indeed, Bingham's *County Election*, which introduced this chapter, was painted about this time.

Despite periodic realignments, the two-party system has continued to dominate American politics. In contrast, the politics of most European countries (Great Britain is an exception) involves a host of small parties that can win elections and influence public policy. Political scientist V.O. Key, Jr., explains this difference by pointing to the general consensus that accompanied this nation's formative years. Many older European countries had over the centuries developed deep divisions along religious, social, and geographic lines. But the United States never had to go through the throes of a Reformation, the exploitation of an insensitive nobility, or the arbitrary reshuffling of boundaries after a war.

The woes of third parties. This does not explain why other parties in later years failed to emerge and play a major, continuing role in American politics. As of 1980, every president for the preceding 120 years was elected as a candidate of one or other of the two major parties. Maine was the only state with an independent governor. Of the 7,458 members of state legislatures, all but six are Democrats or Republicans (excluding Nebraska's nonpartisan assembly).

As can easily be seen in Figure 6-4, third parties have emerged a number of times in American history. But they fail to survive. Or, if they survive, they fail to play any major role in political life. Two of the most successful third parties were the Populist Party of the 1890s and the Progressive Party at the beginning of the twentieth century.

In the early 1890s, farmers, workers, and small businessmen of the West and South organized a party to protest falling prices, lack of money for investment, poor marketing facilities, and crop failures. The Populist Party, or People's Party, advocated unlimited coinage of silver, plenty of paper money, government ownership of all forms of transportation and communication, and a graduated income tax (i.e., the more one earns, the higher the tax rate). James B. Weaver ran as the Populist candidate for president in 1892 and managed to receive over a million votes. The party carried ten seats in the House and five in the Senate. In 1896, the Democratic party adopted the plank of free coinage of silver and nominated William Jennings Bryan for president. Bryan's eloquence captured the bulk of the Populist votes and thereby helped to bring about the collapse of the party.

But some of the more fundamental notions of the Populist Party have persisted. At the core of **populism** was the belief in the possibility of permanent good times and in the natural harmony of social classes (especially farmers, craftsmen, workers, and small businessmen), marred only by the temporary dominance of rich elites. Populism is remarkably critical of the American economic system in general and rejects some key aspects of capitalism. But populism counterbalances its faith in a bigger, more activist government with various devices to ensure greater democratic control and participation.

If the Populists were mainly rural, Progressives were urban. The Progressive Party (also called the Bull Moose Party) split off from the Republicans in 1912. Under the leadership of Theodore Roosevelt, the party advocated advanced (or progressive) social and industrial legislation such as regulation of big business, child labor laws, and female suffrage. In sum, **progressivism** itself was a general tide of change that washed up from cities (where efforts were taken to run government more efficiently and honestly) to the state and federal level. After 1916 they gradually went into decline, though the party attempted revivals in 1924 and 1948.

George Wallace's American Independent party in 1968 is another example of a third party that played a key role in a national election but did not survive. The Prohibition party, founded in 1872, and the Socialist Labor Party, organized in 1877, are examples of third parties that have survived but have never played a key role in elections. In 1980 residents of some states had their choice of half a dozen or more presidential candidates.

The reasons for this short life span of third parties are fairly clear. First, at least one of the two major parties may quickly move to seize the third party's key issue. As George Wallace, the American Independent party candidate in 1968, said, "The third party candidates don't get elected, but their ideas do." Indeed, the two major party candidates that year, Richard Nixon and Hubert Humphrey, not only absorbed Wallace's antigovernment stance. They also absorbed the peace platform of Eugene McCarthy, the antiwar candidate in 1968.

A second reason third parties do not fare well is a not too closely kept secret: The deck is stacked against them. The previously mentioned federal election laws provide for reimbursement of campaign expenses after the election if one receives at least 5 percent of the total vote. The catch is that the third party candidate must compete for that 5 percent under the handicap of rules that limit individual contribution to $1,000. Meanwhile, the government (which, remember, is controlled by the two major parties) has already given each party over $29 million for their campaigns. It is the law. And there are other laws to vex third parties. Federal regulation of the airwaves demands that the stations cover "significant" candidates. But to become a "significant" candidate one needs radio and television exposure.

Finally, and most fundamentally, the Constitution itself encourages two-party politics. One key institutional feature is the single-member legislative district. In each congressional district, only one individual is elected to the legislature. The candidate who gets the most votes in the district wins the legislative seat. This system discourages lasting third-party movements; it gives nothing at all to anybody but the winner—in short, winner takes all. Only a party that has a chance of getting the most votes has any reason for existence. To avoid "throwing their vote away," supporters of third-party candidates tend to switch to one of major party candidates as election day draws near.

(Countries like France and Israel—with **multiparty systems,** i.e., more than two major parties—usually use a system based on **proportional representation.** This is a method of allocating legislative seats to each party in accordance with its share of the total number of votes. Under proportional representation, a party that received only 10 percent of the vote would still get 10 percent of the seats. Proportional representation provides an incentive for splinter groups to persevere. And sometimes they form a coalition government with a larger party when no party gets a majority of the seats in the legislature.)

Party Structure

Figure 6–5 might give you the impression that the parties are as tightly organized. Actually, what we have here is not really a pyramid but a pile of stones shaped like a pyramid. According to one recent count, there were 58,000 separate Democratic or Republican bodies. Moreover, the parties have no dues-paying members, no established bureaucracy, and weak central authority.

The authority of parties, such as it is, derives from selected party members, or **delegates.** They gather from all over the country every four years. At these **national conventions,** they adopt party rules, draft a platform, and nominate candidates for president and vice president.

Control in parties flows from the bottom up rather than top down. Therefore let us begin our inspection of Figure 6–5 at the base. *Since states and parties vary in their organization, the following discussion should be considered as a generalized view.*

Quiz
Name these men

Wide World Photos  United Press International Photo  United Press International Photo

Answers on p. 221.

Precinct, ward, and city. **Precincts** are administrative subdivisions of cities and counties set up for the conduct of elections. The basic unit of the major parties is usually the biennial precinct caucus. This is simply a meeting of all the voters of that party who live in the precinct and care to attend. Attendance at the caucuses is usually (though not always) light. For example, a couple of dozen people out of 500 who vote for that party may bother to attend.

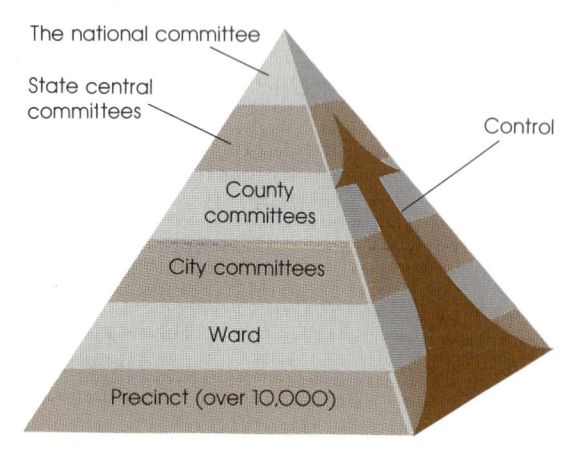

The precinct caucus elects a precinct captain. He or she is responsible for carrying on the party's work in that precinct over the next two years. Despite the growing importance of the electronic media (discussed in Chapter 5), reaching people on a personal basis remains the most effective way of winning votes. This fact makes the precinct captain and block workers, who are responsible for voters in a single block of the precinct, important.

In addition to electing the captain, the precinct caucus selects delegates to represent it at the ward caucus. The **ward** is, of course, the next largest subdivision. It incorporates anywhere from 6 to over 30 precincts. (In some cities, the wards are the districts from which city council members are elected.)

FIGURE 6-5
Party Organization

- The national committee
- State central committees
- Control
- County committees
- City committees
- Ward
- Precinct (over 10,000)

The ward caucuses are often held in the same night as the precinct caucuses. They elect delegates to the county conventions and choose the ward chairman. Sometimes ward caucuses discuss issues of city politics, pass resolutions, and provide instructions for delegates to higher caucuses.

The county convention normally lasts all day. It adopts resolutions on government policies and endorses candidates. Often there is no primary where voters can directly vote for their party's nominee for local government offices (e.g., sheriff and state representative). The caucus itself would then make the nomination. Even more likely, it will elect delegates to the state convention and members to the county central committee. The latter is the party's governing body for the next two years, that is, until the next county convention. Ordinarily the central committee will elect a key figure in county and possibly state politics—the county chairman.

State and national conventions. The state convention runs two or three days. It adopts a state platform, endorses or nominates candidates for statewide office, and elects the highest committee in the state—the state central committee. The committee, which can consist of over 100 members, is responsible for all statewide campaigns, fund raising, and party programs. Ordinarily, it chooses a state chairman and an executive committee for day-to-day activities.

Both parties have a national committee composed of one man and one woman from each of the 50 states, the District of Columbia, and territories. The Republican National Committee, however, adds state chairmen from all states carried by the party in the preceding election. Most states pick committee members at their state conventions.

The powers of the **national chairman** are rather modest. During the campaign, the chairman must compete with the president's own campaign staff and the congressional campaign committees. Between elections, the party is in effect run by the White House (if the party is in there) or by the party leaders in Congress (if the party lost the presidential election). Finally, the chairman's power is diluted by the leaders of various other groups loosely affiliated with his party—for example, the Americans for Democratic Action (Democratic) and Americans for Conservative Action (Republican).

In the early 1970s, both parties initiated reforms to answer the charge that minorities were not adequately represented and that the presidential nominating process was overly influenced by party bosses. In 1972, for the first time, a majority of delegates to the national conventions were picked by voters themselves in direct primaries. This was instead of by state conventions or party leaders. In 1976, the proportion of elected delegates increased to three fourths. In 1980, it rose even higher.

The ordinary voters, rather than party loyalists, now have the loudest voice in choosing the party's nominee. Have these and other changes enhanced or weakened the party system? Some experts think that choosing delegates without regard to their commitment to the party means vesting control over a party in persons who may have little concern for it.

The remainder of this chapter will examine the role political parties play in one of the most important, most exciting, and most confusing aspects of American politics—electing a president.

ELECTING A PRESIDENT

The Electoral System: An Overview

Empty ritual, act of piety, or whatever, the fact remains that the United States is one of the most "electoral" political systems in the world. The number of state and local offices filled by the ballot in America amazes Europeans. Each state chooses its governor and state legislators at the polls; some choose their judges in this manner. Some states also choose important cabinet officers and trivial state officials at the polls. Cities and towns choose every official from mayor to coroner at the polls. Finally, residents of special districts decide at the polls who will represent them on local matters concerning education, water supply, flood control, and the like.

The elections that attract the most interest, however, are for national office. These elections are held at fixed intervals established by the Constitution. A president and vice president are elected every four years. Members of the House are picked every two years. And one third of the members of the Senate voted in every six. In many European democracies this is not quite how things work. In Britain, for instance, general elections must occur at least once every five years. But since the date is not fixed, they may occur much more frequently.

The process of electing candidates for all these office varies from state to state. But generalizations are possible. Most states require that a potential candidate first circulate petitions to be signed by a specified number of registered voters. Then the petition is presented to the appropriate official. This legal act of declaring one's candidacy for public office is called **filing**. It serves to limit the race to serious candidates.

Next, the candidate runs against other candidates of his or her party for the office in a direct primary. These primaries may be either **open** to all voters or **closed** to those who are not party members. In the event no candidate receives a majority of the vote, many southern states require that a **runoff primary** be held for the top two candidates. Most American electoral laws, however, provide for winning by a **plurality vote**. That is, whoever has the most votes among the candidates wins. (This may be even though that candidate has only 30 percent of the total vote.)

Now that the candidate has secured the party nomination, the campaign to win the **general election** begins. It is in this election that voters make their final choice in selecting their public officials. States hold congressional, state, and county elections in the even-numbered years and presidential elections every four years. Typically, these elections are held in November; some states, though, elect some state officials and judges in odd-numbered years, frequently in the spring. Special elections may be called at irregular intervals.

Turning now to the way Americans select presidents, we find things really get complicated. The simplest way to demystify the process is to think of it in terms of how it is presented in Figure 6–6.

The Primary Road

Anywhere from one to two years before Election Day, a candidate will begin to travel around the country getting "exposure." At the same time, he or she tries to raise money and build a staff. Eventually, a formal declaration is made announcing one's candidacy.

The apparent need for an early start concerns some political observers. David Broder of the *Washington Post* has even suggested a "law": "Anybody who wants the presidency so much that he'll spend two years organizing and campaigning for it is not to be trusted with the office."[8] The extraordinarily heavy commitment of time tends to preclude governors and U.S. senators, two traditional sources of political leadership. It explains how Jimmy Carter could capture the Democratic nomination before the 1976 convention and Reagan could do the same well before the Republican convention of 1980. They were, in effect, unemployed.

Soon after the declaration of candidacy, the grind begins. The number of state primaries has mushroomed from 7 in 1960 to 17 in 1968 to 37 in 1980. The rules for primaries vary from state to state and party to party. In general, citizens vote in their party's primary to elect either directly or indirectly (by showing a preference for a presidential candidate) delegates to the national convention. In the past, whole delegations from states occasionally would get to the convention uncommitted. That is, they were not pledged to any of the

**FIGURE 6-6
Running for President**

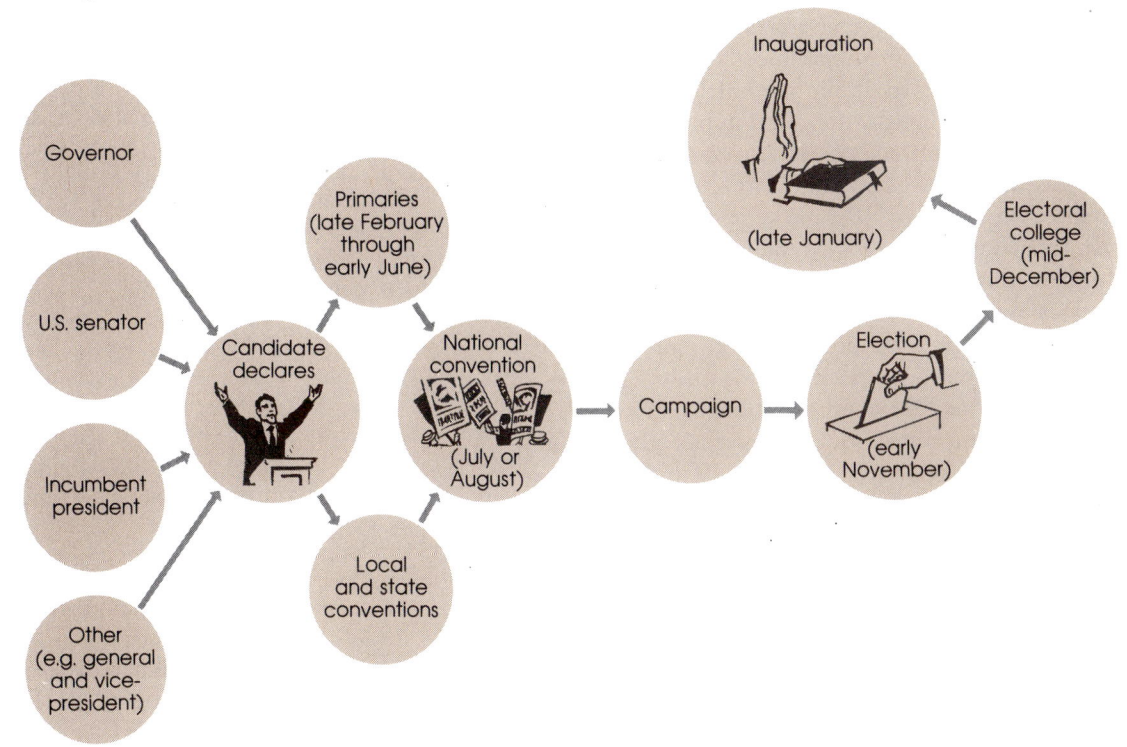

active candidates. New delegate selection rules make this almost impossible to achieve. Consequently, with so many delegates bound by law to vote for the candidate that got the most votes in their district or state, less bargaining goes on at conventions.

Candidates need not run in every primary, though there is pressure to enter as many as possible. Early victories help build momentum for the candidate. They attract early endorsements from other party influentials, thus making it easier to raise money.

This certainly was the way John Kennedy used the primaries in 1960. He went into the Wisconsin primary to show the party leadership that an Easterner could win in a rural Midwest state. Then, he went into West Virginia's primary to show that he, a Catholic, could win in a state that was virtually all Protestant. By this time, with only a few primaries behind him, Kennedy had demonstrated he was "electable." All across the country Democratic governors, mayors, and others who controlled the party started to move in his direction and away from those they were previously supporting (Hubert Humphrey and Lyndon Johnson).

Though early victories—such as New Hampshire in late February—are important, they are not decisive. Later primaries in such big states as New Jersey, Ohio, Texas, Michigan, and California are also important; they send a lot of delegates to the convention.

As you can see in Figure 6-6, a candidate really takes two roads to win delegate votes at his party's national convention. We have just discussed the primary road, where roughly three fourths of the delegates are chosen. But some states choose delegates in party conventions.*

Most often, this process starts in local precincts, where party members meet in caucuses or mass meetings. In 1980, the battle for the Democratic presidential nomination began officially in the Iowa precinct caucuses on January 21. This was followed by the Maine municipal caucuses on February 10.

It takes until June for Maine and Iowa to complete their delegate selection process from the local to the district and state levels. But timing gives the Iowa precinct-level caucuses inordinate importance. Only 50 of the 3,331 delegates to the Democratic national convention came from Iowa. But the winner there gets an enormous publicity boost. In 1976, Iowa put Jimmy Carter on the political map and on the road to the White House. He got close to 29 percent of the vote among 38,500 Democrats who turned out one wintry night. Iowa, like all caucus states, puts a premium on organizational skill and ardent support among party activists.

The National Convention

Just what is a national presidential nominating convention? Here is how Alison Lurie, an observer of the 1980 Democratic Convention, mulled that question:

> This month a peculiar event took place in New York City. Over 25,000 people from all over the country converged on a large indoor arena and remained there for the best part of four days, ill-housed, ill-fed, and often idiotically clothed. They endure conditions of the sort that drive laboratory rats into psychoses: drastic overcrowding, sudden blasts of noise, glaring lights, uncomfortably high temperatures, and (according to many informants) sexual deprivation resulting from exhaustion and round-the-clock lack of privacy.
>
> The official explanation was that 3,331 of these unfortunate people were in Madison Square Garden to choose a presidential candidate (who, as everyone knew, already had been chosen); that another 10,000 people were there to help them choose; and that the additional 11,000 or 12,000 were on hand to record this imaginary choice and associated occurrences. But even a politically naive observer (yours truly) has to assume that more was going on.
>
> According to some experts, the whole convention was a mistake, an anachronism. In bygone years, they said, before the invention of telephones, airplanes, and primaries, it was necessary or at least useful to bring the national and local leaders of a party together every few years to do business; mere stupidity and the difficulty of stopping any large machine once it has been set in motion have preserved the meaningless ritual of a national convention. I am not convinced by this explanation. An event of this size and silliness does not survive just by accident. There are reasons for it. . . .[9]

If the conventions only go through the motions of electing, if all the delegates are prewired to vote for a certain candidate, then what is the reason for these extravaganzas? With the advent of television and the increasing number of primaries, the convention no longer culminates the primaries; it now opens the campaign itself. Thus, both parties try to manage carefully the proceedings. They want to project an image of unity and good sense that viewers will find attractive.

Even the selection of the vice presidential nominee is largely out of the delegates' hands. After a candidate wins the nomination, he huddles with party leaders. They select a candidate who will give geographic or ideological balance to the ticket without, they hope, alienating the party faithful. Reagan's choice of George Bush illustrates the principle nicely. Bush would help in Northeastern states, where Reagan was weakest. Furthermore, Bush was considered less con-

---

* The following states hold conventions to pick delegates: Alaska, Arizona, Colorado, Delaware, Hawaii, Iowa, Maine, Minnesota, Mississippi (Democrats only), Texas (Democrats only), Utah, Virginia, Washington and Wyoming. Arkansas Republicans hold congressional-district and state-committee meetings to select delegates.

servative than Reagan; but he was not too far removed that he would alienate party conservatives such as Sen. Jesse Helms of North Carolina. Most experts say that vice presidential candidates do not swing many votes to the ticket. But one would do well to consider Gerald Ford's choice of Sen. Robert Dole of Kansas. Ford, after his election defeat, indicated that this choice more than anything else cost him the election.

The primaries and the convention reveal quite well the increasing importance of political activists—fired by interests in issues and ideas—in determining party candidates and platform positions. The 1980 presidential conventions, like the preceding two, were attended by delegates ideologically more extreme than the average party members. Thus, while only 21 percent of all Democrats claim to be liberal, 46 percent of the Democratic delegates make that claim. And, while only 41 percent of all Republicans claim to be conservative, 58 percent of Republican delegates make that claim. (*New York Times*/CBS News national poll, August 2–7, 1981).

On the Campaign Trail

After Labor Day the campaigns are well under way. Exactly when the voters make up their minds is debated among experts. Some say it is in early September; others say early October (or one month before Election Day). In any event, few voters are converted by either side during October. The game becomes less one of discussing the great issues of American politics than one of capitalizing on news developments and avoiding gaffes (e.g., ill-considered, off-the-cuff remarks).

Because they can command headlines easily, incumbent presidents have a special advantage. In the fall of 1976, Gerald Ford almost overcame a 20-point deficit in the public opinion polls. He did so not by hitting the campaign trail with vigor but by remaining in the White House and acting "presidential."

Presidential elections differ from the general election pattern in one very important way. The voters do not, strictly speaking, elect the president. The electoral college does.

Every four years, in November, voters vote for presidential electors. The following month, presidential electors representing the winning candidate in each state meet to cast votes for the winning candidate. Although they are supposed to vote for the candidate to whom they are pledged, sometimes they do not.

In January, a joint session of Congress counts these votes. The candidate receiving a majority of electoral votes is elected president. When a strong third-party candidate is in the race, it becomes a real possibility that neither major party candidate will receive a majority. What then?

The House of Representatives decides. This is how it works. Each state delegation votes among itself to see who their favorite is. Then each state, whether big or little, casts one vote. The candidate who gets the vote of majority of the states wins.

Quite clearly, the electoral college can distort the results of the popular vote in a presidential election. Table 6–1 shows what can happen to the popular vote in just two states, California and Wyoming. Candidates can, and have, won the popular vote and lost in the electoral college. In fact, as shown in Table 6–2, 25 out of America's 40 presidents governed without a majority.

The electoral system also influences how presidential candidates conduct their campaigns. Figure 6–7 shows how the United States

TABLE 6–1
Political Effect of Electoral College

	Popular Vote		Electoral Vote	
	Candidate A	Candidate B	Candidate A	Candidate B
California	3,950,000	4,000,000	0	45
Wyoming	110,000	50,000	3	0
Total	4,060,000	4,050,000	3	45

TABLE 6-2
Presidents Who Governed Without Popular Majorities

Years	President	Percentage of Vote
1825–29	Adams	30.5
1841–45	Tyler	None
1845–49	Polk	49.6
1849–50	Taylor	47.3
1850–53	Fillmore	None
1857–61	Buchanan	45.3
1861–65	Lincoln	39.8
1865–69	Johnson	None
1877–81	Hayes	48.0
1881	Garfield	48.3
1881–85	Arthur	None
1885–89	Cleveland	48.5
1889–93	Harrison	47.9
1893–97	Cleveland	46.0
1901–05	Roosevelt	None
1913–17	Wilson	41.8
1917–21	Wilson	49.3
1923–25	Coolidge	None
1945–49	Truman	None
1949–53	Truman	49.5
1961–63	Kennedy	49.7
1963–65	Johnson	None
1969–73	Nixon	43.4
1974–77	Ford	None

looks to a candidate. In the map, the size of each state reflects its electoral importance.

Votes in closely contested states are important because of the winner-take-all provision. Consider the case of candidate A in California; 50,000 votes more and he would have garnered 45 electoral votes more. Votes in big cities are important because pluralities there are crucial to carrying the state. Votes in less populated states are more valuable than votes in the more populous because the number of electoral votes is equal to the state's number of representatives and senators. Little Wyoming may have only three electoral votes; but they are shared by 332,000 people. California's 45 votes, on the other hand, are spread over 19,953,000 people. That means one electoral vote per 110,667 people in Wyoming, one electoral vote per 443,400 in California. A vote for president in Wyoming carries about four times the weight of one cast in California.

In 1980, presidential electors met in state capitals on December 15 to cast their electoral votes. This system is called the **electoral college**. These votes were officially counted in Washington, D.C., on January 6, 1981. A majority of electoral votes—270 of 538—was needed for election as president. On January 20, Reagan, who received nearly 43 million votes, was inaugurated—the last step in the process.

Soon after his election defeat in 1960, Richard Nixon found himself at a luncheon with Ted Sorensen, speechwriter for John F. Kennedy. After a while, the talk at the table turned to JFK's inaugural address.

"I wish I had said some of those things," Nixon remarked.

"Which part?" asked Sorensen. "That part about, 'Ask not what your country can do for you . . . ?'"

"No," said Nixon, "the part that starts, 'I do solemnly swear . . .'"

The 1980 Election: An Analysis

At the very least, the 1980 election results put President Reagan in the congressional driver's seat. Congress was growing more conservative even before the election; Democrats, sensing the country's rightward drift, began abandoning legislation backed by labor, consumers, and public interest lobbies. The 1981 Congress, with Republicans controlling the Senate for the first time since 1954 and House Republicans back to their pre-Watergate strength, will accelerate those trends.

The Republican landslide toppled seven of the Senate's leading liberals. This is not quite the upset that it might appear, since five of the defeated liberals were from traditionally conservative states. In any event, most of them were replaced with extremely conservative Republicans. Republicans gained 12 Senate seats. Democrats dropped from a 59-to-41 Senate majority to a 47-to-53 minority.

The GOP gain of 33 seats in the House

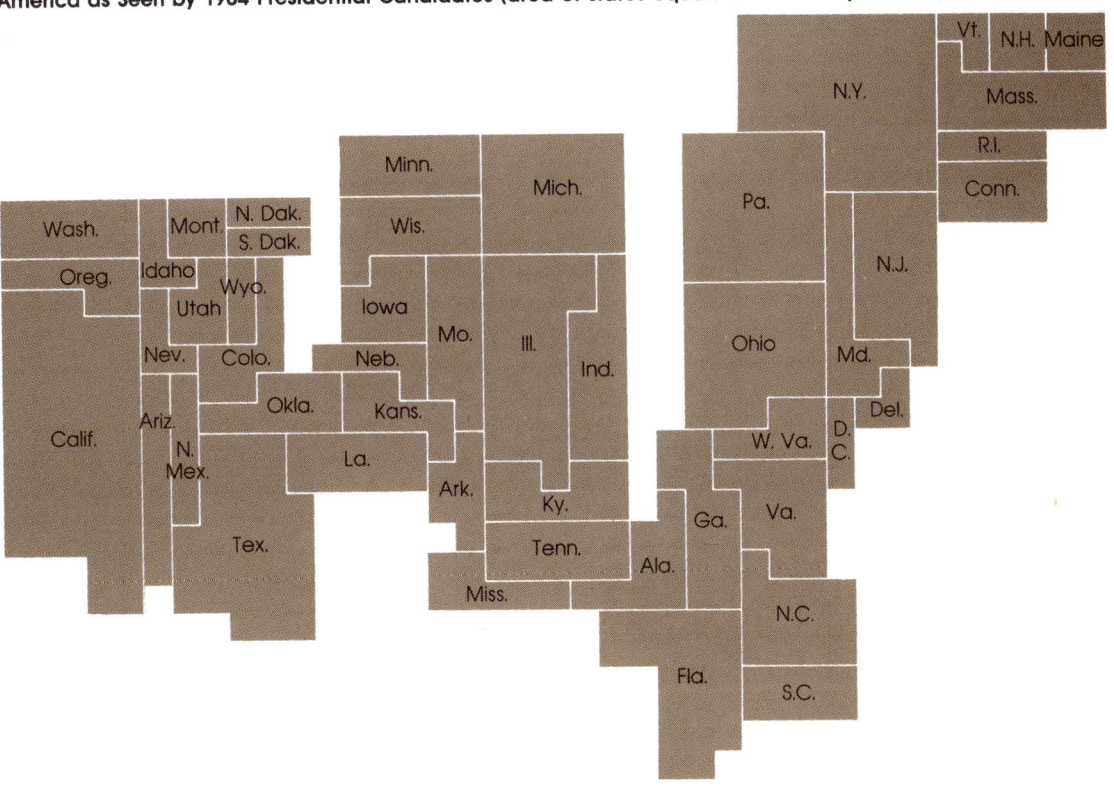

FIGURE 6–7
America as Seen by 1984 Presidential Candidates (area of states equals electoral importance)

was the best Republicans had done since picking up 47 seats in 1966. The 1966 election put the brakes on Lyndon Johnson's Great Society. Democrats fear the 1980 election could mark the beginning of an effort to roll back Great Society programs.

As Table 6–3 confirms, Jimmy Carter suffered critical defections from key groups in the old Democratic coalition. Twenty-seven percent of those describing themselves as liberals, for example, said they had voted for Reagan. Carter had only a narrow edge, 47 percent to 44 percent, among voters from union households. Jewish voters preferred Mr. Carter by only a slim margin, 45 percent to 39 percent. Carter also carried Hispanic Americans by an unimpressive majority for a Democrat, with 54 percent of their votes to 36 percent for Reagan. The only major element of the old Democratic coalition that stayed with Carter in customary proportions was black voters. They provided 21 percent of his popular vote total. Blacks divided 82 percent for Carter and 14 percent for Reagan.

The 1980 election also provides insight into two key questions in the study of American voters: (a) Which issues are most important in deciding how to vote? and (b) When do voters decide about their choice?

The answers to the first question are given in the table below.[10] (Some voters made more than one choice.)

Question	Reagan voters	Carter voters
Balance the budget	26%	14%
Crisis in Iran	9%	21%
Unemployment	20%	29%
Reducing federal income tax	13%	7%
Equal Rights Amendment and abortion	5%	8%
Inflation and the economy	40%	23%
Needs of big cities	1%	4%
U.S. prestige around the world	19%	12%

Reprinted by permission *The Wall Street Journal*

"I'm sorry, but he's asked not to be disturbed. He's reminiscing about the good old days when the incumbent had the *advantage*."

In the 1980 campaign, many candidates apparently assumed they could get elected by using the advantages of incumbency; they could emphasize the special interests of their supporters; and in the case of Democrats, they could rely on high voter identification with the Democratic party label. This strategy seemed to work in 1976 and 1978; it was not enough in 1980. Important Democratic senators like George McGovern, the party's 1972 presidential candidate, and Frank Church, chairman of the Foreign Relations Committee, were defeated.

The answers to the second question—when people decided about their choice—are as follows:

Knew all along (41%)

During the primaries (13%)
During conventions (8%)
Since Labor Day (8%)
In week before election (23%)

TABLE 6–3
How Different Groups Voted for President, 1980

	Carter	Reagan	Anderson
Democrats (43%)	66	26	6
Independents (23%)	30	54	12
Republicans (28%)	11	84	4
Liberals (17%)	57	27	11
Moderates (46%)	42	48	8
Conservatives (28%)	23	71	4
East (32%)	43	47	8
South (27%)	44	51	3
Midwest (20%)	41	51	6
West (11%)	35	52	10
Blacks (10%)	82	14	3
Hispanics (2%)	54	36	7
Whites (88%)	36	55	8
Female (49%)	45	46	7
Male (51%)	37	54	7
Catholic (25%)	40	51	7
Jewish (5%)	45	39	14
Protestant (46%)	37	56	6
Born-again white Protestant (17%)	34	61	4
18–21 years old (6%)	44	43	11
22–29 years old (17%)	43	43	11
30–44 years old (31%)	37	54	7
45–59 years old (23%)	39	55	6
60 years or older (18%)	40	54	4
Education:			
High school or less (39%)	46	48	4
Some college (28%)	35	55	8
College graduate (27%)	35	51	11
Labor union household (26%)	47	44	7
No member of household in union (62%)	35	55	8

Note: Based on 12,782 interviews with voters at their polling places. Shown is how each group divided its vote for president and, in parentheses, the percentage of the electorate belonging to each group.

Source: 1980 election day surveys by *New York Times*/CBS News Poll.

FUTURE FILE

Is the Party Over?

To more than a few political analysts the story of American politics in the 1980s can be summed up in terms of the decline of the political party and the enhanced importance of special interests groups.

In speaking of the "decline of the party," it is helpful to think of the party as consisting of three parts. First is the *party in the electorate*—that is, the number of citizens who say they are Republicans or Democrats. Second is the *party organization,* that loose arrangement headed by a national chairperson, which we discussed in this chapter. Third is the *party in government*—that is, those members of a political party who hold elected office and their leaders. (There is more on this part of the party in Chapter 8.) Throughout the 1970s all three parts seemed to weaken. The percentage of citizens professing to be Republicans and Democrats steadily declined; the number of independents rose. The party organizations diluted their own strength by opening up the primaries and cutting back the influence of long-time party professionals. In the past, parties professional had considerable control over who the nominees of the party would be. The party itself had been a kind of service agency for citizens. It provided jobs, contracts, and social services.

The party clubhouse had been central to community life. Finally, because of numerous reforms after Watergate, party leaders emerged with less control over the rank and file. Members of Congress could vote against the wishes of their party leaders with virtual impunity.

As noted in our analysis of political power in Chapter 4, nature abhors a vacuum. Into the power vacuum created by the weakened parties, emboldened private interest groups charged.

This remarkable rise in the power of special interests groups has led a number of political analysts to speculate that the American party system might be in for hard times, if not collapse. Political candidates, the argument runs, are today far less dependent on political parties. To get elected, politicians only need the financial support of a few interest groups.

Well-intentioned reforms allowed for the liberal use of political action committees. They have made raising cash for candidates less difficult for special interest groups. With cash in hand, the modern candidate can then hire skilled political consultants (or image makers) who develop an advertising campaign selling whatever he or she thinks the voters are buying. Making campaign commercials is only a small

Copyright 1978 G. B. Trudeau. Reprinted with permission of Universal Press Syndicate. All rights reserved.

part of what such advisers do. Of much greater importance is advising the candidate on strategy. In particular, how does the candidate get on the "free media," such as the evening television news?

Sidney Blumenthal writes,

> [Political candidates can do without] such traditional baggage as positions, programs and party endorsement. . . . What no candidate can dispense with, however, is a political consultant. . . . Political consultants are the new directors of the American political drama. They are the permanent residents of the political scene; the politicians are often the transients. Consultants are the new political bosses. They have the personal political contacts, practical campaign experience and vote-catching skills on which old-style party bosses once prided themselves. ("The Candidate Makers," *Politics Today,* March–April 1980, pp. 27–30.)

tioned hotels, candidates for the presidency were chosen in "smoke-filled rooms." Then it was the cigar-chomping party bosses—not the rank and file of the party, and certainly not the people—who decided in closed meetings late at night who would be that party's nominee for the presidency.

In 1968 that approach to selecting candidates began to change. The trend has been to "open up" the process. Voters in 37 primaries were allowed to choose delegates to the national convention committed to a particular candidate. This means that fewer professional politicians will be on the floor of the convention to make bargains; and the few pros that make it there will find they have few votes with which to bargain (since so many delegates have been "locked into" a particular candidate).

Critics of these changes say that it does not produce the strongest, most qualified candi-

Drawing by Lorenz; © 1978 The New Yorker Magazine, Inc.

"I'm sure our firm can handle your campaign, Senator, but first we have to answer the question 'Who are you?'"

In this Future File, we shall consider a couple of trends that might further erode the power of political parties. Then we shall consider three trends that might reverse the process.

Trends that Could Further Weaken the Party System

Changing the way presidents are elected. Once upon a time, in the days before air condi-

dates. "We got FDR and Ike from the smoke-filled room," they say. "And now we get people like Carter and Reagan when the party's political leaders are no longer in control of the selection process."

Defenders of change say that, because democracy is a worthy principle; anything that enhances it must be good. Furthermore, they point to the lackluster series of mostly lackluster presidents running from Martin Van Buren to William McKinley.

Having succeeded in democratizing the nominating process, reformers have turned with renewed vigor on that ancient filter between the citizen and the presidential election—namely, the electoral college. Besides giving an advantage to the small states and large "swing" states, critics of the electoral college system point to a number of other defects. It does not guarantee victory to the candidate who receives more popular votes than his opponents. This is more than a mathematical possibility. It actually happened in 1876 and 1888. It almost happened in 1960 and 1976. In the latter year, a shift of only about 9,000 voters in Ohio and Hawaii would have given the electoral vote to Gerald R. Ford; yet he still would have trailed Jimmy Carter by almost 2 million popular votes. It does not require the electors—that small group of Americans who really elect the president in the month following the general election—to vote for the candidate to whom they are pledged. (This is, however, more of a technical possibility than a standard practice. Of the 20,000 electors since the beginning of the republic, only 10 have been "faithless.") And the system provides that, if no candidate wins the electoral college majority, the election is to be decided in the House of Representatives. There each state delegation, no matter how large or small, has one vote. This further distorts representation of the popular vote.

Consequently, the Senate has given serious consideration to a constitutional amendment to abolish the electoral college; presidents would be elected by direct popular vote, the procedure used for the election of governors. Supporters claim direct election would affirm the principle of "one man, one vote." But the electoral system does tend to blunt single-issue fury. Citizens who oppose gun control or abortion cannot as easily unite nationally to elect, or defeat, a president; they must join, state by state, with other voters moved by other passions. America is a nation of communities. The electoral system reflects that reality. Abolishing the current system would be, moreover, a crushing blow to already wobbly political parties. Why? Because one main reason American political parties continue to exist is to create coalitions across diverse states to make a majority. Without parties, the influence of the media and image makers would become more powerful than ever. Victory would go to those candidates who could most skillfully manipulate television imagery.

Another possible consequence of a national election would be more candidates. Each would be seeking to push the major parties below the 50 percent or 40 percent threshold that some have suggested for victory. Then these minor candidates would try to negotiate a deal during the runoff period. The national election, Senator Orrin Hatch of Utah suggests, would resemble the Boston Marathon. There would be presidential candidates representing every special interest in the country.

Alternatives aside, what is likely to happen in future presidential campaigns? In 1979, Austin Ranney, political scientist and resident scholar at the American Enterprise Institute, offered this view of the future of presidential campaigns.

> My guess is that, in at least its early planning stages, the 1984 Presidential campaign will begin the day after the 1980 election. And my crystal ball tells me that over the next 10 years, the next 20 years, campaigns will become even more media-dominated, less partified, more candidate-entrepreneur kinds of things operating under more stringent financial limitations.
>
> Look if you will at what the Gallup Poll says are the most preferred reforms. Great numbers of people say they want to abolish the Electoral College and go to direct national elections for the President. They want a national initiative and referendum. These are all getting Gallup majorities of 65 to 75 percent. People want more stringent regulation of campaigns, and that would probably mean more public financing of elections. And all of these, it seems to me, are going to carry us more in the direction of direct rule by the people, bypassing or destroying intermediaries like political parties. (*New York Times,* December 2, 1979.)

The wired society. The technology of communications is in a period of revolutionary change. Many new inventions and developments are involved. No aspect of life will remain untouched by telecommunications. It will bring remote medical diagnosis to isolated areas. It will help save millions of gallons of gasoline each year. A study by the Office of Telecommunications Policy concluded that automobile travel for acquisition, exchange, and dissemination of information uses 500 times as much energy in total as would telecommunications.

There is already in existence a Public Response System that would extend democracy, giving people more of a "say in how things are run." This is already being tried in Columbus, Ohio. Warner Brothers' Qube cable system lets subscribers respond via calculator-sized consoles to TV programs.

What if this were someday expanded to a national system? Then the basic function of the party noted at the start of this chapter—namely, filtering and organizing public choices—would be largely eliminated. Individuals could be given relevant background material on an issue, pro and con, then asked to choose. It is unlikely that 100 percent of the citizens would bother to respond. But it is not hard to imagine that better than 53 percent (the percentage who bothered to vote in the 1980 presidential election) would. After all, they would not even have to leave their livingroom nor stand in a line.

But perhaps the most decisive trends in electronics are already in place: the electronic media, public opinion research, and computerized mailing. Candidates find television more effective than formal party organizations in helping them getting elected. With it they can take their message directly to the people. Nor do they need the party to tell them what the citizens are thinking, thanks to public opinion research specialists. Candidates do not even need national parties for the money to compete. Sophisticated direct-mail techniques using computerized lists and covering a wide range of sources (such as PACs) bring in millions of dollars from individual donors. In 1977, one direct-mail specialist, Richard A. Viguerie, raised over $1.5 million for a variety of conservative causes; the Republican National Committee could raise only $8 million. In short, a growing number of candidates need neither a national party nor a precinct captain.

Wide World Photos

Today a primary source of cash for election campaigns are direct-mail entrepreneurs like Richard Viguerie, who can raise vast sums from small contributors. Viguerie keeps 25 million names on 3,000 reels of magnetic tape and sends out 100 million pieces of mail a year. The key to many of these appeals is anger and fear.

Countertrends

Before considering the countertrends that are likely to affect the future of the Democratic and Republican parties, we need to put interest groups and political parties in historical perspective. Is single-issue politics all that new?

Interest groups driven by a single passion that serves as the litmus test of whether to support a particular candidate are hardly new. In the three decades before the Civil War, the abolitionists agitated for the compulsory emancipation of black slaves with all the single-minded intensity and moral outrage as today's National Right to Life movement agitates for a ban on abortions. In the latter part of the

19th century, the Woman's Christian Temperance Unions and the Anti-Saloon League sought the constitutional prohibition of alcoholic beverages. Today the National Organization for Women follows pretty much the same strategy for the Equal Rights Amendment. In short, special interest groups are not new. The National Right to Life Association can trace its origin back to 1871; the Sierra Club can go back almost as far (1892).

Furthermore, writing off political parties has its own history. The Republican party in particular was written off by some after Lyndon Johnson's defeat of Barry Goldwater in 1964. And Watergate was supposedly the final nail in the GOP's coffin.

Yet by June 1981 Republican national chairman Richard Richards was opening the meeting of the Republican National Committee by observing that 1980 might prove to be to the GOP "what 1932 was to the Democratic Party"—the beginning of an era of political dominance in the country. "I think we are on the edge of majority-party status in this country," Richards said. Then he quoted a recent internal party poll indicating that 39 percent of voters asked now said they considered themselves Republicans; 40 percent called themselves Democrats. Richards noted that a year earlier the Democratic lead was 20 percent; and three years before it was 28 percent.

At the same time, when it comes to money, the mother's milk of politics, the Republican party was in excellent shape. Just for openers, party treasurer William J. McManus reported that the Republicans as of May 31, 1981, had $9,373,100 *left* in their till; this was a net increase of more than $8 million since the first of the year and a midyear record after a presidential election. And for 1982, the goal was to raise a net $21 million more. That would be another record at that stage in the four-year political cycle.

One final item: In March 1981, the Supreme Court ruled that national parties did *not* have to recognize delegates selected in open primary states. This could mark a turning away from the "open system" in which party leaders have relatively little control. So much for the party organization. How about the party in government? Because of the public's wish to curb federal spending, members of both parties, for the first time in many years, were beginning to say no to special interest group demands. Old-style special interest politics was suddenly confronted with the Reagan proposal to slash $50 billion from the federal government, with more cuts to follow in later years.

Another trend to watch is the possible attenuation of ethnic politics. In 1980, many candidates for office organized their campaign staffs, speaking schedules, and fund-raising activities around specific ethnic groups. The most elaborate operation was that of Ronald Reagan. He had volunteers working with 26 different ethnic groups. Reagan's advisers also set up a "national council" complete with a separate campaign structure for each ethnic division. This operation was considered important to Reagan's strategy to carry the blue-collar vote of the industrial East and Midwest, where ethnic communities are strong.

The Carter White House had been restructured to respond to ethnic group pressures. Past presidents had had one aide who acted as a link with Spanish-speaking Americans. Carter named a special assistant for Hispanic affairs, with two deputies and a dozen volunteer helpers.

But how deep do ethnic politics run? According to Stephen Thernstrom, editor of the *Harvard Encyclopedia of American Ethnic Groups,* figures on intermarriage prove the limited impact of the ethnic revival.

> The data show that none of the major European immigrant groups has a majority marrying within the group. With Orientals, the figure for marriage to non-Orientals is in the 40-to-60-percent range. So some of these groups may be vanishing within a few generations.
>
> Other evidence comes from two sociologists who have studied social class and ethnicity in Boston and Kansas City, Mo. They did not find ethnicity as significant a factor in people's lives as they had expected. It was of most interest to college students and, secondly, to the highly assimilated and

the affluent who were of the third generation or more. They felt so secure with their American identity that they could afford the luxury of ethnicity. As more people are third generation and secure, it may be that more of them will choose, for a time, to explore their roots. ("Is America's Ethnic Revival a Fad Like Jogging?" *U.S. News & World Report*, November 17, 1980, p. 85.)

In short, Thernstrom thinks that the image of America as a **melting pot** for ethnic groups is still valid: "I know that some people prefer to view the U.S. as a rich stew rather than as a melting pot. That's all right if you recognize that the pieces of meat and vegetables are melting away fairly rapidly."

Chapter Key

Few citizens talk directly to elected officials. Linkage institutions, the subject of this chapter, are required to help translate public opinion into public policy. They get government to listen to private citizens. Interest groups, political parties, and elections are the most important linkage institutions in the United States.

All Americans are not equally prone to join groups. Only about 40 percent of American adults are active members of some kind of organization; only 8 percent belong to a political group. Nevertheless, interest groups in the United States are prolific. Over 14,600 nonprofit national organizations were enumerated as of 1979. Added to these are hundreds of thousands of local, state, and regional associations, plus branch chapters.

National groups can be classified into the types of concerns they represent: business interests (including corporations and trade associations); labor unions; professional associations (including groups like lawyers, doctors, teachers); public interest groups (including environmental and consumer groups); groups representing minorities; and miscellaneous groups (including farmers, veterans, and even public officials.

The techniques and effectiveness of a group's activities are affected by its size (number of members), budget (size of the treasury), status of members, and political skills and contacts of the group's members. The geographic distribution of a group's members can also have an impact on its techniques and effectiveness. Concentrations of group members can be an important factor in elections because our legislatures are chosen geographically. The geographic distribution of members will also influence whether a group seeks access at the state, local, or federal level of government. The essential resource for group influence is its access to one or more decision points in the government structure. The development and cultivation of these access points is the common denominator of virtually all of the political activity of all groups.

The chief job of a lobbyist is to impart information to the decision maker. Lobbyists in Congress tend to concentrate their persuasive powers on a small number of members of committees or subcommittees. They don't try to contact and persuade all legislators. In addition to direct lobbying, interest groups can also have an indirect effect. For example, they may stimulate grass-roots lobbying (such as letter-writing campaigns); they help or hinder candidates (by contributing money or assisting in voter registration and voter turnout drives); and they can participate in the judicial process by filing briefs or sponsoring "test cases."

The largest and best organized minority group in the United States continues to be blacks. Recently one of the most controversial issues involving race has been court-ordered busing. Many black and many white parents oppose busing. But many black leaders tend to think it is necessary to achieve upgraded schools in predominantly black areas. Reverse discrimination to overcome the effects of segregation is also controversial. Other minorities have followed the pattern of the black civil rights movement. Hispanic Americans, especially Mexican-Americans, have taken a new pride in their heritage and have organized to demand economic and legal equality. American Indians enjoy dual citizenship and dual entitlement. But they remain the poorest and the most unemployed minority in the United States. Indians have developed a new pride in Indianness. They now strive for greater control over their resources as a means to elevate their economic standing.

Women were active in slavery protests as early as the 1830s. But they did not organize until the 1880s. Their movement increasingly became a movement for female suffrage. With the ratification of the 19th Amendment in 1920 the movement lost much of its cohesion and drive. Only in the 1960s did women again organize and became active. They have made marked advancements in professions and occupations once essentially closed to women. But they have failed so far in having the Equal Rights Amendment ratified.

Political parties differ from interest groups in four ways: (1) parties are far less numerous; (2) parties focus on a wide range of issues, whereas groups tend to specialize in only a few issues; (3) parties bargain and compromise more than interest groups; and (4) parties nominate candidates.

There are three components of political parties in the United States: the party organization, the party in government, and the party in the electorate. The most important goal of American political parties is to win elections. Unlike Western European parties, America's main political parties have no official system for enrolling members and are not doctrinaire. While seeking to win elections, the parties perform three key functions: they recruit people to run for office; they simplify the voter's choices; and they coordinate the government's policymaking. In a larger sense, parties serve as a means of social control or of restraining social conflict and uniting citizens of varied backgrounds. Indeed, to win votes, the major parties are forced to appeal to many groups.

The system of political parties in the United States has remained quite stable throughout history. One of its most important and most enduring characteristics is that it is a two-party system. Third parties have occasionally emerged for an election or two, but two major parties have consistently dominated American politics. There are several reasons for this. Parents pass on their party identification to their children; this discourages change in the system. American voters tend to be middle-of-the-road on the issues; because the two parties monopolize centrist positions, a third party can find little support. Single-representative districts with plurality elections encourage coalition building by two parties, making victory by a new third party unlikely. Finally, parties may co-opt third-party issues.

The two major parties in the United States have decentralized organizations. The national party organization, which consists of a national committee with respresentatives from each state and a national chairperson, is not very influential. Every four years the party holds a national convention. It nominates the presidential and vice presidential candidates and writes the party's platform. Each of the two major parties has 50 separate state organizations and thousands of largely independent local party organizations. American elections are direct except for the election of the president and the vice president. In this case, voters cast ballots for electors. The electors in turn vote for candidates for whom they are ostensibly pledged.

The first stage in the presidential election process is nomination—that is, a party's endorsement of a candidate for president. The nomination process begins months, even years, before each party's national convention (which is held the summer of presidential election years). Candidates travel the country lining up support in each state. The candidate who is able to win the votes of a majority of the convention delegates wins the nomination. Candidates obtain the support of delegates in two principal ways: through state party caucuses and through presidential primaries. The primary is now the most common route to winning delegates.

A presidential nomination may be decided weeks before the convention. Conventions, though, still have an important role. They unify the party for the presidential campaign. And they adopt a platform upon which the candidate runs. The party's nominee for vice president is also selected at the convention.

The media and money play important roles throughout the process. Some critics charge that the media focuses on the campaign as a game and underplays the issues. The Federal Election Campaign Act of 1974 sought to reform financing. This act limited the size of private contributions. It provided some public funds for campaign expenses and limited the amount candidates could spend. It required financial disclosures by candidates. And it created a federal election commission to enforce compliance with other provisions of the act.

Technically, presidents are formally elected by the electoral college. The electoral college, made up of representatives from each of the 50 states and Washington, D.C., selects the president. If a candidate wins the majority of the popular vote in a state, he is entitled to all of that state's electoral votes. The electoral college system gives large states and urban areas extra influence in presidential campaigns. There have been several proposals to eliminate the electoral college and elect the president by direct popular vote.

During the 1970s, both parties appeared to decline in power. The special interests and media consultants came to play more decisive roles in the selection and election of political candidates. The future of both parties will depend largely on their ability to form broad coalitions and excite the electorate with their ideas.

Answers to Quiz

These are the leading also-rans in the 1980 presidential campaign. Together they had over 8 percent of the vote among them. Barry Commoner (left), candidate of the populist Citizens party, received ¼ of 1 percent of the vote. (Populists advocate an old-fashioned radicalism, deeply rooted in U.S. history. They seek by democratic means to use the power of government to control big business and aid the poor.) Ed Clark (center), candidate of the Libertarian party, received just over 1 percent of the vote. More significantly, perhaps, the party, which believes strongly in the leave-us-alone philosophy of government, was on the ballot in all 50 states. John Anderson, independent and former Republican congressman, received 6.9 percent of the vote. Carter and Reagan charged that Anderson had received much more than 6.9 percent of the media attention.

It is said an Eastern monarch once charged his wise men to invent him a sentence to be ever in view, and which should be true and appropriate in all times and situations. They presented him the words: "And this, too, shall pass away." How much it expresses! How chastening in the hour of pride! How consoling in the depths of affliction! . . . And yet, let us hope, it is not quite true. Let us hope, rather, that by the best cultivation of the physical world beneath and around us, and the best intellectual and moral world within us, we shall secure an individual, social, and political prosperity and happiness, whose course shall be onward and upward, and which, while the earth endures, shall not pass away.

Abraham Lincoln (1859)

PART 3 | Government Institutions

THE KEY TO THIS BOOK

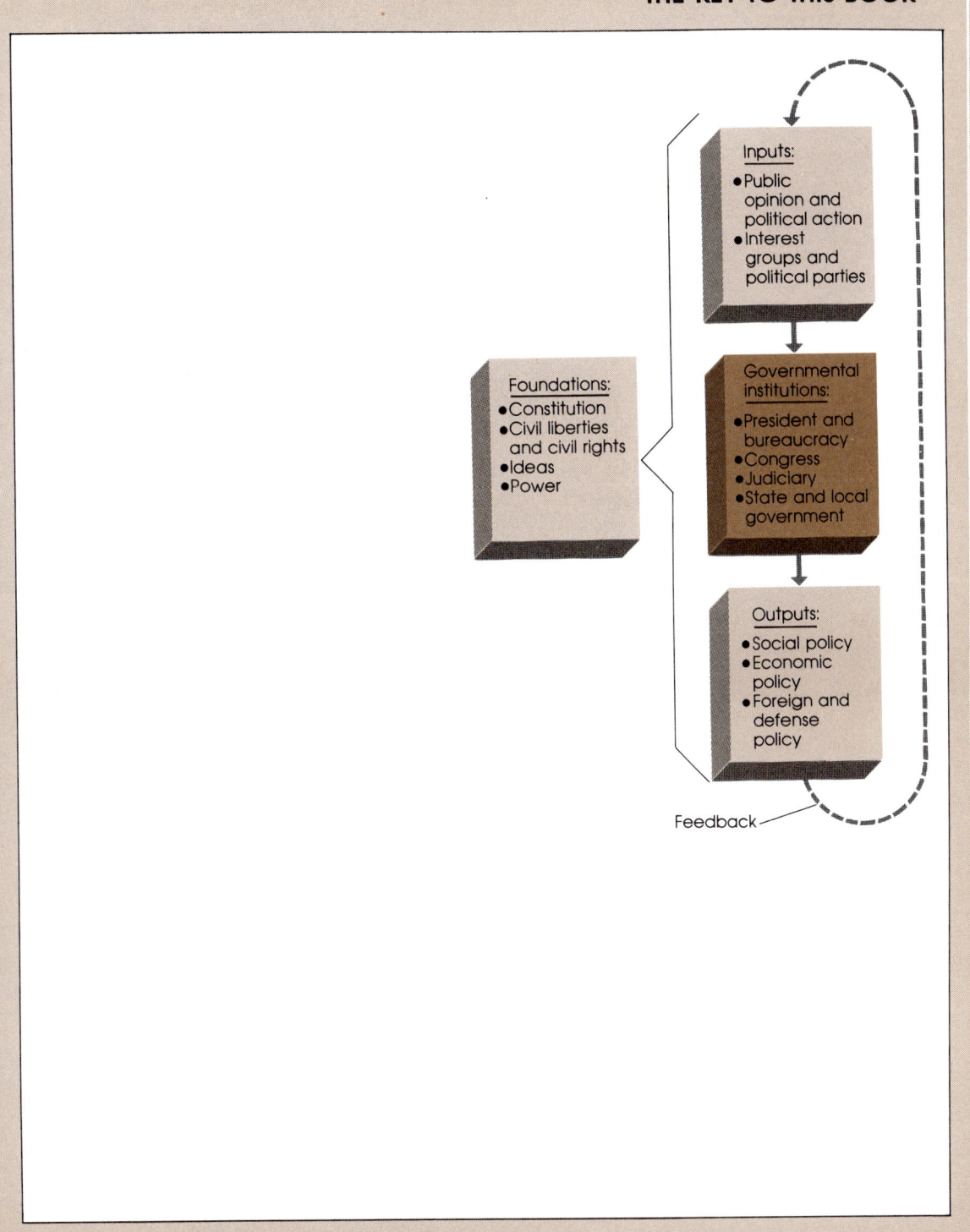

Inputs:
- Public opinion and political action
- Interest groups and political parties

Foundations:
- Constitution
- Civil liberties and civil rights
- Ideas
- Power

Governmental institutions:
- President and bureaucracy
- Congress
- Judiciary
- State and local government

Outputs:
- Social policy
- Economic policy
- Foreign and defense policy

Feedback

Wide World Photos

7 | The Executive Branch: Presidential Leadership and Bureaucratic Management

After studying this chapter you should be able to answer the following questions:

1. How did the modern presidency evolve?
2. What is a critical election?
3. What are the key features of bureaucracy?
4. How is the executive branch organized?
5. What are the stages in policymaking?
6. What is the president's role in the policy process?

Terms you should know:

Administrative Procedures Act
bureaucracy
cabinet
chief executive
civil service
commander in chief
Council of Economic Advisors
critical or realignment election
distributive policies
Executive Office of the President
executive orders
executive privilege
Federal Register
government corporations
Great Society
Hatch Act
impeachment
imperial presidency
implementation
incrementalism
independent regulatory commissions
inherent powers
Jacksonian democracy

Joint Chiefs of Staff
Kitchen Cabinet
legislative veto
merit system
National Security Council
New Deal
New Deal coalition
Office of Management and Budget
Office of Personnel Management
party leader
patronage
Pendleton Act
pocket veto
press secretary
redistributive policies
regulatory policies
Senior Executive Service
spoils system
state of the union
war on poverty
Watergate affair
White House Office

Though a cool, quiet, sunlit place, the president's Oval Office is the ultimate symbol of power in the United States. Here the crucial decisions about peace and war, jobs and health, freedom and equality are made.

The size and tone of the room speak power. Into almost a thousand square feet of gray-green carpet is woven the Great Seal of the United States. Behind an oaken shipboard desk made of the timbers of the old U.S.S. *Resolute*, the flag of the Union stands to the left and the personal purple-and-gold presidential flag to the right. Through the great French windows (about 12 feet high and bulletproof), one can see the Washington Monument to the south and the Lincoln Memorial to the west.

On the desk is an 18-button telephone console. It links the president to, among others, the commanding general of the Strategic Air Command at Omaha and the Commanding General of NATO in his headquarters in Brussels. An amber button controls a direct line to a switchboard that links the President's desk instantly to the desks of the various heads of various critical departments and agencies in the executive branch. A red button controls a special line. It scrambles the president's voice electronically so that only those with a similar button can unscramble it. When the president calls on the red line, he never gets a busy signal. (I use the masculine pronoun only for simplicity, not in an exclusive way.) Any conversations are interrupted automatically and the president speaks.

The president's pay might be modest compared with top corporate executives. But it is not bad: $200,000 plus $50,000 expenses and a $69,630-a-year retirement pension package. Transportation is, of course, provided. At his disposal are Air Force One, more than a dozen Boeing 707s and Lockheed Jetstars, eight VH–3 helicopters, and especially constructed Lincoln Continentals. The sole function of the Special Mission Fleet of the 89th Military Airlift Wing at Andrews Air Force Base is to take the president's staff anywhere on the globe. Housing, too, comes with the job—a 132-room mansion on 18.7 acres (maintained by 30 gardners). For rest and relaxation, there is the 180-acre vacation estate at Camp David served by 150 naval personnel and complete with heated pool, skeet range, and tennis courts. It takes time for one to adjust to this kind of power.

The American presidency is probably the ultimate symbol of power in the world. Even Soviet premier Brezhnev must share some of his power with the other dozen or so members of the Politburo, the most important decision-making organ in the Soviet Union. It is a little hard to imagine that Brezhnev, as general secretary, would look at the other members of the Politburo and say with impunity, as Lincoln once did to his cabinet, when all its members opposed him: "Seven nays, one aye—the ayes have it." Still, one might object that the general secretary does not have to worry about the countervailing power of a Congress and Supreme Court. But just how effective are those two bodies at restraining a determined president? Neither seemed to have the will to resist "military intervention" in Southeast Asia. Nor did they have adequate information on whether the president was using the FBI and IRS legally. But the presidency is not without drawbacks. Just the fact that only three presidents since 1877 have served two full, consecutive terms in office should cause any incumbent concern.

The Constitution is not very specific about the president and the power of the office. It requires that a president be at least 35 years old (the youngest was Theodore Roosevelt, 42); he must be a natural-born citizen (Henry Kissinger is, technically, ineligible); and he must have lived in the United States at least 14 years (although not consecutively). The Constitution also bestows certain formal powers; though, these are permissions, more than actual capabilities. The president is given responsibility for military and foreign policy by virtue of being designated commander in chief and having treaty-making power. (The latter, of course, requires the advice and consent of the Senate.) There is also "the forgotten power" of being able to grant reprieves and pardons. At least it was forgotten until Gerald Ford's pardoning of Richard Nixon. So, as you should know from our discussion of political power in Chapter 4, effective presidents must rely on other resources besides Article II, Sections 2 and 3 of the Constitution, to convince others to act. A number of resources are available: presidential appointments, budgetary allocations, information management, etc.

Other formal sources of power besides the Constitution are statutes (or laws) passed by Congress and the **inherent powers** in any executive office. The latter sources give rise to the 50,000 **executive orders** that have been issued since Washington. They have the effect of law. The president, or **chief executive,** uses these rules or regulations to carry out the provisions of the Constitution, treaties (agreements with foreign governments), and statutes. They are also used to change the organization or procedures of the bureaucracy. For example, in 1948, President Harry S Truman ordered the desegregation of the armed forces.

Thus far, we have been talking mainly about formal powers. But, since the time the Constitutional Convention debated whether to have a president or a king, presidential power has constantly been redefined in practice.

THE EXISTENTIAL PRESIDENCY

Existentialism is not easily defined, which is perhaps one of the reasons it is thrown around so much. But at least one common thread runs through most modern writing about this philosophical doctrine: Human beings are self-creating individuals endowed with a character and goals, *but must choose them by pure acts of decision.* So it is with presidents. They must choose the character and goals of their office. Through practice, they define the office.

One wonders how it could be otherwise. The Constitution is vague and brief when it speaks about the power of the presidency. Accordingly, the 40 men who have occupied the office have felt free to interpret and reinterpret presidential power to accommodate changing circumstances.

Every president has modified the nature of the office in one way or another. But it was not until Franklin Roosevelt that the duties of the presidency underwent real change. It is common to refer to Roosevelt and the eight presidents who have followed as "modern." According to political scientist Fred I. Greenstein, they differ from their "traditional" predecessors in four important ways.[1]

First, the president is active in initiating and seeking to win support for legislative action in Congress. From the start, the Constitution equipped the president with powers to affect legislation. It directs him to inform Congress on the **state of the union,** usually delivered in person as a formal address, and to recommend legislation that he considers necessary and expedient. He may, on extraordinary occasions, convene both houses of Congress or either of them. The president may veto acts of Congress; the latter may override that veto only by a two thirds vote. But today, an evaluation of a president's administration is based in large part upon his success or failure in pushing broad legislative programs through Congress. Because of its size and diversity of interests, Congress is simply not well-equipped to develop broad, complex leadership. Thus, in the modern era, presidents must truly be the **chief legislator.**

Second, by use of the executive order, modern presidents make policy without congressional approval. Third, their staffs have expanded greatly. Finally, in a dangerous, uncertain world, the public expects from modern presidents a higher standard of performance and personal virtue. But the modern presidency clearly has evolved out of the actions and nonactions of the men who have occupied the office.

To understand this development, we must flash back through 200 years of presidential history.

Traditional Presidencies

George Washington. During his two precedent-setting terms, George Washington unified the nation, fostered political harmony, and maintained neutrality in foreign affairs. He also shaped the role of the presidency and pioneered its relations with Congress.

Washington instituted the **cabinet** idea when he began regularly to call together the heads of his four executive departments and the vice president to consult on matters of policy. He also took control of firing officials; this was not mentioned in the Constitution.

He began the practice of withholding his own papers from Congress by claiming **executive privilege**. That is, he claimed the right of executive officials to withhold information from and to refuse to appear before a legislative committee or a court. This privilege is claimed as an inherent executive power under the constitutional separation of powers (see Chapter 2). It was not until 1974 that a legal means could be found by which the president and his staff could be denied executive privilege. In the *United States* v. *Nixon*, the Supreme Court unanimously ordered President Nixon to release recorded tapes that had criminal information on them.

In foreign policy, Washington exerted dominance. He fostered U.S. interests on the North American continent by treaties with Britain and Spain. Yet, until the nation was stronger, he insisted on the maintenance of neutrality. For example, when war broke out between France and England in the wake of the French Revolution, he ignored the pleas of pro-French Jefferson and pro-British Hamilton. Many people encouraged Washington to seek a third term, but he was weary of politics and refused to do so. This set a precedent for a two-term limit that lasted until Franklin Roosevelt's four-term presidency. In his Farewell Address (1796), Washington urged his country to foreswear party spirit and sectional passions. He urged the peo-

---

Quiz

1. Which president lost the popular vote in the general election, but was finally elected by a plurality in the electoral college of just one vote?
2. Who was the first president who had not been a British subject?
3. Which two presidents were journalists by profession?
4. Which vice president became a member of another government's administration after his term?
5. Which vice president shot and killed a political rival while in office?
6. Which two presidents died on the same date?
7. Who was the first president not to be inaugurated in Washington, D.C.?
8. Which famous poet recited one of his works at President John F. Kennedy's inauguration?
9. When did the White House burn down?
10. Who was the only bachelor–not widower– president?
11. When was the first "Ford for President" campaign started?

Answers on p. 260.

ple to avoid entanglement in the wars and domestic policies of other nations.

Thomas Jefferson. Among President Washington's four-member cabinet was Secretary of State Thomas Jefferson. Jefferson eventually resigned because of repeated disagreements with Secretary of the Treasury Alexander Hamilton.

After a brief period of semiretirement, Jefferson returned to politics in 1796, only to lose a close election to John Adams. The Constitution did not then provide separate tickets for the president and vice president. Therefore Jefferson became Adams' vice president. This was despite the fact he was a member of a different party. In 1800, he ran again, this time successfully.

Jefferson's contributions to the development of the presidency were twofold. First, he added yet another role to those already established by the Constitution and by Washington. In addition to being the chief executive, chief legislator, chief diplomat, and commander in chief, the president under Jefferson became **party leader**. During Jefferson's presidency the Federalist party lost power to the Democratic Republicans. Not only did Jefferson organize this party; he also *used it*. That is to say, he cultivated close ties with party members in Congress in order to expedite his legislative program. Since that time, presidents have been expected to influence voters on behalf of their party's candidates. They are expected to make appointments to high executive positions and federal judgships on the basis of party affiliation. And they play an important role in decision making within the party's organization.

Jefferson's other contribution to the development of the presidency was his bold action in foreign relations. During his first term, he deployed naval forces to the Mediterranean to subdue the Barbary pirates. This ended the despised system of paying tribute. Jefferson's greatest achievement in foreign relations was the Louisiana Purchase (1803). This doubled the size of the United States for the ridiculously low price of $16 million. A president cannot conclude a treaty with a foreign nation without the "advice and consent of the Senate." But Jefferson had advised and consented with nobody; he simply bypassed the entire treaty process.

Andrew Jackson. Andrew Jackson was the first chief executive elected from west of the Allegheny Mountains. He was also the first from a state other than Virginia or Massachusetts. The first nonaristocrat, he sought to represent the common man. The general population had been in awe of Washington. They rarely even saw Jefferson. But they knew Jackson was their own man. He would spearhead the change from government by the wealthy few to government by the people. Today the name Jackson is almost synonymous with "fighting friend of the people." This is the spirit of **Jacksonian democracy.**

Jackson combined effectively the roles of chief of party, chief of state, and chief executive. He substantially enhanced the power of the office. Asserting his authority and independence, he refused to yield to Congress or his department heads in policymaking. He wielded strong party leadership and vigorously applied the veto. When one of his major policies was under attack after he left office, Jackson wrote to his successor, Martin Van Buren, "I say, lay on; temporize not, it is always injurious." This sentence neatly summarizes the Jackson style and probably helps to explain the love the people felt for him. To assure a politically loyal bureaucracy, he took one more step toward establishment of a **spoils system.** The idea was to make government more responsive to politics. It did so by permitting the winner of an election to fire officeholders and replace them with politically loyal supporters. These appointments made on the basis of political considerations—**patronage**—were later to be attacked by "reformers" seeking to purify politics and raise the level of competence in the bureaucracy. Still, patronage did give the president a way of ensuring that subordinates carried out the policies the people elected him to formulate. Patronage also gave him another carrot to dangle in front of members of Congress in exchange for their vote on his programs. He trusted his **Kitchen Cabinet,** a group of unofficial advisers, more than his official cabinet.

Abraham Lincoln. Abraham Lincoln was less famous and politically experienced than his leading rivals for the president. But he demonstrated remarkable maturity and statesmanship in the office and immeasurably broadened its scope.

Like Jackson, Lincoln enraged the Congress by sweeping and arbitrary acts that often went beyond Constitutional limits. When the Civil War started, he suspended certain constitutional liberties, spent funds that Congress had not approved, and banned treasonable correspondence from the U.S. mails. He set up limited conscription of young men into the army before Congress authorized it. By proclamation, he threw thousands of people into jail, without a trial, on suspicion of disloyalty. He waited until Congress had adjourned, then issued the Emancipation Proclamation freeing the slaves.

The Lincoln Fix

He was in his plain two-horse barouche, and look'd very much worn and tired; the lines, indeed, of vast responsibilities, intricate questions, and demands of life and death, cut deeper than ever upon his dark brown face; yet all the old goodness, tenderness, sadness, and canny shrewdness, underneath the furrows. (I never see that man without feeling that he is one to become personally attach'd to, for his combination of purest, heartiest tenderness, and native western form of manliness.) By his side sat his little boy, of ten years. There were no soldiers, only a lot of civilians on horseback with huge yellow scarfs over their shoulders, riding around the carriage. . . . They pass'd me once very close, and I saw the President in the face fully, as they were moving slowly, and his look, though abstracted, happen'd to be directed steadily in my eye. He bow'd and smiled, but far beneath his smile I noticed well the expression I have alluded to. None of the artists or pictures has caught the deep, though subtle and indirect expression of this man's face. There is something else there. One of the great portrait painters of two or three centuries ago is needed.

—Walt Whitman, on seeing the president in Washington, D.C., during the war *(Autobiographia).*

One has only to glance at the face of Lincoln "to feel the iron grip of a great man who was not only *in* the force of history (the Civil War was coming willy-nilly, etc.) but *was* a force of history. Not just in hindsight, but then and there, he was

Library of Congress

Abraham Lincoln at 54, photographed by Mathew B. Brady.

so recognized. Without Lincoln, things would not have been a little different, but entirely different. Because of his character, because of his visage . . . because of his *own* sense of history, because even of his triumph, with scars to show, over his physical and emotional self. . . .

One cannot escape Lincoln. Of course he was human, of course luck and happenstance played a role—and anyone can go on from there to list the ifs, buts, and might-have-beens. But still, there is no dissembling the thrust *of* Lincoln *on* history, and one ends up considering not so much any sweep

> of events, great or small, but a particular and overriding human effect—after all other factors have been acknowledged—of *character*.
>
> —Eliot Fremont-Smith in *Village Voice*, October 1–7, 1980, p. 45.
>
> His sad eyes watched and his heart shared the troubles of man adrift, generous and selfish, magnanimous and venal, but adrift, with no compass, a forgotten port, and a strong cold wind. He saw so much so quietly, accepting it without complaint or pretense, and still relishing the strife of the presidency. Like all the important Presidents he expanded the office; but he expanded himself still more. Most men rattle about inside the job; but Lincoln transcended it. Sometimes he seemed about to break its earthly bonds and seize the truth toward which he was groping. But he could not. He knew the vanity of this world. He knew that every secular victory must be soiled. So he could not fulfill himself in politics. And he could find nothing beyond. This is the burden of modern man at his wisest, which may explain why Lincoln was sorrowful.
>
> —Herbert Agar, in *The Price of Union* (Boston: Houghton Mifflin, 1950), p. 438.

The basis of many of these controversial acts was the war powers of the president. War powers are the authority granted to both the president and Congress to protect the nation from its enemies. From where does this authority come? Some of the authority is expressly granted by the Constitution—e.g., Congress can tax and spend for the common defense. Some is inherent in the role of the president as commander-in-chief to do whatever is necessary to protect the nation. Lincoln knew that President Madison had very nearly lost the War of 1812 rather than override the opposition to a draft and a national army. Lincoln would not make the same mistake; he fought to win.

Predecessors of the Modern Presidency: Roosevelt and Wilson

Theodore Roosevelt. The eight presidents who followed Lincoln did little to change the office. Then like a fireball in the night came Theodore Roosevelt. He was venturesome in spirit as well as intellect, flamboyant in personality, and physically energetic. Roosevelt expanded the role of the national government, and with it, the office of the presidency. Unlike Lincoln, Roosevelt won the affection of the American people and symbolized the president's role as leader of the people.

Probably no Congress could be happy with a president like Roosevelt. He had a definite

Library of Congress

Few Republicans have been as effective as Theodore Roosevelt at building and maintaining coalitions. How did he do it? By flattering and appeasing, by making an immense commotion (so that it seemed as if a lot was happening), and by preaching "uplifting" speeches. As he himself explained, there was nothing in these speeches "except a certain sincerity and a kind of commonplace morality which put him *en rapport* with the people."

view about the powers of the presidency. As he explained in a letter: "I think it should be a very powerful office, and I think the President should be a very strong man who uses without hesitation every power that the position yields." In his autobiography, he wrote:

> The most important factor in getting the right spirit in my administration . . . was my insistence upon the theory that the executive power was limited only by specific restrictions and prohibitions appearing in the Constitution or imposed by Congress under its constitutional powers. . . . Under this interpretation of executive power I did and caused to be done many things not previously done by the President and the heads of the departments. I did not usurp power but I did greatly broaden the use of executive power.

In international affairs, Roosevelt followed the principle "Speak softly and carry a big stick." His domestic reform program emphasized regulation of business and trusts, protection of the right of consumers and labor, and advancement of conservation. More than any president before him, he attempted to mobilize public opinion on behalf of his programs. He invented the press conference to take advantage of the emerging mass audience newspapers and magazines. To him, the presidency was a "bully pulpit."

Woodrow Wilson. The expansion in size and scope of national government in the beginning of the 20th century began to change significantly the concept of the presidency. Under Woodrow Wilson, the role of the president as manager was developed. Wilson was one of the first persons to obtain a doctorate in political science from an American university (Johns Hopkins). He was a recognized proponent of progressive reform in government that argued for new forms of efficiency and accountability. Indeed, the discipline of public administration considers Wilson's famous essay "The Study of Administration" as its starting point. Wilson's contention was, "It is getting harder to run a constitution than to frame one." In fact, some of the problems in economic and international affairs encountered by the nation were beyond Wilson's considerable expertise. Still, under Wilson, the framework was laid for a budget office and the machinery to administer the economy (the Federal Reserve system).

The Modern Presidency

When Theodore Roosevelt left office in 1909, the foundation for the modern presidency had been set. When times were quiet, the people seemed to accept an assertion of congressional power and a weakened presidency. But in times of crisis, they turned to the president for decisive leadership. This system worked during World War I when a number of restrictions on the president were shoved aside. For example, Congress authorized President Wilson to fix prices, take over the railroads, manage the communications systems, and control the distribution of food. After the war, Congress took back most of this power. The system worked again in 1933, when Franklin Roosevelt entered the White House and the American people faced an unprecedented economic crisis.

Franklin D. Roosevelt and the New Deal. When Roosevelt came to office, the Great Depression had brought the nation to its knees. Forces were at work that were to generate the cataclysm of World War II. During his unprecedented 12-year stint, Roosevelt greatly expanded presidential authority. He widened government functions and strove to restore economic vigor. He launched an unparalleled program of social welfare and helped lead the country and its allies toward victory over the Axis powers.

Facing a crisis situation, Roosevelt knew that his approach to the presidency should not be that of his predecessor, Herbert Hoover. An astute politician, Roosevelt knew the way the system worked: In times of crisis, the people's preference for weak government gives way to the call for action—for presidential leadership.

Today it seems inconceivable, but many

National Archives

As we shall see in this chapter, presidents play many roles. One of these is **commander in chief,** that is, the chief officer in the armed forces of the United States. In the photo, Franklin Roosevelt is reviewing the fleet from the U.S.S. *Houston* at San Francisco, three years before the United States entered World War II. The two major issues of the Roosevelt administration, according to Henry Steele Commager, were the domestic issue of the extension of government control over the economy and the international issue of the role of America as a world power.

Americans in the 1930s actually enjoyed Roosevelt's impatience with the Supreme Court, which thwarted some of his New Deal legislation. What one senator said of Theodore Roosevelt could also be said of Franklin Roosevelt. "What the boys like about Roosevelt is that he doesn't care a damn for the law." FDR, like many ordinary people suffering through the Great Depression, was convinced that the law, slow and ever obscure, was often an absurdity. "We know," he said, "it takes time to adjust government to the needs of society. But modern history proves that reforms too long delayed or denied have jeopardized peace, undermined democracy and swept away civil and religious liberties. Yes, time more than ever before is vital in statesmanship and in government, in all three branches of it. We will no longer be permitted to sacrifice each generation in turn while the law catches up with life."[2]

Harry S Truman: Consolidation of the modern presidency. Truman was thrust into the presidency by the sudden death of Roosevelt. He entered office at an extraordinary time: the complex and turbulent era ushered in by the conclusion of World War II. He used the atomic bomb against Japan to terminate the war. He contained the spread of communism through collective security alliances and extensive economic aid to war-ravaged and developing countries (the Truman Doctrine and Marshall Plan). He launched a massive airlift that defeated the Soviet Union's blockade of West Berlin. And he militarily resisted North Korea's invasion of South Korea. (See Chapter 14.)

Truman's reputation has grown in recent years. But his performance in office was, at the least, uneven. The Truman years were marked by the beginning of the Cold War with the Soviet Union. There was inflation and slow economic growth. There were government takeovers of private industry and costly nationwide strikes. And even the "limited police action" in Korea was not entirely a popular policy. His leadership was flat and uninspiring; his performance as president frequently generated more disapproval than approval.

But, performance aside, Truman greatly developed the presidency as an institution. Under him, the Bureau of the Budget (which in 1972 became the Office of Management and Budget) became the linchpin of the presidential apparatus. Essentially, the bureau assumed the role of central coordinating mechanism for designing the annual presentations to Congress of the president's program. Under Truman, the White House staff expanded to become a team that could shoulder some of the expanding workload of the presidency staff.

Many of Truman's decisions showed a clear determination to keep the powers of the presidency intact. Though costly to him politically, these tough decisions left little doubt in anyone's mind who the leader of public debate in the United States would be. But what would happen to the modern presidency when another president took office—one who had called for more of a congressional balance?

Dwight D. Eisenhower: Modern Republicanism. Following the more turbulent political events of the Truman administration, the presidency under Dwight D. Eisenhower was a period of relative peace and prosperity. Though economic and international problems abounded, Eisenhower's popularity and personal appeal were high. He negotiated an armistice in Korea. He furthered international disarmament and reduced Cold War tensions. And he inaugurated the U.S. space program. His domestic program of "dynamic conservatism" or "modern Republicanism" emphasized government economy and decentralization of federal projects. This was achieved through cooperation with state and local governments as well as private enterprise. He desegregated the District of Columbia's school system; this had not been done under Roosevelt and Truman. While Eisenhower's record was not unblemished, his decency and competency matched any other president for the previous 60 years.

This is not, however, the conventional view. Closer to the mark is a 1958 cartoon by Herblock. In the water a shark labeled "recession" chases a hapless swimmer. Eisenhower, dressed as a lifeguard, calmly looks on from his tower and says, "Don't get hysterical—I'm watching you all the time." According to Fred I. Greenstein, who has shifted through scores of newly released documents from the Eisenhower administration, this view is pure fiction.[3] Copies of Eisenhower's memos to his assistants make it clear that he was not a do-nothing president. It was he who set policy. The president preferred his staff to have the limelight—particularly when someone had to say no and bear grim news. This strategy, Greenstein contends, "preserved Eisenhower's ability to appear as a benevolent national and international leader."

By appearing to remain above political battles, Eisenhower conserved his "public prestige." By his low-key approach, he avoided "raising expectations about what the President as an individual can ever accomplish." The two presidents who followed him chose different tactics, as we shall see.

John F. Kennedy: The politics of expectations. The youthful John F. Kennedy brought to office a promising vigor, intellect, and style. He urged people to participate in government and commit themselves to the solution of contemporary problems. He inaugurated his "New Frontier" program of domestic reforms and defended minority rights. And he met stern Cold War challenges. But a bullet struck him down 1,037 days into his term, before he could realize many of his aims. He was the first president born in the 20th century and the first Roman Catholic; he was the fourth to be assassinated and the youngest at death.

Our views of Kennedy are still somewhat clouded by the shock of that death in the Dallas afternoon. Let us, therefore, at least begin with the facts. One cold fact is that Kennedy was a very popular president. No subsequent president has matched his record (see Figure 7–1). But facts such as these are inert things. They can be no more than the basis for a more researching line of inquiry. We should ask, (1) What was the source of Kennedy's popularity? and (2) What did Kennedy do with it?

The quickest, surest way a president can give his popularity a boost is by acting in a highly visible manner in the arena of international politics. Certainly this was the case for Kennedy. Not only in crises, such as Cuba, Laos, or Berlin, but in more constructive areas of foreign policy, such as foreign trade (1962) and nuclear test ban treaty (1963), Kennedy constantly appeared before the American people, fully arrayed, as their leader. As British journalist Henry Fairlie observed: "The eyes of the people were turned outward, where they could feel as one, and not inward, where they would be distracted by the normal divisions of a free

FIGURE 7-1
Public Approval of Recent American Presidents*

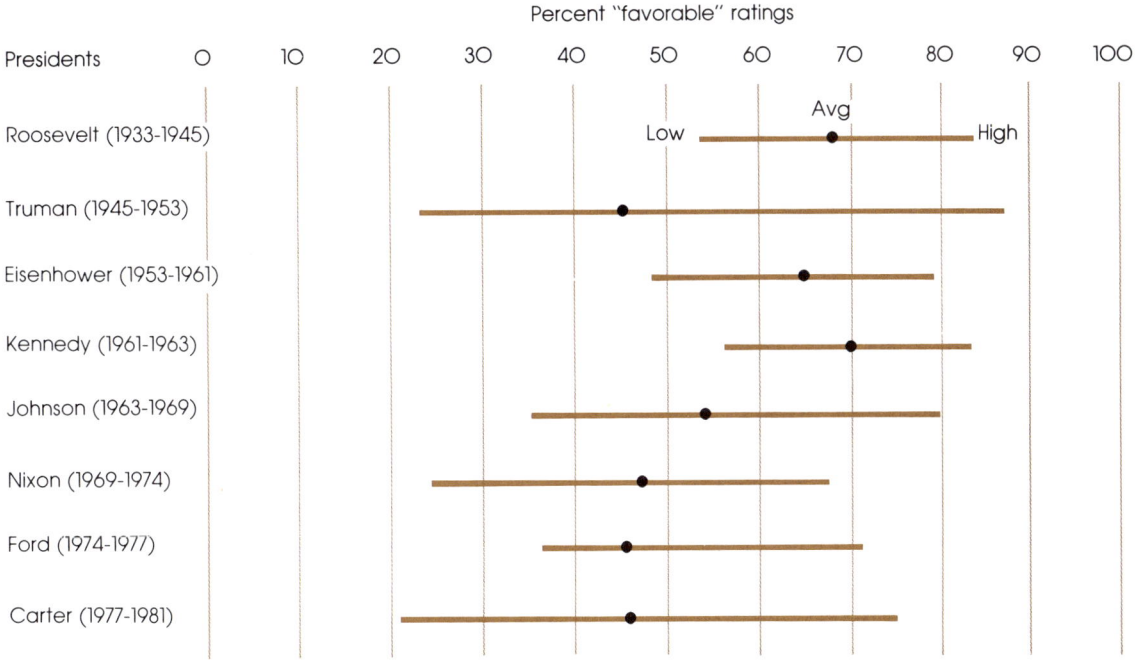

President	Low	Avg	High
Roosevelt (1933-1945)	50	70	85
Truman (1945-1953)	23	45	87
Eisenhower (1953-1961)	48	65	79
Kennedy (1961-1963)	57	70	83
Johnson (1963-1969)	35	55	80
Nixon (1969-1974)	24	49	68
Ford (1974-1977)	37	53	71
Carter (1977-1981)	37	47	75

Note: The percentages are of respondents who answered this question favorably: "Do you approve or disapprove of the way [name of incumbent] is handling his job as President?"

* After two months in office, the current president, Ronald Reagan, had an approval rating of 59 percent.

Source: American Institute of Public Opinion (Gallup Poll).

society. It was by this method, and in this atmosphere, that he practiced the politics of expectation."[4]

But what good is a high level of public support unless it is used as a political resource to do what a leader believes in? Kennedy did not take big risks in domestic policy. In fact, he removed any mention of domestic issues from his inaugural address. Once in office, he waited until popular support developed before acting on his convictions. In short, he avoided domestic battles that he thought he might lose.

As journalist Walter Lippmann observed at the time, the missing element in the Kennedy presidency was the willingness to take the time and trouble to explain, expound, describe, in a word, to teach:

John Kennedy is already proving himself to be an extraordinary chief executive. He has very great gifts of precise analysis and judgment, he has a rare combination of courage and political sophistication. Indeed, he has all the makings of a great president. But if he is to be a great president, he must be not only executive, organizer, politician, and popular leader. He must also be a popular teacher.[5]

Lyndon B. Johnson: War casualty. As we have just seen, Kennedy superbly exercised the inherent powers of the presidency. In his speeches and in his actions, he gave the people an exaggerated picture of what a president and politics could accomplish. Before any disillusionment could set in, however, Kennedy was dead.

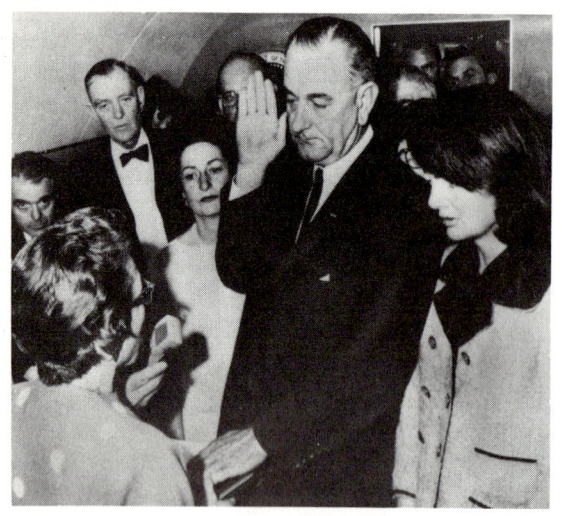

Lyndon Johnson is sworn in as president aboard Air Force One in Dallas on November 22, 1963.

Lyndon Johnson ascended to the presidency upon Kennedy's assassination and won his own term of office by an unprecedented popular majority. He enjoyed more federal legislative experience than any previous chief executive. He was also the first since Andrew Johnson to have come to office from the South. Johnson sought to build a **Great Society** at home while maintaining the nation's role abroad. He made giant strides in civil rights and expanded social welfare programs (many of these were part of his **war on poverty**).

In terms of the evolution of the presidency, three things about the Johnson years are significant. First was the addition of two departments to the president's cabinet: the Department of Housing and Urban Development, to coordinate various federal agencies, and the Department of Transportation, to develop a coordinated national transportation policy.

Second was the 25th Amendment which became part of the Constitution in 1967. It provided procedures by which the vice president could become acting president and procedures for filling the office of vice president if it became vacant. What prompted this adoption was the fact that shortly after the 1966 election Johnson underwent surgery. Part of the amendment was put to use in 1973 when Nixon's vice president, Spiro Agnew, resigned after pleading no contest to criminal charges. President Nixon then nominated Gerald R. Ford as vice president, and he was confirmed by Congress.

It is, however, the third thing about the Johnson years that really stands out. His tenure reveals with stunning clarity how *modern presidents must often face both domestic demands and foreign-policy challenges; a failure in either area can restrict and ultimately destroy the chances of success in the other.* Despite specific campaign pledges not to extend the war in South Vietnam, Johnson steadily increased U.S. intervention after his election in 1964. His support diminished when no end to the combat appeared in sight. With less political support, Johnson's capacity to push forward with his domestic programs was severely compromised. In a nationwide address on March 31, 1968, Johnson declared he would neither seek or accept the Democratic nomination for another term.

Retiring in 1969, Johnson, sad and broken, returned to his Ranch in Texas. Four years later he was dead—himself a political casualty of the Vietnam War, which he had inherited from Kennedy and then expanded. Perhaps because he wanted nothing less than to be a war president, Johnson conducted the war in a very indecisive way.

Richard M. Nixon: The failure of restraint. Richard Nixon's political career was meteoric and filled with vicissitudes. He served in the House of Representatives and Senate. He was a two-term vice president. And he barely lost the presidential race in 1960 and failed to win the California governorship two years later. In 1968, however, he won the presidency, though by a narrow margin. Four years later, he captured a record number of popular votes. Yet, despite notable achievements, particularly in international relations, the so-called **Watergate**

affair brought him to the brink of impeachment and forced him to resign—the first president ever to do so.

What brought about that resignation on August 8, 1974? And to what exactly does the "Watergate affair" refer?

Watergate refers to everything associated with the illegal acts of the Nixon administration. These include breaking into the offices of the Democratic Party National Committee in the Watergate office building in Washington, D.C., on June 17, 1972, wiretapping, stealing documents from the office of a private citizen, and lying to a grand jury.

Why did Nixon resign? The articles of impeachment that the House Judiciary Committee drafted cited several changes. There was a "cover-up"—that is, an illegal obstruction of justice on a grand scale. There was "abuse of power"—that is, a wide range of violations of citizens' constitutional rights. And the president defied congressional subpoenas commanding him to turn over documents and tapes. Nixon had installed a system to tape all his conversations in the Oval Office; without these tapes many believe Nixon could not have been impeached. What the tape did was show quite clearly that Nixon had lied when he previously stated that he had disclosed everything. This inconsistency was probably more damaging than what the tapes said.

One could argue that what occurred in the Nixon White House was pretty routine. Franklin Roosevelt and Lyndon Johnson had used the FBI to harass personal enemies. As John Roosevelt, FDR's youngest son said four months before Nixon's resignation: "I can't understand all the commotion in this case. Hell, my father just about invented bugging. Had them spread all over, and thought nothing of it."[6] John Kennedy's attorney general, Robert F. Kennedy, launched an electronic surveillance of Dr. Martin Luther King, Jr. Alan Dershowitz of the Harvard Law School estimates that 5,000 separate conversations went on tape, violating the privacy of hundreds of innocent King callers and visitors.[7] At least as disturbing were the allegations of President Kennedy's role in assassination plots against foreign leaders, such as Fidel Castro.

Two questions confront us: (1) Why did Nixon not destroy the tapes? and (2) Why was he driven from office for doing nothing more wicked than his predecessors? We can only speculate. But one suspects that Nixon did not destroy the tapes because he really believed himself innocent. As he told David Frost in a television interview in 1977: "When the president does it, that means it is not illegal." For him, *Salus populi suprema lex*—the public will (as interpreted by Richard Nixon) is the highest law.

With respect to the illegal activities of his predecessors, we need to recognize that the scope of Nixon's actions was wider and the context of those actions was different. Bluntly, Nixon went too far. As George F. Will wrote: "Nixon's sin, like all sin, was a failure of restraint. It was the immoderate craving for that which, desired moderately, is a noble goal."[8] Moreover, Nixon was operating at a time when conditions both here and abroad had vastly improved; it is only at times of crisis that the American people seem to want strong presidential leadership.

Ironically, the improved conditions had been to no small extent the fruit of Nixon's labor, especially in matters of foreign policy. The Vietnam War was liquidated, at least in American terms. The road to normalization of relations with China was opened. The framework for detente with the Soviet Union was laid. Much good effort toward a Middle East settlement was achieved. We shall have to wait to see whether historians focus on the dark side or bright side of the Nixon presidency.

With respect to the institution of the presidency, two features of the Nixon years stand out over everything else. As you know from Chapter 2, the Constitution abounds with checks and balances. The ultimate legislative check on presidential power is **impeachment.**

According to the Constitution, the House can bring about impeachment by a majority vote, and the Senate, by a two-thirds vote, can convict and thus remove a president from office. Only one president—Andrew Johnson in 1868—has ever been impeached, but the Senate fell one vote short of convicting him. President Nixon would probably have been the second president impeached (and probably the first convicted) had he not resigned in August 1974 prior to the House vote.

In addition to providing us with a dramatic reminder that Congress has impeachment as a last resort for unrestrained chief executives, the Nixon years resulted in a number of measures designed to control presidential power more tightly. Since Nixon's successor was the first to labor under these tough, new institutional restraints, we shall consider them in our discussion of the Ford presidency.

Gerald R. Ford: An Imperiled presidency?

Gerald Ford assumed office following President Nixon's resignation and quickly restored public confidence. Ford regenerated the spirit of national unity. After serving 25 years in the House of Representatives, he had been appointed as vice president under the 25th Amendment.

Ford was the first chief executive who had never been a candidate in a nationwide election. However, he was also the first to undergo an exhaustive congressional investigation into his qualifications. His prime domestic concern was invigoration of the economy. Abroad, he improved relations with the Soviet Union as well as China. And he spearheaded peacekeeping efforts in the Middle East and southern Africa.

In a speech delivered three years after he left office, Ford argued that we had moved from an **imperial presidency** (as the Nixon White House was called) to an "imperiled" presidency and a too-powerful Congress. In the speech, Ford listed the ways in which the hands of post-Watergate presidents have been tied:

> First, the president is constrained in his ability to impound (i.e., refuse) to spend funds appropriated by Congress—even when an agency is about to squander them.
>
> Second, he is restricted in reorganizing the bureaucracy.
>
> Third, he is restricted in the execution of some laws by the **legislative veto,** which gives Congress the right to cancel day-to-day regulations issued by federal agencies in administering laws already approved.
>
> Fourth, he must report all executive agreements with other countries to Congress.
>
> Fifth, he is at least partially blinded in the conduct of foreign policy by the dismantling of some operations by the Central Intelligence Agency.
>
> Sixth, and perhaps most perilous, he is hobbled by the War Powers Resolution of 1973 (and 70 other limiting amendments) in his ability to react to threats abroad. The president is unable even to *threaten* action. Any president who tests the 1973 act may find that he is no longer commander in chief and that it is up to the Supreme Court to decide whether troops will be committed or withdrawn.[9]

Jimmy Carter: The politics of indecision.

Jimmy Carter was inaugurated as the nation began its third century. He was the first chief executive to come to office directly from the Deep South since well before the Civil War. His only previous elective experience consisted of the governorship of his native Georgia and service in its legislature. But his vigorous presidential campaign dramatically propelled him into national prominence and into the White House. His campaign message was, essentially, this: "I'll never lie to you." In this sense, the ghost of Watergate worked to his advantage. Unfortunately, with the election won, the ghost of Watergate did not leave Carter. It stalked him for four years in Washington—curtailing his powers, expanding congressional powers, and causing general political apathy and mistrust.

Not surprisingly, distrust of President Carter was most visible in Congress. Sen. Henry M. Jackson, a member of Carter's own party, said openly that the president was afflicted by "abulia," an abnormal inability to act or to make decisions. The view was corroborated by former assistants. For instance, speech writer James Fallows charged that Carter was a problem solver who lacked presidential vision and the knack for inspiring people. "He holds explicit, thorough positions on every issue under the sun, but he has no large views of the relations between them, no line indicating which goals (reducing employment? human rights?) will take precedence over which (inflation control? a SALT treaty to control nuclear weapons?)."

Holding no vision larger than the issue at hand, the Carter presidency appeared inconsistent in its handling of such problems as energy, Iran, inflation, Israel, and the Soviet Union. Each zig in domestic policy tended to cancel out whatever progress had been made on the last zag. And zigzagging in foreign policy tended to confuse and even alarm America's allies.

Clark M. Clifford has been watching presidents for 40 years, served under LBJ as secretary of defense, and periodically advised Carter, gave this bittersweet appraisal of the Carter presidency:

> Jimmy Carter was a man who came from nowhere, flashed across the political firmament, had some solid accomplishments in his four years, but ultimately failed to establish a political base. Then the people, at their first opportunity, returned him to Georgia. There was nothing exceptional about it, no new theory of government was presented. It was just one of those rare moments that historians will rack their brains to understand and explain.[10]

Carter was high-minded in purpose. He did his best, conscientiously and honorably. And he cleared the way in many respects for his successor, Ronald Reagan. Perhaps Carter's most memorable achievement was getting elected in the first place. As early as 1972, he had accurately analyzed the mood of the American voter and the significance of the changes in the Democratic party's nominating procedures (which, as we saw in the last chapter, put a premium on campaign skill rather than long party service or experience).

Ronald Reagan. Several major efforts to refocus the presidency appeared quite early in the Reagan administration. It is too early to say whether these efforts will prove successful and lasting. However, viewed from the early 1980s, the ways Ronald Reagan wants to change the office are not hard to make out.

George Tames/NYT Pictures

In early July 1979, President Carter studied energy proposals in the cabinet room in the White House with top advisers. Among those with him were, from left, Treasury Secretary M. Michael Blumenthal, Energy Secretary James R. Schlesinger, and Stuart E. Eizenstat, assistant for domestic affairs. A few days later, President Carter unexpectedly cancelled a nationally televised energy speech at the height of the gasoline shortage and disappeared to Camp David. Thus an unusual personal and political drama engulfed the presidency, as the president met with private citizens to see how he could become a better president. In a conversation that none would soon forget, the president candidly admitted that he had "lost control of the government and did not have real leadership among the people." Afterward, Carter delivered his famous "crisis of confidence" speech, placing the blame for the country's ills squarely on the American people. Then he fired Blumenthal and Schlesinger.

First, he seems to take seriously what political scientists and management experts had been saying for several decades: The office is too big for any one person to manage alone. And he seems to be following the recommended remedy: Delegate authority to strong, competent, and experienced subordinates; concentrate only on the major issues; above all, do not become bogged down in the details of the office and cease to be the chief salesperson for your policies.

Second, Reagan seems to take seriously his campaign promise to cut back—or at least restrict the growth of—federal government. Consequently, he hopes to get states to assume some traditionally federal activities (see Chapter 10).

Third, he uses the office to carry his message to the public. This was no new departure. It is the principle Theodore Roosevelt expounded. (The presidency, Roosevelt said, is a "bully pulpit.") And it is an art Franklin D. Roosevelt and John F. Kennedy refined.

Last, and perhaps most important of all, while wanting to delegate authority to White House subordinates and to governors, Reagan still wants to show that a modern president has sufficient tools to make government work. Consequently, he places extraordinary effort into selling his legislative program to Congress and using his authority as chief executive to overcome congressional road blocks.

By getting Congress to enact the biggest tax and budget cuts in American history, Reagan established his undisputed national leadership in six months and set the American republic on a new economic course. When he took office in January 1981, few political observers thought this possible. What makes this feat so significant is not the fact that it was done despite a Democratic majority in the House, but that it seems to refute the thesis that the modern presidency had become institutionally crippled ("imperiled" in the words of Ford) by a sprawling bureaucracy and disorganized, unresponsive Congress. Certainly the experiences of Nixon, Ford, and Carter gave some credence to that thesis, but Reagan has shown that a president can be bold and purposeful. The worried essays about the breakdown of the machinery of government have stopped.

I should stress that while Reagan has demonstrated that a modern president can still make the system go, this says nothing about the efficacy of his particular goals. Whether the economic and foreign policy goals he seems to be moving toward are the correct goals is a separate issue (which we shall explore in Part IV.)

FUTURE FILE

Was the 1980 Election a "Critical Election"?

An important concept in understanding American politics is that of **critical** or **realignment elections.** Such elections have three characteristics. First, the critical election produces a new majority. More exactly, there is a clear realignment in the social and economic support of the majority and minority blocs. Second, this shift is significant and relatively durable. Third, the creation of a decisive majority has important, lasting political consequences. Let us assume, as we did in Chapter 6, that election outcomes are measures of the ability of citizens to control the direction of government. Then the absence of critical elections or stable majorities indicates a significant limitation in democratic practice. That is to say, "weak" or stalemated administrations cannot be viewed as good when they become the normal pattern of politics. [More elaborate explanations of critical elections can be found in V.O. Key, Jr., "A Theory of Critical Elections," *Journal of Politics* 17 (February 1955): 1–18; Duncan McRae and J. Meldrum, "Critical Elections in Illinois, 1888–1958," *American Political Science Review* 54 (September 1960): 669–83; and W.D. Burnham, *Critical Elections and the Mainsprings of American Politics* (New York: W.W. Norton, 1970).]

Political scientists generally agree that the presidential victories of Thomas Jefferson in 1800, Andrew Jackson in 1828, Abraham Lincoln in 1860, William McKinley in 1896, and Franklin Roosevelt in 1932 were critical elections. These elections served to restructure political alternatives and produce decisive political decisions. For example, the Roosevelt–Democratic victories of 1932 (and 1936) ended a long period of Republican ascendancy. Roosevelt and the Democrats won in 1932 because millions of voters suffering the ruinous consequences of the Great Depression left their old political allegiances to vote for FDR.

What happened in 1980? Was it a critical election? Given the major changes Reagan has initiated (see text), it appears that he is proceeding as if it was. But do the conditions of a critical election obtain? That is, was there a realignment? And if so, will it last?

Certainly, millions of traditional Democrats (who had supported FDR and his Democratic successors) broke their old allegiances in 1980 and voted for Ronald Reagan. Many were reacting to their decline in living standards, the squeeze of inflation and interest rates, and the frustration of American power abroad (as symbolized by the hostage ordeal in Iran). In some instances, they were also protesting the changes in social customs, lifestyles, and community standards condoned or encouraged by liberal legislatures and judges.

How can that be doubted, editor Norman Podhorentz asks,

> When John Lennon, the very embodiment of the 60's counterculture, could say (shortly before his death) that he now wanted "the family [to be] the inspiration for art, instead of drinking or drugs or whatever" . . . or when Tom Hayden, a founder of Students for a Democratic Society, the flagship organization of the New Left, and husband of Jane Fonda, writes in explanation of the defeat of his fellow 'liberals': "Having . . . lost God, the flag, national defense, tax relief, personal safety, and traditional family values to the conservatives, it became more than a little difficult for these liberals to explain why they should be entrusted with the authority to govern." ("The New American Majority," *Commentary*, January 1981.)

In both the urban areas of the Northeast and across the South (the two bases of Roosevelt's New Deal), millions of white Democrats abandoned Carter for Reagan. Many of them also rejected the Democratic senators and representatives they had been returning year after year. This made the election look like more than a mere rejection of Carter.

The Democratic party, since its founding in the 1830s, has been the party of the outsiders: the white South and the non-Yankee, non-WASP minorities, such as Roman Catholics and Jews. In the 1930s, that coalition was joined by black Americans, who were shifting from the Republicans. In the 1970s, one of those large communities came to feel no longer like an outsider; Roman Catholic families of European origin came to identify increasingly, in lifestyle and ideology, with the WASP core culture, traditionally the heart of the Republican party. The reason for this shift is not hard to see. These Catholics had begun to earn the nation's highest incomes after the Jews; both groups in earlier times had been poverty-stricken. Anti-Catholic prejudice, a burning fire in most of American history, has died away since John F. Kennedy's election. Ideas against big government and, as noted above, in favor of traditional moralism have become widespread. Meanwhile, the Democratic party in the 1960s became identified with black America the way it had been identified for many generations with Catholic America. It also became the voice of the new outsiders—Catholics of Latin-American background, women's liberationists, and, in the 1970s, homosexuals. Catholics were no longer outsiders.

The solid Republican West is an electoral

fact, if we allow for some shakiness in the Pacific states. Now the Republican party's dream of a coalition with the South seems at hand. Portions of the once-solid South have spurned the national Democratic candidate in six of the eight postwar presidential elections. In the 1980 election, not only did it give a favorite-son Democratic imcumbent only 12 electoral votes. Also all but two states of the old Confederacy now send Republican senators to Washington. An electoral coalition of the South and West controls 276 electoral votes. This is enough to seal a presidential election without any support at all from the industrial North and Northeast. And the lock will be tightened further when post-Census redistricting awards 14 more electoral votes to the Sun Belt.

But even assuming that there has been a permanent realignment, the question remains whether the 1980 victory is significant. The scope of Reagan's 1980 victory can be summarized as follows:

- Popular vote: About 43.3 million, second largest on record, behind Richard Nixon's 47.2 million in 1972.
- Popular vote percentage: Nearly 51 percent. In the preceding 20 presidential elections, only six winners got a smaller share.
- Electoral vote: 489 to 49, the third widest margin in this century.
- Plurality: About 8.3 million, well above Jimmy Carter's margin of 1.7 million in 1976.

In comparison, Franklin D. Roosevelt received 57.4 percent of the popular vote when he was first elected in 1932. Four years later, when he defeated Alf Landon by an electoral college margin of 523 to 8, he took 60.8 percent of the votes. His popular-vote percentages in his last two terms were 54.7 and 53.3. In order not to sound like I am deprecating Reagan's victory, let me cite some other old statistics. In the 1932 election the voter turnout was exactly as high as it was in 1980; Roosevelt got 30.1 percent of the *eligible electorate*. That is only 3.4 percent more than Reagan. Did Roosevelt have a mandate?

In conclusion, it is premature to read Ronald Reagan's triumph as a certified critical election. But we might say that the election did provide Reagan and the Republicans with a historic opportunity to change American politics. Whether they do will depend on three factors: how well Reagan manages the economy and foreign policy, how the "baby-boom" generation (now between 25 and 35 years of age) vote once they begin to turn out in higher numbers, and how well the Democrats crack the coalition of the new South and West.

Some Lessons for Leaders

To conclude this survey of the presidency, traditional and modern, we might attempt to distill a few common qualifications that can be useful to measure would-be presidents. The idea is to look beyond the issues of the day, for qualifications that are permanent. During presidential campaigns we hear a lot about specific issues. But there are more important qualifications than the ability to take the people down into the valve-and-boiler room of government for a complicated tour of the issues. Demonstrations of technical mastery are not what we are after here.

First, a successful president has a clear idea of what he wants to do. He moves in directions, both here and abroad, that advance this purpose. When does a president stop acting like a statesman? He begins whenever he stops trying to placate or stir up every momentary wish of the people and sets out to make them realize those hidden interests that are attainable and positive. By positive, I mean interests that raise the people to new possibilities, that offer human advancement. Great presidents are great teachers.

What presidents do command is a matchless opportunity for persuasion, if they are gifted enough at speech and timing and can get the nation to listen. "I did not 'divine' what the people were going to think," Teddy Roosevelt said. "I simply made up my mind what they ought to think and then did my best to get them to think it."[11]

They also realize what we said in Chapter 3: Ideas do matter. They have an organizing theory of politics and deeply rooted convictions. They have thought thoroughly how freedom and equality are related, what human nature is, and so forth. Accordingly, they are better able to deal with the shifts and surprises of public affairs. They present specific programs but explain those programs in the context of a sound general theory of how American society should be organized. Then, they consistently pursue the objectives of those programs, recognizing that no great results are ever achieved quickly.

Third, they understand too what we called in Chapter 4 the craft of political power. While President Johnson failed in Vietnam, let us not forget that he was able to gain support for many of his Great Society programs through his extraordinary ability to acquire, maintain, and exercise power. As Abraham Lincoln and Franklin Roosevelt knew, tyranny or anarchy in this republic is more likely to result from the failure of power than the abuse of power. While this expertise need not—and probably should not—be acquired through an entire career in Washington, some responsible Washington experience seems essential.

Fourth, would-be presidents ought to read history, not polls. No one ever accused Harry S Truman of being too scholarly. But few presidents had a keener sense of history.

The same might be said for Lincoln. Quite early, he realized that the slavery issue could not be peaceably resolved. So he proceeded to focus not on that immediate and timeless matter but on the Constitution and the Declaration of Independence: What might these documents mean as definitions of what this country was meant to be? He was perhaps the first president to call explicitly on this history. Lincoln's historical vision dictated his prosecution of the war. It made him, very self-consciously, the most dictatorial president in U.S. history.

Fifth, and finally, a president should have enough self-confidence that he will not feel threatened by having strong, capable people around him. Yet he still must be forceful enough to bring such independent personalities into harmony. As Eisenhower explained:

> The government of the United States has become too big, too complex, and too pervasive in its influence on all our lives for one individual to pretend to direct the details of its important and critical programming. Competent assistants are mandatory; without them the Executive Branch would bog down. To command the loyalties and dedication and best efforts of capable and outstanding individuals requires patience, understanding, a readiness to delegate, and an acceptance of responsibility for any honest errors—real or apparent—those subordinates might make.[12]

Contrary to any impressions you might have gotten from the opening section, the presidency is more than a single individual. It is a system. That is good for us. As a system is can be readily analyzed in two parts—structure and function. That is how biologists are likely to answer you if you ask them what a "digestive system" is.

Whether we are trained biologists or not, we could probably make a fair guess at what the structure and function of a digestive system is. But what is the structure and function of the presidency? I shall give a short answer here. In the next two sections I will elaborate on that answer. The structure of the presidency is, in a word, a **bureaucracy**. The chief function of the presidency is—again, in a word—policy-making.

THE STRUCTURE OF THE PRESIDENCY

The presidency is more than just one individual. Some have described the executive branch as three million people of whom one has been elected. All others are bureaucrats. Newly elected presidents find it difficult, often impossible, to lead the bureaucracy in new directions or away from old ones. This resistance to change is often termed bureaucratic inertia.

Bureaucracy Defined

The ideal of a bureaucracy as a form of organization was outlined in the works of German social scientist Max Weber (1864–1920). Weber maintained that the basis of all bureaucracy is a division of labor or specialization. Thus the Department of Commerce handles the problems of business: the Department of Agriculture handles those of farmers. Similarly, a private company might have one division handle marketing, another manufacturing, and so forth.

Weber also noted that bureaucracies have hierarchical structures or chains of command. This means that lower officials are responsible to and supervised by higher officials. The head of an office reports to the director of a bureau, who reports to a departmental secretary, who reports to the president. Written rules carefully define the authority of all these officials. Finally, Weber maintained that bureaucrats are recruited on the basis not of family and other connections but of competency and experience. Bureaucracy today has a pejorative connotation. But it was a vast improvement over what prevailed in the distant past. Quite frankly, some large-scale undertakings are not possible without some of these characteristics.

For many years, Americans have tended to refer to those who work in government as "bureaucrats." But, as Weber's definition makes clear, private business exhibits many of the characteristics of bureaucracy. Furthermore, many of the civil servants in Washington do not routinely administer programs; rather, they supervise the administration of programs by others. Therefore the term *bureaucrats* is not entirely appropriate. Despite these language problems, we shall, for convenience, refer to the 83 major government agencies that work on more than 1,000 major programs as the bureaucracy.

An Irreverent Look at American Bureaucratic History

1776 In the Declaration of Independence, the American colonists complain bitterly about the abuses of British *bureaucratic* powers: "unjust taxation, the weakening of the independence of the judiciary, the stationing of standing armies, and the extensive use of royal patronage to reward office-seekers at colonial expense."

1789 George Washington hires his nephew to help him with paperwork. If this was nepotism, at least Washington paid his nephew out of his own pocket.

1829 The new politics of the President Jackson era is known as the spoils system. Jackson believed in spoils not because he supported corruption but because he wanted *rotation in office*. He believed that any honest citizen was fit to hold office and that the public had the right to participate in the actual running of government.

A TYPICAL DAY IN THE LIFE OF THE AMERICAN CHIEF EXECUTIVE

Compared to modern presidents, Ronald Reagan does not work long or hard. When in Washington rather than on his California ranch or at nearby Camp David, he is seldom in the office before 8:45 A.M. And it is rare for him to stay there past 6 P.M. He prefers to let his staff and friends do much of the information gathering, planning, listing of options, and following up on past decisions.

This approach to running the executive branch has its advantages and disadvantages. On the plus side, it allows the president to concentrate on public leadership and key issues. The chief executive is not an hourly employee who must punch a time clock. He is paid for his judgment, not his time. His success depends on how he handles social, economic, and foreign policy—not how many hours he has spent on each. Some recent presidents have almost given hard work a bad name.

The disadvantage to this approach is that it can lead to the appearance of inattention to and ignorance of the issues. This can occur at press conferences and at meetings with highly knowledgeable heads of state such as West Germany's Schmidt and Canada's Trudeau. There is also the danger that the president can lose control, especially when the White House organization fails to run smoothly. Less pressure on the chief executive means more responsibility on the staff.

Karl Schumacher / The White House

9 A.M. — Meeting with staff in Oval Office

Michael Evans / The White House

9:30 A.M. — Meeting with Democratic legislators

Michael Evans / The White House

10:15 A.M. — Briefing on day's events by Secretary of State Haig and assistant

Michael Evans / The White House

10:45 A.M. — Meeting with Senator Paul Laxalt, the president's "eyes and ears" in the Senate

Michael Evans / The White House

11:15 A.M. — Interview with the Washington press corps

Bill Fitz-Patrick / The White House

12 NOON — Greeting luncheon guest, the late President Anwar Sadat of Egypt

Michael Evans / The White House

1:30 P.M. — Walking to Cabinet meeting, briefing book in hand

Michael Evans / The White House

1:35 P.M. — Entire Cabinet meets

Karl Schumacher / The White House

2:45 P.M. — Phoning reluctant member of Congress about pending legislation

Michael Evans / The White House

3 P.M. — Meeting with one of many interest groups and advisory committees

Jack Kightlinger / The White House

3:45 P.M. — Catching up on paperwork

Michael Evans / The White House

5 P.M. — Reception for Prince Charles

Therefore, public offices should be rotated. Two consequences follow: (1) rotation tends to favor the party that has won the last election and (2) in order that *any* citizen can hold office, the *form* of government had to change. Accordingly, jobs had to be more narrowly defined, more specialized. In short, government became more machine-like or bureaucratic.

1862 Birth of the federal government's first important agency designed to serve the needs of a particular client, when farmers got a Department of Agriculture. In 1913, unions would get a Department of Labor and business interests—lest they feel neglected—would get a Department of Commerce. In 1978, the Department of Education was created to enhance political representation of teachers in the federal government. Unfortunately, such agencies become relatively free from general political control.

1881 Charles Guitean, a disappointed office-seeker, murders President Garfield. Shortly after the assassination, a letter Guiteau had written to Garfield is discovered. In a single line, it bluntly captures the spirit of the spoils system: "The men that did the business last fall (i.e., worked in your campaign) are the ones to be remembered (i.e., rewarded with a government job)."

1883 Thanks to Guiteau, efforts to establish mechanisms that would reduce the worst outrages of the spoils system move forward rapidly. The reform effort finally culminated in the passage of the **Pendleton Act**. The spoils system was at least partly replaced by a **merit system** in which appointments and promotion are based on more or less objective measures such as tests, experience, and formal education. Implicit in the Pendleton Act were three principles upon which the merit system is based: (1) open competition for available jobs—that is, no group of people should be arbitrarily closed out of being considered for a government; (2) occupational ability—that is, people who are selected should be competent and qualified for the jobs to which they have been appointed; and (3) political neutrality—that is, civil servants should not be obligated to politicians. So it came to pass that the personnel system of federal government became a **civil service system** in which selection and advancement were based on the ability of employees to perform in a politically neutral, competent manner rather than to please politicos intent on reelection.

1887 The first regulatory agency, the Interstate Commerce Commission (ICC), is created. It serves as the model for a long list of alphabet agencies (FTC, FDA, CAB, FCC, and so forth) that purport to protect the public but tend to protect a certain industry (such as trucking or railroads).

1939 The Political Activities Act—better known as the **Hatch Act,** after its sponsor Senator Carl Hatch, a Democrat from New Mexico—prohibits federal employees from using the authority or influence to interfere with an election and prohibits any coercion of public employees to contribute time or money to a candidate or party.

1946 The **Administrative Procedures Act** requires that federal agencies publish advance notice of proposed rule changes in the **Federal Register** and give interested people the opportunity to participate through formal hearings or submissions of written material. The intent of the Act was to prevent bureaucracies from slipping new rules by unsuspecting clients or public interest groups (see Chapter 6). An unintended consequence was the administrative process became more legalistic.

1964 During the Free Speech Movement, Berkeley students complain bitterly about the abuses of the University of California's *bureaucratic* powers: "lack of a say in college government" and "computer-card education." Meanwhile, back at the White House, Lyndon Johnson, protégé of Franklin Roosevelt, is forced to establish a new welfare bureaucracy (Office to Economic Opportunity) *to work around* the calcified apparatus Roosevelt set up for his New Deal.

> **1978** The Civil Service Reform Act recognizes that many high-level positions in the civil services have important policymaking responsibilities and the president ought to have more flexibility in filling them. The law establishes a **Senior Executive Services** (SES) of about 8,000 top federal managers to meet this need. Members of the SES who perform well are eligible for cash bonuses—not surprisingly, a high percentage are deemed to perform well. The act also replaced the Civil Service Commission with the **Office of Personnel Management** (OPM). The latter does most of the hiring for federal agencies. Once hired, a person is assigned a G.S. (General Schedule) rating, ranging from G.S.–1 to G.S.–18.

Just How Big Is the Bureaucracy?

Many Americans might think Weber left out the most important (and loathsome) characteristic of bureaucracy: its size. In the 1830s, the American government bureaucracy consisted of about 300 clerks in four buildings. By the turn of the century, despite a great Civil War, there were still only 26,000 employed. Today there are 3.1 million federal bureaucrats housed in 460,000 buildings.

Whenever people start criticizing the growth of federal government, some government spokesman is apt to respond proudly by letting them know that the number of federal employes has hardly grown at all in the past 30 years. It is well known that this federal payroll figure does not tell the whole story of the government's relationship to the American work force. But in 1979, the weekly magazine *National Journal* took a crack at the hard job of finding out how many workers there actually are who get all or most of their income from the federal government. It came up with the estimate that these "invisible workers" total more than 8 million.

This means that, for every employee who shows up on the federal payroll, there are almost three more government-supported workers who do not. They range from assembly line workers producing military equipment for the Defense Department to public relations consultants for the Department of Energy to schoolteachers financed by HEW grants to managers who run HUD-owned buildings. About 3 million of them, the *National Journal* estimates, provide goods and services to the federal government itself; the other 5 million work for other employers, such as state and local governments, while federal authorities foot the bill. Each of the 8 million, needless to say, has some kind of stake in the persistence of a big and active federal apparatus.

In addition to these "ghost battalions," a couple of other facts ought to be noted if we are to appreciate the scope of the modern bureaucracy. One is that the bureaucracy, along with the president and Congress, helps shape public policy. The other is that the big growth in public employment has occurred in state, county, and local governments. From 1950 to 1978, the number of these employees per 1,000 population increased 117 percent. This reflects the trend for the federal government to coordinate and manage the business of state and local governments.

Bureaucratic Inertia

In physics, as every schoolchild knows, there is the "principle of inertia": Every body persists in a state of rest or state of uniform motion in a straight line, unless compelled by external force to change that state. So it is with those large bodies known as bureaucracies. If they are at rest, they will remain at rest unless a president is willing to make a considerable investment in time and energy to overcome this inertia. Because the required effort is often so great, chief executives sometimes prefer to leave the existing bureaucracy in peaceful slumber and create another bureaucracy to carry out their new policy initiative. The principle of bureaucratic inertia also helps explain why it is so hard for a president to get a bureaucracy to stop what it is doing or to change directions. Business executives who come to Washington with Republican administrations quickly learn this principle. So do the social reformers who come with new Democratic administrations.

agencies, regulatory commissions, and government-owned corporations. (See inside back cover.) We shall consider each of these briefly.

The departments. Today, there are 13 cabinet departments. The relative influence of each department is a function of two factors. First is the department itself. (The Departments of Defense and Health and Human Services are the biggest.) The second is the individuals who head them. (The Department of State was especially influential under Henry Kissinger, as was the Treasury under John Connally.) Over time, the cabinet departments have changed and continue to change in terms of number, size, orga-

---

The Bureaucratic Maw

Once upon a time in Camelot, Robert F. Kennedy was commuting daily through the Virginia countryside and was irritated to see a road sign directing any passing motorist to CIA headquarters at Langley. He complained to his brother the president. "Get somebody to take that sign down," JFK ordered an aide. A call went out to the Interior Department. Days passed. Nothing happened. Bobby repeated his complaint. JFK repeated his order. Again, nothing happened. Finally, exasperated, the president short-circuited the bureaucratic chain of command and put in a direct call to the man in charge of signs in the Virginia exurbs. "This is Jack Kennedy," he said, looking at his watch. "It's 11 o'clock in the morning. I want that sign down by the time the attorney general goes home tonight, and I'm holding you personally responsible." He returned the receiver, still smoking, to its cradle. "I now understand," he said, "that for a president to get something done in this country, he's got to say it three times."

SOURCE: *Newsweek,* January 26, 1981, p. 41.

The power of the bureaucracy to make or break a policy cannot be overemphasized. In some instances, how the bureaucracy chooses to interpret a law is more important to the president's program than what happened in Congress when it was passed.

President as Manager

For convenience, we can group most of the agencies reporting to the president into four categories: departments headed by members of the cabinet, the independent administrative

nization, and responsibility. Yet the idea remains, as originated by Washington's choice of four secretaries (state, treasury, war, and attorney general); the nation's most critical problems and constituencies should be represented in the president's cabinet.

Presidential candidates tend to promise that, if elected, they will rely heavily on their cabinets. Few do. The reasons are varied. Presidents prefer the advice of real experts; most Cabinet officials are more managers or politicians than experts. Gradually, cabinet members tend to become advocates of their individual departments rather than of the president's goals.

The senior administrators of these departments must in practice answer as much to Congress, which votes their departments' funds, as to the president who nominated them. Few other countries have a system in which heads of departments or ministries have, in effect, two separate—and often conflicting—masters.

Contrary to the British system, the American cabinet does not coordinate government programs; nor, for that matter, does the president. Hence there is duplication. For example, there are 77 housing programs under 15 agencies, 100 social service programs, and 20 agencies working in education.

Michael Evans and Bill Fitz-Patrick/The White House

The Reagan Team

1. Alexander Haig, secretary of state
2. Raymond Donovan, secretary of labor
3. Donald Regan, secretary of the treasury
4. Terrel Bell, secretary of education
5. David Stockman, budget director
6. Andrew Lewis, secretary of transportation
7. Samuel Pierce, secretary of HUD
8. William French Smith, attorney general
9. James Watt, secretary of the interior
10. Jeane Kirkpatrick, ambassador to the U.N.
11. Edwin Meese, counselor to the president
12. James Edwards, secretary of energy
13. Malcolm Baldridge, secretary of commerce
14. William Brock, U.S. trade representative
15. Richard Schweiker, secretary of HHS
16. John Block, secretary of agriculture
17. William Casey, director of CIA
18. Caspar Weinberger, secretary of defense

In addition to the 13 major departments, there are numerous **independent agencies** that also answer to the president. Some of the major ones include:

U.S. Postal Service. With more than 650,000 employees, it has the second largest payroll in government.

Community Services Administration. Operates many programs for the nation's poor.

ACTION. Includes the Peace Corps, VISTA, and other citizen-volunteer services for people in need.

National Aeronautics and Space Administration (NASA). Conducts extensive research and directs a variety of manned and unmanned space missions.

General Services Administration. Constructs, maintains, and supplies the huge network of government facilities.

Small Business Administration. Provides advice and financing to new or struggling firms.

United States Information Agency. Conducts informational and cultural programs overseas.

Veterans Administration. Provides health, education, and homeownership services for veterans—plus benefits for their survivors.

Regulatory commissions and government corporations. The executive branch also contains many "independent" agencies or commissions. They are charged with protecting the public by regulating various phases of private business activity. The first was the Interstate Commerce Commission, established in 1887. The largest is the Environmental Protection Agency, with over 12,000 employees. Regulatory bodies cover four general categories: (1) economic regulation of commerce, communications, transportation, and agriculture; (2) regulation of banking and financial activity; (3) environmental, health, safety, and consumer protection regulation; and (4) civil rights and employment regulation. Because regulatory bodies derive their authority from special delegations by the Congress, regulatory agencies serve two often conflicting masters.

Finally, there are about 20 government-owned corporations. They were created to provide some service that could be handled by the private sector but often charge less for their services than the consumer would pay a private-sector producer. Until 1970, when the U.S. Postal Service was created, the largest government corporation was also the oldest—the Tennessee Valley Authority (TVA). It provides electricity, flood control, and recreational facilities to seven southeastern states. Another government corporation, Comsat, sells time sharing on NASA satellites for radio communication. Amtrak is an example of Washington taking over part of a "sick industry" (passenger railroad traffic) and making it into a government corporation.

The Executive Office of the Presidency (EOP). A response of modern presidents to the management problems of the executive branch has been to increase the staff offices of the president. That is to say, to ride herd over the 13 departments and the numerous independent agencies outlined above they have created their own bureaucracy—the Executive Office of the President (EOP). Among the more important agencies in the EOP are the National Security Council (NSC), White House Office, Office of Management and Budget (OMB), Council of Economic Advisers, and Domestic Council. There are three major policy arenas.

First is the area of foreign and defense policy. The **National Security Council** coordinates foreign policy with defense policy. The formal membership includes the president, vice-president, and secretaries of state and defense.

The Central Intelligence Agency, which gathers and interprets vital information on security matters, reports to the NSC. Far from being a hawkish band of adventurers, the Central Intelligence Agency usually develops

The top military adviser on the National Security Council is the chairman of the **Joint Chiefs of Staff**. But high-ranking military officers do not always find it easy to remain true to their convictions. "Their innate awe of the Commander-in-Chief," Henry Kissinger writes, "tempts them to find a military reason for what they consider barely tolerable. They rarely challenge the Commander-in-Chief; they seek excuses to support, not to oppose him." [*White House Years* (Boston: Little, Brown, 1979).] In 1979, the JCS testified before the Senate Foreign Relations Committee on a nuclear arms limitation agreement. From left are Gen. Edward C. Meyer of the Army; Adm. Thomas B. Hayward of the Navy; Gen. David C. Jones, the chairman; Gen. Lew Allen, Jr., of the Air Force; Gen. Robert H. Barrow of the Marine Corps.

The chiefs formally endorsed the agreement with the Soviet Union. But their support wavered under questioning. Such events are rare; high-ranking military officers almost always support firmly the president's position—unless they seek early retirement.

rationales for inaction. No one has ever been penalized for not having foreseen an opportunity. But many careers have been ruined for not predicting a risk. Therefore, the CIA has always been tempted to forecast dire consequences for any suggested course of action.

The president's national security adviser is a post made famous by Henry Kissinger under Nixon. It plays a major role in the council. Ideally, the secretary of state is the president's principal adviser; the security adviser is primarily a senior administrator and coordinator. When the security adviser becomes active in the development and articulation of policy, the effectiveness of the secretary of state is inevitably diminished. As a result, foreign governments are confused. In 1980, largely in reaction to the growing influence of security adviser Zbigniew Brzezinski, President Carter's secretary of state, Cyrus Vance, resigned.

Second is the area of domestic policy. The **White House Office** consists of a number of specialists who are, in effect, organizational extensions of the president. Beginning with Eisenhower, most presidents have designated a chief of staff to run this staff and determine who gets in to see the president. All modern presidents have had a few speech writers; a press secretary, who meets with the media and speaks for the president in his absence; and a staff for congressional relations, which keeps an eye on the progress of presidential high-priority legislation in Congress and, in fact, lobbies members of Congress to support such legislation.

Essentially, the White House Office staff provide a domestic policy staff role. This role has long been a point of contention. In 1970, President Nixon established the Domestic Council under the aegis of the OMB and the White House. The council was to coordinate domestic policy recommendations and preside over interagency review. The Nixon concept (later followed by Ford) was patterned after the NSC model. But it largely fell apart during the Carter administration. Carter wanted more of a regular domestic policy staff. Therefore the Domestic Council was reorganized in 1978. President Reagan has revitalized the original Domestic Council concept somewhat. It remains to be seen, though, how the presidency will organize the coordination of domestic policy matters in the 1980s.

The third and final major policy area is economic. One of the most important agencies in the EOP is the **Office of Management and Budget** (OMB). Its staff of nearly 700 prepares the federal budget each year, prescribes the accounting procedures and guidelines to be used by all federal agencies in drafting their budget requests, monitors their expenditures on a continuous basis, looks for ways to improve the

People working outside the Executive Office of the President see staff agencies such as OMB (left) and CEA (right) in special ways.

management of the agencies, and supervises plans to reorganize the federal bureaucracy. In addition, OMB issues many operating instructions. For example, after Congress adopted the Privacy Act of 1974, OMB told the agencies how to put the law into practice. OMB also screens most forms the federal agencies send out to businesses, individuals, and state and local agencies. It reviews legislation involving federal spending and coordinates the administration's efforts to obtain new legislation. It has a big say on pay raises for federal employees each year. OMB's purview is supposedly economic. But it has a large stake in other areas of domestic policy.

In sum, OMB's job is to make sure the president sees all the implications of any new program and to challenge or improve ongoing programs every year. People who run government programs and special interest groups recognize it as the powerful agency that can wipe out entire projects with a stroke of the pen. As the official nay-sayer, OMB absorbs a lot of criticism that might otherwise be directed at the president.

The **Council of Economic Advisers (CEA)** is usually composed of prominent economists. It provides the president with economic advice on how to *(a)* curb inflation, *(b)* reduce unemployment, and *(c)* preserve growth. Much of this advice is reflected in the economic report it prepares for the president to submit each January to Congress, as required by the Employment Act of 1946. In Chapter 13, we shall consider these three, often contradictory, objectives more closely. In the 1980 presidential campaign, with economic policy a paramount issue, the CEA played a more central role in government than it had in many years.

The invisible deputy: The vice presidency. Given their strategic location in Figure 7–2, why have vice presidents been so ineffective throughout presidential history? Although the vice president is expected to attend cabinet meetings and preside over the Senate (and vote only in case of tie), the role of the office has been largely image with little real substance. Vice presidents have traveled the world and the country representing the presidency. But they have had little effect on the operation of government or policy formulation. The effectiveness of a vice president is largely up to the president. Significantly, President Carter used his vice president, Walter Mondale, perhaps more than any previous presidents had. President Reagan seems to be more or less following

FIGURE 7-2
The Transition of Presidential Power in Crises
Photo by Michael Evans/The White House

National security chain of command under executive order issued first by President Eisenhower

- President
- Defense Secretary
- Chairman, Joint Chiefs of Staff
- Commander of U.S. Forces

Line of succession as set by the Presidential Succession Act of 1947

- Vice President
- House Speaker
- Senate President Pro Tem
- Secretary of State
- Secretary of the Treasury
- Secretary of Defense
- Attorney General
- Secretary of Interior
- Secretary of Agriculture
- Secretary of Commerce
- Secretary of Labor
- Secretary of Health and Human Services
- Secretary of Housing and Urban Development
- Secretary of Transportation
- Secretary of Energy
- Secretary of Education

Early in the Reagan administration Vice President Bush was designated crisis manager. Who would take that post in his absence is not certain. In the photograph, Reagan, who likes to get information orally, is having his weekly lunch with Bush in the Oval Office.

this trend in his use of Vice President George Bush.

The main function of the vice president has been presidential succession. This has probably distorted our image of what makes a successful vice president. A simple test of history trivia will prove the point. Most students can list the nine vice presidents who have succeeded to the presidency. But few can list the nine vice presidents who either died in office (seven) or resigned (two). Succession has provided a number of past controversies; these have been somewhat resolved by the 25th Amendment. Now, when the office of vice president becomes vacant (through death, resignation, or promotion), the president can nominate a new vice president, who then must be confirmed by a majority of both houses of Congress. Of course, in the nuclear age, there remains the eerie possibility that the entire order of presidential succession (president, vice president, Speaker of the House, president pro tem of the Senate, secretary of state, and the remaining cabinet secretaries) could be dispatched with a single stroke. This necessitates, as Secretary of Education Terrell Bell found out hours before President Reagan's inauguration, that at least one member of the Cabinet be in a different location so as to preempt such a possibility. Secretary Bell, as the head of the newest cabinet department, had to stay home.

A more complex matter involves determining whether the president is "disabled" and unable to continue the duties of office. The March 1981 assassination attempt on President Reagan did not result in a disabling injury but very nearly could have. Nonetheless, there was considerable controversy as to who was in charge. The 25th Amendment provides for two procedures to declare presidential disability. The president may notify the Congress in writing directly or the vice president and a majority of the cabinet may provide such written notification. The latter procedure is terminated when the president notifies the Congress of the end of the disability. (This can be disputed, though, by the vice president and a majority of the cabinet.) Should this rather complicated set of events unfold, the Congress must decide the issue directly. There is historical precedent for such a process. Woodrow Wilson suffered a severe stroke in the last year of his presidency, and there remains considerable controversy over both his judgments and who was actually in command of the executive office in this period.

Figure 7–3 provides a helpful, concise con-

Who's in Charge Here?

As President Reagan was undergoing surgery [after an assassination attempt in March 1981], Secretary of State Alexander Haig stood before reporters and television cameras and said, "As of now, I am in control here in the White House, pending return of the vice president, and in close touch with him." Asked who was in authority, Mr. Haig said, "Constitutionally, gentlemen, you have the president, the vice president and the secretary of state, in that order."

Haig, a former White House chief of staff and military commander, may have hoped to reassure the world that the U.S. government was functioning smoothly. But his statements generated confusion about how power and authority are transmitted to others when a president is temporarily unable to function.

To some people in Washington Haig's remarks seemed to imply that Secretary Haig had placed himself in charge of the country, at least temporarily. An aide later explained that all Haig had meant was that until vice president [George Bush] arrived at the White House he, as senior cabinet officer, was in charge of the operations there.

In fact, Haig's recital of the order of succession was erroneous. Neither the U.S. Constitution nor the little-known presidential order establishing

the military chain of command puts the secretary of state third in authority. Article II of the Constitution provides for succession to the presidency by the vice president if the president dies or resigns, or if he is removed from office or in unable to discharge his duties. If neither the president nor the vice president can serve, the Constitution empowers Congress to specify by law "what officer shall then act as President."

By law, the line of succession after the vice president is the Speaker of the House of Representatives, the president pro tempore of the Senate and then the secretary of state, followed by the 12 other officers of the cabinet, in a specified order.

The 25th Amendment to the Constitution, which provides the method for filling a vacancy in the vice presidency, also stipulates how the vice president can assume the powers and duties of the presidency as "acting president."

The amendment, ratified in 1967, was created after the assassination of President Kennedy. Vice President Lyndon Johnson, a man in relatively poor health, had become president, leaving the vice presidency vacant and the succession issue open.

If the president cannot discharge his duties, the amendment provides that he can notify the Speaker of the House and the president pro tempore of the Senate so that the vice president can assume his duties until he is ready to resume them. Similarly, the vice president and a majority of the cabinet can notify congressional leaders in writing of the president's inability to govern. If the president's inability is disputed, Congress must decide by a two-thirds vote of both houses.

Separate from the constitutional procedure, but related to it, is the National Command Authority, a set of rules established by presidential order under which the president exercises his power as commander in chief of the armed forces.

These command rules, based on the National Security Act of 1947, are detailed in secret presidential orders that every President signs at the outset of his administration.

The command authority doesn't establish who succeeds the President in office. Instead, it sets forth the procedure by which the country continues to function—that is, critical decisions can be made—even in the direst of circumstances (such as nuclear attack).

SOURCE: Walter S. Mossberg, *The Wall Street Journal*, April 1, 1981.

---

clusion to this section, which dealt with the bureaucratic structure of the presidency. It also provides an appropriate backdrop for the section on the policy-making function of the presidency, which follows.

Given the size of the executive branch, the president uses the EOP to show that government really can work. Just because he is out of touch with main currents, the president should not think that the announcement of a decision gets the job done. There must be follow-through.

Unfortunately, the administrative system is not well-designed for policy coordination. Few in Washington doubt today the link between foreign policy and economic policy. But, as Figure 7–3 suggests, there are no mechanisms for such coordination. The Treasury Department is primarily responsible for international monetary affairs. Commodity agreements are negotiated by the State Department; but they must be approved by Congress, which is heavily influenced by the Agriculture Department. Matters of trade and investment are handled, variously, by a special trade representative responsible to the president and Congress, and by the Treasury, State, and to some extent, the Commerce Departments. No single individual has a chance to take over foreign economic policy. The linkages between the other policy arenas are even weaker. Consider the problem of illegal aliens in the Southwest; it is an economic, social, and foreign policy problem. Given our current policy coordination capabilities, there is little

FIGURE 7-3
How the President Manages

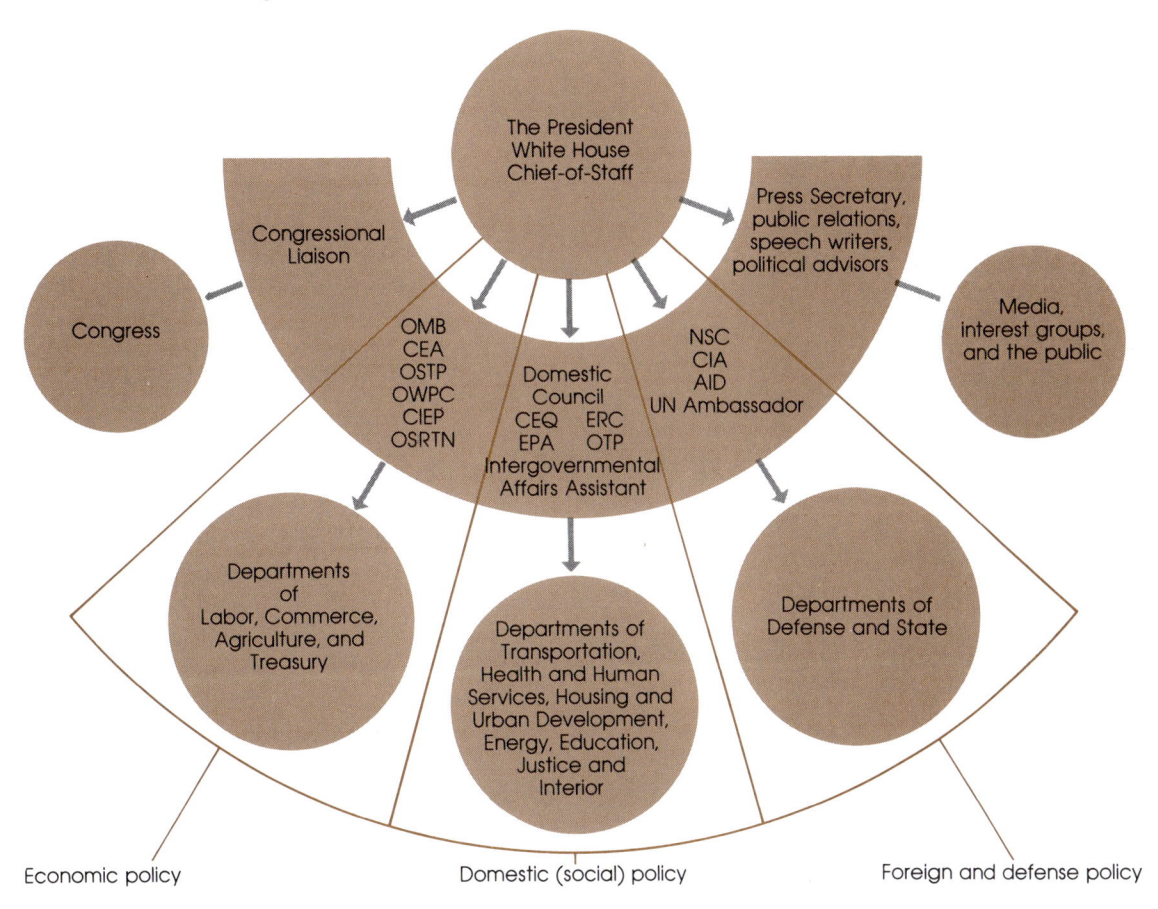

```
                    The President
                    White House
                    Chief-of-Staff
```

Congressional Liaison

Press Secretary, public relations, speech writers, political advisors

Congress

Media, interest groups, and the public

OMB
CEA
OSTP
OWPC
CIEP
OSRTN

Domestic Council
CEQ   ERC
EPA   OTP
Intergovernmental Affairs Assistant

NSC
CIA
AID
UN Ambassador

Departments of Labor, Commerce, Agriculture, and Treasury

Departments of Transportation, Health and Human Services, Housing and Urban Development, Energy, Education, Justice and Interior

Departments of Defense and State

Economic policy — Domestic (social) policy — Foreign and defense policy

chance that any policy will emerge to deal with this set of problems in the near future.

This completes the review of the structure of the presidential system. Now let us consider what its function is.

PRESIDENTIAL POLICYMAKING

Classifying Public Policy

Policy was a word encountered in the opening chapter. There we said it referred to the general direction in which a government wanted to go with respect to some problem. Ideally, a policy is a statement of goals in some order of priority. Major pieces of legislation that come out of Congress are public policies.

We can classify public policies by function or type. The functional classification arranges all legislation according to its purpose; it does not matter which agency administers the program. These functions are indeed meant to be mutually exclusive; in reality this is not always possible. Some major functions are:

Agriculture
Commerce and housing credit
General science, space, and technology

Energy
Natural resources and environment
Transportation
Community and regional development
Education
Training, employment, and social services
Health
Income security
Administration of justice
National defense
International affairs

As we learned in Chapter 4, we can also classify policies by type. One type is **distributive policies**; these attempt to stimulate private activities that citizens or groups would not otherwise undertake. Income tax credits to home owners to better insulate their homes is an example of a distributive policy. Another type is **regulatory policies**; these attempt to set conditions under which private activities operate. Limiting the emissions of pollutants from a petrochemical plant is an example of regulatory policy. A third type is **redistributive policies**; these attempt to benefit one group of citizens at the expense of another. Taxing a dentist to help finance welfare payments to a widow with three children is an example of redistributive policy. (In each of these three definitions, the expression "attempts to" has been used. As we shall see in Part 4, almost all public policies have unintended consequences. Therefore, policymakers can never, and should never, think that a policy will do exactly as it is supposed to do.)

Stages in the Policymaking Process

Policy does not, of course, just suddenly appear in the American political system. It must be developed over many months, even years. Many different people—including the president, members of Congress, lobbyists, bureaucrats, and judges—can be involved in this process. Then, once a policy has been developed, someone, somewhere must *act* so that the goals of the policy will be attained. This task is preeminently that of the bureaucracy.

Policymaking is a protracted process. Therefore it is useful to think of it as occurring in six stages (see Figure 7–4).

Getting on the policy agenda. Unlike the White Queen who told Alice she could sometimes believe as many as six impossible things before breakfast, public policymakers must limit the number of issues they handle. In short, they must set priorities; they must decide what is truly important. They cannot do everything at once.

Of course, what policymakers think is important does not always coincide with what various interest groups think. As you know from Chapter 6, the NAACP was founded in 1909; yet it was unable to get a civil right act passed until 1964. Similarly, a number of private citizens had argued in the 1950s that the United States would face a serious energy squeeze in the 1970s; congressional attention failed to take notice until the Arab oil embargo in 1973.

How then does an issue move from the public agenda to the government agenda? Crises, like the oil embargo or nuclear plant malfunction at Three Mile Island, Pennsylvania, can help. Changes in the dimension of the problem can also help move an issue off the back burner. For example, inflation and unemployment are always problems. But they do not generate heated debates among policymakers until they reach certain threshold levels. (I shall refrain from giving these, since there is a ratchet effect. In other words, once the inflation rate rises from an "acceptable" 6 percent to an "intolerable" 15 percent, bringing it down to 10 percent is considered a victory. Now 10 percent is "acceptable," 15 percent "unsatisfactory," and only 20 percent "intolerable.") Finally, some issues get on the government agenda thanks to the efforts of *policy entrepreneurs*. These are public officials or private citizens who invest their political capital in an issue, such as health

FIGURE 7-4

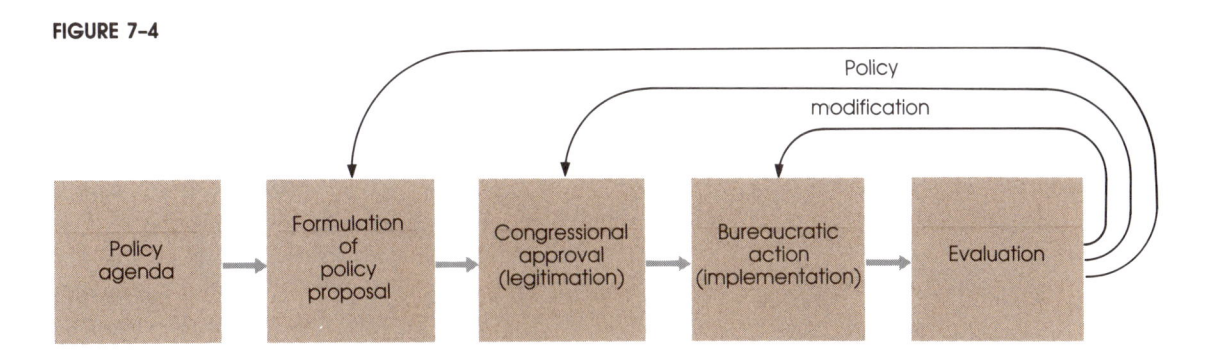

Policy agenda → Formulation of policy proposal → Congressional approval (legitimation) → Bureaucratic action (implementation) → Evaluation

Policy modification (feedback loops from Evaluation to Formulation, Congressional approval, and Bureaucratic action)

insurance or tax cuts, hoping to get a good return (in terms of career, reputation, or power).

Formulating a policy proposal. Once the issue has been catapulted onto, squeezed in, or simply placed on the government agenda, the next stage of the policymaking process begins. The essential question becomes, What shall we do? For any public problem there are numerous alternative strategies available. To meet the energy squeeze, government can emphasize conservation, encourage research, expand production—or some mix of all three. To fight rising unemployment, government can stress training programs, youth unemployment (because it is so high), a reduced minimum wage, tax incentives to industry to hire the hard core unemployed—or some mix of all four.

Most major policy proposals are formulated in the executive branch, usually in the lower levels of an agency. The proposal then works its way upward. It goes across the desk of the departmental secretary and on to the Office of Management and Budget. The OMB insures it is consistent with the president's overall goals. Since 1970, the Office of Management and Budget has chaired a special review mechanism called the Domestic Council. This is essentially an interagency discussion and coordination step for all new legislation and executive policy and regulations. At each juncture, the proposal is carefully analyzed and frequently modified by staffs. For obvious reasons, we call this activity policy analysis. It is the subject of Chapter 12. Only in the most important or controversial proposals does the president become closely involved.

Legitimating the policy. New policies represent, by definition, long-term commitments of the government to some major area of public concern. Therefore they must be approved or adopted by some group outside the bureaucracy. That is why a corporation has a board of directors, a university has trustees, and city has a council. In national government, it is the Congress that fulfills this role. The next chapter considers in detail how Congress goes about legitimizing policies.

The Constitution gives the president powers to affect legislation. Among these are the recommendation of legislative programs through messages to Congress, the veto, and some control over sessions (i.e., when Congress meets). His annual message to Congress is based on the constitutional directive that the president "shall from time to time give to Congress information of the state of the Union, and recommend to their consideration such measures as he shall judge necessary and expedient." The president may choose his time for the message. However, he usually transmits it in January, when the legislative session begins.

Implementing. As any good executive (public or private) knows, somewhere along the policymaking process, plans must translate into work. At some point, talking must stop and acting must start. Once the policy proposal has been legitimated by Congress—in other words, becomes the law of the land—the bureaucracy is charged with the responsibility of attaining the goals of that policy. In short, it must take action to implement the policy. **Implementation** is not a solo performance, however. The courts can become involved in the process. Also, the cooperation of other levels of government is often essential to successful implementation of a policy.

Drawing by Lorenz; © 1981 The New Yorker Magazine, Inc.

"Look, fella, I don't make policy—I just implement it."

Generalization about implementation is not easy. This is because there are so many agencies in the federal government engaged in so many different activities. For example, to control pollution might suggest a number of actions by the relevant agency. First, there could be outright *prohibition* of pollution. Businesses and municipalities would be required to treat fully effluents and sewage before discharge. Second, the agency could set standards by *directive* for everyone that emits pollutants in a region. Third, the agency could give *subsidies and tax rebates* to business firms that invest in new pollution control equipment. Fourth, the agency could apply *direct action* and try to clean up, say, oil spills. Fifth, the agency could *regulate* the kind of pollution control devices that new plants are equipped with; in other words, the government sets the conditions under which private activities operate. (We shall examine the regulatory process much more closely in Chapter 13.)

Evaluation. While implementation is going on, the agency, the White House, and Congress are likely to be monitoring the progress, if any, toward the stated goals of the policy. It is a poor executive indeed who, once a policy is in place, fails to ask the question, How are we doing? In the next chapter we shall see the procedures and staffs that Congress has developed to evaluate bureaucratic operations.

Policy modification. Policies are not set in concrete. An impact of evaluation, therefore, is to develop recommendations on how the original policy, or at least bureaucratic activities, can be modified so that the goals can be achieved as quickly and cheaply as possible.

Chapter Key

The dimensions of the modern presidency have been established by the precedents of previous strong leaders' personalities and responses to crises. Among strong presidents whose terms in office have helped to shape the modern presidency have been George Washington (1789–1797), Andrew Jackson (1829–1837), Abraham Lincoln (1861–1865), Theodore Roosevelt (1901–1909), and Franklin D. Roosevelt (1933–1945). Of all presidents, FDR's impact has been the greatest in terms of shaping the modern presidency. Presidents today, regardless of political philosophy, follow a more Rooseveltian, activist model, as opposed to a more passive model.

- The cumulative effect of the precedents of strong presidents has shaped the public's expectations about how a president should act. The public's belief in the need for a strong presidency has not been altered. This is despite public disillusionment following the Watergate affair and President Nixon's resignation.

In a critical election, there is a clear realignment in the social and economic support of the majority and minority blocs in society. This shift is relatively durable and has lasting political consequences. The new majority is presumed to have mandate for change. Whether the 1980 election was like the critical election of 1932 remains to be seen.

"Bureaucracy" refers to both a way of doing business and the large number of federal government organizations engaged in prescribed tasks. The bureaucratic approach is characterized by (1) a clear division of labor, (2) hierarchical authority patterns, (3) specified job qualifications, and (4) objective administration of rules. Bureaucratic organizations are primarily designed to accomplish goals, not attend to the specific problems of individuals. Therefore, bureaucratic procedures are sometimes viewed as cold and impersonal.

The federal government is the world's largest organization. It has about 4 million civilian and military employees, and the president is its head. He cannot appoint more than a tiny fraction of the government's employees, nor does he always command the personal loyalties even of those people he appoints.

The federal bureaucracy is not organized according to an overall, clear-cut pattern. The 13 cabinet-level departments include the largest bureaucratic organization in government. The regulatory commissions are not directly under presidential control. In trying to manage the vast federal bureaucracy, the president is confronted with a tangled network of entrenched interests. There are those of federal agencies, outside interest groups, and congressional committees. This network is nearly impossible to control. In the face of such obstacles, modern presidents have resorted to acquiring their own White House staff. The Executive Office of the President (EOP) was created in 1939 by President Roosevelt. It has grown to about 5,000. The main components of the EOP are the White House Office, Office of Management and Budget, National Security Council, Domestic Council, Council of Economic Advisers, and Council on Environmental Quality.

Presidents not only execute policy—they also *make it*. Presidents work in three broad policy areas: (1) foreign affairs and national security, (2) economics, and (3) domestic or social policy. Modern presidents place highest priority on foreign policy and national security policy. Domestic policymaking is frequently crowded out of presidents' schedules by the press of demands from the other policy areas.

Within each of these three areas, the president can become involved in any one of the five stages of policymaking: policy agenda, formulation, congressional approval, implementation, and evaluation.

The president and Congress share important powers in the policymaking process. One of the president's most important contributions to the process is his ability to set the congressional legislative agenda. He does so through his State of the Union message, budget message, economic message, and other messages to Congress. Even after legislation has been passed and signed, the president can wield influence over program results. This can be done through personnel appointments, impoundment of funds, and rulemaking authority. The president's popular standing can be an important resource in his dealings with Congress.

Answers to Quiz

1. Rutherford Hayes.
2. Martin Van Buren.
3. Warren G. Harding and John F. Kennedy.
4. John C. Breckinridge became Confederate secretary of war in 1865.
5. Aaron Burr, who as vice president, challenged Alexander Hamilton to a duel and won.
6. John Adams and Thomas Jefferson—July 4, 1826, the 50th anniversary of the signing of the Declaration of Independence.
7. George Washington. (The seat of government was in New York. There was no Washington, D.C., at that time.)
8. Robert Frost.
9. 1814. (The British occupied Washington during the War of 1812 and set fire to the White House.)
10. James Buchanan. (He served as president from 1857 to 1861. He never married.)
11. 1923. (A group of Georgians that year were interested in electing automobile tycoon Henry Ford president and formed a committee. However, Ford didn't want to run for office.)

U.S. Capitol and St. Peter's Church drawn to same scale.

8 The Congressional Balance

After studying this chapter you should be able to answer the following questions:

1. How does the committee system operate?
2. What considerations are most important in determining the role of a legislator?
3. How does a bill become a law?
4. What is the role of Congress in the budgetary process?
5. How does congressional organization help or hinder congressional action?
6. How could Congress change?

Terms you should know:

appropriation
advice and consent
authorization
bill
Budget Message
calendars
case work
caucus
cloture
committee of the whole
conference committee
Congressional Budget and
    Impoundment Act of 1974
constituency
executive oversight
filibuster
fiscal year
gerrymandering
hearing
House Rules Committee
impoundment
iron triangle
issue networks

Joint Committees
legislative oversight
majority leader
markup sessions
McCarthyism
minority leader
parliamentary system
pocket veto
pork barrel
power of the purse
president pro tempore
quorum
rider
select or special committees
seniority system
Speaker of the House
standing committees
subgovernments
sunshine laws
uncontrollable costs
veto
whip

The Capitol of the United States is a landmark known worldwide. Presidents are inaugurated in front of it; members of Congress pose beside it; tourists swarm over it; and artists study it. Within its walls the Congress of the United States deliberates, debates, and decides policies that govern the nation. Computer-linked typewriters stand ready in almost every congressional office; they are programmed with answers to questions that constituents may not have even thought of yet. Most offices also have computer terminals that can spew out facts, figures, correlations, and summaries on almost any conceivable topic. Color television sets, about 425 of them, flicker all over the House side of the Capitol. House debates are covered by TV cameras now; members can watch them from their offices.

Construction of the building began in 1793, when George Washington laid the cornerstone. At the time the process of selecting a design began, the Capitol seemed to many people too ambitious a project for the United States to undertake. America's few architects were mostly self-trained men. Their experience was limited primarily to homes or small-scale public buildings. But when William Trenton, a multi-talented physician living in the Virgin Islands, submitted his design, President Washington was immediately impressed. Washington praised the plan for its "grandeur, simplicity, and beauty of exterior."

As Congress doubled in size and the county spread across the continent, it became obvious that the Capitol would have to be enlarged. In 1850, construction began on two new wings. By late 1857, the House of Representatives moved into its new chamber. In January 1859, the Senate occupied the north wing. But the bulk of the enlarged Capitol dwarfed the old dome.

The decision was made to replace the old dome with one nearly twice as high. The new architect (Thorton had died in 1828) drew on elements in several of the great domes of the Old World—for example, St. Peter's in Rome. The result was the masterpiece that today is instantly recognized worldwide. In the Renaissance, St. Peter's, with its strict geometry, its harmony, its formal serenity, and above all, its high dome, echoed the perfection of the cosmos. But when we consider the Capitol, we see that idea subdued and then boldly fused with more worldly concerns. The Capitol was given enough horizontality to express its dependency on the ground; unlike the towering St. Peter's, the building hugs the soil and fits easily into the landscape.

Throughout the trying first few months of the Civil War, work on the dome went ahead. President Lincoln was personally determined to see the Capitol completed. Once he was asked how he could justify the continued construction of the building; in particular, how could they build the dome, which, like cannonballs, was made of cast iron. Lincoln replied calmly that the work must continue. "If the people see the Capitol going on, it is a sign that we intend the Union shall go on."

But this chapter is not about iron and granite. It is about the men and women who *are* Congress—their relationship to the president, their constitutional powers, their motivations, their tasks, and their leaders.

CONGRESS AND THE PRESIDENT

The founding fathers intended that Congress, along with the judiciary, should balance executive power. The political problem, as they saw it, was to insure that our better selves govern. This is the ultimate purpose of the congressional balance: Refine the impulse of popular government and presidential authority into decent—perhaps even admirable—self-government.

Most modern presidents have found themselves very much balanced. Indeed, most have been exasperated by Congress. Only Franklin Roosevelt and Lyndon Johnson, both coming to office under extraordinary circumstances, can be said to have worked effectively with Congress. By and large, recent presidents have discovered that many of their proposals have received rather unsympathetic treatment in the Congress. This has even been true when the public has largely been in support of such proposals or the president and the Congress are of the same party.

Much of the problem lies outside any president's control. Party discipline has grown weaker over the years. Whereas the president is a national figure, those in Congress are unapologetically local. Representatives, therefore, are more responsive to the 500,000 people who make up their districts than to the president. Furthermore, all members of the House of Representatives and one third of the Senate must run for reelection every two years. This constitutional necessity breeds a natural caution; members of Congress often shy away from controversial legislation. Finally, congressional reaction to the excesses of Vietnam and Watergate created a desire among legislators to keep the presidency more firmly in check.

Congressional action in this past decade has been particularly aggressive in redressing legislative-executive imbalance. For example, there is the War Powers Act of 1973. It requires the president to obtain congressional assent within 60 days of any armed action. The Watergate hearings of 1973 decisively altered the relationship between the president and Congress for decades. And the legislative veto provides the means by which one or both houses of Congress can disapprove executive actions by a simple majority vote. In this chapter we shall examine two more milestones in the march of congressional power. The first is the **Congressional Budget and Impoundment Control Act of 1974.** This act prevents the president from holding up spending of funds approved by Congress. The second is the congressional staff expansion. This has increased congressional resources and expertise for the express purpose of developing and exercising judgments independent of the executive branch.

One could argue that the founding fathers built this tension between the executive and legislative branches into the system. That is not an altogether bad thing. Indeed, the founding fathers devised a system of balance; when one side goes up, the other goes down. Yet one could also argue that, while Congress has popped back up and effectively grabbed power away from the president, so far it has used that power more to block White House initiatives than to exercise constructive leadership. If Congress neither follows the president nor provides its own leadership, it is hard to imagine the ship of state moving anywhere. The founding fathers sought balance, not disarray.

But before we examine questions about the future of the Congress, let us make sure we understand the Congress we have today. What is Congress, anyway? What does it do? How is it organized? And what are the influences on it?

WHAT CONGRESS IS

Congress Is an Institution

You have Article I of the Constitution to thank for the Congress. In the first section, the Constitution vests "all legislative powers" in Congress. The first section establishes a bicameral legislature—that is, a lawmaking body made up of two houses rather than one. The House of Representatives would, presumably, reflect the will of the people; the Senate would serve as a check on it. (To keep the Senate as far removed from the passionate whims of the voting public as possible, the Constitution originally provided for the senators to be elected by state legislatures. This procedure was followed until the passage of the 17th Amendment in 1913.)

The Congress is itself a representational compromise, with senators representing states (two each per state, regardless of size) and representatives population. Section 1 of Article I also provides for an enumeration of the population (or census) every 10 years. This results in a reapportionment of the number of representatives for each state. All states must have at least one representative seat. (Six states have only one—Alaska, Delaware, North and South Dakota, Vermont and Wyoming. California leads with 47.)

There are several differences worth noting between the two houses. The Senate has a special role in foreign policy; all treaties must be approved for ratification by a two thirds vote of the Senate. Also, the Senate must confirm major presidential appointments. Finally, the Senate is more likely to consider the interests of minorities. The reason is that, since they must win elections on a statewide basis; therefore the minority vote for many senators is critical. The House of Representatives has the responsibility for initiating all bills involving revenues or taxes. Both houses share some powers. The House is empowered to bring articles of impeachment against the president; the Senate must try the president, and can convict only with a two thirds vote.

Eight sections of the Constitution granted considerable power to Congress. Among the specific powers granted by the founding fathers are these:

- To spend and tax in order to "provide for the common defense and general welfare of the United States."
- To borrow money.
- To regulate commerce with foreign nations and among the states.
- To declare war, raise and support armies, and provide and maintain a navy.
- To establish post offices and postroads.
- To set up the federal courts under the Supreme Court.
- To initiate constitutional amendments.
- To impeach (House only) and to try impeachments (Senate only).

The final paragraph of Section 8 is particularly important. It authorizes all laws that are "necessary and proper" to carry out the enumerated powers. The Supreme Court in 1819 turned to this clause, sometimes called the "elastic clause," to develop the concept of implied powers.* So, while congressional authority is limited to its delegated powers, Congress can choose *how* it will exercise its authority. An "elastic" construction of the clause has enabled the national government to adapt its powers to the needs of the time without constantly amending the Constitution.

Nor do the powers of Congress end here, for its power also extends to admitting new states, proposing constitutional amendments, ratifying new treaties, and approving presidential appointments.

Back in the days when he was a professor of political science, Woodrow Wilson said that Congress in its committee rooms is Congress at work. It is in the committees of Congress that bills undergo their closest scrutiny. It is there that investigations—including oversight of the executive branch—are conducted. And it is there that the differences in bills passed by each house are reconciled into one version acceptable to both.

To perform these functions, Congress uses four types of committees. Committees that continue from Congress to Congress are called **standing committees.** The subject jurisdictions of these permanent committees are set forth in the rules of each house. Virtually every introduced bill is referred to one or more standing committees, according to the subjects involved. These are the committees that actually review proposed legislation and determine which bills shall be reported to each house.

Currently, there are 22 standing committees in the House; there are 15 in the Senate (see Table 8-1). Most have several subcommittees with specific jurisdictions. Usually a standing committee sends a bill to one of its subcommittees for hearings, review, and recommendations. The bill is then reported to the full com-

---

* The case was *McCulloch v. Maryland* (see Chapter 2).

TABLE 8-1
Standing Committees of the Congress

House Committee	Senate Committee
Agriculture	Agriculture, Nutrition, and Forestry
Appropriations	Appropriations
Armed Services	Armed Services
Banking, Finance and Urban Affairs	Banking, Housing, and Urban Affairs
Budget	Budget
District of Columbia	Commerce, Science, and Transportation
Education and Labor	Energy and Natural Resources
Foreign Affairs	Environment and Public Works
Government Operations	Finance
House Administration	Foreign Relations
Interior and Insular Affairs	Governmental Affairs
Interstate and Foreign Commerce	Human Resources
Judiciary	Judiciary
Merchant Marine and Fisheries	Rules and Administration
Post Office and Civil Service	Veterans' Affairs
Public Works and Transportation	
Rules	
Science and Technology	
Small Business	
Standards of Official Conduct	
Veterans' Affairs	
Ways and Means	

mittee for consideration. Finally, if approved by the full committee, the bill is reported to the full House or Senate.

Standing committees are also responsible for overseeing the operations of the executive departments and agencies under their respective jurisdictions. They usually perform this function by studies. These studies provide Congress with the facts necessary to determine whether the agencies are administering legislation as intended. Congressional studies also help committees identify areas in which legislative action might be needed and the form that action might take.

Other congressional studies are performed by **select or special committees.** These groups are usually established for a limited period. They ordinarily deal with more specific subjects and issues than do the standing committees. For example, in recent years each House has established a select committee on aging to study the multitude of problems that affect the elderly.

Select committees in one house or the other have also studied population problems, narcotics, and Indian affairs. During the past decade, each house has used a select committee to study its own committee system and to recommend improvements. Most select committees may investigate, study, and make recommendations. They may not report legislation, however. But both houses have created a few permanent select committees in recent years and authorized them to report legislation.

Congress uses **joint committees** for investigatory and housekeeping purposes. These are usually permanent bodies composed of an equal number of House and Senate members. Usually joint committees are used to study broad and complex areas over a long time period. An example is the Joint Economic Committee.

The fourth type of committee is the **conference committee.** These are formed to reconcile the differences between the House and Senate when each passes a different version of the same bill. Conference committees are ad hoc joint committees. That is, they are temporary panels appointed to deal with a single piece of legislation. They dissolve upon the completion of that task. Members of both houses serve on each conference committee, and the number of members from each house may be the same. This is not as inequitable as it might seem because the voting in conference committees is by house; its decisions must be approved by a majority of the representatives and a majority of the senators on the committee.

Every member of the House, except the Speaker and minority leader, must serve on at least one standing committee. They, by tradition, serve on none. Senators must serve on at least two standing committees. Counting standing, select, and joint committee assignments, some senators sit on as many as five or six. In the House approximately 90 representatives have only one committee assignment. This is usually because they sit on a particularly busy panel, such as appropriations. All other House members sit on two or three committees. Committee and subcommittee service encourages members to specialize in the subject areas of the panels on which they sit.

Committee sizes vary considerably and sometimes change from Congress to Congress. The House has more than four times as many members as the Senate; therefore its committees are generally larger. In 1980, the largest House committee—appropriations—had 54 members; the largest Senate committee—also appropriations—had 28. Most Senate standing committees have from 14 to 20 members; most House committees from 30 to 45. Traditionally, party ratios on committees correspond roughly to the party ratio in the full chamber.

The committee system was not mentioned in the Constitution. Instead, it evolved slowly over time. Without the system, the Congress would never be able to build up a reservoir of expertise on the wide range of issues that confronts the republic. Without this subdivision of work, members of Congress would find their eight-hour days lengthening into 24-hour ones. They would be desperately trying to familiarize themselves with all the issues on the legislative agenda. No single person working alone could ever learn all about the neutron bomb, an international microwave system, funding for the Export-Import Bank, and so forth.

Congress Is People

When Will Rogers returned from a trip to Washington, D.C., his friends asked him what he thought of Congress. His reply was that half the members were scoundrels and the other half thieves. But he was not worried; it was a good cross section of the country.

This old joke does not quite fit. The average member of Congress differs considerably from the average American. In Congress, there is a disproportionate number of whites, males (only 21 women in 1981), millionaires (16 in the Senate in 1976), Protestants, and lawyers (over half).

Some students of American politics consider such facts very important. But such facts tell us little about what views a member might hold or how they view the work they do.

How the members of Congress spend their days. Some researchers found that a representative's "average day" consisted of hours, 53 minutes in the House chamber, 1:24 in committee work, 3:19 in his or her office, 2:02 in other Washington locations, and 1:40 in other activities. This kind of research has a nice analytical ring to it. But it fails to convey a sense of the extraordinary complexity and unrelenting pressure of the legislative task. It would be better if we could actually follow members for a day. How do they use their staffs, dodge unwelcome lobbyists, generate television exposure, jockey legislation through debates, solve the problems of individuals in their districts (an activity known as **case work**), and so forth? One might have the feeling of riding in a Polaris submarine without instruments. Despite the intense pressure and power, there is often only the slightest idea of where they are going to wind up.

The statistics on the "average day" also blur

differences in how given members of Congress spend their day. Political scientist James L. Payne splits members into two groups. There are "show horses," who neglect their legislative duties in their quest for publicity. And there are "work horses," who quietly but effectively pass bills and attend committee meetings.[1]

Payne took 55 members of the House Banking and Public Works Committee who did not hold committee leadership positions. He compared the number of minutes each representative spent at hearings in 1971–72 with the amount of news coverage received during 1972 in five major newspapers across the country. Ten members received great publicity but attended few hearings. In fact, they averaged 1,343 minutes worth in 1971–72. They included Manhattan Democrat Edward I. Koch (now mayor of New York City), former New York Democrat Bella Abzug, and Philip M. Crane of Illinois (an early candidate for the 1980 Republican presidential nomination). Voters seem to like show horses. The typical one recorded 9.5 percent more votes in 1972 than in 1970; this compares with 2.5 percent gain for the typical work horse. The electorate was cruelest to Republican Fren M. Schwengell of Iowa. His district rewarded his record 7,314 minutes in committee hearings (5½ times as much as the average show horse) by voting him out of office.

Not only does the electorate fail to distinguish those who are working at the job at hand from those who are angling for higher office. Voters are usually unaware of the voting records of these representatives and senators. You can find these in the *Congressional Record* (or in the *Congressional Quarterly Weekly Report*, a private publication). But a trip to the library might not be necessary. Many major daily newspapers print the breakdown of votes on major issues.

The reelection imperative. When first elected, representatives are seldom particularly successful men and women. It is not the physicians and fast-track executives who decide in their mid-30s to run for Congress. Rather, it is those inconspicuous citizens who seek a good job because they do not have one. This observation may seem somewhat harsh. But why then

Quiz
What is going on here?

Hint: These are not silhouettes of the Loch Ness monster, nor do they have anything to do with Star Wars.

Answers on p. 296.

do some members of Congress never return to their districts after defeat? Lawyers of only modest accomplishments are particularly drawn to the House. Not only does the job pay better than their current one. (representatives make $57,500; lawyers average around $35,000.) Even if they lose, the publicity helps their practice. Once elected, their attention turns to the question of how to get reelected.

As we have already seen, voters tend to ignore legislative records. Therefore, if reelection is a representative's chief goal, substantive lawmaking can be deemphasized. Indeed, this should be the case; some policy issues generate political controversy and lead to defeat. To use Sen. Howard Baker's splendid metaphor, "Instead of biting the bullet, they (members of Congress) sort of walk up and 'gum' it a little bit."

When they vote on social legislation, such members do not debate alternative strategies to tackle the problem. Nor do they consider how the legislation might duplicate or undermine previous legislation. What they *do* consider is the computer printout on how much money is going to their district.

As Morris Fiorina of the California Institute of Technology has pointed out, the sheer size and complexity of bureaucracy helps to solidify the electoral connection.[2] The bigger bureaucracy is, the more likely it is to wrong a citizen. Every unfavorable ruling, every delayed Veteran's Administration check, every request for guidance through the bureaucratic maze is, for the legislator, an opportunity to make political capital. Though no one has developed the calculus, it is safe to assume that personal benefits for a constituent are several times more valuable to a politician than television ads.

There are admirable exceptions to this general pattern. Not all members of Congress are driven by the electoral imperative. Many can put national interests above local ones. Others simply find the imperative too onerous and leave Congress altogether. (See box.)

Goodbye to Congress—And All That

For an increasing number of lawmakers, serving in Congress has become more trouble than it is worth. Those leaving include not only persons of retirement age or older. Many are still in their prime. They give various reasons for leaving. But there is a common thread: Service in Congress is more burden than pleasure.

Not long ago, the country-and-western singer Johnny Paycheck had a popular song entitled "Take This Job and Shove It." While Otis G. Pike, a ninth-term congressman from New York was much too urbane to hum that tune to his constituents, he was clearly irritated with the job. Among the irritants cited were the constituents themselves.

> It may be just a sign of old, or at least upper-middle, age, but people bug me more than they used to. They are asking their government to do more for them, and are willing to do less and less for themselves. This is a broad generalization, and surely unfair to many people, but the people who write to their congressman, and there are about 300 a day these days, are more and more demanding, and the demands get more and more shrill.

United Press International Photo

> No one "requests" or "asks" anymore; they "demand." The people who bug me most are people who are absolutely, positively sure that they're right on issues which to me are very close to troubling. I have often wished that I could see issues as clear and simple and one-sided as either doctrinaire liberals or doctrinaire conservatives do. Two thirds of the Congress is completely predictable. It is more difficult being a moderate, being able to see some validity on both sides of an argument, and then having either to try to work out some suitable compromise or to vote for one side or the other. The compromise will be unacceptable to both sides. The vote will be troublesome because you're never all that sure you're right and half the people will be absolutely certain you're wrong. [Extension of Remarks of the Congressional Record, February 14, 1978.]

The shadow lawmakers. No discussion of Congress would be complete without mention of that small army of 13,000 anonymous unelected bureaucrats who staff the committees and offices of the 535 elected members. These shadow lawmakers greatly influence both the drafting and interpretation of legislation that affects every individual in a variety of ways. Indeed, as modern government becomes bigger and more complex, the writing of the nation's laws perforce passes from the hands of the supposed legislators, the numbers of Congress, to their bright and ambitious staff.

How much lawmaking is done by the aides, often with only the sketchiest knowledge of the members of Congress involved, is something every good lobbyist knows. But the public seldom hears about it. The code of silence that governs the back-chamber maneuvering in Congress is almost as sacred as the vow that bound King Arthur's knights. Part of the code is maintaining the fiction that the members do all the work themselves. When you want to know whether a member is for a bill, you may go directly to the member. But when you want to know about technical points, you must go to the staff. For example, many in Washington regard Jonathan Steinberg, chief counsel of the Senate Veterans' Affairs Committee, to be a *surrogate senator*. If one watches him whispering and passing notes to chairman Alan Cranston during committee hearings, it becomes clear why lobbyists for veterans' organizations refer to the Californian as Senator Cranberg.

There is another argument for the expansion of congressional staff. Without them, the House and Senate would simply not have facilities to check the figures of, say, the budgets of the Department of Defense or the Department of Health and Human Services. As agency budgets grow in size and complexity, so the argument goes, more subcommittees with their own staffs of experts must be hired. Thus, the new budget committees of the House and Senate have economists, computers, and other information retrieval systems. They are obviously better equipped to question and challenge the claims and cost overruns put forward by the vast bureaucracy of the executive branch.

CONGRESS IN ACTION

Thus far, we have been viewing Congress from the perspectives of the Constitution and the individual members. Now we want to consider in practical terms how the House and Senate act as a single body. To do that, we need to examine three major functions—making public policy, appropriating funds, and overseeing bureaucracy.

Making Public Policy

Origin of legislation. Legislation originates in several ways. The role of the executive branch or the president as chief legislator has already been mentioned as a very significant source. But the ideas for legislative proposals may come from an individual representative or senator or from any of the executive departments of the government. Or they may come from private organized groups, associations, or individual citizens. However, they can be introduced in their respective houses only by senators and representatives. When introduced, they are referred to the standing committees that have jurisdiction of the subject matter.

Members frequently introduce **bills** that are similar in purpose. In such cases the committee considering them may take one of the bills, adding the best features of the others. Or it may draft an entirely new bill and report it (known as an original bill) in lieu of the others.

The right of petition is guaranteed the citizens of the United States by the Constitution. Many individual petitions and memoranda from state legislatures are sent to Congress. They are laid before the two houses by their respective presiding officers; or they are submitted by individual members of the House and Senate in their respective bodies. They are usually referred to the appropriate committees of the House in which they were submitted. (Under Article I, Section 7 of the Constitution, all bills for raising revenue shall originate in the House of Representatives; but the Senate may propose or concur in amendments, as on other bills.)

Bills to carry out the recommendations of the president are usually introduced by the chairpeople of the committees or subcommittees with jurisdiction of the subject matter. Sometimes the committees themselves may submit and report to the houses original bills to carry out such recommendations.

Nowadays, members of Congress introduce about 25,000 bills during the two-year period that makes up a Congress. Only about 700 become law. To have a reasonable chance of passage, a major bill must be a White House proposal or command the support of a sizable bloc of legislators.

When a committee decides to consider action on a bill, it usually schedules public **hearings**. Until recently, committee chairmen wielded unchallenged authority. They could block or push action on a bill almost singlehandedly. Members today exert more independence.

At public hearings, testimony is taken from the bill's sponsors, administration officials, outside experts, and any special-interest groups that want to be heard.

After concluding the hearings, the committee meets in executive sessions (sometimes referred to as **markup sessions**). In these meetings they discuss the bill in detail and consider amendments that any committee member may wish to offer. Each committee has its own rules of procedure. They generally conform, however, to the rules of the House itself.

By a formal vote, the committee decides whether to report the bill favorably to the House with or without committee amendments. Committees rarely give a bill an unfavorable report. When no action is taken, the bill is in effect killed.*

A committee report must accompany the bill. It sets forth the nature of the bill and reasons for the committee's recommended approval. It spells out specifically the committee amendments. And, in compliance with the rules of each house, the report indicates all changes the bill would make in existing law. Any committee members, individually or jointly, may file additional supplemental or minority views to accompany the majority committee report. The committee report, accompanying the bill, is viewed by the courts and the administrative agencies as the most important document of the Congress' intent in the proposed legislation.

The ways of the two chambers. The House and Senate have different procedures for handling bills once they are approved by committee. Figure 8–1 shows the typical way proposed legislation becomes law. There are more complicated ways. For example, rather than be referred to a single committee in each house, the proposed legislation might be re-

---

* When a bill is stalled in committee, there is a procedure to force the bill onto the floor for consideration by the full House or Senate. In the House, a "discharge petition" must be signed by 218 members. The Senate has a similar device, the discharge resolution. Because members are reluctant to challenge the prerogatives of committees, the discharge rule is rarely used.

ferred to several. And there are simpler ways; for example, some House bills are "privileged" and go directly to the floor from committee. In effect, they bypass the Rules Committee (discussed below). In practice most bills begin as similar proposals in both houses.

Most major House bills go next to the **House Rules Committee.** It decides how a measure will be handled on the floor of the House chamber, where members meet to act on legislation. The Rules Committee allots the time for debate; it also determines whether members will be allowed to amend the bill or simply vote for or against it. In other words, the Rules Committee makes the rules for consideration of a bill. Because the House is larger than the Senate, it needs a traffic cop like the Rules Committee to decide which bills passed by committees can proceed to consideration by the whole House.

The majority leadership of the House consists of the **Speaker,** who is the presiding officer of the House, and the **majority leader.** They decide when to call up a measure for floor action. On some issues, where a strong party position exists, the leaders push hard to round up votes and shape House action; on other issues, they allow others to take the lead.

Procedures in the Senate differ in three fundamental ways. First, bills approved by committee go *directly* to the Senate **calendar** (an agenda of the bills to be considered). Usually, the majority leader decides how and when a particular bill will be considered on the floor. In general, the bill is allowed to remain on the calendar for several days. This enables members to become acquainted with its provisions. In developing the schedule for debate, the majority leader will consult with the minority leader.

The second fundamental difference is that, whereas the House rules make marathon debate difficult, Senate rules make it fairly simple. The rules allow any senator to speak twice on the same day for as long as he or she wishes on any matter before the Senate.

Third, there is no Speaker to act as presiding officer. That job belongs to the vice president, who is president of the Senate. In his absence, the **president pro tempore,** who usually is the senior senator of the majority party, presides or delegates the task to another senator.

To speed action on controversial bills, the majority leader often seeks a "unanimous consent agreement" from the Senate on the time for final votes. Any senator may object and attempt to **filibuster,** or talk a bill to death; then the leadership may resort to **cloture**—a procedure for limiting debate to one hour per senator. Cloture, however, requires the support of 60 senators; it is hard to invoke when the Senate is closely divided.

The vote. Despite these three differences between the House and Senate procedures, there are many similarities. In general, a bill is debated in either chamber at length. The proponents and opponents present their views to acquaint the membership, as well as the general public, with the issues involved; it is all done with a view to arriving at the consensus. Amendments are frequently offered to make the measure conform more with the judgment of the majority. In the course of considering the bill, various parliamentary motions, in both the House and the Senate, may be offered to determine the sentiment of the members with respect to the pending legislation. The measure may be postponed to some future date or referred back to the committee that reported it (not a good sign for proponents).

Finally the general debate concludes and the bill is read for amendments. The question then becomes whether the House or Senate, as the case may be, will pass the bill in its final form. The *Congressional Record* of the day will set forth the verbatim debate on the bill and the disposition made of such amendments as were offered.

According to the Constitution, a majority of the members in each chamber must be present in order to do business. Thus a **quorum** is 218 in the House and 51 in the Senate. Both

FIGURE 8-1
How a Bill Becomes Law*

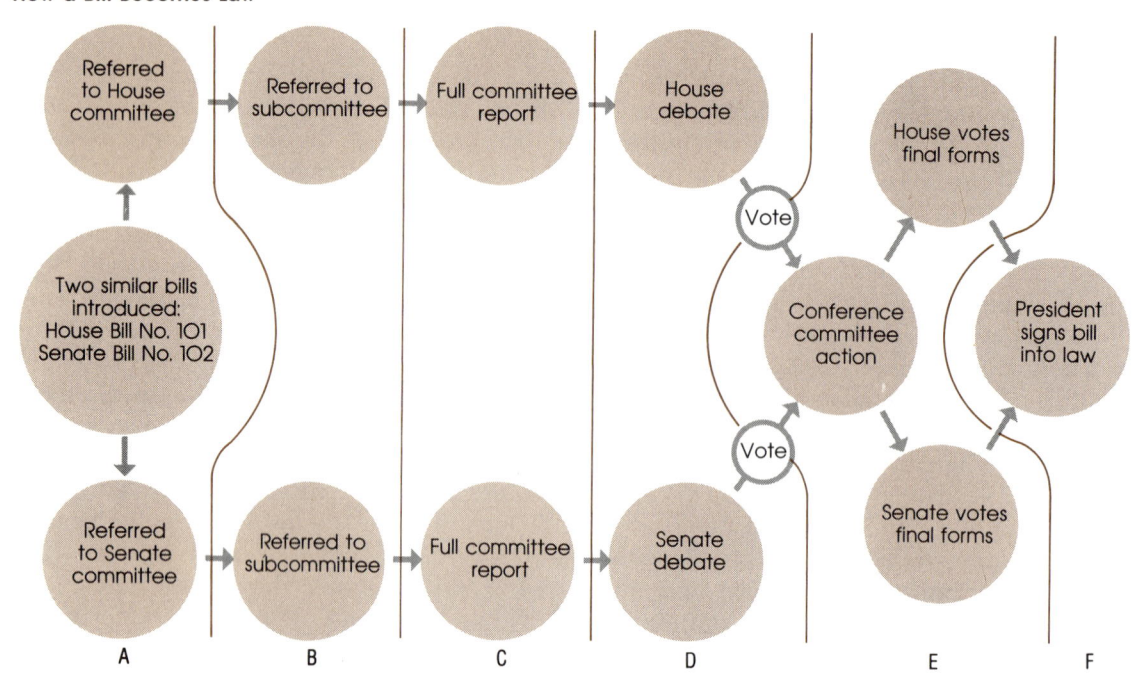

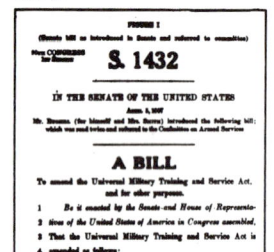

Flow chart stages:
- A: Two similar bills introduced: House Bill No. 101, Senate Bill No. 102 → Referred to House committee / Referred to Senate committee
- B: Referred to subcommittee (House and Senate)
- C: Full committee report (House and Senate)
- D: House debate / Senate debate
- E: Vote → Conference committee action ← Vote; House votes final forms / Senate votes final forms
- F: President signs bill into law

Col. A

Any member of the House or Senate may introduce a bill embodying a proposed law or revision of existing laws, at any time when his respective house in in session. When introduced, the bill will be entered in the Journal of the House, and the title and sponsors of it printed in the *Congressional Record* of that day.

Each bill numbered

Each bill introduced is assigned a number by the clerk of each house and referred to the committee having jurisdiction over the subject matter by the presiding officer, that is, the Speaker of the House or the president of the Senate. Copies of the bill are printed by the Government Printing Office and made publicly available from the congressional document rooms.

Col. B

Acting through its chairman, the committee decides whether a bill should be taken up by the full committee or referred to a subcommittee for its initial consideration.

The deliberative stage

The committee's deliberations are the most important stage of the legislative process. It is here that detailed study of the proposed legislation is made and where people are given the right to present their views in public hearings. When the chairman has set a date for public hearings it is generally announced by publication in the *Congressional Record*.

Copies of the bill under consideration by the committee are customarily sent to the executive departments or agencies concerned with the subject matter for their official views to be presented in writing or by oral testimony before the committee. The number of witnesses, pro and con, heard by the committee is largely dictated by the importance of the proposed legislation and degree of public interest in it.

Testimony heard

The transcript of the testimony taken is available for inspection in the individual committee offices. Quite frequently, dependent on the importance of the subject matter, the committee hearings on a bill are printed and copies made available to the public.

After conclusion of the hearings the committee proceeds to meet in executive sessions—sometimes referred to as "markup" sessions—to discuss the bill in detail and to consider such amendments as any member of the committee may wish to offer. Each committee has its own rules of procedure but they generally conform to the rules of the house itself.

---

* Explanatory notes accompanying each stage are from Robert H. Michel, "How a Bill Becomes a Law," *Congressional Record*, February 17, 1981, pp. E467–8.

Col. C

[Figure III]

The committee vote

By a formal vote of the committee, it decides whether to report favorably to the house the bill with or without committee amendments. A committee report must accompany the bill, setting forth the nature of the bill and reasons for the committee's recommended approval. The report sets forth specifically the committee amendments and, in compliance with the rules of each house, indicates all changes the bill would make in existing law. Any committee member, individually or jointly, may file additional supplemental or minority views to accompany the majority committee report. The committee report, accompanying the bill, is viewed by the courts and the administrative agencies as the most important document as to the intent of the Congress in the proposed legislation.

After reporting

When a bill is reported by the committee it is placed on the appropriate calendar. The majority leadership decides how and when the bill will be considered on the floor. In general the bill is allowed to remain on the calendar for several days to enable members to become acquainted with its provisions.

Col. D

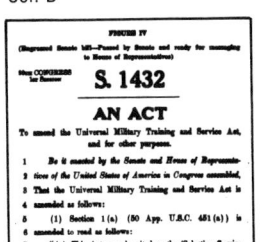

[Figure IV]

In both the House and the Senate innumerable measures of relatively minor importance are disposed of by unanimous consent. In the Senate, where debate is unlimited, major bills are brought up on motion of the majority leader and in the House are called up under a privileged resolution reported from the Rules Committee which fixes the limits of debate and whether amendments may be offered from the floor. The Rules Committee resolution is called a rule for consideration of a bill; a closed rule if no amendments are allowed, as is generally the case in tax bills, and an open rule if amendments can be offered.

Reaching consensus

While there are distant differences between the House and Senate procedures, in general a bill is debated at length with the proponents and opponents presenting their views to acquaint the membership, as well as the general public, with the issues involved, and all with a view to arriving at the consensus. Amendments are frequently offered to make the measure more in conformity with the judgment of the majority. In the course of consideration of the bill there are various parliamentary motions, in both the House and the Senate, which may be offered to determine the sentiment of the members with respect to the pending legislation. The measure may be postponed to some future date or referred back to the committee which reported it.

With the conclusion of general debate and the reading of the bill for amendments, the question becomes whether the House or Senate, as the case may be, will pass the bill in its final form. The *Congressional Record* of the day the bill was under consideration will set forth the verbatim debate on the bill and the disposition made of such amendments as were offered.

Col. E

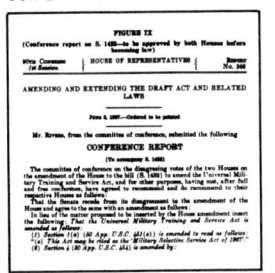

[Figure IX]

After passage

With the passage of a bill by either body it is messaged to the other with the request that they concur. If no action has been taken on the like measure by the body receiving the message the bill is usually referred to the appropriate committee of that body for consideration. Hearings are again held and the bill reported for floor action. On relatively minor or noncontroversial matters the Senate or the House accepts the measure as messaged to it by the other body.

If there are substantial differences between the House and Senate versions of a given bill, the measure is sent to a conference committee which is appointed by the Speaker and the president of the Senate from the ranking committee members of each body having original jurisdiction over the bill. The object of the conference committee is to adjust the differences between the two bodies, and to report back to each its agreement. The report of the conference committee must be in writing and signed by those agreeing thereto and must have the signature of the majority of the conferees of each house.

Conference report

The report of the conference committee cannot be amended and must be accepted or rejected by each house as it stands. If either house finds itself unable to accept the conference committee report a further conference is usually requested.

Col. F

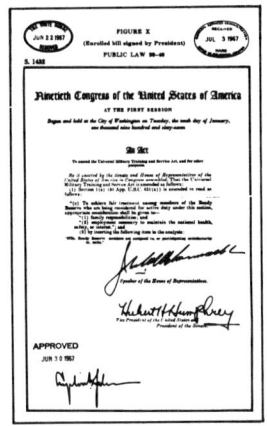

[Figure X]

When the bill has been agreed to in identical form by both bodies a copy of the bill is enrolled, signed by the Speaker and by the president of the Senate, for presentation to the president. The bill becomes law with the president's signature of approval, or it may become law without his signature if he does not return it, with his objections, to the Congress within 10 days of its presentation to him.

If the president should return the bill, with his objections, to the originating body of the Congress, his veto may be overridden by two thirds of both the House and Senate respectively voting to have the measure become law the president's objections to the contrary notwithstanding. Both the president's veto message and a record of the vote of the individual members in the motion to override are required by the Constitution and set forth in the *Congressional Record*.

chambers often proceed with fewer than a quorum unless challenged by a member. In the Senate, votes are cast by voice. If a roll-call vote is demanded, each senator's name is called out; each responds "yea" or "nay." In the House, roll-call votes are recorded electronically. Each member carries a wallet-size voting card. When one end of the card is inserted in one of 44 voting terminals in the House chamber, a "nay" vote is recorded; the other end records a "yea." A computer flashes a running tally of the vote on a lighted scoreboard. The vote of each member is also projected on the chamber wall.

Once a bill has passed one house, it is sent to the other. Frequently, the House and Senate pass different versions of a bill. When this happens, a **conference committee** of senators and representatives must resolve the differences. The "conference agreement"—the compromise version—must then be passed again by both houses before it is sent to the president for signing.

When the bill has been agreed to in identical form by both bodies, a copy of the bill is enrolled—signed by the Speaker and by the president of the Senate—for presentation to the president. The bill becomes law with the president's signature of approval; or it may become law without his signature if he does not return it, with his objections, to the Congress within 10 days of its presentation to him.

Suppose the president should return the bill, with his objections, to the originating body of Congress. This **veto** (which means "I forbid" in Latin) may be overridden by two thirds of both the House and Senate, respectively. They vote to have the measure become law, the president's objections to the contrary notwithstanding. One third plus one of the members of *either* house supporting the president's view means the veto prevails. Thus Congress overrides few vetoes. Presidents use the *threat* of a veto to shape legislation while Congress is still deliberating it.

The **pocket veto** also provides the president with additional power. If, at the end of the legislative session, the president holds a piece of legislation for 10 days without signing or vetoing it for—and Congress adjourns during that time—the bill does not become law.

Lobbying. In Chapter 6, we said that one of the major functions of interest groups was lobbying. That is, they seek to secure favorable action from a legislature or bureaucracy. Congressional lobbyists in particular have a dismal image because of periodic scandals. The "Abscam" scandal of 1979 is a case in point.

In the Abscam Scandal, FBI intermediaries offered large bribes to dozens of members of Congress in return for special favors. Perhaps the most notorious case was that of Representative Michael ("Ozzie") Myers, a three-term Democrat from Philadelphia. Although he was videotaped taking $50,000 from undercover agents, he told the House ethics committee that he was just "play acting." The tapes were, however, appalling. They showed Myers boasting, with profanity, that he could get legislation passed to help a nonexistent Arab sheik. It was so appalling, in fact, that the full House voted to expel him from Congress. The last time such a drastic measure was taken was when three members were ousted for treason. (They had joined the Confederacy in 1861.) Most members of Congress manage to stay carefully within legal bounds when dealing with lobbyists. But the corruption exposed in scandals like Abscam shows that bribery is an ever-present possibility.

Nevertheless, lobbying is a necessary and legitimate function. It is necessary because members of Congress often need the additional information for decision making; it is legitimate because all citizens have the right to "petition" their government (in the words of the Constitution). What can individuals do to make their voices heard more effectively in the Capitol?

First, they can analyze the positions of their members of Congress and their staff. A member of Congress will vote on literally thousands of

In October 1980, millions of Americans got to watch on television Democratic congressman Michael Myers (second from left) of Pennsylvania accept a $50,000 payoff from an FBI agent posing as a representative of an Arab sheik during an undercover operation. Of the six House members convicted of or awaiting trial on bribery charges, five (including Myers) were defeated in the November 1980 elections.

legislative matters every year. No single human being could possibly absorb all the information needed to vote intelligently on every piece of legislation encountered. Typically, members are left with two sources of information: their legislative staffs and lobbyists.

The legislative staff in a congressional office will research and analyze each bill under consideration. The staff will track the history of the legislation and its impact on constituents in the member's district. The staff will analyze constituent mail and phone calls to develop a tally of favorable versus unfavorable constituent response. Staff reports will determine if pressure groups, especially pressure groups within the district, expressed interest in the legislation. Based on these inputs, a summary of pros and cons and staff recommendations will be presented to the member to help decide on the pending legislation. The staffs that develop these laborious studies are incredibly overworked. Therefore they welcome input from sources outside of government, particularly comments from responsible lobbyists.

Therefore, individuals seeking to be more effective at lobbying will provide their members of Congress with concise, first-rate, accurate information. You can fool some of the people some of the time, but you cannot fool a savvy legislator very often. And you do so only at considerable peril for your future interests.

The effective lobbyist may be your media stereotype who wines and dines the influential and massages assorted power brokers. But he or she must be a source of reliable and timely information and skilled at the use of the "softsell" to be successful. A good lobbyist can provide technical expertise as well as political savvy to members and their staff. The successful lobbyist will identify emerging coalitions and know how to indulge the inevitable trade making that characterizes the political process. A lobbyist who has proven helpful to a member of Congress can become a confidant and a valuable proponent of the member's political aspirations. (Remember the reelection imperative.)

A good lobbyist also recognizes the importance of getting specific commitments. For example, a lobbyist visits a senator to solicit federal money for marine biology research. The senator's response: "Why, yes, I've always been in favor of science. When the pending legislation comes up, I'll certainly vote pro-science." The lobbyist might think he has a firm commitment, but the senator is free to vote any way he pleases. He could vote against the legislation on the grounds it did not go far enough. The point of this example is that good lobbyists specify the bill and whether they want a yes or no vote. They also watch to see that the senator does not add any crippling amendments in the relative privacy of committee.

A Profile of Lobbyist Liz Robbins

Late Tuesday night, outside the Senate chamber, a weary Sen. Pete Domenici spotted Elizabeth Robbins prowling the halls. He threw up his hands in mock frustration and sighed: "You've done us in with your lobbying on this one, Lizzie."

The Senate Budget Committee chairman was talking about a dispute over Medicaid funding between House and Senate budget conferees. The object of his compliment was the woman who is probably Washington's most successful lobbyist for federal aid for social services.

Her clients include the California cities of San Francisco and Berkeley, the Michigan state legislature, and, in special cases, New York City and Oneida County, N.Y. In the Medicaid dispute, she helped the State of Michigan escape a loss of about $40 million in aid in the coming fiscal year.

Even in a time of social-service cut-backs, Miss Robbins is a force in the legislative process. Much of her activity is defensive, aimed at preventing cutbacks or at reshaping budget proposals to meet her clients' interests.

In a year when liberal lobbyists aren't doing well, Miss Robbins is doing better than most.

Rarely does a day pass when she isn't outside the House or Senate chamber, looking a bit disheveled, frequently a bit frantic, and always carrying volumes of material on arcane subjects, such as "The Matching Formula for Title 20."

Sometimes, she'll flag a lawmaker with a polite "Senator" or "Mister Chairman." Usually, however, it's more like, "Hey Chris, we're going to move that amendment in conference tomorrow," or "Tom, we got some problems on the cap." Whatever the greeting, most pay attention to Liz Robbins.

"Liz Robbins knows every button to push for almost every member," says Rep. Charles Wilson, the Texas Democrat who heads the newly formed Sunbelt Council that frequently competes with Miss Robbins' Northern industrial-state clients for federal money.

She is also a refutation of some myths about Washington lobbyists. While exaggerated stories abound about a few high-living women who call themselves lobbyists, Liz Robbins is considered as straight-laced as she is straightforward. She has a staff of only five, and lacks the fancy limousines and unlimited expense accounts of the high-powered corporate lobbyists.

Instead, she capitalizes on a willingness to put in many 16-hour days, on her personal contacts with hundreds of well-placed staffers and lawmakers, and on an extraordinary knowledge of some complex subjects.

"She has a remarkable ability to really help members understand the practical effects of decisions they are making," says Sen. Thad Cochran, a conservative Mississippi Republican. "And she never misleads you."

It isn't easy, especially this year, for the 35-year-old lobbyist and her clients. She lost an effort to increase funds for day care and disabled children. And her habit of talking governmentese—there are lots of "glitches" and "minimum matches" in her conversation—confounds some lawmakers.

But she has plenty of political pragmatism and ingenuity. Earlier this year, she persuaded House Budget Committee Chairman James Jones (D., Okla.) to give a dinner party for one of her clients, Mayor Diane Feinstein of San Francisco. The advantages were reciprocal; for Jim Jones, a moderately conservative Democrat with ambitions for higher office, a chance to entertain a big-city mayor and for Diane Feinstein, an opportunity to get to know an influential congressman.

Miss Robbins, unlike some liberal lobbyists, devotes a lot of time to cultivating conservatives. Even when she doesn't get their votes, she figures she softens their opposition. "I don't know of anybody up here who doesn't like and respect her," says Sen. Orrin Hatch, the conservative Republican from Utah.

SOURCE: Albert R. Hunt, "Lobbyist Liz Robbins Is Moving Force in Fight for U.S. Aid to Social Services," *The Wall Street Journal* (July 31, 1981).

Appropriating Funds

You may find it odd that a description of the executive budget process is found in a legislative chapter. The annual federal budget is considered by many to be the executive branch's most important decision-making process. The president has the responsibility for proposing a federal budget in January. (This must be done within 15 days of the start of the legislative session.) To assist in putting his **Budget Message** together, there are the staffs of Office of Management and Budget (OMB), the Treasury Department, and the Council of Economic Advisers (CEA). OMB, in consultation with departments and agencies, draws up a proposed budget; the Treasury and CEA try to make economic projections (including what the revenue will be). The president sends the final budget proposals—as *recommended expenditures* for various programs and tax totals—to Congress for congressional review.

But the federal budget process is an example of what is termed a *weak executive–strong legislative* budgeting system. This means more power, legally and politically, lies with the legislative branch. Some state governments follow a *strong executive–weak legislative* budget system; the governor holds the power. There are several critical differences. First concerns the legal requirement to balance the budget. States must do this; the federal government has only done so eight times since World War II. Then there are the rights to line-item veto and to impounding funds.

The line-item veto empowers an executive to reject any legislated spending increase (termed appropriations) *over* what was recommended in the original budget. Some governors can; presidents cannot. **Impoundment** is executive action taken to withhold funds that have been legally obligated. There are many reasons for and past examples of impoundment. These include emergencies, such as wars, changing situations, and illegal actions taken by potential beneficiaries. But when President Nixon impounded federal budget funds appropriated by Congress because of "fiscal conditions," the Congress fought back and put strict limits on impoundments by executives.

Money is, therefore, the stuff of modern politics. In American government its allocation is the source of almost all power. In 1981, the budget of the federal government was over $600 billion. Every year, not surprisingly, such a huge budget is fought over. The budget submitted by the Reagan administration for 1982 generated a war of massive proportions because it proposed $85 billion in cutbacks.

Congress tries to get its act together. Thanks largely to OMB, the president is able to make unified, comprehensive budgetary decisions and recommendations. Only in recent years, however, has Congress had a similar capability. The division of Congress into two chambers and each chamber, in turn, into a number of committees made such a unified look difficult, if not impossible. It was as if you considered your own household budget in terms of separate decision packages. How much do I want to spend this year on housing? How much on food? On transportation? On entertainment? Of course, we do not make decisions in such an isolated fashion. We first try to establish an overall budget ceiling based largely on our expected income. Then, within that limit, we try to decide how much we can spend within each category. Suppose we decide we "must" spend a certain amount on transportation; then we know that it must come out of some other category, or somehow our income must be increased.

Until the passage of the **Congressional Budget and Impoundment Act of 1974,** congressional appropriations committees tended to violate this commonsense approach. For example, the subcommittee on agricultural appropriations simply asked what would be desirable for the farmers, then recommended that. With each committee operating this way, it is not surprising that, when all the recommendations were put together, the sum was greater than almost any single member of Congress would wish for. What the 1974 act did was to unify the budgetary process. It requires that, four months after the president has made his budgetary recommendations, Congress adopts a tentative federal budget. It sets targets or ceilings in 14 areas of public policy as well as an overall budgetary ceiling. Congress votes on a final budget each September. To aid Congress in this task are the Congressional Budget Office (see box) and two new budget committees, one in each house.

How well has the new budgetary process worked? While it has forced Congress to take a more comprehensive and long-range view of federal spending, it has failed in at least two respects. First, the process has failed to bring spending levels in line with revenue; in other words, the federal government has spent more than it has taken in through taxes every year

---

What Is the Congressional Budget Office?

In a major effort to reassert its constitutional authority over the Federal budget, the Congress in 1974 enacted a comprehensive budget reform measure, the Congressional Budget and Impoundment Control Act of 1974 (Public Law 93–344). The Budget Act set up a process whereby each year the Congress determines the appropriate level of Federal revenues, spending, and debt, and the size of the deficit through the passage of two concurrent resolutions on the budget.

Each spring, the Congress formulates and adopts a concurrent resolution setting budget targets for the fiscal year to begin on the coming October 1st. In September, the Congress reviews the detailed spending and revenue decisions it has made since the first resolution in the form of individual bills. It then arrives at and adopts a second concurrent resolution, reconfirming or changing the totals in the spring resolution. While the first resolution sets targets, the second establishes an actual ceiling on spending and a floor for revenues. If subsequent adjustments are required by changing circumstances, the Congress can enact additional concurrent resolutions.

The Budget Act created three new entities: Budget Committees in both the House and the Senate and the Congressional Budget Office (CBO). CBO is a nonpartisan organization mandated to provide the Congress with budget-related information and with analyses of alternative fiscal, budgetary and programmatic policies. The office does not make recommendations on mat-

Wide World Photos

Alice M. Rivlin, director, Congressional Budget Office.

ters of policy; its principal tasks are to present the Congress with options for consideration and to study the possible budgetary ramifications of those options.

CBO's specific responsibilities include: estimates of the five-year budgetary costs of proposed legislation, inflation impact analyses of proposed legislation, tracking of Congressional budgetary actions against preset budget targets (scorekeeping), periodic forecasts of economic trends and alternative fiscal policies, studies of programmatic or policy issues that affect the Federal budget, and an annual report on major budgetary options.

SOURCE: *The Capitol*, 8th ed. (Washington, D.C.: U.S. Government Printing Office).

since passage of the Budget Reform Act. Second, even though the act extends the period of time Congress has to develop a new budget, Congress still tends to run out of time. In such cases, it must pass stopgap resolutions to keep government going at last year's level.

The power of the purse. When Congress allocates money, using the president's budget as a guideline, it does so in two ways.

First is **authorization**. This basic substantive legislation, enacted by Congress, sets up or continues the legal operation of a federal program or agency. An example is seen in the ordering of a nuclear submarine. Once the decision has been made to build, initial expenses might be quite small; costs rise to a peak in only the second or third year of construction. Such legislation is normally a prerequisite for subsequent appropriations; but it does not usually provide the authority for an agency to spend money.

Second is **appropriation**. This is the budget authority that does permit agencies to incur obligations and make payment. It is the estimated amount to be spent in the current fiscal year on a particular project. Congress appropriates funds for all projects. Actual outlays have in recent years been relatively less than the administration or Congress had expected; when the economy is sluggish, government departments are, it seems, unable to spend all the money allotted to them. Of course, recent executive practices of "freezing" certain outlay categories during the year account for much of this.

Often provisions unlikely to pass on their own merits are attached to an appropriation bill. Such provisions are called **riders** for the simple reason they "ride" through the legislative process on the back, so to speak, of some vital piece of legislation. Presidents, who, as we said above, do not have an item veto, must either take the bill with the rider or reject the entire package. Not surprisingly, popular kinds of riders are **pork-barrel** items, such as costly federal projects, grants, and contracts available to cities, businesses, and other institutions in a member's district.

Congressional control is, in fact, limited. The great bulk of the budget—75 percent—goes to **uncontrollable costs.** These include social security, federal pensions, and payment of interest on the public debt. In addition, the cost of some programs written into the law cannot be cut without changing the law. The amount of money spent is not determined by Congress. It is set by the number of people using the programs—e.g., welfare benefits and medical assistance for the elderly and poor. This means, of course, that the fraction—25 percent—about which there is some discretion is all the more bitterly fought over.

Thus the president really has no independent, formal power either to raise taxes or authorize the spending of money. He can only advise—though some presidents, like Johnson and Reagan, can be very convincing in the "advice" they offer. Only Congress can appropriate funds and determine how much is to be spent and where. Congress jealously guards this absolute power. Congressional committees pick over every aspect of the president's budget.

United Press International Photo

The powers of a committee to investigate are sometimes effective, sometimes frightening. Senator Joseph McCarthy used the committee on government operations to mount his infamous anticommunist campaign of the 1950s. For years there was a house committee on "un-American activities." McCarthy's adversary, Joseph Welch, the army's special counsel, looks skeptical. So notorious was this investigation that the term **McCarthyism** has come to refer to any groundless, reckless charges made against innocent individuals.

Overseeing the Bureaucracy

We have seen two main areas of congressional responsibility: policymaking and budgeting. A third area of responsibility is investigation or **executive oversight**.

Much of the focus for executive oversight comes from the various committees in the Congress. The powers of a committee to investigate are widespread. In 1973, Sen. Sam Ervin helped expose the intricate web of Watergate in a Senate select committee. The House Judiciary Committee held hearings on Richard Nixon's impeachment. Sen. Frank Church more recently chaired a committee to investigate the CIA. Not all are successful, however. A bitterly divided house committee investigated the assassinations of John Kennedy and Martin Luther King, Jr. And some committees would have trouble justifying their staff or budgets.

A case could be made that the oversight function should be given more emphasis, even if this were to come at the expense of the legislative function. The argument goes like this.

Congress simply does not keep a close enough eye on the bureaucracies it creates. Senator Rudy Boschwitz of Minnesota suggests that these bureaucracies are like businesses that Congress creates, funds, and expands. Therefore, congressional committees should act as sort of boards of directors to see that these bureaucratic enterprises operate as Congress intended. Relatively little time is spent doing this—despite the enormous sums of money involved.

In fairness, however, it must be pointed out that Congress has its own investigative agency—the General Accounting Office (see box). Furthermore, during the Nixon and Ford years, House committees increased considerably the time spent in oversight activities.

What Is the General Accounting Office?

Finding ways to run the Federal Government—a $600 billion enterprise—more efficiently, effectively and economically is the task of the U.S. General Accounting Office.

The General Accounting Office came into existence as an independent, nonpolitical arm of the Congress in 1921 when the Budget and Accounting Act was enacted.

GAO's basic purposes are:

- To assist the Congress, its committees and its Members as much as possible in carrying out their legislative and oversight responsibilities, consistent with the agency's role as an independent, nonpolitical agency.
- To audit and evaluate the programs, activities and financial operations of Federal departments and agencies and make recommendations toward more efficient and effective operations.
- To carry out financial control and other functions with respect to Federal Government programs and operations including accounting, legal and claims settlement work.

GAO's primary internal objective is to perform all of its functions as effectively, efficiently, economically and promptly as possible.

Government has become much more complex since the Congress established GAO almost 60 years ago. The needs of the Congress for help have grown and will continue to grow.

This agency's greatest contribution is to provide answers to questions such as:

- Where are there opportunities to eliminate waste and the inefficient use of public money?
- Are Federal programs, whether administered directly by the Federal Government or through other organizations, such as the United Nations, or through State and local governments, achieving their objectives?
- Are there other ways of accomplishing the objectives of these programs at lower costs?

> Are funds being spent legally and is the accounting for them adequate?
>
> Using such information, Members of Congress are in a better position to make decisions concerning Government programs—whether the issue is continuing an innovative education program, acquiring a major weapons system for the Defense Department or providing development assistance for a foreign country.
>
> Concerns are being voiced in the Congress and elsewhere about the apparent decrease of confidence in the Government, particularly in the Government's ability to make programs effective and to serve well those individuals and groups for whom public funds are spent. Greater attention is also being focused on the accountability of Government officials to taxpayers. Thus it is more important than ever that the public be aware of the work of GAO as an organization with principal concern for fiscal integrity and the economical and effective management of Government programs.
>
> In the past years, GAO's professional staff—numbering 4,200—has been expanded to include engineers, mathematicians, statisticians, computer specialists, economists, business and public administrators, and even a medical doctor.
>
> During fiscal year 1978, the agency issued 1,136 audit reports and special studies, addressed to the Congress, its committees or Members, or to heads of departments and agencies. Copies of these reports are available to the public through GAO's Distribution Section, Room 1518, 441 G Street, NW, Washington, D.C. 20548.
>
> GAO provides information to the Congress by testifying before Congressional committees; holding informal briefings on agency problems for committees, Members and staffs; assigning staff members to work on Congressional committees; and providing legal opinions and comments on pending legislation.
>
> In addition, the Office undertakes reviews of major Government programs on its own initiative. Although GAO is authorized to investigate all matters relating to the receipt, disbursement, and application of public funds (with some exceptions), the policy is to review programs, activities, or functions of direct interest to the Congress and the public.
>
> SOURCE: *The Capitol*, 8th ed. (Washington, D.C.: U.S. Government Printing Office).

POWER WITHIN CONGRESS

Thus far in this chapter, we have looked at how Congress exercises power within the American political system. We have noted its recent efforts to curb some of the president's power. Finally, we have considered the constitutional bases of congressional power: policymaking, budgeting, and oversight.

In this section, we want to lift back that massive dome and peek inside the Capitol to see who within Congress holds the power.

Like the external appearance of a building, floor plans can speak too. Consider the now standard plan of the suburban home with its three bedrooms off a corridor. What could this possibly tell us? It tells of adult Americans' belief about children's relationship to their parents, the privilege of privacy, and the need for easy access to the common goods of the house (the kitchen). In another society, the children might have to pass through the parents' room to reach theirs.

The same kind of analysis might be applied to Congress. Unlike the floor plan of the White House, the layout of the Capitol reveals no single center of power. After exploring its two chambers, its long corridors and winding passages, its many offices and hearing rooms, and its ornate rotundas and galleries, the visitor concludes that, at best, Congress has many decision centers—or, at worst, it has none.

This discussion is important to both presidents and lobbyists. Presidents who come in with contempt for Congress, thinking they can bulldoze their way through, are doomed to legislative failure.

Inexperienced lobbyists and bureaucrats can make an equally fatal error. They take out the formal organizational chart of Congress, try to figure out who is in charge, and then make a deal with those individuals. Unfortunately for them, Congress is a more fragmented, complex place than their chart suggests. For example,

FIGURE 8-2
Party Leadership in Congress, 1981-1982

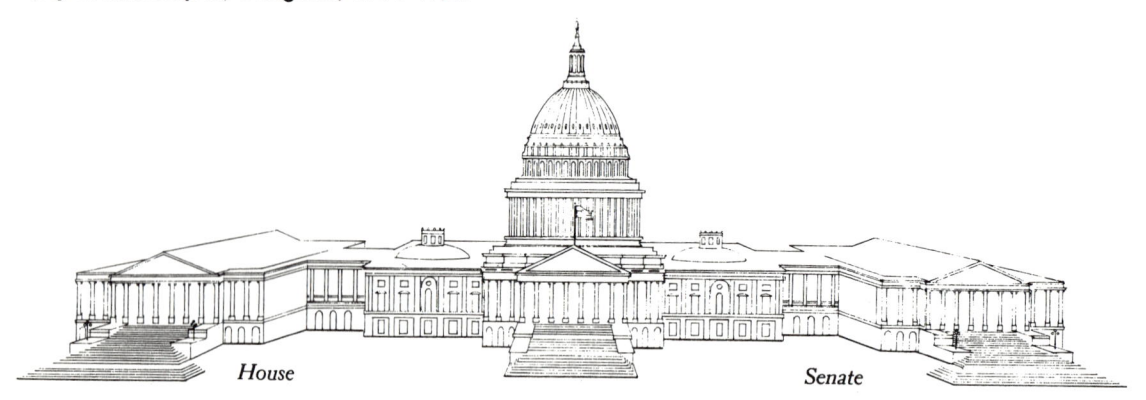

House	Senate
Speaker Thomas P. O'Neill, Jr. (Mass.)	Majority Leader Howard K. Baker, Jr. (Tenn.)
Majority Leader Jim Wright (Tex.)	Whip Ted Stevens (Alaska)
Whip Thomas S. Foley (Wash.)	Chairman of the Policy Committee† John Tower (Tex.)
Chairman, Steering and Policy Committee Thomas P. O'Neill, Jr. (Mass.)	Chairman of the Committee on Committees* Jake Garn (Utah)
Minority Leader Robert H. Michel (Ill.)	**Minority leader** Robert C. Byrd (W.Va.)
Whip Trent Lott (Miss.)	**Whip** Alan Cranston (Calif.)
Chairman, Committee on Committees* Robert H. Michel (Ill.)	**Chairman of the Policy Committee†** Robert C. Byrd (W.Va.)
Chairman, Republican Policy Committee† Richard B. Cheney (Wyo.)	**Chairman of the Steering Committee*** Robert C. Byrd (W.Va.)

Note: The majority party for each chamber appears on the top and positions held by Democrats are shown in color. So you can readily see that the Democratic party controls the House, while the Republican party controls the Senate.
* Committee that assigns party members to standing committees.
† Committee that helps party leader schedule legislation.

one reason why President Jimmy Carter's 1980 energy legislation moved so slowly was that jurisdiction over this area was fragmented between 83 different House committees and subcommittees.

Even more perplexing to the newcomers is the power held by certain members of Congress who hold no exalted formal positions of authority. This was especially true in the old Democratically controlled Senate. But we must not let all this talk about fragmentation and complexity obscure one elemental fact. The *formal* leadership positions in the House and Senate are still very powerful indeed (see Figure 8–2).

House Leadership

At the beginning of each Congress, the leadership of the House of Representatives is elected. The Constitution authorizes the House to elect a Speaker. Each party **caucus** also elects its party leader.* Under the tradition of the two-party system in this country, the leader of the party with the most members becomes the majority leader. The **minority leader** is invariably the member nominated by the minority party for the Speaker.

It would do no violence to the truth to call the Speaker of the House the second most powerful office holder in the U.S. government, surpassed only by the president. In fact, the Presidential Succession Act of 1947 places the Speaker second in line in succession to the presidency. He is behind only the vice president, whose assumption to that office is required by the Constitution.

The House majority leader works very closely with the Speaker in developing the party's position on major policy issues. Historically, the majority leader almost always has represented a different geographic area of the country from the Speaker. The role is to consult with committee chairmen and urge them to move legislation that the party considers important.

Each party also appoints a whip and assistant whips. They assist the floor leader in execution of the party's legislative program. The main job of the whips is to survey party members on a pending issue and give the floor leader an accurate estimate of the support or opposition expected on a bill. The term **whip** refers to the responsibility of these members to pressure the other members of their party to the floor for key votes.

In recent years the majority party has revitalized the caucus of its members. The chairman of the caucus, elected by party colleagues, has become an important part of the leadership structure.

Usually considered as part of the leadership are the chair positions of the 22 committees of the House. Until the congressional reforms in 1975 the chair achieved status solely by virtue of seniority. Currently, they are elected by the majority party caucus, by secret ballot. Committee chairs are nominated by the Steering and Policy Committee. This committee is composed of House leaders, their nominees, and members elected by the caucus on a regional basis.

Senate Leadership

The Constitution requires that the vice president be the president of the Senate. The vice president is frequently not present in the Senate, except in the case of a close vote that may end in a tie. Therefore the Senate elects a president pro tempore. By custom, in recent decades, it has the most senior majority member of the Senate. The president pro tempore is a key member of his party's policymaking body.

---

* The word *caucus* probably comes from the Indian word *cau-cau-a-su*, meaning adviser. It simply means a private meeting of members of a political organization for the purpose of choosing officers or deciding upon joint action on pending policy questions. In an era of simple issue politics, this latter function has become much stronger. Name an interest and some member of Congress will form a caucus. In 1979, there were 19. They were organized on ethnic, geographic, and economic bases.

He usually designates a more junior senator to preside over daily sessions in his place. The president pro tempore also has the responsibility for the Legislative Counsel, a group of legal specialists who assist senators in drafting bills.

Since the turn of the century, the Senate has by custom developed the position of majority leader as a parallel in power to Speaker of the House. The real leader of the Senate is the majority leader. This is the legislative strategist position that also exercises considerable influence on committee assignments.

In cooperation with their party organization, each leader is responsible for the achievement

---

A PROFILE OF SPEAKER OF THE HOUSE TIP O'NEILL: Like an Irish bartender, contemplating a customer who's had one too many, House Speaker Thomas O'Neill is about to face up to an unpleasant duty. What he has to do in this congress, jokes a sympathetic colleague, is "get a six-foot, eight-inch drunk to go home."

The drunk in this analogy is the Democratic party. For almost a half-century the party has used federal spending as its dry martini, its scotch on the rocks; ever-increasing spending has enabled the party to woo diverse interest groups and cement them into a political alliance.

But now the national anti-spending mood is forcing the Democrats on the wagon—or, more accurately, toward the wagon. With growth in the nondefense budget slowing, and with outlays for some programs actually shrinking in real terms, the party is being forced to set priorities among its many client groups. . . .

The prospect isn't appetizing, least of all for a party leader like Tip O'Neill, whose instincts and political philosophy are the products of a freer-spending era. . . .

Tip O'Neill remains a liberal Democrat in a House growing steadily more conservative; a product of old-style ward and neighborhood politics in a House growing steadily less orthodox.

At age 66, a white-maned, shambling bear of a man, he presides over one of the youngest, least-experienced Houses in decades. Of the 433 sitting members, 200 have served in Washington only four years or less. It is also an atomized House, increasingly resistant to leadership.

The power of the committee chairmen has been drastically reduced by internal reforms, even as the power of special interest groups has been rising. What the combination means, in practical terms, is that even the lowliest freshman is now a power unto himself, often more responsive to his constituents and the interest groups that bankrolled his campaign than to the Speaker or the president of the United States. . . .

This is a strident, polarized House; if it once had a center, a pivotal group of reasonable, accommodating members who saw things whole, that center is fast disappearing. Its members seem ever more prone to stake out rigid positions geared to fit 30-second television interviews and two-page press releases. The Speaker himself is an instinctively partisan Democrat. But in dealing with his fellow Democrats, his instaincts remain those of an earlier time: stay loose, don't lock yourself in, work things out in the backroom.

SOURCE: Dennis Farney, *The Wall Street Journal,* April 5, 1979.

of the legislative program. They manage the order in which legislation moves to passage and expedite noncontroversial legislation. They keep members of their party informed regarding pending business. Each leader is an ex-officio member of their party's policymaking and organizing body. Each is aided by an assistant leader, called the whip, as in the House, and by the majority or minority secretary, who are professional staff administrators but not members of the Senate.

The two major parties in the Senate are organized differently. The Republican senators form the Republican Conference, which elects the majority leader and deals with procedural matters. The Conference Committees nominate committee chairmen and assign party members to committees. They also elect the Republican Policy Committee, which handles the research and policy determination function of the party.

The Democrats have a caucus that nominates the minority leader, elects the Steering Committee, and approves Steering Committee nominations for committees. The Steering Committee assigns party members to committees. The Democratic Policy Committee develops legislative policy and positions.

Alternative Perspectives on Congressional Power: Iron Triangles, Rubber Triangles, and Issue Networks

The iron triangle model. Viewed from the perspective of an elected official outside Wash-

---

A PROFILE OF SENATE MAJORITY LEADER HOWARD H. BAKER (R–TENN.): A bright and diligent legislator, Howard Baker's rise to majority leader with the Republican capture of the Senate in 1980 has been fairly rapid. Baker was born into a political family. (His father was a seven-term congressman; his mother completed the term when his father died in 1964.) He married the daughter of Sen. Everett Dirkson, the long-time Republican leader and a Senate minority leader. Elected to the Senate in 1966 on his second try, his "family ties" resulted in considerable public attention and excellent committee positions. He was co-chair of the Watergate investigation committee. His calm and determined manner on the committee vaulted him into national prominence as he persisted in trying to determine the real extent of President Nixon's culpability. His subsequent work in foreign affairs, especially on the SALT II treaty, cemented his reputation. He was elected minority leader in 1977 and became the first Republican Senate majority leader in more than a quarter century—and one of the few Republican leaders elected from east of the Mississippi.

Baker says he will strive to make the Senate a deliberative body again, rather than "a bunch of elected bureaucrats" who pass "1,000 – page bills." That comment is probably an indirect criticism of Senator Robert C. Byrd, the former Democratic majority leader, who excelled in fashioning agreements that limited debate. "I'd like to see us restore the nature of the Senate as a great debating institution," Baker says. "Our committees report too much legislation and we pass too many laws. We don't need more laws. We need less laws." (*New York Times*, December 3, 1980)

George Tames/NYT Pictures

Senators Howard H. Baker, Jr., left, the majority leader, and Robert C. Byrd, the minority leader, conferring in a hallway at a pause in Senate proceedings.

ington, D.C., it often seems as if "iron triangles" run and maintain federal programs. And, like iron, they are not easily penetrated.

To simplify, one side of the triangle is made up of the relevant congressional subcommittee staff. The number of subcommittees runs quite high (157 in the House, 101 in the Senate); so too does the potential number of iron triangles. The second side consists of that section of the federal bureaucracy charged with administering the program. The lobby supporting the program completes the figure.

The power of triangles is that they write the laws and regulations and run the programs. Triangles come in various sizes and strengths. Some, such as the "sugar triangle," are particularly sturdy.

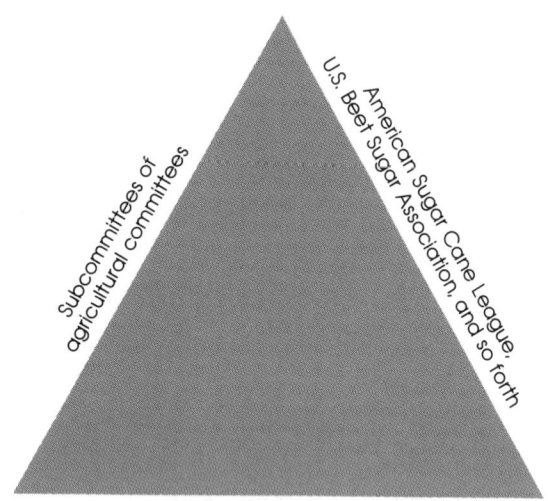

Sugar division of Department of Agriculture

(Subcommittees of agricultural committees; American Sugar Cane League, U.S. Beet Sugar Association, and so forth)

Clearly, these **subgovernments** dominate many areas of public policy. The relationship among the three elements is, in a word, cozy. Because some federal agencies have developed such cozy relations with the industry they are supposed to regulate, political scientists sometimes refer to the former as **captured agencies**. (In the language of power politics presented in Chapter 4, we would say such agencies have been co-opted.)

Not only do agencies and industry share information; they also share personnel. Professionals move freely back and forth through the **revolving doors** that connect the three sides. Members of Congress—preoccupied, as we have seen with constituent services—cannot devote much time to shaping the activities of these triangles. The president is too short on technical information and political appointees to intervene effectively. And the public finds that it just does not have the incentives, much less the expertise, to lobby against the special interests. By default, the iron triangle prevails.

Rubber triangle model. Recently, some young theorists have been studying a new version of the triangle. Since around 1970, a number of new federal agencies have been created that do not have ties with a single industry. This makes it almost impossible for cozy relationships to develop.

Three good examples of these newer agencies are the Environmental Protection Agency, Occupational Safety and Health Administration (OSHA), and Equal Employment Office. Their responsibilities cut across virtually all industries. When an OSHA inspector finds fire extinguishers too high off the ground or handrails painted the wrong color in a sugar beet factory, they are far less sympathetic to the industry's position; they simply do not spend enough time with any one industry to develop empathy. They want compliance with OSHA regulations.

The link between Congress and such agencies is hardly made of carbon steel. For example, Congress and their staffs sitting on the relevant health and safety subcommittees must be sympathetic to the complaints from business, especially those that provide jobs and dollars to their states and districts. But they are also under the watchful eye of unions and environmental groups who see sympathy as "selling out" to business.

In short, the iron triangle is only a partial explanation of American politics in the 1980s. At worst, it tends to make us look for one small, autonomous group exerting power over the rest of us to make public policy. This makes the iron triangle model downright misleading.

Issue networks. Many policy initiatives of the last 20 years seemed to occur without the emergence of any dominant, all-powerful actors. Who controlled, and is controlling, national policy on abortion, income redistribution and other welfare measures, consumer protection, or energy? When we look too hard for the powerful, we tend to overlook "the many whose webs of influence provoke and guide the exercises of power."[3] These webs, Hugh Hecto calls "issue networks."

> Issue networks comprise a large number of participants with quite variable degrees of mutual commitment or of dependence on others in their environment; in fact, it is almost impossible to say where a network leaves off and its environment begins. Iron triangles and subgovernments suggest a stable set of participants coalesced to control fairly narrow public programs which are in the direct economic interest of each party to the alliance. Issue networks are almost the reverse image in each respect. Participants move in and out of the networks constantly. Rather than groups united in dominance over a program, no one, as far as one can tell, is in control of the policies and issues. Any direct material interest is often secondary to intellectual or emotional commitment. Network members reinforce each other's sense of issues as their interests, rather than (as standard political or economic models would have it) interests defining positions on issues.
>
> Issue networks operate at many levels, from the vocal minority who turn up at local planning commission hearings to the renowned professor who is quietly telephoned by the white House to give a quick "reading" on some participant or policy.[4]

Unfortunately, it is difficult to describe the exact appearance of an issue network. Like Bigfoot and flying saucers, no one has yet taken a clear picture of one. At any given time only part of the network may be active. Through time the various connections may intensify or fade among policy intermediaries and the executive and congressional bureaucracies. A clear picture seems impossible.

FUTURE FILE

Congress 2001

Composition

The makeup of Congress will become more diverse, younger, and southwestern.

Ethnic minorities, who were once shut out of legislative office, will expand their footholds. In 1953, the house of Representatives had only two black members and one Hispanic member. The Senate had one Hispanic member and no blacks. Neither the House nor Senate had any members of Oriental descent. Today, the number of black legislators stands at 17 in the House and zero in the Senate. The Senate now has no one of Spanish descent, but the House has five. Two Orientals now serve in the House; three serve in the Senate. If this growth rate holds, the house in the year 2001 will have at least 31 blacks and Hispanics. But if the growth rate matches population trends, the House will have over twice that number.

Women, too, will gain in legislative power. In 1953, there were 12 women in the House; today there are 19. In the Senate, women have had ups and downs. In 1953, they held one seat, that of Margaret Chase Smith, Republican of Maine, who was defeated in 1972. Today, there are two women in the Senate. Nevertheless, assuming the trends hold in the House, there should be at least 22 women in Congress by 2001.

Congressional critics picture the institution as a collection of aging mossbacks. But while the average age in the United States is rising, Congress is getting younger every year. When the 96th Congress convened in 1978, the average age in the House and Senate was 49.5 years. This was the lowest figure in more than 30 years. It was the first Congress since World War II whose average age was below 50.

This trend is likely to hold for several reasons. The switch from party-based to individually based campaigning has made almost any complacement incumbent potentially vulnerable to a young, ambitious, well-financed newcomer. The key to reelection now is good constituent service. It is an uninteresting and relentless task that many members find increasingly unpleasant as they grow older.

There has been a growing mobility of the electorate, increased use of television, and rise of special interest groups. These all mean that outsiders can ignore the established structure and appeal directly to the voters. One sort of outsider is the *celebrity candidate*; this is someone who has made a name in another field and enters politics with enormous name recognition. The classic example is Bill Bradley. He is the former basketball player for the New York Knicks who beat the party-backed candidate in the Democratic primary in New Jersey. Another form of outsider is the candidate who springs directly from a special interest organization.

The safest forecast about the future composition of Congress is that the Republican party will probably add more seats in the House because of the way new district lines are being drawn. Specifically, the population shift between 1970 and 1980 was from the northern Frost Belt to the more conservative Sun Belt, and from traditionally Democratic big cities to suburbia.

Predicting what the numbers mean in political terms is more risky. Arguably, if the G.O.P. controlled both houses of Congress, the right wing of the party would have more influence than it did in 1981–82. Reagan might have a difficult time curbing their more extravagant goals in such areas as school prayer, environmental protection, and abortion.

Size

Congress is a big enterprise. In fact, it is elephantine. The Senate budget for fiscal year 1981 was greater than the budget of 74 countries. The Capitol police force is bigger than the army of Luxembourg.

But the important statistic concerns the continued growth of congressional staff. In 1972, there were 2,426 Senate aides and 913 Senate committee staffers; there were 5,280 House aides and 783 House committee staffers—a grand total of 9,402. By 1976, that total had jumped to 13,272. But, as we know from Professor Parkinson, bureaucracies do not grow linearly but geometrically. At that rate, we could see an army of about 150,000 strong by 2001.

Besides the issue of how to pay all these salaries, what makes this trend alarming is that

Air Photographics, Inc.

At nightfall, the lights come up in the Rayburn House Office Building. Glasses tinkle and laughter rings out from congressional receptions for constituents and lobbyists. Capitol Hill is like a convention hotel at that hour, lighthearted and bustling.

Sometimes congressional quarters are on a lavish scale. For example, Senator William Proxmire has observed that the new Senate Office Building "would make a Persian prince green with envy."

already many members of Congress feel that they spend their days responding to staff. Staffs compete against other staffs; members are caught up in the crossfire, extra work, and meetings.

Because of these larger staffs, legislation is written in much greater detail.

Reforming Reform

Senator Roscoe Conkling (1829–88) of New York once said about the good-government enthusiasts of his day: "When Dr. Johnson defined patriotism as the last refuge of a scoundrel, he was unconscious of the then underdeveloped capabilities and uses of the word *reform.*" Mr. Conkling would not be surprised to see that his successors in the U.S. Congress have now reformed the government enough to be driving some of the best people out of it and threatening the performance of those that are left.

Eugene McCarthy and James Kilpatrick provide this whimsical picture of reform:

> The Reform comes in various guises. The most familiar include the Needed Reform, the Imperative Reform, and the Too Long Delayed Reform. In every guise, however, Reforms share this common fate—their lives will be short and their permanent effects will be few.
>
> Like the vipers described in the ancient Bestiaries, Reforms and Reformers tend to be destroyed by their own progeny.
>
> The Reform may be ostensibly respected, but is seldom truly loved. The Reform goes abroad like a parson who has just hit the Listerine jug, smelling faintly of piety and antisepsis. The Reform is diligent and persistent and almost always worse than the condition just Reformed.
>
> Reforms may be found in widely varying terrains, from the humblest home to the most sophisticated corporation. Ordinarily, of course, they are encountered in governmental situations, where the power of law may be imposed in their behalf. Early in 1978, President Carter succeeded Ralph Nader as the most vigorous proponent of Reform in Washington.
>
> In the usual course of events, Reforms are spawned by elections in which Reform candidates seek to displace the politicians in power. Mr. Dooley, the eminent Chicago bartender, knew all about this. "A rayformer," said Mr. Dooley, "thinks he was ilicted because he was a rayformer, whin th' truth iv th' matther is he was ilicted because no wan knew him."
>
> As Mr. Dooley might also have observed, such election contests have a dual purpose. The first, as to the opposition, is to throw their rascals out. The second, closer home, is to throw our rascals in. [Eugene McCarthy and James Kilpatrick, *A Political Bestiary* (New York: McGraw-Hill, 1979).]

In the wake of Watergate, Congress attempted to "reform" itself in a variety of ways. To reduce the power of committee chairman and the **seniority system** (whereby first choice of committee position, etc., goes to the longest-serving member), the number and influence of subcommittees was increased. Members of Congress were limited as to outside income and required to make complete disclosure of wealth. **Sunshine laws** were passed at every level of government. These require that practically all meetings of all official bodies be open to public view. And the House and Senate breathed new life into their ethics committees, which were established in the 1960s.

The political appeal of such measures is undeniable. Who would want to be against reform? "In our system of politics," noted political author Theodore H. White suggests, "anything that can be described as virtuous automatically enlists the support of all high-minded people, most of the media and all those pressure groups that respond to the call of virtue as Pavlov's dog to his bell." (Quoted in Dennis Farney, "Congress, Fragmented and Fractrous, Gets Less and Less Done," *The Wall Street Journal*, December 14, 1979.)

And yet, this ethical revolution has not been an unmitigated success.

Ironically, these reforms stem from a kind of egalitarian revolution led by Rep. Morris Udall and other Democrats. As the young turks of the early 1970s, they pushed through a series of House rules revisions that weakened committee chairmen and gave more power to subcommittee chairmen and individual members. But since then, many of the young turks themselves have become committee chairmen. Udall, for example, is chairman of the House Interior Committee. From this new vantage point, they are asking, "Did we go too far?"

"The older I get, the wiser I get," says a wry Mo Udall today. He still defends most of the changes; but he talks of "Udall's Fourth Law," which is: "Every reform always carries consequences you don't like" [*The Wall Street Journal* (May 3, 1979.)] For example, chairmen no longer can ram bad bills through the House. But neither can they block bad bills churned out by their increasingly autonomous subcommittee chairmen. Now the oil companies win over the environmentalists in Udall's committee. Thus, the turmoil and hubbub of floor debate, instead of the committee meeting, is where more and more controversial legislation is finally being shaped. One consequence of the rules changes is that it is becoming harder and harder to control or direct the House.

Otis Pike (see earlier box, "Goodbye to Congress—And All That") had trouble finding the logic in an ethics rule that limits outside income: "If I take those 191 days when Congress was not in session and go junketing all around the world at your expense, I am ethical. If I go home and work in my law office, I am unethical. There were loopholes for certain professions. If I write a book, I am ethical. If I write wills or deeds, I am unethical. If I get $100,000 a year sitting on my butt and collecting dividends, interests, rents, and royalties, I am ethical. If I work and earn $10,000, I am unethical." (Extension of Remarks of the *Congressional Record*, February 14, 1978.)

When it comes to making rules for themselves and investigating of each other, members of Congress are less than effective. The Senate, for example, cannot get any of its members to volunteer for its ethics committee any more; the committee's investigations of Senators Brooke and Talmadge turned out to be nasty enterprises that brought the committee members only resentment from their fellow lawmakers. Even if the investigation is thorough and honest, it is difficult for the public to accept it as being conducted in good faith. The public is skeptical of any self-investigation.

One possible solution is to separate the investigative function from the prosecutional function. The investigation could be done by an independent commission—that is, a group of people not appointed by the branch under investigation. The commission would have the authority to conduct a full investigation and find out the facts. Thus, it could turn them over to a prosecutor, which might be part of Congress.

Other legislators, and many bureaucrats, question also the logic of the sunshine laws. Because they penalize candor and compromise and reward aggressive "grandstanding," some now question whether they provide the best way to run a school board, university department, trade union, government agency, or congressional committee.

Fusing the Legislative and Executive Powers

The most far-reaching, serious proposal to change Congress calls for the adoption of a **parliamentary system** of government. To see how such a system might work, we need look no further than British cabinet government; it fuses rather than separates legislative and executive powers.

The legislative branch of British government is Parliament. Like the Congress, it is bicameral, consisting of a popularly elected House of Commons and a nonelected House of Lords. The former is, however, the more powerful by far. The leaders of the majority party in Commons are joined by the leaders of the same party in Lords to form "the Government." In other words, whichever party gets a majority of the seats in Commons wins not only the legislature but also the executive.

The Government governs the country only as long as its leaders—the prime minister and the cabinet—maintain the support of the House of Commons. The Commons can at any time vote the cabinet out of office or force it to resign by defeating it on a major policy issue. In such cases, a government could call for another election in an effort to regain its strength in the Commons.

The cabinet, as we said, is a group of top party leaders, most of whom head particular administrative departments or ministries while retaining their seats in Commons. Given this fusion of executive and legislative branches in Britain, prime ministers have considerable experience before attaining that office. Unlike the American system, one must work one's way up in the party; there are no alternative routes, such as governor or general. (The average prime minister has served 25 years of prior service in Parliament.)

This arrangement tends to foster party discipline. If one rebels against the party leaders, one is unlikely to receive appointments to the lesser offices in which one can demonstrate having the ability necessary for higher political office. The arrangement also lacks all the intricate checks and balances of the American system. Therefore it also tends to strengthen the executive in dealing with the legislature. The cabinet, not some Speaker or majority leader or rules committee, determines what matters are to be considered and how much time is to be allotted to each. Unlike the American practice, only the cabinet can propose to raise and spend money.

All members of Parliament (MPs) are expected to vote the way their party instructs them to, regardless of personal attitudes. When MPs rebel on an issue of sufficient importance or frequently enough, they may be expelled from the party in Parliament. Thus they risk their political careers. This behavior does not stem from a lack of political courage. Rather, it comes from a recognition that failing to vote with one's party can help that party lose a crucial vote. In that event, a new election must be held with the possibility that the opposition party becomes the new government. Party loyalty also comes from a recognition that one is not elected because of any personal attributes but because of the party label. People vote for a MP in order to give a particular party a majority in Parliament.

Would this work in the United States? Surely not as well. In a large, heterogenous country like the United States, political issues are often more regional than national. Constituents in the United States might not like such close adherence by their representatives to the stands of national leaders. The British government concentrates power well. It has far less trouble ramming through needed legislation than the American system. Such a system fixes responsibility as well. No handful of perverse legislators can thwart the government's program. When things do not get done or do not work well, they know who to blame.

The Challenge Congress Cannot Escape

Thus far we have been exploring internal alterations that Congress might experience. But Congress does not operate in a vacuum. When the founding fathers outlined the structure and functions of Congress, they gave it "all legislative powers herein granted."

Thus a crucial question is, What kinds of external forces will reshape the legislative agenda in the future? Surely a new and rapidly changing technology will present Congress with many problems and opportunities.

The fundamental challenge that all these technologies present to Congress is, *How do we capitalize on the benefits of new technology while holding the costs and risks to a bare minimum?* Historically, Americans have looked mostly at the central effects of a new technology (that is, those results it is expected to have); they have ignored its side effects. Those days are over.* Now the motto is "proceed with caution."

In terms of public policy, three technologies will be particularly important to Congress over the next two decades. They are energy conversion, biomedicine, and telecommunications. Chapters 12 and 13 touch on these complex issues; we only mention them here.

Perhaps Congress, like the average Ameri-

---

* Without trying to be too precise about when those days ended, we might consider congressional rejection of the SST (supersonic transport) in 1972 as symbolic that they were on the wane. It was probably the first time Congress had ever said no to a technologically feasible project. Subsequently, the British and French experience with the Concorde seems to vindicate the wisdom of the decision.

can, is a little ambivalent about this brave new world. It is worth recalling that the Capitol itself (like so much American architecture) attempted, on the one hand, to be modern and, on the other, to hold back the onward sweep of modernist destiny. Thus the use of iron in its dome was praised as forward-thinking. But the form of the dome, with its obvious historical reference, was condemned as dated.

Ambivalent or not, Congress enters America's third century perhaps more sure of its true nature and balancing role in government than the American corporation is of its nature and role in society. As William Hubbard, a practicing architect in Virginia, reminds us, "the mute, sleek corporate style offers an institution respectability and chic at an economical price, but that very muteness also offers a tempting route around the task of self-examination." In contrast, Congress and the Capitol were consciously conceived by minds sure of their intentions. Fortunately.

Chapter Key

Committees and subcommittees are the key policy-making bodies in Congress. Only by dividing work among specialized committees can Congress keep pace with the increasing volume and complexity of its workload.

There are more than 300 committees and subcommittees in the House and Senate. There are many types of committees in Congress—for example, standing and temporary, authorizing and fiscal, joint, and conference. The standing committees, which are permanent, are the work horses of Congress.

The seniority system awards committee chairmanships to majority-party committee members with the most years of service. Congressional reforms in the 1970s changed the way seniority is applied and resulted in wider distribution of committee chairmanships. Jurisdiction has accrued to committees as bills were assigned to them and precedents built up. Not surprisingly, jurisdictional rivalries and entanglements among the committees are common. In Congress, politics is property.

Legislators differ widely on how they perceive and carry out their congressional role. Some see themselves as "errand runners"; they devote most of their time to constituency service. "Workhorses" place primary emphasis on legislation and policymaking. Legislators differ also in their views of how to represent their constituencies. Some follow their own conscience in making decisions; others rely on instructions from the voters.

The House and Senate have each determined their own rules of procedure that set the stage for how a bill becomes a law. Of the thousands of bills introduced in Congress each session, only a small percentage become law. The critical phase of a bill's life occurs during committee deliberation.

If a bill is reported by committee, it must get to the floor of the House or Senate. The House relies on several legislative calendars and the Rules Committee to schedule when, if, and under what conditions bills are taken to the floor; the Senate usually calls bills up by unanimous consent. Thus, the House Rules Committee is very powerful.

Floor debate is the most visible part of the lawmaking process. It is not usually substantively important; the arguments have all been covered in committee. Floor debate serves mainly to put members' positions on the public record before the floor vote is taken. A bill must repeat the same procedure of committee deliberation, scheduling, floor debate, and vote in both houses before it can be sent to the president. If the House and Senate versions of a bill differ, a conference committee must work out the differences.

The raising and spending of money for government programs lie at the core of congressional powers. The House Ways and Means Committee is responsible for originating all tax legislation. (It also has jurisdiction over a variety of other matters.) The Senate counterpart, the Finance Committee, plays a significant but secondary role.

The spending power granted in Article I, Section 8—"The power of the purse"—is Congress' most potent weapon in overseeing the executive branch. Each year, agency heads must appear before House and Seante appropriations subcommittees to justify their budget requests and answer questions about their programs.

In 1974, Congress felt a need to reduce the fragmentation in its revenue and spending responsibilities and to compete with the president's budgeting capabilities. Therefore it instituted a new budget process with the passage of the Budget and Impoundment Control Act. This act established procedures for Congress to determine national budget priorities. It also created, among other things, House and Senate budget committees, the Congressional Budget Office, a timetable for new budgeting procedures, and a mechanism for controlling presidential impoundments. The point of the new budgeting process was to get Congress to consider all of its revenue and spending programs as a whole rather than piecemeal. Nevertheless, Congress continued to spend billions more than it collected in taxes.

Committees represent dispersed or decentralized power. Congressional parties and their leaders, on the other hand, represent the primary centralizers of congressional power. Party leaders—the Speaker, majority leaders, minority leaders, and whips—work with party bodies (the Democratic caucus and Republican conference) to regulate the flow of legislation, muster support for bills, and select committee members and chairmanships. Party leadership has traditionally been stronger and more vigorous in the House than in the Senate. Strong leadership in the Senate has been the exception, not the rule.

The political parties form the most stable and important grouping in Congress. Party loyalty, though not strong, is still the leading determinant of how members will vote in both houses. Many forces tug at members' party loyalties, however. These forces include constituency, interest groups, state delegations, regional differences, and ideology.

The bureaucracy supporting Congress has grown enormously since the 1950s; it numbered almost 39,000 in 1976. The support staff for Congress includes members' personal staff, staff for congressional committees, housekeeping staff, and supporting agencies. These support agencies do legislative research, handle requests from legislators, analyze the impact of pending bills, and assist in congressional oversight.

The 1980s are likely to witness several important changes in Congress. The 1980 census gives more representation to western and southern states. This should give Congress a more conservative complexion than in the preceding decade. It is also likely that some of the reforms of the 1970s to make Congress more democratic will be "reformed." The number of women members is likely to increase.

Answers to Quiz
(See page 269)

The figure on the left is New York state's rambling 33rd state senate district; the one on the right is California's 69th assembly district. They are prime examples of how politicians struggle for control of the map.

Now that population figures from the 1980 census are available, most states are beginning to redraw the boundaries of congressional and state legislative districts. The process is called **reapportionment** or **redistricting**, and the law requires that it take place every 10 years. Its intent is to see that each person's vote counts equally. To accomplish this, there must be an equal number of people in each legislative district, and the count must reflect the latest population figures.

Despite its tremendous importance, redistricting has always been little publicized and little understood by the general public. Instead, it has been a complex and private numbers game often used by officeholders to enhance their chances for reelection and the power of the majority party. Reapportionment analysts say this happened in 1971 when many state legislators shifted district boundaries to include incumbents' supporters, while placing solid blocks of unsympathetic voters elsewhere.

Since incumbent security is so crucial to those in charge, the other implications of redistricting may be regarded as secondary. For example, minority communities have been sliced up during reapportionment so that their votes can be used to help incumbents in neighboring areas. Minority groups believe this is one reason they have failed to elect many of their own representatives. State legislators also tend to slice up populous cities and counties to prevent local politicians from gaining a constituency to back them for seats in state legislatures or Congress. As a result, urban areas are often hampered in their efforts to influence legislation.

Two other important issues are at stake as well: There is the question of whether the new districts will properly reflect the recent population growth of the suburbs and smaller, outlying cities or be designed to protect the declining political power of some big cities. Will the new computer technology help draw more equitable districts or will it be used to tilt the votes in favor of those already in power?

Some political theorists believe that when politicians manipulate reapportionment to draw safe districts for themselves, the public suffers. Individual voters and so-called special interest groups have more influence with officeholders who do not have safe districts. This is how democracy is designed to work, they say. In a position of relative insecurity, politicians are forced to be responsive to the wishes of the voters. Furthermore, when officeholders are worried about reelection, they work harder to get support and campaign contributions from important groups in their districts.

Other experts say that, at least in the case of congressional representatives, safe districts help legislators build seniority on committees. This, they contend, leads to more benefits for constituents.

As most of us learned in high school government classes, the word **gerrymander** refers to the misshapen district that often results when legislators attempt to manipulate district lines. It was named for Massachusetts Governor Elbridge Gerry, who signed a bill in 1811 creating a district to help his party stay in power. It was shaped like a winged monster and came to be called "a gerrymander." To correct this kind of abuse, many states began requiring that districts be compact, contiguous, accessible to voters and that they follow county boundaries. Despite these restrictions, another kind of abuse developed called *malapportionment*. The term refers to gross disparities between the number of people in one district and another. In the 1960s the U.S. Supreme Court acted to end district inequality by ruling that legislative districts must contain equal populations.

The court's rulings ended state restrictions on gerrymandering, and the 1971 reapportionment created some strangely misshapen districts. Reapportionment expert Dr. Alan Heslop of California's Rose Institute explained, "Now if districts sprawl across the map and dip for population into communities far distant from each other, if they crisscross county and city boundaries, even if they are connected only by artificial corridors and cut by mountain ranges, so long as they are equal in population, they are probably legal."

In the past, reapportionment has been shunned by the public and the press as too boring or complex for the average person. But this year things may be different. Outraged by what they perceive as an unfair reapportionment in 1971, many will be more vocal about abuses this time. A number of academic groups are studying the implications of proposed reapportionment plans to let the public know what their impact will be. Other groups, such as ethnic communities, business, labor, city and county officials, and professional organizations, are much more sensitive to the process and ready to agitate if they feel they are being cheated out of a fair voice in government.

SOURCE: "Will Public Outcry Bring About Fair Redistricting?" *CAP Reports*, May 1971.

Philadelphia Museum of Art/The W. P. Wilstach Collection

9 | The Judiciary: A Citizen's Guide

After studying this chapter you should be able to answer the following questions:

1. What are the basic functions of law in the U.S. political system?
2. What are the major sources of judicial power?
3. How is the federal court system organized?
4. How do strict and loose interpretations of the Constitution differ?
5. What is the adversary system?
6. What is the function of judges, lawyers, and juries in the U.S. legal system?
7. How might America become a less litigious society?

Terms you should know:

adjudication
administrative law
adversary system
age of majority
amicus curiae brief
assault
beyond a reasonable doubt
bond
civil law
common law
concurring opinion
contract
court of appeals
criminal law
defendant
depositions
discovery
dissenting opinion
district courts
equity
error of law
felonies
fraud
judicial activism versus judicial restraint
judiciary

jurisdiction
justice of the peace
larceny
majority opinion
misdemeanors
open-housing laws
parole
plaintiff
plea bargaining
political question doctrine
precedent
private law
public law
real property
remedy
senatorial courtesy
small claims court
solicitor general
standing
stare decisis
statutory law
tort
trial versus appeal courts
writ of certiorari

Thomas Jefferson called it a "talkative and dubious trade." Caricaturist Honoré Daumier portrayed it as incisively in pictures as Jefferson did in words. Yet the legal profession is deeply enmeshed in the political development of the American republic. The world's longest-lived democracy is based on the "rule of law." Many of America's outstanding political leaders from the founding fathers onward have been lawyers. As you know from Chapter 2, one of the cornerstones of the American system of government is an independent **judiciary**. (The term *judiciary* refers to all the courts and judges in the United States—federal and state.)

Today, no nation has as many lawyers, either in relative or absolute terms, as America. The French have only one tenth as many lawyers per capita; and the state of Ohio alone has more lawyers than all of Japan. Perhaps Jefferson should have written "talkative, dubious, *and numerous.*"

The idea upon which this chapter is based that law deserves a place in a liberal education. Many political questions, if not resolved in a reasonably short time by either the executive or legislature, become judicial questions. The customs and technicalities of the legal profession seep through the walls of the law schools and courts to permeate American politics and society. Hence, one cannot understand American politics without understanding the controversies, ideas, and even language of judicial proceedings.

Though we sometimes may be inclined to think of law as a negative force—abolishing this, restraining that—it is actually a positive force. The end of law is to preserve and enlarge on some very important ideas discussed in Chapter 3—freedom and equality, for example. Where there is no law, there is no freedom. "For liberty is," John Locke wrote, "to be free from restraint and violence from others." Because of this function, minorities have often turned to courts for protection when elected officials have failed to respond to their pleas.

Several other important judicial functions might be noted. As we saw in Chapter 1, all political relationships involve conflict. It is a primary function of the courts to settle these disputes. Working within a framework of laws, judges administer the process through which these conflicts are peacefully resolved. As we saw in Chapter 2, the Constitution divides and balances political power. In particular, the founding fathers set up a federal system in which a national and many state governments could operate at the same time over the same territory. An important function of the judiciary is to serve as head umpire when questions develop between officials in this system. When disputes arise, judges sorting out who has the authority to act and who does not. And as we saw in Chapter 4, the power of political symbols is not to be taken lightly. When President Andrew Jackson remarked, "Mr. Justice Marshall has made his decision; now let him enforce it," he seemed to epitomize the view that the Supreme Court is powerless. But judges personify both the law itself and society's values (impartiality, reason, fairness, etc.). Often we say someone is as sober as a judge or invoke the blindfolded figure holding up the scales of justice; we are giving testimony to the fact that judges, in their black robes and on their benches, are performing a function that transcends any individual judge.

This chapter is designed to explain simply and briefly what that machinery is and how it functions. First, it takes a look at the way the law is—What are its sources and how is it classified? The chapter then sketches the structure and operations of the federal and state courts and their relationship to each other. Here particular emphasis will be placed on the powerful influence of the Supreme Court in American government. Finally, it traces, step by step, a typical lawsuit with a view to showing how the adversary process works. The roles of litigants, lawyers, judges, jurors, police, and interest groups are explained.

One final point. To become a more perceptive interpreter of American politics is not, however, the only reason why citizens might undertake to learn a little more about judicial functions. To a far greater extent than the executive or legislative branches, the judiciary impinges on their lives. The list is as long as it is obvious. Getting married, suing for divorce, busing schoolchildren, buying a house, handling a traffic accident or traffic violation, suing for unpaid bills, starting a business, serving on a jury, and probating a will (i.e., processing an inheritance through courts) are just some of the ways a citizen can become involved in the machinery of justice.

WHAT THE LAW IS

Law, as you could probably infer from the quotation by Locke given a moment ago, is simply a uniform system of rules to govern or prescribe certain behavior for everyone living within a given area. The courts, of course, interpret law.

The technical name for this power to interpret and apply the law is **adjudication**. One citizen says that a law prohibiting disturbance on a public beach means that people cannot ride their motorcycles up and down the beach. Another citizen says that this law means that the police department must only insure that rioting on the beach does not occur. What does the law really mean? Adjudication will tell us.

But to better understand the nature of adjudication and to lay a basis for understanding how the courts operate, we need to examine the idea of judicial power. From where does the authority to interpret the law come?

Sources of Judicial Power

Constitutional law. In Chapter 2 we learned that the Constitution, as interpreted by the Supreme Court, is the supreme law of the land. The sweep of the Constitution is broad. It covers government power and individual rights. But it obviously does not apply to all potential conflicts that might arrive in American society. Constitutional law is, therefore, the U.S. Constitution plus the thousands of decisions made by the Court when it has had to reinterpret the meaning of such vague phrases as "interstate commerce" or "due process of law."

Common law. To varying degrees, the legal systems of most English-speaking nations of the world have been influenced by **common law,** derived from England. The roots of common law, or judge-made law, are found in the early Middle Ages. At that time local courts decided cases by applying custom and reason to everyday disputes. In common law, judges were bound by certain civilized assumptions, such as "all men were equal before the law." Judges also had recourse to precedent; that is, they could look to the recorded reasoning of other judges in similar cases. Thus, over the years, thousands of judicial decisions became fused together to form one, coherent system. The maxim that reflects this fundamental principle of precedent is **stare decisis** ("let the decision stand"). It is from the English common law that the American legal system evolved.

Equity and statutory law. Common law can contrast with equity and statutory law.

Equity is that branch of law designed to provide a remedy where common law does not apply. Common law is concerned largely with granting of damages *after* a wrongful act. But what about situations in which damages after the fact are not meaningful? In situations where unique solutions to unusual problems are required, a court can grant equitable relief through "specific performance" or "injunction." Here are examples of each term.

> The court may *order* that something be done. A seller may be ordered to convey title to a buyer of a property in accordance with the terms of a contract.
>
> The court may *enjoin* a party from breaking a contract under certain conditions. A basketball player who did not want to play with his NBA team could be enjoined by that team from playing for a rival team

in the ABA league, if he were still under contract to the NBA team.

Unlike common law and equity, **statutory law** is made by legislation. Because governments from city councils to the Congress legislate on so many subjects, the scope of statutory law is exceedingly broad. Federal laws currently in force are collected in the United States Code, which is kept up-to-date with annual supplements and is revised every six years. Many states have collected and classified their statutes, including pertinent judicial decisions, under the title *Compiled Laws*. Codes collect all related laws under a subject heading for easy reference use.

The Biases of Judges

Figure 9–1 summarizes what we have been saying about the sources of American law. In addition, it attempts to highlight the role that the biases of judges plays in determining how the various sources of law will be brought to bear on a particular legal question.

FIGURE 9-1
The Structure of American Law

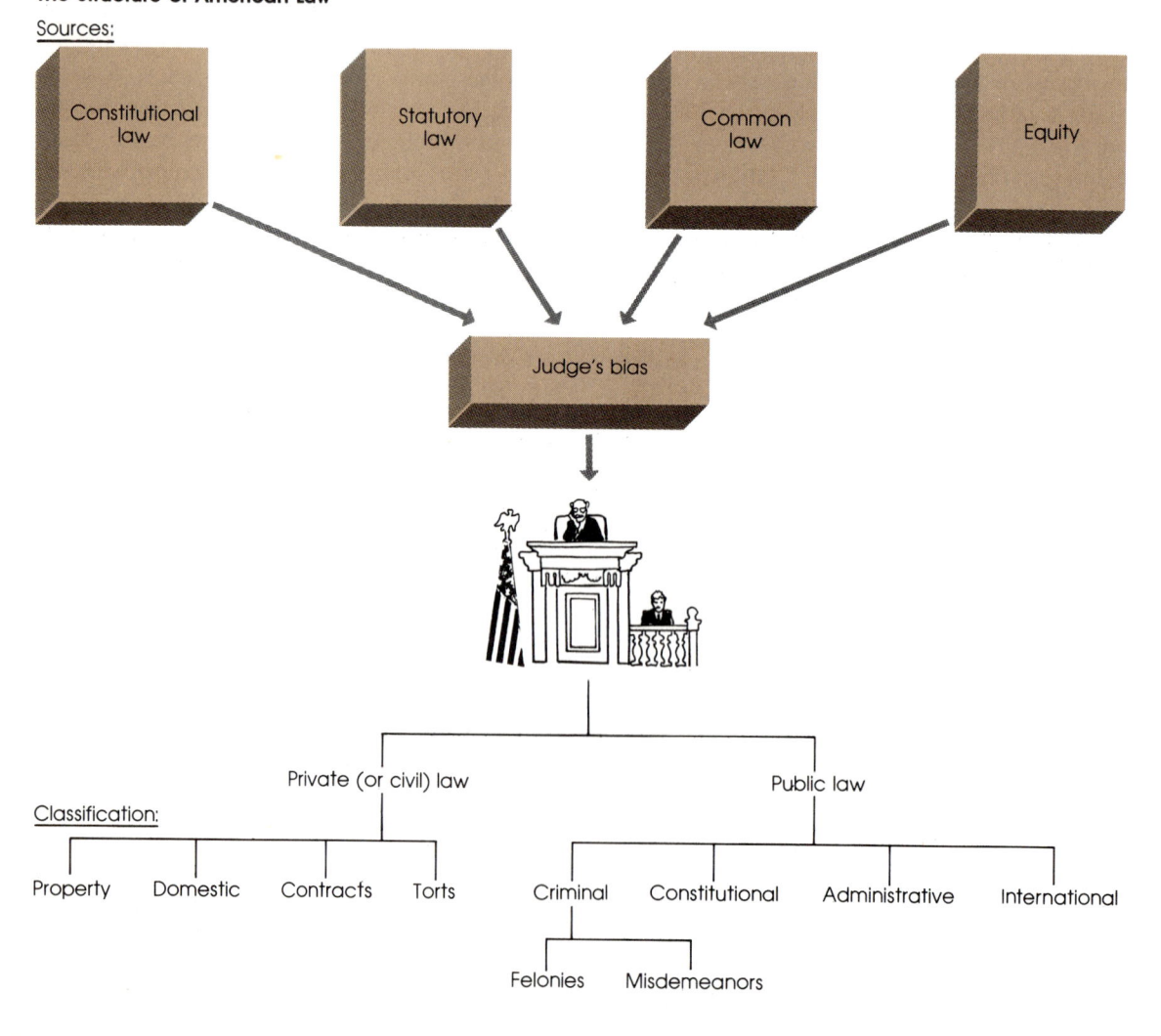

Sources: Constitutional law, Statutory law, Common law, Equity → Judge's bias →

Classification:
- Private (or civil) law: Property, Domestic, Contracts, Torts
- Public law: Criminal (Felonies, Misdemeanors), Constitutional, Administrative, International

There is a persistent myth, first articulated by Chief Justice Marshall, that "courts are mere instruments of the law and can will nothing." But courts have always consisted of men and women with political views; often they have been appointed and confirmed by politicians, often with specific goals in mind. They have had to make decisions in the context of history and politics. Philosophy, sociology, economics, and their own values have helped determine their decisions. Contrary to Marshall, judicial interpretation of the law involves more than the discovery of unambiguous truths. Closer to the mark perhaps is Chief Justice Charles Evans Hughes' remark: "The Constitution is what the judges say it is." Though some may deplore these words, they reveal what is perhaps an inevitable outcome of the judicial process. As the great judge Benjamin N. Cardozo once explained:

> There is in each of us a stream of tendency, whether you choose to call it philosophy or not, which gives coherence and direction to thought and action. Judges cannot escape that current any more than other mortals. All their lives, forces which they do not recognize and cannot name, have been tugging at them—inherited instincts, traditional beliefs, acquired convictions; and the resultant is an outlook on life, a conception of social needs . . . which, when reasons are nicely balanced, must determine where choices shall fall. In this mental background every problem finds its setting. We may try to see things as objectively as we please. Nonetheless, we can never see them with any eyes except our own. . . .[1]

In addition, summarizing the sources of law and highlighting the role of the judge's biases, Figure 9-1 shows you how law is classifed.

Classification of Laws

A convenient way to divide the rules of law is into **private law** and **public law.** Broadly speaking, private law includes all rules relating to private persons; that is, it deals with the relationships between one individual and another. Private law is sometimes called **civil law.** (Civil law can also refer to the legal systems of many modern European countries. This meaning of the term is quite different than the usage here.)

The chief branches of private law or civil law are shown in Figure 9-1. The law of property deals with the ownership and possession of land. All land, with everything permanently fixed to it, is known as **real property.** All movable property is personal property. (Articles of personal property are generally called "chattels.") The law of property also deals with inheritance and with rights over such things as trademarks, patents, or copyrights.

The laws of domestic relations regulate such relationships as marriage, parenthood, and guardianship.

Because it forms the basis of all business transactions, the law of **contracts** is very important to modern society. For a contract to be binding and enforceable, it must involve "consideration." This is the lawyers' way of saying that it must be entered into "for money or money's sake." There must also be mutual consent—"a meeting of the minds"—by the parties. The parties must be competent, not morons or infants. And, to be enforceable by a court, contracts must be for lawful purposes, despite the misleading jargon by "hit men."

The law of **torts** deals with wrongful actions for which the injured party can claim money to compensate for personal injury. Tort law in the United States operates through court actions for trespass, nuisance, ultrahazardous risks, negligence, conversion, deceit, slander and libel, privacy, interference with trade or employment, and abuse of government power and process. When someone makes a false statement to you, intending you to rely upon it, **fraud** (or misrepresentation) has occurred. The chief **remedy** for all these torts is money damages.*

---

* A single act can sometimes be both tort and a crime. For example, a candidate firebombing his opponent's campaign headquarters could be sued by the property owner for damage done to the building and could also be prosecuted for the crime of arson.

Quiz

Most introductions to American politics, when they get to the law and the courts, concentrate on individual rights and liberties, history and theory, the court system, and criminal law.

But the most probable way in which American law and courts will impinge on us is in the areas of consumer law, family law, and housing law. This quiz is designed to see what you know about "street law" (that is, everyday law).

1. If you order dinner in a restaurant and come down with ptomaine poisoning, do you have a claim in damages against the owner of the restaurant?

2. What can you do if you are denied credit?

3. Horror stories about billing disputes are not uncommon in our computerized society: Sometimes your monthly bill shows a charge for an item you returned (or never bought); it charges you for late payment when you paid on time; it bills you twice for the same item; and so forth. How do you talk back to a computer?

4. Jill puts Jack through medical school. On graduation day, Jack introduces Jill to Sue and says he wants a divorce and that he plans to marry Sue. Can Jill assert a property right in Jack's medical degree—which, after all, she paid for?

5. What obligations do parents have towards their children?

6. Is an apartment lease a contract?

7. What rights do these black apartment hunters have?

Mario Ruiz

8. Who are these couples and what are their pictures doing in this quiz?

Globe Photos, Inc.

Frank Edwards/Fotos International

Criminal law is the body of law that defines criminal offenses, establishes the procedures for apprehending, charging, and trying suspected offenders; it also fixes the penalties and methods of treatment applicable to convicted offenders. The distinction between criminal law and tort law is hard to draw. Roughly speaking, a tort is a private injury; a tort suit is primarily to obtain compensation from the wrongdoer for injuries sustained by the victim. In contrast, a crime, even though it may (and ordinarily does) involve injury to some individual, is considered an offense against society as a whole.

Criminal offenses are divided into **misdemeanors** and **felonies**. Misdemeanors carry a penalty of one year or less in prison; felonies carry a penalty of a prison term of more than one year. The precise character of each varies from state to state and is defined by law. Felonies generally include murder, arson, robbery, aggravated **assault,** and forgery. When someone takes your property without your consent, **larceny** has occurred. When considerable money or value is involved, it is called grand larceny. Misdemeanors may include such offenses as traffic violations, petty theft, disorderly conduct, and gambling. They are generally tried by "summary process," without indictment by a grand jury or trial by jury.

Chapters 2 and 11 deal with constitutional law. **Administrative law** concerns procedures before government agencies. Chapter 7 discussed a few of the more important of these procedures.

Finally, international law provides rules governing relations among nations and between governments and foreign nationals. Today treaties and other international agreements are the most important source of international law. Some theorists reject the concept of international law; they see it as a flimsy and piecemeal structure painfully inadequate to deal with the crucial problems of the modern world. They hold that some sovereign authority with enforcing agencies must exist if law is to be meaningful. Be that as it may, interdependence of the world community is forcing more and more problems into the arena of international law. Examples include terrorism, hijacking, space, Antarctic claims, refugees, frozen assets, and seabed mining.

THE STRUCTURE AND OPERATIONS OF THE JUDICIARY

The judicial system in the United States is highly fragmented and decentralized. Figure 9–2 will give you some idea of what I mean.

One dimension of this fragmentation we have already considered—namely, that cases can involve either civil or public law. In civil disputes, the **plaintiff** brings suit against the **defendant** and has the burden of proof. Trial judges try to reduce disagreements to a minimum and arrive at out-of-court settlements. Among the cases involving public law, criminal cases are especially important because of their

FIGURE 9–2
American Judicial System—Decentralized and Fragmented

number, penalties (literally life and death), publicity, and relative complexity.

Figure 9–3 gives a simplified version of the general steps taken in civil and criminal cases. (Civil and criminal cases are tried separately and can never be combined.) Not all roads to the Supreme Court are shown. For example, prisoners who claim that their constitutional rights have been violated can seek release from jail by direct appeal to the high court. Writ of certiorari, discussed later in the chapter, is another shortcut.

Almost 170,000 civil cases begin each year in the district courts, but only 11 percent are decided by trial. About 30,000 criminal cases began in federal courts, but only 18 percent are decided by trial. The vast majority of civil and criminal cases are decided by either an agreement between the parties or a guilty plea.

Over 20,000 appeals are filed each year to the 11 circuit courts. In the American judiciary, appeals are relatively easy. Therein lies a major reason trials can drag on for years.

The American legal system is also fragmented into a second and third dimension. Because of federalism, the United States has dual federal and state courts. Most legal matters that affect everyday life are handled by state courts. California state courts, for example, handled about 15 million cases last year. By contrast, 198,000 civil and criminal cases were begun in all federal trial courts in 1980.

Each court system, in turn, is divided into **trial courts,** which have original jurisdiction, and **appellate courts.** The trial court judge determines the law that applies to a specific case. The appellate judge assesses case records and decides upon the appropriate law applicable to

FIGURE 9–3
Main Roads to the Supreme Court

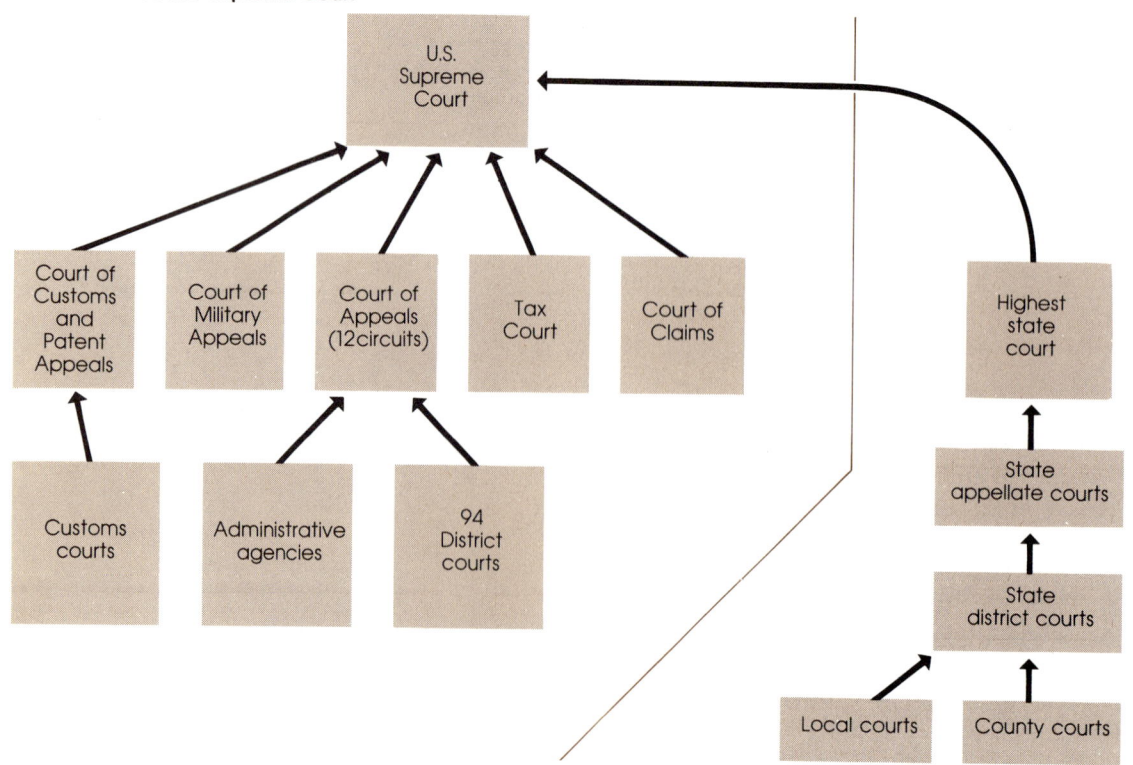

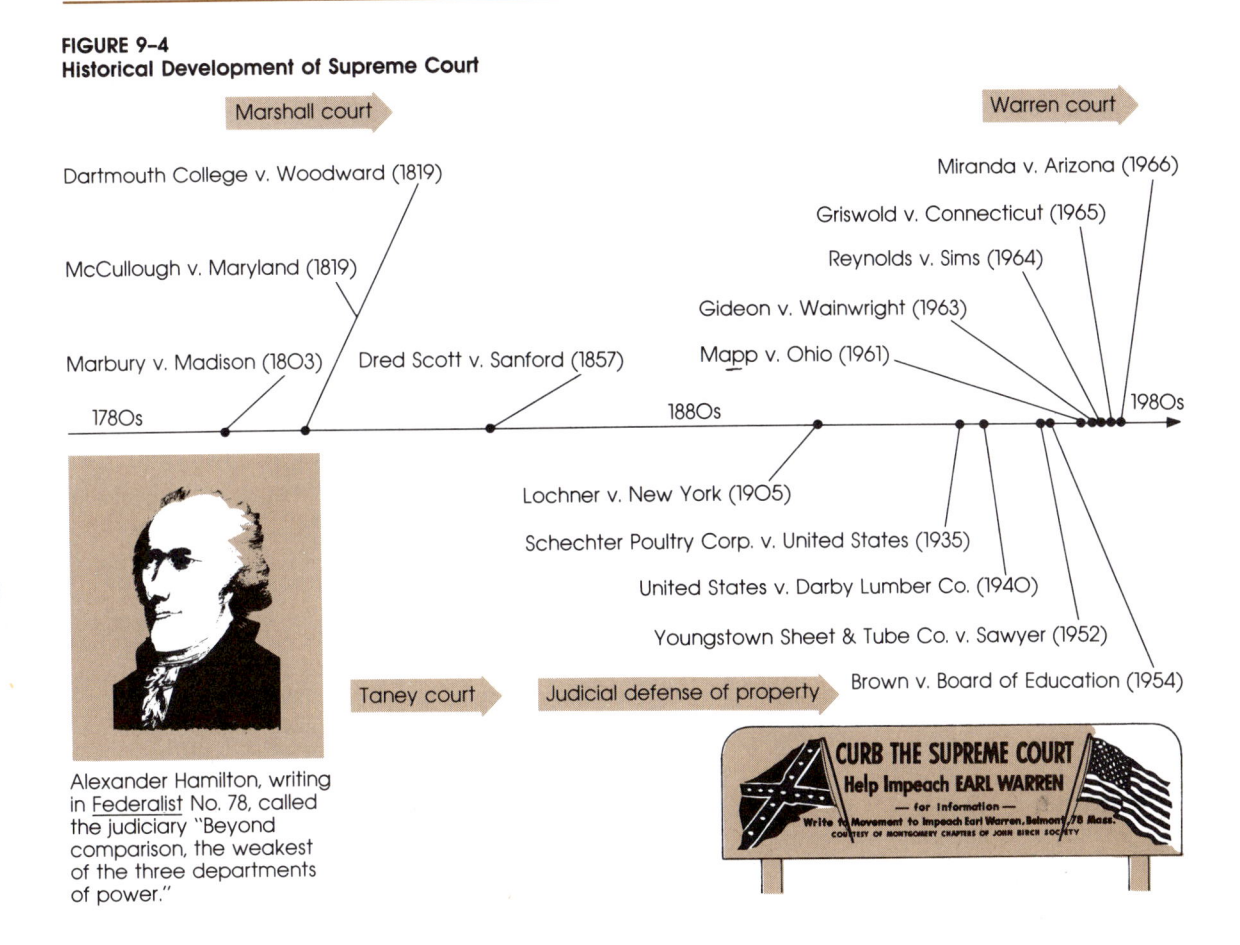

FIGURE 9–4
Historical Development of Supreme Court

Marshall court
- Dartmouth College v. Woodward (1819)
- McCullough v. Maryland (1819)
- Marbury v. Madison (1803)

Taney court
- Dred Scott v. Sanford (1857)

Judicial defense of property
- Lochner v. New York (1905)
- Schechter Poultry Corp. v. United States (1935)
- United States v. Darby Lumber Co. (1940)
- Youngstown Sheet & Tube Co. v. Sawyer (1952)
- Brown v. Board of Education (1954)

Warren court
- Miranda v. Arizona (1966)
- Griswold v. Connecticut (1965)
- Reynolds v. Sims (1964)
- Gideon v. Wainwright (1963)
- Mapp v. Ohio (1961)

Timeline: 1780s — 1880s — 1980s

Alexander Hamilton, writing in *Federalist* No. 78, called the judiciary "Beyond comparison, the weakest of the three departments of power."

CURB THE SUPREME COURT — Help Impeach EARL WARREN — for information — Write to Movement to Impeach Earl Warren, Belmont, 78 Mass. COURTESY OF MONTGOMERY CHAPTERS OF JOHN BIRCH SOCIETY

---

the facts of a case. He or she does so by consulting trial records and briefs and arguments presented by the lawyers of the case.

Figure 9–4 and the following boxed discussion provide an historical overview of the Supreme Court, the only court specifically mentioned in the Constitution. The Court has been a real political force in the American system of government.

The remainder of the section shall consider the structure and operation of state judiciary. We shall examine the elaborate structure Congress has established at the federal level under the Supreme Court. This examination will culminate with an inside look at how the modern Supreme Court functions. We shall also analyze the long-standing controversy of whether the Court should be active or restrained.

Inside the Federal Court System

The **jurisdiction** (i.e., authority to hear and decide a case) of federal courts is limited. As you know from Chapter 2, they deal with the interpretation of federal laws, treaties, or the Constitution. But, as you are also aware from Chapter 2, their rulings in such cases can have a sweeping effect. As John Leonard of the *New York Times* has acutely said of the Supreme Court, this particular committee votes on how the rest of us would be obliged to behave when it comes to abortion, busing, and pornography. In short,

Historical Development of the Supreme Court in a Nutshell

Hamilton believed that the judiciary was the least dangerous branch. It had "neither force nor will but merely judgement." But the power to adjudicate proved to be the power to profoundly shape public policy. In Figure 9-4, you see some of the more important court cases, out of thousands, that have shaped public policy in the United States.

Basically, the nine cases above the time line represent decisions in which the Supreme Court expanded national power or individual liberties. The five cases below the time line represent decisions in which the Court protected states rights or private property.

Marbury v. *Madison* (1803), which was discussed in Chapter 4, arose from William Marbury's claim to be a justice of the peace. The Court firmly established the constitutional, rather than the legislative, source of Supreme Court jurisdiction; it also entrenched the principle of judicial review—the right of the Court to declare laws unconstitutional. In *McCullough* v. *Maryland* (1819), discussed in Chapter 2, the Court held that the chartering of a National Bank of the U.S. was a "necessary and proper" means of achieving the effective exercise of powers delegated to Congress by the Constitution. By its broad interpretation, the Court widened the range of actions that could be initiated by the federal government. In a dramatic reversal of earlier opposition to President Franklin Roosevelt's New Deal legislation, the Court in *U.S.* v. *Darby Lumber Co.* (1940) upheld the Fair Labor Standard Act of 1938. That act provided for the fixing of minimum wages (for men) and maximum hours for employees in an industry whose products were shipped in interstate commerce.

Brown v. *Board of Education* (1954) was an early milestone in the Warren Court's activism in the areas of desegregation, voting, and law enforcement. The Court held that in the field of public education the "separate but equal" doctrine established by *Plessy* v. *Ferguson* (1896) was not justified; separating schoolchildren of similar age and qualifications solely on the basis of race may inflict irreparable psychological damage. *Brown* opened an era of civil rights initiatives by the courts and by Congress (see Chapter 11). In *Mapp* v. *Ohio* (1961), the Court held that evidence produced as a result of a search or seizure violating the Fourth Amendment must be excluded from state criminal trials. In *Gideon* v. *Wainwright* (1963), the Court held that indigent criminal defendants in felony cases are entitled to counsel appointed by the state. After ruling in *Baker* v. *Carr* (1962) that federal courts could hear cases involving alleged unequal apportionment of state legislative districts, the Court held in *Reynolds* v. *Sims* (1964) that both chambers of a state legislature must be apportioned by population—one man, one vote—and that there is a presumption of unconstitutionality for any system that deviates from the norm of equal representation. In *Griswold* v. *Connecticut* (1965), the Court for the first time decided the merits of a constitutional challenge to state anti-birth control laws; it struck down a Connecticut statute prohibiting the sale of contraceptives, on the grounds that enforcing the law against married couples violated a right of marital privacy. Griswold illustrates the ability of the Court to "discover" a right (e.g., privacy) not explicitly spelled out in the Constitution. In *Miranda* v. *Arizona* (1966) the Court held that the Fifth Amendment bars the use in court of statements that stem from custodial interrogation without procedural safeguards to protect the accused against self-incrimination. These include his right to remain silent, his right to the presence of counsel, and his right to have counsel appointed if he cannot afford a lawyer.

But there are other chapters of a different sort in the evolution of the Supreme Court. Let us begin with the first case below the time line. The Court ruled in *Dartmouth College* v. *Woodward* (1819) that a legislature may not interfere in the affairs of a private corporation unless the legislature, in granting a corporate charter, reserves the right to amend that charter at some later date. *Dartmouth College* reflected the high measure of protection 19th-century judges were willing to extend to property. In *Dred Scott* v.

Sandford (1857), the Court held that Congress could not prohibit slavery without violating the due process clause of the Fifth Amendment and citizens' property rights. In *Lochner* v. *New York* (1905), the Court held that a New York state law limiting bakers to a 60-hour workweek was an unconstitutional abridgement of the right of contract. Thus a constitutional provision (14th Amendment) intended to secure the rights of newly freed slaves was transformed into a buttress of laissez-faire capitalism. *Schechter Poultry Corp.* v. *U.S.* (1935) was one of several decisions striking at New Deal measures. In it the Court invalidated National Recovery Administration codes established to regulate minimum wages, maximum hours, collective bargaining, and unfair competition. The Court held that the codes constituted an excessive delegation of legislative power to the executive and an unconstitutional exercise of the congressional commerce power.

In *Youngstown Sheet & Tube Co.* v. *Sawyer* (1952), the Court held invalid the action of President Truman in seizing the country's steel industry during the Korean War without authority from Congress—regardless of wartime emergencies.

Is there any pattern in the evolution of the Supreme Court? Speaking very roughly, we might say that it has passed through three periods. In the first, which lasted until the end of the Civil War, the Court asserted the supremacy of the federal government. In the second, which lasted until the beginning of Franklin Roosevelt's New Deal, the major issue concerned the relationship between government and the economy. In the third period, the Court, especially under Chief Justice Earl Warren, reversed itself somewhat by limiting the freedom of business to act as it wished. At the same time, the Court expanded a number of personal freedoms.

---

this committee has taken the deciding of many momentous national issues out of the hands of the people. The Constitution established the Supreme Court; it also authorized Congress to establish from time to time such inferior courts as seemed necessary. Since 1891, the United States has had two systems of lower courts. Today there are 94 district courts (with each state having at least one) and 12 judicial circuits (with one court of appeals in each circuit).

District courts hear both civil and criminal cases. These include cases in which a citizen of one state sues a citizen of another state. They review some actions by administrative agencies (see Chapter 7), enforce federal laws, and supervise bankruptcy proceedings and the naturalization of aliens. The courts of appeals hear cases from the district courts, the federal regulatory commissions (see Chapter 7), and some of the specialized courts. Congress has established several special courts. Among these are:

Court of Claims. Established in 1851, this court hears claims of private individuals against the government. For example, on June 30, 1980, the Supreme Court upheld the largest award ever granted by the U.S. Court of Claims. The high court ruled that the federal government must pay the Sioux Indian nation more than $100 million for Black Hills land taken from the tribe in 1877 in part as retribution by Congress for the massacre of General George Custer and his cavalry regiment at Little Bighorn. Both sides agreed that the Sioux were entitled to the 1877 fair market price of the land. At issue was whether 103 years of interest, at 5 percent a year, was to be heaped on top of that sum. The Supreme Court said yes.

Tax Court. The Tax Court is the federal body to which taxpayers can take disputes that they think haven't been satisfactorily resolved by the appeals division of the IRS. Other federal courts—namely the federal district courts and the Court of Claims—also hear tax disputes. But to use those courts, the taxpayer must first pay the disputed amount, request a refund, and wait for the IRS to refuse it; the Tax Court, in contrast, will hear cases where IRS-determined deficiencies are still outstanding. Of course, most disgruntled taxpayers prefer to litigate without having to pay first. So, they take their disputes to the Tax Court. And they do that by suing the commissioner of the IRS in Tax Court to "redetermine" what the IRS has deemed a deficiency.

- Court of Customs and Patent Appeals. Established in 1909, this court reviews appeals from decisions of the Customs Court, the Patent Office (in the Department of Commerce), and the Tariff Commission (see Chapter 13). Thanks to this court the district and circuit courts need not struggle with such issues as who was really first to discover the laser. But some questions—e.g., Can life be patented?—get passed on to the Supreme Court. (The answer, incidentally, is yes. This 1979 decision delighted General Electric, which had developed an oil-slick-digesting bacterium through recombinant DNA technology.)

- Court of Military Appeals. Traditionally, Americans have expressed open concern over the standards and procedures of military justice. As one wiseacre put it, military justice is to justice as military music is to music. So, in 1950, Congress established the Uniform Code of Military Justice. This was an attempt to strengthen the rights of persons in court-martial proceedings, yet still meet the needs of military discipline. The Court of Military Appeals, which reviews court-martial decisions, is a part of that reform effort.

As Figure 9–3 makes plain, the ultimate court is the Supreme Court. Most of its business concerns appeals from lower courts. But it can act as a trial court in disputes between states or in cases involving ambassadors, consuls, and other representatives of foreign governments. Appeals must present a "substantial federal question" to qualify for review. Examples of cases that would meet this rule are: *(a)* when a federal court of appeals has held a federal or state law to be in violation of the Constitution, and *(b)* when the highest court in a state has held a treaty or federal law invalid or has upheld a state law that had been challenged as a violation of federal law. In rare cases—such as the suit to obtain the White House tapes of President Nixon—the Supreme Court may ask that a case brought in a lower court be sent up immediately.

In civil cases, litigants may obtain a Supreme Court review by asking the Court to issue a **writ of certiorari** to the lower court. For the writ to be issued, at least four of the nine judges must think the case should be reviewed. Less than 15 percent of these requests are granted.

The Supreme Court in action. From October through June the Supreme Court works. This eight-month term is divided into sittings and recesses, which alternate at two-week intervals. During sittings, the justices hear oral arguments, announce opinions, and rule on motions to admit lawyers to represent their clients before the Court; during recesses, they do all other court work.

As we saw in the last chapter, subordinate power—such as exercised by the congressional staff—can be very powerful indeed. But the most powerful subordinates in U.S. government may be the 32 clerks who serve the justices of the Supreme Court. They advise and draft opinions for the justices. They screen appeals out of the thousands that the Court receives each year; they help determine the 3 percent that will be heard. That is gatekeeping with a vengeance. Sometimes they even write the opinion, as this anecdote about Justice Thurgood Marshall, from Bob Woodward's and Scott Armstrong's *The Brethren*, reveals:

> . . . a clerk once pointed out, "You said that the right to privacy must go further than the home."

"No," Marshall retorted. He had never said that.

"Yes," the clerk insisted.

"No, never," Marshall was sure. "Show me." The clerk brought the bound opinions. Marshall read the relevant section.

"That's not my opinion. That's the opinion of a clerk from the prior term," he declared.[2]

The final decision to grant an appeal or writ of certiorari is made in a secret conference with only the justices present. In an address to the Cincinnati Bar Association in 1979, Justice Potter Stewart provided an inside look at this process and Supreme Court Decision making in general. (For excerpts, see box.)

Yoichi R. Okamoto/Photo Researchers, Inc.

Behind closed doors: Burger lunching in chambers with staffer Mark Cannon.

Wide World Photos

After 191 years of what some observers would call male chauvinism, a woman was finally appointed to the Supreme Court. In a historic decision, President Reagan's first nomination to the Supreme Court was Judge Sandra D. O'Connor, an Arizona appeals court judge and former Stanford Law School classmate of Justice Rehnquist. Judge O'Connor replaced Potter Stewart, who had decided to retire.

Bill Fitz-Patrick/The White House

The U.S. Supreme Court. President Ronald Reagan poses with the Supreme Court after the swearing in of Justice Sandra Day O'Connor in September 1981. From left to right are Justices Harry A. Blackmun, Thurgood Marshall, and William J. Brennan, Jr., Chief Justice Warren E. Burger, President Reagan, and Justices Sandra Day O'Connor, Byron R. White, Lewis F. Powell, Jr., William H. Rehnquist, and John Paul Stevens.

Inside the Supreme Court

I came to the Court at the beginning of the 1958 term. In that term the aggregate of the cases on the calendar numbered about 1,800. In the term that ended last July we had to deal with over 4,500 cases—an increase of 150 percent. How does the Court manage such a huge volume of cases? The answer is that since 1925 we have had the authority to screen the cases and select for argument and decision only those which, in our judgment, raise the most important and far-reaching questions. By that device we select annually only about 200 cases in all.

Each Justice receives copies of every certiorari petition and response. Each Justice, without consultation with his colleagues, reaches his own tentative conclusion whether the petition should be granted or denied. The first consultation comes at the Court conference at which the case is listed for discussion on the agenda. We sit in conference almost every Friday during the term. Those conferences begin at 9:30 and continue through the day, except for a half-hour recess for lunch. Only the Justices are present. There are no law clerks, no stenographers, no secretaries, no pages—just the nine of us. The conferences are held in an oak-paneled room with one wall lined with books from floor to ceiling. Over the mantel of the marble fire-place at one end hangs the only picture—a portrait of Chief Justice John Marshall. In the middle of the room stands a rectangular table, large enough for the nine of us. Upon entering, each of us shakes hands with his colleagues. This handshake tradition originated many years ago. It is a symbol that harmony of aims, if not of views, is the Court's guiding principle. Each of us has his own copy of the agenda of the cases to be considered, and each has done his homework and noted on his copy his tentative view in every case as to whether review on the merits should be granted or denied.

The Chief Justice begins the discussion of each case. Then discussion proceeds down the line by seniority until each Justice has spoken. Voting goes the other way, if there is any need for a formal vote following the discussion. When any case receives four votes for review, certiorari is granted, and that case is then transferred to the Argument List. This "Rule of 4" is not written down anywhere, but it is an absolutely inflexible rule.

Oral argument ordinarily takes place about four months after the petition for certiorari is granted. Each party used to be allowed one hour for argument, but in recent years we have limited oral argument to half an hour a side in almost all cases. Counsel submit their briefs and record in sufficient time for the distribution of one set to each Justice two or three weeks before the argument. We follow a schedule of two weeks of argument, followed by two weeks of recess for opinion writing and the study of petitions for review. The Friday conference discussion of the dozen or so cases that have been argued that week follows the same procedure described for the discussion of certiorari petitions, but, of course, the discussion of an argued case is generally much more extended. Not until the discussion is completed and a vote is taken is the opinion assigned. The senior member of the majority designates one of his colleagues or sometimes himself to write the opinion of the Court. This means that the Chief Justice assigns the opinions in those cases in which he has voted with the majority, and the senior associate Justice in the majority assigns the opinions in all other cases. The dissenters agree among themselves who will write the dissenting opinion. But each Justice is free to write his own individual opinion, concurring or dissenting.

The writing of an opinion is not easy work. It always takes weeks, sometimes months. When the author of an opinion for the Court has completed his work, he sends a printed copy to each member, those in dissent as well as in the majority. Often some of those who voted with him at the conference will say that they want to reserve final judgment pending circulation of the dissent. It is a common experience that drafts of dissenting opinions change votes, even enough votes to become the majority. Before everyone has finally made up his mind, a constant interchange goes on while we work out the final form

> of the Court opinion. There was one case this past term in which I circulated 10 printed drafts before one was finally approved as the opinion of the Court. The point is that each Justice, unless he disqualifies himself in a particular case, passes on every piece of business. The Court does not function by means of committees or panels. The process can be a lonely, troubling experience for fallible human beings conscious that their best may not be adequate to the challenge. A Justice does not forget how much may depend on his decision. He knows that it may affect the course of important social, economic and political currents.
>
> Unlike Congressional or White House decisions, Americans demand of their Supreme Court that the written and oral arguments of the issues be completely open to the public, and that its decisional process produce a written opinion, the collective expression of a majority of the Justices, setting forth the reasons that led them to the decision they reached. These opinions are the exposition, not just to lawyers, to legal scholars and to other judges, but to our society, of the basis upon which the result in any case rests.
>
> SOURCE: Potter Stewart, "Inside the Supreme Court," *New York Times*, October 1, 1979.

Once a case is accepted for review, the parties usually submit briefs. Only 5 percent argue the case orally in the high-ceilinged court room on the main floor of the Court's impressive marble building. Pomp and tradition is the order of the day. For example, some lawyers wear striped trousers and tailcoats when they are making arguments at a lectern in front of the justices. The federal government is represented by the **solicitor general,** the third-ranking officer in the Department of Justice. Interested parties not directly involved may submit written briefs or even oral arguments. Such parties are called "friends of the court" or **amicus curiae.**

The Court usually issues a written opinion explaining its decision. For example, on July 25, 1981, the Supreme Court, by a 6–3 vote, affirmed that women are exempt from registration for the draft. Writing for the six-man majority, Justice William Rehnquist held that the courts must defer to Congress' "broad and sweeping power over national defense and military affairs, and perhaps in no other area has the court accorded Congress greater deference." This opinion, for obvious reasons is called the **majority opinion.** If the vote had been 9–0, it would have been the **unanimous opinion.** Writing for the three-man minority, Thurgood Marshall said the ruling "excludes women from a fundamental civil obligation."

This opinion is called the **dissenting opinion.** A fourth kind of opinion, **concurring opinion,** occurs when one or more justices agree with the majority but for a different reason, which they wish to express.

Activism versus self-restraint. Judges can take one of two approaches to their decision making. **Activists** use their position to promote desirable social ends. Today, activists acclaim the Court's new and grander conception of its role; they assert its power to revise the Constitution, bypassing the cumbersome procedure prescribed by Article V of the Constitution. Advocates of **judicial self-restraint** try to set personal philosophy aside and defer to the legislative and excutive branches, which are elected by the people. They acclaim that nowhere are the justices given the authority to bypass Article V, which reserves to the people the exclusive right to amend the Constitution. In their view, the Court has not merely been acting as a "legislature" rather than a court, but even worse. It is acting as a continuing constitutional convention; it usurps a function reserved for the people. Were the people to become aware that the Court is imposing its own values on them—as activists unabashedly acknowledge—they would insist on deciding their own destiny.

Without entering into the question of whether the judges are imposing their values, this much is clear. In recent years, federal courts have become forums for the redress of all sorts of injustices in life. Boston's elected school committee refused to bus schoolchildren; the local federal judge did it himself, right down to approving the bus routes. A federal judge in Alabama ruled that inadequate mental-health care is unconstitutional; he listed 84 minimal standards, right down to the supply of hot water at 110°F. These are but two of many examples.

The fundamental problem, according to some constitutional scholars, is that the judiciary has usurped general government powers on the grounds that the 14th Amendment gives them that authority. Several decades ago, Justice Oliver Wendell Holmes expressed his concern.

> As the decisions now stand, I see hardly any limit but the sky to the invalidation of (the constitutional rights of the states) if they happen to strike a majority of this Court for any reason as undesirable. I cannot believe that the amendment was intended to give us carte blanche to embody our economic or moral beliefs in its prohibitions.[3]

The nub of the controversy between activism and self-restraint is whether the American people want a "living Constitution." In Chapter 2 it was more or less suggested that this was a good idea. Quite clearly, the Court has become increasingly sensitive to public opinion; it is inclined to measure the success of its decisions by their effects upon society; and it is responsive to changing political conditions. (These are the "felt necessities of the time" in the words of Justice Holmes.) Before overturning the "living Constitution" for one strictly interpreted, it is useful to review the advantages to American society of the former. Moreover, one must remember the enormous growth of the executive and legislative branches and the influence of special interest groups over each. These factors raise some doubt as to whether society is best served by a literal, strict reading of the Constitution.

The story is told of a famous law professor who began his constitutional law course by warning his students not to read the Constitution; it would only confuse them. So there you have the spirit of the activists' position in its purest form. Don't fuss over what the Constitution says; just do what you (the judge) think is right.

Is there not some middle ground between such an extreme activist's position and a strict interpretation? Of course there is. It works like this: The words of the Constitution are always the starting point. But judges can mold these words to be in accord with changes in the American polity's ideas about justice. In the larger sense, this is what the founding fathers *meant*. What we should not forget—and what we should remember from Chapter 3—is that the founding fathers were men of ideas. More specifically, they were imbued with the belief in natural law; accordingly, they accepted the notion of a higher law protecting certain natural rights and having precedence over mere positive law. As Prof. Thomas Grey of Stanford University has pointed out, the Ninth Amendment ("The enumeration in the Constitution, of certain rights, shall not be construed to deny or disparage others retained by the people") could mean that there remain "unwritten but still binding principles of higher law."

Inside the State System

Though the federal judicial system gets the most publicity, the state judicial systems handle the most cases. To briefly characterize these 50 systems is impossible. In the first place, the laws differ from state to state (see Table 9–1). In the second place, the organization of state judicial systems varies widely. In some states, civil and criminal cases are handled in separate courts; in others, they are handled by one court. In some states, the highest court is called the supreme court; in others, the court of final resort is called the court of appeals or supreme court of errors. In 20 states, there is an interme-

FUTURE FILE

Reagan and the Supreme Court

When Jimmy Carter left the White House in January 1981, he suffered the dubious distinction of being the first president since Andrew Johnson (1865–69) not to have made a single appointment to the U.S. Supreme Court. Still, in less than four years, he was able to reshape the federal courts by naming to coveted lifetime seats more judges than any other president in history (over one third of the federal jurists sitting today.) He appointed more women, blacks, and Hispanics than all other presidents combined; he appointed a higher percentage of members of his own party than any president in this century except Woodrow Wilson (see table); and he appointed large numbers of liberals likely to accentuate the activist course of the federal bench.

Percentage of Federal Judges Belonging to Same Party as the President Who Appointed Them

Carter (D)	97.8%
Roosevelt (D)	96.4%
Johnson (D)	95.2%
Eisenhower (R)	95.1%
Nixon (R)	93.7%
Truman (D)	93.1%
Kennedy (D)	90.9%
Hoover (R)	85.7%
Ford (R)	81.2%

SOURCE: Basic data from Henry J. Abraham, University of Virginia.

What kind of justices is Ronald Reagan likely to appoint and what effect will they have on Supreme Court decision making between now and the turn of the 21st century? The first part of that question is easy.

When Reagan was governor of California, he appointed competent conservatives to the state bench. Most likely, if he is elected president and survives the five elderly Supreme Court justices (Reagan himself is over 70), he would repeat the pattern. If he were to serve two full terms, by the time he left office in 1989 the Court could consist of eight Republicans and one conservative Democrat, Justice Byron White, appointed by President Kennedy in 1962.

What difference this will make is not as easy to say as one might think. In 1969, conservative Richard M. Nixon nominated Warren Burger to succeed Earl Warren as chief justice. How was the Warren Court, which had been a force for liberal reform in American life, changed? Characterizing the performance of the Supreme Court over the past decade is difficult.

According to some liberal voices in the press, the Burger Court has been a disaster. But the record of the Burger over the last 10 years does

United Press International Photo

Rites of passage: Exit Earl Warren, enter Nixon and Burger.

not support the charge that it is a particularly conservative body. Nor has it been guided by the spirit of Richard Nixon. Consider these important decisions:

> The Pentagon Papers case, rejecting the Nixon administration's attempt to stop publication of a secret history of the Vietnam war.
>
> *United States* v. *Nixon,* ordering the president to hand over White House tapes needed by the Watergate special prosecutor.
>
> The case of Allan Bakke, deciding that universities may weigh the race of applicants as a factor but not an exclusive one in deciding whether to admit them. (This does not support the charge that the Burger court is a reactionary body, or one guided by the spirit of Richard Nixon.)
>
> *Roe* v. *Wade,* holding that state laws restricting abortions during the early months of pregnancy were an unconstitutional invasion of a woman's privacy.

Indeed, the Roe decision is one of the most radical in the history of the Court. The Court, in effect, struck down anti-abortion laws in all 50 states. Four Warren Court holdovers joined three Nixon appointees to hold that a woman's "right to privacy" precludes practically all regulation of abortion. Justice Blackmun, one of the Nixon appointees, wrote the decision. The Court promulgated a complicated set of rules that seemed at first glance to allow some restrictions; but the bottom line was that, if a woman could find one doctor willing to say the abortion was necessary for her health (including mental health), an abortion could be performed even in the ninth month of pregnancy. Justice Byron White, a Warren Court "liberal," denounced the decision as an "exercise in raw judicial power." He was joined by Justice Rehnquist, the only one of the "conservatives" to dissent.

The Roe decision tested the limits of all the theories of judicial power. The decision was not based on tradition; the authors of the constitutional provision the Court was "interpreting" would surely have disagreed. Nor was the basis consensus; *Roe* struck down 50 state laws. Nor was the basis reason; the Court itself admitted that reasonable people differ on the humanity of the fetus. Nor was the basis consistency; the Court still allowed that states could constitutionally prohibit the destruction of dogs and draft cards and punish you for smoking marijuana or performing consensual homosexual acts in the privacy of your home.

The only possible basis therefore seems to be the values of the judges. This brings us back to the question of the Reagan Court. Will those who applauded judicial activism during the Warren Court begin to insist on strict interpretation when and if the Court becomes thoroughly Reaganized?

Before we peer too deeply into the future, a backward glance is helpful. Richard Nixon was not the only president who tried and failed to pick justices who would follow his ideological line. At the turn of the century, Theodore Roosevelt checked the antitrust views of Oliver Wendell Holmes before appointing him; Sen. Henry Cabot Lodge of Massachusetts assured the president that Holmes agreed on the idea of stopping the power of big business. No sooner was Holmes on the Court than he voted against the government in a major antitrust case. Roosevelt wrote to Lodge: "I have seen more backbone in a banana."

diate appellate tribunal between the trial court and the court of final resort; in the other 30 states, cases can move from the trial court directly to the court of final resort.

States call the lowest courts in their judicial hierarchy by a variety of names: municipal court, police court, magistrate's court, justice of the peace, family court, probate court, small claims court, traffic court, juvenile court, court of common pleas, and so forth. Let us take a brief look at only two of these minor courts.

The **justice of the peace** has existed in the

TABLE 9-1
Penalties for Possession of Marijuana in the 50 States (the first offense)

I. The Decriminalized States[1]

State	Maximum Fine Imposed	Maximum Amount in Possession[2]
Oregon	$100	1 oz.[3]
Alaska	$100	1 oz.[4]
Maine	$200	Any
Colorado	$100	1 oz.
California	$100	1 oz.
Ohio	$100	100 grams[3]
Minnesota	$100	1½ oz.
Mississippi	$250	1 oz.
North Carolina	$100	1 oz.
New York	$100	25 grams

II. Light Penalty States: Less than Six-Month Maximum Jail Term, up to $500 Fine

State	Maximum Amount in Possession
Hawaii	1 oz.
Illinois	2.5 grams
Kentucky	Any
Nebraska	1 lb.
New Mexico	1 oz.
Pennsylvania	30 grams
South Carolina	1 oz.
South Dakota	1 oz.
Washington	4 oz.

III. Six-Month Maximum Jail Term, up to $500 Fine

State	Maximum Amount in Possession
Illinois	2.5 to 10 grams
Louisiana	Any
Massachusetts	Any
New Jersey	25 grams
Texas	2 oz.
Utah	Any
Vermont	Any

IV. Six-Month Maximum Jail Term, up to $1,000 Fine

State	Maximum Amount in Possession
Iowa	Any
South Carolina	Over 1 oz.
West Virginia	Any
Wyoming	Any

V. Up to One-Year Jail Term, up to $500 Fine

State	Maximum Amount in Possession
Arkansas	Any
Rhode Island	Any
Wisconsin	Any

VI. Up to One-Year Jail Term, up to $1,000 Fine

State	Maximum Amount in Possession
Alabama	Any
Connecticut	4 ozs.
Florida	5 grams
Georgia	1 oz.
Hawaii	1 oz. to 1 kilogram
Idaho	3 oz.
Illinois	10 to 30 grams
Maryland	Any
Michigan	Any
Missouri	35 grams
Montana	60 grams
New Hampshire	1 lb.
N. Dakota	Any
Oklahoma	Any
South Dakota	Over 1 oz.
Tennessee	Any
Virginia	Any
D.C.	Any

VII. Heavy Penalty States

State	Maximum Amount in Possession	Penalty
Arizona	Any	0-1 year county jail and/or $1,000 or 1-10 years in state prison and/or $50,000
Connecticut	Over 4 oz.	0-5 years/$2,000
Delaware	Any	0-2 years/$500
Florida	Over 5 grams	0-5 years/$5,000
Indiana	30 grams	1 year/$5,000
Kansas	Any	1 year/$2,500
Nevada	1 oz.	1-6 years/$2,000

[1] The common elements of the decriminalization laws are that minor marijuana violations are punished by fines without imposition of jail sentences; a traffic-like citation is authorized, not an arrest; there is no permanent criminal record.
[2] Greater amounts bring heavier penalties.
[3] Some states use the gram measurement, some use the ounce. 1 oz. = 28.35 grams, 1 lb. = 453.59 grams, 2.2 lbs. = 1 kilogram.
[4] 1 oz. in public, any amount in private.
Source: NORML, 2317 M Street, N.W. Washington, D.C. 20037

United States almost without change since colonial times. This judicial officer, who need not be a lawyer, is authorized to hear and settle civil actions involving small amounts of money. He or she may hold preliminary hearings for felonies to determine whether a person should be held for trial in a higher court. And he or she may try traffic violations and misdemeanors.

Critics charge that the fee system leads to corruption and biased judgments. The speed trap for nonresidents is a notorious example of this possibility. In urban areas, the trend has been to replace judges by municipal courts.

Supporters say that **small claims** courts, like the JP system provides an inexpensive way of dispensing justice in petty cases. In 1976, for example, New York City's small claims courts had to deal with 70,000 cases—consumers suing merchants for lost or damaged goods or for poorly performed services, landlords and tenants battling over unpaid rents or unreturned security deposits, and a host of other money disputes with one thing in common: They involved $1,000 or less. Legal experts generally feel the New York City small claims courts dispense justice fairly, quickly, and efficiently.

Not so everywhere. Eight states do not even have special procedures for dealing with small claims; half a dozen others have the courts only in the biggest cities. Procedures vary widely. Some courts, for instance, permit the use of attorneys; others do not.

Many of these courts, critics say, are in awkward locations or function at hours when people cannot get to them. Nor do the courts seem to be the streamlined "people's courts" anticipated when they were created. Court procedures remain too complex and cases too protracted to facilitate the swift resolution of grievances. Another criticism is that small claims courts are often "collection agencies" for businesses.

THE ADVERSARY PROCESS

A lawsuit is not unlike a boxing match: the disputant (or litigants) are the backers; their lawyers, the fighters; the judge, the referee; the order of procedure, the rounds (see Figure 9–5). And the media of course covers the contest. Books instructing attorneys how to win trials are replete with the language of battle: "To *destroy* the witness it is necessary to . . ."; "the double-edged *sword*—cross examination"; "to *demolish* the effectiveness of the key witness. . . ." Presumably, truth and justice emerge more readily through this adversary process—opposing parties presenting their best arguments and try to discredit the other side's case—than in any other process.

We shall critically evaluate that view later. But first we want to understand how the process works.

Reprinted by permission *The Wall Street Journal*

"And don't go off whining to some higher court!"

Trial court judges determine the law that applies to a specific case; appellate judges review trial decisions. Usually appellate judges assess case records and decide upon the appropriate law applicable to the facts of a case by consulting trial records and briefs and arguments presented by the lawyers of the case. Very few appeals are taken—less than 10 percent of the average.

The right to appeal is not constitutionally guaranteed. However, it is provided for by legislation for almost all cases. (Important exception: The government may not appeal a case in which the defendant has been acquitted.)

FIGURE 9-5
Basic Steps in a Trial

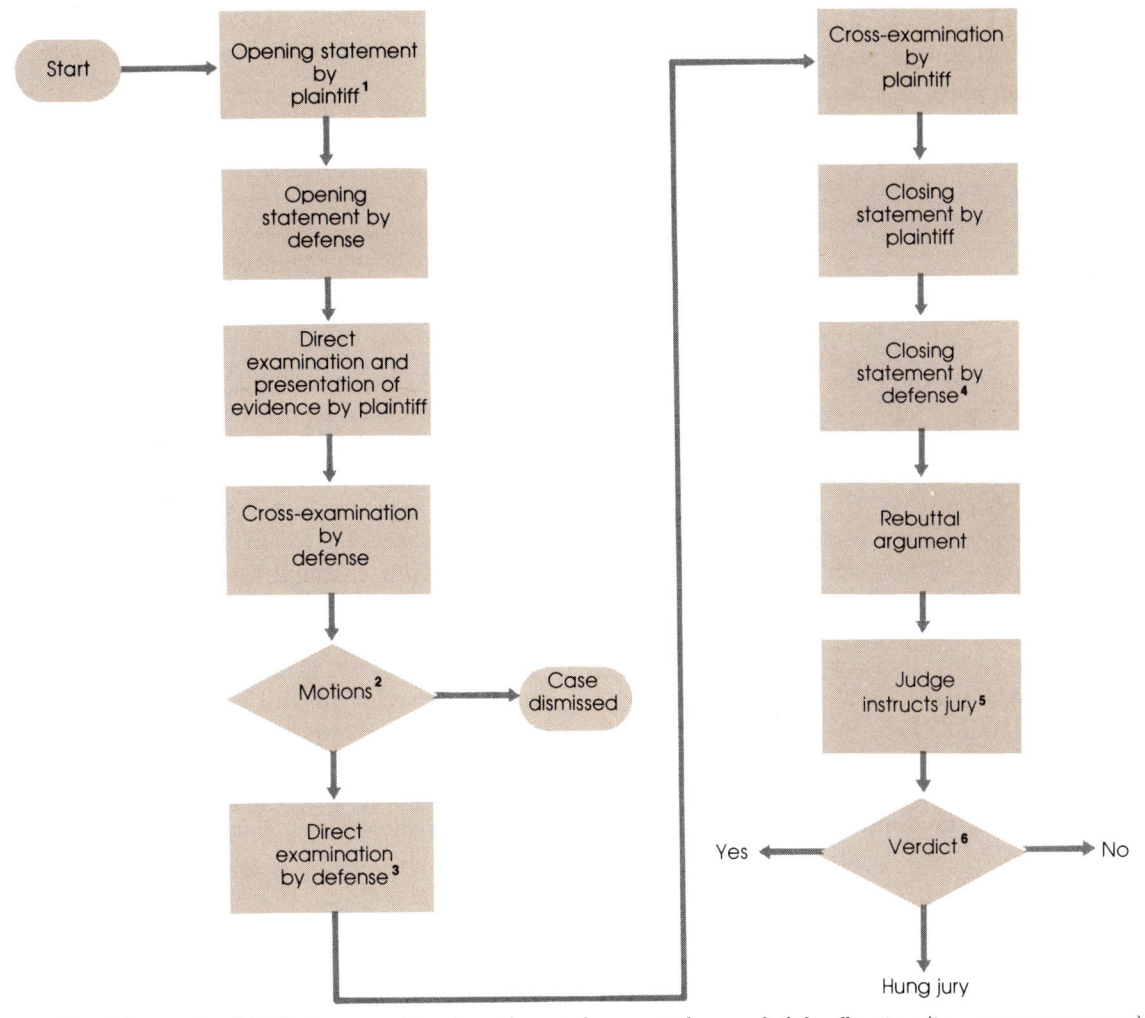

[1] In civil cases, the plaintiff attorney explains the evidence to be presented as proof of the allegations (i.e., unproven statement) in the complaint. In criminal cases, the prosecutor does this.
[2] If the plaintiff's basic case has not been established from the evidence introduced, the judge can end the case by granting the defendant's motion to dismiss.
[3] Defense questions its witnesses.
[4] Defense asks for a finding of "not guilty" in criminal cases or "for defendant" (in civil cases).
[5] Finally the judge's instructions, sometimes called the charge, come to aid the jury in reaching its verdict. The judge instructs the jury in the law governing the case and reviews the evidence. The authority of the judge to comment on the facts of a case, as distinguished from the law involved, varies from state to state; federal judges have wide latitude. An important part of the charge deals with the burden of proof resting upon the prosecution. The jurors are told that the accused starts out with a presumption of innocence; they cannot convict unless satisfied of guilt beyond a reasonable doubt. If the judge is careless in his charge, or shows bias, the case may be overturned by a higher court.
[6] In most states, a unanimous decision is required one way or the other. If the jury cannot reach a unanimous decision, it is said to be a *hung jury;* the case may then be tried again.

Essential Elements in a Trial

Every trial has two essential elements: establish the facts of the case; find the legal rule that applies. In a jury trial, the jury decides questions of fact; the judge questions of law.

Facts of the case. Discovering what actually occurred, or what did not occur but should have, is not easy. You have probably heard of laboratory experiments in which a group of subjects are shown a picture or film of a crime being committed and then asked to describe what they saw. Few eyewitnesses observe accurately; most "see" what they expect to see. But all believe what they describe to be the true version.

One bystander at a traffic accident stated that she had seen a car drive through a crowded street at 50 miles an hour. Unable to shake her testimony, the lawyer cross-examining her finally asked how fast she walked. Her reply: 20 miles per hour. In short, eyewitnesses accounts are not as strong a kind of evidence as you might think. For spectacular proof that even eyewitnesses can be mistaken, consider the case of Adolf Beck (see box).

Thus, circumstantial evidence can sometimes be more useful than direct evidence. In fact, without circumstantial evidence many criminal prosecutions could not take place. In crimes such as murder objective eyewitnesses are often unavailable. As one judge and former prosecuting attorney observed,

> Circumstantial evidence is not a vague, amorphous thing, as popularly conceived, which, chameleon-like can change in varying connotations to suit the occasion. It is, in truth, an essential component of legal procedure, and I assert unequivocally and emphatically that when it is available in adequate measure there is no more convincing or trustworthy proof.

If a civil case goes to trial, the plaintiff must prove his or her case by a "preponderance of evidence"; that is, he or she must offer more evidence than the defendant. Because the stakes are higher in a criminal case, (namely, a person's freedom), so too is the standard of evidence. In a criminal case, the prosecution has the burden of proving the defendant "guilty beyond a reasonable doubt."

There is a scene in the film *Monty Python and the Holy Grail* in which a group of medieval villagers are about to throw someone suspected of witchcraft into a lake. Since witches are supposed to float, the defendant will only be found innocent if she drowns. Luckily, modern juries

---

The Strange Case of Adolf Beck

Adolf Beck was tried in England in 1896 for a series of embezzlements. His claimed plan of operation was as follows: Posing as a titled man of wealth, he would strike up an acquaintance with a woman and persuade her that she should come to live with him either as his housekeeper or as his mistress. In making arrangements, he would suggest that her clothes and jewelry were not adequate to her approaching new status and give her a check to purchase new clothes, and he would borrow a ring so that he would have the measurements for ordering better jewelry. Occasionally, he would also take along a bracelet to be repaired and sometimes he would borrow change for cabfare. The articles and money were never returned; the checks bounced; the man disappeared. No fewer than ten of the victims (eyewitnesses of course) positively identified Beck as the embezzler, and he was convicted. Upon his release from prison, another series of embezzlements following the same pattern occurred, and again Beck was arrested and convicted, this time in 1904. Then while Beck was in jail, the real embezzler was caught—an entirely different man, but one who looked and dressed very much like Beck. Beck was pardoned.

SOURCE: Delmar Karlen, *The Citizen in Court* (Hinsdale, Ill.: Dryden Press, 1964), p. 149.

do not rely on such superstitions to become convinced beyond a reasonable doubt. But the process is not without subjectivity.

Juries believe—not without reason—that self-interest often leads people to falsify testimony in their own favor; the greater the interest, the greater this tendency to shade the truth. Because their interest is less apparent, witnesses for the prosecution (e.g., handwriting experts, accountants, and ballistics experts) are given more credence. The demeanor of witnesses—their tone of voice and body movements—and the corroboration of other witnesses can also affect juries.

Juries also look for consistency and a capacity to remember and describe crucial events. Attorneys try to undermine both during cross-examination (see box).

Finally, juries consider inherent probability. The Abscam trials (see Chapter 8) illustrate this concept nicely. Many explanations were given by members of Congress for why they accepted thousands of dollars from FBI undercover agents; many did not have the ring of truth. (For example: "I was conducting my own investigation"; "I didn't plan to spend it.")

The American legal system has many rules governing the types of evidence that may be given and the procedures to be followed in court. The more important safeguards of individual rights were discussed in Chapter 3. Some rules, however, do not involve deep philosophical questions; rather, they involve plain common sense. For example, only qualified experts can express opinion; and all documents admitted as evidence must be verified to be authentic.

The Tactical Goals of Cross-Examination

Cross-examination also has specifically tactical goals. These include obtaining helpful and discrediting harmful testimony; discrediting the witness; laying a foundation for impeachment of the witness; and laying a foundation for an objection to "incompetent" testimony.

A basic query recommended by most of the manuals, and aimed at discrediting those who testify adversely, is "To whom have you talked about this case?" The trap, of course, is that the witness has necessarily talked at least with the attorney who called him. But he may believe that talking to others about testimony is forbidden or invalidates the testimony. Or else he assumes that the question reasonably excludes the calling attorney. His "No one" therefore permits the cross-examiner to pounce. The witness has been caught in a lie, the lawyer cries, and his entire testimony must be discounted—whatever it may be.

Another basic setup question attempts to capitalize upon the myth of perfect recall. For instance, of an event that occurred some 20 years before: "In what month was that?"—"Oh, you *think* it was May or June. You mean you don't *know*?"—"Well, which was it, then?"—"Ah, you're *not sure*? Your testimony is, then,— *you don't remember*?"

The point, Goldstein instructs, is that "the more times . . . the lawyer can make the witness say 'I don't remember,' the better will be the psychological effect." For, explains Ehrlich in *The Lost Art of Cross-Examination*, "It is impossible in a court of law to place confidence in the evidence of a witness who can be reduced in cross-examination to saying 'I do not remember.' "

The examiner's manner is often more important than the substance of his question. The approach may be verbal, tonal, or silent altogether. A grin, eyebrow lift, or "listen-to-that" shrug toward Bench or jury box may invite emotional conspiracy. The dismissing of a witness with "That will be all!" in triumphant tone may pretend that damaging testimony was instead a coup. Another device is to address a witness as "Sir" or "Madame" in a heavy sneer that, if verbalized outside the courtroom's permissive ground, would approach slander.

SOURCE: Anne Strick, *Washington Monthly*, January 1977, pp. 21–22.

Applicable rule. Despite the apparent simplicity of the top portion of Figure 9–1, finding the correct legal rules to apply is often a complex task. American law is subject to constant change through new decisions (some 30,000 a year) and new statutes (at least 10,000 a year); regular and prompt supplementation and updating are required. At the same time, American law is marked by a quest for stability. (Recall the doctrine of **stare decisis**). American law also derives from many federal agencies and from a variety of jurisdictions (the federal government, 50 states, and a host of local counties, cities, and towns); this multiplies the sources of law considerably. The components of American law differ in their relative authority. Some are binding; others are only persuasive in various degrees; and some lack any formal legal force. Finally, since the forms of American law are issued chronologically (rather than by subject), finding the law applicable to a particular factual situation requires some research.

The most important sources of law are the federal and state statutes and appellate court decisions. The sources relevant to any problem may range from the first enactment of American legislative bodies in the 1790s to yesterday's decisions, statutes, and rulings. The earliest sources retain their legal effect until expressly overruled or repealed; accordingly, they are not to be ignored.

Once the relevant rules have been distilled from the ocean of law, the judge must establish their precise significance. Few rules are entirely free of ambiguity.

In some cases, the judge will decide that no rule exists that covers the dispute at hand. Then the judge must decide the case according to more general principles of law. That decision will form a precedent that is binding, in certain circumstances, on judges trying similar cases in the future.

One example will help underline the extent to which changing conditions and ethical ideas can require changes in the law. In the first decade of this century the ownership of automobiles began to rise. The courts were confronted with an essentially new problem. What happens if the product is defective? Can the owner sue the manufacturer, even though he bought the product from a dealer? At the time, only manufacturers of articles inherently dangerous (e.g., dynamite) were liable to the actual users. Thus, manufacturers of stagecoaches were not liable—but then stagecoaches could not go 50 miles per hour. Precedents drawn from the days of stagecoaches and carriages did not fit the automobile. New principles were required.

So it is every time the color of a case does not match the colors of any previous case. As Benjamin N. Cardozo (the judge who helped refashion tort law for the automobile) explained, "It is when the colors do not match . . . when there is no decisive precedent, that the serious business of the judge begins." In fashioning the law of the litigants in a particular case, the judge will be fashioning it for others. So the judge's job boils down to this and little more: Decide the comparative importance of logic, history, custom, and efficiency in advancing the welfare of society.

Formal Participants in a Trial

Litigants. Litigants (the defendant and the plaintiff) activate the adversary process. Therefore it is with them that we begin. As we have seen, in criminal cases governments bring charges against defendants, and in civil cases plaintiffs bring actions against defendants.

A simple example will help you see how a civil case begins. Harvey Wallbanger goes to Fast Eddie's house for a party. Harvey has too much to drink and knocks over Eddie's Optonica RT-6905 recorder. It costs Eddie $500 to repair the system. Harvey, in crashing into it, suffers a concussion.

Eddie files a complaint against Harvey in a small claims court for $500 in damages. Harvey promptly denies it was his fault; he makes a counterclaim against Eddie for $600. According to Harvey, he bumped his head because Eddie's floor was slippery. Now he is claiming damages for medical bills, lost wages, and pain and suffering.

Both men's attorneys now make motions for pretrial discovery. The term **discovery** refers to finding out about the case of your adversary before the case goes to trial. Attorneys "discover" what evidence the other side has by asking questions and obtaining documents. The first step in discovery usually involves **depositions.** A deposition is the oral testimony of one of the parties or of a witness. It is taken under oath before a notary public; then it is reduced to typewritten pages after the testimony has been transcribed; finally, it is bound and filed with the court, with a copy given to each side. Depositions serve three main purposes:

To find out what the person whose deposition is being taken will say.

To learn as much as can be learnt about the case prior to trial.

To pin the witness down to a written, sworn statement from which he cannot deviate at trial without having to explain his inconsistencies to the judge or jury.

To preserve testimony of a witness who might not be around at the time of trial.

A trial will be held about eight weeks after Eddie's complaint was filed.

Litigation requires more than money. It also requires toughness. The witness stand has been called the "slaughterhouse of reputation." Judge Learned Hand was once moved to remark that "as a litigant, I should dread a lawsuit beyond almost anything else short of sickness and death." (If you seek examples whereof the judge speaks, reread the preceding box. Or, better yet, sit in on a rape trial—you will soon find yourself wondering whether the woman or the man is on trial.)

Lawyers. There are over 450,000 lawyers in the United States. Around 15 percent are government lawyers who work for the various federal, state, or local agencies. For example, U.S. district attorneys, who are nominated by the president and confirmed by the Senate, are located in each state. The office is highly sought by the politically ambitious. Another 15 percent work for various corporations, unions, or trade associations. A small number of lawyers work for public interest or legal aid organizations. An even smaller number are law professors, judges, or elected officials.

Unlike Perry Mason, most lawyers rarely go to court. The practice of law usually involves giving advice to clients, drafting legal opinions or briefs, negotiating settlements, drafting contracts and wills, and appearing before government bodies. In the United States, lawyers are called the bar. Most states require all practicing attorneys to belong to the state's bar association.

Three of the most important matters a person needs to know in this legalistic society are when to get a lawyer, how to find a lawyer, and what to ask a lawyer. Even senior executives of giant corporations sometimes are less than savvy when it comes to knowing these matters. Unfortunately, many people see a lawyer only after they get in trouble. The best time to see one is, of course, *before* the problem arises—an ounce of prevention, and all that.

More specifically, people should consult a lawyer when they find themselves in a situation like Harvey's above—that is, when defending a criminal charge or bringing a civil suit. Other situations include buying or selling a home (more on this later), setting up a business (with nearly 14 million firms in the United States, hardly a rare event), obtaining a divorce and adoption of a child (more later), making a will, signing an important contract, and handling accidents involving personal injury or property damage.

There are several ways to find the right lawyer to help you. One is through the recommendation of a judge, a banker, or an acquaintance (especially someone who has had a similar problem satisfactorily resolved). Another is to take a look at the *Martindale-Hubbell Law Directory;* it is available in most public libraries. This directory lists most but not all lawyers in private practice; it tells when they were born, where they went to law school, how long they have been in practice, what professional associations they belong to, and what kind of clients they represent. The lawyers are also rated by the publisher on the basis of first-hand evaluations compiled from confidential questionnaires sent to lawyers in each community. The publisher uses two scales. The first consists of A (excellent), B (good), C (average), and no rating (usually in the case of lawyers recently admitted to practice). The second rates the lawyer's reputation for honesty, integrity, etc.; he or she gets either a V (very high) or no rating. A–V is the highest rating. A third way to find a lawyer is to call a lawyer referral service in your community; it maintains a list of lawyers who specialize in certain areas. Anyone who calls the referral service will be told the amount of the initial consultation fee and will be given the name of a lawyer for an appointment. If additional legal service is needed, the fee is subject to agreement between the lawyer and the client.

A recent U.S. Supreme Court decision gave attorneys the right to advertise. Thanks to that decision, citizens now have a fourth way to find a lawyer—legal clinics. With advertising to build high volume for their streamlined operations, the clinics reasoned, they could dispense cut-rate legal services to a middle class that was steadily being priced out of the market. To a degree they have succeeded. The clinics provide satisfactory low-cost services in areas that call for little legal analysis and much form processing; this includes simple wills and uncontested divorces involving childless marriages. But when the problems are more complex, when the legal job cannot be done by the numbers, legal clinics—which tend to rely on young, inexperienced attorneys—are often the wrong place to go for advice. And for tough jobs they frequently cost as much as their traditional competition. There are some bargains available, however.

Once you have found a lawyer, the Georgetown University Law Center recommends you get answers to the following questions:

- What is the lawyer's fee? Is the client required to pay a flat fee or by the hour? Is a retainer (down payment) required? What about a contingent fee in which the lawyer gets paid only if he or she wins your case?
- Has the lawyer ever handled cases like this before? If so, with what results?
- Will the lawyer provide you with copies of all correspondence and documents prepared on your behalf?
- Will the lawyer keep you informed of any new developments in your case and talk to you in "plain English"?
- How much personal attention will you get? If the lawyer is a member of a law firm, is he or she the person who will actually do your legal work?

If you are not satisfied with the answers, shop around.

Judges. Judges have considerable discretion—if not outright legislative powers. Therefore, selecting and removing them are matters of great import in the United States. There is considerable merit to the proposition that the most lasting and far-reaching effect a president can have on the course of the American republic is in the judges he appoints.

Presidents nominate, and the Senate must confirm, all federal judges. Usually, a president will observe **senatorial courtesy** when he appoints someone such as a district judge. This requires him to first obtain approval of the senators from the state, if they are of his political party. The FBI screens each prospective nominee.

States choose judges either by election, gubernatorial appointment, or legislative selection. Increasingly, states are changing to a merit system of selection. Elected state judges may be impeached and, in some states, removed by a special panel of judges. Congress may impeach federal judges.

What is it like to be a judge? Well, it does have prestige, and everyone stands up when he or she enters. Perhaps best of all a judge is allowed to interrupt two highly talkative lawyers whenever the urge strikes. The job has certain disadvantages, however. Cases are occasionally extremely boring. But almost all cases are hard. If the case were an easy one, it probably would never have come to trial.

Above all, a judge is expected to remain free of prejudice and not to impose any personal visions of justice. As Irving R. Kaufman, chief judge of the Manhattan-based U.S. Court of Appeals for the Second Circuit, expressed it, "self-restraint is the very soul of judicial impartiality. The ideal is to have the losing party feel that he is not the victim of the judge, but simply the objective of a process that is the same for all."

Jury.* Why does the U.S. system of justice include these nonprofessionals? To many, trial by jury seems expensive and inefficient. According to Nicholas B. Katzenbach, former U.S. attorney general and now general counsel for IBM, "The better your case, the better off you are with a judge. The weaker your case, the better off you are with a jury."[4]

Cases in which a judge could have reached a verdict in 30 minutes can take juries over 30 hours to reach. "Being a juror was a terrible thing," recalls one of the 10 men and two women who convicted Juan Corona in 1973 on 25 separate counts of first-degree murder.

> I'm not smart and I'm not educated, and I don't know if it's right to put a person like me in a position of being the judge. It was awful. I had to think like I've never thought before. I had to try and understand words like justice and truth. . . . If it hadn't been for [the foreman of the jury] I don't know what we would have done. He didn't finish high school, you know . . . why do they make people like us the judges?[5]

---

* This subsection discusses only a trial jury, or petit jury. A grand jury is a body of 12 to 23 members who hear evidence presented by the prosecuting attorney against persons accused of a serious crime. If indicted by the grand jury, the person goes to trial; if not, he or she goes free.

Juries must be randomly selected. Up to now, most courts have obtained their pools of potential jurors from voter registration lists. But critics say that registered voters amount to only 60 to 70 percent of the eligible population.

Lawyers for both sides in the process try to select a fair and impartial jury. Of course, the defense also wants a sympathetic one. Each side has a specific number of peremptory challenges; each side may challenge an unlimited number of prospective jurors with good cause (for example, knowledge of case and prejudices). Some questions are routine: Where do you work? What do you like to do in your spare time? Have you ever been the victim of a crime? Have you ever served on a jury? Do you remember reading anything about this case?

When asked by either side, judges may grant a change of venue—i.e., transfer the case to another judicial district.

To repeat: Trial juries *determine* the facts in civil and criminal cases and determine how the law should be applied in individual cases. Hence, jurors have a passive role during the trial. The trial judge instructs the jury in the law applying to the case in point.

In criminal cases, federal courts require unanimous verdicts; state courts require either unanimous verdicts or majority verdicts. However, the Supreme Court has ruled that unanimous verdicts are required in capital cases.

As the quote by a juror in the Corona trial suggests, the jury system is not perfect. In fact, in reaching their final decision, the jury had to, as do many trial juries, overcome a single holdout. When the holdout finally gave in, the other jurors could not be sure whether she had really changed her mind or merely yielded to the pressures—or possibly even voted "guilty" at last because she feared her sister would no longer feed the cats she had left at home.

In complex civil cases, the jury system is found guilty of shortcomings of a different sort. A growing number of lawyers, legal scholars and defendants in civil cases argue that jurors simply lack the knowledge and the background to rule on the complex issues now facing them with increasing regularity. Consider this snipped testimony from the MCI–AT&T trial:

> Attorney: "Why were the revenues being placed in jeopardy?"
>
> Witness: "The major reason is, as I said, the breadth of services that we felt—well, for instance, 50 percent of the market, more than 50 percent of the market was being foreclosed in the refusal to FX and CCSA interconnect. There are additional parameters. There was the double connection at the double loops of the terminal to the customers premises under certain circumstances."

Opponents of juries in complex civil cases use jargon-filled testimony like this to argue

FIGURE 9–6
Bird's-Eye View of the Criminal Justice System

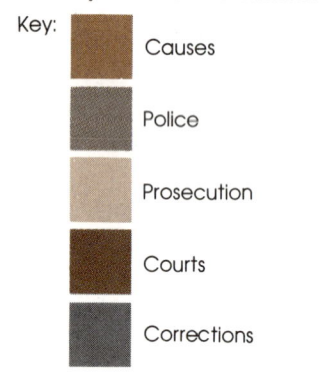

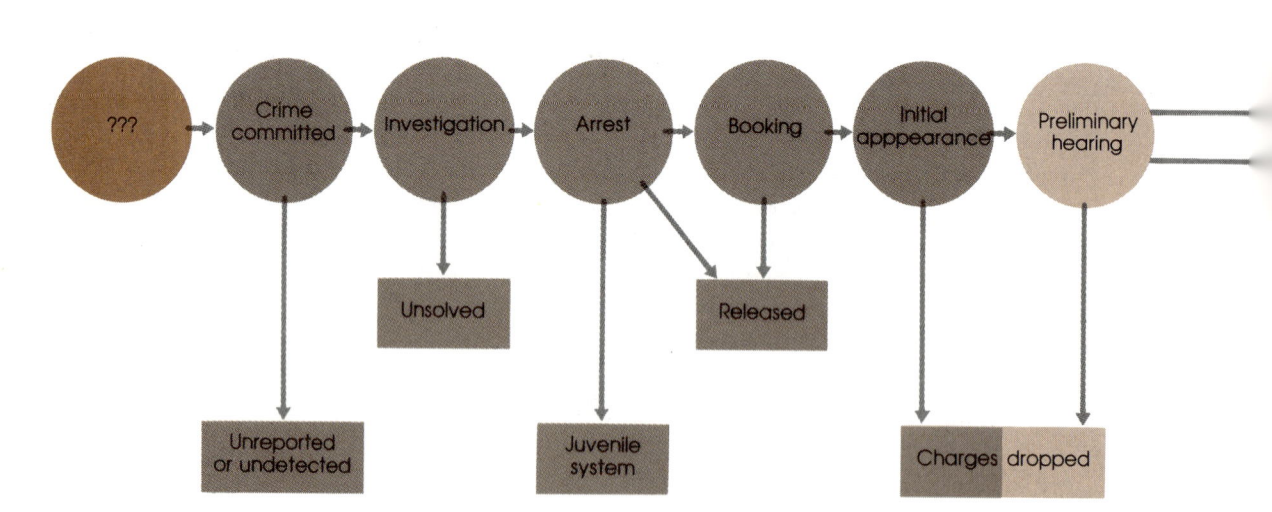

Key:
- Causes
- Police
- Prosecution
- Courts
- Corrections

??? → Crime committed → Investigation → Arrest → Booking → Initial appppearance → Preliminary hearing

- Investigation → Unsolved
- Crime committed → Unreported or undetected
- Arrest → Juvenile system
- Arrest → Released
- Booking → Released
- Initial appppearance → Charges dropped
- Preliminary hearing → Charges dropped

that, as civil cases grow more technical, particularly those in antitrust and patent law, juries aren't capable of deciding them on their legal merits. Accordingly, Chief Justice Burger has since appointed a committee to study alternatives to the jury system in complex cases. Proposals have ranged from the creation of "blue-ribbon" juries to a constitutional amendment removing the current guarantee of a jury trial for anyone requesting it in a civil case.

The Criminal Justice System

The founding fathers wrote that "Governments are instituted among men" to secure "life, liberty, and the pursuit of happiness." When they

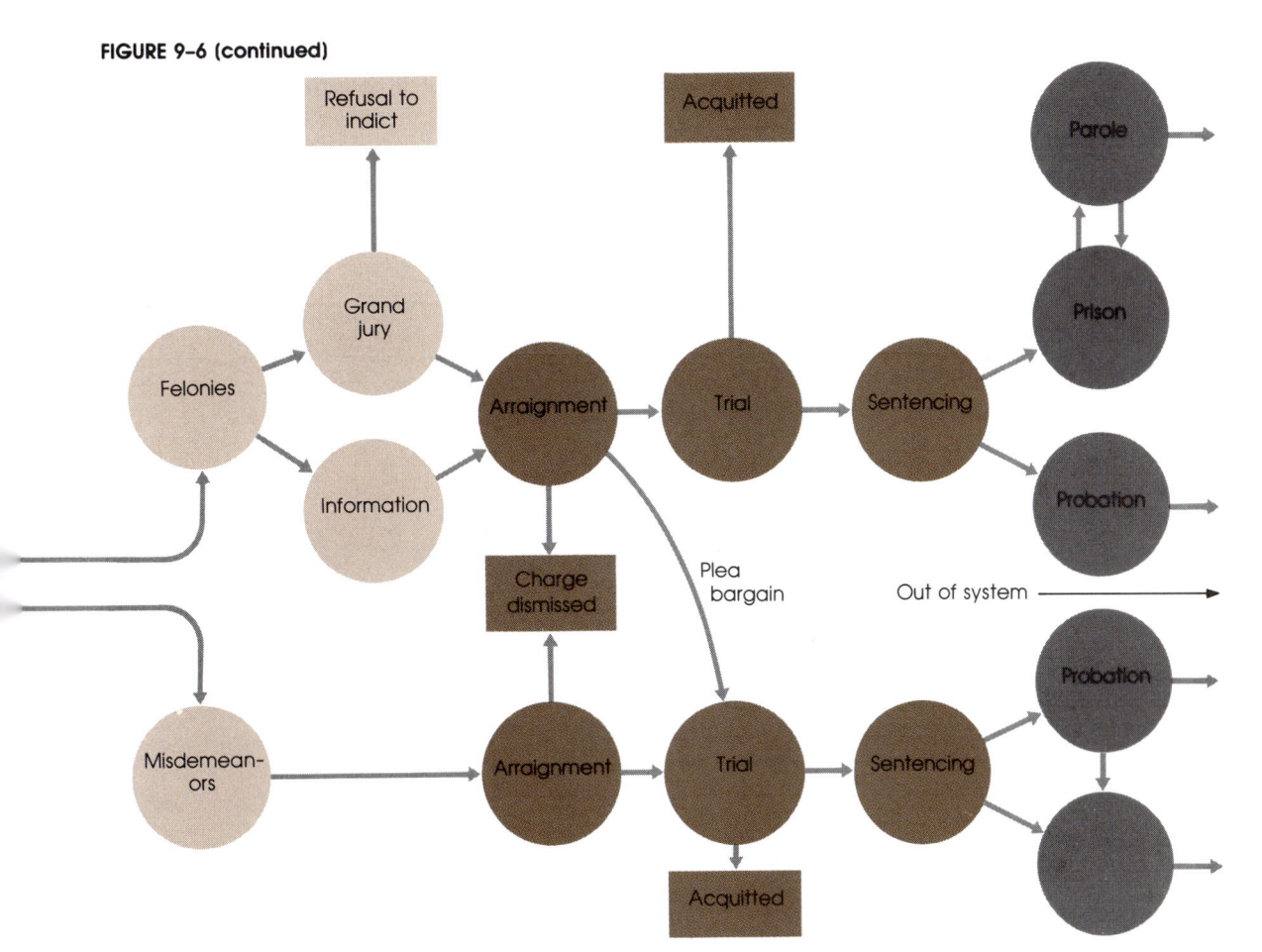

FIGURE 9-6 (continued)

This chart provides a simplified overview of a complex process—the way cases move through the American criminal justice system. But the most significant feature does not appear—the relative volumes of cases disposed of at various points in the system. Ponder these figures:

In 1976, there were 5,266 serious crimes for each 100,000 citizens.
Only half of all serious crimes are ever reported to police.
Of crimes reported, a suspect is arrested in only 19 percent of cases. (Only Kojak always gets his man or woman.)
Only half of all suspects arrested are ever convicted.
Only a quarter of those convicted ever "do time"—1.5 percent of all those who commit a crime.
Jails are full—over a quarter of a million prisoners in 1978.
Half of the prisoners are age 17–29, though this group is only 23 percent of the population.

said this they were making plain that criminal justice entails one of the most basic purposes of government.

A system, you should recall from Chapter 1, is a collection of interrelated parts. The structure of the American criminal justice system appears in Figure 9–6. (If you have not been watching many police shows on television lately and are puzzled by some of the terms in Figure 9–6, you might find the glossary helpful.) But you should also recall that every system can be described in terms of function as well as structure. In the case of the criminal justice system, describing a structure is a lot easier than describing its function.

Some would say the function of the system is to preserve order and, especially, to protect property. Others would say the chief function is to preserve justice and, especially, to protect the rights of the accused and guilty. Still, others would argue the real function of the system is to preserve legitimacy and, especially, to insure that wrongdoers do not go unpunished.

Why so little consensus on the chief function of the criminal justice system? A large part of the answer, I suspect, lies in the differing views of crime. Without a consensus on the nature of crime, it is not surprising that citizens differ with respect to the priorities of the criminal justice system. (See Chapter 12.)

FUTURE FILE

Delegalizing America

"We may be on our way to a society overrun by hordes of lawyers hungry as locusts."

Warren Burger,
chief justice of the
U.S. Supreme Court

The Problem

This chapter can be summed up in five words: America is a litigious society. America already supports two thirds of all the lawyers on the planet; its law school assembly lines now churn out almost one lawyer every 21 minutes. By 1984, there should be about 800,000 lawyers. If present trends continue, 100 years from now there will be one lawyer for every 43 persons—7 million lawyers in all.

Currently only one fourth of all adults have ever retained a lawyer. However, by 1985, 10 to 20 million people might be covered by prepaid legal plans. These comprehensive, prepaid legal plans will likely bring about some changes:

- People may seek advice before they get into trouble rather than retain a lawyer afterwards.
- Lawyers may become people oriented, acting as counselors on personal problems that have become legal problems.
- People may handle many of their own problems with lawyers as educators.
- Lawyers' salaries may be set by dues-paying clients.

Laws and lawsuits are also growing. Lawrence Tribe of Harvard Law School writes:

> In 1977, the legislative bodies at the federal, state, and local levels enacted approximately 150,000 new laws, and each of these new laws, on the average, required the issuance of ten new regulations. Between 1969 and 1972, the case load of the federal courts (corrected for the increase in population) rose by half. If the federal appellate case load, which accounts for only 10

percent of all federal cases, continues to grow as it has in the past decade, over one million federal appellate cases a year will flood the courts by the year 2010. ("Too Much Law, Too Little Justice—An Argument for Delegalizing America," *Atlantic,* July 1979.)

Jerold S. Auerbach, a professor of history at Wellesley College, writes:

> In the future, each American will receive a law degree at birth, followed immediately by a court calendar date for his or her inevitable appearance as a litigant. Now that disgruntled sports fans sue referees, children sue their parents, parishioners sue clergymen, and even non-divorcing spouses sue each other (as, for example, when a husband neglected to shovel snow and his wife slipped and injured herself), litigation has become an inevitable stage in the life cycle—slightly beyond adolescence but before maturity. ("Welcome to Litigation," *New Republic,* January 17, 1981.)

Technology supports these seemingly impossible trends. For example, telecommunication may enable attorneys to work out of their homes using combined telephone-television units to communicate with courts and interview clients. Juries could be selected and impaneled for home viewing of televised trials. Votes would be cast by punching a key on the computer. A judge, also using a computer, could enter relevant variables and get predictions on the outcomes of various sentences.

These trends in law will be very expensive. Already legal fees in the United States are more than $25 billion a year. Government policy in effect finances the litigious society since much of that $25 billion is tax-deductible.

Aside from these out-of-pocket expenses, there is a deeper problem: Too much law can breed disrespect for the law. Tribe writes: "Frustrated citizens naturally distrust an expensive, inefficient, frequently incomprehensible nonsystem that often seems contrived to serve lawyers rather than law. The scale of despair is alarming."

Consider probate laws. Since everyone dies someday, no one can avoid the probate system. Because of its complexity, dying is an expensive business. In fact, most families have to pay a lawyer eight times as much as the undertaker. The process can drag out an average of two to five years. In the end, lawyers can take up to 30 percent of an estate or inheritance. But it need not be this way. In Great Britain probate costs average one hundredth the amount they do in the United States, and the process lasts one seventeenth as long.

The answer to the problem of an increasingly litigious society comes in two forms. One is piecemeal; the other is radical. One attacks the branches of the American legal system; the other attacks the roots. Let us begin with the branches.

Simplify and Arbitrate

In theory, the most obvious solution is cut back the barrage of red tape and legal mumbo-jumbo. A committee of legal scholars has already drafted model legislation that would greatly reduce the time and expense of probate. Surely, out of the 450,000 legal minds now in the United States, similar committees could be formed to simplify laws governing the buying and selling of property, running a simple business, getting a divorce, adopting a child, settling a contested insurance claim, and the like. Already some have authorized private no-fault auto insurance; this insurance automatically compensates injury victims without forcing them to go to court to prove fault.

But there is a hitch in the theory. With few exceptions, the state legislatures that must pass on these kinds of reform bills refuse to do so. The reason is that it would take billions of dollars from the lawyers who control—who are—the legislatures.

HALT (Help Abolish Legal Tyranny) is a new, nonprofit organization to lobby for legal reform. The address of this public interest group is 10 E. Street, S.E., Washington, D.C. 20003. "The notion that ordinary people want black-robed judges, well-dressed lawyers and fine-paneled courtrooms as the setting to resolve their disputes isn't correct," Chief Justice Warren Burger says. "People with problems, like people with pains, want relief, and they want it as quickly and inexpensively as possible." HALT agrees.

Now legal experts and groups like the American Bar Association and the Justice Department are promoting the idea of resolving minor disputes through informal mechanisms, usually *mediation* or *arbitration*. (Under the latter, the parties agree in advance to be bound by the arbitrator's decision.) The basic idea is age-old; primitive societies have long relied on local officials or even family members to resolve problems between individuals.

One can also avoid lawyers by suing in a small claims court (it might be called conciliation court, justice of the peace, or magistrate's court, depending on city and state). One pays a filing charge that is usually less than 10 dollars and argues his or her own case in front of a judge or arbitrator. The presentation of the case may take only a few minutes (but chances of winning improve if one spends time organizing facts and rehearsing a concise presentation).

At the filing office, the form is simple. All that is needed, in addition to names and addresses of both parties, is the amount one is suing for (usually less than $1,000) and a few words about the reason for the suit. When the form is accepted, a date for a court appearance is set and a summons is sent by certified mail to the other party.

Being angry at someone is not grounds for a suit. The question should be: "Has the other party caused me to suffer monetary damages through intentional behavior, negligence, or breach of a contract?" And the first step should be to give the other party advance warning by stating the complaint in a brief letter. The notice might bring an offer to settle.

Rethinking the Adversary System

Some students of the American judiciary think they have found and isolated the virus causing the fever. It is not sentencing, parole, plea bargaining, or juries; rather, it is that trial-by-battle procedure we call the adversary system.

There are plenty of examples of how the adversary system can lead to distorting truth and degrading citizens. The adversary system is perhaps cruelest in rape cases; there it often sounds as if the woman raped is herself on trial. A more common example of this perverse cruelty is found in divorce cases. In the courtroom, parents are forced to blame one another for what went wrong. The result is often a lifelong mutual animosity, which can hardly be healthy for the children involved. In proceedings involving complex issues such as nuclear safety and polychlorinated biphenyls (PCBs), or even relatively simple ones involving an auto accident, the adversary system operates on the absurd premise that one party has to be entirely to blame; economics do not matter. The reality is often quite different. Sometimes several parties must share responsibility, and economic trade-offs are often central in the quest for justice. The point is that the system focuses all subtleties into absurd, artificial choices of guilty-or-innocent, yes-or-no, either-or.

Therefore, some critics would like to see a more European type of judiciary. Disputes would be handled chiefly by judges. The overriding goal would be justice and truth, even if some procedural niceties had to be omitted. Judges, not lawyers, would take responsibility for protecting each party's rights, as do some small claims courts. In trying to get to the heart of the Watergate affair, Judge John Sirica at times brushed aside a number of procedural niceties that, some say, encrust the adversary system. The European style is by no means unprecedented in American government.

The major problem with this retooling of the American judiciary is that it goes against the current of American history and culture. That current is particularly long and deep. Madison said of Americans "the latent causes of faction are . . . sown in the nature of man" and proceeded with the other founding fathers to design a government based on this premise. If the premise happens to be correct, then I guess the national disposition is for this trial-by-battle procedure, flawed though it may be.

THE JUDICIARY AND PARADOXES OF POLITICAL POWER

In Chapter 7, we saw how excesses of the Nixon White House lead to accusations that the United States now had an imperial presidency. Going on the assumption that was the case, Congress in the mid-1970s took a number of steps to restore the balance. Regardless of who was imperial, it was clear that the size and reach of both branches had increased substantially.

I do not know whether Newton's Third Law of Motion (for every action there is an equal and opposite reaction) is as valid in politics and government as it is in space and time. But it might be. For as the executive and legislative branches have increased their powers, so too has the judiciary. Indeed, not long ago Senator Daniel Patrick Moynihan of New York was speaking of an "imperial judiciary." Proving or disproving this proposition is not easy; there is no calculus of judicial power. Therefore, in this concluding section, I shall do no more than try to recap some of the key aspects of judicial power in America. Toward that end, we might play with the following four paradoxes.

More Is Less

Early in our inquiry we observed that the concept of judicial review is uniquely American. What other democratic nation has invested a small unelected body with the power to overturn the collective will of 536 elected officials (that is, both chambers of Congress plus the president)? The concept of judicial review—to declare null and void legislation and executive action that it, the Court, deems unconstitutional—seems cold, austere, absolute, final. Nor is the modern Court squeamish about using it. In fact, between 1789 and 1978, the Court struck down 136 provisions of federal law and almost 800 state laws as unconstitutional.[6]

Yet relatively few of these, especially since 1937, have had broad national significance. Typical of this pattern was one of its more recent uses of judicial review, *Leary* v. *United States* (1969). In that case, the Court struck down the Marijuana Tax Act which required dope dealers to register with the Internal Revenue Service and pay a tax on their sales.

It would appear that the Supreme Court would rather use finesse than wheel out heavy artillery when facing issues of major national importance. Awesome power apparently imposes self-restraint among those wishing to retain it.

Few Are More Political Than the Nonpolitical

To understand this paradox, you need to know a couple more things about how the Supreme Court operates. Unlike legislatures, courts cannot initiate remedial action to solve social problems; they must wait for someone else to bring the case to them.

The Supreme Court cannot rule on just anything, either. The parties must be in actual conflict, not just seeking advice from the court about some contemplated action. Further, one of the parties must have **standing,** that is, an individual must have a sufficient personal interest in the controversy, and that interest or right he or she wants defended must be legally protected. But even a case meeting these conditions will not be resolved in a court if it involves a **political question.** Such questions might involve whether the president acted correctly in recognizing a foreign government or, as in *Colegrove* v. *Green* (1946), whether congressional districts were too unequal in population.

The thrust of these various rules of operation seems clear: The scope of Court action is carefully narrowed and restrained—especially with respect to political questions.

And yet, who is it that decides whether a question is "political"? The Court, of course. Cynics might say that this allows the Court to sidestep issues that are too controversial until such time that it is ready to act. In any event, sixteen years after the *Colegrove* decision the Court, in *Baker* v. *Carr*, declared population differences unconstitutional.

Some critics of the Court maintain that today there seems to be virtually no issue—political or other—outside the sphere of judicial power. Lino A. Graglia of the University of Texas Law School is one such critic:

> What at this time, in our system of government, are the actual effective limits on what our judges can do? Specifically, what are the limits on what the Supreme Court can do, acting in the name of constitutional law? We know that judges can order the reapportionment of our legislatures, state and federal; remove most restrictions on the availability of abortion and on the distribution of materials historically considered obscene; prohibit prayers and devotional Bible reading in public schools; and require the transportation of public school children in order to increase racial mixing in the schools. And we now know that a judge can even require that a neutered male be permitted to compete in the women's division of the United States Open Tennis Tournament. The British Parliament, it used to be said, can do anything but make a man a woman; this limitation it appears, does not apply to our judges. The list could easily be extended, but this is surely enough to show that the question is a serious and important one.[7]

Professor Graglia might have added to his list that judges can also detail standards of operation of prisons and mental hospitals, require communities to build fewer roads (to protect jobs), and establish how much teachers shall be paid and how firefighters will be selected.

No Political Institution Is More Powerful than Those Without Claws

Conventional wisdom says that a major limit to federal courts is their lack of an enforcement arm. Yes, they can declare this or that illegal, but they must depend on the executive to ensure compliance. Recall President Andrew Jackson's remark, "John Marshall has made his decision, now let him enforce it."

And yet, it is also worth recalling that dramatic photograph in Chapter 4. When President Eisenhower ordered the army to Little Rock to enforce the Supreme Court decision on school desegregation, he was doing no more than what virtually all chief executives have done: upholding his oath of office by supporting the law of the land. I can think of no major instance to the contrary.

While No Political Actors Set a Higher Value on Judicial Restraint than Members of Congress, None Have Been Less Concerned with Its Realization

Generally speaking, Congress does not like judicial activism. Jealously guarding its prerogatives, a large number of the members of Congress look with disfavor on courts "legislating." The pages of the *Congressional Record*, speeches before the Rotary Club, and testimony at hearings are filled by members sounding the alarm about this harmful trend.

And yet, despite a formidable arsenal to check judicial activism, members do very little. I shall not try to develop an institutional or psychological explanation for why this is so. Rather, let us merely note what weapons are available to save the Republic from an incipient imperial judiciary.

First, the Senate can alter the composition of the judiciary by the kinds of appointments it confirms and by impeaching judges it deems activists. Second, the Constitution gives Congress the power to alter the number of judges. Third, in collaboration with the states, Congress can amend the Constitution. Fourth, it can simply rewrite the law to make it acceptable to the Court.

If you want to see the most awesome weapon available to Congress, read Article III, Section 2, paragraph 2 of the Constitution (in Appendix A). What this passage seems to say is that Congress can decide what the entire jurisdiction of the lower courts and appellate jurisdiction of the Supreme Court shall be. For example, Congress could conceivably take any issue—except those for which the Constitution provides original jurisdiction—entirely out of the Court's jurisdiction.

I do not mean to suggest that Congress has not used, or tried to use, these tools. For example, it has repassed laws declared unconstitutional over thirty times. But the puzzling thing is why, given congressional grumbling over judicial activism, it has practiced so much "congressional restraint."

Chapter Key

Contempt and ingratitude toward the legal system is a grave fault. It ignores the long arduous growth of an institution to which we owe our ease and privileges. The law is yet another example of ideas at work in the restless complexity of human life. The legal profession is easy to ridicule, as Daumier's prolific output of etchings testifies. But as an attempt to mold coherent, sturdy conceptions of what justice is, law is nothing less than a triumph of human intelligence.

American courts are a central feature of the governing apparatus in the United States. Courts are involved continuously in the interpretation of law, although the extent of judicial aggressiveness in interpreting the law has varied over time. By their power of interpretation of law, courts in effect make law.

Policies and laws made by judicial and nonjudicial sources are similar in that both deal with the same kinds of broad issues—distribution of the benefits and protections of government, regulation of private activity, and adjusting social conflict. Courts are the major public institutions in America that use formal processes to resolve conflict peaceably. Courts deal only with real cases in which two parties have a real difference of opinion. They generally consider only cases in which the alleged injury to one of the parties has already occurred.

Law—the source of judicial power—is the set of rules of conduct that a government uses to control society. Law becomes established either by custom or by enactment by a lawmaking body. It may be classified as civil or criminal law. Civil law involves offenses committed by a private individual, corporation, or group against another individual, corporation, or group. Criminal law involves offenses that a government interprets as being against the public interest. Constitutions embody constitutional law; legislative bodies enact statutory law; executive departments and agencies issue administrative law; and judges create common law.

The United States has a large and complex judicial system, of which the federal courts are only a portion. Each of the 50 states has a variety of trial courts and appellate courts. The federal court system has a three-level organization (one Supreme Court, 12 courts of appeals, and 94 district courts), plus a number of special courts. The system is decentralized and fragmented by jurisdictive authority and by federalism. Federal district courts, courts of appeal, and the Supreme Court have jurisdiction in both civil and criminal cases. Most state courts have jurisdiction in both civil and criminal cases; but some states have separate criminal and civil appellate systems. The federal and state judicial systems are separate. Only cases involving a federal question may be appealed from a state's highest court to the Supreme Court.

The states have a far greater variety of trial courts than the federal government. Special state courts handle such matters as divorce and probate cases. Magistrate and municipal courts and justices of the peace may hear minor civil and criminal cases. State and federal trial courts settle about 90 percent of the cases they hear. States have appellate court systems similar to the federal system. The state system usually contains intermediate appellate courts and a state supreme court, which is the court of last appeal (except for those relatively few cases carried to the U.S. Supreme Court).

The long debate of judicial activism versus judicial restraint is grounded in concerns about the proper role of unelected judges in a representative democracy. There is no single, proper resolution to this debate. The Supreme Court has varied in the issue areas it has addressed; however, since 1864 it has been quite active with exception of the 1936–1953 period.

The United States utilizes an adversary system that requires each side in a case of law to present its best arguments with a judge or jury deciding the issue.

Judges in America play a more active role in our political life than in other democracies. Although bound by procedural requirements, including *stare decisis*, they have to exercise discretion. Lawyers represent clients, but they do far more than just appear in court trials. In fact, a large percentage of lawyers have duties that do not require that they appear in court. They file legal briefs, draft contracts and wills, advise clients on tax matters, and appear before government bodies. The nonprofessionals in the American judicial system are the jurors who serve on grand juries and on trial, or petit, juries. The grand jury is usually composed of up to 23 people. It hears preliminary evidence in secret to decide if an indictment should be handed down against a person accused of a crime. The trial jury is usually made up of 12 people. It decides—on the basis of evidence presented in individual cases—what the facts are and how the law will be applied in both civil and criminal cases.

The number and costs of law suits in the United States are growing. As a result, many citizens, businesses, and unions are settling their disputes through mediation or arbitration. Based on the experience of other industrialized countries (including England), it is clear that American law could be vastly simplified. Improvement in the administration of federal courts has become a major political issue, as has the improvement of the operations of the Department of Justice and federal prosecutors.

Answers to Quiz
(see page 304)

1. A warranty is a statement of fact concerning the quality or character of goods sold made by the seller to induce the sale. There are two types of warranties. An express warranty is one made either orally or in writing by the seller to the buyer. An implied warranty is one imposed by law; it has nothing to do with any statement made by the seller. In this case, the implied warranty of fitness for human consumption has been breached; you have a claim in damages against the owner of the restaurant.

2. The Equal Credit Opportunity Act of 1975 says that a creditor must tell a consumer why he or she was turned down. Under the Fair Credit Reporting Act of 1971, you have a right to request the credit or to reveal the credit bureau that supplied the report. This means, in effect, that consumers have the right to learn the nature of information in their credit files. If you discover false, misleading, incomplete, irrelevant information, you can require the credit bureau to recheck its information and correct the errors. Finally, if still not convinced that your right has been handled fairly, you may complain to the Federal Trade Commission or sue the bureau in court.

3. Fortunately, the Fair Credit Billing Law provides a billing-dispute resolution procedure. It must be followed by every business that uses credit or charge cards. The law requires that within 60 days of receipt of the disputed bill, you send the company written notification that you are contesting the bill. Here's a sample letter:

   > Dear Sir or Madam:
   >
   > This request is being made pursuant to Section 226.14 of Regulation Z under the Fair Credit Billing Law.
   > (Statement saying why you believe a billing error has occurred and how much the error is for.)
   > Please send me copies of documentary evidence of my indebtedness.
   >
   > Sincerely,
   >
   > Your Name

   It is a good idea to send the letter by certified mail; and, of course, be sure to include your account number.

   Incidentally, the Fair Debt Collection Practices Act of 1978 protects you from abusive and unfair collection practices by professional debt collectors (but not from creditors collecting their own bills). When phone calls or letters become unreasonable and harrassing, consumers should report it to the FTC or their local consumer protection agency.

4. All property acquired by either Jack or Jill is called community property. Each spouse owns a half interest in such commonly held property. Unfortunately for Jill, courts hold that education and training are not part of the marriage estate subject to division upon divorce. While the court may offer alternative compensation to Jill, it will probably reject Jill's property right in her husband's degree. Jill should have had an agreement or contract—namely, that she would put Jack through school so they would both some day enjoy a better life—formally articulated *before* her marriage to Jack.

   The reason courts do not recognize property rights on a degree is that a degree—unlike, say, stocks and bonds or a house—cannot be transferred or exchanged. Since the property cannot be converted into cash as another form of property in the marketplace, its value is highly speculative.

   The particular remedy that a court may use to attempt to compensate for this injustice to Jill depends upon the particular state laws. For example, the court may award her a rather substantial award of alimony or divide the marital property unequally, giving a disproportionate share to Jill, who made the contribution to the education. But Jack has a loophole. He might be able to escape his obligations by declaring bankruptcy. The purpose of federal bankruptcy laws is to allow a bankrupt person to start life afresh without debts.

5. The law requires the parents to support their children, depending on the parent's wealth and the children's needs. This requirement extends until emancipation, or when the youth reaches the **age of majority**. State law sets this age and allows for exceptions—such as getting married or becoming (with parental consent) self-supporting.

   Children, in turn, must obey the reasonable commands of their parents and may be required to turn over any earnings to their parents. Parents may decide where their children live and go to school, what religion they practice, when they come home at night, who they see. Parents have a right to discipline their children, though not with excessive force. In short, as long as parents do not neglect or abuse their children, courts are reluctant to interfere in parent-child relations.

   Parents are not liable if their children injure someone, destroy property, or steal. Many states, however, punish parents who contribute to the delinquency of a child. And, if the court finds a child has been continually disobedient or has been beyond control of the parents, it may declare a PINS or CHINS (a person or child in need of supervision). In such cases, the court removes the youth from the home. A court can also remove a child when parents have injured or mistreated a child.

6. Because the lease must contain all the requirements of a contract, it is a contract. First, the parties to the lease—namely, the landlord and the tenant—must be capable of entering into a valid contract. Second, there must be consideration—that is, something of value offered or received, which constitutes the reason for making the contract. In the case of a lease, the consideration is the rent paid by the tenant and the possession of the premises given by the landlord. Finally, the subject matter of the lease must be lawful. Thus, a contract to lease an opium den is void.

7. Since 1968, federal law (the Fair Housing Act) prohibits housing discrimination. Unfortunately, Congress failed to give the Department of Housing and Urban Development sufficient tools to enforce such **open housing laws**. In 1977, for instance, officials estimate that 2.5 million acts of real-estate discrimination took place; about 3,400 complaints reached HUD. The agency worked out compromises in 277 cases; 70 people actually obtained the housing they were originally denied.

   Generally speaking, the rights of a tenant—black or white—are somewhat less than those of the landlord. The latter may enter an apartment without permission to demand payment of rent. They may seize a tenant's household goods when the latter fails to pay rent. They have no obligation to return a deposit, unless expressly provided for in the receipt. They may evict tenants if the latter damage the premises or create a nuisance. Ordinarily, the tenant, not the landlord, has the duty to make repairs to the leased premises. Even when the landlord says that the rooms are "clean" and the tenant, upon moving in, finds insects or mice, the landlord has no obligation. (Clean only means that the apartment was swept and scoured.) But, if the lease says that the landlord will provide heat, then the landlord must do so. Otherwise, a tenant can move out and recover any expenses.

   Sometimes tenants may want to form an organization or association. In some states, tenants have the legal right to withhold their rent if the landlord will not make repairs. If repairs are not made by the date, the rent money should be placed in a bank account.

8. The couple on the left is Lee Marvin and Michelle Triola Marvin; the couple on the right is Nick Nolte and Karen Ecklund. Their

pictures are in the quiz because they are examples of a new type of "divorce" case. When a man (or woman) decides to leave a live-in girlfriend (or boyfriend) who is not a spouse, can the girlfriend (or boyfriend) sue? To see how the courts handle such cases, let us consider a hypothetical example.

Jill Smith moves in with Jack Davis. Although they never obtain a marriage license or have a formal marriage ceremony, they live as husband and wife. Jill even signs her name Jill Davis. Are they legally married? If Jill and Jack live in a state that allows common law marriage, they probably are. These states are Alabama, Colorado, Georgia, Idaho, Iowa, Kansas, Montana, Ohio, Oklahoma, Pennsylvania, Rhode Island, and South Carolina. The time required to create a valid common law marriage varies from only a day to a year or more.) In such states, Jack and Jill would need a divorce from a court before they could marry someone else.

Unlike a contract, marriage is a status fixed by laws. In an ordinary contract, the parties are free to modify the terms of the agreement or even cancel the contract altogether. But in marriage, the parties may not modify the terms of the nuptial contract. They cannot, for example, mutually agree to dissolve the marriage and wed other spouses except in accordance with the law. In a contract, the only test is one of mental capacity. In marriage, however, certain physical capacity is also required. The husband, for example, must be physically able to consummate the union—i.e., be able to have sexual intercourse with his wife. Otherwise, the marriage may be dissolved by annulment.

U.S. Geological Survey EROS Data Center

10 Government at the Grass Roots

After studying this chapter you should be able to answer the following questions:

1. What are the pros and cons of federalism?
2. What are the major activities of the states?
3. How do federal officials cooperate with state and local constituencies in passing and administering federal laws?
4. Who has the power in state and local governments?
5. Why are American cities suffering? What can be done about it?
6. Which activities do you think are best done at the state or local level rather than national?

Terms you should know:

bicameral legislatures
block grants
categorical grant-in-aid
city charter
city manager
commission form of government
councils of government
county government
general revenue sharing
home rule
intergovernmental lobby
intergovernmental relations

item veto
matching funds
patronage
progressive tax
proportional tax
Proposition 13
regressive tax
special districts
states' rights
Sun Belt versus Snow Belt
urban homesteading
zoning

At this very moment the U.S. government may be taking your picture—or at least one of the building in which you are reading this sentence. NASA and the U.S. Geological Survey (USGS) photograph the world from 610 to 19,716 meters overhead. Landsat satellites provide even loftier pictures from 920 kilometers up. (These photographs are available from EROS Data Center, Sioux Falls, South Dakota, 57198, for a price.) This chapter is not about aerial photography, however. It is about government at the grass roots.

Consider the photograph of San Francisco, which perhaps you recognized, at the beginning of this chapter. You can probably identify parks, roads, ships, and the like. If you know the city well, you might even point out the historic Barbary Coast, Japantown (the forgotten Asian cousin of Chinatown), Mission Delores, the Cannery, and Pier 39. But something else is in the picture—less visible but not less real. It is layers of government.

The last three chapters basically dealt with a single government—the national one. In this chapter, we shall be dealing with 80,000 governments. In addition to the 50 states, we need to consider about 3,000 counties, 18,500 cities, 17,000 townships, 16,000 school districts, and 40,000 special-purpose agencies. Actually, San Francisco is less of a government jungle than many other cities. For example, unlike most other large California cities, it has a consolidated city-county government.

The theme of this chapter can be easily stated: It is impossible to fully understand American politics without considering the complexities of federalism. Supporting this theme requires neither recondite reasoning nor farfetched examples. (Perhaps, that is why it is so often ignored by otherwise perceptive students of American politics.) Consider:

> The issue of state responsibilities and restraints reverberates through the seven articles of the Constitution. The very words *state* or *states* appear more than 90 times; the word *nation*, in reference to the United States of America, never appears. The Constitution carefully lists what the three branches of the national government can and cannot do. The 10th Amendment, however, rivets into the document the right of each state to proceed with anything it desires—provided it is neither delegated to the United States nor prohibited by the Constitution.

In short, to grasp the origin and abiding location of political power in the United States, one must consder the 50 states, from whence that power flows. The powers of the central government, as James Madison pointed out in the Virginia Convention in 1787, came from "the people as composing thirteen sovereignties." That is to say, the powers came from the states.

John C. Calhoun, vice president from 1825 to 1832, was probably the last American statesman to do any primary political thinking. And the kingpin in his political system was the role of states and other units in government. Since government by numerical majorities was inherently unstable, he argued that it be replaced with "government by the whole community." To Calhoun this meant a government that would represent organically both majority and minority. Therefore, society should not be governed by counting heads; it should be governed by considering the great economic interests and geographical units of the nation.

This was hardly the first time a brilliant theory was put to ignoble purposes. Why ignoble? Concerned over the growing number of free states, Calhoun demanded an amendment to the Constitution in the form of the requirement for a "concurrent majority." He saw this as a way of insuring the long-term survival of slavery in the southern states.

A year after Calhoun's death, relations between the national and state governments became an even greater source of political conflict. The Civil War had begun.

In 1936, the Supreme Court declared Franklin Roosevelt's first Agricultural Adjustment Administration unconstitutional on the grounds that the regulation of agriculture belonged to the states.

By 1980, regional politics had become greater than at any time since the Civil War. Only this time it was not North versus South, but East versus West.

The issues as well as battle lines are new: energy, urban policy, and land use. The East consumes energy; the West produces it. The cities of the East are declining, and they want federal aid to maintain the quality of life. The cities of the West are growing, and they want federal aid to handle the problems of growth. Westerners also want greater control over federal land in their states. Named for the bush that abounds in the area, the Sagebrush Rebellion began as a fight over the federal government's vast land holdings. (Forty-five percent of California and 87 percent of Nevada are federally owned. Put together all the millions of acres of federally owned land and you would have an area the size of the entire United States east of the Mississippi River, plus Texas and Louisiana.) Now it extends to federally financed water projects, government red tape, and the 55-mile-per-hour speed limit. This conflict—pitting ranchers, loggers, miners, and other westerners against eastern power centers—will be a major political issue for at least the next 10 years.

Photos by Jana Burkhalter

The spark that ignited the Sagebrush Rebellion was the 1976 Federal Land Policy and Management Act. The act says that public land must be kept in perpetual trust by the federal government and not turned over to state and local residents. In 1980, the Bureau of Land Management told Gerald and Barbara Chaffin that their house, near Midwest, Wyoming, which was 47 years old, had been illegally built on government land. They were ordered to either remove all traces of the house or face a prison sentence and fine. Unable to pay for its removal, the Chaffins were forced to burn it.

From the preceding survey, it should be clear that the image of federalism as two government spheres, each rotating perfectly in its own separate orbit, touching but never overlapping, has little basis in historical fact. From the beginning, there has been a blurring and a mixing. Nevertheless, the dual structure remains, and a full understanding of the concept of federalism is essential to any understanding of how the American republic works.

FEDERALISM: PRO AND CON

The Critics

Given the geography and population of the United States, it is doubtful that any management consultant would recommend the current government divisions. Leon D. Epstein of the University of Wisconsin explains:

> Fifty states are probably too many, and some of them are so small, so poor, or so incoherent geographically as to be handicapped in exercising governmental authority and in mobilizing political participants. We are all familiar with the inherent difficulties faced by states so small in area as Rhode Island, so small in population as Wyoming, or so poor as Mississippi; and we observe that even a state as large and prosperous as New Jersey suffers from an identity problem because much of its population belongs to either the New York or the Philadelphia metropolitan area and so receives its news primarily from daily papers and television stations that are outside New Jersey itself. Perhaps no other heavily populated state is similarly limited with respect to state news, but several states have substantial numbers of people living in places that belong socially and economically, not just for news, to metropolitan centers in adjacent states. Cases in point are much of New Hampshire in relation to Boston; northwestern Indiana in relation to Chicago; northwestern Wisconsin in relation to the twin cities of Minnesota; Kansas City, Kansas, in relation to Kansas City, Missouri; and East St. Louis, Illinois, in relation to St. Louis, Missouri. Markets do not always coincide with states.[1]

Another line of criticism is that states are indecisive, antiquated, timid, and ineffective. They are uninterested in their cities and generally unresponsive to new problems. William Riker, a political scientist, declares that "the main effect of federalism since the Civil War has been to perpetuate racism."[2] There is some truth in this. State politicians who opposed national civil rights action did so on the grounds of **states' rights**. This is a doctrine that called for an interpretation of the Constitution that would place limits on the federal assumption of implied powers and give expanded interpretation to the reserved powers of the states (see Chapter 2).

The Defenders

To the charge that states are not rational units, several points might be made. First, it is a sweeping generalization. Four states have fewer than a million people; but most have the population, the geographic size, and resources to make moderately impressive nations. Indeed, a few, such as California and Texas, have several industries any one of which would make many a nation wealthy. Enterprises of this scale would seem to require governing.

Second, geographers and economists may be able to design a more rational arrangment, but they would have to overlook tradition. Effective state government is more than a linear programming problem; it involves more than just trying to optimize the instrument of popular government subject to certain constraints. People have grown accustomed to states. And, because a sense of community is a keystone of political well-being, that tradition is probably worth preserving. Edmund Burke put it this way: "To be attached to the subdivision, to love the little platoon we belong to in society, is the first principle (the germ as it were) of public affections. It is the first link in the series by which we proceed towards a love to our country, and to mankind."[3]

What Burke is saying is that the county commissioners in Wyoming are accessible in ways that bureaucrats stationed in Washington or in regional headquarters are not. When Gerald and Barbara Chaffin speak to the commissioner, they do so with a real sense of participation and community; they speak to him opposing their removal from their home as a fellow citizen in the community of Midwest, Wyoming. When the Chaffins travel to the Bureau of Land Management in Washington, by contrast, they feel a sense of insecurity. In this world of strangers, they stand subdued. It is the concentration of all power into one body that, in Jefferson's words, "has destroyed the liberty and rights of man in every government which has ever existed under the sun."

Why not then use the city as the basis for a decentralized, popularly based authority? The main problem is that cities do not have the resources for dealing with problems such as mass transportation, pollution, health, and welfare. Moreover, their boundaries are even more haphazard—more irrational, if you will—than the states.

To the charge that the states have been unwilling to face problems, the states are only guilty in part. Since the 1970s, advocates of states' rights are no longer associated with stifling civil rights. In fact, liberal-minded environmentalists in energy-producing states often oppose national efforts to increase energy supply on the grounds of states' rights.

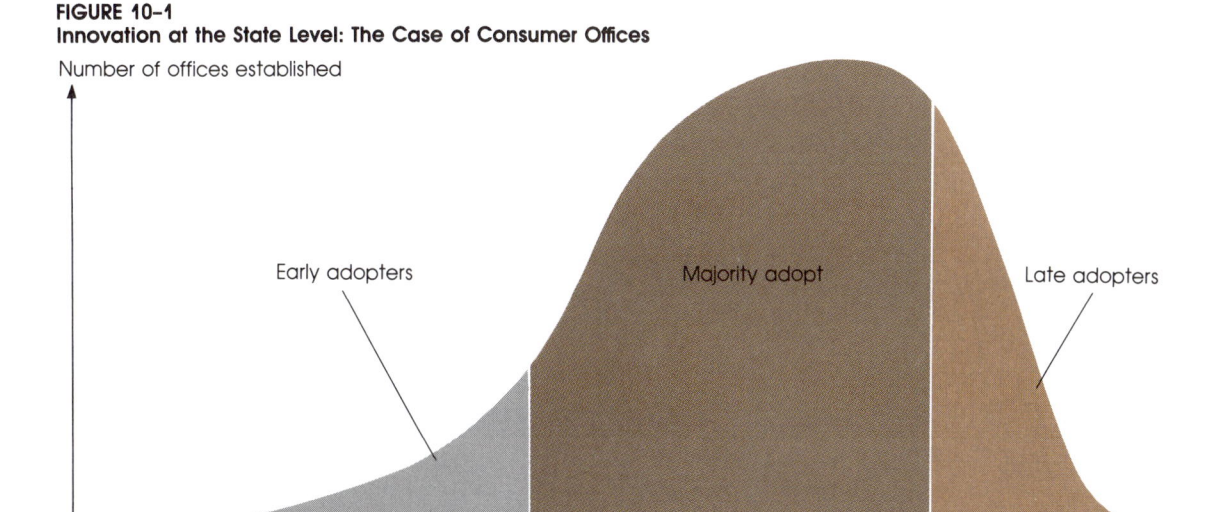

FIGURE 10-1
Innovation at the State Level: The Case of Consumer Offices

The Consumer Product Safety Commission established as an independent federal regulatory agency

By plotting the number of states that established an office of consumer affairs between 1957 and 1974 and drawing a normalized curve, a fairly typical pattern for innovation at the state level emerges. First are the early innovators: New York (1957), New Jersey (1960), Illinois (1961), Washington (1961), Massachussetts (1963), California (1965), Connecticut (1965), Delaware (1965), and Iowa (1965). The laggards usually come two to six years behind the majority: Alabama (1972), North Dakota (1972), Ohio (1972), Utah (1972), Montana (1973), Wyoming (1973), Tennessee (1973), Mississippi (1974), and South Dakota (1974).

Source: Based on data from Graham T.T. Molitor, "How to Anticipate Law-Making Action," paper delivered at the Public Affairs Council Conference, Mayflower Hotel, Washington, D.C., June 23, 1977.

The positive case for the states is that they can serve as laboratories for experimentation. A number of states have been more innovative than the federal government in such areas as voter registration, no-fault auto insurance, consumerism, environment, free-fare transit, and banning throwaway cans (see Figure 10–1). Furthermore, there is a case to be made for diversity. Why should every state have exactly the same laws with regard to right-to-work laws, business taxation, and capital punishment? Why should New Jersey, New York, and Massachusetts have to create state universities comparable to those of California, Michigan, and Wisconsin—states where there are fewer great private universities? The point is that, because conditions and traditions differ from state to state, there is a case for innovation and diversity rather than national uniformity.

In sum, the objective of federalism, as conceived by the founding fathers, was to assure citizens the best of both worlds. The nation was given a central government with enough power to act boldly on truly national interests, yet not so powerful that it would swallow up the administration of local interests. De Tocqueville put it even more concisely. The federal system combined the advantages of "magnitude and littleness of nations."

WHAT STATES DO

The Growth in Spending and Employment

Despite the notoriety of big government at the federal level, growth by state and local government has been even faster. Federal spending rose by 395 percent between 1960 and 1978;

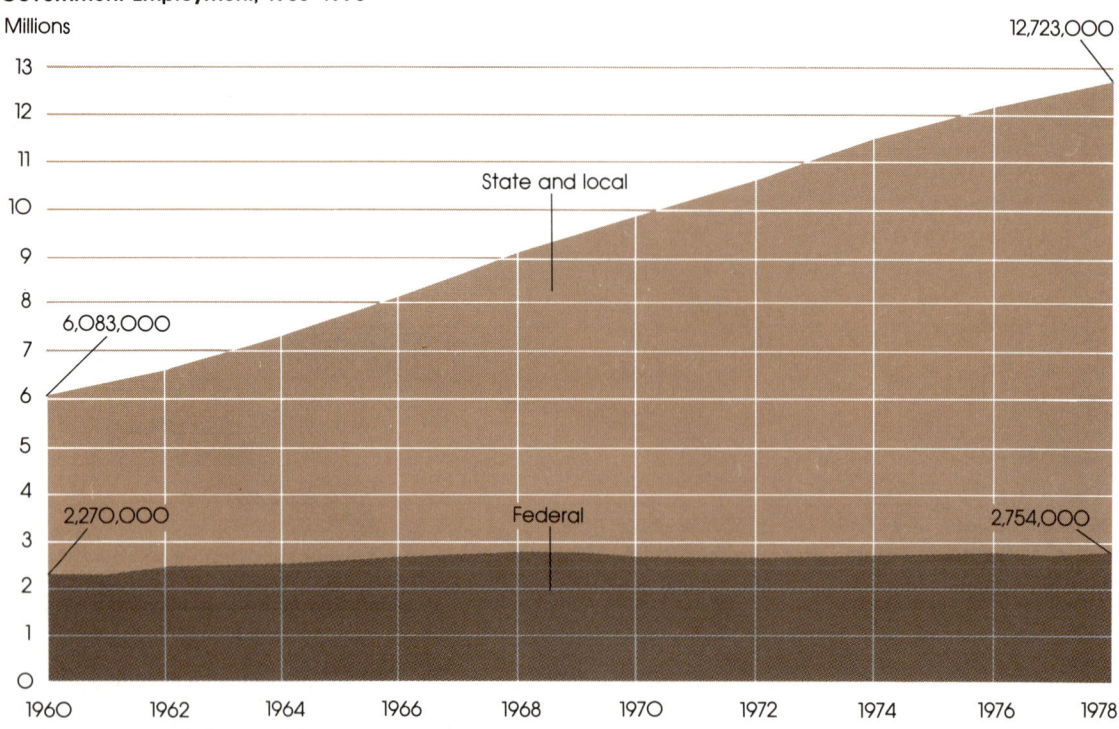

FIGURE 10–2
Government Employment, 1960–1978

Source: *Statistical Abstract of the United States, 1980*, p. 318.

state and local spending rose 502 percent. The employment figures are even more striking. During the same period, federal government employment rose only 21 percent; state and local rose 109 percent (see Figure 10–2). Today, one of every six jobholders in California works for state or local government.

The pressure for state and local governments to expand is tremendous. Many jurisdictions are collecting taxes and increasing their budgets faster than the general economy is growing. Taxpayers have begun to launch moves to limit the amount government can tax.

Why such a sharp rise in state and local expenditures? Most of the rise can be explained in terms of inflation, population growth, and public demand. When the consumer price index (see Chapter 13) rises 102 percent in 10 years in a city, that city either raises its budget or stops paving the streets. Moreover, if that city is in the South or West, it probably experienced a population increase; this translates into more spending. Let's look at one of the more extreme cases. Since 1972 the population of Harris County, Texas, has increased nearly 20 percent. That is the equivalent of adding a city the size of Cincinnati to the county.

Compounding this pair of trends is a third: the insatiable demand for services (by the same people who complain about taxes, one suspects). Political leaders at the state and local levels, like those in Washington, find it hard to say no to these demands. Thus San Francisco added 16 new departments in 10 years. In 1979, its board of supervisors created a new Office of Child Care at a cost of $64,800 a year. (This was despite there being a $12.8 million child care operation already in operation within the school system.) The trend is the same in other cities.

Perhaps another explanation for this rise can be cited. Congress and the federal bureaucracy are inducing state and local officials to expand services and controls. Most of the programs are developed on a national level. They are either mandated or are made so attractive on a matching funds type of setup that it is politically impossible for states or localities to decline. For example, if you have a chance to pay only part of the bill to offer water and sewage-treatment facilities and systems to a rural area, how can you refuse? Who wouldn't put up $20,000 (10 percent) to get $180,000 (90 percent)? Not many mayors—that much seems clear.

Sources of Funds

States finance their governments with revenue raised from taxes, funds secured from the federal government (more on this later), and borrowed money.

State taxes tend to be regressive. Any tax that takes away a smaller and smaller percentage of additional income, as income rises, is **regressive tax.** Under a **proportional tax,** as an individual's income goes up so do his or her taxes in exactly the same proportion. Under a **progressive tax,** the more a person makes the higher the rate of taxation.*

The typical state relies primarily on sales, motor fuels, and income taxes. Six states have no individual income tax at all; several collect only small amounts from it. Five states have no general sales tax. Local governments rely primarily on property taxes.

Because states and cities vary in their tax systems, where you live and work can cut your bill for state and local taxes by over 50 percent. For example, people who made from $50,000 to $100,000 could figure on paying more than $10,000 in state and local taxes in New York state; they could expect to pay only about a seventh as much in Wyoming. At the lower

---

* An example might help clarify the difference. Under either a proportional tax system or a progressive tax system, a person making $20,000 might be taxed at a 20-percent rate. Thus he pays the government $4,000. If his income rises to $50,000 under a proportional system, he is still taxed at a 20-percent rate—only now he must pay $10,000. If his income rises to $50,000 under a progressive system, however, he will be taxed at a higher rate, say, 30 percent. Therefore, he must now pay $15,000.

end of the economic ladder—people earning between $10,000 and $15,000—Massachusetts and its localities levied the heaviest load—more than $1,600; Louisiana imposed the lightest—just $557. Generally, state and local levies tend to be highest in the Northeast—except for New Hampshire, which uses low taxes to lure industry from its New England neighbors.

Which states deal most gently with the wealthy? The difference between the amount paid by the most and least affluent groups is $742 in Wyoming, $1,290 in Tennessee, and $1,298 in Texas. On the other hand, people in the top category paid $8,561 more than those in the low group in New York; they paid $6,391 more in Minnesota; and they paid $6,368 more in Wisconsin.

Of course, states and localities with heavier taxes sometimes provide greater services. In general, they are likely to spend the most per capita on health, education, and welfare. They also tend to have the highest average incomes.

In 1978, many political observers thought they saw the beginnings of a national "tax revolt." In that year, the voters of California adopted **Proposition 13,** a measure designed to cut local property taxes sharply. The leader of the revolt, Howard Jarvis, had defied the old cliché, "You can't fight city hall." State officials had warned that the tax cut would cut deeply into spending for schools and city services, but voters listened to Jarvis and passed Proposition 13 by nearly a 2-to-1 margin. Tax revolt fever then spread to other states—including politically liberal states like Massachusetts. In the November 1978 elections, twelve other states passed some form of limitation on spending or taxes. Today, several years afterwards, it seems that tax cut fever has run its course at the state level.

Scope of State Activities

The Book of States, which is published every two years, gives us a sense of what state governments spend all this revenue on. Most recently, it presents major state services under seven headings:

- Education (public schools, post-secondary schools, and library agencies).
- Transportation (highways, aviation, mass transit, and automobile insurance).
- Human services (health, public assistance, and a host of other programs).
- Public protection (criminal justice, prisons, state police, consumer protection, public utility regulation, and the national guard).
- Housing and development (including planning).
- Natural resources (conservation, outdoor recreation, forestry, agriculture, and energy).
- Labor relations (personnel system, employment relations, and employment security).

In addition to the major services noted above, states regulate individuals, businesses, and even local governments. Among subjects of state legislation are elections, public lands, animal health, food regulation, workmen's compensation, grain warehouses, barbers, medical societies, funeral directors, oil inspection, bingo control, banks, savings and loan associations, insurance, partnerships, corporations, marriage, contracts, automobiles, trucks, snowmobiles, real estate, landlord-tenant relations, mortgages, and criminal acts. Whether you have to be eighteen or nineteen years old to drink beer, whether state police looking for drugs can plant wiretaps in your home, and whether you can hire a farmworker to use a hoe with a handle less than four feet in length are a few of the specific questions a state legislature might address.

THE CONCEPT OF INTERGOVERNMENTAL RELATIONS

Traditionally, federalism is concerned with the allocation of power between a central government (Washington, D.C.) and regional governments (the 50 states). But now we must widen our perspective. To do that requires the introduction of a new concept. This concept must comprise not only federal-state relationships but also every conceivable government relationship—state–state, state–local, local–local, and federal–local. That concept is **intergovernmental relations.**

Since it will be impossible to examine every facet of intergovernmental relations in the United States, in this section only two will be emphasized.

State–Local Relationships

Earlier it was indicated that state law even establishes local governments and prescribes their functions. This power vested in a local unit of government by a state is called **home rule.** The city or county under home rule has control over its local problems, provided it does not violate the state constitution or the general laws of the state. In a sense, home rule interjects an element of federalism into state–local relations. As Burke would no doubt argue, home rule thereby strengthens democracy and increases citizen interest.

Despite home rule, local governments have lost power to state governments. The number of state employees has grown faster than the number of city employees. Similarly, state expenditures have grown faster than city expenditures. Even more revealing, about one third of all local government expenditures are accounted for by the states. Today, there are more state controls over local government and more local officials carrying out state policies. In short, the general trend of state–local relationships is characterized by centralization.

State–National Relationships

Importance of Washington. Regardless of how much local officials believe that their power is being eroded by state government, it is Washington that Leon Epstein sees as "the main actor in altering the distribution of power in the federal system."[4]

Several reasons for this redistribution of power can be cited. The most obvious, but not the most significant, is that, in the last half of the 20th century, the American republic has become, largely through technological advances, a much more interrelated society. At the same time, the major problems—pollution and energy shortages are prime examples—transcend state boundaries. To that extent, federal action is required.

Secondly, the federal government is better or at least more efficient than state governments at raising revenue. Accordingly, the dependency of state and, especially, local governments on federal aid has increased.

Consider the city of Tulsa, Oklahoma, which has a self-image of free enterprise and independence. Yet it received more than $48 million in direct federal grants in 1978. Twenty-seven percent of Tulsa's services of the kind that cities traditionally provide, such as protection of property, community health and environment, transportation, and general administration of government, came from Washington. But very few people realize this fact. The importance of federal dollars to Tulsa is obscured by the existence of layers of separate trusts or authorities—for urban renewal and other services. These receive federal money, but their finances are often hidden from the public and at times from elected officials. The Tulsa Urban Renewal Authority, for example, receives federal community development grants through the city; however, it reports no financial data in the city budget. Although cities vary widely in their structure, what has happened in Tulsa is typical of many expanding cities. It is one example of how, in only a decade, a new form of government has emerged. It is so complex and so fragmented that much of it eludes the public view.

The interesting question is, Does this financial dependence of states and cities on the federal government means that Washington has increased its control over regional and local governments? To answer that question, we need to dig a little deeper into the subject of federal aid. *How* that aid is distributed has a lot to do with the control that comes with it.

Categorical, block grants, and general revenue sharing. One way the federal government can distribute aid is by providing grants for specific purposes. In 1980, 78 percent of the fiscal aid it gave to state and local governments was through this method, which is called the **categorical grant-in-aid**. Through a jungle of almost 500 separate categorical programs, the national government supports such activities as agricultural research, mental health facilities, vocational training, and highway maintenance. Frequently, these programs clash with or duplicate each other. Boston, for example, must file 72 separate applications through scores of agencies, each with its own criteria, for redevelopment of three city neighborhoods.

This method interjects a certain amount of conflict into the federal system. The conflict is between professional programs specialists and elected officials (see Figure 10–3). Each column represents an alliance among like-minded program specialists, regardless of the level of government in which they serve. Elected officials at the state and local levels resent the autonomy of these vertical program bureaucracies. Let me make this point as concretely as possible. A big-city mayor may nominally have authority over her director of public health. Yet, on a day-to-day basis, the director is more likely to be in communication with his counterparts at the state capitol and in Washington, D.C. Moreover, it is probably those state and federal officals that talk his language and that can help him do his job.

One further point about these vertical bureaucratic alliances: Because each one is independent from every other one, interagency competition—rather than coordination—becomes a way of life. Mayors look on helplessly as their cities become battlegrounds for federal agencies.

FIGURE 10–3
A Model of Federalism

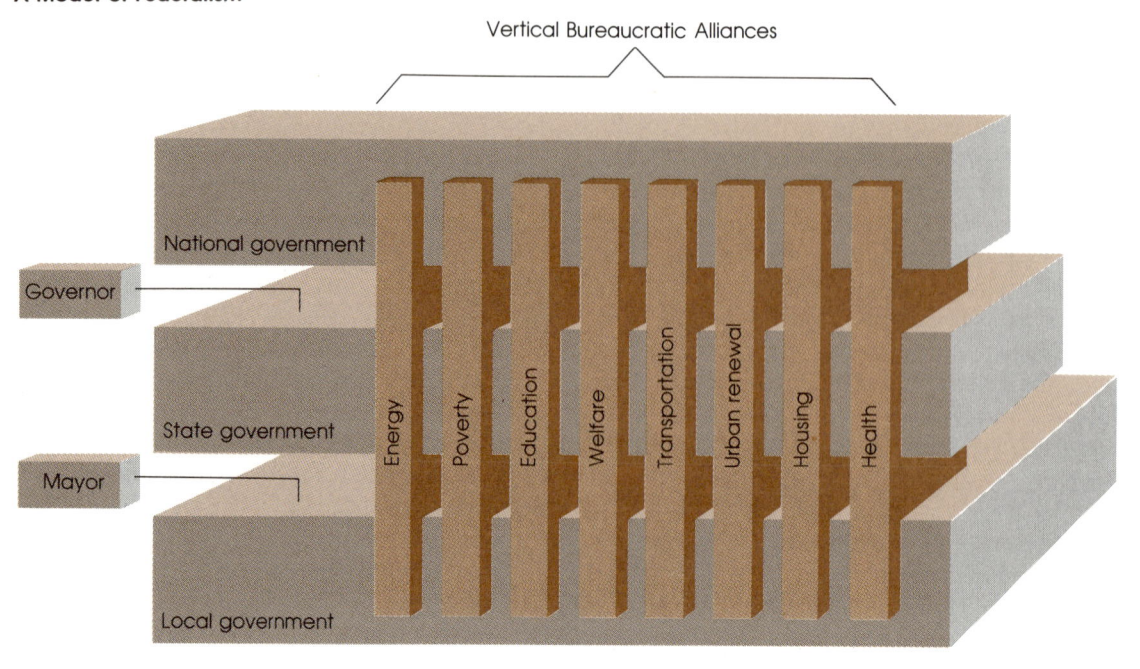

As a response to the redundancy, duplication, and conflict that can sometimes attend categorical grants, the Nixon administration began to consolidate several of them into single **block grants.** These grants (sometimes called special revenue sharing) were devoted to a general purpose. For example, the community development block grant funds provide assistance directly to local governments. Recipients have considerable freedom in selecting projects for this purpose, so long as they are within the general guidelines of community development. In 1980, block grants accounted for about 11 percent of all federal aid programs.

The third method of distributing federal aid, **general revenue sharing** (GRS), is virtually without strings. First adopted in 1972, the GRS program was the centerpiece of the Nixon administration's "New Federalism." It does not have even the broad focus of block grants. In 1980, GRS accounted for about 11 percent of all federal aid programs.

As he promised in his 1980 campaign, President Reagan seems intent on cutting the tangle of state-federal relations and, eventually, returning power to state governments. The cutting has concentrated on the categorical grants. Enactment of all the cuts he recommended in 1981 would have shrunk these many special-interest intergovernmental programs from 29 percent to 18 percent of the federal government.

Particularly important to state and local officials is the way these programs are cut. They figured that with less federal overhead and interference they could get the same results with 10 percent less spending. In 1981, President Reagan held them to more than their word; among other actions, he consolidated 45 education programs into two block grants with a 20 percent cut.

The politics of fiscal federalism. Both liberals and conservatives have opposed GRS. The former see it as a move away from programs they have traditionally favored. Under GRS, state and local officials are free to spend the monies however they see fit. This means less money for welfare and mental health programs and more for police cars and tennis courts. In short, GRS is not targeted nearly as well as categorical grants to the needy. Conservatives, who certainly have nothing against police or tennis, point to the big budget surpluses of some (though not all) states. They question the wisdom of the federal government, itself running a continuous deficit, ladling out billions of dollars to states.

There is a very interesting political alignment over revenue sharing. To the extent GRS cuts down the influence of the federal bureaucracy in the lives of people, President Reagan is for it. But, as a conservative, he wants a balanced budget, which means the less GRS the better.

The federal bureaucracy favors categorical grants; they give it more influence than GRS. Similarly, members of Congress favor categorical grants; they provide a clear-cut vehicle for maintaining the support of special interest groups.

States and local governments are for GRS because it gives them more influence. Indeed, if *all* federal funds were suddenly converted into GRS, the vertical program bureaucracies in Figure 10–3 would melt away; the lives of governors and mayors would become less troubled. But any governor or mayor's support for GRS is based on the assumption that his or her area gets an adequate slice of the GRS pie (see box).

One could argue that it is this tension between (1) vertical program bureaucracies and (2) governors and mayors that has become the driving force of fiscal federalism. Samuel Beer of Harvard goes even further: The recent inexorable growth in government is primarily due to demands (i.e., lobbying) of groups *within* government, not the citizenry at large.[5]

The politics of fiscal federalism raise a couple of serious questions about American politics. How can government spending be controlled if both the federal bureaucracy and this **intergovernmental lobby** continue to call for more money? Second, how can the American repub-

Slicing the Federal Pie

With jobs declining and social service costs rising, New York's political leaders such as Mayor Edward Koch, Suffolk County's John Klein, and Senator Patrick Moynihan have lined up with other **Snow Belt** states of the Northeast to demand more federal assistance. Indeed, syndicated columnist Joseph Kraft suggests that fiscal federalism is changing the Empire State's politics: The political culture of New York Democrats, until very recently, tended to favor brilliant, sharp-tongued lawyers of a moralistic cast. They would go to Congress, ensconce themselves in the judiciary committees, and go after anyone straying from the straight and narrow in the White House, the Pentagon, the Central Intelligence Agency, or the FBI ("Changing Their Tune," *Houston Post*, September 4, 1980).

The financial crisis in New York City and the decline of Buffalo and mill towns along the Erie Canal changed that. In 1976, Pat Moynihan was elected by promising he could get more federal money for New York.

Moynihan argues that the states of the South and West—the **Sun Belt,** win the tally of who gets what back from federal taxes (see table at right). But, as we have seen repeatedly in this book, statistics must always be scrutinized. The thinly populated western states traditionally rank high because of highway construction grants and

Jack Manning/NYT Pictures

What States Receive in Return for Each Tax Dollar That Goes to Washington, D.C.

New Mexico	$1.91
Mississippi	$1.58
Alaska	$1.45
Virginia	$1.41
Tennessee	$1.39
South Dakota	$1.38
Maine	$1.32
North Dakota	$1.31
Hawaii	$1.30
Utah	$1.29
Missouri	$1.25
Alabama	$1.25
Arkansas	$1.25
Idaho	$1.21
Arizona	$1.21
Montana	$1.19
Maryland	$1.18
Vermont	$1.18
South Carolina	$1.16
Massachusetts	$1.13
Kentucky	$1.12
West Virginia	$1.12
Georgia	$1.11
Florida	$1.11
Washington	$1.10
Oklahoma	$1.09
Colorado	$1.06
Nebraska	$1.06
Rhode Island	$1.05
Louisiana	$1.05
Connecticut	$1.02
California	$ .98
North Carolina	$ .97
Kansas	$ .95
New York	$ .95
Texas	$ .93
New Hampshire	$ .92
Nevada	$ .92
Pennsylvania	$ .92
Wyoming	$ .91
Oregon	$ .87
Minnesota	$ .85
Iowa	$ .76
Wisconsin	$ .74
Illinois	$ .73
Delaware	$ .73
Ohio	$ .71
Indiana	$ .70
New Jersey	$ .69
Michigan	$ .66

shared revenues from federal land holdings. For example, the Rocky Mountain states have the lowest regional population density, extensive federal land holdings, and, until recently, the highest per capita aid. But this difference has diminished in recent years as Federal human resource programs have grown relative to physical resource programs.

lic impose upon public expenditure any coherent policy, any set of priorities reflecting "an overall view of national needs"? The bureaucracy is too specialized and the intergovernmental lobby too regionally oriented for such a view.

How much federal control? Earlier I raised the question of whether federal aid to states and cities means federal control of those governments. Now we can begin to answer it.

The intergovernmental lobby—made up of mayors, governors, school principals, county highway commissioners, local police chiefs, and many others interested in federal funds—has been successful at getting more aid with fewer strings. This seems to undermine somewhat the notion that the federal government controls the states. Masters should be made of sterner stuff.

The intergovernmental lobby is not the only termite gnawing away at the theory of federal control. Another is the reluctance of the federal government to withdraw money from a jurisdiction that fails to comply with the numerous rules about how the money is to be spent. And even if some bureaucrat decided he or she would do so—and weather the firestorm that would surely come from that region's senators and representatives—the state or local government might think "So what?" After all, with

FIGURE 10-4
Federal Mandates Imposed on Local Governments

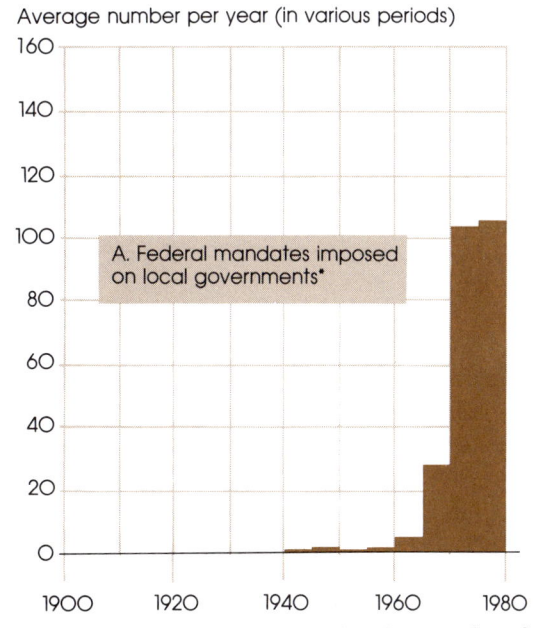

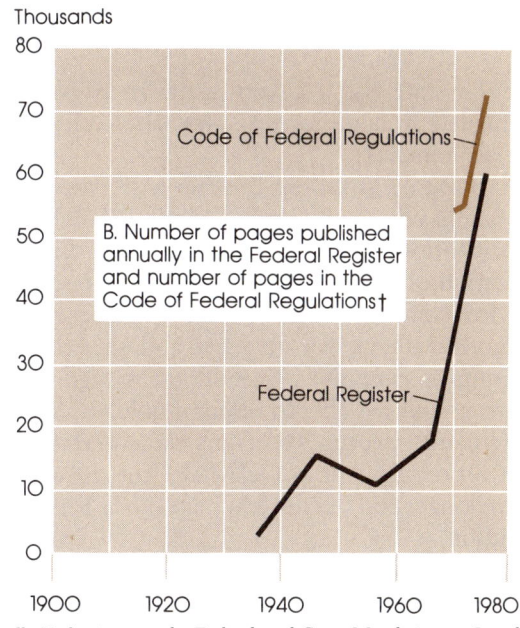

Sources: The information for the first chart was derived from Lovell, Katherine, et al., *Federal and State Mandating to Local Government: Impact and Issues*, 1979 draft, p. 71. The sources of the second chart were Morris P. Fiorina, *Congress: Keystone of the Washington Establishment*, 1977, p. 93, and the Public Interest, Number 47, New York, NY, National Affairs Inc., Spring 1977, p. 50.

all the duplication of grants in the federal bureaucracy, there would probably be alternative sources to tap.

Suppose we dismiss the theory that federal aid equals federal control. We still cannot dismiss the theory that the federal government has in recent years tightened its grip on government at the grass roots (Figure 10–4). We need only recall from the last chapter the role of the judiciary, especially the Supreme Court, in telling state prisons and local school districts how to spend their budgets, to appreciate in concrete terms the role of the judiciary in federalism.

INSTITUTIONAL MODERNIZATION

It would be wrong to view the problems of states and cities as exclusively a problem of public finance. Emphasis must also be given to improving the capacity of states, cities, and counties to exercise power. Because state government roughly parallels national government, our chief focus will be on city government.

The States

Each state has a government. In it power is divided among executive, legislative, and judicial branches.

State constitutions are the basic law at the state level. Anyone concerned with why the institutions of state government need modernization should look at these documents first. Most state constitutions fragment executive authority among departments and set stringent limits on executive power. Therefore, governors are not always able to respond boldly to citizen demands. Because voters may amend state constitutions (except in Delaware), the documents are longer and less flexible than the U.S. Constitution.

Governors. Except for the roles of chief diplomat and symbolic leader, governors fill many of the roles a president does. Governors are even commanders in chief of their state national guards; the president, though, can nationalize guard units whenever necessary.

Certainly, governors are the chief executives of their states. It is true, though, that they usually must share a greater proportion of their power with other elected executive department officials. In fact, lieutenant governors, secretaries of state, attorneys general, and state treasurers may even be from a different party than the governor. The civil service systems mandate merit (not political views) for selecting and promoting career public officials. This further limits a governor's control over the executive branch.

In any event, governors can be quite influential in shaping state policy. They can issue executive orders, deliver state of the state messages to their legislatures, exercise their veto powers (except in North Carolina), and disperse political patronage. In 43 states, a particularly effective tool is available—the **item veto**. This is a power that not even the president has. It allows governors to veto specific provisions in a money bill they find otherwise satisfactory.

New York, Illinois, and Hawaii have probably given their governors the most formal authority, while Texas and West Virginia have allowed their chief executives the least. But, as we learned in Chapter 4, power depends at least as much on the *person* as the position. Few political observers would call Bill Clements of Texas and Jay Rockefeller of West Virginia weak governors.

Governors serve either two-year or four-year terms. Most are limited to two terms.

Legislatures. Again, rough comparison to national government counterparts are appropriate. Except for Nebraska's single house, all states have **bicameral legislatures** (two chambers), like the U.S. Congress. Leadership positions within state legislatures parallel Congress, too.

Therefore, it is easier to note exceptions than similarities. Presidents pro tempore in state senates generally have far more power than their counterparts in the U.S. Senate. Seniority in state legislatures is less important in determining committee assignments and chairmanships. State legislators usually do not make a career of serving in their legislatures.

Among the special interest groups, school teachers and labor are particularly effective. In the last decade, as the scope and influence of state action has risen, business lobbyists have begun to pay more attention than ever to the state legislatures.

As with structure and procedures, the behavior and motivation of state legislators closely parallels that of members of Congress. Keenly interested in reelection, state legislators spend a great deal of time providing services to constituents. (For example, they make sure the branches from an elm tree are picked up after an ice storm.) And they spend much time making sure they vote "correctly" on the handful of critical votes they face each year. (For example, should a prison be built in their district?) Pork barrels abound in state capitols. They range from state funding for a national track and field hall of fame to subsidizing a chronically flooded historical site. Such projects are often lumped together; few could pass standing alone. And, finally, there are the grandstand bills. These are pieces of pretentious legislation that have no chance of passage but show the folks back home that *their* representative is really trying.

Political parties. Despite the gains of the Republican party in the 1980 elections at the federal level, the party did only fair at the state level. Republicans picked up just half of the 400 seats they hoped to gain, and they won control of only a handful of state legislative chambers. This does not bode well for the future of the G.O.P., since there will be fewer good potential candidates in the Republican "farm system" than party leaders desired, and less control over reapportionment.

After the 1980 election, this is how party control of state legislatures looked:

Democrats Control Both Houses in 29 States:

Oregon	Florida
California	Georgia
Nevada	Tennessee
Texas	Kentucky
New Mexico	North Carolina
Oklahoma	South Carolina
Minnesota	West Virginia
Wisconsin	Maryland
Missouri	Delaware
Arkansas	Connecticut
Louisiana	Rhode Island
Mississippi	Virginia
Alabama	New Jersey
Michigan	Hawaii
Massachusetts	

Republicans Control Both Houses in 15 States:

Montana	Indiana
Idaho	Pennsylvania
Arizona	Wyoming
Utah	Vermont
Colorado	Kansas
North Dakota	New Hampshire
South Dakota	Iowa

Neither Party Controls Both Houses in 5 States:

Washington	Ohio
Illinois	Maine
New York	Nebraska
Alaska	

In 1980, Republicans riding the Reagan tide won seven of 13 gubernatorial contests and sliced Democratic control of statehouses to its lowest point in a decade. The results gave the Republican party 23 governorships and cut the Democrats to 27. But G.O.P. officials controlled both legislative and executive in only 12 states.

Obviously, the effectiveness of many of these Republican governors in shaping state policy is undermined by the relative dominance by Democrats of state legislatures (as noted above).

Local Government

Institutional setting. As pointed out earlier, there are nearly 80,000 units of local government in the United States distributed among five categories—municipalities, counties, towns and townships, school districts, and special districts.

In 1979, local governments spent 233 billion

dollars, equal to 43 percent of federal spending. About half of that went to pay 9.4 million employees. The 1979 ratio of 1 local-government worker for every 23 Americans compares with about 1 for every 53 residents in 1940.

Education remains local government's biggest expense—in 1979 comprising 37.8 percent of total budgets. Other major items, were utilities (11.4 percent of all expenditures), health and hospitals (6.2 percent), public welfare (5 percent), highways (4.9 percent), and sanitation (4.9 percent).

Figure 10–5 shows the three basic forms of city government in the United States. But organizational charts seldom tell the full story about who has the power to decide.

Most of the nation's largest cities are mayor–council cities (see Figure 10–5A). The earliest form of American municipal government, it follows American tradition of separating legislative and executive powers. Mayor and council are elected separately. The mayor is elected by all of the city's voters; members of the council may be elected at large (by all the city's voters) or by wards (specific election districts). "Strong" mayors have authority over the executive agencies of city government; they exercise substantial power over budget making; and they may have a veto over council actions. "Weak" mayors share control of the executive with other elected city officials (e.g., city attorney and collector comptroller); they have less budget-making power and lack veto power.

The **commission form of city government** combines legislative and executive powers in a small body (see Figure 10–5B). The mayor sits on the commission, first among equals; the commissioners may take turns holding the office. The individual commissioners are responsible for the operation of specific city departments and agencies. Unanimity of members on policy is often difficult to achieve. American cities are widely abandoning the commission system.

In the council–manager form of government, the elected council decides policy (see Figure 10–5C). The **city manager** is a professional appointed by the council. He or she has the re-

FIGURE 10-5
Forms of City Governments

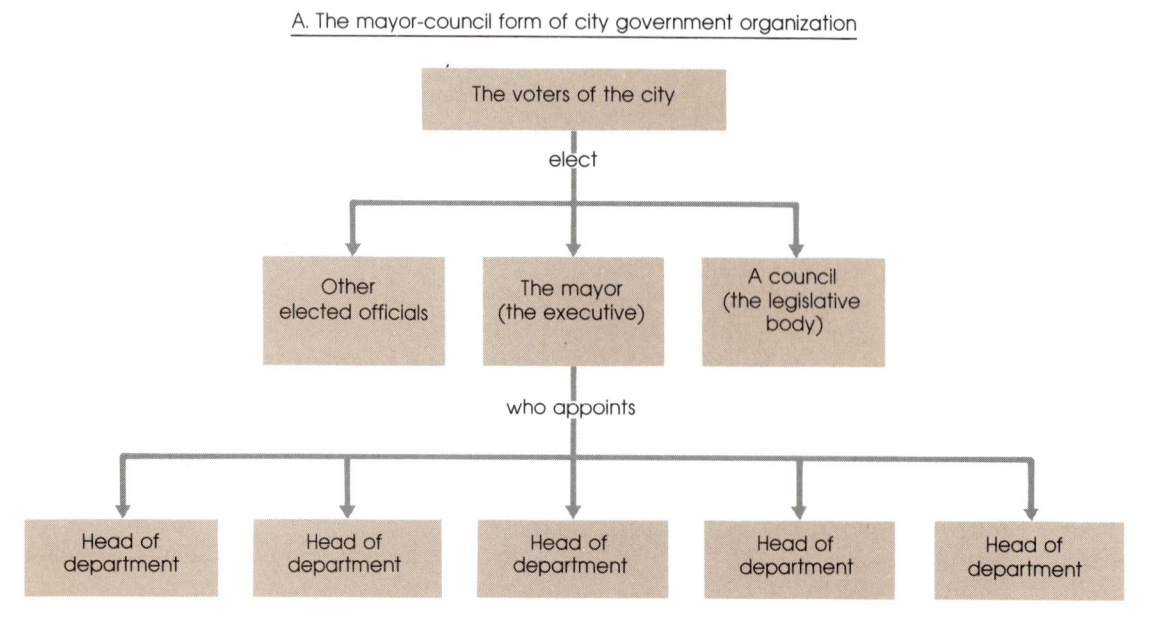

A. The mayor-council form of city government organization

```
                The voters of the city
                         |
                       elect
         ┌───────────────┼───────────────┐
         ▼               ▼               ▼
      Other           The mayor        A council
   elected officials (the executive) (the legislative
                                         body)
                         |
                    who appoints
     ┌──────────┬────────┼────────┬──────────┐
     ▼          ▼        ▼        ▼          ▼
  Head of   Head of   Head of   Head of   Head of
 department department department department department
```

FIGURE 10-5 (continued)

B. The comission form of city government organization

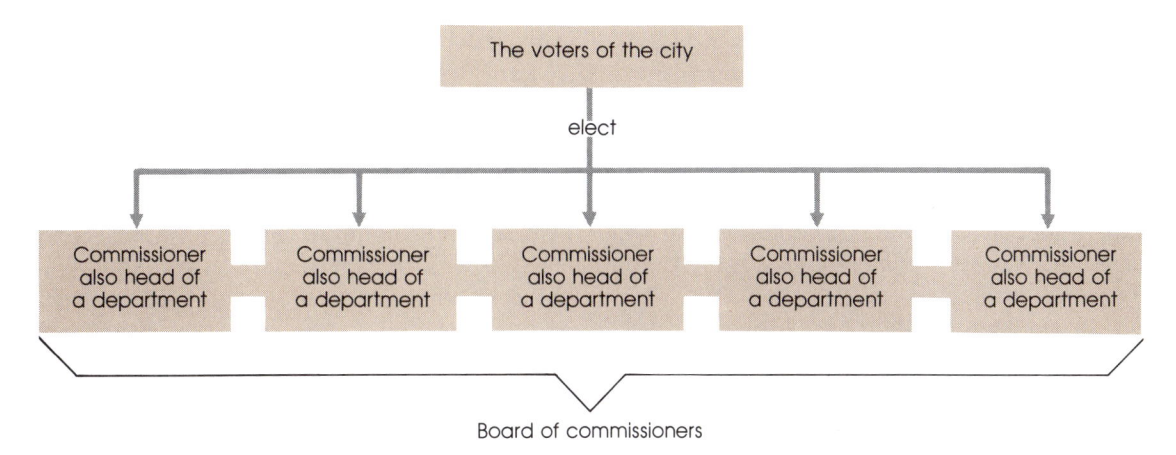

```
The voters of the city
        │
      elect
        │
┌───────┬───────┬───────┬───────┐
▼       ▼       ▼       ▼       ▼
Commissioner  Commissioner  Commissioner  Commissioner  Commissioner
also head of  also head of  also head of  also head of  also head of
a department  a department  a department  a department  a department

Board of commissioners
```

C. The city manager form of city government organization

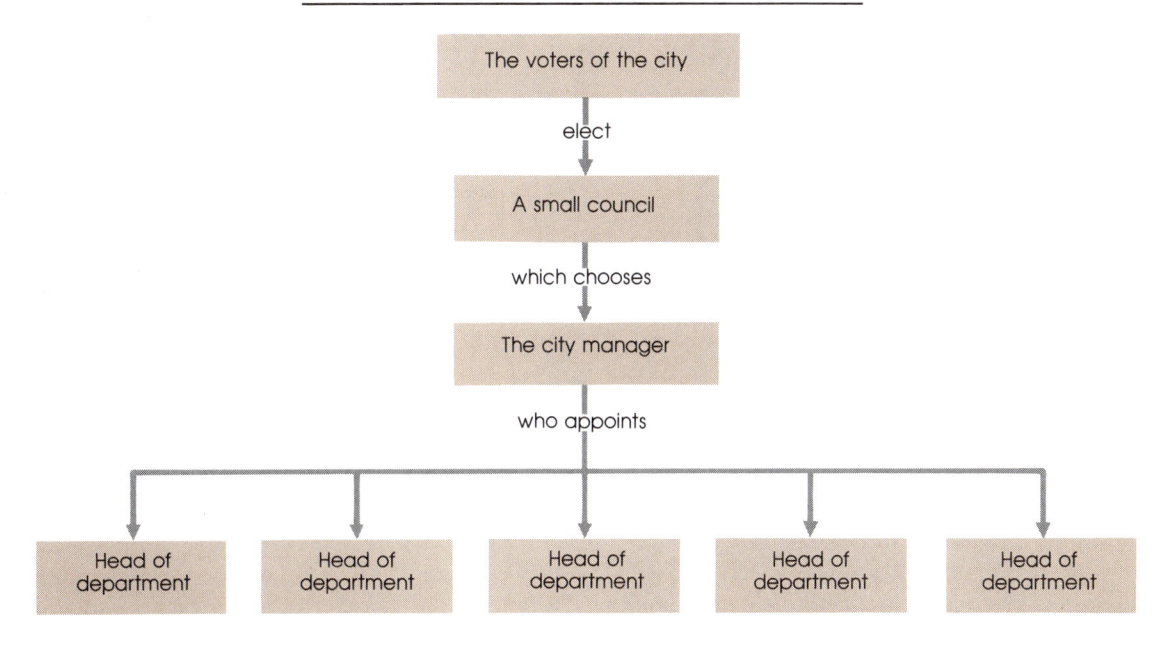

```
The voters of the city
        │
      elect
        ▼
   A small council
        │
   which chooses
        ▼
  The city manager
        │
   who appoints
        │
┌───────┬───────┬───────┬───────┐
▼       ▼       ▼       ▼       ▼
Head of  Head of  Head of  Head of  Head of
department department department department department
```

sponsibility for executive administration. The manager has the power to hire and fire personnel of most major city departments within limits set by any existing merit system. For cities of 5,000 to 500,000 residents, this is the fastest growing form of government.

Though cities may be the best-known form of local government, counties house the most Americans. Nearly 90 percent of the population lives in 3,042 counties. The traditional functions of counties have been law enforcement, judicial administration, road construction and maintenance, the keeping of public records, welfare, and, in some areas, administration of schools. But counties today, particularly in urban areas, also have assumed duties once performed mainly by overburdened municipalities.

County government comes in several forms, but the most popular is the commission form, used in 79 percent of the nation's counties. Voters elect a board of commissioners whose members have both legislative and executive powers. The commissioners, sometimes called supervisors, share power with other elected officials such as the sheriff, prosecutor, clerk, and coroner.

While the number of counties has held steady, the number of towns and townships—created to serve defined areas without regard to population—has dropped to under 17,000, or 2,000 fewer than 35 years ago. Township government, once the centerpiece of rural life, has declined in much of the Midwest and Middle Atlantic area. But the New England town has remained a vital form of local government that still features the town meeting, at which voters assemble to decide such issues as taxes, budgets, and bond issues.

In contrast to townships, **special districts** are growing rapidly. Excluding school districts—which, strictly speaking, are a form of special district—the number of units has jumped from 8,299 in 1942 to nearly 26,000 today. They range from the Port Authority of New York and New Jersey—which runs tunnels, bridges, airports, and the World Trade Center on an annual budget of nearly one billion dollars—to tiny districts dealing with historic preservation and mosquito control.

Two factors account for the growth of special districts. First, they generally are not bound by tax and debt limits that states often set for other forms of local government. Second, they allow several neighboring jurisdictions to spread out the cost of expensive services (such as sewers). But there is a price in all this: Because special districts fragment local government, they make the coordination of services difficult.

Problems of urban life. Since World War I, the United States has been an urban nation. Today, almost 75 percent of all Americans live on 2 percent of the land area. A majority of them crowd the 276 areas defined as metropolitan areas by the U.S. government. Most of the nation's wealth and most of the social, cultural, educational, and political forces are centered in its cities. Thus the condition and future of the American federal system—indeed, the republic—depends on the viability of urban areas.

What are the problems that must be managed to insure that long-term viability? The nation's urban areas suffer many specific deficiencies. Included among them are: inadequate housing, congestion and ineffective transportation, pollution (not only of air and water but also of the land itself as the solid wastes of a throwaway society mount steadily), lack of open spaces for recreational purposes, crime and delinquency, and declining standards in central city schools.

In big-city slums, life is today often worse than it was in the 1960s, when riots ripped through them. Black unemployment in 1981 was nearly double the rate for blacks in the 1960s. Almost 40 percent of all black teenagers in the job market are unemployed. Many observers find the inner cities filled with an unhealthy mixture of cynicism, anger, disillusionment, and frustration. The consequence could be either riots (as occurred in Miami in 1980) or implosion (with crime, alcoholism, ghetto alienation, and despair growing steadily). In short, many blacks in the inner cities feel they have no stake in society.

There are three basic reasons such problems persist. First, and most obvious, the national economy has not performed well for the past decade. The riots of the 1960s came at a time of heightened aspirations for all blacks. These aspirations were brought about by a booming economy and gains of the civil rights movement.

Second, while most government revenues are those of the national government, solutions to urban problems for the most part must be paid for by state and local governments. Their less responsive revenue systems have left them behind rising demands for expenditures. Problems to be met in education, law enforcement, and sanitation are among the severest in inner cities.

Third, even if sufficient funds were available, solutions to urban problems would remain difficult. Urban America lacks the governmental institutions to act effectively. The system of local government in the United States has changed little from that of 17th-century England, from which it was adopted. Today, counties, cities, and towns fragment power in metropolitan areas. Clearly, this makes the management of large-scale, complex problems nearly impossible. A "typical" metropolitan area has some 90 units of general and special purpose government; this "typical" area includes two counties, 13 townships, 21 municipalities, 18 school districts, 31 special districts or authorities, 3 or 4 federally supported planning districts, and 1 regional council of governments (see Figure 10–6).

With all this proliferation, there is little match between the extent of the urban problems to be solved and the power of government jurisdictions to solve them. States are now in the process of reversing the trend. But they have been slow to use their legal, administrative,

FIGURE 10–6

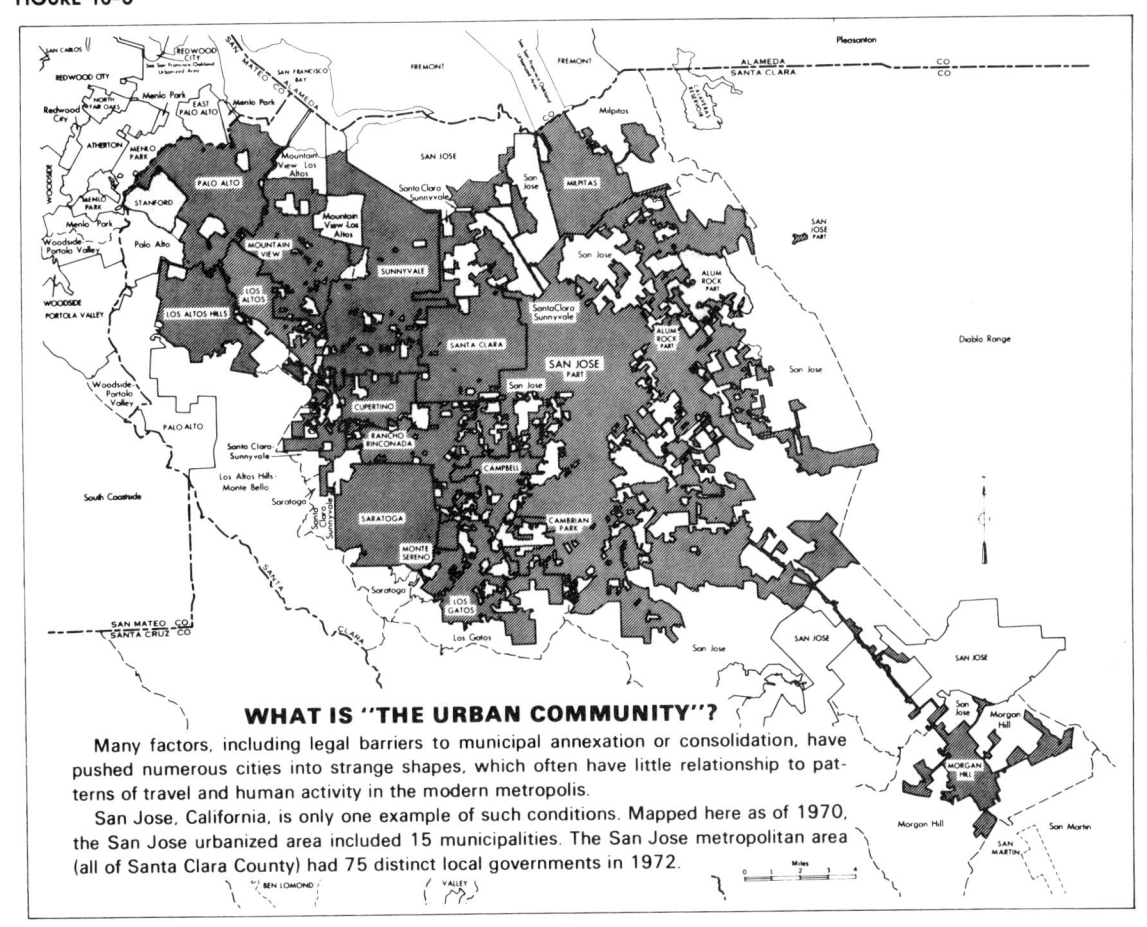

WHAT IS "THE URBAN COMMUNITY"?

Many factors, including legal barriers to municipal annexation or consolidation, have pushed numerous cities into strange shapes, which often have little relationship to patterns of travel and human activity in the modern metropolis.

San Jose, California, is only one example of such conditions. Mapped here as of 1970, the San Jose urbanized area included 15 municipalities. The San Jose metropolitan area (all of Santa Clara County) had 75 distinct local governments in 1972.

Advisory Commission on Intergovernmental Relations (1976).

and fiscal powers to rationalize urban government. Over the years, they have generally restricted annexation powers, while tolerating unrestricted incorporation procedures. Nor have the states for the most part been quick to alleviate such urban problems within their reach as inner city and suburban fiscal disparities, the general weakness of county governments, and chaotic local land use practices.

The federal government has tried to strengthen the multijurisdictional focus of its many grant programs. It has done so by instituting procedures requiring review and comment by state and area officials on applications in grant programs. The major vehicle for this coordination are **councils of government** (COG). Yet many federal departments and agencies continue to ignore the economic, migrational, and locational implications of their operations within metropolitan areas. Several federal programs have actually added to the proliferation of metropolitan organizations.

The politics of urban America. The conventional wisdom is that city politicians try to balance local special interest groups to ensure their reelection. Certainly, this was true of machine politics. It attracted votes and controlled elections by offering social services, patronage, and favors to the urban masses. But today, political machines and bosses are less prominent.

Increasingly active in American city politics today are conservative reformers and liberal reformers.[6] The former act to achieve greater efficiency, rather than to balance special interests against each other. The latter tend to act to extend democratic participation. If this analysis is correct, urban groups must do more than merely vote, as in the old days of political machines, to protect their interests. Because reformers will sometimes act counter to the balance of forces, every group must seek the power to make policy.

This tendency is increasingly evident in the "neighborhood movement." These movements have appeared in cities as diverse as San Antonio, Chicago, Cleveland, Atlanta, Baltimore, Dallas, and Boston. They are reshaping political life in state after state. Their names are a jungle of abbreviations and acronyms: AID (Against Investment Discrimination) in Brooklyn; NWBCCC (North West Bronx Community and Clergy Coalition); CBBB (Citizens to Bring Broadway Back) in Cleveland; ROBBED (Residents Organized for Better and Beautiful Environmental Development) in San Antonio; PAR (Playland Area Residence) in Council Bluffs, Iowa; UWE–COACT (United West End–Citizens Organization Acting Together) in Duluth, Minn.; and so on.

Coalitions of neighborhood groups have won passage of strong legislation on such issues as bank mortgage lending practices. At the national level, the neighborhood lobby has succeeded in winning a series of laws and regulatory changes. These changes are intended to restrict the actions of big government and big business on residential areas. At the local level, these community groups may oppose school busing, make alliances with black homeowners, and patrol against criminals simultaneously. Some neighborhood activists have helped form a major base for a new generation of urban politicians. Many, however, have stayed away from political involvement.

Small, unstructured, decentralized, activist, and basically nonideological, the neighborhood movement may be one of the forces helping to fashion the politics of the 1980s. In any event, through involvement, formerly silent people are learning that they can exercise some control over their lives.

What can we call this tendency of urban groups, especially among underrepresented groups such as blacks and the poor, to take a direct hand in policy formulation? Yates aptly names it "street-fighting pluralism."[7] Its consequences should not be ignored. Bluntly, it means that the weak, fragmented administrative capacity of modern cities is experiencing political overload. It means that new policy initiatives are ripped apart in the fight between rival political interests.

FUTURE FILE

Urban Catastrophe or Urban Renaissance?

The City in Science Fiction

Science fiction gives us a range of possibilities and a warning about matters we perhaps do not take seriously enough. One would not have to survey science fiction literature long to find warnings for urbanites. Early science fiction predicted cities replete with spaghetti bowl networks of elevated highways and monorails carrying Buck Rogers-style automobiles around and through gleaming mile-high towers; contemporary science fiction novels are totalitarian nightmares of pollution and alienation.

In John Brunner's *Shock Wave Rider,* machines have taken over. Chicago has become in effect one giant computer. The plot concerns a robot that finds some frozen human beings in tubes and tries to figure out what use they ever could have had. The message here is that cities are dehumanizing and impersonal.

Overpopulation is another typical theme. In

NASA

City of the future? NASA artist's concept of the interior of a huge space colony. Stationed a quarter of a million miles from earth and constructed almost entirely of ore mined from the moon, the colony would contain a population of 10,000. The inhabitants would live and work in an earth-like environment inside a vast wheel more than a mile in diameter. Trees, grassy parks, birds, even streams and ponds, would help provide a familiar setting. Beneath the upper living area would be a level of offices, stores, service buildings, as well as facilities for light industry.

The World Inside by Robert Silverberg, the hero lives in ChiPitt, a dense megalopolis stretching from Chicago to Pittsburgh. Every acre of open land must be farmed to provide food for the world's burgeoning populace.

In Harry Harison's *Make Room! Make Room!*—the basis of the movie *Soylent Green*—older people are exterminated to ease crowding. The hero discovers his city's disturbing solution to the food problem—the bodies of the elderly are being made into food.

The whole world is a city in Silverberg's *Getting Across*. Somebody has stolen the computer program that runs everything. The characters struggle to find manual methods to run the air conditioning and get rid of garbage and discover their police are robots. It is our urban world gone mad.

In *City* by Clifford D. Simak, the opposite has happened. Cities have vanished altogether. This story is written from the standpoint of a man who has never experienced cities. He wonders what in the world they could have been and why people would have lived that way.

The City According to the Experts

According to urban experts, the reality of cities of the future is more prosaic than science fiction would have us believe. Less beset by the social problems of the 1960s and 1970s, future cities will be rebuilt to be more efficient and livable places. Already a number of trends are working to ease the pressure on cities. The migration of poor people into major cities has stopped; the size of families is declining; the teenage population is shrinking, which means less crime; the work force is also shrinking, which means a greater availability of jobs.

But neither technology nor events will generate a massive migration from the suburbs back to the cities. In 30 years or so our big cities will have become small or medium-sized, with few exceptions. Silverberg's ChiPitt (Chicago to Pittsburgh) is such an exception. Other "supercities" might include BosWash (Boston to Washington) and San San (San Francisco to San Diego).

One reason a full-scale revival of big U.S. cities seems unlikely is technology. New forms of transportation and communication are destroying many of the time and money savings that dense central cities offered. Faster, cheaper, transportation and newer, more versatile telecommunication let businesses operate over wider areas.

Another reason a full-scale revival seems unlikely is social. Many Americans believe the disadvantages of urban life—higher prices, more crime, etc.—outweigh such advantages as diversity and cultural richness. The process of suburbanization did not occur against anyone's will.

Finally, there is no reason to assume that the big cities of the Sun Belt will continue to grow and prosper while those of the Snow Belt de-

Wide World Photos

Within the remnants of some older cities, young-to-middle-aged affluent whites want to be near their downtown offices. Therefore, they are forming vibrant kernels for the cities of the next century. The question of what will happen to the poor whites, blacks, and Hispanics—who are being squeezed out of their old neighborhoods (above)—remains unresolved. Nevertheless, it is clear that the economic and social organization of the American city is undergoing fundamental change. By the early 1980s, the onset of the future city has become visible.

cline. The competitive edge of the South and West is already eroding. Many of its areas are arid, with insufficient water to sustain both farming and industry. Labor costs are approaching northern levels. The rise of an advanced electronics industry in rural New England shows that northern industrial decline need not be inevitable when the flow of federal funds to the cities is slowed. Cities such as Houston, Miami, and Atlanta now have greater social drawbacks than Minneapolis. Industries tend to go where the environment is most pleasant, which usually means away from cities—whether they are in the South, West, or North—to areas with recreational opportunities.

Political Decisions

It is worth recalling at this point Aristotle's observation that politics is the master science. Political decisions—as much as any economic, technological, or social trends—will shape the city of tomorrow. Whether cities become important centers of their regions will hinge on how much federal and state governments put forward a consistent urban policy to deliberately strengthen the city.

New initiatives. One of the most important anthropologists of the 20th century, Bronislaw Malinowski, tells us about the beliefs of the Trobriand Islanders of Melanesia. This tribe believed that the gods of the rain forest would destroy their villages unless appeased by animal sacrifices and the ritual destruction of property. For the last few decades, many urban experts seemed to have held similar superstitions. They believed American cities would be destroyed unless the gods were appeased by the ritual expansion of government social programs. Malinowski never reported how many pigs were sacrificed or how many artifacts were burned. The Office of Management and Budget, though, knows how much government has spent on urban development projects and jobs programs (such as CETA—Comprehensive Employment and Training Act). Between 1967 and 1980, the amounts were $76 billion and $67 billion.

Yet these same experts argue that cities today are worse off than ever. At least, the Trobriand Islanders could claim success. No village was ever lost to an angry rain forest god.

In what follows, we will look at what new initiatives might be tried, and might even work, to combat the ills of American cities. But regardless of what is tried in the next two decades, one fact is certain: America's cities can never be healthy until the economy is healthy. Inner-city residents and suburbanites alike can have neither dignity nor earning power if they do not have jobs. When reading the eight suggestions that follow, please keep this in mind: The greatest contribution government can make to curing the ills of the city is to curb inflation, end recession, and put people to work. (This awesome task is the subject of Chapter 13.)

Suggestion 1: Public policy should protect and foster mediating structures. Sociologists Peter L. Berger and Richard John Neuhaus define "mediating structures" as those institutions closest to the control and aspirations of most Americans. Examples are family, neighborhood, church, voluntary association, and ethnic and racial subcultures (*To Empower People* [Washington, D.C.: American Enterprise Institute, 1978]). Public policy should not only foster and protect these institutions, it should also use them to advance legitimate social goals in the areas of education and child care, criminal justice, housing and zoning, welfare and social services, and health care.

Take the family. What happens when public policy comes to be perceived as contradicting the meaning and values that family life embodies? What happens, for example, "when welfare policies have the effect of disrupting the family rather than helping to hold it together; or when the educational system imposes a worldview on children that is inimical to the values of the families from which they came; or when the health delivery system deprives the parents of handicapped children of decision and choice?" The results, according to Berger and Neuhaus, is a sense of powerlessness, anger, and more negative feelings about American governments.

By reversing these trends, government can

restore the mediating function to the family. This would be good for two reasons. First, mediating institutions provide a place where the individual knows who he or she is and can feel at home in a sometimes troublesome world. Second, a mediating institution "provides meanings and values by which the larger society appears to be something more than a practical arrangement." This second function, though subtle, is especially important in a democracy. Unless government has a meaningful relationship with mediating institutions such as family, church, neighborhood, or subculture, government either claims all values for itself or becomes valueless.

Suggestion 2: Improve the productivity in delivery of services. Improving productivity—or efficiency—simply means to increase output or results for the same amount of resources used. For example, it may once have taken a crew of three to handle trash pickup; with mechanical help it might require only two. Several government agencies can purchase goods in bulk and receive a discount. Or they can merge communication centers and crime laboratories. Police departments can use civilians or reserves to handle routine chores. The list of possibilities is limitless.

Suggestion 3: Contract with private firms. A number of cities, among them San Francisco, have begun contracting out some or all of their park maintenance and recreational services to private firms. Rochester, New York, contracts out its street maintenance, building maintenance, vehicle maintenance, and parking garages. Envirotech, Inc., of Menlo Park, California, operates wastewater treatment plants on a guaranteed-performance basis. Municipal computer services in such cities as Newark, New Jersey, and Torrance, California, as well as Orange County, California, have been turned over entirely to a private firm, Computer Sciences Corporation.

The basic question about contracting is who can provide a given service cheaper—government or business?

Suggestion 4: Create two-tiered government. The lack of balance between a city and its suburbs is one of the major causes of urban decline. Few cities are better off than their suburbs (Richard Nathan and Paul Dommel, "Understanding the Urban Predicament," *Brookings Bulletin*, Nos. 1 and 2 [1977]). The boundaries of the unhealthiest cities have remained largely unchanged for several generations. In contrast, newer and "healthier" cities such as Phoenix and Houston *have* been able to expand geographically. They have thereby increased their "resource base."

Therefore, federal subsidies without structural relief may have only a limited effect. Ailing cities should realign their function, if not their boundaries, to share in the wealth of more affluent areas. For example, Portland, Oregon, recently established a regional government. It embraces parts of three counties and has the power to do such things as to scatter low-income housing and to order a community to accept a garbage dump. If it works as planned, the Portland area is headed for a two-tiered government of the kind that has been held up as a goal for urban areas that spread over several jurisdictions. One level would be municipal, county, and other local jurisdictions providing such basic services as police protection and schools. The other would be the regional government; it would have authority in land use, transportation, air and water quality, water supply, sewerage, waste disposal and cultural activities. One level would preserve local autonomy. The other would coordinate financial policy. Voters would send representatives to both the local and regional jurisdictions.

Such attempts have gone nowhere in some cities (Rochester, Denver, and Tampa). However, the governments of Los Angeles City and Los Angeles County and of Miami and Dade County come close to the two-tiered ideal.

Suggestion 5: Lift regulations from inner-city areas to boost development. Dubbed "enterprise zones" by proponents, the concept is relatively straightforward: Remove most zoning, taxation, and fedeal and local business regulations from carefully defined inner-city districts. The upshot, in the eyes of the proponents, would be to encourage new industrial and commercial development, including jobs, in those same areas. One key criterion for the zone, however, would be that firms must employ at least 50 percent of their work force from the zone area to qualify for most of the various tax reductions. Other firms with a smaller percentage of the work force from the area would have more limited tax advantages.

President Reagan made the enterprise zone one of the cornerstones of his urban political agenda. But support for the special zones goes beyond the Republican party. An unusual coalition of blacks, conservative economists, socialists, urban planners, and liberal officeholders is taking shape to push a bold new effort to save central cities from urban blight. In fact, a version of the concept in the House of Representatives is cosponsored by conservative New York Republican Jack Kemp and liberal Democrat Robert Garcia. (Garcia's district encompasses the South Bronx, one of the most blighted urban areas in the United States.) The bill's sponsors estimate it would cost $1.4 billion in lost federal revenue in a year. They say, however, some of the money might be returned to the Treasury through increased income-tax revenues from people who get new jobs. Proponents say the zones would be less costly and more effective than stop-and-go federal jobs programs.

Suggestion 6: Manage growth. Residential growth management means that a city consciously steers new residential growth into urban areas that are already served by public facilities and city staff. By maximizing the use of existing fire stations, libraries, and parks, and their presently employed staff, a city can achieve greater efficiency. Also, substantial savings result from not having to build and staff prematurely in remote and sparsely populated parts of the city.

Actually, this suggestion is nothing but an extension of the older concept of **zoning.** For decades, state and local government have tried to control land use through a policy that specifies acceptable and unacceptable uses of land. Zoning regulates the location of industry and apartments and specifies various construction requirements.

Suggestion 7: Invest to upgrade the labor force. When minority youths cannot get jobs, everyone suffers. The effects are lost productivity; taxes for welfare, medical care, social services; crime and the costs of police, courts, and prisons; and cynicism and distrust among those who have been rejected from the world of work. Excess unemployment costs the nation, by conservative estimates about $200 billion a year in lost output alone.

Black Teenage Unemployment (over a quarter century)

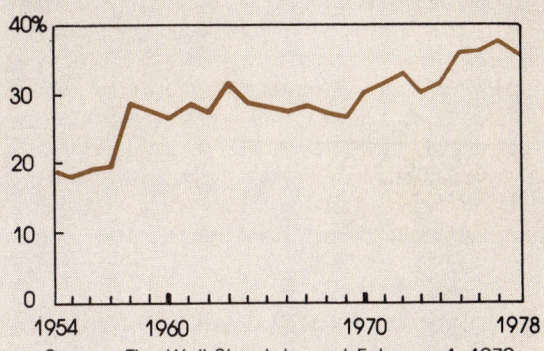

Source: *The Wall Street Journal,* February 1, 1979, p. 40.

In the past, the federal governments major line of attack on unemployment was the use of CETA. It provides states and municipalities with funds to hire the unemployed for public service jobs, such as playground supervisors or road crew laborers. CETA funding doubled during the Carter presidency, to more than $11 billion in fiscal year 1979. The program, however, was at best a stopgap substitute for welfare. It took the jobless off the streets but did not prepare them for permanent employment. Much of the money was spent on programs like scraping graffiti off telephone poles rather than skill training for specific jobs. In 1981, the new Reagan Administration made deep cuts in CETA funding.

What is to be done? Aside from the overarching task of getting the American economic machine back on track, other lines of attack on high unemployment are possible. One is cheap and quick; the other is expensive and long-term.

The quick, cheap solution is to lower, remove, or restructure the minimum wage. To the extent that federal law pegs all wages at a certain level, business firms do not hire millions of men and women with limited skills. A large body of evidence reveals a statistically significant rise in unemployment associated with a rise in the minimum wage level or coverage. One study, for example, found that a 1 percent increase in the wage reduces the teenage share of employment by 0.3 percent (Finis Welch, "Minimum Wage Legislation in the U.S.," *Economic Inquiry*, September 1974).

The other solution is for the United States to view the work force as a form of "capital." It must be trained and retrained on a continuing basis to supply the changing spectrum of sophisticated skills needed by a high-technology nation. West Germany, for example, gives every adult the right to up to two years of full-time training or retraining. Needless to say, this labor force investment policy is quite different from the low-skill CETA program.

Suggestion 8: Encourage voluntarism. Suppose government were to meet every need that can be identified—for mental illness, drug abuse, child care, nursing homes, training programs, etc. It would have to triple existing government activity at the state, local, and federal level.

Consider police activity. How many police would have to be hired to insure adequate safety? There is an alternative. Citizens could assume a greater degree of responsibility for their own defense and protection. For example, in Santa Ana, California, a police chief inaugurated a community-oriented police program. It involved the community, through neighborhood meetings and block captains, in their own security along with the activities of the police. In New York City, Curtis Sliwa formed the Guardian Angels to patrol the subways. Their approach is a show of numbers and uniforms rather than physical force. Sliwa's troops wear red berets as they patrol for six or eight hours each night on the subway trains in four boroughs and in Central Park. They travel in groups of from 6 to 20 and carry no weapons. As of mid-1981, the Guardian Angels numbered 142—males and females, blacks, whites, Hispanics, and Orientals, ages 16 to 28.

Governor Edmund G. Brown, Jr., of California put the case for voluntarism this way during a speech in 1977:

> There is no substitute for neighborhoods, for mutual-support systems in the private sector. Whether it be neighbors who know each other, who have some responsibility for someone other than themselves and their family—you can't get away from it. The idea that you can put it on government, if you want to, is going to triple your taxes because then you have to hire a full-time person who doesn't have the commitment involved in it that you would do that kind of work.
>
> That's my simple message: that voluntarism is not a luxury, it is a necessity for a civilized society that wants to truly meet its human needs. And we have to expand it in a dramatic way across a broad front of government and human activity. We have to find some way to recreate the spirit of neighborliness and mutual self-support that existed before the mobility and the anonymity and increasing information flow that has been the product of this very prosperous society.

By way of conclusion, I should like to return to one of the central themes of this book—power. In a sense, to study federalism is to study where and how a nation concentrates its political power. Today, as in colonial times, many Americans think that too much responsibility is on the shoulders of national leaders, especially the president. One way to change this situation

Wide World Photos

Guardian Angels on patrol in a New York City subway train.

for the better, they argue, is to transfer some of that power to the leaders of local communities.

These Americans agree with Alexis de Tocqueville's insistence that "intermediate" authorities, which impose themselves between Washington and the people, often constitute the sort of authorities people respect. Tocqueville never traveled far enough nor lived long enough to visit that most compelling and magical of places, San Francisco. But I think it is the sort of thing he had in mind, despite its illogical design. While few American communities have Victorian architecture, perpetual autumn climate, breathtaking beauty, and cosmopolitan urbanity, to Tocqueville such communities are all the real foundations of freedom.

Chapter Key

Federalism exists when two or more levels of government rule the same people, with each level having at least one area in which it sets policy independently of the other. Federalism was originally justified as a means of preventing tyranny; it was a price to be paid for a union of large and small states. This is perhaps the major reason the West German constitution established a strong federal system after World War II. Had there been one in place before the war the rise of Hitler probably would have been more difficult. We may say that there are few Hitlers stalking the land today; but we must also remember that the founding fathers were not designing a system for a single day, a single decade, or even a century.

A debate in contemporary federalism concerns the administrative effectiveness of a federal system. Because of the federal system there is often confusion caused by the existence of diverse state laws and added layers of bureaucracy. But federalism can be defended on the grounds that in a large nation diverse laws are necessary. Further, the states can act as laboratories of democracy. They can test ideas that, if successful, could be copied on a national level. The states also provide a training ground for many of our national leaders.

Despite increased dependence on federal aid, state and local governments are still important policymakers. They regulate much economic activity. State laws regulate the chartering of corporations and the licensing of barber shops; and set rates for insurance and phone service and electricity. Counties and cities control land use through zoning laws. Many states have established laws to protect consumers and environment. The four major functions of state and local government (at least in terms of spending) are education, public welfare, transportation, and health care.

State and local governments get about one fifth of their funds from federal grants-in-aid, block grants, and revenue sharing. The federal government formulates the basic policy for which grants-in-aid funds will be used; state and local governments, though, administer the programs. Either state, local, or federal officials may initially propose programs for grants-in-aid funding. The federal government provides block grants to state and local governments for broad functions; state and local officials, though, have more discretion on how to use the funds than they have with grants-in-aid. Under the revenue sharing program, state and local administrators have even more discretion in selecting and administering programs.

Who has the power in state and local governments? In contrast to the federal government with its 536 elected officials (537 if one counts the vice president), power is dispersed among 490,265 state and local officials. This dispersion plus fragmented parties makes access easier but change harder.

Unlike the federal Constitution, state constitutions tend to be poorly written, poorly organized, and fairly inflexible documents. To varying degrees, state legislatures control constitutional change. Existing arrangements tend to preserve the status quo. The 1970s did witness, however, a number of political reforms and modernization efforts in state legislatures. Today most legislatures are more accountable to the people and better prepared to handle the public policy issues. Direct legislative procedures, especially the initiative petition, are a prominent part of the legislative process, especially in the West. Other direct procedures, such as the referendum and the recall, are also available to voters in some states.

Governors are playing increasingly complex roles in the federal system. Among their formal powers, designing the state budget and appointing people in the state administration and court system are the most important.

Because constitutional power is vested in the states, cities, towns, and counties act as agents of the state. The most common forms of government at the city level are the mayor–council or the council–manager (city manager) plans. Mayor–council governments generally have a strong mayor and partisan city elections and operate with a ward system. City–manager cities generally select the mayor from the council and operate with at-large and nonpartisan election arrangements. The most common form of government at the county level is the commission. Finally, the past few decades have witnessed a tremendous growth in the number of special districts formed to provide special-purpose functions for several communities in an area.

Few things in America last forever. What many people see as the crisis of the cities is largely a shift of population—from the city to suburbs, from the Northeast to the South and West. Nevertheless, a number of things can be done to improve the quality of urban life, other than using federal funds as an artificial life support system. Among the suggestions are these: Foster mediating structures (e.g., voluntary associations); improve productivity of city administration; create a two-tiered government; encourage "enterprise zones" in central city districts; and upgrade the labor force.

Coda: Coping with Government

cō′ da, n. [from Latin *cauda*, tail.] a passage of more or less independent character introduced after the completion of the essential parts of a composition, so as to form a more definite and satisfactory conclusion.

Liberty means responsibility. That is why most men dread it.

George Bernard Shaw

© BEELDRECHT, Amsterdam/ VAGA, New York. Collection Haags Gemeentemuseum

The three levels of American government loom large in most of our lives. You experience local government when you try to get heavy trash collected, a traffic light installed, or a nude modeling studio closed (or reopened). You experience state government when you stand in line to get a driver's license. You experience federal government when you pry loose your grandmother's overdue social security check or pay someone to prepare your income tax return.

Faced with this growing presence, one can do one of three things: Submit to government edicts; trust elected officials and Common Cause to reform bureaucracy; or learn to cope with bureaucrats and their encroachments.

The first alternative is tempting. The average American wants to avoid the bounce game. You become a bouncee when your phone call is shunted indiscriminately from one government agency to another—accompanied by that maddening refrain, "Oh, we can't handle that in this office. You need to speak to . . ."

The second alternative is as appealing as it is naive. Proposals to reform the bureaucracy are as regular and frequent as the full moon. One of the oldest is to reshuffle the boxes on the organization chart. This activity is not called reshuffling, however; it's reorganizing. The Carter years treated the Americans to not only a lot of rhetoric about reorganizing; we also heard a lot about sunset laws and zero-based budgeting. Essentially, both of these new reforms did the same thing: They required bureaucracies to periodically justify their programs and very existence. What bureaucrat worth half his or her salt could not do that?

So, we are left with the third alternative—proclaiming a declaration of independence from the government bureaucrat. Coping requires, above all, that we keep in mind that it is the people and not the bureaucrats that are the source of power in this republic. The Constitution begins "We the people . . ."; it does not begin "We the planning analysts, schemes routing specialists, managers of creative services, social priorities specialists, suggestions' awards administrators, fringe benefit specialists, confidential assistants to the confidential assistant, etc." Government, therefore, exists for the people, not vice versa. You are in charge.

This section is blatantly action oriented. Nevertheless, before a citizen storms the citadel, there are a couple of facts worth understanding about a government agency. First, who are the people in it? Second, why do they do what they sometimes do?

Reprinted by permission The Wall Street Journal

"Something the Consumer Protection Agency will let me keep."

Who Are the Bureaucrats?

Most federal employees (about 61 percent) obtain their jobs through the civil service system. Until the Pendleton Act of 1883, federal employees got their jobs through **patronage.** They were hired and promoted based on whether they knew the right people. New presidents staffed the government with friends and allies.

The Pendleton Act began to change that by establishing a civil service system based on the idea of merit. Using entrance exams and promotion ratings, the system would produce administration by people of talent to survive presidents of either party. Meanwhile, at the state level, a similar trend was taking place. State civil service commissions were established; control over personnel was generally taken away from governors. In effect, these commissions tried to insulate state personnel from state political parties. In 1978, this reform was reformed as Congress passed legislation to set up the Office of Personnel Management (OPM). The office has detailed rules about hiring, promotion, working conditions, and firing. When one position opens, OPM will send the agency a list of three names to choose from. The person hired is assigned a GS (General Schedule) rating from GS–1 to GS–18.

About 39 percent of the civilian employees are not appointed on the basis of qualifications designed or approved by OPM. Most of these "excepted" employees are appointed on a nonpartisan basis by various agencies that have their own merit-based appointment systems. These include Postal Service employees, FBI agents, intelligence agents, foreign service officers in the State Department, and doctors in the Public Health Service and the Veterans' Administration.

A few very top federal employees still obtain their jobs through presidential appointment. In his aptly titled book *A Government of Strangers*, Hugh Heclo estimates that there are about 300 of these top policymaking jobs.[1] (These include cabinet secretaries, undersecretaries, assistant secretaries, and bureau chiefs.) There are also about 2,000 lesser jobs. (These are "Schedule C" jobs for executive assistants, special aides, and confidential secretaries.) The average undersecretary or assistant secretary only lasts about 22 months. Heclo therefore argues that few ever get to know their subordinates very well. Consequently, the senior civil servants, who have been there longer and know the complexities of the job better, retain considerable power.

The existence of these kinds of jobs outside the merit system is evidence of a continuing need for presidents to have competent personnel who can help them compile a record of effective political action. Similarly, at the state and local levels, there is the beginnings of a trend toward the reestablishment of appointive powers in the hands of governors and mayors.

Few observers, for example, would say that Chicago today is a better managed city than it was under Mayor Daley, where patronage was rife. Without discounting the achievements of the civil service reform, the argument for patronage can be summarized thus. It gives an elected official a chance to fulfill the promises made to the voters. If, after two or four years, those promises are not fulfilled because the chief executive appointed cronies, then the voters vote him or her out. They cannot fob off their failures on the bureaucracy, which is literally their bureaucracy. Advocates of patronage maintain it is more likely to produce responsive government than elaborate civil service systems. Critics say the price, in terms of corruption and incompetency, is too high.

Bureaucratic Pathologies

Rather than criticize the government bureaucracy in the abstract, or compare it against some ideal standard that has never existed in this world, it seems more fruitful to compare it with something concrete and in this world. The obvious standard for comparison is a business firm.

The most important difference between government and business organizations is the absence in the former of dollar measure. In a profit-oriented business, the dollar provides an overall measure of both effectiveness (the extent to which the organization accomplishes its goals) and efficiency (the relationship between expenses and output). In contrast, government lacks a satisfactory, single, overall measure of performance.

This absence is a serious management problem. The output of the State Department is "diplomacy"; the output of the Department of Defense is "readiness to defend the interest of the United States"; the output of a state university is "enlightenment." Without a single criterion, how do managers know that one expenditure in their organization is better than another? How do they know if the benefits even exceed the expenditure? How does an organization that lacks a good measure of performance delegate important decisions to lower-level managers? Not surprisingly, many problems must be resolved in Washington or in state capitals rather than in regional or local offices.

A second difference between government and business is that the latter can change its strategy if management so decides. But managers in government have far less flexibility in responding to changing conditions. For example, a city is expected to provide certain services for its residents—education, police protection, welfare, etc. It can make decisions about the amount of these services, but cannot decide to discontinue them.

Furthermore, government bureaucracies must provide services as directed—often in minute detail—by an outside agency (e.g.,—a city council, a state legislature, or Congress). In contrast, corporate boards of directors tend to be composed of fairly like-minded individuals. (No one ever defined Congress as 535 like-minded individuals.) It is clear which body would be easier for a manager to deal with.

In a government bureaucracy, top management also finds that its employees are insulated by virtue of job security and rules. Career civil servants know they will outlast the term of office of the elected or appointed chief executive. Thus they may be able to drag their heels long enough on projects they dislike so that a new management will take over and possibly rescind the project.

Third, government bureaucracies must obtain all, or almost all, of their financial support from sources other than revenues from services rendered. In these organizations, there is no direct connection between services received and resources provided. Accordingly, the bureaucracy expends considerable energy in getting the legislature (or wherever its source is) to expand its budgets; businesses, meanwhile, expend their energies trying to please their customers and cut operating expenses. If high profits can be a mark of distinction in the business, a big budget can serve the same purpose in the bureaucrats' world.

In a business organization, new clients are an opportunity vigorously sought after; in some government bureaucracies, the new client may be only a burden. This negative attitude towards clients gives rise to complaints about the poor service and surly attitude of bureaucrats. Customers in a MacDonalds are more likely to hear "please" and "thank you" than visitors to the Immigration and Naturalization Service.

Fourth, in many bureaucracies, the important people are professionals (e.g., physicians, engineers, combat commanders, teachers, and pilots). Professionals often have motivations that are inconsistent with efficient use of resources. They judge success by the standards of their profession, not the principle of efficiency. Bluntly, they tend to look down on managers and give inadequate weight to the costs of their decisions.

Finally, bureaucracies are under more political influence than business. They are responsible to the electorate or to a legislative body. Therefore, decisions result from multiple—often conflicting—pressures. That is a major reason one part of the federal government supports agricultural research in growing tobacco while another part supports educational programs to stop smoking. That is why one part tries to reclaim land for farming while another part pays farmers not to use perfectly suitable land.

Elected officials cannot function if not elected. In order to be elected, they favor satisfying the immediate needs of their constituents. Yet satisfying these needs may not be in the constituents' long-run best interest. Nor may it be in the best interest of the larger body of citizens. These pressures tend to induce an emphasis on highly visible, short-term goals.

Political pressures, plus the restrictive statutes passed by legislative bodies, tend to inhibit bold, decisive action. Instead, a civil service syndrome develops: You need not produce success, just avoid making major mistakes. This mindset helps explain the bureaucrat's alleged love of red tape. It also can help us understand James H. Boren's Laws of the Bureaucracy: (1) When in doubt, mumble; (2) when in trouble, delegate; (3) when in charge, ponder.[2]

Citizen Action

Now you have some idea who the bureaucrats are and why they behave the way they do. We can next consider how individuals can deal with them.

Know what you want. Suppose you want to be identified as an intelligent activist, not a mere complainer. Then you must clearly identify and define in your own mind *the problem*. You need to know how the situation got the way it did (the history of it) and who is affected by the situation, both favorably and unfavorably. Next, you need to determine what should be done about the problem. Consider a variety of solutions. Think through these alternative solutions until you are convinced the best one really lies within the purview of government bureaucracy.

At this point, you need to locate exactly where in the machinery of government the relevant source of authority is. Who allowed the problem to come into existence? Who has the authority to change the situation? This analysis will tell you where to start.

It is frustrating not to know whom to call or what number to ask for. Thus, directories are useful. If you are dealing with the federal government, a handy, general one is *The United States Manual*. It will provide comprehensive information on agencies of the legislative, judicial, and executive branches. Almost any library should have a recent copy. Most agencies have lawyers who will give you the agency's legal position on an issue.

What if you are interested in a problem on a continuing basis? Then it is worth the trouble to obtain a telephone directory of the personnel of the agency or its regional office. With your agency directory in hand, call Washington. (Call person-to-person at noon D.C. time.

When the person you want is out, and hope they return your call on their own line.) Standard Federal Administrative regions were set up to achieve more uniformity in the location and geographic jurisdictoin of federal field offices. They provide a basis for better coordination among agencies and federal–state–local governments. A map showing the standard boundaries is printed below.

The serious activists will get on the agency's mailing list by giving it their address. They will even make it a habit to call key agency people once a month to keep informed on latest developments. Most agencies have libraries that are useful sources of information. For activists outside Washington, D.C., and outside the regional headquarters city indicated on the map, a Federal Information Center may be housed in a nearby public or university library. This is a depository of agency documents, studies, environmental impact statements, etc. Specialized newsletters, published on a variety of subjects, are another source of information. They are usually very expensive, but offer thorough coverage of ongoing rules, regulations, meetings, and so forth (e.g., *Air and Water News*).

Under the Freedom of Information Act, all federal agencies must make available almost any record or documents properly requested by the public. If an agency does not do so, or makes no response within 10 days, the person requesting the information has the right to bring suit in federal court to compel compliance. (For more on this act, and many other sources of information, see Appendix C.)

I have dwelled on these sources of information because you should be able to state clearly and accurately the basis of your grievance, the legal principle involved, and the precise remedy the agency should take. Furthermore, you need to know whom to call or write. Otherwise you are forced to start at the top and hope the letter or inquiry will trickle down the layers of the bureaucracy and reach the right bureau-

Standard Federal Regions

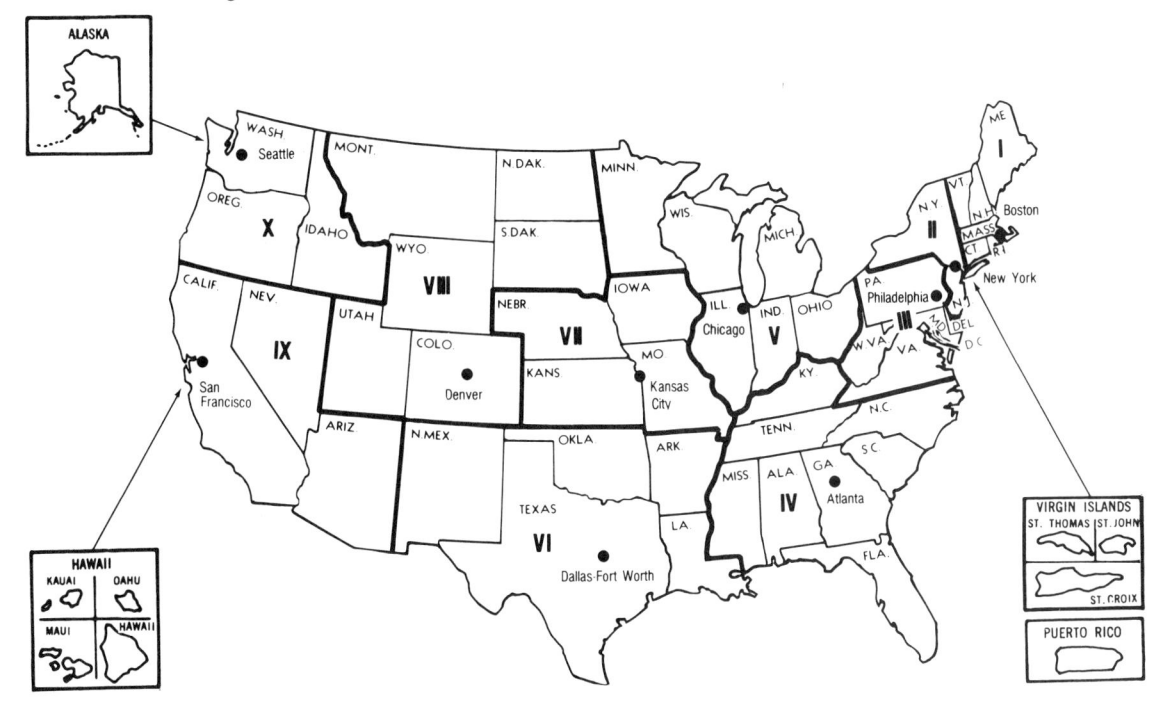

crat. Not only is this time consuming; it also antagonizes lower-level functionaries and solidifies their stubbornness.

Know the rules of the game. Congressional legislation provides agencies with broad powers. With these powers in hand, bureaucrats begin spelling out in rules and regulations what citizens can and cannot do. (See Schema.)

This rulemaking process is often long and complicated. A lawyer's expertise is usually required to master the procedural maze and technical requirements imposed by federal agencies. Even so, the average citizen in most cases has a chance to be heard before a new regulation goes into effect. But this presupposes that our hypothetical citizen knows the rules by which the game is played. More specifically, it requires knowledge of petitions, the *Federal Register*, rulemaking and regulations, and public hearings and meetings. In the discussion that follows, the focus will be on federal agencies. The basic procedures, though, are roughly the same for state agencies and city councils.

Any citizen may petition a regulator agency to issue, change, or withdraw a rule. For example, in 1978, the National Wildlife Federation submitted a 21-page petition for rulemaking under the Fish and Wildlife Coordination Act and the National Environmental Policy Act to the Departments of the Army and the Interior and the Council on Environmental Quality. The petition was for the issuance of regulations to reduce the loss of fish and wildlife to water resources projects.

After the petition is filed, it is studied to see if it is complete. It is also checked to see if the agency has jurisdiction over the request. Then, it is routed to the technical staff, which collects data—pro and con—pertinent to the petition. Based on this information, the staff makes a series of recommendations to the commission.

If the petition is granted, the staff, with public input, proposes a rule for approval by the commission. This is published in the *Federal Register* to allow for public comments, usually due within 30 to 60 days.

The technical staff evaluates the comments. It then decides if any changes are needed in the proposed rule changes and makes a final decision. The rule is then published in the *Federal Register* and has the effect of law.

Tactical consideration. Of all the ways of reaching a bureaucrat, the least desirable is a telephone call. In such a case, you and your complaint becomes only a disembodied voice miles away. The best approach, therefore, is face-to-face. Now you are a real person with a real problem.

When you visit an agency, bring all essential documents with you and state the problem concisely. From the earlier discussion of bureaucratic pathology, you should appreciate the futility of shouts or threats. Use the wrong approach and the bureaucrats and their agency draw the wagons in a circle.

If you cannot make a personal visit, the next best approach is a businesslike letter. Be sure to state the problem and your remedy. Enclose copies of all relevant documents.

The importance of good documentation when dealing with bureaucracy cannot be overemphasized. Put into writing any oral promises the bureaucrat makes.

In the event you feel a fair solution has still not been obtained, several options remain open. You can complain to a bureaucrat's superiors; or, better yet, have your representative from your district complain for you. Remember: Congress determines an agency's budget; bureaucrats listen with great attention to its members.

With this chapter we come to the end of Part 3. Many of the problems that we have examined in Parts 2 and 3 are complex and interwoven. Here are the main ones.

A declining faith of Americans in the fairness, integrity, and competence of their political institutions. This is well reflected in the decline in the number of people who show confidence enough in democracy to bother to vote.

The intolerable length of the nominating and campaign procedures, which often have nothing to do with the realities of governing.

The growing power of the media and pollsters and the trivialization of a long election process.

The relative weakness of the political parties.

The radical increase in the number, professionalism, and potency of special interest groups.

A weakened presidential capacity for leadership. This was caused in part by Vietnam and Watergate, by a large, sprawling bureaucracy, and by strained congressional relations.

The fragmentation of the congressional leadership, coupled with the new aggressiveness of individual members of Congress.

The growing involvement of the courts as a second legislative body in program administration. This problem increases as Congress avoids tough issues, such as school desegregation and prison reform.

The mounting costs and delays in the delivery of public services as the complexities of federalism increase.

Schema: The American Policy Formulation System

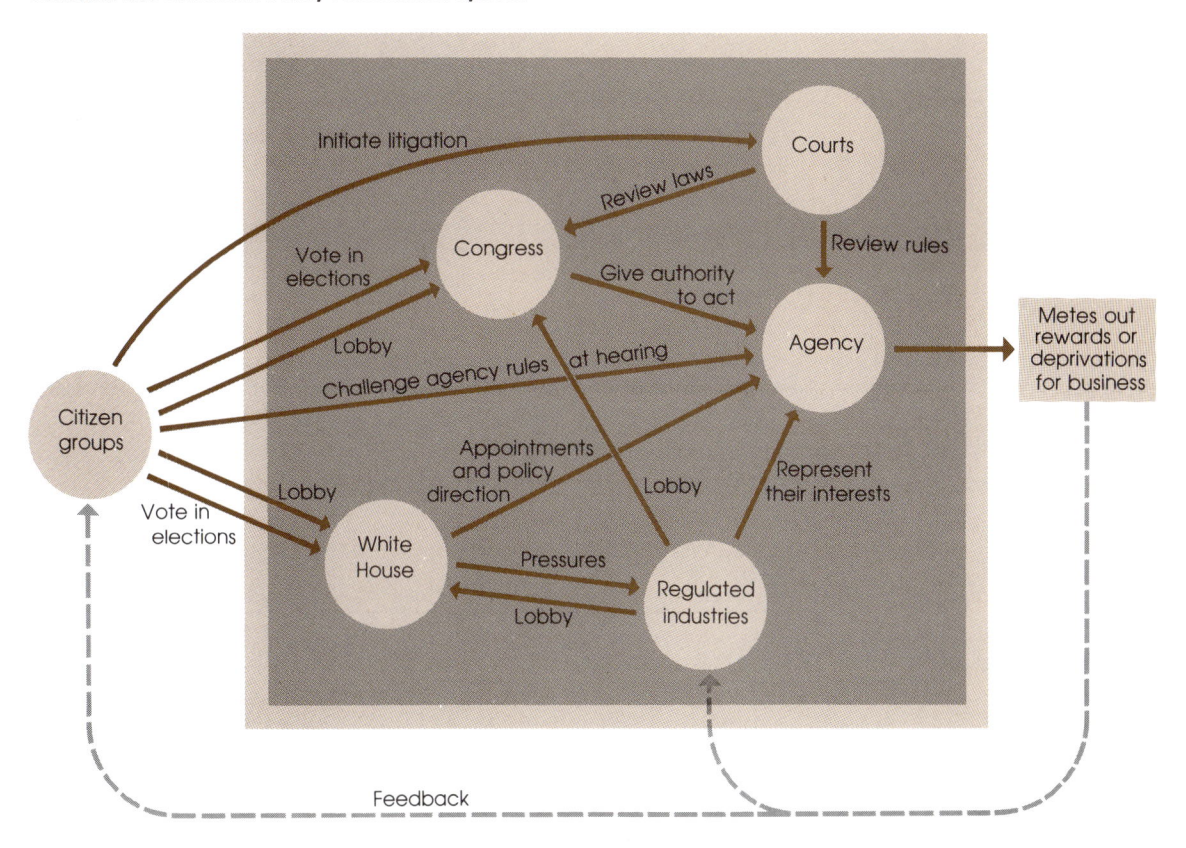

The growing belief among conservatives that Washington has entered areas it has no constitutional authority to, and among liberals that the presidents and Congress have become, in effect, mayors and city councils. Consequently, Washington has become so overloaded it cannot carry out its prime functions (for example, conducting foreign affairs, managing the economy, enforcing civil rights, and overseeing national concerns that cannot be handled locally). Both conservatives and liberals now seem to share the belief that the United States is too diverse for highly centralized government programs. This is particularly true because both population and political centers have become decentralized.

Against the backdrop of these political and institutional trends and events, government tries to formulate and implement public policy. The disturbing fact is this: Even if the trends and events were somehow wiped away overnight, the policymakers would still face staggering domestic, economic, and global challenges.

> This is the crisis of the 20th century: The state is becoming ever stronger and we have the paradox that to defend themselves from Soviet expansionism, to defend democracy, the Western Nations are becoming steadily less democratic. There are external capitulations such as defending Pinochet (in Chile) and Somoza (in Nicaragua), and internal violations, such as Watergate.
>
> Octavio Paz (1979)

PART 4 | Outputs of the Political System

THE KEY TO THIS BOOK

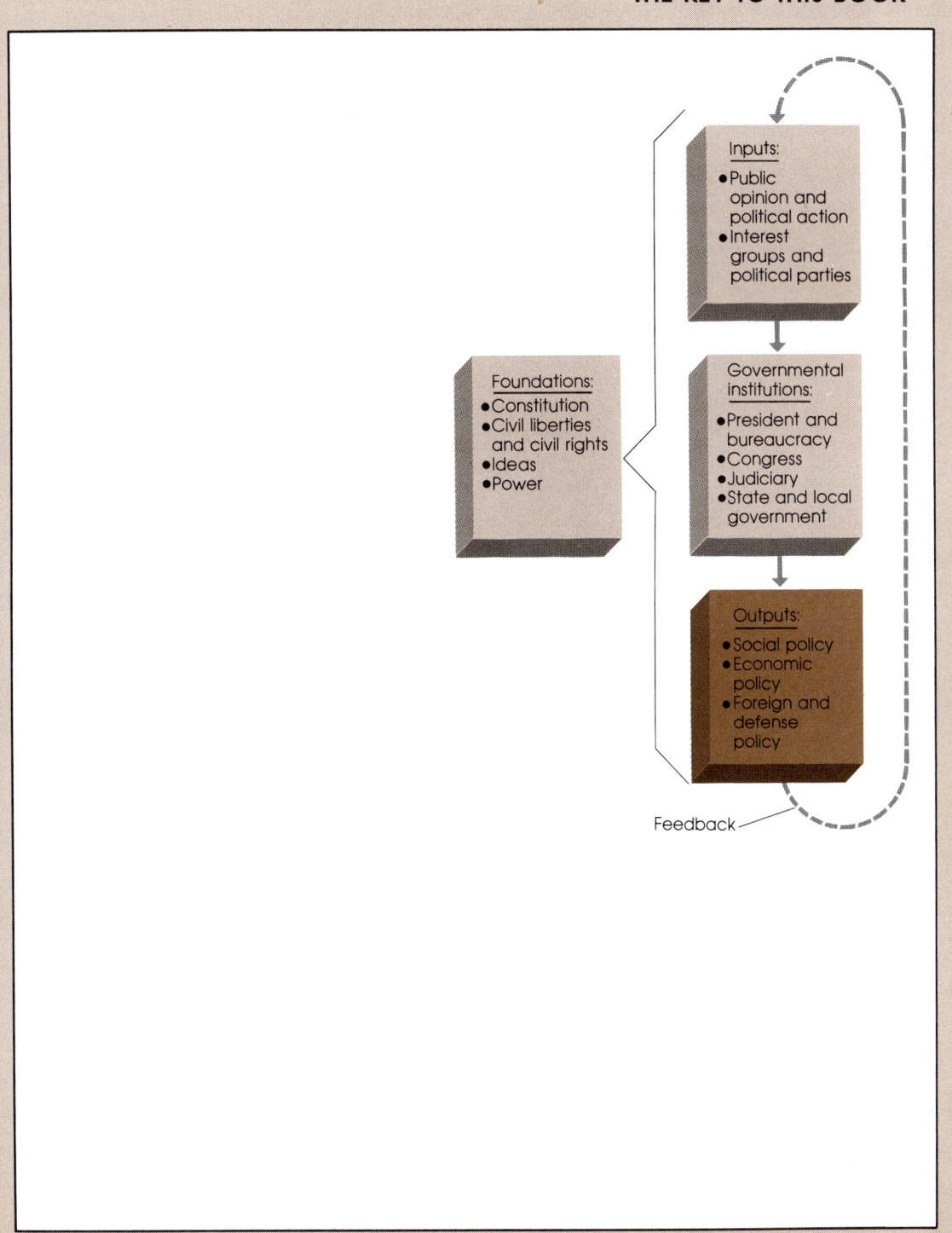

Inputs:
- Public opinion and political action
- Interest groups and political parties

Foundations:
- Constitution
- Civil liberties and civil rights
- Ideas
- Power

Governmental institutions:
- President and bureaucracy
- Congress
- Judiciary
- State and local government

Outputs:
- Social policy
- Economic policy
- Foreign and defense policy

Feedback

Library of Congress

IN THIS TEMPLE
AS IN THE HEARTS OF THE PEOPLE
FOR WHOM HE SAVED THE UNION
THE MEMORY OF ABRAHAM LINCOLN
IS ENSHRINED FOREVER

11 | Civil Liberties and Civil Rights

After studying this chapter you should be able to answer the following questions:

1. What do we mean by civil liberties and civil rights?
2. What freedoms are protected by the First Amendment?
3. What are the rights of the accused?
4. Why is the protection of privacy and autonomy becoming an increasing concern?
5. What were the major victories and setbacks in the blacks' long struggle for equality?
6. Viewed from the 1980s, how close has American society come to realizing the goal of "equality in freedom"?

Terms you should know:

affirmative action
at-large voting
Bakke case
bill of attainder
civil liberties
civil rights
Civil Rights Act of 1964
"clear and present danger"
confidentiality of sources
de jure versus de facto segregation
double jeopardy
due process clause
equal protection clause
exclusionary rule
ex post facto laws
fairness doctrine
14th Amendment
free exercise clause
Fullilove v. *Fultznick*
Gideon v. *Wainwright*
Gitlow decision
Griswold v. *Connecticut*
indictment

Jim Crow Laws
libel
literacy test
Mapp v. *Ohio*
Miranda case
naturalization
19th Amendment
obscenity
Palko test
Pentagon Papers case
Plessy v. *Ferguson*
prior restraint
probable cause
procedural rights
reverse discrimination
right to privacy
Roe v. *Wade*
separate but equal doctrine
single-member district
Voting Rights Act of 1965
Weber v. *Kaiser Aluminum Co.*
writ of habeas corpus

Many nations are products of historical events or ethnic affinities. But this is not particularly true in the case of the United States. At the very moment of the nation's birth, the founding fathers *decided* what kind of nation they would establish. To be sure, they took care of various structural arrangements—How would laws be passed?, How would presidents be elected?, and so forth. But they were really after larger game. They asked themselves, What would distinguish America from all other nations in the world in the year 1776? What would be its contribution to the art of nation building?

In three words, Hans J. Morgenthau gives the answer the founding fathers arrived at: equality in freedom.[1] That is to say, the founding fathers tried to design a nation that would do more than just provide for the safety and economic well-being of its citizens. One of the chief purposes of American politics would be to insure freedom from permanent political domination and the opportunity for all to compete equally for power.

As one might expect, this great purpose is reflected most sharply in the thought and character of those Americans who, by preference and by training, were most political. It is difficult to think of a famous American as thoroughly and completely the politician as Abraham Lincoln. His entire adult life, except for a brief period of law practice, was absorbed by politics. As one of his contemporaries wrote after Lincoln's death, "It was in the world of politics that he lived. Politics was his life, newspapers his food, and his great ambition his motive power."[2]

There can be little doubt that Lincoln had a full awareness of this purpose in American politics. Nowhere perhaps was that awareness more clearly revealed than in his words spoken on February 22, 1861, in Independence Hall in Philadelphia:

> I have never had a feeling politically that did not spring from the sentiments embodied in the Declaration of Independence. . . . I have often inquired of myself, what great principle or idea it was that kept this Confederacy so long together. It was not the mere matter of the separation of the colonies from the mother land; but something in that Declaration giving liberty, not alone to the people of this country, but hope to the world for all future time. It was that which gave promise that in due time the weights should be lifted from the shoulders of all men, and that all should have an equal chance. This is the sentiment embodied in that Declaration of Independence. . . . I would rather be assassinated on this spot than to surrender it.[3]

Therefore, one of the central themes of this book in general and this chapter in particular is that a cornerstone of American politics—from the colonial period through the civil rights movement of the 1960s to the contemporary problems of economics, technology, and global relations—has been the achievement of equality in freedom. The compactness of the concept calls for elaboration.

Freedom is conceived here as being a minimization of political control. The founders were well agreed on this. As John Hancock put it, "Security to the persons and properties of the governed is so obviously the design and end of civil government, that to attempt a logical proof of it would be like burning (candles) at noon to assist the sun in the enlightening of the world."[4] When we speak of this kind of freedom—freedom *against* government—we usually think of freedom of religion, freedom of speech, freedom of assembly, and freedom of the press. This kind of freedom is frequently referred to as **civil liberties**.

But freedom as civil liberties signifies little if a person is discriminated against by fellow citizens. To be meaningful, civil liberties must be coupled with **civil rights**. When one is denied equal opportunity in education, jobs, housing, and the right to vote (because of race, religion, national origin, or sex) protection from government must lose some of its luster. A society of equal opportunity is, on the other hand, a society in which no person has a fixed station into which he or she is bound; it is a society of vertical mobility.

Therefore, we shall use the term *civil rights* to refer to the rules against all forms of discrimination (especially racial ones); *civil liberties* will refer to all other constitutional guarantees of individual freedom. Because the two concepts are so intertwined, we shall treat them together in this chapter. We will use the label *equality in freedom* to underscore this interrelationship.

Lincoln's formulation of the concept of equality is worth a careful reading. At Springfield, Illinois, he put it this way:

> The founders meant to set up a standard maxim for free society, which would be familiar to al¹, and revered by all; constantly looked to, constantly labored for, and even though never perfectly attained, constantly approximated, and thereby constantly spreading and deepening its influence and augmenting the happiness and value of life to all people of all colors everywhere. The assertion that "all men are created equal" was of no practical use in effecting our separation from Great Britain; and it was placed in the Declaration not for that, but for future use.[5]

Lincoln brings out here an important point about the concept of achieving equality. He indicates that equality is to be pursued "even though never perfectly attained." To say that a major aim of American politics is the achievement of equality in freedom is not to imply that either equality or freedom has been achieved. Nor is it to imply that the thrust of American politics has been unswervingly in that direction. Thus, an important trait of the ideal of equality in freedom in American politics is that it is not susceptible to complete and permanent realization. It is in the very nature of its dynamics that, as soon as it nears realization, new conditions spoil its full achievement. American political history, therefore, moves somewhat in the fashion of a cycle: Achievement is followed by crisis, to be followed again by achievement.

In this chapter, we shall focus on civil liberties and civil rights as formal procedures that are essential to achieving equality in freedom. We shall take up civil liberties first and closely explain the Bill of Rights (see Chapter 2). We shall then review what has and has not been done concerning the condition of blacks, women, and other minorities to reaffirm the American purpose. Finally, we shall consider some of the reasons it is unlikely that equality in freedom can even be achieved in a clearcut, universally accepted manner. Like the North Star, equality in freedom is more a guide than a destination.

CIVIL LIBERTIES: THE QUEST FOR FREEDOM

First Amendment Freedom

Freedom of religion. As interpreted by the courts, two guarantees are given to the individual with respect to religious freedom. First, neither Congress nor a state legislature may "make any law respecting an establishment of religion." This means that no law may be passed that favors one church over another, establishes an official church to which all Americans must subscribe or support, or requires religious belief or religious nonbelief. Second, no law may validly interfere with the "free exercise" of one's religion. This clause assures that each citizen is guaranteed freedom to worship by individual choice.

The Court's modern interpretation of the **establishment clause,** as the first guarantee is called, has supplied the notions of voluntarism and neutrality as constituting the mortar of this "wall of separation between Church and State." Government activity that has the purpose or primary effect of advancing or inhibiting religion, or that results in excessive government entanglement with religion, is prohibited. Court decisions in this area are not easily categorized. But the courts have been extremely reluctant to permit any government involvement with private elementary and secondary schools. It has determined that students there are more impressionable. Thus they are more liable to be coerced than university-level students.

In interpreting the **free exercise clause,** as the second guarantee is called, the courts have held that, if the purpose or effect of a statute is to impede the observance of religion, or to discriminate among them, then the free exercise of religion is abridged. Indeed, the Supreme Court recently established that only a compelling government interest can legitimize a statute that restricts the free exercise of religion.

In this regard, it is clear that no statute can validly impinge upon religious thoughts—that is, religious belief devoid of conduct. Moreover, by applying the compelling interest test, the Court has assured that forms of conduct based on religious belief are to receive increasing protection. Thus, when a Seventh-Day Adventist was fired for refusing to work on Saturdays (her holy day), the Court ruled that she was fully entitled to unemployment benefits. Similarly, Amish parents were held to be protected in their refusal to send their children beyond the eighth grade to public schools; the state interest in requiring the two years of additional mandatory schooling failed to outweigh the legitimate devotion of the Amish to their tenets. These forms of conduct based upon religious belief have been held to be protected by the free exercise clause. But not all activity can be protected by claims of religious belief. Practitioners of polygamy, snake handling, and the ceremonial use of drugs take note.

Americans have never found it easy to draw the line separating church and state. In recent years, the broad boundaries established by the U.S. Constitution have become increasingly blurred, complicated, and emotional.

Perhaps the best known, most controversial church-state question that has faced the Supreme Court concerns prayer in school. In 1963, the Court declared unconstitutional a Pennsylvania law calling for reading a few verses from the Bible each day in public schools. Although teachers were not to comment on the verses and students could be excused from the reading, the Court ruled that the First Amendment required government to be strictly neutral in matters of religion. Stipulating "the Holy Bible" seemed to show a preference. Many people were outraged that the Court would "take God out of the schools." But, as you know from Chapter 9, Court decisions are not self-enforcing; consequently, many school boards tend not to follow the spirit of the 1963 decision.

One of the most serious breaches of church-state separation in recent years, many observers believe, occurred in 1978. That year California's attorney general took over the financial supervision of Herbert W. Armstrong's Worldwide Church of God. The basis of the takeover was a series of unproven allegations of fiscal mismanagement made by a few former members of the church. This action was the logical outcome of the increasingly widespread notion that churches—as tax-exempt organizations—are ultimately "owned" by the public. Government has also tried to control religious fundraising, especially by fringe groups like Dr. Moon's Unification Church and the International Society for Krishna Consciousness, whose young members blanket public places such as airports and state fairs to solicit funds as well as potential converts.

While government agencies have failed in their efforts to curb such solicitation, larger churches are concerned. The government's eagerness to control fringe groups could lead to efforts to establish a uniform law requiring the registration of all religious groups who want to solicit funds from the public.

"I esteem it above all things necessary," Locke wrote in his *Letter Concerning Toleration*, "to distinguish exactly the business of civil government from that of religion, and to settle the just bounds that lie between the one and the other. . . . The commonwealth," Locke continued, "seems to me to be a society of men constituted only for the procuring, preserving, and advancing their own civil interests."

A church is "a voluntary society of men, joining themselves together of their own accord in order to . . . [worship] God in such manner as they judge acceptable to Him, and effectual to the salvation of their souls."

Locke's doctrine of the separation of church and state—which is, of course, embodied in the First Amendment—is not easily interpreted in a nation where citizens have diverse conceptions of religion. In the discussion of freedom of religion, perhaps more than anywhere else, ideas seem to determine all other opinions. If one thinks that religious freedom is to "be esteemed above all things necessary," then one is likely to hold the view that the state should show a compelling reason for trading off religion's First Amendment rights for some other value. On the other hand, if one holds the view that the church does not enhance the commonwealth, then one is likely to hold the view that the church is frequently subverting public morals.

Freedom of speech. No doubt a good number of contemporary defenders of free speech long for the good old days. Back then the issue involved the rights of nice guys like Eugene V. Debs, the American labor organizer, and James Joyce, author of *Ulysses*. But today the issue of free speech seems to involve an altogether different breed. It involves American storm troopers bedecked in swastikas, machine-gun-wielding Klansmen, and last but not least, the editor of *Hustler* magazine.

Freedom of speech is explicitly established in the First Amendment. The English common law concept of freedom of speech meant freedom from **prior restraint** (i.e., effort to censor a publication before it goes to press). Present American theory of freedom of speech generally establishes both freedom from prior restraint and freedom from subsequent punishment for the exercise of these rights. Some Supreme Court justices, in fact, have suggested that freedom of speech is absolute. But a majority of the Court has always maintained that it must be balanced against other legitimate interests.

Justice Oliver Wendell Holmes, Jr., gave the classic statement of this position in 1919: "The most stringent protection of free speech would not protect a man in falsely shouting fire in a theater and causing a panic." Holmes offered a **clear and present danger** test for speech. When speech provokes a clear and present danger to people, government can restrain free speech. In short, the Court has attempted to preserve the greatest degree of expression—consistent with the protection from overriding and compelling government interests.

Central to the concept of freedom of speech is the freedom of individual belief. Recognizing

United Press International Photo

Bill Wilkinson is the Imperial Wizard of the Invisible Empire, one of many factions of an increasingly militant Ku Klux Klan. He is attending a "sacred" cross-burning ceremony in Scotland, Connecticut. Staunch civil libertarians argue that First Amendment rights should not be just for poets and other "good guys."

this, the Supreme Court has held that the right to associate with those who hold beliefs compatible to one's own, in order to further those beliefs, must receive basic protection. The principal way to convey one's beliefs is through actual expression. Generally citizens may speak out freely on any subject. They may exercise this right verbally, by parading, by wearing buttons, by flying flags and banners, and in a variety of other ways. They may, in short, advocate any idea they desire, no matter how unpopular or alien. Even advocacy of the use of force or violation of law can be punished *only where it is directed to inciting or producing imminent lawless action and is likely to incite or produce such action.** Abusive or profane language also is protected, unless it is directed to a specific individual and tends to incite that person to violence.

Engaging in "symbolic speech" such as wearing black armbands or using a flag in certain ways—for instance, sewed to the seat of your Levis—receives similar First Amendment protection. On the other hand, more physical actions, such as burning draft cards, may be banned or punished. The Court reasoned that if all action—murder, arson, rape—could be excused on the grounds that someone was trying "to send a message," then the First Amendment could become a kind of license to kill.

Therefore, it is the nature of a particular activity, combined with the environment in which it is undertaken, that determines whether it really is "symbolic speech" deserving First Amendment protection. In this determination, the Court examines whether there is an intention to communicate and an audience capable of understanding. The gravity of the government's interest also must be weighed. If the government is trying to regulate content, it requires a compelling justification. Or is it merely attempting to regulate time, place, or manner of speech? These factors will determine whether the activity is protected "speech" or unprotected "conduct."

Organized institutions, like individuals, are guaranteed freedom of expression. This not primarily for their own benefit. It is for their contribution to furthering a free interchange of ideas in our democratic society. That a profit may be derived from managing a newspaper, for example, does not lessen the guarantee. Furthermore, this protection extends beyond political expression. It also includes discourse on practically any subject of some serious social value.

Does this include **obscenity** or hardcore pornography? Certain forms of expression are deemed without "serious" social importance; thus they may go unprotected by the First Amendment. But not all expression dealing with sex is obscene. The Court has held that expressions that, by the standards of the local community and taken as a whole, appeal to a prurient interest in sex, portray sexual conduct in a patently offensive way, and do not have serious literary, artistic, political, or scientific value, may be classified as obscene.* Ordinances

---

* In *Dennis* v. *United States* (1951), the Supreme Court upheld the conviction of 11 Communist party leaders for conspiring to teach and advocate the violent overthrow of the government. The Court held that it was not necessary for the government to wait until the conspiracy ripened into action before it could say there was a "clear and present danger." *Yates* v. *United States* (1957) modified this ruling, however. In the *Yates* case, the Court said that a distinction must be drawn between urging people to *believe* in something and urging them to actually *do* it. Obviously, this ruling made prosecution harder to come by.

* In *Miller* v. *California* (1973), the Supreme Court established a basic test for determining obscenity: Would the "average person," applying contemporary community (i.e., local not national) standards find that the work, taken as a whole, appeals to prurient interest in sex, portrays sexual conduct in a patently offensive way as defined by law, and lacks serious artistic, political, or scientific value. In reaching this decision, the Court rejected the earlier view that obscenity meant "utterly without redeeming social value." The Court also refused to accept the position that the entire problem of obscenity could be eliminated by simply limiting access to pornographic material to consenting adults.

restricting the locations of theaters specializing in films exhibiting "specified sexual activities" or "specified anatomical areas" are permissible.

Defamation or slander is another class of expression that has been deemed devoid of any serious social value. There is one basic exception to this classification. Because of the importance of comment upon issues affecting government, the Court has carefully restrained government remedies for allegedly defamatory speech or **libel** (written defamation) in regard to public officials, candidates for public office, and some public figures. In order to recover damages for defamatory comment, public figures must prove that it was uttered with actual malice.

Freedom of assembly is also crucial to freedom of expression. The assembly clause adds little to the protection of the rights to assemble, picket, or parade that would not already be protected by the speech clause. But it does reaffirm the breadth of the rights that are guaranteed.

The right to petition is designed to enable citizens to communicate with their government without hindrance. It assures their right to present individual views both orally and in writing. It also embraces his right to travel to the seat of government.

Freedom of the press. Should a magazine be free to publish an article on how to make a hydrogen bomb? That difficult question lay at the heart of a suit the federal government brought in 1979 against *Progressive* magazine. What made the question so difficult was that the press has a special place in America's heritage. (Recall from Chapter 2 how press pamphlets by Thomas Paine—especially his *Common Sense*—and by Samuel Adams helped to ignite the American Revolution.) The Court realizes the value of an unrestrained press to American society. Therefore it has been very reluctant to sanction government censorship of the press or management of the news. Prior restraints upon the press have come to the Court with such a heavy presumption of invalidity that the Supreme Court has *never* upheld them. Suppression before publication is perhaps the gravest possible denial of free speech and press.

In the *Progressive* case, the government sought to suppress before publication an article entitled "How a Hydrogen Bomb Works." It contained secret and restricted data "and would help other nations develop" such a bomb. In the view of U.S. District Court judge Robert W. Warren of Milwaukee, the conflict boiled down to freedom of the press versus national security: "A mistake in ruling against the *Progressive* will seriously infringe cherished First Amendment rights. A mistake in ruling against the United States could pave the way for thermonuclear annihilation for us all." Thus Warren became the first federal judge to exercise "prior restraint."

In some respects, the *Progressive* case resembles the legal controversy over the **Pentagon Papers.** On June 13, 1971, the *New York Times* published the first installment of a series on how the United States got involved in Vietnam. It was based on a classified study by the Department of Defense. Afterwards, the Nixon administration moved swiftly to suppress it; the administration claimed the series damaged national security. But the Supreme Court upheld the paper's right to continue publication, because the government had failed to demonstrate a threat to national security.

Recent trends indicate some weakening of the guarantee of freedom of the press. Publications' liability for defamation has been broadened. In the case *Herbert* v. *Case* (1979), for example, the Supreme Court ruled that a journalist being sued for libel by a public figure may be compelled to disclose what he was thinking (was it malice?) at the time the offending report was being composed. Other recent decisions have done the following:

> Sanctioned unannounced police searches (with a warrant) of newsrooms for evi-

dence in criminal cases *(Zurcher v. Stanford Daily).*

Ruled that a reporter's promise to protect the identity of a confidential news source may be overridden by a judge who wants to examine his notes and files.

Held that police may obtain from telephone companies' lists of reporters' long-distance calls, in effect giving them a roster of the reporters' sources.

The broadcast media operates within a somewhat different constitutional framework than the printed press. Television and radio station owners are licensees of scarce frequencies. Therefore they have been held subject to government regulation in a number of areas. They must, for example, guarantee equal time to reply to editorial attacks as well as provide fairness in treating issues. Government regulation cannot, however, go so far as to require broadcasters to accept paid political or public issues advertising—as long as issues are presented fairly by that station.

Television and radio broadcasters have the Federal Communications Commission and its **fairness doctrine** to contend with. This doctrine requires that broadcasters who give air time to political candidates must make available "equal time" to their opponents. No such requirement applies to newspapers, which, under the First Amendment, are free to make their own editorial judgments as to what is worth covering and how to cover it. The rationale for the distinction is that there is room for only a limited number of radio and television stations on the broadcast spectrum, while there is no limit on the number of newspapers that can be printed. The scarcity of broadcast opportunities thus mandates federal enforcement of fairness.

Thus far in this section we have been discussing the protections provided by the First Amendment: freedom of religion, speech, press,

Quiz

What is going on here?

(a) Medical examination
(b) Invasion of his privacy
(c) Invasion of her privacy
(d) Investigative reporting

Bill Ray, Life magazine; © 1963 Time, Inc.

Answers on p. 413.

and assembly. In a nutshell, this important amendment helps ensure that citizens are free to participate in the political process. In the second half of the section our focus will shift. Now we want to discuss the protections against arbitrary police and court action that are found in Amendments 4 through 9.

Rights of Accused

Freedom in equality was a major aim of the founding fathers. However, they did not lose sight of the need for public order. To maintain that order, they knew that some public officials would have to be given the power to seize property and punish citizens. In this section, we shall see how carefully this power was parceled out and restricted.

In addition to the freedoms discussed earlier in the chapter, the Constitution has "baked into it" the rights of people accused of a crime. Essentially, these rights provide citizens with protection against arbitrary actions by public officials. Sheriffs are prohibited from pistol whipping citizens into confessions; judges are not allowed to hold midnight trials in dark basements. Under the Constitution, a person cannot be deprived of life, liberty, or property, except under well-defined procedures. Justice Felix Frankfurter once expressed the rationale behind the important theme of American law. "This history of liberty," he said, "has largely been the history of observance of procedural safeguards."

In this section, we shall look at **procedural rights,** particularly those specified in the Fourth through Ninth Amendments.* But first we must note several individual rights that appeared not in the Bill of Rights but in the Constitution as originally adopted.

Constitutionally mandated procedures.
Article I, Section 9, clause 2 reads: "The privilege of the unit of habeas corpus shall not be suspended, unless when in cases of rebellion or invasion the public safety may require it."

This clause secures to the Congress the power to suspend, or to authorize the president to suspend, the privilege of the writ upon a declaration of national emergency. A suspension of habeas corpus is probably tenable only when the courts are physically unable to function because of war, invasion, or rebellion. But what exactly is a **writ of habeas corpus?**

Originally, the writ of habeas corpus was a pretrial device that enabled people imprisoned pursuant to executive order to attack the legality of their detention. Subsequently, the concept of the writ has been expanded by the Supreme Court. Now anyone whose freedom has been officially restrained may now petition a federal court to test whether that restraint was legally imposed. In this manner of use, it has become an important means of post-conviction attacks upon criminal convictions in state and federal courts. The Court has recently curtailed the availability of this device in state convictions. This was done by requiring full compliance with and exhaustion of state remedies before permitting the issuance of a writ of habeas corpus from a federal court.

Habeas corpus is a vital safeguard against unlawful imprisonment. Therefore it is unusual that it is explicitly mentioned only in the context of its suspension. Nowhere in the Constitution is this right affirmatively conferred. Nevertheless, there is a long-standing statutory authorization to federal courts to exercise the habeas corpus power.

Article I, Section 9, clause 3 prohibits the passage of any **bill of attainder.** A bill of attainder historically is a special act of a legislature that declares that a person or group of persons has committed a crime. It also imposes punishment without a trial by court. Under the constitutional system of separation of powers, only courts may try a person for a crime or impose

---

* It is useful to distinguish procedural rights from substantive rights. The latter guarantees are essential for personal liberty—for example, freedom of speech. The former are concerned with the methods by which these rights are protected.

punishment for violation of the law. Section 9 restrains Congress from passing bills of attainder; Section 10 restrains the states.

Article I, Section 9, clause 3 and Article I, Section 10, clause 1 prohibit the federal government and the states from enacting any criminal or penal law that makes unlawful any act that was not a crime when committed. Such laws are termed **ex post facto laws.** These two clauses also prevent the imposition of a greater penalty for a crime than that in effect when the crime was committed. But laws that retroactively determine how a person is to be tried for a crime may be changed, as long as no important rights are lost. Laws are not ex post facto if they make the punishment less severe than it was when the crime was committed.

Article III of the Constitution outlines the structure and power of the federal court system. It establishes a federal judiciary, which helps maintain the rights of American citizens. Article III, Section 2 also contains a guarantee that the trial of all federal crimes, except cases of impeachment, shall be by jury. The Supreme Court has interpreted this guarantee as containing exceptions for "trials of petty offenses," cases rightfully tried before court-martial or other military tribunal, and some cases in which the defendant has voluntarily relinquished his right to a jury.

Treason is the only crime defined by the Constitution (Article III, Section 3). The precise description of this offense reflects an awareness by the founders of the danger that persons holding unpopular views might be branded traitors. Recent experience in other countries with prosecutions for conduct loosely labeled "treason" confirms the wisdom of the authors of the Constitution in expressly stating what constitutes this crime and how it shall be proved.

Fourth Amendment: Search and seizure. May police stop a car at random to look at a driver's identification? In 1979, the Supreme Court said no, unless the police have some objective reason to suspect that the law has been broken.

Briefly, this was the case: In 1976, a police officer in Delaware stopped William Prouse at random. The officer was checking for unlicensed drivers and unregistered cars. He found neither, but he did find a bag of marijuana. Prouse was then arrested for possession.

The court reasoned that the random checking of drivers probably contributes only slightly to highway safety. In any event, the benefit is not enough to outweigh the Fourth Amendment prohibition of unreasonable searches and seizures. Writing for the majority, Justice Byron White called random checks of certain individuals by police" an unsettling show of authority." People have as much right to expect privacy in their cars as in their homes.

The Fourth Amendment protects the individual and his property from "unreasonable" searches and seizures. It does so by generally prohibiting government acts that invade one's "reasonable" expectation of privacy. This provision applies both to arrests of a person and to searches of his person or property for evidence. In practice, however, the Court treats arrests and searches quite differently.

For example, a police officer may make a warrantless arrest in a public place (including the entrance hall of a home) when a person is suspected of committing either a felony or a misdemeanor in the officer's presence. But the Court has held that, barring special circumstances, a search is unreasonable unless preceded by a valid warrant issued upon **probable cause.**

Probable cause is a fairly important concept in criminal law. The basic idea is this: It is improper for a warrant to be issued based upon the mere opinion of an officer, unsupported by any facts. Something must have occurred, or some facts must exist that are known to the officer requesting a warrant, that would reasonably cause the officer to believe that a crime had been committed and that evidence important to that crime is in the place to be searched. Officers cannot go on a "fishing expedition" because they think they may find something illegal there. Without reasonable cause for believing this—other than personal suspicions—reasonable or probable cause does not exist. If officers illegally search someone, the evidence found cannot be used in court. This **exclusionary rule** means that nothing—even the proverbial smoking gun—can be used as evidence unless it was lawfully obtained. In *Mapp v. Ohio* (1961), the Supreme Court said the rule applied to state trials as well as federal ones.

Despite the distinction between arrests and searches, the Court normally encourages warrants in either instance. This reflects the fact that the warrant process is a valuable safeguard of Fourth Amendment rights. For example, a warrant must be issued by a neutral magistrate (i.e., a civil officer with power to administer the law) who is able to determine whether probable cause exists.

The circumstances in which searches may be conducted without a warrant are limited. A search without a warrant (but still with probable cause) may be valid where:

Consent is voluntarily given by the individual whose person or property is to be searched. As we have seen, automobiles—which, unlike a home, are mobile—may be subject to warrantless searches.

Persons have been lawfully arrested. If the arrest occurs in a home, however, a valid search is limited to the body of arrestees and the area immediately around them from which they might be able to obtain a weapon.

Persons are detained but not arrested. Generally, though, frisks are permissible only to discover weapons endangering the officer.

Persons are entering the United States, but only when conducted reasonably near the nation's borders or points of entry.

Materials are in "plain view."

For years the Court adhered to the view that electronic surveillance—such as wiretapping—was neither a search nor a seizure. But now the Court holds that the Fourth Amendment requires observance of the warrant requirement in this circumstance. In 1968, Congress buffered this holding by enacting an extensive law on the subject. Subsequently the president argued that he is permitted to authorize electronic surveillance on the basis of national security without regard to the Fourth Amendment or the 1968 statute. This has been rejected by the Court in a case involving domestic subversive investigations. (The Court did, however, refrain from addressing this question when applied to the activities of foreign powers within or without this country.)

Enforcement of the Fourth Amendment by the courts has generally been effected through the controversial exclusionary rule. It provides that no evidence—however reliable—is admissible in court if it has been obtained in violation of the Fourth Amendment. The principal purpose of the rule is to deter violations of the amendment.

The Fifth Amendment: Self-incrimination, due process, and much more. Let us now consider the case of Barry Floyd Braeseke. In 1978, Braeseke told Mike Wallace on national television, witnessed by 30 million Americans, how he had killed his mother, father, and grandfather in their home two years earlier. He said he had been using the drug PCP ("angel dust"). He came downstairs with a rifle and shot each member of the family in the back. Though convicted of murder in 1977, the California Supreme Court in 1979 overturned that conviction. Why? Had he been informed of his rights to an attorney, as required by *Gideon v. Wainwright* (1963)? Yes. Had he been informed of his right to remain silent, as required by *Miranda v. Arizona* (1966)? Yes.

According to court records, here is what happened. After the shootings, Braeseke voluntarily went to the police. Seeing blood on his clothing, they told him he was a suspect and then informed him of his rights. At first, he said he did not want to talk about the crime until he had seen an attorney; but while being booked and fearing a night in jail, he changed his mind. He told the police sergeant he wished to speak "off the record." Again, he was told he could remain silent, though any information would be appreciated.

Braeseke then confessed in detail. Several hours later, he confessed again to the deputy prosecutor. According to tapes of the interrogation, the deputy prosecutor read him his rights four times and asked 30 times if he understood them. Braeseke answered yes 30 times. What then was the catch?

According to California's high court, there was not "proof beyond a reasonable doubt" that Braeseke had made a "knowing and intelligent" waiver of his right to silence before making two separate confessions of the murders. The police sergeant should have informed Braeseke that "there could be no such thing as an off-the-record discussion." And, since the second confession was a product of the first, it was no good either.

What the Braeseke case illustrates is this: The Fifth Amendment guarantees that no person shall be compelled to be a witness against himself or herself in a criminal proceeding in a federal court. This right has been extended through the due process clause of the 14th Amendment (discussed below) to apply to criminal proceedings in state courts as well. The basic assumption underlying the self-incrimination clause is that no one is obliged to provide answers to questions tending to convict oneself of a crime.

The Court's reasoning stems in part from fears of physical or mental coercion when an individual is interrogated in the custody of the police. Some 40 years before *Braeseke*, Justice Felix Frankfurter wrote a decision throwing out the confession and conviction of a man who had been interrogated for five straight nights by a team of police officers. "There comes a point," Frankfurter wrote, "when this court should not be ignorant as judges of what we know as men." While the case was quite the opposite of *Braeseke*, some political observers today would suggest that the wheels of justice have been turned almost completely around since then.

In addition to ruling out self-incrimination, the Fifth Amendment does something even more basic. It expresses one of the fundamental ideas of American justice: **due process of law.** (A due process clause is also found in the 14th Amendment as a restraint upon state governments.) The due process clause affords protection against arbitrary and unfair procedures in judicial or administrative proceedings that affect the personal and property rights of a citizen. Timely notice of a hearing or trial that adequately informs the accused of the charges against him or her is a basic concept included in "due process." The opportunity to present evidence in one's own behalf before an impartial judge or jury, to be presumed innocent until proven guilty by legally obtained evidence, and to have the verdict supported by the evidence presented are other rights repeatedly recognized to be within the protection of the due process clause.

The Fifth Amendment contains three other clauses worth noting. These concern the grand jury, double jeopardy, and just compensation.

Before a person is tried in federal court for an "infamous" crime, he or she must first be **indicted** or accused by a grand jury (see Chapter 9). The grand jury's duty is to make sure that there is probable cause to believe that the accused person is guilty. This prevents a person from being subjected to a trial when there is not enough proof that he has committed a crime.

An infamous crime is a felony (a crime for which a sentence of more than one year's imprisonment can be given) or a lesser offense that can be punished by confinement in a penitentiary or at hard labor. An indictment is not required for a trial by court-martial or other military tribunal. The constitutional requirement of grand jury indictment does not apply, however, to trials in state courts.

The **double jeopardy** clause prevents the retrial in either state or federal court of an individual after he or she already has been placed in "jeopardy." Jeopardy applies not only after a prior conviction or acquittal but also in jury trials once the jury is sworn and in trials without juries once the introduction of evidence has begun. Thereafter, if for some reason the trial is terminated, a second trial is barred, except in limited circumstances (e.g., jury deadlocks).

The double jeopardy clause will offer no protection where conduct violates both federal and state law; the offender may be prosecuted in the courts of both jurisdictions. Neither does the clause prevent the multiple prosecution of a suspect for conduct that constitutes more than one offense. Furthermore, if a defendant obtains a reversal of a conviction and is retried, the clause does not prevent an increase of penalty if he or she is reconvicted.

Finally, the Fifth Amendment requires that, whenever government takes an individual's property (this power is called *eminent domain*), the property acquired must be taken for public use, and the full value thereof paid to the owner as *just compensation*. Thus the government cannot take property from one person simply to give it to another.

Sixth Amendment: Criminal and civil trials. The Sixth Amendment sets forth specific rights guaranteed to persons facing criminal prosecution in federal courts—and in state courts by virtue of the 14th Amendment.

The right to speedy and public trial requires that the accused be brought to trial without unnecessary delay, and that the trial be open to the public. Intentional or negligent delay by the prosecution may prejudice defendants' rights to defend themselves. Such delays have been held as grounds for dismissal of the charges. The Supreme Court has ruled that delay in prosecution was not justified by the defendant's confinement on an earlier conviction; one should be temporarily released for purposes of trial on the latter charge.

Trial by an impartial jury supplements the earlier guarantee contained in Article III of the Constitution. The requirements that the jury have 12 members and that it must reach a unanimous verdict were derived from common law (see Chapter 9); they are not specifically accorded by the Constitution. In fact, the Supreme Court has ruled that state juries need not be composed of 12 members. It has actually approved a state statutory scheme providing for only six. Moreover, the Court has ruled that jury verdicts in state courts need not necessarily be unanimous. The right to jury trial does not apply to trials for petty offenses, which the Supreme Court has suggested as those punishable by six months' confinement or less. In trials where a jury is used it must be impartially selected; no one can be excluded from jury service merely because of his race, class, or sex.

The Sixth Amendment also requires that defendants be notified of the particular factual nature of the crimes of which they have been accused. Therefore they may have an opportunity to prepare a defense. This also means that the crime must be established by statute beforehand. Thus all persons are on public notice as to the existence of the prohibition. The statute must not be so vague or unclear that it does not inform people of the exact nature of the crime. Generally, the accused is entitled to have all witnesses against him or her present their evidence orally in court. Moreover, the accused is entitled to the aid of the court in having compulsory process issued, usually a subpoena. This orders into court as witnesses those persons whose testimony is desired at the trial.

Finally, the Sixth Amendment provides a right to be represented by counsel. For many years, this was interpreted to mean only that the defendant had a right to be represented by a lawyer if he or she could afford one. But in *Gideon* v. *Wainwright* (1963), the Supreme Court held that the amendment imposes an affirmative obligation. The federal and state governments must provide legal counsel at public expense for those who could not afford it, so that their cases might be adequately represented to the court. The Supreme Court has held that this right extends even to cases involving "petty offenses," if there is a chance that a jail sentence might result. The poor have this right at any "critical stage of the adjudicatory process." In addition, they have the right to a free copy of their trial transcript for purposes of appeal of their conviction.

The Seventh Amendment applies only to federal civil trials and not to civil suits in state courts. Except as provided by local federal court rules, if a case is brought in a federal court and a money judgment is sought which exceeds $20, the party bringing the suit and the defendant are entitled to have the controversy decided by the unanimous verdict of a jury.

Eighth Amendment: Bail and punishment. William James Rummel is a Texas prisoner who had been convicted of three nonviolent crimes that netted him $230.11. This was his criminal career in a capsule:

1964—Purchased $80 worth of automobile tires on a stolen credit card.
1969—Forged a rent check for $29.36.
1972—Cashed a $120.75 check without completing the repair work for which the check was advanced.
Sentence—Life.

The reason Rummel was given a life sentence is that Texas law mandates it upon the third felony conviction. State laws for "habitual offenders" are not uncommon; the Texas law though, does remove any discretion from the judge. Rummel and his attorney have appealed this sentence on the grounds that it is a violation of the Eighth Amendment. This amendment states that "cruel and unusual punishments" shall not be inflicted.

This clause not only bars government from imposing punishments that are barbarous and inhumane. It also forbids, as the Supreme Court had announced, punishments that society's "evolving standard of decency" would mark as excessive. It also bars punishment that is disproportionate to the offense committed, based on the facts of the particular case.

The Court recently held that the use of the death penalty as a punishment for murder does not necessarily constitute cruel and unusual punishment. Nevertheless, it did strike down mandatory death sentences for certain crimes. The Court required that attention be focused on the defendant, the crime itself, and similarly situated defendants. These considerations notwithstanding, the Court's primary emphasis upon the discretion of the jury is somewhat inconsistent with its 1972 landmark decision, which struck down the death penalty because of the arbitrary, capricious, and racist manner in which it was usually applied by juries.

Finally, punishment for narcotics addiction has been held to be cruel and unusual. The grounds are that addiction is an illness; therefore it cannot be properly categorized as a crime.

The Eighth Amendment also prohibits excessive *bail* and fines. Traditionally, bail has meant payment by the accused of an amount of money specified by the court to insure his or her presence at trial. An accused released from custody who fails to appear for trial forfeits the bail to the court.

This amendment does not specifically provide that all citizens have a "right" to bail; it only states that bail will not be excessive. A right to bail has, however, been recognized in common law and by statute since 1791. In 1966, Congress enacted the Bail Reform Act. This act provided for pretrial release of persons accused of noncapital crimes. Congress thus sought to end pretrial imprisonment of defendants who could not afford to post money bail. Such defendants were, in effect, confined only because of their poverty. The act also discouraged the traditional use of money bail. It did so by requiring the judge to seek other means likely to insure that the defendant would appear when trial was held.

Whether bail, when available, is excessive or not will depend upon the facts of each particular case. In a few instances, as when a capital offense such as murder is charged, bail may be denied altogether.

Now I want you to think of an individual who has very little interest in participating in the political process (as you know from Chapter 5, such individuals number in the millions). For such an individual, the First Amendment would probably not be a matter of great concern. Let us further assume that this apolitical animal is a law-abiding citizen—does not even get parking tickets, returns library books promptly, and so forth. So, the preceding discussion of the rights of the accused is about as relevant to him as an analysis of Jupiter's moons. Question: What in the Bill of Rights could possibly interest such a person? The answer, I suspect, is found below.

Protection of Privacy and Autonomy

The Ninth Amendment reflects the view that the powers of government are limited by the rights of the people. Just because certain rights of the people are listed in the Constitution, one should not infer that government has license to trample on other rights. Indeed, as we shall see in a moment in the *Gitlow* case, some justices sought to change the Ninth Amendment's status to one of positive affirmation and protection of the right to privacy.

The idea that an individual has an inherent right to be left alone by the government is not something that can be pointed to directly to the Constitution. But perhaps this is only because privacy is like the air we breath. It is so pervasive one could argue that virtually all the civil liberties thus far considered—freedom to speak your mind, to practice your religion, to assemble with those you choose, and to be protection from unreasonable searchers and self-incrimination—are aspects of privacy. In any event, with the 1965 decision in **Griswold v. Connecticut,** the Supreme Court read into the Constitution a broader "right to privacy."

In that decision, the Court struck down a Connecticut law that forbade counseling married couples to use contraceptive devices as an invasion of marital privacy. In the years since, privacy has proven one of the most difficult rights to interpret. The reasons seem to stem from two facts. First is the very pervasiveness of the concept. And second are the developments in electronic technology. These developments provide us with ever more sophisticated ways of spying on each other and ever more efficient ways of collecting personal data.

What does privacy mean to you? To a California gym teacher, it meant in 1975 the right to pose as a nude magazine centerfold without threat of losing his job. (No doubt many Americans would consider such public exposure quite the opposite of privacy.)

A number of legal scholars contend that the most remarkable opinion of the Supreme Court under Warren Burger, who became chief justice in 1969, is in this emerging zone of personal autonomy and lifestyle. The opinion came in ***Roe* v. *Wade*** (1973). Here the Court held that the 14th Amendment's due process clause protects a woman's right, as a matter of privacy, to decide whether to have an abortion. In *Roe*, the scope of the "privacy" right is carried well beyond that declared in *Griswold* in two important respects. The latter case was more concerned with privacy in the traditional sense. For example, the intimacy of the marital bedroom. In *Roe*, however, the concern was personal autonomy; that is, it dealt with the right to make and carry out the abortion decision without government interference. Second, the nature of competing state interests differed significantly in the two cases. In *Griswold*, the state had to show that a persuasive interest was served by regulating the contraceptive practices of married couples—no small task. But in *Roe* the state was in a far more powerful position. It could claim that, in preventing abortions, it was protecting an incipient life (the fetus). Nevertheless, the Court held that a woman, in consultation with her physician, has an absolute right to decide to have an abortion in the

Wide World Photos

This photograph shows Oliver Sipple (the man wearing the light jacket on the extreme left) seconds after spoiling Sara Jane Moore's assassination attempt on President Ford. Afterwards, Sipple became a hero. But the publicity also revealed that he was a member of San Francisco's homosexual community. Sipple sued several newspapers for invading his privacy.

first trimester of pregnancy and a qualified right thereafter.

Clearly, the concept of privacy has moved beyond the right to be left alone in one's livingroom. In his dissenting opinion from a ruling by the U.S. Court of Appeals in Richmond, Virginia, that upheld a state sodomy statute, the late Judge J. Braxton Craven, Jr., provided one of the better attempts at defining this expanded concept of privacy. "This freedom," he wrote, "may be termed more accurately 'the right to be let alone,' or personal autonomy, is simply 'personhood.'" Definitions aside, the issue of privacy, as reflected in decisions like *Roe*, continues to be controversial.

CIVIL RIGHTS: THE QUEST FOR EQUALITY

To restate the central theme of this chapter: The purpose of American politics is achieving equality in freedom. In the preceding pages, we have examined the bedrock freedoms guaranteed by the Constitution. In the pages that follow, we shall look at how those freedoms have not been equally shared by all Americans. We shall also look at what efforts have been made to do something about this inequality in freedom. We shall begin with the black's struggle for equality; it is the most conspicuous struggle and, in many respects, provided the inspiration for those that came after.

Blacks in America: The Great Contradiction

From slavery to emancipation. Apparently, blacks in early America took the words of the Declaration of Independence quite seriously. Consider the names they chose when they were allowed to join the Continental Army: Cuff Freedom, Dick Freedom, Ned Freedom, Peter Freeman, Cuff Liberty, Jeffrey Liberty, Pomp Liberty. It is unlikely that they failed to note the irony of fighting a war under the banner of liberty and equality.

Even as the founders drafted that inspired framework for a free society, the Constitution, they continued to condone slavery. We can be fairly certain they were not altogether comfortable with such contradictions. Why else would they resort to such euphemisms as "other persons" when the word *slave* was what they really meant?

Successive generations sought to resolve this great contradiction. Sometimes the initiatives ended in disaster, as in the case of Dred Scott.

Essentially, the case involved the issue of the status of slavery in the federal territories. In 1834, Dred Scott, a Negro slave, was taken by his master from Missouri, a slave state, to Illinois, a free state, and then to the Wisconsin territory, where slavery was prohibited by the Missouri Compromise. Sometime after Scott was taken back to Missouri, he sued for his freedom. His grounds were that residence in a free state and then a free territory had ended his bondage. In a badly divided opinion, the Court ruled the blacks could not become citizens of the United States nor were they entitled to the rights and privileges of citizenship.

The great failure of this decision lay in pitting the Constitution itself against the very purpose of American politics: equality in freedom. As Don E. Fehrenbacher has perceptively pointed out, the founders were actually trying to write *two* constitutions—one for their own time, the other for the ages.[6] They viewed slavery "bifocally"; that is, it was plainly visible at their feet but disappeared when they lifted their eyes toward the future. The founders wrote a constitution for a free people that allowed for slavery to be permitted locally but not sanctioned nationally.

The Dred Scott decision was a disaster because it spread the problem of slavery from one region of the country to the entire country. At the same time, the decision put freedom on the defensive for the first time in the young country's history. But the anti-slavery forces were not about to accept as final that blacks could not be citizens and that Congress had no power to set limits on slaveholding in the territories. What was needed they thought was a constitutional amendment to overcome the Court's ruling. As it turned out, the antislavery forces were too optimistic. It took a civil war costing 365,000 lives and not one but three consitutional amendments—the 13th, 14th, and 15th.

The 13th and 14th amendments. The 13th Amendment prohibits slavery in the United States. It was held that certain state laws were in violation of this amendment; they, in effect, jailed a debtor who did not perform his financial obligations. The Supreme Court ruled, however, that selective service laws authorizing the draft for military duty are not prohibited by this amendment.

The first sentence of the 14th Amendment overrules the *Dred Scott* decision: "All persons born or naturalized in the United States . . . are citizens of the United States and of the state wherein they reside." But the amendment had effects that went far beyond knocking down the *Dred Scott* decision. In particular, it provided the means by which the Bill of Rights could be applied to the states: No state shall "deprive any person of life, liberty, or property without due process of law."

The due process clause requires government to observe a number of restraints. Before action can be taken to deprive individuals of their basic liberty or property, they must be given notice and an opportunity to be heard before an impartial tribunal under conditions that enforce fairness. For example, public school teachers who have a reasonable expectation of tenure must be given the opportunity to have a hearing before they are dismissed. The same requirement applies before a public school student may be dismissed or suspended. Also, criminal defendants are protected from prosecution under vague statutes. Every element necessary to establish their culpability must be proved beyond a reasonable doubt. Due process also insures that prosecutors may not conceal evidence favorable to defendants. It protects the rights of convicted persons, requiring fair treatment of them in prison. In addition, the Court has begun to apply the notion of due process to those committed to or confined in mental institutions. Finally, as a function of due process, juvenile defendants are now afforded procedures tailored both to protect them and to preserve the uniqueness of the system of juvenile justice.

The 14th Amendment also prohibits a state from making unreasonable or arbitrary distinctions among persons as to their rights and privileges: "No state shall . . . deny to any person within its jurisdiction the equal protection of the laws." The aim here is to prevent a State from depriving a minority group, no matter how small or unpopular, its rights. Like the founders, the Court, under the **equal protection clause,** seeks to prevent tyranny rule by the majority.

Finally, in addition to providing these protections to American citizens, the 14th Amendment states who is a citizen. The condition of membership in the republic is an important

FIGURE 11-1
Extending the Bill of Rights to the 50 States

Beginning with ***Gitlow v. New York*** (1925), the Supreme Court began to use the due process clause of the 14th Amendment as a conduit through which the Bill of Rights guarantees could be applied to the states.

In 1937, Justice Cardozo formulated the doctrine, known as the **Palko test,** which distinguished between such rights as (a) the First Amendment freedoms and (b) indictment by a grand jury or trial before a jury in a civil case. According to Cardozo, the former rights were so fundamental that no state could be permitted to violate them. But replacement of the latter rights by other procedures at the state level could be permitted. The Palko doctrine was not to last, however.

By the 1960s, the Supreme Court had broadened the interpretation of the 14th Amendment to limit state actions in most areas in which the founding fathers in 1791, had banned federal action.

Einstein's Theory of Citizenship

The 14th Amendment to the Constitution defines American citizenship: "All persons born or naturalized in the United States, and subject to the jurisdiction thereof, are citizens of the United States and of the state wherein they reside." Citizenship is therefore based mainly on one's place of birth *(jus soli)*. So, persons born in the United States are American citizens regardless of the their parents' citizenship. (Only one exception to the rule: children born to foreign ambassadors.)

But a person may acquire citizenship in two other ways. One is though blood relations *(jus sanguinis)*. A child born of an American parent living abroad is an American citizen at birth, provided one citizen parent has been present in the United States before the child's birth. The other way a person can become an American citizen is through the legal process of **naturalization.** Following the footsteps of millions of other men and women, this is the path the great Einstein traveled. How and why is worth retelling.

During his lifetime, Albert Einstein was a citizen of three countries: Germany (at birth and again at 34), Switzerland (at 22), and finally America (at 61). To him, citizenship was a matter not of birth but of moral choice. In a nation that denied the freedom of the human mind and spirit, citizenship was not worth having. Towards the end of his life, Einstein was drawn inevitably to the United States—"a country where political liberty, toleration and equality of all citizens before the law is the rule."

The naturalization procedure itself provides proof of America's dedication to that purpose. Clearly, the procedure is designed to foster the "Americanization" of the alien. An individual 18 years of age or older may be naturalized after meeting certain qualifications. These include: (1) residence in the United States for five years; (2) the ability to read, write, and speak English; (3) proof of good moral character; (4) knowledge of the history of and attachment to the principles of American government; (5) neither advocacy of communism nor other subversive or totalitarian organizations; and (6) taking of an oath of allegiance to the United States and renunciation of allegiance to one's former country. The Immigration and Naturalization Service of the Department of Justice handles the details; a federal judge administers the examination and oath.

Some would say that these efforts to measure moral standards and political view are excessive. Why the curiosity about personal views on the ethical basis of authority? Why, in America, the land of the free, are immigrants asked what they think of freedom?

Gilbert Chesterton, an English writer who visited the United States in 1921, suggests an answer: "America, with its ambition of combining the most disparate ingredients in one republic, had to have a mold of some kind." I would like

Wide World Photos

> to pause to let the meaning of those words sink in. We must not become so preoccupied with the dark and ugly moments of ethnic relations in America that we lose sight of the obvious: America has assimilated an extraordinary variety of ethnic groups. As the editors of the *Harvard Encyclopedia of American Ethnic Groups* put it, "The capacity of the United States to absorb so many different people and to forge binding ties among them is . . . incredible." The variety is indeed astonishing. The *Encyclopedia* has entries on Albanians, Assyrians, Bosnian Muslims, Cape Verdeans, Copts, Cossacks, Frisians, Kurds, Maltese, Manx, Tatars, and Turkestanis—to name only some of the more exotic ethnic groups that have found their way to the United States. But to get back to Professor Einstein . . .
>
> On October 1, 1940 in a court in Trenton, New Jersey, Albert Einstein and his daughter became American citizens. The act was a commitment to an idea; it was not an identification with some race or nationalistic movement. Of nationalism Einstein said: "Nationalism is an infantile disease. It is the measles of Mankind."

matter. Citizenship is an office; it carries with it certain powers and responsibilities. The box concerning Einstein's theory of citizenship explains how citizenship is acquired and retained.

From Jim Crow to Linda Brown. Despite a bloody civil war and three constitutional amendments, the great contradiction remained. The blacks' quest for equality had not ended. In many ways, the real struggle had just begun.

Southern legislatures began to pass **Jim Crow laws** that required segregation of blacks and whites. Blacks were deemed "unfit to vote, to serve on juries, to drink from whites' water fountains, to worship in whites' churches, and so on and so on, from birth through life and into death, barred from white funeral parlors and white cemeteries, forever unworthy."[7] For more than six decades, not only did the baser side of human nature prevail; it was the law, the expression of the body politic.

All obstacles to these odious laws were removed by a decision of the Supreme Court, ***Plessy* v. *Ferguson*** (1896). This decision upheld a state law requiring segregation to the races in public transportation. The Court held that under the equal protection clause of the 14th Amendment, a state could provide "separate" facilities for blacks as long as they were "equal."

This doctrine remained in effect until the early afternoon of May 17, 1954. On that day, Earl Warren, a new chief justice of the United States, decided whether the Reverend Oliver Brown's daughter Linda, a fifth grader, had a right to go to the school of her choice. Linda Brown was black; the Topeka, Kansas, school she wanted to attend was white.

The case had troubled the nine judges of the court for more than two years. And the outcome of *Brown* v. *Board of Education of Topeka, Kansas*, broadcast that afternoon in 34 languages around the world, would resound like few rulings before or since. "We conclude," the court decreed unanimously, "that in the

Elliott Erwitt/Magnum Photos, Inc.

Separate but not-so-equal water fountains.

field of public education the doctrine of 'separate but equal' has no place."

Though a great landmark, *Brown* v. *Board of Education* was more the culmination of a train of events than a sudden bolt from the blue. During the two decades before *Brown*, the foundations of legalized racial discrimination had begun to weaken. In 1947, Jackie Robinson broke the color line in baseball. In 1948, the Supreme Court forbade the enforcement of restrictive clauses that kept blacks out of white neighborhoods. In that same year President Truman ordered immediate desegregation of the armed forces. In 1950, the Supreme Court held in *Sweatt* v. *Painter* that Texas could not satisfy the 14th Amendment simply by establishing a separate law school for Negroes.

The *Brown* decision, like *Sweatt*, attempted to grapple with the subtle, intangible effects of segregation. In the *Brown* decision, the Court took judicial notice of the view that putting black children in separate schools "generates a feeling of inferiority . . . that may affect their hearts and minds in a way unlikely ever to be undone." This decision appeared to turn largely on recent findings of social scientists and statisticians regarding the adverse psychological effects that segregation had upon schoolchildren. Yet one wonders, Is this the best grounds for attacking segregation by race? A stronger, clearer reason, it would seem, is that racial segregation contradicts the language of the Declaration of Independence—that "all men are created equal."

The civil rights movement. The Supreme Court had decided; now local school authorities and federal district courts would have to enforce the decision. Given the years of segregation and Jim Crow laws, enforcement would not be easy. Moving cautiously, the Supreme Court in 1955 said only that desegregation was to proceed "with all deliberate speed."

The first major showdown came in 1957 at Little Rock's Central High School. Arkansas governor Orval Faubus had sought to prevent nine black students from entering the school. President Eisenhower faced essentially two choices. He could let Faubus' personal opposition to *Brown* stand in the way of the legal rights of black schoolchildren; or he could exercise his constitutional powers. By sending a thousand Army paratroopers to Little Rock, he chose to enforce the law.

The second act in the drama, which began in 1962, seemed much like the first. A federal court had ordered a black student, James Meredith, be enrolled in a southern school, the all-

Carl Iwasaki, *Life* magazine; © Time, Inc.

In *Brown* v. *Board of Education of Topeka, Kansas,* the Supreme Court concluded "that in the field of public education, the doctrine of 'separate but equal' has no place." With those words, segregation laws in the 17 states that had them were declared unconstitutional. A companion decision rendered the same afternoon, *Bolling* v. *Sharpe,* struck down segregation in Washington, D.C. Linda Brown could go to school wherever she wanted.

> **Quiz**
>
> **Who is this woman?**
>
> Wide World Photos

Answer on p. 403.

white University of Mississippi. This time, however, violence broke out. Only after 14,000 federal troops had arrived and two people had been killed was peace restored.

The next year the scene and tempo changed. Martin Luther King led a massive, peaceful March on Washington. President Johnson successfully urged Congress once again, after a long hibernation on racial matters, to act. The results were the **Civil Rights Act of 1964** and the **Voting Rights Act of 1965**. The 1964 act made discrimination against any group in hotels, motels, and restaurants illegal. It also forbade many kinds of job discrimination. The 1965 act prohibited literacy tests and other devices designed to limit voting by blacks.

Section 5 of the 14th Amendment furnished Congress ample power to do what Johnson thought necessary. Besides the two mentioned acts, a number of significant pieces of legislation have been passed under this positive grant of authority. Among other guarantees, such legislation has established the right to be free from racial discrimination in public dining facilities, in transportation facilities, and in the operation of public recreational facilities; the right of equality of opportunity to hold public employment, to be free from racial discrimination in government housing, and to be free from purposeful discrimination by city authorities in their official relations.

In 1968, the Court also began to rouse itself once again. In *Green* v. *County Board of New Kent County* (Virginia), it spoke of an *affirmative* duty to eliminate discrimination "root and branch." Also the Court decreed that a school board must develop a plan that promises to work. Three years later, under a new chief justice, Warren Burger, the Supreme Court reaffirmed the power of federal courts to order schools to integrate. Among the remedies available were redrawing attendance zones and requiring the busing of students.

But a major reversal of these trends occurred in 1974. In *Milliken* v. *Bradley*, the Court limited a federal court's power to order busing across school district boundary lines to achieve integration. Such busing could occur only where there had been past practices of racial discrimination or where district lines had been deliberately drawn to provide for segregated schools. The decision overturned a major cross-county busing order in Detroit. It gave strong support to the concept of the neighborhood school. Thus the Court drew a distinction between segregation imposed by state law and segregation resulting from housing patterns. The former is known as *de jure* segregation; the latter is *de facto* segregation.

Martin Luther King, Jr., asserted the need for legislative and judicial actions to the struggle for civil rights. But he also recognized how laws and other institutions in American politics "work to throw more and more responsibility on the consciences of the individuals." He thought that "the ultimate solution to the race problem lies in the willingness of men to obey the unenforceable." Until that glorious time, however, King would settle for an expansion of existing civil rights laws: "Morality cannot be legislated, but behavior can be regulated. Judicial decrees may not change the heart, but they can restrain the heartless."

Members of the football team at a high school in St. Louis greet one of 17 buses carrying black students to school on the first day of court-ordered desegregation in 1980. The extent of integration in the public schools is a matter of debate, much of which centers on the definition of an "integrated" school unit. The U.S. Civil Rights Commission has concluded that, in 1977, 46 percent of the nation's black schoolchildren still attended schools that were "at least moderately segregated," even though the number was down sharply from 76 percent in 1968. Progress towards integration has been far more promising in higher education.

Today, almost 30 years after the Supreme Court ruled in favor of Linda Brown, virtually all of America's largest urban school systems are more racially imbalanced than ever. Despite increased court-ordered busing, the outlook is for more segregation—not less. What happened?

Powerful demographic forces that extend beyond the reach of court decisions appear to be dooming the goal of improved racial balance in schools. In almost every big urban school district, the proportion of whites continues to fall rapidly. For example, in Los Angeles, the proportion of whites in the school district fell from 56 percent in 1966 to 29 percent in 1980; less than 14 percent is the projection for 1987. In Detroit, whites were 50 percent in 1970; in 1980, they constitute less than 20 percent.

Consequently, there are simply not enough white children to go around.

But this exodus of whites is not the only population shift that has affected desegregation. Large numbers of Hispanic immigrants are moving into many cities. This trend throws previously planned programs out of kilter.

Many civil rights activists argue that the only way urban schools can be integrated in the face of these population shifts is to merge city schools with suburban districts. Then children could be bused back and forth in so-called metropolitan busing plans. But the outlook for such plans does not appear good. First, they arouse enormous opposition from suburbanites. And second, the courts have been reluctant to go along with the concept unless given explicit evidence that suburban districts have been systematically guilty of past discriminatory practices.

The Politics of Equality

"Beyond opportunity." Since the coming of Franklin Roosevelt and the New Deal, the concept of equality of results has filled the political air in the United States. The Depression changed the way Americans viewed government. What was once a passive enterprise became an engine of salvation from despair and violence. It protected what savings were left in banks; it gave jobs to the hungry; it helped the aged. Faced with mass suffering and the collapse of an economy, President Roosevelt, the consummate pragmatist, tried one tool after another. Government was becoming a bestower of benefits. The welfare state had arrived, though no one called it by that name. If people were unemployed, then they were *entitled* to government help. If people wanted decent food, clothing, and housing, then government had an *obligation* to guarantee those rights. The notion of an economy built by rugged individualists, free of government intervention, rushed out the back door.

The concept of equality of results really came into prominence in the early 1960s. In an important speech in 1965, President Lyndon Johnson explained why equality of results should be distinguished from the older idea of equality of opportunity. The time had come, he said, for government programs to help blacks move "beyond opportunity":

> You do not take a person who, for years, has been hobbled by chains and liberate him, bring him to the starting line of a race, and then say you are free to compete with all the others, and still just believe that you have been completely fair. Thus it is not enough just to open the gates of opportunity. All our citizens must have the ability to walk through those gates. This is the next and more profound stage of the battle for civil rights. We seek not just freedom but opportunity. We seek not just legal equity but human ability, not just equality as a right and a theory but equality as a fact and equality as a result.[8]

In time, the ideas expressed in Johnson's speech proved overly optimistic. Many Americans did not accept willingly the notion that race could and should be explicitly recognized as a way of identifying who had what claims on government. The mounting cost of the War in Vietnam, a slowing down in economic growth, and a growing realization about the complexity of social intervention all conspired to blunt the thrust of Johnson's speech. Let us take a closer look at what went happened.

Voting Rights Act of 1965. The Voting Rights Act of 1965 was the fourth modern attempt—after the Civil Rights Acts of 1957, 1960, and 1964—at ensuring the rights of southern blacks to vote. This was a traditional concern of civil rights advocates: access to the ballot. But this idea suggested another: The federal government should guarantee the right to maximum political effectiveness, the right to equal electoral *results*.

The key provisions of the Voting Rights Act of 1965 is that it suspended literary tests and other devices in all states and political subdivisions with a voting registration or turnout of

> **Answer to Quiz (See page 400)**
>
> On the afternoon of December 1, 1955, Rosa Parks, a black seamstress, took a bus ride that became a milestone of the civil rights movement. Defying the custom and law of Montgomery, Alabama, she refused to give up her seat to a white man. She was arrested. Within days, thousands of local blacks forged a year-long boycott that left buses virtually empty. It was from that boycott that a 26-year-old black preacher named Martin Luther King, Jr., became known nationally as the resonant voice of black protest against racial discrimination. Rosa Parks is an extraordinary example of what ordinary Americans can do. She is also a reminder that, though the simple decencies of life may seem banal to many people, they owe their enjoyment of those decencies to the bravery of previous generations.

less than 50 percent. Furthermore the act forbids, in those same jurisdictions, the start of any new "voting qualifications or prerequisite to voting" without the approval of the attorney general or the District of Columbia court.

But in time the act took on a quite different meaning. It became more than simply a means of making sure that the ban on literacy tests stuck; it became the instrument to ensure electoral effectiveness of minorities. What brought this all about was the Supreme Court's 1969 decision in *Allen* v. *Board of Elections*.*

The *Allen* decision must be distinguished from the epic *Baker* v. *Carr*, which established in 1962 a constitutional right to equal representation for equal numbers. The Supreme Court's concern in the *Allen* decision was the poor representation of interests and racial groups among elected officials—not inequalities in the weight of individual voters. The *Allen* decision established the necessity for equality among groups in the results of an election. For example, if all members of a city council had to be elected on a citywide basis, this might make the election of a black candidate difficult in a city that had a white majority. Whereas if the members were elected from various parts of the city, then a black candidate would have a much better chance of being elected.

Now the test is not "one man–one vote"; it is whether the group to which that person belongs is "underrepresented" in the system. "Group power, not individual worth," Abigail M. Therstrom writes, "is made the measure of political equity."[9]

Bakke to Fullilove. More recent Supreme Court cases also address the issue of whether slots should be assigned on the basis of race or ethnicity. As we saw earlier in this chapter, efforts to deal with racial discrimination after the *Brown* decision focused on purification of the process; that is, that dealt with insuring the access of blacks to the ballot, to schools, to opportunity. But slowly the focus shifted to results. The federal government began to insist on **affirmative action** (setting ethnic and sex quotas for employment and promotion) by public and private institutions. National policy had moved beyond preventing discrimination to using quotas and direct action to achieve balance.

---

* The case involved several statutory amendments to electoral procedures in Mississippi. The most important of these involved a switch from **single-member districts** to **at-large voting** for county supervisors. The issue is somewhat complex. In a single-member district, a single representative is chosen, usually by a plurality vote ("winner take all") by subdivisions of an entire government unit. In an at-large election, voters of the entire government unit (in this case, a county) elect members of the entire body (in this case, supervisors). Election of supervisors at large, it is argued, does not "mirror" local interests as well as the district system; hence, minority groups, who often cannot muster enough countrywide support to win, are not represented in proportion to their strength in the voting population. The party or race of the majority captures all contested seats.

A symbol of the shift, coming approximately a quarter century after *Brown*, was the Supreme Court's 1978 decision in **Regents of California v. Bakke.** The University of California at Davis had a special admissions program for minority applicants to its medical school. Allan Bakke had scored higher on the entrance examination than all of the special admissions candidates. He filed suit alleging that his exclusion violated his rights under the 14th Amendment, which says that no state will deny "equal protection of the laws." Five justices voted to require Davis to admit Bakke. He was the first Norwegian-American ever to win a race-discrimination case in the Supreme Court. But five justices also asserted that universities might use race as one factor among many other factors in the admissions process. So special admissions programs won, too.

Unsatisfied, some argue that the use of racial quotas creates divisions in socitey. But if law schools ignored race and went purely by test scores, the percentage of blacks among first-year law students would drop from about 5 percent to between 1 and 2 percent. Somehow it is hard to think of such results as creating less division within American society.

Not long after the *Bakke* decision, the Supreme Court faced another tough case. Brian Weber was a white employee at the Kaiser Aluminum Company in Gramercy, Louisiana. He had sued both his employer and his union over a voluntary affirmative action plan they negotiated in 1974. The company had never been found guilty of past discrimination. However, it feared that federal affirmative action enforcement officials might come after it in the future, threatening lawsuits and tying up government contracts. So, in agreement with the union, it set up a special training program for high-paying skilled crafts jobs. Fifty percent of the program's places were reserved for minority group members. Weber could not make it into the program; blacks with lower seniority did. Weber sued, claiming racial discrimination of a kind explicitly forbidden by the 1964 Civil Rights Act.

Like Bakke, **Weber v. Kaiser Aluminum Co.** (1979) was upheld all the way through the Court of Appeals. But, unlike Bakke, the Supreme Court overturned the circuit court decision and ruled against him. The Kaiser–United Steelworkers of America plan did not involve state action. Therefore the case did not raise issues of the equal protection clause of the Constitution. The crux of the issue was only whether the Civil Rights Act forbade voluntary efforts of the type used by Kaiser. The Court concluded that it did not.

The majority opinion, written by Justice

Copyright 1977 *The Washington Star.* Reprinted with permission of Universal Press Syndicate. All rights reserved

Laboratory analyst Brian Weber at entrance to Kaiser facility in Gramercy, La.

William Brennan, relied on what he saw as the "spirit" of the job-bias provisions of the 1964 Civil Rights Act.

> It would be ironic indeed if a law triggered by a nation's concern over centuries of racial injustice and intended to improve the lot of those who had been victims of discrimination constituted the first legislative prohibition of all voluntary, private race-conscious efforts to abolish traditional patterns of racial segregation and hierarchy.

The decision was widely hailed as a victory of major proportions by civil rights advocates. They saw it as a breakthrough that dismissed the basic notion of **reverse discrimination.** It gave the green light to companies that want to bring in more employees who are members of minority groups, but who had hesitated out of fear of legal retribution by white applicants and employees.

Two years after the ambiguous *Bakke* case and one year after the carefully limited *Weber* case, the Supreme Court upheld for the first time a congressionally enacted affirmative action program. In another important decision, the Court endorsed the power of Congress to award federal benefits on the basis of race. *Fullilove* v. *Fultznick* (1980) was a powerful constitutional statement likely to become a potent tool for racial minorities seeking, in the words of Chief Justice Burger, "to achieve the goal of economic opportunity."

The debate over affirmative action. A majority of Americans approve of government actions to help disadvantaged groups catch up, especially when those groups have been clearly discriminated against. But, when government actions attempt to provide preferential treatment for those groups, approval melts away quite rapidly. The reason for the unpopularity of **affirmative action** by government is that it is intended to discriminate on behalf of those in specific groups—although, to be sure, that group was discriminated against in the past. Interestingly, both blacks and whites oppose this kind of "reverse discrimination."*

Virtually every effort to introduce preferential treatment meets opposition. In February 1981, the editorial board of the prestigious Harvard Law Review voted to reserve four spaces for black students who had very good but not outstanding records. After two weeks of bitter controversy, the Review changed its mind. If a liberal institution such as Harvard fights to preserve its merit principle, one can understand the bitterness that decisions like *Weber* and *Fullilove* create among blue-collar workers.

But one should also try to understand the *ideas* behind affirmative action. Basically, the intent of such programs is to establish fairness or justice. As we know from Chapter 3, justice is really more than equality. Based on past experiences, a *fair* treatment of some groups may not mean *equal* treatment of all groups. Let me put this as strongly as I can. To make individual liberty the overriding value can only be acceptable in a society that has never violated this value in the past. Can it be fair for a society that has practiced group discrimination to sud-

---

* A 1974 Gallup poll found that 96 percent of all Americans said a job or promotion should go to the best qualified person regardless of race. Among blacks, 83 percent agreed.

denly say, "OK, now we are going to be a society based on individual performance. Therefore, we cannot have reverse discrimination"? Would that be fair to those groups that had experienced discrimination?

One further point. As anyone who has pondered government aid to the textile industry and farmers knows, government is already heavily engaged in helping groups. And make no mistake about it: Any action by government to help one group is likely to be at the expense of some other group—at least to a degree.

To make the preceding arguments is not to say that all is well with affirmative action. Rather, it is to say that a legitimate rationale for such programs in terms of fairness does exist. Whether affirmative action is an effective method to overcome the income differences between racial and ethnic groups in the United States is a separate question (which we shall address in the next chapter).

EQUALITY IN FREEDOM: AN ASSESSMENT OF AMERICA IN THE 1980s

Erma "Tiny" Motton is a black mother of five in rural Missouri. She felt so demeaned by welfare that she took two jobs to put herself through high school, then college. Now she can respect herself.

> Tiny's a long way of bein' out of the pocket, but just like an ant, I'm wigglin' hard. You know I'm there. What the dream means to me is for my children to be able to live anywhere they want to, even be able to come back home where they were born and raised, and get a good job, hold their head high. Not given something because they're black, and not something taken away from them because they're black. But given something because they're a man and they deserved it. That's my American Dream. I do believe something's stirring.[10]

What is one to make of such a statement, found in Studs Terkel's *American Dreams: Lost and Found?* Some would no doubt argue that it provides eloquent testimony that the republic is still progressing towards ever greater equality in freedom. Others, less hopeful, would ask why, at this late date in the republic's history, Tiny Motton must take two jobs to put herself through high school and college. Perhaps the most judicious interpretation is to say that at least the ideal—if not the reality—of equality in freedom continues to be a part of the American political culture. It resonates as much in Tiny Motton's words as it did in Independence Hall that February morning in 1861 when Lincoln spoke.

An assessment of equality in freedom may be approached from two directions. We can take the comparative approach: How well America is doing in comparison with yesterday? Or we can look at the facts and—the hard part—try to understand what they mean.

Historical Perspective

Reading today's newspaper and watching the evening news distorts the reality of contemporary race relations in the United States. Simply put, from a historical perspective, conditions have improved vastly. In 1830, Congress passed a law requiring all Indians east of the Mississippi River to move, under Army escort, to the "Indian Territory" west of the river. Today Indian groups are winning victory after victory in the white man's courts (see Chapter 9). In the late 1800s, Chinese and Japanese were viewed with disdain. In the 1940s, Franklin Roosevelt ordered the army to remove all Japanese-Americans from their homes in California and place them to "relocation centers." Today these groups—not white Anglo-Saxons Protestants—are among America's most prosperous ethnic groups (see box). There is also a significant absence of racial, religious, or ethnic resistance and protest to new groups coming to these shores. Historically unprecedented is the absence of any significant protest by American citizens in general or labor unions in particular to the recent admission of thousands of Indo-Chinese, Cubans, and Haitians. In the 1850s,

The Fallacy of a National Average

Anglo-Saxons are not pace setters in income, occupations, or education. Americans of Jewish, Japanese, Polish, Chinese, or Italian ancestry make more money. While the image of the WASP is one of old families in elite enclaves, the reality also includes desperately poor people scattered along hundreds of miles of the Appalachians, and others scattered throughout the whole range of American incomes and occupations.

The idea of a "national average" is as misleading as the idea of a WASP majority. Most people are not average. Variations in income from one group to another are common, and income variations among age brackets, or among cities, are even larger than income variations among ethnic groups. The national average is nothing more than a statistical amalgamation of all these wide-ranging diversities. The idea that it is a norm or a standard—that any statistical deviation from it is both unusual and suspicious, and that we would all be the same except for the sins of "society"—is arbitrary political rhetoric.

The incomes of so-called ethnic minorities do not line up below the mythical national norm but range on both sides of the statistical average. For example, the following American ethnic groups earned the following percentages of the national average in family income, at the time of the most recent census (*Essays and Data on American Ethnic Groups*, Urban Institute, 1978.)

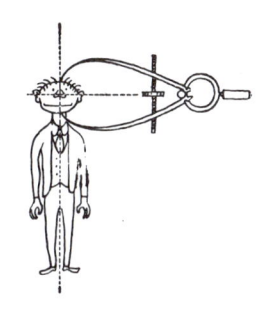

Ethnicity	Income
Jewish	172%
Japanese	132
Polish	115
Italian	112
Chinese	112
German	107
Anglo-Saxon	107
Irish	103
National Average	100
Filipino	99
West Indian	94
Mexican	76
Puerto Rican	63
Black	62
Indian	60

SOURCE: Thomas Sowell, "Myths about Minorities." Reprinted from *Commentary*, August 1979, pp. 33–34. By permission; all rights reserved.

---

the Boston police department fought against hiring—of all things—Irishmen. In the 1930s, Cornell University's medical school had a strict quota to limit the number of Jewish students. Today not only are there thousands of Irish police and Jewish physicians; there are also thousands of Irish and Jewish political leaders.

Until 1870 and 1920, respectively, blacks and women did not have a constitutionally guaranteed right to vote. Today the number of blacks and women elected officials approaches 20,000—though the figures for both groups remains disproportionately low (see Tables 11–1 and 11–2).

Education is no longer the sole privilege of the wealthy; it is a right of all. In 1966, the median number of years of school completed by blacks was 10; by 197, the number reached 12.3. (In the same span, the comparable figure for whites rose only from 12.3 to 12.6 years.) Along the same line, a study by New York's Conference Board shows that, in a recent six-year period, "the number of black college students more than doubled . . . from 520,000 to 1,000,000."[11] This gain far exceeds a 35 percent rise in overall college enrollment in the same six years. In 1978, 20.1 percent of black youths ages 18 to 24 were enrolled in college;

TABLE 11-1
Black Elected Officials by Office, 1970 to 1979

Year	Total	U.S. and State Legislatures*	City and County Offices†	Law Enforcement‡	Education§
1970 (Feb.)	1,472	182	715	213	362
1972 (Mar.)	2,264	224	1,108	263	669
1973 (Apr.)	2,621	256	1,264	334	767
1974 (Apr.)	2,991	256	1,602	340	793
1975 (Apr.)	3,503	299	1,878	387	939
1976 (Apr.)	3,979	299	2,274	412	994
1977 (July)	4,311	316	2,497	447	1,051
1978 (July)	4,503	316	2,595	454	1,138
July 1979	4,584	315	2,647	486	1,136

(As of July 1979, no black elected officials had been identified in Idaho, Montana, North Dakota, South Dakota, Utah, Vermont, or Wyoming.)
 * Includes elected state administrators and directors of state agencies.
 † County commissioners and councilmen, mayors, vice mayors, aldermen, regional officials, and other.
 ‡ Judges, magistrates, constables, marshals, sheriffs, justices of the peace, and other.
 § College boards, school boards, and other.
 Source: Joint Center for Political Studies, Washington, D.C., *National Roster of Black Elected Officials*, annual. (Copyright.)

TABLE 11-2
Women Holding Public Offices, by Office, 1975 to 1979

Year	Total	State Judiciary*	U.S. and State Legislature	County Commission	Mayoralty	Townships and Local Councils
1975	7,089	92	629	456	566	5,365
1977	11,392	110	714	656	735	9,195
1979	14,364	177	787	958	998	11,461

 * Covers all major state appellate courts and trial courts.
 Source: Center for the American Woman and Politics, The Eagleton Institute of Politics, Rutgers University, New Brunswick, New Jersey, *National Information Bank on Women in Public Office.*

this compared with 25.7 percent for whites. As we have seen in this chapter, laws and customs that once excluded or segregated various minority groups have been reduced or abolished.

In addition, there have been dramatic changes in attitudes toward minorities, particularly blacks. Gallup polls over a 21-year period reveal progressively pro-black attitudes. In 1958, 42 percent of those polled would have voted for a "well-qualified" black as president; in 1978, 81 percent said they would do so. A Harris study of attitudes in 1963 and 1978 showed that white opposition to blacks' moving into their neighborhoods dropped from 62 to 39 percent.

What progress has been made in securing equal rights for women? The United States was the first country to admit women into any of the professions; teaching was the first profession to include women. Still, it was not until 1920 that the **Nineteenth Amendment** was adopted, granting women the right to vote.

In 1923, a constitutional amendment to guarantee equal rights for women was unsuccessfully introduced in Congress. This amendment was reintroduced every year thereafter until 1972 when Congress passed the Equal Rights Amendment (ERA). To become law, three fourths of the states (i.e., 38) must ratify it. The deadline for ratification, already extended once, was 1982.

While the prospects for the amendment itself shriveled, Congress and the courts were conscientiously ratifying its provisions *de facto*. The Equal Pay Act of 1963 covered some women workers; a 1972 amendment to it extended coverage to the professions. The Civil Rights Act of 1964 was amended by Congress in 1972 to include Title VII; this statute bans sex discrimination by institutions receiving federal funds (i.e., virtually everybody but the corner grocer). The fallout from that statute has been enormous. The Equal Employment Opportunity Commission (EEOC) recently declared even an office "pass" to be "sex harassment" litigable as discrimination. Title IX of the 1972 Higher Education Act prohibits sex discrimination in intercollegiate sports, etc. At the same time, state legislatures have been grinding out statutes to "equalize" everything from inheritance laws to poolrooms. Some states have added their own ERAs to their state constitutions.

But also important to ERA advocates are recent court decisions in which the Fifth and 14th Amendments have been construed to prohibit sex discrimination under the equal protection clause.

Over the last few years, laws attacking discrimination have involved more and more groups. The employment problems of older workers—who can be displaced by technological change and often have trouble finding new employment—also pose serious questions of equality for American society. In 1967, Congress passed the Age Discrimination in Employment Act. This law, amended in 1978, prohibits most employers, employment agencies, and labor unions from discriminating in employment against those between the ages of 40 and 70. The Rehabilitation Act of 1973 was an attempt

United Press International Photo

In common political usage, the term *minority* refers to Hispanics, Puerto Ricans, and Native Americans—in short, all those groups that are nonwhite and usually poor. Because the term has such an oppressed underdog connotation, it is preferred by a group even when that "minority" is a majority. The word is applied to women crusading for equal rights—although in 1976 women were 51.2 percent of the U.S. population.

In recent years, the term has extended to other groups with no basis in either race or gender, but who consider themselves discriminated against. Among these "newest" minorities are the aged, handicapped, children, mentally retarded, drug addicts, and homosexuals. In New York City and other cities, gay activists are lobbying for more police protection, as the crimes against them rise.

to provide legal equality for the handicapped. The law says, "No otherwise qualified handicapped individual . . . shall, solely by reason of his handicap, be excluded from participation in, be denied the benefit, or be subjected to discrimination under any program or activity receiving federal financial assistance." Despite strong feelings on the part of many Americans that homosexuality is immoral or even evil, gay rights is gaining ground as a civil rights issue. Homosexuals say they routinely are subjected to not only social stigmatization but to widespread abuses, ranging from job and housing bias to police brutality. Two states—California and Pennsylvania—have banned employment bias against homosexuals. Fifty cities and counties—ranging from large ones like New York, Detroit, Seattle, Boston, Washington, and San Francisco to heartland American locales like Iowa City and Yellow Springs, Ohio—have passed ordinances banning at least some forms of discrimination against gay people.

What Are the Facts and What Do They Mean?

The status of liberty. As you know from Figure 9–4, the Supreme Court under Chief Justice Earl Warren strengthened the right of criminals during the 1960s. It would be wrong to say, as does the cartoon, that the Burger Court has made hash out of our liberties. Yet there can be little doubt that the Burger Court has, over the past decade, revised the impact of many earlier decisions. For example, people accused of crimes are no longer automatically entitled to trials by juries of 12 members; trial judges are no longer required to instruct the jury that the accused is presumed innocent; the jury can convict with a less-than-unanimous verdict; poor people, accused of nonpetty crimes, do not necessarily have a right to a free lawyer; your bank and telephone records can be seized by the government without your knowledge; and newspaper reporters can be jailed for protecting their sources of information.

The revisions of the Burger Court, are likely to continue as President Reagan replaces retiring liberal judges with more conservative ones. These revisions may be summarized this way:

The expansion of the rights of suspects partially forged by the Warren Court has been dismantled through a series of decisions that have sharply limited these rights in the streets, in interrogation rooms, in police lineups, and in the courts.

Conflicts between an individual and the government have been resolved in favor of government.

A "new" constitutional right—the right to privacy—has been created. In *Griswold* and subsequent cases, the Court held that women have a right to make their own private decisions about conception and giving birth. In *Roe v. Wade*, the Burger Court extended this freedom from government interference.

What all this means depends largely on what political ideas you hold important. There is no need at this point to recapitulate Chapter 3, which was on the force of ideas. But it would be wrong to dismiss these trends as some sort of mindless drift towards totalitarianism. A more useful explanation is that we are witnessing more stress on certain ideas than others. Consider the Burger Court's tendency to resolve conflicts between the right of a fair trial of an individual (even the criminally convicted) and the right of the press to know and publish the truth; the Court has ruled mainly against the press. The Burger Court may be far less concerned about the rights of suspects than the Warren Court was; but it has been far *more* concerned about their rights when the press has been on the other side.

The status of equality. The next logical step in our assessment should be to look at how wealth and income are distributed in the United States. How are they distributed between blacks and whites and among all Americans? That is an issue that will be tackled in the next chapter, which is far more analytical than this one. So, fasten seatbelts.

Chapter Key

Though scholars might debate the purpose of American politics, a guiding assumption of this book is that "equality in freedom" is of central importance. For that reason, this chapter precedes the other three policy chapters. This does not mean that social, economic, and national security are less important. All three areas are essential to the survival of the American republic—indeed, to the survival of any modern nation. But to say that the purpose of American politics is national security is like saying that the purpose of life is eating; it confuses necessary functions with goals.

Equality in freedom has been the most constant theme in American politics. It can be traced from colonial times through the thoughts and deeds of Abraham Lincoln and Martin Luther King, Jr., right down to the present. If people around the world have historically looked to America as an example, they have not done so for its social programs, economic system, or armed forces. Rather they look to America as a sometimes flawed but nonetheless imperishable symbol of equality in freedom.

The Constitution describes the powers that the federal government has. The Bill of Rights describes limits on the government's power over its citizens. Those limits constitute the citizens' protections against government; they are known as civil liberties. When we speak of civil rights, we are referring to the question of whether every American has the opportunity to take part fully in the political system established by the Constitution.

The First Amendment states that no church shall be officially supported by the federal government and that citizens shall be free to exercise their religious belief. On the basis of these guarantees, the Supreme Court has outlawed prayer in public schools and most forms of government aid to church-related schools. It has permitted people to avoid military service on religious grounds. Yet it has denied individuals the right to some practices (such as polygamy) that were justified on religious grounds.

Other freedoms necessary to a democracy are the freedom of speech and press, the right to petition the government and to assemble peaceably, and the freedom of association and dissent. The Supreme Court has tried to balance its decisions in cases involving freedom of speech between maintaining liberty for citizens and maintaining public order. Justice Oliver

Wendell Holmes first announced the clear-and-present danger doctrine; the Supreme Court has generally tried to abide by that precedent. The Court has tended to oppose efforts by the government to impose prior restraint on speech and upon conduct considered a symbolic form of speech (e.g., marchers and demonstrations).

The difficulty of defining pornography has limited the effectiveness of laws and court rulings attempting to regulate obscene material. Conflicts persist between First Amendment press rights and the Sixth Amendment guarantee of a fair trial. The freedom the press enjoys to report the news does not extend to its rights to get the news. But the Freedom of Information Act of 1966 has opened many government sources previously closed to individual citizens, reporters, and groups. Recent decisions have not supported reporters claims that the right to protect news sources is central to a genuinely free press.

Americans have the right to privacy. However, police officials have the right to encroach on that privacy if they believe a crime has been committed and if they believe evidence is in danger of being destroyed. Generally the Warren Court increased protection against unreasonable searches; the Burger Court has limited them. Neither federal nor state law enforcement officials may use warrantless electronic surveillance except in cases involving national security. The Court has extended the right of privacy to include control over the use of one's body.

The Constitution includes protections against unreasonable search and seizure, self-incrimination, and cruel and unusual punishment. It guarantees the right to trial and the right to counsel. In recent years, the courts have ruled that illegally seized evidence may not be used in a trial. Also, any defendant accused of a crime for which jail is the punishment has the right to a lawyer. And an accused person must be told of his or her rights and may have a lawyer present during questioning.

The 14th Amendment defines national and state citizenship. Broad interpretation of the amendment, combined with additional congressional law, has extended its provisions far beyond its original purpose of granting citizenship to former slaves. The 14th Amendment also restricts state control over American citizens. The Constitution gave power to establish voting standards to the states. However, constitutional amendments, court decisions, and congressional laws have shifted much of that power to the federal government.

The Fifth and 14th Amendments guarantee Americans due process and equal protection under the law. They apply to both state and federal governments. The courts specifically guard the equal protection clause by giving extra scrutiny to cases that fall within constitutionally suspect classifications—i.e., laws classifying people on basis of race, religion, economic standing, and in some cases, sex.

Slavery for blacks in America officially ended with the Civil War. But southern states soon passed laws and altered constitutions to disenfrachise former slaves. The 14th Amendment granted full citizenship to blacks, and Congress passed the Civil Rights Acts to remedy this. However, in 1883 the Supreme Court declared the Civil Rights Act of 1875 unconstitutional; it violated the 14th Amendment by placing restrictions on individuals and private business. Rigid segregation became the rule since blacks were largely denied the right to vote. Jim Crow laws requiring separate public accommodations for the races spread throughout the southern and border states. In *Plessy* v. *Ferguson* (1896), the Supreme Court in effect upheld the Jim Crow laws by ruling that separate but equal facilities were consistent with the 14th Amendment. Fifty-eight years later *Brown* v. *Board of Education* reversed the *Plessy* ruling for educational facilities. It inaugurated a period of advancement in the black drive for equality. Presidents Eisenhower and Kennedy used federal power to enforce the *Brown* decision. Black leaders and organizations embarked on a period of demonstrations and protests for equal access to public private facilities. After Congress passed the Civil Rights Act of 1964, other acts and programs beneficial to the black cause followed.

Answer to Quiz

(b) In 1963, two reporters for *Life* magazine visited the home of A. A. Dietemann. One of the reporters, acting as if she were a patient, described imaginary cancer symptoms to Dietemann, who had no medical training and would later be described by a court as a quack. While Dietemann spoke with his "patient," his words were carried by a small radio transmitter in the reporter's purse to a parked car where an assistant district attorney listened. Meanwhile, the second reporter in Dietemann's house secretly took pictures.

Shortly thereafter, the "doctor" was arrested for practicing medicine without a license. Dietemann then sued *Life* for invasion of privacy. According to the Court, which ruled in his favor, Dietemann's "den was a sphere from which he could reasonably expect to exclude eavesdropping newsmen."

Ansel Adams

12 | How to Analyze Public Policy

After studying this chapter you should be able to answer the following questions:

1. Why is defining the problems of society so difficult?
2. What is the relationship between goals and strategies?
3. What are the potential costs, benefits, and risks in a public policy?
4. Why is it important to consider the distribution of costs and benefits?
5. In considering political feasibility, about what should the policy analyst be most concerned?
6. What are some of the things that can go wrong during the implementation of a policy?
7. Why is the evaluation of public policy both important and difficult?

Terms you should know:

Aid to Families with Dependent Children
alternatives
cost-benefit analysis
cost-effectiveness analysis
direct and indirect benefits
direct and indirect costs
Economic Opportunity Act of 1964
environment impact statement
evaluation
Family Assistance Plan of 1969
guaranteed annual income
guns and butter
income distribution
incrementalism

Job Corps
marginal analysis
medicaid
medicare
opportunity cost
policy analysis
rehabilitation
retribution
Social Security Act of 1935
subsidies
tax expenditure
trade-off
transfer payment

"If we can land a man on the moon, why can't we solve our social problems here on earth?" It was a frequent question around 1970, when the United States was in fact landing astronauts on the moon yet experiencing frustration arising from riots and decay in its major cities.

This incongruity between triumph in space and failure on earth is not hard to explain. No one lives between Cape Canaveral and Mare Tranquillitatis, site of the first manned lunar landing. This 250,000-mile stretch of space without property owners, truculent mayors, consumer groups, militant minorities, public-interest lawyers, or conspiring business executives is a social planner's dream.

The differences between planning a complex technical project like landing men on the moon and a social-economic project like creating jobs for the unemployed in Oakland could not be sharper. The two tasks are as different as playing chess with ivory pieces and playing croquet with live hedgehogs for balls and live flamingoes for mallets. The game of chess might require more intelligence; but at least, once the king's bishop has been moved, it will stay put. In our wonderland game of croquet, however, that assumption does not hold: Everything is alive with a will of its own. So it is with social programs.

This chapter will show you how to think systematically about public policy. The suggested approach can be applied to all public policies—civil liberties and rights, social, economic, foreign, and defense. However, the focus of this chapter will be chiefly on social policies.

If size is any indication, social policies constitute an extremely important part of what government does. In 1980, the federal government spent about $564 billion. About one fourth of that sum went to defense and international affairs. And a little over 11 percent went to paying interest on the national debt. (Governments, like people, have to pay for the money they borrow.) Most of the remaining billions went to social programs.

But let us be more specific. Social programs may be grouped in terms of the following 12 functions. (You can get some sense of their relative importance from the numbers in parentheses, which are the percentage of the total federal budget devoted to each.)

Income security (33.9 percent)*
Health (10.0 percent)
Energy (1.4 percent)
Administration of justice (less than 1 percent)
Transportation (3.5 percent)
Education and training (5.4 percent)
Environment and natural resources (2.3 percent)
Science, space, and technology (1.0 percent)
Veterans benefits (3.7 percent)
Commerce and housing credit (1.0 percent)
Community and regional development (1.5 percent)
Agriculture (less than 1 percent)

This chapter will also show you how to think more deeply about contemporary issues; how to probe behind surface events; how to *analyze* public policy. To "analyze" means to "decompose," "break down," "separate the whole into component parts." Given something as complex as a major public policy, analysis seems a reasonable road to a better understanding of that policy. One might be inclined to say that analysis is the thinking person's approach to the headlines. The thinking person does not stop with the facts presented. He or she tries to get behind the headlines and determine what they really mean.

But what are the components of a public policy? Can a public policy such as the Clean Air Act of 1972 be analyzed in the same way a chemist analyzes a compound or mixture? Figure 12–1 suggests that it can.

---

* Included here are programs designed to assure a reasonable income for poor Americans and to insure against loss of family income due to unemployment, retirement, disability, or death.

FIGURE 12-1
Steps in Policy Analysis

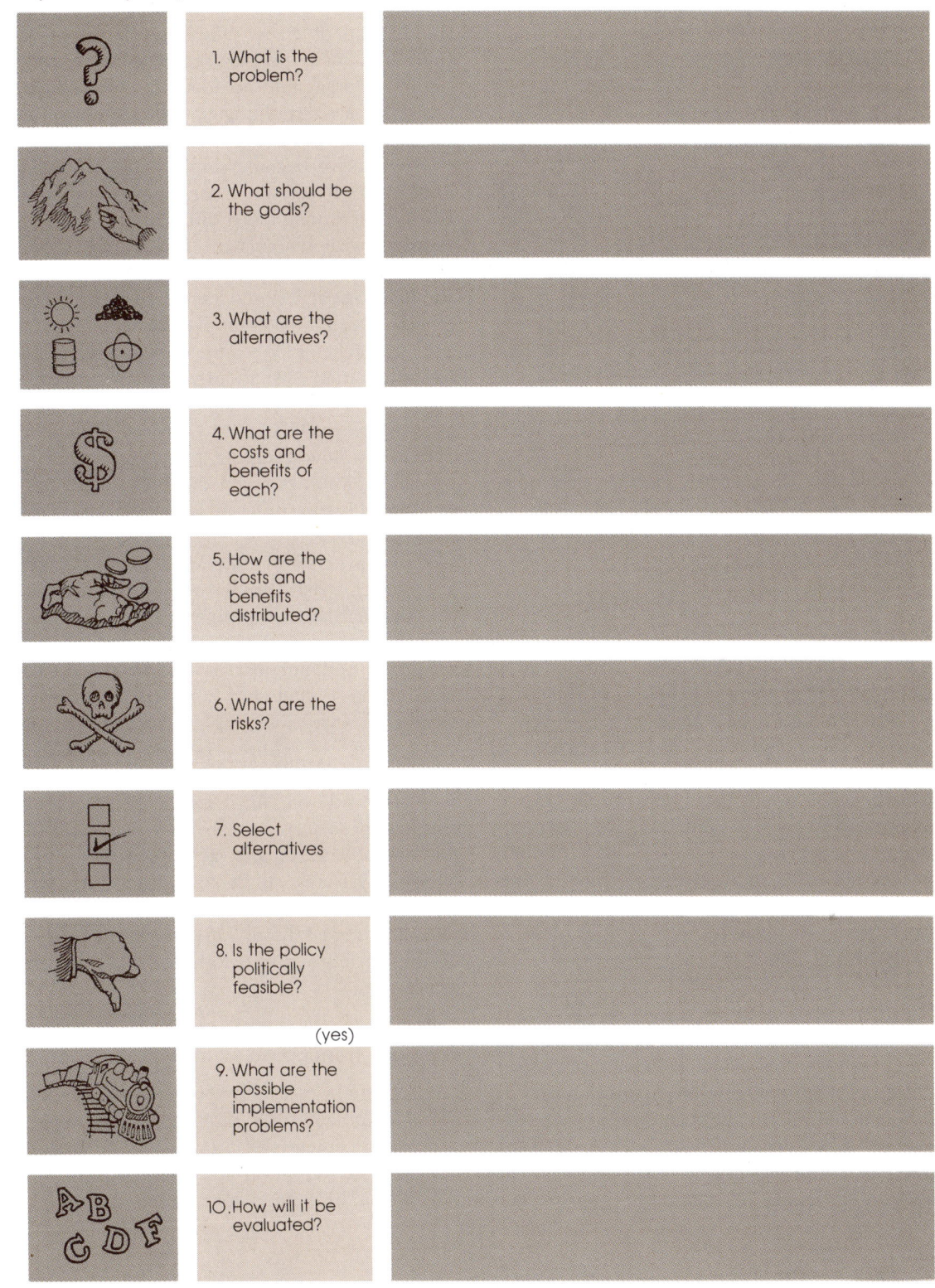

1. What is the problem?

2. What should be the goals?

3. What are the alternatives?

4. What are the costs and benefits of each?

5. How are the costs and benefits distributed?

6. What are the risks?

7. Select alternatives

8. Is the policy politically feasible?
(yes)

9. What are the possible implementation problems?

10. How will it be evaluated?

Understanding the fundamentals of policy analysis can help you see behind the headlines. In government, however, policy analysis is an ingredient in the play of power. Above, Senator Edward Kennedy uses a chart and statistics to discuss one of his favorite issues—tax reform.

This chapter will elaborate on Figure 12–1 in some detail. For each step, one, two, or three examples will be given. At the end of the chapter, you will find a quiz that lets you try your hand at the analysis of a policy proposal. If the chapter has served its purpose, your insights into the issue should be much deeper than if you tried to tackle it now. Also, your analysis of the issue should be more sophisticated than what is normally found in the morning or evening news.

1. WHAT IS THE PROBLEM?

The first question to ask about any proposed action by government is, What problem does it address? A policy can never be very successful if the problem is ill-defined or misunderstood.

Social and economic problems are *not* self-evident. They do not arrive on the desks of bureaucrats and legislators with neatly typed labels. They must be defined. People expect the Bureau of Labor Statistics (BLS) to tell them how many people are unemployed in the United States. But no formula can precisely fit everyone's idea of how to define and measure unemployment. If the wife of an $80,000-a-year executive becomes bored with civic work and decides to seek paid work at a fashion magazine, is she unemployed until hired? If her son registers with his college employment bureau for a Saturday job to earn money to buy gas for his Porsche, should he be counted in the official estimate of unemployed Americans? If a young bachelor looked for work unsuccessfully for more than two months until he became discouraged and quit looking, is he still classified as unemployed? Because there is a range of opinion on how to define unemployment, BLS regularly publishes seven distinct employment ratings reflecting different concepts of joblessness.

Policymakers and concerned citizens should also take care that they have not misunderstood the true nature of a problem. Like the skilled physician, they want to treat the real cause of an illness and not just its symptoms. By the same token, they do not want to fall into what I call the "root cause trap." Some say that the "root cause" of crime is poverty, poor education, substandard housing and health care, and so forth, and that until these conditions are eliminated society can do nothing about the crime problem. This is, at best, a half truth. Many physicians might think that the "root cause" of cancer is genetic, but few would argue that until a breakthrough in genetic engineering occurs, society can do nothing for cancer patients.

Example 1: Income Security

Let us begin by considering the simple question, *What is poverty?* Despite years of research, wide disagreement still prevails among specialists over the definition and causes of poverty. Poverty can be defined, for example, in absolute terms: "It takes X dollars per year for a nonfarm family of four to live decently. Anything less than X is poverty." But what are the "basic needs" of a family—just food, clothing, shelter, and health care? What is a "decent" level for these needs?

Assume that X could be determined with mathematical precision and be accepted universally by the public. Even then some specialists would not be satisfied. To them, the real problem of poverty is how one is doing in comparison to those around him. If you make $50,000 per year but live in a community of millionaires, this school of thought maintains that you are in poverty. Admittedly, this view has been stated in rather extreme terms. But it is not quite as absurd as it might seem. As human beings, we are very sensitive to relative incomes. Consider the case of two young lawyers hired by the same law firm. Both attended equally prestigious law schools and made similar grades. Yet one lawyer is payed $27,900 and the second receives $28,000. That $100 can seem enormous to the first lawyer. "Man is not just a blind glob of idling protoplasm," social psychologist Ernest Becker wrote in *The Denial of Death*, "but a creature with a name who lives in a world of symbols and dreams and not merely matter. His sense of self-worth is constituted symbolically, his cherished narcissism feeds on symbols, on an abstract idea of his own worth."

Different concepts of the causes of poverty suggest different remedies. Some specialists think the causes are individual—lack of motivation, lack of the right gene, instability of the family structure, etc. At the opposite pole are the sociologists and anthropologists. The former see poverty primarily as a "situational" problem characterized by misfortune. The latter believe a large segment of the poor is caught in a self-perpetuating "culture of poverty." Whatever put them there, millions of people find themselves trapped in a cycle that apparently has no beginning and no end:

Thus, a legacy of poverty passes from one generation to the next. But some research suggests that poverty is less permanent. One study found that only one fourth of the families stayed poor five years in a row.

Example 2: Health

Now let us turn to the question, *What is health?* The fastest-rising proportion of the GNP is devoted to health care.* Some political leaders charge that this rise is due to "waste" in the hospitals. But a careful analysis of hospital cost sheets could reveal that the primary source of

---

* Total health outlays for the nation increased 70 percent, and federal outlays rose 97 percent between 1973 and 1977. Between 1970 and 1980, hospital costs grew almost 2½ times as fast as the cost of living. Health absorbed 8.9 percent of gross national product in 1977 and will claim 13 cents out of every nondefense budget dollar in 1980. Americans work an average of more than one month a year to pay for their health care.

Yet such sums are modest compared with what the national health bill might come to by the year 2000. Health now costs the country $150 billion annually; some estimates put the end-of-the-century figure at $1 trillion a year.

Trends in Population Below the Poverty Level

In 1971, the United States passed a milestone. In that year the federal government's expenditures for transfer of income and wealth between individuals and institutions exceeded, for the first time, the federal government's expenditures for the purchase of goods and services to conduct its direct business—national defense, operation of the national forest and park system, certain kinds of research, operation of the federal airway system, and the like.

What effect did this remarkable shift, combined with the growth of jobs and income in the private sector, have on poverty in the United States? The public perception is that welfare has been a "dismal failure." People believe millions of Americans are still no better off than the migrant mother of the 1930s. They are wrong. In terms of the key goals the welfare system was set up to accomplish—namely, providing the basic necessities of human life—it must be evaluated as a smashing, total success. As Alice Rivlin, director of the Congressional Budget Office, said, "The nation has come a lot closer to eliminating poverty than most people realize" (quoted in Mark R. Arnold, "We're Winning the War on Poverty," *The National Observer*, [February 19, 1977], p. 1.)

Lester C. Thurow, an economics professor at MIT and a *Newsweek* columnist, agrees:

> While general poverty, officially defined as any four-person family with an annual income of less than $7,386, has fallen from 22 percent of the population in 1959, to 12 percent in 1979, elderly poverty has plunged from 35 percent to 15 percent during the same period. Where there was once a large gap, there is now only a small gap.
>
> The mean per-capita income of the elderly is now only 6 percent below that of the entire population, and the elderly have a higher average net worth.[1]

Thurow also thinks government programs such as food stamps, medicare, and medicaid have succeeded in significantly reducing some of the main hardships associated with poverty:

> Twenty years ago, a national nutrition commission found evidence of widespread malnutrition. [In 1978] a similar commission could find no significant malnutrition. . . . Medicare and medicaid have also succeeded in meeting their basic goals. Today it is difficult, if not impossible, to find individuals that need medical care but are not getting it.[2]

Martin Anderson reports that, when one considers all benefits that families receive as well as income, only 3 percent of the American population was poor in 1975 (*Welfare: The Political Economy of Welfare Reform in the United States* [Stanford, Calif.: Hoover Institute, 1977]). The last 3 percent will be harder to eliminate. Included here are those who, like the "bag ladies" one sees poking through trash along many city streets, stubbornly refuse institutional aid. Their only goal seems to be complete independence.

Library of Congress

waste is not just maladministration, technological "frills," or "overutilization" of hospitals by patients and physicians. It is also a massive overlay of federal, state, and local regulation that makes hospitals one of the nation's most regulation-burdened industries. In New York state, a recently released survey based on 1976 results found hospitals ruled by no fewer than 164 regulatory agencies, including 40 at the federal level.

The United States is already well advanced towards a system of "free" hospital care; over 90 percent of costs have been socialized through public and private insurance schemes. Without doubt, this has lowered the incentive to keep costs low. That is to say, because more and more Americans have their medical bills paid indirectly, they have less incentive to shop around for low-cost medical care. Costs also have been pushed up by general inflation, malpractice lawyers, and federal policies (e.g., the Hill-Burton Act, which has encouraged overexpansion).

As with the issue of poverty, the experts on health care disagree on the character of the problem. Some think the causes of ill health are rooted in the individual. The control of communicable disease does depend largely on broad changes in the environment. But control of the present major health problems in the United States depends directly on modification of individual living habits (see box).

Example 3: What Is the "Energy Crisis"?

Finally, let us consider the question, *What is the "energy crisis"?* The U.S. energy situation is exceedingly complex in certain specifics.[3] But it is not hard to understand in broad terms.

Energy demand. Figure 12–2 shows that the total energy consumed in the United States has been rising steeply since 1940. If we simply extrapolated—i.e., assumed a continuation of the upward growth curve of the past four decades—the line would go off the top of the chart (note dashed line).

Fortunately, that will not happen. Population growth is slowing, which should mean that the rate of growth in energy consumption should slow. At the same time, the population is getting older, which should mean less consumption per person, since older people tend to use less energy than younger people on the average.

Economic and technological trends should also help slow the rate of growth in energy consumption. More of the U.S. economy is de-

---

Why Some Experts Think Health Is Not a Purely Public Problem

Studies show that the following basic health habits significantly increase life expectancy:

1. Three meals a day at regular times and no snacking.
2. Breakfast every day.
3. Moderate exercise two or three times a week.
4. Adequate sleep (seven or eight hours a night).
5. No smoking.
6. Moderate weight.
7. No alcohol or only in moderation.

John H. Knowles, president of the Rockefeller Foundation and a physician, comments:

> A 45-year-old man who practices 0 to 3 of these habits has a remaining life expectancy of 21.6 years (to age 67), while one with 6 to 7 of these habits has a life expectancy of 33.1 years (to age 78). In other words, 11 years could be added to the life expectancy at age 65 between 1900 and 1966.... The health status of those who practiced all seven habits was similar to those 30 years younger who observed none [*Doing Better and Feeling Worse: Health in the United States* (New York: Norton, 1977), p. 61].

FIGURE 12-2
U.S. Energy Consumption and Supply

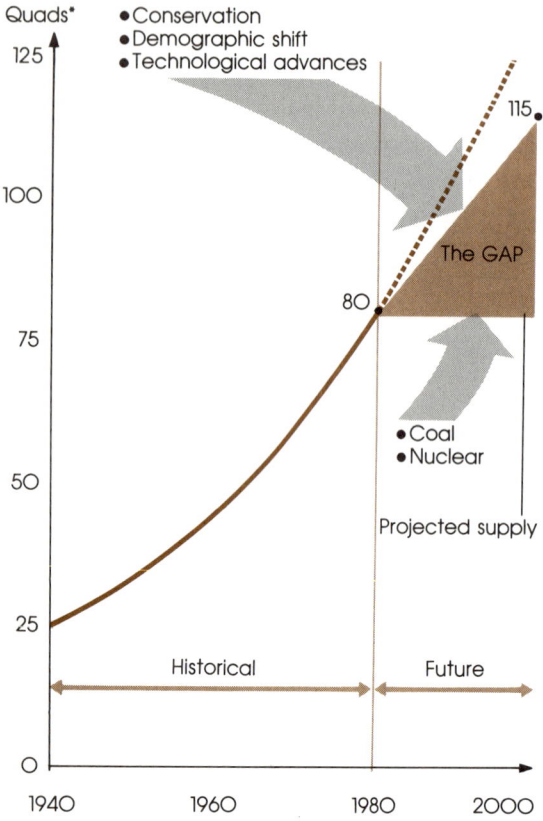

Quads*
- Conservation
- Demographic shift
- Technological advances

115 (The GAP)
80
● Coal
● Nuclear
Projected supply

Historical | Future
1940   1960   1980   2000

*A quad is a quadrillion BTU's—British Thermal Units. It just gives us a convenient number to talk about, like yards on a football field. A quad is 7½ billion gallons of gasoline, enough to run 10 million automobiles for a year. Or it is 45 million tons of coal; that's a string of railroad cars stretching from Seattle to New York—and back. Viewed another way, a quad is about the total energy used by a city of 1 million people every three years.

voted to services than energy-intensive manufacturing. (Industry accounted for about three eighths of energy consumption in 1980.) Telecommunications can substitute for some travel and transportation costs. Why fly when you can have a "teleconference"?

Conservation measures—e.g., insulation in houses and buildings, better burners, lighter cars, and more efficient energy conversion technology—can also yield big reductions in national energy consumption. But this reduction will not come cheaply. A true national commitment to energy conservation will require perhaps a half trillion dollars. Unless oil-exporting nations make an effort to drop the world price, industrial countries undoubtedly will continue in this direction.

Figure 12-2 gives an optimistic projection of how much energy will be consumed in the United States in the year 2000. The estimate of 115 quads comes from the Resources for the Future.

Energy supply. Now we come to the crux of the problem: What are the prospects for the U.S. economy to supply that much energy? As a glance at Table 12-1 will show, the prospects are not very good. Let us assume that oil and gas can maintain current levels and that hydroelectric energy can be expanded moderately. That leaves the nation 53 quads short. In contrast, the potential prospects for coal, nuclear, and solar energy are much brighter than oil, gas, and hydroelectric. But they are riddled with political and technological uncertainties.

Coal. The 1973 Arab oil embargo inspired big new mining projects that only now are beginning to produce coal. But the increase in mining capacity has not been matched by the increase in demand. Some coal analysts see supply and demand coming into balance by 1983.

Beyond 1983, most observers see a bright

TABLE 12-1
U.S. Energy Production Projection (quads)

Source	1980 Consumption Quads	Percent	Production Outlook for 2000 (expert's consensus)
Oil	37	47	Down slightly
Natural gas	20	27	Flat
Hydroelectric	3	4	Up slightly
Coal	14	17	Up
Nuclear	3	4	?
Other*	1	1	Up
Total	78	100	

* Includes solar heating systems, biomass (the burning of wood and agricultural wastes), geothermal (using heat from beneath the earth's surface), and the comparatively small contributions from windmills, etc.

future. Electric utilities probably will use more coal, because of higher oil prices, uncertainty over natural gas supplies, and the political problems of nuclear power. Coal exports also should grow as Europe and the Far East move away from dependence on oil.

While the known quantities of coal in the United States are vast (according to the Brookings Institute, 400 years worth), coal is expensive to transport and creates pollution when burned.

Nuclear power. Even more than the oil and coal industries, nuclear power is so mired in political controversy that any long-range forecasts may well be short-circuited by the next day's headlines. In the aftermath of the Three Mile Island mishap, the Nuclear Regulatory Commission stopped issuing new construction and operating licenses. Today, several new nuclear plants stand idle; they cannot generate power for lack of operating licenses.

President Reagan asserts that the United States cannot shut the door on nuclear energy. Even so, its immediate future seems bleak. Besides the uproar over safety, the escalating cost of nuclear plants is narrowing their economic advantage over coal-burning facilities. The possibility of uranium-fuel shortages within the next few decades stirs doubts. Problems of storing nuclear wastes, some of which will remain dangerous for millenia, have not been resolved.

But, despite the current problems, nuclear power will probably play an important role in the 1980s. In the United States, 70 nuclear power plants are already operating; in addition, construction licenses have been granted for about 90 more. Nevertheless, nuclear power seems certain to fall short of the ambitious goals once discussed by its proponents. Only a decade ago, enthusiasts envisioned as many as 1,000 nuclear plants in the United States by the year 2000. Now, with the Energy Department estimating only 152 to 173 nuclear plants operating in 1990, that goal seems wide of the mark.

The federal government could enhance the acceptability of nuclear power by making specific arrangements to take responsibility for waste disposal. Furthermore, regulators could reemphasize ongoing efforts towards careful plant design, "defense in depth" to lessen effects if accidents do occur, and a set of institutional arrangements that separate the diagnosis of potential hazards from the responsibility to pay for correcting them.

While the U.S. nuclear program is lagging, some foreign nations are pushing ahead. The Soviet bloc plans to increase its nuclear generating capacity by 1990. In Western Europe, it is expected that nuclear power will provide 30 percent of its electricity in 1985, up from 10 percent in the late 1970s.

Solar power. Compared with coal and nuclear power, solar energy technology is—at least for the near future—primitive. We cannot expect renewable sources of energy like solar power to become important supplies until sometime in the 21st century. In fact, there could be a danger in spending too much on such programs, since capital to meet today's energy problems is limited. To the extent that we divest funds into inefficient—though politically popular—projects, we limit the funds that can go into more immediately useful programs.

How much of U.S. energy needs could be derived from solar energy by the year 2000? Estimates vary widely. Different analysts work with different definitions of solar energy and some have a strong bias for or against solar energy. In an effort to simplify the matter, the Department of Energy divided solar energy into three major groups: heating and cooling of buildings, fuels from biomass (plant matter, including wood and waste), and solar electric (e.g., windmills, ocean thermal electric, and solar cells). The Energy Project at the Harvard Business School estimates that, given reasonable incentives, solar power could provide about 21 quads by the turn of the 21st century.

The preceding discussion of the U.S. energy crisis stressed two things. The crux of the problem is to close the gap between the need for energy and the capacity to produce it. In closing that gap a number of strategies are available but, surrounding each, are uncertainties.

Of course, there are many other ways to define the problem. A couple of simple yet important ones appear in the box below.

2. WHAT SHOULD THE GOALS BE?

Once the problem has been defined, the analysis turns to an examination of goals. The idea is to decide the *general* direction of government

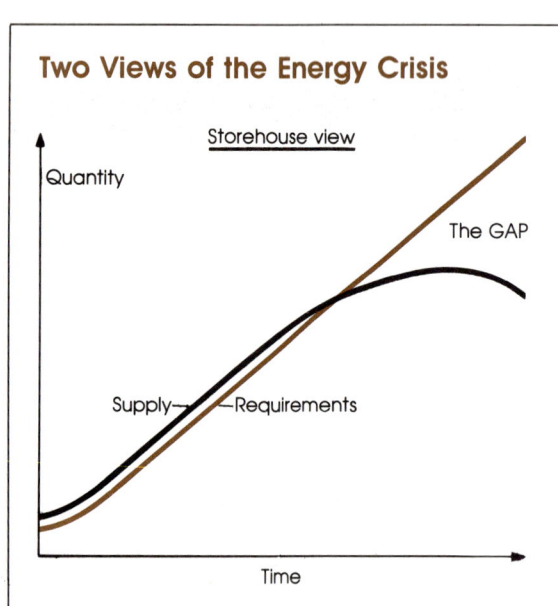

Two Views of the Energy Crisis

Storehouse view

[Graph showing Quantity vs. Time with Supply and Requirements curves diverging, labeled "The GAP"]

Cost-price view

[Graph showing Cost-price vs. Quantity with Demand and Supply curves]

The "storehouse" view is generally held by geologists, mining engineers, and others in the mineral industry; [it was the basis of Figure 12–2. The storehouse view] assumes that for any given material there are a limited number of deposits containing a sufficient concentration of the mineral to be useful to man. Once these have been exploited the store will be empty, but before we reach that point it will become more and more difficult to find suitable deposits. Such a view is often colored by the physical and geologic uncertainties encountered in the daily search for ore, and assumes that the technologic and economic circumstances of the past will be repeated in the future. There is also a tendency to develop, through extrapolation, a requirement figure for future demand which when compared with the limited supply usually results in dire warnings of catastrophe. The warnings may be right, but the method assumes a world of mechanical trends in which people march to the edge of disaster like lemmings.

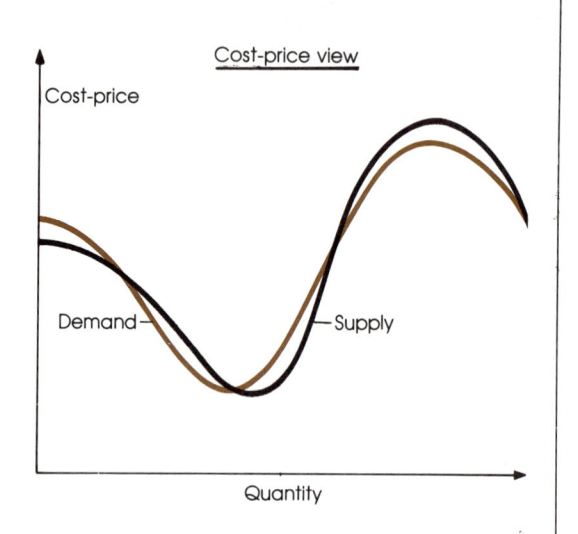

On the other extreme are the cost-price types, who assume that as price goes up, consumption will drop. Mineral resources for all practical purposes are unlimited in terms of demand, and are in fact only defined by cost rather than by a physical limitation. Under this view mineral resources need not be considered finite in the sense of ultimate exhaustion. Advocates of the cost concept would view shortages as a short-term phenomenon and would insist that society can get what it wants by bringing marginal properties into production or through the development of substitutes as prices rise. In any case, costs would continue to decline through the introduction of new technology.

SOURCE: Congressional Research Service, *Are We Running Out? A Perspective on Resource Scarcity* (Washington, D.C.: U.S. Government Printing Office, August 1980).

policy with respect to the problem or issue at hand.

If goals are to be effective they should exhibit certain characteristics. First, they should be achievable. Grandiose goals can lead to high expectations at first, followed by resentment and distrust when they are not attained. Second, goals should be clear and provide a sense of direction. Third, goals should be constantly rethought. It is the appropriateness of the goals, more than the size of the budget, that determines the results. Finally, goals should be *used*. They should help structure the actions of government. For each action, the acid test becomes: How does this step further the attainment of our goals?

Example 1: Health

The 1981 federal budget set three broad goals in health policy: to contain or limit the costs of medical care; to expand and improve medical services for the poor; and to pay more attention to preventing disease and disability. Goals, we said, should be achievable. Cost containment, the dominant goal, may not be—at least through direct limitations on the rate of increase in the price of routine hospital services. Hospitals can easily compensate for any decrease in revenues from routine services. They simply raise the price of other services and induce doctors to prescribe more services.

Example 2: Energy

The most frequently heard goals for an American energy policy are conservation and increased exploration. While some goals can be in conflict, this pair is not. Most thoughtful students of energy policy would advocate both goals but vary as to the relative importance, or priority, to be given to each. According to Daniel Yergin of the Harvard Business School, a meaningful energy conservation goal should build on these three principles. First, prices of energy should reflect the true costs of energy.

Courtesy of General Motors Corporation

Why be modest? The 1959 Cadillac Eldorado.

Second, government should provide financial incentives so that conservation measures have a fair chance against imported oil. Third, government should conduct an education campaign to make clear the problems associated with imported oil and the possibilities of conservation.

These principles would be applied in various ways to different parts of the economy. For example, with automobile manufacturing, Yergin recommends the following: Regulatory policies applied with flexibility are most effective; higher gasoline efficiency should be pursued vigorously; buses and carpools should be stimulated; and perhaps free public transportation should be attempted in a few cities. Gas prices should show real increases.[4]

The goal of increased exploration builds on different assumptions. Perhaps the central one is that the world is *not* running out of oil.

In 1948, proven world reserves of crude oil (excluding those in the communist countries) amounted to only 62.3 billion barrels. By 1972, this figure had increased better than ninefold. During this same period, known reserves in the United States and Canada more than doubled. But the biggest growth was in the Third World. Thanks to new technology, proven reserves in the Middle East jumped from 28.5 billion barrels in 1947 to 355 billion in 1972. Significantly, the amount of proven reserves has been rising, not falling, compared to the current rate of consumption.

There are approximately 600 prospective pe-

Culver Pictures

Is there still oil in them thar hills?

troleum basins in the world. Of these, 160 are commercially productive; 240 are partially or moderately explored; the remaining 200 are essentially unexplored.

3. WHAT ARE THE ALTERNATIVE STRATEGIES THAT WILL HELP ATTAIN THESE GOALS?

Any goal, of course, has a number of alternative strategies that can contribute to its successful attainment. Policymakers need to consider as many of them as time and money permit.

Example 1: Income Security

The range of programs designed to reduce poverty, however defined, is overwhelming. There are *direct income programs* that pay money directly to individuals. Some of these are social insurance. The individual, and perhaps his or her employer, pays a certain amount into a fund to draw upon at some future date as the need arises. Social security, unemployment compensation, and worker's compensation are examples. Other direct income programs are known as public assistance—e.g., **Aid to Families with Dependent Children (AFDC)**.

Another category of welfare programs provides direct services. Food stamps, medicare (for aged), medicaid (for poor), and housing assistance are among the biggest such programs.

There are also programs that provide indirect services (e.g., education, employment and affirmative action programs training), and indirect income (e.g., economic development of depressed areas).

Some welfare experts have advocated replacing programs such as AFDC with a **guaranteed annual income** or negative income tax. This plan would, in effect, put a floor under the incomes of all families. President Nixon endorsed the concept in his Family Assistance Plan. Although the proposal passed the House, it failed in the Senate. The great strength of the idea is that it eliminates the need for a large welfare bureaucracy. Its weakness is the uncertain effect it would have on a person's desire to work, despite the plan's built-in incentives to work.

One of the latest alternatives is the Community Services Administration's effort to help establish labor-intensive business enterprises in poor areas. Aided by public and private capital, dozens of these community development councils have been formed, some with notable success. In Harlem, residents own and operate a multimillion-dollar business in real estate, home improvements, and auto-parts manufacturing. In Mississippi, a similar company makes blue jeans for a major retail chain.

Example 2: Health

If government regulation of health costs is not the most appropriate way to tackle rising cost, then what is? Costs are rising because patients and their doctors demand these newer, more expensive services when a large part of the cost is offset by insurance. Martin Feldstein of Harvard University offers this example:

> Some simple but striking numbers will illustrate what the growth of insurance has done. In 1950, when the average cost per patient day was $16, private insurance and government programs paid for half of hospital bills. This meant that, on average, the net cost to a patient for a day of care was about $8. By 1979, many hospitals will have a cost per day of $250. But with 90 percent of this cost paid by public and private insurance, the net cost to the patient will be only $25.
>
> Moreover, since the general consumer price level has roughly tripled since 1950, this $25 in 1979 can only buy about as much as $8 could in 1950. The growth of insurance means that, in real terms, the net cost to the patient at the time of illness has not changed at all during the past 30 years. As a result, consumer demand maintains the pressure for an ever-increasing expenditure on hospital care.[5]

Solving the health cost problem may be difficult. But it is surely not impossible. One alternative is to provide tax incentives for individuals to purchase private insurance. This would make them more cost-conscious. Another alternative is to encourage health maintenance organizations. HMOs, as they are called, provide health services at a prepaid flat rate. The incentive is to keep the patient well and out of the hospital rather than, as in fee-for-service insurance, to give them extensive treatment.

Example 3: Administration of Justice

Frustrated by the apparent inability of the criminal justice system to control crime, some experts argue that punishment or **retribution** ("an eye for an eye") should be stressed at the expense of general political and social reform. This view, of course, runs roughshod over many ideas fundamental to a liberal society (see Chapter 3).

But is it really necessary to pull the system up by the roots? Why not chop a branch here and encourage the growth of another there? A complete description of the possibilities is beyond the scope of this book. But here are a few, brief alternatives:

Court reform. Case loads have doubled in the past 10 years, but the number of judges has increased by only 25 percent. This has led to crowded court dockets, case backlogs, and lengthy pretrial delay. Largely because of the need to lighten court loads, an estimated 90 percent of felony cases nationwide are now handled by plea bargaining. The result is that many serious criminals get off with light sentences. More judges, prosecutors, public defenders, clerks, and courtrooms are urged to expedite the trial and assure the conviction of dangerous criminals.

Career criminals. In New York, public outcry followed the arrest and conviction of Charles Yuki for the strangling of Karin Schlegel on a Greenwich Village rooftop. Yuki had been imprisoned in 1966 for killing a New York model, Susan Reynolds, after sexually abusing her and mutilating her body with a razor. Seven years after his sentencing for the Reynolds slaying, Yuki had been released by the New York State Parole Board from his maximum 15-year sentence for manslaughter. He killed Miss Schlegel only 14 months later. Yuki could be eligible for parole again in about 10 years. About

70 percent of adults arrested for serious crimes are repeaters. One new law enforcement effort, currently operating in about 18 cities, seeks to identify these habitual offenders (called "career criminals"), prosecute them swiftly, and assure that the longest prison sentences possible are imposed. Many authorities believe that corralling the sizable group of hard-core offenders and locking them up for long periods should greatly reduce the crime rate. Of course, such programs must be designed with a careful eye toward safeguarding the constitutional rights of those labeled as career criminals.

Juvenile justice. The juvenile courts are even more badly glutted than adult courts. This is largely because of the variety of problems handled by them. One widely accepted reform proposal would be to remove from their jurisdiction the so-called status offenders—i.e., youths who have committed no crimes but are troublesome to parents, neighbors, or schools (such as truants or runaways). Status offenses now account for about 40 percent of the caseload of the juvenile courts. Another main target of criticism in the juvenile justice system is the training schools that have been breeding grounds for further criminal activity. The recidivism rate of offenders who are sent to training schools is an overwhelming 80 percent. Many reformers now believe that penal institutions for juveniles should be done away with in favor of alternatives, such as group or foster homes.

Sentencing. Given that 80 percent of violent crime is caused by criminals between the ages of 15 and 25, some suggest mandating a minimum sentence of 10 years for anyone in this age group found guilty of a violent crime. The purpose would be simply to protect society. It would not be revenge or rehabilitation, though rehabilitation efforts should not be stopped. At the same time, under this plan, show the nonviolent first offender *maximum mercy*; allow every chance at probation.

White-collar crime. Crooked executives, corrupt government officials, and thieving employees—those guilty of the economic offenses known as white-collar crime—are currently causing financial losses in this country in excess of $40 billion annually. Many experts believe that there should be an end to leniency for these criminals; they feel that stricter penalties, particularly more prison sentences, must be imposed. It is believed by many that strict penalties serve as a strong deterrent to white-collar criminals. Punishment of such criminals pro-

United Press International Photo

A policeman in New York City plays volleyball with community youngsters in a public-relations program with the goal of dispelling mistrust of police. As the cartoon suggests, police in some cities place less stress on such goals.

Mike Peters in *Dayton Daily News*

motes more general confidence in the fairness of the legal system.

Community-level actions. Studies indicate that low-income people are more likely to commit a crime in a large slum than outside it. Therefore government should help those who still live there to leave. Studies also show that a stable family structure reduces crime; therefore, government welfare policies should not reward desertion. Fathers who desert should be found and held accountable. Schools should be better integrated with actual employment opportunities and youth unemployment reduced. Police should establish better relations with the community they serve.

Jail and prison reform. Most experts agree that prisons in their present form cannot **rehabilitate** many prisoners. Many believe that there should be greater use of community-based treatment (probation, halfway houses, intermittent sentences to be served on weekends, etc.), restitution programs, and fines. Long incarceration in big prisons should be reserved for high-risk offenders who cannot be safely controlled in other ways. Many reformers also believe that rehabilitation efforts are wasted unless freely chosen. Therefore, rehabilitation programs, which are now usually mandatory, should be made voluntary. One quick way to reduce crowded conditions is to release perpetrators of victimless crimes—e.g., alcoholics and prostitutes. Their problem is their own, not society's; they need help, not jail. Finally, the training and career opportunities of guards should be upgraded.

4. WHAT ARE THE TOTAL COSTS AND BENEFITS OF EACH ALTERNATIVE?

The key word in this question is *total*, for government action has *indirect* as well as direct consequences. It is the indirect, less visible effects that make inflation so pernicious—though Americans tend to focus their concern mainly on the rising price of gas, food, and the like.

If a state highway department builds a highway through the edge of a city, there are **direct costs**: asphalt, wages, land, etc. But there are also **indirect costs**: community dislocation, accidents during construction, and aesthetics (as beautiful old homes and landmarks crumble before the construction team's bulldozers).

Similarly, we can find **direct and indirect benefits** in the project. The former would include—at least in the short run—reduced congestion. Since a driver's time is worth something (maybe $5 per hour, maybe $40), this benefit can be measured. Indirect benefits might include reduced traffic fatalities, since a new six-lane highway should be safer than an old two-lane road.

Indirect costs are usually borne by third parties—that is, people who neither carried out the project nor benefit from it. A classic example is a municipal airport. The people who live by it bear the noise pollution but are not necessarily the heaviest users of air travel.

Economists do not look at costs quite in the same way the rest of us do. To them the true value of a good or service is not simply the price tag on it; the true value—the **opportunity cost**—is what one has to forego in order to purchase it. For example, what is the price of a college education? Let us see. Four years of school times tuition, room and board, books, etc. (say, $8,000) gives us a grand total of $32,000. But an economist would say that the income given up in order to attend school must be figured in as well. So, the true cost of a college education might be closer to $80,000 ($32,000 plus four years times $12,000 in salary given up each year). Similarly, the opportunity cost of devoting a given amount of resources to national defense is not devoting those resources to social welfare or vice versa. This is the nub of the so-called **guns and butter** debate. Because some resources must always be given up to produce goods or provide services, economists are fond saying, "There is no such thing as a free lunch."

In the examples below we shall be concerned

mainly with costs rather than benefits. The main reason is that costs are often harder to see. Later in the chapter we shall note several benefits from various government policies (see, for example, step 8 in Figure 12–1).

Example 1: Health

Government policymakers have tended to misunderstand the true nature of the rising costs of health. Inflation means the cost of buying a pound of butter is higher than it was 10 years ago. But the 10-year rise in costs of one day in a hospital is not necessarily all inflation. The reason is that 1975 butter is exactly the same as 1985 butter, but a day in the hospital in 1975 is not the same as a day spent in 1985.

Today's hospital care is more complex, more sophisticated, and more effective than it was 10 years ago. As Robert M. Heyssel, executive vice president and director of the Johns Hopkins Hospital notes:

> We are not paying for iron lungs and orthopedic repair of polio-damaged limbs. Pneumonia does not kill 30 percent of its victims.
>
> But we are paying for kidney transplants, total hip replacements, coronary bypass procedures, and radiation treatments, along with sophisticated emergency care of severe trauma patients. A day in a cancer hospital can cost up to $600. Each new medical or scientific breakthrough improves the quality and the outcome of care, but in most instances the cost of care rises proportionately.[6]

Health care provides many excellent examples of why it is important, when analyzing costs, to focus on the aggregate effect of a government program. We should avoid viewing policy decisions exclusively in terms of individuals—that is, unless we have unlimited resources.

Consider the implications of the decision by the federal government to pay for hemodialysis treatments nationwide. (Hemodialysis is the process of removing blood from an artery, purifying it, adding vital substances, and returning it to a vein. It is used most frequently with

Dan McCoy/Black Star

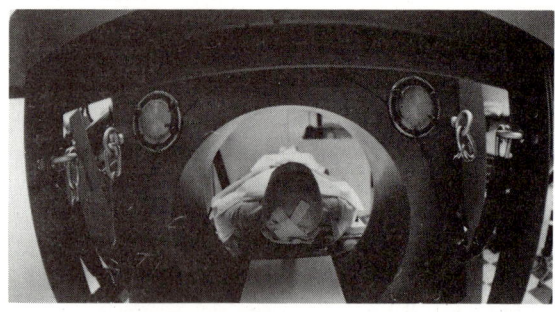

The computerized axial tomography (CAT) scanner is a powerful diagnostic device. It allows physicians to see cross-sections of the human body to detect disorders. In 1896, an X-ray machine cost $50. Today's CATs start at $700,000.

kidney patients.) Today the bill runs around $2 billion annually.

What will happen when artificial lungs and hearts are readily available? Two more very large groups of people now dying from chronic illnesses will then live. But this will happen only if their fellow citizens are willing to pick up the huge and growing tab for this treatment.

The limitation on new technology has already begun. Some hospitals today, for example, are not eligible for a CAT scanner. There is little doubt that the new equipment will be welcomed by physicians. Yet how will society possibly pay the bill? Where are the billions, possibly trillions, of dollars going to come from?

Example 2: Energy

To summarize our earlier discussion of the energy problem, oil, gas, and hydroelectric alone will leave the United States with an energy shortage of 53 quadrillion BTUs in the year 2000. A reasonable estimate for solar energy is 21 quads. Thus, the United States must either (a) expand coal and nuclear energy production by 32 quads, (b) import 15 million barrels a day, or (c) do without. There are no other options.

The indirect costs of importing and doing

without must be appreciated. To import 15 million barrels of oil a day—twice the current levels—would likely drive world oil prices even higher. Next, it would enormously upset an already precarious balance of trade (see p. 488). Finally, to these potential costs of increased oil imports must be added social and political risks. Inflation at home would be even worse and foreign policy would be largely dictated by OPEC.

Equally unpleasant is simply doing without 32 quads. Consider this: In 1973 a mere one-quad shortage triggered the biggest recession the United States had experienced in 40 years. With much less than a 1-quad shortage of gas during the winter of 1976–1977, thousands of plants were closed and millions of workers lost their jobs. A quad shortage would mean more than economic dislocations. It would require massive cutbacks in social programs. It would cause divisions as interest groups struggled over a shrinking pie. It would require more physical labor by the work force. And it would seriously undermine national defense.

Many areas of public policy are closely related. This is especially true of energy and transportation. Read the boxed article below and you will see why. You will also learn a little more about how policy analysts try to capture all the costs and benefits of a public policy.

The Costs of Going 55

The campaign to educate us about the benefits of the 55-mph limit has been strident and persistent. Somehow this new wonder drug, the 55 limit, is supposed to cure our national energy problem, save lives and cause us all to pursue a more virtuous existence. But wonder drugs often have unfortunate side effects, and this one is no exception. I want to focus your attention on some of these undesirable side effects.

The major cost associated with the 55-mph limit is an enormous chunk of wasted travel time. Specifically, it costs about 102 man-years of extra travel time to save one life. In contrast to this considerable cost, the energy savings associated with the 55-mph limit are so trivial that we could get about the same conservation effect by simply assuring that everyone kept his tires properly inflated. (Consider the whimsical implications of this fact: imagine an elite sidewalk Pressure Patrol, armed with air gauges, ticketing cars for low tire pressure.)

There is another way of evaluating the costly side effects of the 55-mph wonder drug: the value of time. The principle is simple: time is money, and studies have shown that commuters are willing to pay up to 42 percent of an hour's wage to save an hour of travel time. Thus, when transportation analysts measure the benefits of new subway systems, like BART or METRO, they count up the number of travel hours that would be saved by the transit improvement, and then multiply by the value of time to compute a dollar measure of the benefits. The same principle can also be used to assign a dollar cost to the extra travel time caused by slowing down traffic. When we do this we find that the 55-mph limit causes enough of a traffic slowdown to waste about $6 billion worth of travel time per year.

Saving Lives

The National Highway Traffic Safety Administration says we save about 4,500 lives per year because of the 55-mph limit. Hence, it costs about $1.3 million per life saved. Is this a bargain, or are there other social policies that might save more lives for less money? Well, it has been estimated that placing a smoke detector in every home in the U.S. would save about as many lives in total as the 55-mph limit, and would cost only $50,000 to $80,000 per life saved; or more kidney-dialysis machines could save lives for only about $30,000 per life; or additional mobile cardiac-care units cost only about $2,000 per life saved; and there are even a great number of highway improvements that can be made, through reducing roadside hazards, which cost only about

$20,000 to $100,000 per life saved. At a cost of $1.3 million per saved life, the 55-mph limit is hardly a bargain.

For a more humane way of calculating the cost of the 55-mph limit, we might compare the 2,710 million extra travel hours (from lower travel speeds) to the reduction in fatalities. This shows that it costs 102 man-years of wasted time to save one life. Yes, that means 102 years of extra time riding around in your automobile in order to save one life. Now, I confess to some trouble keeping up with the latest theological notions as to the nature of hell, but 102 years traveling in an automobile fits my personal notion of that place rather closely.

Energy Conservation

Where does all this leave us? We now see that the 55-mph limit is an incredibly expensive way to save lives, and that there are cheaper and more effective means of reducing our national death rate. We now see that the 55-mph limit has only an insignificant effect on energy conservation: even the most optimistic government estimates say that it saves only about 1 to 2 percent of our gasoline consumption. This is an effect so trivial that we can do as well be switching to radial tires, or by changing spark plugs at more regular intervals, or by keeping our tires at the proper pressure.

If we want to save transportation energy, there is a much more effective way to do so. Instead of focusing so much of our attention on a misguided speed limit that saves only 1 to 2 percent of our gasoline, let's look at some changes that could save 50 percent of our gasoline. The average car in the U.S. now gets about 15 miles per gallon. But the showrooms are full of cars that can double or triple this efficiency. If we could persuade only 4 percent of the drivers to switch from conventional cars to fuel-efficient cars we would have made a bigger contribution to saving energy than was accomplished by the 55-mph limit.

How could we get people to drive smaller cars? Well, there are two traditional approaches to influencing human behavior: (1) we can pass a new *law* and make the desired behavior compulsory—the method so beloved of dictators, lawyers, and old-fashioned liberals; or (2) we can increase the *incentives* for buying fuel-efficient cars—the method favored by economists, psychologists, and other suspicious characters.

A New Scheme

Since I am a card-carrying member of the second group, let me advocate an incentive scheme. Suppose we reward the drivers of fuel-efficient cars by allowing them to drive faster: a 55-mph limit for gas guzzlers and a 65-mph limit (traffic permitting) for economy cars. Issue two kinds of license plates so that the police would have no trouble telling the two classes apart; permit the differential speeds only on uncongested highways.

Would this kind of reward, getting to drive faster, provide enough of an incentive to cause people to switch car types? Well, 20 years of traffic research aimed at trying to predict why commuters chose one mode of travel over another, or one route over another, all confirm one straightforward rule: the fastest mode gets all the people. There is no question that the chance to drive faster would make a really significant impact on relative market shares of gas guzzlers vs. fuel-efficient cars.

The point is simple: if we are going to insist on manipulating the speed limit to affect energy consumption, then let's at least manipulate it in an effective way.

SOURCE: Charles A. Lave, in *Newsweek* (October 23, 1978), p. 37.

5. WHO PAYS? WHO BENEFITS?

It is hard to think of any government action that benefits and costs every citizen equally. The thinking person will always want to ask, Now who will this program *really* benefit and how much? Who will have to pay for it and how much? That line of questioning might end in a surprise or two.

This step (step 5 in Figure 12–1) is likely

to become even more important in the next decade. As growth in the American economy slows, the economic pie becomes more fixed in size. What that means is this: In order for me to get a larger slice, someone else—perhaps you—must take a smaller one. If the middle class began to resist welfare programs in the mid-1970s, it was largely because the economic pie, from which they were financed, ceased to grow as rapidly as it had in the 1960s.*

Public policy affects the distribution of costs and benefits in many ways. Some are subtle; some are not. A sales tax is a nonsubtle way in which costs are distributed. But **tax expenditure** is a more subtle way. Commonly referred to as loopholes, tax expenditures represent the difference between what the government actually collects in taxes and what it would have collected without special exemptions. Tax expenditures are the way government encourages certain activities. Thus, if a business hires hard-to-employ workers it may be eligible for a tax deduction for training expenses.

When the cities of Boulder, Colorado, and Palm Springs, California, say that certain kinds of structures cannot be built within the city limits, they are engaging in a subtle form of benefit distribution. For example, if these cities require a fixed structure of a specific size using certain kinds of building materials, it might not be possible for lower middle class families to have the benefit of living in either place.

A more pervasive, less subtle way in which benefits are distributed are **transfer payments.** These are cash payments, or things with cash value, that a government takes from A and gives to B. A large percentage of government expenditure falls under this heading. Social security payments, welfare benefits, veterans' assistance, and farm subsidies are all among the most conspicuous cash transfer payments.

The distribution of benefits and costs, of course, can be examined along other dimensions besides income levels—sex, age, region, and race. Can you think of how different kinds of medical research might affect each group?

Perhaps the most useful way to examine the distribution of costs and benefits is in terms of politics. Different programs tend to be associated with different kinds of politics. For example:

Programs like social security and school lunches—which many pay for and many benefit from—we might call "mass appeal programs."

Programs like those designed to reduce air pollution—which few pay for and many benefit from—we might call "public interest programs." These are called public interest programs because of their close association with the political efforts of the public interest groups (discussed in Chapter 6).

Programs like those designed to regulate interstate commerce—which few pay for and few benefit from—we might call "special interest programs." These programs, of course, are closely associated with the lobbying of special interest groups (also discussed in Chapter 6).

Programs like those which give special favors in the form of cash payments, called **subsidies,**—which many pay for but few benefit from—we might call "iron triangle programs." These programs are usually the product of the political dynamics of those political subsystems called iron triangles in Chapter 8. Federal subsidies to the milk industry are a prime example.

So far so good. But determining who actually benefits from and who actually pays for a particular government program is not always easy. As the following two examples demonstrate, our initial perception of who benefits may not always be accurate.

---

* One might ask how then Franklin Roosevelt was able to start the welfare programs of his New Deal in the midst of a depression. The answer is it was a shoestring operation. In 1980, spending on food stamps alone equaled FDR's entire federal budget for 1939.

Example 1: Education

Suppose, for example, a state decides that all its school districts will be funded equally (so many dollars per student); it does not matter how rich or poor a particular district happens to be. This decision would seem quite clearly to benefit the little schoolchildren of the state, especially those in poorer neighborhoods. This "obvious" interpretation of who really benefits may or may not be correct. One must also consider that the main (but not the only) budget item for a school district is teacher salaries. It hardly seems farfetched to suppose that the teachers in the less affluent district will have fatter paychecks. Who are these teachers? The typical schoolteacher is probably a married, white female—in short, a member of a middle- or upper-middle-class household. Her husband is likely to be employed also, with an upper-middle-level income. Thus, a major beneficiary is not necessarily the group that the state legislature or courts had in mind when the decision was made.

Example 2: Transportation

Consider the suggestion by one candidate for the U.S. Senate that the New York City subways should be "free." What he really meant was that people in Tulsa, Omaha, and elsewhere should pay for it through federal subsidies even more than they already are paying. Or consider the federal loan guarantee to Chrysler Corporation. What that action could amount to was that taxpayers employed by the furniture industry could be required to help maintain the wages of automobile workers who earn over twice as much as they do. Or consider the request of lobbying groups for the handicapped for a $230,000 bus equipped with hydraulic wheelchair lift that will give them access guaranteed by the Rehabilitation Act of 1973. Many handicapped say they do not want *special* transportation; it carries a mark of inferiority. To lift this "stigma" they want the rest of the taxpayers to spend nearly a half billion dollars a year to build the modified bus. Here we have a tough trade-off that can never be resolved in purely economic terms.

6. WHAT ARE THE RISKS?

This step is closely related to measuring the size and distribution of the costs of a public policy. Some public policies entail high and dangerous risks. Careful analysis requires that such risks be assessed.

For the benefits of convenience, you are willing to ride in an automobile and take a 1-in-5,000 chance of being killed any given year. Would you exchange the risk of only 1 in 750,000 for the benefits of a nuclear plant? According to the Nuclear Regulatory Commission, if the United States were to abandon nuclear power, it would cost the nation $60 billion to replace plants now in place and an estimated $9.8 billion a year in higher electric costs. Questions like this one have long concerned policymakers and citizens. But today the debate seems to have reached gale force, thanks to troubles like those at the Three Mile Island nuclear facility.

Given the relative affluence of American society, some have advocated zero risks. Others assert that refusal to take certain risks does more than just preclude the benefits of technological options for future generations; it may signal the decline and fall of the American republic (see box).

We might compromise and use the 1-in-5,000 risk of being killed in an auto accident as a kind of cutoff point. If some beneficial public policy had a higher risk factor (say, 1-in-4,000), it would be rejected. But if the risk were less (say, 1-in-6,000), the policy would be adopted.

What this approach to risk ignores is the distribution of risk. The risk of automobile fatalities is fairly evenly distributed throughout society; the risk from nuclear accidents is not. More important, the risk from nuclear accidents is

Paralysis in a Risk-Free Society: An Opinion

The desire to build a risk-free society has always been a sign of decadence. It has meant that the nation has given up, that it no longer believes in its destiny, that it has ceased to aspire to greatness, and has retired from history to pet itself. . . .

I turn from the notion of a risk-free society to the epic of Homer, to the magnificent testimony to a people's will in the Old Testament, to the sagas of the Vikings and the daring of the Elizabethans, and there is not a hint of a safety regulation in one of them. But turn nearer to hand. It was not just the wretched and oppressed who came to America, but the wretched and the oppressed who would risk. It was the strong, and not the weak, who came, and then still came. They did not ask if the Mayflower was seaworthy—it was a miserable hulk even for its times—and into our own century they still got onto tubs that might break apart to cross an ocean. What I feel most in America now is the ever more constricted sinews of a country that was made by such people.

Soft and swaddling are the constraints—do not do this because it might hurt you; even worse, it might make you feel "uncomfortable"—but they are binding the spirit of a great people like a fetter.

This draining pusillanimity runs into personal as well as into social relationships. The American people are being cajoled into talking to each other as I used to think that only a few people talked to their indoor plants. . . . What is "wrong" with America can be put quite simply. With a Ralph Nadar at the head of a wagon train, no one would have made it across the plains, none would have crossed the Rockies, and no immigrant would have pushed noisomely out of the gutter.

SOURCE: Henry Fairlie, *Washington Post* (July 22, 1979).

---

nonvoluntary; riding in an automobile is more a matter of individual choice. For this reason, some would also object to the government's ban a few years ago of saccharin, even though the synthetic sweetener seems to cause tumors in rats. If diabetics want to run the "risk" of using saccharin, why not let them?

How then does one think intelligently about risks? The first key word is **trade-offs.** Trade-off simply means that to get more of one value, such as safety, one must take less of some other value. Consider the ban of the pesticide DDT. DDT is toxic to animals and human beings. But it also offered the best hope of eliminating malaria in certain countries and of controlling insect plagues that destroy crops in countries where starvation is endemic. In sum, there are potential dangers if future governments assume vast amounts of control over risk management. Individual judgment and choice would be replaced by government action that wards off evils automatically before they materialize.

The other key word in thinking about risk is *comparative.* In speaking of the risk of policy, it is often a good idea to ask oneself, "In comparison to what?" In other words, one way to determine how risky alternative A is might be to compare its risks to those associated with B.

Example: Energy

Herbert Inhaber, in a controversial article appearing in *Science,* compared the risk to human health from five conventional energy sources (coal, oil, natural gas, nuclear, hydroelectricity) and six "nonconventional" energy sources (solar-thermal electric, solar photovoltaic, solar space heating, methanol, wind, and ocean thermal). The entire cycle for producing energy was considered, not just part. Here are some of his current estimated ranges of deaths for a specified energy output (10 gigawatts).

Coal	40–1,600
Oil	20–1,400
Wind	120–230
Solar, space heating	80–90
Uranium	2½–15
Natural gas	1–4

The important point is that risk assessment is a young discipline. Also it is filled with enormous problems in collecting and comparing data. Inhaber comments:

> The risk to human health from nonconventional sources can be as high as, or even higher than, that of conventional sources. This result is produced only when the risk per unit of energy is considered, rather than the risk per solar panel or windmill. The risk from nonconventional energy sources derives from the large amount of material and labor needed, along with their backup and storage requirements.

7. SELECT AN ALTERNATIVE OR SET OF ALTERNATIVES

After a careful examination of the alternatives, the time of decision arrives. Which alternative or combination of alternatives seems most likely to attain the goals established in step 2? In making this decision, policymakers have two basic approaches available.

The first approach is **incrementalism**. Policymakers do not have to consider every possible alternative until they find the best. In practice, they usually lack the time and money for such an exhaustive consideration of alternatives. So, they tend to stick with what they have been doing or make slight—"incremental"—adjustments in it. While this approach might not lead to the ideal solution, it is less likely to be strongly resisted.

A good example of incremental policy making is the **medicare** program which became law in 1965. Rather than provide a comprehensive medical-care insurance like that offered in most Western European countries, medicare was limited to medical expenses for the aged. Medicare was able to pass Congress because it represented only an incremental change in existing government assistance to the aged and was set up on a basis similar to the well-established social security program.

The second approach is rational policymaking. This approach requires that the values of the decision makers be carefully defined and then all alternatives be examined. Finally, the alternative that seems to offer the best chance of realizing those values most fully is selected.

One way to think of the difference between these two approaches to selecting an alternative is that incrementalism is a highly political approach and something like a rule of thumb. The rational policymaking is the more academic approach and closer to the scientific method. Frequently we see elements of both in the formulation of a public policy.

Policymakers following the rational approach have several tools available. A couple of these tools are fairly popular and worth noting: cost-benefit analysis (CBA), and cost-effectiveness analysis (CEA). We shall illustrate CBA by seeing how it can be applied to the regulation of business. Then, we shall illustrate CEA by seeing how it can be applied to such diverse areas of public policy as highway safety and health care.

Example 1: Environment

The idea of CBA is simple: Add all the costs and all the benefits. If the latter exceeds the former, procede. For example, in a study released in 1979 by the Environmental Protection Agency, the financial benefits from cleaning up the air appeared to be greater than the cost of removing one major form of air pollution. The study said that, as of 1977 the United States was spending $6.7 billion annually on government-required controls for pollution from power plants, factories, and other nonautomotive sources. Yearly benefits from the improved air were estimated at $8 billion, a figure based on such items as more time on the job and increased productivity by those who suffered from air pollution. One can draw a reasonable conclusion that the health benefits alone from cleaning up air pollution appear to be substantially more than (the cost of) controlling particles and all other pollutants from stationary sources.*

Of course CBA can be applied to all kinds of regulation, not just environmental.

What are the total costs of regulation? The figures most frequently used by politicians, economists, and business-executives were developed by Murray Weidenbaum. At the time he was director of the Center for the Study of American Business at Washington University in St. Louis. In 1976, Weidenbaum and his colleagues found that the compliance costs to business for regulations issued by several dozen agencies totaled $62.9 billion. Those agencies had operating budgets totaling $3.2 billion that year. Thus the ratio of compliance costs to agency budgets was 20 to 1.

Weidenbaum and his associates applied the 20-to-1 ratio to the projected increases in agency budgets. They projected a figure of about $100 billion for 1980—a figure often used by Ronald Reagan in the 1980 presidential campaign. Under the formula, the 1982 figure would be nearly $150 billion.

What do these costs consist of? Filling out forms for government bureaucrats—paperwork—accounts for about one quarter of the costs. Installing new equipment and changing procedures accounts for the bulk of the rest.

Needless to say, most of these costs are passed on to the consumer in the form of higher prices.

In 1981, Murray Weidenbaum became chairman of President Reagan's Council of Economic Advisers. His cost-benefit analysis approach to regulation draws heavy criticism from people in the consumer movement. Some say Weidenbaum underestimates the benefits of regulation.

Mark Green and Norman Waitzman, for instance, report new estimates of the benefits of social regulation in the 1981 edition of their book *Business War on the Law: An Analysis of the Benefits of Federal Health Safety Enforcement*. For four major agencies, Green and Waitzman say, the benefits in 1978 were $37.1 billion; in 1985 the benefits will be $94.1 billion.* The potential benefits, if all the problems dealt with by the regulations were eliminated, would be $226 billion.

Example 2: Transportation

CEA differs from CBA in two important respects. First, it does not require that all benefits be converted in dollars. As you can see in Table 12–2, alternative highway safety measures can be compared in terms of lives saved. Second, and this is a weakness of CEA, it does not capture all the costs and benefits. For example, highway safety programs have not one but a variety of objectives. They include fewer injuries, less human suffering, and less property damage. However, cost-effectiveness analysis generally requires comparing the costs of attaining a single objective. Thus, in some cases, cost-benefit analysis may be a more effective approach than cost-effectiveness analysis.

---

* Actually, CBA is not quite this simple. For one thing, costs and benefits of a program or project occur over time. Therefore, it is necessary to convert these downstream costs and benefits into present value. (As you no doubt realize, $1,000 five years from now will be worth much less than $1,000 today. You merely have to put $1,000 in a bank for five years to see that.) The technique policy analysts use to reduce these downstream costs and benefits is called discounting.

* The four agencies and the ratios of their benefits to their costs in 1978 were, according to Green and Waitzman, as follows:

Occupational Safety and Health Administration	1.49
Environmental Protection Agency	1.03
National Highway Safety Administration	1.50
Food and Drug Administration	3.50

TABLE 12-2
Twelve Ways to Reduce Traffic Fatalities

Measure	Dollars per Fatality Forestalled
Mandatory safety belt usage	$ 506
Highway construction and maintenance practices	20,000
Upgrade bicycle and pedestrian safety curriculum offerings	20,400
Nationwide 55-mph speed limit	21,200
Guardrails	34,100
Pedestrian safety information and education	36,800
Motorcycle rider safety helmets	53,300
Citizen assistance of crash victims	209,000
Warning letters to problem drivers	263,000
Roadway lighting	936,000
Bridge widening	3,460,000
Roadway alignment and gradient	7,680,000

Source: U.S. Department of Transportation, *National Transportation: Trends and Choices* (Washington, D.C.: U.S. Government Printing Office, 1976), p. 99.

Example 3: Health

Does the second apple you eat give you as much satisfaction as the first? Probably not. And it is likely that the third will provide even less satisfaction than the second did. We often refer this as "diminishing returns." Economists use a closely related concept in their analysis of public policy—**marginal analysis**.

Marginal analysis is an important concept in both CBA and CEA. In other words, when thinking about public policies, we should be interested in marginal benefits. Since the term *marginal* means additional, marginal benefits refers to those benefits that result from a one-unit change in inputs. In public policy, those inputs are usually dollars.

Let us see how such marginal information might be used to determine the preferred mix of disease control programs. Assume we can determine, as in the following table, the number of lives saved by different expenditures on disease A and disease B:

	Expenditures	Lives Saved
Disease A	$ 500,000	360
	1,000,000	465
Disease B	$ 500,000	200
	1,000,000	270

If we only knew the effect of spending $1 million, we might opt for a program in which all of our money was spent on controlling disease A; we could save 465 lives instead of 270 if we spent it all on disease B. Similarly, if we only knew the effects of programs of a half million dollars, we would probably prefer A; we would save 360 lives rather than only 200 lives.

But suppose we knew the results for expenditures of both a half million dollars and $1 million in each program. We would quickly see that spending half of our money in each program was better than putting it all in one program, assuming that we had $1 million available.

Our calculations would be:

Expenditures	Lives Saved
$1,000,000 on A	465
$1,000,000 on B	270
$1,000,000 {$500,000 on A-360, $500,000 on B-200}	560

Marginal information should also help you see why pouring additional money into a program, *once a certain point has been reached*, becomes unwise. (As Figure 12-3 shows, more

FIGURE 12-3
Marginal Contribution of Medical Care to Health in United States (Generalized)

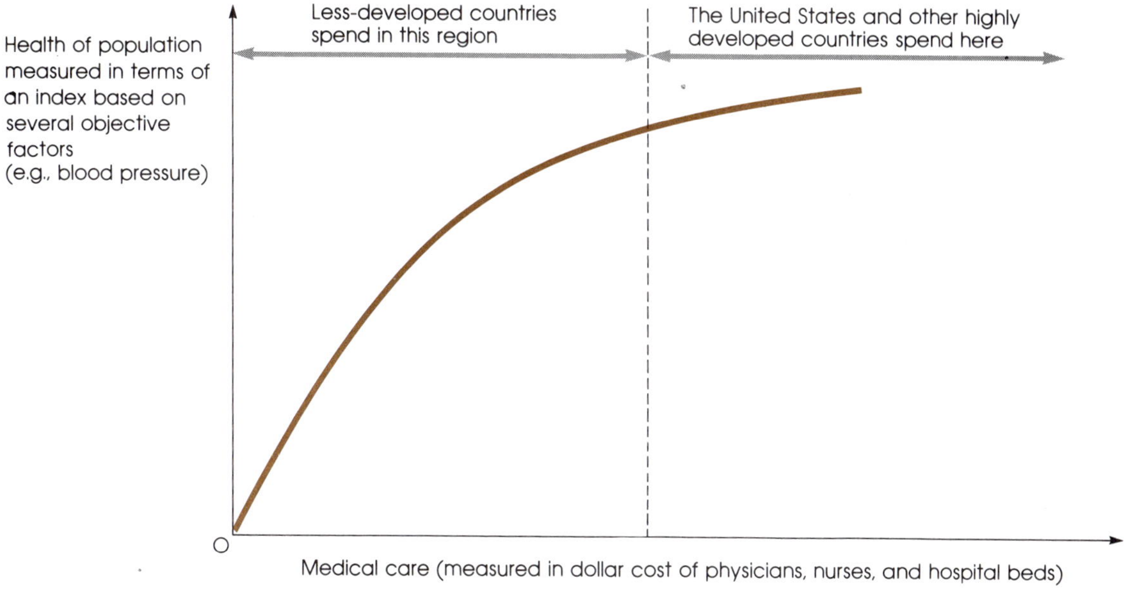

Health of population measured in terms of an index based on several objective factors (e.g., blood pressure)

Less-developed countries spend in this region

The United States and other highly developed countries spend here

Medical care (measured in dollar cost of physicians, nurses, and hospital beds)

physicians, nurses, hospitals, and the like make little contribution to the health of the population in modern nations.) In contrast, breakthroughs in medical technology and efforts to prevent illness *are* cost effective. Nevertheless, the Department of Health and Human Services devotes less than 3 percent of its budget to prevention. Apparently, rapid increases in medicare and medicaid costs leave little room for such programs.

8. IS THE POLICY POLITICALLY FEASIBLE?

Eventually, the analysts must confront the issue of political feasibility. Who is in favor of the policy? Who is against it? Can the opposition be won over? Can the policy proposal be modified to make it more salable? Many of the proposals that might have sailed through the first seven steps crack on this rock.

While few navigation charts are available, the principles noted in earlier chapters on political power (in particular, Chapter 4) are clearly relevant to assessing and enhancing political feasibility. When a proposal cannot be refurbished to make it acceptable, the analyst must go back a step in his or her analysis and select other alternatives. This might be the case with social security, one of the most troublesome social policies of the 1980s.

Example: Income Security

Over the past four decades, social security, a kind of group insurance operated by the government and set up by the **Social Security Act of 1935**, has provided protection against the loss of income that usually comes with old age or the death or disability of a breadwinner. Most workers in the United States are required to buy social security protection with money deducted from their wages and matched by employer contribution.

Taxes deducted today are used almost immediately to pay benefits to retired workers and others currently on social security; the future benefits for today's workers will come from taxes paid in the future by their children and grandchildren. Today's workers are complaining the most loudly about social security. To keep the social security fund from going broke, Congress in 1977 voted sharp increases in payroll taxes for employees, employers, and the self-employed.

But even the higher tax rates probably will not cure the system's financial problems. For the coming 75 years, according to government studies, the major social security fund that pays benefits to the elderly and survivors and the one that pays to the disabled show a projected combined deficit of roughly $800 billion. What this means is that what will be paid out will exceed what will be paid in by nearly a trillion dollars.

This long-term deficit results from Congress's failure to take into account the "graying" of the U.S. population that is expected early in the next century. As Americans born in the post-World War II baby boom grow old and retire, fewer and fewer workers will support more and more beneficiaries. The illustration shows how the number of people receiving benefits compared to workers paying social security taxes is increasing. The best guess is that the retirement and survivors fund will be broke by 2028; the part of medicare that pays hospital bills will run out of money as early as 1992.

Congress is in a bind. The younger workers complain about the system's increasing burden; beneficiaries complain that their monthly checks are too small to provide an adequate living. Here are five options along with their political implications:

1. *Cut payroll taxes.* Bigger federal deficit and hence more inflation. Would push system closer to bankruptcy, which would upset beneficiaries.
2. *Cut payroll taxes and benefits.* When Carter made this proposal early in 1979, Congress was flooded with angry protests; several groups, with names like Save Our Security (SOS), sprang to fight proposal.
3. *Cut payroll taxes, benefits, and use income-tax money as source of revenue.* Use of income taxes is controversial; it challenges the philosophy of social security—the link between a worker's benefits and the amount of payroll tax he or she paid.
4. *Cut payroll taxes, benefits, and use sales-tax money as source of revenue.* A national sales tax would be inflationary.
5. *Cut payroll taxes and future benefits.* In 1981, the Reagan administration proposed cutting benefits to those who retire early at age 62, but not cutting benefits to those already receiving them. Sweeteners in this proposal were directed at younger workers, who would pay fewer taxes, and at older retirees, who would be able to earn as much as they wished without having their benefits reduced.

Not without reason, the social security system has been described as a way the old can legally mug the young. But virtually any move

Reprinted with permission

[Cartoon by Benson, 5-15-81, The Arizona Republic / Washington Post Writers]

to change the existing system will set off political shock waves.

9. WHAT ARE THE POSSIBLE IMPLEMENTATION PROBLEMS?

Implementation means to carry out, accomplish, fulfill, produce, and complete. One of the greatest difficulties in government today is implementing public policy. There are two fundamental reasons this is so. First, implementing public policy requires the cooperation of many participants. These participants are located in various agencies and frequently not even a part of the government. Second, Murphy's Law does apply: If anything can go wrong, it will. But implementation will go more smoothly if, early in the formulation of policy, policymakers consider some of the reasons for failure.

More specifically, policymakers should try to keep the number of participants to a bare minimum. Then they must provide an attractive set of incentives for the remaining participants. Furthermore, they must engage in a "what if" exercise. In other words, they have to try to think of what could go wrong and how the policy could be modified to take care of such contingencies.

Example 1: Energy

The Congress has passed a measure whereby the government will subsidize initial coal gasification plants until the process proves economically viable. Vast quantities of coal will be turned into gas and then into liquid fuel (synthetic fuels). What happens when the ideal site for such a plant is near a residential area? No doubt, local citizens will oppose the prospect of air pollution and water shortages (the process uses a lot of water); the rumble of coal trains will be heard at all hours of the day and night; there will be the danger of fire; and traffic will increase. That kind of opposition has prevented the construction of scores of nuclear plants and oil refineries in recent years. But some form of cash compensation could pave the way.

Residents within a 10-mile radius of the synthetic fuel plant would be paid to endure it. That is only fair; the residents are being reimbursed in effect for a burden they bear that will benefit society as a whole. Thus, cash compensation—not bribery—is one technique by which controversial policy can be implemented in a free society.

Example 2: Transportation

In 1974, the Emergency Highway Energy Conservation Act was signed into law. It established 55 mph as the maximum legal highway speed in the United States. Under the legislation, states that fail either to establish a 55-mph speed limit or to certify certain levels of enforcement will be penalized by the loss of a portion of their gasoline-tax funds. Administration of the law is in the hands of two agencies of the Department of Transportation. The National Highway Traffic Safety Administration oversees enforcement by the states; the Federal Highway Administration collects and analyzes speed-control and speed-monitoring data.

Over the first several years after passage, opposition to the law grew. This was despite studies claiming that tens of thousands of lives have been saved and billions of gallons of fuel conserved as a result of the law. Even now, the Department of Transportation says that California, Texas, New Mexico, Montana, Wyoming, Arizona, and Nevada are not complying with 1978 legislation requiring that at least 40 percent of drivers go no faster than 55 mph.

The article in the box will give you some idea why a seemingly straightforward plan like the 55-mph speed limit has not been fully implemented.

Drive to Modify 55 mph Speed Limit Pits Western Motorists against Bureaucrats

Leno Menghini, superintendent of the Wyoming Highway Department, thinks the 55 m.p.h. speed limit "is probably all right" in principle. It's just that "we Western states are different and shouldn't be required to comply as rigidly as other states."

A lot of Westerners agree. And now that the Republican Party has sought to make the limit a campaign issue, a lot of officials from Western states have some suggestions about how to focus the debate.

Democrats describe the Republican platform's call for repeal as a step backward that would cost lives and fuel. But the officials in Western states say the important question is whether, and where, drivers obey the limit and whether Washington should be playing enforcer by cutting federal highway funds to states that don't measure up.

Safe at 80

"Some of your Eastern states are so congested it's difficult to drive faster than 55," says Richard Shafer, chief of the Arizona Highway Patrol. "But here the roads were designed to be safe at 80, and people who travel the roads know it."

Even in the East, officials doubt that most drivers are going to stop speeding, especially with gasoline so plentiful. "People obey the law only if they think they're going to be arrested," says Thomas Smith, superintendent of the Maryland state police. The problem, he adds, is that the perceptions vary widely around the country.

Federal figures confirm regional variations in compliance. In Maryland, 28.9 percent of the state's drivers exceeded the 55 m.p.h. limit in the nine months ended June 30. In Georgia the figure was 38 percent and in Virginia 41.7 percent. But head west and the story changes. Nevada had 60.3 percent exceeding the limit, while Utah had 65.3 percent. Arizona 65.5 percent and California 67.3 percent.

Losing Highway Funds

Money is at stake. For the fiscal year ending in October, states must have a 40 percent compliance record or they will lose 5 percent of their federal highway funds. State officials monitor the

> speeds with federal overseers checking them. Last year, with a 30 percent requirement, all states passed. But this year—and next, when the requirement rises to 50 percent—a lot of states may lose out.
>
> The Transportation Department says that states could improve their compliance with better enforcement. It cites figures indicating growing support for the limit nationally, with 49 percent of interstate drivers speeding in this year's first half, down from 54.2 percent a year ago.
>
> But the Westerners think that's unfair. "We're trying to crack down on speeders, and we think we're doing a good enforcement job," says Mr. Menghini of Wyoming. "But with 100 miles between towns, we just don't have the manpower." Already, he says, police have had to ignore other traffice problems to concentrate on catching speeders. "But we just can't catch everybody," he says, "and the speeders know that."
>
> **Cancels the Savings**
>
> So the federal sanctions rankle. "There are an awful lot of people in the state who resent the feds holding this over our heads," says Clifford McCorkle, a Republican state senator from Nevada. "It's blackmail." Other state officials argue that cutting highway funds is counterproductive because it means more dangerous roads, canceling out the savings in lives that the lower speed limit brings.
>
> "It's another in a long line of examples of Washington rules being applied equally to different states, and it's silly," says a Midwestern state senator who seeks repeal of the law or the sanctions. "Our people will speed more, and our police will catch fewer of them. That's just common sense. But not to Washington."
>
> SOURCE: Lawrence Rout, *The Wall Street Journal* (August 11, 1980).

10. HOW WILL RESULTS BE EVALUATED?

In private enterprise, this question is generally answered by looking at the balance sheet. But in government not everything can be put into dollars. This fact should not become an excuse for ignoring measurable public policies. In fact, there is much that can be measured—reading levels of third graders, tons of solid waste removed, reductions in energy consumption, percentage of minorities in middle-level management, etc.

Evaluation seeks to answer the question, Did we accomplish what we planned? Did we solve, or at least adequately deal with, the problem? Did we create new problems?

The concern in government with evaluation is a recent phenomenon. It reflects both a change in the scope and sophistication of government activities and a new mood in the public. Since the 1960s, governments have been involved in a much greater range of complex programs and activities. Many of these programs are aimed at critically modifying and altering the behavior patterns of the society at large. These efforts, often labeled "social intervention," have been met by an increasingly reinforced belief that governments are largely failing in these areas. As Charles Schultze notes in his book *The Public Use of Private Interest*, the public no longer believes that the Great Society approach to problem-solving works.[7] That approach consists mainly of an unflappable belief that social or economic problems can be solved via some new type of federal program. Indeed much of the public now believes the reverse; that is, they feel most government programs don't work and essentially involve nothing more than "throwing money at problems." The disenchantment of which Schultze speaks has been helped by the development of new evaluation processes. These processes have generated considerable evidence that many government programs are indeed ineffective.

It is reasonable to demand that programs have an effect on problems—and the right problems at that. Simply put, the most basic objective of a program evaluation is to measure the impact of a program on its target problem. So, evaluation as an administrative process seems totally logical. After all, what organization would not want to possess information that essentially tells it where it is on its chosen path?

Yet, the fact remains that government organizations may resist evaluation. Aaron Wildavsky has suggested in his work "The Self-Evaluating Organization" that organizations stress stability while evaluation harbors continued change. Hence, resistance to evaluation is inevitable.[8] Wildavsky questions the capacity and desire of organizations to accept evaluation and change. Evaluations tend to be preoccupied with the more negative aspects of organizational performance. This negative dimension can be traced back centuries. French court auditors used to only submit lists of errors found; a "perfect" performance was rewarded with a blank report. This often creates an environment where the administrators being evaluated dislike the process; they naturally dislike getting bad report cards. No wonder many administrators take the tactic of noncooperation, especially for outside evaluations. Noncooperation is accomplished by providing minimal information to evaluators. More than one evaluator has had to conduct studies of programs with little available data or statistics. Yet they find the agency rebuttal to the final evaluative study replete with vast statistical data, not previously offered.

Example 1: Transportation

Do high school driving courses save lives? According to Leon Robertson, a senior research associate at Yale University's Institute for Social and Policy Studies, high school driver education courses actually *increase* traffic deaths. Such courses allow many more teenagers to be on the road, who otherwise would have to wait until they were age 18 to drive.

Robertson examined the records of 8,000 drivers and compared the traffic fatality rates in 27 states with driver education. He found such courses had no effect on the individual teenage driver's chances of being involved in a fatal crash. Raising the driving age to 18, he estimated, would prevent at least 2,000 fatal crashes.

Example 2: Income Security

Have transfer payments made Americans more equal? Table 12–3 would seem to indicate a considerable amount of inequality of income in the United States (though not much more than in other industrialized democracies). But, as I warned you in Chapter 1, statistics can be misleading. Not only that; the very concept of inequality is ambiguous. Let us see why evaluation is so hard here.

First, the data in Table 12–3 ignore noncash income, such as food stamps, subsidized housing, **medicaid** (a federally supported state program for poor people unable to qualify under medicare but in need of medical services). **The Economic Opportunity Act of 1964** also provides services rather than money for the poor: a **Job Corps** for young persons chronically unemployed; literacy programs to teach English; a Neighborhood Youth Corps to provide work experience; a work-study program to subsidize college students from poor families; and a Community Action Program to allow poor to help

TABLE 12–3
Distribution of Aftertax Income in the United States and Other Industrialized Countries

The Poorest 10 Percent of Households Get:		The Richest 10 Percent of Households Get:	
France	1.4 %	Sweden	18.6 %
Spain	1.5	Netherlands	21.8
Australia	1.6	Norway	21.9
Canada	1.6	Britain	23.9
United States	1.7	Canada	24.7
Britain	2.4	Australia	25.2
Norway	2.4	United States	26.1
Sweden	2.6	Japan	27.8
Japan	2.7	Spain	28.5
Germany	2.8	France	30.5
Netherlands	3.2	Germany	30.6

Source: Organization for Economic Cooperation and Development, 1976.

plan the programs designed to benefit them. For the poor, these things matter greatly.

Second, family size has decreased steadily over the years. Consequently, the families in the bottom 20 percent contain fewer individuals to be supported by the 5.4 percent of income. Therefore, members of these families are today better off than they were in 1947.

Third, as Morton Paglin of Portland State University has pointed out, the people in 1947 who were poor are not the same people who were poor in 1952 or poor today. A significant portion of the unequal income at any given moment derives from the unequal ages and therefore the unequal earning power of the people involved. Young high school graduates do not make as much money as their parents; pensioners do not make as much as they did during their peak earning years. Both young and old are concentrated in the lower end of income distribution.

Fourth, the share of income going to the top 20 percent of households actually represents more labor today than in 1947. The reason is that today a much higher percentage of these top-income families have two earners. (Among the bottom fifth, the reverse is true.)

Yet even with these four qualifications our analysis of **income distribution** is not beyond criticism. For example, income may be a poor standard for comparison. It is usually based on salaries; but a great deal of the wealth of the upper 20 percent comes from nonsalary sources, such as rents, dividends, and interest (see Table 12–4). In contrast, the bottom 20 percent have virtually all their wealth coming from salaries or government benefits.

Suppose we could arrive at a reasonably accurate picture of how income (or wealth) is distributed in the United States. The question would still remain whether that is the way it ought to be distributed. Serious egalitarians would be concerned about *any* inequalities. Faculty salaries may range from a low of $18,000 to a high of $40,000. Certainly no other society in history has had a narrower range of income

TABLE 12–4
Personal Wealth—Percent Share of Top One Percent of Population: 1922 to 1972

Year	Percent
1922	31.6
1929	36.3
1933	28.3
1939	30.6
1945	23.3
1949	20.8
1953	24.3
1954	24.0
1956	26.0
1958	23.8
1962	22.0
1965	23.4
1969	20.1
1972	20.7

Note: Persons 21 years and over counted.
Source: *Statistical Abstract of the U.S., 1980*, p. 471.

(the "richest" only make 2.2 times more than the "poorest"). Yet, as any college administrator can tell you, within this range, professor A can become very animated when he learns that professor B makes a mere $100 a year more.

Inequality in society is usually defended on one of two grounds. First, some inequality is necessary to provide incentives for risk taking and hard work.* Second, if one of the major functions of government is to protect property, citizens should have the right to do with their wealth as they please—which may include passing it on to their children.†

Thus far we have been looking at economic equality irrespective of race. But the issue of

---

* Lester Thurow makes the interesting observation that the distribution of income among white males is much more equal than among all other workers. Since this equality does not seem to affect the incentives of white males, then the U.S. government might safely establish a distribution of earnings for everyone "that is no more equal than that which *now* exists for fully employed white males" [*The Zero Sum Society* (New York: Basic Books, 1980), p. 201].

† The argument for property, which goes back at least as far as John Locke, has been updated by Robert Nozick (see Chapter 3).

economic inequality between blacks and whites is an important one. It was raised briefly towards the end of the last chapter. Now we need to take a second, longer look at it.

Three years after the Civil Rights Act of 1964 (discussed in Chapter 11), the median income of all black families as a percentage of median white income was .59. The percentage climbed for five years, fell briefly, and then arose again, reaching a high of nearly 62 percent of white median income in 1975. But since that time, as you can see in Figure 12–4, the trend went down and never returned to the 1975 peak. The other trend in Figure 12–4 shows a steady climb in the median income of black husband-wife families where the wife was in the labor force. In 1978, such families earned about 85 percent of what similar white familes earned.

The Civil Rights Acts of 1964 and 1965 appear to have had little effect on the money income of *individual* blacks. Here are the ratios of median income of blacks to whites for a 23-year period:

Year	Percent
1955	67%
1960	57
1965	73
1970	68
1975	67
1978	67

The data upon which these calculations are based do not include the growing black male "underclass." Therefore an evaluation of overall black economic progress is probably biased. The gap is probably even larger than the percentages above indicate.

What other factors would distort our evaluation? According to Thomas Sowell of UCLA, one of the most obvious factors for differences in income among ethnic groups is that some groups work more than others.

FIGURE 12–4
Comparisons of Median Family Income by Race, 1967–1978

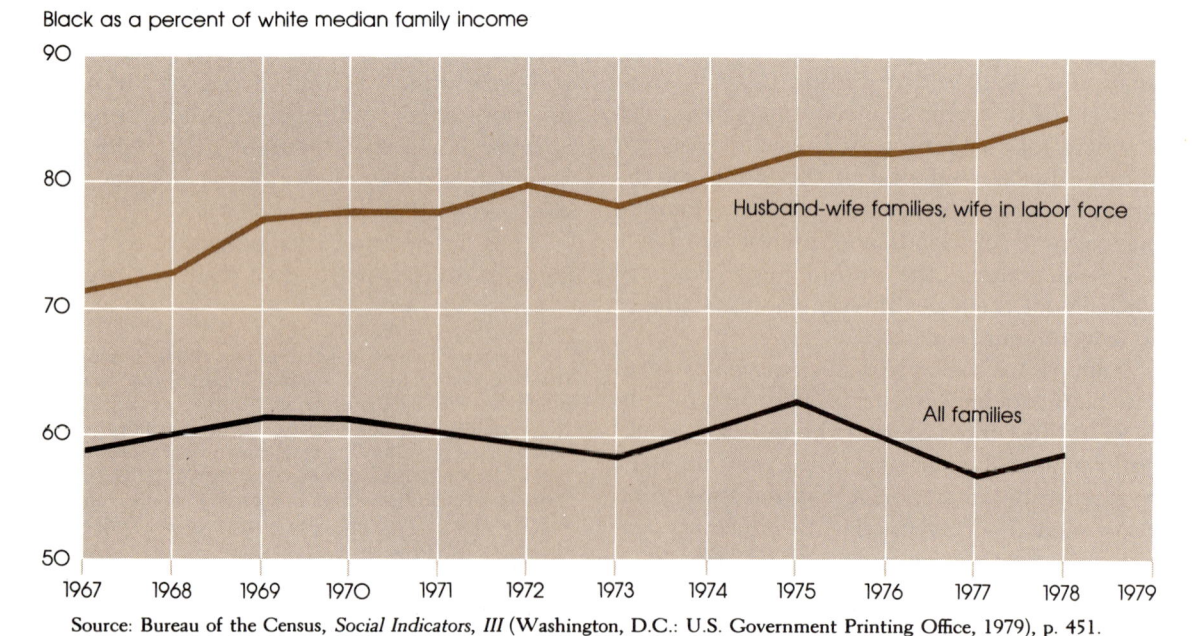

Black as a percent of white median family income

Source: Bureau of the Census, *Social Indicators, III* (Washington, D.C.: U.S. Government Printing Office, 1979), p. 451.

About one fifth of Chinese-American families have three or more people working. Among Puerto Ricans the proportion is less then half that. When it comes to families with one working, it is the Puerto Ricans who are first and the Chinese who are last. Most ethnic groups fall somewhere between these extremes.[9]

According to Sowell, another obvious factor routinely ignored is age. The average age of blacks is some six years below that of whites. "This is a country where income differences among age brackets are even greater than income differences among races and ethnic groups. For this reason, differences in age (experience) among ethnic groups will obviously affect income."[10] Table 12–5 shows how vast these age differences are. Such differences make any meaningful comparisons between ethnic groups exceedingly difficult, if not impossible.

Educational, geographic, and cultural differences also militate against such comparisons. For example, Jews not only are older than Puerto Ricans, but average 70 percent more education. Therefore, it is not surprising to find Jews well represented in the high-paying occupations, which typically require experience and education. It is simply fallacious to say that the difference in income between Jews and Puerto Ricans can be explained entirely in terms of discrimination.

And where one lives has an even greater effect on income disparities among ethnic groups.

> Virtually every American ethnic group has its own peculiar pattern of geographical distribution, reflecting historical happenstance and cultural preference. . . . Even an ideal society, with zero discrimination, would not produce equal incomes for its various ethnic groups as long as they were distributed geographically in different ways.[11]

Once we recognize the effect of geography, we can begin to understand such paradoxes as the fact that Puerto Ricans earn more than blacks nationally, while at any given location blacks earn more. The answer is easy: Half the black population lives in the low-income South; most Puerto Ricans live in the high-income Northeast.

The point of the preceding evaluation was twofold. First, it is important to recognize the gains and losses made by blacks and other minorities in the last several years. Second, it is important to recognize the limitations—even crudeness—of many statistical measures.

Example 3: Administration of Justice

Have law enforcement agencies helped to control crime or is the crime rate increasing? Contrary to the popular view, crime in the United States has not increased appreciably in the last decade. It has remained remarkably stable. Reported crime, though, has risen sharply. Any evaluation of law enforcement in the United States must be clear on these distinctions.

Data on people who are crime victims are available from many sources. The *Uniform Crime Reports for the United States*, published by the FBI, and the criminal victimization surveys conducted by the Bureau of the Census for the Law Enforcement Assistance Administration are the most informative.

TABLE 12–5
Median Age (In Years) of Persons by Ethnic Origin

Ethnicity	Age
Jewish	46
Polish	40
Irish	37
German	36
Italian	36
Anglo-Saxon	34
Japanese	32
Total United States	28
Chinese	27
Black	22
American Indian	20
Mexican	18
Puerto Rican	18

Source: U.S. Bureau of the Census, *Current Population Reports*, series P-20, 1978.

The *Uniform Crime Reports* present data on incidents actually reported to police departments nationwide. From 1960 to 1978, the rates of both violent and property crimes grew about threefold. Since 1975, however, the rate of increase for rape and aggravated assault has declined, while both the murder and robbery rates themselves have actually declined. By 1978, the rates of property crimes (burglary, larceny-theft, and motor vehicle theft) had been reduced.

Although the rapid growth in violent and property crime rates reported by the police to the FBI from 1960 to 1978 is a justifiable cause for concern, the average annual percent change in the rates for these offenses were notably higher between 1965 and 1970 than they were for the 1970-to-1978 period. The national homicide rate (that is, the number of murders each year per 100,000 people) has fluctuated between 10 and 11 for the last decade.

These data imply that the rate of reported crime is either leveling off or diminishing for some offenses. Nevertheless, the incidence of violent and property crimes—which is certainly higher than the rates of reported crime cited here—poses a very real threat to the personal safety of many citizens.

The Bureau of the Census developed the National Crime Survey program for the LEAA to clearly define the magnitude and nature of selected forms of criminal victimization in the United States. Based on continuing surveys of a representative national sample of households and businesses, this program provides comprehensive data on crime and its victims. Since 1973, data have been collected from individuals on victimizations resulting from rape, robbery, assault, personal larceny, and such household offenses as burglary, household larceny, and motor vehicle theft. (See Table 12–6.)

One of the most fascinating aspects of these victimization data is the remarkable stability in the various rates during the six-year period ending in 1978. This relative lack of fluctuation seems to dispel the theory held by many that crime is on the upswing. On the contrary, these data suggest that citizens today are not falling victim to criminal acts more frequently than they were a few years ago.

One of the most attractive features of the National Crime Survey program is its ability to provide data on the volume of certain crimes which are not brought to the attention of law enforcement authorities. Information obtained from victimization surveys covering 1973 to 1978 indicates that a significant portion of criminal activity was not reported to the police. For example, in 1978, somewhat less than one half of all personal crimes of violence included in

TABLE 12–6
Victimizations Reported and Unreported to Police: 1973–1978

Type of Crime	1973	1974	1975	1976	1977	1978
	Number Reported (thousands)					
Rape	153 (49%)	161 (52%)	154 (56%)	145 (53%)	154 (58%)	171 (49%)
Robbery	1,087 (52)	1,174 (54)	1,147 (53)	1,111 (53)	1,083 (56)	1,038 (51)
Assault	4,002 (44)	4,064 (45)	4,272 (45)	4,344 (48)	4,664 (44)	4,732 (43)
Personal crimes of theft	14,761 (22)	15,610 (25)	16,294 (26)	16,519 (27)	16,933 (25)	17,050 (25)
Burglary	6,432 (47)	6,655 (48)	6,744 (49)	6,663 (48)	6,765 (49)	6,704 (47)
Household larceny	7,506 (25)	8,866 (25)	9,223 (27)	9,301 (27)	9,418 (25)	9,352 (24)
Motor vehicle theft	1,335 (68)	1,342 (67)	1,433 (71)	1,235 (70)	1,297 (68)	1,365 (66)

Note: Percentage columns reveal what proportion of the true crime rate has been reported to police. For example, in 1973, the Census Bureau's survey found that the 153,000 reported rapes were only 49 percent of the true number.

Source: Bureau of the Census, *Social Indicators*, III (Washington, D.C.: U.S. Government Printing Office, 1979), p. 249.

the victimization surveys were brought to police attention.

Thus, a careful evaluation of crime in the United States leads to the conclusion that the reported rate of many crimes is growing at a decelerated pace; victimization rates from most violent and household crimes have remained fairly constant during the mid-1970s. If the general population perceives the prevalence of crime as an ever-growing problem, does it really matter what the reported statistics show? It is a rare event when one can read a newspaper or listen to a newscast that does not mention some significant criminal incident. The media constantly feed the public information about the latest murders, rapes, and robberies. When people hear the grim details of these brutal crimes, it is very difficult to console them with the fact that the rate of murder per 100,000 population has not increased significantly in the last several years. One particularly gruesome incident makes a lasting impression on people. Feelings cannot be counterbalanced by mere statistics that appear to paint a picture of hope.

Drawing by Chas. Addams; © 1979 The New Yorker Magazine, Inc.

For reasons explained in the text, public perceptions about crime vary markedly from the responses one might expect after an evaluation of only the reported statistics. Recently, the general population has expressed a feeling of increasing uneasiness and anxiety with the volume of crime. Furthermore, they have called for stricter punishment of those who threaten individual safety. If this is how people perceive their plight, one can reasonably expect their actions to reflect these concerns. Their apprehensions may be expressed by consciously avoiding certain high-crime areas, eliminating nighttime strolls through the neighborhood, installing extra security locks on doors and windows at home, buying handguns for protection, etc.

The most exciting and important thing about policy analysis remains to be said. Today there is much talk about broadening the concept of liberal education. But something is missing in much of this talk: Students must know how to act, how to use this knowledge. Jean Mayer, president of Tufts University, had something of this in mind when he said that students "need to learn to coordinate widely disparate pieces of information to form the basis of decision making, and they need to learn how to make a decision. The ability to arrive at complex decisions should be the hallmark of the educated person. Indeed, it should be what education, as opposed to instruction or training, is all about." (*Chronicle of Higher Education*, November 8, 1976)

This insight charges policy analysis with transcendent importance. Why? Because decision making—choosing one course of action over others—is the vital center of policy analysis. To analyze public policy is to come to understand that we cannot have everything at the same time, facile political slogans notwithstanding. To analyze public policy is to understand, to weigh political, economic, ethical, and even esthetic factors before leaping to any isolated actions called "solutions." To study public policy is to understand that there are costs and risks—financial and human, foreseen and unforeseen—in every decision. But, let us face it: Today we are not very good at these things.[12]

Quiz

Analyze this policy: Legalization of marijuana

Drug bust in Miami

Wide World Photos

Virtually all Americans agree that recent federal efforts to control illegal drugs are ineffective. The United States retail market for narcotics was an estimated $57 billion in 1978, rose to $78 billion in 1979, and is still growing. The Drug Enforcement Administration (DEA) administrator estimates that there are 100,000 to 150,000 people involved in smuggling marijuana alone.

As an exercise in policy analysis, consider this proposal: legalization of marijuana.

To help structure your analysis, let me suggest you pay particular attention to the following questions:

1. What would be the costs and benefits? (Give answer in types, not dollars.)

2. How would the costs and benefits be distributed?

3. What are the risks?

4. Is the proposal politically feasible?

5. What are possible implementation problems?

6. What other alternatives are there—besides legalizing marijuana or giving DEA a bigger budget?

Answer on p. 452.

Chapter Key: Steps in Policy Analysis

?	1. What is the problem?	The true nature of problems facing society is seldom self-evident. Consequently, defining the problem might constitute up to 40 percent of the total time in an analysis. For example, is the "energy crisis" economic (prices too low), political (war in the Middle East), or physical (scarce resources)?
	2. What should be the goals?	Policies should be more than a collection of furtive actions. They should have goals, i.e., general statements of where we want to go. For example, a goal for national energy policy might be to emphasize conservation, increased production, or new technology
	3. What are the alternatives?	For each goal several alternative strategies or projects should be considered.
$	4. What are the costs and benefits of each?	The costs and benefits – both direct and indirect – of each alternative should be assessed.
	5. How are the costs and benefits distributed?	How the costs and benefits are distributed among citizenry is important. Possible categories are geographic region, income level, sex, age group, and race.
☠	6. What are the risks?	Many public policies entail uncertainties. For example, a new drug causes cancer, a dam breaks, a tanker spills oil. What is the probability (1 in 100? 1 in 10,000? 1 in a million?) that something could go wrong?
☑	7. Select alternatives	With the costs, benefits, and risks of each alternative estimated, select the most attractive.
👎	8. Is the policy politically feasible?	Can the policy's goals and the strategies for attaining them be sold in the political arena? Who will be for them? Against? How might they be modified to make them more politically attractive?
	(yes) 9. What are the possible implementation problems?	What difficulties might be encountered in carrying out the policy?
ABCDF	10. How will it be evaluated?	How will the success of the policy be measured?

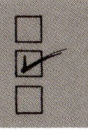

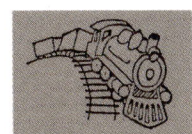

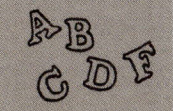

Answers to Quiz

What follows should not be thought of as THE ANSWER; in policy analysis, there can never be a definitive solution. Rather, let us think of what follows as simply notes towards one possible analysis of the proposal to legalize marijuana.

1. The major benefit from legalization is probably the revenue that federal and state government would collect from an excise tax on marijuana. If government taxed the difference between the cost of producing a pound of prerolled and prepackaged marijuana cigarettes (one estimate is about $8.00 a pound) and the current street price ($700), the total annual revenue could be over $3 billion. In comparison, the cigarette industry paid $6 billion in taxes in 1978, while the liquor industry paid $10.5 billion.

    Other benefits are less tangible. One is the reduced paranoia experienced by users of marijuana. The other is the plant's therapeutic potential. Today about 12,000 cancer patients use tetrahidrocannabinol (THC)—the active ingredient in marijuana—to relieve the violent nausea and vomiting that accompany chemotherapy. Glaucoma victims smoke it to ease pressure on their eye. The plant is also being studied as a possible aid to people stricken with epilepsy, acute migraine, or multiple sclerosis.

    The costs of legal marijuana will be examined in the answer to question 3, along with risks.

2. Contrary to popular wisdom, there is little evidence that the tobacco industry is gearing up for legalized marijuana. To be sure, they have the physical ability to move quickly into this area if the laws were changed. But they are already under considerable pressure from health and consumer groups. Therefore they have thus far carefully avoided any association with the marijuana issue.

    Groups that would surely benefit from legalization would be the paraphernalia "industry," (some claim it includes 1,200 manufacturers and 300 distributors), farmers (in California, illegal marijuana runs close to grapes as the leading cash crop), and the fertilizer industry.

    Who would be adversely affected? Wider use of marijuana could possibly siphon off some liquor business. And legalization in the United States would most certainly affect the cash flow of some countries, such as Jamaica, Mexico, and Colombia.

3. Tests show that marijuana interacts with the body in subtler ways than alcohol, morphine, and many other substances. Research indicates that marijuana may affect ovulation, sperm production, and adolescent hormonal balance. Because tampering with these functions is risky, some scientists are deeply worried. Reese Jones of the Langley Porter Psychiatric Institute in San Francisco says, "Not long ago I wouldn't have guessed just how complicated marijuana is. Now we're finding out, and it could be only a matter of time before the dangers become manifest. After all, it took 60 years of steady cigarette smoking in the United States before doctors realized that there was a connection between lung cancer and cigarettes." (Quoted in *Discovery*, August 1981, p. 17)

    Because marijuana affects a user's response time and sense of spatial relations, traffic accidents would likely increase. (Some users, like some drunks, *think* they drive better stoned.)

    Intangible costs should not be ignored. Chronic marijuana use clearly has effects on the personality. When a smoker is high, his or her intellectual abilities—particularly the memory—plummet. Observers ranging from psychiatrists to parents to peers have noticed that people who smoke several joints a day often lack motivation to work, study, exercise, or indeed do much more than sit and listen to music.

4. The political feasibility of legal marijuana is a crucial factor in the analysis. First, a Republican Senate would have to vote to

either amend or withdraw from an international treaty on drug regulation (the Single Convention on Narcotic Drugs). Next, Congress would have to vote on the legalization, regulation, and taxation of what many Americans still think of as the "killer weed." Finally, states and countries would still retain the option to ban or further restrict sales.

5. The implementation of the proposal could probably best be handled by the U.S. Bureau of Alcohol, Tobacco and Firearms. This is the tax-collection unit of the Treasury Department.

6. One alternative to legalization is to focus on the flow of dollars from the illegal sale of marijuana. In 1979, for example, Treasury officials noticed a suspicious $3.3 billion cash surplus in Florida banks. The resources of the less-than-effective Drug Enforcement Administration could be linked to those of the Internal Revenue Services, the FBI, and the Treasury Department. The FBI could take over the DEA's domestic drug investigations; the U.S. Customs Service, a Treasury agency, would handle overseas intelligence and border operations. This makes sense, since many drug kingpins are also organized crime figures.

Other alternatives to legalization include increasing payments to informants, giving customs agents greater authority to stop departing travelers suspected of carrying unreported cash, and allowing the navy and air force to share information on suspicious aircraft and ship.

John Thoeming/Dorsey Press; (inset) Library of Congress

13 | The Government and the Economy

After studying this chapter you should be able to answer the following questions:

1. Why is it impossible to separate politics and economics?
2. What are the various ways a nation's wealth can be measured?
3. How does a market system operate?
4. What are the ways a market system can fail to work?
5. What are the major tools available to government to manage the economy?
6. What are the major economic issues facing the United States in the 1980s? What are the leading theories on how to cope with these issues?
7. Why can we not consider the U.S. economy separate from the world economy?

Terms you should know:

appropriate technology
comparative advantage
consumer price index
deficits
deregulation
expansion
FDA
Federal Reserve Board
fiscal policy
free rider effect
gross national product
ICC
incomes policy
industrial policy
inflation
monetary policy
monopoly
multinational corporation
National Labor Relations Board
neo-Keynesians

Occupational Health and Safety Administration (OSHA)
oligopoly
productivity
public and private goods
public debt
Keynesians
recession
spillovers
stagflation
supply-side economics
supply and demand laws
surplus
tariff
tax expenditures
third world
trade surplus and trade deficit
"uncontrollable" expenditures
wage-price controls

Monopoly is the most popular board game every designed—at least that is what my friends, who keep up with such things, tell me. In any event, Monopoly is not a bad introduction to economics.

If several players, rather than one player, want to buy a piece of property I own (say, Boardwalk), their demand drives up the price. If there is a player in the game who has an obsession about owning railroads, then I will make an extra effort to acquire the B&O or Reading. I can then, in turn, supply him with it. And thanks to the chance cards—with their friendly little messages about inheritance taxes and the like—Monopoly continues to remind us that the government affects economic activity. For instance, having paid my taxes, I have insufficient funds to acquire the B&O railroad.

Yet there is one profound lesson about economics that Monopoly does not teach. In the game, the players seek their own advantage until the ruthless competition drives all but one player from the game. In the real world of economics, men and women seek their own advantage but are led at the same time and quite unintentionally to advance the interests of others.

To understand this paradox we must consider that masterwork of economic thought, *The Wealth of Nations* (1776). Its author was Adam Smith, whose portrait has been superimposed upon the picture of the Monopoly board. Smith explained the mechanism that reconciles the chaos inherent in a society filled with individuals pursuing their self-interest. The protective mechanism is competition. Each individual, in trying to better his or her condition in life, benefits society as a whole. Smith explained how several manufacturers seeking customers are forced to keep their prices down, close to their production costs. He further explained how the competitive mechanism constantly forces labor and investment into more and more profitable areas. What makes these areas profitable is that they are satisfying some consumer demand. Thus competition is a self-correcting mechanism, which forces the makers of buggy whips into more useful areas.

Finally, and perhaps most important, this acquisitive drive is the key to the growth of a nation. How else can one explain the extraordinary postwar growth of a nation with virtually no natural resources—Japan?

Economics can be a demanding subject. Therefore a few stakes ought to be driven into the ground at the outset. Then we can see better the terrain we shall be covering in this chapter.

The first is an obvious one. We shall note some of the ways economics, the focus of this chapter, and American politics, the theme of this book, are related.

Second, we shall develop some understanding of what the wealth of a nation consists and how that wealth is measured.

Third, we shall want to take a closer look at exactly how competition is harnessed for the benefit of society as a whole. This will require that we understand how the market system works. We shall also note how the American economic engine can malfunction.

Malfunctioning engines require mechanics. So, in the fourth section of the chapter, we shall meet the master mechanic—the federal government. We shall discover what tools are available to policymakers when they try to get better performance from the American economy.

Fifth, we shall consider the major economic issues facing the United States in the 1980s. We shall also consider ideas about how best to overhaul the economy.

In the final section of the chapter, we shall cast our searchlight beyond the national boundaries to consider how the international economy affects things at home. This section will also serve as a bridge to the final chapter of the book, which looks at American foreign policy.

REDISCOVERING THE LINKS BETWEEN POLITICS AND ECONOMICS

How do political decisions influence economic decisions and vice versa? Without trying to chalk out a complete answer, a few crucial connections, past and present, are worth noting.

In Chapter 2 a thoroughgoing economic interpretation of the American Revolution was rejected. But it would be wrong to say that economic considerations played either no part or a very minor part in what happened. The fact that merchants decided they needed a central government to protect their economic interests certainly was a factor in propelling the colonies towards a more unified state. (Hence: economic conditions → political results.)

By 1914, the U.S. economic system was producing the same volume of economic goods as Britain, Germany, and France combined. Many reasons might be given for this growth. But the really decisive factor was the free constitution (political condition) and its enthusiastic acceptance by the waves of emigrants from authoritarian states. (Hence: political conditions → economic results.)

Workable solutions to inflation are neither abstract nor difficult to pinpoint. One solution is restraint—in consumption, in government spending programs, in living beyond our means

FIGURE 13-1
President Carter and the Economy

As all presidents are well aware, the public tends to hold them responsible for the economy. The chart below shows that economic expectations of the public and Carter's approval rating declining together. The upward blip in Carter's score in late 1978 reflects the Egypt-Israel peace agreements he helped negotiate.

Source: *The Wall Street Journal* (August 26, 1980).

458 UNDERSTANDING AMERICAN POLITICS

Reprinted by permission of the Chicago Tribune–New York News Syndicate, Inc.

by borrowing, in the extension of credit, in the regulatory demands the government puts on the economy. Each of these restraints will affect different groups and in different amounts. Generally speaking, the more influential of these groups are likely to complain and try to get the policy changed. (Hence: economic problems → political problems.)

American presidents can and do manipulate the economy for their political advantage. Though contemporary literature on the political economy of inflation is scant, Edward R. Tufte of Yale University, in his book, *Political Control of the Economy*, has provided statistical evidence that in election years (even-numbered) the party in power tends to hit the economic accelerator.[1] More specifically, Tufte found that, in recent years, real disposable personal income (i.e., what is left over after taxes) in this country has regularly experienced growth spurts because of economic "hormones" administered in election years. These "hormones" are principally tax cuts and transfer payments; the latter consist of veterans', old age, survivors, disability, and health insurance benefits, including social security. Tufte's fascinating evidence suggests that there is a "four-year presidential cycle of high unemployment early in the term followed by economic stimulation, increasing prosperity, and reduced unemployment late in the term."[2] (Hence: political events → economic conditions.)

Finally, the 1980 presidential election as much as any in recent history turned on economic issues. The new president made economic problems almost the sole concern of his first year in office, even letting a number of pressing problems in foreign affairs go untended. (Hence: economic problems → political decisions.)

MEASURING AMERICA'S WEALTH

How Big Is the U.S. Economy?

One way to measure the size of U.S. economic production is to add together the value of all the goods and services produced in one year. The total is called the **gross national product** (GNP). We constantly see and hear references to this total in the news as a yardstick of production. The GNP does not include do-it-yourself activities, such as housework or home gardening. Nor does it measure things like the quality of the environment—a point to which we shall return in a moment.

In 1979, the American GNP was over $2,369 billion. Its size was greater than those of the

Used with permission of the McGraw-Hill Book Company

FIGURE 13-2
Gross National Product, Selected Years, 1960-1979

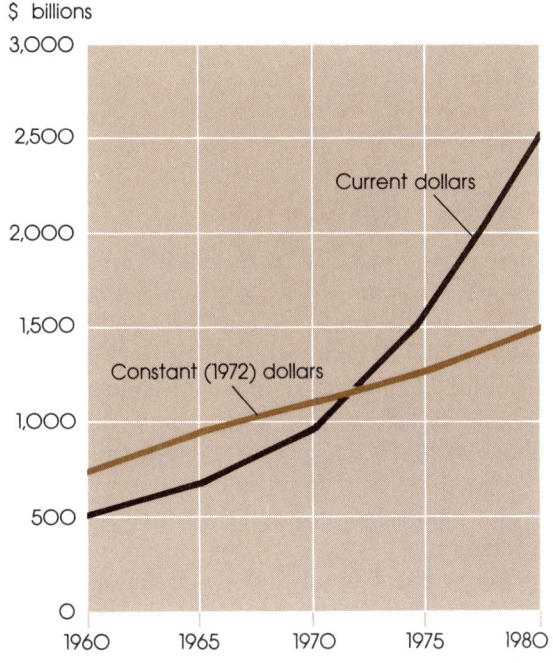

$ billions

[Line graph showing GNP from 1960 to 1980, with Current dollars rising from about 500 in 1960 to 2,500 in 1980, and Constant (1972) dollars rising from about 750 to 1,500.]

Source: *Statistical Abstract of the United States, 1980.* Tables 725 and 727.

USSR, West Germany, and France combined. This overwhelming figure can be better understood by thinking of it as about $10,745 worth of goods and services per American.

Figure 13–2 show you how the American GNP has increased over the years.

When population growth is taken into account, the GNP per person is still seven times its value of 100 years ago.

Throughout this time, American output of goods and services per person has remained the highest of the world's major industrial nations. Below are a few international comparisons for 1978, with the United States assigned a rating of 100.

Some smaller nations, such as Sweden, Switzerland, and Kuwait, did as well or better in national output per person than the major industrial nations listed below.

Of course, one has to realize that output per person is simply one of the many factors that determine standard of living. One must also consider what affects the quality of lives as well—such as how clean the air is, how clean the water is, or how much leisure time we have. Still, GNP is useful as a measure of some of the things an economy provides that affect how well we live.

Today many questions are asked about our GNP and its growth. Some people feel that there should be little or no economic growth, in order to conserve natural resources. Others say the United States should continue to increase production and employment, even at some cost to the environment. Clearly these are critical choices.

Other Measures

Several new measurements—popularly known as "social indicators"—were born of experts'

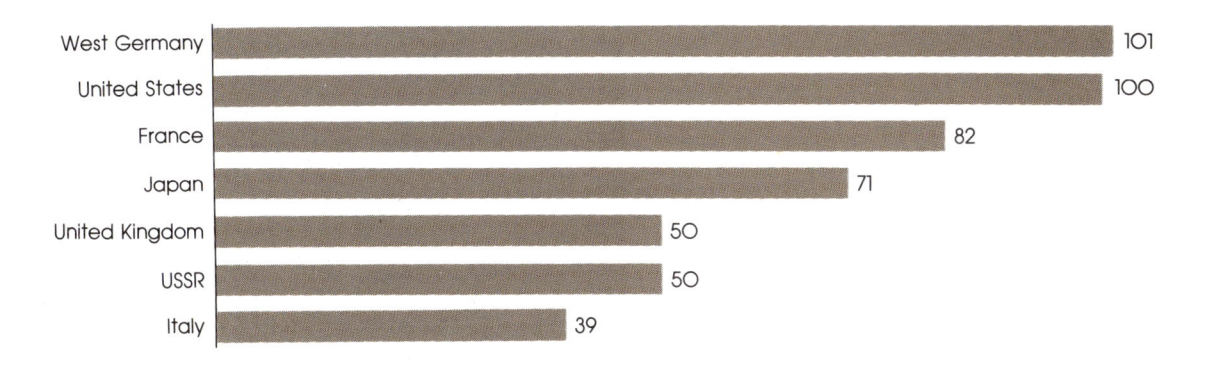

Country	Rating
West Germany	101
United States	100
France	82
Japan	71
United Kingdom	50
USSR	50
Italy	39

dissatisfaction with the use of gross national product (GNP) and other conventional economic yardsticks to gauge progress in the countries of Asia, Africa, and Latin America. It was widely felt that use of the GNP overemphasized aggregate economic growth and neglected the needs of poor majorities within developing societies.

Efforts have been made by the United Nations and various development institutions to devise social indicators that can measure the quality of life of impoverished Third World populations. A case in point is the physical quality of life index (PQLI). This is a unique system that was introduced in 1977 to show how GNP figures fail to reflect the true living standards of Third World majorities. Devised by the Overseas Development Council, the PQLI combines infant mortality, life expectancy, and literacy rates into a simple, easily understood number. The results it yields can be surprising.

FIGURE 13-3
Physical Quality of Life Index

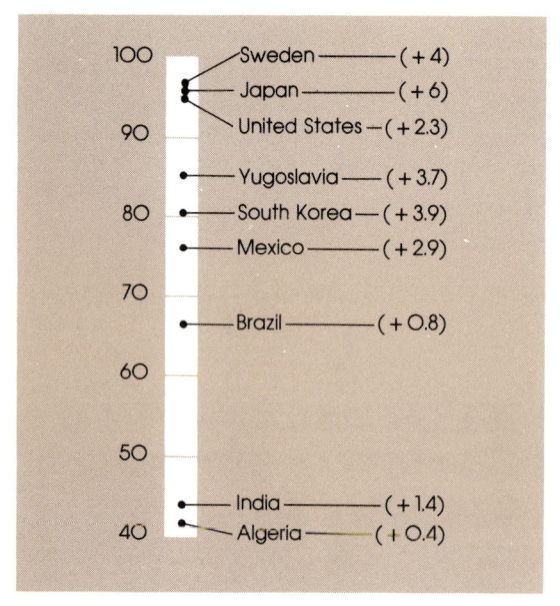

Score	Country	Change
100	Sweden	(+4)
	Japan	(+6)
90	United States	(+2.3)
	Yugoslavia	(+3.7)
80	South Korea	(+3.9)
	Mexico	(+2.9)
70	Brazil	(+0.8)
60		
50		
	India	(+1.4)
40	Algeria	(+0.4)

Note: Percentage change in index from 1964 to 1975 is shown in parenthesis; for Brazil the period of change is 1960–1970.

Source: David Morris, *Measuring the Condition of the World's Poor: The Physical Quality of Life Index* (Pergamon Press, 1979).

For example, Sri Lanka has a low per capita GNP of $200; however, its rating on the PQLI (82 on a scale of 100) is almost as high as that of Washington, D.C. (88). Qatar's score of 31, on the other hand, makes one wonder where its staggering per capita wealth of $11,400 is being spent.

The Real Nature of Wealth

One of the reasons Adam Smith wrote *The Wealth of Nations* was to debunk a common fallacy of the times. It was believed that the wealth of any country could be increased by introducing or by detaining in it a large quantity of gold and silver. To Smith's mind, this made about as much sense as an attempt to increase the good cheer of families by forcing them to keep an unnecessary number of spoons in their kitchens.

Today the United States may be operating under another fallacy: the illusion that resources and capital are the real sources of wealth. George Gilder writes:

> This fallacy is one of the oldest of economic delusions, from the period of empire when men believed that wealth was land, to the period of mercantilism when they fantasized that it was gold, to the contemporary period when they suppose it is oil; and our citizens clutch at real estate and gold as well. But economists make an only slightly lesser error when they add up capital in quantities and assume that wealth consists mainly in machines and factories.[3]

Consider oil, for example. There was no real demand for oil until the automobile existed. Oil was not thought of as a "resource" until the automobile made it useful. The wealth of Arabia was created in a garage in Dearborn, Michigan. Capital ventures—risks taken on an unknown future—create wealth. Human will, imagination, creativity, and risk-taking create wealth.

Is there a single word that will encapsulate all four terms? I think there is. The word is *technology*. It is in new technology (more than anywhere in the economy that we can see) that imagination, creativity, and boldness will come together to create new wealth.

Let me try to express the idea as a proposition: *In the 21st century, the wealth (and power) of nations will be chiefly predicated on the excellence of their technology.*

The most vivid example of how this proposition works is the case of the German chemist Fritz Haber. Early in this century, one of the outstanding problems chemists faced was finding a practical use for the enormous amounts of free nitrogen in the air. Nitrogen and hydrogen under pressure form ammonia, which could then be converted easily into fertilizer or explosives. Karl Bosch turned this laboratory experiment into an industrial operation.

Today, the production of nitrogen not only is a major branch of the fertilizer industry; it is a most important segment of the chemical industry as a whole. World production of nitrogen by the late 1970s was well over 50 million tons annually. The Haber process is still used, in principle, today.

The point of the story is to illustrate how certain scientific breakthroughs (Haber) and technological breakthroughs (Bosch) can be "pyramided" into giant industries. Similar stories could be told for other modern industries (e.g., synthetic fibers, plastics, transistors, penicillin). In every case the pattern would be the same. If one wants to know the long-range future of the U.S. economy, the fundamental question one must ask is, What does the future of American technology look like?

FUTURE FILE

Where Is American Technology Headed?

Defining Technology

The term *technology* has two meanings. First, it can refer to what humans make to feed, clothe, house, transport, and defend themselves and to communicate with each other. Thus, the first type of technology consists of machinery, contrivances, devices, materials, structures, and other artifacts. In short, it consists of hardware.

The term *technology* can also refer to procedures, processes, or techniques that lead to a particular result. In this sense, citizen participation, educational methods, management styles, planning techniques, problem solving, and working arrangements are all technologies. Like hardware, this software can have profound social, economic, and political effects.

Technology as hardware is often thought of as following two separate, but converging, lines of development. One of these might be called macroengineering. Under this heading would come space exploration, nuclear research, manufacturing in space stations, mining the ocean floor (for manganese nodules), sea farming, MX missile production (Chapter 14), desert irrigation, and semisubmersible floating platforms (upon which large numbers of people can live). What these seven examples have in common is that they are all big, expensive, and politically explosive. Who should farm the ocean floor? Can a space station declare independence? How do we farm the ocean intensively enough to curb global starvation but intelligently enough to preserve the ecological balance? Can we even afford to build an MX missile system?

The other line of development followed by hardware shows that technology need not be large and expensive to have a profound social

NASA

impact. The windmill was probably at least as important as the Homestead Act in making it possible for Americans to earn a living on the raw plains. John Deere's plow, with a revolving blade and steel moldboard, allowed these settlers to cut through the heavy, matted sod of the prairie that would break an ordinary plow. And barbed wire helped redraw the political geography of a large part of the United States and turned cowboys into ranchers.

Today, there is much talk about **appropriate technology.** It is designed on a more human scale, responds better to local and community needs, and damages the environment less. Where capital is scarce and labor cheap, more labor-intensive technologies might be considered. What works in Pittsburg will not necessarily be good for Bombay. In developing this concept, E.F. Schumacher, in his book *Small Is Beautiful,* attacked many of the basic premises of macroengineering (New York: Harper & Row, 1973).

The fundamental challenge that all technology presents government decision makers is *how to capitalize on the benefits of new technology while holding the costs and risks to a bare minimum.* Historically, Americans have looked mostly at the central effects of a new technology. (That is, they looked at those results it is expected to have.) They ignored its side effects. Those days are over.* Now the motto is "Proceed with caution."

In terms of public policy, three technologies will be particularly important to Congress over the next two decades. They are energy conversion, biomedicine, and electronics. Chapter 12 dealt in part with the issue of energy; therefore, we shall consider only biomedicine and electronics here.

The Next Two Decades

Biological-medical technology. The next two decades will be exciting times in biological and medical technology. Advances in x-ray scanning devices will make earlier diagnosis of tumors possible. Computerized X-ray machines will provide color television pictures of most human organs (see picture on p. 430). More effective anticancer and heart disease treatments will be found. In 10 to 15 years, dentists believe they will be able to vaccinate infants against tooth decay.

While the list of possible biomedical breakthroughs is long, the most revolutionary ad-

---

* Without trying to be too precise about when those days ended, we might consider congressional rejection of the SST (supersonic transport) in 1972 as symbolic that they were on the wane. It was probably the first time Congress had ever said no to a technologically feasible project. Subsequently, the British and French experience with the costly Concorde seems to vindicate the wisdom of the decision.

vances are occurring in the area of genetic research. During World War II, biochemists became increasingly aware that nucleic acids were the instruments whereby physical characteristics were inherited. It was deoxyribonucleic acid (DNA) of the chromosomes, they concluded, that was the key chemical of life. In a classic paper published in 1953, Francis Crick, a British physicist, and James Watson, a young American biochemist, suggested that the DNA molecule consisted of a double helix (the shape, that is, of what is usually called a spiral staircase). This new look of the DNA molecule opened up many fruitful avenues of research.

Physicians are already testing unborn babies for hundreds of genetically caused diseases. By the end of the 1980s, they could be performing these tests on a massive scale. Perhaps by the end of the century, all genetic diseases could be eliminated.

Within about 25 years, gene therapy may be able to eliminate certain genetic diseases. Physicians will be able to cut out "bad" genes and insert fresh genetic information in their place. Already, genetic material from animals and man have been inserted into bacteria. The result is an organism endowed with the characteristics of two unrelated species. This line of research should eventually lead to the implantation of insulin genes into the body cells of diabetics, enabling them to produce their own insulin without the necessity of daily shots.

Genetic-engineering techniques can produce not only new drugs. One scientist at General Electric has already developed a strain of bacteria that eats up industrial oil spills. And many scientists are trying to engineer a new strain of bacteria that would live in the roots of crops, virtually eliminating the need for fertilizer, and new plants that are resistant to weedkillers and that combine the nutritional value of two or more plants. The ultimate effect of genetic engineering on the chemical and pharmaceutical industries could be similar to the effect of the transistor on the electronics industry.

Broadly speaking, cloning is asexual reproduction that results in a genetic duplicate of the original organism. Scientists began cloning in 1952 by substituting the genetic material from one cell of an animal into the nucleus of an egg obtained from a female of the same species. So far, the most success has been with amphibians.

Today cloning helps scientists to better understand genetic diseases and the secrets of aging. By cloning prize-winning livestock, ranchers will be able to produce tastier, heartier animals.

The public policy issues raised by the new biomedical technology are staggering. How well-prepared is American society for a significantly extended human life span? Will citizens with certain defective genes be forbidden to marry? Will expectant mothers be required to fill out reports on their fetuses? Will harmful new forms of life be developed, either accidently or otherwise? Since the cloning technique could eventually be extended to humans, what guidelines will be needed?

Electronics. In 1840, Samuel Morse obtained a patent for the first telegraph. He then managed to persuade a reluctant Congress into appropriating $30,000 in 1843 to build a telegraph line from Baltimore to Washington, D.C. It was built in 1844 and it worked. Morse's first message was, "What hath God wrought?"

No message could be more prophetic. Today, we are on the threshold of a new development—technological revolution that links communications such as telephone and television devices with computers. This new communications system allows for the transmission of data and interaction between persons or between computers through cables, microwave relays, or satellites. This breakthrough could lead to the replacement of paper money for purchases made in stores by an electronic funds transfer system. Most households would have access to information banks and retrieval systems. Documents would be sent and stored electronically; paper would cease to exist in offices. In sum, telecommunications will represent the essential commercial foundation of the next century—comparable to the railroads and harbors of the 19th century.

Assuming these and other technological developments will continue, what can we say about their political consequences?

For one thing, the wealth of the United States and other advanced industrial countries might be centered around the production, distribution, and consumption of information. By the year 2000, the world could see a high-technology cartel imposing an information embargo on the new industrialized nations.

And, as information becomes more important in world wealth, protection of this information will become more of a concern. Most western countries today consider the free flow of information as valuable as a free flow of trade. Viewing information as a resource may require a major shift in economic and political thinking. For example, advances in information storage technology, such as new optical disks and worldwide data transmission networks, indicate that huge data bases will soon be available. Information could easily become a major commodity, traded like grain.

Increased reliance on telecommunications can, of course, reduce the need for face-to-face meetings. This means less travel. And less travel means less energy consumption. A study by the Office of Telecommunications Policy concluded that automobile travel for acquisition, exchange, and dissemination of information uses 500 times as much energy in total as would telecommunications.

Computers will continue to get smaller and faster. Some experts predict that by 1990 computers the size of a basketball will do more than today's largest. By the end of the 1980s, we should also see supercomputers up to 100 times faster than today's most powerful models. Such trends doubtlessly will accelerate the computerization of society. Even the humblest household gadgets will have their own "brains."

Already computers sometimes help replace physicians in the making of diagnoses. Some computers even help design themselves. Such systems are forerunners of the new "knowledge engineering" industry that will emerge in the next decade.

Technological Adolescence

The United States still remains the world leader in technology. Despite the growing intensity of competition from Japan and Western Europe, it is likely to continue to play a leading role. A recent study of the National Research Council estimates that U.S. basic research "constitutes somewhat more than one third of the world total." The report goes on to warn, however, that the United States may lose its lead "if support of research as a fraction of GNP continues to decline as it rises in some countries that are some of our most successful competitors."

The American public seems to recognize almost intuitively these new realities. In 1978, Lou Harris took a poll to see what factors Americans thought contributed to "America's present greatness." In order of importance, this is what he found: "rich, natural resources," "a hard-working people," "scientific research," "industrial know-how," and "technological genius."

And when the people surveyed were asked to look ahead, they were convinced the United States will depend more on scientific research, industrial know-how and technological genius, and work.

In 1979, *U.S. News & World Report* updated their 1976 survey of public opinion of the ability of 25 institutions and groups to get things done, and on their honesty, integrity, and dependability. Science and technology, a new addition to the list, was rated highest in both performance and dependability.

In contrast to the public's favorable view of technology, a deep distrust of technology runs among certain intellectual elites. These technology skeptics dismiss many of the advances made by technology. In fact, they doubt technology's potential for improving the lot of mankind. They base their opinions on arguments such as the following:

Our century-long addiction to technology has produced much to regret and much cause for caution. In physical terms, we have grown to need massive quantities of energy that produce waste heat and pollutants cumulatively injuring our biosystem at an accelerating rate. Technology has produced a world of people expecting accouterments, comforts, and goods.

Technology concentrated in a few originating nations has produced populations and expectations of wealth throughout the world. These populations cannot foreseeably be fed because of resource and invironmental limitations of the planet. Also, the imbalance threatening catastrophic conflict is made more deadly by technology.

Technology is too often employed to temporarily remedy nontechnological problems. The problems don't go away; they just grow in scale, often requiring more drastic solutions later.

There is a dangerous unpredictability in the combined effects of multiplying and accelerating technologies on societies and environments.

The trend has been for high technologies to shape social organization to fit their supply and operational needs, thus massing, organizing, and dehumanizing people.

Examples of the above concerns are said to abound. They range from the imminent death of Lake Erie, to the cancer risks of common industrial chemicals, the hazards of radiation, and environmental pollution by oxides of nitrogen, to the ugliness of electronic transmission lines, highways, big dams, and similar massive structures.

Technology advocates counter these arguments and examples with the following:

The claims of antitechnologists in many cases are not supported by specific evaluations.

Technological progress always has and will continue to have costs. But these are more than offset by the benefits to society. Technology is a human product; like everything human, it wears the Janus face of good and bad at once. This makes the task of assessing new technology all the more tedious and difficult—but all the more necessary.

Reprinted by permission of the Chicago Tribune–New York News Syndicate, Inc.

- The problems that can be attributed to modern technology require a thorough technological understanding of their nature rather than quick intuitive prohibitions.
- Continued productivity gains are essential. They are needed to maintain a stable social and economic climate in the face of rising material needs and expectations. These can be realized primarily through advanced technology.
- Many problems that appear to stem from technology may, in fact, stem from human behavior. An example is refusal to clean up sewage and other wastes.
- There is a case that the techniques that will ultimately emerge in competitive marketplaces will be the most cost-effective and least hazardous ones. When the market fails to reflect social values or safety considerations, recourse to political and legal remedies is readily available.

Can we have it both ways? There are two extremes. There are those who want to return to lifestyles with less dependence on technology; and there are those who equate any restrictions on technology as downright un-American. But a reasonable middle road can be found. In brief, it consists of (a) greater government support for technology coupled with (b) more intelligent assessment and monitoring of new technologies.

Governments can cultivate a nation's technological basis by providing either directly (through contracts, grants, or loans) or indirectly (through tax write-offs and less regulation) more financial incentives to invest in research and development—especially basic research. Unless the changes occur, many companies will continue to invest the bulk of their capital in the acquisition of other firms or cosmetic changes in existing products.

Government also needs to develop a consistent, long-range policy for controlling the transfer of technological information to communist countries, as well as to companies in Western Europe and Japan. A closely related area is patent protection. The translation of research and development into new products is a complex and risky business. For example, it now takes an average of eight years and $57 million in research and development costs before a new pharmaceutical product can be brought to market. The U.S. patent system allows 17 years on a patent. With eight years spent before marketing, the effective life of that patent is only nine years. This substantially increases the risk involved in developing a new pharmaceutical. If a company can't be assured of a reasonable flow of profits from its new products, there will be no money for new research into cures for diseases, such as cancer and arthritis.

The politics of technology. Can the American political system make the kinds of complex scientific and technological decisions that will be called for increasingly in the decades ahead? In the field of energy, for example, people with only minimal competence speak from highly emotional points of view. Emotionally, one may love the idea of solar energy. But what will it cost? How long will it take to develop a cost-effective solar cell? How difficult will it be to get solar power on a large scale? What environmental dangers might it pose? These are all issues that must be resolved if we are to have an intelligent political discussion of the issue.

Today many of these decisions are made through the adversary process in courts (see Chapter 10). In this system, there must be a winner and a loser; trade-offs and side effects tend to get slighted. If we believe in democracy, then we must find a better forum for effective discussions of highly technological issues. Once there is a clear consensus on what science and technology say about an issue, the political process can yield the value judgment.

A technological decision need not be zero-sum game in which one party's gain is another's loss. The more America avails itself of the potentials of science and technology, the more it finds itself in a variable-sum game; all players gain by making mutual concessions.

A big step in this direction would be a mutual reduction in military preparations. Today, nations invest nearly 10 percent of the world's total gross national product and more than 25 percent of its technical talent in armaments. This is nearly half as much as the world's total investment in productive enterprises. It is a prime drain of resources that could be channeled into future technological developments in energy, medicine, transportation—and space.

HOW THE AMERICAN ECONOMIC ENGINE WORKS—AND FAILS TO WORK

Supply and Demand

The core idea of pure market economics is "Scarcity creates value." Just think of gold. If there is a limited supply of something (gold mines are few) and it is desirable (gold has many uses, is pretty, and provides security in an uncertain world), then the value of the item is bid up. On the other hand, if the item is plentiful, such as air, then it is free or has little value in the economic sense.

Many factors determine the demand for gasoline at the corner station. (How far does one travel? How often does one have to travel? What is the gas mileage of the vehicle one owns? How rich is the one who owns the car?) Setting aside all these individual situations, two things in general are clear. If gas prices double, use will decline; if gas prices are cut in half, the opposite will happen.

Now let us look at matters from the side of the oil company. A higher price provides both an incentive and the money to expand the amount produced. With more gas available at the higher price, inventories begin to accumulate. (This is because the consumers have already cut back on their consumption.) Now, if the gas station has an inventory of gas that it cannot sell, the price will come down and provide an incentive to buy for more frivolous uses. It costs the gas station owner to hold an inventory. Conversely, if the price is high, the gas station owner will try to sell more gas to take advantage of the potential profits. Figure 13–4 illustrates how these automatic adjustments of supply to demand occur in a free market. Indeed, the figure illustrates perhaps the most fundamental law in economics: Scarcity creates value.

The figure also illustrates a couple of ways this ideal situation can be upset. For instance, government can intervene and not allow producers to raise their prices to the market clearing price. When prices are frozen below that price, shortages and long gas lines (or lines for whatever is being controlled) become a way of life.

Producers themselves can also upset the ideal situation. This occurs when there is one very large producer, a **monopoly,** or a small number of firms that account for a large proportion of output, an **oligopoly.** In either case, the result is the same—market domination rather than competition. When prices begin to rise, the monopolists and oligopolists are not forced to increase their production; customers either buy from them or do without. By freezing production levels, monopolies or oligopolies are able to keep prices artificially high.

A simple market economy can be thought of as a continuous flow around a closed loop (see Figure 13–5). Businesses pay wages, rent, interests, and dividends to the public. The public spends the income in payment to businesses for finished goods and services. This demand, in turn, leads businesses to hire workers to produce more goods and services for the public and to pay more in wages. The continuous flow of labor and products (outside loop) is matched by a counterflow of money (inside loop).

The price system (described earlier, in Figure 13–4) guides the whole arrangement. Note that there are two markets in Figure 13–5. In the top one, people exchange money for goods or

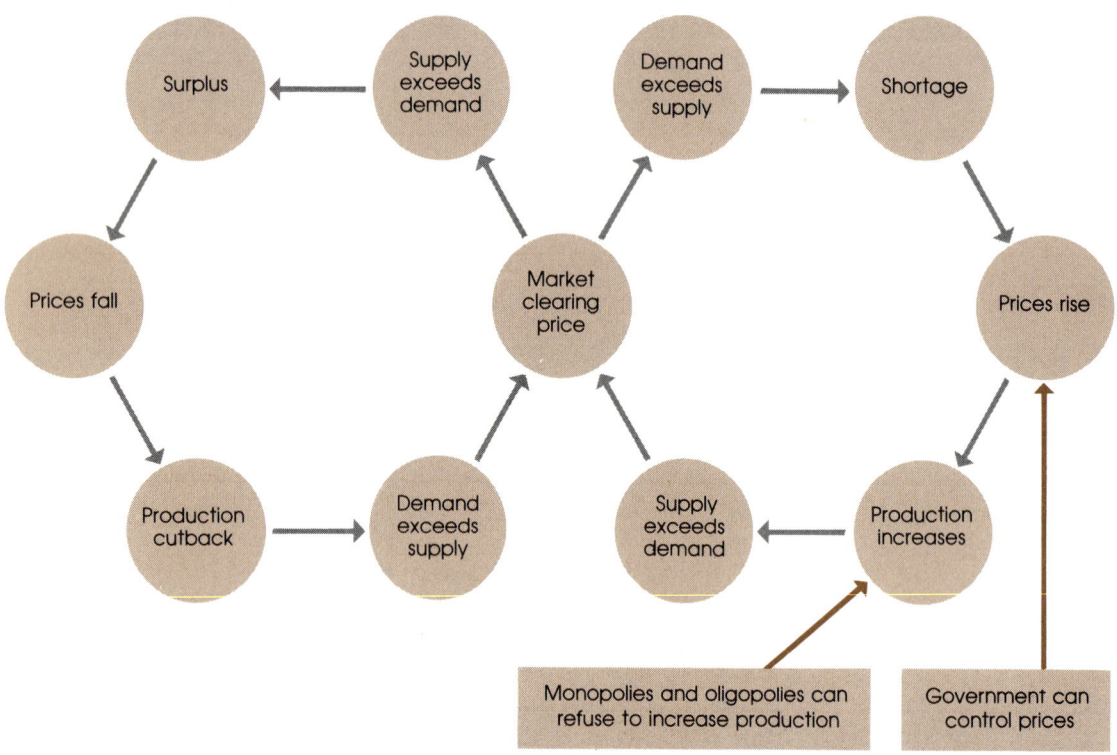

FIGURE 13-4
How a Free Market Adjusts Supply to Demand

The market clearing price is also called the equilibrium price, or the price at which there is no tendency for change. Consumers seem satisfied with the quantity they are buying at the price; suppliers seem satisfied with the amount they can sell at that price.

services. In the bottom one they exchange their labor services, use of land and capital, and entrepreneurial skill for payment from business. The exchange rate is called, of course, price.

Virtues of the Market

The system illustrated in Figure 13-4 has a number of advantages over a centrally controlled system such as the one found in socialist countries. It is based on voluntary compliance; it avoids the high costs of information needed in a centrally planned economy; it is efficient; and along with other societal institutions, it provides a check on government power.

Voluntary. The market is based on the mutual advantage of each party. In a command system, capitalist transactions between consenting adults would have to be outlawed. Market arrangements minimize the need for coercion as a means of social organization.

A market does not rely on the compassion, brotherly love, and cultural solidarity of the citizens. It harnesses what is a more prevalent motive—material self-interest—to promote the common good. The way a market system gets consumers to conserve gas is not through appeals to patriotism; it is through higher prices.

Hard-to-get information. A second advantage of the market is that it reduces the need

FIGURE 13-5
Circular Flows of Money and Products

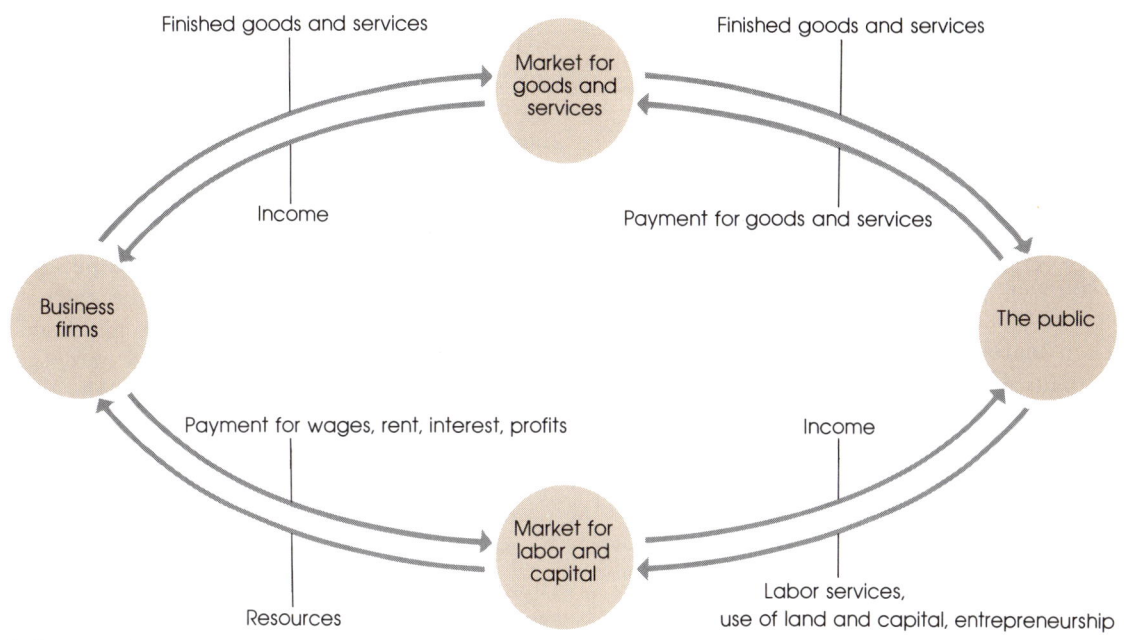

In the market for goods and services, the public exchanges money for finished products and firms exchange products for money. In the market for labor and capital, the public exchange their resources for money and firms exchange money for resources.

for hard-to-get information. Suppose some government bureau was charged with the responsibility for making sure New York City was adequately supplied with all the goods and services that its residents might need on September 15, 1984.

What kinds of information would that bureau need to measure the needs of the residents, and then to price properly all the goods and services that should be available that day? Then, for each good and service—for each bagel and baby pacifier—decisions must be made on inputs. How much wheat flour, how much plastic, what colors, etc.?

Finally, how should the goods be distributed within the city? How many bagels to the shop on the corner of Eighth Avenue and 79th Street? How many pink baby pacifiers to Brooklyn? It is enough to drive the toughest bureaucrat to early retirement. Yet every day (weekends and holidays included) the market makes millions of such decisions with few hitches.

Efficiency. That a capitalist system can deliver the goods—that it is *efficient* arrangement—is seldom disputed. As Marx and Engels conceded in the *Communist Manifesto*, capitalism "has created more massive and colossal production forces than have all the preceding generations together." In the United States, business configurations are hardly loved; but when the Roper Organization, in December 1978, asked Americans to compare business competence with government competence, business received positively glowing marks. Which is run more *efficiently?* Business—by nearly 8 to 1.

Through higgling and bargaining, the free market encourages specialization according to the principle of **comparative advantage.** Specialization refers to the division of productive activities among persons and regions. In such a system no one individual or area is totally self-sufficient. For example, an individual may specialize in turquoise jewelry or nuclear physics. A nation may specialize in the production of straw hats or computers.

But specialization would hardly be efficient if the people making the turquoise jewelry lacked manual dexterity and an artistic eye; likewise if those specializing in nuclear physics lacked mathematical ability. Similarly, it does not seem efficient for the United States to make straw hats (good though they might be) while Panama makes computers (which they could). The principle of comparative advantage comes into play. Each individual and country should specialize in some goods or services in which they are *relatively* more efficient—and trade for the others. The key word here is *relative*. If I had written *absolute* instead, then we could not explain why the best lawyer in town should not also do his or her own typing—if he or she happened to also be the best typist in town. (Not a silly example at all: William Howard Taft, the 27th president, was an extraordinarily fast stenographer.)

The market encourages specialization and comparative advantage; thus it increases the general welfare. The virtue of the market is not that it creates a harmonious society; it is that it reduces irksome toil through the phenomenon of economic growth.

A check on government. Most Americans are suspicious of single concentrations of power. Their preference, it would seem, is to have many centers of power. This diffusion creates the "space" in which individual liberty can survive and prosper. Privately owned companies are, therefore, consistent with the founding fathers' concept of checks and balances. Would the Watergate investigation have been as aggressive—or even have occurred—had the *Washington Post* merely been a bureau within some Department of Information?

How the Engine Fails to Work

Like any engine, however well engineered, the market from time to time requires certain adjustments. What are the conditions that justify government decision makers peering under the hood with wrench in hand?

Spillovers. Certain economic activities create certain costs or **spillovers** that are not paid for fully by the producers. In such cases, market operations will not be efficient. This is because these external costs do not enter the calculations on which production decisions are based. Chemical emissions from industrial activities are examples of external effects that justify government intervention to compensate for the market's tendency to impose costs on innocent bystanders who are neither producers nor consumers.*

Public goods. Markets tend to produce more **private goods** (such as food, autos, hair spray, and socks) than **public goods** (such as schools, parks, security, and clean streets). The fundamental difference between private goods and public goods is that the former is divisible; that is, you can enjoy your auto and I can enjoy my socks. In contrast, clean streets and national defense are things we both benefit from.

The market system favors private goods because they are easier to produce, package, and sell. It slights public goods because they are hard to sell to individual customers; this is a **free rider effect.** That is to say, since everyone shares public goods, each individual thinks, "If I don't pay for my share of public television, it won't matter because I *know* someone else will contribute."

Viewed from the perspective of society as a whole this situation is inefficient. If there were no free public education, it would not mean the disappearance of education in the United States. But it would mean a much

---

* Economists call these external effects "externalities." They are the same thing as the indirect costs discussed in the last chapter.

higher illiteracy rate; and consequently, we would have a less prosperous nation.

Some consider the distribution of goods and services that occurs under capitalism an example of market failure. In this view, a more equal income is a particular type of public good. Outcomes that diverge from the socially preferable distribution are likely to be considered market failures. In short, the pursuit of profits by individual firms does not necessarily lead to the most total benefits for society. But determining where that point of maximum benefits lies is not easy. How does one compare the benefits from equity, clean air, better educated minds, and a richer culture with private goods such as a vacation, a house, a book, and a new pair of shoes?

Lack of competition. Earlier, we noted that monopolies and oligopolies can turn the classic law of supply and demand upside down. In such cases, government has a good reason to act in the public interest to restore competitive conditions.

Sometimes monopolies—such as electric utilities and, in the past, the telephone company—are desirable; it is more efficient to have just one firm supply the good or service than several. Not surprisingly, such firms are regulated and cannot raise their prices without approval by a public board.

Not all monopolies are justified, of course. For example, according to the Department of Agriculture, American consumers are probably paying more than $16 billion a year in overcharges on food due to industry concentration. Or take the case of blockbuster record albums. Many record companies raise the list price for some of their most popular artists' new releases by dollars once the record sells over a million copies.

Lack of information. In addition to competition, an ideal market system assumes that producer and buyer have adequate information. Buyers in particular, must know what their choices are—that is, everything that is available at various prices—and what they are really getting for the price.

In a complex, technological society, these conditions are not always attainable in a completely unfettered market. How many products can be tested by the consumer? You might buy a new brand of beer and find it too bitter. So you never buy it again. And, if sufficient beer drinkers also find it too bitter, the company will either have to change the product or go broke. The market system works.

But what about some new drug? Powerful drugs have powerful side effects; some are downright dangerous. Since it is unreasonable to expect consumers to have home laboratories, the federal Food and Drug Administration insures quality and safety for consumers.

HOW GOVERNMENT MANAGES THE ECONOMY

In the last section, we saw how a simple market system works. We saw that consumers and businesses make decisions in the American economic system through the mechanism of the price system. We also noted four ways the system can fail—or, at least, not work to the maximum benefit of society as a whole. Now let us see how government tries to fix the system.

Government Activities Today

Since the Constitution was written, the United States has grown enormously; so, too, has the government's role and responsibility. There are six major areas in which government units, on the federal, state, and local levels, are involved in the economy. Five of these are:

Providing public goods such as highways, national defense, and education.

Regulation—that is, the promotion of fair economic competition and the protection of public health and safety (see Box, "Ninety-Five Years of Government Regulation").

Ninety-Five Years of Government Regulation

The oldest of all regulatory agencies is the **Interstate Commerce Commission,** created in 1887. At first, its chief mission was to keep markets open by doing battle with railroad firms which had combined in an effort to reduce competition. Such combinations are known as trusts. Since the 1930s, however, the ICC's principal concern has been to limit entry into the transportation industry and to maintain a balance among existing transportation carriers (railroads, trucks, bus lines, etc.). Some critics have accused the ICC of holding back technological advances that might upset this balance.

The year 1914 marked another milestone in regulatory history. In that year, the Federal Trade Commission was created to curb unfair trade practices, protect consumers, and maintain competition. In addition, Congress passed the Clayton Act which provided the Antitrust Division of the Justice Department additional power to insure competition. Today the FTC protects consumers against products and services (from life insurance to auto repair) that do not perform as the consumer expects.

The shock of the Depression and the rapidity of technological change led to some fundamental rethinking of the relationship between government and the economy. In 1931, the **Food and Drug Administration** was created to establish regulations concerning the purity, safety, and labeling accuracy of certain foods and drugs. More typical of what happened during the 1930s were the Federal Communications Act of 1934 and the Civil Aeronautics Act of 1938. The 1934 act set up the Federal Communications Commission to license civilian radio and television communications and to license and set rates for interstate communication by wire (especially telephone). The 1938 act was an effort to make the airline industry both orderly and predictable. But there was no chaos in industry in 1938. Indeed, it appears that the airline industry wanted the law to prevent future chaos.

The 1930s and President Roosevelt's New Deal were also a time of change in the government's relationship with labor unions. In particular, Congress passed the National Labor Relations Act of 1935 (often called the Wagner Act). The act guaranteed workers the right to collective bargaining—that is, the right for workers to have representatives of their unions negotiate with management on pay and working conditions. To oversee these negotiations and to control "unfair labor practices," the act created the **National Labor Relations Board.** What constitutes fair or unfair practices, Congress left to the NLRB to define. It is this kind of delegation of authority that gives many federal agencies a formidable source of power in the political system.

The 1970s saw a dramatic change in both the number and nature of regulatory agencies. While the 1930s could claim 11 new agencies, the 1970s witnessed the creation of 20 new regulatory agencies. Among these were the following:

1970: Environmental Protection Agency (EPA) to develop environmental quality standards, approve state environmental plans, and rule on the environmental impact of various projects.

1971: Occupational Safety and Health Administration (OSHA) to provide for the regulation of safety and health standards in workplaces.

1972: Consumer Product Safety Commission (CPSC) to provide for mandatory product safety standards and for planning of hazardous substances.

What makes these newer agencies fundamentally different than earlier agencies like the ICC and FCC is that they tend to regulate *across* industry lines. For example, the OSHA regulates the transportation industry, the communications industry, the chemical industry, and so forth. As a consequence, the cozy relationships that might arise between the ICC and the trucking industry are quite unlikely.

Whether this is good or bad, it is not easy to say. Certainly the cozy relationship between regulator and industry can result in less service and more cost to the public. This is chiefly because the industry is protected from new competition. On the other hand, when an agency regulates across industry lines it can lose sight of the real costs it is imposing on the firm. For example, on OSHA regulation might say that all ladders must be painted yellow and be 17 inches from the wall. When a large chemical company—with red and white ladders 16 inches from the wall—must comply in all its plants, we are talking about a considerable expense that may have only the slightest connection to worker safety. Ultimately, it is the public, as consumers, that must pay for the regulation, as the company passes the cost on in terms of higher prices.

Recognizing the inherent limitations in both types of regulation (namely, industry specific and cross-industry regulation), government by the late 1970s was moving towards **deregulation.** The first major step occurred in 1978 with the loosening of control over airline routes and rates, a move applauded by both liberals and conservatives. And, in 1981, the government began to make progress toward partial deregulation of the communication industry in general and the massive American Telephone and Telegraph ("Ma Bell") in particular.

- Promotion of economic growth, employment, and low inflation rates through various economic policies and programs.
- Direct support to individuals through programs to reduce hardships for individuals who can not meet their minimum needs because of special circumstances or lack of employment.
- Direct support to companies through programs designed to reduce risk and provide certain services. For example, the Department of Commerce provides business with useful information, protects the patents of new inventions, and subsidizes the American merchant marine by several hundred million dollars a year. The Small Business Administration aids small companies through such services as financial counseling and various loan programs (see Box, "Taking Care of (Small) Business").

Taking Care of (Small) Business

The Small Business Administration (SBA) was established in 1953 to aid, counsel, assist, and protect the interests of small businesses. Since many small businesses face financing problems, the SBA helps small business owners gain access to capital and credit. It maintains an active loan program and has recently concentrated on loans to women, minorities, and Vietnam War veterans. Most SBA loans are made from funds supplied by local private banks unde. the SBA guarantee program. In effect, the SBA becomes the small businessperson's cosigner on the loan.

The SBA runs training programs and provides consulting services aimed at improving the management skills of small business owners, potential owners, and managers. Two of its programs are SCORE and ACE. SCORE is the Service Corps of Retired Executives. ACE is the Active Corps of Executives. These two groups provide volunteer counseling to small business owners. The SBA publishes a wide variety of practical guides for small businesses. Many of these guides, such as "Management Aids for Small Manufacturers," are available without charge from any of the SBA's local offices.

The SBA is also concerned about the long-range competitive welfare of small business. It conducts studies on the current and future problems and needs of the small business community and makes recommendations to other federal agencies. Part of its function is to make sure that small businesses receive a fair portion of government purchases, contracts, and subcontracts.

SOURCE: *U.S. Government Manual, 1977/78*, pp. 625–30.

These functions cost money—which brings us to the sixth area in which governments are involved in the economy. To carry them out in 1978, federal, state, and local governments spent about $524 billion. All of this must be paid for with money raised in two basic ways: by taxing individuals and businesses, and by borrowing. In some cases we pay more directly for the public services we get. Bridge tolls, postage, and tuition charges at public universities are examples of "user charges"; the money raised in these ways helps pay for some of the costs of these services. Figure 13–6 shows you the major categories of expenditure for the federal government and its sources of income.

The nondefense part of the budget has been rising rapidly in recent years. Since 1960 federal payments to individuals multiplied 11.8 times. For comparison, defense spending rose only 2.8 times. Another comparison that may help put the growth in payments to individuals in perspective: Spending on food stamps alone in 1980 equaled Franklin Roosevelt's entire federal budget in 1939.

Three concepts are particularly useful in helping us make sense of such big budgets: **uncontrollables, entitlements,** and **deficit.**

To a large extent, decisions made in previous years determine the size of the nondefense budget for the years ahead. Such expenditures are relatively "uncontrollable" because they can only be altered if the basic legislation authorizing such spending is changed. Today over three quarters of the budget is "uncontrollable."

To understand entitlements we need to go back to Lyndon Johnson's landslide election of 1964. Supported by a liberal Congress, Johnson set out to complete the unfinished work of the

FIGURE 13–6
Federal Budget—Percent Distribution by Function, 1970 and 1980

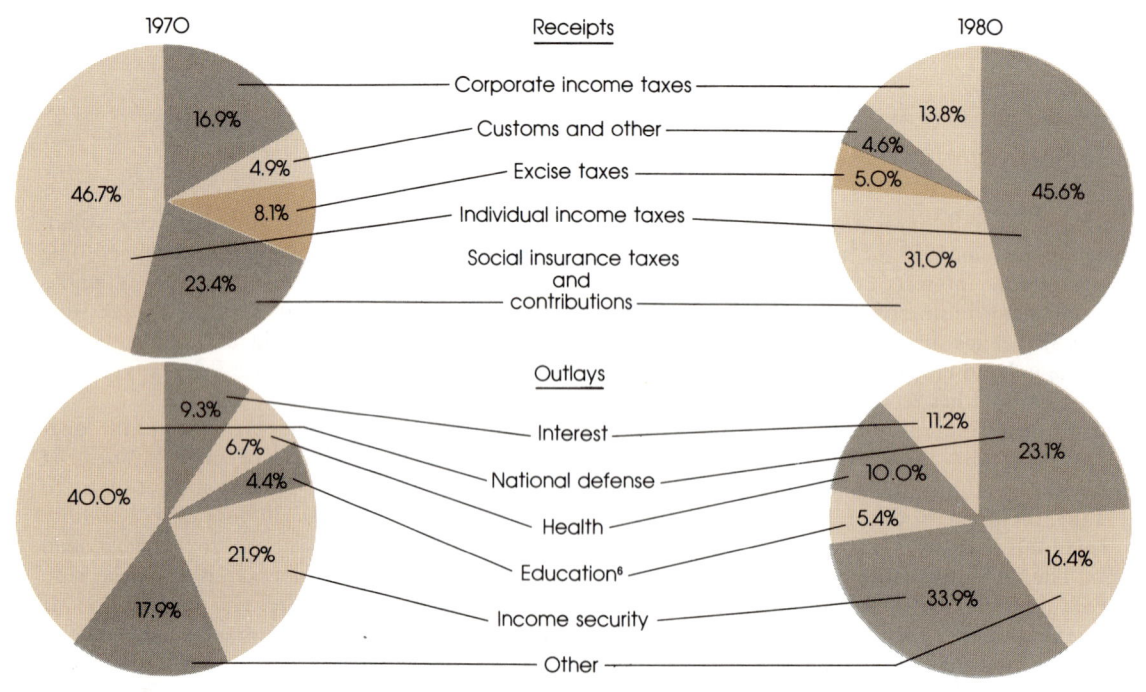

1970 Receipts 1980

- Corporate income taxes — 1970: 16.9%; 1980: 13.8%
- Customs and other — 1970: 4.9%; 1980: 4.6%
- Excise taxes — 1970: 8.1%; 1980: 5.0%
- Individual income taxes — 1970: 46.7%; 1980: 45.6%
- Social insurance taxes and contributions — 1970: 23.4%; 1980: 31.0%

Outlays

- Interest — 1970: 9.3%; 1980: 11.2%
- National defense — 1970: 40.0%; 1980: 23.1%
- Health — 1970: 6.7%; 1980: 10.0%
- Education† — 1970: 4.4%; 1980: 5.4%
- Income security — 1970: 21.9%; 1980: 33.9%
- Other — 1970: 17.9%; 1980: 16.4%

* Other includes gift taxes and other receipts.
† Includes training, employment, and social services.
Source: Chart prepared by U.S. Bureau of the Census.

New Deal. In doing so, he engaged the federal government in many new areas. At first, the aim was to help those who could not help themselves, but eventually aid was extended to a wide spectrum of interest groups. New programs and agencies were hastily created without thinking through the consequences. Subsequent Congresses not only authorized specific amounts for programs but also signed several blank checks or "entitlement" programs such as workers compensation, food stamps, and black lung assistance.

Today entitlement programs are the largest category of uncontrollable spending. The reason is that expenditures for them keep rising as the number of eligible persons rises (500,000 a year for social security) or that the average level of benefits rises automatically (as prescribed by the law). These open-ended programs made up nearly one half of the federal budget in 1982.

Anyone who keeps watch over his or her own budget will see from Figure 13-7 that the total spending by the federal government for 1978 was greater than the taxes collected by about $40 billion. The $40 billion difference is called a deficit. Government deficits are financed by borrowing from—and paying interest to—financial institutions and other investors.

Over the 20-year period from 1960 through 1980, the federal government had deficits in 19 years (see Figure 13-7). The consequences of deficits and **surpluses** (taxes greater than spending) at the federal level will be discussed later.

Balancing the Economy[4]

As you probably realize by now, an important factor making the American economic system work is the "law" of supply and demand. It is not really a law, of course; it is an explanation of the factors determining how much of each product and service is produced, and how those goods and services are distributed.

When we buy less than our economy is producing, eventually production goes down and unemployment increases. When our purchases increase, this demand results in business expansion and higher employment.

Supply and demand forces ultimately determine the levels of production and employment in our economy. But, as we shall see, certain steps can be taken to influence what these levels will be. It is now a responsibility of the federal government, as established by the Employment Act of 1946, "to promote maximum employment, production, and purchasing power."

Maintaining both stable prices and high employment, however, is difficult in a free society. Wages tend to increase when available workers are in short supply, and prices of goods tend to rise when demand outstrips supply.

Ups and downs of the economy. Over the years, the U.S. economy has grown at a remarkable rate. But in this process there have been periods of **expansion** and periods of **recession**. These alternating ups and downs mean that our national goal of high employment is not always achieved.

The economy expands and contracts because our total spending changes. Many factors can cause this, including the introduction of new technologies, the availability of investment funds, changing national economic policies, crop failures, wars, and public confidence in our economic future. There are many more. All these factors directly affect the economy.

Let us pursue the matter of public confidence a little further. When economic times are "good," individuals, businesses, and many governments feel more confident about the future; therefore they spend more. An individual might buy a new car or decide to buy a home. A company may decide the time is right to build a new factory or install new equipment. A local government may build a new school.

Expenditures like these are not made every day. When spending occurs in surges because of increased public confidence, this stimulates the economy for a period of time. When such

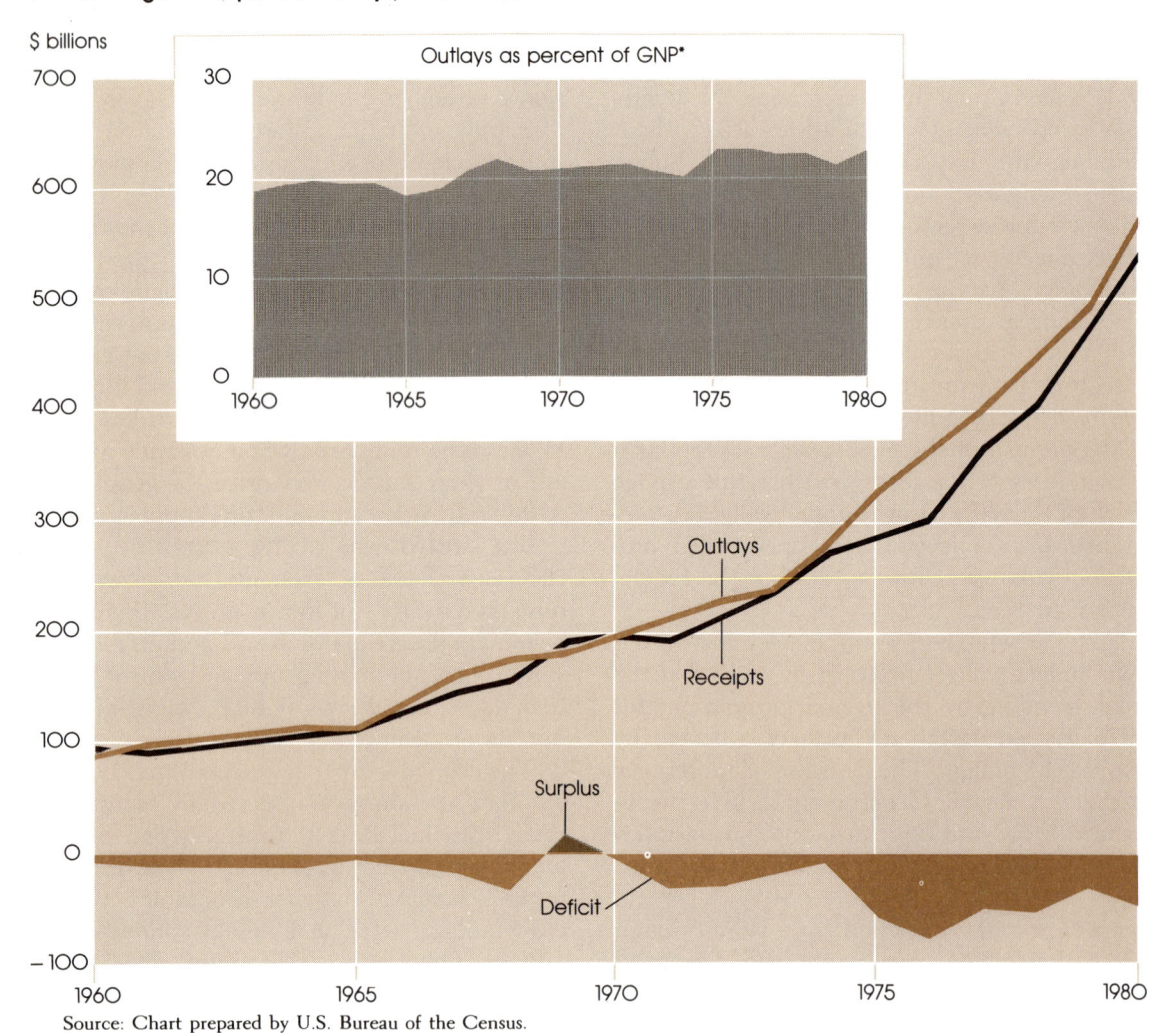

FIGURE 13-7
Federal Budget Receipts and Outlays, 1960 to 1980

Source: Chart prepared by U.S. Bureau of the Census.

spending slows down, this contributes to a slowing down of the economy.

These economic ups and downs have varied widely in the past, and federal government policies often have attempted to moderate their adverse impacts. However, there are so many complex forces at work in our economy, and the timing of government policies is so critical, that unexpected results can occur.

Fiscal policies. The taxing and spending policies of the federal government are called fiscal policies.

Federal spending can be increased to keep overall demand at a high level if private spending is low. And federal spending can be restrained to reduce overall demand when dmand is higher than our total production.

Government tax policies can also be changed

to help balance the economy. Federal tax cuts and rebates can be used to stimulate the economy in a recession—as was done in 1981—or tax increases may be used to help dampen excessive demand.

Whether the federal government has a surplus (spending less than taxes) or a deficit (spending greater than taxes) depends on how fiscal policy is used to meet the needs of the economy and how the economy performs.

Monetary policy. The Federal Reserve system has responsibility for controlling our nation's "money supply." The money supply is the total of all coins and currency in circulation, plus checking accounts held by individuals and businesses. This control is called monetary policy, which is another way to lessen the adverse effects of economic swings.

The supply of money has an important influence on spending and production, and banks play a central role in this process. By changing the money supply, the Federal Reserve—also called "the Fed"—affects the amount of money that banks can lend to individuals and businesses to spend. In simplest terms, the Federal Reserve generally makes money more available when total spending is considered too low, and less available when total spending is too high. These actions directly influence interest rates throughout our economy.

This section has set forth some of the most important tools the federal government has available to manage the economy. In the next section, we take a look at three economic issues facing the United States in the 1980s: inflation, productivity, and industrial policy. (Unemployment, at least as important an issue as this trio, was dealt with in Chapter 10. Moreover, to the extent decision makers can successfully manage inflation, productivity, and industrial policy, unemployment should become less troublesome.)

We shall not be content with a quick look at these issues. We also want to examine the great debate surrounding what is to be done about them. Are the tools discussed in this section adequate for the management of these economic issues? Or do policymakers need new tools—and new ideas?

THE AMERICAN ECONOMY IN THE 1980s: ISSUES AND IDEAS

Three Crucial Issues

Inflation. Inflation means a rise in the general level of prices. Nobody wants inflation. However, it has become all too familiar in the world today.

Prices of most goods and services have increased significantly over recent years. Prices often go up as the quality of the goods and services we buy improves. But, in general, price increases that are not accompanied by improved quality are called inflationary.

When inflation occurs, each dollar we have buys fewer goods and services. Between 1967 and 1980, the ability of our dollar to purchase these goods and services went down by about 59 percent.

Inflation has at least three basic causes: (1) Consumers, businesses, and governments spend too heavily on available goods and services, creating a high demand; (2) Costs of production rise and producers try to maintain profit levels; (3) A lack of competition between producers exists.

The burdens of inflation tend to fall more heavily on those who live on incomes that remain the same or rise more slowly than prices. This can include many workers and retired people. The only way these people can cope with rising prices is to buy less; this reduces their living standards.

Economists by no means agree on how to measure inflation. The most commonly used measure is the consumer price index. The CPI is a comparative index that states today's prices against prices in 1967. When the consumer price index rises, a staggering amount of public and private spending rises along with it, pulling inflation up all the more.

For example, union members with cost-of-living adjustment clauses in their contracts get pay increases that vary with the index. The index also triggers increases in the amount of federal expenditures—federal employees' pension benefits, social security benefits, food stamps (which are tied to the food components of the index), and more. Government expenditures rise by about $1.5 billion for every one-point jump in the consumer price index.

Technically, the index compares the overall price of a "market basket" of goods and services with the 1967 prices of roughly the same items. With the base year 1967 given a rating of 100, we are told the consumer price index rose to 242.5 in April 1980. Most economists agree, however, that the index exaggerates the actual rate of inflation. Their main objections is this: The exact selection of the different goods and services in the consumer price index are based on a consumer expenditures survey taken in 1972. That survey does not very accurately reflect what we buy now.

When high inflation occurs along with high unemployment we have a condition called **stagflation**. The late American economist Arthur Okum developed an index of economic discomfort to measure this relatively new problem. The discomfort index is the sum of the inflation and unemployment rates; Figure 13–8 divides three decades into four year periods and shows the average discomfort index. Note the stability of the index from 1950 to 1969. Note, too, the trade-off between unemployment and inflation. If one went up, the other went down—hence, the basic stability in the discomfort index. This trade-off ceased to hold during the 1970s. (See cartoon on p. 479.)

Productivity. This important concept is not hard to define. Technically, productivity is a figure obtained by dividing the country's total output (gross national product adjusted for inflation) by the total labor input (number of worker hours). This yields a rough measure of how efficiently a country produces goods and services. Since 1960, U.S. productivity has increased at an average annual rate of about 2 percent. In 1974, it declined by 3.0 percent. As you can see in Figure 13–9, since 1965, hourly compensation has increased at a much faster pace than productivity.

The reasons for the sluggish growth in productivity are varied and have little to do with how hard people work. One reason is that the United States has failed to reinvest much of its GNP in new plants and technology (see Figure 13–10). Another reason is that the United States has more of a service- and information-based economy. Productivity gains are harder in these sectors than in the industrial sector (Figure 13–11).

Figure 13–12 shows the vicious circle that connects productivity to inflation and economic stagnation.

FIGURE 13-8
Discomfort Index

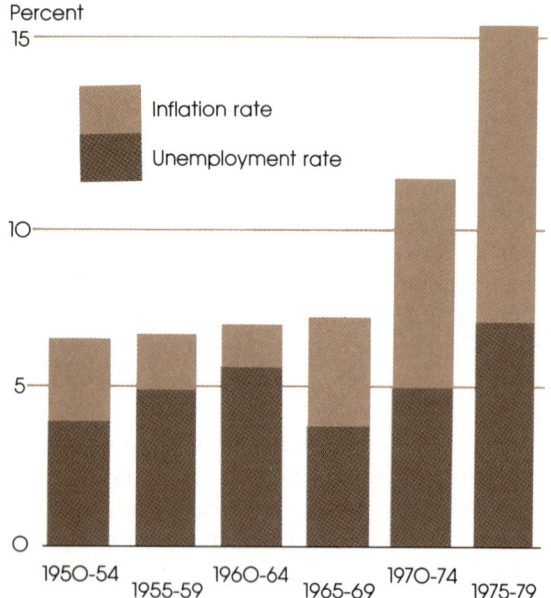

Source: U.S. Bureau of Labor Statistics, *Monthly Labor Review* and *Handbook of Labor Statistics*, annual.

Auth in *The Philadelphia Inquirer*

Since the end of the 1960s, the U.S. economy has had simultaneous bouts of high employment and severe inflation. New situations require new words. Economists have labeled this new situation stagflation, indicating economic stagnation and simultaneous inflation.

Can you explain why the headlines in the cartoon read "Fed Tightens Money Supply"? According to theory, this is the way monetary policy should work: When inflation is high, reduce or tighten the money supply. While this will cause some rise in unemployment, it should also bring inflation rates down. In period of stagflation, however, that trade-off does not seem to work well. High unemployment coexists with high inflation—regardless of what monetary theory and economics textbooks say.

Industrial policy. Some politicians and academics maintain that the United States needs to develop an **industrial** policy. This basically means that the federal government should stop protecting backward industries. The Japanese have a national policy of closing "sunset" industries and opening "sunrise" industries. The United States protects sunset industries, such as steel, shipping, textiles, shoes, sugar, and cheese; this keeps workers and resources locked into low-productivity work. Import barriers support such ailing industries as steel and textiles. Some troubled firms, such as Chrysler, are propped up by federal bailouts. The hidden price is a perpetuation of inefficiency.

In the 1980s, international competition will become even more vigorous. The upper level of developing countries—Brazil, South Korea, and Taiwan in particular—are building up steel industries that will combine low wages with the latest technology. If the United States is not to turn into a society whose people exist by taking in each other's laundry, the older sunset industries must be replaced by the newer sunrise industries, such as semiconductors (where output per person rose a phenomenal 115 percent between 1975 and 1979), energy conversion, oceanography, industrial applications of space, and molecular biology.

Workers in the sunset industries will need incentives to accept new products and processes. If American workers had greater job se-

FIGURE 13-9
Compensation and Productivity—Annual Rates of Change in Total Private Economy, 1960 to 1979

Source: Chart prepared by U.S. Bureau of the Census.

curity, technical progress would seem less like a threat to their livelihood and more like an opportunity. Many workers in other countries show less concern than Americans about technological change; they know it does not jeopardize jobs. Here government policy can play an important role.

Not all economists agree that government should develop an industrial policy. How, they ask, can bureaucrats in Washington know which industries are truly sunrise industries? Who in Washington in the 1940s would have thought IBM and computers were going to be winners—or, more recently, minicomputers and semiconductors? These critics would favor a more indirect approach: investment tax credits and government support for basic research.

Economists like Lester C. Thurow of MIT argue that the U.S. government should aid promising industries for competitive reasons. As he recently explained:

> Everybody agrees that computer chips and robots and all the things that will flow from them are a growth area in the economy.
> But our semiconductor industry is in the process of shifting from relatively low to relatively high capital-intensive technologies. The traditional American way is to finance that change out of retained earnings, which means it's going to be slow.
> The Japanese strategy is to infuse their semiconductor industry with massive, indirect government loans—letting their firms scale up to this new capital-intensive technology much

FIGURE 13-10
Productivity and Investment: Cross-National Comparison

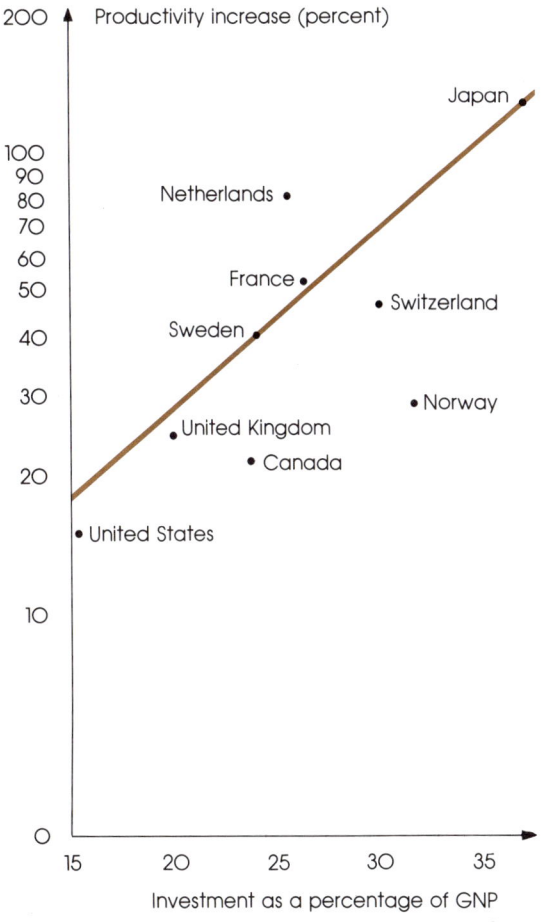

[Scatter plot with Y-axis "Productivity increase (percent)" ranging from 0 to 200 (log scale showing 10, 20, 30, 40, 50, 60, 70, 80, 90, 100, 200) and X-axis "Investment as a percentage of GNP" ranging from 15 to 35. Data points: United States (~15, ~18); United Kingdom (~23, ~25); Canada (~25, ~22); Sweden (~23, ~40); France (~25, ~50); Netherlands (~23, ~80); Norway (~30, ~30); Switzerland (~30, ~55); Japan (~35, ~150). A trend line runs from lower-left to upper-right.]

Note: American industry faces a new economic problem: a decline in productivity. Usually a measure of the man-hours expended in turning out goods and services, productivity is often seen today in terms of how fast industry is able to increase its output against the hours worked. Its growth is largely a function of investment in new technology allowing industry to operate more efficiently.
Source: Bureau of Labor Statistics, *Handbook of Labor Statistics*; United Nations, *Statistical Yearbook*.

more rapidly, Japanese firms then can learn how to use that technology before the rest of the world gets it, and drive everybody out of the business. If they're going to do it that way, then you have to do it, too, simply for competitive reasons. If you don't, you're going to lose.[5]

What Is to Be Done?

Arthur Lewis of Princeton, a Nobel Prize winner in economics, tells the story of an interdisciplinary conference at which an economist had asserted that economics was the oldest profession. "Oh, no," a sociologist replied, "ladies of pleasure have the oldest profession."

"Wrong," a physician interjected. "Since God took a rib from Adam and created Eve, surgery is the oldest profession."

"I beg to differ," an engineer said. "Since God created an orderly universe out of chaos, engineering is the oldest profession."

"But who do you suppose created the chaos?" the economist asked.

As we shall see in the discussion that follows, chaos does indeed seem to be the state of economics today. Current problems of high unemployment and high inflation—what we termed stagflation—have baffled economists. This is because conventional economic theory said that an imperfect market system could be managed by careful fiscal and monetary planning. To stimulate demand to fight unemployment, government should spend more, even if that meant running a deficit. To restrain demand to lower inflation, government should cut back on spending and follow a tight money policy. But when the 1974–1975 recession raised unemployment to 8.5 percent and still left the United States with 6 percent inflation, economists began to rethink economic theory. Basically two groups emerged. The first group we can call the supply-side economists. The second group we can loosely call the neo-Keynesian economists. This group names itself after British economist John Maynard Keynes, who influenced President Franklin Roosevelt during the Great Depression.

Now let us see the ideas that these two groups of economists advocate.

Supply-siders. In a nutshell, this group believes that inflation is the result of consumer demand exceeding supply. The best way to cure

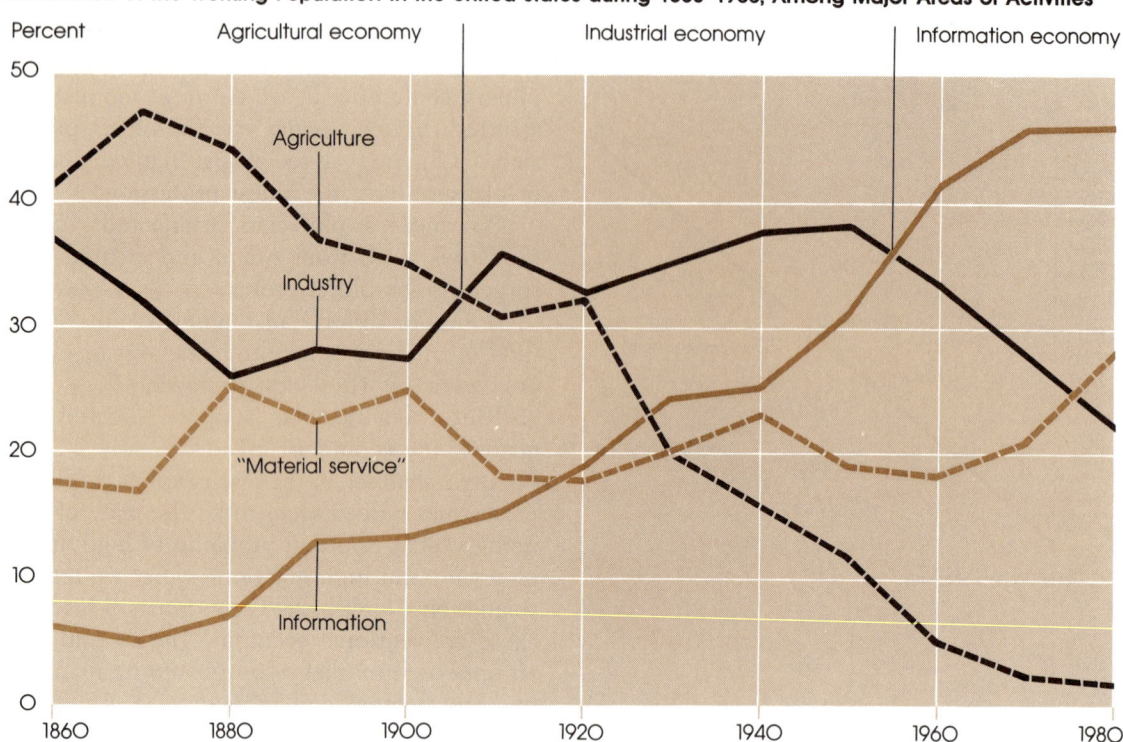

FIGURE 13-11
Distribution of the Working Population in the United States during 1860-1980, Among Major Areas of Activities

Source: Marc Uri Porat, "The Information Economy," Office of Telecommunications, U.S. Department of Commerce, Special Publication 77-12, 1977, p. 121.

inflation, therefore, is for the government to follow policies that will increase supply.

Several of these policies have already been suggested in this chapter:

Increase tax incentives to business for research and investment.

Limit government spending.

Encourage saving.

Lower income taxes.

Reduce burdensome government regulations.

A central idea of the supply-siders was foreshadowed by Adam Smith: "High taxes . . . frequently afford a smaller revenue to government than what might be drawn from more moderate taxes."

How do we explain this paradox? How can a cut in taxes result in an increase in revenue? The answer is that heavy taxes limit the output of an economy; they act as a brake on business. Since government revenues are a percent of output, anything that increases output should increase revenues. This is basically what happened in the United States from 1962 through 1965. During that period, federal tax rates for businesses and individuals were reduced in the total by about $20 billion. During the same period, budget revenues rose $22.5 billion.

High taxes make investment by business and individuals less attractive. And, as we saw in Figure 13-10, low investment seems to go hand in hand with low productivity rates. In comparison to other capitalist countries, U.S. taxes on

FIGURE 13-12
Inflation–Productivity–Economic Stagnation: The Vicious Circle

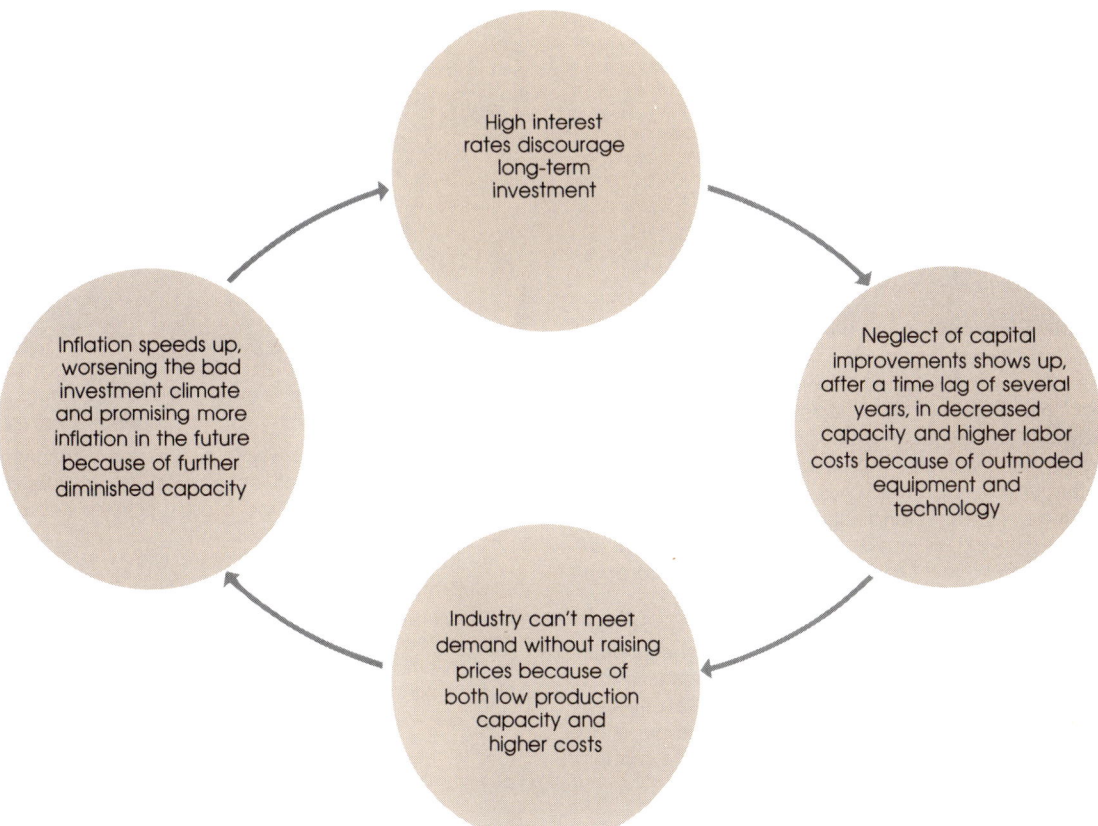

```
        High interest
        rates discourage
        long-term
        investment

Inflation speeds up,                    Neglect of capital
worsening the bad                       improvements shows up,
investment climate                      after a time lag of several
and promising more                      years, in decreased
inflation in the future                 capacity and higher labor
because of further                      costs because of outmoded
diminished capacity                     equipment and
                                        technology

        Industry can't meet
        demand without raising
        prices because of
        both low production
        capacity and
        higher costs
```

investment are relatively high, while *overall* taxes are relatively low. In 1976, for instance, the United States taxed returns on investments at a rate eight times higher than Sweden and about four times higher than Germany and Japan. The U.S. tax system allow far less generous depreciation of new technology. American taxes on business profits are about double those among European competitors. Indeed, Sweden and Germany exempt many large and profitable businesses from all taxes on profits. In recent years, taxes have been growing in the United States 80 percent faster than inflation and 20 percent faster than personal income. In fact, for 15 years taxes—the price of government— have been the fastest-rising major cost in the economy.

High taxes (and government regulation) also drive more and more people into the so-called underground economy. The underground economy may be vastly bigger than was suspected several years ago. It may be growing even more swiftly than was supposed. Regarding size, it now appears that the underground economy may come to as much as 27 percent of the gross national product—about $700 billion. That sum is larger than the reported gross national product of France. In the last decade, Edgar L. Feige of the University of Washington reckons that the economy has grown at

484 UNDERSTANDING AMERICAN POLITICS

Library of Congress

The Great Depression resulted not in a political revolution but rather in an economic one. The real makers of the revolution were the intellectuals, spearheaded by John Maynard Keynes. Guided capitalism, Keynes argued to Franklin D. Roosevelt, could work where unfettered free enterprise failed. Conventional wisdom suggested a cutting back in wages and spending during a recession. Keynes turned this upside down and insisted on increased government spending to give people more purchasing power.

In reality, Roosevelt's administration talked more than acted to stimulate a sick economy. On the eve of World War II, unemployment still stood at 14 percent. It took the war to restore the economy to health. Nevertheless, the brilliance and persuasiveness of Keynes did spark the New Deal and lay the foundations of the modern welfare state.

United Press International Photo

In the period of just five years, supply-side economics progressed from "voodoo economics" to presidential policy. In an even shorter time, it lost its partisan Republican character.

President Reagan above urges Congress to "act forcefully" to cut $41 billion in government spending and enact tax reductions worth $1,500 to a middle-income family of four over the next three years. But the idea was not simply to increase total disposable income. Rather it was to increase the incentives of workers and investors to supply additional goods and services to the market.

roughly triple the rate at which the official gross national product has expanded.

Neo-Keynesians. Another group of economists offers a different explanation for inflation. Whenever the price of any product—for example, oil or pinto beans—goes up, inflation will occur unless other prices and incomes fall. But in the modern U.S. economy prices and wages do not fall. The reason is the structure of the private economy and the policies of government.

Large corporations and big labor unions have the power to stop their prices or wages from falling. Corporate executives know they have

---

Was Alexander Hamilton a Supply-Sider?

"[Many taxes] prescribe their own limit, which cannot be exceeded without defeating the end proposed—that is, an extension of the revenue. When applied to this object, the saying is as just as it is witty that, in political arithmetic, two and two do not always make four. If [taxes] are too high, they lessen the consumption; the collection is eluded; and the product to the treasury is not so great as when they are confined within proper and moderate bounds."

Federalist No. 21

more profits to lose from cutting prices than from cutting output. According to the neo-Keynesians, as long as the cutbacks in production are small and brief, corporate executives can "informally coordinate" such cutbacks with their industrial competitors. When the number of competing firms in an industry are few—e.g., the top four firms account for 80 percent of the sales—economists say an oligopoly exists. When foreign competition threatens to force down prices, big business runs to Washington for protection.

In the modern American economy, wages are probably even less likely to fall than prices. Professional sports provides an excellent microcosm of the structure of rigid wages in any industrial operation. Lester C. Thurow writes:

> One superstar gets a large wage increase, and this leads other superstars to break their existing contracts for higher wages. With superstar wages rising, lesser players demand and get large wage increases. Each threatens to use his power to disrupt the team and lower his own productivity if his demands are not met. Wages rise and owners pass the burdens onto consumers in the form of higher ticket prices. While the wage structure and bargaining of sporting teams is more visible than most, it is by no means unique. What goes on there goes on in a milder form throughout our complex interrelated economy.[6]

What then is the neo-Keynesians' cure? In brief, they favor an **incomes policy** that would allow the government to weigh conflicting claims on income openly and decide accordingly. They admit that such a policy would be difficult to carry out in a society filled with well-organized interest groups. But, they say, the U.S. policymakers have only that and continued inflation between which to choose.

Closely related to the incomes policy approach are **wage and price controls.** Price controls are nothing new in the American political economy. During the earliest days of the nation, Puritans imposed a code of wage and price limitations. Violators of the code were considered as bad as "adulterers and whoremongers." Even before the Declaration of Independence, the Continental Congress had set price ceilings.

During World War II, Congress passed the Price Control Act of 1942 which set up the Office of Price Administration. On August 15, 1971, President Nixon, by executive order,

Quiz

It is no closely guarded secret that there is a general lack of understanding in the United States of how the economy works. Whether this state of affairs contributes to the problem outlined in this chapter, I am not prepared to say. But I would venture the opinion that ignorance of economics affects one's understanding of American politics.

1. What is the relationship between growth in money supply and inflation?
2. What percent of sales, on the average, does business get back as profit?
3. Is "overall environmental quality" in the United States declining or improving?
4. Do economists generally agree or disagree that wage and price controls are an effective way of dealing with inflation?
5. Is the United States running out of raw materials and entering an "age of scarcity"?
6. What are the most important federal laws protecting the consumer?

Answers on p. 493.

froze prices, rents, wages, and salaries for 90 days. These controls, which were a rare instance of peacetime controls, were to last, in some form, until April 30, 1974.

A milder form of wage and price control is for the president to appeal to business and labor to exercise restraint in increasing wages and prices. We refer to this practice of persuasion as "jawboning." A somewhat stronger measure is the setting of voluntary "guidelines."

Generally speaking, wage and price controls during periods of rapidly rising inflation are politically attractive: Nixon no doubt benefited in the 1972 election from his actions, and Carter might have done better in the 1980 election had he done the same. But many economists doubt their efficacy. Controls tend to distort the normal allocation of resources. Decisions that were arrived at by millions of buyers and sellers in the marketplace are taken over by government bureaucracy. The problems are considerable. For example, cars and cabbages sell at different prices at different times of the year, how does government make these adjustments? Can a resort hotel charge more over Labor Day? Is Halloween candy a seasonal product? Is honey a "raw" food and therefore exempt from regulation or a "processed" food and therefore subject to regulation? In the lumber industry, if a company cuts one eighth of an inch off plywood sheets has a "service" been performed, thereby making the company eligible for a price increase?

Another problem with controls is, when prices are held below world market value, U.S. producers export more abroad. This leads to shortages at home and even more inflation. Controls can also be unfair. High technology companies, with rising productivity, find it hard to reward their employees at rates above some across-the-board ceiling.

Yet another problem is that price controls seem only to delay rather than prevent inflation. When the controls of World War II were removed, inflation jumped over 50 percent in less than three years. When Nixon finally lifted controls—after the 1972 election—prices went up to 8.8 percent in 1973 and 12.2 percent in 1974. A crude analogy would be that the imposition of wage and price controls is like putting a heavy lid on a pot which was boiling over. That might stop the spillover, but only turning off the fire will stop the buildup of heat. Proponents of controls would say that what makes this analogy crude is that it ignores the possible psychological effects of a sudden abatement of inflation on buyers and sellers. To the extent controls alter an individual's expectation about future changes in prices, they are effective. (For example, union leaders will not ask for a 12 percent increase in wages if they know that inflation will only rise 4 percent.)

THE GLOBAL CONNECTION

Thus far in this chapter, we have been focusing on the U.S. economy as if it were a closed system, shut off from the rest of the world. While this approach may have simplified discussion, it distorts economic reality. The fact is the United States is becoming ever more interdependent economically with the rest of the world.

Several elements in this interdependence are worth highlighting: international trade, the multinational corporation, and lesser developed countries.

International Trade

Trade with other nations is essential to the economic well-being of the United States. International trade permits a nation to apply more of its work and resources to activities where it can do a better job than other nations. It also allows other nations to be successful where they can do a better job than we can.

A country can have a production advantage because of the availability of certain raw materi-

FIGURE 13-13
U.S. Dependence on Foreign Resources (1979 figures)

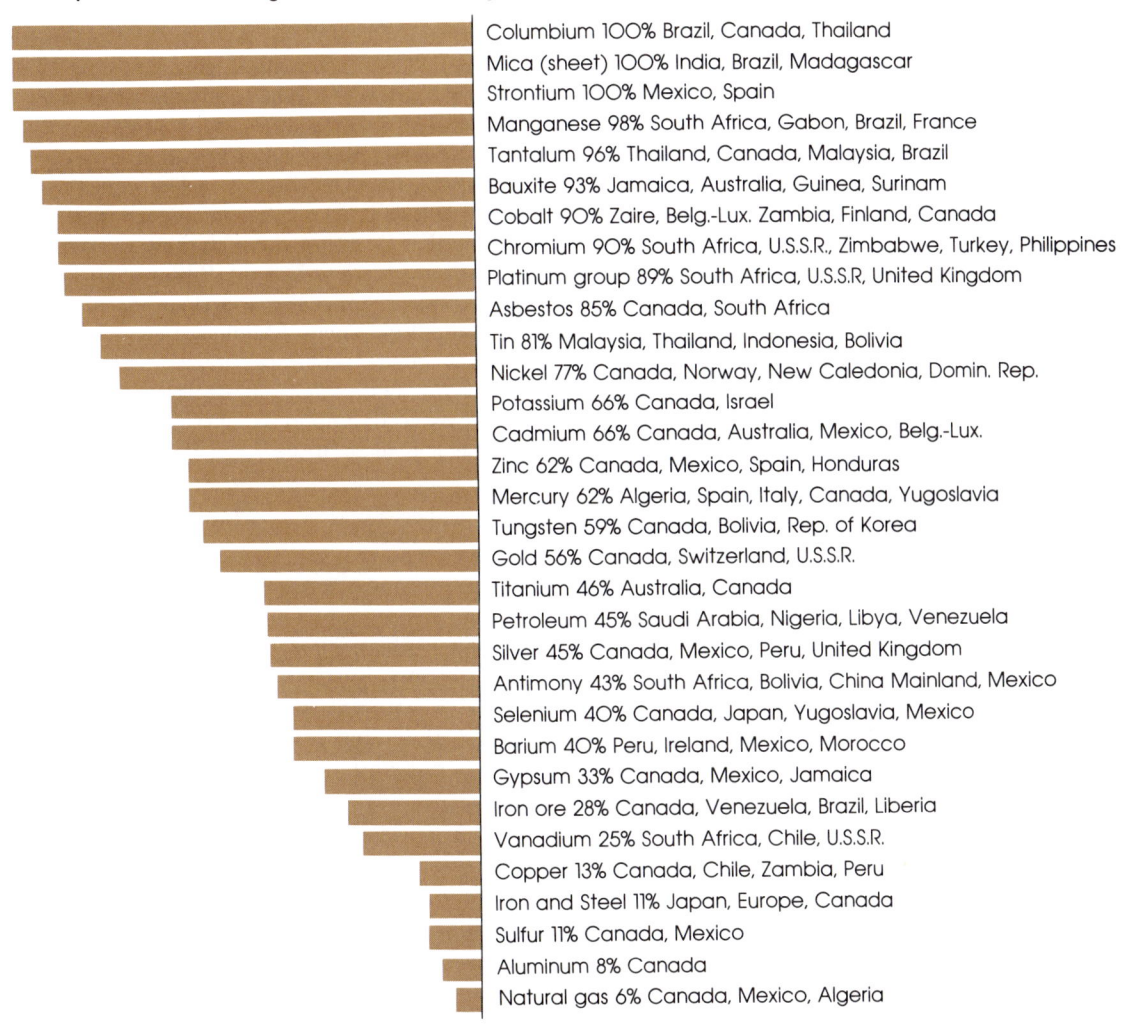

Columbium 100% Brazil, Canada, Thailand
Mica (sheet) 100% India, Brazil, Madagascar
Strontium 100% Mexico, Spain
Manganese 98% South Africa, Gabon, Brazil, France
Tantalum 96% Thailand, Canada, Malaysia, Brazil
Bauxite 93% Jamaica, Australia, Guinea, Surinam
Cobalt 90% Zaire, Belg.-Lux. Zambia, Finland, Canada
Chromium 90% South Africa, U.S.S.R., Zimbabwe, Turkey, Philippines
Platinum group 89% South Africa, U.S.S.R, United Kingdom
Asbestos 85% Canada, South Africa
Tin 81% Malaysia, Thailand, Indonesia, Bolivia
Nickel 77% Canada, Norway, New Caledonia, Domin. Rep.
Potassium 66% Canada, Israel
Cadmium 66% Canada, Australia, Mexico, Belg.-Lux.
Zinc 62% Canada, Mexico, Spain, Honduras
Mercury 62% Algeria, Spain, Italy, Canada, Yugoslavia
Tungsten 59% Canada, Bolivia, Rep. of Korea
Gold 56% Canada, Switzerland, U.S.S.R.
Titanium 46% Australia, Canada
Petroleum 45% Saudi Arabia, Nigeria, Libya, Venezuela
Silver 45% Canada, Mexico, Peru, United Kingdom
Antimony 43% South Africa, Bolivia, China Mainland, Mexico
Selenium 40% Canada, Japan, Yugoslavia, Mexico
Barium 40% Peru, Ireland, Mexico, Morocco
Gypsum 33% Canada, Mexico, Jamaica
Iron ore 28% Canada, Venezuela, Brazil, Liberia
Vanadium 25% South Africa, Chile, U.S.S.R.
Copper 13% Canada, Chile, Zambia, Peru
Iron and Steel 11% Japan, Europe, Canada
Sulfur 11% Canada, Mexico
Aluminum 8% Canada
Natural gas 6% Canada, Mexico, Algeria

als, a favorable climate, lower wages, or more advanced manufacturing processes.

When goods and services can be produced with relative efficiency, they are competitive in the world marketplace. They offer value that cannot be obtained elsewhere, so other nations buy and import them. This creates jobs and opportunities at home. The products of the agriculture, aerospace, and computer industries are examples of goods that the U.S. exports because of its superiority in producing them.

International trade also permits the United States to obtain raw materials and foods that are not available in sufficient supply. One obvious example would be petroleum; others can be seen in Figure 13-13.

Detroit Doubletalk?

To buy an American-made automobile seems like nothing less than patriotic duty these days. If all those people now purchasing foreign cars would "buy American," the auto companies contend, some of the 200,000 jobless auto workers made parts into their own vehicles.

There probably is "something foreign in everything" that the domestic companies turn out, concedes a Ford Motor Company executive. The parts list for some current and future U.S. autos has a global flavor: engines from West Germany and Japan, brakes from Brazil, clutches from France, and so on, from Spain to Singapore.

Just like American car buyers, U.S. car makers are finding that some foreign products are cheaper. Or better. Or more readily available. Faced with fierce competition and a fast-changing market, U.S. auto makers are scrambling to save time and money as they race to bring out the new small cars their customers crave.

But to some, that makes the industry's cry for limits on imported cars seem like a plea for a double standard. Many American parts makers complain that Detroit is doing to them just what customers are doing to Detroit. Edward Schalon, a parts-company executive and chairman of the Motor and Equipment Manufacturers Association trade group, isn't too sympathetic. "They can't have it both ways," he declares, asserting that the issue of import competition "isn't as simple as it is made to be."

SOURCE: Leonard M. Apcar, *The Wall Street Journal*, May 14, 1980.

The size and mix of U.S. international trade for 1979 are shown below:

1979 Imports and Exports ($ billions)

Category	Imports	Exports
Foods, feeds, and beverages	17.4	29.8
Industrial supplies and materials	109.9	57.8
Capital goods, except automotive	24.6	58.1
Automotive vehicles and parts	25.6	17.4
Consumer goods (nonfood)	30.6	12.6
	211.5	182.1

The table shows that, in 1979, industrial supplies accounted for 52 percent of imports, primarily due to price increase by the Organization of Petroleum Exporting Countries (OPEC). Also, agricultural products represented almost 16 percent of total exports; this we can easily see the importance of food production to international trade.

Even in 1776, the United States was a major trading nation. Today, it is the world's leading trader; West Germany is second and Japan third.

The American economy has become more and more interrelated with the economies of other nations, and we have seen a dramatic growth of its international trade. From 1967 to 1979, the value of U.S. exports rose almost 600 percent and imports rose by almost 800 percent.

When the value of exports is less than the value of our imports, we have what is called a **trade deficit**. This means extra dollars end up in those countries from which we imported. The reverse is true when we have a **trade surplus**.

A trade deficit or surplus is one of the factors that determines the dollar's value abroad. Other factors include domestic and foreign interest rates, inflation rates, and expectations about the future. In general, the prices we pay for imports change as the supply of and demand for U.S. dollars change in the world's economy.

Exchange rates have to be set up to make easy international trade possible. They do so by setting the amounts at which different currencies can be traded for each other. There are different ways exchange rates can work.

They can be fixed. The relative values of

different currencies then depend on the amount of some agreed-on material such as gold that each note is backed by. Or they can be managed or "pegged." In various forms, this system has governed international monetary dealings since 1944. It allows rates to fluctuate, but only within fairly narrow boundaries set by national governments. If speculation or trade conditions threaten to alter a country's currency value drastically, the government can intervene to offset the trend—buying up or selling its own currency on world markets until the exchange value returns to its pegged rate.

Many factors determine the demand for a given currency. If there is a great, worldwide demand for, say, German cars, people will want to exchange their currencies for deutsche marks in order to pay German auto manufacturers. So, the mark's value will go up relative to other currencies. On the other hand, suppose Washington follows a tight monetary policy that keeps inflation low and maintains high real interest rates. Then foreign investors will want to profit from the high rate of return they can get by investing in the U.S. economy.

Multinational Corporations

Another element bringing about economic interdependence is the **multinational corporation** (MNC). One seventh of the world's gross national product is created by MNCs; more of them based in the United States than any other nation.

Basically, the MNC is characterized by two elements. First, it has a manufacturing base or investment in at least one country other than its home country. And second, it has a managerial philosophy regarding management, marketing, production, and finance that is global in nature. Thus, all decision making considers not only the domestic economy and competition but also the global positions of the firm. Most of the large corporations in the world today are multinational.

Symbolic of the huge network of MNCs is the new line of "global cars." Ford Fiesta has windshields from Oklahoma, carburetors from Northern Ireland, spark plugs from England, wheels from Belgium, bumpers from West Germany, and is put together in Spain. Ford currently has 22 overseas plants, followed closely by GM's 21 factories in Europe alone. GM also has joint ventures in Japan, Kenya, Korea, Iran, Yugoslavia, and South Africa. How does a national government go about regulating such activities?

In many ways, the multinational corporation is a natural phenomenon. As businesses grow and expand, they begin to sell their products or services to ever-increasing markets. Eventually, some of these markets become international in scope. At first, most companies establish an overseas branch or subsidiary. This subsidiary usually has a manager who carries the title of vice president for international operations. Soon the company finds its sales abroad increasing at a far greater rate than its sales at home. So the company begins to expand its international operations. However, instead of adding more plants in the same foreign country, the corporation opens offices in other countries. In effect, the company begins to view the world in the same way it used to view the home country. Where before it routinely made decisions about locating plants in New York and California, now it routinely makes the same decisions about locating plants in London and Tokyo.

Obviously, the potential for the misuse of power—both political and economic—is substantial for MNCs. Sometimes, too, the potential becomes reality. In the early 1970s, rumors (later to be confirmed) abounded about an attempt at an overthrow of the Chilean government by IT&T. And many people were of the impression that some kinds of conspiracy existed among the oil companies when, in 1973–1974, the nation suffered serious gasoline shortages. Finally, many Americans were appalled in the mid-1970s, when it was revealed that many U.S. business firms had engaged in bribery. Almost lost in the discussion was the fact that in many countries "bribes" are an accepted business practice.

It would be wrong to conclude that MNCs are all bad. In general, they have made major contributions to the quality of life throughout the world. One may sometimes be appalled at this lack of patriotism. But MNCs are a balance against the passions of nationalism that have occasioned so many wars in the past two centuries. In the **Third World** countries of Asia, Africa, and Latin America, MNCs can provide perhaps the best opportunity for advancement based on merit.

In sum, the degree of economic interdependence in increasing. We see proof in the fact that international trade has risen almost twice as fast as world production; international capital flows have expanded even more rapidly. The internationalization of economic life cannot be reversed except at great economic—and political—cost. Consequently, government policies and international institutions for collective decision making need to be improved.

FUTURE FILE

Persistence of Poverty in Less Developed Countries

Despite rapid economic growth in the less developed countries (LDCs), the bulk of their population and, indeed, of the world's population still live in abject poverty.

In 1980, for the first time, the U.S. government added its voice to the chorus of those deeply distressed about the global future. *The Global 2000 Report to the President* gives these warnings:

> The gap between richest and poorest will have increased. By every measure of material welfare the study provides—per capital GNP and consumption of food, energy, and minerals—the gap will widen. For example, the gap between the GNP per capita in the LDCs and the industrialized countries is projected to grow from about $4,000 in 1975 to about $7,900 in 2000. Great disparities within countries are also expected to continue.
>
> The environment will have lost important life-supporting capabilities. By 2000, 40 percent of the forest still remaining in the LDCs in 1978 will have been razed. The atmospheric concentration of carbon dioxide will be nearly one third higher than preindustrial levels. Soil erosion will have removed, on the average, several inches of soil from croplands all over the world. Desertification (including salinization) may have claimed a significant fraction of the world's rangeland and cropland. Over little more than two decades, 15 to 20 percent of the earth's total species of plants and animals will have become extinct—a loss of at least 500,000 species.

United Press International Photo

If the fertility and mortality rates projected for 2000 were to continue unchanged into the 21st century, the world's population would reach 10 billion by 2030. Thus anyone with a present life expectancy of an additional 50 years could expect to see the world population reach 10 billion. This same rate of growth would produce a population of nearly 30 billion before the end of the 21st century.

As with most government reports, the recommendations were quite general.

The time for action to prevent this outcome is running out. Unless nations collectively and individually take bold and imaginative steps toward improved social and economic conditions, reduced fertility, better management of resources, and protection of environment, the world must expect a troubled entry into the 21st century.

When reading such doomsday reports, several things ought to be recognized.

First, contrary evidence could be cited about what the trends are. Here are some examples of the less publicized "good news":

Per capita food production in the world has been increasing at roughly 1 percent yearly (see United Nations, Food and Agriculture Organization, *Production Yearbook*). Even in LCDs, food production has increased subtantially; India has food in storage.

Since World War II, the number of famines has declined dramatically. Because of improved roads, only a 10th as many people died of famine in the third quarter of the 20th century as in the last quarter of the 19th, when there were far fewer people (see "Famine" in *Encyclopaedia Britannica*). Ironically, it was increased population density and improvements in technology that helped produce the better roads.

Improvements in the standard of living in some countries with a high birth rate come slow. But many countries have combined great gains in their standard of living with a high birth rate. In short, careful analysis of the data shows little relationship between birth rates and standard of living.

Are we running out of farmland? In the United States, all land used for urban areas and roads totals less than 3 percent of land area. The increase from 1920 to 1970 was 0.00025 percent of total land annually (see Barlowe, *Land Resource Economics*, p. 50). Moreover, millions of acres are converted every year to efficient cropland by draining swamps and irrigating deserts.

Second, in addition to the affluent oil exporters, some LDCs are developing strong, growing, and broadly based economies. This category includes Brazil (which is an emerging industrial power), Korea, Malaysia, Mexico, the Phillipines, and several smaller economies. In short, the LDCs are not all in the same boat. Economic progress is possible where sensible economic policies are followed.

Third, the major problems that developing countries have to resolve are domestic, not foreign, ones. Many of these problems are self-inflicted: forced collectivization of farming, expulsion of the most productive groups (for instance, the Chinese in Vietnam and Indonesians or Asians in East Africa), suppression of private trade and industry, restrictions on MNCs, refusal to kill animals for protein, and prohibiting women from taking paid work (as in many Moslem countries). Focusing on foreign threats and causes, however, does serve to keep the attention of the people away from the failures of their leaders.

Finally, international economic policies by the United States and other developed countries can assist in solving some of these problems, though only to a limited extent. As a percentage of the GNP of a developing country, foreign aid is at best a fraction of one percent. If correctly targeted—for example, to starving people—even such slight amounts could have a great impact. Unfortunately, *official*—as opposed to private—aid often does not go to those skeletal figures. It goes to their rulers, whose spending policies are determined by their own personal and political priorities.

New Realities

Past economic successes and current failures provide U.S. policymakers with three lessons. First, every nation, even the United States, has lost a large degree of control over its economy. This is the meaning of the growing economic interdependence of the world. The increased movement of goods, people, ideas, and capital across national boundaries has been a major factor behind the rapid and sustained economic expansion of the postwar period. It has also been a source of problems, since economic developments in a major country cannot be kept from having an impact on others.

Second, with its economic welfare increasingly determined by developments abroad, each nation has an interest in the economic policies of others. It follows that the institutions for international consultation and collaboration to meet common economic problems are essential.

National economic policies must take account of their repercussions on other countries. And effective international coordination of economic policies includes not only such staples as foreign trade, exchange rates, and the balance of payments; more important, it includes broad domestic economic matters, such as the reduction of unemployment and control of inflation.

Finally, the role of the United States is crucial. The overwhelming size of its economy and the international importance of the dollar means that it is responsible for much of world economic development, good or bad. Furthermore, no other nation has the economic power that it does. The United States is still the only real economic superpower. It is the nation best able to take the initiative.

In the chapter that follows, we shall see how this global interdependence occurs in other important areas besides economics.

Chapter Key

Since the founding of the American republic, political and economic considerations have been closely linked. Presidential elections are generally influenced more by economic issues than any other.

When Adam Smith wrote *The Wealth of Nations* in 1776, the conventional wisdom was that gold was the ture measure of a nation's wealth. (Smith, with his customary good sense, rejected this notion.) Today gross national product (GNP) is the most frequently used measure. But a growing number of economists question whether the sum of all the goods and services a nation produces in a year is a satisfactory measure of the quality of life of a nation. Perhaps the true wealth of a modern nation is the will, creativity, and entrepreneurship of its people—in short, its technological base. How else can one explain the Japanese success?

A market system harnesses the competitive impulses of millions of individuals to produce goods and services that benefit everyone—though not equally. When business produces too much, the resulting surplus drives prices down. When consumers demand a certain product, the price rises. Rising prices, in turn, encourage more and better production by business. All these operations assume certain conditions—e.g., a competitive market in which there are no monopolies.

The federal government attempts to manage economic condition through fiscal and monetary policy. The former refers to government spending and taxing; the latter refers to government control of the money supply.

In the last decade, the U.S. economy has been racked by high inflation and high unemployment—in a word, stagflation. There is little consensus among economists regarding how this came about it and the best way to solve it. Supply-side economists argue that stagflation is the result of high taxes and burdensome government regulation. Neo-Keynesians argue that the structure of the market has fundamentally changed; big corporations can resist price decreases and big labor can demand wage increases unjustified by their output.

The benefits derived from foreign trade, which Smith put forward in 1776, are even truer today:

> Between whatever places foreign trade is carried on, they all of them derive two distinct benefits from it. It carries out that surplus part of the produce of their land and labour for which there is no demand among them, and brings back in return for it something else for which there is a demand. It gives a value to their superfluities, by exchanging them for something else, which may satisfy a part of their wants, and increase their enjoyments. . . . By opening a more extensive market for whatever part of the produce of their labour may exceed the home consumption, it encourages them to improve its productive powers, and to augment its annual produce to the utmost, and thereby to increase the real revenue and wealth of the society.

Answers to Quiz (see page 485)

1. Monetary growth is a major factor determining the rate of inflation over the longer term. As the chart on p. 494 shows, ups and downs in monetary growth have been followed by corresponding ups and downs in inflation. The interval between changes in money and subsequent changes in inflation has varied but averaged roughly two years.

   Relatively few people even understand what money is (currency in circulation plus commercial bank demand deposits), or how it is created. Moreover, many people believe that the way to lower interest rates is for the central bank—the Federal Reserve system—to increase the supply of credit by creating more money. In fact, economists now know that though an easy-credit policy may lower interest rates temporarily, it soon will increase inflation and prompt *higher* interest rates.

   The public's ignorance in this regard makes it difficult for politicians and government officials to follow a more sensible economic policy.

2. Cartoons like the one on p. 495 perpetuate misunderstanding by the public of the level of business profits and of the function of profits in the economy. Surveys of the public indicate that people on average figure that a profit rate of 10 percent on sales would be reasonable. The public believes, however, that business is getting something like a 27 percent or 28 percent return on sales. In fact, the average profit on sales is more like 4 percent to 5 percent. Nor does the average person comprehend the need for business to be profitable enough to continue the investment programs that create jobs and provide the goods demanded by consumers.

   Another way to think about profits is in

Inflation Follows Money

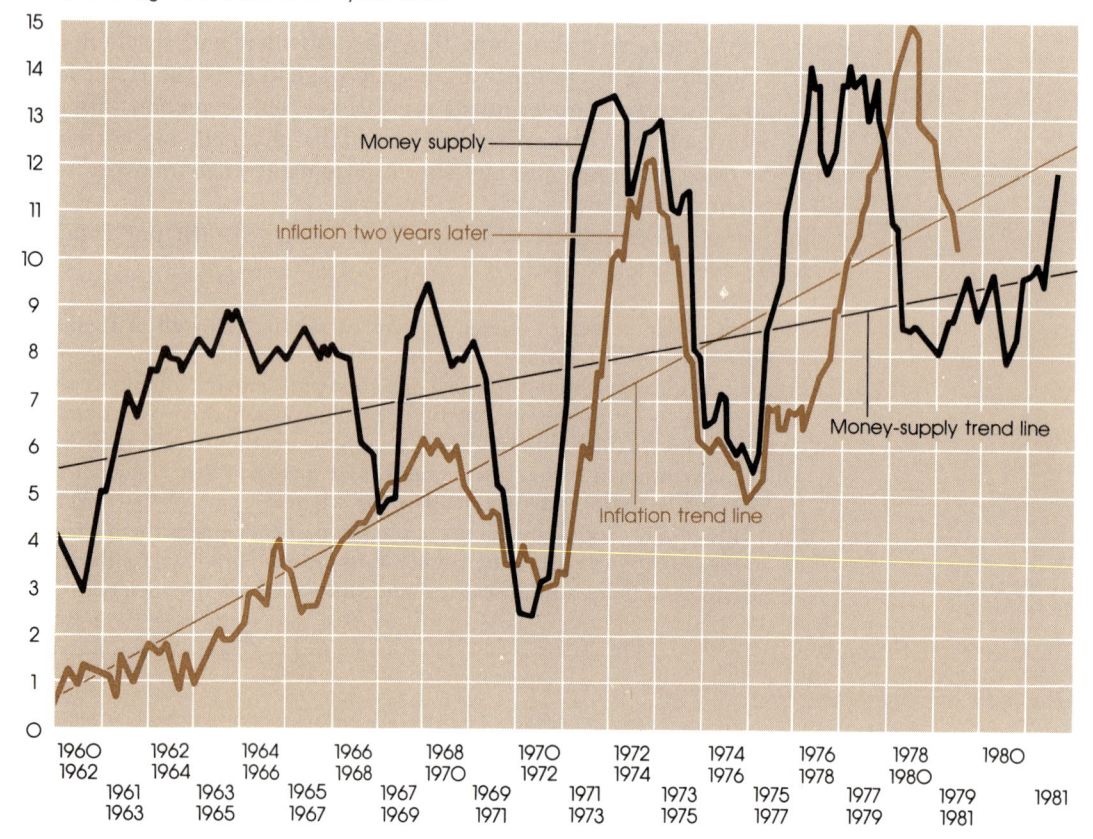

Percent change from same month year earlier

[Chart showing Money supply and Inflation two years later from 1960 to 1981, with Money-supply trend line and Inflation trend line, y-axis 0 to 15]

Money supply: M–2-Currency, checkable and other demand deposits, savings and small time deposits.
Inflation: Consumer price index.
Source: *Newsweek* (June 15, 1981), p. 80.

terms of a single company. For example, in 1979 Mobil Oil Corporation had about $47.9 billion in sales. Here is what they did with all of those billions:

47.9	Sales
−29.5	Payments to suppliers
−11.7	Taxes to government
− 3.6	Wages to employees
3.1	Left for investment and return to investors

But $3.1 billion is still a lot of money by anyone's standard. Where did it go? A total of $2.6 billion was reinvested in the business in order to find and develop new energy sources and provide for other products and services. The remaining $500 million was paid in dividends to 270,000 shareholders—including pension funds, mutual funds, and insurance companies—who put up the capital. It was the cost of using their money.

By Don Wright; © 1979 *Miami News.* Reprinted by permission of Special Features

> **PLEASE NOTE:** IN ORDER TO PROTECT SMALL OR IMPRESSIONABLE CHILDREN OR PERSONS WHO MIGHT OBJECT BECAUSE OF WHAT THEY CONSTRUE TO BE BAD TASTE, THE FOLLOWING DISGUSTING, **OBSCENE** STATEMENTS HAVE BEEN PRINTED UPSIDE DOWN.
>
> TEXACO INC.—81% INCREASE IN PROFITS
> GULF OIL CO.—61% INCREASE IN PROFITS
> MARATHON OIL—107% INCREASE IN PROFITS
> EXXON—37% INCREASE IN PROFITS

3. The official data of the Council on Environmental Quality concerning major air pollutants show sharp improvements in the last decade. With respect to water, "major improvements in the quality of polluted streams have been documented." The fish catch in Lake Erie, long ago said to be "dead" by Barry Commoner, has been increasing. The most important indicator of environmental quality is life expectancy: it continues to rise, and at an increasing rate; it gained 2.1 years from 1970 to 1976, compared with a gain of only 0.8 years during the entire 1960s.

4. The vast majority of economists in the United States and abroad agree that wage and price controls are not the way to deal with inflation. Such controls have been tried in numerous industrial countries; they have done little or nothing to trim inflation over the long run. Yet surveys consistently indicate that a majority of the public favors wage and price controls. Pressures on presidents to impose them are considerable. The temporary relief from rising prices and the illusion that "somebody is doing something" generally gives him a boost in the popularity.

5. Julian L. Simon of the University of Illinois thinks not. He explains:

   The only meaningful measure of scarcity in peacetime is the cost of the good in question. The cost trends of almost every natural resource—whether measured in labor time required to produce the energy, in production costs, in the proportion of our incomes spent for energy, or even in the price relative to other consumer goods—have been downward over the course of recorded history.

   An hour's work in the United States has bought increasingly more of copper, wheat, and oil (representative and important raw materials) from 1800 to the present. . . . These trends imply that the raw materials have been getting increasingly available and less scarce relative to the most important and most fundamental element of life, human worktime.

   Not only are the relative prices of raw materials falling but also the service we get from them is increasing. A single communications satellite, for example, can provide more and better services than the thousands of tons of copper that go into a conventional telephone network. (*Science*, June 27, 1980, p. 1435).

6. Congress has passed a number of laws over the years to protect consumers' interests. Some federal agencies with responsibilities for carrying out these laws have been around for decades. Examples are the Federal Trade Commission and the Food and Drug Administration.

   In the past, consumer law emphasized the idea of *caveat emptor* ("let the buyer beware"). In other words, the consumer was expected to look for unfair sales practices and suffer the consequences if he or she got less than expected. Today, however, the law has shifted the emphasis to what some authorities would call the idea of "let the *seller* beware." For instance, a program was announced in 1971 requiring advertisers to be able to support advertising claims of product performance, safety, quality, or comparative price.

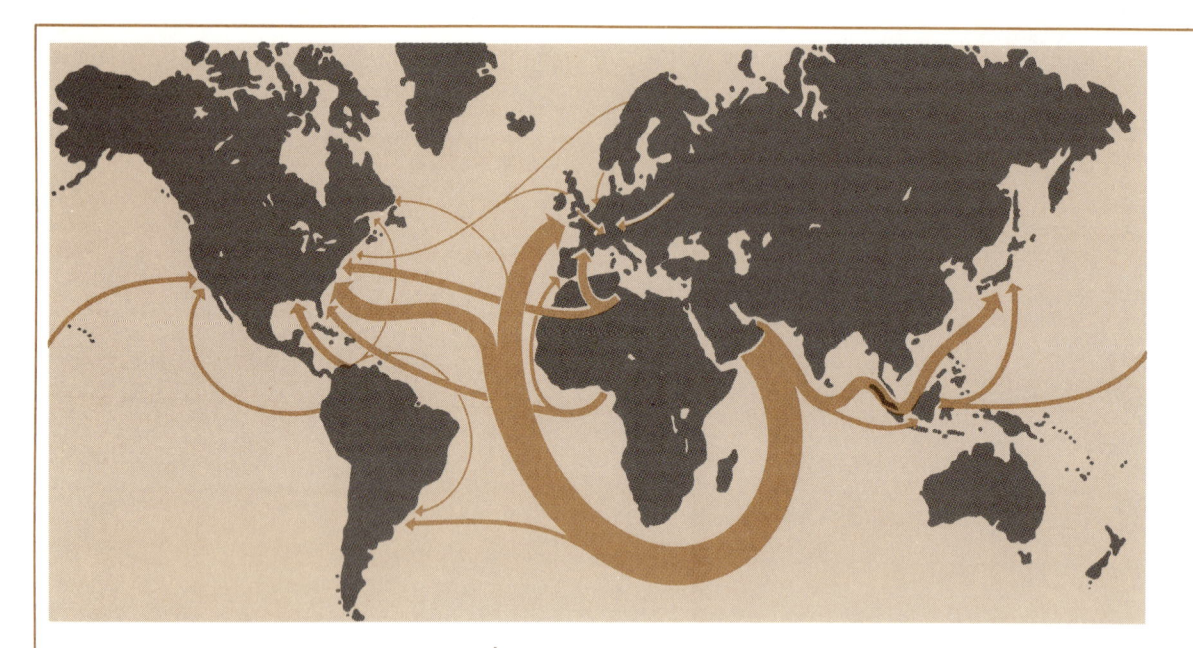

14 America in an Interdependent World

After studying this chapter you should be able to answer the following questions:

1. What do you think are the five or six events that have most shaped the perception Americans have of the world?
2. Who makes American foreign policy?
3. How might we classify approaches to foreign policy exhibited by these decision makers?
4. What do you think are the five or six most critical spots on the global for American foreign policy?
5. Who makes national security policy?
6. What are the problems in trying to assess national security?
7. How is peace preserved?

Terms you should know:

apartheid
appeasement
balance of power
Bay of Pigs
bipartisan
Blockade of West Berlin
brinkmanship
Central Intelligence Agency (CIA)
cold war
colonial power
containment
Cuban missile crisis
detente
deterrence
escalation
Farewell Address (Washington's)
the good neighbor policy
Gulf of Tonkin Resolution
gunboat diplomacy
hawks and doves
Iranian revolution
Iron Curtain
isolationism

Korean conflict
limited war
linkage
Marshall Plan
massive retaliation
Monroe Doctrine
national interest
Nixon Doctrine
North Atlantic Treaty Organization (NATO)
nuclear proliferation
Organization of Petroleum Exporting Countries (OPEC)
Pearl Harbor
Pentagon
Soviet Afghanistan invasion
Strategic Arms Limitations Talks (SALT)
terrorism
triad
Truman Doctrine
United Nations
Vietnam war
War Powers Act
Yalta Conference

500 UNDERSTANDING AMERICAN POLITICS

Oliver Wendell Holmes, wounded three times in the Civil War, used to thunder a century ago about "this smug, oversafe corner of the world . . . a little space of calm in the midst of the tempestuous, untamed streaming of the world," so far removed from most human want and anguish. But now it is changing. Today, distant events quickly touch the lives of every American. An oil tanker goes down in the Straits of Hormuz and the price of a Fleetwood Mac album in Manhattan goes up. (Rising oil prices increase the price of vinyl for records.) Rainfall in the Soviet Union declines and the price of bread in Wichita, Kansas, shoots up. Even cowboys are affected. To save on the cost of diesel fuel, thousands of cattle in South Dakota are now driven rather than trucked to the stockyards. Interdependence is increasing, especially as resources become scarcer.

Equally important perhaps is the economic interdependence. Americans have invested $135 billion abroad; foreigners have invested $27 billion in America. More ominous, the United States has made more than $70 billion worth of loans to the Soviet Union and Eastern Europe. If, at any moment, the Soviet Union wanted to play havoc with the U.S. economy, they would not need to take over the Middle East oil fields; they would only need to announce their refusal to pay back existing loans. A catastrophe of equal proportions for Japan would be the sudden closure of the American market to their exports.

Advances in telecommunications and transportation are also forces shaping a more interdependent world. Each year 8 million Americans jet themselves abroad, while 5 million foreigners vist the United States. American citizens each year send a billion pieces of mail, 50 billion telephone calls, and 200,000 students abroad. According to a 1977 study by the Union of International Associations, there are over 52,000 identifiable, interlocking relationships and cross-linkages among some 1,857 transnational organizations.

Wide World Photos

Cultures are now more and more penetrated by each other. In 1980, Pope John Paul II visited Africa. As shown above, the Pope is giving communion to a girl at service in Kisangani, Zaire. In Nairobi, the Pontiff urged all Africans to guard against losing their independence.

Although there is much talk in the West about the forces of Islam, African Christians of all denominations are doubling in numbers every 12 years. By the end of the century, there may be over 350 million professing African Christians. That would be the largest single group within the global Christian community, exceeding in numerical importance even the Latin Americans.

Technological advances also gave the United States a new neighbor—the Soviet Union. The shortest and best routes between the Old World and New World are no longer via the Pacific and Atlantic; rather they are over the North Pole. The buffer of the oceans—which had once made America such a "smug, oversafe corner of the world"—has vanished. The security problems raised by having such a powerful new neighbor are beyond anything Holmes could have dreamt. Accordingly, U.S. defense strategy shifted from an eastward, transatlantic orientation to one based on a distant early warning system (DEW line) arrayed across Canada.

The point that we are more interdependent today than ever before seems beyond argument. Nevertheless, Americans and their leaders (with exceptions like John F. Kennedy and Richard M. Nixon) appear singularly ill-informed about global affairs. When Jimmy Carter took office

> ### A Truly Open Mind
>
> In February 1981, when William P. Clark appeared before the Senate Foreign Relations Committee for confirmation as deputy secretary of state, the following exchange occurred:
>
> **Sen. Joseph Biden:** Can you tell me who is the Prime Minister of South Africa?
>
> **William P. Clark:** No, sir, I cannot.
>
> **Biden:** Can you tell me who the Prime Minister of Zimbabwe is?
>
> **Clark:** It would be a guess.
>
> **Biden:** What are the countries in Europe, in NATO, that are most reluctant to go along with theater nuclear-force modernization?
>
> **Clark:** I am not in a position . . . to categorize them.
>
> **Biden:** Can you tell us, just from the accounts in the newspapers, what is happening to the British Labor Party these days?
>
> **Clark:** I don't think I can tell with specificity what is happening in the British Labor Party today.

in 1976, he knew little about diplomatic history or economic geography. Had he been asked prior to his election to give the approximate location of Namibia or Minsk, I doubt his answer would have been very close to the mark. The criticism probably carries even more weight in the case of Ronald Reagan—who, after all, never had the benefit of a Naval Academy education.

This chapter should help you better understand these and other issues. But its chief aim is twofold. First, it is to make you aware of how international events affect "domestic" troubles (e.g., inflation, recession, energy, pollution, human rights, racial troubles, poverty, education, research science, technology, business, labor, food, transportation, population, culture, communication, terrorism, revolution, law enforcement, arms, narcotics, religion, ideology). The second aim is to make you aware of how domestic politics influence government action in the world arena.

Not surprisingly, the chapter uses interdependence as its organizing theme. In the first half, we shall consider the political connection between the United States and the rest of the world. In the second half, we shall consider the strategic or military connection. There is, of course, an economic connection between the United States, and the rest of the world. But we explored this very important interrelationship at the end of the last chapter. (See pp. 486–92.)

Drawing by Peter Arno; © 1938, 1966 The New Yorker Magazine, Inc.

"Hey, Jack, which way to Mecca?"

Generally speaking, neither American citizens nor their leaders have a good grasp of the interdependence of the world and the disparate cultural, demographic, geographic, economic, and political forces that fill it. It was true in 1938, and it is true today—despite greater interdependence.

THE POLITICAL CONNECTION

Important Events in the Growth of American Foreign Policy

Political interdependence has a somewhat longer history than economic interdependence. In this section, you will see that thinking and acting about political relations with other countries has occupied the American republic since Washington's presidency. It is hoped you will also begin to see how earlier presidents could put foreign relations on the back burner and why no president since World War II has had that option.

We saw in Chapter 5 how the past experiences of individuals shape their view of the political world; we called this phenomenon socialization. Nations, like people, develop collective memories over time and these memories influence current behavior. Suppose you want to know why many people in Mexico and Central America tend to resent the American government, no matter how benign any particular administration may be towards them. You need only recall the long record of frequent U.S. intervention in the Caribbean and Central America. Past events etched themselves into a nation's consciousness—sometimes so deeply that it is hard for governments to understand current events (much less future trends) properly.

Therefore, it is important to study the following chronology with some care. It is essential background to what follows.

1796

In his **Farewell Address,** George Washington suggested basic principles that should govern the nation's conduct. He warned of the dangers of sectional factions and of party and foreign alliances. He did not use the famous phrase "entangling alliances." (It came from Jefferson's first inaugural.) However, he did beg the nation to "steer clear of permanent alliances with any portion of the foreign world." Temporary agreements were understandable; but Washington devoted a long section to the evils of playing favorites with foreign powers.

1823

During his annual message to Congress in 1823, President James Monroe declared American opposition to any European intervention in the affairs of the American continents. The true originator of the **Monroe Doctrine,** however, was Monroe's tough-minded secretary of state, John Quincy Adams. Over the years, the doctrine became one of the basic tenets of American foreign policy.

1890

A convergence of forces turned the United States into a **colonial power.** New views of national self-interest that emphasized geography and military might had great influence. Many Americans opposed intervention in foreign spheres such as the Philippines. But advocates argued forcefully that, if the United States did not step in, some of the great powers would. Indeed, during this period, the European powers were carving up Africa and establishing Asian and Pacific markets.

The United States had matured industrially and was already a force in world markets. To politicians, press, and the public, it seemed that national interest dictated that America, too, should flex her muscles abroad. Critics call this policy **gunboat diplomacy.**

1917

On October 23, in trenches near Nancy, France, a gun of the American Expeditionary Force fired the first American shot into German lines. With that, the United States truly entered world history. But the United States' involvement in World War I and the postwar peace conferences was followed by a policy of

Quiz
What is wrong with this map?

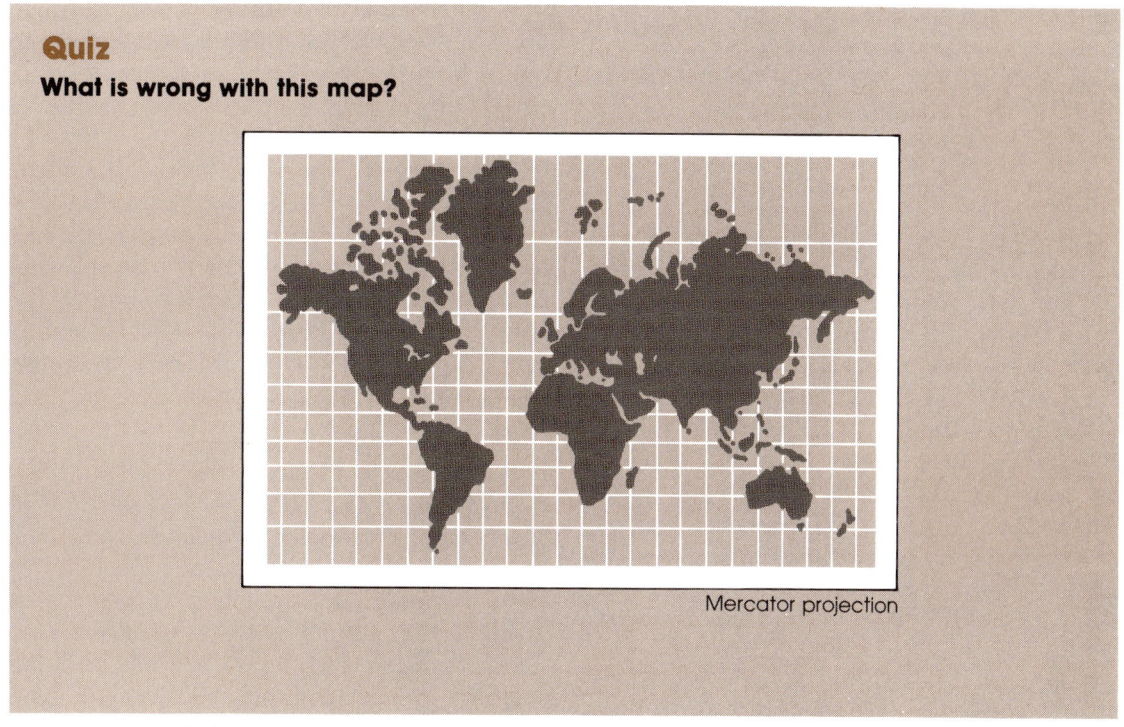

Mercator projection

Answer on page 534.

isolationism or noninvolvement in the affairs of other nations.

1933

In his first inaugural address, President Franklin Roosevelt announced his dedication to a new principle: **the good neighbor policy.** In practice, this policy meant that the United States would treat Latin-American nations as a friend and equal—not as the "Colossus of the North," or "Yankee imperialist." The creation later (in 1948) of the regional organization, the Organization of American States (OAS), institutionalized this policy and linked it to the Monroe Doctrine (1823).

1938

Hitler, alleging mistreatment of several million persons of German descent living in part of Czechoslovakia, demanded that Czechoslovakia cede the Sudetenland to Germany. Although the Czech government was willing to hang tough, British Prime Minister Neville Chamberlain granted almost all of Hitler's demands by the **Munich Agreement.** This left Czechoslovakia defenseless. Chamberlain returned to England a popular hero, announcing that he had achieved "peace in our time." When Hitler proceeded to swallow the rest of Czechoslovakia six months later, Chamberlain's **appeasement** strategy was definitely repudiated. Munich remains a potent (though not always valid) symbol of the dangers of not facing up to unpleasant realities.

1941

On December 7, Japan bombed the United States naval base at **Pearl Harbor.** The following day, the United States declared war on Japan and isolationism was virtually dead. The Japanese decision was brilliantly executed but fundamentally rash; they could never hope to defeat a fully mobilized America.

1945

World War II was followed by a new era termed the **cold war**. The origins of the cold war are still controversial. Some historians blame President Truman for hostility towards Soviet Russia and Stalin; others blame him for being too yielding. The argument really goes back at least to the **Yalta Conference** in February 1945, where President Franklin Roosevelt and Stalin made major concessions. FDR wanted Stalin to make war on Japan as soon as Germany was defeated. Stalin agreed because Britain and the United States offered part of Sakhalin (originally taken from Russia by Japan in 1905). In addition, Outer Mongolia would stay within the Soviet orbit. Actually, the Yalta terms ultimately restricted Stalin: by August 1945, the Red Army had advanced far into Manchuria and could have claimed chunks of distant China and Korea. In fact, Stalin kept his word on this; the Red Army evacuated Manchuria.

What did the West "concede" to Stalin in Europe? At the time of Yalta, the Russians were already occupying Poland and were sweeping across Central Europe. Stalin wanted Poland as a safe satellite or buffer against Germany and the West. Churchill and FDR did all they could short of force. They exacted a pledge that Stalin would allow the Poles to hold "free elections." However, elections never materialized.

The Senate ratified the **United Nations** charter with only two nay votes in July 1945. FDR had prepared the way by bipartisan consultation weeks before his death, not wishing to repeat Woodrow Wilson's mistakes in establishing the League of Nations. The main problem at San Francisco in June had been the Soviet Union's acceptance. Stalin and his allies were outnumbered in voting power, so he insisted on veto rights for the great powers in the Security Council (as did the United States). After Truman intervened personally, a compromise was hammered out. Over the years, the Security Council performed poorly, with many Soviet vetoes and much big-power rivalry. The important work of the U.N. was performed by its various scientific and humanitarian subagencies, such as UNESCO (social and cultural contacts), WHO (world health), UNICEF (children), and the International Court of Justice.

1946

Soviet scientists raced to perfect their own atomic bomb. The United States did not, in fact, practice atomic blackmail at this time; the remarkable Baruch Plan of June 1946 offered international sharing and control of atomic knowledge. Stalin was suspicious that the control body, like the U.N., would be dominated by the United States and its allies. Mutual suspicions bred an atomic arms race. Baruch is said to have coined the phrase *cold war* at this time. Its companion phase, the **Iron Curtain**, was coined by Baruch's close friend, Winston Churchill, in a speech at Fulton, Missouri. The so-called Iron Curtain grew by degrees. Communist political systems were established first in Poland and Rumania. Finland kept control of its own domestic policy, but was forced to do nothing to offend the Soviet Union in foreign policy. In Yugoslavia, Tito created a communist regime in 1945–46, though he split with Stalin in 1948. Communism was triumphant in Bulgaria in 1946, Hungary in 1947. Czechoslovakia was secured for communism by a coup in 1948. The Soviet zone of East Berlin was of course rigidly communist.

1947

The policy of **containment** arose in 1947 and dominated U.S. foreign policy down to the 1970s. Containment came into existence in response to unstable conditions in the Eastern Mediterranean. By 1947 the British hold in Greece and Palestine was weak. Britain was financially unstable, having lost her world trading position during the war. She could no longer afford to keep forces in the Near East. In 1947, a year of grave financial crisis at home, and England announced her withdrawal from Greece and Palestine. The United States stepped into the power vacuum. President Truman asked Congress for aid to Greece and Turkey on the grounds that "We shall not realize our objectives unless we are willing to help free peoples to maintain their free institutions and their national integrity against aggressive movements that seek to impose on them totalitarian regimes." The **Truman Doctrine** marked the first official acceptance of the containment philosophy.

President Truman persuaded Congress to pass a plan for massive economic aid to rebuild Europe, the **Marshall Plan.** Critics have said the plan was designed to assure U.S. domination of the Western economies. But more powerful motivations were at work: to save Europe from crippling economic ills and possible starvation. World War II had arisen out of such conditions following the first world conflict. (The plan was named after Truman's secretary of state, George C. Marshall, who had announced it in a public speech.)

1948

Inherent in the Truman Doctrine (1947) was the idea of a Western military alliance. Churchill's "Iron Curtain" (1946) hinted at it; the Marshall Plan (1947), though economic, looked toward a future Western European Union, which America strongly favored. A European military alliance, without the United States, was signed at Brussels in 1948 by Britain, France, Belgium, Luxembourg, and the Netherlands. A government for West Germany, the Federal Republic, was organized in 1948 after East-West negotiations on a German peace treaty broke down. Russian fears of a revived Germany, possibly armed by the West, were fully aroused. For these and whatever other motives, Stalin ordered the **West Berlin blockade** on April 1, 1948. All roads leading to the city were cut off at the East German and East Berlin borders. The aim was unclear—probably to squeeze the Allies out of West Berlin altogether and strengthen the Soviet hold on East Germany.

The U.S. and British air forces began a complex airlift to keep West Berlin alive. By September 1948 they were airlifting 4,000 tons of supplies a day. Between June 1948 and May 1949, when the highways were reopened, they shipped 3 million tons in 300,000 flights. Stalin's experiment in confrontation had failed; the president had managed the crisis without war. For Truman the blockade was another proof of the need to be "tough" (within reasoned limits) to the Russians; "appeasement," the alleged lesson of Munich (1938), never pays.

Out of the airlift came the formation of a new, military alliance including the United States—the **North Atlantic Treaty Organization.** Senate ratification of the treaty was organized by a bipartisan group especially briefed by President Truman. NATO was the logical military accompaniment to the Marshall Plan (1947). It assured Western Europe's defense against possible Soviet aggression. It also gave the United States added security. The long-term outcome of the cold war was that Europe was now two hostile camps; and each had an extra-European power as protector.

1949

Mao Tse-tung drove Chiang Kai-chek off the Chinese mainland onto the island of Formosa and established the **People's Republic of China** in September 1949. The United States, of course, did not recognize Red China and insisted on the Nationalist Chinese being represented in the U.N. This situation lasted until 1971 when President Nixon's visit to China was announced. In January 1950 a State Department paper blamed Chiang for his own defeat. Meanwhile, the Soviet Union developed its own atom bomb in 1949.

1950

In the predawn light of June 25, 1950, seven infantry divisions, support units, and an armored brigade crossed from North into South Korea over the 38th parallel and began the Korean War. Truman took action within hours. A special session of the U.N. Security Council, with the Russians being absent, voted 9 to 0 to condemn communist North Korean aggression. Seoul, South Korea's capital, fell within three days. On June 27 the council asked U.N. member nations to take military action to defend South Korea. The Russians were still boycotting meetings. America was at war again. Because it was fought without employing all major weapons (e.g., nuclear) and for objectives other than the complete defeat of the enemy (e.g., return to status quo), the **Korean conflict** was a **limited war**. Others would follow.

1954

In practice, the foreign policy of President Eisenhower and his secretary of state, John Foster Dulles, did not differ markedly from Truman's. Tough policy declarations were part of Dulles' idea of the power politics game of **brinkmanship**—to push your rival to the very "brink" of war to test his resolution and reactions. **Massive retaliation** was an economic policy as well as a possible military strategy. By concentrating resources on nuclear weapons systems, Dulles, Eisenhower, and Defense Secretary Charles Wilson hoped to cut the defense budget and save on the high costs of conventional warfare, with its large numbers of men and items of equipment.

1961

Despite events in the rest of the world, revolutionary sentiment in Latin America remained low. The one exception, which had momentous consequence, was Cuba. Many Cubans viewed the United States as the real power behind the dictator Batista, who came to power in 1952. Although the U.S. government disapproved of Batista and cut off aid to him in 1957, Fidel Castro had begun a guerrilla campaign against Batista. In 1959, Castro became prime minister of revolutionary Cuba. He described his regime as "humanistic" and not communist.

But Castro did not receive U.S. economic aid. Gradually, he moved towards Marxist solutions for Cuba's grave economic and social problems. Partly influenced by the Argentine radical Che Guevara, Castro began a sweeping reform program. U.S. firms were expropriated with little pretense at genuine compensation. Relations with the United States deteriorated throughout 1959 while Castro wooed Russia. In one of his last presidential actions, Eisenhower broke diplomatic relations with Castro. A CIA-aided counterrevolutionary invasion of Cuba was being planned. The invasion in April at the **Bay of Pigs** was a disaster. It was inadequately supported from the air, and based incorrectly on the wishful notion that the Cuban people were ready to rise up en masse against Fidel Castro.

1962

Khrushchev installed intermediate and long-range missiles on Cuba. They were targeted at U.S. cities and located only 90 miles from the U.S. shore. The **Cuban missile crisis** was a dangerous game of brinkmanship, though the United States also had sites in Italy and Turkey, close to the Soviet border. Soviet sites in Cuba were first photographed by high-flying U-2 spy planes on October 14. For Kennedy, the installations were a direct provocation to U.S. leadership in the Americas since the USSR had not placed missiles in foreign nations before. For six terrifying days the world hung on the brink of war. The president resisted military pressure for invasion of Cuba or immediate bombing of the missile sites; rather he settled for a naval blockade of Cuba, calling it a "quarantine." (A blockade is an act of war.) Khrushchev eventually agreed to remove the Soviet missiles from Cuba; Kennedy promised that the United States would not reinvade the island. A face-saving solution was found for both sides.

1963–1969

The day after the Bay of Pigs fiasco, Kennedy had asked for a report on Vietnam and the state of the Diem government. Diem had little support among the peasants of South Vietnam; his large force of 250,000 troops seemed incapable of putting down a mere 15,000 communists in the winter of 1961. The Diem government began to falter in 1963. Diem's wholesale persecution of Buddhists, his favoritism towards Catholics, and his refusal to apply internal reforms, gravely weakened his control at a time of advances by the Viet Cong, the communist rebels. On November 1, 1963, a coup by generals led to the murder of Diem. (This was an event of which Kennedy apparently had prior knowledge and in which apparently there was CIA involvement.)

When Lyndon Johnson became president there were 6,000 Americans in Vietnam. Increasingly, Viet Cong and North Vietnamese attacked South Vietnam. LBJ promised in October 1964, "We are not about to send American boys nine or ten thousand miles away from home to do what Asian boys ought to be doing for themselves." That promise came to nought. Pentagon documents show that as early as September 1964, before the election, contingency plans existed to bomb parts of North Vietnam in the new year. For almost three months LBJ held back. Then, after Viet Cong successes, he unleashed the "Rolling Thunder" bombing campaign that began on February 13, 1965.

Authority for escalation was claimed under the **Gulf of Tonkin Resolution** passed by Congress in 1964. This gave the White House power to "take all necessary measures to repel any armed attack against the forces of the United States and to prevent further aggression." The resolution was based on an alleged incident of August 2 in which two U.S. destroyers were said to have been fired on in international waters off North Vietnam. (It is now known that a Gulf of Tonkin type of resolution was prepared by a White House aide *before* the alleged incident took place.)

In South Vietnam a series of weak governments followed the murder of Diem—eight changes in 19 months. In June 1965 General Thieu became president, with Air Marshall Ky, the dapper, suave, bitter anticommunist as premier. U.S. air raids on North Vietnam were extended as far as Hanoi, the capital, and further north. U.S. soldiers escalated their involvement in June, beginning "search and destroy" mission. U.S. troop strengths mounted to 74,000. Organized demonstrations against U.S. involvement in the war began in October 1965 at home. The nation was becoming deeply divided over the **Vietnam War.**

At the peak of U.S. involvement, in 1968, there were half a million troops in Vietnam (536,000). U.S. casualties were mounting and more bombs were falling. The Joint Chiefs of Staff still demanded more and more troops and bombs. They wished to bomb Hanoi, the harbor of Haiphong, and other targets; they also wished to invade neighboring Laos and Cambodia and close North Vietnamese ports with air-laid mines. (Some of these actions President Nixon later carried out.)

In the communists' "Tet" (holiday) offensive of February 1968, Saigon itself was threatened. The 1968 Tet offensive was a military defeat for the Viet Cong; but it was perceived as a massive American defeat by newspapers and television. What is remarkable is that the people who were in the best position to know better (Johnson's staff) also believed it to be a defeat.

In 1972, under President Nixon, the pullout from Vietnam began—after nine years and 50,000 American dead. Called "peace with honor," the terms were essentially those the communists had demanded in 1964. Some critics called the pullout the first U.S. military surrender in its 200-year history. But this is not

Despite the long years of guerrilla warfare, South Vietnam was ultimately conquered by an external force between December 1974 and April 1975. This was a totally conventional campaign: the North Vietnam Army (NVA) beat the Army of the Republic of Vietnam (ARVN). Notwithstanding all of the analyzing, the war in Vietnam came down to this: Would the North conquer the South, or would it not? The final events in early 1975 attested to the truth of three axioms: an army with ample military supplies (NVA) has a major advantage over an army that is ill supplied; an army on the defensive (ARVN) finds it extremely difficult to stage a deliberate retreat; and a nation with little experience at losing (USA) does not exit in a very orderly manner.

quite accurate. When South Vietnam fell to the forces from North Vietnam in 1975, U.S. combat forces had been out of the fighting for two years.

1969

President Richard Nixon and his chief strategist, Henry Kissinger, decided that the United States would follow the same policy in other parts of the world that it had in South Vietnam. That is, they would build up local forces to the point where they could assume responsibility for the defense of their own country and then supply them with necessary military aid.

The United States would thereby avoid direct limited war involvements. Thus the Truman Doctrine gave way to the **Nixon Doctrine**. This policy went hand in hand with another policy. It was called **detente** (from the French word for "loosening"). Detente was heralded as the beginning of a new era in the relations between the United States and the Soviet Union. In this new era, a "structure of peace" would be built; cooperation between the two superpowers would replace "confrontation." Negotiations would proceed to limit the proliferation of strategic nuclear weapons. Nixon and Kissinger believed that a combination of surrogate forces (i.e., the armed forces of regional allies rather than American forces) and positive economic and political incentives would restrain Soviet adventurism.

Negotiations between the Soviet Union and the United States—aimed at controlling strategic nuclear weapons systems—began in Helsinki in 1969. In this first series of **Strategic Arms Limitations Talks** (SALT), agreement was reached on limiting missile delivery systems for five years. There was no agreement, though, on the number of nuclear warheads in each missile. Agreement was also reached to limt the number of antiballistic missile (ABM) defense systems to two in each country. Negotiations to conclude SALT II agreements to set firm limits on major weapons' systems to avoid a runaway arms race were concluded by the Carter administration; they were not ratified by the Senate, though. (In Spring 1982, the Reagan administration planned to begin renegotiating the treaty, but with emphasis on reductions rather than limitations.)

1973

The Middle East War of 1973 produced for the first time, an Arab oil embargo against Western nations that supported Israel. This newfound unity, combined with a rise in world demand for oil, served to expand the membership of the **Organization of Petroleum Exporting Countries** (OPEC), an intergovernmental cartel, to limit oil supplies and maintain prices at agreed levels.

1979

Shah Mohammed Reza Pahlavi was driven out of Iran on January 16, as a prime minister appointed by him tried desperately to mediate the demands of several militant groups who were united in only one goal, to bring the Iranian monarchy to an end. The focal point of revolt was Ayatollah Khomeini. He was the leader of the Shiite Moslem sect who had been exiled from Iran by the Shah. The dramatic return of Ayatollah Khomeini to Teheran on February 1 brought down the short-lived government. It also opened the door to hundreds of brief trials and summary executions for civilians and military officials who had supported the Shah.

Khomeini appointed another moderate prime minister, Mehdi Barzagan. A new constitution was written. It had the effect of making the Shiite Moslem hierarchy both the religious and temporal leaders of the country. This proposition did not sit well with other Moslem sects that comprise the majority of Iran's population.

A situation of considerable concern for the United States became an outright crisis on November 4 when Iranian radicals surprised the U.S. embassy, occupied the grounds, and took American diplomats as hostages. The radicals demanded the return of the Shah for trial as the only condition for release. Not until January 1981 were the 52 hostages released.

People will argue for years about what the lessons of Iran are—just as they have over Vietnam. American support for the Shah was an example of the Nixon Doctrine (1969) in action. In the early 1970s the British were pulling out of the Persian Gulf; the Soviets were in Egypt; and Soviet influence was mounting in Iraq. A power vacuum was developing in the Middle East that some nation—preferably favorable to the United States—had to fill. Iran seemed of extraordinary strategic importance at that time. Indeed, in 1973, during the Middle East war, Iran was the only country that did not join the oil embargo, that continued to supply our friends with oil, and that did not permit overflights of Soviet airplanes.

Also in 1979, in a series of lightning strokes, troops of the Soviet Union occupied Afghanistan. The **Soviet Afghanistan invasion** shook the very foundation of President Carter's conception of the Soviet Union in general. No matter how this extraordinary move was interpreted, it was not compatible with the notion that the Soviet Union favored maintaining the status-quo. Even if the Russians were acting defensively to prevent the overthrow of a client state on their own border, the sending of Soviet—not Cuban or East German but Soviet—troops to a country outside the Warsaw Pact represented a new phase of Soviet foreign policy.

1981

After more than a year of turmoil, the government of Poland declared martial law and put an end to the only free trade union in the communist world, Solidarity. Because it feared that the democratic reform movement could grow and spread over the rest of Eastern Europe, the Soviet Union had put heavy pressure on Poland's Communist rulers to get tough.

NYT Pictures

Afghan rebels made available this document, which they say was the Soviet ID card of Private Yuri A. Borovik, a soldier killed in Afghanistan's Badakhshan province. In 1980, coffins for the Russian war dead were said to be arriving daily in Moscow, Odessa, and the cities of Central Asia. According to Western intelligence estimates, 3,000 to 5,000 Soviet soldiers may have been killed or wounded. But no one in the West knows for sure; the Soviet government released no casualty figures on its "limited military contingent" in Afghanistan. In a country that normally conceals news and airline crashes from its own people, this is not too surprising.

Although the Soviets did not intervene directly, they probably would have if they thought it necessary. Why? The countries of Eastern Europe are economically useful and, more important, form a land buffer against military attack. Throughout Russian history, European armies have invaded through Poland.

Despite the martial law, Poles are not likely to abandon their drive for greater economic and political reform—a trend which presents a major worry to Soviet rulers for the 1980s.

MAKING SENSE OF AMERICAN REACTION TO WORLD EVENTS

Policymakers interpret events such as those described in the last eight pages in various ways. From such events, they generalize about America's political connection. Rather than try to catalog every species of generalization, let me suggest creating a grid. Upon this grid, theoretically at least, every foreign policy decision maker could be placed (see Figure 14–1).

Morality and Pragmatism in American Foreign Policy

Everyone who has helped to shape American foreign policy has had to answer the question of how foreign policy should serve moral ends. In a dangerous and often hostile world, to what extent should the United States champion equality and freedom?

The question has by no means a single, unequivocal answer. Some point to Woodrow Wil-

FIGURE 14–1
The Foreign Policy Grid

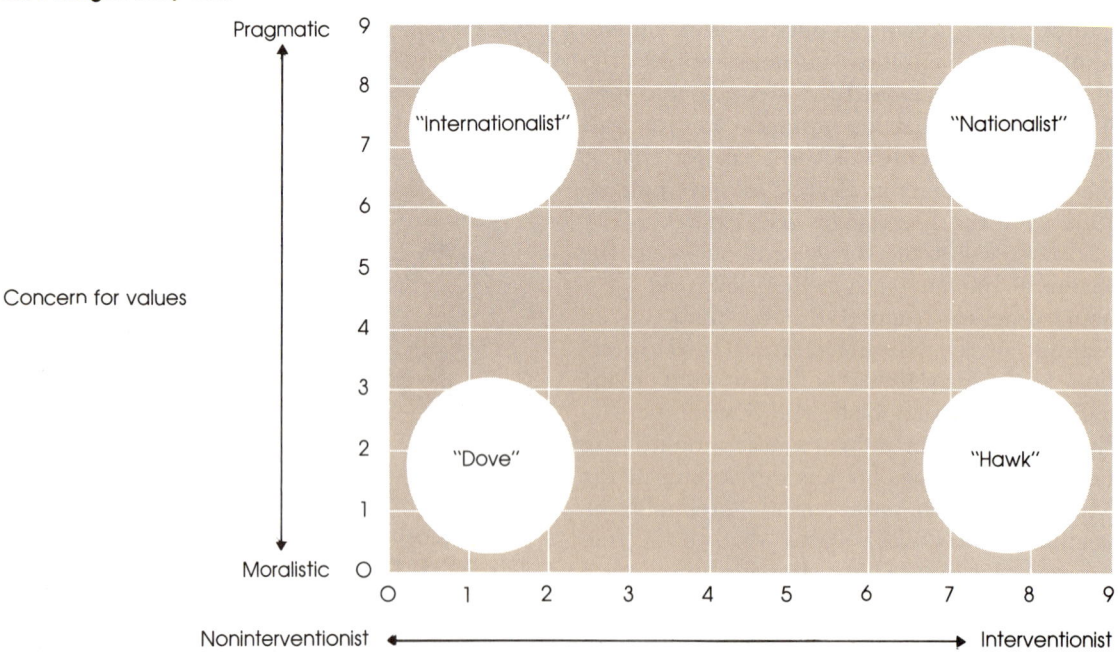

By using a graphic grid format, which has a horizontal axis indicating one's orientation towards the use of force and a vertical axis locating one's concern for values, decision makers in foreign affairs can be placed at one of the 81 available positions. Each position registers one's relative orientation towards value and force. Grid scores can be used as the point of departure for a discussion of various foreign policies. The four ideal types indicated on the grid are explained in the text.

son's call for "self-determination for all nations" and efforts to "make the world safe for democracy." With Wilson American foreign policy began to shift away from pragmatism towards morality. Before him, the prevailing attitude seemed to be that not all peoples—everywhere, at all times—could be expected to embody the ideals of Western constitutional democracy.

The tension between morality and pragmatism remains. To pursue the basic principles of human rights in foreign relations seems worthwhile and noble. But generally speaking, Americans are also a pragmatic people, common sensical, undogmatic, flexible; they want things to work. Therefore, most American foreign policy has attempted to pursue justice, freedom, equality, and progress within the context of survival and its practical necessities.

The results, to the purists, may not be entirely satisfactory. The United States sends arms to Pakistan, a nation where the legal code still permits the public flogging of criminals and where political opposition is outlawed. Richard Nixon, long-time anticommunist, opens the door to mainland China, once virulently anti-American. And all modern presidents negotiate with the Soviet Union, despite its mischief abroad and often brutal repression at home.

As a generalization, we can say that most shapers of American foreign policy have avoided both extreme moralism and extreme realism. They have tried to integrate some concept of human rights into alliances, military and economic aid programs, cultural exchanges, and treaties. Realism in foreign policy is seldom pushed to its hard-headed limit. For example, while some policymakers may turn their heads when another country fails to provide adequate medical care for its citizens or to allow them the right to participate in self-government, certain forms of human rights violations are not likely to be ignored. Among these I would include torture of political opponents, prohibition of emigration, violation of religious freedom, and persecution of certain racial groups. I want to emphasize that American policymakers have not always spoken out against these human rights violations. But when they do, American foreign policy seems most consistent with the ideas of the founding fathers.

Intervention and Nonintervention in American Foreign Policy

There is another dimension to foreign policy. It concerns the particular instruments of force and the readiness to use them.

American policymakers have held different views about the use of force in world politics. Some follow the historical "City on the Hill" ideal: America's chief mission is not to change the world through direct means; it is to concentrate on creating the best kind of society here at home and thereby serve as an example. The spirit was very much at the core of George McGovern's unsuccessful 1972 presidential campaign. "Come home, America" was one of his campaign's major themes.

Another kind of spirit also rejects meddling in the affairs of other countries. But it does want to make the world safe for democracy by trying to create a hospitable environment. This spirit was found in such presidents as Woodrow Wilson and Jimmy Carter.

An entirely different spirit from the first two was suggested by the ancient Greek biographer Plutarch. It occurs in his harsh description of the citizens of Syracuse. "They had forgotten they were able to make things happen around them rather than always wait for things to happen to them." In the context of foreign policy, the message is clear: The art of foreign policy is to prevent situations from occurring in which adversaries like the Soviet Union and allies like Israel continue to act without fear of American sanctions.

Policymakers sharing this spirit will *not* reject the use of the various instruments of direct action in their pursuit of foreign policy objectives. Some will, however, require clearer indications than others that intervention is (a) appropriate and (b) workable.

What are the various instruments short of

a nuclear strike? In descending order of seriousness, they are:

1. Commitment of American troops and demand for unconditional surrender of enemy.
2. Limited war.
3. Sending unconventional forces, such as advisers, marines, or paratroopers.
4. Using proxies (the Nixon Doctrine).*
5. Covert operations such as by CIA.
6. Economic sanctions.
7. Verbal condemnation (Now we are on the left-hand side of the horizontal scale in Figure 14–1).

A Few Examples

Now let us see how the grid works by considering a few examples. Figure 14–1 suggests four general approaches to foreign policy. For convenience, I have named these as follows:

Dove—moralistic, noninterventionist

Hawk—moralistic, interventionist

Internationalist—pragmatic, noninterventionist

Nationalist—pragmatic, interventionist

Thus, **doves** and **hawks** have at least one thing in common: purity of motives. Both speak in emotional slogans. The doves call for abstinence from world affairs. In the 1920s they did so because they thought the United States was too good for it. In the 1960s they did so because they thought the United States was violating the right of self-determination of developing nations (that is, it was trying to determine what kind of government these countries could and could not have). Similarly, the hawks call for crusades and excessive commitments. They reject any attempt to relate ends to means and commitments to capacities. Their attitude can be summarized as "We won't stand for it." Indeed, one reason the Vietnam debate of the late 1960s and early 1970s grew so bitter was that both supporters and critics of involvement viewed the war purely in moral terms.

What makes the nationalists and internationalists different from the hawks and doves is that nationalists and internationalists attempt to adjust to the world as it really is. The internationalists may be thought of as the dove position leavened by some theory of international politics and rational calculation of how American action affects the future.

For instance, internationalists might observe restraint in responding to a Soviet ploy. But this action is not because intervention is immoral. It is because they envisage the building of a new international order that would, in the end, make Soviet cooperation inevitable and question the effectiveness of force in the modern world. Furthermore, the internationalist would argue that constant response to Soviet mischief would jeopardize the creation of strong ties in the Third World. In short, the idea is to accommodate and direct forces of change rather than to see each change in the status quo as a setback for the United States.

The nationalist may be thought of as the hawk position leavened by a rational calculation of **national interest.** Unlike the hawk, the nationalist draws a line between areas of vital interest and areas of peripheral interest. Again, Vietnam provides a good example. Hans J. Morgenthau, Walter Lippmann, and other distinguished observers of American foreign policy found nothing morally wrong with using force of arms to save South Vietnam from communism. However, they did question whether vital U.S. interests were at stake in Southeast Asia. Their conclusion: The stakes were not high enough to justify the costs and risks.

Central to this pragmatic way of thinking is the assumption that political equilibrium in a group of states may be maintained if power is distributed among them so that no state or combination of states may gain ascendency over

---

* Proxies are persons who act for another. The United States used Iran during the Shah's reign. Today the Soviet Union uses Cuban and East German troops in Africa.

"We will wipe them out! The nation voted for the Islamic republic and everyone should obey. If you do not obey, you will be annihilated." So said the Ayatollah Khomeini in September 1979 about his opponents. The case that Iran is better off under Khomeini than the Shah is not persuasive. In purely economic terms, the answer must be no. In political terms, however, the answer is more problematic. While the Shah's Iran was no Middle Eastern Camelot, there were some freedoms. In the new Islamic republic, there are none for groups like the Kurdish prisoners above. According to Amnesty International, by October 1981, 3,350 people had been put to death since Khomeini came to power in February 1979. And, in June 1981, the nation's first and only popularly elected president, Abolhassan Bani-Sadr, was dismissed and went into hiding as mobs called for his death.

the rest. Nationalists say this **balance-of-power** theory of international politics provides a realistic view of the world. International society is made up of many nations harboring antagonism toward one another. The Soviet Union may have temporary successes in the Middle East or Africa; but this must be objectively weighed against less firm support from Eastern European allies and very badly deteriorated relations with China.

REGIONAL SURVEY

A long time ago many a schoolchild solved the mystery of spelling the word *geography* with this sentence: George Eliot's old grandson rode a pig home yesterday. Apparently some of America's strategic thinkers need to go back to school for some lessons of their own, starting at just about that level. Or, at least, so one might judge from what is being said about defense problems in Africa, the Persian Gulf, Korea, Eastern Europe, and just about everywhere. Therefore, to round out our discussion of the political connection in foreign policy, we also need a quick global tour.

Two countries, Canada and Great Britain, need little introduction. They are not only our closest allies but the bonds of a shared heritage, a common language, and with one, the longest unguarded border on the globe, make the Canadian–British–American relationship unique. Yet there are many problems. Economic independence from the United States, the French separatist movement in Quebec, and national energy disputes between East and West are very significant issues for Canada. Britain has immense economic and organizational difficulties, a separatist movement in Scotland, terrible violence in Northern Ireland, and increasing problems with immigration and racial discrimination. These problems cannot be lightly dismissed. But they are ones that Americans understand very well and share to a great extent. After all, we have serious economic difficulties, major problems with racial discrimination and immigration, a separatist movement in Puerto Rico (and some say Texas), and sharp interregional rivalries. But the political institutions for the United States, Britain, and Canada are strong enough to ensure that the debate is on policy issues and appropriate actions, not establishing new forms of government or new states. It is the other areas on the globe where we should focus our regional survey.

Latin America

A good starting point might be the closest neighbor of the United States, Latin America. Generalizations about large regions are usually hazardous. But it does seem possible to recognize four common themes that run through Latin America.

CUBA–The crucial question underlying Cuba's release of thousands of political prisoners in 1980 was whether Castro's revolution had finally run aground. His record of failure is apparent also in Cuba's humiliating dependence on $3 billion in annual Soviet aid and in the plague of shortages in a mismanaged single-crop economy. Cuba has made little progress in its campaign to win full diplomatic recognition from the United States. Cuban troop and military aid involvements as Soviet surrogates in Africa, and now in Central America, are of grave importance to the United States.

EL SALVADOR–Incidents staged by three active guerrilla groups keep the country in turmoil as a condition of civil war exists. There are still other troubled nations in Central America. In Guatemala there is continuous open warfare between leftist guerrillas and rightist vigilantes who claim they are protecting the country in the absence of any strong action by President Romeo Lucas Garcia. In Honduras, the poorest nation in Central America, the military rulers have reacted to criticism of their support for the now-departed Somoza regime in Nicaragua by severe action against labor and peasant organizations.

JAMAICA–In 1980, Jamaican citizens voted overwhelmingly for Edward Seaga for prime minister. Seaga promised to resurrect free enterprise. The defeat of incumbent Michael Manley and his "democratic socialism" was a major strategic blow to Castro. Castro had closely advised Manley and was making small but steady inroads into the politically vulnerable Caribbean.

MEXICO–One of the most sensitive issues is U.S. treatment of the thousands of Mexican nationals who enter the United States illegally each year in search of employment. (Reports are that there are as many as 12 million illegal aliens in the United States.)

Another major issue is U.S. access to the substantial oil and gas reserves being developed in Mexico. The Mexican government, however, has not rushed to develop its production capacity. It has also taken a cool position toward committing a substantial portion of its production to the United States. Three key questions for the 1980s:

Will Mexico, now potentially one of the world's largest oil producers, join OPEC?

Will the newfound wealth cause instability among Mexico's 60 million population, as it has in Iran?

If the United States is to rely on Mexican oil, what political demands may Mexico make in return?

VENEZUELA–A significant creation of the 1960s, Venezuelan democracy has about it some elements of plutocracy. Overall, though, it has been a great achievement for Latin America. Its "heavy" oil deposits equal the world's known conventional deposits.

NICARAGUA–In 1979, the regime of President Anastasio Somoza was toppled by an old coalition of left-leaning guerrillas and disgruntled businessmen. Somoza showed excesses in denying human rights and in turning major portions of the nation's economy to his personal benefit. This left him with little popular support. Once Somoza left the country and resigned as president, however, the United States offered its assistance to the new regime. So far, it seems to be resisting the efforts of its more radical elements to turn Nicaragua into a left-leaning state.

BRAZIL–Its military president, General Figueiredo (fifth in a line that began in 1964), has promised eventual democracy and free expression for the nation. Brazil's battle against impoverishment through oil costs and general inflation continues. Economic and population pressures grow worse and strikes are chronic. Testing of a nuclear device and development of a space program are imminent.

CHILE–Since the downfall of Marxist president Salvador Allende in 1973, the tide of international criticism has risen. Chile's economy, though, was relatively stable, thanks to free-market policies. Defenders of Chile point out that the U.N. Human Rights Commission says the country's human rights record has improved. Also, the government of General Pinochet is respected by a majority of Chileans, primarily because it brought order after the chaos of the Allende regime.

ARGENTINA–Military rule over the country since 1976 has been a hard one. The government has a very poor human rights record. The regime has effectively slowed the rate of inflation.

URUGUAY–The military regime here is considered the toughest in all of Latin America. Uruguay's badly intimidated newspapers are beginning to print mild criticism of the government. Public assemblies of more than five people–even to attend a soccer game–are banned unless police permission is given in advance. The military regime has accomplished substantial progress in economic areas, however. There is relatively full employment and the economy has achieved a substantial growth rate.

The first is Latin America's Western orientation; it shares the same cultural roots as the United States. This historical reality implies that the United States might develop more of a special relationship with Latin America— not unlike the one America has had with Europe for centuries. The second theme is a commitment to radical economic growth—many leaders expect their countries' GNPs to rise in the 1980s at a rate two or three times that of the industrialized nations. This means that the critical diplomatic issues will be trade, technology, and investment. A third theme is the commitment—except for Cuba—to private enterprise.

The fourth theme is less encouraging. It involves the continuing anti-U.S. feelings of Latin American intellectuals and exportation of revolution by Cuba. The Reagan administration is convinced that Castro is sending arms to leftist guerrillas in Central America. In Nicaragua, for example, an increasingly authoritarian Sandinista regime is building the strongest army in the area. Thus far, however, the administration has been largely unsuccessful in getting other Latin American countries to resist this trend. Given these circumstances, U.S. alternatives appear limited.

Europe

During the early 1980s, the ten nations of the European Economic Community continued to share broad aims with the United States. But they became more equal partners in the Western alliance. Combined, they surpassed the United States in gross national product.

But they continue to look to Washington for leadership. Some 300,000 U.S. troops remain stationed in Europe as part of the Atlantic defense alliance to deter Soviet aggression. Yet leadership does not mean dominance, as the Reagan administration quickly learned.

President Reagan had begun his term by denouncing the Soviets as "liars" and "cheats," with whom the United States could not decently do business. But this belligerent attitude stirred protests in Western Europe. European allies began to insist that they could go through with the planned modernization of nuclear arms only if the United States agreed to talk to the Soviets about an arms reduction. The Reagan administration was forced to comply.

While communist parties in Western Europe still fare badly in elections, two socialist leaders did emerge in the early 1980s. In Greece, premier Andreas Papandreou hinted that he may curtail his country's role in NATO's military activities. But in France, President Mitterrand was the first in Europe to accuse the Soviets of "interfering" in Poland and to call the martial law "repression." Mitterrand's position was much closer to Reagan's than any other European leader.

Middle East

Rumbles shake the countries of the Middle East every day and underscore U.S. dependency on oil from the region. Accordingly, developing a Mideast policy and figuring a way to project U.S. power into the region is an urgent priority for the 1980s.

The crisis in Iran (1979), civil war in Lebanon, and assassination of Egyptian president Anwar Sadat and election of Hosni Mubarak are only some examples of the chaos sweeping over the Moslem world. These events threaten the stability of allies and set the stage for more Russian initiatives in the region. The lack of progress on the Palestinian issue is perhaps the most disruptive force.

What is the Palestinian issue? After World War II, the victorious Western powers created the state of Israel as a homeland for the Jews surviving persecution. But to create that historic homeland, millions of Palestinians were displaced from *their* homeland. Today, Palestinians live in camps near Israeli borders. They have established dozens of organizations committed to the destruction of Israel. The Palestinian Liberation Organization (PLO) is the best known of these. Thus far, Egypt and Israel have been unable to negotiate self-rule for the more than 1 million Arabs living on the West Bank land taken from Jordan by Israel. Without progress on this issue, moderate Arabs like Jordan's King Hussein, the Saudis, and other conservative Arabs will grow impatient.

NORTHERN IRELAND—There seems to be no end to terrorism by the Irish Republican Army in its drive to unify Ulster with Ireland. About 13,000 British troops remain in the region, which for 10 years has been torn by strife at a cost of more than 1,900 lives.

POLAND—This is he most self-assertive of the nations under Soviet domination. As one of the most ardently Catholic nations in Europe, Poland experienced profound inspirataion from the visit of the first Polish Pope, John Paul II. In 1980, thousands of Polish workers demanded and obtained formal recognition of their right to bargain with government.

RUMANIA—Under President Ceaucescu, this nation defies Soviet domination with U.S. encouragement.

ITALY—Writer Luigi Barzini describes his country as "a glorious, gilded galleon with holes in the hull that sits in the mud. It can't go anywhere, but then again it can't sink either." Like many other observers of the Italian political scene, Barzini is convinced that the country will not be able to sail out of the political mud unless a strong party-probably socialist but not communist-can rally a true majority in parliament. Without that kind of consensus, they say, Italy will continue to wander from one political extreme to another. That extremism is typified by the kidnapping and murder of former premier Aldo Moro in 1978. Despite the political uncertainty, Italian industry is relatively strong; the Italian armed forces form the keystone of the defense of NATO's southern flank.

FRANCE—The role the French armed forces are willing to assume in any future attack against NATO remains as much an enigma as it has been since the late President Charles DeGaulle stripped them out of the NATO order of battle.

WEST GERMANY—The year 1979 marked the 30th year of the Federal Republic of Germany. It has been perhaps the most prosperous and dignified period in Germany's history. But problems remain. A small but highly vocal neo-Nazi movement, a radical left, 2 million imported laborers, and high labor costs all exist. The concept of reunification with Communist East Germany may seem unrealistic. But it remains a distant but still pursued goal.

TURKEY—Turkey's 1974 invasion of the Island of Cyprus strained relations with the United States. It also caused the withdrawal of Greek forces from active participation in NATO. (Cyprus contains Greek ethnic areas.) Turkey is an important base for monitoring Soviet compliance with arms control treaties. In 1980, amidst political and religious violence, the military took over the government.

SPAIN—Premier Adolfo Suarez steadfastly maintains that his long-term goal is for Spain to become a member of NATO. Yet his government was a participant in the conference of "nonaligned" nations held in Havana in 1979. The nation has turned increasingly to democratic rule since the death of Francisco Franco in 1975. However, the centuries-old feud between Spanish Basques and the rest of Spain continues. The Basque drive for regional autonomy has been carried out in an atmosphere of tension, marked by frequent acts of terrorism.

HUNGARY—The communist leader of Hungary, Janos Kadar, has been supervising what he calls a "new economic mechanism" since 1968. Hungary now trades more with the West than with all of its partners in the Soviet bloc. Over a million Westerners visited Hungary in 1978; 355,000 Hungarians journeyed to the West. U.S. relations with Hungary have improved to the point that Hungarian exporters have been granted "most favored nation" status for trading with the United States.

YUGOSLAVIA—In 1980, President Tito (see Chapter 4) died at the age of 88. The new leadership is committed to continuing his independent brand of communism and his policy of nonalignment and to maintain ties with the United States.

Quiz
Name them:

1.
2.
3.
4.
5. United Press International Photos

Answers on p. 535.

East and South Asia

Asia is beginning to come alive economically and militarily. Along the strip of coastal Asia, one can find the greatest economic successes of the Third World—Taiwan, South Korea, Hong Kong, and Singapore.

Of all Asia's unknowns, China remains the biggest. In mid-1979 China announced the findings of its 1977 census. It showed a population of almost 950 million. This is almost a fourth of the world's total population, 3.7 times as many people as in the Soviet Union and more than four times the population of the United States. The bulk of the Chinese population is still committed to the production of food; there is very little opportunity for upward mobility. Nevertheless, its desire to achieve industrial growth is reflected in a recent law that, for the first time, permits foreign companies to enter into joint ventures with Chinese partners. This law even allows foreigners to take the profit from the ventures out of the country in hard cash rather than in trade goods or credits.

American-Chinese relations illustrate well how presidents sacrifice ideology to pragmatism (a point made in our discussion of the foreign

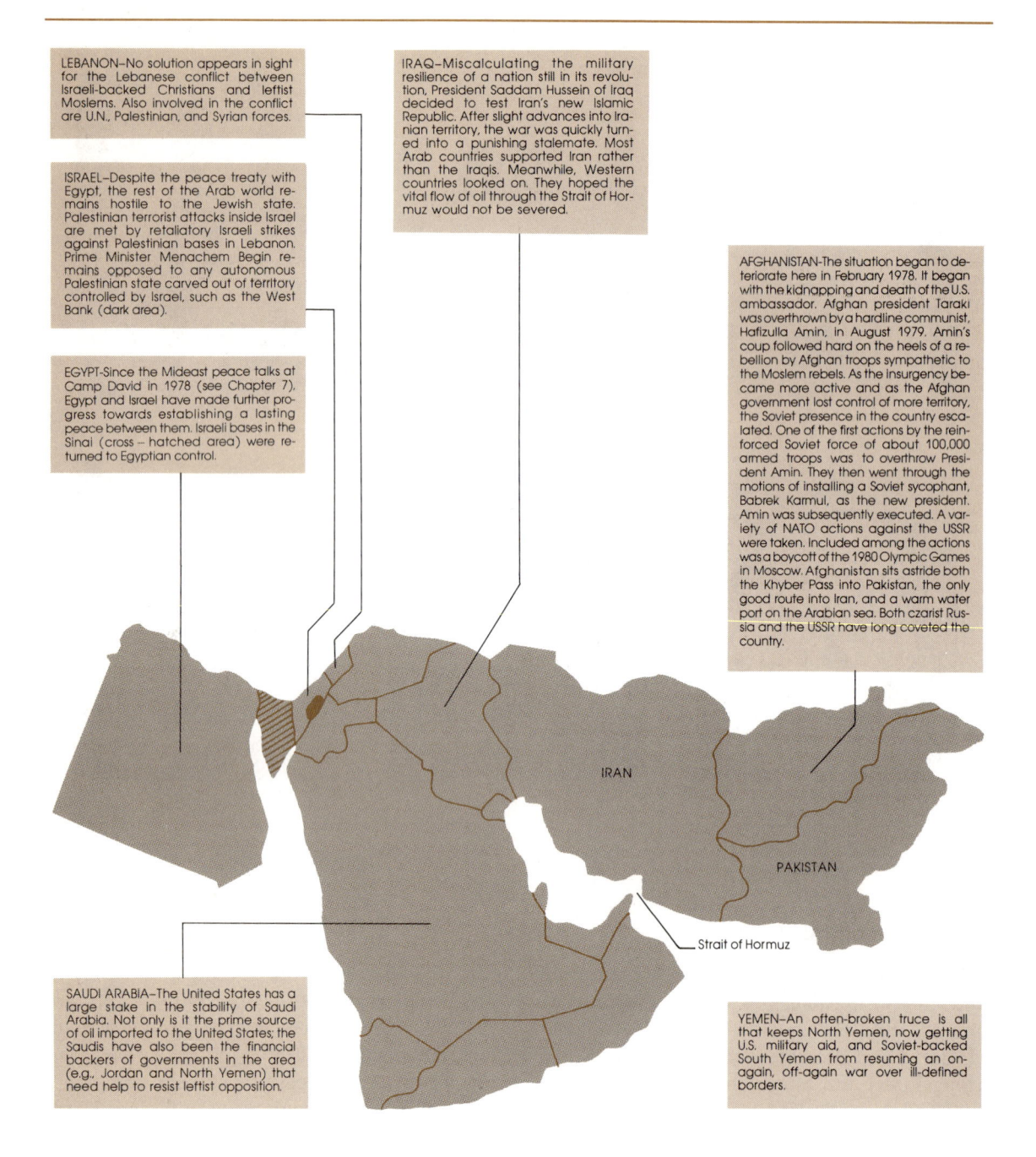

LEBANON–No solution appears in sight for the Lebanese conflict between Israeli-backed Christians and leftist Moslems. Also involved in the conflict are U.N., Palestinian, and Syrian forces.

IRAQ–Miscalculating the military resilience of a nation still in its revolution, President Saddam Hussein of Iraq decided to test Iran's new Islamic Republic. After slight advances into Iranian territory, the war was quickly turned into a punishing stalemate. Most Arab countries supported Iran rather than the Iraqis. Meanwhile, Western countries looked on. They hoped the vital flow of oil through the Strait of Hormuz would not be severed.

ISRAEL–Despite the peace treaty with Egypt, the rest of the Arab world remains hostile to the Jewish state. Palestinian terrorist attacks inside Israel are met by retaliatory Israeli strikes against Palestinian bases in Lebanon. Prime Minister Menachem Begin remains opposed to any autonomous Palestinian state carved out of territory controlled by Israel, such as the West Bank (dark area).

AFGHANISTAN–The situation began to deteriorate here in February 1978. It began with the kidnapping and death of the U.S. ambassador. Afghan president Taraki was overthrown by a hardline communist, Hafizulla Amin, in August 1979. Amin's coup followed hard on the heels of a rebellion by Afghan troops sympathetic to the Moslem rebels. As the insurgency became more active and as the Afghan government lost control of more territory, the Soviet presence in the country escalated. One of the first actions by the reinforced Soviet force of about 100,000 armed troops was to overthrow President Amin. They then went through the motions of installing a Soviet sycophant, Babrek Karmul, as the new president. Amin was subsequently executed. A variety of NATO actions against the USSR were taken. Included among the actions was a boycott of the 1980 Olympic Games in Moscow. Afghanistan sits astride both the Khyber Pass into Pakistan, the only good route into Iran, and a warm water port on the Arabian sea. Both czarist Russia and the USSR have long coveted the country.

EGYPT–Since the Mideast peace talks at Camp David in 1978 (see Chapter 7), Egypt and Israel have made further progress towards establishing a lasting peace between them. Israeli bases in the Sinai (cross – hatched area) were returned to Egyptian control.

IRAN

PAKISTAN

Strait of Hormuz

SAUDI ARABIA–The United States has a large stake in the stability of Saudi Arabia. Not only is it the prime source of oil imported to the United States; the Saudis have also been the financial backers of governments in the area (e.g., Jordan and North Yemen) that need help to resist leftist opposition.

YEMEN–An often-broken truce is all that keeps North Yemen, now getting U.S. military aid, and Soviet-backed South Yemen from resuming an on-again, off-again war over ill-defined borders.

Will Japan be stronger in the 1980s? (Above: cadets at Japanese military academy)

policy grid). When Reagan became president, he wanted to improve diplomatic and military ties with Taiwan. But mainland China considers Taiwan really a part of their country. To give Taiwan the military aid it wants would jeopardize relations with Peking. For compelling strategic reasons (e.g., China keeps about 50 Soviet divisions tied down on its western border), Reagan decided to let relations with China take precedence over better links with Taiwan.

Africa

Not until the end of the Ford administration did the events in Africa seem very immediate to the concerns of U.S. foreign policy. What had happened? First was the intervention of Cubans to decide the outcome of civil war in Angola. Second was the awakening of American policymakers to the ominous drift towards racial war in South Africa. The Carter administration assigned an unprecedented priority to African problems.

For that reason, President Carter never really faced in Africa the problem President Reagan does. Throughout the continent, rightly or wrongly, black Africans perceive Reagan as a hard-nosed conservative more interested in the Soviet Union and NATO than African issues (e.g., economic development, trade, hunger, refugees, and South Africa).

The issue of what exactly the strategic significance of Africa is for U.S. national interests has never really been resolved. Is the continent to be a new battleground for the Cold War? Are the new nations there unique and essentially independent of Soviet-American ambitions? Is the continent a place where the United States should demonstrate dramatically its commitment to human rights or exercise power politics? Given the complexity of the continent, clear-cut answers do not flow easily.

As the map underscores, the difficulties Africa presents to American foreign policy makers are many and challenging. Still, a few common themes are discernable: personal rule rather than constitutional rule; weak civil service and governmental corruption; conflict between tribes; arbitrary national boundaries (drawn back in the colonial era); and a tendency to call on outside assistance to resolve problems government leaders cannot or will not resolve. There are, of course, encouraging exceptions to all these themes. Several are noted on the map.

THE STRATEGIC CONNECTION

Defense, or national security, is another aspect of global interdependence. It is closely linked to the political connection; indeed, it is highly artificial for policymakers to try to separate the two. To speak of a problem as "purely military" or "purely political" is inaccurate, if not foolish.

National security is also an exceedingly complex subject. This is partly a function of the technical issues surrounding defense policy; it is also partly a function of the acronyms and abbreviations that defense experts are fond of using. For example, various cruise missiles are called "alcoms," "slickems," and "glickems"—for the ALCM (air-launched cruise missile), SLCM (sea-launched), and GLCM (ground-launched). MIRV and MARV, as we shall soon see, are not a team of comedians; they are systems for multiple warheads.

To cut through some of this complexity, it seems a good idea to pose four basic questions.

CHINA—Despite a successful test of an intercontinental ballistic missile in 1979, the overall strategic position of China is not good. Intelligence and academic experts think China faces the prospect of military encirclement by the Soviet Union. To the South, the Soviets have established a military presence on China's southern flank through the use of naval and air facilities in Vietnam. To the North, the Russians have strengthened their ground forces along the 4,000 mile frontier with China. These forces are estimated at 45 divisions (or 450,000 men). To the East is the Soviet Union's Pacific Fleet with eight missile cruisers and 75 submarines.

SOUTH KOREA—U.S. Pressure is needed to keep the military-civilian hierarchy on the road to democracy following the assassination in 1979 of President Park Chung Hee. Strains exist between the forces favoring rapid reform and those intent on maintaining an authoritarian regime. This strain could tear apart the nation, long a key anticommunist outpost.

JAPAN—Japan's relations with the United States in the 1970s centered more on the economic than on the military. Japanese prime ministers and American presidents continued to work toward a better balance of trade between the two countries. (U.S. imports of Japanese goods exceeded exports to Japan by $12 billion in 1978.)

Japan has been under U.S. pressure to spend more on its own defense. In 1980, a blue-ribbon panel recommended that they boost their military budget by $1.7 billion — about 20 percent. The panel said there had been a perceptible decline in U.S. military supremacy in the world and in the U.S. will to defend its allies. The comprehensive national security study group called Japan's self-defense force obsolete; it would be unable to defend the country "for one or two weeks . . . until the United States Army can come to Japan."

INDIA—The return to power of former prime minister Indira Gandhi could once again move India away from the United States, closer to Russia. But there is a bigger worry for the United States. Both India and Pakistan, bitter enemies in South Asia, appear to be on the verge of manufacturing atomic weapons, in defiance of American attempts to eliminate the danger of nuclear proliferation.

THAILAND—Tensions between Thailand and Cambodia have eased. But minor skirmishes still occur, and their border is closed. Within Thailand, an estimated 10,000 Communist guerrillas operate in mountain and border areas. The government is opposing them with social and economic programs for the region's population rather than by military force.

KAMPUCHEA (CAMBODIA)—The first communist government was installed on April 17, 1975. At that time, Cambodia had a population between 7 million and 9 million people. Today, according to U.S. Census Bureau estimates, the country has 4.8 million. Thus the Cambodian population declined by at least 30 percent over five years as the new government tried to "create a new society."

Vietnamese troops drove into Cambodia in 1978 and set up a new communist government. They are still fighting to eliminate remaining forces of the ousted Pol Pot regime. China is helping the defeated premier; Russia is backing Vietnam. Regardless of the outcome of the fighting, Cambodia remains a human tragedy of profound dimensions.

TAIWAN—After the trauma of normalization of relations between the United States and the People's Republic of China and the concurrent withdrawal of recognition of the Republic of China on Taiwan, trade between the United States and Taiwan has returned to normal; in fact, it hardly faltered. Apparently, the indirect assurances made to Taiwan that the United States would continue to look out for the interests of its former ally have been strong enough to sustain good commercial relations.

PHILIPPINES—Moslem guerrillas of the separatist Moro National Liberation Front continue to press their seven-year campaign in the southern Philippines. President Marcos's efforts to negotiate a peace have failed. Opponents to his martial-law regime are injecting more anti-Americanism into their campaign to restore parliamentary rule. The United States has large military bases located in the Philippines. Therefore America will have to be wary of the effects of potential civil upheaval.

14 / AMERICA IN AN INTERDEPENDENT WORLD

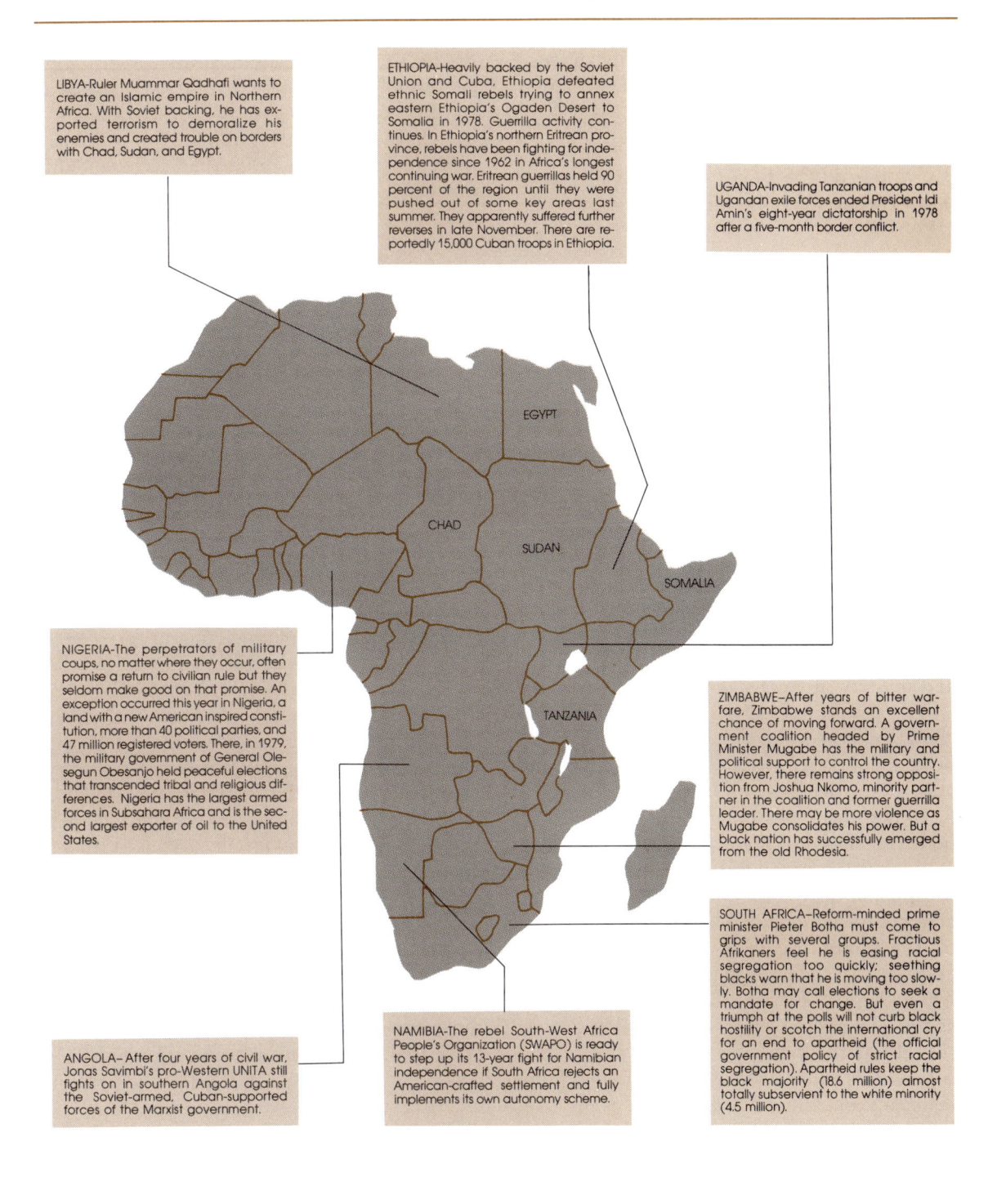

LIBYA—Ruler Muammar Qadhafi wants to create an Islamic empire in Northern Africa. With Soviet backing, he has exported terrorism to demoralize his enemies and created trouble on borders with Chad, Sudan, and Egypt.

ETHIOPIA—Heavily backed by the Soviet Union and Cuba, Ethiopia defeated ethnic Somali rebels trying to annex eastern Ethiopia's Ogaden Desert to Somalia in 1978. Guerrilla activity continues. In Ethiopia's northern Eritrean province, rebels have been fighting for independence since 1962 in Africa's longest continuing war. Eritrean guerrillas held 90 percent of the region until they were pushed out of some key areas last summer. They apparently suffered further reverses in late November. There are reportedly 15,000 Cuban troops in Ethiopia.

UGANDA—Invading Tanzanian troops and Ugandan exile forces ended President Idi Amin's eight-year dictatorship in 1978 after a five-month border conflict.

NIGERIA—The perpetrators of military coups, no matter where they occur, often promise a return to civilian rule but they seldom make good on that promise. An exception occurred this year in Nigeria, a land with a new American inspired constitution, more than 40 political parties, and 47 million registered voters. There, in 1979, the military government of General Olesegun Obesanjo held peaceful elections that transcended tribal and religious differences. Nigeria has the largest armed forces in Subsahara Africa and is the second largest exporter of oil to the United States.

ZIMBABWE—After years of bitter warfare, Zimbabwe stands an excellent chance of moving forward. A government coalition headed by Prime Minister Mugabe has the military and political support to control the country. However, there remains strong opposition from Joshua Nkomo, minority partner in the coalition and former guerrilla leader. There may be more violence as Mugabe consolidates his power. But a black nation has successfully emerged from the old Rhodesia.

SOUTH AFRICA—Reform-minded prime minister Pieter Botha must come to grips with several groups. Fractious Afrikaners feel he is easing racial segregation too quickly; seething blacks warn that he is moving too slowly. Botha may call elections to seek a mandate for change. But even a triumph at the polls will not curb black hostility or scotch the international cry for an end to apartheid (the official government policy of strict racial segregation). Apartheid rules keep the black majority (18.6 million) almost totally subservient to the white minority (4.5 million).

NAMIBIA—The rebel South-West Africa People's Organization (SWAPO) is ready to step up its 13-year fight for Namibian independence if South Africa rejects an American-crafted settlement and fully implements its own autonomy scheme.

ANGOLA—After four years of civil war, Jonas Savimbi's pro-Western UNITA still fights on in southern Angola against the Soviet-armed, Cuban-supported forces of the Marxist government.

Then we can indicate how experts of differing stripes would respond. These are the questions:

1. Who makes American foreign policy?
2. Who is number one?
3. What do the Soviet leaders really want?
4. How are wars prevented?

Who Makes American Foreign Policy?

The insiders. As you know from the historical surveys found at the beginning of Chapter 7, the president's role in formulating and executing foreign policy has continued to expand since Washington's administration. As more nations appeared on the map and the connections between them grew in complexity and scope, presidents found themselves spending larger and larger chunks of time on foreign affairs. Reports on events in foreign countries filter into the State Department daily from more than 250 U.S. foreign-service posts. One of the first things the president does each morning is receive a briefing on the latest diplomatic and military situations around the world.

The Constitutional basis of the president's central role in foreign policy has surfaced repeatedly in earlier chapters. But we may profitably review that basis.

Under the Constitution, the president is both the chief executive and the commander-in-chief of the armed forces. He has the power to appoint many key officials who help him conduct foreign policy. Through interpretation of the Constitution by the courts, he has emerged as the undisputed chief diplomat. Through force of circumstance, he has emerged as the only elected official in a position to view the global situation in a comprehensive and coherent manner. Moreover, with a huge bureaucracy and billions of dollars at his disposal, he has an overwhelming advantage in shaping the course of American foreign policy. Let us consider some of the bureaucracy that helps the president in the conduct of foreign policy.

The National Security Council was created during the Truman administration to bring together all the administrative heads involved in foreign policy. The purpose of the council was to help the president coordinate foreign policy. When serious crises erupt (like those noted at the start of the chapter), the president may call the council into an immediate session for advice.

The effectiveness of the NSC depends largely on how the president chooses to use it and who his national security adviser is. During the Nixon years, the NSC was headed by Henry Kissinger and was very influential in shaping foreign policy. Seeking to avoid the conflicts that occurred during the Carter administration between the national security adviser and the Secretary of State, Ronald Reagan appointed low-keyed Richard Allen. Nevertheless, in 1982, Reagan was forced to replace Allen with William P. Clark (see p. 501). Not only had Allen not worked well with Secretary of State Alexander Haig, but he had also been widely criticized for several possible illegal activities and ineffectiveness in running the NSC staff. Reagan now had an opportunity to restore the NSC to its original use: providing the president with a wide range of facts and informed opinions and helping him coordinate foreign policy.

In recent years, the State Department's role in foreign policy making has declined. Perhaps the best explanation for its decline is that it is divided geographically (a bureau for African affairs, another for European, still another for Latin American, and so forth). The State Department is also divided by functions: a bureau for the United Nations, one for intelligence and research, etc. This fragmentation often makes speaking with a consistent, coherent voice difficult. Meanwhile, the role of the Department of Defense (DOD) has risen. Again, organization might be the answer: It is big, yet tightly organized; its voice carries weight.

In terms of our foreign policy grid, how might we classify the top brass at the **Pentagon** (the huge five-sided building in Washington, D.C., that is headquarters of the U.S. armed forces)? According to Richard Betts, who studied the advice given to the president by the joint chiefs of staff in his *Soldiers, Statesmen, and Cold War,* they are only slightly more likely to be hawks than civilian advisers. According to Betts, some army generals even show definite dovish tendencies.

Established in 1947, the CIA has also steadily increased its influence in foreign affairs relative to the State Department.

A final insider in making foreign policy is Congress. While the role of Congress has fluctuated since World War II, it is safe to say that after the winding down in Vietnam in the early 1970s, Congress moved to assert its authority over the president. A prime example was the **War Power Act of 1974,** which limited to 60 days the time a president could commit troops overseas without Congressional approval. About the same time, Congress also reasserted its power over the CIA, which had involved itself in many questionable activities. In 1981, however, some of these tightened controls over the CIA (for example, prohibitions against wiretapping American citizens within U.S. borders) were loosened.

It is unlikely that Congress can ever come to play a role close to that of the president. For one thing, it is far more fragmented than the State Department. For another, its members are inclined to favor short-term solutions over long-term ones and to favor their constituents over the national interest. Thus, Congress will tend to side with Greece over Turkey when the two countries are in conflict. Although Turkey is infinitely more important to U.S. strategic concerns, there are likely to be far more Greek-American voters than Turkish-American voters in a Congressional district.

The outer circle. In addition to the president, the NSC, the State Department, DOD, CIA, and Congress, there are a number of other organizations and groups that from time to time affect foreign policy decisions. The Department of Commerce, Department of Agriculture, and multinational corporations (see Chapter 13) have an obvious interest in international trade. Likewise, the Treasury Department is concerned with international monetary agreements and international drug traffic.

The media, public opinion, and American allies also influence the way in which the insiders make foreign policy. The case could be made that it as not until these forces shifted that government policy regarding the Vietnam War shifted. Because Johnson Secretary of Defense Robert McNamara ignored the role of media and public opinion in foreign policy, he made surely one of the most inane remarks ever recorded by a major American political figure—namely, that America could, if necessary, fight a war in Asia indefinitely.

Who Is Number One?

It is first of all vital to recognize the enormity of the Soviet arms drive. In military investment—procurement and construction—the Soviets have outspent the United States by 50 percent to 80 percent over the last half decade. The aggregate margin of spending since 1972 by the Soviets is about $100 billion.

Next, it is vital to recognize that a comparison of Soviet and American military power provides only one perspective on an issue of relative strength. Why not add NATO defenses to American and Eastern European defenses to Soviet (as is done in Table 13–3)? Such a comparison is not nearly as disturbing as a straight American-Soviet comparison.

Finally, it is vital to recognize that military power should not be seen only in terms of hardware, weapons systems, bodies, or spending. Military power consists of many tangibles and intangibles. For instance:

Population. The long-term strength of a nation requires a steady and secure military force. The drop in the number of Slavs and the sharp rise in the number of Muslims coming of military age already represents a serious problem for the Soviet military. The absolute number of young Soviets will decline during the

1980s and 1990s. Therefore conscription quotas will become increasingly difficult to fulfill. By 1983, according to Murray Feshback of the U.S. Bureau of the Census, it is quite possible that the Soviet armed forces will experience something akin to a labor shortage.

Geography. Unlike the United States, the Soviet Union is surrounded by hostile countries, uncertain allies, and unstable regimes.

Natural resources. Both the United States and the Soviet Union are relatively self-sufficient, although the Soviet Union is more so.

Industrial capacity. The United States and its allies enjoy a big edge here (see Table 14–1). Experts now put the Soviet economic growth rate at 2 percent, the lowest since World War II. Some Western observers suggest that the Soviet Union may actually have entered the beginning of a long phase of negative economic growth. In any event, the prospects for prolonged zero rates of growth, and even for negative growth, will increase over the 1980s and 1990s as production problems intensify.

Mobility. As the Prussian military theorist Karl von Clausewitz noted three centuries ago, one of the first principles of warfare is getting the maximum number of troops to the decisive point of battle. That requires mobility. If the United States was helpless to influence events in the Persian Gulf, it was not because it lacked the troops; it was because they were too far away and too hard to move.

Skill. The point is that armies vary widely in skill, leadership, and organizational effectiveness. These qualities are not easily measured. Nonetheless they are highly relevant to any comparison of military strength.

Will. The perception of resolve and a willingness to use force if necessary is another intangible ingredient in the military power of a nation.

Intelligence. This ingredient has nothing to do with the Stanford-Binet Intelligence Scale or college boards. It refers to knowing what a

TABLE 14–1
Military Resources of Nato, Warsaw Pact, and People's Republic of China

Resources	NATO	Warsaw Pact	People's Republic of China
Population	554,800,000	365,700,000	900,000,000
GNP (billions)	$3,367	$1,240	$309
Military spending (billions)	$175	$139	$23–28
Military manpower	4,900,000	4,580,000	4,300,000
Strategic nuclear weapons*	9,400	4,500	2007
Tactical nuclear weapons†	22,000?	15,000?	n.a.
Tanks	25,250+	59,000	9,000
Antitank missiles	200,000+	n.a.	n.a.
Other armor vehicles	48,000+	62,000+	3,500
Heavy artillery	11,400+	22,600+	20,000
Combat aircraft	8,900+	10,400	5,900
Helicopters	12,300	4,550	350
Major surface warships	522	247	22
Attack submarines (all types)	211	239	66

n.a. = not available.

* Strategic nuclear weapons are those capable of attacking Soviet territory or the continental United States. The range and payload of intercontinental ballistic missiles (ICBMs) has increased dramatically since the 1950s. Russia deploys missiles (SS-16s) with much larger warheads than America. But America has a greater number of multiple warheads and her missiles are considered to be more accurate than those of Russia.

† Tactical nuclear weapons are relatively short-range. Both the United States and Soviet Union have them stationed in Europe. The armory of tactical nuclear weapons consists of short- and medium-range missiles capable of carrying nuclear, biochemical, or conventional warheads. Missiles are constantly being improved and new types introduced with greater payload, range, and flexibility. The Soviet Frog 7 and the American MGM 52C Lance represent the new generation of tactical missiles. They are capable of high mobility on wheeled or tracked carriers.

Source: Department of Defense, International Institute for Studies, Center for Defense Information.

Wide World Photos

The aborted rescue mission in Iran in 1980 raised questions about organizational effectiveness of American forces. (The charred wreckage and abandoned helicopter, with secret documents left on it, are being examined by Iranians in picture.)

These questions deal with the maintenance of helicopters and other equipment, the adequacy of aircraft conceived in the 1950s for operations in the 1980s, the accuracy of intelligence reports and the operational planning that limited the visible military force to 90 men. "If you want to find out what's wrong with your outfit, try it out on something important," has been an axiom of sergeants since the time of the Roman legions. Some friendly critics of the American military say that it has not carried a single major successful military operation since the Inchon landing in the Korean War over 30 years ago.

Jim Moore/Liaison

In April 1777, General George Washington issued this order: "Put none but Americans on guard tonight." By the end of the 1970s, few wise foreigners found comfort in the fact that America was on guard for the free world. This perception of a lack of will to support allies weakens a nation's strength. Above, one wise foreigner concerned about U.S. vacillation, Morocco's King Hassan II, listens carefully to President Carter for signs.

nation's prospective enemies are doing, or are about to do, and using covert means (as opposed to direct military intervention) to achieve objectives in the world; in short, it refers to espionage. Every day, around the world, espionage games are being played out between U.S. and Soviet intelligence services. These spying operations can become crucial when a U.S.–Soviet crisis arises, such as the recent commotion over Soviet troops in Cuba or Cuban involvement in Central America. But even when relations are calm, both sides are quietly working to place "moles," penetration agents, within the opposing spy service, and to pry loose the other side's most vital secrets.

What concerns many U.S. intelligence ex-

perts is growing evidence that the Russians have been winning this covert war. They cite examples of an aggressive Soviet espionage effort. Over the years it has compromised U.S. spy-satellite technology, penetrated CIA security, and subverted the agency's operations. These experts contend that new controls on U.S. counterintelligence, such as have been discussed by Congress, could further weaken U.S. defenses against Soviet spies. According to former CIA director Richard Helms: "You can say what you like about the Russians: that their agricultural system doesn't work or that they're too bureaucratic. But there's no country in the world that understands intelligence better. The KGB is a damned good organization."

Technological sophistication. There is little question that the United States has the technological edge over the Soviet Union in weapons. Some critics make several charges, however. American defense planners put too much faith in technology. Some technology can become not only too expensive (which means

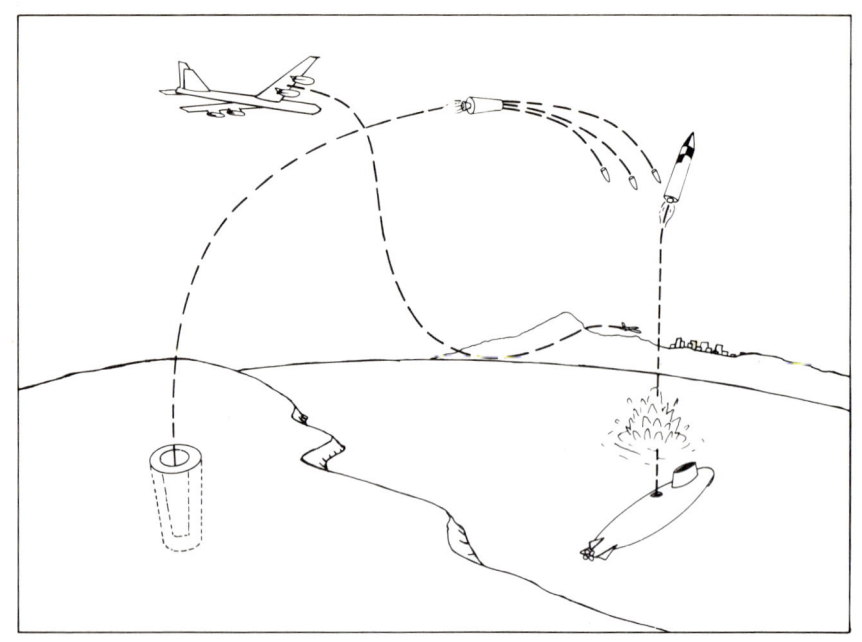

This drawing suggests how the so-called **triad** of ICBMs, submarine-launched missiles, and strategic bombers, which constitute U.S. strategic forces, would work. The basic land-based Minuteman missile still known by its initials, ICBM (intercontinental ballistic missile)—is fired from its silo with its multiple warheads. The MIRV (multiple independent reentry vehicle) system greatly enhances the ICBMs capacities by providing them with a cluster of warheads, each independently targeted. Used in large numbers, they can swamp enemy defenses and destroy widely separate targets. The even more advanced MARV can have its course adjusted after launch.

Just two of the relatively invulnerable Poseidon submarines—less than 4 percent of America's total nuclear force—carry enough warheads to destroy every large and medium-size city in the Soviet Union. Recently, the United States began a new era in submarines by launching the *Ohio,* the first of a planned fleet of 13 Trident subs. The *Ohio* is staggering 560 feet long.

The Boeing B-52 Stratofortress remains the backbone of the U.S. Strategic Air Command. The eight-engine bomber was originally designed to carry four thermonuclear bombs in internal weapons bays. In the drawing, a cruise missile with nuclear warhead is launched from the B-52 and flies low to penetrate enemy territory under radar screens. The cruise missile enters enemy territory at over 500 mph and under 100 feet; its sophisticated computer guidance system offers a relatively cheap offensive weapon that can hit targets with almost pinpoint accuracy, examine the landscape below and to the sides of its flight path, perform computerized terrain analysis, search for landmarks using the techniques of pattern recognition, and compare these results to its own internal maps. It can plot its own courses and home in on their targets with dazzling accuracy. Thanks to the new science of robotics and artificial intelligence, cruise missiles strike within centimeters of their intended destinations.

The Rockwell International B-1 bomber is about two thirds the size of the B-52 but newer and more sophisticated. The U.S. Air Force has proposed it as a replacement for the B-52 and hopes to build a force of 244 B-1s. By 1981, four prototypes had been built and President Reagan was calling for full production.

Military force does not always translate itself into political influence. This has been said many times. But it would be wrong to ignore the fact that in the coming years arms will weigh heavily on the balance of destiny. Or, as the American author Dannon Runyon put it: "The race is not always to the swift nor the battle to the strong, but that's the way to bet."

fewer weapons), but also too complicated to work under combat conditions. Such critics favor smaller ships capable of operating independently over huge aircraft carriers and accompanying task forces; weapons that are simple, easily maintained, and reliable are favored over those that are costly and complicated.

What Do the Soviet Leaders Really Want?

Mind reading is an impossible but necessary task in the design and conduct of foreign policy. And no minds are more worth trying to probe than those of the top leaders in the Kremlin. Among those who have given some thought to this question, two broad and conflicting views have emerged.

In the first view, the Kremlin leaders are seen as a group of quite ordinary men. Because of their advanced age, they are not given to rash adventure and starting wars. Their chief concerns are the defense and economic development of their country. Because they care more about appearances than reality and have an obsession about secrecy, they are sometimes difficult to deal with.

Adherents of this view also believe that commercial and technical exchanges with the Soviet Union encourage the growth and influence of a modernizing and liberalizing element in Soviet society that eventually will take control of Soviet government. In short, the Soviet Union's essential national interests coincide with the interests of the Western industrial countries. Indeed, the really serious division in the world of the future will not be between East and West but between the rich and the poor.

Then there is the second view. These conservative, old gentlemen who sit in the Kremlin are true believers in Marx and Lenin. Yes, they will sacrifice material concerns and human rights to this revolutionary and visionary political ideology. Adherents of this view offer the following evidence:

> From 1974 to 1980, Angola, Ethiopia, Afghanistan, South Yemen, Mozambique, Laos, Cambodia, and South Vietnam have all been brought under Soviet control or under control of those, like Castro, who owe their survival in part to the Soviets.
>
> Most terrorist groups use Soviet bloc weapons. They get training in Warsaw Pact countries or Mideast nations like South Yemen or PLO-controlled Lebanon. And they find sanctuary in the same places.

U.S. Air Force Photos

U.S. Phantom II jets routinely track Soviet air reconnaisance missions over the North Atlantic. Just how closely is illustrated by these recently released Air Force photos. Left, a crewman in the tail gunner's seat of a Soviet Tu95 "Bear," a bomber converted for reconnaissance. Right, two Phantoms fly right alongside the Soviet plane.

In fact, modern terrorism is a form of "warfare by remote control" by these countries and groups.

"The Soviets are the most powerful opponents of liberty on earth today," Senator Daniel P. Moynihan writes. Moreover, their political ideology sanctions this opposition. Moynihan explains:

> They are singled out by the force of their ideology which, since the passing of Nazism and the eclipse of fascism as a school of political thought . . . remains the only major political doctrine that challenges human rights *in principle*. When the authoritarian regimes of the Right violate human rights nowadays, they generally do so not in the name of a different political creed but in the name of national security. They must torture, they say, to uproot guerrillas and terrorists; or they must keep political prisoners to protect themselves against armed subversion from without and within. Unlike the Soviets and their ideological progeny in other countries ruled by Marxist-Leninist regimes, these right-wing regimes do not deride liberty as a "bourgeois" illusion. They commit abominations in practice; the Communist countries commit abominations on principle. Anyone who cares about human rights will know what type of abomination is the more destructive of those rights.[1]

One does not have to be an unreconstructed Cold Warrior to see something sinister in this pattern of human right violations, expansionism, and exploitation of terror. But there is an element of truth to the other view. It is hard to believe that some grand design for world conquest can charge generation after generation of Soviet leadership. Unlike the great religions of the world, the life span of revolutionary political doctrines is relatively short. Moreover, it is an objective fact that the Soviet Union has low productivity, economic stagnation, and potentially restive and even antagonistic neighbors. In short, the Soviet leaders have cause for pessimism. In this context, their military buildup is not surprising. Unfortunately, and this is the nub of the matter for U.S. relations with the Soviets in the 1980s, a nation that is militarily strong but economically weak is the most dangerous kind.

How Are Wars Prevented?

The costs of war. As we have seen in this section, the two superpowers spend staggering sums on arms. If one adds to those billions the costs of weapons produced for the growing international arms trade, how much money are we looking at? A conservative estimate is that each year over $200 billion is spent worldwide on weapons procurement. That is more than $500 million a day.

Quite a lot of money, to be sure. But that figure assumes no shots are fired between the superpowers. If they are, then we are really talking about big—incalculable—costs. In 1979, a grim doomsday scenario was released by the Office of Technology Assessment. In it a "limited" nuclear attack by only 10 Soviet multiwarhead missiles, aimed at crippling the American energy supply, might be able to knock out 64 percent of U.S. oil refining capacity. It could kill 5 million people and decimate such major cities as Houston, Philadelphia, Los Angeles, and Chicago.

A counterattack of similar scope by the United States would result in far fewer Russian deaths—about 1.45 million. But it would wipe out 73 percent of Soviet refining capacity and 16 percent of oil storage capacity.

An all-out exchange of strategic nuclear warfare between those nations would end with more dead Americans than Soviets. But both societies would be reduced to a primitive level. Up to 165 million Americans could die in such a clash, the study found. And the survivors would live under conditions that would be "the economic equivalent of the Middle Ages." The Soviets would suffer fewer casualties, because their warheads are larger and therefore more deadly than their U.S. counterparts. But the other effects of an all-out nuclear conflagration would be just as severe.

The causes of war. The OTA report is sobering reading indeed. Yet academics have paid relatively little attention to the nature and causes of war. Until we understand that better, the study of international relations theory will remain in its present state of infancy.

Here are a few general theories about the causes of international violence among states that provide some insight:

Failure to maintain the balance of power or an adequate **deterrence.** An "adequate" deterrence may be defined as a military capability so strong that any attacking nation would fear destruction by retaliation.

The innate aggressive drive thought to exist in humans.

The unchecked expansion of great power. (Munich [1938] is the classic example.)

The dynamics of capitalism. (This is the classic Marxist explanation. Needing new markets, capitalist nations carve up the Third World. In the modern version, it runs like this: Industrialists make profit from wars; therefore, they encourage wars.)

The belief that war is inevitable.

Recurring patterns of history.

The tendency for small-scale disagreements to snowball into major conflict; this process is termed **escalation.**

Inadvertence, or the tendency for some relatively small incident, not at the center of things, in a highly unstable situation to trigger a world war.

Recently, Nigel Calder has suggested at least three specific ways—intentionally or not—the two superpowers might enter nuclear war.[2] The first is by the proliferation or acquisition of nuclear weapons by powers that don't at present possess them. Some of these countries are likely to prove just aggressive enough to use nuclear weapons for selfish, stupid, or last-ditch reasons. Given the growing list of possibility (Israel versus the Arab block, Pakistan versus India, South Africa versus neighbors, China versus India, etc.), this way to nuclear war is probably the most likely.

The second way is through the escalation of a European crisis. Calder points to a "mismatch" between NATO and Soviet doctrine. NATO provides for the "controlled" use of tactical nuclear weapons against targets within the Central European battlefield should the conventional defense look like it is collapsing. Soviet doctrine, on the other hand, regards any use of nuclear weapons as a signal that the gloves are off; it would be justification for hitting the whole Western European area with perhaps 2,000 high-yield warheads. That would be in part the fault of Western Europe, Calder argues. They have failed to make the financial and personal sacrifices necessary to build a conventional army that could stop a Russian invasion.

The third way a nuclear war might arise is through concern over the safety of the early warning system. The precious half hour (or 20 minutes) between the time a Soviet attack is launched and an American president can respond in kind is assured by an elaborate system of radar screen, earthbound and airborne, now supplemented by satellite scanners. Of the two, the satellites recently have become the more important. Both superpowers are therefore hypersensitive to technical developments—currently in laser and particle-beam weapons—that threaten to interfere with those earth-circling early-warning stations. "As a result, any actual or imagined interference with these 'fences' may itself provoke war, thus compromising the very safety they are designed to safeguard."[3]

The SALT debate. In 1979, the Carter administration completed. Strategic Arms Limitation Talks (SALT) with the Soviet Union. President Carter contended that the agreement would blunt the Russian challenge while leaving the United States free to proceed with essential weapons programs. Critics insisted that the agreement would freeze the United States into a position of strategic inferiority. The Reagan

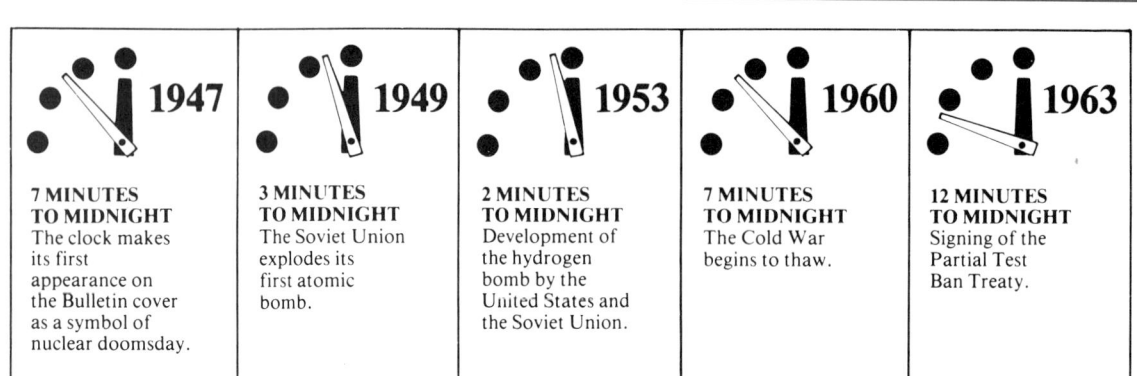

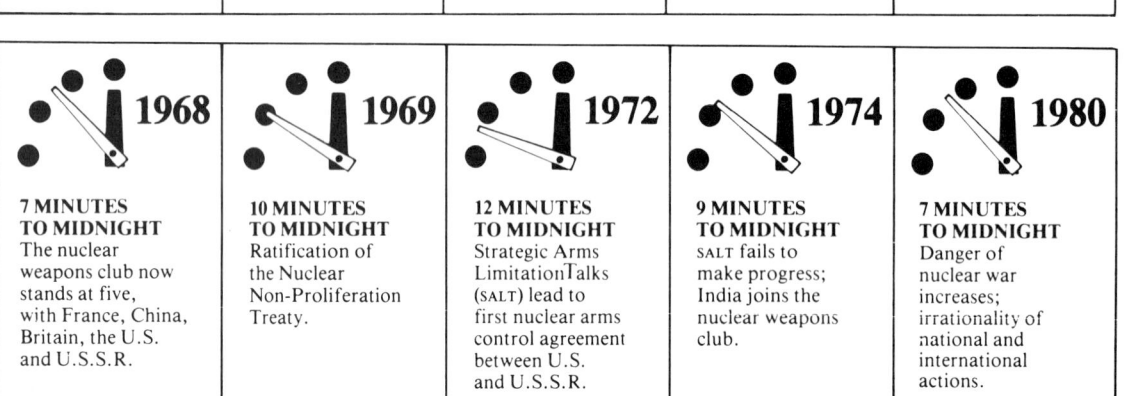

1947	**1949**	**1953**	**1960**	**1963**
7 MINUTES TO MIDNIGHT The clock makes its first appearance on the Bulletin cover as a symbol of nuclear doomsday.	**3 MINUTES TO MIDNIGHT** The Soviet Union explodes its first atomic bomb.	**2 MINUTES TO MIDNIGHT** Development of the hydrogen bomb by the United States and the Soviet Union.	**7 MINUTES TO MIDNIGHT** The Cold War begins to thaw.	**12 MINUTES TO MIDNIGHT** Signing of the Partial Test Ban Treaty.
1968	**1969**	**1972**	**1974**	**1980**
7 MINUTES TO MIDNIGHT The nuclear weapons club now stands at five, with France, China, Britain, the U.S. and U.S.S.R.	**10 MINUTES TO MIDNIGHT** Ratification of the Nuclear Non-Proliferation Treaty.	**12 MINUTES TO MIDNIGHT** Strategic Arms LimitationTalks (SALT) lead to first nuclear arms control agreement between U.S. and U.S.S.R.	**9 MINUTES TO MIDNIGHT** SALT fails to make progress; India joins the nuclear weapons club.	**7 MINUTES TO MIDNIGHT** Danger of nuclear war increases; irrationality of national and international actions.

Since 1947, *The Bulletin of the Atomic Scientists* has featured on its cover a "doomsday clock" with hands posed a few minutes before midnight—thus symbolizing humanity hovering on the edge of nuclear destruction.

administration insisted that the treaty required further negotiations with the Soviets.

Three key issues are at the heart of the SALT debate:

1. The potential vulnerability of the land-based ICBMs. In recent years, the Soviet Union has deployed a new force of larger, increasingly accurate ICBMs. By 1983, theoretically, a third of this developing force could destroy the bulk of America's 1,000 ICBMs in their silos plus perhaps half the American submarines and strategic bombers. Thus the logic of second-strike deterrence—the idea that neither side would attack first as long as it was convinced that it would be destroyed in turn—might no longer hold.*

---

* The descriptive acronym for this balance of terror concept is MAD—"mutual assured destruction."

If correct, the possible consequences are not bright. Now the Soviet Union may very well be able to destroy the U.S. weapons at their launch places and still have a surplus in hand. That being the case, an American president must now consider whether his punitive second strike—with the few missiles he has left—is a choice he wishes to make. He might want to overlook the assault and sue for peace with American cities still intact.

2. How to monitor compliance. This would be achieved by relying on spy satellites and electronimonitoring stations. But critics claim that with the loss of key U.S. monitoring stations in Iran, it is impossible to verify Soviet performance.

3. The role of **linkage.** The Reagan administration has made it clear that they believe in linkage. That is, they intend to link ratifica-

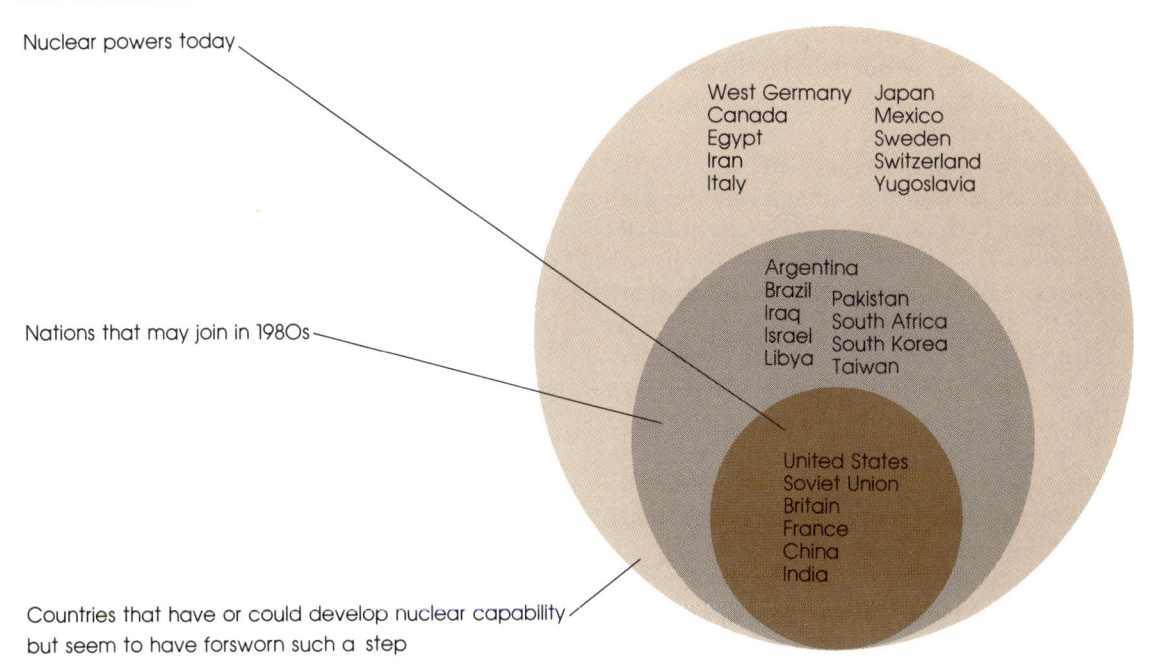

Nuclear powers today:
- United States
- Soviet Union
- Britain
- France
- China
- India*

Nations that may join in 1980s:
- Argentina
- Brazil
- Iraq
- Israel
- Libya
- Pakistan
- South Africa
- South Korea
- Taiwan

Countries that have or could develop nuclear capability but seem to have forsworn such a step:
- West Germany
- Canada
- Egypt
- Iran
- Italy
- Japan
- Mexico
- Sweden
- Switzerland
- Yugoslavia

* Has exploded nuclear device, but is not known to have developed atomic weapons.
Source: Arms Control Association, Washington, D.C.

tion of the SALT treaty to evidence of Soviet good behavior internationally—for example, in Ethiopia, Poland, Afghanistan, Angola and the Middle East.

Outlook. In 1981, President Reagan decided to abandon a plan President Carter had supported. Essentially the plan was to place a number of the latest type American ICBMs, called MX missiles, underground in a few Western states. Because these missiles would be on tracks, they would be mobile. Thus, American strategists could move them around underground over large areas. In this giant shell game, the Soviets could never be exactly sure where all the missiles were; hence, the MX mobile ICBM plan would reduce the Soviet threat to American land-based missiles.

Fearing costs and perhaps political reaction from Western states, Reagan opted instead for placing the new MX missile in silos that currently hold the older Titan missiles. In making this decision, Reagan seemed to be dropping the notion that the United States was going to be terribly vulnerable to Soviet missiles in the first half of the 1980s. In a sense, he was correct. The window of vulnerability was really opened in 1949, when the United States lost its nuclear monopoly.

On November 30, 1981, nuclear arms control talks between the United States and the Soviet Union reopened in Geneva, Switzerland, with NATO nations listening in. The focus of the negotiations was European continental-range (intermediate) nuclear weapons.* The United States wanted to concentrate initially on the most accurate, penetrating, and swift—and therefore most threatening—weapons, the land-based missiles. The Soviet Union wanted to include American nuclear-armed aircraft and submarines.

The present intermediate-range nuclear balance in Europe is more than 2-to-1 in favor of the Soviet Union (International Institute for

* This encompasses a range from about 750 to 5,000 kilometers (465 to 3,100 miles).

Strategic Studies figures). The figures for the most threatening weapons, the longer-range land-based missiles, show an even greater disparity of almost 50–to–1.

At the beginning of the Geneva talks, the Soviet Union proposed a "moratorium," which would freeze present levels—and present Soviet superiority. The United States countered with a "zero option" which would have the Russians dismantle all their SS–20s, SS–4s and SS–5s in return for NATO's not installing those planned new missiles in 1983 as planned.

Obviously, neither side will accept the other side's proposal. This is to be expected. The proposals are mere opening positions for the INF (intermediate-range nuclear forces) talks that will be long and hard.

One final point, and it is an important one. *No defense policy can provide real national security unless it is connected to serious arms control talks.* I say that for several reasons. The most obvious one is that an unending race on both sides for military superiority or nuclear invulnerability can bring little true security. Second, only by limiting the Soviet arsenal will U.S. intelligence have a basis for counting and judging what the Soviets are doing. Third, the fewer missiles the Soviets have, the less vulnerable are American land-based missiles, submarine pens, and air bases. Only progress on arms control will reduce the pressure in Western Europe for unilateral disarmament, which might eventually spread to the United States. Unilateral disarmament means one side lays down its arms while the other side does as it pleases. That, at least to me, is not security. Yet failure to pursue arms control can conceivably lead a democracy in precisely that direction.

At this writing, the Reagan administration is preparing itself for the opening of START—strategic arms reduction talks—as early as Spring 1982. Whether Reagan can negotiate and then get through the Senate the strategic arms reduction treaty he says he wants remains to be seen. If there is any cause for hope in this grim analysis, it is the possibility that only a tough-talking Reagan could get away with such a treaty in the same way that only anticommunist Nixon could go to Communist China. Such paradoxes are the stuff of history.

Chapter Key

Numerous events have helped to shape American foreign policy in the last several decades. But the most important ones are tied, one way or another, to the Soviet Union. The continuing competition between the two superpowers remains the decisive factor in understanding U.S. foreign policy.

A couple other axes around which American foreign policy takes place are worth sketching. There is a West-versus-West axis, that is, the United States against Japan and West Germany. This rivalry is almost entirely economic. Next, there is a North-versus-South axis between the older, Western industrialized nations such as the United States and the rising tides of new nations, the so-called LDCs. This rivalry is basically economic (concerning the price of raw materials and the terms of long-term loans), but to some extent it also involves political and ideological issues.

By using a grid format, with a horizontal axis indicating an individual's orientation towards the use of force and a vertical axis indicating his or her concern for values, a rough classification of American decision makers in foreign policy is possible. Those who are moralistic and noninterventionist are "doves." Those who are moralistic and interventionists are "hawks." Those who are pragmatic and noninterventionists are "internationalists." Finally, those who are pragmatic and interventionists are "nationalists."

Foreign policy makers must formulate and implement policies toward other nations in an environment of public opinion, media attention, interest-group activity, and electoral politics. The importance of these factors will vary depending on the type of policy under consideration. In general, the level of public knowledge about foreign policies is low; media attention of foreign policy is limited.

In foreign and military affairs, the president carries the burden of leadership. He, with help from other agencies in the executive branch, is responsible for day-to-day relations with foreign nations. The president is aided in the conduct of foreign affairs by the secretary of state, the National Security Council, and other officials in the Departments of State and Defense.

The broader task of formulating foreign policy is shared with Congress. Congress has some constitutionally granted prerogatives in foreign policy. Congressional involvement in foreign policy has been increasing. This is because the interdependence of international economies has increased, domestic policies overlap into foreign policy areas, spending for foreign policies has increased, and Congress has reasserted its initiative following the Vietnam War. In addition to confirming a large number of presidential appointments to the Foreign Service and ratifying treaties (Senate only), the appropriations process allows Congress to influence foreign policy. And Congress exercises war powers jointly with the president. One continuing dilemma limiting Congress' role in foreign policy making is that Congress speaks with many voices, and nearly always in uncoordinated fashion.

The Department of State is the agency with chief responsibility for implementing the United States' foreign policy. Organized by geography and function, the core State Department staff is the diplomatic corps; they staff U.S. embassies and missions abroad. Unlike other domestic agencies, the State Department lacks a vocal domestic constituency. The secretary of defense, a civilian, oversees a defense establishment of more than 3 million military and civilian personnel; he also oversees an annual budget of more than $100 billion. The Defense Department includes separate departments for each of the armed services. (Traditionally they have been jealous rivals.) The Defense Department spends an enormous amount of money procuring goods and services to support its policies. Spying has traditionally been a part of military operations. The CIA is the principal modern-day spy agency for the government.

"War is not merely a political act," Karl von Clausewitz wrote in 1832, "but also a political instrument, a continuation of political relations, a carrying out of the same by other means." Perhaps in the next century the human race can eliminate this particular political instrument. Meanwhile, American foreign policy decision makers will have to cope with the world as it is.

National security is an expensive, complicated business. Clearly it involves

Answer to Map Quiz

The two maps below may help you see how the traditional world maps seriously distorts our perception of the world. The polar-centered map (left) shows that the Soviet Union is closer to the United States than you might think. The other map shows the continents in their correct proportions and the equator in the middle. Thus we can see that Europe is considerably smaller than South America and the Soviet Union is not quite so huge. Note too how China "gains" in size. Could this help explain some of the Russian nervousness about the Chinese?

The study of the influence of geography on politics, national power, and foreign power of a nation is called **geopolitics.** While the subject is mostly ignored by American universities, I hope this quiz has given you some appreciation of its relevancy.

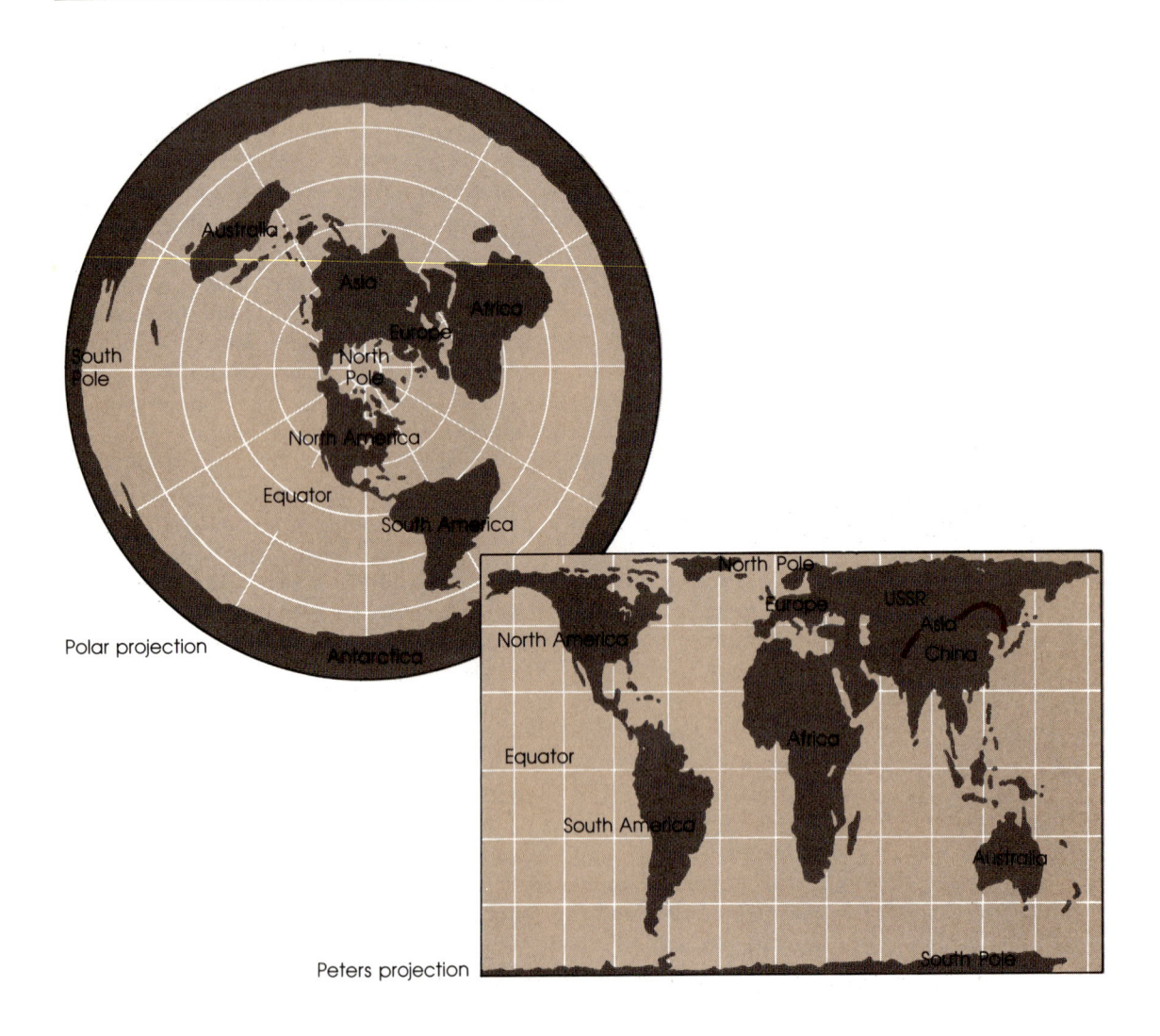

Polar projection

Peters projection

many factors other than military weapons. How much the United States should pay to deter war and achieve certain foreign policy goals is a hotly debated subject. And hanging over the entire debate is the question of how to prevent the use of nuclear weapons, which are spreading to more and more countries.

The early 1980s witnessed a renewed concern about military preparedness in the United States. Across the Atlantic, American allies watched and hoped that this concern could go hand-in-hand with strategic arms limitation talks. It was precisely this hope, and this policy, that John F. Kennedy had expressed at his inauguration in 1960: "Let us never negotiate out of fear, but let us never fear to negotiate."

Answers to Quiz (see page 517)

1. Helmut Schmidt, chancellor of West Germany, and Prime Minister Margaret Thatcher of Britain—leaders of two very important American allies. In fact, Schmidt—who is known in West Germany as Der Macher ("The doer" or "fixer")—has emerged as one of the most influential and respected Western leaders.

2. Yasir Arafat, leader of the Palestine Liberation Organization.

3. Lech Walesa, leader of Solidarity, a Polish worker organization. Possibly the biggest grass roots anticommunist workers' movement that the Soviet empire has seen since its expansion into Europe at the end of World War II. In late 1981, it was crushed by elements of the Polish military and Walesa was put under house arrest.

4. Pierre Elliot Trudeau, who came out of retirement in 1979 to become Canada's prime minister once again. The fundamental problem he faces: the pressure within French-speaking Quebec province for political independence from other provinces.

5. Socialist François Mitterrand, president of France. France is certainly America's oldest ally—and perhaps most temperamental.

Epilogue

Around 1912 a young boy set out alone in a raft on the Minnesota headwaters of the Mississippi. Fifteen years later, that same boy would set out alone in a silvery plane from a muddy field in New York. Thirty-three hours afterwards, Charles Lindbergh—that imperishable symbol of the American adventure—would land in Paris.

Today aviation, even space exploration, seems commonplace. "The average American," journalist George F. Will recently noted, "is so jaded that he is unmoved by the idea of exploring beyond the thin atmosphere of this tiny cinder that orbits in a corner of a solar system in the whirl of the universe."[1] Indeed, the most important political conflict may no longer be between black and white, rich and poor, or conservative and liberal. Rather, the decisive political struggle today may be between those who want to preserve industrial society (or even restore the preindustrial arts of weaving and pottery) and those who are ready to advance beyond it. Will the American republic enter tomorrow with confidence and creativity? I can pose no question more crucial than that.

The purpose of this epilogue is not prophecy. But there are a few indicators of how that question might be resolved in the years ahead.

First, the experiences of Watergate (Chapter 7) and Vietnam (Chapter 14) are now held

The Charles A. Lindbergh Papers, Yale University Library

in better perspective. With respect to the former, we recognize that high-minded reforms, what Swinburne called the sexless orgies of morality, can have unintended consequences. We better recognize now the drawback to becoming so inebriated with virtue that quiet competency and experience cease to be important requirements for public service. With respect to Vietnam, yes, we recognize the limits of power. But we also recognize that, in an interdependent world, America cannot retreat to its shoreline. The fears and hopes of future years for millions of people in the world are tied to the fate and strength of America.

Another indication of how America may enter the future involves our knowledge about how to control the effects of technology on the environment. While these are still rudimentary, they are getting better. At a minimum, we know that technology undirected by the higher imagination is perilous to everybody. But we also appreciate how the development of new technology, the protection of the environment, and the condition of the economy are intertwined; and we appreciate why none of these three issues should become our only concern.

A third indication of how America may enter the future is that economists are becoming optimistic. Analysts seem confident that the nation's economic performance will improve steadily as inflation and unemployment decline and productivity and growth rise. Economists base their forecast on a number of favorable trends. One of these trends was touched on a moment ago: Because the United States has made substantial progress in cleaning up the environment, relatively fewer resources in the 1980s will have to be diverted to such purposes from productive activities.

Perhaps the most important trend is demographic. The postwar "baby boom" generation, which flooded the labor market with unskilled new workers in the 1970s, will be moving into its most productive years. At the same time, the influx of inexperienced teenagers and women into the labor force will slacken.

Favorable government investment policies will reinforce this demographic trend. As capital investment (in new plants, new machines, etc.) increases in the 1980s, productivity should be given another boost. That this trend will enhance economic conditions can hardly be doubted: In 1980, the United States had the highest percentage of obsolete plants and lowest capital investment (as percentage of GNP) of any major industrial nation.

Few economists believe that these trends *guarantee* economic prosperity. President Reagan's promise of a huge military buildup with extensive tax cuts could lead to record deficits. The prospect of $100 billion to $150 billion deficits could reinforce inflation.

Finally, politics provides us with clues as to how America will enter tomorrow. I readily admit that a survey of the contemporary American political system might be discouraging. But let us not be confused by appearances, by shadows dancing on the wall of the cave. The system was only a few years old when Congressman Fisher Ames of Massachusetts made the following accurate statement about democracy. He said a monarchy is like a great ship—"You ride with the wind and tide in safety and elation, but by and by you strike a reef and go down. Democracy is like a raft: You never sink, but damn it, your feet are always in the water."

America has continued to seethe with political activity. In his 1982 State of the Union address, President Reagan proposed turning back to the states and local governments 40 programs costing nearly $50 billion. Most governors favored the redistribution of power from Washington back to them (Chapter 10). As governance becomes more complex and as regional problems remain different, the delegation of power makes sense. At the national level, the composition of the Senate changed dramatically in 1980 and reapportionment effected similar changes in the House (Chapter 8). A new politics has emerged. Meanwhile single-issue groups (Chapter 6) remain aggressively at work at all levels of government. Possibly, when they attain more participation in leadership, they will become convinced that they at least have power—a recognition that is a prerequisite of restraint and responsibility.

The American public itself, for reasons indicated a moment ago, became frustrated with government performance in the late 1960s and

70s. Still, Americans are not antigovernment. They continue to want and expect a vigorous—but not wasteful—government. They want a better-working—not an absence of—government. Reagan (or any conservative president) would probably do well to balance his rhetoric about the problems of big government (which are real enough) with the articulation of a larger national purpose. As Everett C. Ladd, director of the University of Connecticut's Roper Center, recently put it: "Americans are a highly public people. When something goes wrong, the public wants to come together to solve the problem."[2]

What all this political activity demonstrates, I think, is America's enormous capacity to constantly remake itself, to adjust to changing conditions. Not swiftly, not neatly—but slowly and surely.

In sum, I think there are indications that the next two decades will bring another surge of American inventiveness and reaffirmation of its own values. The American adventure—that spirit symbolized by the young boy on the raft—goes on.

Appendix A: The Constitution of the United States

The Preamble

We the People of the United States, in Order to form a more perfect Union, establish Justice, insure domestic Tranquility, provide for the common defence, promote the general Welfare, and secure the Blessings of Liberty to ourselves and our Posterity, do ordain and establish this Constitution for the United States of America.

Article I—The Legislative Article

Legislative power

Section 1. All Legislative Powers herein granted shall be vested in a Congress of the United States, which shall consist of a Senate and House of Representatives.

House of representatives: composition; qualification; apportionment; impeachment power

Section 2. The House of Representatives shall be composed of Members chosen every second Year by the People of the several States, and the Electors in each State shall have the Qualifications requisite for Electors of the most numerous Branch of the State Legislature.

No Person shall be a Representative who shall not have attained to the Age of twenty five Years, and been seven Years a Citizen of the United States, and who shall not, when elected, be an Inhabitant of that State in which he shall be chosen.

Representatives and direct Taxes shall be apportioned among the several States which may be included within this Union, according to their respective Numbers, which shall be determined by adding to the whole Number of free Persons, including those bound to Service for a Term of Years, and excluding Indians not taxed, three fifths of all other Persons. The actual Enumeration shall be made within three Years after the first Meeting of the Congress of the United States, and within every subsequent Term of ten Years, in such Manner as they shall by Law direct. The Number of Representatives shall not exceed one for every thirty Thousand, but each State shall have at Least one Representative; and until such enumeration shall be made, the State of New Hampshire shall be entitled to chuse three, Massachusetts eight, Rhode-Island and Providence Plantations one, Connecticut five, New-York six, New Jersey four, Pennsylvania eight, Delaware one, Maryland six, Virginia ten, North Carolina five, South Carolina five, and Georgia three.

When vacancies happen in the Representation from any State, the Executive Authority thereof shall issue Writs of Election to fill such Vacancies.

The House of Representatives shall chuse their speaker and other Officers; and shall have the sole Power of Impeachment.

Senate: composition; qualifications; impeachment trials

Section 3. The Senate of the United States shall be composed of two Senators from each State, chosen by the Legislature therof, for six Years; and each Senator shall have one Vote.

Immediately after they shall be assembled in Consequence of the first Election, they shall be divided as equally as may be into three Classes. The Seats of the Senators of the first Class shall be vacated at the Expiration of the second Year, of the second Class at the Expiration of the fourth Year, and of the third Class at the Expiration of the sixth Year, so that one third may be chosen every second Year; and if Vacancies happen by Resignation, or otherwise, during the Recess of the Legislature of any State, the Executive thereof may make temporary Appointments until the next Meeting of the

Legislature, which shall then fill such Vacancies.

No Person shall be a Senator who shall not have attained to the Age of thirty Years, and been nine Years a Citizen of the United States, and who shall not, when elected, be an Inhabitant of that State for which he shall be chosen.

The Vice President of the United States shall be President of the Senate, but shall have no Vote, unless they be equally divided.

The Senate shall chuse their other Officers, and also a President pro tempore, in the Absence of the Vice President, or when he shall exercise the Office of the President of the United States.

The Senate shall have the sole Power to try all Impeachments. When sitting for that Purpose, they shall be on Oath or Affirmation. When the President of the United States is tried, the Chief Justice shall preside: And no Person shall be convicted without the Concurrence of two thirds of the Members present.

Judgment in Cases of Impeachment shall not extend further than to removal from Office, and disqualification to hold and enjoy any Office of honor, Trust or Profit under the United States: but the Party convicted shall nevertheless be liable and subject to Indictment, Trial, Judgement and Punishment, according to law.

Congressional elections: time; place; manner

Section 4. The Times, Places and Manner of holding Elections for Senators and Representatives, shall be prescribed in each State by the legislature therof; but the Congress may at any time by Law make or alter such Regulations, except as to the Places of chusing Senators.

The Congress shall assemble at least once in every Year, and such Meeting shall be on the first Monday in December, unless they shall by Law appoint a different Day.

Powers and duties of the houses

Section 5. Each House shall be the Judge of the Elections, Returns and Qualifications of its own Members, and a Majority of each shall constitute a Quorum to do Business; but a smaller Number may adjourn from day to day, and may be authorized to compel the Attendance of absent Members, in such Manner, and under such Penalties as each House may provide.

Each House may determine the Rules of its Proceedings, punish its Members for disorderly Behaviour, and, with the Concurrence of two thirds, expel a Member.

Each House shall keep a Journal of its Proceedings, and from time to time publish the same, excepting such Parts as may in their Judgment require Secrecy; and the Yeas and Nays of the Members of either House on any question shall, at the Desire of one fifth of those Present, be entered on the Journal.

Neither House, during the Session of Congress, shall, without the Consent of the other, adjourn for more than three days, nor to any other Place than that in which the two Houses shall be sitting.

Rights of members

Section 6. The Senators and Representatives shall receive a Compensation for their Services, to be ascertained by Law, and paid out of the Treasury of the United States. They shall in all Cases, except Treason, Felony and Breach of the Peace, be privileged from Arrest during their Attendance at the Session of their respective Houses, and in going to and returning from the same; and for any Speech or Debate in either House, they shall not be questioned in any other Place.

No Senator or Representative shall, during the Time for which he was elected, be appointed to any civil Office under the Authority of the United States, which shall have been created, or the Emoluments whereof shall have been encreased during such time; and no Person holding any Office under the United States, shall be a Member of either House during his Continuance in Office.

Legislative powers: bills and resolutions

Section 7. All Bills for raising Revenue shall originate in the House of Representatives; but the Senate may propose or concur with Amendments as on other Bills.

Every Bill which shall have passed the House of Representatives and the Senate, shall, before it become a Law, be presented to the President of the United States. If he approve he shall sign it, but if not he shall return it, with his Objections to that House in which it shall have originated, who shall enter the Objections at large on their Journal, and proceed to reconsider it. If after such Reconsideration two thirds of that House shall agree to pass the Bill, it shall be sent, together with the Objections, to the other House, by which it shall likewise be reconsidered, and if approved by two thirds of that House, it shall become a Law. But in all such Cases the Votes of both Houses shall be determined by Yeas and Nays, and the Names of the Persons voting for and against the Bill shall be entered on the Journal of each House respectively. If any Bill shall not be returned by the President within ten Days (Sunday excepted) after it shall have been presented to him, the Same shall be a Law, in like Manner as if he had signed it, unless the Congress by their Adjournment prevent its Return, in which Case it shall not be a Law.

Every Order, Resolution, or Vote to which the Concurrence of the Senate and House of Representatives may be necessary (except on a question of Adjournment) shall be presented to the President of the United States; and before the Same shall take Effect, shall be approved by him, or being disapproved by him, shall be repassed by two thirds of the Senate and House of Representatives, according to the Rules and Limitations prescribed in the Case of a Bill.

Powers of Congress

Section 8. The Congress shall have Power To lay and collect Taxes, Duties, Imposts and Excises, to pay the Debts and provide for the common Defence and general Welfare of the United States; but all Duties, Imposts and Excises shall be uniform throughout the United States;

To borrow Money on the credit of the United States;

To regulate Commerce with foreign Nations, and among the several States, and with the Indian Tribes;

To establish an uniform Rule of Naturalization, and uniform Laws on the subject of Bankruptcies throughout the United States;

To coin Money, regulate the Value thereof, and of foreign Coin, and fix the Standard of Weights and Measures;

To provide for the Punishment of counterfeiting the Securities and current Coin of the United States;

To establish Post Offices and post Roads;

To promote the Progress of Science and useful Arts, by securing for limited Times to Authors and Inventors the exclusive Right to their respective Writings and Discoveries;

To constitute Tribunals inferior to the supreme Court;

To define and punish Piracies and Felonies committed on the high Seas, and Offences against the Law of Nations;

To declare War, grant Letters of Marque and Reprisal, and make Rules concerning Captures on Land and Water;

To raise and support Armies, but no Appropriation of Money to that Use shall be for a longer Term than two Years;

To provide and maintain a Navy;

To make Rules for the Government and Regulation of the land and naval Forces;

To provide for calling forth the Militia to execute the Laws of the Union, suppress Insurrections and repel Invasions;

To provide for organizing, arming, and disciplining, the Militia, and for governing such Part of them as may be employed in the Service of the United States, reserving to the States respectively, the Appointment of the Officers, and the Authority of training the Militia according to the discipline prescribed by Congress;

To exercise exclusive Legislation in all Cases whatsoever, over such District (not exceeding ten Miles square) as may, by Cession of particular States, and the Acceptance of Congress, become the Seat of the Government of the United States, and to exercise like Authority over all Places purchased by the Consent of the Legislature of the State in which the Same shall be for the Erection of Forts, Magazines, Arsenals, dock-Yards, and other needful Buildings;-And

To make all Laws which shall be necessary and proper for carrying into Execution the foregoing Powers, and all other Powers vested by this Constitution in the Government of the United States, or in any Department or Officer thereof.

Powers denied to Congress

Section 9. The Migration or Importation of such Persons as any of the States now existing shall think proper to admit, shall not be prohibited by the Congress prior to the Year one thousand eight hundred and eight, but a Tax or duty may be imposed on such Importation, not exceeding ten dollars for each Person.

The Privilege of the Writ of Habeas Corpus shall not be suspended, unless when in Cases of Rebellion or Invasion the public Safety may require it.

No Bill of Attainder or ex post facto Law shall be passed.

No Capitation, or other direct, Tax shall be laid, unless in Proportion to the Census or Enumeration herein before directed to be taken.

No Tax or Duty shall be laid on Articles exported from any State.

No Preference shall be given by any Regulation of Commerce or Revenue to the Ports of one State over those of another: nor shall Vessels bound to, or from, one State be obliged to enter, clear, or pay Duties in another.

No Money shall be drawn from the Treasury, but in Consequence of Appropriations made by Law; and a regular Statement and Account of the Receipts and Expenditures of all public Money shall be published from time to time.

No Title of Nobility shall be granted by the United States: And no Person holding any Office of Profit or Trust under them, shall, without the Consent of the Congress, accept of any present, Emolument, Office, or Title, of any kind whatever, from any King, Prince, or foreign States.

Powers denied to the states

Section 10. No State shall enter into any Treaty, Alliance, or Confederation; grant Letters of Marque and Reprisal; coin Money; emit Bills of Credit; make any Thing but gold and silver Coin a Tender in Payment of Debts; pass any Bill of Attainder, ex post facto Law, or Law impairing the Obligation of Contracts, or grant any Title of Nobility.

No State shall, without the Consent of the Congress, lay any Imposts or Duties on Imports or Exports, except what may be absolutely necessary for executing its inspection Laws: and the net Produce of all Duties and Imposts, laid by any State on Imports or Exports, shall be for the Use of the Treasury of the United States; and all such Laws shall be subject to the Revision and Control of the Congress.

No State shall, without the Consent of Congress, lay any Duty of Tonnage, keep Troops, or Ships of War in time of Peace, enter into any Agreement or Compact with another State, or with a foreign Power, or engage in War, unless actually invaded, or in such imminent Danger as will not admit of delay.

Article II—The Executive Article

Nature and scope of presidential power

Section 1. The executive Power shall be vested in a President of the United States of America. He shall hold his Office during the Term of four Years, and, together with the Vice President, chosen for the same term, be elected, as follows:

Each State shall appoint, in such Manner as the Legislature thereof may direct, a Number of Electors, Equal to the whole Number of Senators and Representatives to which the State may be entitled in the Congress: but no Senator or Representative, or Person holding an Office of Trust or Profit under the United States, shall be appointed an Elector.

The Electors shall meet in their respective States, and vote by Ballot for two Persons, of whom one at least shall not be an Inhabitant of the same State with themselves. And they shall make a List of all the Persons voted for, and the Number of Votes for each; which List they shall sign and certify, and transmit sealed to the Seat of the Government of the United States, directed to the President of the Senate. The President of the Senate shall, in the Presence of the Senate and House of Representatives, open all the Certificates, and the Votes shall then be counted. The Person having the greatest Number of Votes shall be the President, if such Number be a Majority of the whole Number of Electors appointed; and if there be more than one who have such Majority, and have an equal Number of Votes, then the House of Representatives shall immediately chuse by Ballot one of them for President: and if no Person have a Majority, then from the five highest on the List the said House shall in like Manner chuse the President. But in chusing the President, the Votes shall be taken by States, the Representation from each State having one Vote; A quorum for this Purpose shall consist of a Member or Members from two thirds of the States, and a Majority of all the States shall be necessary to a Choice. In every Case, after the Choice of the President, the Person having the greatest Number of Votes of the Electors shall be the Vice President. But if there should remain two or more who have equal Votes, the Senate shall chuse from them by Ballot the Vice President.

The Congress may determine the Time of chusing the Electors and the Day on which they shall give their Votes; which Day shall be the same throughout the United States.

No Person except a natural born Citizen, or a Citizen of the United States, at the time of the Adoption of this Constitution, shall be eligible to the Office of President; neither shall any Person be eligible to that Office who shall not have attained to the Age of thirty five Years, and been fourteen Years a Resident within the United States.

In Case of the Removal of the President from Office, or of his Death, Resignation, or Inability to discharge the Powers and Duties of the said Office, the Same shall devolve on the Vice President, and the Congress may by Law provide for the Case of Removal, Death, Resignation or Inability, both of the President and Vice President, declaring what Officer shall then act as President, and such Officer shall act accordingly, until the Disability be removed, or a President shall be elected.

The President shall, at stated Times, receive for his Services a Compensation, which shall neither be encreased nor diminished during the Period for which he shall have been elected, and he shall not receive within that Period any other Emolument from the United States, or any of them.

Before he enter on the Execution of his Office, he shall take the following Oath or Affirmation:- "I do solemnly swear (or affirm) that I will faithfully execute the Office of President of the United States, and will to the best of my Ability, preserve, protect and defend the Constitution of the United States."

Powers and duties of the president

Section 2. The President shall be Commander in Chief of the Army and Navy of the United States, and of the Militia of the several States, when called into the actual Service of the United States; he may require the Opinion, in writing, of the principal Officer in each of the executive Departments, upon any Subject relating to the Duties of their respective Offices, and he shall have power to grant Reprieves and Pardons for Offences against the United States, except in Cases of Impeachment.

He shall have Power, by and with the Advice and Consent of the Senate, to make Treaties, provided two thirds of the Senators present concur; and he shall nominate, and by and with the Advice and Consent of the Senate, shall appoint Ambassadors, other public Ministers and Consuls, Judges of the supreme Court, and all other Officers of the United States, whose Appointments are not herein otherwise provided for, and which shall be established by Law; but the Congress may by Law vest the Appointment of such inferior Officers, as they think proper, in the President alone, in the Courts of Law, or in the Heads of Departments.

The President shall have Power to fill up all Vacancies that may happen during the Recess of the Senate, by granting Commissions which shall expire at the End of their next Session.

Section 3. He shall from time to time give to the Congress Information of the State of the Union, and recommend to their Consideration such Measures as he shall judge necessary and expedient; he may, on extraordinary Occasions, convene both Houses, or either of them, and in Case of Disagreement between them, with Respect to the Time of Adjournment, he may adjourn them to such Time as he shall think proper; he shall take Care that the Laws be faithfully executed, and shall Commission all the Officers of the United States.

Impeachment

Section 4. The President, Vice President and all civil Officers of the United States, shall be removed from Office on Impeachment for, and Conviction of, Treason, Bribery, or other High Crimes and Misdemeanors.

Article III—The Judicial Article

Judicial power, courts, judges

Section 1. The judicial Power of the United States, shall be vested in one supreme Court, and in such inferior Courts as the Congress may from time to time ordain and establish. The Judges, both of the supreme and inferior Courts, shall hold their Offices during good Behaviour, and shall, at stated Times, receive for their Services, a Compensation, which shall not be diminished during their Continuance in Office.

Jurisdiction

Section 2. The judicial Power shall extend to all Cases, in Law and Equity, arising under this Constitution, the Laws of the United States, and Treaties made, or which shall be made, under their Authority; to all Cases affecting Ambassadors, other public Ministers and Consuls; to all Cases of admiralty and maritime Jurisdiction; to Controversies to which the United States shall be a Party; to Controversies between two or more States; between a State and Citizens of another State; between Citizens of different States; between Citizens of the same State claiming Lands under Grants of different States, and between a State or the Citizens thereof, and foreign States, Citizens or Subjects.

In all Cases affecting Ambassadors, other public Ministers and Consuls, and those in which a State shall be Party, the supreme Court shall have original Jurisdiction. In all the other Cases before mentioned, the supreme Court shall have appellate Jurisdiction, both as to Law and Fact, with such Exceptions, and under such Regulations as the Congress shall make.

The Trial of all Crimes, except in Cases of Impeachment, shall be by Jury; and such Trial shall be held in the State where the said Crimes shall have been committed; but when not committed within any State, the Trial shall be at such Place or Places as the Congress may by Law have directed.

Treason

Section 3. Treason against the United States, shall consist only in levying War against them, or in adhering to their Enemies, giving them Aid and Comfort. No Person shall be convicted of Treason unless on the Testimony of two Witnesses to the same overt Act, or on Confession in open Court.

The Congress shall have Power to declare the Punishment of Treason, but no Attainder of Treason shall work Corruption of Blood, or Forfeiture except during the Life of the Person attainted.

Article IV—Interstate Relations

Full faith and credit clause

Section 1. Full Faith and Credit shall be given in each State to the public Acts, Records, and judicial Proceedings of every other State. And the Congress may by general Laws prescribe the Manner in which such Acts, Records and Proceedings shall be proved, and the Effect thereof.

Privileges and immunities; interstate rendition

Section 2. The Citizens of each State shall be entitled to all Privileges and Immunities of Citizens in the several States.

A Person charged in any State with Treason, Felony, or other Crime, who shall flee from Justice, and be found in another State, shall on Demand of the executive Authority of the State from which he fled, be delivered up, to be removed to the State having Jurisdiction of the Crime.

No Person held to Service or Labour in one State, under the Laws thereof, escaping into another, shall, in Consequence of any Law or Regulation therein, be discharged from such Service or Labour, but shall be delivered up on Claim of the Party to whom such Service or Labour may be due.

Admission of states

Section 3. New States may be admitted by the Congress into this Union; but no new State shall be formed or erected within the Jurisdiction of any other State; nor any State be formed by the Junction of two or more States, or Parts of States, without the Consent of the Legislatures of the States concerned as well as of the Congress.

The Congress shall have Power to dispose of and make all needful Rules and Regulations respecting the Territory or other Property belonging to the United States; and nothing in this Constitution shall be so construed as to Prejudice any Claims of the United States, or of any particular State.

Republican form of government

Section 4. The United States shall guarantee to every State in this Union a Republican Form of Government, and shall protect each of them against Invasion; and on Application of the Legislature, or of the Executive (when the Legislature cannot be convened) against domestic Violence.

Article V—The Amending Power

The Congress, whenever two thirds of both Houses shall deem it necessary, shall propose Amendments to this Constitution, or, on the Application of the Legislatures of two thirds of the several States, shall call a Convention for proposing Amendments, which, in either Case, shall be valid to all Intents and Purposes, as Part of this Constitution, when ratified by the Legislatures of three fourths of the several States, or by Conventions in three fourths thereof as the one or the other Mode of Ratification may be proposed by the Congress; Provided that no Amendment which may be made prior to the Year One thousand eight hundred and eight shall in any Manner affect the first and fourth Clauses in the Ninth Section of the first Article; and that no State, without its Consent, shall be deprived of its equal Suffrage in the Senate.

Article VI—The Supremacy Article

All Debts contracted and Engagements entered into, before the Adoption of this Constitution, shall be as valid against the United States under this Constitution, as under the Confederation.

This Constitution, and the Laws of the United States which shall be made in Pursuance thereof; and all Treaties made, or which shall be made, under the Authority of the United States, shall be the supreme Law of the Land; and the Judges in every State shall be bound thereby, any Thing in the Constitution or Laws of any State to the Contrary notwithstanding.

The Senators and Representatives before mentioned, and the Members of the several State Legislatures, and all executive and judicial Officers, both of the United States and of the several States, shall be bound by Oath or Affirmation, to support this Constitution; but no religious Test shall ever be required as a Qualification to any Office or public Trust under the United States.

Article VII—Ratification

The Ratification of the Conventions of nine States, shall be sufficient for the Establishment of this Constitution between the States so ratifying the Same.

Done in Convention by the Unanimous Consent of the States present the Seventeenth Day of September in the Year of our Lord one thousand seven hundred and Eighty seven and of the Independence of the United States of America the Twelfth. In witness whereof We have hereunto subscribed our Names.

THE BILL OF RIGHTS

[The first 10 Amendments were ratified December 15, 1791, and form what is known as the Bill of Rights]

Amendment 1—Religion, Speech, Assembly, and Politics

Congress shall make no law respecting an establishment of religion, or prohibiting the free exercise thereof; or abridging the freedom of speech, or of the press; or the right of the people peaceably to assemble, and to petition the Government for a redress or grievances.

Amendment 2—Militia and the Right to Bear Arms

A well regulated Militia, being necessary to the security of a free State, the right of the people to keep and bear Arms, shall not be infringed.

Amendment 3—Quartering of Soldiers

No Soldier shall, in time of peace be quartered in any house, without the consent of the Owner, nor in time of war, but in a manner to be prescribed by law.

Amendment 4—Searches and Seizures

The right of the people to be secure in their persons, houses, papers, and effects, against unreasonable searches and seizures, shall not be violated, and no Warrants shall issue, but upon probable cause, supported by Oath or affirmation, and particularly describing the place to be searched and the persons or things to be seized.

Amendment 5—Grand Juries, Self-Incrimination, Double Jeopardy, Due Process, and Eminent Domain

No person shall be held to answer for a capital, or otherwise infamous crime, unless on a presentment or indictment of a Grand Jury, except in cases arising in the land or naval forces, or in the Militia, when in actual service in time of War or public danger, nor shall any person be subject for the same offence to be twice put in jeopardy of life or limb; nor shall be compelled in any criminal case to be a witness against himself, nor be deprived of life, liberty, or property, without due process of law; nor shall private property be taken for public use, without just compensation.

Amendment 6—Criminal Court Procedures

In all criminal prosecutions, the accused shall enjoy the right to a speedy and public trial, by an impartial jury of the State and district wherein the crime shall have been committed, which district shall have been previously ascertained by law, and to be informed of the nature and cause of the accusation; to be confronted with the witnesses against him; to have compulsory process for obtaining witnesses in his favor, and to have the Assistance of Counsel for his defence.

Amendment 7—Trial by Jury in Common Law Cases

In Suits at common law, where the value in controversy shall exceed twenty dollars, the right of trial by jury shall be preserved, and no fact tried by a jury, shall be otherwise reexamined in any Court of the United States, than according to the rules of the common law.

Amendment 8—Bail, Cruel and Unusual Punishment

Excessive bail shall not be required, not excessive fines imposed, nor cruel and unusual punishments inflicted.

Amendment 9—Rights Retained by the People

The enumeration in the Constitution, of certain rights, shall not be construed to deny or disparage others retained by the people.

Amendment 10—Reserved Powers of the States

The powers not delegated to the United States by the Constitution, nor prohibited by it to the States, are reserved to the States respectively, or to the people.

PRE-CIVIL WAR AMENDMENTS

Amendment 11—Suits Against the States

[Ratified February 7, 1795]

The Judicial power of the United States shall not be construed to extend to any suit in law or equity, commenced or prosecuted against one of the United States by Citizens of another State, or by Citizens or Subjects of any Foreign State.

Amendment 12—Election of the President

[Ratified July 27, 1804]

The Electors shall meet in their respective states and vote by ballot for President and Vice-President, one of whom, at least, shall not be an inhabitant of the same state with themselves; they shall name in their ballots the person voted for as President, and in distinct ballots the person voted for as Vice-President, and they shall make distinct lists of all persons voted for as President, and of all persons voted for as Vice-President, and of the number of votes for each, which lists they shall sign and certify, and transmit sealed to the seat of the government of the United States, directed to the President of the Senate;-The President of the Senate shall, in the presence of the Senate and House of Representatives, open all the certificates and the votes shall then be counted;-The person having the greatest number of votes for President, shall be the President, if such number be a majority of the whole number of Electors appointed; and if no person have such majority, then from the persons having the highest numbers not exceeding three on the list of those voted for as President, the House of Representatives shall choose immediately, by ballot, the President. But in choosing the President, the votes shall be taken by states, the representation from each state having one vote; a quorum for this purpose shall consist of a member or members from two-thirds of the states, and a majority of all the states shall be necessary to a choice. And if the House of Representatives shall not choose a President whenever the right of the choice shall devolve upon them, before the fourth day of March next following, then the Vice-President shall act as President, as in the case of the death or other constitutional disability of the President.-The person having the greatest number of votes as Vice-President, shall be the Vice-President, if such number be a majority of the whole number of Electors appointed, and if no person have a majority, then from the two highest numbers on the list, the Senate shall choose the Vice-President; a quorum for the purpose shall consist of two-thirds of the whole number of Senators, and a majority of the whole number shall be necessary to a choice. But no person constitutionally ineligible to the office of President shall be eligible to that of Vice-President of the United States.

CIVIL WAR AMENDMENTS

Amendment 13—Prohibition of Slavery

[Ratified December 6, 1865]

Section 1. Neither slavery nor involuntary servitude, except as a punishment for crime whereof the party shall have been duly convicted, shall exist within the United States, or any place subject to their jurisdiction.

Section 2. Congress shall have power to enforce this article by appropriate legislation.

Amendment 14—Citizenship, Due Process, and Equal Protection of the Laws

[Ratified July 9, 1868]

Section 1. All persons born or naturalized in the United States, and subject to the jurisdiction thereof, are citizens of the United States and of the State wherein they reside. No State shall make or enforce any law which shall abridge the privileges or immunities of citizens of the United States; nor shall any State deprive any person of life, liberty, or property, without due process of law; nor deny to any person within its jurisdiction the equal protection of the laws.

Section 2. Representatives shall be apportioned among the several States according to their respective numbers, counting the whole number of persons in each State, excluding Indians not taxed. But when the right to vote at any election for the choice of electors for President and Vice President of the United States, Representatives in Congress, the Executive and Judicial Officers of a State, or the members of the Legislature thereof, is denied to any of the male inhabitants of such State, being twenty-one years of age, and citizens of the United States, or in any way abridged, except for participation in rebellion, or other crime, the basis of representation therein shall be reduced in the proportion which the number of such male citizens shall bear to the whole number of male citizens twenty-one years of age in such State.

Section 3. No person shall be a Senator or Representative in Congress, or elector of President and Vice President, or hold any office, civil or military, under the United States, or under any State, who having previously taken an oath, as a member of Congress, or as an officer of the United States, or as a member of any State legislature, or as an executive or judicial officer of any State, to support the Constitution of the United States, shall have engaged in insurrection or rebellion against the same, or given aid or comfort to the enemies thereof. But Congress may by a vote of two-thirds of each House, remove such disability.

Section 4. The validity of the public debt of the United States, authorized by law, including debts incurred for payment of pensions and bounties for services in suppressing insurrection or rebellion, shall not be questioned. But neither the United States nor any State shall assume or pay any debt or obligation incurred in aid of insurrection or rebellion against the United States, or any claim for the loss or emancipation of any slave; but all such debts, obligations and claims shall be held illegal and void.

Section 5. The Congress shall have power to enforce, by appropriate legislation, the provisions of this article.

Amendment 15—The Right to Vote

[Ratified February 3, 1870]

Section 1. The right of citizens of the United States to vote shall not be denied or abridged by the United States or by any State on account of race, color, or previous condition of servitude.

Section 2. The Congress shall have power to enforce this article by appropriate legislation.

TWENTIETH-CENTURY AMENDMENTS

Amendment 16—Income Taxes

[Ratified February 3, 1913]

The Congress shall have power to lay and collect taxes on incomes, from whatever source derived, without apportionment among the several States, and without regard to any census or enumeration.

Amendment 17—Direct Election of Senators

[Ratified April 8, 1913]

The Senate of the United States shall be composed of two Senators from each State, elected by the people thereof for six years; and each Senator shall have one vote. The electors in each State shall have the qualifications requisite for electors of the most numerous branch of the State legislatures.

When vacancies happen in the representation of any State in the Senate, the executive authority of such State shall issue writs of election to fill such vacancies: *Provided,* That the legislature of any State may empower the executive thereof to make temporary appointments until the people fill the vacancies by election as the legislature may direct.

This amendment shall not be so construed as to affect the election or term of any Senator chosen before it becomes valid as part of the Constitution.

Amendment 18—Prohibition

[Ratified January 16, 1919]

Section 1. After one year from the ratification of this article the manufacture, sale, or transportation of intoxicating liquors within, the importation thereof into, or the exportation thereof from the United States and all territory subject to the jurisdiction thereof for beverage purposes is hereby prohibited.

Section 2. The Congress and the several States shall have concurrent power to enforce this article by appropriate legislation.

Section 3. This article shall be inoperative unless it shall have been ratified as an amendment to the Constitution by the legislatures of the several States, as provided in the Constitution, within seven years from the date of the submission hereof to the States by the Congress.

Amendment 19—For Women's Suffrage

[Ratified August 18, 1920]

The right of citizens of the United States to vote shall not be denied or abridged by the United States or by any State on account of sex. Congress shall have power to enforce this article by appropriate legislation.

Amendment 20—The Lame Duck Amendment

[Ratified January 23, 1933]

Section 1. The terms of the President and Vice President shall end at noon on the 20th day of January, and the terms of Senators and Representatives at noon on the 3d of January, of the years in which such terms would have ended if this article had not been ratified; and the terms of their successors shall then begin.

Section 2. The Congress shall assemble at least once in every year, and such meeting shall begin at noon on the 3d day of January, unless they shall by law appoint a different day.

Section 3. If, at the time fixed for the beginning of the term of the President, the President elect shall have died, the Vice President elect shall become President. If a President shall not have been chosen before the time fixed for the beginning of his term, or if the President elect shall have failed to qualify, then the Vice President elect shall act as President until a President shall have qualified; and the Congress may by law provide for the case wherein neither a President elect nor a Vice President elect shall have qualified, declaring who shall then act as President, or the manner in which one who is to act shall be selected, and such person shall act accordingly until a President or Vice President shall have qualified.

Section 4. The Congress may by law provide for the case of the death of any of the persons from whom the House of Representatives may choose a President whenever the right of choice shall have devolved upon them, and for the case of the death of any of the persons from whom the Senate may choose a Vice President whenever the right of choice shall have devolved upon them.

Section 5. Sections 1 and 2 shall take effect on the 15th day of October following the ratification of this article.

Section 6. This article shall be inoperative unless it shall have been ratified as an amendment to the Constitution by the legislatures of three-fourths of the several States within seven years from the date of its submission.

Amendment 21—Repeal of Prohibition

[Ratified December 5, 1933]

Section 1. The eighteenth article of amendment to the Constitution of the United States is hereby repealed.

Section 2. The transportation or importation into any State, Territory, or possession of the United States for delivery or use therein of intoxicating liquors, in violation of the laws thereof, is hereby prohibited.

Section 3. This article shall be inoperative unless it shall have been ratified as an amendment to the Constitution by conventions in the several States,

Amendment 22—Number of Presidential Terms

[Ratified February 27, 1951]

Section 1. No person shall be elected to the office of the President more than twice, and no person who has held the office of President, or acted as President for more than two years of a term to which some other person was elected President shall be elected to the office of the President more than once. But this Article shall not apply to any person holding the office of President when this Article was proposed by the Congress, and shall not prevent any person who may be holding the office of President, or acting as President, during the term within which this Article becomes operative from holding the office of President or acting as President during the remainder of such term.

Section 2. This article shall be inoperative unless it shall have been ratified as an amendment to the Constitution by the legislatures of three-fourths of the several States within seven years from the date of its submission to the States by the Congress.

Amendment 23—Presidential Electors for the District of Columbia

[Ratified March 29, 1961]

Section 1. The District constituting the seat of Government of the United States shall appoint in such manner as the Congress may direct:

A number of electors of President and Vice President equal to the whole number of Senators and Representatives in Congress to which the District would be entitled if it were a State, but in no event more than the least populous State; they shall be in addition to those appointed by the States, but they shall be considered, for the purposes of the election of President and Vice President, to be electors appointed by a State; and they shall meet in the District and perform such duties as provided by the twelfth article of amendment.

Section 2. The Congress shall have power to enforce this article by appropriate legislation.

Amendment 24—The Anti-Poll Tax Amendment

[Ratified January 23, 1964]

Section 1. The right of citizens of the United States to vote in any primary or other election for President or Vice President, for electors for President or Vice President, or for Senator or Representative in Congress, shall not be denied or abridged by the United States or any State by reason of failure to pay any poll tax or other tax.

Section 2. The Congress shall have power to enforce this article by appropriate legislation.

Amendment 25—Presidential Disability, Vice Presidential Vacancies

[Ratified February 10, 1967]

Section 1. In case of the removal of the President from office or of his death or resignation, the Vice President shall become President.

Section 2. Whenever there is a vacancy in the office of the Vice President, the President shall nominate a Vice President who shall take office upon confirmation by a majority vote of both Houses of Congress.

Section 3. Whenever the President transmits to the President pro tempore of the Senate and the Speaker of the House of Representatives his written declaration that he is unable to discharge the powers and duties of his office, and until he transmits to them a written declaration to the contrary, such powers and duties shall be discharged by the Vice President as Acting President.

Section 4. Whenever the Vice President and a majority of either the principal officers of the executive departments or of such other body as Congress may by law provide, transmit to the President pro tempore of the Senate and the Speaker of the House of Representatives their written declaration that the President is unable to discharge the powers and duties of his office, the Vice President shall immediately assume the powers and duties of the office as Acting President.

Thereafter, when the President transmits to the President pro tempore of the Senate and the Speaker of the House of Representatives his written declaration that no inability exists, he shall resume the powers and duties of his office unless the Vice President and a majority of either the principal officers of the executive department or of such other body as Congress may by law provide, transmit within four days to the President protempore of the Senate and the Speaker of the House of Representatives their written declaration that the President is unable to discharge the powers and duties of his office. Thereupon Congress shall decide the issue, assembling within forty-eight hours for that purpose if not in session. If the Congress, within twenty-one days after receipt of the latter written declaration, or, if Congress is not in session, within twenty-one days after Congress is required to assemble, determines by two-thirds vote of both Houses that the President is unable to discharge the powers and duties of his office, the Vice President shall continue to discharge the same as Acting President; otherwise, the President shall resume the powers and the duties of his office.

Amendment 26—Eighteen-Year-Old Vote

[Ratified June 30, 1971]

Section 1. The right of citizens of the United States, who are eighteen years of age or older, to vote shall not be denied or abridged by the United States or by any State on account of age.

Section 2. The Congress shall have the power to enforce this article by appropriate legislation.

Appendix B: Two Selections from *The Federalist*

The Federalist Papers are not only the most influential commentary ever written on the U.S. Constitution. They are also a starting point for some of the major American political thinking of today. This appendix allows you to see why by examining two of the 85 papers that James Madison, Alexander Hamilton, and John Jay wrote in support of the Constitution (see Chapter 2). Madison is the author of both: No. 10 is an elegant essay on representation; and No. 51 is an essay on checks and balances and the separation of powers.

Footnote on "faction." By "faction," Madison, like other founding fathers, meant any group assembled for the promotion of its own private interests at the expense of the public. Factions were part of the price paid for the liberty that went with republican government. What Madison sought and found in a republic of large size was a way not to prevent factions but to frustrate them. It was not a question of letting them fight it out until the biggest or best won. What Madison wanted was a deadlock of all private interests to make way for public virtue. This is the way it works: When a nation encourages the interplay of many different interests, the net effect is to *block them all*. Thus, above the squabble over self-interest, the true interest of the people may shine. Or so went Madison's theory of government.

10
MADISON

The Size and Variety of the Union as a Check on Faction

To the People of the State of New York:
Among the numerous advantages promised by a well-constructed Union, none deserves to be more accurately developed than its tendency to break and control the violence of faction. The friend of popular governments never finds himself so much alarmed for their character and fate, as when he contemplates their propensity to this dangerous vice. He will not fail, therefore, to set a due value on any plan which, without violating the principles to which he is attached, provides a proper cure for it. The instability, injustice, and confusion introduced into the public councils, have, in truth, been the mortal diseases under which popular governments have everywhere perished; as they continue to be the favorite and fruitful topics from which the adversaries to liberty derive their most specious declamations. The valuable improvements made by the American constitutions on the popular models, both ancient and modern, cannot certainly be too much admired; but it would be an unwarrantable partiality, to contend that they have as effectually obvi-

ated the danger on this side, as was wished and expected. Complaints are everywhere heard from our most considerate and virtuous citizens, equally the friends of public and private faith, and of public and personal liberty, that our governments are too unstable, that the public good is disregarded in the conflicts of rival parties, and that measures are too often decided, not according to the rules of justice and the rights of the minor party, but by the superior force of an interested and overbearing majority. However anxiously we may wish that these complaints had no foundation, the evidence of known facts will not permit us to deny that they are in some degree true. It will be found, indeed, on a candid review of our situation, that some of the distresses under which we labor have been erroneously charged on the operation of our governments; but it will be found, at the same time, that other causes will not alone account for many of our heaviest misfortunes; and, particularly, for that prevailing and increasing distrust of public engagements, and alarm for private rights, which are echoed from one end of the continent to the other. These must be chiefly, if not wholly, effects of the unsteadiness and injustice with which a factious spirit has tainted our public administrations.

By a faction, I understand a number of citizens, whether amounting to a majority or minority of the whole, who are united and actuated by some common impulse of passion, or of interest, adverse to the rights of other citizens, or to the permanent and aggregate interests of the community.

There are two methods of curing the mischiefs of faction: the one, by removing its causes; the other, by controlling its effects.

There are again two methods of removing the causes of faction: the one, by destroying the liberty which is essential to its existence; the other, by giving to every citizen the same opinions, the same passions, and the same interests.

It could never be more truly said than of the first remedy, that it was worse than the disease. Liberty is to faction what air is to fire, an aliment without which it instantly expires. But it could not be less folly to abolish liberty, which is essential to political life, because it nourishes faction, than it would be to wish the annihilation of air, which is essential to animal life, because it imparts to fire its destructive agency.

The second expedient is as impracticable as the first would be unwise. As long as the reason of man continues fallible, and he is at liberty to exercise it, different opinions will be formed. As long as the connection subsists between his reason and his self-love, his opinions and his passions will have a reciprocal influence on each other: and the former will be objects to which the latter will attach themselves. The diversity in the faculties of men, from which the rights of property originate, is not less an insuperable obstacle to a uniformity of interests. The protection of these faculties is the first object of government. From the protection of different and unequal faculties of acquiring property, the possession of different degrees and kinds of property immediately results; and from the influence of these on the sentiments and views of the respective proprietors, ensues a division of the society into different interests and parties.

The latent causes of faction are thus sown in the nature of man; and we see them everywhere brought into different degrees of activity, according to the different circumstances of civil society. A zeal for different opinions concerning religion, concerning government, and many other points, as well of speculation as of practice; an attachment to different leaders ambitiously contending for pre-eminence and power; or to persons of other descriptions whose fortunes have been interesting to the human passions, have, in turn, divided mankind into parties, inflamed them with mutual animosity, and rendered them much more disposed to vex and oppress each other than to co-operate for their common good. So strong is this propensity of mankind to fall into mutual animosities, that where no substantial occasion presents itself, the most frivolous and fanciful distinctions have been sufficient to kindle their unfriendly passions and excite their most violent conflicts. But the most common and durable source of factions has been the various and unequal distribution of property. Those who hold and those who are without property have ever formed distinct interests in society. Those who are creditors, and those who are debtors, fall under a like discrimination. A landed interest, a manufacturing interest, a mercantile interest, a moneyed interest, with many lesser interests, grow up of necessity in civilized nations, and divide them into different classes, actuated by different sentiments and views. The regulation of these various and interfering interests forms the principal task of modern legislation, and involves the spirit of party and faction in the necessary and ordinary operations of the government.

No man is allowed to be a judge in his own cause, because his interest would certainly bias his judgment, and, not improbably, corrupt his integrity. With equal, nay with greater reason, a body of men are unfit to be both judges and parties at the same time; yet what are many of the most important acts of legislation, but so many judicial determinations, not indeed concerning the rights of single persons, but concerning the rights of large bodies of citizens? And what are the different classes of legislators but advocates and parties to the causes which they determine? Is a law proposed concerning private debts? It is a question to which the creditors are parties on one side and the debtors on the other. Justice ought to hold the balance between them. Yet the parties are, and must be, themselves the judges; and the most numerous party, or, in other words, the most powerful faction must be expected to prevail. Shall domestic manufactures be encouraged, and in what degree, by restrictions on foreign manufactures? are questions which would be differently decided by the landed and the manufacturing classes, and probably by neither with a sole regard to justice and the public good. The apportionment of taxes on the various descriptions of property is an act which seems to require the most exact impartiality; yet there is, perhaps, no legislative act in which greater opportunity and temptation are given to a predominant party to trample on the rules of justice. Every shilling with which they overburden the inferior number, is a shilling saved to their own pockets.

It is in vain to say that enlightened statesmen will be able to adjust these clashing interests, and render them all subservient to the public good. Enlightened statesmen will not always be at the helm. Nor, in many cases, can such an adjustment be made at all without taking into view indirect and remote considerations, which will rarely prevail over the immediate interest which one party may find in disregarding the rights of another or the good of the whole.

The inference to which we are brought is, that the *causes* of faction cannot be removed, and that relief is only to be sought in the means of controlling its *effects*.

If a faction consists of less than a majority, relief is supplied by the republican principle, which enables the majority to defeat its sinister views by regular vote. It may clog the administration, it may convulse the society; but it will be unable to execute and mask its violence under the forms of the Constitution. When a majority is included in a faction, the form of popular government, on the other hand, enables it to sacrifice to its ruling passion or interest both the public good and the rights of other citizens. To secure the public good and private rights against the danger of such a faction, and at the same time to preserve the spirit and the form of popular government, is then the great object to which our inquiries are directed. Let me add that it is the great desideratum by which this form of government can be rescued from the opprobrium under which it has so long labored, and be recommended to the esteem and adoption of mankind.

By what means is this object attainable? Evidently by one of two only. Either the existence of the same passion or interest in a majority at the same time must be prevented, or the majority, having such coexistent passion or interest, must be rendered, by their number and local situation, unable to concert and carry into effect schemes of oppression. If the impulse and the opportunity be suffered to coincide, we well know that neither moral nor religious motives can be relied on as an adequate control. They are not found to be such on the injustice and violence of individuals, and lose their efficacy in proportion to the number combined together, that is, in proportion as their efficacy becomes needful.

From this view of the subject it may be concluded that a pure democracy, by which I mean a society consisting of a small number of citizens, who assemble and administer the government in person, can admit of no cure for the mischiefs of faction. A common passion or interest will, in almost every case, be felt by a majority of the whole; a communication and concert result from the form of government itself; and there is nothing to check the inducements to sacrifice the weaker party or an obnoxious individual. Hence it is that such democracies have ever been spectacles of turbulence and contention; have ever been found incompatible with personal security or the rights of property; and have in general been as short in their lives as they have been violent in their deaths. Theoretic politicians, who have patronized this species of government, have erroneously supposed that by reducing mankind to a perfect equality in their political rights, they would, at the same time, be perfectly equalized and assimilated in their possessions, their opinions, and their passions.

A republic, by which I mean a government in which the scheme of representation takes place, opens a different prospect, and promises the cure for which we are seeking. Let us examine the points in which it varies from pure democracy, and we shall comprehend both the nature of the cure and the efficacy which it must derive from the Union.

The two great points of difference between a democracy and a republic are: first, the delegation of the government, in the latter, to a small number of citizens elected by the rest; secondly, the greater number of citizens, and greater sphere of country, over which the latter may be extended.

The effect of the first difference is, on the one hand, to refine and enlarge the public views, by passing them through the medium of a chosen body of citizens, whose wisdom may best discern the true interest of their country, and whose patriotism and love of justice will be least likely to sacrifice it to temporary or partial considerations. Under such a regulation, it may well happen that the public voice, pronounced by the representatives of the people, will be more consonant to the public good than if pronounced by the people themselves, convened for the purpose. On the other hand, the effect may be inverted. Men of factious tempers, of local prejudices, or of sinister designs, may, by intrigue, by corruption, or by other means, first obtain the suffrages, and then betray the interests, of the people. The question resulting is, whether small or extensive republics are more favorable to the election of proper guardians of the public weal; and it is clearly decided in favor of the latter by two obvious considerations:

In the first place, it is to be remarked that, however small the republic may be, the representatives must be raised to a certain number, in order to guard against the cabals of a few; and that, however large it may be, they must be limited to a certain number, in order to guard against the confusion of a multitude. Hence, the number of representatives in the two cases not being in proportion to that of the two constituents, and being proportionally greater in the small republic, it follows that, if the proportion of fit characters be not less in the large than in the small republic, the former will present a greater option, and consequently a greater probability of a fit choice.

In the next place, as each representative will be chosen by a greater number of citizens in the large than in the small republic, it will be more difficult for unworthy candidates to practise with success the vicious arts by which elections are too often carried; and the suffrages of the people being more free, will be more likely to centre in men who possess the most attractive merit and the most diffusive and established characters.

It must be confessed that in this, as in most other cases, there is a mean, on both sides of which inconveniences will be found to lie. By enlarging too much the number of electors, you render the representative too little acquainted with all their local circumstances and lesser interests; as by reducing it too much, you render him unduly attached to these, and too little fit to comprehend and pursue great and national objects. The federal Constitution forms a happy combination in this respect; the great and aggregate interests being referred to the national, the local and particular to the State legislatures.

The other point of difference is, the greater number of citizens and extent of territory which may be brought within the compass of republican than of democratic government; and it is this circumstance principally which renders factious combinations less to be dreaded in the former than in the latter. The smaller the society, the fewer probably will be the distinct parties and interests composing it; the fewer the distinct parties and interests, the more frequently will a majority be found of the same party; and the smaller the number of individuals composing a majority, and the smaller the compass within which they are placed, the most easily will they concert and execute their plans of oppression. Extend the sphere, and you take in a greater variety of parties and interests; you make it less probable that a majority of the whole will have a common motive to invade the rights of other citizens; or if such a common motive exists, it will be more difficult for all who feel it to discover their own strength, and to act in unison with each other. Besides other impediments, it may be remarked that, where there is a consciousness of unjust or dishonorable purposes, communication is always checked by distrust in proportion to the number whose concurrence is necessary.

Hence, it clearly appears, that the same advantage which a republic has over a democracy, in controlling the effects of faction, is enjoyed by a large over a small republic,—is enjoyed by the Union over the States composing it. Does the advantage consist in the substitution of representatives whose enlightened views and virtuous sentiments render them superior to local prejudices and to schemes of injustice? It will not be denied that the representation of the Union will be most likely to possess these requisite endowments. Does it consist in the greater security afforded by a greater variety of parties, against the event of any one party being able to outnumber and oppress the rest? In an equal degree does the increased variety of parties comprised within the Union, increase this security. Does it, in fine, consist in the greater obstacles opposed to the concert and accomplishment of the secret wishes of an unjust and interested majority? Here, again, the extent of the Union gives it the most palpable advantage.

The influence of factious leaders may kindle a flame within their particular States, but will be unable to spread a general conflagration through the other States. A religious sect may degenerate into a political faction in a part of the Confederacy; but the variety of sects dispersed over the entire face of it must secure the national councils against any danger from that source. A rage for paper money, for an abolition of debts, for an equal division of property, or for any other improper or wicked project, will be less apt to pervade the whole body of the Union than a particular member of it;

in the same proportion as such a malady is more likely to taint a particular county or district, than an entire State.

In the extent and proper structure of the Union, therefore, we behold a republican remedy for the diseases most incident to republican government. And according to the degree of pleasure and pride we feel in being republicans, ought to be our zeal in cherishing the spirit and supporting the character of Federalists.

PUBLIUS

51
MADISON

Checks and Balances

To the People of the State of New York:
To what expedient, then, shall we finally resort, for maintaining in practice the necessary partition of power among the several departments, as laid down in the Constitution? The only answer that can be given is, that as all these exterior provisions are found to be inadequate, the defect must be supplied, by so contriving the interior structure of the government as that its several constituent parts may, by their mutual relations, be the means of keeping each other in their proper places. Without presuming to undertake a full development of this important idea, I will hazard a few general observations, which may perhaps place it in a clearer light, and enable us to form a more correct judgment of the principles and structure of the government planned by the convention.

In order to lay a due foundation for that separate and distinct exercise of the different powers of government, which to a certain extent is admitted on all hands to be essential to the preservation of liberty, it is evident that each department should have a will of its own; and consequently should be so constituted that the members of each should have as little agency as possible in the appointment of the members of the others. Were this principle rigorously adhered to, it would require that all the appointments for the supreme executive, legislative, and judiciary magistracies should be drawn from the same fountain of authority, the people, through channels having no communication whatever with one another. Perhaps such a plan of constructing the several departments would be less difficult in practice than it may in contemplation appear. Some difficulties, however, and some additional expense would attend the execution of it. Some deviations, therefore, from the principle must be admitted. In the constitution of the judiciary department in particular, it might be inexpedient to insist rigorously on the principle: first, because peculiar qualifications being essential in the members, the primary consideration ought to be to select that mode of choice which best secures these qualifications; secondly, because the permanent tenure by which the appointments are held in that department, must soon destroy all sense of dependence on the authority conferring them.

It is equally evident, that the members of each department should be as little dependent as possible on those of the others, for the emoluments annexed to their offices. Were the executive magistrate, or the judges, not independent of the legislature in this particular, their independence in every other would be merely nominal.

But the great security against a gradual concentration of the several powers in the same department, consists in giving to those who administer each department the necessary constitutional means and personal motives to resist encroachments of the others. The provision for defence must in this, as in all other cases, be made commensurate to the danger of attack. Ambition must be made to counteract ambition. The interest of the man must be connected with the constitutional rights of the place. It may be a reflection on human nature, that such devices should be necessary to control the abuses of government. But what is government itself, but the greatest of all reflections on human nature? If men were angels, no government would be necessary. If angels were to govern men, neither external nor internal controls on government would be necessary. In framing a government which is to be administered by men over men, the great difficulty lies in this: you must first enable the government to control the governed; and in the next place oblige it to control itself. A dependence on the people is, no doubt, the primary control on the government; but experience has taught mankind the necessity of auxiliary precautions.

This policy of supplying, by opposite and rival interests, the defect of better motives, might be traced through the whole system of human affairs, private as well as public. We see it particularly displayed in all the subordinate distributions of power, where the constant aim is to divide and arrange the several offices in such a manner as that each may be a check on the other—that the private interest of every individual may be a sentinel over the public rights. These inventions of prudence cannot be less requisite in the distribution of the supreme powers of the State.

But it is not possible to give to each department an equal power of self-defence. In republican government, the legislative authority necessarily predominates. The remedy for this inconveniency is to divide the legislature into different branches; and to render them, by different modes of election and different principles of action, as little connected with each other as the nature of their common functions and their common dependence on the society will admit. It may even be necessary to guard against dangerous encroachments by still further precautions. As the weight of the legislative authority requires that it should be thus divided, the weakness of the executive may require, on the other hand, that it should be fortified. An absolute negative on the legislature appears, at first view, to be the natural defence with which the executive magistrate should be armed. But perhaps it would be neither altogether safe nor alone sufficient. On ordinary occasions it might not be exerted with the requisite firmness, and on extraordinary occasions it might be perfidiously abused. May not this defect of an absolute negative be supplied by some qualified connection between this weaker department and the weaker branch of the stronger department, by which the latter may be led to support the constitutional rights of the former, without being too much detached from the rights of its own department?

If the principles on which these observations are founded be just, as I persuade myself they are, and they be applied as a criterion to the several State constitutions, and to the federal Constitution, it will be found that if the latter does not perfectly correspond with them, the former are infinitely less able to bear such a test.

There are, moreover, two considerations particularly applicable to the federal system of America, which place that system in a very interesting point of view.

First. In a single republic, all the power surrendered by the people is submitted to the administration of a single government; and the usurpations are guarded against by a division of the government into distinct and separate departments. In the compound republic of America, the power surrendered by the people is first divided between two distinct governments, and then the portion allotted to each subdivided among distinct and separate departments. Hence a double security arises to the rights of the people. The different governments will control each other, at the same time that each will be controlled by itself.

Second. It is of great importance in a republic not only to guard the society against the oppression of its rulers, but to guard one part of the society against the injustice of the other part. Different interests necessarily exist in different classes of citizens. If a majority be united by a common interest, the rights of the minority will be insecure. There are but two methods of providing against this evil: the one by creating a will in the community independent of the majority—that is, of the society itself; the other, by comprehending in the society so many separate descriptions of citizens as will render an unjust combination of a majority of the whole very improbable, if not impracticable. The first method prevails in all governments possessing an hereditary or self-appointed authority. This, at best, is but a precarious security; because a power independent of the society may as well espouse the unjust views of the major, as the rightful interests of the minor party, and may possibly be turned against both parties. The second method will be exemplified in the federal republic of the United States. Whilst all authority in it will be derived from and dependent on the society, the society itself will be broken into so many parts, interests and classes of citizens, that the rights of individuals, or of the minority, will be in little danger from interested combinations of the majority. In a free government the security for civil rights must be the same as that for religious rights. It consists in the one case in the multiplicity of interests, and in the other in the multiplicity of sects. The degree of security in both cases will depend on the number of interests and sects; and this may be presumed to depend on the extent of country and number of people comprehended under the same government. This view of the subject must particularly recommend a proper federal system to all the sincere and considerate friends of republican government, since it shows that in exact proportion as the territory of the Union may be formed into more circumscribed Confederacies, or States, oppressive combinations of a majority will be facilitated; the best security, under the republican forms, for the rights of every class of citizens, will be diminished; and consequently the stability and independence of some member of the government, the only other security, must be proportionally increased. Justice is the end of government. It is the end of civil society. It ever has been and ever will be pursued until it be obtained, or until liberty be lost in the pursuit. In a society under the forms of which the stronger faction can readily unite and oppress the weaker, anarchy may as truly be said to reign as in a state of nature, where the weaker individual is not secured against the violence of the stronger; and as, in the latter state, even the stronger individuals are prompted, by the uncertainty of their condition, to submit to a government which may protect the weak as well as themselves; so, in the former state, will the more powerful factions or parties be gradually induced, by a like motive, to wish for a government which will protect all parties, the weaker as well as the more powerful. It can be little doubted that if the State of Rhode Island was separated from the Confederacy and left to itself, the insecurity of rights under the popular form of government within such narrow limits would be displayed by such reiterated oppressions of factious majorities that some power altogether independent of the people would soon be called for by the voice of the very factions whose misrule had proved the necessity of it. In the extended republic of the United States, and among the great variety of interests, parties, and sects which it embraces, a coalition of a majority of the whole society could seldom take place on any other principles than those of justice and the general good; whilst there being thus less danger to a minor from the will of a major party, there must be less pretext, also, to provide for the security of the former, by introducing into the government a will not dependent on the latter, or, in other words, a will independent of the society itself. It is no less certain than it is important, notwithstanding the contrary opinions which have been entertained, that the larger the society, provided it lie within a practical sphere, the more duly capable it will be of self-government. And happily for the *republican cause*, the practicable sphere may be carried to a very great extent, by a judicious modification and mixture of the *federal principle*.

PUBLIUS

Appendix C: Acquiring Information More Efficiently

This appendix builds on two assumptions—one old, the other modern. The old one was concisely put by Sir Francis Bacon in 1597: "Knowledge is power." The modern one is that Americans are in the midst of an information deluge, powered largely by the stunning advances in microelectronics.

The table below is designed to provide a convenient guide to the list of sources that follows it. For those who want more than provided in the appendix, *The National Directory of Addresses and Telephone Numbers* (Bantam Books, 666 Fifth Ave., New York, New York, 10019; $14.95) is an excellent place to look. This reference book provides the 50,000 most wanted numbers in the United States listed alphabetically and by category.

One other general observation. While most of the sources given in this appendix are national organizations, many have counterparts at the state and local levels. For example, most states have a Consumer Protection Division in

For These CONCERNS...	Call or write these SOURCES...
Citizen action	1, 2, 3, 4, 5
Civil rights and discrimination	6, 7, 8, 9, 10, 11, 12, 13, 14, 15, 16, 17
Consumer affairs	1, 2, 18, 19, 20, 21, 22, 23, 24, 25, 26, 27, 28, 29
Courts	32, 33
Credit	30, 31
Crime prevention	34, 35, 36, 37, 38
Financial and business assistance	43, 44, 45, 46, 47, 48, 49, 50, 51, 52
Government employment	10, 39, 40, 41, 81
Information rights	86
Legal services	53, 54, 55, 56, 57
Lobbying	58
Media	59, 60, 61, 62, 63, 64, 65
Political action	66, 67, 68, 69, 70, 71, 72, 73, 74, 75, 76
Volunteerism	77, 78, 79, 80, 81, 82, 83, 84
Voting records of members of Congress	85

their office of the attorney general. And the Yellow Pages of any major city have an entry "Legal Aid" for those seeking legal services.

If you need information on any of the programs or services of the federal government, visit, telephone, or write the nearest Federal Information Center (FIC) in your area. They will search their own resources, or provide the proper referral, so you can get the answers or publications that you need. A free pamphlet, updated periodically, listing the local FICs, may be picked up at your nearest FIC office or from FIC, General Services Administration, Washington, D.C., 20405.

1. **National PIRG Clearinghouse**
   1329 E Street, N.W., Suite 1127
   Washington, D.C. 20004

2. **Citizen Action Group**
   Public Citizen
   1346 Connecticut Avenue, N.W. #1209
   Washington, D.C. 20036

3. **National Association of Neighborhoods (NAN)**
   1901 Que Street, N.W.
   Washington, D.C. 20009

4. **National Community Development Association (NCDA)**
   1620 Eye Street, N.W., Suite 503
   Washington, D.C. 20006

5. **Department of Housing and Community Development**
   1325 G Street, N.W., Room 904
   Washington, D.C. 20005

6. **Office of Civil Rights**
   H.E.W. North Building
   330 Independence Avenue, S.W.
   Washington, D.C. 20201

7. **American Civil Liberties Union (ACLU)**
   22 East 40th Street
   New York, N.Y. 10016

8. **Operation P.U.S.H.**
   930 East 50th Street
   Chicago, Ill. 60615

9. **Equal Employment Opportunity Commission**
   2401 E Street, N.W.
   Washington, D.C. 20506

10. **U.S. Department of Labor**
    Employment Standards Administration
    Washington, D.C. 20210

11. **U.S. Department of Housing and Urban Development**
    451 7th Street, S.W.
    Washington, D.C. 20410

12. **National Association for the Advancement of Colored People (NAACP)**
    1790 Broadway
    New York, N.Y. 10019

13. **National Urban League**
    500 East 62nd Street
    New York, N.Y. 10021

14. **American Jewish Committee**
    Institute of Human Relations
    165 East 56th Street
    New York, N.Y. 10022

15. **Anti-Defamation League of B'nai B'rith**
    315 Lexington Avenue
    New York, N.Y. 10016

16. **NOW Legal Defense and Educational Fund**
    9 West 57th Street
    New York, N.Y. 10019

17. **National Conference of Christians and Jews (NCCJ)**
    43 West 57th Street
    New York, N.Y. 10019

18. **Council of Better Business Bureaus**
    1150 17th Street, N.W.
    Washington, D.C. 20036

19. **Federal Trade Commission**
    Pennsylvania Ave at 6th St., N.W.
    Washington, DC 20580

20. **The Food and Drug Administration**
    5600 Fishers Lane
    Rockville, Md. 20852

21. **U.S. Consumer Product Safety Commission**
    1111 18th St., N.W.
    Washington, D.C. 20207

22. **Consumer Federation of America**
    State and Local Organizing Project
    1012 14th Street, N.W.
    Washington, D.C. 20005

23. **Office of Consumer Affairs**
    U.S. Department of Health, Education, and Welfare
    621 Reporters Building
    Washington, D.C. 20201

24. **Office of Consumer Inquiries**
    U.S. Food and Drug Administration (FDA)
    U.S. Department of Health, Education, and Welfare

5600 Fishers Lane
Rockville, Md. 20857

25. **Office of the Ombudsman Consumer Affairs Division**
U.S. Department of Commerce
Washington, D.C. 20230

26. **Office of Public Information**
Federal Trade Commission (FTC)
6th Street and Pennsylvania Avenue, N.W.
Washington, D.C. 20580

27. **U.S. Consumer Product Safety Commission**
5401 Westbard Avenue
Washington, D.C. 20207

28. **Center for the Study of Responsive Law**
P.O. Box 19367
Washington, D.C. 20036

29. **Consumers' Research Inc.**
Bowerstown Road
Washington, N.J. 07882

30. **Bureau of Consumer Protection**
Federal Trade Commission
Washington, D.C. 20850

31. **National Foundation for Consumer Credit, Inc.**
1819 H Street, N.W.
Washington, D.C. 20006

32. **Supreme Court of the United States**
Office of the Clerk
1st and East Capitol Streets, N.E., Room 17
Washington, D.C. 20543

33. **Federal Mediation and Conciliation Service**
2100 K Street, N.W.
Washington, D.C. 20427

34. **National Neighborhood Watch Program**
National Sheriffs' Association
1250 Connecticut Avenue, N.W.
Washington, D.C. 20036

35. **National Association of Citizens Crime Commissions**
1336 Hickory Street
Waukegan, Ill. 60085

36. **U.S. Department of Justice**
Federal Bureau of Investigation
Washington, D.C. 20535

37. **National Alliance for Safer Cities**
165 East 56th Street
New York, N.Y. 10022

38. **Office of Community Anti-Crime Program**
Law Enforcement Assistance Administration (L.E.A.A.)
U.S. Department of Justice
633 Indiana Avenue, N.W.
Washington, D.C. 20531

39. **Office of Personnel Management**
1900 E Street, N.W.
Washington, D.C. 20415

40. **Equal Employment Opportunity Commission (EEOC)**
2401 E Street, N.W.
Washington, D.C. 20506

41. **Employment Standards Administration**
Office of Information and Consumer Affairs
U.S. Department of Labor
Washington, D.C. 20210

42. **Foundation Center**
888 Seventh Avenue
New York, N.Y. 10019

43. **Aid to Families with Dependent Children (AFDC)**
Assistance Payments Administration
U.S. Department of Health, Education, and Welfare
Washington, D.C. 20201

44. **Social Security Administration**
U.S. Department of Health, Education and Welfare
6401 Security Boulevard
Baltimore, Md. 21235

45. **Food Stamp Program**
U.S. Department of Agriculture
Food and Nutrition Service (FNS)
500 12th Street, S.W., #650
Washington, D.C. 20250

46. **National Center for Productivity and Quality of Working Life**
Washington, D.C. 20036

47. **Internal Revenue Service (IRS)**
U.S. Department of the Treasury
111 Constitution Avenue, N.W.
Washington, D.C. 20226

48. **U.S. Department of Commerce**
14th Street between Constitution Avenue Street, N.W.
Washington, D.C. 20230

49. **U.S. Small Business Administration (SBA)**
1441 L Street, N.W.
Washington, D.C. 20416

50. **Business and Professional Women's Foundation**
2012 Massachusetts Avenue, N.W.
Washington, D.C. 20036

51. **Chamber of Commerce of the United States**
1615 H Street, N.W.
Washington, D.C. 20062

52. **The Conference Board**
845 Third Avenue
New York, N.Y. 10022

53. **Legal Services Corporation**
733 15th Street, N.W.
Washington, D.C. 20005

54. **Legal Services Corporation**
National Clearinghouse for Legal Services
500 North Michigan Avenue, Suite 1940
Chicago, Ill. 60611

55. **Standing Committee on Lawyer Referral Service**
American Bar Association
1155 East 60th Street
Chicago, Ill. 60637

56. **American Bar Association (ABA)**
1155 East 60th Street
Chicago, Ill. 60637

57. **Women's Legal Defense Fund**
1424 16th St. N.W.
Washington, D.C. 20036

58. **The Congressional Quarterly, Inc.**
1414 22nd St., N.W.
Washington, D.C. 20037
Publishes a guide to the thousands of organizations that lobby in Washington.

59. **Federal Communications Commission (FCC)**
Consumer Assistance Office
Washington, D.C. 20554

60. **Media Access Project**
1912 N Street, N.W.
Washington, D.C. 20036

61. **Morality in the Media, Inc.**
487 Park Avenue
New York, N.Y. 10022

62. **National Advertising Review Board (NARB)**
845 Third Avenue
New York, N.Y. 10022

63. **National Citizens Committee for Broadcasting (NCCB)**
1028 Connecticut Avenue, N.W.
Washington, D.C. 20036

64. **National News Council**
One Lincoln Plaza
New York, N.Y. 10023

65. **Women Against Violence in Pornography & Media (WAVPM)**
2112 Channing Way
Berkeley, Calif. 94704

66. **Federal Government Information Sources for the Public**
To find out the status of current federal legislation, you need to know the number, author, or subject of the bill in question. A computerized system in Washington, D.C., will then provide you with information on its status. You can find out those numbers by dialing (202) 555-1212 (Washington, D.C., information) and asking for the telephone numbers of the House Bill Status Office or the Senate Bill Status Office.

67. **The mailing addresses for Congress are:**
Senator _____
Senate Office Building
Washington, D.C. 20510
Representative _____
House Office Building
Washington, D.C. 20515

68. **Democratic National Committee**
1625 Massachusetts Avenue, N.W.
Washington, D.C. 20036

69. **Republican National Committee**
310 First Street, S.E.
Washington, D.C. 20003

70. **Common Cause**
2030 M Street, N.W.
Washington, D.C. 20036

71. **Council of State Governments**
Iron Works Pike
Lexington, Ky. 40511

72. **National Association of Counties (NACo)**
1735 New York Avenue, N.W.
Washington, D.C. 20006

73. **National League of Cities (NLC)**
1620 Eye Street, N.W.
Washington, D.C. 20006

74. **United States Conference of Mayors**
1620 Eye Street, N.W.
Washington, D.C. 20006

75. **National Federation of Republican Women**
310 First Street, S.E.
Washington, D.C. 20003

76. **National Organization for Women (NOW)**
425 13th Street, N.W.
Washington, D.C. 20004

77. **American National Red Cross**
17th and D Streets, N.W.
Washington, D.C. 20006

78. **Association of Junior Leagues, Inc. (AJL)**
825 Third Avenue
New York, N.Y. 10022

79. **National Center for Voluntary Action (NCVA)**
1214 16th Street, N.W.
Washington, D.C. 20036

80. **The Salvation Army**
120 West 14th Street
New York, N.Y. 10011

81. **ACTION**
Washington, D.C. 20525

82. **Volunteers of America**
National Headquarters
340 West 85th Street
New York, N.Y. 10024

83. **National Information Center on Volunteerism (NICOV)**
P.O. Box 4179
Boulder, Colo. 80306

84. **Alliance for Volunteerism**
1214 16th Street, N.W.
Washington, D.C. 20036

85. **Senate Journal and House Journal** daily record the votes taken. But for an analysis of individual voting records you might want to write:
For a liberal perspective:
Americans for Democratic Action,
1411 K St., N.W.
Washington, D.C. 20005
For a conservative perspective:
American Conservative Union, Suite 400,
316 Pennsylvania Avenue, S.E.
Washington, D.C. 20003
For a labor perspective:
American Federation of Labor & Congress of Industrial Organizations,
815 16th St., N.W.
Washington, D.C. 20006
For a business perspective:
National Association of Businessmen, Inc.
1000 Connecticut Avenue
Washington, D.C. 20036

86. The Freedom of Information Act applies only to documents held by the administrative agencies of the executive branch of the federal government. It does not apply to information maintained by the legislative and judicial branches. The executive branch includes executive departments and offices, military departments, government corporations, government controlled corporations, and independent regulatory agencies. All records in possession of these entities must be released to you upon request unless the information falls within one of the nine specific and narrowly drawn categories.

Among other things, the act grants public access to final opinions and orders of agencies, policy statements and interpretations not published in the Federal Register, administrative staff manuals, and government records that affect the public. Presidential papers have not been considered government records and have therefore not been required to be disclosed under the act.

There are many government documents that may be of interest to you. For example:

Reports compiled by the Department of Health, Education, and Welfare concerning conditions in federally supported nursing homes.

Data collected by the Agriculture Department regarding the purity and quality of meat and poultry products and the harmful effects of pesticides.

Records of regulatory agencies concerning such matters as airpollution control programs, the adverse effects of television violence, and the safety records of airlines.

Test results maintained by departments and agencies concerning the nutritional content of processed foods, the efficacy of drugs, and the safety and efficiency of all makes of automobiles.

Consumer complaints registered with the Federal Trade Commission regarding interstate moving companies, corporate marketing practices, and faulty products.

Some government documents may be of interest to you for more personal reasons. For example:

If you have worked for a federal agency or government contractor, or have been a member of any branch of the armed services, the federal government has a file on you.

If you have participated in any federally financed project, some agency has a record.

If you have been arrested by local, state, or federal authorities and your fingerprints were taken, the Federal Bureau of Investigation retains a record of the arrest.

If you have applied for a government subsidy for farming purposes or have received veteran's benefits—such as mortgage or education loans, employment opportunities, or medical services—the government has a file on you.

If you have lost your home or business in a natural disaster and accepted government loan assistance, participated in any federally funded project, or received medicare or social security benefits, there is a government file on you.

All this and more is available to you under the Freedom of Information Act. The FOIA does not obligate federal agencies to do research for you. For example, you cannot expect the agency to analyze documents or to collect information it does not have. However, if the information is on record—a document, a tape recording, a computer printout—the act can help you get it.

The only information that may be withheld under the act is that which falls within nine designated categories.

Locating records. To obtain the information you desire, you should first determine which agency is most likely to have it. The U.S. Government Manual lists all federal agencies and describes their functions. In addition, it usually lists their local and regional office addresses and telephone numbers. The Manual can be found in most libraries, and can be purchased for $6.50 by writing to the Superintendent of Documents, U.S. Government Printing Office, Washington, D.C. 20402. The Congressional Directory can also be of use since, like the manual, it lists the administrators of the various agencies. This too is available in most public libraries and can be purchased from the Government Printing Office for $6.50.

If you are unable to obtain a copy of the manual and are unsure of the location of the record or records you want, you should write to the agency you think is most likely to have them. In most cases, if the agency doesn't have the record, it will forward your letter to the appropriate source or tell you whom to write.

If you have reason to believe that a local or field office of a federal agency has the information you are seeking, it may also be helpful to contact that office with regard to your request. Most states have local federal offices, which are listed in the telephone books of the major cities. Or you can use the regional federal telephone books, which list the agencies operating in each area along with the names and titles of the policy-level employees. These books can usually be obtained at cost from the regional offices.

Making a request. When you have accumulated as much information about the record you want as is conveniently available, write a letter. It should be directed to the head of the agency whose address can be found in the Government Manual, the Congressional Directory, or in the list provided in this handbook. Or, you can write to the FOIA officer of the agency. However, if your telephone calls have uncovered the official directly responsible for the record you want, write to that official. In any event, it is always a good idea to write "Freedom of Information Request" on the bottom left-hand corner of the envelope.

Identify the records you want as accurately as possible. Although you are not required under the FOIA to specify a document by name or title, your request must "reasonably describe" the information sought. The more specific and limited the request, the greater the likelihood that it will be processed expeditiously. This could also result in savings in the cost of searching fees. (See section on fees.)

One of the principal differences between the FOIA and previous laws is that the individual seeking information is not required to demonstrate a need or even a reason for wanting it. But in some instances the probability of getting the information you desire may be enhanced by explaining your reasons for requesting it. Agency officials have the discretionary power to release files even where the law does not require it, and they may be more inclined to disclose information which could be withheld if they understand the uses to which it is to be put.

The House-Senate conference report on the 1974 amendments to the FOIA made it clear that Congress intended that "fees should not be used for the purpose of discouraging requests for information or as obstacles to disclosure of requested information."

Pursuant to the act, each agency is required to publish a uniform schedule of fees covering all the divisions of the agency. These fees may not exceed the actual costs of searching for and copying the requested documents. Moreover, agencies cannot charge for reviewing documents to determine whether all or portions of them should be withheld. Searching fees run around $5 per hour. The average charge for copying is 10¢ a page for standard size copies of 8 × 11 inches and 8 × 14 inches. Many agencies do not charge anything where the aggregate cost is less than $3 or $4.

If you want a waiver or reduction of the fees, you might benefit by stating your reasons for requesting the information since the act provides that agencies can waive or reduce fees when "furnishing the information can be considered as primarily benefiting the general public." They also have the option to disregard charges for indigent requesters. Another way to save money on reproduction expenses is to ask to see the documents at the agency rather than having copies made. Most agencies will be glad to make the necessary arrangements for this.

Here is a sample request letter:

Agency head or FOIA Officer
Title
Name of Agency
Address of Agency
City, State, Zip Code
     Re: Freedom of Information Act
       Request.
Dear ----------:
 Under the provisions of the Freedom of Information Act, 5 U.S.C. 522a, I am requesting access to (identify the records as clearly and specifically as possible).

If there are any fees for searching for, or copying, the records I have requested, please inform me before you fill the request. (Or: . . . please supply the records without informing me if the fees do not exceed $ _____.)
[Optional] I am requesting this information (state the reason for your request if you think it will assist you in obtaining the information.)
[Optional] As you know, the act permits you to reduce or waive fees when the release of the information is considered as "primarily benefiting the public." I believe that this request fits that category and I therefore ask that you waive any fees.

If all or any part of this request is denied, please cite the specific exemption(s) which you think justifies your refusal to release the information, and inform me of the appeal procedures available to me under the law.

I would appreciate your handling this request as quickly as possible, and I look forward to hearing from you within 10 days, as the law stipulates.

     Sincerely,

     Signature
     Name
     Address
     City, State, Zip Code

Requirements for agency responses. Federal agencies are required to respond to all requests for information within 10 working days (excluding Saturdays, Sundays, and holidays) after receipt of the request. If you are in a hurry to get the material, you might want to send your letter by certified mail and ask for a return receipt so you will know when the 10 days have run out. If you haven't received a reply by the end of that time (be sure to allow for the return mail), you can write a followup letter or telephone the agency to inquire about the delay.

If an agency runs into difficulty in meeting the 10-day time requirement due to "unusual circumstances," it must inform you in writing that an extension—not to exceed 10 more working days—will be required. Moreover, should your request be denied, the agency must tell you the reasons for the denial and advise you to whom you can appeal within the agency. It must also give you the names and addresses of those responsible for denying the request.

In most cases, agencies will do their best to respond within the designated time periods. However, they may sometimes fail to meet the 10-day guidelines due to substantial backlogs of requests. While it is your right to contest this in court, you should also realize that the government's failure to comply with the prescribed time limits may not of itself constitute a basis for the release of the records you seek.

Appendix D: A Brief Guide to Federal Statutory Forms and Judicial Reports

The first published official text of a statute is issued in a pamphlet or single sheet called a *slip law*. You can request a copy from the appropriate congressional clerk, from an individual member of Congress, or from the Superintendent of Documents, U.S. Government Printing Office.

At the end of each session of Congress, slip laws are accumulated, corrected, and issued in bound volumes known as the official *Statutes at Large* for that session. These are cited by volume and page. For example, "72 Stat 962" refers to page 962 of volume 72 of the *Statutes at Large*.

Since the *Statutes at Large* are a chronological collection of all private and public laws of one session of Congress, they are not very convenient to use, if, say, a researcher wanted to quickly finding out what laws were in effect concerning the protection of the environment. Fortunately, the law is codified (that is, systematically arranged) in the *U.S. Code*. This publication, arranged by subject matter, is fully revised every six years. Between revisions, annual cumulative supplements are issued. U.S. Code citation works a little differently than the *Statutes at Large*. For example, here is a U.S. Code citation: 42 U.S.C. 4907. The 42 refers not to the volume but to the title or subject matter (in this case, "Public Health and Welfare"); the 4907 refers not to the page but to the section (in this case, the labeling of products).

Courts interpret law. Thus, the sources to which a researcher can turn for case reports merit some explanation. The following explanation is from Victor G. Rosenblum and A. Didrick Castberg's *Cases on Constitutional Law*, (Homewood, Ill.: Dorsey Press, 1973):

> There are three primary sources for the complete reports of the Supreme Court decisions. The official government source is the *United States Reports*. The initials "U.S." between the volume and page numbers of the case identify the source: e.g., 347 U.S. 483 refers to the case beginning on page 483 of volume 347 of the *United States Reports*. Prior to 1875, the name of the reporter was used in place of "U.S." Thus the citation for *Marbury* v. *Madison*, 1 Cranch 137 (1803), refers to page 137 of volume 1 of Cranch's series of reports. The second widely used source for the text of Court decisions is the *Lawyers Edition* of the United States Supreme Court Reports, published by the Lawyers Cooperative Publishing Company and cited by the initials "L.Ed." between volume and page numbers. The third source, the *Supreme Court Reporter*, published by West Publishing Company, is cited as "Sup. Ct." Thus, *Brown* v. *Board of Education* would be cited 347 U.S. 483, 74 Sup. Ct. 693, and 98 L.Ed. 591 (1954).

Another source, especially valuable when one seeks the text of an opinion prior to its publication in the above volumes, is *United States Law Week*, published by the Bureau of National Affairs of Washington, D.C., immediately after the decision is handed down by the Court. The source is cited by the initials "L.W." and is usually found in articles and books discussing very recent cases.

The cases are generally referred to by the names of the litigants: Brown versus the Board of Education of Topeka, Kansas, where Brown is the party bringing the case against the Board of Education. Brown, variously called the "plaintiff," "appellant," and "petitioner," has lost the case in the lower court and is appealing to the Supreme Court. The Board of Education, the "defendant," "appellee," and "respondent," has won the case in the lower court and seeks to have the Supreme Court sustain the ruling of that court.

Glossary

Absentee requirement If a qualified voter because of travel, illness, or military obligations is unable to cast a ballot at the poll on election days, state laws have provisions to allow absentee voting. Generally, these voters must obtain ballots within a specified period preceding the election, mark it, and return it notarized to the proper official.

Access points Times and places within the policymaking process that are especially good for promoting one's point of view.

Accountability The principle according to which officials are held responsible for their actions by those who elected or appointed them. "Faceless bureaucracy" is a way of charging that there is no accountability.

Acquittal The formal determination by a court that the accused is not guilty of the offense as charged.

Act A legislature-passed statute or law. It may be called either by its official title (e.g., Labor Management Relations Act) or by the name of the legislators who sponsored it (e.g., Taft-Hartley Act).

Activists Individuals who are extensively and vigorously involved in political activity, either within or outside the party system, but who do not run for office.

Adjudication The act of settling a dispute judicially. This may occur in administrative agencies (e.g., the Interstate Commerce Commission) or courts.

Administrative law The body of law controlling authority and procedures of administrative agencies in their dealings with private interests. Administrative law also involves court review of how government agencies make and apply rules. Regulations made by bureaucratic agencies have the binding power of laws passed by Congress.

Administrative Procedures Act A major law, passed in 1946, requiring that regulatory agencies publicize their operations, give notice of proposed rules, and permit persons to testify. The act also provides standards for judicial review of agency decisions.

Adversary system The notion that justice emerges most readily from the clash of opposing views in a trial.

Advise and consent The Constitution allows the president to make treaties and appoint personnel subject to the "advice and consent" of the Senate.

Advisory committee Commissions composed of outsiders who are not government employees, whose function is to advise the government on how the bureaucracy should operate. Advisory committee members are often very sympathetic to the interests of the agencies they are advising.

Affirmative action The requirement, imposed by law or administrative regulation, that an organization (public and private) take steps to increase the number or proportion of minorities in its membership.

Age of majority The age (usually 18 or 21) when a person becomes an adult as specified by state law. It gives the individual both the rights and responsibilities of adulthood.

Agency An administrative division of a government set up to carry out certain laws.

Agenda A list of specific items of politically relevant issues to be considered at a legislative session, conference, or meeting.

Agenda setting The process by which certain items are put on or kept off an agenda.

Aid to Families with Dependent Children (AFDC) A major public assistance program that provides payments to low-income families with dependent children. States set benefit levels and eligibility requirements, though federal government partly finances it.

Alienation A sense of estrangement from society or one's work; a feeling of powerlessness to affect social change.

Alternatives The various courses of action from among which a government decision maker chooses in order to achieve certain goals or objectives.

Amendment An alteration or addition to a bill, motion,

GLOSSARY   G-1

or constitution. Congressional bills may be amended at virtually any point before they are passed; Article 5 of the Constitution specifies how constitutional amendments may be proposed.

Amicus curiae **brief** Written arguments filed in a court where a case is pending by groups or individuals who are not directly involved in the case but who have an interest in the outcome. These groups are referred to as "friends of the court."

Antifederalists Men who opposed adoption of the U.S. Constitution framed in 1787. After the Constitution was ratified, many of them became supporters of Thomas Jefferson and opponents of Alexander Hamilton and other Federalists.

Antitrust A policy that opposes the concentration of power in one of a few firms at the expense of competition.

Apartheid Policy of racial segregation against blacks and other of colored descent living in South Africa.

Appeal A legal proceeding in which a case is carried from a lower court to a higher court for review or reexamination.

Appeasement The policy of trying to avoid conflict by injudicious and unilateral concessions that weaken those who make them and often hurt third parties.

Appellate courts Those courts in which appeals of lower court decisions are heard. In the federal court system, the 11 Courts of Appeals and the Supreme Court are appellate courts.

Apportionment The determination of the number of congressional representatives each state shall elect.

Appropriate technology The idea that the latest, most complex technology might not be the most suitable of everyone everywhere.

Appropriation A bill actually granting an agency permission to spend funds in specified amounts for purposes that Congress has authorized.

Aristocracy A form of government in which an elite or privileged upper class rule.

Arraignment A legal proceeding at which a defendant enters a plea. For a misdemeanor, this is also the defendant's initial appearance where the judge informs the defendant of the charges and sets the bail.

Articles of Confederation The first national constitution, drafted in 1777 but not ratified by all states until 1781. It was superseded by the U.S. Constitution in 1788 because of shortcomings in its content, especially the supremacy of states and the weakness of the national government.

Assault An intentional physical attack, or a threat of attack with the apparent ability to carry out the threat so that the victim feels in danger.

Assimilation The process by which a minority is absorbed into the dominant social group. When a group is assimilated, its members lose their distinctiveness—as if thrown (voluntarily) into a "melting pot."

At-large voting Electing a member of a body by voters of an entire unit rather than of a subdivision. U.S. senators are elected at large from each state. Representatives may be elected from a congressional district in their state if it is so divided, or at large by all the voters of their state, as in the cases of Alaska, Delaware, North Dakota, Vermont, and Wyoming.

Authoritarianism A form of government in which individual liberty is held as completely subordinate to the authority of the state, which itself is centered in one person or small groups. This form is opposite to democracy, which places ultimate authority in the people.

Authority The power or right to issue commands and punish for violations by virtue of rank or position.

Authorization A bill giving permission to begin or continue a government program. While an authorization bill may grant permission to spend a certain sum of money, that money does not ordinarily become available unless it is also appropriated.

Backlash Any sudden and forceful recoil, especially the reaction by whites against black advancement when its results directly affect them, such as in job competition.

Bail Money put up as security by the accused to obtain release from jail while awaiting trial. The purpose of bail is to assure the court that the defendant will return for trial.

Balance-of-payments deficit Total payments made to foreign nations by U.S. citizens and the U.S. government are higher than total receipts from foreign sources.

Balance of power In international relations, the strategy of organizing a combination of states to hold in check any state that might otherwise come to dominate.

Baker v. *Carr* A 1962 Supreme Court case decision that required the boundary lines of state legislative districts to be drawn so that they are nearly equal in population.

Bakke case By a five-to-four majority the Supreme Court upheld in 1978 the constitutionality of "affirmative action" programs not involving explicit quotas.

Bargaining chip In negotiations, the strategy of having certain goods (e.g., a weapons system) that are developed only to be "given up" for the express purpose of getting a similar concession from the other side.

Battery Any intentional unlawful, or unconsented to physical contact by one upon another.

Bay of Pigs invasion A 1961 invasion of Cuba by Cuban refugees who were armed and trained by the CIA. Intended to overthrow Fidel Castro and liberate the island, the invasion was instead a disaster.

Behavioral science Those sciences that study the behavior of humans and animals—e.g., psychology.

Beyond a reasonable doubt The standard used by judges or juries for convicting a defendant in a criminal case. It does not mean "convinced 100 percent," but does mean there are no reasonable doubts as to guilt."

Bicameral legislatures A lawmaking body made up of two houses. All states now have bicameral legislatures, except Nebraska (which has a unicameral form).

Bill A written proposal submitted to the House and Senate for consideration and ratification to become a law.

Bill of attainder A law that declares a person, without a trial, to be guilty of a crime. Article I, Sections 9 and 10, of the Constitution forbids such acts.

Bill of rights The first 10 amendments to the Constitution proposed by the First U.S. Congress soon after the ratification of the Constitution in 1788. The Bill of Rights gave formal recognition to the rights and liberties of the individual in the American system.

Bipartisan A concept of American foreign policy that holds that both major political parties should support the president's foreign policies. Bipartisanship flourished after World War II.

Block grants Allocations of money from the national government to states and localities to be used for broad purposes specified in statutes and regulations. There are fewer federal government restrictions on recipients of block grants than on recipients of **categorical grants**.

Blockade of West Berlin On April 1, 1948, Stalin ordered all roads leading to West Berlin cut off. His aim was to squeeze the Allies out of West Berlin. The United States and British forces responded with an airlift to keep the city alive.

Blue-ribbon panel A committee chosen on basis of expertise to investigate some complex, important issue. Presidents have appointed such committees to give the image of "action."

Bond A mandatory insurance or obligation. A bail bond is the money a defendant pays to secure release from jail before trial.

Bourgeois In Marxist theory, the middle class opposed to the wage-earning class or proletariat.

Boycott An organized refusal to deal with a person, organization, or nation in order to bring about policy changes by pressures.

Brinkmanship A national security policy based on the idea that a nation must be willing to risk total war in order to force an adversary to back down in a confrontation.

Brokerage politics The adjustment of the claims of interest groups in the political process in the attempt to secure harmonization of those claims.

Budget A formal statement estimating the planned or anticipated costs of operations and the revenues available for a specified length of time, such as the federal budget for a fiscal year.

Budget and Impoundment Control Act of 1974 The act that established a more coherent congressional budget process.

Budget message A statement of estimated income and expenses of the government. The president is responsible for preparing it and delivering it to Congress annually.

Bureaucracy An organization of offices or positions arranged hierarchically (i.e., everyone has a boss to report to) and operating according to rules rather than personal relations. As used in the text, the departments and agencies of the executive branch.

Cabinet A decision-making body, never mentioned in the Constitution, composed of the heads of executive departments (e.g., secretary of agriculture and selected members of the White House staff.

Calendar An agenda of the bills to be considered in committees or chambers of a legislature.

Capitalism An economic system based on private ownership of the means of production and on a market economy.

Captured agency A regulatory agency that has been co-opted by the client groups it was intended to regulate, so that it protects the client groups' interests rather than the public interest.

Case work Work that members of Congress do for individual constituents.

Categorical grants-in-aid Financial aid from the federal government to the states that must be spent for specific categories of activities.

Caucus A meeting of partisans or party leaders, closed to the public, to discuss and decide party positions. Caucuses are only rarely used today to select candidates for elective office.

Censorship Broadly, any government restrictions on speech or writing. More precisely, government restrictions on expression before they are disseminated. Except in time of war or national emergency, prior restraint upon freedom of speech or of the press is ordinarily forbidden.

Central Intelligence Agency The agency established by the National Security Act of 1947 with responsibility for consolidating the government's intelligence activities and information.

Centrist Someone whose political philosophy falls roughly between left and right, conservative and liberal; a middle-of-the-roader; a moderate.

CETA Abbreviation for the Comprehensive Employment and Training Act of 1973, a major special revenue-sharing program for government employment and training programs.

Charisma An extraordinary quality possessed by persons that is thought to give them a unique quality. In politics, this personal appeal becomes the source of authority.

Chief executive The president's constitutionally derived role as head of the executive branch of government, including most of the federal bureaucracy.

Citizen participation An administrative principle found in some government programs that allows the people (clients) who are directly affected by government services to have a voice in how the programs are operated.

Citizenship According to Aristotle, citizenship always meant participation in public affairs. The modern notion is less intimate and more legal. It is defined in the 14th Amendment of the Constitution thus:

"All persons born or naturalized in the United States, and subject to the jurisdiction thereof, are citizens of the United States and of the state wherein they reside." Citizenship is based mainly on one's place of birth *(jus soli)* but may be acquired through naturalization and, under cicumstances defined by Congress, through blood relation *(jus sanguinis)*.

City charter A local government "constitution" or basic law granted to it by the state.

City manager A professional administrator to act as chief executive who is appointed by the city council in one form of city government.

Civil disobedience A strategy advocated by Gandhi in the 1930s and Martin Luther King, Jr., in the 1960s. By refusing (often nonviolently) to obey what they consider unjust laws, the police and judicial machinery of the state is so overloaded, the laws can no longer be applied. It requires a relatively benevolent government to work effectively.

Civil law Law that is not criminal law. The term also denotes law that is not derived from the common law. Many European nations do not let judges "make" law, but instead confine them to applying complicated statutes covering every imaginable contingency to specific cases. The body of such statutes is called the civil law. Civil law, in this sense, is of Roman origin; the common law is of Anglo-Saxon origin.

Civil liberties The freedoms of speech, press, religion, and petition, together with freedom from arbitrary arrest and punishment.

Civil rights The rights of citizens to vote, to receive equal treatment before the law, and to share equally with other citizens the benefits of public facilities regardless of race, sex, or national background.

Civil Rights Act of 1964 A law making discrimination against any group in public accommodations such as hotels and restaurants illegal. It also forbade many kinds of job discrimination.

Civil service system The personnel system of the federal government. Established in 1883, it provides for selection and advancement based on merit, not politics. Most federal civilian employees are covered by the civil service system.

Class A specific stratum of society. Marx identified classes in relationship to the means of production and predicted increasing class conflict under capitalism.

Class action suit A lawsuit in which one or more persons sue as representatives of a larger group in a similar situation.

Clear and present danger A rule raised by the Supreme Court to measure the permissible bounds of free speech. In 1919, Oliver Wendell Holmes put the test this way: "The question in every case is whether the words used are used in such circumstances and are of such a nature as to create a clear and present danger that they will bring about the substantive evils that Congress has a right to prevent. It is a question of proximity and degree."

Closed primary versus open primary A closed primary is an election restricted to party members. An open primary is an election in which voters do not have to declare their party identification but choose in the voting booth the ballot of the political party in whose primary contest they want to vote.

Coalition building Combining two or more factions or parties for the purpose of achieving some political goal. An example is the coalition sometimes formed in Congress between southern Democrats and Republicans.

Cold war The tensions between the United States and the USSR (and their allies) that have characterized post-World War II era.

Colonialism A form of imperialism based on maintaining sharp distinctions, often expressed in law, between the ruling nation and the subordinate or colonial population. The United States (itself once a colony) was not purely an observer during the revival of the race for colonies in the late 19th and early 20th century. Since World War II, the term *neocolonialism* has been used to refer to the predominance of the economy and culture of former colonial power over a newly independent nation. See **imperialism.**

Command economies An economic system based on public or worker ownership of the means of production and on some central mechanism for distributing goods and services—in short, socialism.

Commander in chief The role of the president as head of the armed forces.

Commerce clause A clause in Article I of the Constitution that grants to Congress the authority to regulate commerce with foreign nations and among the states.

Commission form of government City government in which a small board of elected commissioners serves both as a legislative council and as heads of the city departments.

Committee of the whole The members of the House of Representatives organized into a committee for the consideration of bills and other matters. In order to expedite business and to avoid the formal requirements of its regular sessions (e.g., having a quorum of one half the membership).

Common law The body of legal principles governing rights and duties of persons, developed in England and the United States from judges' decisions rather than legislative action. It may vary from state to state and, of course, can be superseded by statute.

Comparative advantage The principle upon which free trade in the global economy is justified. Even if the United States can make straw hats more efficiently than Panama, the two countries should specialize in products in which they have the greatest *relative* efficiency. Thus, if the United States makes computers and Panama hats, trade will be mutually profitable to both nations.

Competition An essential condition for the proper operation of a market economy. Requires rivalry among sellers for customers.

Compromise Concessions made by policymaking participants that result in a mutually acceptable policy position that all participants support.

Concurrent powers Authority shared by both the state and national governments (e.g., the power to tax and to maintain courts).

Concurring opinion A written opinion of one or more judges that supports the conclusions of a majority of the court but for different reasons.

Confederation A political system in which states or regional governments retain ultimate authority, except for those powers they specifically delegate to a central government.

Conference committees A special joint committe of the House and Senate that reconciles differences between the versions of a bill that passes the two houses of Congress.

Conflict A situation in which two or more people (or groups) seek scarce resources or propose contradictory principles.

Conflict of interest When officials act in a way that might be thought to benefit themselves. For example, a member of Congress might introduce a bill that would benefit some firm in which he had a financial interest.

Congressional Budget and Impoundment Act of 1974 This act created a mechanism through which Congress could monitor the economic impact of its decisions. Established were the House and Senate Budget Committees and the Congressional Budget Office. The act also restricted presidential powers to impound funds.

Connecticut Compromise The agreement reached at the Constitutional Convention that Congress would consist of two chambers: the House of Representatives, in which the size of state delegations would be fixed according to population; and the Senate, in which each state, regardless of population, would be represented equally.

Consensus Agreement on broad elements of national purpose and rules of the game.

Conservatism A political philosophy stressing the importance of careful thought before making changes in policies and institutions, the need for preserving traditional values, the preservation of a strong defense, and the primacy of merit over equality.

Constituency The residents of a legislator's district.

Constitutionalism Adherence to the idea of government based on fundamental laws and principles that prescribe the nature, functions, offices, and limits of a government. A constitution may be written (as in the United States) or unwritten (as in Great Britain).

Consumer price index A statistical measure of the average of prices of a specified set of goods and services purchased by wage earners in urban areas. A sustained rise in the CPI indicates inflation.

Containment A feature of American foreign policy following World War II that sought to limit the spread of communism and Soviet influence.

Continental Congress An association of representatives of the American colonies that first met in 1774 to protest British oppressions. The Continental Congress became the principal organ of national government under the **Articles of Confederation.**

Contract A legally enforceable agreement between two or more people to do a certain thing in exchange for payment in some form. This payment is called "consideration."

Cooling-off period Any provision to postpone a strike or other forceful action during conflict resolution in order to give the parties an additional opportunity to mediate their differences.

Co-optation The conversion of opposition by absorption. This strategy says, in effect, if you cannot defeat the opposition, then flatter them into joining you.

Correlation A statistical measure of the strength of the relationship or association that exists between two separate factors. A high correlation means there is a strong relationship present (such as the one that exists between one's level of education and rate of political participation).

Cost-benefit analysis A feature of some budget decision-making procedures that weighs the benefits a program proposes to achieve against the costs of the program and selects alternative programs on the basis of most benefits gained for dollar cost.

Council of Economic Advisers A trio of economists appointed by the president to advise him on how to "maintain employment, production, and purchasing power" and to assist him in preparing economic reports.

Criminal law Law that defines crime against the public order.

Critical or realignment election A presidential election that produces a new majority, marks a shift that is pronounced and relatively durable, and has important political consequences. Perhaps five such elections have occurred in American political history.

Cross-cutting cleavages The concept that individual voters in an election are influenced by a variety of factors that can affect their voting preference in conflicting ways.

Cuban missile crisis For 13 days in 1962, the United States and the Soviet Union came as close as ever to nuclear war. The cause was the Soviet government's decision to locate offensive nuclear missiles in Cuba.

Deal A political trade of favors or support. For example, in 1876, Samuel J. Tilden, the Democratic candidate for president, won more votes than Rutherford B. Hayes, the Republican candidate. But 185 electoral votes were necessary for a majority and Tilden had only 184. So, a deal was struck: The Democrats would give the election to Hayes if the Republicans would withdraw federal troops from the "carpetbag states in the South."

Declaration of Independence The document adopted by the Continental Congress on July 4, 1776, formally severing ties between the American colonies and England. Drafted by Thomas Jefferson, the Declaration is an eloquent statement of American political principles, though largely derived from English philosopher John Locke.

De jure versus de facto segregation De jure segregation is required by law; de facto segregation results from housing patterns.

Delegate or expressed power Powers expressly granted to the national government by the Constitution. These powers, found in Article I, Section 8, include the authority to provide for the common defense, to coin money, and to regulate commerce.

Delegates An elected representative who seeks to enact his or her constituents' preferences and to serve their interest as they define it, not as he or she does.

Democracy Government in which ultimate authority resides in the people and provides free and frequent elections.

Dennis decision In 1951, the Supreme Court permitted the government to jail several American Communist party leaders under the Smith Act.

Deposition A statement under oath, taken down in writing, to be used in court in place of the spoken testimony of the witness.

Deregulation The act or process of removing regulations or restrictions to free an industry from government regulation.

Detente Relaxation of tensions—even conciliation—with another nation.

Deterrence The assumption that, if a nation's military capabilities are strong enough, no other nation will attack for fear of being destroyed by retaliation.

Dillon's rule The principle that a city is legally dependent on the state for its authority.

Diminishing marginal utility After a certain point, the increase in total benefit of a government program becomes smaller as more money is spent on the program.

Direct and indirect benefits Direct benefits are the intended and primary results of a program. Indirect benefits are beneficial side-effects. The space program, for example, led to the development of new medical techniques.

Direct costs The costs that are paid for by the agency running a program. Unlike indirect costs, they are not passed off to third parties.

Discharge petition A method House members may use to take a bill away from a committee and turn it over to full House consideration after 30 days.

Discovery The pretrial process of exchanging information between the opposing sides.

Dissenting opinion An opinion of one or more judges that disagrees with the majority opinion.

Distributive policy Domestic government policy that promotes certain kinds of private activity through provision of subsidies. Subgovernments are very important in decision making in the distributive policy area.

District courts One of the 95 federal courts of "original jurisdiction," where most federal cases begin. It is the only federal court where trials are held, juries are used, and witnesses are called.

Double jeopardy The guarantee in the Fifth Amendment to the Constitution that one may not be tried twice for the same crime.

Due process clause The Fifth and 14th Amendments require that any person involved in a legal dispute have a fair hearing or trial. No law or procedure can be arbitrary or unfair.

Economic opportunity act of 1964 An act intended to overcome the causes of poverty by encouraging programs of education and training for employment; it was the centerpiece of President Johnson's **war on poverty.**

Economic system The arrangement within a society that determines how goods and services will be produced and distributed.

Elastic clause Clause in Article I, Section 8 of the Constitution that gives Congress power to "make all laws which shall be necessary and proper" for executing the expressed or enumerated powers.

Electoral college Refers to the way the president and the vice president of the United States are elected. The electoral college is made up of electors chosen by the voters of each state. The electors for the candidates for president and vice president have won a plurality of the popular vote in their states. The votes of the electors are counted in a joint system of Congress in January following each presidential election.

Elite theory A model of politics that suggests a small group of people exercise disproportionate influence on the making of public policy.

Eminent domain The constitutional power for the state to take private property, provided that it is taken for a public purpose and that just compensation is awarded.

Enfranchisement The act or process of admitting a person or group to citizenship, especially the right to vote.

Enlightenment A cultural period (early 17th to beginning of 19th century) distinguished by efforts to make human reason the absolute ruler of life. It took its start in England from Newton and Locke, spread to Europe, and eventually to Jefferson and the founding fathers.

Entitlement programs Government programs such as social security that transfer benefits (especially money) automatically to persons that happen to be members of certain groups.

Entrapment An act by law enforcement officials to induce a person to commit a crime that the person would not have committed otherwise.

Enumerated powers Those powers explicitly stated in the Constitution.

Environment impact statement An assessment (required by law) of the effect any new project or program will have on the environment.

Equal protection clause A requirement of the 14th Amendment that state laws may not arbitrarily discriminate against persons.

Equal Rights Amendment The proposed 27th Amendment, which provides "Equality of rights under the law shall not be denied or abridged by the United States or any state on account of sex."

Equity This concept emerged as a body of law in England to overcome the perceived limits of the common law in cases where it did not provide an adequate remedy.

Error of law A mistake made by a judge in legal procedures or rulings during a trial that may allow the case to be appealed.

Escalation An acceleration of military activity in preparation for or during an armed conflict.

Establishment clause First Amendment clause that forbids the passage of any law "respecting an establishment of religion."

Evaluation An assessment of program performance and accomplishments usually compared to some previously specified standards.

Exclusionary rule A legal rule that prohibits illegally obtained evidence from being used against a defendant on trial.

Executive agreements Agreements made by the president with the heads of foreign countries, often after secret negotiations, that have the force of treaties but that do not require Senate approval. In this century, executive agreements have been used more often than treaties.

Executive interpretation One of the ways the Constitution has managed to change over time. Different presidents have interpreted its meaning differently.

Executive Office of the President The collection of staff and agencies that report directly to the president and help the president manage the federal bureaucracy.

Executive orders Rules or regulations issued by presidents, governors, or other administrative authorities that have the effect of law.

Executive privilege The claimed right of executive officials to withhold information from the legislature or courts on the grounds that the information is confidential and would damage the national interest.

Expansion An increase in the rate of overall business activity (as indicated by changes in total income, employment, and prices). It is the opposite of a recession.

Expatriation The act of banishing a person from his native country. Also, the withdrawing of one's allegiance to one's country.

Ex post facto laws A law that "after the fact" makes an act criminal.

Express warranty A statement of fact or a demonstration concerning the quality or performance of goods offered for sale.

Externalities Economically speaking, externalities are costs or benefits not taken into account in a transaction or a system of transactions. In this usage, the right of an industry to pollute a stream (i.e., a "free good") when such pollution is not charged against the cost of doing business would be an externality.

Fairness doctrine A policy of the FCC that requires radio and television stations to air different sides of controversial issues and to provide equal time to opposing political candidates.

Family Assistance Plan of 1969 The Nixon proposal for a nationwide guaranteed minimum income.

Farewell address A monument of American oratory delivered by Washington at the end of his second term. (He refused to run for a third term and set a precedent unbroken until Franklin Roosevelt.) The address contained the warning for the United States against "permanent alliances" with foreign powers.

Fascism A political ideology and mass movement that acquired considerable power in Europe between World War I and World War II. It emphasized nationalism, order, and government planning. Because of fascism's close association with Adolf Hitler, the term is today used somewhat imprecisely by radicals to attack opponents.

Federal Aviation Administration (FAA) This agency became a part of the Department of Transportation in 1967. It is charged with regulating air commerce to foster aviation safety, promoting civil aviation and a national system of airports, achieving efficient use of navigable air space, and developing and operating a common system of air traffic control and air navigation for both civilian and military aircraft.

Federal Communication Commission (FCC) A federal agency responsible for regulating the radio and TV outlets, as well as interstate and foreign communications by wire, cable, and satellite.

Federal Election Campaign Act of 1971 Legislation designed to reform and strengthen the regulation of campaign spending (a subject not addressed by Congress in the previous half century). The legislation was amended in 1974 and 1976.

Federal Election Campaign Amendments of 1974 Amendments passed by Congress following the Watergate affair that established limits on campaign contributions and expenditures, required disclosure of campaign finances, and provided for public financing of presidential campaigns.

Federal Election Commission A six-member body established by the 1974 amendments to the federal campaign finance law to administer the complex campaign finance provisions of that law.

Federal Register A lengthy bulletin published daily by the government that contains, among other things, the text of all regulations issued by executive agencies.

Federal Reserve Board Created by Congress in 1913 to regulate the lending practices of banks, "the Fed" is crucial in affecting the supply of money and credit in the U.S. economy.

Federalism A system of government characterized by a constitutional sharing of powers between a national government and subnational units of government.

The Federalist Papers Articles written in support of RATIFICATION of the Constitution by Alexander Hamilton, John Jay, and James Madison. These articles were a primary persuasive tool of Federalists in the fight to ratify the Constitution; even today they remain a significant statement of American political thought.

Federalists Proponents of the federal (national) system of government and of the Constitution drafted in Philadelphia in 1787.

Felonies Serious crimes punishable by a prison sentence of a year or more.

Filibuster A delaying or obstructionist tactic by which a single senator, or a group of senators, can hold the floor through marathon speechmaking, thereby preventing a vote.

Finesse A strategy of applying only as much power as necessary to obtain an objective. One does not use a sledgehammer to kill a fly; in politics, such brazen displays of power can induce counterattacks.

Fiscal policy Efforts to manage the economy by altering the level of government spending and taxation. Government tries to run a surplus (take in more by taxation than it spends) when there is inflation and to run a deficit (spent more than it takes in by taxes) when there is a recession.

Fiscal year An annual accounting period for the federal government that begins October 1 and ends the following September 30.

Fourteenth Amendment This important post-Civil War amendment defines citizenship and restricts the power of states in their relations with their residents. In particular, it forbids states from depriving any person of life, liberty, or property without due process of law or from denying any person equal protection of the law. Since 1925, it has been used by courts to extend many Bill of Rights freedoms to the states.

Fraud Any deception, lie, or dishonest statement made to cheat someone.

Free exercise clause Because the United States is a nation with diverse religious groups, the First Amendment prohibits government from interfering in the free exercise of religion. Still, snake-handling, polygamy, and a few other exercises are prohibited.

Free-rider problem Public goods (such as clean air) often have the free-rider problem, in which an individual, when asked, will claim that he does not want the good in question because he hopes that in this way he will get the good but that others will pay for it. He attempts to get a free ride.

Free trade Commercial transaction between countries with a minimum of government interference, such as tariffs and other fees imposed on products cross borders. See **comparative advantage.**

Full faith and credit Article IV, Section I of the Constitution requires states to honor the civil rulings of other states: "Full faith and credit shall be given in each state to the public acts, records, and judicial proceedings of every other state."

Gatekeepers The persons in the journalism trade who made the decisions about what material will be included in print and in broadcasts as news.

General Election An election to fill public offices. See **primary election.**

General revenue sharing A program begun in 1972 that returns billions of federal tax dollars to states and localities on the basis of a complex formula. There are very few restrictions on how the recipients may spend this money.

Geopolitics The assumption that a nation's geography and natural resources are the most important factors determining its foreign policy.

Gerrymandering The deliberate alignment of voting district lines in order to favor a party or segment of the electorate.

Gideon v. *Wainwright* Since this 1963 Supreme Court decision, all persons subject to any kind of police interrogation must be represented by a lawyer.

Gitlow decision In 1925, the Supreme Court ruled that freedom of the press and of speech must also be protected by states.

GNP Gross national product, an economic indicator of the current market value of all goods and services produced in the United States in a year.

Goal An outcome of a public policy that a decision maker prefers to some other outcome.

The good neighbor American policy towards Latin America initiated by President Franklin Roosevelt in the early 1930s. Marked a change from the role of the United States as "Big Brother" in Latin America.

G.O.P. Nickname of the Republican Party; G.O.P. stands for "Grand Old Party."

Government That part of society that set goals and takes measures to attain those goals.

Government of laws The concept that laws override the wants of public officials. Hence, all public officers in the United States take oaths not to support some leader but to "defend and protect the Constitution."

Grand jury A group of people who hear preliminary evidence to decide if there is sufficient reason to formally charge a person with a crime.

Grandfather clause A provision that only those who could demonstrate that their father or grandfather had voted were exempt from strict literacy tests and property requirements that limited the franchise. The aim was to keep blacks from voting. Today it refers to any legal provision protecting persons having some right or benefit from changes in that right or benefit.

Grant-in-aid Allocations of money from the national government to state and local governments to be utilized for specific purposes, spelled out by statute or administrative regulations.

Great Society The slogan of the administration of President Lyndon B. Johnson.

Griswold **v.** ***Connecticut*** In 1965, the Supreme Court struck down a law that forbade counseling married couples to use contraceptives. The Court argued that such a law was an invasion of the right to privacy protected by the First and Ninth Amendments.

Group theory A theory of the political process that holds that groups form spontaneously in response to their members' mutually perceived threats or opportunities, and that public policy is largely the result of bargaining among these groups. See **elite theory**.

Guaranteed annual income See **family assistance plan**.

GULAG An acronym for the Soviet slave labor camps, which entered the English language with the publication of Alexander Solzhenitsyn's *The Gulag Archipelago* in 1973.

Gulf of Tonkin resolution A congressional resolution passed in 1964 that authorized President Johnson to take all necessary measures to protect American forces in Vietnam. The war in Vietnam rapidly escalated following this point.

Gunboat diplomacy Use of military forces to control the politics of smaller states by intimidation.

Guns and butter The idea that there is no such thing as a free lunch. If a nation wants a bigger army, it will have to give up consumer goods—and vice versa. In the language of economics, it is expressed by the production possibility curve.

Hatch act Law that barred federal employees from active participation in politics.

Hatchetman The associate of a political leader who performs the unpleasant assignment of attacking the opposition and firing employees (thus allowing the leader to appear "above politics").

"Hawks" and "doves" Hawks are public officials who take a bellicose approach to foreign affairs; doves are more pacific.

Hearing A session of a legislative body in which witnesses present testimony on matters under consideration by the committee.

Historical materialism The cornerstone of Marx's theory of history. The mode of production determines the general character of social, political, and spiritual life. Hence, historical development is largely determined by economic conditions.

Home rule A form of local political autonomy drafted by a city in the form of a "home-rule charter." Once approved by the state it cannot be changed by the state legislature.

Honeymoon period A period of high public expectations and popular support of the president and of usually cordial relations between the president and Congress that characterizes the beginning of every president's term.

House Rules Committee A powerful standing committee that provides the special rules under which specific bills will be debated, amended, and considered by the House. The committee also controls the flow of bills from committees to the floor for consideration.

Human rights The idea that each person is born with the moral claim on some political freedom. In recent years, some American politicians have argued that the United States should put pressure on those governments that deny these claims to their residents.

ICC The Interstate Commerce Commission was created as an independent establishment by the act to regulate commerce of February 4, 1887, now known as the Interstate Commerce Act. The commission's authority has been strengthened and the scope of its jurisdiction has been broadened by subsequent legislation. Surface transportation under the commission's jurisdiction includes railroads, trucking companies, bus lines, freight forwarders, water carriers, transportation brokers, and express agencies.

Ideology A belief system that is tightly organized, logical, and that includes a program of action for implementing the beliefs. Examples of political ideologies are **communism** and **fascism**.

Image The impression that a public figure attempts to convey of himself or herself. With the emergence of television, public relations, and professional marketing, image building in politics has become more important. In politics, the perception of power can be almost as important as the reality of power.

Immunity Protected from some legal action such as being sued.

Impeach A formal accusation against a public official by the lower house of a legislative body. Impeachment is merely an accusation, not a conviction.

Imperial presidency Reference to the growth of presidential powers and the exaggerated pomp and isolation of presidential lifestyles that has characterized the evolution of the presidency since the 1930s.

Imperialism In general, the extension of the power of a state, usually by conquest, over other territories. See **colonialism**.

Implementation The activities undertaken to transform government policy statements (which are expressions of intent about dealing with perceived problems) into tangible actions. Implementation activities include acquisition, interpretation, organization, and provision of benefits.

Implied powers Authority possessed by the national government by inference from those powers expressly delegated to it in the Constitution. For example, the national government's power to draft persons into the armed forces is inferred from its delegated power to raise armies and navies. See **delegated powers**.

Income distribution The percentage of total annual income by group. For example, the top 10 percent of households may receive 30 percent of the total income, while the bottom tenth only 3 percent; hence a measure of inequality.

Incomes policy Efforts by government to insure that

money incomes from wages, salaries, rents, and dividends do not rise so fast as to set up cost inflation.

Incrementalism A model of policymaking that suggests that government decision makers are likely to only make slight (or incremental) modifications on previous policy rather than sweeping revisions.

Incumbent The person currently in office.

Independent regulatory commission Agencies independent of the executive branch that are designed to regulate some important aspect of the economy. See **Federal Communications Commission**, **Interstate Commerce Commission**, and **Federal Reserve Board**.

Indictment An accusation issued by a grand jury stating that a person is charged with a crime.

Indirect cost See **externalities**.

Industrial policy Generally, efforts by government to support those industries that seem to have the most promising future and therefore highest potential contribution to the nation's well-being. Can also mean efforts to prop-up ailing industries.

Inflation A time of generally rising prices for goods and services.

Information society A society in which a majority of workers are involved in neither agriculture nor manufacturing but rather in the creation, processing, and storage of information. Clearly this is the direction in which most Western industrialized countries are headed.

Inherent powers Those powers inherent in the federal government by virtue of its being a nation. For example, although the Constitution does not say that the government can acquire territory, the United States has grown considerably since 1787.

Initiative A procedure whereby citizens can propose legislation or constitutional amendments and refer the decision to popular vote by obtaining the required number of signatures on a petition.

Injunction An order by a court that a party to a judicial process act or cease acting in a certain manner.

Institutionalization The process whereby people come to expect that an individual or institution will act in certain predictable ways under given situations.

Institutions Technically, a well-established and structured pattern of relationships that is accepted as a fundamental part of society and that exists over time.

Interest groups An organization that seeks to influence the formulation and implementation of public policy. Though it does not directly offer candidates for election, an interest group does support those who are favorable to its cause.

Intragovernmental lobby Those organizations consisting of state and local officials and federal bueaucrats that pressure the federal policymakers for more programs to benefit them and their constituencies.

Iranian revolution In 1979, Shah Mohammed Reza Pahlavi, the proAmerican head of Iran, was driven from his throne. Eventually, Iran became an Islamic state, highly unstable and anti-american.

Iron curtain The barrier to communication and travel between the people in the Soviet bloc countries and the West that permits the communist regime to operate relatively free from outside criticism.

Iron law of oligarchy The principle that within any large organization eventually some small group of people must emerge who hold a disproportionate amount of power.

Iron triangle The hypothesized relationship among an interest group, the bureau that dispenses benefits to the interest group's members, and the congressional committee or subcommittee whose members oversee the bureau and have the interest group's members as part of their constituency and electoral coalition. This coalition is often seen as opposed to actions that would harm any of its members.

Isolationism A policy of avoiding foreign entanglements, characteristic of American foreign policy until World War II.

Issue networks According to Hugh Heclo, these webs composed of many participants influence the formulation of public policy in specific areas (such as consumer protection).

Item veto The power of an executive to disapprove parts of a bill rather than the total bill. The president does not have this power, but most state governors do.

Jacksonian democracy An era of popular rule beginning in the 1820s with Jackson's emergence as a political leader in the 1820s when the common man became increasingly involved in politics.

Jim Crow laws Legislation designed to discriminate against blacks, especially in the South.

Job Corps A program, authorized by the Economic Opportunity Act of 1964, that enables jobless youths from 16 to 21 to work and study at training centers or in conservation camps. The Job Corps was inaugurated as part of the Johnson administration's **war on poverty**.

Johnson treatment President Lyndon Johnson's technique of badgering, dickering, and overpowering people in person-to-person persuasion.

Joint Chiefs of Staff The head of the military services, plus a chairman from one of the services, all of whom are appointed by the president. The Joint Chiefs serve as military and foreign policy advisers to the president, the secretary of defense, and the National Security Council.

Joint committees Legislative committees composed of members of both houses.

Judicial activism versus judicial restraint The continuing debate about the proper role of the courts in making public policy. Activists prefer a judiciary that is self-consciously and vigorously involved in making public policy; restrainers prefer that the determination of public policy is not the responsibility of the courts.

Judicial review The principle, established in the 1803 Supreme Court decision in *Marbury* v. *Madison*, that the Supreme Court has the authority to review the laws and actions of Congress and the states in light of their conformance with the Constitution of the United States.

Judiciary The system of courts of justice.

Jurisdiction Authority vested in a court to hear and decide certain types of cases.

Justice According to Aristotle, the proper balance between liberty and equality; fairness.

Justice of the peace A judicial officer empowered to try minor civil and criminal cases (e.g., traffic violations).

Keynesians Economists and public officials who believe that, by controlling aggregate demand, government can manage the economy. This approach to fiscal policy was advocated by John Maynard Keynes (1883–1946).

Kitchen Cabinet Informal advisers to the president who do not hold formal positions on the White House staff but who have the president's ear.

Korean conflict In 1950, communist North Korea (later backed by China) invaded pro-American South Korea. The war dragged on until 1953.

Labor theory of values Marx, who borrowed this idea from John Locke (of all people), argued that the true value of an product is determined by the labor (measured in time) that was required to produce it. It serves as the theoretical basis for his explanation of how capitalists exploit workers.

Laissez-faire An economic doctrine emphasizing little or no government intervention in the economy; based on Adam Smith's assumption that, if everyone competes in pursuit of his own self-interest, all will benefit. From a French phrase meaning "let alone."

Lame duck A person, legislature, or administration that has been defeated in an election but still holds office for a period of time. For example, after Ronald Reagan defeated Jimmy Carter, Carter was a lame duck president from November until January, when Reagan was inaugurated.

Larceny The unlawful taking of someone else's property with the intent to steal it.

Leadership The ability to use power not as an end in itself but as a means to some goal outside one's self.

Leak The disclosure of information concerning newsworthy government activity through unofficial channels.

Legislative oversight Congressional monitoring of executive branch activities, particularly the implementation of programs legislated by Congress and administered by the bureaucracy.

Legislative veto A form of legislative oversight in which the executive branch is required to give notice to Congress before taking certain actions.

Leverage Indirect pressure that can be brought to bear on political decision makers and convention delegates. For example, A can use B, who is a close friend of C, to influence C for him.

Libel To defame or injure a person's reputation, usually by a published writing; often punishable under criminal law.

Liberalism A political philosophy originated in the 18th century and associated with the idea of freedom, economic and political.

Liberty The concept of liberty covers a wide variety of individual freedoms (e.g., religious, political, and speech). Fundamental perhaps is the freedom of individuals to come and go as they please. Philosophers such as Locke and Rousseau developed the idea of individuals possessing certain natural rights that could not be taken away by the state. See **Civil liberties**, **Civil rights**, **Human rights**, and **Bill of Rights**.

Limited war Military conflict limited either by terrain, the weapons used, or the objectives pursued. The **Korean War** and **Vietnam War** were limited. World War II was total war.

Linkage In international politics, a negotiating strategy that requires progress in one area before progress in another area can occur. For example, the United States might try to establish linkage between arms control with the Soviet Union and the Soviet invasion of Afghanistan.

Litigation Pursuing a case or claim in the judicial process.

Lion and fox According to Machiavelli, effect leaders should combine the strength of the lion and the craftiness of the fox. But, like Franklin Roosevelt, they must know when each behavior is appropriate.

Lobbying Acting as an agent for a group that seeks to bring about the passage or defeat of legislative bills, to influence their contents, or to influence administrative actions.

Logrolling Vote trading by elected representatives in support of each other's bills.

Machine A centrally led state or local party organization that rewards members with material benefits. See **patronage**.

Majority leader (floor leader) A member of the majority party in the House and Senate selected by the majority party in caucus or conference who helps frame party strategy and keep members in line.

Managed news Information carefully selected and distributed to the media by government in order to present as favorable a picture of what it is doing, as in the case of national security issues, to confuse the foreign adversary.

Mandamus, Writ of An order issued by a court to compel performance of a specified act. For example, if a contract is not fulfilled as agreed upon, a writ of mandamus will be issued to order its enforcement. (Mandamus is Latin for "we command.")

Mapp v. Ohio In 1961, with this landmark case, the Supreme Court broadened the requirement that warrants must be obtained before searches can be made, though it did not bar all searches without a warrant.

Marbury v. Madison (1803) An 1803 Supreme Court case decision, significant because it was the first Supreme Court decision to declare a law of Congress unconstitutional. In writing the decision for the

Court, Chief Justice John Marshall established the principle of judicial review.

Market economies An economic system in which the major means of production are privately owned and the distribution of good and services occurs chiefly through a market that reconciles supply and demand. In short, capitalism or free enterprise.

Mark-up Revising a legislative proposal in a committee.

Marshall Plan Recognizing the importance of a strong Europe, America gave aid to the countries of Europe to help them rebuild after World War II.

Marxism An interpretation of the political process resting on the belief that political events reflect the clash of economic classes.

Matching funds A requirement of some federal aid programs that states and localities put up some specified share of funds in order to receive federal funds.

Mass media Means of communication that have large audiences, standardized communications, and concentrated ownership and control. For example, TV, radio, and newspapers.

Maoism The Marxist philosophy of Mao Tse-Tung, former Chinese leader. Essentially, Mao argued for "uninterrupted revolution" and the decisive role of will in history.

Massive retaliation In international politics, the strategy of threatening to meet foreign military challenges with all-out nuclear attack.

McCarthyism Refers to Sen. Joe McCarthy's investigations into communist infiltration of the U.S. government during the early 1950s and his often groundless charges against innocent individuals of being communist sympathizers.

McCulloch v. Maryland (1819) In 1819, Supreme Court established the doctrine of national supremacy and the doctrine that the **implied powers** of the national government are to be generously interpreted.

Mean The average position in a distribution.

Median The position in a distribution for which there are as many observations above it as below it.

Medicaid A federal-state matching fund program enacted in 1965 that reimburses health care personnel who provide health services to eligible recipients.

Medicare A government program that provides medical insurance for the elderly as part of the social security program. Medicare was an extremely controversial policy of a redistributive nature that required years to achieve legitimation.

Melting pot See **assimilation**.

Merit system The selection or promotion of government employees on the basis of demonstrated merit rather than on the basis of political patronage. See also **civil service**.

Military-industrial complex An alleged relationship among military officers, industrialists, politicians, and citizens whose interests are furthered by government defense spending.

Minority leader (floor leader) Party leader in each house elected by the minority party.

Miranda case In 1966, the Supreme Court overturned the conviction of Ernesto A. Miranda who had kidnapped and raped an 18-year-old woman. The Court held that prior to any questioning, a person must be warned that he or she has the right to remain silent and to the presence of an attorney.

Misdemeanor A crime not as serious as a felony for which judges may impose short prison terms or monetary fines.

Mistrial A trial in which a legal error is made or a jury is unable to reach a unanimous verdict.

Mixed economy An economy that contains elements of **command economies** and **market economies.**

Model A simplified picture or reconstruction of reality developed in order to help one understand that reality better.

Monarchy A form of government in which the supreme power is actually or (as in the case of modern-day Great Britain) nominally lodged in a king or queen.

Monetarists Economists and politicians who think that **monetary policy** is an effective way to fight **inflation** and **recession.** The basic idea is to use "tight money" with the former and "loose money" with the latter.

Monetary policy Government policy that alters the money supply and the availability of credit in order to manage the economy.

Monopoly A public or private firm that alone produces a good or service for which there are no close substitutes.

Monroe Doctrine In 1823, President James Monroe declared that the United States would oppose any European intervention in the affairs of the Americas.

Muckrakers Investigative newspaper journalists active at the turn of the 20th century who documented and exposed social and economic problems and political corruption; their stories led to progressivist reforms.

Multilateral treaty A treaty among *three* or more countries.

Multinational corporation Business corporations that are registered and operate in several countries.

Multiparty system A political system (such as the French) with three or more major political parties.

National chairman Each major party has a national committee to direct and coordinate its activities during the four years between national party conventions. Each committee ratifies the presidential nominee's selection of a national chairman, who acts as spokesman for his party.

National convention A meeting, held every four years, by each major party to select presidential and vice presidential candidates and write a **platform.**

National interest The concept that, in the conduct of foreign policy, the overriding concern should be the security and well-being of the United States—not the protection of special interests in the United States, not the unqualified support of certain allies, and not the advocacy of certain moral principles.

National Labor Relations Board An independent agency created by the National Labor Relations Act of 1935 (Wagner Act), as amended by the acts of

1947 (Taft-Hartley Act), 1959 (Landrum-Griffin Act), and 1974. The act affirms the right of employees to self-organization and to bargain collectively through representatives of their own choosing or to refrain from such activities. The act prohibits certain unfair labor practices by employers and labor organizations or their agents and authorizes the board to designate appropriate units for collective bargaining and to conduct secret ballot elections to determine whether employees desire representation by a labor organization.

National Security Council This council was established by the National Security Act of 1947. By the Reorganization Plan of 1949, the council was placed in the Executive Office of the President. It is chaired by the president and its members include the vice president and the secretaries of state and defense. The chairman of the Joint Chiefs of Staff serves as military adviser to the council; the director of the Central Intelligence Agency is its intelligence adviser. The function of the council is to advise the president with respect to the integration of domestic, foreign, and military policies relating to national security.

Natural law A "higher law" that is supposedly universally valid and therefore natural. In this sense, they are opposed to the positive law of the state.

Naturalized citizen A person born in one country who becomes a citizen of another.

Necessary and proper clause See **elastic clause.**

Negligence A **Tort** arising because of negligence occurs as the result of an "omission to do something which a reasonable man, guided by those ordinary considerations which ordinarily regulate human affairs, would do, or the doing of something which a reasonable and prudent man would not do."

Neo-Keynesians or post-Keynesians A group of economists who maintain that it is the structure of the private economy and policies of the U.S. government that are the primary causes of inflation.

The new class A conservative version of elite theory. It consists of relatively young persons whose positions are the result not of wealth or business but of their education and technical skills. They tend, according to the theory, to be of liberal outlook and to dominate the mass media.

New Deal A phrase used to describe the policies of President Franklin Roosevelt's first administration (1933–37) aimed at recovering the United States from the Great Depression.

New Deal Coalition The electoral coalition engineered by Democrats in 1932 that put Franklin D. Roosevelt and the Democrats in the White House. The New Deal coalition seemed reasonably stable until 1980.

New Jersey Plan A plan for a single-house Congress submitted to the Constitutional Convention of 1787 representing the views of the small states and states' rights advocates; a counterproposal to the **Virginia Plan.**

Nineteenth Amendment An amendment adopted in 1920 that prohibits states from denying the right to vote to women.

Nixon Doctrine The foreign policy proclaimed by Nixon after Vietnam that sought to maintain U.S. involvement in global politics but to require allies to bear more of the manpower burden of their own defense.

Nolo contendere Latin phrase meaning "no contest." A defendant's plea to criminal charges that does not admit guilt but also does not contest the charges. It is equivalent to a guilty plea, but it cannot be used as evidence in a later civil trial for damages based on the same set of facts.

Nonviolence See **civil disobedience.**

North Atlantic Treaty Organization (NATO) The alliance of certain North American and European nations, established under the North Atlantic Treaty of 1949, to create a single unified defense force to safeguard the security of the North Atlantic area.

Nuclear proliferation The growth in the number of nations that possess atomic or hydrogen bombs.

Nullification A doctrine expounded by advocates of extreme **States' rights.** It held that they have the right to declare null and void any federal law that they deem unconstitutional.

Obscenity A work or expression that depicts sexual conduct in a patently offensive way as outlined by specific legislation or judicial interpretations; lacks serious literary, artistic, political, or social value.

Occupational Safety and Health Administration (OSHA) This agency, established pursuant to the Occupational Safety and Health Act of 1970 (84 Stat. 1590), develops and promulgates occupational safety and health standards, develops and issues regulations, conducts investigations and inspections to determine the status of compliance with safety and health standards and regulations, and issues citations and proposes penalties for noncompliance with safety and health standards and regulations.

Office of Management and Budget OMB is the agency within the Executive office of the President that is responsible for preparing the federal budget every year and for central clearance of legislative proposals from federal agencies.

Office of Personnel Management (OPM) Set up in 1978, this office administers a merit system for federal employment, which includes recruiting, examining, training, and promoting people on the basis of their knowledge and skills, regardless of their race, religion, sex, political influence, or other nonmerit factors. OPM's role is to ensure that the federal government provides an array of personnel services to applicants and employees.

Oligarchy A form of government in which political power is exercised by a small group of people, usually self-selected.

Oligopoly A market situation in which (a) there are few sellers of a product or services and (b) the chances of price fixing and other anticompetitive activities are ripe.

Open-housing laws Legislation designed to overcome segregation in housing. The federal Fair Housing

Act of 1968 forbids discrimination because of a person's race, color, sex, national origin, or religion. This law covers the rental, sale, or financing of privately owned houses and apartments with four or more units. An executive order also prohibits discrimination in federally owned, operated, or assisted housing, including public housing. Some states and cities have passed even tougher laws that prohibit discrimination in sale of homes.

Opinion leader Persons or groups whose opinions on issues and policies are especially valued and who therefore influence the opinions of others.

Opportunity cost The cost of a program or project measured not in terms of dollars but in terms of what was given up (What opportunities were for gone) in order to carry it out.

Organization of Petroleum Exporting Countries (OPEC) A group of major oil-producing countries that are joined together in a cartel to try to limit oil supplies and maintain prices at agreed levels.

Oversight The attempt by Congress to ensure that the executive branch bureaucracy is efficiently doing what Congress authorized it to do.

Pacifist One who believes that war is always unjustifiable.

Palko case In 1937, the Supreme Court ruled the **Double jeopardy** provision of the Fifth Amendment does *not* apply to the states through the 14th Amendment.

Pardon The granting of a release from the punishment or legal consequences of a crime by the proper executive authority before or after conviction.

Parliamentary system A political system in which the legislature selects the executive head of the government (usually called the prime minister).

Parole Release from prison before the full sentence has been served, granted at the discretion of a parole board.

Participatory democracy A system of government in which all or most citizens participate directly in deciding the things that affect their lives.

Partisanship Refers to the strength of one's identification with a political party. There are strong partisans, weak partisans, and many in between.

Party identification The sense of attachment of loyalty one feels for a political party.

Patronage The exchange of rewards—jobs, contracts, franchises, favors—given by political leaders and organizations to supporters and friends. See **spoils system.**

Pearl Harbor On December 7, 1941—"a day that would live in infamy," in the words of President Roosevelt—while negotiations were going on with Japanese representatives in Washington, Japanese carrier-based planes swept in without warning on U.S. military installations at this land-locked harbor in Hawaii.

Pendleton Act (Civil Service Reform Act of 1883) Law establishing job-related competence as the primary basis for filling national government jobs; created the U.S. Civil Service Commission to oversee the new "merit" system. The commission was replaced in 1978 with the **Office of Personnel Management.**

Pentagon The five-sided building across the Potomac River from Washington, D.C., that houses the central agencies of the Defense Department and headquarters for the navy, army, air force, and marines.

Pentagon Papers case A secret compilation of documents on the conduct of 743) the Vietnam War prepared by the Defense Department. Leaked to the press in 1971, the Pentagon Papers showed that government officials had deliberately misled the public about the war.

Plaintiff In civil law, the person who initiates the lawsuit or brings an action to court.

Plans List of objectives and the actions required to attain them. Governments develop plans to carry out policies.

Platform Declaration of the principles and positions held by a political party (and its candidates for office) that is drafted at the **party convention.**

Plea bargaining Negotiations in a criminal case between a prosecutor and a defendant and his attorney. Guilty plea is often exchanged for a lesser charge or a lesser sentence.

Ploy A maneuver to achieve an objective without revealing the ultimate goal.

Pluralism See elite theory.

Plurality vote The largest number of votes won by a candidate in an election for a public office in which there are three or more candidates.

Pocket veto The power of the president to kill a bill without taking any action (if Congress adjourns *sine die* within 10 days of sending the bill to the president).

Policy The authoritative statements of intentions or goals made by the government for dealing with perceived problems and the actions taken by the government to implement its statements of intent.

Policy analysis The application of systematic research techniques to a policy proposal in order to create a more optimum policy.

Policy formulation The stage in the policy process in which alternative proposals for dealing with a perceived problem are examined and debated by participants. Formulation includes activities of information gathering, alternative development, advocacy, and decision.

Political action committee A committee set up by a special-interest group, especially a corporation or labor union, that raises and gives campaign contributions on behalf of the organization or group it represents.

Political culture A broadly shared set of ways of thinking about how politics and governing ought to be carried out.

Political parties An organization that runs candidates for election.

Political question doctrine A view developed by the Supreme Court holding that certain constitutional issues cannot be decided by the courts, but are to be decided by the executive or legislative branches. For example, the court accepts presidential power to recognize foreign governments.

Political science The systematic study of politics.

Political socialization A process by which people come to have political beliefs, attitudes, preferences, and values.

Political system Those elements in society that interact over political issues. Thus, political systems is a broader concept than government, but somewhat less than society.

Politico An officeholder who is concerned primarily with reelection.

Poll tax The mandatory payment of a fee by a voter in order to be qualified to vote in the United States; poll taxes had been levied by some states in order to prevent black citizens from voting.

Populism The promotion of political ends by appealing to people to exercise direct pressure on government. What the "people" want becomes the ultimate test of morality, justice, and even art. Populists tend to believe in **elite theory.**

Pork barrel Reference to the distribution of benefits to special groups or constituencies that characterize some committees' work.

Positive law Unlike natural law, positive law is established by legislature or other government authority.

Poverty-level income An income figure, determined periodically by government officials and adjusted for family size, that defines in a technical and narrow sense what "poor" means. To be eligible for many government programs, applicants' incomes must be below the poverty-level figure.

Power The capacity of one person to influence the behavior of another.

Power base A politician's foundation of support. One of the most curious things about President Carter was his apparent lack of any hard-core support.

Power of the purse The traditional legislatively controlled power to tax and spend public funds.

Precedent The judicial practice that decisions in previous cases are and should be very important determinants of subsequent court decisions. The Latin term *stare decisis* (literally, "let the decision stand") refers to the rule of precedent.

Precincts For election purposes, cities and counties are divided into precinct polling districts.

Preliminary hearing Pretrial proceeding at which the prosecutor must prove that a crime was committed and establish the probable guilt of the defendant. If the evidence presented does not show probable guilt, the judge may dismiss the case.

Preponderance of the evidence The standard used by judges or juries in finding for the plaintiff in a civil (noncriminal) action. The preponderance-of-the-evidence standard requires that the plaintiff's complaint has a greater than 50–50 chance of being true. See **beyond a reasonable doubt.**

Presentment The initial appearance in felony cases, at which time defendants are informed of the charges against them and advised of their rights.

President pro tem Officer elected by the Senate to preside in the absence of the vice president. An honor, but not an important position.

Press secretary The White House Office staff official who meets with the media and speaks for the president in the president's absence.

Primary An election prior to the general election in which voters select the candidates who will run on each party's ticket. Primaries are also used to choose convention delegates. See **closed primary versus open primary.**

Prior restraint An effort to censor a publication before it goes to press.

Private law Legislation to aid a particular person rather than classes of citizens or all of the citizens considered together. For example, a member of the Congress might pass a private bill to simplify the process for a particular alien trying to gain entry into the United States.

Productivity Output per hour of labor. It is measured by dividing total output in a nation by labor hours employed. Increases in productivity are measured by the percent change in productivity from year to year.

Profit In popular parlance, profit is the difference between the cost of producing something and the price it fetches in the marketplace. Economists find the concept much more complex. To some, it is one of the costs of doing business, in the sense that a company must have a profit to induce people to invest in the company and bear the risk. Others say profit is a special category of high temporary earnings resulting from innovation and entrepreneurship. To Marxists, profit is the morally unjustified markup over labor costs. See **labor theory of value.**

Programs Specific sets of actions to be taken in the implementation or carrying out of a **plan.**

Progressive A liberal who prefers not to be called a liberal.

Progressive tax Taxation that takes a larger share from higher incomes than from lower incomes. The federal income tax is mildly progressive.

Proletariat The working class as distinguished from the propertied class, the bourgeoisie, or the nobility.

Property That which a person owns. While Locke, like Marx, believed that the earth is the common possession of mankind, he also asserted that the conditions of human life require labor and that labor necessarily introduces private property. For individuals to effectively use things, Locke argued, they must *own* them. Hence government should protect the rights of property.

Proportional representation An electoral system of allocating seats in a legislature so that each political party is given a percentage of seats roughly equivalent to its electoral strength. Not used in American elections for national offices, but used in several European systems.

Proportional system See **proportional representation.**

Proposition 13 A referendum provision passed by California voters in the spring of 1978 to set strict limits to the possible increases in local property taxes.

Pseudo event "Media events" planned or planted so that they can be reported.

Public and private goods Those goods whose consumption by one person does not lessen the amount available to other persons, once the good is produced. Examples of public goods are national defense and radio and TV signals. A private good, in contrast, tends to benefit one person exclusively—for example, a pair of socks. A market economy is far better at producing private goods than public goods.

Public bill A legislative bill that deals with matters of general—as opposed to private—concern. Opposite to a private bill. See **private law.**

Public debt The value of all outstanding federal government bonds, notes, and other securities—in other words, how much the federal government owes.

Public interest group An interest group that supports a cause in which the members have no direct financial interest.

Public law A law that deals with general legislative concerns and affects the public at large.

Public opinion Preferences held by people on a significant issue.

Public opinion poll An attempt to determine **public opinion.**

Public policy A general statement of where a government wants to go; a major piece of legislation; a statement of goals in order of priority.

Quorum The minimum number of members who must be in attendance to allow business to be conducted in the House or Senate. Although normally a majority of all members is needed for a quorum, in the House a minimum of 100 members allows the House to conduct business as a **committee of the whole.**

Random sample A group whose members have been selected by social scientists or poll takers at random that is representative of the larger population being studied.

Ratification The act of confirming by expression of consent or approval. Can apply to the ratification of the Constitution of 1787, by the original 13 states, to ratification of treaties with foreign countries by senate, or to ratification of an constitutional amendment by the Senate.

Realigning election See **critical election.**

Realist-idealist dichotomy Two ways of viewing international relations. The realist is concerned with the balance of power among nations and the interest of his own nation; the idealist is concerned with morals and principles and the interests of all humanity.

Realpolitik Conducting international relations on the basis of power rather than appeals to morality and world opinion.

Recall Removal of an official from office before the end of his term.

Recession A economic downturn. More precisely, two quarters (six months) in which the **gross national product** has failed to grow.

Redistributive policy Domestic government policy that attempts to shift wealth, rights, or other things among social or racial groups.

Referendum A direct election in which citizens choose a public policy without the immediate intervention of elected officeholders.

Referent power When B does what A wishes because B deeply respects A and wants to be apart of what A does, we say A has referrent power.

Registration Appearance before an official during a certain period of time before an election, in order to be eligible to vote. See **absentee ballot.**

Regressive tax Taxation that takes an equal amount or percent from all taxpayers regardless of their incomes. Sales taxes are regressive (they take a fixed percent from everyone) and have more impact on low-income people than wealthier people. See **progressive tax.**

Regulatory policies Government policies designed to control the behavior of, or set the operating conditions for, business, unions, or similar organizations.

Rehabilitation The goal of sentencing criminals to programs that attempt to reform them so they will not commit another crime.

Remedy What is done to compensate for an injury or to enforce some right.

Reprivatization Turning over to business certain functions (e.g., trash collection) now done by government bureaucrats in the hope of achievening greater efficiency.

Republican government A form of government in which much decision-making power is exercised by elected officers and representatives, who are responsible to the people and who govern according to law. See *Federalist Paper* No. 10.

Reserved powers Under the 10th Amendment, powers not delegated to the national government nor prohibited to the states by the Constitution are reserved for the state.

Restitution A court order in which convicted persons are required to pay back or otherwise compensate the victim for their crime.

Retribution The goal of sentencing criminals to inflict harm on them in proportion to the harm they have done. Punishment for its own sake, not for **rehabilitation.**

Reverse discrimination Discrimination in favor of those groups previously discriminated against. Its aim is to overcome the effects of previous discrimination and bring more people into the mainstream of American life.

Revolving door The movement of private-sector managers or interest group officials to government and vice versa. For example, an oil executive goes to the Federal Energy Administration, a consumer advocate goes to the Consumer Product Safety Commission, and a defense contractor becomes deputy secretary of defense.

Rider A provision added to an important bill (such as defense) but not necessarily relevant to the bill's purpose. The hope behind this strategy is that the provision (often bluntly designed to aid special interests) will thus "ride" through the legislative process.

Runoff primary An election held when no candidate in a previous election received a required percentage of the total votes cast.

Sampling error The degree to which the sample is distorted and does not represent the "polling universe" to be measured.

Select or special committees A legislative committee established for a limited time period and for a special purpose.

Senior executive service With the passage of the **civil service act of 1978**, Congress created a Senior Executive Service (SES) of about 8,000 top federal managers who could be hired, fired, and transferred more easily than ordinary civil servants. The aim was to give the president more flexibility.

Seniority system Method of awarding committee chairmanships to members with the longest continuous service on the committee.

Separate-but-equal doctrine In *Plessy v. Ferguson* (1896), the Supreme Court ruled that a state could provide separate but equal facilities for blacks.

Separation of power The conscious division of government power into separate branches—executive, legislative, and judicial—to prevent a concentration of all powers in the same hands. See *Federalist Paper No. 51*.

Shays' rebellion During the critical 10-year period after the Revolutionary War ended, this rebellion in western Massachusetts stirred deep fears of anarchy and helped to move the thoughts of many early Americans towards establishing a stronger central government.

Single-issue politics The idea that contemporary American politics is dominated by groups with very narrow interests and that, as a consequence, public interest (that is, the interest of the whole political community) suffers.

Small claims court A court that handles civil claims for small amounts of money. People usually represent themselves rather than hire an attorney.

Social contract A hypothesized agreement by which—according to Hobbes, Locke, Rousseau, Rawls, Nozick, and other philosophers—individuals have united and formed a state. The idea serves as a criterion to determine whether the consent of the governed might be assumed.

Social Security Act of 1935 The basic social welfare legislation of the **New Deal** embodying social insurance, public assistance, and child health and welfare services.

Socialism See **command economies.**

Sociobiology The study of all aspects of social behavior in animals, from ants to man; ethology.

Solicitor general Official in the department of justice who conducts cases on behalf of the United States before the Supreme Court.

Sovereign Having supreme and independent authority in government as possessed or claimed by a state or community.

Soviet Afghanistan invasion In 1980, shortly after the fall of the Shah of Iran, nearly 100,000 Soviet troops entered Afghanistan in order to protect the pro-Soviet regime in Kabul (the nation's capital) from widespread opposition among the people. This event seemed to change dramatically President Carter's conciliatory attitude towards the Soviet Union.

Speaker of the House The member of the majority party in the House of Representatives who is selected by the party to preside over sessions of the House.

Spillovers See **externalities.**

Split ticket A ballot cast by a voter who chooses candidates from more than one party.

Spoils system The award of government jobs (spoils) to political supporters and friends of the victory. See **patronage.**

Stagflation An economic condition characterized by high inflation and slow growth (which means relatively high unemployment).

Standing Status in a court to bring a lawsuit to it. For example, an individual must ordinarily show personal harm in order to sue.

Standing committee A permanent legislative committee that considers legislation within a certain subject area.

Stare decisis The practice of standing by precedent in judicial decision making. Rather than disturb settled points, judges will base their decisions on similar cases already decided.

State of nature According to many political philosophers, the hypothesized condition that exists prior to the state. See **social contract.**

State of the Union Message An annual presidential message to Congress containing presidential proposals for new and existing government programs that require congressional legislation.

States' rights Opposition to the national government's power at the expense of state power or authority. Its basis is the **Tenth Amendment.**

Statistics The science that deals with the collection, classification, analysis, and interpretation of numerical data and that provides convient ways to speak about aggregates of disparate elements (such as members of state legislatures).

Statute of limitations A legislative act that establishes a time limit within which lawsuits may be brought or crimes prosecuted.

Statutory law Laws created by the members of a legislature. It also includes treaties and executive agreements.

Step-by-step A negotiating strategy that proceeds cautiously, seeking small agreements by both sides rather than one sudden and comprehensive solution.

Stewardship An activist conception of the presidency advanced by Theodore Roosevelt, which holds that the president can do anything that is not expressly prohibited by the Constitution.

Strategic Arms Limitations Talks Negotiations between the United States and Soviet Union over the reduction of nuclear weapons.

Strategy An overall plan of maneuvers for obtaining a

Subgovernments The close relationships among congressional subcommittee members, executive agency officials, and interest group representatives ("cozy triangles") that characterize a large portion of domestic policymaking.

Subpoena An order that commands a witness to appear and give testimony, "under penalty" for not complying.

Subsidies Cash payments from the government to recipients to induce desired behavior. A subsidy may be made directly or indirectly through allowable deductions.

Suffrage The right to vote in elections.

Sun Belt versus Snow Belt The conflict between Southern and Western states, on the one hand, and Northern states, on the other, about how natural resources and tax revenue should be allocated.

Sunset legislation Legislation that would require agencies and programs to return periodically to Congress (for example, every three to five years) to obtain renewed authorization. Those not renewed would automatically expire.

Sunshine laws Laws requiring that meetings of agencies or government units be open to the public.

Supply and demand, law of The quantity *demanded* of a good or service goes up when its price goes down and vice versa. As the price, and hence the rate of return of **profit,** goes up for a good or service, producers will want to supply more. See **market economies.**

Supply-side economies The theory that the best approach to overcome economic difficulties such as **stagflation** is through government policies that help increase the supply of goods and services. Tax cuts and deregulation are critical elements in this approach.

Supremacy clause Article VI of the Constitution provides that the Constitution, federal laws, and all treaties are the supreme law of the land. See ***McCulloch v. Maryland.***

Survey research A method used by many social scientists to learn some things about a large population (called a "universe") by asking questions and collecting data about a smaller group (called a "sample") that has been chosen to be representative of the larger group. Polling organizations like Gallup and Harris and many political science teachers are among the users of survey research methods.

Systems analysis An approach to understanding complex phenomena. For example, American political life can be conceived of as a system—that is, a collection of interrelated components. government institutions become a mechanism for converting citizen inputs into outputs (namely, public policy).

Targeting In political campaigns, the candidates try to concentrate their time and money on those areas that will yield the highest return in votes. In the formulation and implementation of public policy, government officials try to make sure that the benefits of programs fall directly on those parts of the community that are most in need of help.

Tariff Duties or customs imposed by government on imports or exports.

Tax expenditures Taxes deliberately not levied by the government in order to subsidize special groups—for example, homeowners. These unlevied taxes constitute revenues deliberately foregone by the government.

Technology assessment A method of trying to anticipate all the major effects of a new technology and to take measures to mitigate the most adverse effects.

Tenth Amendment According to some people, this amendment tells what happens when state and federal power collide. It states: "The powers not delegated to the United States by the Constitution, nor prohibited to the states, are reserved to the states respectively, or to the people." But in *U.S.* v. *Darby* (1941), the Supreme Court said that the amendment merely asserts that the states have independent powers of their own.

Terrorism The activity of using terror (e.g., threat of death) to change the policies of a government. Essentially, the weapon of a minority that has no chance of success by persuasion.

Third parties Minor political parties that espouse ideas that major parties have not addressed. Third parties can affect the outcome of presidential elections.

Third World A sweeping term that includes the 100-plus nations of Asia, Africa, and Latin America. The term comes from the idea that the First and Second Worlds are the free industrial countries of the west and the communist bloc countries; all else is the Third World. Some argue that there are really three groups in the Third World: countries on the verge of industrialization (e.g., South Korea and Singapore); countries that are oil rich (e.g., Saudia Arabia); and countries that are extremely poor (e.g., Bangladesh).

Torts A breach of some obligation causing harm or injury to someone; a civil wrong, such as negligence or libel.

Totalitarianism A form of government in which a small group of people or one person not only maintains absolute political control (generally through the use of terror) but also tries to control all aspects of social life.

Trade association A kind of **interest group** that represents many firms all in the same line of business.

Trade deficit and trade surplus When a country buys from abroad more than it sells, it runs a trade deficit. If it sells more than buys, it runs a surplus.

Trade-off A compromise that often must be made between to divergent but necessary values of goods. See **guns and butter** and **opportunity costs.**

Transfer payment Income paid by the government to recipients through a variety of direct cash payments or in-kind services.

Treaty of Versailles The agreement reached in 1919 that terminated World War I. The outstanding American figure is the negotiations leading to the treaty was President Wilson.

Truman Doctrine In 1947, President Truman adopted a policy that called for the United States to aid Greece and Turkey and to fight communist expansion. See **containment**.

Tyranny Arbitrary or unrestrained use of power by government authorities.

"Uncontrollable" expenditures Spending that has been mandated by previous statutory commitments that in the short run cannot be altered. "Uncontrollables" have been taking a growing share of the budget.

Unitary government Unlike a federal system, a centralized government in which local or state governments exercise only those powers given to them by the central government.

United Nations International organization created in 1945 and headquartered in New York City. Its General Assembly is composed of all member nations (about 150), but the seat of real power is the 15-member Security Council.

Utilitarianism The theory that takes the ultimate good to be the greatest happiness of the greatest number and defines the rightness of public policy in terms of its contribution to the general happiness.

Utopia An imaginary human paradise and important concept in the development of political ideas from Plato's *Republic* to modern socialist writers.

Variable-sum game A circumstance in which two or more people, with their interests partially in conflict, work out a solution in which each gains at least some of what they want. It is the opposite of a zero-sum game, where the gain of one participant is the loss of the other.

Veto The constitutional power granted to the president that allows him to refuse to sign a bill passed by Congress into law; a vetoed bill can become law if two thirds of each house of Congress votes to override the veto.

Vietnam War Although Lyndon Johnson promised during the 1964 presidential campaign he would not "send American boys" to Vietnam, within a couple of years he had a half million there. Richard Nixon obtained a peace treaty in 1973, but by 1975 the capital of South Vietnam was captured by troops from the North. While American troops were never technically defeated, the experience demonstrated the problems facing a democracy that tries to fight a protracted limited war.

Virginia Plan Proposal in the Constitutional Convention of 1787 that provided for a strong legislature with representation in each house determined by population.

Volatility Changeability; prominent characteristic of American public opinion.

Voter turnout The proportion of the voting-age population that votes in presidential elections.

Voting Rights Act of 1965 Legislation passed by Congress to guarantee the rights of all citizens to register and to vote freely in state and federal elections.

Wage-price controls An attempt to slow the rate of inflation by requiring government approval of major price increases and wage settlements.

War on poverty The label President Johnson applied to the federal government's efforts to combat poverty in America. Many of these programs were enacted in the 1964 Economic Opportunity Act.

War Powers Act Legislation passed by Congress in 1973 that seeks to place limits on the president's power to wage war by requiring that he notify Congress immediately whenever U.S. troops are committed abroad. Congress may require troop withdrawal within 60 to 90 days of notification if it disapproves of the action.

Watergate affair Illegal acts carried out by officials in the Nixon administration and subsequent efforts by Nixon to cover up what happened. It ended with the resignation of Nixon and the succession to the presidency of vice president Gerald R. Ford.

Welfare state A government that seeks to ensure minimum benefits for all of its citizens by extensive programs, such as those that provide education, housing, medical care, minimum wages, job security, old-age assistance, and special help for the handicapped. By adopting the principles of the welfare state, many of the inequities of a capitalist economy have been reduced.

Wesberry* v. *Sanders A 1964 Supreme Court case decision that required Georgia to redraw the borders of congressional districts so that they would be nearly equal in population. This decision advanced the concept of one person, one vote implicit in Article I of the Constitution.

Whips Assistants to the majority and minority leaders in both houses who are liaisons between the leaders and the rank-and-file party members.

White House Office A collection of presidential staff, many of whom are housed in the White House, who provide policy advice and other services to the president.

Writ of certiorari Using this procedure, a petitioner tells the Supreme Court why it should be interested in a case. This writ literally requires that the lower court (whose decision the petitioner is appealing to) send a certified record of the case to the Supreme Court.

Writ of habeas corpus Court order requiring jailers to explain to a judge why they are holding a prisoner in custody. Its purpose is to prevent illegal arrests and unlawful imprisonment.

Yalta Conference Meeting in February 1945 at Yalta, Crimea, USSR, of British prime minister Winston

Churchill, President Roosevelt, and Soviet Premier Joseph Stalin. Plans were made for dividing Germany into four zones of occupation and for trials of Nazi leaders. Roosevelt was later critized for many of the concessions made to Stalin (e.g., giving him Chinese territory without informing China).

Yates decision In 1957, a majority of the Supreme Court tried to distinguish between the expression of a philosophical belief and advocacy of an illegal act. Only the latter was punishable.

Youngstown Sheet and Tube Co.* v. *Sawyer (1952) Supreme Court decision striking down President Truman's **Executive order** that authorized seizure of steel mills.

Notes

Chapter 1

1. *Politics: Who Gets What, When, How?* (Cleveland: World, 1958).
2. Herbert Agar, *The Price of Union* (Boston: Houghton Mifflin, 1966), p. 22.
3. *Time*, June 25, 1979.
4. David J. Garrow, *Protest at Selma* (New Haven, Conn.: Yale University Press, 1980).
5. Thomas Hobbes, *The Leviathan*, Book I, Chapter 13.
6. *Congressional Record* (July 19, 1979), p. S9908.
7. Michael Oakeshott, "Political Education," inaugural address delivered at the London School of Economics, March 6, 1951.
8. James David Barber, *The Presidential Character* (Englewood Cliffs, N.J.: Prentice-Hall, 1972).
9. Outstanding illustrations of systems analysis in political science are David Easton, *Framework for Political Analysis* (Englewood Cliffs, N.J.: Prentice-Hall, 1965); and Karl W. Deutsch, *The Nerves of Government* (New York: Free Press, 1966). For numerous examples of how systems analysis can heighten our understanding of many phenomena, see Joel de Rosnay, *The Macroscope* (New York: Harper & Row, 1975).
10. Robin Fox, *The Red Lamp of Incest* (New York: Dutton, 1980). The most comprehensive treatment of sociobiology is Edward O. Wilson, *Sociobiology* (Cambridge, Mass: Harvard University Press, 1975).
11. Leo Strauss, speech at the University of Chicago, June 6, 1959.
12. Agar, *The Price of Union*, pp. 632–33.
13. Kenneth O'Donnell and David Powers, *Johnny, We Hardly Knew Ye* (Boston: Little, Brown, 1970).
14. Richard E. Newstadt, *Presidential Power* (New York: New American Library, 1964).
15. Charles Peters, "A Platform for the Eighties," *Washington Monthly*, February 1979.
16. Clinton Rossiter and James Lare, eds., *The Essential Lippman* (New York: Random House, 1963).

Chapter 2

1. George F. Will, *The Pursuit of Happiness, and Other Sobering Thoughts* (New York: Harper & Row, 1978), p. 239.
2. Bernard Law Montgomery, *A History of Warfare* (New York: World, 1968), p. 321.
3. For insight into the complexities of the Articles of Confederation, see William F. Swindler, "Our First Constitution: The Articles of Confederation," *American Bar Association Journal*, February 1981.
4. Daniel Boorstin, *The Genius of American Politics* (Chicago: University of Chicago Press, 1953), pp. 71–73.
5. *Dialogues of Alfred North Whitehead*, as recorded by Lucien Price (Boston: Little, Brown, 1954). The other occasion was the work of Augustus, the first Roman emperor (27 B.C.–14 A.D.), which saved Rome from bankruptcy and the wornout ideas of the old patrician class.
6. David Hackett Fischer, *Historian's Fallacies* (New York: Harper & Row, 1970), pp. 74–78 and 210. For additional criticism of Beard's thesis, see Martin Diamond, "The Declaration and the Constitution: Liberty, Democracy, and the Founders," *Public Interest* 41 (Fall 1975); and Jack P. Greene, "The Reappraisal of the American Revolution in Recent Historical Literature," in Greene, *The Reinterpretation of the American Revolution, 1763–1789* (New York: Harper & Row, 1968).
7. William Gladstone, letter to the committee in charge of the celebration of the centennial anniversary of the American Constitution, July 20, 1887.
8. Herbert Storing, "The Problem of Big Government," in *A Nation of States*, ed. Robert Goldwin (Chicago: Rand McNally, 1975), pp. 83–84.
9. Will, *The Pursuit of Happiness*.
10. James Madison, *The Federalist* 10.
11. Richard Rovere, "Affairs of State," *The New Yorker* (March 19, 1979), p. 138.
12. Rudolf Arnheim, *The Dynamics of Architectural*

Form (Berkeley: University of California Press, 1977), pp. 145–46.

Chapter 3

1. Hans J. Morganthau, *The Purpose of American Politics* (New York: Vintage Books, 1964).
2. I *Corinthians* 12, 4–8.
3. Robert A. Dahl, *After the Revolution?* (New Haven, Conn.: Yale University Press, 1970), pp. 59–63.
4. Joseph A. Schumpeter, *Capitalism, Socialism and Democracy* (New York: Harper Torchbooks, 1962); Robert A. Dahl, *A Preface to Democratic Theory* (Chicago: University of Chicago Press, 1956).
5. Dahl, *A Preface*, p. 269.
6. Samuel Beer, "In Search of a New Public Philosophy," in *The New American Political System*, ed. Anthony King (Washington, D.C.: American Enterprise Institute, 1978).
7. Daniel Bell, "Meritocracy and Equality," *Public Interest* 29 (Fall 1972), p. 40.
8. *The New York Times*, February 20, 1979.
9. Ibid.
10. The discussion of Rawls' philosophy is based on John Rawls, *A Theory of Justice* (Cambridge, Mass.: Harvard University Press, 1971).
11. Dworkin interview with Bryan Magee, in *Men of Ideas* (New York: Viking Press, 1979).
12. The discussion of Nozick's philosophy is based on Robert Nozick, *Anarchy, State, and Utopia* (New York: Basic Books, 1974).
13. Edmund Burke, *Selected Writing of Edmund Burke*, ed. W.J. Bate (New York: Modern Library, 1960).
14. George F. Will, *The Pursuit of Happiness, and Other Sobering Thoughts* (New York: Harper & Row, 1978).
15. Karl R. Popper, *The Open Society and Its Enemies*, 2 vol. (New York: Harper Torchbooks, 1962).
16. *U.S. News & World Report*, December 10, 1979, pp. 57–58.

Chapter 4

1. Edmund S. Morgan, *The Genius of George Washington* (New York: W. W. Norton, 1980).
2. Theodore White, *The Making of the President, 1960* (New York: Atheneum House, 1961).
3. Rowland Evans and Robert Novak, *Lyndon B. Johnson: The Exercise of Power* (New York: New American Library, 1966).
4. James MacGregor Burns, *Leadership* (New York: Harper & Row, 1978).
5. Morris Janowitz, *The Last Half-Century: Societal Change and Politics in America* (Chicago: University of Chicago Press, 1978), p. 511.
6. Theodore Lowi, "American Business, Public Policy, Case Studies and Political Theory," *World Politics* 16 (1960); 541–63.
7. Peter Bachrach and Morton S. Baratz, "Two Faces of Power," *American Political Science Review*, March 1962, pp. 121–22.
8. *Newsweek*, February 16, 1981.
9. Richard M. Pious, *The American Presidency* (New York: Basic Books, 1979).
10. John P. Kotter, "Power, Dependence and Effective Management," *Harvard Business Review*, July–August 1977, p. 131.
11. Richard Sennett, *Authority* (New York: Alfred A. Knopf, 1979).
12. Herbert Agar, *The Price of Union* (Boston: Houghton Mifflin, 1966), pp. 634–35.
13. Kotter, "Power," p. 136.
14. Agar, *The Price of Union*, p. 661.
15. Evans and Novak, *Lyndon B. Johnson*, pp. 100–101.
16. James MacGregor Burns, *Roosevelt: The Lion and the Fox* (New York: Harcourt, Brace & World, 1956), p. 284.
17. Evans and Novak, *Lyndon B. Johnson*, p. 112.
18. Pious, *The American Presidency*, Chapter 2.
19. Saul Alinsky, *Rules for Radicals* (New York: Random House, 1971).
20. Edward Banfield, *Political Influence* (New York: Free Press, 1965), pp. 37–42.
21. This interpretation of King's strategy is based on David J. Garrow, *Protest at Selma* (New Haven, Conn.: Yale University Press, 1980).
22. *Saturday Review* (April 3, 1965).
23. Jeff Greenfield, *Playing to Win* (New York: Simon & Schuster, 1980).
24. Theodore White, *The Making of the President, 1960* (New York: Atheneum House, 1961), p. 369.
25. Agar, *The Price of Union*, p. 409.
26. Burns, *Roosevelt*, p. 285.
27. Henry S. Kissinger, *The White House Years* (Boston: Little, Brown, 1979).
28. William Shakespeare, *Julius Caesar*, Act IV, Scene 3, lines 218–221.
29. Burns, *Roosevelt*, p. 284.
30. L.R. Pondy, "Organizational Conflict: Concepts and Models," *Administrative Science Quarterly*, September 1967, pp. 296–320.
31. Kissinger, *The White House Years*.
32. Murray Edelman, *The Symbolic Use of Politics* (Urbana, Ill.: University of Illinois Press, 1964), p. 123.
33. E.E. Schattschneider, *Semi-Sovereign People* (New York: Holt, Rinehart & Winston, 1961), p. 68.
34. The discussion of hand gestures is drawn from Desmond Morris, *Manwatching* (New York: Abrams, 1977).
35. Alinsky, *Rules for Radicals*.

Chapter 5

1. Kenneth Keniston, Young Radicals (New York: Harcourt Brace Jovanovich, 1968).
2. Robert Coles, "What Children Know About Politics" (a series), New York Review of Books (February 20, March 6, and March 20, 1975).
3. Robert D. Hess and Judith V. Torney, *The Development of Political Attitudes in Children* (New Haven, Conn.: Yale University Press, 1965).

4. *The New York Times* (May 31, 1980).
5. Ben J. Wattenberg and David Gergen, "American— A Storehouse of Public Opinion," in U.S. Department of Commerce, Bureau of the Census, *Reflections of America: Commemorating the Statistical Abstract Centennial* (Washington: D.C.: U.S. Government Printing Office, 1980).
6. Samuel P. Huntington, "Postindustrial Politics: How Benign Will It Be?" *Comparative Politics*, January 1974.
7. James David Barber, *Pulse of Politics* (New York: W. W. Norton, 1980).
8. This section's title is the title of David Halberstam's book (New York: Alfred A. Knopf, 1980); he also provided the CBS and *Washington Post* anecdotes.
9. Ben Stein, *The View from Sunset Boulevard* (New York: Basic Books, 1979).
10. Ibid.
11. Herbert J. Gans, *Deciding What's News* (New York: Pantheon Books, 1979).
12. Ernest W. Lefever, *TV and National Defense: An Analysis of CBS News* (Boston: Institute for American Strategy Press, 1974).
13. The concept of the pseudoevent is fully developed in Daniel J. Boorstin, *The Image* (New York: Harper & Row, 1964).
14. For a systematic look at which groups are most and least involved in the voting process, see Raymond E. Wolfinger and Steven J. Rosenstone, *Who Votes?* (New Haven, Conn.: Yale University Press, 1980).
15. The subsection on nonvoting is based largely on an article of the same title by Kenneth L. Adelman, *The Wall Street Journal*, October 15, 1980.
16. The Costikyan quote and the *Time*/CBS reference are from Norman Podhoretz, "The New American Majority," *Commentary*, January 1981.
17. *The Washington Post*, November 6, 1980.
18. William Safire, *Safire's Political Dictionary* (New York: Random House, 1978), p. 384.
19. See Ronald W. Clark, *Einstein* (New York: Avon Books, 1971) for the complete story on Einstein's famous letter.

Chapter 6

1. Diagram suggested by Robert G. Meadow, *Politics as Communication* (Norwood, N.J.: Ablex, 1980).
2. Alexis de Tocqueville, *Democracy in America*, trans. Henry Reeve (New York: Schocken, 1961), vol. 2, p. 128.
3. This analysis is based on Tom Bethell, "Taking a Hard Look at Common Cause," *The New York Times Magazine*, August 24, 1980.
4. Thomas Sowell, "Myths about Minorities," *Commentary*, August 1979, pp. 33–37.
5. Francis G. Hutchins, "The New Indian Offensive," *New Republic*, August 30, 1980, pp. 14–17.
6. Charles Ackess, *Abigail Adams: An American Woman* (Boston: Little, Brown, 1979).
7. Ibid.
8. Paul Dickson, *The Official Rules* (New York: Delacorte Press, 1979), p. 19.
9. Alison Lurie, "Return of the Ship of Fools," *New Republic*, August 30, 1980, p. 17.
10. 1980 Election Day surveys by *The New York Times*/CBS News Poll.

Chapter 7

1. Fred I. Greenstein, "Change and Continuity in the Modern Presidency," in *The New American Political System*, ed. Anthony King, (Washington, D.C.: American Enterprise Institute, 1978), pp. 80–82.
2. Franklin D. Roosevelt, address in Washington, D.C., on Constitution Day, September 17, 1937.
3. Fred I. Greenstein, "Eisenhower as an Activist President: A Look at New Evidence," *Political Science Quarterly*, Winter 1979–80, pp. 575–99.
4. Henry Fairlie, *The Kennedy Promise* (New York: Doubleday, 1973), p. 273.
5. Clinton Rossiter and James Lare, eds., *The Essential Lippmann* (New York: Random House, 1963), p. 273.
6. Bob Considerie, *The Boston Herald-American*, May 25, 1973.
7. *The New York Times*, March 9, 1975.
8. George F. Will, *The Pursuit of Happiness, and Other Sobering Thoughts* (New York: Harper & Row, 1978), p. 223.
9. Greenstein, "Change and Continuity," pp. 80–82.
10. *The New York Times*, January 8, 1981.
11. Clinton Rossiter and James Lare, eds., *The Essential Lippmann* (New York: Random House, 1963), p. 273.
12. Greenstein, "Change and Continuity," p. 84.

Chapter 8

1. James L. Payne, "Show Horses and Work Horses in the U.S. House of Representatives," *Polity*, Spring 1980.
2. Morris Fiorina, *Congress—Keystone of the Washington Establishment* (New Haven, Conn.: Yale University Press, 1977).
3. Hugh Heclo, "Issue Networks and the Executive Establishment," in ed. Anthony King, *The New American Political System* (Washington, D.C.: American Enterprise Institute, 1978), p. 102.
4. Ibid.

Chapter 9

1. Benjamin Nathan Cardozo, "The Nature of the Judicial Process," in *Selected Works of Benjamin Nathan Cardozo* (New Haven, Conn.: Yale University Press, 1947).

2. Bob Woodward and Scott Armstrong, *The Brethren: Inside the Supreme Court* (New York: Simon & Schuster, 1980).
3. Raoul Berger, *Government by Judiciary: The Transformation of the Fourteenth Amendment* (Cambridge, Mass.: Harvard University Press, 1975).
4. *The Wall Street Journal*, June 9, 1980.
5. Victor Villasenor, *The People vs. Juan Corona* (Boston: Little, Brown, 1977).
6. P. Allan Dionisopolous, "Judicial Review in the Textbooks," *DEA News* 11 (Fall 1976).
7. Lino A. Graglia, "The Supreme Court's Abuse of Power," reprinted in *Congressional Record* (June 19, 1981), p. S6589.

Chapter 10

1. Leon D. Epstein, "The Old States in a New System," in ed. Anthony King, *The New American Political System* (Washington, D.C.: American Enterprise Institute, 1978), p. 325.
2. Ibid., p. 154.
3. Edmund Burke, *Selected Writing of Edmund Burke*, ed. W.J. Bate (New York: Modern Library, 1960).
4. Epstein, "The Old States," p. 361.
5. Samuel Beer, "Federalism, Nationalism, and Democracy in America," *American Political Science Review*, March 1978, pp. 5–44.
6. David Greenstone and Paul Peterson, *Race and Authority in Urban Politics* (New York: Russell Sage Foundation, 1973).
7. Douglas Yates, *The Ungovernable City* (Cambridge, Mass.: MIT Press, 1977).

Coda

1. Hugh Heclo, *A Government of Strangers* (Washington, D.C.: Brookings Institution, 1977).
2. Quoted in Paul Dickson, *The Official Rules* (New York: Delacorte Press, 1977), p. 17.

Chapter 11

1. Hans J. Morganthau, *The Purpose of American Politics* (New York: Vintage Books, 1964).
2. Ibid.
3. Ibid.
4. John Herman Randall, Jr., *The Making of the Modern Mind* (New York: Columbia University Press, 1976), p. 346.
5. Quoted in Morganthau, *The Purpose of American Politics*.
6. Don E. Fehrenbacher, *The Dred Scott Case: Its Significance in American Law and Politics* (New York: Oxford University Press, 1978).
7. Lois D. Rice and Albert B. Fitt, "25 Years after Brown," *The New York Times*, May 13, 1979.

8. Quoted in *The Vantage Point* (New York: Holt, Rinehart & Winston, 1971), p. 166.
9. Abigail Therstrom, "The Odd Evolution of the Voting Rights Act," *Public Interest*, Winter 1980, pp. 49ff.
10. Quoted in Studs Terkel, *American Dreams: Lost and Found* (New York: Pantheon Books, 1980).
11. U.S. Office of Civil Rights, *Racial and Ethnic Enrollment Data from Institutions of Higher Learning*, biennial.

Chapter 12

1. "There Are Solutions to Our Economic Problems," *The New York Times*, August 10, 1980, p. 30.
2. Ibid.
3. Data used in this analysis comes chiefly from five sources: U.S. Department of Energy publications; Robert Stobaugh and Daniel Yergin, ed., *Energy Future* (New York: Random House, 1979); Sam H. Schurs, et al., *Energy in America's Future* (Baltimore: Johns Hopkins University Press, 1979); Arthur Bueche, "The Hard Truth About Our Energy Future," Paper delivered to the Western Conference of Public Service Commissioners, in Seattle, Washington, June 11, 1979; and a series of Shell Oil papers dealing with the national energy outlook.
4. Yergin in Stobaugh and Yergin, *Energy Future*.
5. Martin Feldstein, "Consequences of Hospital Controls," *The Wall Street Journal*, April 12, 1979.
6. Robert M. Heyssel, "The Cost of Health," *The New York Times*, July 16, 1979.
7. Charles Schultz, *The Public Use of Private Interest* (Washington, D.C.: Brookings Institution, 1977).
8. Aaron Wildavsky, "The Self-Evaluating Organization," in *Speaking Truth to Power* (Boston: Little Brown, 1979), pp. 212–37.
9. Thomas Sowell, "Myths about Minorities," *Commentary*, August 1979.
10. Ibid.
11. Ibid.
12. Grover Starling, *The Politics and Economics of Public Policy* (Homewood, Ill.: Dorsey Press, 1979).

Chapter 13

1. Edward R. Tufte, *Political Control of the Economy* (Princeton, N.J.: Princeton University Press, 1978).
2. Ibid.
3. George Gilder, *Wealth and Poverty* (New York: Basic Books, 1980).
4. This discussion is based on U.S. Department of Commerce, *The American Economic System*, n.d.; available through the Advertising Council, Inc.
5. "There Are Solutions to Our Economic Problems," *The New York Times*, August 10, 1980, p. 29.
6. Lester Thurow, *The Zero Sum Society* (New York: Basic Books, 1980), p. 58.

Chapter 14

1. Daniel Moynihan, "The Politics of Human Rights," *Commentary*, August 1977, p. 23.
2. Nigel Calder, *Nuclear Nightmares: An Investigation into Possible Wars* (New York: Viking Press, 1979).
3. Ibid.

Epilogue

1. George F. Will, *The Pursuit of Happiness and Other Sobering Thoughts* (New York: Harper & Row, 1978), p. 33.
2. Quoted in *Christian Science Monitor*, January 3, 1982.

To Explore Further

General, Historical, Theoretical, and Reference

The Federalist Papers (Many editions available).
The Essential Lippmann, ed. Clinton Rossiter and James Lare (Vintage).
William Safire, *Safire's Political Dictionary* (Random House).
Herbert Agar, *The Price of Union* (Houghton Mifflin).
Karl W. Deutsch, *The Nerves of Government* (Free Press).
Statistical Abstract of the United States (Yearly government publication).

Public Opinion and Political Action

Robert S. Erikson and Norman G. Luttbeg, *American Public Opinion* (Wiley).
Everett Carll Ladd, Jr., *Where Have All the Voters Gone?* (Norton).
Michael J. Robinson, "Television and American Politics, 1956–76," *The Public Interest* (Summer 1977).
Paul Weaver, "The New Journalism and the Old," *The Public Interest* (Spring 1974).

Government Institutions

Richard E. Neustadt, *Presidential Power* (Wiley).
Richard M. Pious, *The American Presidency* (Basic Books).
Robert G. McCloskey, *The American Supreme Court* (University of Chicago Press).
The New American Political System, ed Anthony King (AEI).
Lee P. Arbetman et al., *Street Law.* (West)

Public Policy

Lester Thurow, *The Zero Sum Society* (Basic Books).
George Gilder, *Wealth and Poverty* (Basic Books).
For analysis of public policy issues with a liberal slant, see publications by the Brookings Institute. For the conservative slant, see those by the American Enterprise Institute.

Index

A

Abortion, 393
Abraham, Henry J., 315
Abscam scandal, 276
   trials, 321
Absentee ballot, 173
Abzug, Bella, 269
Access points, 116
ACTION, 249
Active Corps of Executives (ACE), 473
Active-negative types, 14
Active-positive types, 14
Activism, 313, 332
Adams, Abigail, 195
Adams, John, 39, 52, 124, 229
Adams, Samuel, 385
Adams, Sherman, 43
Adenauer, Konrad, 128
Adjudication, 301
Administrative law, 305
Administrative Procedures Act, 245
Adversary process, 318, 322, 330
Affirmative action, 403–6
Afghanistan, Soviet invasion, 509
Agar, Herbert, 231
Age Discrimination in Employment Act, 409
Agenda, 113, 149
Agnew, Spiro, 236
Agricultural Adjustment Administration, 341
Agriculture, Department of, 245, 254
Aid to Families with Dependent Children (AFDC), 426
Alinsky, Saul, 121, 139
Allen, Richard, 121, 522
Allen v. Board of Elections, 403
Alliteration, 135
Amending the Constitution, 56–62
   Bill of Rights, 56–57
   constitutional convention, 58
   current proposals, 57–58
American Agricultural Movement, 192
American Bar Association, 330
American Civil Liberties Union, 190
American Enterprise Institute, 176
American Farm Bureau Federation, 190
American Federation of Labor–Congress of Industrial Organizations (AFL–CIO), 187, 189
American Independent Party, 202, 203
American Indians; *see* Indians, American
American League to Abolish Capital Punishment, 189
American Legion, 190
American Medical Association, 189
American Petroleum Institute, 197
American Revolution, 35–41
Americans for Conservative Action, 205
Americans for Democratic Action, 205
Ames, Fisher, 537
Amicus curiae, 313
Amtrak, 249
Anarchy, 73
Anderson, Clinton, 118–19
Anderson, John, 167, 174–75
Anderson, Martin, 420
Anglo-Saxon Protestants, 406–7
Animal behavior, 16
Antifederalists, 45
Anti-Saloon League, 217
Antitrust Division of Justice Department, 472
Apcar, Leonard M., 488
Appeasement, 503
Appellate courts, 306, 309
   states, 316
Appropriate technology, 462
Appropriation, 281
Appropriations committees, 279
Arab oil embargo, 508
Arbitration, 330
Arendt, Hannah, 8 n
Aristocracy, 73
Aristotle, 4, 25, 71, 72–74, 85, 361
Arms control talks, 529, 532
Armstrong, Herbert W., 382
Armstrong, Scott, 310
Arnheim, Rudolf, 62
Arnold, Mark, 420
Aron, Raymond, 94
Articles of Confederation, 41–43
Association of Community Organizations for Reform Now (ACORN), 190
Attainder, bill of, 387
Auerbach, Jerold S., 329
Australia, federalism, 48
Authoritarian form of government, 8
   nations' distribution along continuum of democracy-authoritarianism, 9
Authority, 6
Authorization, 281
Autonomy, right of, 393–94

B

Bachrach, Peter, 113
Backlash, 129
Bagdikian, Ben, 168
Bail, 392–93
Bail Reform Act, 392
Baker, Howard K., Jr., 270, 284, 287
Baker, James A., III, 121
Baker, Russell, 22
Baker v. Carr, 172, 308, 332, 403
Bakke, Allan, 316, 404
Baktiar, Shahpour, 509

Balance-of-power theory, 513
Banfield, Edward, 122
Bar, 323
Baratz, Morton S., 113
Barber, David, 14
Barber, James D., 167
Bargaining chips, 133
Barrett, Nancy S., 81
Baruch Plan, 504
Barzagan, Mehdi, 509
Bay of Pigs, 506, 507
Beard, Charles A., 47, 48
Beck, Adolf, case of, 320
Becker, Ernest, 419
Beer, Samuel, 79, 349
Begin, Menachem, 132
Behavioral science, 13–14
Bell, Daniel, 80
Bell, Terrell, 253
Bennis, Warren, 160
Berger, Peter L., 361
Berlin blockade, 505
Betts, Richard, 623
Bicameral legislature, 352
Bill, 272
   amendments, 273
   to carry out presidential recommendations, 272
   committee, 272–73
   conference committee, 276
   debate, 273
   enrolled, 276
   hearings, 272
   original, 272
   privileged, 273
   voting, 276
Bill of attainder, 387
Bill of Rights, 49, 56, 81, 381
   extension to states, 395, 396
Bingham, George Caleb, 184, 192
Biology, 15–16
Black, Hugo, 62
Black Leaders in Conflict, 75
Blackmun, Harry A., 311, 316
Blacks, 44, 163, 193
   civil rights movement, 392–402
   elected officials 1970–79, 408
   equality of results, 402–6
   Jim Crow laws, 398.
   median income, 446
   slavery to emancipation, 394–95
   unemployment, 356
Blake, William, 68
Block grants, 349
Blue-ribbon jury, 327
Blue-ribbon panel, 139
Blumenthal, Sidney, 149 n, 214
Bohr, Niels, 179
Bolling v. Sharpe, 399
The Book of States, 346
Boorstin, Daniel, 45, 170

Boren, James H., 370
Bosch, Karl, 461
Boschwitz, Rudy, 282
Boston Massacre, 35, 38
Bourgeois ideology, 96
Bradley, Bill, 290
Bradley, Tom, 189
Braeseke, Barry Floyd, 389–90
Braestrip, Peter, 166
Brand, Stewart, 160
Brazil, 479
   federalism, 48
Brennan, William J., Jr., 311, 405
The Brethren, 310–11
Brezhnev, Leonid, 226
Bribery, 276
Briefs, 313
Brinkmanship, 506
Britain, 505, 513
Brock, Bill, 70
Broder, David, 11, 206
Brown, Edmund G., Jr., 364
Brown v. Board of Education of Topeka, Kansas, 75, 197, 308, 398–99
Brunner, John, 359
Bryan, William Jennings, 202
Brzezinski, Zbigniew, 121, 250, 522
Buber, Martin, 74
Buckley, William F., 113
Budget; *see* Federal budget
Budget Message, 279
Bull Moose Party (Progressive Party), 202
Bureau of the Budget, 233
Bureau of Indian Affairs, 195
Bureau of Labor Statistics (BLS), 418
Bureau of Land Management, 341, 343
Bureaucracy, 243, 244–45
   business compared, 369–70
   chains of command, 244
   citizen action, 370–73
   congressional responsibility to oversee, 282–83
   defined, 244
   Executive Office of Presidency, 249–51
   history, 244–46
   inertia, 246–47
   laws of, 370
   pathologies, 369–79
   president as manager, 247
   regulatory commissions and government corporations, 249
   reorganization, 367
   size, 246
Burger, Warren, 311, 315, 327, 328, 329–30, 393, 400, 405, 410
Burke, Edmund, 89–90, 342–43
Burnham, W. D., 241
Burns, James McGregor, 108
Business interest groups, 186–87
Business Roundtable, 187

Byrd, Robert C., 284, 297
Byrne, Jane, 130

C

Cabinet, 228
Calendar of the Senate, 273
Calhoun, John C., 61, 340
Campaign organization, 129–30
Campaign Reform Act, 197
Canada, 513
Cannon, Mark, 311
Cant, 135
Capital investment, 537
Capitalism, 9, 84
Captured exchanges, 288
Cardozo, Benjamin, 303, 322
Carson, Johnny, 172
Carter, Jimmy, 5, 6, 23, 70, 106, 128, 129, 130, 132, 137, 139, 150, 156, 167, 171, 175, 194, 206, 208, 211, 215, 241, 250, 285, 315, 500, 509, 511, 519, 529
Case work, 268
Castberg, A. Didrick, 566
Castro, Fidel, 98, 237, 506
Castroism, 98
Catchwords, 135
Categorical grant-in-aid, 348
   targeting, 349
Caucus
   party, 208, 285, 287
   precinct, 204
   ward, 205
Celebrity candidate, 290
Census, 265
Central Intelligence Agency, 238, 249, 250, 523
CETA; *see* Comprehensive Employment and Training Act
Chaffin, Barbara and Gerald, 341, 343
Chamber of Commerce, 187
Chamberlain, Neville, 503
Charisma, 117
Chattels, 303
Chavez, Ceasar, 194
Checks and balances, 52, 53, 556–58
Cheney, Richard B., 284
Chesterton, Gilbert, 397
Chiang Kai-chek, 505
Chicano, 193
Chief executive, 227
Chief legislator, 227
Chief of staff for the president, 250
Child labor laws, 58–59
China, 100
   American foreign policy, 517–19
   Maoism, 98
   normalization of relations, 237
Christian heritage, 74–75
Chrysler Corporation, 479
Churchill, Winston, 119, 504

CIA; see Central Intelligence Agency
Cicero, 92
Cinema, 169
Circumstantial evidence, 320
Cities, 343
  black unemployment, 356
  enterprise zones, 362–63
  future, 359–64
  governmental forms, 354–55
  lack of governmental institutions, 357
  metropolitan areas, 357
  political decisions, 361–64
  politics, 358
  slums, 356
  zoning, 363
Citizenship, 71, 395, 397–98
City, 360
Civil disobedience, 74, 88
Civil law, 303, 305, 306, 322
  evidence, 320
  jury system, 325–26
  Supreme Court review, 310
Civil liberties, 8, 380–81
  freedom of press, 385–87
  freedom of religion, 381–83
  freedom of speech, 383–85
  privacy and autonomy, 393–94
  rights of accused, 387–93
Civil rights, 380–81, 394–406
  affirmative action, 403–6
  Blacks, 394–406
  equality of results, 402–6
  Fourteenth Amendment, 395–96, 400
  school desegregation, 398–402
  Thirteenth Amendment, 395
Civil Rights Act of 1964, 400, 404–5, 409, 446
Civil rights movement, 399–402
Civil Service Reform Act, 246
Civil service system, 245, 368, 369
Claims, Court of, 309
Clark, William P., 501, 522
Class action suits, 196–97
Clean Air Act of 1972, 416–17
Clifford, Clark M., 239
Closed primary, 206
Closed society, 92
Closet vote, 151–52
Cloture, 273
Coal, 422–23
Coalition building, 129
Code words, 135
Coercive power, 115–16
Cold war, 233, 234, 504
Colegrove v. Green, 331, 332
Coles, Robert, 155
Command economies, 9
Commander in chief, 231, 233
Commerce clause, 58, 59
Commission form of city government, 354–55

Committees of Congress, 266–68
  appropriations, 279
  bills, 272
  chair positions, 285
  executive oversight, 282
  executive sessions, 272
Common Cause, 189–90, 197
Common law, 301
Communications Act of 1934, 21
Communism, 504
Communist Manifesto, 469
Communities Organized for Public Service (COPS), 129
Community development councils, 426–27
Community Power Structure, 111
Community Services Administration, 249, 426
Comparative advantage, 470
Compensatory action, 162
Competition, 471
Compiled Laws, 302
Composition, fallacy of, 108
Comprehensive Employment and Training Act (CETA), 361, 363–64
Compromise, 133
Computers, 464
Comsat, 249
Conciliation court, 330
Concurrent majority, 340
Concurrent powers, 50
Concurring opinion, 313
Conference agreement, 276
Conference Board, 187, 407
Conference committee, 267–68, 276, 287
Conflict, 4–6
  courts, 300
  resolution through negotiation, 130–34
  techniques, 131–32
  scarce resources, 109
Congress, U.S., 53
  budgeting; see Federal budget
  committees, 266–68
  Constitution, 265–66, 272
  differences between the two houses, 266
  executive oversight, 282–83
  federal agencies, 288
  foreign policy, 523
  future issues, 289–94
  legislation, 271–77
  party leadership, 284
  power, 283–94
  president, 264–65
  quorum, 273–74
  reelection imperative, 269–70
  reform, 291
  size, 290–91
  staff, 265
  voting records, 269
  working habits, 268–69
Congress of Racial Equality, 193

Congressional Budget and Impoundment Control Act (1974), 265, 279–80
Congressional Budget Office, 280
Congressional Quarterly Weekly Report, 209
Congressional Record, 269, 273, 332
Congressional staff, 265, 271, 277
Congressional studies, 267
Conkling, Roscoe, 291
Connally, John, 247
Connecticut Compromise, 44
Connection power, 116
Conscription, 23
Consensus, 4, 6
Conservatism, 70, 78, 88–92
  philosophical, 90
  similarity to liberalism, 88–89
Constituents, 149, 270–71, 277
Constitution, U.S., 24–25, 539–50
  amendment process, 56–58
  assessment, 47–48
  change in perspective, 60–62
  commerce clause, 58
  customs and practices of political parties, 59
  distribution of power, 50–51
  equal protection clause, 58
  executive interpretation, 58, 59
  federalism, 48
  influences, 45–46
  judicial interpretation, 58–59
  liberal versus strict construction, 60
  political philosophy, 46
  power, 109
  ratification, 44
  representative government, 55–56
  separation of powers, 52–54
Constitutional Convention (1787), 43–48, 227
Constitutional convention for purpose of amendment, 58
Constitutional law, 301
Constitutionalism, 73
Consumer advocacy, 190
Consumer offices, 343
Consumer price index (CPI), 477–78
Consumer Product Safety Commission, 472
Containment policy, 504–5
Continental Congress, 35, 37
  first, 35, 37–39
  second, 40
Contracts, 303
Contrapuntal phrases, 135
Coolidge, Calvin, 15
Cooling-off period, 134
Cooke, Janet, 169, 170
Co-optation, 133
Cornwallis, George, 41
Correlation, 13
Cortes, Ernesto, Jr., 129

Cost-benefit analysis (CBA) of public policies, 429–34, 436–39
   education, 434
   energy, 430–31
   environment, 436–37
   health, 430, 438–39
   transportation, 434, 437–38
Cost-effectiveness analysis (CEA), 436
   health, 438–39
   transportation, 437–38
Cost-of-living adjustment clauses in union contracts, 478
Costikyan, Edward, 176
Council of Economic Advisers (CEA), 249, 251, 279
Council-manager form of city government, 354–55
Councils of government (COG), 358
Counsel, right to, 391
County, 355–56
   commission, 356
   function, 355–56
   government, 356
   supervisors, 356
County central committee, 205
County convention, 205
Court of Appeals, 306, 309
Court of Claims, 306, 309
Court of Customs and Patent Appeals, 306, 310
Court of Military Appeals, 306, 310
Court reform, 427
Courts, 303; *see also specific courts*
Crane, Philip M., 269
Cranston, Alan, 284
Craven, J. Braxton, Jr., 394
Crime rate, 447–49
   public perceptions, 449
Criminal and civil trials, 391–92
   counsel, 391
   jury trial, 391
Criminal law, 305, 306, 320, 322, 326–28
   chief function of the system, 328
   unanimous verdict in trials required, 325
Critical election, 240–42
Cronkite, Walter, 166, 172
Cross-cutting cleavages, 185
Cuba, 100, 506
Cuban missile crisis, 506
Cuban refugees, 193
Cultural equality, 80
Culture of poverty, 419
Currency demand, 489
Curtis, Charlotte, 160
Czechoslovakia, 504

D

Dahl, Robert A., 78–79, 96, 106, 107, 111
Daley, Richard, 129, 130, 369
Dallas, 112
Daniel Shay's Rebellion, 42–43

Dartmouth College v. *Woodward*, 308
De facto segregation, 401
De jure segregation, 401
Debs, Eugene V., 383
Declaration of Independence, 37, 38–40, 45, 70–71, 73–74, 76–77
Defamation, 385
Defendant, 305, 320, 322
Defense policies; *see* National security
Delegated power, 50
Delegates, 203
Democracy, 6, 7–8, 22–23, 78–79, 92
   direct, 7–8
   leading to egalitarianism, 73
   nations' distribution along continuum from democracy to authoritarianism, 9
   representative, 8
   socialist economic systems, 10
Democratic party, 199–201, 241
   state legislatures control, 353
Democratic Policy Committee, 287
Democratic-Republican party, 200
Demographics, 164–65
   trends, 537
Deng Xiaoping, 518
Dennis v. *United States*, 384 n
Department of Agriculture, 245, 523
Department of Commerce, 245, 523
Department of Defense (DOD), 247, 522
Department of Education, 189, 245
Dependence power, 116
Deposition, 323
Dershowitz, Alan, 237
Detente, 508
Dewey, Thomas, 138
Direct democracy, 7–8, 55
Discharge petition or resolution, 272 n
Discomfort index, 478
Discovery, 323
Disraeli, Benjamin, 13, 126
Dissenting opinion, 313
Distribution of goods and services, 471
Distributive policies, 110–11, 256
District attorney, 323
   U.S., 323
District courts, 309
Divorce cases, 330
Dobrynin, Anatol, 108
Dole, Robert, 209
Domenici, Peter, 278
Domestic Council, 249, 250, 257
Domestic relations, law of, 303
Dommel, Paul, 362
Double jeopardy, 390–91
Dove, 512, 523
Downs, Anthony, 176
Dred Scott v. *Sandford*, 308–9, 394–95
Due process, 390, 395
Dulles, John Foster, 506

Dworkin, Ronald, 86–87, 92
Dynamic conservatism, 234

E

E Pluribus Unum: The Formation of the American Revolution, 47
East-West regional conflict, 341
Easterlin, Richard, 164
An Economic Interpretation of the Constitution of the United States, 47
Economic liberty, 83
Economic Opportunity Act of 1964, 444
Economic systems, 9–11
   capitalism, 9
   mixed, 10
   relation to politics, 10–11
   socialism, 10
   welfare state, 10
Economics, 11
   link with politics, 457–58
   market; *see* Market economy
   nature of wealth, 460–61
   scarcity, 467
   U.S. economy; *see* U.S. economy
Edelman, Murray, 134
Edey, Maitland, 16 n
Education, 346, 407–8
   cost-benefit analysis, 434
   local government expense, 354
Egalitarianism, 73
Eighth Amendment, 392–93, 546
Einstein, Albert, 98, 179, 397–98
Eisenhower, Dwight D., 15, 111, 122, 140, 175, 243, 332, 399, 506
   presidency, 234
Elastic clause of Constitution, 50, 266
Electoral college, 209
   abolishing, 215
Electoral system, 205, 209–10
Elite theory of power, 109–14, 111–14
Emancipation Proclamation, 230
Eminent domain, 391
   compensation, 39
Empirical method, 73
Employment Act of 1946, 475
Endangered Species Act, 190
Energy policies
   conservation, 432
   cost-benefit analysis, 430–32
   demand, 421–22
   goals, 425–26
   implementation problems, 441–42
   risks, 435–36
Enfranchisement, 196
Engels, Friedrich, 469
Enlightenment, 68
Enterprise zones, 362–63
Entitlement programs, 80, 474–75
Entitlement theory of justice, 88

Environment
  cost-benefit analysis, 436–37
  effects of technology, 537
Environmental Defense Fund, 196
Environmental Protection Agency, 190, 196, 249, 288, 436, 472
Environmental values, 5
Epstein, Leon D., 342
Equal Employment Office, 288
Equal Employment Opportunity Commission (EEOC), 409
Equal opportunity, 79, 81
Equal Pay Act of 1963, 409
Equal protection clause, 395, 398
  sex discrimination, 409
Equal Rights Amendment (ERA), 22, 196, 217, 408–9
Equality, 78, 79–81
  excess of, 85
  politics of, 402–6
Equality in freedom, 380–81, 394
  historical perspective, 406–10
  status of liberty, 410–11
Equality of opportunity, 162, 402
Equality of outcome, 80, 81, 402–6
Equilibrium price, 468
Equity, 301
Ervin, Sam, 282
An Essay Concerning Human Understanding, 76
Establishment clause, 381
Ethnic groups
  income disparities, 447
  median age, 447
Ethnic politics, 217–18
Ethnology, 16
Eurocommunism, 515
Europe, 515
European Economic Community, 515
Evidence
  circumstantial, 320
  direct, 320–21
Ewald, William Bragg, Jr., 122
Ex post facto laws, 388
Exchange rates, 488–89
  pegged, 489
Exclusionary rule, 389
Executive interpretation, 58, 59
Executive Office of the Presidency (EOP), 249, 254
Executive order, 227
Executive oversight, 282
Executive privilege, 54, 228
Existential presidency, 227–44
Existentialism, 227
Expert power, 116
Exploitation, 94
Expressed powers, 50
Externalities, 470 n

F
Factions, 184, 551–56
Fainsod, Merle, 8 n
Fair Labor Standards Act (1938), 59, 308
Fairlie, Henry, 234, 435, 537
Fairness doctrine, 386
Fallows, James, 239
Family, 154–55, 361
Family Assistance Plan, 426
Farney, Dennis, 286, 291
Fascism, 93
Faubus, Orville, 399
Federal agencies, 372–73
Federal budget, 279–81
  appropriation, 281
  authorization, 281
  Congress, 279–81
  deficit, 474
  entitlements, 474–75
  nondefense, 474
  Office of Management and Budget, 279
  recommended expenditures, 279
  surplus, 475
  uncontrollable costs, 281, 474
Federal Communications Act, 472
Federal Communications Commission, 386, 472
Federal courts, 306, 388
  jurisdiction, 307
  lack of enforcement power, 332
Federal Election Campaign Act, 197
Federal government
  aid to local governments, 351–52, 358
  councils of government, 358
  employment, 345
  spending, 344
Federal Highway Administration, 442
Federal Information Center (FIC), 560
Federal judiciary, 54
Federal Land Policy and Management Act, 341
Federal Register, 245, 372
Federal Reserve System, 232, 477
Federal Statutory Forms, 566–67
Federal Trade Commission, 472
Federal Voting Rights Act, 125–26
Federalism, 41–42, 48, 50–52, 340–52
  Constitution, 340
  criticism of, 342
  defense, 342–44
  fiscal, 349, 351
  intergovernmental relations, 346–52
  model, 348
  objective, 344
The Federalist Papers, 45, 68, 75, 78, 130, 551–58
Federalist Party, 45, 200
Federation of State, County and Municipal Workers, 189
Fehrenbacher, Don E., 395

Feige, Edgar L., 483
Feldstein, Martin, 427
Felony, 305
Fifteenth Amendment, 172, 547
Filibuster, 273
Filing for candidacy, 206
Fiorina, Morris, 270, 351
First Amendment, 381, 383, 386, 545
Fiscal federalism, 349, 350
Fiscal policies, 476–77, 481
Fiscal year, 280
Food and Drug Administration, 472
Force, 6
  distinguished from power, 108
Ford, Gerald, 138, 171, 209, 215, 227, 236, 282, 394
  presidency, 238
Foreign policy
  Africa, 519
  Asia, 517–19
  colonialism, 502
  containment, 504–5
  decisions made by small group, 112
  Europe, 515
  history, 502–10
  intervention and nonintervention, 511–13
  Jefferson, 229
  Kennedy, 234
  Latin America, 513–15
  Middle East, 515
  morality and pragmatism, 510–11
  national interest, 512
  national security; *see* National security
  policymaking, 522–23
  Roosevelt, Theodore, 232
  Truman, 233
  Washington's presidency, 228–29
Formal authority, 120
Fort Sumter, 125
Fourteenth Amendment, 390, 395, 396, 397, 398, 400, 547
Fourth Amendment, 388–89, 545
  enforcement by exclusionary rule, 389
Fox, Robin, 16
France, federalism, 48
Frankfurter, Felix, 387, 390
Franklin, Benjamin, 39, 68, 106
Fraud, 303
Free exercise clause, 382
Free market, 84–85
Free rider effect, 470
Freedom, 380
Freedom of individual belief, 383
Freedom of Information Act, 83, 371, 563–64
Freedom of the press, 385–87
  confidentiality of sources, 386
  recent trends, 385–86
Freedom of religion, 381–83
  establishment clause, 381

Freedom of speech, 73, 383–85
 defamation or slander, 385
 obscenity, 384
 organized institutions, 384
Fremont-Smith, Eliot, 231
Friend of the court, 313
Frost, David, 237
Fullilove v. Fultznick, 405
Furtive fallacy, 47

G

Game plans, 119
Gandhi, Mahatma, 121
Gans, Herbert J., 170
Garcia, Robert, 363
Gardner, John W., 189
Garfield, James, 245
Garn, Jake, 284
Garth, David, 159
Gatekeepers, 166
General Accounting Office, 282–83
General election, 206
General revenue sharing (GRS), 349
 targeting, 349
General Schedule (GS) rating, 368
General Services Administration, 249
George, Alexander, 14 n
Gergen, David, 161
German Federal Republic, 50
Germany, federalism, 48
Gerry, Elbridge, 296
Gerrymander, 296
Getting Across, 360
Gideon v. Wainwright, 308, 389, 391
Gilbert, Felix, 46
Gilder, George, 460
Ginsberg, Allen, 177
Gitlow v. New York, 393, 396
Gladstone, William, 48
The Glass Bead Game, 127
The Global 2000 Report to the President, 490
GM citizen action organizations, 190–91
Goel, M. L., 177
Goldwater, Barry, 175
Good neighbor policy, 503
Gould, Stephen Jay, 18
Government
 defined, 7
 economics, 9
 forms of, 7–9
 principles of government policies, 23–24
 public policy, 9
 study of politics, 20–22
Government corporations, 249
Government documents, information on, 563–64
Government institutions, 26
Government of laws, 96
Government of men, 96

Government-owned corporations, 249
Government programs, 24
 aid to local governments, 351–52, 358
Governors, 352
Graglia, Lino A., 332
Grand jury, 325, 390
Grass-roots pressure, 197
Great Compromise, 44
Great Depression, 232–33, 484
Great Society, 236, 243
Greeley, Horace, 119
Green, Mark, 437
Green v. County Board of New Kent County, 400
Greenfield, Jeff, 126
Greenstein, Fred I., 227, 234
Grey, Thomas, 314
Griswold v. Connecticut, 308, 393, 410
Gross national product (GNP), 458–59
Guaranteed annual income, 426
Guardian Angels, 364
Guitean, Charles, 245
GULAG, 99
Gulag Archipelago, 99
Gulf of Tonkin Resolution, 507
Gunboat diplomacy, 502
Guns and butter debate, 429

H

Habeas corpus, 387
Haber, Fritz, 461
Haig, Alexander, 108, 253, 522
Haldeman, Robert, 119
HALT (Help Abolish Legal Tyranny), 329
Hamilton, Alexander, 45, 47, 68, 106, 130, 200, 229, 307, 308, 484, 551
Hammer v. Dagenhart, 59
Hand, Learned, 323
Hand gestures, 137–38
Handicapped, legal equality for, 409–10
Happiness, 73–74
Harding, Warren G., 14
Harper v. Virginia Board of Elections, 62
Harvard Encyclopedia of American Ethnic Groups, 398
Harvard Law Review, 405
Hassan II, King, 525
Hatch, Carl, 245
Hatch, Orrin, 215
Hatch Act, 245
Hatchetman, 122
Hawk, 512, 523
Hayakawa, S. I., 126
Hayden, Tom, 99, 241
Health care policies
 cost-benefit analysis, 430, 438–39
 cost-effectiveness analysis, 438–39
 goals, 425
 problem assessment, 419, 421
 strategies, 427
 technology, limits on, 430

Health and Human Services, Department of, 247
Health maintenance organizations (HMOs), 427
Hearing, 272
Heclo, Hugh, 289, 368
Helms, Jesse, 209
Helms, Richard, 525
Hemingway, Ernest, 127
Hemodialysis, 430
Henry, Patrick, 43
Herbert v. Case, 385
Heslop, Alan, 296
Hesse, Hermann, 127
Heyssel, Robert M., 430
Higher Education Act, 409
Hill-Burton Act, 421
Hispanics, 164–65, 193–94
Historical materialism, 93
History, 11–13
Hitler, Adolf, 503
Hobbes, Thomas, 6, 72, 75, 92
Holmes, Oliver Wendell, 314, 316, 383, 500
Home rule, 347
Homosexuality, 410
Honeymoon period, 128
Hoover, Herbert, 232
Hospital care, 421
Hostage crisis in Iran, 509
Hough, Jerry F., 8 n
House of Representatives, 206, 209, 265–66
 leadership, 273, 285, 286
 revenue raising, 272
 Rules Committee, 273
 Steering and Policy Committee, 285
Housing and Urban Development, Department of, 236
Hughes, Charles Evans, 62, 303
Humphrey, Hubert, 129, 203, 207
Hungary, 504
Hunt, Albert R., 278
Hunter, Floyd, 111
Huntington, Samuel P., 167

I

"I see" construction, 136
ICBMs, 530–31
Ideas, 68–100, 243
 Aristotle, 71–74
 Judaic and Christian tradition, 74–75
 Locke, 75–78
 role in politics, 68–70
 shaping Declaration of Independence and Constitution, 70–78
 shaping global policies, 92–100
Ideologies, 92–93
Illegal aliens, 254
Image, 138

Immigration and Naturalization Service, 397
Impeachment, 53
 Congress, 266
 Constitution, 237–38
 Johnson, Andrew, 238
 Nixon, 237
Imperial judiciary, 331
Imperial presidency, 238, 331
Imperialism, 96, 97
Implementation of policy, 257–58
Implied powers, 50, 60, 266
Impoundment, 279
Income distribution, 444–45
Income security policies
 evaluation, 444–47
 political feasibility, 439–40
 problem assessment, 418–19
 strategies, 426–27
Incomes policy, 485
Incrementalism, 436
Independent agencies, 249
Independents, 174
India, federalism, 48
Indians, American, 194–95, 406
 activism, 195
 assimilation, 195
 autonomy, 195
 termination, 195
Indictment, 390
Indirect costs, 470 n
Inflation, 21, 477–78
 causes, 477
 government deficits, 537
 measuring, 477–78
 political economy of, 458
 solutions, 457
 supply-side economics, 481–84
Information, 464
 agency response requirements, 565
 federal government, 360
 locating records, 564
 making request, 564–65
 sources of, 559–65
Inherent powers, 50, 227
Initiative, 55, 171
Inner cities, 356–57
Inputs for the political system, 25–26
Institutions, 26
Intelligence operations, U.S. and Soviet compared, 525
Interdependence of nations
 American foreign policy; see Foreign policy
 defense; see National security
 political connection, 502–19
 strategic connection, 519–32
 trade connection; see International trade

Interest groups, 111, 184–99
 business, 186–87
 criticisms, 184–85
 enhanced performance, 213
 labor, 187–89
 lobbying, 276
 minorities, 192–96
 political parties influenced, 216–17
 professional associations, 189
 public interest groups, 189–90
 state governments, 353
Intergovernmental lobby, 349, 351
Intergovernmental relations, concept of, 346–52
 state-local relationships, 347
Interlocking elements, 115
International Commerce Commission (ICC), 245
International law, 305
International Society for Krishna Consciousness, 382
International trade
 deficit, 488
 exchange rates, 488–89
 imports and exports, 488
 surplus, 488
 U.S. dependence on foreign resources, 487
Interstate commerce, 58
Interstate Commerce Act of 1887, 58
Interstate Commerce Commission, 249, 472
Iran, hostages, 509
Iron Curtain, 504, 505
Iron Law of Oligarchy, 107
Iron triangle model, 287–88
Isolationism, 503
Issue networks, 289
Item veto, 352

J

Jackson, Andrew, 229, 241, 244, 300, 332
Jackson, Henry M., 238
Jackson, Jesse, 193, 194
Jacksonian democracy, 229
Jail and prison reform, 429
Janowitz, Morris, 110
Japan
 industrial policy, 479
 war with United States, 503–4
Japanese-American internment in World War II, 406
Jarvis, Howard, 346
Jawboning, 486
Jay, John, 45, 551
Jefferson, Thomas, 14, 39–40, 43, 47, 61, 68, 71, 72, 74, 76, 106, 124, 200, 241, 300
 presidency, 229
Jeopardy, 391
Jim Crow laws, 398

Job Corps, 444
Johanson, Donald, 16 n
Johnson, Andrew, 238, 315
Johnson, Lyndon, 14, 79, 107, 108, 118, 120, 129, 170, 175, 207, 211, 237, 243, 245, 254, 264, 400, 402, 474, 507
 presidency, 235–36
Joint chiefs of staff, 250
Joint committees of the Congress, 267–68
Jordan, Barbara, 44
Joyce, James, 383
Judaic heritage, 74–75
Judges, 324–25
 selection of, 324
Judicial activism, 313, 332
Judicial circuits, 309
Judicial reports, 566–67
Judicial review, 54, 58, 125, 331
Judiciary, 300
 biases of judges, 302–3
 classification of laws, 303–5
 European type, 330
 federal system, 307, 309–10
 political power, 331–32
 selection of judges, 324–25
 sources of power, 301–2
 state system, 314, 316–18
 structure and operations, 305–18
 Supreme Court: see Supreme Court
Jujitsu, 122
Jury, 321–27
 blue-ribbon, 327
 trial, 325, 391
Just law, 74
Justice, 78, 85–88
Justice, administration of
 community action, 428
 court reform, 427
 habitual criminals, 427–28
 jail and prison reform, 429
 juvenile justice, 428
 public policy evaluation, 447–49
 sentencing, 428
 white-collar crime, 428
Justice of the peace, 316–17, 330
Juvenile justice, 395, 428

K

Kant, Immanuel, 72
Karlen, Delmar, 320
Katzenbach, Nicholas B., 325
Kaufman, Irving R., 325
Keeton, William T., 17
Kefauver, Estes, 118–19
Kemp, Jack, 363
Keniston, Kenneth, 154
Kennedy, Edward, 5, 6, 47, 113, 137, 138, 155, 167, 418

Kennedy, John F., 14, 18, 107, 118–19, 126, 128, 130, 134, 137, 138, 149, 155, 175, 207, 210, 240, 241, 254, 500, 506, 507
  Nixon debate, 119–20
  presidency, 234–35
Kennedy, Joseph, Jr., 155
Kennedy, Joseph P., Sr., 155
Kennedy, Robert, 107, 155, 237
Key, V. O., 175, 202, 241
Keynes, John Maynard, 68, 481, 484
Khomeini, Ayatollah, 12, 509
Khrushchev, Nikita, 97
Kilpatrick, James, 291
King, Martin Luther, Jr., 6, 69, 74, 75, 79, 117, 125–26, 193, 237, 400, 401
Kingship, 73
Kirkland, Lane, 187
Kissinger, Henry, 128, 129, 133, 226, 247, 508, 522
Knowledge as political resource, 120
Knowles, John H., 421
Koch, Edward, 120, 189, 269, 350
Korean War, 233, 234, 506
Kosciusko, Thaddeus, 40
Kosygin, Alexsei N., 108
Kotter, John P., 117, 118
Kraft, Joseph, 350
Ku Klux Klan, 383

L

La Raza Unida Party, 194
Labor
  interest groups, 187
  training, 363
  unions, 187–89
  viewed as capital, 363
Lacqueur, Walter, 169
Ladd, Everett C., Jr., 161–62
Lafayette, Marquis de, 40
Landon, Alfred, 128
Language, 134–40
  nonverbal communication, 137–40
  political speeches, 134–37
Larceny, 305
Lasswell, Harold, 5, 14, 15, 106
Latin America, 514–15
Latin Americans, in United States, 93
Lave, Charles, 432
Law, 300
  classification, 303–5
  common, 301
  constitutional, 301
  delegalization of America, 328–30
  judicial interpretation, 303
  relevant rules, 322
  sources, 322
  structure of American law, 302
Law Enforcement Assistance Administration, 447

Lawyers, 323–24, 328–29
  advertising, 324
Leadership, 108
League of United Latin American Citizens, 194
Leak, 121–22
Leary v. United States, 331
Lefever, Ernest, 116
Legal clinic, 324
Legislation, 271–83
  budget, 279–81
  committee hearings, 272–73
  conference agreement, 276
  debate, 273
  difference in procedures between House and Senate, 272
  origin, 271
  statutory law, 302
  voting, 276
Legislative Counsel, 286
Legislative oversight, 282
Legislative veto, 238, 265
Legitimacy, 6
Legitimate power, 116, 118
Lenin, Vladimir Ilich Ulyanov, 97
Leninism, 97
Leonard, John, 307
Less developed countries (LDCs), 490–91
"Letter from Birmingham Jail," 74
Lewis, Andrew, 40
Lewis, Anthony, 160
Lewis, Arthur, 481
Lewis, Robert, 81
Libel, 385
Liberalism, 78, 84, 88, 93
  similarity to conservatism, 88–89
Libertarian, 88
Liberty, 78, 81–88
  economic, 83–85
  excess of, 85
  political, 81–83
Liddell Hart, B. H., 134
Limited war, 506
Lincoln, Abraham, 72, 79, 119, 127, 134, 222, 241, 243, 380, 381
  presidency, 230–31
Lindbergh, Charles, 536
Lindblom, Charles, 11
Line-item veto, 279
Linkage, 530–31
Lion and the fox theory of political power, 106
Lippman, Walter, 176, 235, 512
Lipset, Seymour Martin, 162
Literary Digest, 150
Litigation, 196–97
Little Rock Central High School, desegregation, 399
Lobbying, 177–78, 197, 276–78

Local government, 353–64
  city government forms, 354–55
  county government, 355–56
  expenses, 354
  special districts, 356
  townships, 356
  urban problems, 356–57
Lochner v. New York, 309
Locke, John, 75–78, 92, 300, 382, 383, 445 n
Lodge, Henry Cabot, 316
Logrolling, 116
Loose construction of Constitution, 60, 62
Lopez Portillo, Jose, 132
Lott, Trent, 284
Louisiana Purchase, 61, 229
Lovell, Katherine, 351
Lower courts, 309
Lowi, Theodore, 110
Lubell, Sam, 167
Lurie, Alison, 208
Lynd, Helen, 111
Lynd, Robert, 111

M

McCarthy, Eugene, 203, 291
McCarthy, Joseph, 84, 167, 281
McCarthyism, 281
McCorkle, Clifford, 443
McCulloch v. Maryland, 60–61, 308
McDonald, Farrect, 47
McGovern, George, 511
McKinley, William, 5, 6, 241
McManus, William J., 217
McNamara, Robert, 523
McRae, Duncan, 241
Machiavelli, Niccolo, 106, 118, 127, 140
Machine politics, 130, 358
Madison, James, 45, 47, 106, 124, 184, 231, 551–58
Magistrate's court, 330
Mailer, Norman, 101–2
Majority leader, 273, 284, 286
Majority opinion, 313
Majority rule, 8, 79
Make Room! Make Room! 360
Making of the President, 1960, 107
Malapportionment, 297
Malinowski, Bronislaw, 361
Malthus, T. R., 11
Mandatory death sentence, 392
Mandel, Ruth, 141
Manipulation, 7
Mao Zedong (Tse-tung), 98, 505
Maoism, 96, 98
Mapp v. Ohio, 308, 389
Marbury, William, 124, 308
Marbury v. Madison, 54, 124, 308
Marcus Aurelius, 90
Marginal voters, 176

Marijuana, state penalties for possession, 317
Marijuana Tax Act, 331
Market clearing price, 468
Market economy, 9, 10, 84, 89, 467
  distribution of goods, 471
  failures, 470–71
  information lack, 471
  public goods not produced, 470
  spillovers, 470
  uncompetitive, 471
  virtues, 468–70
    check on government, 470–71
    efficiency, 469
    information, 468–69
    specialization, 469–70
Markup sessions, 272
Marshall, George C., 505
Marshall, John, 60–61, 124, 303
Marshall, Thurgood, 310, 311, 313
Marshall Court, 58
Marshall Plan, 233, 505
Martindale-Hubbell Law Directory, 323
Marx, Karl, 89, 92, 93–100, 469
  compared to Newton, 93, 96
Marxism, 93–100
  alienation, 94–95
  fragmentation of, 96–99
  historical materialism, 93–94
  labor theory of value, 94
  after Marx, 97–98
Mass media; see Media
Massive retaliation policy, 506
Mayor-council form of city government, 354
Mayors, 348, 349, 354
Mean income, 14
Media, 152, 159, 166–71
  accuracy, 168–69
  adversary relationship, 166–67
  competition, 168
  criticism, 168–71
  political campaign, 168
  political information regulator, 166
Median, 14
Mediating structures, 361–62
Mediation, 330
Medicaid, 444
Meese, Edwin, 121
Melting pot, 218
Meredith, James, 399–400
Merit system, 245
Metaphor, 136
Metropolitan area, 357
Mexican-American Political Association, 194
Mexican-Americans, 193
Michel, Robert H., 274, 284
Michels, Robert, 107
Middle East, 515
Middletown in Transition, 111

Milbrath, Lester W., 177
Military-industrial complex, 111
Mill, John Stuart, 84, 92
Miller v. *California,* 384 n
Millett, Kate, 4
Milliken v. *Bradley,* 400
Mills, C. Wright, 110–12
Minimum wage, 363
Minogue, Kenneth, 94, 96
Minorities, 163, 409
  Blacks; see Blacks
  Hispanics, 164–65, 193–94
  Indians; see Indians, American
  legislative office, 289
  national party conventions, 205
  women; see Women
Minority leader, 284
Minority rights, 8, 86
Minority rule, 79
Miranda v. *Arizona,* 308, 389
Misdemeanor, 305
Mixed economy, 10
Molitor, Graham T. T., 343
Monarchy, 75
Mondale, Walter, 251–52
Monetary policy, 111–12, 477, 481
Money as political resource, 120
Money supply, 477
Monopoly, 467
Monroe, James, 47, 200, 502
Monroe Doctrine, 502, 503
Montesquieu, Charles, 46, 92
Monteux, Pierre, 117
Montgomery, Bernard, 41
Moore, Sara Jane, 394
Moral law, 74
Moral Majority, 192
Morgan, Edmund S., 106, 139
Morgan, J. Pierpont, 133
Morgenthau, Hans J., 380, 512
Morison, Samuel Eliot, 34
Morris, Desmond, 137
Morris, Gouverneur, 44, 46, 134
Morse, Samuel, 463
Mossberg, Walter S., 254
Motton, Erma "Tiny," 406
Moynihan, Daniel P., 6, 331, 350, 528
Mugabe, Robert, 100–101
Multinational corporations, 489–90
Multiparty systems, 203
Munich agreement, 503
Murrow, Edward R., 167, 172
Myers, Michael (Ozzie), 276–77
Myrdal, Gunnar, 157
The Myth of the Independent Voter, 176

N

Nader, Ralph, 122, 129, 160, 190–91
Nathan, Richard, 362
National Aeronautics and Space Administration (NASA), 249

National Association for the Advancement of Colored People (NAACP), 193
National Association of Black Manufacturers, 81
National Association of Counties, 192
National Association of Manufacturers, 187
National chairman of political party, 205
National Command Authority, 254
National Conference of State Legislatures, 192
National Congress of Neighborhood Women, 196
National convention, 203, 205
  minority representation, 205
National Education Association (NEA), 189
National Environmental Act of 1969, 9
National Governors' Conference, 192
National Highway Traffic Safety Administration, 431, 442
National interest, 512
National Labor Relations Act (Wagner Act), 472
National Labor Relations Board, 472
National League of Cities, 192
National Organization for Women (NOW), 196, 217
National Recovery Administration, 309
National Right to Life Association, 217
National security
  comparison of U.S. and Soviet military power, 523–24
  Geneva talks, 531–32
  policymakers, 522–23
  SALT debate, 529–31
  technical issues, 519
  war prevention, 528–32
National Security Act of 1947, 254
National security chain of command, 252
National Security Council, 249, 522
National Women's Political Caucus, 196
Nationalism, 93, 398
Nationalist China, 505
Native Americans; see Indians, American
NATO; see North Atlantic Treaty Organization
Natural law, 68, 72
Natural rights theory, 86
Naturalization, 397
Necessary and proper clause of Constitution, 50
Negative income tax, 426
Nehru, Jawaharlal, 121
Neighborhood movement, 358
Nelson, Garrison, 111
Neo-Keynesian economists, 481, 484–86
Neo-Marxism, 96
Nesbet, Robert, 163
Neuhaus, Richard John, 361
New class, 113

New Deal, 232–33
"New Federalism," 349
"New Frontier" program, 234
New Jersey Plan, 43–44
New Journalism, 169, 170
New Left, 96–99
New Testament, 74
New York Times, 158, 168, 170, 385
News management, 170–71
Newton, Isaac, 68, 95, 96
Nie, Norman H., 177
Nigeria, federalism, 48, 50
1980 election, 240–42
Nineteenth Amendment, 172, 196, 408, 548
Ninth Amendment, 393–94, 546
Nixon, Richard, 14, 15, 113, 119, 166, 175, 203, 227, 250, 279, 282, 315, 316, 426, 485, 500, 505, 507, 508, 511
    Kennedy debate, 119–20
    presidency, 236–38
Nixon Doctrine, 508, 509
Nonresolutions, 133–34
Nonviolence, 121, 126
North Atlantic Treaty Organization (NATO), 505
    military resources, 524
Northwest Ordinance, 42
Nozick, Robert, 82, 88, 445 n
Nuclear power, 423
Nullification, doctrine of, 61

O

Oakeshott, Michael, 13
Obligation power, 116, 118
Obscenity, 384
Occupational Safety and Health Act (OSHA), 190, 288, 472
O'Connor, Sandra D., 311
Office of Economic Opportunity, 245
Office of Management and Budget (OMB), 233, 249, 250–51, 257, 279, 361
Office of Personnel Management (OPM), 246, 368
Office of Price Administration, 485–86
Office of Technology Assessment, 528
Office of Telecommunications Policy, 464
Okun, Arthur, 478
Oligarchy, 73
Oligopoly, 467, 485
O'Neill, Thomas P., Jr., 116, 284, 286
Open primary, 206
Open societies, 92
Opinion leaders, 158
Opportunity cost, 429
Organization of American States (OAS), 503
Organization of Petroleum Exporting Countries (OPEC), 488, 508
Outputs of the political system, 26

Overseas Development Council, 460
Oxymoron, 136

P

Paglin, Morton, 445
Paine, Thomas, 5, 6, 106, 385
Palestinian issue, 515
Palestinian Liberation Organization (PLO), 515
Palko test, 396
Pardon, 227
    Nixon, 227
    presidential power, 227
Paris, Peter J., 75
Parks, Rosa, 193
Parliament, 292–93
Parliamentary system, 292
Participatory democracy, 79
Partisanship, 174
Party convention, 208
Party identification, 174, 175
Party leadership, 229, 284
Pascal, Blaise, 141
Passive-negative type, 15
Passive resistance, 69
Patronage, 229, 368, 369
Patton, George, 117
Payne, James L., 269
Peace Corps, 249
Pearl Harbor, 503
Pendleton Act (1883), 245, 368
Pentagon, 522
Pentagon Papers, 316, 385, 507
People's Republic of China, 505
Percy, Charles, 115
Pericles, 144
Persuasion, 116
Peters, Charles, 23
Petit jury, 325
Petition, right of, 272
Philosophy, 3
Physical quality of life index (PQLI), 460
Pike, Otis G., 270–71, 292
Pious, Richard M., 116, 120
Plaintiff, 305, 320, 322
Plans, 9
Platforms, 199
Plato, 4, 25, 71, 72, 89, 92
Plessy v. Ferguson, 308, 398
Ploy, 121
Pluralism theory of power, 109–14
    critique of, 111–14
Pluralistic elite, 110
Plurality vote, 206
Plutarch, 511
Pocket veto, 276
Podhoretz, Norman, 241
Pointer phrases, 136
Poland, 504
Policy, 255
Policy agenda, 113, 149, 256–57

Policy entrepreneurs, 256–57
Politburo, 226
Political action
    lobbying, 177–78
    polling; see Polls
    voting, 171–77
    writing public officials, 178–80
Political action committees (PACs), 190, 197–98
Political activism, 167–68
    Indians, 195
Political behavior, model for analysis, 152–53
Political campaigns, interest groups, 197–99
Political consultant, 214
Political Control of the Economy, 458
Political culture, 153, 157–65
    determines public opinion, 157
    population, 164
        age structure, 164
        ethnic distribution, 164–65
    in transition, 161–65
Political jujitsu, 122–24
Political liberties, 83
Political parties, 184
    control of state legislatures, 353
    decline in importance, 213
    electorate, 213
    evolution of, 201
    functions, 199–200
    government, 213
    interest groups, 216–18
    organization, 213
    platforms, 199–200
    structure, 203–5
    telecommunication, effect on, 216
    third, 202–3
    trends to strengthen, 216–18
    trends that could weaken, 214–16
    two-party system, 200–203
Political party identification, 155
Political question doctrine, 331
Political resources, 120
Political science, 11, 68
    definition, 107
Political socialization
    family, 154
    lifetime process, 156–57
    school, 155–56
    significant events, 156
Political speech writing, 135–37
Political strategy and tactics, 119–30
    building institutions, 129–30
    goals, 119–20
    language and symbols, 134–40
    marshalling resources, 120–22
    political jujitsu, 122–28
    resolving conflict through negotiations, 130–34
    timing considerations, 128–29

Political theory, 69
Politics
  conflict, 4–6
  consensus, 4, 6
  critical-thinking development, 16–17
  definition, 4
  power, 6–7, 17–20
  relation to economics, 10–11
  role of ideas, 68–70
  understanding government, 20–22
Polls
  advice to candidates, 149
  ideology of Americans, 159–61
  interpreting, 149–52
  sample size, 149–50
  types of questions, 150, 152
  volatility, 150–51
Pope John Paul II, 500
Popper, Karl, 92
Populism, 202
Populist Party, 202
Pork barrel, 281, 353
Pornography, 86
Portland, Oregon, 362
Positive rights, 80
Post hoc ergo propter hoc fallacy, 13
Poverty
  causes, 419
  defined, 418
  less developed countries, 490–91
  programs to reduce
    Aid to Families with Dependent Children, 426
    direct income, 426
  trends in population below poverty level, 420
Powell, Lewis F., 311
Power, 6–7
  defined, 106
  importance of, 109
  necessity for, 140–41
  political strategies and tactics to acquire, 119–30
  resolving conflict through negotiation, 130–34
  role in American politics, 106–9
  sources of, 115–19
  study of politics, 17–20
Power, 121
Power base, 130
The Power Elite, 110
Precedent, 322
Precinct, 204
  caucus, 204
Preferential treatment, 162
Presidency, 52
  commander in chief, 231
  election; *see* Presidential election
  existential, 227–44
  as manager, 247–55
  modern, 227, 232–40

Presidency—*Cont.*
  party leader, 229
  pay, 226
  persuasion, 243
  policymaking; *see* Presidential policymaking
  powers
    to affect legislatures, 227, 257
    constitutional, 226–27
    formal sources, 226–27
    inherent, 227
    war, 231
  public approval of, 235
  structure of, 244–55
  traditional, 227, 228–31
President pro tempore, 273, 285–86
  state senate, 352–53
Presidential election, 205–18
  campaign, 209
  candidate selection changes, 214
  electoral system, 205–6
  national convention, 208–9
  1980 election analysis, 210–12
  primary, 206–8
Presidential management, 247–55
Presidential policymaking, 244
  agenda, 256–57
  classification of, 255–56
  evaluation, 258
  formulating proposals, 257
  implementing, 257
  legitimating, 257
  modification, 258
  stages in, 256–58
Presidential succession, 252–54
Presidential Succession Act of 1947, 252, 285
Press, freedom of; *see* Freedom of the press
Press secretary, 250
Pressure groups, 184, 277
Price, 468
Price Control Act of 1942, 485
Primary, 206–8
The Prince, 118, 140
Prior restraint, 383, 385
Prison reform, 429
Privacy, rights of, 393–94, 410
Private goods, 470
Private law, 303
Private property, 162
Probable cause, 388–89
Probate laws, 329
Procedural rights, 387
Productivity, 478–79, 481
Professional Air Traffic Controllers Organization (PATCO), 189
Professional associations, 189–90
Programs, 9
Progress, belief in, 162
Progressive, 385
Progressive Party (Bull Moose Party), 202

Progressive tax, 345
Progressivism, 202
Prohibition Party, 203
Proletariat, 93
Property, 75
Property law, 303
Proportional representation, 203
Proportional tax, 345
Proposition 13, 345, 346
Prouse, William, 388
Proxies, 512 n
Pseudo-events, 170
Psychoanalytical theory, 13–14
Public goods, 470
Public interest groups, 189–90
Public-land policy, 42
Public law, 303
Public opinion
  analysis of individual political behavior, 152–53
  influence on political leaders, 148–49
  political culture as determinant, 157
  polls; *see* Polls
Public policy, 9, 23–24
  classification by type, 256
  functional classification, 255
  shaping, 246
Public policy analysis
  cost-benefit analysis, 429–34, 436–39
  direct and indirect, 429
  evaluation, 443–50
  goals, 424–26
  implementation problems, 441–42
  incrementalism, 436
  political feasibility, 439–40
  problems addressed, 418–24
  rational policymaking, 436
  risk analysis, 434–36
  selecting alternatives, 436–39
  strategies, 426–29
Public relations campaigns, 197
Public Response System, 216
Puerto Ricans, 193
  income, 447
Punishment, 392–93
PUSH for excellence, 193

Q–R

Quorum, 273
Radicalism, 93
Rae, Douglas, 81
Rafshoon, Gerald M., 120
Randolph, A. Philip, 127
Random sample, 149
Ranney, Austin, 215
Rape cases, 330
Rather, Dan, 170, 172
Rational policymaking, 436
Rawls, John, 85–86, 88

Reagan, Ronald, 12, 15, 70, 117, 132, 149, 151, 165, 175, 192, 206, 210, 217, 241, 253, 311, 315–16, 349, 365, 423, 437, 484, 501, 519, 529, 532
  presidency, 239–40
Real property, law of, 303
Realignment elections, 240
Reapportionment, 266, 296
Recall, 55, 171
Recession, 475
Recombinant DNA molecule research, 463
Redistributive policies, 111, 256
Reelection imperative, 269–70
Referendum, 55, 171
Referent power, 117
Regents of California v. Bakke, 404
Registration, 173
Regulatory agencies, petitioning, 372–73
Regulatory commissions, 249
Regulatory policies, 111, 256
Rehabilitation Act of 1973, 409
Rehnquist, William H., 311, 313, 316
Religion, freedom of; see Freedom of religion
Representative form of government, 34, 55–56, 78, 95
Representatives; see House of Representatives
Republican Conference, 287
Republican Party, 199–202, 241–42
  organization in Senate, 287
  state legislatures, 353
Republican Policy Committee, 287
Reserved powers, 50
Retribution, 427
Revenue sharing, 349
Reverse discrimination, 405–6
Revolution, 46
Reward power, 117
Reynolds v. Sims, 308
Rhetoric, 137
Richards, Richard, 217
Rider, 281
Rights of accused, 387–93
  constitutionally mandated procedures, 387–88
  Fifth Amendment, 389–91
  Fourth Amendment, 388–89
  right to counsel, 391
Riker, William, 342
Risk analysis of public policy, 434–36
  comparative, 435
  energy policy example, 435–36
  trade-offs, 435
Rivlin, Alice M., 280, 420
Robbins, Liz, 278
Robertson, Leon, 444
Robinson, Jackie, 399
Rockefeller, David, 113
Roe v. Wade, 316, 393, 410

Rogers, Will, 268
Roll-call vote, 276
Roman Catholics, 241
Roosevelt, Franklin Delano, 14, 106, 120, 127, 128, 138, 166, 180, 199, 227, 237, 240, 241, 243, 264, 308, 309, 341, 406, 481, 484, 503, 504
  presidency, 232–33
Roosevelt, Theodore, 5, 6, 17, 18, 117, 118, 120–21, 133, 187, 202, 226, 240, 243, 316
  presidency, 231–32
Rosenblum, Victor G., 566
Rosenman, Samuel L., 129
Rousseau, Jean Jacques, 89, 92
Rout, Lawrence, 443
Rovere, Richard, 58
Rubber triangle model, 288
Rule of law, 72–73, 300
Rules Committee, 273
  House, 273
Rumania, 504
Rummel, William James, 392
Runoff primary, 206
Ruskin, John, 69
Russell, Bertrand, 71

S

Sachs, Alexander, 180
Sadat, Anwar, 132
Safe Drinking Water Act, 190, 196
Safire, William, 8 n
Sagebrush Rebellion, 341
St. Augustine, 74
St. Ignatius Loyola, 140
St. Thomas Aquinas, 74
Sales tax, 433
SALT; see Strategic Arms Limitations Talks
Sampling error, 150
Scarcity, 467
Schalon, Edward, 488
Schattschneider, E. E., 134
Schechter Poultry Corp. v. U.S., 309
Schedule C jobs, 368
Schlafly, Phyllis, 196
Schmidt, Helmut, 515
School districts, 356
School prayer, 382
School segregation, 398–402
Schultze, Charles, 443
Schumpeter, Joseph, 78–79, 96
Schwengell, Fren M., 269
Science, 95, 98
Scully, Vincent, 62
Search and seizure, 388
Segregation, 74–75, 398–402
  de jure and de facto, 401
  population shifts, 401–2
Select committee, 267–68
Self-incrimination, 389–91

Selma protest march, 125–26
Senate of the United States, 206, 265
  calendar, 273
  leadership, 285–87
  procedures for handling bills, 272
Senatorial courtesy, 324
Senior Executive Services (SES), 246
Seniority system, 291
Sennett, Richard, 117
"Separate but equal" doctrine, 308, 398–99
Separation of Church and State, 381
Separation of powers, 52–54, 95
Service Core of Retired Executives (SCORE), 473
Seventeenth Amendment, 265, 547–48
Seventh Amendment, 392, 545–46
Sex discrimination, 409
Shah Mohammed Reza Pahlavi, 8, 12, 509
Shaw, George Bernard, 367
Shay's Rebellion, 42–43
Sherman Anti-Trust Act (1890), 58
Shock Wave Rider, 359
Sierra Club, 189, 217
Silverberg, Robert, 360
Simak, Clifford D., 360
Sipple, Oliver, 394
Sirica, John, 330
Slander, 385
Slavery, 394–95
Sliwa, Curtis, 364
Small Business Administration, 249, 473
Small claims courts, 318, 330
Smith, Adam, 84, 456, 460, 482
Smith, Margaret Chase, 289
Sneer words, 137
Snow Belt, 350, 360–61
Social contracts, 75, 78
Social indicators, 459–60
Social policies, 416
  programs grouped by function, 416
Social rights, 80
Social Security Act of 1935, 439–40
Socialism, 10, 84
Socialist Labor Party, 203
Sociobiology, 16, 17
Socrates, 91
Solar power, 423–24
Solicitor general, 313
Solzhenitsyn, Alexander, 99–100
Somatarchy, 15–16
Sorensen, Ted, 210
South Korea, 479
Southern Christian Leadership Conference (SCLC), 193
Sovereignty, 48
Soviet Union, 70
  Afghanistan invasion, 509–10
  arms buildup, 523
  arms control, 528–32
  detente, 237

Soviet Union—*Cont.*
  foreign policy, 527–28
  geography, 524
  industrial capacity, 524–27
  Marxism after Marx, 97–98
  natural resources, 524
  population, 523–24
Sowell, Thomas, 407, 446–47
Spain, market economy, 10
Speaker of the House, 273, 284, 285, 286
Special committee of the Congress, 267–68
Special districts, 356
Special interest groups; *see* Interest groups
Special revenue sharing, 349
Specialization, 469–70
Spillovers, 470
Spoils system, 229, 244
Stagflation, 478, 479, 481
Stalin, Joseph, 97, 504
Stalinism, 97
Standard Federal Regions, 371
Standing committees of the Congress, 266–67
Standing to sue, 331
Stare decisis, 301, 322
State central committee, 205
State constitutions, 45, 352
State convention, 205
State courts, 306, 314, 316–18
State Department, 247, 254, 522
State-local relationship, 347
State-national relationships, 347–52
State of nature, 75
State of the Union, 227
States, 4
  constitutional rights, 340
  constitutions, 352
  demand for services from, 345
  federal control, 351
  federal mandates imposed, 351
  government unit, 342–44
  governors, 352
  growth in spending and employment, 344
  legislatures, 352–53
    party control, 353
  return from federal taxes, 350
  services rendered, 346
  sources of funds, 345–46
  state-local relationships, 347
  state-national relationships, 347–52
States rights, 61, 342
Statistical inference, 13–14
Statistics, 13
Statutes at Large, 566
Statutes of limitations, 195
Statutory law, 301–2
Steering and Policy Committee, 285, 287
Stein, Ben, 169
Steinberg, Jonathan, 271

Step-by-step negotiations, 132
Steuben, Frederick von, 40
Stevens, John Paul, 311
Stevens, Ted, 284
Stewart, Potter, 313
Stockman, David, 116
Stop ERA movement, 196
Storing, Herbert J., 52
Strategic Arms Limitations Talks (SALT), 508, 529–31
Strategic concessions, 132–33
Street-fighting pluralism, 358
Strick, Anne, 321
Strict construction of Constitution, 60–61, 62
Strong executive–weak legislative budget system, 279
Student Non-Violent Coordinating Committee, 96, 193
Students for a Democratic Society (SDS), 96
Subcommittees, 266–67
Subgovernments, 288
Suburban school districts, 402
Suffrage, 196
Summary process, 305
Sun Belt, 165, 350, 360–61
Sunrise industries, 479, 480
Sunset industries, 479
Sunshine laws, 291
Supply-side economics, 481–84
Supremacy clause, 50
Supreme Court, 52–55
  activism, 313–14
  activities, 310–16
  clerks, 310–11
  historical development, 307, 308–9
  main roads to, 306
  Reagan, 315–16
  usurpation of powers, 313–14
Surplus value, 94
Surrogate senator, 271
Survey research, 13
Suspects, rights of, 411
Sweatt v. Painter, 399
Sweden, 10
Switzerland, federalism, 48
Symbolic speech, 384
Symbols, 134, 138, 139
Systems analysis, 15

T

Taft, William H., 14
Taiwan, 479
Targeting, 121
Tariff Commission, 310
Tax courts, 306, 309–10
Tax expenditure, 433
Tax Foundation, Inc., 21
Taxation without representation, 35

Taxes, 482–84
  investment, 482–83
Technology, 460–67
  appropriate, 462
  biological-medical, 462–63
  criticisms of, 464–66
  definition, 461
  electronics, 463–64
  politics of, 466–67
  U.S. leadership, 464
  U.S. and Soviet Union compared, 525–27
Telecommunications, 216, 464
Television and radio, 21, 166, 216
  freedom of the press, 386
  political activism, 167–68
Tennessee Valley Authority, 249
Terkel, Studs, 406
Texas Constitution, 62
Thernstrom, Stephen, 217, 218
Therstrom, Abigail M., 403
Third parties, 202–3
  candidates, 209
Third World
  multinational corporations, 490
  physical quality of life index, 460
Thirteenth Amendment, 395, 546–47
Thompson, Hunter A., 170
Three Mile Island, 256
Thurow, Lester C., 420, 445 n, 480, 485
Tillich, Paul, 74
Time, 158
Tito, Josip Broz, 98, 504
Titoism, 98
Tocqueville, Alexis de, 157, 161, 186, 344, 364
Torts, 303, 305
Totalitarian form of government, 8
Tower, John, 284
Town meeting, 55, 356
Township, 356
Trade associations, 187
Trade deficit and surplus, 488
Trade-offs in public policy, 435
Transfer payments, 433, 444
Transportation, Department of, 236, 442–43
Transportation policies
  cost-benefit analysis, 434
  cost-effectiveness analysis, 437–38
  evaluation, 444
  implementation, 444
Treason, 388
Treasury Department, 254, 279, 523
Treaties, 305
Trenton, William, 264
Trial, 318–30
  basic steps, 319
  cross-examination, 321
  establishing facts, 320–21
  finding applicable rule, 322

INDEX I-13

Trial—*Cont.*
  formal participants, 322
  juries, 321
  lawyers, 322–24
  litigants, 322
  right to, 391–92
  verdict, 325
Trial balloon, 121–22
Trial courts, 306
Trial jury, 325
Tribe, Lawrence, 328
Trotsky, Leon, 98
Trotskyism, 98
Truman, Harry, 14, 20, 55, 127, 138, 227, 243, 309, 399, 504, 505
  presidency, 233–34
Truman Doctrine, 233, 505
Tufte, Edward R., 458
Tulsa, Oklahoma
  state-national relationship, 347
  Urban Renewal Authority, 347
Twenty-fifth Amendment, 236, 254, 549
Twenty-fourth Amendment, 172, 549
Twenty-sixth Amendment, 172, 550
Two-tiered government, 362
Two Treatises of Government, 75

U

Udall, Morris K., 178–79, 291–92
Unanimous opinion of Supreme Court, 313
Uncontrollable costs, 281
Underground economy, 483–84
Unemployment, 363
Unification Church, 382
Uniform Code of Military Justice, 310
Uniform Crime Reports for the United States, 447
Unilateral disarmament, 532
Unitary system, 48, 50
United Auto Workers, 187
United Mine Workers, 187
United Nations, 504
U.S. Conference of Mayors, 192
U.S. v. Darby, 59, 308
U.S. economy; *see also* Market economy
  budget; *see* Federal budget
  deregulation, 473
  expansion and recession, 475–76
  fiscal policies, 476–77
  government management, 471–77
  gross national product, 458–59
  industrial policy, 479–81
  inflation, 477–78
  international trade, 486–92
  monetary policies, 477
  multinational corporations, 489–90
  price system, 467–68
  productivity, 478–79
  regulation, 472–73
  small business, 473

U.S. Economy—*Cont.*
  social indicators, 459–60
  supply and demand, 467–68, 475
  virtues of market system, 468–70
United States Information Agency, 249
United States Law Week, 567
United States Manual, 370
United States v. Nixon, 54, 228, 316
U.S. Postal Service, 249
Urban League, 193
Urban life; *see* Cities
Utilitarianism, 86
Utopia, 92

V

Van Buren, Martin, 229
Vance, Cyrus, 522
Variable-sum game, 131 n
Venue, change of, 324
Verba, Sidney, 177
Verdicts, 325
Veterans Administration, 249
Veterans of Foreign Wars (VFW), 190
Veto
  item, 352
  legislative, 238, 265
  line-item, 279
  pocket, 276
  presidential, 227
Vice president, 209, 251–53, 254
  presidential succession, 285
  Senate president, 273
Vietnam War, 236, 237, 507–8, 536
Viguerie, Richard A., 216
Virginia Plan, 43
Vista, 249
Voluntarism, 364
Voter turnout, 175
Voting, 171–77
  electoral turnout, 172–73
  nonvoting, 175–77
  party-line, 174–75
  presidential elections, 176
  qualifications, 402
  voter characteristics, 173, 175–76
Voting Rights Act of 1965, 172, 193, 400, 402–3

W

Wage and price controls, 485
Wage and price guidelines, 486
Wagner Act (National Labor Relations Act), 472
Waitzman, Norman, 437
Wallace, George, 155, 202, 203
Wallace, Mike, 389
War
  causes, 529
  costs, 528
  prevention, 528–32
War on Poverty, 79, 236

War Powers Act of 1973, 238, 265
War Power Act of 1974, 523
Ward, 204
  caucus, 205
Warrant, 288–89
Warrantless arrest, 388
Warren, Earl, 52, 309, 315, 410
  school desegregation, 398
  Warren court, 308
Warren, Robert W., 385
Warsaw Pact, military resources, 524
Washington, George, 5, 6, 40, 45, 106, 127, 134, 139, 244, 247, 264, 525
  Farewell Address, 61, 228, 502
  presidency, 228–29
Washington Post, 168, 169, 170
WASP, 407
Water Pollution Control Act, 190
Watergate scandal, 236–37, 265, 282, 536
Wattenberg, Ben J., 161
Weak executive–strong legislative budgeting system, 279
Wealth of Nations, 84, 456, 460
Weathermen, 96
Weaver, James B., 202
Weber, Brian, 404–5
Weber, Max, 244
Weber v. Kaiser Aluminum Co., 404–5
Weidenbaum, Murray L., 24 n, 437
Welch, Finis, 363
Welch, Joseph, 281
Welfare legislation, 112
Welfare state, 10, 89, 402
Wells, H. G., 13
Wershba, Joseph, 167
Wesberry v. Sanders, 172
West Germany, 505
Whip, 284, 285, 287
White, Byron R., 311, 315, 316, 388
White, Theodore, 107, 126, 159, 291
White, William Allen, 14, 117
White-collar crime, 428
White House Office, 249, 250
  staff, 250
Whitehead, Alfred North, 47
Whitman, Walt, 230
Who Governs: Democracy and Power in the American City, 111
Wholesale price index (WPI), 612
Wickard v. Filburn, 59
Wicksell, K., 424 n
Wildavsky, Aaron, 444
Wildcat banks, 98 n, 259
Wilkinson, Bill, 383
Will, George F., 90, 237, 536
Willett, Thomas, 652 n
Wilson, Charles, 506
Wilson, Woodrow, 14, 54, 253, 266, 315, 510–11
  presidency, 232
Winner-take-all provisions, 210

Witnesses, 320–21
Wolfe, Thomas, 162
Woman's Christian Temperance Union, 217
Women
  enfranchisement, 196
  Equal Rights Amendment, 408–9
  legislative power, 289
  movement, 195–96
  in public office, 408
  role in society, 163
  suffrage, 196, 407, 408
Women's Legal Defense Fund, 196
Woodward, Bob, 310
The World Inside, 360
World War I, 181, 502–3
World War II, 503–4
World-wide Church of God, 382
WPI; *see* Wholesale price index
Wright, Jim, 204
Writ of certiorari, 310, 311
Writ of Mandamus, 124

Y–Z

Yalta Conference, 504
Yates v. United States, 384 n
Yergin, Daniel, 425
Youngstown Sheet and Tube Co. v. Sawyer, 55, 309
Yugoslavia, 100, 504
Zero-sum game, 118, 131
Zimbabwe, 100–101
Zinger, 137
Zoning, 363
Zurcher v. Stanford Daily, 386

This book has been set CAP, in 10 and 9 point Avanta, leaded 2 points. Part numbers are 18 and 36 point Avant Garde Gothic Book; chapter numbers are in Avant Garde Gothic Extra Light. Part and chapter titles are 36 and 24 point Avant Garde Gothic Book, respectively. The overall size of the type area is 36½ by 48½ picas.